THE WORLD'S BEST.

WHIT BURNETT editor of *The World's Best*

AUTHOR OF

The Maker of Signs, short stories, Harrison & Smith, 1934.

The Literary Life and The Hell With It, essays, Harper & Bros., 1938.

Immortal Bachelor (with John Pen), Robert Burns novel, Story, 1942.

EDITOR OF

A *Story* Anthology (with Martha Foley), Vanguard Press, 1933.

Story in America (with M. F.), Vanguard Press, 1934.

The Flying Yorkshireman, novellas (with M. F.), Harper, 1938.

This Is My Best, 93 greatest living American authors in their best, Dial Press, 1942.

Two Bottles of Relish, fantasies, Dial Press, 1943.

The Seas of God, stories of the human spirit, J. B. Lippincott, 1944.

Eighteen Great Modern Stories, Avon, 1944.

Time to Be Young, stories of youth, Lippincott, 1945.

The *Story* Pocket Book, Pocket Books, 1945.

American Authors Today, high school reader (with Charles Slatkin), Ginn & Co., 1947.

STORY: The Fiction of the Forties (with Hallie Burnett, co-editor of *Story*), E. P. Dutton, 1949.

The World's Best, 105 greatest living authors in their most representative works, Dial Press, 1950.

Story Magazine, devoted to the short story, 1931-1948.

105 GREATEST LIVING AUTHORS

PRESENT

The World's Best

STORIES · HUMOR · DRAMA · BIOGRAPHY

HISTORY · ESSAYS · POETRY

Edited by

WHIT BURNETT

The Dial Press · New York · 1950

CONTENTS

****

Foreword by WHIT BURNETT   **xi**

I. THE AMERICAS
UNITED STATES

EUGENE O'NEILL: *The Hunted: Act Four* (drama)   3

ERNEST HEMINGWAY: *The Snows of Kilimanjaro*
(short story)   16

SINCLAIR LEWIS: *An Assemblage of Husbands and Wives*
(novel units)   38

ROBERT FROST: *Six New England Poems* (poetry)   52

JOHN STEINBECK: *Easter Sunday: Sea of Cortez* (essay)   61

CARL SANDBURG: *Abraham Lincoln Speaks at Gettysburg*
(biography)   77

EDNA ST. VINCENT MILLAY: *Twelve Sonnets* (poetry)   98

THORNTON WILDER: *From a Journal-Letter of Julius Caesar*
(novel unit)   104

JOHN DEWEY: *The Unity of the Human Being* (philosophy)   111

JOHN DOS PASSOS: *Art and Isadora* (biography)   124

PEARL BUCK: *Fighting Angel* (biography)   131

VAN WYCK BROOKS: *Edwin Arlington Robinson* (criticism)   141

H. L. MENCKEN: *The Poetry of Christianity* (essay)   148

WILLIAM FAULKNER: *Sunday Morning at the Compsons*
(novel unit)   155

MAXWELL ANDERSON: *A Faith in the Theater* (essay)   173

EDGAR LEE MASTERS: *Five From Spoon River* (poetry)   184

ARCHIBALD MACLEISH: *Poems* (poetry)   188

UPTON SINCLAIR: *The Hog Squeal of the Universe*
(novel unit)   196

ROBERT SHERWOOD: *The Titans Meet at Teheran* (history)   204

v

JOHN GUNTHER: *Death Be Not Proud: The Graduation*
(biography)   221
WILLIAM ROSE BENÉT: *Four Poems* (poetry)   225
CARL VAN DOREN: *Franklin and French Ladies* (biography)   228
ERSKINE CALDWELL: *Yellow Girl* (short story)   237
ROBINSON JEFFERS: *Three Poems* (poetry)   248
JAMES THURBER: *More Alarms at Night* (short story)   250
DOROTHY CANFIELD FISHER: *A Drop in the Bucket*
(short story)   255
JAMES BRANCH CABELL: *Is of Southern Ladies* (biography)   268
JOHN P. MARQUAND: *Yoicks—and Away* (novel unit)   279
JOHN HERSEY: *Moment of Judgment* (novel unit)   297
RICHARD WRIGHT: *American Hunger* (autobiography)   303
VINCENT SHEEAN: *Valediction to Churchill* (essay)   309
WILLIAM L. SHIRER: *The Prisoners at Nuremberg* (history)   314

CANADA

MAZO DE LA ROCHE: *Death of a Centenarian* (novel unit)   323
MORLEY CALLAGHAN: *Rigmarole* (short story)   333

MEXICO

MARIANO AZUELA: *The Under Dogs* (novel units)   339

SOUTH AMERICA

GABRIELA MISTRAL: *Three Poems* [first English translation]
(poetry)   349
PABLO NERUDA: *Summits of Macchu Picchu* [first English
translation]   (poetry)   355
EDUARDO MALLEA: *Pillars of Society* (novel unit)   368

II. THE BRITISH ISLES

ENGLAND

T. S. ELIOT: *Burnt Norton* (poetry)   393
ALDOUS HUXLEY: *The Tillotson Banquet* (short story)   400

Contents   **vii**

W. Somerset Maugham: *Truth, Beauty and Goodness*
                                        (autobiography)   420
John Masefield: *Three Poems* (poetry)   431
E. M. Forster: *The Trial* (novel unit)   435
Bertrand Russell: *Education* (essay)   447
Walter de la Mare: *Two Poems* (poetry)   457
V. Sackville-West: *The Duchess Dresses for Dinner*
                                        (novel unit)   466
Hilaire Belloc: *Heroic Poem in Praise of Wine* (poetry) 472
W. H. Auden: *The Massacre of the Innocents* (poetry)   479
Julian Huxley: *The Uniqueness of Man* (essay)   490
Edith Sitwell: *Five Poems* (poetry)   502
Noel Coward: *Hands Across the Sea* (drama)   510
Siegfried Sassoon: *The Weald of Youth* (autobiography) 529
J. B. Priestley: *The Grand Canyon* (essay)   536
Winston Churchill: *Dunkirk: The Miracle of the*
                            Evacuation   (history)   541
Rebecca West: *The Meaning of Treason* (essay)   548
C. E. M. Joad: *Decadence* (philosophy)   556
Graham Greene: *The Hint of an Explanation* (short story) 566
Arnold J. Toynbee: *Civilization on Trial* (essay)   577

SCOTLAND

A. J. Cronin: *Birth* (novel unit)   587

IRELAND

Lord Dunsany: *Business in Ireland* (essay)   592
Sean O'Casey: *The Plough and the Stars* (drama)   599
Padraic Colum: *Five Poems* (poetry)   618
Elizabeth Bowen: *The Easter Egg Party* (short story)   623
Liam O'Flaherty: *The Challenge* (short story)   634

III. EUROPE

FRANCE

André Gide: *Fruits of the Earth and New Fruits* (essay) 645
Jules Romains: *On the College Roof* (novel unit)   655

ANDRÉ MAUROIS: *The Kingdom of God* (autobiography)   670
ANDRÉ MALRAUX: *The Essential Problems* (novel unit)   677
JACQUES MARITAIN: *Art and Beauty* (essay)   685
FRANÇOIS MAURIAC: *Thérèse and the Doctor* (novel unit)   696
JEAN COCTEAU: *Proust and Laughter* (essay)   714
PAUL CLAUDEL: *The East I Know: Here and There* (essay)   720
JEAN-PAUL SARTRE: *The Art of Prose* (criticism)   726
ST. JOHN PERSE: *The Snows* (poetry)   731
ALBERT CAMUS: *Sentence of Death* (novel unit)   736
COLETTE: *Reading and Writing* (autobiography)   747
LOUIS ARAGON: *Poems in War Time* (poetry)   750

GERMANY

THOMAS MANN: *The Masters of Buddenbrooks* (novel unit)   757
ERICH REMARQUE: *Darkness in Paris* (novel unit)   797
ALBERT SCHWEITZER: *Out of My Life and Thought*
      (autobiography)   809
ALBERT EINSTEIN: *Science and Life* (essays)   824

SWITZERLAND

HERMANN HESSE: *Within and Without* [first English
      translation]   (short story)   830

NORWAY

SIGRID UNDSET: *The Loss and the Healing* (novel unit)   841
KNUT HAMSUN: *The Wonderful New Machine* (novel unit)   852

DENMARK

ISAK DINESEN: *The Pearls* (short story)   862
JOHANNES V. JENSEN: *Columbus in the Trade Wind*
      (novel unit)   876

FINLAND

FRANS EEMIL SILLANPÄÄ: *The Night of the Harvest Festival*
      (novel unit)   889

ICELAND

HALLDÓR LAXNESS: *An Icelandic Pioneer* (novel unit)   898

ITALY

BENEDETTO CROCE: *Soliloquy of an Old Philosopher* (essay)   912
IGNAZIO SILONE: *The Seed Beneath the Snow* [first English translation]   (novel units)   919

SPAIN

GEORGE SANTAYANA: *Normal Madness* (essay)   936
JOSÉ ORTEGA Y GASSET: *The Coming of the Masses* (essay)   945
SALVADOR DE MADARIAGA: *Dedicated to Women* (essay)   951
PIO BAROJA: *Youth and Egolatry* (autobiography)   959

HOLLAND

PIERRE VAN PAASSEN: *Uncle Kees Protests* (biography)   965

GREECE

ANGELOS SIKELIANOS: *Two Poems* (poetry)   971

HUNGARY

ARTHUR KOESTLER: *Apage Satanas* (novel unit)   977
FERENC MOLNÁR: *Liliom's Return* (drama)   993

RUSSIA

IVAN BUNIN: *The Gentleman from San Francisco* (short story)   1008
MIKHAIL SHOLOKHOV: *Civil War* (novel unit)   1029
ILYA EHRENBURG: *The Storm* (novel units)   1044

IV. ASIA

CHINA

LIN YUTANG: *The End of Living Is Living Itself* (essay)   1059
HU SHIH: *The Civilizations of the East and West* (essay)   1066

INDIA

JAWAHARLAL NEHRU: *Time in Prison* (autobiography)   1078
SRI AUROBINDO: *The Life Divine: The Present Evolutionary
                          Crisis*   (essay)   1093

BIOGRAPHIES AND BIBLIOGRAPHIES   1109
ACKNOWLEDGMENTS   1160
LISTS OF BALLOT SIGNERS   1169
INDEX OF AUTHORS   1181
INDEX OF TITLES   1183

A FOREWORD IN THE FORM OF A REPORT

****

To THE 105 world authors whose writings make up the contents of this book,

To THE 96 distinguished authors who voted for their contemporaries,

To THE 30 officers of the European P.E.N. Clubs (Poets, Editors and Novelists) who marked, signed and returned their ballots,

To THE 36 members of the P.E.N. in the United States,

To THE 70 editors of the *Columbia Dictionary of Modern European Literature* who balloted,

To THE 24 editors of magazines, literary journals, etc.,

To THE 31 book reviewers of newspapers, magazines and radio,

To THE 121 Presidents of American colleges and others in the field of education who balloted for their choices in this volume,

To THE 108 librarians in the United States who did likewise,

To THE 22 miscellaneous public figures who balloted,

To THE 23 bookstore personnel in American cities who balloted,

To THE 82 subscribers to *The Saturday Review of Literature* who balloted as a cross section of the general reading public, and

To all good discerning readers who may have this book in hand,

LADIES AND GENTLEMEN:

First, let me thank you — for your patience. It has taken a long time to complete the task we all began, so confidently, three full years ago.

The task, you will remember, was to find out from the best readers of our day who were the most important living writers of our time.

It sounded like a simple, direct project. It wasn't.

But through your cooperation, and dealings with authors and agents, publishers and translators, mails and deaths, permissions,

Russians, copyrights and space, I am able at last to hand you the results of our collaboration.

It is an assemblage of 105 of the most distinguished living authors in the world, selected, in the main, through balloting in many countries among reading individuals, 643 of whom signed and returned their ballots nominating the authors now brought together, for the first time in any language, in this book.

In the following pages I respectfully submit some details of what kind of a book this is; who is in it, where the authors come from and how the book was assembled. I would like also to compare briefly the balloting from different groups; and to say why such a book in the world today, in English, has its value; and what are some of the overtones and meanings in the book.

THE PERIOD

It is, of course, a book of a period, as there have been other books, like *Don Quixote,* or *Gargantua and Pantagruel,* or further back, the *Decameron,* which were period books. And the greatest writers of a period take on the lights and shadows of their time. But this is not a one-man book — in editing or in writing. It contains 105 of the most representative writers of today. There is no Shakespeare in it, no Keats nor Milton. It does not go back to the Elizabethans, nor does it include the writers who have functioned in our time but now are dead. It is a book of writers now living, men and women who, in their individual and creative ways, have had an influence of greatness on their day.

"Formerly the century was a unit," writes J. Donald Adams, the critic, "when generalizations were made about the temper of a period, and the character of the literature that was produced within its boundaries." "We now," he adds, "like to generalize in decades." Roughly, this is a book of the last three decades; and true to its times, with two world wars and violent tremors in our lives, it contains the work of artists in participation in and withdrawal from "the age's capacity for being eloquent on the unspeakable."*

If it was a period, it began under the influence of relativity and the general discovery of the depths of the subconscious. If it has a boundary at this time, perhaps it is bounded by a prospect of consciousness

---

*Charles Poore, *New York Times,* on *Story: The Fiction of the 'Forties,* Whit and Hallie Burnett, *Dutton,* 1949.

and maturity. And some may find meaning in the fact that the man who promulgated the theory of relativity at the beginning of the period now, at mid-century, has announced a new integration, in the theory of the unified field.

If the world is shrinking in our times, it was always somewhat shrunken to the intelligent man's size when it came to good literature. For the best writing of one country has crossed, in times past, to other lands and other languages. "World literature," says Professor Albert Guérard* of Stanford University, "begins not in the graduate school, but in the nursery. . . . Our children do not object to the Grimm Brothers because they were Germans, to Charles Perrault because he was French, to Hans Christian Andersen because he was a Dane. . . ." The day when there was one great book in all languages, the Bible — a part of World Literature — has given way to the day when there are many books in many languages.

This is a book in one language. That it was undertaken in America, at this time, is not as strange as it seems. What is remarkable, to me, is how few translations were required to represent most of the great continental authors. Their best was already in English. My chief trouble was in finding some of these books. And it is here the anthologists serve a little-known function. The publishers allow many great books to go out of print. It is up to the anthologist to find them.

Stature, and a body of work, something to say which has been found valid across the frontiers of an artist's own land — these were some of the bases for the nomination of the authors in this book.

Its contributors are not young writers. They are authors whose literary output has been substantial enough to win them public acceptance not only in their own countries but throughout the world. Some are in their eighties. Many are in their fifties or sixties. Few were world prominent before the First World War. Many emerged in the twenties, and all have been creating their books, wherever they are, in Paris, in London, in Iceland, or in India, during the last thirty years, maturing with the decades. But among the older trees are the new growth. *The Jungle* of its day is here, and so is *The Wall*. The philosophers may reach back into the years for a distilled representation of their thought, or like Croce, sum up today the spirit of the past. The historians, like Toynbee, also look into the future.

*Preface to World Literature, Henry Holt & Co., 1940, 1947.

THE COUNTRIES OF THE AUTHORS

Twenty-three countries are represented as follows:

The United States	32 authors
England	20
France	13
Ireland	5
Germany	4
Spain	4
Russia	3

The following countries are represented by two each: Canada, Chile, China, Denmark, Hungary, India, Italy, Norway.

The following countries, one author each: Argentina, Finland, Greece, Holland, Iceland, Mexico, Scotland, Switzerland.

If, with thirty-two out of 105 authors, Americans are found most numerous, it must be admitted the book was oriented from America, where the balloting was most extensive and where many who signed the ballots said they read only English. Conceivably, had this project been conducted by a French editor and predominantly French or European selectors, the book might have had a greater proportion of French or German authors. For those who think there should be more Americans, I can only refer them to an earlier, purely American assemblage, *This Is My Best,* which contained ninety-three authors many of whom, no doubt — but for the rest of the world — might have graced these pages.

The British Isles were next, numerically, with twenty authors from England, five from Ireland and one from Scotland. France was next with thirteen, Germany four, Spain four, and Russia three. Eight countries are represented with two authors each and eight more countries with one author each.

I have appended charts to this report. One shows the fifty world authors* most heavily voted upon by all eleven groups of selectors combined, in the order of the votes. All living authors in the first fifty, with a few exceptions to be cited, are included in the book, together with more than fifty others, most of whom were within the 100 most voted upon. In the cases where this is not true the inclusion of some is due to their having been written in on many ballots; or,

*The ballots sent to the selectors contained the names of 457 authors — 146 from North America, 266 from Europe (and Russia), twenty-two from Asia and Australasia, eight from Asia Minor, ten from South America, and five from Africa.

not widely known to the public, they were deemed most important
by authorities in their countries and literatures.

THE 50 MOST VOTED UPON

As the greatest living writers in the world

Voting Strength: 658

		Votes
1.	George Bernard Shaw (Ire.)	539
2.	Thomas Mann (Ger.)	524
3.	Eugene O'Neill (U.S.)	508
4.	Ernest Hemingway (U.S.)	466
5.	Sinclair Lewis (U.S.)	453
6.	Sigrid Undset (Nor.)	452
7.	George Santayana (Sp.)	436
8.	T. S. Eliot (Eng.)	435
9.	Aldous Huxley (Eng.)	434
10.	Robert Frost (U.S.)	432
11.	John Steinbeck (U.S.)	427
12.	W. Somerset Maugham (Eng.)	424
13.	Carl Sandburg (U.S.)	414
14.	Willa Cather* (U.S.)	409
15.	Edna St. V. Millay (U.S.)	403
16.	John Masefield (Eng.)	393
17.	André Gide (Fr.)	382
18.	Maurice Maeterlinck (Bel.)	377
19.	Thornton Wilder (U.S.)	373
20.	John Dewey (U.S.)	368
21.	John Dos Passos (U.S.)	365
22.	Jules Romains (Fr.)	358
23.	Benedetto Croce (It.)	342
24.	Pearl Buck (U.S.)	332
25.	E. M. Forster (Eng.)	328
26.	Van Wyck Brooks (U.S.)	324
27.	Arnold J. Toynbee (Eng.)	318
28.	Erich Maria Remarque (Ger.)	313
29.	Bertrand Russell (Eng.)	311
30.	Charles and Mary Beard (U.S.)	307
31.	H. L. Mencken (U.S.)	306
32.	Sholem Asch (U.S.)	305
33.	Walter de la Mare (Eng.)	300
34.	Knut Hamsun (Nor.)	293
35.	André Maurois (Fr.)	290
36.	William Faulkner (U.S.)	287
37.	Lin Yutang (Chi.)	280
38.	Maxwell Anderson (U.S.)	278
39.	Rebecca West (Eng.)	277

*Willa Cather died after the ballots were prepared.

40. André Malraux (Fr.)   276
41. Arthur Koestler (Hun.)   268
42. Edgar Lee Masters (U.S.)   264
43. Archibald MacLeish (U.S.)   255
44. Hilaire Belloc (Eng.)   253
45. Jacques Maritain (Fr.)   250
46. W. H. Auden (Eng.)   249
47. Lord Dunsany (Ire.)   247
48. José Ortega y Gasset (Sp.)   245
49. Noel Coward (Eng.)   243
50. Upton Sinclair (U.S.)   240
51. J. B. Priestley (Eng.)   237

THE FIRST TEN WORLD AUTHORS

*Nominated on the largest number of ballots
in eleven different groups of readers*

List No. 1: 96 authors
1. Mann
2. Shaw
3. Eliot, O'Neill
4. Lewis
5. Hemingway
6. Maugham
7. Huxley
8. Forster
9. Faulkner, Frost
10. Gide

List No. 2: 30 European
P.E.N. (officers of the Poets,
Editors and Novelist Clubs of
Europe)
1. Shaw
2. Gide
3. Lewis
4. Dos Passos, Huxley, Steinbeck, Undset
5. Mann, Maeterlinck
6. Buck, Duhamel, Hemingway
7. Romains
8. O'Neill, Wilder
9. Ehrenburg, Eliot, Priestley
10. Belloc, Croce, De la Mare, Maugham, Mauriac

List No. 3: 36 P.E.N., U.S.
1. Shaw
2. Mann, Hemingway
3. Millay, Cather
4. Huxley
5. Undset, O'Neill, Maugham, Sandburg
6. Santayana
7. De la Mare, Frost
8. Eliot, Masefield, Lewis
9. Russell, Faulkner
10. Wilder

List No. 4: 70 editors of the
Columbia (University) *Dictionary of Modern European Literature*
1. Shaw
2. Croce
3. Mann, O'Neill
4. Gide
5. Hemingway, Lewis
6. Santayana
7. Eliot
8. Steinbeck
9. Maeterlinck, Undset
10. Huxley

List No. 5: 24 Editors
1. Shaw

2. Mann, Lewis, Hemingway, O'Neill, Santayana
3. Sandburg
4. Eliot
5. Huxley, Koestler, Maugham, Mencken, Millay
6. Dos Passos, Toynbee
7. Faulkner, Gide, Romains
8. Cather, Dewey, Frost, MacLeish, Maeterlinck, Malraux, Sherwood, Undset
9. Lin Yutang, Thurber, White, Wilder
10. Anderson, Asch, Brooks, Coward, Forster, Steinbeck, West

List No. 6: 31 reviewers

1. Shaw
2. Huxley, Santayana
3. Lewis, Undset
4. Dos Passos, Hemingway, Mann, O'Neill, Sandburg, Steinbeck
5. Eliot, Forster, Maugham
6. Frost, Mencken
7. Asch, Masefield
8. Brooks, Dewey
9. Buck, Millay, Thurber, Toynbee
10. Beerbohm, Faulkner, Gide, Remarque, Sinclair

List No. 7: 121 college presidents and educators

1. Masefield
2. Cather, Sandburg
3. O'Neill
4. Mann, Undset
5. Millay
6. Shaw
7. Frost
8. Noyes, Santayana
9. Belloc, Eliot
10. Brooks, Lewis

List No. 8: 108 U.S. librarians
1. Mann
2. Shaw
3. Undset

4. O'Neill
5. Sandburg
6. Cather
7. Frost
8. Masefield
9. Millay
10. Hemingway, Steinbeck

List No. 9: 22 miscellaneous public figures

1. Shaw
2. Steinbeck
3. Hemingway, Huxley
4. Mann, Maeterlinck
5. Beard, Toynbee, West
6. Dewey, Maugham
7. Cather, Faulkner, Forster, Gide, Lewis, Millay, Undset
8. Asch, Caldwell, Cocteau, Dos Passos, Frost, Gunther, Thurber, Wilder
9. Anderson, Beerbohm, Brooks, Croce, Eliot, Feuchtwanger, Ghandi, Lin Yutang, Malraux, Masefield, Molnár, Morley, Nehru, Waugh
10. Adamic, Angell, Aragon, Auden, Hamsun, Hecht, Hellman, J. Huxley, Jeffers, Koestler, MacLeish, Maurois, Mencken, Odets, Shirer, Sholokhov, Silone, Simonov, Sinclair, Van Paassen, E. B. White, Wright

List No. 10: 23 bookstore personnel

1. Shaw
2. Mann
3. Maugham
4. Hemingway
5. O'Neill, Brooks, Dewey
6. Huxley, Mencken, Sandburg, Toynbee
7. Cather, Dos Passos, Frost, Millay, Steinbeck, Undset
8. Gide, Lin Yutang
9. Asch, Eliot, Romains, Santayana, West
10. Nehru, Peattie, Remarque

List No. 11: 82 *Saturday Review of Literature* readers
1. Shaw
2. O'Neill
3. Frost
4. Millay, Sandburg
5. Mann, Maugham
6. Santayana
7. Masefield
8. Cather
9. Buck, Hemingway, Lewis
10. Steinbeck

There are ninety-three men and twelve women authors. The United States and England have three women each: Pearl Buck, novelist, Dorothy Canfield Fisher, novelist, and Edna St. Vincent Millay, poet, from America; V. Sackville-West, novelist, Edith Sitwell, poet, and Rebecca West, novelist and journalist, England. Of the twelve women in the book, three are poets; the other nine are most generally known as fiction writers.

Thirty-eight of the authors are represented by fiction — novel units or short stories; eighteen by poetry, twenty-four by essays on literature, philosophy; science, etc., four by plays, seven by biography, eight by autobiography, three by history and two by criticism. Since poets are usually represented by more than one selection, there are more complete selections — 165 — than authors.

THE 105 AUTHORS BY COUNTRIES

The United States   32 (29 men, 3 women) alphabetical order

Maxwell Anderson, playwright; William Rose Benét, poet; Van Wyck Brooks, critic; Pearl Buck, novelist; James Branch Cabell, novelist; Erskine Caldwell, novelist; John Dewey, philosopher; John Dos Passos, novelist; William Faulkner, novelist; Dorothy Canfield Fisher, novelist; Robert Frost, poet; John Gunther, journalist-historian; John Hersey, novelist; Ernest Hemingway, novelist; Robinson Jeffers, poet; Sinclair Lewis, novelist; Archibald MacLeish, poet; John P. Marquand, novelist; Edgar Lee Masters, poet; H. L. Mencken, critic; Edna St. Vincent Millay, poet; Eugene O'Neill, playwright; Carl Sandburg, poet and biographer; Vincent Sheean, novelist and journalist; Robert Sherwood, playwright and biographer; William L. Shirer, journalist-historian; Upton Sinclair, novelist; John Steinbeck, novelist; James Thurber, essayist; Carl Van Doren, biographer; Thornton Wilder, novelist; Richard Wright, novelist.

England   20 (17 men, 3 women)

W. H. Auden, poet; Hilaire Belloc, poet; Winston Churchill, historian; Noel Coward, playwright; Walter de la Mare, poet; T. S.

Eliot, poet; E. M. Forster, novelist; Graham Greene, novelist; Aldous Huxley, novelist; Julian Huxley, essayist; C. E. M. Joad, philosopher; John Masefield, poet; W. Somerset Maugham, novelist; J. B. Priestley, novelist; Bertrand Russell, philosopher; V. Sackville-West, novelist; Siegfried Sassoon, biographer; Edith Sitwell, poet; Arnold J. Toynbee, historian; Rebecca West, novelist and journalist.

France 13 (12 men, 1 woman)

Louis Aragon, poet; Albert Camus, novelist; Paul Claudel, poet; Jean Cocteau, poet and essayist; Colette, novelist; André Gide, critic and essayist; André Malraux, novelist; Jacques Maritain, theologian and philosopher; François Mauriac, novelist; André Maurois, novelist and biographer; St.-John Perse, poet; Jules Romains, novelist; Jean-Paul Sartre, novelist and critic.

Ireland 5 (4 men, 1 woman)

Elizabeth Bowen, novelist; Padraic Colum, poet; Lord Dunsany, storyteller; Liam O'Flaherty, novelist; Sean O'Casey, playwright.

Germany 4

Albert Einstein, essayist; Thomas Mann, novelist; Erich Maria Remarque, novelist; Albert Schweitzer, philosopher.

Spain 4

Pio Baroja, novelist; Salvador de Madariaga, essayist; José Ortega y Gasset, philosopher; George Santayana, philosopher.

Russia 3

Ivan Bunin, novelist; Ilya Ehrenburg, journalist and novelist; Mikhail Sholokhov, novelist.

Eight Countries 16 (2 from each)

Canada: Morley Callaghan, novelist; Mazo de la Roche, novelist.
Chile: Gabriela Mistral, poet; Pablo Neruda, poet.
China: Hu Shih, philosopher; Lin Yutang, novelist and essayist.
Denmark: Isak Dinesen, short story writer; Johannes V. Jensen, novelist.
Hungary: Arthur Koestler, novelist; Ferenc Molnár, playwright.
India: Sri Aurobindo, poet and philosopher; Jawaharlal Nehru, historian and biographer.
Italy: Benedetto Croce, philosopher; Ignazio Silone, novelist.
Norway: Knut Hamsun, novelist; Sigrid Undset, novelist.

Eight Countries **8** *(1 from each)*

Argentina: Eduardo Mallea, novelist.

Finland: Frans Eemil Sillanpää, novelist.

Greece: Angelos Sikelianos, poet.

Holland: Pierre van Paassen, novelist.

Iceland: Halldór Laxness, novelist.

Mexico: Mariano Azuela, novelist.

Scotland: A. J. Cronin, novelist.

Switzerland: Hermann Hesse, novelist.

THE AMERICANS*

The American author who was on more ballots than any other American was the dramatist Eugene O'Neill. He was third in the world voting, following Bernard Shaw, first, and Thomas Mann, second.

The Americans who followed O'Neill were two novelists, Ernest Hemingway, fourth, and Sinclair Lewis, fifth. The New England poet, Robert Frost, was tenth in order of the most balloted upon; John Steinbeck, novelist, eleventh.

The other Americans in the first fifty were Carl Sandburg, poet, thirteenth; Edna St. Vincent Millay, poet, fifteenth; Thornton Wilder, novelist, nineteenth; John Dewey, philosopher, twentieth; John Dos Passos, novelist, twenty-first; Pearl Buck, novelist, twenty-fourth; Van Wyck Brooks, critic, twenty-sixth; H. L. Mencken, critic, thirty-first; William Faulkner, novelist, thirty-sixth; Maxwell Anderson, playwright, thirty-eighth; Edgar Lee Masters, poet, forty-

*BALLOTING IN THE PAST

*Authors have selected their favorite works in times past, both in America (for the editor Ray Long, once) and earlier in England. And the balloting idea which helped assemble the American collection *This Is My Best* in 1942 has also been utilized to test the public standing of authors, even though no book was the outcome.

Balloting in 1942 among librarians, critics and subscribers to *The Atlantic Monthly, Harper's* and *The New Yorker* magazine for inclusions in the all-American volume *This Is My Best* showed Carl Sandburg on the largest number of ballots, John Steinbeck next, Eugene O'Neill third, Ernest Hemingway fourth, Willa Cather fifth, Pearl Buck sixth, Edna St. Vincent Millay seventh, Sinclair Lewis eighth, Christopher Morley ninth, Carl Van Doren tenth, Robert Frost eleventh, Thornton Wilder twelfth, H. L. Mencken thirteenth, Edna Ferber fourteenth and George Santayana fifteenth.

In 1936 *The Colophon,* the book collector's quarterly, asked its readers what ten American authors then living had the best chance of being considered classics by the reading public of the year 2000. Sinclair Lewis received 332 votes, first place; Willa Cather, with 304, second. Eugene O'Neill was third; Edna St. Vincent Millay, fourth; Robert Frost, fifth; Theodore Dreiser, sixth; James Truslow Adams, seventh; George Santayana, eighth;

second; Archibald MacLeish, poet, forty-third; Upton Sinclair, novelist, fiftieth.

Fourteen others account for the American section of thirty-two, the other Americans within the 100 most voted upon being, Carl Van Doren, Robinson Jeffers, Erskine Caldwell, John Hersey, John Gunther, Robert E. Sherwood, William Rose Benét, James Thurber, Dorothy Canfield Fisher, James Branch Cabell, John P. Marquand, Vincent Sheean, William L. Shirer and Richard Wright.

NOBEL PRIZE WINNERS

Twelve of the fifteen* winners of the Nobel Prize Award for Literature, given annually for the most distinguished idealistic work to "persons who shall have contributed most materially to benefit mankind," are represented, plus Sigrid Undset, of Norway, who chose her selection before her death. Maurice Maeterlinck, the Belgian, balloted on his contemporaries, but died before he made his own choice.

Of the Nobel Prize winners, ten are men: Ivan Bunin, novelist, Russia; André Gide, poet, essayist, novelist, France; Knut Hamsun, novelist, Norway; Hermann Hesse, novelist, Switzerland; Johannes V. Jensen, novelist, Denmark; Sinclair Lewis, novelist, the United States; Thomas Mann, novelist, Germany; Eugene O'Neill, playwright, the United States; Frans Eemil Sillanpää, novelist, Finland; and T. S. Eliot, poet, England.

The three women Nobel Prize winners are Sigrid Undset, novelist, Norway, winner of the 1928 award; Pearl Buck, novelist, the United

---

Stephen Vincent Benét, ninth; and James Branch Cabell, tenth. (It is interesting that six of the ten living fourteen years later were voted among the first 100 in *THE WORLD'S BEST* poll, and five, Lewis, O'Neill, Millay, Frost and Santayana among the first fifteen.)

The oldest ballot I know on the American great was shown to me recently by Lawrence White, the Dante translator, at his home in Smithtown, Long Island. It was a poll taken April 12, 1884 by J. L. and J. B. Gilder, Editors of *The Critic and Good Literature*, listing votes on "forty immortals" of the day for a possible American Academy. Oliver Wendell Holmes with 130 votes led the list, James Russell Lowell, next with 128; John Greenleaf Whittier, third, with 125. Fourth was George Bancroft, William Dean Howells, fifth. Francis Bret Harte was eighth and Henry James with eighty-six votes was thirteenth, just after George W. Cable in the voting order. Mark Twain got less votes than Edmund Clarence Stedman or Richard Grant White who were ninth and tenth, respectively. Mark Twain was fourteenth with 84 votes, and Walt Whitman, with 76, was twentieth.

*Jacinto Benavente (1866–, Spain), dramatist, received a negligible number of nominations; concerning Roger Martin du Gard (1881–,

States, 1938; and Gabriela Mistral, poet, Chile, winner of the 1945 award.

What is especially interesting is that, no matter what group of voters is counted, the first fifty most heavily voted upon authors were everybody's choice.* There was merely a difference in relative position. The French writer Gide was the second most generally voted upon with the European P. E. N. Clubs, for example, while he was eleventh with the American P. E. N. Club members, fourth with the *Columbia Dictionary* editors and thirty-fifth with the general readers of *The Saturday Review of Literature*.

THE SHAW - BURNETT LETTERS

The man who received the honor of nomination from our Academy of Readers on more ballots than any other living writer — he was listed for inclusion on 82.3 percent of the balloting — was the great Irish non-cooperator, G. Bernard Shaw, about one percent ahead of Thomas Mann, the German novelist, with 81.6 percent of the balloting. Shaw was first with eight out of eleven groups; Mann first with the authors themselves and American librarians; and John Masefield, Poet Laureate of England, was listed most numerously by the college presidents and educators.

I regret to report, in all frankness, that the man more people inclined to think should be in the book than any other one author is such an individualist that he refuses to appear in company with his peers, even when they vote for him. When the winners of the Nobel Prize for literature were anthologized recently, Mr. Shaw,

---

France) best known for his many-volumed novel of a French family, *Les Thibaults,* neither he, the editor, nor his publishers were able to arrive at a literarily satisfactory self-contained unit from this highly integrated work, so he was omitted.

Turning to other omissions, it should be mentioned that the Beards (thirtieth on the ballot list) were omitted after the death of Charles Beard; Sholem Asch (thirty-second on the ballot list) declined to participate on the ground that he was too busy.

*To the statistical-minded, the editor must say that in the final selection of the authors he has been influenced by the judgments of the best authorities available. Thus he has considered the ballots by the editors of the *Columbia Dictionary of Modern European Literature* of greater selective weight than those of relatively anonymous balloters in more average reading groups. While there are 643 ballot signers, there is a combined voting strength equalling 658, seventy signed (four unsigned) *Columbia Dictionary* voters counting double and those in the average reader fields counting one-half. While this made practically no difference in the order of the first fifty voted upon, it tended to give a greater selective value to recognized authorities in the European field in the *second* group of fifty authors included in the volume.

such a winner, declined that time also. I wrote Mr. Shaw the results of the selections made by his admirers. I said he was first with the combined vote of eleven groups of selectors. Mr. Shaw replied in ink, on a penny pink post-card: "You class me as one of the HUNDRED BEST. I am humiliated. I thought I was one of the ten best."

Again I explained that he was not only one of the hundred best, he was one of the ten best, and like Abou ben Adhem, his name led all the rest. He wrote that he did not care to pick out anything of his work.

I consulted his producers and his critics. Lawrence Langner, of the Theatre Guild, and George Jean Nathan, men who differ theatrically, merged in a happy coincidental opinion that the best and most representative piece of writing by Shaw or any other dramatist today was the Inquisitor's Scene in *Saint Joan*. I wrote that this opinion might soften the dramatist's labor of self-selection. He replied he did not want to have it taken out of context, and his contracts with his American publishers "do not admit of such dismemberment."

I consulted his American publishers who were not at all adamant; indeed, they were quite cooperative. And I so wrote the dramatist. The next response was a letter from Mr. Shaw's London solicitor, advising me of the law of copyright.

It is pleasanter to record that among other great men of letters, Thomas Mann, George Santayana, and Thornton Wilder, for instance, the spirit and the will were less stand-offish. Thomas Mann's comment on his work from *Buddenbrooks* tells its own story; and George Santayana, an elderly and retired man now, living in Rome, carefully edited and cut his own fragment because he thought it might be too long for the number of other great writers he imagined would be included in the book. To them and a hundred other authors of great generosity and friendliness, the editor owes his thanks.

Readers looking for "firsts" may be particularly grateful to at least four of the authors who have provided for this volume work never before translated into English. Ignazio Silone's wife translated for the first time several fragments never included in the American edition of *The Seed Beneath the Snow*. The Nobel Prize Winner, Hermann Hesse, of Switzerland, chose a hitherto untranslated short story. Pablo Neruda, of Chile, is represented by one of his longest and latest poems which Angel Flores has here translated for the first time. Another Nobel Prize Winner, Gabriela Mistral, of Chile, whose poetry has been considered extremely difficult to carry over from one language to another, is also represented by a first presentation in English of three of her longest, finest poems.

SCOPE OF THE BOOK

It was the hope of the editor that in a volume including literary men from all parts of the world, the resulting variety of men and works would not tend to make a patchy, fragmentary book. To this end, authors were not materially limited in the length of their selections. The selections have a stature and magnitude reflective of their authors. They say what they have to say, in the way the author wanted to say it, with no abridgement of a unit; the pieces are whole.

Thus, from all this, it must be seen this is not one man's compilation of many different writers. It is the tacit judgment of hundreds of discerning readers appraising writers for values they seek in art and life. Essentially a book of individual artists, coming to grips with life on the terms of thinking and creating human beings, it is a book of moral and artistic responsibility. And from the way the authors made the selections to represent them, it is a book, it seems to me, of splendid affirmations.

It is many views on the lives of man: as a farmer in Halldór Laxness' Icelandic wilderness, or as a peon in Azuela's Mexico; it is man as a figure in his times, Sandburg's Lincoln, Van Doren's Franklin, or Columbus, Roosevelt, or Schweitzer; it is man in war, with Sholokhov, Sikelianos, Remarque and Malraux; it is man as a thinking animal, speculating by the sea of Cortez, in the heart of Africa, or London; it is civilization seen in perspective by a Toynbee, Croce, Ortega y Gasset, a Julian Huxley, a Dewey and a Russell; and it is many created characters moving through the fictions of their creators, demonstrating in their actions the meaning of their lives.

It is the life of the mind and the promptings of the spirit, and notes from the worlds of the poets. It is a musician in Africa, building a hospital and working out a philosophy of a reverence for life; a Negro in the back streets of Chicago learning how to read. It is a poet in a snow storm, writing to his wife; a Chinese musing on the ends of living, an Indian on the divine in man; and a Broadway playwright expounding his faith in the art of the theater.

There is a love of the place of birth, the native land, in Neruda's

Chile and Frost's New England, the countryside of Finland, and the Greece of a poet. There is an essay on The Uniqueness of Man. Another on Women in War, on Education, on The Poetry of Christianity, on Treason, on Truth, Beauty and Goodness. And there is man facing death, in Camus, Koestler, Hemingway and Gunther.

It is not my place to point out the virtues in the individual writings in this book. They will be found by the reader himself. And in a volume where so many reflective men have commented on their works, I feel no further comment of mine is pertinent.

A number of patient persons, besides the signers of the ballots,* were involved in this project. Only the modesty of matrimony, which will be understood by all true bookmen, prevents me from expressing as fully as I might my indebtedness to Hallie Southgate Burnett, for her extensive reading and sound discerning help. I have tried to thank personally all the hard-working publishers' editors, and these include the staff of The Dial Press, especially Herbert Mordana, Fred Reinfeld and Ethel Pushkoff, whose aid and advice were considerable.

To the Reader then, let us commend this book and the authors who share in it.

　　　　　　　　　　　　　　Respectfully submitted,

　　　　　　　　　　　　　　　　WHIT BURNETT,

　　　　　　　　　　　　　　　　　Editor.

Setauket, Long Island,
May 15, 1950

*A list of the names on the signed ballots appears in the Acknowledgments at the end of this volume.

I

✳✳✳

THE AMERICAS

✳✳✳

UNITED STATES · 3

CANADA · 323

MEXICO · 339

SOUTH AMERICA · 349

EUGENE O'NEILL

****

Act Four of the trilogy Mourning Becomes Electra *has been selected as representative of the work of Eugene O'Neill, America's most outstanding playwright.* Mourning Becomes Electra *is a work which has been called "the most ambitious ever attempted by an American playwright" (Barrett H. Clark). It was put on by the Theatre Guild October 26, 1931, the thirty-fourth work of his produced, and such is the vitality of the piece that sixteen years later it was transcribed to the screen. A modern retelling of a Greek legend, played against a background of post Civil War South and New England, the play grew out of the dramatist's preoccupation with the problem as he has explained it in a diary note: "Is it possible to get modern psychological approximation of Greek sense of fate into such a play, which an intelligent audience of today, possessed of no belief in gods or moral retribution, could accept and be moved by?" Act Four of* The Hunted, *from* Mourning Becomes Electra, *plays in the semi-darkness aboard a ship tied at a Boston wharf. Christine Mannon, following the poisoning of her husband, has come to see her lover, Captain Adam Brant, and to warn him that something has gone wrong in the murder—that her daughter Lavinia now suspects her and Brant. While she is in this scene, her daughter Lavinia and her son Orin are watching and listening at a cabin skylight, awaiting their revenge for their father's death. This scene was selected with the aid of Mr. O'Neill's chief editor (at Random House) and long-time personal friend, Saxe Commins, who considers this choice an excellent one from the body of O'Neill's work, in that it is "an entity and reads as if it were an independent one-act play."*

****

The Hunted: Act Four

The stern section of a clipper ship moored alongside a wharf in East Boston, with the floor of the wharf in the foreground. The vessel lies

*with her bow and amidships off left and only the part aft of the
mizzenmast is visible with the curve of the stern at right. The ship
is unloaded and her black side rises nine or ten feet above the level
of the wharf. On the poop deck above, at right, is the wheel. At left
is the chart room and the entrance to the companionway stairs leading below to the cabin. At extreme left is the mizzenmast, the lowest
yard just visible above, the boom of the spanker extending out above
the deck to the right. Below the deck the portholes show a faint light
from the interior of the cabin. On the wharf the end of a warehouse
is at left front.*

It is a night two days after Act Two—the day following EZRA
MANNON'S *funeral. The moon is rising above the horizon off left
rear, its light accentuating the black outlines of the ship.*

*Borne on the wind the melancholy refrain of the capstan chanty
"Shenandoah," sung by a chantyman with the crew coming in on
the chorus, drifts over the water from a ship that is weighing anchor
in the harbor. Half in and half out of the shadow of the warehouse,
the* CHANTYMAN *lies sprawled on his back, snoring in a drunken
slumber. The sound of the singing seems to strike a responsive chord
in his brain, for he stirs, grunts, and with difficulty raises himself to
a sitting position in the moonlight beyond the shadow.*

*He is a thin, wiry man of sixty-five or so, with a tousled mop of
black hair, unkempt black beard and mustache. His weather-beaten
face is dissipated, he has a weak mouth, his big round blue eyes are
bloodshot, dreamy and drunken. But there is something romantic,
a queer troubadour-of-the-sea quality about him.*

CHANTYMAN. (*listens to the singing with critical disapproval*) A
hell of a chantyman that feller be! Screech owls is op'ry singers compared to him! I'll give him a taste of how "Shenandoah" ought t'
be sung! (*He begins to sing in a surprisingly good tenor voice, a bit
blurry with booze now and sentimentally mournful to a degree, but
still managing to get full value out of the chanty*)

>   *"Oh, Shenandoah, I long to hear you—*
>   *A-way, my rolling river!*
>   *Oh, Shenandoah, I can't get near you—*
>   *Way—ay, I'm bound away*
>   *Across the wide Missouri!*

>   *"Oh, Shenandoah, I love your daughter*
>   *A-way, my rolling river!"*

(*He stops abruptly, shaking his head—mournfully*) No good! Too drunk to do myself jestice! Pipe down, my John! Sleep it off (*He sprawls back on his elbows—confusedly*) Where am I? What the hell difference is it? There's plenty o' fresh air and the moon fur a glim. Don't be so damn pertic'lar! What ye want anyways? Feather-bed an' a grand piany? (*He sings with a maudlin zest*)

> "A bottle o' wine and a bottle o' beer
> And a bottle of Irish whiskey oh!
> So early in the morning
> The sailor likes his bottle oh!"

(*He stops and mutters*) Who'll buy a drink fur the slickest chantyman on the Western or any other damn ocean? Go to hell then! I kin buy it myself! (*He fumbles in his pants pocket*) I had it in this pocket—I remember I put it there pertic'lar—ten dollars in this pocket—(*He pulls the pocket inside out—with bewildered drunken anger*) By Christ, it's gone! I'm plucked clean! (*He struggles to a sitting position*) Where was I last? Aye, I remember! That yaller-haired pig with the pink dress on! Put her arm around me so lovin'! Told me how fine I could sing! (*He scrambles unsteadily to his feet*) By Christ, I'll go back an' give her a seaboot in her fat tail that'll learn her—! (*He takes a step but lurches into the shadow and leans against the warehouse*) Hard down! Heavy gales around Cape Stiff! All is sunk but honor, as the feller says, an' there's damn little o' that afloat! (*He stands against the warehouse, waiting for the sway-ing world to subside.*

The companionway door on the poop deck of the vessel is opened and ADAM BRANT *comes cautiously out. He looks around him quickly with an uneasy suspicious air. He is dressed in a merchant captain's blue uniform. Satisfied that there is no one on the deck, he comes to the rail and stares expectantly up the wharf, off left. His attitude is tense and nervous, and he keeps one hand in his coat pocket. The* CHANTYMAN *loses his balance, lurches forward, then back against the warehouse with a thump.* BRANT *leaps back from the rail startledly, jerking a revolver from his coat pocket—then leans over the rail again and calls threateningly*).

BRANT. Who's there? Come out and let me have a look at you or by God I'll shoot!

CHANTYMAN. (*stares up, startled in his turn and momentarily sobered—hastily*) Easy goes, shipmate! Stow that pistol! I'm doin' you no harm. (*He lurches out into the moonlight—suddenly pugnacious*) Not that I'm skeered o' you or your shooter! Who the hell are you to be threatenin' the life of an honest chantyman? Tryin' to hold me up, air ye? I been robbed once tonight! I'll go to the police station and tell 'em there's a robber here—

BRANT. (*hastily, with a placating air*) No harm meant. I'm skipper of this vessel and there have been a lot of waterfront thieves around here lately. I'm lacking a watchman and I've got to keep my weather eye open.

CHANTYMAN. (*again momentarily sobered—touching his forehead*) Aye—aye, sir. Mind your eye. I heer'd tell robbers broke in the "Annie Lodge's" cabin two nights back. Smashed everything and stole two hundred dollars off her skipper. Murderous, too, they be! Near beat the watchman's brains out! (*Then drunken pugnaciousness comes over him again*) Think I'm one o' that gang, do ye? Come down out o' that and I'll show ye who's a thief! I don't give a damn if ye air a skipper! Ye could be Bully Watermann himself an' I'd not let you insult me! I ain't signed on your old hooker! You've got no rights over me! I'm on dry land, by Christ, and this is a free country and—(*His voice has risen to a shout.* BRANT *is alarmed that this uproar will attract someone. He puts the pistol back in his pocket hastily and peers anxiously down the wharf. Then he interrupts the* CHANTYMAN's *tirade by a sharp command*).

BRANT. Stow your damned jaw! Or, by the Eternal, I'll come down and pound some sense in your head!

CHANTYMAN. (*automatically reacts to the voice of authority— quietly*) Aye—aye, sir. (*Then inconsequentially*) You ain't needin' a chantyman fur your next vi'ge, are ye, sir?

BRANT. I'm not sailing for a month yet. If you're still out of a job then—

CHANTYMAN. (*proudly*) You don't know me, that's plain! I'm the finest damn chantyman that ever put a tune to his lip! I ain't lookin' fur berths—they're lookin' fur me! Aye! Skippers are on'y too glad to git me! Many's a time I've seed a skipper an' mates sweatin' blood to beat work out of a crew but nary a lick could they git into 'em till I raised a tune—and then there'd be full sail on her afore ye knowed it!

BRANT. (*impatiently*) I'm not doubting your ability. But I'd advise you to turn in and sleep it off.

CHANTYMAN. (*not heeding this—sadly*) Aye, but it an't fur long, steam is comin' in, the sea is full o' smoky tea-kettles, the old days is dyin', an' where'll you an' me be then? (*Lugubriously drunken again*) Everything is dyin'! Abe Lincoln is dead. I used to ship on the Mannon packets an' I seed in the paper where Ezra Mannon was dead! (BRANT *starts guiltily. The* CHANTYMAN *goes on maudlinly*) Heart failure killed him, it said, but I know better! I've sailed on Mannon hookers an' been worked t' death and gotten swill fur grub, an' I know he didn't have no heart in him! Open him up an' you'd find a dried turnip! The old skinflint must have left a pile o' money. Who gits it, I wonder? Leave a widder, did he?

BRANT. (*harshly*) How would I know? (*Changing the subject calculatingly*) What are you doing here, Chantyman? I'd expect a man with your voice would be in a saloon, singing and making merry!

CHANTYMAN. So I would! So I would! But I was robbed, sir—aye —an' I know who done it—a yaller-haired wench had her arm around me. Steer clear o' gals or they'll skin your hide off an' use it fur a carpet! I warn ye, skipper! They're not fur sailormen like you an' me, 'less we're lookin' fur sorrow! (*Then insinuatingly*) I ain't got the price of a drink, that's why I'm here, sir.

BRANT. (*reaches in his pocket and tosses him down a silver dollar*) Here!

CHANTYMAN. (*fumbles around and finds the dollar*) Thank ye, sir. (*Then flatteringly*) It's a fine ship you've got there, sir. Crack sail on her and she'll beat most of 'em—an' you're the kind to crack sail on, I kin tell by your cut.

BRANT. (*pleased; glancing up at his ship's lofty rig*) Aye! I'll make her go right enough!

CHANTYMAN. All you need is a good chantyman to help ye. Here's "Hanging Johnny" fur ye! (BRANT *starts at this. The* CHANTYMAN *suddenly begins to sing the chanty "Hanging Johnny" with sentimental mournfulness*)

> *"Oh, they call me Hanging Johnny*
> *Away—ay—i—oh!*
> *They says I hangs for money*
> *Oh, hang, boys, hang!"*

BRANT. (*harshly*) Stop that damned dirge! And get out of here! Look lively now!

CHANTYMAN. (*starting to go*) Aye—aye, sir. (*Then resentfully*) I see ye ain't got much ear fur music. Good night.

BRANT. (*with exasperated relief*) Good night. (*The* CHANTYMAN *goes unsteadily off left, between the warehouse and the ship. He bursts again into his mournful dirge, his voice receding*)

"They say I hanged my mother
Away—ay—i—oh!
They say I hanged my mother
Oh, hang, boys, hang!"

(BRANT, *standing by the rail looking after him, mutters a curse and starts pacing up and down the deck*) Damn that chanty! It's sad as death! I've a foreboding I'll never take this ship to sea. She doesn't want me now—a coward hiding behind a woman's skirts! The sea hates a coward! (*A woman's figure dressed in black, heavily veiled, moves stealthily out from the darkness between the ship and the warehouse, left. She sees the figure on the deck above her and shrinks back with a stifled gasp of fear.* BRANT *hears the noise. Immediately his revolver is in his hand and he peers down into the shadows of the warehouse*) Who's there?

CHRISTINE. (*with a cry of relief*) Adam!

BRANT. Christine! (*Then quickly*) Go back to the gangplank. I'll meet you there. (*She goes back. He hurries along the deck and disappears off left to meet her. Their voices are heard and a moment later they enter on the poop deck, from left. She leans against him weakly and he supports her with his arm around her*) I have to bring you this way. I bolted the door to the main deck.

CHRISTINE. I was so frightened! I wasn't sure which ship! Some drunken man came along singing—

BRANT. Aye. I just got rid of him. I fired the watchman this morning so I'd be alone at night. I was hoping you'd come soon. Did that drunk see you?

CHRISTINE. No. I hid behind some boxes. (*Then frightenedly*) Why have you got that pistol?

BRANT. (*grimly*) I was going to give them a fight for it—if things went wrong.

CHRISTINE. Adam!

BRANT. By God, you don't think I'll ever let them take me alive, do you?

CHRISTINE. Please, please! Don't talk of that for a moment! Only hold me close to you! Tell me you love me!

BRANT. (*harshly*) It's no time! I want to know what's happened! (*Then immediately repentant he kisses her—with rough tenderness*) Don't mind me! My nerves are gone from waiting alone here not knowing anything but what I read in the papers—that he was dead. These last days have been hell!

CHRISTINE. If you knew what they have been for me!

BRANT. There's something gone wrong! I can read that in your face! What is it, Christine?

CHRISTINE, (*falteringly*) Vinnie knows—! She came into the room when he was dying! He told her—

BRANT (*harshly*) God! What is she going to do? (*Then, without giving her time to answer his question, he suddenly looks around uneasily*) Christine! How did you get away? She'd suspect you weren't going to your father's now. She followed you once before—

CHRISTINE. No. It's all right. This morning Orin said his cousins, the Bradfords, had invited him and Vinnie to visit them overnight at Blackridge and he was taking Vinnie with him because he thought a change would bring her back to her senses. I've made him think she's out of her head with grief—so he wouldn't listen to her—

BRANT. (*eagerly*) And he believes that?

CHRISTINE. (*weakly*) Yes—he does—now—but I don't know how long—

BRANT. Ah!

CHRISTINE. So I told him by all means to go. It gave me the chance I wanted to come to you. They went this morning. They don't know I've gone and even after they've found out they can't prove where I went. I can only stay a little while, Adam—we've got to plan—so many things have happened I couldn't foresee—I came to warn you—

BRANT. Ssshh! Come below in the cabin! We're fools to be talking out here. (*He guides her with his arm around her through the door to the companionway stairs and closes it quietly behind them.*

A pause in which the singing of the crew on the ship in the harbor comes mournfully over the water.

Then ORIN *and* LAVINIA *come in stealthily along the deck from the left. She is dressed in black as before. He wears a long cloak over his uniform and has a slouch hat pulled down over his eyes. Her manner is cold and grim.* ORIN *is holding in a savage, revengeful rage. They approach the cabin skylight silently.* ORIN *bends down by it to listen. His face, in the light from the skylight, becomes distorted with jealous fury.* LAVINIA *puts a restraining hand on his arm.*

The scene fades out into darkness. Several minutes are supposed to elapse. When the light comes on again, a section of the ship has been removed to reveal the interior of the cabin, a small compartment, the walls newly painted a light brown. The skylight giving on the deck above is in the middle of the ceiling. Suspended in the skylight is a ship's compass. Beneath it is a pine table with three chairs, one at rear, the other two at the table ends, left and right. On the table is a bottle of whiskey, half full, with a glass and a pitcher of water.

Built against the right wall of the cabin is a long narrow couch, like a bunk, with leather cushions. In the rear wall, at right, is a door leading into the captain's stateroom. A big sideboard stands against the left wall, center. Above it, a ship's clock. Farther back is a door opening on the alleyway leading to the main deck. The companionway stairs lead down to this alleyway.

There is a lighted lamp on the sideboard and a ship's lantern, also lighted, at the right end of the table.

In the cabin, BRANT *is seated at the right of table,* CHRISTINE *to the rear of it. Her face looks haggard and ageing, the mouth pinched and drawn down at the corners, and her general appearance, the arrangement of her hair and clothes, has the dishevelled touch of the fugitive. She is just finishing her story of the murder and the events following it. He is listening tensely.*

On the deck above, ORIN *and* LAVINIA *are discovered as before, with* ORIN *bending down by the transom, listening).*

CHRISTINE. When he was dying he pointed at me and told her I was guilty! And afterwards she found the poison—

BRANT. (*springing to his feet*) For God's sake, why didn't you—

CHRISTINE. (*pitifully*) I fainted before I could hide it! And I had planned it all so carefully. But how could I foresee that she would come in just at that moment? And how could I know he would talk to me the way he did? He drove me crazy! He kept talking of death! He was torturing me! I only wanted him to die and leave me alone!

BRANT. (*his eyes lighting up with savage satisfaction*) He knew before he died whose son I was, you said? By God, I'll bet that maddened him!

CHRISTINE. (*repeats pitifully*) I'd planned it so carefully—but something made things happen!

BRANT. (*overcome by gloomy dejection, sinks down on his chair again*) I knew it! I've had a feeling in my bones! It serves me right, what has happened and is to happen! It wasn't that kind of revenge I had sworn on my mother's body! I should have done as I wanted —fought with Ezra Mannon as two men fight for love of a woman! (*With bitter self-contempt*) I have my father's rotten coward blood in me, I think! Aye!

CHRISTINE. Adam! You make me feel so guilty!

BRANT. (*rousing himself—shamefacedly*) I didn't mean to blame you, Christine. (*Then harshly*) It's too late for regrets now, anyway. We've got to think what to do.

CHRISTINE. Yes! I'm so terrified of Vinnie! Oh, Adam, you must promise me to be on your guard every minute! If she convinces Orin you are my lover—Oh, why can't we go away, Adam? Once we're out of her reach, she can't do anything.

BRANT. The "Flying Trades" won't be sailing for a month or more. We can't get cargo as soon as the owners thought.

CHRISTINE. Can't we go on another ship—as passengers—to the East—we could be married out there—

BRANT. (*gloomily*) But everyone in the town would know you were gone. It would start suspicion—

CHRISTINE. No. Orin and Vinnie would lie to people. They'd have to for their own sakes. They'd say I was in New York with my father. Oh, Adam, it's the only thing we can do! If we don't get out of Vinnie's reach right away I know something horrible will happen!

BRANT. (*dejectedly*) Aye. I suppose it's the only way out for us now. The "Atlantis" is sailing on Friday for China. I'll arrange with her skipper to give us passage—and keep his mouth shut. She sails at daybreak Friday. You'd better meet me here Thursday night. (*Then with an effort*) I'll write Clark and Dawson tonight they'll have to find another skipper for the "Flying Trades."

CHRISTINE. (*noticing the hurt in his tone—miserably*) Poor Adam! I know how it hurts you to give up your ship.

BRANT. (*rousing himself guiltily—pats her hand—with gruff tenderness*) There are plenty of ships—but there is only one you, Christine!

CHRISTINE. I feel so guilty! I've brought you nothing but misfortune!

BRANT. You've brought love—and the rest is only the price. It's worth it a million times! You're all mine now, anyway! (*He hugs her to him, staring over her head with sad blank eyes*).

CHRISTINE. (*her voice trembling*) But I'm afraid I'm not much to boast about having—now. I've grown old in the past few days. I'm ugly. But I'll make myself beautiful again—for you—! I'll make up to you for everything! Try not to regret your ship too much, Adam!

BRANT. (*gruffly*) Let's not talk of her any more. (*Then forcing a wry smile*) I'll give up the sea. I think it's through with me now, anyway! The sea hates a coward.

CHRISTINE. (*trying pitifully to cheer him*) Don't talk like that! You have me, Adam! You have me! And we will be happy—once we're safe on your Blessed Islands! (*Then suddenly, with a little shudder*) It's strange. Orin was telling me of an island—(*On the deck above,* ORIN, *who has bent closer to the transom, straightens up with a threatening movement.* LAVINIA *grips his arm, restraining him*).

BRANT. (*with a bitter, hopeless yearning*) Aye—the Blessed Isles —Maybe we can still find happiness and forget! (*Then strangely, as if to himself*) I can see them now—so close—and a million miles away! The warm earth in the moonlight, the trade winds rustling the coco palms, the surf on the barrier reef singing a croon in your ears like a lullaby! Aye! There's peace, and forgetfulness for us there—if we can ever find those islands now!

CHRISTINE. (*desperately*) We will find them! We will! (*She kisses him. A pause. Suddenly she glances frightenedly at the clock*) Look at the time! I've got to go, Adam!

BRANT. For the love of God, watch out for Vinnie. If anything happened to you now—!

CHRISTINE. Nothing will happen to me. But you must be on your guard in case Orin—Good-bye, my lover! I must go! I must! (*She tears herself from his arms but immediately throws herself in them again—terrifiedly*) Oh! I feel so strange—so sad—as if I'd never see you again! (*She begins to sob hysterically*) Oh, Adam, tell me you don't regret! Tell me we're going to be happy! I can't bear this horrible feeling of despair!

BRANT. Of course we'll be happy! Come now! It's only a couple of days. (*They start for the door*) We'll go by the main deck. It's shorter. I'll walk to the end of the wharf with you. I won't go further. We might be seen.

CHRISTINE. Then we don't have to say good-bye for a few minutes yet! Oh, thank God! (*They go out to the alleyway,* BRANT *closing the door behind him. A pause. On the deck above* ORIN *pulls a revolver from under his cloak and makes a move, as if to rush off left down to the main deck after them.* LAVINIA *has been dreading this and throws herself in his way, grasping his arm*).

ORIN. (*in a furious whisper*) Let me go!

LAVINIA. (*struggling with him*) No! be quiet! Ssshh! I hear them on the main deck! Quick! Come to his cabin! (*She urges him to the companionway door, gets him inside and shuts the door behind them. A moment later the door on the left of the cabin below is opened and they enter*).

LAVINIA. He's going to the end of the wharf. That gives us a few minutes. (*Grimly*) You wanted proof! Well, are you satisfied now?

ORIN. Yes! God damn him! Death is too good for him! He ought to be—

LAVINIA. (*sharply commanding*) Orin! Remember you promised not to lose your head. You've got to do everything exactly as we planned it, so there'll be no suspicion about us. There would be no justice if we let ourselves—

ORIN. (*impatiently*) You've said all that before! Do you think I'm a fool? I'm not anxious to be hanged—for that skunk! (*Then with bitter anguish*) I heard her asking him to kiss her! I heard her warn him against me! (*He gives a horrible chuckle*) And my island I told her about—which was she and I—she wants to go there—with him! (*Then furiously*) Damn you! Why did you stop me? I'd have shot his guts out in front of her!

LAVINIA. (*scornfully*) Outside on deck where the shot would be sure to be heard? We'd have been arrested—and then I'd have to tell the truth to save us. She'd be hanged, and even if we managed to get off, our lives would be ruined! The only person to come off lucky would be Brant! He could die happy, knowing he'd revenged himself on us more than he ever dared hope! Is that what you want?

ORIN. (*sullenly*) No.

LAVINIA. Then don't act like a fool again. (*Looks around the cabin calculatingly—then in a tone of command*) Go and hide outside. He won't see you when he passes along the alleyway in the dark. He'll come straight in here. That's the time for you—

ORIN. (*grimly*) You needn't tell me what to do. I've had a thorough training at this game—thanks to you and Father.

LAVINIA. Quick! Go out now! He won't be long!

ORIN. (*goes to the door—then quickly*) I hear him coming. (*He slips out silently. She hurriedly hides herself by the sideboard at left, front. A moment later* BRANT *appears in the doorway and stands just inside it blinking in the light. He looks around the cabin sadly*).

BRANT. (*huskily*) So it's good-bye to you, "Flying Trades"! And you're right; I wasn't man enough for you! (ORIN *steps through the door and with the pistol almost against* BRANT's *body fires twice.* BRANT *pitches forward to the floor by the table, rolls over, twitches a moment on his back and lies still.* ORIN *springs forward and stands over the body, his pistol aimed down at it, ready to fire again*).

LAVINIA. (*stares fascinatedly at* BRANT's *still face*) Is he—dead?

ORIN. Yes.

LAVINIA. (*sharply*) Don't stand there! Where's the chisel you brought? Smash open everything in his stateroom. We must make it look as if thieves killed him, remember! Take anything valuable! We can sink it overboard afterwards! Hurry! (ORIN *puts his revolver on the table and takes a chisel that is stuck in his belt under his cloak and goes into the stateroom. A moment later there is the sound of splintering wood as he pries open a drawer*).

LAVINIA. (*goes slowly to the body and stands looking down into* BRANT'S *face. Her own is frozen and expressionless. A pause.* ORIN *can be heard in the stateroom prying open* BRANT'S *desk and scattering the contents of drawers around. Finally* LAVINIA *speaks to the corpse in a grim bitter tone*) How could you love that vile old woman so? (*She throws off this thought—harshly*) But you're dead! It's ended! (*She turns away from him resolutely—then suddenly turns back and stands stiffly upright and grim beside the body and prays coldly, as if carrying out a duty*) May God find forgiveness for your sins! May the soul of our cousin, Adam Mannon, rest in peace! (ORIN *comes in from the stateroom and overhears the last of her prayer*).

ORIN. (*harshly*) Rest in hell, you mean! (*He comes to her*) I've pried open everything I could find.

LAVINIA. Then come along. Quick. There's your pistol. Don't forget that. (*She goes to the door*).

ORIN. (*putting it in his pocket*) We've got to go through his pockets to make everything look like a burglary. (*He quickly turns* BRANT'S •*pockets inside out and puts the revolver he finds, along with bills and coins, watch and chain, knife, etc., into his own*) I'll sink these overboard from the dock, along with what was in his stateroom. (*Having finished this, he still remains stooping over the body and stares into* BRANT'S *face, a queer fascinated expression in his eyes*).

LAVINIA. (*uneasily*) Orin!

ORIN. By God, he does look like Father!

LAVINIA. No! Come along!

ORIN. (*as if talking to himself*) This is like my dream. I've killed him before—over and over.

LAVINIA. Orin!

ORIN. Do you remember me telling you how the faces of the men I killed in the war came back and changed to Father's face and finally became my own? (*He smiles grimly*) He looks like me, too! Maybe I've committed suicide!

LAVINIA. (*frightenedly—grabbing his arm*) Hurry! Someone may come!

ORIN. (*not heeding her, still staring at* BRANT—*strangely*) If I had been he I would have done what he did! I would have loved her as he loved her—and killed Father too—for her sake!

LAVINIA. (*tensely—shaking him by the arm*) Orin, for God's sake, will you stop talking crazy and come along? Do you want us to be found here? (*She pulls him away forcibly*).

ORIN. (*with a last look at the dead man*) It's queer! It's a rotten dirty joke on someone! (*He lets her hustle him out to the alleyway*).

CURTAIN

ERNEST HEMINGWAY

****

*The selection by Ernest Hemingway will find some critics calling
attention to the fact that of all the pieces in this book this one has
certainly been reprinted before. In the winter of 1947, Bennet Cerf
in* The Saturday Review of Literature, *reported that Mr. Hemingway
told a friend, "I must be slipping. No new anthology containing my*
Snows of Kilimanjaro *has been publlished in almost four days."*

Like the other well-recognized piece in this book, Ivan Bunin's
The Gentleman From San Francisco, The Snows of Kilimanjaro
*represents its author at a high point of writing. Each author con-
siders his story the one which best represents his style and thought.
If there is any argument, the critics will have to take it up with the
author, whose choice in these instances the editor has not disputed.*

*"I think," Mr. Hemingway's comment was characteristically
laconic, "you might as well re-print* The Snows of Kilimanjaro."
*And, regarding his balloting on his contemporaries, he added,
"please do* not *publish any list or tabulation of writers I did* not *vote
for—nor publish my ballot in its entirety."—E.H.*

****

The Snows of Kilimanjaro

*Kilimanjaro is a snow-covered mountain 19,710 feet high, and is
said to be the highest mountain in Africa. Its western summit is
called the Masai "Ngàje Ngài," the House of God. Close to the
western summit there is the dried and frozen carcass of a leopard.
No one has explained what the leopard was seeking at that altitude.*

"THE MARVELOUS THING is that it's painless," he said. "That's how
you know when it starts."

16

"Is it really?"

"Absolutely. I'm awfully sorry about the odor though. That must bother you."

"Don't! Please don't."

"Look at them," he said. "Now is it sight or is it scent that brings them like that?"

The cot the man lay on was in the wide shade of a mimosa tree and as he looked out past the shade onto the glare of the plain there were three of the big birds squatted obscenely, while in the sky a dozen more sailed, making quick-moving shadows as they passed.

"They've been there since the day the truck broke down," he said. "Today's the first time any have lit on the ground. I watched the way they sailed very carefully at first in case I ever wanted to use them in a story. That's funny now."

"I wish you wouldn't," she said.

"I'm only talking," he said. "It's much easier if I talk. But I don't want to bother you."

"You know it doesn't bother me," she said. "It's that I've gotten so very nervous not being able to do anything. I think we might make it as easy as we can until the plane comes."

"Or until the plane doesn't come."

"Please tell me what to do. There must be something I can do."

"You can take the leg off and that might stop it, though I doubt it. Or you can shoot me. You're a good shot now. I taught you to shoot, didn't I?"

"Please don't talk that way. Couldn't I read to you?"

"Read what?"

"Anything in the book bag that we haven't read."

"I can't listen to it," he said. "Talking is the easiest. We quarrel and that makes the time pass."

"I don't quarrel. I never want to quarrel. Let's not quarrel any more. No matter how nervous we get. Maybe they will be back with another truck today. Maybe the plane will come."

"I don't want to move," the man said. "There is no sense in moving now except to make it easier for you."

"That's cowardly."

"Can't you let a man die as comfortably as he can without calling him names? What's the use of slanging me?"

"You're not going to die."

"Don't be silly. I'm dying now. Ask those bastards." He looked over to where the huge, filthy birds sat, their naked heads sunk in the hunched feathers. A fourth planed down, to run quick-legged and then waddle slowly toward the others.

"They are around every camp. You never notice them. You can't die if you don't give up."

"Where did you read that? You're such a bloody fool."

"You might think about some one else."

"For Christ's sake," he said, "that's been my trade."

He lay then and was quiet for a while and looked across the heat shimmer of the plain to the edge of the bush. There were a few Tommies that showed minute and white against the yellow and, far off, he saw a herd of zebra, white against the green of the bush. This was a pleasant camp under big trees against a hill, with good water, and close by, a nearly dry water hole where sand grouse flighted in the mornings.

"Wouldn't you like me to read?" she asked. She was sitting on a canvas chair beside his cot. "There's a breeze coming up."

"No thanks."

"Maybe the truck will come."

"I don't give a damn about the truck."

"I do."

"You give a damn about so many things that I don't."

"Not so many, Harry."

"What about a drink?"

"It's supposed to be bad for you. It said in Black's to avoid all alcohol. You shouldn't drink."

"Molo!" he shouted.

"Yes Bwana."

"Bring whiskey-soda."

"Yes Bwana."

"You shouldn't," she said. "That's what I mean by giving up. It says it's bad for you. I know it's bad for you."

"No," he said. "It's good for me."

So now it was all over, he thought. So now he would never have a chance to finish it. So this was the way it ended in a bickering over a drink. Since the gangrene started in his right leg he had no pain and with the pain the horror had gone and all he felt now was a great tiredness and anger that this was the end of it. For this, that now was coming, he had very little curiosity. For years it had obsessed him; but now it meant nothing in itself. It was strange how easy being tired enough made it.

Now he would never write the things that he had saved to write until he knew enough to write them well. Well, he would not have to fail at trying to write them either. Maybe you could never write them, and that was why you put them off and delayed the starting. Well he would never know, now.

"I wish we'd never come," the woman said. She was looking at him holding the glass and biting her lip. "You never would have gotten anything like that in Paris. You always said you loved Paris. We could have stayed in Paris or gone anywhere. I'd have gone anywhere. I said I'd go anywhere you wanted. If you wanted to shoot we could have gone shooting in Hungary and been comfortable."

"Your bloody money," he said.

"That's not fair," she said. "It was always yours as much as mine. I left everything and I went wherever you wanted to go and I've done what you wanted to do. But I wish we'd never come here."

"You said you loved it."

"I did when you were all right. But now I hate it. I don't see why that had to happen to your leg. What have we done to have that happen to us?"

"I suppose what I did was to forget to put iodine on it when I first scratched it. Then I didn't pay any attention to it because I never infect. Then, later, when it got bad, it was probably using that weak carbolic solution when the other antiseptics ran out that paralyzed the minute blood vessels and started the gangrene." He looked at her, "What else?"

"I don't mean that."

"If we would have hired a good mechanic instead of a half baked kikuyu driver, he would have checked the oil and never burned out that bearing in the truck."

"I don't mean that."

"If you hadn't left your own people, your goddamned Old Westbury, Saratoga, Palm Beach people to take me on——"

"Why, I loved you. That's not fair. I love you now. I'll always love you. Don't you love me?"

"No," said the man. "I don't think so. I never have."

"Harry, what are you saying? You're out of your head."

"No. I haven't any head to go out of."

"Don't drink that," she said. "Darling, please don't drink that. We have to do everything we can."

"You do it," he said. "I'm tired."

Now in his mind he saw a railway station at Karagatch and he was standing with his pack and that was the headlight of the

Simplon-Orient cutting the dark now and he was leaving Thrace then after the retreat. That was one of the things he had saved to write, with, in the morning at breakfast, looking out the window and seeing snow on the mountains in Bulgaria and Nansen's Secretary asking the old man if it were snow and the old man looking at it and saying, No, that's not snow. It's too early for snow. And the Secretary repeating to the other girls, No, you see. It's not snow and them all saying, It's not snow we were mistaken. But it was the snow all right and he sent them on into it when he evolved exchange of populations. And it was snow they tramped along in until they died that winter.

It was snow too that fell all Christmas week that year up in the Gauertal, that year they lived in the woodcutter's house with the big square porcelain stove that filled half the room, and they slept on mattresses filled with beech leaves, the time the deserter came with his feet bloody in the snow. He said the police were right behind him and they gave him woolen socks and held the gendarmes talking until the tracks had drifted over.

In Schrunz, on Christmas day, the snow was so bright it hurt your eyes when you looked out from the weinstube and saw every one coming home from church. That was where they walked up the sleigh-smoothed urine-yellowed road along the river with the steep pine hills, skis heavy on the shoulder, and where they ran that great run down the glacier above the Madlener-haus, the snow as smooth to see as cake frosting and as light as powder and he remembered the noiseless rush the speed made as you dropped down like a bird.

They were snow-bound a week in the Madlener-haus that time in the blizzard playing cards in the smoke by the lantern light and the stakes were higher all the time as Herr Lent lost more. Finally he lost it all. Everything, the skischule money and all the season's profit and then his capital. He could see him with his long nose, picking up the cards and then opening, "Sans Voir." There was always gambling then. When there was no snow you gambled and when there was too much you gambled. He thought of all the time in his life he had spent gambling.

But he had never written a line of that, nor of that cold, bright Christmas day with the mountains showing across the plain that Barker had flown across the lines to bomb the Austrian officers' leave train, machine-gunning them as they scattered and ran. He remembered Barker afterwards coming into the mess and starting to tell about it. And how quiet it got and then somebody saying, "You bloody murderous bastard."

Those were the same Austrians they killed then that he skied with later. No not the same. Hans, that he skied with all that year, had been in the Kaiser-Jagers and when they went hunting hares together up the little valley above the saw-mill they had talked of the fighting on Pasubio and of the attack on Pertica and Asalone and he had never written a word of that. Nor of Monte Corno, nor the Siete Commum, nor of Arsiedo.

How many winters had he lived in the Voralberg and the Arlberg? It was four and then he remembered the man who had the fox to sell when they had walked into Bludenz, that time to buy presents, and the cherry-pit taste of good kirsch, the fast-slipping rush of running powder-snow on crust, singing "Hi! Ho! said Rolly!" as you ran down the last stretch to the steep drop, taking it straight, then running the orchard in three turns and out across the ditch and onto the icy road behind the inn. Knocking your bindings loose, kicking the skis free and leaning them up against the wooden wall of the inn, the lamplight coming from the window, where inside, in the smoky, new-wine smelling warmth, they were playing the accordion.

"Where did we stay in Paris?" he asked the woman who was sitting by him in a canvas chair, now, in Africa.

"At the Crillon. You know that."

"Why do I know that?"

"That's where we always stayed."

"No. Not always."

"There and at the Pavillion Henri-Quatre in St. Germain. You said you loved it there."

"Love is a dunghill," said Harry. "And I'm the cock that gets on it to crow."

"If you have to go away," she said, "is it absolutely necessary to kill off everything you leave behind? I mean do you have to take away everything? Do you have to kill your horse, and your wife and burn your saddle and your armour?"

"Yes," he said. "Your damned money was my armour. My Swift and my Armour."

"Don't."

"All right. I'll stop that. I don't want to hurt you."

"It's a little bit late now."

"All right then. I'll go on hurting you. It's more amusing. **The only thing I ever really liked to do with you I can't do now.**"

"No. That's not true. You liked to do many things and everything you wanted to do I did."

"Oh, for Christ sake stop bragging, will you?"

He looked at her and saw her crying.

"Listen," he said. "Do you think that it is fun to do this? I don't know why I'm doing it. It's trying to kill to keep yourself alive, I imagine. I was all right when we started talking. I don't mean to start this, and now I'm crazy as a coot and being as cruel to you as I can be. Don't pay any attention, darling, to what I say. I love you, really. You know I love you. I've never loved any one else the way I love you."

He slipped into the familiar lie he made his bread and butter by.

"You're sweet to me."

"You bitch," he said. "You rich bitch. That's poetry. I'm full of poetry now. Rot and poetry. Rotten poetry."

"Stop it, Harry, why do you have to turn into a devil now?"

"I don't like to leave anything," the man said. "I don't like to leave things behind."

It was evening now and he had been asleep. The sun was gone behind the hill and there was a shadow all across the plain and the small animals were feeding close to camp; quick dropping heads and switching tails, he watched them keeping well out away from the bush now. The birds no longer waited on the ground. They were all perched heavily in a tree. There were many more of them. His personal boy was sitting by the bed.

"Memsahib's gone to shoot," the boy said. "Does Bwana want?"

"Nothing."

She had gone to kill a piece of meat and, knowing how he liked to watch the game, she had gone well away so she would not disturb this little pocket of the plain that he could see. She was always thoughtful, he thought. On anything she knew about, or had read, or that she had ever heard.

It was not her fault that when he went to her he was already over. How could a woman know that you meant nothing that you said; that you spoke only from habit and to be comfortable? After he no longer meant what he said, his lies were more successful with women than when he had told them the truth.

It was not so much that he lied as that there was no truth to tell. He had had his life and it was over and then he went on living it again with different people and more money, with the best of the same places, and some new ones.

You kept from thinking and it was all marvellous. You were equipped with good insides so that you did not go to pieces that way, the way most of them had, and you made an attitude that you cared nothing for the work you used to do, now that you could no longer do it. But, in yourself, you said that you would write about these people; about the very rich; that you were really not of them but a spy in their country; that you would leave it and and write of it and for once it would be written by some one who knew what he was writing of. But he would never do it, because each day of not writing, of comfort, of being that which he despised, dulled his ability and softened his will to work so that, finally, he did no work at all. The people he knew now were all much more comfortable when he did not work. Africa was where he had been happiest in the good time of his life, so he had come out here to start again. They had made this safari with the minimum of comfort. There was no hardship; but there was no luxury and he had thought that he could get back into training that way. That in some way he could work the fat off his soul the way a fighter went into the mountains to work and train in order to burn it out of his body.

She had liked it. She said she loved it. She loved anything that was exciting, that involved a change of scene, where there were new people and where things were pleasant. And he had felt the illusion of returning strength of will to work. Now if this was how it ended, and he knew it was, he must not turn like some snake biting itself because its back was broken. It wasn't this woman's fault. If it had not been she it would have been another. If he lived by a lie he should try to die by it. He heard a shot beyond the hill.

She shot very well this good, this rich bitch, this kindly caretaker and destroyer of his talent. Nonsense. He had destroyed his talent himself. Why should he blame this woman because she kept him well? He had destroyed his talent by not using it, by betrayals of himself and what he believed in, by drinking so much that he blunted the edge of his perceptions, by laziness, by sloth, and by snobbery, by pride and by prejudice, by hook and by crook. What was this? A catalogue of old books? What was his talent anyway? It was a talent all right but instead of using it, he had traded on it. It was never what he had done, but always what he could do. And he had chosen to make his living with something else instead of a pen or a pencil. It was strange, too, wasn't it, that when he fell in love with another woman, that woman should always have more money than the last one? But when he no longer was in love, when he was only lying, as to this woman, now, who had the most money of all, who had all the money there was, who had had a husband and children, who had taken lovers and been dissatisfied with them, and who loved him dearly as a writer, as a man, as a companion and as a proud possession; it was strange that when he did not love her at all and was lying, that he should be able to give her more for her money than when he had really loved.

We must all be cut out for what we do, he thought. However you make your living is where your talent lies. He had sold vitality, in one form or another, all his life and when your affections are not too involved you give much better value for the money. He had found that out but he would never write that, now, either. No, he would not write that, although it was well worth writing.

Now she came in sight, walking across the open toward the camp. She was wearing jodhpurs and carrying her rifle. The two boys had a Tommy slung and they were coming along behind her. She was still a good-looking woman, he thought, and she had a pleasant body. She had a great talent and appreciation for the bed, she was not pretty, but he liked her face, she read enormously, liked to ride and shoot and, certainly, she drank too much. Her husband had died when she was still a comparatively young woman and for a while she had devoted herself to her two just-grown children, who did not need her and were embarrassed at having her about, to her stable of horses, to books, and to bottles. She liked to read in the evening before dinner and she drank Scotch and soda while she read. By dinner she was fairly drunk and after a bottle of wine at dinner she was usually drunk enough to sleep.

That was before the lovers. After she had the lovers she did not drink so much because she did not have to be drunk to sleep. But the lovers bored her. She had been married to a man who had never bored her and these people bored her very much.

Then one of her two children was killed in a plane crash and after that was over she did not want the lovers, and drink being no anæsthetic she had to make another life. Suddenly, she had been acutely frightened of being alone. But she wanted some one that she respected with her.

It had begun very simply. She liked what he wrote and she had always envied the life he led. She thought he did exactly what he wanted to. The steps by which she had acquired him and the way in which she had finally fallen in love with him were all part of a regular progression in which she had built herself a new life and he had traded away what remained of his old life.

He had traded it for security, for comfort too, there was no denying that, and for what else? He did not know. She would have bought him anything he wanted. He knew that. She was a damned nice woman too. He would as soon be in bed with her as any one; rather with her, because she was richer, because she was very pleasant and appreciative and because she never made scenes. And now this life that she had built again was coming to a term because he had not used iodine two weeks ago when a thorn had scratched his knee as they moved forward trying to photograph a herd of waterbuck standing, their heads up, peering while their nostrils searched the air, their ears spread wide to hear the first noise that would send them rushing into the bush. They had bolted, too, before he got the picture.

Here she came now.

He turned his head on the cot to look toward her. "Hello," he said.

"I shot a Tommy ram," she told him. "He'll make you good broth and I'll have them mash some potatoes with the Klim. How do you feel?"

"Much better."

"Isn't that lovely? You know I thought perhaps you would. You were sleeping when I left."

"I had a good sleep. Did you walk far?"

"No. Just around behind the hill. I made quite a good shot on the Tommy."

"You shoot marvellously, you know."

"I love it. I've loved Africa. Really. If *you're* all right it's the most fun that I've ever had. You don't know the fun it's been to shoot with you. I've loved the country."

"I love it too."

"Darling, you don't know how marvellous it is to see you feeling better. I couldn't stand it when you felt that way. You won't talk to me like that again, will you? Promise me?"

"No," he said. "I don't remember what I said."

"You don't have to destroy me. Do you? I'm only a middle-aged woman who loves you and wants to do what you want to do. I've been destroyed two or three times already. You wouldn't want to destroy me again, would you?"

"I'd like to destroy you a few times in bed," he said.

"Yes. That's the good destruction. That's the way we're made to be destroyed. The plane will be here tomorrow."

"How do you know?"

"I'm sure. It's bound to come. The boys have the wood all ready and the grass to make the smudge. I went down and looked at it again today. There's plenty of room to land and we have the smudges ready at both ends."

"What makes you think it will come tomorrow?"

"I'm sure it will. It's overdue now. Then, in town, they will fix up your leg and then we will have some good destruction. Not that dreadful talking kind."

"Should we have a drink? The sun is down."

"Do you think you should?"

"I'm having one."

"We'll have one together. *Molo, letti dui whiskey-soda!*" she called.

"You'd better put on your mosquito boots," he told her.

"I'll wait till I bathe . . ."

While it grew dark they drank and just before it was dark and there was no longer enough light to shoot, a hyena crossed the open on his way around the hill.

"That bastard crosses there every night," the man said. "Every night for two weeks."

"He's the one makes the noise at night. I don't mind it. They're a filthy animal though."

Drinking together, with no pain now except the discomfort of lying in one position, the boys lighting a fire, its shadow jumping on the tents, he could feel the return of acquiescence in this life of pleasant surrender. She *was* very good to him. He had been cruel and unjust in the afternoon. She was a fine woman, marvellous really. And just then it occurred to him that he was going to die.

It came with a rush; not as a rush of water nor of wind; out of a sudden evil-smelling emptiness and the odd thing was that the hyena slipped lightly along the edge of it.

"What is it, Harry?" she asked him.

"Nothing," he said. "You had better move over to the other side. To windward."

"Did Molo change the dressing?"

"Yes. I'm just using the boric now."

"How do you feel?"

"A little wobbly."

"I'm going in to bathe," she said. "I'll be right out. I'll eat with you and then we'll put the cot in."

So, he said to himself, we did well to stop the quarrelling. He had never quarrelled much with this woman, while with the women that he loved he had quarrelled so much they had finally, always, with the corrosion of the quarrelling, killed what they had together. He had loved too much, demanded too much, and he wore it all out.

He thought about alone in Constantinople that time, having quarrelled in Paris before he had gone out. He had whored the whole time and then, when that was over, and he had failed to kill his loneliness, but only made it worse, he had written her, the first one, the one who left him, a letter telling her how he had never been able to kill it. . . . How when he thought he saw her outside the Regence one time it made him go all faint and sick inside, and that he would follow a woman who looked like her in some way, along the Boulevard, afraid to see it was not she, afraid to lose the feeling it gave him. How every one he had slept with had only made him miss her more. How what she had done could never matter since he knew he could not cure himself of loving her. He wrote this letter at the Club, cold sober, and mailed it to New York asking her to write him at the office in Paris. That seemed safe. And that night missing her so much it made him feel hollow sick inside, he wandered up past Taxim's, picked a girl up and took her out to supper. He had gone to a place to dance with her afterward, she danced badly, and left her for a hot Armenian slut, that swung her belly against him so it almost scalded. He took her away from a British gunner subaltern after a row. The gunner asked him outside and they fought in the street on the cobbles in the dark. He'd hit him twice, hard, on the side of the jaw and when he didn't go down he knew he was in for a fight. The gunner hit him in the body, then beside his eye. He swung with his left again and landed and the gunner fell on him and grabbed his coat and tore the sleeve off and he clubbed him twice behind the ear and then smashed him with his right as he pushed away. When the gunner went down his head hit first and he ran with the girl because they heard the M. P.'s coming. They got into a taxi and drove out to Rimmily Hissa along the Bosphorus, and around, and back in the cool night and went to bed and she felt as over-ripe as she looked but smooth, rose-petal, syrupy, smooth-bellied, big-breasted and needed no pillow under her buttocks, and he left her before she was awake looking blousy enough in the first daylight and turned up at the Pera Palace with a black eye, carrying his coat because one sleeve was missing.

That same night he left for Anatolia and he remembered, later on that trip, riding all day through fields of the poppies that they raised for opium and how strange it made you feel, finally, and all

*the distances seemed wrong, to where they had made the attack
with the newly arrived Constantine officers, that did not know a
god-damned thing, and the artillery had fired into the troops and
the British observer had cried like a child.*

*That was the day he'd first seen dead men wearing white ballet
skirts and upturned shoes with pompoms on them. The Turks had
come steadily and lumpily and he had seen the skirted men running
and the officers shooting into them and running then themselves and
he and the British observer had run too until his lungs ached and
his mouth was full of the taste of pennies and they stopped behind
some rocks and there were the Turks coming as lumpily as ever.
Later he had seen the things that he could never think of and later
still he had seen much worse. So when he got back to Paris that time
he could not talk about it or stand to have it mentioned. And there
in the cafe as he passed was that American poet with a pile of
saucers in front of him and a stupid look on his potato face talking
about the Dada movement with a Roumanian who said his name
was Tristan Tzara, who always wore a monocle and had a headache, and, back at the apartment with his wife that now he loved
again, the quarrel all over, the madness all over, glad to be home,
the office sent his mail up to the flat. So then the letter in answer
to the one he'd written came in on a platter one morning and when
he saw the handwriting he went cold all over and tried to slip the
letter underneath another. But his wife said, "Who is that letter
from, dear?" and that was the end of the beginning of that.*

*He remembered the good times with them all, and the quarrels.
They always picked the finest places to have the quarrels. And why
had they always quarrelled when he was feeling best? He had never
written any of that because, at first, he never wanted to hurt any
one and then it seemed as though there was enough to write without
it. But he had always thought that he would write it finally. There
was so much to write. He had seen the world change; not just the
events; although he had seen many of them and had watched the
people, but he had seen the subtler change and he could remember
how the people were at different times. He had been in it and he
had watched it and it was his duty to write of it; but now he never
would.*

"How do you feel?" she said. She had come out from the tent
now after her bath.

"All right."

"Could you eat now?" He saw Molo behind her with the folding table and the other boy with the dishes.

"I want to write," he said.

"You ought to take some broth to keep your strength up."

"I'm going to die tonight," he said. "I don't need my strength up."

"Don't be melodramatic, Harry, please," she said.

"Why don't you use your nose? I'm rotted half way up my thigh now. What the hell should I fool with broth for? Molo bring whiskey-soda."

"Please take the broth," she said gently.

"All right."

The broth was too hot. He had to hold it in the cup until it cooled enough to take it and then he just got it down without gagging.

"You're a fine woman," he said. "Don't pay any attention to me."

She looked at him with her well-known, well-loved face from *Spur* and *Town and Country,* only a little the worse for drink, only a little the worse for bed, but *Town and Country* never showed those good breasts and those useful thighs and those lightly small-of-back-caressing hands, and as he looked and saw her well-known pleasant smile, he felt death come again. This time there was no rush. It was a puff, as of a wind that makes a candle flicker and the flame go tall.

"They can bring my net out later and hang it from the tree and build the fire up. I'm not going in the tent tonight. It's not worth moving. It's a clear night. There won't be any rain."

So this was how you died, in whispers that you did not hear. Well, there would be no more quarrelling. He could promise that. The one experience that he had never had he was not going to spoil now. He probably would. You spoiled everything. But perhaps he wouldn't.

"You can't take dictation, can you?"

"I never learned," she told him.

"That's all right."

There wasn't time, of course, although it seemed as though it telescoped so that you might put it all into one paragraph if you could get it right.

There was a log house, chinked white with mortar, on a hill above the lake. There was a bell on a pole by the door to call the

*people in to meals. Behind the house were fields and behind the
fields was the timber. A line of lombardy poplars ran from the
house to the dock. Other poplars ran along the point. A road went
up to the hills along the edge of the timber and along that road he
picked blackberries. Then that log house was burned down and all
the guns that had been on deer foot racks above the open fire place
were burned and afterwards their barrels, with the lead melted in
the magazines, and the stocks burned away, lay out on the heap of
ashes that were used to make lye for the big iron soap kettles, and
you asked Grandfather if you could have them to play with, and
he said, no. You see they were his guns still and he never bought
any others. Nor did he hunt any more. The house was rebuilt in
the same place out of lumber now and painted white and from it
porch you saw the poplars and the lake beyond; but there were
never any more guns. The barrels of the guns that had hung on the
deer feet on the wall of the log house lay out there on the heap of
ashes and no one ever touched them.*

*In the Black Forest, after the war, we rented a trout stream and
there were two ways to walk to it. One was down the valley from
Triberg and around the valley road in the shade of the trees that
bordered the white road, and then up a side road that went up
through the hills past many small farms, with the big Schwarzwald
houses, until that road crossed the stream. That was where our
fishing began.*

*The other way was to climb steeply up to the edge of the woods
and then go across the top of the hills through the pine woods, and
then out to the edge of a meadow and down across this meadow to
the bridge. There were birches along the stream and it was not big,
but narrow, clear and fast, with pools where it had cut under the
roots of the birches. At the Hotel in Triberg the proprietor had a
fine season. It was very pleasant and we were all great friends. The
next year came the inflation and the money he had made the year
before was not enough to buy supplies to open the hotel and he
hanged himself.*

*You could dictate that, but you could not dictate the Place Con-
trescarpe where the flower sellers dyed their flowers in the street
and the dye ran over the paving where the autobus started and the
old men and the women, always drunk on wine and bad marc; and
the children with their noses running in the cold; the smell of dirty
sweat and poverty and drunkenness at the Cafe des Amateurs and
the whores at the Bal Musette they lived above. The Concièrge who
entertained the trooper of the Garde Républicaine in her loge, his*

horse-hair-plumed helmet on a chair. The locataire across the hall who husband was a bicycle racer and her joy that morning at the Crémerie when she had opened L'Auto and seen where he placed third in Paris-Tours, his first big race. She had blushed and laughed and then gone upstairs crying with the yellow sporting paper in her hand. The husband of the woman who ran the Bal Musette drove a taxi and when he, Harry, had to take an early plane the husband knocked upon the door to wake him and they each drank a glass of white wine at the zinc of the bar before they started. He knew his neighbors in that quarter then because they all were poor.

Around that Place there were two kinds: the drunkards and the sportifs. The drunkards killed their poverty that way; the sportifs took it out in exercise. They were the descendants of the Communards and it was no struggle for them to know their politics. They knew who had shot their fathers, their relatives, their brothers, and their friends when the Versailles troops came in and took the town after the Commune and executed any one they could catch with calloused hands, or who wore a cap, or carried any other sign he was a working man. And in that poverty, and in that quarter across the street from a Boucherie Chevaline and a wine co-operative he had written the start of all he was to do. There never was another part of Paris that he loved like that, the sprawling trees, the old white plastered houses painted brown below, the long green of the autobus in that round square, the purple flower dye upon the paving, the sudden drop down the hill of the rue Cardinal Lemoine to the River, and the other way the narrow crowded world of the rue Mouffletard. The street that ran up toward the Panthèon and the other that he always took with the bicycle, the only asphalted street in all that quarter, smooth under the tires, with the high narrow houses and the cheap tall hotel where Paul Verlaine had died. There were only two rooms in the apartments where they lived and he had a room on the top floor of that hotel that cost him sixty francs a month where he did his writing, and from it he could see the roofs and chimney pots and all the hills of Paris.

From the apartment you could only see the wood and coal man's place. He sold wine too, bad wine. The golden horse's head outside the Boucherie Chevaline where the carcasses hung yellow gold and red in the open window, and the green painted co-operative where they bought their wine, good wine and cheap. The rest was plaster walls and the windows of the neighbors. The neighbors who, at night when some one lay drunk in the street, moaning and groaning *in that typical French* ivresse* *that you were propaganded to believe did not exist, would open their windows and then the murmur of talk.*

"Where is the policeman? When you don't want him the bugger is always there. He's sleeping with some concierge. Get the Agent." Till some one threw a bucket of water from a window and the moaning stopped. "What's that? Water. Ah, that's intelligent." And the windows shutting. Marie, his femme de mènage, protesting against the eight-hour day saying, "If a husband works until six he gets only a little drunk on the way home and does not waste too much. If he works only until five he is drunk every night and one has no money. It is the wife of the working man who suffers from this shortening of hours."

"Wouldn't you like some more broth?" the woman asked him now.

"No, thank you very much. It is awfully good."

"Try just a little."

"I would like a whiskey-soda.".

"It's not good for you."

"No. It's bad for me. Cole Porter wrote the words and the music. This knowledge that you're going mad for me."

"You know I like you to drink."

"Oh yes. Only it's bad for me."

When she goes, he thought, I'll have all I want. Not all I want but all there is. Ayee he was tired. Too tired. He was going to sleep a little while. He lay still and death was not there. It must have gone around another street. It went in pairs, on bicycles, and moved absolutely silently on the pavements.

No, he had never written about Paris. Not the Paris that he cared about. But what about the rest that he had never written?

What about the ranch and the silvered gray of the sage brush, the quick, clear water in the irrigation ditches, and the heavy green of the alfalfa. The trail went up into the hills and the cattle in the summer were shy as deer. The bawling and the steady noise and slow moving mass raising a dust as you brought them down in the fall. And behind the mountains, the clear sharpness of the peak in the evening light and, riding down along the trail in the moonlight, bright across the valley. Now he remembered coming down through

* *Drunkenness.*

*the timber in the dark holding the horse's tail when you could not
see and all the stories that he meant to write.*

*About the half-wit chore boy who was left at the ranch that time
and told not to let any one get any hay, and that old bastard from
the Forks who had beaten the boy when he had worked for him
stopping to get some feed. The boy refusing and the old man saying
he would beat him again. The boy got the rifle from the kitchen and
shot him when he tried to come into the barn and when they came
back to the ranch he'd been dead a week, frozen in the corral, and
the dogs had eaten part of him. But what was left you packed on a
sled wrapped in a blanket and roped on and you got the boy to help
you haul it, and the two of you took it out over the road on skis,
and sixty miles down to town to turn the boy over. He having no
idea that he would be arrested. Thinking he had done his duty and
that you were his friend and he would be rewarded. He'd helped to
haul the old man in so everybody could know how bad the old man
had been and how he'd tried to steal some feed that didn't belong
to him, and when the sheriff put the handcuffs on the boy he
couldn't believe it. Then he'd started to cry. That was one story he
had saved to write. He knew at least twenty good stories from out
there and he had never written one. Why?*

"You tell them why," he said.

"Why what, dear?"

"Why nothing."

She didn't drink so much, now, since she had him. But if he lived
he would never write about her, he knew that now. Nor about any
of them. The rich were dull and they drank too much, or they
played too much backgammon. They were dull and they were repe-
titious. He remembered poor Julian and his romantic awe of them
and how he had started a story once that began, "The very rich are
different from you and me." And how some one had said to Julian,
Yes, they have more money. But that was not humorous to Julian.
He thought they were a special glamorous race and when he found
they weren't it wrecked him just as much as any other thing that
wrecked him.

He had been contemptuous of those who wrecked. You did not
have to like it because you understood it. He could beat anything,
he thought, because no thing could hurt him if he did not care.

All right. Now he would not care for death. One thing he had
always dreaded was the pain. He could stand pain as well as any
man, until it went on too long, and wore him out, but here he had

something that had hurt frightfully and just when he had felt it breaking him, the pain had stopped.

He remembered long ago when Williamson, the bombing officer, had been hit by a stick bomb some one in a German patrol had thrown as he was coming in through the wire that night and, screaming, had begged every one to kill him. He was a fat man, very brave, and a good officer, although addicted to fantastic shows. But that night he was caught in the wire, with a flare lighting him up and his bowels spilled out into the wire, so when they brought him in alive, they had to cut him loose. Shoot me, Harry. For Christ sake shoot me. They had had an argument one time about our Lord never sending you anything you could not bear and some one's theory had been that meant that at a certain time the pain passed you out automatically. But he had always remembered Williamson, that night. Nothing passed out Williamson until he gave him all his morphine tablets that he had always saved to use himself and then they did not work right away.

Still this now, that he had, was very easy; and if it was no worse as it went on there was nothing to worry about. Except that he would rather be in better company.

He thought a little about the company that he would like to have.

No, he thought, when everything you do, you do too long, and do too late, you can't expect to find the people still there. The people are all gone. The party's over and you are with your hostess now.

"It's a bore," he said out loud.

"What is, my dear?"

"Anything you do too bloody long."

He looked at her face between him and the fire. She was leaning back in the chair and the firelight shone on her pleasantly lined face and he could see that she was sleepy. He heard the hyena make a noise just outside the range of the fire.

"I've been writing," he said. "But I got tired."

"Do you think you will be able to sleep?"

"Pretty sure. Why don't you turn in?"

"I like to sit here with you."

"Do you feel anything strange?" he asked her.

"No. Just a little sleepy."

"I do," he said.

He had just felt death come by again.

"You know the only thing I've ever lost is curiosity," he said to her.

"You've never lost anything. You're the most complete man I've ever known."

"Christ," he said. "How little a woman knows. What is that? Your intuition?"

Because, just then, death had come and rested its head on the foot of the cot and he could smell its breath.

"Never believe any of that about a scythe and a skull," he told her. "It can be two bicycle policemen as easily, or be a bird. Or it can have a wide snout like a hyena."

It had moved up on him now, but it had no shape any more. It simply occupied space.

"Tell it to go away."

It did not go away but moved a little closer.

"You've got a hell of a breath," he told it. "You stinking bastard."

It moved up closer to him still and now he could not speak to it, and when it saw he could not speak it came a little closer, and now he tried to send it away without speaking, but it moved in on him so its weight was all upon his chest, and while it crouched there and he could not move, or speak, he heard the woman say, "Bwana is asleep now. Take the cot up very gently and carry it into the tent."

He could not speak to tell her to make it go away and it crouched now, heavier, so he could not breathe. And then, while they lifted the cot, suddenly it was all right and the weight went from his chest.

It was morning and had been morning for some time and he heard the plane. It showed very tiny and then made a wide circle and the boys ran out and lit the fires, using kerosene, and piled on grass so there were two big smudges at each end of the level place and the morning breeze blew them toward the camp and the plane circled twice more, low this time, and then glided down and levelled off and landed smoothly and, coming walking toward him, was old Compton in slacks, a tweed jacket and a brown felt hat.

"What's the matter, old cock?" Compton said.

"Bad leg," he told him. "Will you have some breakfast?"

"Thanks. I'll just have some tea. It's the Puss Moth you know. I wont be able to take the Memsahib. There's only room for one. Your lorry is on the way."

Helen had taken Compton aside and was speaking to him. Compton came back more cheery than ever.

"We'll get you right in," he said. "I'll be back for the Mem. Now I'm afraid I'll have to stop at Arusha to refuel. We'd better get going."

"What about the tea?"

"I don't really care about it you know."

The boys had picked up the cot and carried it around the green tents and down along the rock and out onto the plain and along past the smudges that were burning brightly now, the grass all consumed, and the wind fanning the fire, to the little plane. It was difficult getting him in, but once in he lay back in the leather seat, and the leg was stuck straight out to one side of the seat, where Compton sat. Compton started the motor and got in. He waved to Helen and to the boys and, as the clatter moved into the old familiar roar, they swung around with Compie watching for warthog holes and roared, bumping, along the stretch between the fires and with the last bump rose and he saw them all standing below, waving, and the camp beside the hill, flattening now, and the plain spreading, clumps of trees, and the bush flattening, while the game trails ran now smoothly to the dry waterholes, and there was a new water that he had never known of. The zebra, small rounded backs now, and the wildebeeste, big-headed dots seeming to climb as they moved in long fingers across the plain, now scattering as the shadow came toward them, they were tiny now, and the movement had no gallop, and the plain was as far as you could see, gray-yellow now and ahead old Compie's tweed back and the brown felt hat. Then they were over the first hills and the wildebeeste were trailing up them, and then they were over mountains with sudden depths of green-rising forest and the solid bamboo slopes, and then the heavy forest again, sculptured into peaks and hollows until they crossed, and hills sloped down and then another plain, hot now, and purple brown, bumpy with heat and Compie looking back to see how he was riding. Then there were other mountains dark ahead.

And then instead of going on to Arusha they turned left, he evidently figured that they had the gas, and looking down he saw a pink sifting cloud, moving over the ground, and in the air, like the the first snow in a blizzard, that comes from nowhere, and he knew the locusts were coming up from the South. Then they began to climb and they were going to the East it seemed, and then it darkened and they were in a storm, the rain so thick it seemed like flying through a waterfall, and then they were out and Compie turned his head and grinned and pointed and there, ahead, all he could see, as wide as all the world, great, high, unbelievably white in the sun, was the square top of Kilimanjaro. And then he knew that there was where he was going.

Just then the hyena stopped whimpering in the night and started to make a strange, human, almost crying sound. The woman heard it and stirred uneasily. She did not wake. In her dream she was at the house on Long Island and it was the night before her daughter's debut. Somehow her father was there and he had been very rude. Then the noise the hyena made was so loud she woke and for a moment she did not know where she was and she was very afraid. Then she took the flashlight and shone it on the other cot that they had carried in after Harry had gone to sleep. She could see his bulk under the mosquito bar but somehow he had gotten his leg out and it hung down alongside the cot. The dressings had all come down and she could not look at it.

"Molo," she called, "Molo! Molo!"

Then she said, "Harry, Harry!" Then her voice rising, "Harry! Please, Oh Harry!"

There was no answer and she could not hear him breathing.

Outside the tent the hyena made the same strange noise that had awakened her. But she did not hear him for the beating of her heart.

SINCLAIR LEWIS

****

THORVALE FARM
WILLIAMSTOWN, MASS.

DEAR WHIT:

Naturally, I'm pleased to be included with the lambs. I think the selection that would best represent me would be from the beginning of Cass Timberlane *to the bottom of page 17, because it establishes fairly completely an American city and a serious American citizen . . . or instead of Chapter One in* Cass, *use Trock, Virga-Allan, and Claywheels. I think the best order would be Virga (1), Claywheels (2), Trock (3), but arrange 'em as you like.*

Ever,

RED

****

An Assemblage of Husbands and Wives

VIRGA VAY & ALLAN CEDAR

ORLO VAY, the Chippewa Avenue Optician, Smart-Art Harlequin Tinted-Tortus Frames Our Specialty, was a public figure, as public as a cemetery. He was resentful that his profession, like that of an undertaker, a professor of art, or a Mormon missionary, was not appreciated for its patience and technical skill, as are the callings of wholesale grocer or mistress or radio-sports-commentator, and he tried to make up for the professional injustice by developing his personal glamor.

He wanted to Belong. He was a speaker. He was hearty and public about the local baseball and hockey teams, about the Kiwanis Club, about the Mayflower Congregational Church, and about all war drives. At forty-five he was bald, but the nobly glistening egg of his face and forehead, whose arc was broken only by a pair of Vay Li-Hi Bifocals, was an adornment to all fund-raising rallies.

38

He urged his wife, Virga, to co-operate in his spiritual efforts, but she was a small, scared, romantic woman, ten years his junior; an admirer of passion in technicolor, a clipper-out of newspaper lyrics about love and autumn smoke upon the hills. He vainly explained to her, "In these modern days, a woman can't fritter away her time daydreaming. She has to push her own weight, and not hide it under a bushel."

Her solace was in her lover, Dr. Allan Cedar, the dentist. Together, Virga and Allan would have been a most gentle pair, small, clinging, and credulous. But they could never be openly together. They were afraid of Mr. Vay and of Allan's fat and vicious wife, Bertha, and they met at soda counters in outlying drug stores and lovingly drank black-and-whites together or Jumbo Malteds and, giggling, ate ferocious banana splits; or, till wartime gasoline-rationing prevented, they sped out in Allan's coupe by twilight, and made shy, eager love in mossy pastures or, by the weak dashlight of the car, read aloud surprisingly good recent poets: Wallace Stevens, Sandburg, Robert Frost, Jeffers, T. S. Eliot, Lindsay.

Allan was one of the best actors in the Masquers, and though Virga could not act, she made costumes and hung about at rehearsals, and thus they were able to meet, and to stir the suspicions of Bertha Cedar.

Mrs. Cedar was a rare type of the vicious woman; she really hated her husband, though she did not so much scold him as mock him for his effeminate love of acting, for his verses, for his cherubic mustache, and even for his skill with golden bridgework. She jeered, in the soap-reeking presence of her seven sisters and sisters-in-law, all chewing gum and adjusting their plates, that as a lover "Ally" had no staying-powers. That's what *she* thought.

She said to her mother, "Ally is a bum dentist; he hasn't got a single rich patient," and when they were at an evening party, she communicated to the festal guests, "Ally can't even pick out a necktie without asking my help," and on everything her husband said she commented, "Oh, don't be silly!"

She demanded, and received, large sympathy from all the females she knew, and as he was fond of golf and backgammon, she refused to learn either of them.

Whenever she had irritated him into jumpiness, she said judiciously, "You seem to be in a very nervous state." She picked at him about his crossword puzzles, about his stamp-collection, until he screamed, invariably, "Oh, let me *alone*!" and then she was able to say smugly, "I don't know what's the matter with you, so touchy about every little thing. You better go to a mind-doctor and have your head examined."

Then Bertha quite unexpectedly inherited seven thousand dollars and a house in San Jose, California, from a horrible aunt. She did not suggest to her husband but told him that they would move out to that paradise for chilled Minnesotans, and he would practise there.

It occurred to Allan to murder her, but not to refuse to go along. Many American males confuse their wives and the policeman on the beat.

But he knew that it would be death for him to leave Virga Vay, and that afternoon, when Virga slipped into his office at three o'clock in response to his code telephone call of "This is the Superba Market and we're sending you three bunches of asparagus," she begged, "Couldn't we elope some place together? Maybe we could get a little farm."

"She'd find us. She has a cousin who's a private detective in Duluth."

"Yes, I guess she would. Can't we *ever* be together always?"

"There is one way—if you wouldn't be afraid."

He explained the way.

"No, I wouldn't be afraid, if you stayed right with me," she said.

Dr. Allan Cedar was an excellent amateur machinist. On a Sunday afternoon when Bertha was visiting her mother, he cut a hole through the steel bottom of the luggage compartment of his small dark-gray coupé. This compartment opened into the body of the car. That same day he stole the hose of their vacuum-cleaner and concealed it up on the rafters of their galvanized-iron garage.

On Tuesday—this was in February—he bought a blue ready-made suit at Goldenkron Brothers', on Ignatius Street. He was easy to fit, and no alterations were needed. They wanted to deliver the suit that afternoon, but he insisted, "No, hold it here for me and I'll come in and put it on tomorrow morning. I want to surprise somebody."

"Your Missus will love it, Doc," said Monty Goldenkron.

"I hope she will—when she sees it!"

He also bought three white-linen shirts and a red bow-tie, and paid cash for the lot.

"Your credit is good here, Doc—none better," protested Monty.

Allan puzzled him by the triumphant way in which he answered, "I want to keep it good, just now!"

From Goldenkrons' he walked perkily to the Emporium, to the Golden Rule drug store, to the Co-operative Dairy, paying his bills in full at each. On his way he saw a distinguished fellow-townsman, Judge Timberlane, and his pretty wife. Allan had never said ten words to either of them, but he thought affectionately, "There's a couple who are intelligent enough and warm-hearted enough to know what love is worth."

That evening he said blandly to his wife, "Strangest thing happened today. The University school of dentistry telephoned me."

"Long distance?"

"Surely."

"Well!" Her tone was less of disbelief than of disgust.

"They're having a special brush-up session for dentists and they want me to come down to Minneapolis first thing tomorrow morning to stay for three days and give instruction in bridge-work. And of course you must come along. It's too bad I'll have to work from nine in the morning till midnight—they do rush those special courses so—but you can go to the movies by yourself, or just sit comfortably in the hotel."

"No—thank—*you*!" said Bertha. "I prefer to sit here at home. Why you couldn't have been an M.D. doctor and take out gall-bladders and make some real money! And I'll thank you to be home not later than Sunday morning. You know we have Sunday dinner with Mother."

He knew.

"I hope that long before that I'll be home," he said.

He told her that he would be staying at the Flora Hotel, in Minneapolis. But on Wednesday morning, after putting on the new suit at Goldenkrons', he drove to St. Paul, through light snowflakes which he thought of as fairies. "But I haven't a bit of real poet in me. Just second-rate and banal," he sighed. He tried to make a poem, and got no farther than:

> *It is snowing,*
> *The wind is blowing,*
> *But I am happy to be going.*

In St. Paul he went to the small, clean Hotel Orkness, registered as "Mr. A. M. Romeo & wife," asked for a room with a double bed, and explained to the clerk, "My wife is coming by train. She should be here in about seventeen minutes now, I figure it."

He went unenthusiastically to the palsied elevator, up to their room. It was tidy, and on the wall was an Adolph Dehn lithograph instead of the fake English-hunting-print that he had dreaded. He kneaded the bed with his fist. He was pleased.

Virga Vay arrived nineteen minutes later, with a bellboy carrying her new imitation-leather bag.

"So you're here, husband. Not a bad room," she said indifferently.

The bellboy knew from her indifference and from her calling the man "husband" that she was not married to him, but unstintingly in love. Such paradoxes are so common in his subterranean business that he had forgotten about Virga by the time he reached his bench in the lobby. Six stories above him, Virga and Allan were lost and blind and quivering in their kiss.

Presently she said, "Oh, you have a new suit! Turn around. Why, it fits beautifully! And such a nice red tie. You do look so young and cute in a bow-tie. Did you get it for me?"

"Of course. And then—I kind of hate to speak of it now, but I want us to get so used to the idea that we can just forget it—I don't want us to look frowsy when they find us. As if we hadn't been happy. And we *will be*——we are!"

"Yes."

"You're still game for it?"

"With you? For anything."

He was taking off the new suit; she was tenderly lifting from her bag a nightgown which she had made and embroidered this past week.

They had all their meals in the room; they did not leave it till afternoon of the next day. The air became a little close, thick from perfume and cigarette smoke and the bubble baths they took together.

Late the next afternoon they dressed and packed their bags, completely. He laid on the bureau two ten-dollar bills. They left the luggage at the foot of their bed, which she had made up. She took nothing from the room, and he nothing except a paper bag containing a bottle of Bourbon whisky, with the cork loosened, and a pocket anthology of new poetry. At the door she looked back, and said to him, "I shall remember this dear room as long as we live."

"Yes. . . . As long as we live."

He took his dark-gray coupé out of the hotel garage, tipping an amazed attendant one dollar, and they drove to Indian Mounds Park, overlooking the erratic Mississippi. He stopped in the park, at dusk, and said, "Think of the Indians that came along here, and Pike and Lewis Cass!"

"They were brave," she mused.

"Brave, *too!*" They nervously laughed. Indeed, after a moment of solemnity when they had left the hotel, they had been constantly gay, laughing at everything, even when she sneezed and he piped, "No more worry about catching pneumonia!"

He drove into a small street near by and parked the car, distant from any house. Working in the half-darkness, leaving the engine running, he pushed the vacuum-cleaner hose through the hole in the bottom of the luggage compartment, wired it to the exhaust pipe, and hastily got back into the car. The windows were closed. Already the air in the car was sick-sweet with carbon monoxide.

He slipped the whisky bottle out of the paper bag and tenderly urged, "Take a swig of this. Keep your courage up."

"Dearest, I don't need anything to keep it up."

"I do, by golly. I'm not a big he-man like you, Virg!"

They both laughed, and drank from the bottle, and kissed lingeringly.

"I wonder if I could smoke a cigarette. I don't *think* C_2O_2 is explosive," he speculated.

"Oh, sweet, be careful! It *might* explode!"

"Yes, it—" Then he shouted. "Listen at us! As if we cared if got blown up now!"

"Oh, I am too brainless, Allan! I don't know if you'll be able to stand me much longer."

"As long as we live, my darling, my very dear, oh, my dear love!"

"As long as we live. Together now. Together."

His head aching, his throat sore, he forgot to light the cigarette. He switched on the tiny dashlight, he lifted up the book as though it were a bar of lead, and from Conrad Aiken's "Sea Holly" he began to read to her:

> *It was for this*
> *Barren beauty, barrenness of rock that aches*
> *On the seaward path, seeing the fruitful sea,*
> *Hearing the lark of rock that sings ——*

He was too drowsy to read more than just the ending:

> *Stone pain in the stony heart,*
> *The rock loved and labored; and all is lost.*

The book fell to the seat, his head dropped, and his arm groped drowsily about her. She rested contentedly, in vast dreams, her head secure upon his shoulder.

Harsh screaming snatched them back from paradise. The car windows were smashed, someone was dragging them out . . . and Bertha was slapping Virga's face, while Bertha's cousin, the detective, was beating Allan's shoulders with a blackjack, to bring him to. In doing so, he broke Allan's jaw.

Bertha drove him back to Grand Republic and nursed him while he was in bed, jeering to the harpies whom she had invited in. "Ally tried to—you know—with a woman, but he was no good, and he was so ashamed he tried to kill himself."

He kept muttering, "Please go away and don't torture me."

She laughed.

Later, Bertha was able to intercept every one of the letters that Virga sent to him from Des Moines, where she had gone to work in a five-and-ten-cent store after Orlo had virtuously divorced her.

"Love! Ally is learning what that kind of mush gets you," Bertha explained to her attentive women friends.

PERRY & BERNICE CLAYWHEEL

PERRY CLAYWHEEL, superintendent of schools of Grand Republic and president of its small Junior College, was an enterprising and liberal educator. He fought to have the meager salaries of his teachers increased, and every summer he read several books.

He admired and even liked his lily-pale consort, Bernice, but he was almost impotent to make love to her, and they had no children.

Bernice, that prim wanton, was no nymphomaniac. She said, extraordinarily often, "I think All Those Things are too much discussed." But she did have a normal longing for passion, and she went shyly tripping to Dr. Drover.

"I'm sure you'll believe me, Doctor, when I tell you that I entirely disapprove of immorality, and still more of showing bad taste. But what can I do? My husband leaves me so dissatisfied that sometimes I can't think of anything else, and I'm afraid I'll go crazy. What do you advise?"

"Why don't you try to do your job right and get him interested? You probably scare him off."

"You mean the arts of love?"

"Huh? Yuh, I guess you could call it that."

"To me, Doctor, that would be sordid, and unmodern, like a slave-woman. I must have romance—all the beauty that the movies make an effort to show. I deserve it! And if Perry can't give it to me —— It isn't that I want an 'affair,' but if I don't have one, I'm afraid I'll go crazy. I feel so nervous. But if I, uh, go with a man of my own social class, I'm afraid it will get out, and honestly, I wouldn't want to jeopardize my husband's important position. And if I picked up some common person, I'd be terrified of blackmail. Tell me, Doctor—I'm dreadfully ashamed to even ask this, but are there—uh—places where women can go, as there are places where men go?"

"No! Besides, I don't know what you're talking about. That's a problem you'll have to work out by yourself," snapped the virtuous Dr. Drover.

Both Bernice and Dr. Drover regarded themselves as persons who had learned the facts of life.

When she was in this wretched way of feeling, she took some papers for her husband to Bradd Criley. It was late in the afternoon, a rainy October afternoon, and Mr. Criley's stenographer had gone. He remembered, with surprise, that just then he had no affair on whatever, except for an interest in Jinny Timberlane which that fractious girl had never permitted to go beyond flirtation. He looked at Bernice and thought how lovely she was, shining in the putrescent autumn light. He led her to the leather couch and kissed her.

Even with his professional experience, he was surpised by the way in which she instantly went to pieces. She cried "Oh!" and almost smothered him with her reaching arms, and seemed about to eat him up. "Is she hot!" he thought.

They met half a dozen times in a month, and he told himself— indeed, he rather hinted to his friend Dr. Drover—that he was a public benefactor. Bernice asked him whether they were "really doing the right thing," and he assured her—at first—that it was "necessary for her health."

What began to bore him, what made him cut the affair off even more quickly than usual, was the fact that Bernice kept moaning, "Oh, lover, we oughtn't to be doing this to Perry."

"Where do you get that 'we'?" he protested, first to himself but presently to her, and she wept enough, she acted badly enough, so that he was able to break it off with quite a show of indignation.

Now Perry Claywheel had been convincing himself that he was becoming a better lover, recently. There was a teacher, not too young, who thought fairly well of him—not that they did anything really wrong, you understand.

On the night after Bernice's first visit to Bradd, Perry had turned to her, in their golden-oak double bed, with a slight quiver of rapture, but she had said sharply, "Oh, not tonight. Anyway, it's not good for you."

He protested that it *was* good for him, and that he longed for her, and as she continued to refuse him, with more and more resentment, as though he were a preposterous stranger, he could think of nothing but his desire to be with her. He trembled with conceptive agony that, in his humiliation, was not uncolored with madness.

He did not try to persuade her again. However he might long for her imaginatively, in her presence he became powerless. He had a shameful feeling that he was not quite a man, that his failure was incurable.

He was afraid of her, though he still wanted her to think of him as a possible lover for some time in the future, when she should have got over this curious triumphant mood of hers, which he could not understand. Looking about Grand Republic, he suspected that many husbands were afraid of their wives, quiveringly trying to placate those small tyrants. He wondered if there was any country save America in which a large share of the men were frightened continuously by their own wives.

With all this, he became irritable at school, snapping at the teachers, accusing the pupils, and he no longer enjoyed the intellectual card-cataloging and small prides of his job. He just did not enjoy anything, not even the sight of Bernice and her beauty, for she was suddenly changing, and becoming drab and hesitant, uninteresting even to the young men who delivered groceries and with whom she had once laughed in the kitchen.

When Bernice finally hinted to him that she was willing to return to his embraces, he said bleakly that he had no longer any desire. But he never knew what he owed to Bradd Criley, a man well spoken of for his geniality.

NORTON TROCK

IN SO VAST a city as Grand Republic, with so ancient a history—going clearly back 20,000 years to the first known traces of Indian occupation—there were too many varieties of marriage even to index. Stuart Vogel, the county agricultural agent, and his wife, a skillful high-school teacher, deserve a whole treatise. They met at night, courteous and cheerful, to share in cooking the dinner, in reading plays for the next Masquers production.

They had one sort of "modern marriage," and Norton and Isabel Trock another, also modern.

Before her death, ten years ago, the elder Mrs. Trock often said to the other ladies in hotel lounges with tapestries that she had proved it was all nonsense, this offensive contemporary notion that

it was bad for an only son to have a widow mother hovering over
him. Look at her boy Norton, that neat and handsome young
banker. He had been frail, as a boy, and had shown the sweetest
old-fashioned manners, like a little prince, and so neat about hanging up his clothes, yet look at him now: he was a fine swimmer, a
splendid boxer, a correct duck-shot—and all the girls were crazy
about him.

Then she died.

After her death, it was obvious to her older friends that she had
been right. At forty-eight, Norton was president of the Blue Ox
National Bank, in which Mr. Boone Havock was chief stockholder.
He had two bonny children, and his wife, Isabel, though not too
bright and not especially pretty, had the same daintiness as Norton's
mother.

He had always, since the age of three, called his mother "Sweetheart," so that it had become her pet name among the choice little
set of the more fastidious matrons of Grand Republic, who embroidered altar cloths and explained that they were of pure English
descent.

Sweetheart's husband had not been popular with these ladies. He
called himself a wholesale chemist, but as a matter of fact he was in
the liquor. business. He was a coarse, red, bristling, man, without
taste in altar cloths. Fortunately he died when Norty, as Sweetheart
called him, was only five years old, and fortunately he left them
almost six thousand dollars a year.

Sweetheart thought of moving to New England or France or
Fiesole or the Monterey Peninsula, but she could not sell the house,
like a dark stone prison, which her husband had inconsiderately
built, and the "wholesale chemist business" needed her shrewd eye.

But Sweetheart and Norty did travel, always the two of them
together and always first class. They were not lonely, for they had
each other; they could sit talking, lightly laughing, about their
fellow-travelers, possibly malicious but always well-bred, from after
dinner till after midnight.

She sent Norty to school in Connecticut and to that small but
thoroughly sound and Christian college, Toplady. She always rented
a cottage for herself near the institution, and Norty lived with
her and was spared the coarser associations with the rough male
students. But she saw to it that he did not fail to become manly;
she had private teachers for him in boxing, riding, swimming,
tennis, and bridge; and though vulgar competitors hinted that he
won by nasty little tricks, she crowed that he did win. He was also a

pianist, and sang French lyrics over which his mother, a broad-minded woman, looked shocked but giggled in an advanced manner.

After his college, they had a leisurely two years abroad, during which they rode on camels and looked up at but did not climb the First Pyramid. For two months they stayed at the loveliest pension in Florence, filled with the most cultured in American and English womanhood. In Lausanne they met an earl. In Canterbury, England, Sweetheart bought a pair of lilac-colored kid slippers, with his help, as usual, and they had to laugh at the strange affection he had for these slippers. "Do put them on, Sweetheart dearest," he begged, almost every evening. He preferred them even to her gold slippers.

He did have the best taste, pointed out Sweetheart.

For three months they had a flat on the Left Bank in Paris and Norty had a friendship with several exiled American poets and novelists that was surprisingly vivid, considering how shaggy their necks were and how many naughty words they used in the books they had published privately.

Sweetheart watched their capital deftly, and when it was diminished to the danger point, Norty and she reluctantly returned to Grand Republic, to the morose stone house, and he started as a clerk in the Blue Ox Bank. He was good. He liked figures. They were impersonal and dependable, they partook of the divine, and yet they could be mastered as the crude, inappreciative people about him could not be.

Naturally, his mother and he lived together, while he looked for a wife, with the assistance of the love, the industry, and the remarkable intuition of Sweetheart. Together they inspected every available girl in Radisson County and in the better (yet not too vulgarly rich) sections of St. Paul, Duluth, Winona, and Minneapolis.

He would go earnestly calling on these buds, he would play the piano and sing the French songs, and stay till ten, at which hour his mother would telephone him, even if it was long-distance, to remind him that he had had a headache that afternoon.

Sweetheart always asked the girl candidates at the house, and was kind to them, and asked tactful questions about their stand on homemade puddings, Republicanism, and the reservation of the Host. She had one special test for the chicks. She showed them the bowl of shaving soap which she imported from St. James's Street, London, for Norty, and if the girl laughed or looked puzzled, it was evident that she was a crude provincial.

The young ladies always failed to snare Prince Charming. Without his mother being so intrusive as to point it out, Norty saw for himself that they could never be counted on to warm his pajamas or scrape the mud off his shoes or go out in the kitchen and cook guinea hen or listen to his reading aloud of Ronald Firbank, as Sweetheart could.

Some dozens of girls proved unfit. Norty said, "Sweetheart, I think this whole country has become coarsened and vulgarized. Democracy is all right as an ideal, but why must all the young ladies today be so ribald and impertinent? There aren't any more girls like you, dearest."

"I'm afraid that's true, but let's not give up hope," said Sweetheart.

"Oh, I just don't care one bit about *any* of them!" Norty cried petulantly, and kissed her.

They remained together all evening, every evening. They were invited to dinner together. Norty grew—not older; he could never, in the lulling spell of Sweetheart's tenderness, grow older, but he did grow less young. Sweetheart sometimes said (but laughingly)· that he seemed a little bald, and his waistcoat (not his "vest") was more robin-like. He chuckled once, and said that he was catching up to her in age. Some day he would be able to marry her.

Sweetheart thought that was sweet of him, but she worried over it for a couple of days, then hinted. Sorry, but wasn't that remark possibly in bad taste?

He almost cried.

Each year he was neater. He trained Ed Oleson to cut his hair more precisely; his trousers hung even better; there was less danger of anyone finding a cigarette crumb on his sleeve; and to take care of the long-vexing, often-discussed question of how to keep shoelaces and black dress-ties really neat in his top highboy drawer, Sweetheart and he spent two week-ends building an intricate nest of tiny cardboard compartments, which she lined with gold tea-chest paper, kissing each one as she finished it.

"Imagine finding any *young* woman who would give such attention to my needs!" he shrieked.

"Oh, don't say that!" she said, with satisfaction.

She was tireless in trying to coax him out of his moods of violent depression which seemed to increase every year.

She died quickly, of an embolism, in his arms.

It was thought by his friends—who happened, most of them, to be women of his mother's age and understanding—that Norty would go mad.

Dr. Roy Drover coarsely advised him to "marry the first cutie that makes a grab at you when you tickle 'em." Norty was not offended by Dr. Drover's masculine brutality, as you might have expected. Indeed, he came into the doctor's office frequently, and invited him to the house for a drink. The clumsy doctor was embarrassed by these offers of friendship, and growled, "Say, I'm not a nosy psychiatrist that wants to hang around his patients," and the justly offended Norty cut him off. No, sir, Drover might beg all he wanted to, but he was finished with the dull oaf.

After some weeks Norty found an aide and companion; Larry Drome, a large young man who had been a truck-driver, policeman, soldier, sailor. He had once been imprisoned for burglary, but that had been a mistaken-identity case, explained Larry.

He became Norty's chauffeur, valet, and companion at gin-rummy. Together they took motor trips into the Arrowhead forest, and shared a cottage. Someone said that he had seen them together in Los Angeles, and that Norty was introducing his handsome friend as "Major Drome," but that was probably a lie. You know how small-city people talk.

But the talk spread, like honey on your wrist.

The directors of the Blue Ox National, particularly Mr. Havock, thought well of Norton Trock as a banker. He was first vice-president now, in charge of personnel and of loans. He picked careful assistants, and he could refuse a loan, or call one, with tact. They wanted to make him president, but they were perturbed by rumors, probably spread by his rivals.

Mr. Havock had never heard of Krafft-Ebing or Stekel, but he had run construction-camps filled with hoboes, ex-convicts, and mess boys. While he had never been educated into the history of Greek and Roman culture and morals, also he had never been educated out of a knowledge of hobo culture and morals. He had Norty for dinner, along with Isabel Avondene, cousin of Stella. He had noted that Isabel looked rather like Sweetheart. After dinner, when the two men were alone, with cigars and bootlegged white mule, which Boone preferred to brandy, as being stronger, Boone spoke:

"Nort, we want you to be president of the Blue Ox. But we have to have a man who is a church member and a family-man—you know, beyond criticism. Why don't you marry Izzy Avondene?"

"I don't know that I——"

"You heard me!"

Norty wanted to be a sound husband. He sent his chauffeur, Larry—a rough fellow who might have offended his virginal wife—

off to live in a boarding-house. Isabel and he had bedrooms at opposite ends of a rather long corridor, but he did go in to see her, nervously but politely.

They acquired two children in four years, but after that Norty never again entered her bedroom, and he found it was "just too ghastly inconvenient for poor Larry to tramp through all that snow before he drives me to the bank in the morning." He installed Larry again in an attic room of his large house, and again went off canoeing with him.

Isabel consulted Dr. Drover, who was cross.

"Doctor, I loathe talking about such intimate things, but I think I'm going a little crazy. I have such improper thoughts and I don't seem to be able to control them, and I've tried to talk with our rector, but he isn't of much help. My husband never—uh—he never comes near me any more—at night, I mean. He's always so nice and pleasant and he seems quite fond of me, and he's *so* good about playing with the children and entertaining my relatives and so on, but——I do miss something."

"Did you—uh—did you enjoy it when—when he used to come to you?"

"I was beginning to, I'm afraid."

"I'm not a mental doc, Isabel. I much prefer what surgery I can get. But I can tell you this: Don't worry. You women never understand how hard we husbands work, and it's just that Nort gets all tired out, slaving away in that big bank, and so he hasn't—he hasn't much left for you. Uh. He'll be all right again when the pressure lets up. Now skip along, and don't be so impatient with the poor fellow."

When she had gone, Dr. Drover thought, "Poor fellow, rats! Poor *girl*! Nothing I can do. Wonder if these Chicago sex-sharks do really know anything? I must ask some time, when I'm at a medical convention."

Unlike Bernice Claywheel, Isabel Trock could not frisk with Bradds and lusty farmhands. After all, she was an Avondene! Whenever she was distressed by lewd thoughts, she prayed. It did not seem to help. So, from having too little of natural human sinfulness, she became as pale and bewildered and hermit-like as the oracular doctor's wife, Lillian, from having too much.

But Norty was blithe and rosy.

ROBERT FROST

****

It would be a very false pose for me to pretend to know what I have done best. Any choice I made would mean little or nothing an hour after I had made it. Every new moon I could get up something entirely new. By the time my friend Whit Burnett had completed all the anthologies he could think of, I should have been in them with nearly everything I ever wrote. After all, what I have published represents a pretty strict essential selection as it is in my seven or eight books. But if I may be permitted to put forward a few that I have lately been looking fondly back over as deserving more attention than they get, let me seize the chance to name these.

ROBERT FROST

****

Six New England Poems

THE NEED OF BEING VERSED
IN COUNTRY THINGS

THE HOUSE had gone to bring again
To the midnight sky a sunset glow.
Now the chimney was all of the house that stood,
Like a pistil after the petals go.

The barn opposed across the way,
That would have joined the house in flame
Had it been the will of the wind, was left
To bear forsaken the place's name.

No more it opened with all one end
For teams that came by the stony road
To drum on the floor with scurrying hoofs
And brush the mow with the summer load.

The birds that came to it through the air
At broken windows flew out and in,

Their murmur more like the sigh we sigh
From too much dwelling on what has been.

Yet for them the lilac renewed its leaf,
And the aged elm, though touched with fire;
And the dry pump flung up an awkward arm;
And the fence post carried a strand of wire.

For them there was really nothing sad.
But though they rejoiced in the nest they kept,
One had to be versed in country things
Not to believe the phoebes wept.

THE MOUNTAIN

THE MOUNTAIN held the town as in a shadow.
I saw so much before I slept there once:
I noticed that I missed stars in the west,
Where its black body cut into the sky.
Near me it seemed: I felt it like a wall
Behind which I was sheltered from a wind.
And yet between the town and it I found,
When I walked forth at dawn to see new things,
Were fields, a river, and beyond, more fields.
The river at the time was fallen away,
And made a widespread brawl on cobble-stones;
But the signs showed what it had done in spring:
Good grass-land gullied out, and in the grass
Ridges of sand, and driftwood stripped of bark.
I crossed the river and swung round the mountain.
And there I met a man who moved so slow
With white-faced oxen in a heavy cart,
It seemed no harm to stop him altogether.

'What town is this?' I asked.

'This? Lunenburg.'
Then I was wrong: the town of my sojourn,
Beyond the bridge, was not that of the mountain,
But only felt at night its shadowy presence.
'Where is your village? Very far from here?'

'There is no village—only scattered farms.
We were but sixty voters last election.
We can't in nature grow to many more:
That thing takes all the room!' He moved his goad.
The mountain stood there to be pointed at.
Pasture ran up the side a little way,
And then there was a wall of trees with trunks;
After that only tops of trees, and cliffs
Imperfectly concealed among the leaves.
A dry ravine emerged from under boughs
Into the pasture.

     'That looks like a path.
Is that the way to reach the top from here?—
Not for this morning, but some other time:
I must be getting back to breakfast now.'

'I don't advise your trying from this side.
There is no proper path, but those that *have*
Been up, I understand, have climbed from Ladd's.
That's five miles back. You can't mistake the place:
They logged it there last winter some way up.
I'd take you, but I'm bound the other way.'

'You've never climbed it?'

     'I've been on the sides,
Deer-hunting and trout-fishing. There's a brook
That starts up on it somewhere—I've heard say
Right on the top, tip-top—a curious thing.
But what would interest you about the brook,
It's always cold in summer, warm in winter.
One of the great sights going is to see
It steam in winter like an ox's breath,
Until the bushes all along its banks
Are inch-deep with the frosty spines and bristles—
You know the kind. Then let the sun shine on it!'

'There ought to be a view around the world
From such a mountain—if it isn't wooded
Clear to the top.' I saw through leafy screens
Great granite terraces in sun and shadow,

Shelves one could rest a knee on getting up—
With depths behind him sheer a hundred feet;
Or turn and sit on and look out and down,
With little ferns in crevices at his elbow.

'As to that I can't say. But there's the spring,
Right on the summit, almost like a fountain.
That ought to be worth seeing.'

                     'If it's there.
You never saw it?'

               'I guess there's no doubt
About its being there. I never saw it.
It may not be right on the very top:
It wouldn't have to be a long way down
To have some head of water from above,
And a *good distance* down might not be noticed
By anyone who'd come a long way up.
One time I asked a fellow climbing it
To look and tell me later how it was.'

'What did he say?'
                 'He said there was a lake
Somewhere in Ireland on a mountain top.'

'But a lake's different. What about the spring?'

'He never got up high enough to see.
That's why I don't advise your trying this side.
He tried this side. I've always meant to go
And look myself, but you know how it is:
It doesn't seem so much to climb a mountain
You've worked around the foot of all your life.
What would I do? Go in my overalls,
With a big stick, the same as when the cows
Haven't come down to the bars at milking time?
Or with a shotgun for a stray black bear?
'Twouldn't seem real to climb for climbing it.'

'I shouldn't climb it if I didn't want to—
Not for the sake of climbing. What's its name?'

'We call it Hor: I don't know if that's right.'

'Can one walk around it? Would it be too far?'

'You can drive round and keep in Lunenburg,
But it's as much as ever you can do,
The boundary lines keep in so close to it.
Hor is the township, and the township's Hor—
And a few houses sprinkled round the foot,
Like boulders broken off the upper cliff,
Rolled out a little farther than the rest.'

'Warm in December, cold in June, you say?'

'I don't suppose the water's changed at all.
You and I know enough to know it's warm
Compared with cold, and cold compared with warm.
But all the fun's in how you say a thing.'

'You've lived here all your life?'

                                        'Ever since Hor
Was no bigger than a—' What, I did not hear.
He drew the oxen toward him with light touches
Of his slim goad on nose and offside flank,
Gave them their marching orders and was moving.

THE ROAD NOT TAKEN

Two ROADS diverged in a yellow wood,
And sorry I could not travel both
And be one traveler, long I stood
And looked down one as far as I could
To where it bent in the undergrowth;

Then took the other, as just as fair,
And having perhaps the better claim,
Because it was grassy and wanted wear;
Though as for that the passing there
Had worn them really about the same,

And both that morning equally lay
In leaves no step had trodden black.
Oh, I kept the first for another day!
Yet knowing how way leads on to way,
I doubted if I should ever come back.

I shall be telling this with a sigh
Somewhere ages and ages hence:
Two roads diverged in a wood, and I—
I took the one less traveled by,
And that has made all the difference.

THE GRINDSTONE

HAVING a wheel and four legs of its own
Has never availed the cumbersome grindstone
To get it anywhere that I can see.
These hands have helped it go, and even race;
Not all the motion, though, they ever lent,
Not all the miles it may have thought it went,
Have got it one step from the starting place.
It stands beside the same old apple tree.
The shadow of the apple tree is thin
Upon it now, its feet are fast in snow.
All other farm machinery's gone in,
And some of it on no more legs and wheel
Than the grindstone can boast to stand or go.
(I'm thinking chiefly of the wheelbarrow.)
For months it hasn't known the taste of steel,
Washed down with rusty water in a tin.
But standing outdoors hungry, in the cold,
Except in towns at night, is not a sin.
And, anyway, its standing in the yard
Under a ruinous live apple tree
Has nothing any more to do with me,
Except that I remember how of old
One summer day, all day I drove it hard,
And someone mounted on it rode it hard,
And he and I between us ground a blade.

I gave it the preliminary spin,
And poured on water (tears it might have been);
And when it almost gayly jumped and flowed,
A Father-Time-like man got on and rode,
Armed with a scythe and spectacles that glowed.
He turned on will-power to increase the load
And slow me down—and I abruptly slowed,
Like coming to a sudden railroad station.
I changed from hand to hand in desperation.
I wondered what machine of ages gone
This represented an improvement on.
For all I knew it may have sharpened spears
And arrowheads itself. Much use for years
Had gradually worn it an oblate
Spheroid that kicked and struggled in its gait,
Appearing to return me hate for hate;
(But I forgive it now as easily
As any other boyhood enemy
Whose pride has failed to get him anywhere).
I wondered who it was the man thought ground—
The one who held the wheel back or the one
Who gave his life to keep it going round?
I wondered if he really thought it fair
For him to have the say when we were done.
Such were the bitter thoughts to which I turned.

Not for myself was I so much concerned.
Oh no!—although, of course, I could have found
A better way to pass the afternoon
Than grinding discord out of a grindstone,
And beating insects at their gritty tune.
Nor was I for the man so much concerned.
Once when the grindstone almost jumped its bearing
It looked as if he might be badly thrown
And wounded on his blade. So far from caring,
I laughed inside, and only cranked the faster,
(It ran as if it wasn't greased but glued);
I'd welcome any moderate disaster
That might be calculated to postpone
What evidently nothing could conclude.
The thing that made me more and more afraid
Was that we'd ground it sharp and hadn't known,

And now were only wasting precious blade.
And when he raised it dripping once and tried
The creepy edge of it with wary touch,
And viewed it over his glasses funny-eyed,
Only disinterestedly to decide
It needed a turn more, I could have cried
Wasn't there danger of a turn too much?
Mightn't we make it worse instead of better?
I was for leaving something to the whetter.
What if it wasn't all it should be? I'd
Be satisfied if he'd be satisfied.

THE GIFT OUTRIGHT

THE LAND was ours before we were the land's.
She was our land more than a hundred years
Before we were her people. She was ours
In Massachusetts, in Virginia,
But we were England's, still colonials,
Possessing what we were still unpossessed by,
Possessed by what we now no more possessed.
Something we were withholding made us weak
Until we found out that it was ourselves
We were withholding from our land of living,
And forthwith found salvation in surrender.
Such as we were we gave ourselves outright
(The deed of gift was many deeds of war)
To the land vaguely realizing westward,
But still unstoried, artless, unenhanced,
Such as she was, such as she would become

ONE STEP BACKWARD TAKEN

NOT ONLY sands and gravels
Were once more on their travels,
But gulping muddy gallons
Great boulders off their balance
Bumped heads together dully
And started down the gully.
Whole capes caked off in slices.

I felt my standpoint shaken
In the universal crisis.
But with one step backward taken
I saved myself from going.
A world torn loose went by me.
Then the rain stopped and the blowing
And the sun came out to dry me.

JOHN STEINBECK

****

Although it is usually impossible to obtain any comment on his own work from Mr. Steinbeck, the following excerpt from Sea of Cortez, *a Leisurely Journal of Travel and Research, is the author's own selection of his writing which in his estimation best represents his style and thought.* Sea of Cortez *is a large book, part of it containing a scientific appendix of the marine animals of the Panamic Faunal Province compiled by E. F. Ricketts, the biologist with whom Steinbeck joined in a unique scientific fishing expedition, the details of which constituted* Sea of Cortez.

****

Easter Sunday: Sea of Cortez

THE BEACH was hot and yellow. We swam, and then walked along on the sand and went inland along the ridge between the beach and a large mangrove-edged lagoon beyond. On the lagoon side of the ridge there were thousands of burrows, presumably of large land-crabs, but it was hopeless to dig them out. The shores of the lagoon teemed with the little clicking bubbling fiddler crabs and estuarian snails. Here we could smell the mangrove flowers without the foul root smell, and the odor was fresh and sweet, like that of new-cut grass. From where we waded there was a fine picture, still reflecting water and the fringing green mangroves against the burnt red-brown of the distant mountains, all like some fantastic Doré drawing of a pressed and embattled heaven. The air was hot and still and the lagoon rippleless. Now and then the surface was ringed as some lagoon fish came to the air. It was a curious quiet resting-place and perhaps because of the quiet we heard in our heads the children singing in the church at La Paz. We did not collect strongly or very efficiently, but rather we half dozed through the day, thinking of old things, each one in himself. And later we discussed manners of thinking and methods of thinking, speculation which is not stylish any more. On a day like this the mind goes outward and touches in all directions. We discussed intellectual methods and approaches, and we thought that through inspection of thinking technique a kind of purity of approach might be consciously achieved—that non-teleological or "is" thinking might be substituted in part for the usual cause-effect methods.

The hazy Gulf, with its changes of light and shape, was rather like us, trying to apply our thoughts, but finding them always pushed and swayed by our bodies and our needs and our satieties. It might be well here to set down some of the discussions of non-teleological thinking.

During the depression there were, and still are, not only destitute but thriftless and uncareful families, and we have often heard it said that the country had to support them because they were shiftless and negligent. If they would only perk up and be somebody everything would be all right. Even Henry Ford in the depth of the depression gave us his solution to that problem, "Everybody ought to roll up his sleeves and get to work."

This view may be correct as far as it goes, but we wonder what would happen to those with whom the shiftless would exchange places in the large pattern—those whose jobs would be usurped, since at that time there was work for only about seventy percent of the total employable population, leaving the remainder as government wards.

This attitude has no bearing on what might be or could be if so-and-so happened. It merely considers conditions "as is." No matter what the ability or aggressiveness of the separate units of society, at that time there were, and still there are, great numbers necessarily out of work, and the fact that those numbers comprised the incompetent or maladjusted or unlucky units is in one sense beside the point. No causality is involved in that; collectively it's just "so"; collectively it's related to the fact that animals produce more offspring than the world can support. The units may be blamed as individuals, but as members of society they cannot be blamed. Any given individual very possibly may transfer from the underprivileged into the more fortunate group by better luck or by improved aggressiveness or competence, but all cannot be so benefited whatever their strivings, and the large population will be unaffected. The seventy-thirty ratio will remain, with merely a reassortment of the units. And no blame, at least no social fault, imputes to these people; they are where they are "because" natural conditions are what they are. And so far as we selfishly are concerned we can rejoice that they, rather than we, represent the low extreme, since there must be one.

So if one is very aggressive he will be able to obtain work even under the most sub-normal economic conditions, but only because there are others, less aggressive than he, who serve in his stead as potential government wards. In the same way, the sight of a half-wit should never depress us, since his extreme, and the extreme of his kind, so affects the mean standard that we, hatless, coatless, often bewhiskered, thereby will be regarded only as a little odd. And similarly, we cannot justly approve the success manuals that tell our high school graduates how to get a job—there being jobs for only half of them!

This type of thinking unfortunately annoys many people. It may especially arouse the anger of women, who regard it as cold, even brutal, although actually it would seem to be more tender and understanding, certainly more real and less illusionary and even less blaming, than the more conventional methods of consideration. And the value of it as a tool in increased understanding cannot be denied.

As a more extreme example, consider the sea-hare *Tethys*, a shell-less, flabby sea-slug, actually a marine snail, which may be seen crawling about in tidal estuaries, somewhat resembling a rabbit crouched over. A California biologist estimated the number of eggs produced by a single animal during a single breeding season to be more than 478 million. And the adults sometimes occur by the hundred! Obviously all these eggs cannot mature, all this potential cannot, *must not,* become reality, else the ocean would soon be occupied exclusively by sea-hares. There would be no kindness in that, even for the sea-hares themselves, for in a few generations they would overflow the earth; there would be nothing for the rest of us to eat, and nothing for them unless they turned cannibal. On the average, probably no more than the biblical one or two attain full maturity. Somewhere along the way all the rest will have been eaten by predators whose life cycle is postulated upon the presence of abundant larvae of sea-hares and other forms as food—as all life itself is based on such a postulate. Now picture the combination mother-father sea-hare (the animals are hermaphroditic, with the usual cross-fertilization) parentally blessing its offspring with these words: "Work hard and be aggressive, so you can grow into a nice husky *Tethys* like your ten-pound parent." Imagine it, the hypocrite, the illusionist, the Pollyanna, the genial liar, saying that to its millions of eggs *en masse,* with the dice loaded at such a ratio!

Inevitably, 99.999 percent are destined to fall by the wayside. No prophet could foresee which specific individuals are to survive, but the most casual student could state confidently that no more than a few are likely to do so; any given individual has *almost* no chance at all—but still there is the "almost," since the race persists. And there is even a semblance of truth in the parent sea-hare's admonition, since even here, with this almost infinitesimal differential, the race is still to the swift and/or to the lucky.

What we personally conceive by the term "teleological thinking," as exemplified by the notion about the shiftless unemployed, is most frequently associated with the evaluating of causes and effects, the purposiveness of events. This kind of thinking considers changes and cures—what "should be" in the terms of an end pattern (which is often a subjective or an anthropormorphic projection): it presumes the bettering of conditions, often, unfortunately, without achieving more than a most superficial understanding of these conditions. In their sometimes intolerant refusal to face facts as they are, teleological notions may substitute a fierce but ineffectual attempt to change conditions which are assumed to be undesirable, in place of the understanding acceptance which would pave the way for a more sensible attempt at any change which might still be indicated.

Non-teleological ideas derive through "is" thinking, associated with natural selection as Darwin seems to have understood it. They imply depth, fundamentalism, and clarity—seeing beyond traditional or personal projections. They consider events as outgrowths and expressions rather than as results; conscious acceptance as a desideratum, and certainly as an all-important prerequisite. Non-teleological thinking concerns itself primarily not with what should be, or could be, or might be, but rather with what actually "is"—attempting at most to answer the already sufficiently difficult questions *what* or *how*, instead of *why*.

An interesting parallel to these two types of thinking is afforded by the microcosm with its freedom or indeterminacy, as contrasted with the morphologically inviolable pattern of the macrocosm. Statistically, the electron is free to go where it will. But the destiny pattern of any aggregate, comprising uncountable billions of these same units, is fixed and certain, however much that inevitability may be slowed down. The eventual disintegration of a stick of wood or a piece of iron through the departure of the presumably immortal electrons is assured, even though it may be delayed by such protection against the operation of the second law of thermodynamics as is afforded by painting and rustproofing.

Examples sometimes clarify an issue better than explanations or definitions. Here are three situations considered by the two methods.

A. *Why are some men taller than others?*

Teleological "answer": because of the underfunctioning of the growth-regulating ductless glands. This seems simple enough. But the simplicity is merely a function of inadequacy and incompleteness. The finality is only apparent. A child, being wise and direct, would ask immediately if given this answer: "Well, why do the glands underfunction?" hinting instantly towards non-teleological methods, or indicating the rapidity with which teleological thinking gets over into the stalemate of first causes.

In the non-teleological sense there can be no "answer." There can be only pictures which become larger and more significant as one's horizon increases. In this given situation, the steps might be something like this:

(1) Variation is a universal and truly primitive trait. It occurs in any group of entities—razor blades, measuring rods, rocks, trees, horses, matches, or men.

(2) In this case, the apropos variations will be towards shortness or tallness from a mean standard—the height of adult men as determined by the statistics of measurements, or by common-sense observation.

(3) In men varying towards tallness there seems to be a constant relation with an underfunctioning of the growth-regulating ductless glands, of the sort that one can be regarded as an index of the other.

(4) There are other known relations consistent with tallness, such as compensatory adjustments along the whole chain of endocrine organs. There may even be other factors, separately not important or not yet discovered, which in the aggregate may be significant, or the integration of which may be found to wash over some critical threshold.

(5) The men in question are taller "because" they fall in a group within which there are the above-mentioned relations. In other words, "they're tall because they're tall."

This is the statistical, or "is," picture to date, more complex than the teleological "answer"—which is really no answer at all—but complex only in the sense that reality is complex; actually simple, inasmuch as the simplicity of the word "is" can be comprehended.

Understandings of this sort can be reduced to this deep and significant summary: "It's so because it's so." But exactly the same words can also express the hasty or superficial attitude. There seems to be no explicit method for differentiating the deep and participating understanding, the "all-truth" which admits infinite change or expansion as added relations become apparent, from the shallow dismissal and implied lack of further interest which may be couched in the very same words.

B. *Why are some matches larger than others?*

Examine similarly a group of matches. At first they seem all to be of the same size. But to turn up differences, one needs only to measure them carefully with calipers or to weigh them with an analytical balance. Suppose the extreme comprises only a .001 percent departure from the mean (it will be actually much more) ; even so slight a differential we know can be highly significant, as with the sea-hares. The differences will group into plus-minus variations from a hypothetical mean to which not one single example will be found exactly to conform. Now the ridiculousness of the question becomes apparent. There is no *particular* reason. It's just so. There may be in the situation some factor or factors more important than the others: owing to the universality of variation (even in those very factors which "cause" variation), there surely *will* be, some even predominantly so. But the question as put is seen to be beside the point. The good answer is: "It's just in the nature of the beast." And this needn't imply belittlement; to have understood the "nature" of a thing is in itself a considerable achievement.

But if the size variations should be quite obvious—and especially if uniformity were to be a desideratum—then there might be a particularly dominant "causative" factor which could be searched out Or if a person must have a stated "cause"—and many people must, in order to get an emotional understanding, a sense of relation to the situation and to give a name to the thing in order to "settle" it so it may not bother them any more—he can examine the automatic machinery which fabricates the products, and discover in it the variability which results in variation in the matches. But in doing so, he will become involved with a larger principle or pattern, the universality of variation, which has little to do with causality as we think of it.

C. *Leadership.*

The teleological notion would be that those in the forefront are leaders in a given movement and actually direct and consciously lead the masses in the sense that an army corporal orders "Forward march" and the squad marches ahead. One speaks in such a way of church leaders, of political leaders, and of leaders in scientific thought, and of course there is some limited justification for such a notion.

Non-teleological notion: that the people we call leaders are simply those who, at the given moment, are moving in the direction behind which will be found the greatest weight, and which represents a future mass movement.

For a more vivid picture of this state of affairs, consider the movements of an ameba under the microscope. Finger-like processes, the pseudopodia, extend at various places beyond the confines of the chief mass. Locomotion takes place by means of the animal's flowing into one or into several adjacent pseudopodia. Suppose that the molecules which "happened" to be situated in the forefront of the pseudopodium through which the animal is progressing, or into which it will have flowed subsequently, should be endowed with consciousness and should say to themselves and to their fellows: "We are directly leading this great procession, our leadership 'causes' all the rest of the population to move this way, the mass follows the path we blaze." This would be equivalent to the attitude with which we commonly regard leadership

As a matter of fact there are three distinct types of thinking, two of them teleological. Physical teleology, the type we have been considering, is by far the commonest today. Spiritual teleology is rare. Formerly predominant, it now occurs metaphysically and in most religions, especially as they are popularly understood (but not, we suspect, as they were originally enunciated or as they may still be known to the truly adept). Occasionally the three types may be contrasted in a single problem. Here are a couple of examples

(1) Van Gogh's feverish hurrying in the Arles epoch, culminating in epilepsy and suicide.

Teleological "answer": Improper care of his health during times of tremendous activity and exposure to the sun and weather brought on his epilepsy out of which discouragement and suicide resulted.

Spiritual teleology: He hurried because he innately foresaw his imminent death, and wanted first to express as much of his essentiality as possible.

Non-teleological picture: Both the above, along with a good many other symptoms and expressions (some of which could probably be inferred from his letters), were parts of his essentiality, possibly glimpsable as his "lust for life."

(2) The thyroid-neurosis syndrome.

Teleological "answer": Over-activity of the thyroid gland irritates and over-stimulates the patient to the point of nervous breakdown.

Spiritual teleology: The neurosis is causative. Something psychically wrong drives the patient on to excess mental irritation which harries and upsets the glandular balance, especially the thyroid, through shock-resonance in the autonomic system, in the sense that a purely psychic shock may spoil one's appetite, or may even result in violent illness. In this connection, note the army's acceptance of extreme homesickness as a reason for disability discharge.

Non-teleological picture: Both are discrete segments of a vicious circle, which may also include other factors as additional more or less discrete segments, symbols or maybe parts of an underlying but non-teleological pattern which comprises them and many others, the ramifications of which are n, and which has to do with causality only reflectedly.

Teleological thinking may even be highly fallacious, especially where it approaches the very superficial but quite common *post hoc, ergo propter hoc* pattern. Consider the situation with reference to dynamiting in a quarry. Before a charge is set off, the foreman toots warningly on a characteristic whistle. People living in the neighborhood come to associate the one with the other, since the whistle is almost invariably followed within a few seconds by the shock and sound of an explosion for which one automatically prepares oneself. Having experienced this many times without closer contact, a very naïve and unthinking person might justly conclude not only that there was a cause-effect relation, but that the whistle actually caused the explosion. A slightly wiser person would insist that the explosion caused the whistle, but would be hard put to explain the transposed time element. The normal adult would recognize that the whistle no more caused the explosion than the explosion caused the whistle, but that both were parts of a larger pattern out of which a "why" could be postulated for both, but more immediately and particularly for the whistle. Determined to chase the thing down in a cause-effect sense, an observer would have to be very wise indeed who could follow the intricacies of cause through more fundamental cause to primary cause, even in this largely man-made series about which we presumably know most of the motives, causes, and ramifications. He would eventually find himself in a welter of thoughts on production, and ownership of the means of production, and economic whys and wherefores about which there is little agreement.

The example quoted is obvious and simple. Most things are far more subtle than that, and have many of their relations and most of their origins far back in things more difficult of access than the tooting of a whistle calculated to warn bystanders away from an explosion. We know little enough even of a man-made series like this—how much less of purely natural phenomena about which also there is apt to be teleological pontificating!

Usually it seems to be true that when even the most definitely apparent cause-effect situations are examined in the light of wider knowledge, the cause-effect aspect comes to be seen as less rather than more significant, and the statistical or relational aspects acquire larger importance. It seems safe to assume that non-teleological is more "ultimate" than teleological reasoning. Hence the latter would be expected to prove to be limited and constricting except when used provisionally. But while it is true that the former is more open, for that very reason its employment necessitates greater discipline and care in order to allow for the dangers of looseness and inadequate control.

Frequently, however, a truly definitive answer seems to arise through teleological methods. Part of this is due to wish-fulfillment delusion. When a person asks "Why?" in a given situation, he usually deeply expects, and in any case receives, only a relational answer in place of the definitive "because" which he thinks he wants. But he customarily accepts the actually relational answer (it couldn't be anything else unless it comprised the whole, which is unknowable except by "living into") as a definitive "because." Wishful thinking probably fosters that error, since everyone continually searches for absolutisms (hence the value placed on diamonds, the most permanent physical things in the world) and imagines continually that he finds them. More justly, the relational picture should be regarded only as a glimpse—a challenge to consider also the rest of the relations as they are available—to envision the whole picture as well as can be done with given abilities and data. But one accepts it instead of a real "because," considers it settled, and, having named it, loses interest and goes on to something else.

Chiefly, however, we seem to arrive occasionally at definitive answers through the workings of another primitive principle: the universality of quanta. No one thing ever merges gradually into anything else; the steps are continuous, but often so very minute as to seem truly continuous. If the investigation is carried deep enough, the factor in question, instead of being graphable as a continuous process, will be seen to function by discrete quanta with gaps or synapses between, as do quanta of energy, undulations of light. The apparently definitive answer occurs when causes and effects both arise on the same large plateau which is bounded a great way off by the steep rise which announces the next plateau. If the investigation is extended sufficiently, that distant rise will, however, inevitably be encountered; the answer which formerly seemed definitive now will be seen to be at least slightly inadequate and the picture will have to be enlarged so as to include the plateau next further out. Everything impinges on everything else, often into radically different systems, although in such cases faintly. We doubt very much if there are any truly "closed systems." Those so called represent kingdoms of a great continuity bounded by the sudden discontinuity of great synapses which eventually must be bridged in any unified-field hypothesis. For instance, the ocean, with reference to waves of water, might be considered as a closed system. But anyone who has lived in Pacific Grove or Carmel during the winter storms will have felt the house tremble at the impact of waves half a mile or more away impinging on a totally different "closed" system.

But the greatest fallacy in, or rather the greatest objection to, teleological thinking is in connection with the emotional content, the belief. People get to believing and even to professing the apparent answers thus arrived at, suffering mental constrictions by emotionally closing their minds to any of the further and possibly opposite "answers" which might otherwise be unearthed by honest effort— answers which, if faced realistically, would give rise to a struggle and to a possible rebirth which might place the whole problem in a new and more significant light. Grant for a moment that among students of endocrinology a school of thought might arise, centering upon some belief as to etiology—upon the belief, for instance, that all abnormal growth is caused by glandular imbalance. Such a clique, becoming formalized and powerful, would tend, by scorn and opposition, to wither any contrary view which, if untrammeled, might discover a clue to some opposing "causative" factor of equal medical importance. That situation is most unlikely to arise in a field so lusty as endocrinology, with its relational insistence, but the principle illustrated by a poor example is thought nevertheless to be sound.

Significant in this connection is the fact that conflicts may arise between any two or more of the "answers" brought forth by either of the teleologies, or between the two teleologies themselves. But there can be no conflict between any of these and the non-teleological picture. For instance, in the condition called hyperthyroidism, the treatments advised by believers in the psychic or neurosis etiology very possibly may conflict with those arising out of a belief in the purely physical cause. Or even within the physical teleology group there may be conflicts between those who believe the condition due to a strictly thyroid upset and those who consider causation derived through a general imbalance of the ductless glands. But there can be no conflict between any or all of these factors and the non-teleological picture, because the latter includes them—evaluates them relationally or at least attempts to do so, or maybe only accepts them as time-place truths. Teleological "answers" necessarily must be included in the non-teleological method—since they are part of the picture even if only restrictedly true—and as soon as their qualities of relatedness are recognized. Even erronous beliefs are real things, and have to be considered proportional to their spread or intensity. "All-truth" must embrace all extant apropos errors also, and know them as such by relation to the whole, and allow for their effects.

The criterion of validity in the handling of data seems to be this: that the summary shall say in substance, significantly and understandingly, "It's so because it's so." Unfortunately the very same words might equally derive through a most superficial glance, as any child could learn to repeat from memory the most abstruse of Dirac's equations. But to know a thing emergently and significantly is something else again, even though the understanding may be expressed in the self-same words that were used superfically. In the following example* note the deep significance of the emergent as contrasted with the presumably satisfactory but actually incorrect original naïve understanding. At one time an important game bird in Norway, the willow grouse, was so clearly threatened with extinction that it was thought wise to establish protective regulations and to place a bounty on its chief enemy, a hawk which was known to feed heavily on it. Quantities of the hawks were exterminated, but despite such drastic measures the grouse disappeared actually more rapidly than before. The naïvely applied customary remedies had obviously failed. But instead of becoming discouraged and quietistically letting this bird go the way of the great auk and the passenger pigeon, the authorities enlarged the scope of their investigations until the anomaly was explained. An ecological analysis into the relational aspects of the situation disclosed that a parasitic disease, coccidiosis, was endemic among the grouse. In its incipient stages, this disease so reduced the flying speed of the grouse that the mildly ill individuals became easy prey for the hawks. In living largely off the slightly ill birds, the hawks prevented them from developing the disease in its

* *Abstracted from the article on ecology by Elton,* Encyclopaedia Britannica, *14th Edition, Vol. VII, p. 916.*

full intensity and so spreading it more widely and quickly to otherwise healthy fowl. Thus the presumed enemies of the grouse, by controlling the epidemic aspects of the disease, proved to be friends in disguise.

In summarizing the above situation, the measure of validity wouldn't be to assume that, even in the well-understood factor of coccidiosis, we have the real "cause" of any beneficial or untoward condition, but to say, rather, that in this phase we have a highly significant and possibly preponderantly important relational aspect of the picture.

However, many people are unwilling to chance the sometimes ruthless-appearing notions which may arise through non-teleological treatments. They fear even to use them in that they may be left dangling out in space, deprived of such emotional support as had been afforded them by an unthinking belief in the proved value of pest control in the conservation of game birds: in the institutions of tradition; religion; science; in the security of the home or the family; or in a comfortable bank account. But for that matter emancipations in general are likely to be held in terror by those who may not yet have achieved them, but whose thresholds in those respects are becoming significantly low. Think of the fascinated horror, or at best tolerance, with which little girls regard their brothers who have dispensed with the Santa Claus belief; or the fear of the devout young churchman for his university senior who has grown away from depending on the security of religion.

As a matter of fact, whoever employs this type of thinking with other than a few close friends will be referred to as detached, hard-hearted, or even cruel. Quite the opposite seems to be true. Non-teleological methods more than any other seem capable of great tenderness, of an all-embracingness which is rare otherwise. Consider, for instance, the fact that, once a given situation is deeply understood, no apologies are required. There are ample difficulties even to understanding conditions "as is." Once that has been accomplished, the "why" of it (known now to be simply a relation, though probably a near and important one) seems no longer to be preponderantly important. It needn't be condoned or extenuated, it just "is." It is seen merely as part of a more or less dim whole picture. As an example: A woman near us in the Carmel woods was upset when her dog was poisoned—frightened at the thought of passing the night alone after years of companionship with the animal. She phoned to ask if, with our windows on that side of the house closed as they were normally, we could hear her ringing a dinner bell as a signal during the night that marauders had cut her phone wires preparatory to robbing her. Of course that was, in fact, an improbable contingency to be provided against; a man would call it a foolish fear, neurotic. And so it was. But one could say kindly, "We can hear the bell quite plainly, but if desirable we can adjust our sleeping arrangements so as to be able to come over there instantly in case you need us," without even stopping to consider whether or not the fear was foolish, or to be concerned about it if it were, correctly regarding all that as secondary. And if the woman had said apologetically, "Oh, you must forgive me; I know my fears are foolish, but I am so upset!" the wise reply would have been, "Dear person, nothing to forgive. If you have fears, they *are;* they are real things and to be considered. Whether or not they're foolish is beside the point. *What* they are is unimportant alongside the fact *that* they are." In other words, the badness or goodness, the teleology of the fears, was decidedly secondary. The whole notion could be conveyed by a smile or by a pleasant intonation more readily than by the words themselves. Teleological treatment which one might have been tempted to employ under the circumstances would first have stressed the fact that the fear was foolish—would say with a great show of objective justice, "Well, there's no use in *our* doing anything; the fault is that *your* fear is foolish and improbable. Get over that" (as a judge would say, "Come into court with clean hands"); "then if there's anything *sensible* we can do, we'll see," with smug blame implied in every word. Or, more kindly, it would try to reason with the woman in an attempt to help her get over it—the business of propaganda directed towards change even before the situation is fully understood (maybe as a lazy substitute for understanding). Or, still more kindly, the teleological method would try to understand the fear causally. But with the non-teleological treatment there is only the love and understanding of instant acceptance; after that fundamental has been achieved, the next step, if any should be necessary, can be considered more sensibly.

Strictly, the term non-teleological thinking ought not to be applied to what we have in mind. Because it involves more than thinking, that term is inadequate. *Modus operandi* might be better—a method of handling data of any sort. The example cited just above concerns feeling more than thinking. The method extends beyond thinking even to living itself; in fact, by inferred definition it transcends the realm of thinking possibilities, it postulates "living into."

In the destitute-unemployed illustration, thinking, as being the evaluatory function chiefly concerned, was the point of departure, "the crust to break through." There the "blame approach" considered the situation in the limited and inadequate teleological manner. The non-teleological method included that viewpoint as correct but limited. But when it came to the feeling aspects of a human relation situation, the non-teleological method would probably ameliorate the woman's fears in a loving, truly mellow, and adequate fashion, whereas the teleological would have tended to bungle things by employing the limited and sophisticated approach.

Incidentally, there is in this connection a remarkable etiological similarity to be noted between cause in thinking and blame in feeling. One feels that one's neighbors are to be blamed for their hate or anger or fear. One thinks that poor pavements are "caused" by politics. The non-teleological picture in either case is the larger one that goes beyond blame or cause. And the non-causal or non-blaming viewpoint seems to us very often relatively to represent the "new thing," the Hegelian "Christ-child" which arises emergently from the union of two opposing viewpoints, such as those of physical and spiritual teleologies, especially if there is conflict as to causation between the two or within either. The new viewpoint very frequently sheds light over a larger picture, providing a key which may unlock levels not accessible to either of the teleological viewpoints. There are interesting parallels here: to the triangle, to the Christian ideas of trinity, to Hegel's dialectic, and to Swedenborg's metaphysic of divine love (feeling) and divine wisdom (thinking).

The factors we have been considering as "answers" seem to be merely symbols or indices, relational aspects of things—of which they are integral parts—not to be considered in terms of causes and effects. The truest reason for anything's being so is that it *is*. This is actually and truly a reason, more valid and clearer than all the other separate reasons, or than any group of them short of the whole. Anything less than the whole forms part of the picture only, and the infinite whole is unknowable except by *being* it, by living into it.

A thing may be *so* "because" of a thousand and one reasons of greater or lesser importance, such as the man oversized because of glandular insufficiency. The integration of these many reasons which are in the nature of relations rather than reasons is that he *is*. The separate reasons, no matter how valid, are only fragmentary parts of the picture. And the whole necessarily includes all that it impinges on as object and subject, in ripples fading with distance or depending upon the original intensity of the vortex.

The frequent allusions to an underlying pattern have no implication of mysticism—except inasmuch as a pattern which comprises infinity in factors and symbols might be called mystic. But infinity as here used occurs also in the mathematical aspects of physiology and physics, both far away from mysticism as the term is ordinarily employed. Actually, the underlying pattern is probably nothing more than an integration of just such symbols and indices and mutual reference points as are already known, except that its power is *n*. Such an integration might include nothing more spectacular than we already know. But, equally, it *could* include anything, even events and entities as different from those already known as the vectors, tensors, scalars, and ideas of electrical charges in mathematical physics are different from the mechanical-model world of the Victorian scientists.

In such a pattern, causality would be merely a name for something that exists only in our partial and biased mental reconstructings. The pattern which it indexes, however, would be real, but not intellectually apperceivable because the pattern goes everywhere and is everything and cannot be encompassed by finite mind or by anything short of life—which it is.

The psychic or spiritual residua remaining after the most careful physical analyses, or the physical remnants obvious, particularly to us of the twentieth century, in the most honest and disciplined spiritual speculations of medieval philosophers, all bespeak such a pattern. Those residua, those most minute differentials, the 0.001 percentages which suffice to maintain the races of sea animals, are seen finally to be the most important things in the world, not because of their sizes, but because they are everywhere. The differential is the true universal, the true catalyst, the cosmic solvent. Any investigation carried far enough will bring to light these residua, or rather will leave them still unassailable as Emerson remarked a hundred years ago in "The Oversoul"—will run into the brick wall of the *impossibility* of perfection while at the same time insisting on the *validity* of perfection. Anomalies especially testify to that framework; they are the commonest intellectual vehicles for breaking through; all are solvable in the sense that any *one* is understandable, but that one leads with the power *n* to still more and deeper anomalies.

This deep underlying pattern inferred by non-teleological thinking crops up everywhere—a relational thing, surely, relating opposing factors on different levels, as reality and potential are related. But it must not be considered as causative, it simply exists, it *is*, things are merely expressions of it as it is expressions of them. And they *are* it, also. As Swinburne, extolling Hertha, the earth goddess, makes her say: "Man, equal and one with me, man that is made of me, man that is I," so all things which are *that*—which is all— equally may be extolled. That pattern materializes everywhere in the sense that Eddington finds the non-integer *q* "number" appearing everywhere, in the background of all fundamental equations,* in the sense that the speed of light, constant despite compoundings or subtractions, seemed at one time almost to be conspiring against investigation.

The whole is necessarily everything, the whole world of fact and fancy, body and psyche, physical fact and spiritual truth, individual and collective, life and death, macrocosm and microcosm (the greatest quanta here, the greatest synapse between these two), conscious and unconscious, subject and object. The whole picture is portrayed by *is,* the deepest word of deep ultimate reality, not shallow or partial as reasons are, but deeper and participating, possibly encompassing the Oriental concept of *being.*

And all this against the hot beach on an Easter Sunday, with the passing day and the passing time. This little trip of ours was becoming a thing and a dual thing, with collecting and eating and sleeping merging with the thinking-speculating activity. Quality of sunlight, blueness and smoothness of water, boat engines, and ourselves were all parts of a larger whole and we could begin to feel its nature but not its size.

* The Nature of the Physical World, *pp. 208-10.*

CARL SANDBURG

****

DEAR MR. BURNETT:
You might use for THE WORLD'S BEST *if you like, Chapter 44, Volume II,* Abraham Lincoln: the War Years, *titled "Abraham Lincoln Speaks at Gettysburg."*

Yours,

CARL SANDBURG

****

Abraham Lincoln Speaks at Gettysburg

A PRINTED INVITATION came to Lincoln's hands notifying him that on Thursday, November 18, 1863, exercises would be held for the dedication of a National Soldiers' Cemetery at Gettysburg. The same circular invitation had been mailed to senators, congressmen, the governors of Northern States, members of the Cabinet, by the commission of Pennsylvanians who had organized a corporation through which Maine, New Hampshire, Vermont, Massachusetts, Rhode Island, Maryland, Connecticut, New York, New Jersey, Pennsylvania, Delaware, West Virginia, Ohio, Indiana, Illinois, Michigan, Wisconsin, and Minnesota were to share the cost of a decent burying-ground for the dust and bones of the Union and Confederate dead.

In the helpless onrush of the war, it was known, too many of the fallen had lain as neglected cadavers rotting in the open fields or thrust into so shallow a resting-place that a common farm plow caught in their bones. Now by order of Governor Curtin of Pennsylvania seventeen acres had been purchased on Cemetery Hill, where the Union center stood its colors on the second and third of July, and plots of soil had been allotted each State for its graves.

The sacred and delicate duties of orator of the day had fallen on Edward Everett. An eminent cultural figure, perhaps foremost of all distinguished American classical orators, he was born in 1794, had

been United States Senator, Governor of Massachusetts, member of
Congress, Secretary of State under Fillmore, Minister to Great
Britain, Phi Beta Kappa poet at Harvard, professor of Greek at
Harvard, President of Harvard. His reputation as a public speaker
began in the Brattle Street Unitarian Church of Boston. Two volumes of his orations published in 1850 held eighty-one addresses,
two more volumes issued in 1859 collected one hundred and
five speeches. His lecture on Washington, delivered a hundred and
twenty-two times in three years, had in 1859 brought a fund of
$58,000, which he gave to the purchase and maintenance of Mount
Vernon as a permanent shrine. Other Everett lectures had realized
more than $90,000 for charity causes. His wife was Charlotte Gray
Brooks, daughter of Peter Chardon Brooks, first of American marine
and life-insurance millionaires. Serene stars had watched over their
home life and children until tragedy crept in, and Edward Everett's
wife was sent to a private retreat, incurably insane. A life-long
friendship took root between him and her father; they shared a sorrow; when Peter Brooks died in 1849 Everett wrote a eulogistic biography. No ordinary trafficker in politics, Everett had in 1860 run
for Vice-President on the Bell-Everett ticket of the Constitutional
Union party, receiving the electoral votes of Virginia, Kentucky,
and Tennessee.

The Union of States was a holy concept to Everett, and the
slavery issue secondary, though when president of Harvard from
1846 to 1849 he refused to draw the color line, saying in the case of
a Negro applicant, Beverly Williams, that admission to Harvard
College depended on examinations. "If this boy passes the examinations, he will be admitted; and if the white students choose to withdraw, all the income of the College will be devoted to his education." Not often was he so provocative.

On the basis of what Everett had heard about Lincoln he wrote
in his journal shortly before the inauguration in '61 that the incoming President was "evidently a person of very inferior cast of character, wholly unequal to the crisis." Then on meeting the new
President he recorded that he found him of better stuff than he had
expected. As a strict worshiper of the Constitution and the Union
he was drawn toward Lincoln's moderate slavery policy, writing to
critics after the Administration had lost in the '62 fall elections, "It
is my purpose to support the President to the best of my ability."
Speaking publicly as a man of no party, and as the leading founder
of the Mount Vernon memorial to George Washington, he trusted
he would offend no candid opponent by saying that the main objec-

tion against Mr. Lincoln, "that personally he lacks fixedness of purpose," might on precisely the same grounds be brought against George Washington and his Administration. The President's "intellectual capacity" had been proved in his debates with Douglas. "He is one of the most laborious and indefatigable men in the country," said Everett, "and that he has been able to sustain himself under as great a load of care as was ever laid upon the head or the heart of a living man is in no small degree owing to the fact that the vindictive and angry passions form no part of his nature and that a kindly and playful spirit mingles its sweetness with the austere cup of public duty."

In September of '62 Lincoln wrote a note of introduction for Everett's use on a trip to Europe, saying Everett's visit, because of his reputation, was "sure to attract notice, and may be misconstrued." Therefore the President saw fit to say that Everett "bears no mission from this government, and yet no gentleman is better able to correct misunderstandings in the minds of foreigners in regard to American affairs." With a pleasant salutation, Lincoln ended this note: "While I commend him to the consideration of those whom he may meet, I am quite conscious that he could better introduce me than I him in Europe."

Serene, suave, handsomely venerable in his sixty-ninth year, a prominent specimen of Northern upper-class distinction, Everett was a natural choice of the Pennsylvania commissioners, who sought an orator for a solemn national occasion. When in September they notified him that the date of the occasion would be October 23, he replied that he would need more time for preparation, and the dedication was postponed till November 19.

Lincoln meanwhile, in reply to the printed circular invitation, sent word to the commissioners that he would be present at the ceremonies. This made it necessary for the commissioners to consider whether the President should be asked to deliver an address when present. Clark E. Carr of Galesburg, Illinois, representing his State on the Board of Commissioners, noted that the decision of the Board to invite Lincoln to speak was an afterthought. "The question was raised as to his ability to speak upon such a grave and solemn occasion. . . . Besides, it was said that, with his important duties and responsibilities, he could not possibly have the leisure to prepare an address. . . . In answer . . . it was urged that he himself, better than any one else, could determine as to these questions, and that, if he were invited to speak, he was sure to do what, under the circumstances, would be right and proper."

And so on November 2 David Wills of Gettysburg, as the special agent of Governor Curtin and also acting for the several States, by letter informed Lincoln that the several States having soldiers in the Army of the Potomac who were killed, or had since died at hospitals in the vicinity, had procured grounds for a cemetery and proper burial of their dead. "These grounds will be consecrated and set apart to this sacred purpose by appropriate ceremonies on Thursday, the 19th instant. I am authorized by the Governors of the various States to invite you to be present and participate in these ceremonies, which will doubtless be very imposing and solemnly impressive. It is the desire that after the oration, you, as Chief Executive of the nation, formally set apart these grounds to their sacred use by a few appropriate remarks."

Mr. Wills proceeded farther as to the solemnity of the occasion, and when Lincoln had finished reading the letter he understood definitely that the event called for no humor and that a long speech was not expected from him. "The invitation," wrote Clark E. Carr, "was not settled upon and sent to Mr. Lincoln until the second of November, more than six weeks after Mr. Everett had been invited to speak, and but little more than two weeks before the exercises were held." . . . .

The Gettysburg speech was shaping at the same time that Lincoln was preparing his annual message to Congress, assembling it in less than three weeks. In that message he would point to "actual commencement of work upon the Pacific railroad," his own act of fixing an initial point being the most tangible part of the commencement.

When Lincoln boarded the train for Gettysburg on November 18, his best chum in the world, Tad, lay sick abed and the doctors were not sure what ailed him. The mother still remembered Willie and was hysterical about Tad. But the President felt imperative duty called him to Gettysburg.

Provost Marshal General James B. Fry as a War Department escort came to the White House, but the President was late in getting into the carriage for the drive to the station. They had no time to lose, Fry remarked. Lincoln said he felt like an Illinois man who was going to be hanged and as the man passed along the road on the way to the gallows the crowds kept pushing into the way and blocking passage. The condemned man at last called out, "Boys, you needn't be in such a hurry to get ahead, there won't be any fun till I get there."

Flags and red-white-and-blue bunting decorated the four-car

special train. Aboard were the three Cabinet members, Nicolay and Hay, Army and Navy representatives, newspapermen, the French and Italian Ministers and attachés. The rear third of the last coach had a drawing-room, where from time to time the President talked with nearly everyone aboard as they came and went. Henry Clay Cochrane, lieutenant of Marines, noted:

"I happened to have a *New York Herald* and offered it to Mr. Lincoln. He took it and thanked me, saying, 'I like to see what they say about us.' The news was about Burnside at Knoxville, Grant and Sherman at Chattanooga and Meade on the Rapidan, all expecting trouble. He read for a little while and then began to laugh at some wild guesses of the paper about pending movements. It was pleasant to see his sad face lighted up. He was looking sallow, sunken-eyed, thin, care-worn and very quiet. He returned the paper remarking among other things that when he had first passed over that road on his way to Congress in 1847 he noticed square-rigged vessels up the Patapsco River as far the Relay House and now there seemed to be only small craft.

"At the Calvert Street Station Secretary Seward began to get uneasy as we approached Baltimore. Upon reaching the Calvert Street Station in Baltimore all was quiet, less than two hundred people assembled, among them women with children in arms. They called for the President. He took two or three of the babies up and kissed them which greatly pleased the mothers. General Schenck and staff joined us and soon after the President went forward in the car and seated himself with a party of choice spirits, among whom was Mayor Frederick W. Lincoln of Boston, not a kinsman. They told stories for an hour or so, Mr. Lincoln taking his turn and enjoying it. Approaching Hanover Junction, he arose and said, 'Gentlemen, this is all very pleasant, but the people will expect me to say something to them tomorrow, and I must give the matter some thought.' He then returned to the rear room of the car."

An elderly gentlemen got on the train and, shaking hands, told the President he had lost a son at Little Round Top at Gettysburg. The President answered he feared a visit to that spot would open fresh wounds, and yet if the end of sacrifice had been reached "we could give thanks even amidst our tears." They quoted from his unburdening to this old man: "When I think of the sacrifices of life yet to be offered, and the hearts and homes yet to be made desolate before this dreadful war is over, my heart is like lead within me, and I feel at times like hiding in deep darkness." At one stop a little girl lifted to an open window thrust a bunch of rosebuds into the car. "Flowerth for the Prethident." Lincoln stepped over, bent down, kissed her face. "You are a little rosebud yourself."

Nearing Gettysburg, Hay noted the President in a little talk with Wayne MacVeagh (lawyer and chairman of the Pennsylvania Republican Central Committee) about Missouri affairs. "MacV. talked Radicalism until he learned he was talking recklessly." MacVeagh brought up the Edwards case as though it were hardly any credit to the Administration. "The President disavowed any knowledge of the Edwards case." Bates had said to Lincoln, as indeed Lincoln had said to Hay, "that Edwards was inefficient and must be removed for that reason." It seemed, however, to be an uppermost matter in MacVeagh's mind and he thrust at the President about it and enjoyed doing so. It was precisely the sort of matter that professional politicians heading State central committees sought opportunity to bring up.

At sundown the train pulled into Gettysburg and Lincoln was driven to the Wills residence, Seward to the Harper home fronting on the public square. A sleepy little country town of 3,500 was overflowing with human pulses again. Private homes were filled with notables and nondescripts. Hundreds slept on the floors of hotels. Military bands blared till late in the night serenading whomsoever. The weather was mild and the moon up for those who chose to go a-roaming. When serenaders called on the President for a speech, he made again one of those little addresses saying there was nothing to say. "In my position it is sometimes important that I should not say foolish things. [A voice: "If you can help it."] It very often happens that the only way to help it is to say nothing at all. Believing that is my present condition this evening, I must beg of you to excuse me from addressing you further."

The crowd didn't feel it was much of a speech. They went next door with the band and blared for Seward. He spoke so low that Hay could not hear him, but he opened the stopgaps of patriotic sentiment, saying in part, "I thank my God for the hope that this is the last fratricidal war which will fall upon the country which is vouchsafed to us by Heaven—the richest, the broadest, the most beautiful, the most magnificent, and capable of a greater destiny than has ever been given to any part of the human race." What more could a holiday crowd ask for on a fair night of moonlit November? Seward gave them more and closed: "Fellow citizens, good night." It was good night for him but not for them. They serenaded five other speakers.

Something of the excess spirit of the evening was set down in Hay's diary. He with MacVeagh and others went out to the Lutheran Theological Seminary, ate from a chafing dish of oysters, then a real supper, loafed around the courthouse where Lamon was holding a meeting of his marshals, then hunted up John W. Forney, a Democrat born and raised in near-by Lancaster, editor of the *Intelligencer and Journal* there, later editor of the *Washington Union,* defeated for United States Senator from Pennsylvania by Simon Cameron. As a Douglas Democrat editing the *Philadelphia Press,* Forney was credited as much as anyone except Douglas with splitting the Democratic party in 1860 and giving the election to Lincoln. Forney's newspaper, the *Sunday Morning Chronicle* in Washington, had in 1862 become a daily paper, an Administration organ, a defender and expositor of Lincoln.

"Before I ever saw or knew Mr. Lincoln," said Forney to friends, "he wrote me a letter directly after his election in 1860 thanking me for what he was pleased to call my service in resisting the Buchanan administration, and proffering a friendship which never abated. When I was defeated for Clerk of the House in March, 1861, Mr. Lincoln called upon a number of Senators and asked them to vote for me for Secretary of that body. When Stonewall Jackson was killed, and one of my assistant editors spoke kindly, Lincoln wrote to me commending the tribute to a brave adversary. . . . I recommended Horace Greeley for Postmaster-General, because dear old Horace, four years before, without knowing that I had fallen from grace under Mr. Buchanan, recommended me for that office. But as Lincoln had selected Seward for Secretary of State from New York, he could not, of course, appoint Greeley from the same State, and so he replied, and that proposition fell." Trends and manipulations in the Senate often came quickly to Lincoln through Forney, whose information and counsel were freely given when the President asked for it on the hundreds of visits Forney made to the White House. That Forney was a storyteller full of anecdotes, and a philosopher of so wide a tolerance that he was intimate with both the righteous and the wicked, did not lessen his charm for Lincoln. Hay had seen him often at the White House.

"We found Forney," Hay wrote of this Wednesday evening in Gettysburg . . . "and drank a little whiskey with him. He had been drinking a good deal during the day and was getting to feel a little ugly and dangerous. He was particularly bitter on Montgomery Blair. MacVeagh was telling him [Forney] that he pitched into the Tycoon coming up and told him some truths. He [Forney] said the

President got a good deal of that from time to time and needed it. . . . He talked very strangely. Referring to the affectionate and loyal support which he and Curtin had given to the President in Pennsylvania, with references . . . to favors shown the Cameron party whom they regard as their natural enemies." The party went out, heard Lincoln, heard Seward speak to the serenaders, "Forney and MacVeagh . . . still growling about Blair." They picked up Nicolay. "We went back to Forney's room . . . and drank more whiskey. Nicolay sung his little song of the 'Three Thieves' and we then sung John Brown. At last we proposed that Forney should make a speech and two or three started out . . . to get a band to serenade him."

And Forney sat growling quietly. The band arrived with a crowd and newspaper reporters. "Hay, we'll take a drink!" said Forney. Somebody commanded prudence. "I am always prudent," said Forney sternly. The crowd shouted as he opened the door. "My friends," said Forney, "these are the first hearty cheers I have heard tonight. You gave no such cheer to your President down the street. Do you know what you owe to that great man? You owe your country—you owe your name as American citizens." Forney black-guarded the crowd for its apathy, diverged to his own record; he had been for Lincoln in his heart in 1860; open advocacy was not as effectual as the course he took in dividing the most corrupt organization that ever existed, the pro-slavery Democratic party. "He dwelt at length on this question," noted Hay, "and then went back to the eulogy of the President, that great, wonderful mysterious inexplicable man who holds in his single hands the reins of the republic; who keeps his own counsels; who does his own purpose in his own way, no matter what temporizing minister in his Cabinet sets himself up in opposition.... And very much of this." MacVeagh and another speaker held forth. John Russell Young of the *Philadelphia Press* remarked as to Forney: "That speech must not be written out yet. He will see further about it when he gets sober." They went upstairs with Forney, sang "John Brown" again, went home and called it a night.

At dinner in the Wills home that evening Lincoln met Edward Everett, a guest under the same roof, and Governor Curtin and others. About ten o'clock he was in his room, with paper and pencil ready to write, when he sent a colored servant down for Judge Wills to come up. Still later, about eleven o'clock, he sent the colored servant down again for Judge Wills, who came up and heard Lincoln request to see Mr. Seward. Judge Wills offered to go and bring Seward from next door at the Harpers'. "No, I'll go and see him," said Lincoln, who gathered his sheets of paper and went for a half-hour with his Secretary of State.

Whether Seward made slight or material alterations in the text on the sheets was known only to Lincoln and Seward. It was midnight or later that Lincoln went to sleep, probably perfectly clear in his mind as to what his speech would be the next day. The one certainty was that his "few appropriate remarks," good or bad, would go to an immense audience. Also he slept better for having a telegram from Stanton reporting there was no real war news and "On inquiry Mrs. Lincoln informs me that your son is better this evening."

Fifteen thousand, some said 30,000 or 50,000, people were on Cemetery Hill for the exercises the next day when the procession from Gettysburg arrived afoot and horseback representing the United States Government, the Army and Navy, governors of States, mayors of cities, a regiment of troops, hospital corps, telegraph-company representatives, Knights Templar, Masonic Fraternity, Odd Fellows, and other benevolent associations, the press, fire departments, citizens of Pennsylvania and other States. They were scheduled to start at ten o'clock and at that hour of the clock Lincoln in a black suit, high silk hat, and white gloves came out of the Wills residence and mounted a horse. A crowd was on hand and he held a reception on horseback. At eleven the parade began to move. The President's horse seemed small for him, as some looked at it. Clark E. Carr, just behind the President, believed he noticed that the President sat erect and looked majestic to begin with and then got to thinking so that his body leaned forward, his arms hung limp, and his head bent far down.

A long telegram sent by Stanton at ten o'clock from Washington had been handed him. Burnside seemed safe though threatened at Knoxville, Grant was starting a big battle at Chattanooga, and "Mrs. Lincoln reports your son's health as a great deal better and he will be out today."

The march of the procession of military and civic bodies began. "Mr. Lincoln was mounted upon a young and beautiful chestnut horse, the largest in the Cumberland Valley," wrote Lieutenant Cochrane. This seemed the first occasion that anyone had looked at the President mounted with a feeling that just the right horse had been picked to match his physical length. "His towering figure surmounted by a high silk hat made the rest of us look small," thought Cochrane. At the President's right Seward and Blair rode their horses, at his left Usher and Lamon. In the next rank were six horses with the secretaries Nicolay and Hay, Provost Marshal General Fry, Lieutenant Cochrane, and military officers. Cochrane rode "a mischievous brute that required much attention to keep him from getting out of line to browse on the tail of the President's horse." The President rode "easily, bowing occasionally to right or left," noted Cochrane, while Seward lacked dignity, his trousers working up over the shoe tops to show his homemade gray socks. Seward was "entirely unconscious" that the Secretary of State looked funny—and nobody really cared. In the town of Gettysburg men with wounds still lingered in hospitals. And many flags along the main street were at half-mast for sorrow not yet over.

Minute guns spoke while the procession moved along Baltimore Street to the Emmitsburg Road, then by way of the Taneytown Road to the cemetery, where troop lines stood in salute to the President.

The march was over in fifteen minutes. But Mr. Everett, the orator of the day, had not arrived. Bands played till noon. Mr. Everett arrived. On the platform sat Governors Curtin of Pennsylvania, Bradford of Maryland, Morton of Indiana, Seymour of New York, Parker of New Jersey, Dennison of Ohio, with ex-Governor Tod and Governor-elect Brough of Ohio, Edward Everett and his daughter, Major Generals Schenck, Stahel, Doubleday, and Couch, Brigadier General Gibbon and Provost Marshal General Fry, foreign Ministers, members of Congress, Colonel Ward Hill Lamon, Secretary Usher, and the President of the United States with Secretary Seward and Postmaster General Blair immediately at his left.

The United States House chaplain, the Reverend Thomas H. Stockton, offered a prayer while the thousands stood with uncovered heads.

"O God, our Father, for the sake of Thy Son, our Saviour, inspire us with Thy spirit, and sanctify us. . . . By this altar of sacrifice and on this field of deliverance—on this mount of salvation—within the fiery and bloody line of these munitive rocks, looking back to the dark days of fear and trembling, and to the rapture of relief that came after, we multiply our thanksgiving, and confess our obligations to renew and perfect our personal and social consecration to Thy service and glory. . . Bless the efforts to suppress this rebellion. . . . As the trees are not dead, though the foliage is gone, so our heroes are not dead though their forms have fallen—with their personality they are all with Thee, and the spirit of their example is here. It fills the air, it fills our hearts, and long as time shall last it will hover in these skies and rest on this landscape. . . ."

The chaplain prayed as a master of liturgy and a familiar of sacred literature. The *Philadelphia Press* said that with the prayer "there was scarcely a dry eye in all that vast assemblage," while the *Cincinnati Daily Gazette* reporter wrote his observation: "The President evidently united in this adjuration in all the simplicity of his soul, and the falling tear declared the sincerity of his emotions."

Benjamin B. French, officer in charge of buildings in Washington, introduced the Honorable Edward Everett, orator of the day, who rose, bowed low to Lincoln, saying, "Mr. President." Lincoln responded, "Mr. Everett."

The orator of the day then stood in silence before a crowd that stretched to limits that would test his voice. Beyond and around were the wheat fields, the meadows, the peach orchards, long slopes of land, and five and seven miles farther the contemplative blue ridge of a low mountain range. His eyes could sweep them as he faced the audience. He had taken note of it in his prepared and rehearsed address. "Overlooking these broad fields now reposing from the labors of the waning year, the mighty Alleghanies dimly towering before us, the graves of our brethren beneath our feet, it is with hesitation that I raise my poor voice to break the eloquent silence of God and Nature. But the duty to which you have called me must be performed;—grant me, I pray you, your indulgence and your sympathy." Everett proceeded, "It was appointed by law in Athens," and gave an extended sketch of the manner in which the Greeks cared for their dead who fell in battle. He spoke of the citizens assembled to consecrate the day. "As my eye ranges over the fields whose sods were so lately moistened by the blood of gallant and loyal men, I feel, as never before, how truly it was said of old that it is sweet and becoming to die for one's country."

Northern cities would have been trampled in conquest but for "those who sleep beneath our feet," said the orator. He gave an outline of how the war began, traversed decisive features of the three days' battles at Gettysburg, discussed the doctrine of State sovereignty and denounced it, drew parallels from European history, and came to his peroration quoting Pericles on dead patriots: "The whole earth is the sepulchre of illustrious men." The men of nineteen sister States had stood side by side on the perilous ridges. "Seminary Ridge, the Peach-Orchard, Cemetery, Culp, and Wolf Hill, Round Top, Little Round Top, humble names, henceforward dear and famous,—no lapse of time, no distance of space, shall cause you to be forgotten." He had spoken for an hour and fifty-seven minutes, some said a trifle over two hours, repeating almost word for word an address that occupied nearly two newspaper pages, as he had written it and as it had gone in advance sheets to many newspapers.

Everett came to his closing sentence without a faltering voice: "Down to the latest period of recorded time, in the glorious annals of our common country there will be no brighter page than that which relates THE BATTLES OF GETTYSBURG." It was the effort of his life and embodied the perfections of the school of oratory in which he had spent his career. His erect form and sturdy shoulders, his white hair and flung-back head at dramatic points, his voice, his poise, and chiefly some quality of inside goodheartedness, held most of his audience to him, though the people in the front rows had taken their seats three hours before his oration closed.

The Baltimore Glee Club sang an ode written for the occasion by Benjamin B. French, who had introduced Everett to the audience. The poets Longfellow, Bryant, Whittier, Lowell, George Boker, had been requested but none found time to respond with a piece to be set to music. The two closing verses of the ode by French immediately preceded the introduction of the President to the audience:

> Great God in Heaven!
> Shall all this sacred blood be shed?
> Shall we thus mourn our glorious dead?
> Oh, shall the end be wrath and woe,
> The knell of Freedom's overthrow,
>   A country riven?
>
> It will not be!
> We trust, O God! thy gracious power
> To aid us in our darkest hour.
> This be our prayer—"O Father! save
> A people's freedom from its grave,
>   All praise to Thee!"

Having read Everett's address, Lincoln knew when the moment drew near for him to speak. He took out his own manuscript from a coat pocket, put on his steel-bowed glasses, stirred in his chair, looked over the manuscript, and put it back in his pocket. The Baltimore Glee Club finished. The specially chosen Ward Hill

Lamon rose and spoke the words "The President of the United States," who rose, and holding in one hand the two sheets of paper at which he occasionally glanced, delivered the address in his high-pitched and clear-carrying voice. The *Cincinnati Commercial* reporter wrote, "The President rises slowly, draws from his pocket a paper, and, when commotion subsides, in a sharp, unmusical treble voice, reads the brief and pithy remarks." Hay wrote in his diary, "The President, in a firm, free way, with more grace than is his wont, said his half dozen words of consecration." Charles Hale of the *Boston Advertiser*, also officially representing Governor Andrew of Massachusetts, had notebook and pencil in hand, took down the slow-spoken words of the President, as follows:

Fourscore and seven years ago, our fathers brought forth upon this continent a new nation, conceived in liberty and dedicated to the proposition that all men are created equal.

Now we are engaged in a great civil war, testing whether that nation—or any nation, so conceived and so dedicated—can long endure.

We are met on a great battle-field of that war. We are met to dedicate a portion of it as the final resting place of those who have given their lives that that nation might live.

It is altogether fitting and proper that we should do this.

But, in a larger sense, we cannot dedicate, we cannot consecrate, we cannot hallow, this ground. The brave men, living and dead, who struggled here, have consecrated it, far above our power to add or to detract.

The world will very little note nor long remember what we say here; but it can never forget what they did here.

It is for us, the living, rather, to be dedicated here, to the unfinished work that they have thus far so nobly carried on. It is rather for us to be here dedicated to the great task remaining before us; that from these honored dead we take increased devotion to that cause for which they here gave the last full measure of devotion; that we here highly resolve that these dead shall not have died in vain; that the nation shall, under God, have a new birth of freedom, and that government of the people, by the people, for the people, shall not perish from the earth.

In a speech to serenaders just after the battle of Gettysburg four and a half months before, Lincoln had referred to the founding of the republic as taking place "eighty odd years since." Then he had hunted up the exact date, which was eighty-seven years since, and phrased it "Fourscore and seven years ago" instead of "Eighty-seven years since." Also in the final copy Lincoln wrote "We have come" instead of the second "We are met" that Hale reported.

In the written copy of his speech from which he read Lincoln used the phrase "our poor power." In other copies of the speech which he wrote out later he again used the phrase "our poor power." So it was evident that he meant to use the word "poor" when speaking to his audience, but he omitted it. Also in the copy held in his hands while facing the audience he had not written the words "under God," though he did include those words in later copies which he wrote. Therefore the words "under God" were decided upon after he wrote the text the night before at the Wills residence.

The *New York Tribune* and many other newspapers indicated "[Applause.]" at five places in the address and "[Long continued applause.]" at the end. The applause, however, according to most of the responsible witnesses, was formal and perfunctory, a tribute to the occasion, to the high office, to the array of important men of the nation on the platform, by persons who had sat as an audience for three hours. Ten sentences had been spoken in five minutes, and some were surprised that it should end before the orator had really begun to get his outdoor voice.

A photographer had made ready to record a great historic moment, had bustled about with his dry plates, his black box on a tripod, and before he had his head under the hood for an exposure, the President had said "by the people, for the people" and the nick of time was past for a photograph.

The *New York Times* reporter gave his summary of the program by writing: "The opening prayer by Reverend Mr. Stockton was touching and beautiful, and produced quite as much effect upon the audience as the classic sentences of the orator of the day. President Lincoln's address was delivered in a clear loud tone of voice, which could be distinctly heard at the extreme limits of the large assemblage. It was delivered (or rather read from a sheet of paper which the speaker held in his hand) in a very deliberate manner, with strong emphasis, and with a most business-like air."

The *Philadelphia Press* man, John Russell Young, privately felt that Everett's speech was the performance of a great actor whose art was too evident, that it was "beautiful but cold as ice." The *New York Times* man noted: "Even while Mr. Everett was delivering his splendid oration, there were as many people wandering about the fields, made memorable by the fierce struggles of July, as stood around the stand listening to his eloquent periods. They seem to have considered, with President Lincoln, that it was not what was *said* here, but what was *done* here, that deserved their attention. . . . In wandering about these battlefields, one is astonished and indignant to find at almost every step of his progress the carcasses of dead horses which breed pestilence in the atmosphere. I am told that more than a score of deaths have resulted from this neglect in the village of Gettysburg the past summer; in the house in which I was compelled to seek lodgings, there are now two boys sick with typhoid fever attributed to this cause. Within a stone's throw of the white-washed hut occupied as the headquarters of General Meade, I counted yesterday no less than ten carcasses of dead horses, lying on the ground where they were struck by the shells of the enemy."

The audience had expected, as the printed program stipulated, "Dedicatory Remarks, by the President of the United States." No eloquence was promised. Where eloquence is in flow the orator must have time to get tuned up, to expatiate and expand while building toward his climaxes, it was supposed. The *New York Tribune* man and other like observers merely reported the words of the address with the one preceding sentence: "The dedicatory remarks were then delivered by the President." These reporters felt no urge to inform their readers about how Lincoln stood, what he did with his hands, how he moved, vocalized, or whether he emphasized or subdued any parts of the address. Strictly, no address as such was on the program from him. He was down for just a few perfunctory "dedicatory remarks."

According to Lamon, Lincoln himself felt that about all he had given the audience was ordinary garden-variety dedicatory remarks, for Lamon wrote that Lincoln told him just after delivering the speech that he had regret over not having prepared it with greater care. "Lamon, that speech won't *scour*. It is a flat failure and the people are disappointed." On the farms where Lincoln grew up as a boy when wet soil stuck to the mold board of a plow they said it didn't "scour."

The near-by *Patriot and Union* of Harrisburg took its fling: "The President succeeded on this occasion because he acted without sense and without constraint in a panorama that was gotten up more for the benefit of his party than for the glory of the nation and the honor of the dead. . . . We pass over the silly remarks of the President; for the credit of the nation we are willing that the veil of oblivion shall be dropped over them and that they shall no more be repeated or thought of."

The *Chicago Times* held that "Mr. Lincoln did most foully

traduce the motives of the men who were slain at Gettysburg" in his reference to "a new birth of freedom," the *Times* saying, "They gave their lives to maintain the old government, and the only Constitution and Union." He had perverted history, misstated the cause for which they died, and with "ignorant rudeness" insulted the memory of the dead, the *Times* alleged: "Readers will not have failed to observe the exceeding bad taste which characterized the remarks of the President and Secretary of State at the dedication of the soldiers' cemetery at Gettysburg. The cheek of every American must tingle with shame as he reads the silly, flat, and dish-watery utterances of the man who has to be pointed out to intelligent foreigners as the President of the United States. And neither he nor Seward could refrain, even on that solemn occasion, from spouting their odious abolition doctrines. The readers of the *Times* ought to know, too, that the valorous President did not dare to make this little journey to Gettysburg without being escorted by a bodyguard of soldiers. For the first time in the history of the Country, the President of the United States, in traveling through a part of his dominions, on a peaceful, even a religious mission, had to be escorted by a bodyguard of soldiers. . . . It was fear for his own personal safety which led the President to be escorted as any other military despot might go." In the pronouncement of a funeral sermon Mr. Lincoln had intruded an "offensive exhibition of boorishness and vulgarity," had alluded to tribal differences that an Indian orator eulogizing dead warriors would have omitted, "which he knew would excite unnecessarily the bitter prejudices of his hearers." Therefore the *Chicago Times* would inquire, "Is Mr. Lincoln less refined than a savage?"

A Confederate outburst of war propaganda related to Lincoln and the Gettysbury exercises was set forth in a *Richmond Examiner* editorial, and probably written by its editor, Edward A. Pollard, taking a day off from his merciless and occasionally wild-eyed criticism of President Jefferson Davis of the Confederacy. And the *Chicago Times,* which seldom let a day pass without curses on Lincoln for his alleged suppression of free speech and a free press, reprinted in full the long editorial from the *Examiner.* "The dramatic exhibition at Gettysburg is in thorough keeping with Yankee character, suited to the usual dignity of their chosen chief," ran part of the editorial scorn. "Stage play, studied attitudes, and effective points were carefully elaborated and presented to the world as the honest outpourings of a nation's heart. In spite of shoddy contracts, of universal corruption, and cruel thirst for southern blood, these people have ideas . . . have read of them in books . . . and determined accordingly to have a grand imitation of them. . . . Mr. Everett was equal to the occasion. He 'took down his Thucydides,' and fancied himself a Pericles commemorating the illustrious dead. The music, the eloquence, the bottled tears and hermetically sealed grief, prepared for the occasion, were all properly brought out in honor of the heroes, whom they crimp in Ireland, inveigle in Germany, or hunt down in the streets of New York.

"So far the play was strictly classic. To suit the general public, however, a little admixture of the more irregular romantic drama was allowed. A vein of comedy was permitted to mingle with the deep pathos of the piece. This singular novelty, and deviation from classic propriety, was heightened by assigning this part to the chief personage. Kings are usually made to speak in the magniloquent language supposed to be suited to their elevated position. On the present occasion Lincoln acted the clown."

This was in the customary tone of the *Chicago Times* and relished by its supporting readers. Its rival, the *Chicago Tribune*, however, had a reporter who telegraphed (unless some editor who read the address added his own independent opinion) a sentence: "The dedicatory remarks of President Lincoln will live among the annals of man."

The *Cincinnati Gazette* reporter added after the text of the address, "That this was the right thing in the right place, and a perfect thing in every respect, was the universal encomium."

The American correspondent of the London *Times* wrote that "the ceremony was rendered ludicrous by some of the sallies of that poor President Lincoln. . . . Anything more dull and commonplace it would not be easy to produce."

Count Gurowski, the only man ever mentioned by Lincoln to Lamon as his possible assassin, wrote in a diary, "Lincoln spoke, with one eye to a future platform and to re-election."

The *Philadelphia Evening Bulletin* said thousands who would not read the elaborate oration of Mr. Everett would read the President's few words "and not many will do it without a moistening of the eye and a swelling of the heart." The *Detroit Advertiser and Tribune* said Mr. Everett had nobly told the story of the battle, "but he who wants to take in the very spirit of the day, catch the unstudied pathos that animates a sincere but simple-minded man, will turn from the stately periods of the professed orator to the brief speech of the President." The *Providence Journal* reminded readers of the saying that the hardest thing in the world is to make a good five-minute speech: "We know not where to look for a more admirable speech than the brief one which the President made at the close of Mr. Everett's oration. . . . Could the most elaborate and splendid oration be more beautiful, more touching, more inspiring, than those thrilling words of the President? They had in our humble judgment the charm and power of the very highest eloquence."

Later men were to find that Robert Toombs of Georgia had in 1850 opened a speech: "Sixty years ago our fathers joined together to form a more perfect Union and to establish justice. . . . We have now met to put that government on trial. . . . In my judgment the verdict is such as to give hope to the friends of liberty throughout the world."

Lincoln had spoken of an idea, a proposition, a concept, worth dying for, which brought from a Richmond newspaper a countering question and answer, "For what are we fighting? An abstraction."

The *Springfield Republican* had veered from its first opinion that Lincoln was honest but "a Simple Susan." Its comment ran: "Surpassingly fine as Mr. Everett's oration was in the Gettysburg consecration, the rhetorical honors of the occasion were won by President Lincoln. His little speech is a perfect gem; deep in feeling, compact in thought and expression, and tasteful and elegant in every word and comma. Then it has the merit of unexpectedness in its verbal perfection and beauty. We had grown so accustomed to homely and imperfect phrase in his productions that we had come to think it was the law of his utterance. But this shows he can talk handsomely as well as act sensibly. Turn back and read it over, it will repay study as a model speech. Strong feelings and a large brain were its parents—a little painstaking its *accoucheur*."

That scribbler of curious touch who signed himself "The Lounger," in *Harper's Weekly* inquired why the ceremony at Gettysburg was one of the most striking events of the war. "There are graveyards enough in the land—what is Virginia but a cemetery?—and the brave who have died for us in this fierce war consecrate the soil from the ocean to the Mississippi. But there is peculiar significance in the field of Gettysburg, for there 'thus far' was thundered to the rebellion. . . . The President and the Cabinet were there, with famous soldiers and civilians. The oration by Mr. Everett was smooth and cold. . . . The few words of the President were from the heart to the heart. They can not be read, even, without kindling emotion. 'The world will little note nor long remember what we say here, but it can never forget what they did here.' It was as simple and felicitous and earnest a word as was ever spoken. . . . Among the Governors present was Horatio Seymour. He came to honor the dead of Gettysburg. But when they were dying he stood in New York sneeringly asking where was the victory promised for the Fourth of July? These men were winning that victory, and dying for us all; and now he mourns, *ex officio,* over their graves."

Everett's opinion of the speech he heard Lincoln deliver was written in a note to Lincoln the next day and was more than mere courtesy: "I should be glad if I could flatter myself that I came as near to the central idea of the occasion in two hours as you did in two minutes." Lincoln's immediate reply was: "In our respective parts yesterday, you could not have been excused to make a short address, nor I a long one. I am pleased to know that, in your judgment, the little I did say was not entirely a failure."

At Everett's request Lincoln wrote with pen and ink a copy of his Gettysburg Address, which manuscript was auctioned at a Sanitary Fair in New York for the benefit of soldiers. At the request of George Bancroft, the historian, he wrote another copy for a Soldiers' and Sailors' Fair at Baltimore. He wrote still another to be lithographed as a facsimile in a publication, *Autographed Leaves of Our Country's Authors.* For Mr. Wills, his host at Gettysburg, he wrote another. The first draft, written in Washington, and the second one, held while delivering it, went into John Hay's hands to be eventually presented to the Library of Congress.

After the ceremonies at Gettysburg Lincoln lunched with Governor Curtin, Mr. Everett, and others at the Wills home, held a reception that had not been planned, handshaking nearly an hour, looking gloomy and listless but brightening sometimes as a small boy or girl came in line, and stopping one tall man for remarks as to just how high up he reached. At five o'clock he attended a patriotic meeting in the Presbyterian church, walking arm-in-arm with old John Burns, and listening to an address by Lieutenant Governor-elect Anderson of Ohio. At six-thirty he was on the departing Washington train. In the dining-car his secretary John Hay ate with Simon Cameron and Wayne MacVeagh. Hay had thought Cameron and MacVeagh hated each other, but he noted: "I was more than usually struck by the intimate jovial relations that existed between men that hate and detest each other as cordially as do these Pennsylvania politicians."

The ride to Washington took until midnight. Lincoln was weary, talked little, stretched out on one of the side seats in the drawing-room and had a wet towel laid across his eyes and forehead.

He had stood that day, the world's foremost spokesman of popular government, saying that democracy was yet worth fighting for. He had spoken as one in mist who might head on deeper yet into mist. He incarnated the assurances and pretenses of popular government, implied that it could and might perish from the earth. What he meant by "a new birth of freedom" for the nation could have a thousand interpretations. The taller riddles of democracy stood up out of the address. It had the dream touch of vast and furious events epitomized for any foreteller to read what was to come. He did not assume that the drafted soldiers, substitutes, and bounty-paid privates had died willingly under Lee's shot and shell, in deliberate consecration of themselves to the Union cause. His cadences sang the ancient song that where there is freedom men have fought and sacrificed for it, and that freedom is worth men's dying for. For the first time since he became President he had on a dramatic occasion declaimed, howsoever it might be read, Jefferson's proposition which had been a slogan of the Revolutionary War—"All men are created equal"—leaving no other inference than that he regarded the Negro slave as a man. His outwardly smooth sentences were inside of them gnarled and tough with the enigmas of the American experiment.

Back at Gettysburg the blue haze of the Cumberland Mountains had dimmed till it was a blur in a nocturne. The moon was up and fell with a bland golden benevolence on the new-made graves of soldiers, on the sepulchers of old settlers, on the horse carcasses of which the onrush of war had not yet permitted removal. The *New York Herald* man walked amid them and ended the story he sent his paper: "The air, the trees, the graves are silent. Even the relic hunters are gone now. And the soldiers here never wake to the sound of reveille."

In many a country cottage over the land, a tall old clock in a quiet corner told time in a tick-tock deliberation. Whether the orchard branches hung with pink-spray blossoms or icicles of sleet, whether the outside news was seedtime or harvest, rain or drouth, births or death, the swing of the pendulum was right and left and right and left in a tick-tock deliberation.

The face and dial of the clock had known the eyes of a boy who listened to its tick-tock and learned to read its minute and hour hands. And the boy had seen years measured off by the swinging pendulum, and grown to man size, had gone away. And the people in the cottage knew that the clock would stand there and the boy never again come into the room and look at the clock with the query, "What is the time?"

In a row of graves of the Unidentified the boy would sleep long in the dedicated final resting-place at Gettysburg. Why he had gone away and why he would never come back had roots in some mystery of flags and drums, of national fate in which individuals sink as in a deep sea, of men swallowed and vanished in a man-made storm of smoke and steel.

The mystery deepened and moved with ancient music and inviolable consolation because a solemn Man of Authority had stood at the graves of the Unidentified and spoken the words "We cannot consecrate—we cannot hallow—this ground. The brave men, living and dead, who struggled here, have consecrated it far above our poor power to add or detract. . . . From these honored dead we take increased devotion to that cause for which they gave the last full measure of devotion."

To the backward and forward pendulum swing of a tall old clock in a quiet corner they might read those cadenced words while outside the windows the first flurry of snow blew across the orchard and down over the meadow, the beginnings of winter in a gun-metal gloaming to be later arched with a star-flung sky.

EDNA ST. VINCENT MILLAY

****

DEAR MR. BURNETT:
As I read over the introduction I did for your This Is My Best *it seems to me that it would do for the new book.*

WILLIAM ROSE BENÉT

Another rereading of work by this poet, that has for many years sustained rereading many times, has led me to the belief that it would be best to represent her by the finest of her sonnets, and leave the culling of her lyrics for a later day. It is hard to sacrifice such poems from Second April, *one of the most beautiful of her books (first published over twenty years ago), as "Elegy Before Death," "Weeds," "The Poet and His Book," and "Exiled." In these lyrics, as elsewhere throughout her career, there are immortal lines, as well as an extraordinary—and inspired—faithfulness of natural observation. The last line of "Weeds"—"The Blood too bright, the brow accurst"—is as amazing as any line to be found among the Elizabethans. In another vein, her need for the ocean off the coast of Maine, as expressed in "Exiled," in its second through its sixth verses, as perfectly conveys everything noted by the senses in a particular scene as any poem we have in the language.*

The limitations of the reviewers of Miss Millay's poetry in the sonnet form have spoken for themselves. The fact is that she remains today the greatest living master of the sonnet in the English language. It may be a form that future poetry will discard or expand into something unrecognizable. She has accepted its convention, in the main, though she has also experimented with final heptameter lines and with sonnets in tetrameter. Accepting that convention, she has filled the form again and again with new force and fire, with great wit, emotion, and a marvelous dexterity of art that conceals art. Her work has sometimes been assailed as a nostalgic for the classical and mediaeval, traditional in phraseology, unmodern in idiom. One of the greatest of her sonnets introduces again the much-used myth of Endymion, but in a new and passionately actual instance. Being an artist and a lover of beauty she has never desired to destroy the art of the past, like the modern vandal. She has but turned it to her own great uses. She has lived vividly in the present world, as must be amply apparent to anyone with intelligence, and in the realm of the imagination she is fitted to discourse with the deathless dead.

WILLIAM ROSE BENÉT

****

Twelve Sonnets

I SHALL FORGET you presently, my dear,
So make the most of this, your little day,
Your little month, your little half a year,
Ere I forget, or die, or move away,
And we are done forever; by and by
I shall forget you, as I said, but now,
If you entreat me with your loveliest lie
I will protest you with my favourite vow.
I would indeed that love were longer-lived,
And oaths were not so brittle as they are,
But so it is, and nature has contrived
To struggle on without a break thus far,—
Whether or not we find what we are seeking
Is idle, biologically speaking.

CHERISH you then the hope I shall forget
At length, my lord, Pieria?—put away
For your so passing sake, this mouth of clay,
These mortal bones against my body set,
For all the puny fever and frail sweat
Of human love,—renounce for these, I say,
The Singing Mountain's memory, and betray
The silent lyre that hangs upon me yet?
Ah, but indeed, some day shall you awake,
Rather, from dreams of me, that at your side
So many nights, a lover and a bride,
But stern in my soul's chastity, have lain,
To walk the world forever for my sake,
And in each chamber find me gone again!

PITY me not because the light of day
At close of day no longer walks the sky;
Pity me not for beauties passed away
From field and thicket as the year goes by;
Pity me not the waning of the moon,
Nor that the ebbing tide goes out to sea,
Nor that a man's desire is hushed so soon,
And you no longer look with love on me.
This have I known always: Love is no more
Than the wide blossom which the wind assails,
Than the great tide that treads the shifting shore,
Strewing fresh wreckage gathered in the gales:
Pity me that the heart is slow to learn
What the swift mind beholds at every turn.

EUCLID alone has looked on Beauty bare.
Let all who prate of Beauty hold their peace,
And lay them prone upon the earth and cease
To ponder on themselves, the while they stare
At nothing, intricately drawn nowhere
In shapes of shifting lineage; let geese
Gabble and hiss, but heroes seek release
From dusty bondage into luminous air.
O blinding hour, O holy, terrible day,
When first the shaft into his vision shone
Of light anatomized! Euclid alone
Has looked on Beauty bare. Fortunate they
Who, though once only and then but far away,
Have heard her massive sandal set on stone.

ON HEARING A SYMPHONY
OF BEETHOVEN

SWEET SOUNDS, oh, beautiful music, do not cease!
Reject me not into the world again.
With you alone is excellence and peace,
Mankind made plausible, his purpose plain.
Enchanted in your air benign and shrewd,
With limbs a-sprawl and empty faces pale,
The spiteful and the stingy and the rude
Sleep like the scullions in the fairy-tale.

This moment is the best the world can give:
The tranquil blossom on the tortured stem.
Reject me not, sweet sounds! oh, let me live,
Till Doom espy my towers and scatter them.
A city spell-bound under the aging sun,
Music my rampart, and my only one.

    Moon, that against the lintel of the west
Your forehead lean until the gate be swung,
Longing to leave the world and be at rest,
Being worn with faring and no longer young,
Do you recall at all the Carian hill
Where worn with loving, loving late you lay,
Halting the sun because you lingered still,
While wondering candles lit the Carian day?
Ah, if indeed this memory to your mind
Recall some sweet employment, pity me,
That with the dawn must leave my love behind,
That even now the dawn's dim herald see!
I charge you, goddess, in the name of one
You loved as well: endure, hold off the sun.

    Love is not all: it is not meat nor drink
Nor slumber nor a roof against the rain;
Nor yet a floating spar to men that sink
And rise and sink and rise and sink again;
Love can not fill the thickened lung with breath,
Nor clean the blood, nor set the fractured bone;
Yet many a man is making friends with death
Even as I speak, for lack of love alone.
It well may be that in a difficult hour,
Pinned down by pain and moaning for release,
Or nagged by want past resolution's power,
I might be driven to sell your love for peace,
Or trade the memory of this night for food.
It well may be. I do not think I would.

Hearing your words, and not a word among them
Tuned to my liking, on a salty day
When inland woods were pushed by winds that flung them
Hissing to leeward like a ton of spray,

I thought how off Matinicus the tide
Came pounding in, came running through the Gut,
While from the Rock the warning whistle cried,
And children whimpered, and the doors blew shut;
There in the autumn when the men go forth,
With slapping skirts the island women stand
In gardens stripped and scattered, peering north,
With dahlia tubers dripping from the hand:
The wind of their endurance, driving south,
Flattened your words against your speaking mouth.

EVEN in the moment of our earliest kiss,
When sighed the straitened bud into the flower,
Sat the dry seed of most unwelcome this;
And that I knew, though not the day and hour.
Too season-wise am I, being country-bred,
To tilt at autumn or defy the frost:
Snuffing the chill even as my fathers did,
I say with them, "What's out tonight is lost."
I only hoped, with the mild hope of all
Who watch the leaf take shape upon the tree,
A fairer summer and a later fall
Than in these parts a man is apt to see,
And sunny clusters ripened for the wine:
I tell you this across the blackened vine.

OH, SLEEP forever in the Latmian cave,
Mortal Endymion, darling of the Moon!
Her silver garments by the senseless wave
Shouldered and dropped and on the shingle strewn,
Her fluttering hand against her forehead pressed,
Her scattered looks that trouble all the sky,
Her rapid footsteps running down the west—
Of all her altered state, oblivious lie!
Whom earthen you, by deathless lips adored,
Wild-eyed and stammering to the grasses thrust,
And deep into her crystal body poured
The hot and sorrowful sweetness of the dust:
Whereof she wanders mad, being all unfit
For mortal love, that might not die of it.

THE SECOND OF TWO SONNETS
IN MEMORY OF SACCO AND VANZETTI

WHERE can the heart be hidden in the ground
And be at peace, and be at peace forever,
Under the world, untroubled by the sound
Of mortal tears, that cease from pouring never?
Well for the heart, by stern compassion harried,
If death be deeper than the churchmen say,—
Gone from this world indeed what's graveward carried,
And laid to rest indeed what's laid away.
Anguish enough while yet the indignant breather
Have blood to spurt upon the oppressor's hand;
Who would eternal be, and hang in ether
A stuffless ghost above his struggling land,
Retching in vain to render up the groan
That is not there, being aching dust's alone?

ONLY the diamond and the diamond's dust
Can render up the diamond unto Man;
One and invulnerable as it began
Had it endured, but for the treacherous thrust
That laid its hard heart open, as it must,
And ground it down and fitted it to span
A turbaned brow or fret an ivory fan,
Lopped of its stature, pared of its proper crust,
So Man, by all the wheels of heaven unscored,
Man, the stout ego, the exuberant mind
No edge could cleave, no acid could consume,—
Being split along the vein by his own kind,
Gives over, rolls upon the palm abhorred,
Is set in brass on the swart thumb of Doom.

THORNTON WILDER

****

During the Nineteenth Century the novelists seem never to have been troubled by the claim to omniscience which is at the base of their art. First signs of discomfort in regard to it appeared in Flaubert and Turgeniev. It became acute in Henry James and now in some form or other undermines the self-confidence of all storytellers. Are readers believing that our stories are "true" and in what sense do we believe them ourselves?

This is the crisis of the novel. Writers for the stage are not confronted by it.

The assumption of omniscience is no less present in writing for the theatre, but once the action is passing upon the stage we are not aware of the narrator who is presenting it to us. A novel may be described as "everything pertinent to our understanding of an action or a series of actions" and throughout a novel we are aware that an all-knowing intelligence is recounting to us this pertinent matter. On the stage, however, it is always "now"; no intervening editorial voice is present; and in a very dramatic sense our seeing is believing.

In The Ides of March *I tried to dispense with the fictional narrator. When one purports to recount the thoughts of a Caesar, a Cicero, and a Catullus, the claim to omniscience becomes doubly preposterous. All art is pretense but the pretense of the historical novel is particularly difficult to swallow. I therefore moved the pretense over to a different terrain: I pretended to have discovered a large collection of letters and documents written by these notable persons. I attempted to coerce belief by submitting a sort of apparatus of historical method and scholarship. It all "looks" more credible than if I had written a running narrative full of such phrases as "Caesar remembered their first meeting" and "Cleopatra concealed her anger." But more important from the point of view of credibility was the fact that I had approached the effect of the theatre. Each of the letters and documents is in the present tense; no narrator is heard describing the whole action as having taken place in the past. As on the stage each speech rises from the actors in an immediate spontaneity—as their "time" on the stage becomes*

104

our "time" in the audience—so in a novel-in-letters each document tends to give the impression of a speech, a cry, at which we are present.

I am far from pretending that this affords a solution to the problem of the novel. The novel-in-letters runs into other difficulties, difficulties so great that the form can only be the vehicle for a very limited type of story. Time is a sense in which I did not seriously attempt to cope with them, as Richardson did. I begged the question by surrounding my work with a veil of irony, offering it as a sort of parody of historical scholarship. I begged the question in that I not so much asked the reader to "believe" me as to "play this game" with me.

THORNTON WILDER

****

From a Journal-Letter of Julius Caesar

977. [*On the enmity felt toward him by Cato, Brutus, and Catullus.*] I called on Cato on the day commemorating his great ancestor's services.

As I have told you before, writing to you has a strange effect on me; I find myself examining matters which I do not otherwise consider. The thought that came to my pen that moment and which I was about to reject is this:

Of the four men whom I most respect in Rome three regard me with mortal enmity. I mean Marcus Junius Brutus, Cato, and Catullus. It is very likely that Cicero would also be pleased to miss me. There is no doubt about all this; many letters reach me which were not intended for my eyes.

I am accustomed to being hated. Already in early youth I discovered that I did not require the good opinion of other men, even of the best, to confirm me in my actions. I think there is only one solitude greater than that of the military commander and of the head of the state and that is the poet's—for who can advise him in that unbroken succession of choices which is a poem? It is in this sense that responsibility is liberty; the more decisions that you are forced to make alone, the more you are aware of your freedom to choose. I hold that we cannot be said to be aware of our minds save under responsibility and that no greater danger could befall mine than that it should reflect an effort to incur the approval of any man, be it a Brutus or a Cato. I must arrive at my decisions as though they were not subject to the comment of other men, as though no one were watching.

And yet I am a politician: I must play the comedy of extreme deference to the opinion of others. A politician is one who pretends that he is subject to the universal hunger for esteem; but he cannot successfully pretend this unless he is free of it. This is the basic hypocrisy of politics and the final triumph of the leader comes with the awe that is aroused in men when they suspect, but never know for certain, that their leader is indifferent to their approval, indifferent and a hypocrite. What?—they say to themselves—: what? can it be that there is absent from this man that serpent's nest which is lodged within us all and which is at once our torture and our delight—the thirst for praise, the necessity of self-justification, the assertion of one's self, cruelty, and envy? My days and nights are spent amid the hissing of those serpents. I once heard them in my own vitals. How I silenced them there I do not know, though the answer to that question, as put to Socrates, exceeds all other questions in interest.

It is not by reason of such serpent's nests, I think, that I am hated by a Marcus Brutus, a Cato, and by this poet. It is indeed from their minds that they hate me and from their views of government and freedom. Even if I brought them up to the place I hold and showed them the world stretched out as one can only see it from here; even if I could split open my skull and show them the experience of my lifetime, so many hundredfold closer to men and government than theirs has been; even if I could read with them, line by line, the texts of the philosophers to whom they cling, and the histories of the countries from which they draw their examples; even then I could not hope to clear their eyes. The first and last schoolmaster of life is living and committing oneself unreservedly and dangerously to living; to men who know this an Aristotle and a Plato have much to say; but those who have imposed cautions on themselves and petrified themselves in a system of ideas, them the masters themselves will lead into error. Brutus and Cato repeat liberty, liberty, and live to impose on others a liberty they have not accorded to themselves—stern, joyless men, crying to their neighbors: be joyful as we are joyful; be free as we are free.

Cato is not educable. Brutus I have sent to Hither Gaul as governor, to school. Octavius is beside me, seeing all the traffic of state; I shall soon send him out into the arena.

But why should Catullus hate me? Can great poets generate indignations out of sentiments acquired in old textbooks? Are great poets stupid in everything except poetry? Can they form their opinions from the table conversation of the Aemilian Draughts and Swimming Club?

I confess, my dear friend, that I am astonished by a weakness that I feel awakening in me, a delirious weakness: oh, to be understood by such a one as Catullus and to be celebrated by his hand in verses that would not soon be forgotten.

978. [*On a principle of banking.*]

979. [*On some conspiratorial activities in Italy agitating for his assassination.*]

980. Do you remember where Redhead Scaevola asked us to go hunting with him the summer we returned from Greece? The second wheat there promises very well. [*This is a financial tip, obliquely stated in order not to alert their several secretaries.*]

981. *On the poverty of adjectives which discriminate color in the Greek language.*]

982. [*On a possible abolition of all religious observances.*] Last night, my noble friend, I did something which I have not done for many years: I wrote an edict; reread it; and tore it up. I indulged an uncertainty.

These last few days I have been receiving unprecedentedly absurd reports from the disembowelers of birds and the auditors on thunder. Moreover, the Courts and the Senate have been closed for two days because an eagle let fall an untidy mess within an arrow's flight of the Capitol. My patience was drawing short. I refused to perform myself the ceremonial of propitiation, to mime the frightened self-abasement. My wife and my very servants looked at me askance. Cicero deigned to advise me that I should comply with the expectations of popular superstition.

Last night I sat down and wrote the edict abolishing the College of Augurs and declared that henceforward no days were to be regarded as unlucky. I wrote on, giving to my people the reasons for this action. When have I been happier? What pleasures are greater than those of honesty? I wrote on and the constellations glided before my window. I disbanded the College of Vestal Virgins; I married the daughters of our first houses and they gave sons and daughters to Rome. I closed the doors of the temples, of all our temples except those of Jupiter, I tumbled the gods back into the gulf of ignorance and fear from which they came and into that treacherous half-world where the fancy invents consolatory lies. And finally the mo-

ment came when I pushed aside what I had done and started to
begin again with the announcement that Jupiter himself had never
existed; that man was alone in a world in which no voices were
heard than his own, a world neither friendly nor unfriendly save as
he made it so.

And having reread what I wrote I destroyed it.

I destroyed it not for Cicero's reasons—not because the absence of
a state religion would drive superstition into clandestine forms and
still baser practices (that is already taking place); not because so
sweeping a measure would disrupt the social order and leave the
people in despair and dismay like sheep in a snowstorm. In certain
orders of reform, the dislocations caused by gradual change are almost as great as those caused by a total and drastic alteration. No, it
was not the possible repercussions of the move which arrested my
hand and will; it was something in and of myself.

In myself I was not certain that I was certain.

Am I sure that there is no mind behind our existence and no mystery anywhere in the universe? I think I am. What joy, what relief
there would be, if we could declare so with complete conviction. If
that were so I could wish to live forever. How terrifying and glorious
the role of man if, indeed, without guidance and without consolation he must create from his own vitals the meaning for his existence
and write the rules whereby he lives.

You and I long since decided that the Gods do not exist. Do you
remember the day that with finality we agreed upon that decision
and resolved to explore all its consequences—sitting on the cliff in
Crete, throwing pebbles into the sea, counting porpoises? We took
a vow never to allow our minds to offer entrance to any doubt upon
this matter. With what boyish lightheartedness we concluded that
the soul was extinguished at death. [*The English language cannot
reproduce the force of this phrase in Caesar's Latin where the very
cadence expresses a poignancy of renunciation and regret. The recipient of the letter understood that Caesar was referring to the death
of his daughter Julia, the wife of Pompey, the overwhelming loss of
his life. Mamilius Turrinus was with him when the news of her
death reached Caesar's headquarters in Brittany.*]

I thought I had not relapsed from all the strictness of these asser-
tions. There is only one way, however, to know what one knows and
that is to risk one's convictions in an act, to commit them in a
responsibility. In drawing up the edict last night and in foreseeing
the consequences that would ensue, I was driven to examine myself
most strictly. All the consequences I would most gladly face, certain

that the truth would ultimately fortify the world and all that are in it, but only if I were certain that I was certain.

Some last hesitation arrests my hand.

I must be certain that in no corner of my being there lingers the recognition that there is a possibility of a mind in and behind the universe which influences our minds and shapes our actions. If I acknowledge the possibility of one such mystery, all the other mysteries come flooding back: there are the Gods who have taught us what is excellent and who are watching us; there are our souls which are infused in us at birth and which outlive our death; there are the rewards and punishments which furnish a meaning to our slightest action.

Yes, my friend, I am not accustomed to irresolution and I am irresolute. You know how little I am given to reflection; whatever judgments I arrive at I arrive at I know not how, but instantaneously; I am not adept at speculation, and since the age of sixteen I have regarded philosophy with impatience, as a tempting but fruitless exercise of the mind and as a flight from the obligations of immediate living.

It seems to me that there are four realms in which, with dread, I see in my life and in the life about me, the possibility of this mystery:

The erotic—have we not explained away too easily all that accompanies the fires that populate the world? Lucretius may be right and our jesting world wrong. I seem to have known all my life, but to have refused to acknowledge that all, all love is one, and that the very mind with which I ask these questions is awakened, sustained, and instructed only by love.

Great poetry—poetry is indeed the principal channel by which all that most weakens man has entered the world; there he finds his facile consolations and the lies that reconcile him to ignorance and inertia; I count myself second to no man in my hatred of all poetry save the best—but great poetry, is that merely the topmost achievement of the man's powers or is that a voice from beyond man?

Thirdly, a moment that accompanies my illness and whose intimation of greater knowledge and happiness I cannot hastily dismiss. [*This sentence is evidence of the unbounded confidence that Caesar felt in his correspondent. Caesar never permitted any reference to be made to his attacks of epilepsy.*]

And, finally, I cannot deny that at times I am aware that my life and my services to Rome seem to have been shaped by a power beyond myself. It may well be, my friend, that I am the most irre-

sponsible of irresponsible men, capable long since of bringing upon
Rome all the ills that a state can suffer, but for the fact that I was
the instrument of a higher wisdom that selected me for my limitations and not for my strength. I do not reflect, and it may be that
that instantaneous operation of my judgment is no other than the
presence of the *daimon* within me, which is a stranger to me, and
which is the love which the Gods bear to Rome and which my
soldiers worship and the people pray to in the morning.

A number of days ago I wrote you in arrogance; I said that, respecting no man's good opinion, I was not interested in any man's
advice. I come to you for counsel. Think over these things and give
me all your thought when I see you in April.

In the meantime I scan all that passes without and within me,
and particularly love, poetry, and destiny. I now see that I have
been putting these questions all my life, but one does not know what
one knows, or even what one wishes to know, until one is challenged
and must lay down a stake. I am challenged; Rome is requiring
some new enlargement of me. My time grows short.

JOHN DEWEY

****

*My selection is an article which will be found beginning on p. 817
of Ratner's* Philosophy of John Dewey, *The Modern Library, 1939
(other title of volume being* Intelligence in the Modern World, *pp.
819-835). It was originally an address before the Annual Meeting
of the College of Physicians at St. Louis in 1937.*

JOHN DEWEY

****

The Unity of the Human Being

WE HAVE NO WORDS that are prepared in advance to be fit for framing and expressing sound and tested ideas about the unity of the human being, the wholeness of the self. If we ask an economist "What is money?" the proper official reply is that it is a medium of exchange. The answer does not stand in the way of a great deal of money being accumulated by using it to obstruct the processes of exchange. Similarly, we say that words are a means of communicating ideas. But upon some subjects—and the present one falls in this class—the words at our disposal are largely such as to *prevent* the communication of ideas. The words are so loaded with associations derived from a long past that instead of being tools for thought, our thoughts become subservient tools of words.

The meanings of such words as soul, mind, self, unity, even body, are hardly more than condensed epitomes of mankind's agelong efforts at interpretation of its experience. These efforts began when man first emerged from the state of the anthropoid ape. The interpretations which are embodied in the words that have come down to us are the products of desire and hope, of chance circumstance and ignorance, of the authority exercised by medicine men and priests as well as of acute observation and sound judgment.

Physicists had in the beginning a like problem. They are solving it by the invention of technical terms and a technical language. Symbols have, in principle, only the meanings that are put upon them because of special inquiries engaged in. It will be a long time before anything of this sort will be accomplished for human beings. To expel traditional meanings and replace them by ideas that are products of controlled inquiries is a slow and painful process.

Doubtless advance is possible, and will be made, by invention of words that are not charged with the debris of man's past experience. But it is also possible that this process cannot be carried with safety as far as it can be with physical things. Our technical terms might easily represent such artificial constructions that they would fail to help us in dealings with human beings—with the John Smiths and Susan Joneses with whom we rub elbows in daily life.

The words in which I try to communicate ideas to you are, then, at best, but means of stimulating personal observation and reflection. This statement holds even of the phrase "the unity of the human being." At first, the words have only a meaning derived from a contrasting effect. The idea of man as an integral whole is projected against a background of beliefs about man which are chiefly of emotional origin and force; against belief in a dualism that was the expression of religious and moral institutions and traditions.

The phrase "unity of man" has at first, accordingly, a negative meaning. It expresses a way of *not* talking about soul *and* body, body *and* mind. The word "unity" is a protest against the canonized dualism expressed in the presence of the word "and." Nevertheless, the split expressed in this word is so engrained in our emotional and intellectual habits that no sooner have we consciously rejected it in one form than it recurs in another. The dualism is found today even among those who have abandoned its earlier manifestations. It is shown in separations made between the structural and the functional; between the brain and the rest of the body; between the central nervous system and the vegetative nervous system and viscera; and most fundamentally, between the organism and the environment. For the first of each of these pairs of terms—structure, brain, organism—retains something of the isolation and alleged independence that used to belong to the "soul" and the "mind" and later to "consciousness."

While it is necessary to advance from the negative meaning of the phrase "the unity of man" the idea of unity also has its perils. For it has taken on associations during centuries of philosophic discussion that make it a dangerous word. It has become almost an invitation to set an abstraction in place of concrete phenomena. You and I can easily think of comprehensive systems—psychiatric, therapeutic, philosophical and psychological—suggested in the first place by undoubted facts, which under the protecting shield of the idea of unity, have been built up so as to force the facts, disguising and distorting them. At the present time there is a revulsion against the endless splitting up of human beings into bits. It is going on with respect to cells, structures and organs, sensations, ideas, reflexes; and with respect to atoms and electrons. The phrase "unity of man" is a protest against analysis of man into separate ultimate elements, as well as against the traditional split into body and soul. But it is easier, much easier, to set up the idea of unity in a vague way, than it is to translate it into definite facts.

"Unity of the human being" only indicates, at best, a point of view, and the point of view has no meaning save as it is used as a vantage point from which to observe and interpret actual phenomena.

We often hear such phrases as the unity of a family, the unity of a nation. These phrases stand for something. Yet in the history of social and political speculation, men have allowed the words to take the bit in their teeth and run away from inquiry into the actual facts to which they refer. These instances of the use of "unity" may, however, provide a suggestion from which it is safe to set out. Whatever else the unity is or is not, it at least means the way in which a number of different persons and things work together toward a common end. This *working together* exists in action, operation, not as a static object or collection of objects. It is the kind of unity that seems to me to give the clew to understanding the unity of the human being.

We can recognize and identify a man as a single object, a numerical unit, by observation which marks out boundaries, as we note that the bounded object moves as a whole. In that way you recognize me as a single object standing here on the stage before you. That is the way in which we recognize a rock, tree or house as a single object, as a unity and whole. But that which makes a rock a single whole is the interaction of swarms of molecules, atoms, and electrons; its unity is an affair of the way elements work together. The boundaries by which we mark off a human being as a unit are very different from the energies and organization of energies that make *him* a *unified human being*. We can observe the boundaries at a single moment. We can grasp the unity only, so to speak, longitudinally—only as something that goes on in a stretch of time. It is not found in any number of cross-sectional views.

Nevertheless, if we could look into the minds of our neighbors, I think we should not be much surprised to find in them quite frequently the notion that a man exists within the boundaries which are visible, tangible, and observable. In a word, the man is identified with what is underneath his skin. We incline to suppose that we would know all about him if we could find out everything that is happening in his brain and other parts of his nervous system: in his glands, muscles, viscera, heart and lungs and so on.

Now up to a certain point we are on the right track, provided we emphasize sufficiently the interaction, the working together, of all these diverse processes. We can get a better idea of the unity of the human being as we know more about all these processes and the way they work together, as they check, and stimulate one another and bring about a balance. But the one positive point I wish to present is that while this is necessary it is not enough. We must observe and understand these internal processes and their interactions from the standpoint of their interaction with what is going on outside the skin—with that which is called the *environment*—if we are to obtain a genuine conception of the unity of the human being.

Our attitude with respect to this matter is a strange mixture. In special points we take for granted the inclusion of the conditions and energies that are outside the boundaries set by the skin. No one supposes for a moment that there can be respiration without the surrounding air; or that the lungs are anything more than organs of interaction with what is outside the body. No one thinks of separating the processes of digestion from connection with foodstuffs derived by means of other organs from the environment. We know that eye, ear and hand, and somatic musculature, are concerned with objects and events outside the boundaries of the body. These things we take for granted so regularly and unconsciously that it seems foolish to mention them. Physiologists at least recognize that what is true of breathing and digestion holds also of the circulation of fluids that goes on entirely within the body, although the connecction of these processes with environing conditions is a stage more indirect. The structure and processes of the central nervous system do not have that immediate connection with the outside world that the peripheral neural structures have.

Yet an authority upon the anatomy and physiology of the nervous system recently used these words: "Every movement is the result of the messages which pass from the central mass of nerve cells to the muscles, and the outgoing messages are varied according to the reports submitted by the sense organs. These show what is happening in the world outside, and the nervous system must evolve a plan of action appropriate to the occasion."*

That movements affected by the muscles have to do, directly and

* *N. Adrian,* Harvard Tercentenary Publications, *vol. I, p. 4.*

indirectly, with activities of seeking, defense, and taking possession of energies of the outside world is obvious. The central nervous system has the function of evolving the plans and procedures that take effect in dealing with outside conditions as they are reported through sense organs—and I suppose it would be admitted that these reports vary, depending upon what the body was doing previously in connection with outside conditions.

In other words, with respect to every special set of organic structures and processes, we take it for granted that things beyond the body are involved in interaction with those inside the body, and that we cannot understand the latter in isolation. This states a fact so generally recognized as to be a commonplace. The strangeness of the mixture of which I spoke consists in the fact that while we recognize the involvement of conditions external to the body in all organic processes, when they are taken one by one, we often fail to recognize and act upon the idea as an inclusive principle by which to understand the unity of man and the disorders which result from disruption of this unity.

Whole philosophical systems have been built up, for example, by treating thinking, especially in so-called abstract ideas, as having no connection with the activities the body executes in the environment in use and enjoyment of the conditions it presents. There is many a mathematician who would be shocked if he were told that his constructions had anything to do with activities carried on in the environment. Yet we know that neural structures and processes developed in control and use of the environment are the organs of all thinking. Even some who call themselves behaviorists, who pride themselves on their strictly scientific attitude, have identified the behavior about which they talk with the behavior of the nervous system in and by itself. Having, for example, identified thought with language—a position for which much may be said—they go on to locate language in the vocal cords, ignoring the transaction of communication in which, directly and indirectly, other human beings take part. It may even be that on occasion physicians think of diseases, and even psychical disorders, as something that goes on wholly inside the body, so that they treat what goes on outside as, at most, an external cause rather than a constituent and interacting factor in the disease.

At all events, there is a good deal of description and interpretation in many fields in which the structural and static lord it over the active and functioning. Whenever we find this to be the case we may be sure that some structure of the body has been described and interpreted in isolation from its connection with an activity in which an environment plays an integral part.

On the other hand, when physicians proceed to regulate the diet, sleep and exercise of patients, when they inquire into and give advice about their habits, they are dealing with the "use of the self" in its active functional connection with the outside world. What, then, I am urging is simply the systematic and constant projection of what is here involved into all our observations, judgments and generalizations about the unity and the breakdowns of unity of human beings. For its implications are that all beliefs and practices which gratuitously split up the unity of man have their final root in the separation of what goes on inside the body from integrated interaction with what goes on outside.

This abstract principle becomes concrete as soon as one thinks not of environment in general, but of the human environment—that which is formed by contacts and relations with our human fellows. Psychiatrists have made us familiar with disturbances labeled "withdrawal from reality." They have pointed out the role of this withdrawal in many pathological occurrences. What are these withdrawals but cases of the interruption or cessation of "the active operative presence of environing conditions in the activities of a human being"? What are the resulting pathological phenomena but evidences that the self loses its integrity *within itself* when it loses integration with the medium in which it lives?

It is only necessary to think of those mild instances of withdrawal, forming ordinary day-dreaming and fantasy building, to appreciate that the environment which is involved is human or social. When a person builds up not only a systematized delusion of wealth but engages in a day-dream in which he has come into possession of a large sum of money, it is not the physical money he is thinking of, but the prestige and power it gives him over his fellows. If a fantasy becomes habitual and controlling, it brings about, sooner or later, retraction from even the physical environment. But these withdrawals from physical surroundings originate in disturbances of relationship with the human environment. They go back to such things as pettings and coddlings, personal rejections, failure to win recognition and approvals, fear of those in authority, frustration of hope and desire by social conditions.

We may then anticipate a time when our entire traditional psychology will be looked upon as extraordinarily one-sided in its exclusive concern with actions and reactions of human beings with their physical surroundings to the neglect of interpersonal relation-

ships. We have, to be sure, reached a point where we have chapters
and books entitled "social psychology." But we are far from having
reached the point in which it is seen that the whole difference between animal and human psychology is constituted by the transforming effect exercised upon the former by intercourse and association with other persons and groups of persons. For, apart from unconditioned reflexes, like the knee-jerk, it may be questioned whether
there is a single human activity or experience which is not profoundly affected by the social and cultural environment. Would we
have any intellectual operations without the language which is a
social product? As for our emotional life, permit me to cite two
passages written by a physician: "Contact with human beings is the
stimulus that elicits emotional and visceral reactions. It is not the
clatter of railways and motors, this 'fast hurrying age in which we
live' so often spoken of; it is rather the pride, the envy, the ambition,
the rage, the disappointment, the defeat that develop in purely
human relations that stir the viscera"; and again: "There is an immense amount of hokum uttered about the psychological tensions
caused by our swiftly moving era, as though the telephone, the radio,
and the electric refrigerator were instruments that could swerve the
viscera. The emotional life does not actually hinge on machinery but
on the type of response to living situations, situations that for the
most part are created by human contacts."*

I do not believe I am going beyond the implications of these passages when I say that the operation of "living situations created by
human contacts" is the only intelligible ground upon which we can
distinguish between what we call the *higher* and the *lower* (the
physical on one side and the ideal and "spiritual" on the other) in
human experience. The occurrence of a sensation, for example, may
be described as an interaction between certain neural processes and
certain vibrations. The principle involved here is the same in animals
and in man. But the *significance* of a quality of red depends upon
the part it plays in the customary uses and enjoyments of the social
group of which a person is a member. To a bull, its presence is a
purely physiological stimulus. For a child, it may be that a dress,
worn perhaps only on a festal occasion or a ribbon worn for adornment in the presence of others, is that which fixes the significance
of red. When we wait in an automobile for a traffic light to turn, red
is still a physiological stimulus. But it has its *significance* in terms of
adaptation of the behavior of individuals to one another. The emotional importance of red in a red, white and blue flag to a patriotic

* *Houston,* The Art of Treatment, *pp. 348-349; p. 450.*

American citizen is surely not native in physiological structure.

Examples do not *prove* the principle laid down. But I do believe that reflection upon these and similar cases will show that the only verifiable basis we have for marking off the experiences that have practical, emotional and intellectual significance from those which do not is the influence of cultural and social forces upon internal physiological processes.

At least, what I have said is a challenge to produce any instance of an experience having so-called ideal or even "spiritual" meaning that cannot be accounted for on this ground. Otherwise we must have recourse to the old division between soul and body. Take the case of those who revolt against the old dualism, and who because of their revolt imagine they must throw away and deny the existence of all phenomena that go by the names of "higher," intellectual and moral. Such persons exist. They suppose they are not scientific unless they reduce everything to the exclusively somatic and physiological. This procedure is a conspicuous instance of what must happen when observation, description and interpretation of human events are confined to what goes on under the skin to the exclusion of their integrated interaction with environmental conditions, particularly the environment formed by other human beings. Knowledge of strictly somatic organs and processes is certainly necessary for scientific understanding of "higher" phenomena. But only half-way science neglects and rules out the other factor.

We may reject the traditional dualism. In my conviction we should reject it. We cannot be scientific save as we seek for the physiological, the physical factor in every emotional, intellectual and volitional experience. As more is known of this factor, more intellectual capital and more resources of control are at our command. In the case of the physician especially is it so true as to be a truism, that the more anatomical, chemical and immunological information he has, the better prepared is he for his work. And it is also true that our knowledge of social relations and their effects upon native and original physiological processes is scanty and unorganized in comparison with the physical knowledge at command.

But in view of the role played by human contacts and relations in developing and sustaining the emotional and intellectual quality of human experience on one side, and in bringing disturbance and disorder into it on the other, this fact is all the more reason for devoting constant attention to the as yet relatively unknown factor in the case of every human being who comes under observation. This need cannot be met by knowledge of even the most up-to-date scientific psychology which now exists. For, unfortunately, this psychology suffers for the most part from exactly the one-sided concern in question: the failure to take into account the operations and effects of relationships between human beings.

To me, a layman, it appears that physicians have a unique opportunity for building up just the kind of knowledge that is now so largely lacking. Physicians are the persons who have the most direct, intimate and continued contact with the living situations in which the problem is most acutely present. Since the decline of the influence of priest and pastor, no other professional body is in a position to make such a contribution and render such a service—though it should be acknowledged that the group of teachers also has an opportunity of which it fails to take adequate advantage. I am impressed, as every one else naturally is, with the now oft-made statement that at least one-half of those who consult physicians are suffering from ailments having a strictly neural basis and that show psychopathological traits. Indeed, this statement seems to me to be actually a great under-statement of the seriousness of the situation.

For the conception of good health is so vague that most persons do not go to see a physician until their ailments have become rather extreme. No one knows how many who do not come suffer loss of energy, efficiency and happiness because of difficulties that have a psychic aspect. A fair guess would be, I take it, that this group includes in some degree, everybody. If the factor of human relationships is as fundamental in production of these disorders, slight and intense, as we now have reason to believe is the case, it is impossible to over-state the extent or the importance of the concrete body of knowledge physicians can build up.

At this point, I must invite your attention again to the dubious and controversial state in which the whole matter of so-called higher mental state finds itself, and the disastrous consequences that ensue. In saying this, I am not referring to controversies between philosophers and psychologists about the relations of the mental and physical—controversies that pass under the names of interactionism, parallelism, materialism, etc. I think these are of no great practical importance save as they reflect certain divisions of a more practical kind that are rife. There are some who are so impressed with the influence of mind upon body, and with opportunities for exploiting those whose troubles have a marked psychic phase, that they form special cults, while there are others who react to the opposite extreme. They will have as little to do with anything that cannot be located and described in some specific lesion or specific somatic process. The respective views and practices of the two groups supply ammunition the one to the other. It is this situation which gives practical point to the search for the unity of the human being, and that justifies presentation of the view that unity and its breakdowns must be sought for in the interactions between individual organisms and their environment, especially that of human associations.

In this connection may be cited some rather simple facts which indicate that there is nothing mystical or metaphysical in acknowledgment of the "higher" functions when they are interpreted by the view that has been set forth. When one of us steps on the toes of his neighbor in a crowded place, we offer regrets—since otherwise we are likely to subject ourselves to sour looks, irritation and resentment. A strictly physical event has taken place, but even from an ordinary common-sense point of view, the physical is not the whole of the matter. The presence of a personal relation introduces a qualifying factor.

If I stub my toe on an object left lying on a public street my response is quite different from that which happens if I stub it on the root of a tree in climbing a mountain. In the first case, I feel the object has no business there, that somebody has been careless, that something ought to be done about such things. A personal element has modified an otherwise purely physical reaction. In the second case, I may suffer equal or greater pain, but if the pain should be partly that of irritation, the irritation is directed at my own awkwardness. Again, I can hardly imagine anyone thinking that the pain a child suffers from colic is of the same quality as the agony of torture a sensitive child suffers from an act of injustice or unkindness at the hands of some one from whom he expects different treatment.

Sentimentalists put the pain a dog suffers in undergoing an act of vivisection on the same level with what a parent suffers who has lost a child. To other people, this attitude seems to display rather extraordinary callousness towards distinctively human pain—a pain that is what it is because the processes of the human organism have been profoundly affected by relations with another human being.

The point illustrated by these simple instances is that the whole ground for the difference between a sensation and an emotion seems to lie in the absence or presence of a response coming from another human being. Persons acquire likes and dislikes for physical objects and physical scenes. But upon the strictly physical level—meaning by that, one in which a human relation plays no part—a dislike is expressed by simple rejection, as, say, one "doesn't like olives or castor oil." When the rejection is accompanied by emotion, even a layman suspects there is something back of it. When such cases are studied it is found, practically without exception, that the object rejected is of a kind that has been socially "conditioned," as the term goes. The strong stirring of emotional interest that most people experience when revisiting, after a lapse of years, the scenes of their childhood is called out by the fact that these scenes were not merely the theatrical stage and properties of early activities, but have entered so intimately into personal relations with father and mother, brother and sisters and playmates, that it is impossible to draw a line and say the influence of the physical ends *here* and that of the social begins *there*.

It may be assumed, I suppose, that all students of biology and physiology now take it for granted that there is no recollection apart from a modification of neural structure undergone in consequence of an earlier experience. But would any one attempt to read off from even the most minute and thorough study of the structure of the modified neural cells and the chemical processes going on in them, what the nature of the earlier experience was? I imagine not; I also imagine that there are few indeed who think any possible future development of knowledge will enable this result to come to pass, making it possible to reconstitute a past experience on the basis of what can be observed about an organic structure. What is relied upon is personal contact and communication; while personal attitudes, going deeper than the mere asking of questions, are needed in order to establish the confidence which is a condition for the patient's telling the story of his past. The organic modification is there—it is indispensable. Without it the patient would not be able to recall past incidents. But this is not enough. The physical fact has to be taken up into the context of personal relations between human being and human being before it becomes a fact of the living present.

Intellectual operations are discriminative. They bring things to a focus, to a point, down, as we say, to brass tacks. But when we are angry or depressed, we are mad or sad all over. A *physical* pain may be more or less definitely and accurately localized. But while we may feel severe local burnings and constrictions in the case of severe grief, there is also a *total* experienced response which occurs. It operates through organic structures, especially the viscera. But if it were referred exclusively to them, to the exclusion of a relation to another human being, it would not *be* grief.

I remember as a child trying to reinstate on a hot summer's day, the experience of a day in winter—not just to recall intellectually that it was cold, but to recover the actual feeling. Naturally, I never succeeded, and I was not aware that if I had succeeded it would have been an hallucination. What I was attempting, was, however, hardly more difficult than it is, when we are experiencing an intense emotion, to procure or permit the introduction of ideas associated with another mood. Elation and strong hope take such possession of us that we cannot entertain ideas that suggest the possibility of failure as long as the emotions last. The person depressed with melancholy has no room for any idea connected with success or vital hope.

Now it may be doubted whether there is any idea, no matter how intellectual and abstract, that is not tinged, if not dyed, with the emotion that arises from the total response of the whole organism to its surroundings. The cases, then, of the influence of emotions upon somatic conditions, even to the extent of producing neuroses in some cases and creating astonishing recoveries in other cases, have nothing mystical or metaphysical about them. They are expressions of the regulative force exercised over partial organic processes by the whole of which they are part.

I have given a number of illustrations which by themselves are commonplace rather than weighty. The principle they are intended to illustrate is, however, of the utmost importance. For, as I have suggested, disruption of the unity of the self is not limited to the cases that come to physicians and institutions for treatment. They accompany every disturbance of normal relations of husband and wife, parent and child, group and group, class and class, nation and nation. Emotional responses are so total as compared with the partial nature of intellectual responses, of ideas and abstract conceptions, that their consequences are more pervasive and more enduring. I can, accordingly, think of nothing of greater practical importance than that the psychic effects of human relationships, normal and abnormal, should be the object of continued study, including among the consequences the indirect somatic effects.

We cannot understand the conditions that produce unity in the human being and conditions that generate disruptions of this unity until the study of the relations of human beings to one another is as alert, as unremitting and as systematic as the study of strictly physiological and anatomical processes and structures has been in the past. The plea is not for any remission on the side of the latter. But we need to recover from the impression, now widespread, that the essential problem is solved when chemical, immunological, physiological and anatomical knowledge is sufficiently obtained. We cannot understand and employ this knowledge until it is placed integrally in the context of what human beings do to one another in the vast variety of their contacts and associations. Until the study is undertaken in this spirit, neglect will continue to breed and so support belief in the soul, and in mental processes supposed to be wholly independent of the organism and of somatic conditions. The consequences produced by this belief will not be confined to errors of theory. The practical outcome is division and conflict in action where unity and coöperation of social effort are urgently required.

I may rephrase what I have said by saying that the fine old saying "A sound mind in a sound body" can and should be extended to read "A sound human being in a sound human environment." The mere change in wording is nothing. A change in aims and methods of working in that direction would mean more than any of us can estimate. Is there anything in the whole business of politics, economics, morals, education—indeed in any profession—save the construction of a proper human environment that will serve, by its very existence, to produce sound and whole human beings, who in turn will maintain a sound and healthy human environment?

This is the universal and all-embracing human task. Its first phase cannot be turned over to politicians alone, and the second phase cannot be turned over to parents, preachers and teachers alone. It is not the peculiar business of any special calling. Yet perhaps there is none who is more intimately concerned with aiding production of sound individual human beings than the physician. There is none who has as much opportunity as he has to observe the effects of disturbed and disordered human relations in production of warped and divided personalities. The situations with which physicians deal are not artifically produced in laboratories. They are nevertheless sufficiently extensive and varied to provide conditions of control like those of the laboratory.

I cannot help thinking that the idea of preventive medicine and of public health policies has bearing and application upon the point made. Because of the unity of the human being, because of the inextricable intertwining of the physical and psychical in his make-up, the work of preventing disease and disorders is not completely done when the physical conditions of sanitation, pure water, and milk supply, sewage disposal, and healthy homes have been attended to. The social conditions that make for the production of unified, effective, reasonably happy human beings and their opposites, come into the picture also. We may solve the problems of dualism and monism satisfactorily in theory, and yet not have touched the sore spots in society and in individuals, and this is the place where they have to be resolved practically.

JOHN DOS PASSOS

****

VIRGINIA

The biographies in USA *were meant as illustrative panels, portraits of typical or important personalities of the time, intended to interrupt, and by contrast to give another dimension to the made-up stories which are the body of the book, much as the portraits of saints illustrated and reinforced the narrative in the* retablos *of early church painting.*

JOHN DOS PASSOS

****

Art and Isadora

IN SAN FRANCISCO in eighteen seventy-eight Mrs. Isadora O'Gorman Duncan, a highspirited lady with a taste for the piano, set about divorcing her husband, the prominent Mr. Duncan, whose behavior we are led to believe had been grossly indelicate; the whole thing made her so nervous that she declared to her children that she couldn't keep anything on her stomach but a little champagne and oysters; in the middle of the bitterness and recriminations of the family row,

into a world of gaslit boardinghouses kept by ruined southern belles and railroadmagnates and swinging doors and whiskery men nibbling cloves to hide the whiskey on their breaths and brass spittoons and four-wheel cabs and basques and bustles and long ruffled trailing skirts (in which lecturehall and concertroom, under the domination of ladies of culture, were the centers of aspiring life)

she bore a daughter whom she named after herself Isadora.

The break with Mr. Duncan and the discovery of his duplicity turned Mrs. Duncan into a bigoted feminist and an atheist, a passionate follower of Bob Ingersoll's lectures and writings; for God read Nature; for duty beauty, *and only man is vile.*

Mrs. Duncan had a hard struggle to raise her children in the love of beauty and the hatred of corsets and conventions and manmade

124

laws. She gave piano-lessons, she did embroidery and knitted scarves and mittens.

The Duncans were always in debt.

The rent was always due.

Isadora's earliest memories were of wheedling grocers and butchers and landlords and selling little things her mother had made from door to door,

helping hand valises out of back windows when they had to jump their bills at one shabbygenteel boardinghouse after another in the outskirts of Oakland and San Francisco.

The little Duncans and their mother were a clan; it was the Duncans against a rude and sordid world. The Duncans weren't Catholics any more or Presbyterians or Quakers or Baptists; they were Artists.

When the children were quite young they managed to stir up interest among their neighbors by giving theatrical performances in a barn; the older girl Elizabeth gave lessons in society dancing; they were westerners, the world was a goldrush; they weren't ashamed of being in the public eye. Isadora had green eyes and reddish hair and a beautiful neck and arms. She couldn't afford lessons in conventional dancing, so she made up dances of her own.

They moved to Chicago. Isadora got a job dancing to *The Washington Post* at the Masonic Temple Roof Garden for fifty a week. She danced at clubs. She went to see Augustin Daly and told him she'd discovered

the Dance

and went on in New York as a fairy in cheesecloth in a production of *Midsummer Night's Dream* with Ada Rehan.

The family followed her to New York. They rented a big room in Carnegie Hall, put mattresses in the corners, hung drapes on the wall and invented the first Greenwich Village studio.

They were never more than one jump ahead of the sheriff, they were always wheedling the tradespeople out of bills, standing the landlady up for the rent, coaxing handouts out of rich philistines.

Isadora arranged recitals with Ethelbert Nevin

danced to readings of Omar Khayyám for society women at New-
port. When the Hotel Windsor burned they lost all their trunks and
the very long bill they owed and sailed for London on a cattleboat
to escape the materialism of their native America.

In London at the British Museum
they discovered the Greeks;
the Dance was Greek.
Under the smoky chimneypots of London, in the sootcoated
squares they danced in muslin tunics, they copied poses from Greek
vases, went to lectures, artgalleries, concerts, plays, sopped up in a
winter fifty years of Victorian culture.
Back to the Greeks.

Whenever they were put out of their lodgings for nonpayment of
rent Isadora led them to the best hotel and engaged a suite and sent
the waiters scurrying for lobster and champagne and fruits outof-
season; nothing was too good for Artists, Duncans, Greeks;
and the nineties London liked her gall.
In Kensington and even in Mayfair she danced at parties in
private houses,
the Britishers, Prince Edward down,
were carried away by her preraphaelite beauty
her lusty American innocence
her California accent.

After London, Paris during the great exposition of nineteen hundred. She danced with Loïe Fuller. She was still a virgin too shy to
return the advances of Rodin the great master, completely baffled by
the extraordinary behavior of Loïe Fuller's circle of crack-brained
invert beauties. The Duncans were vegetarians, suspicious of vulgarity and men and materialism. Raymond made them all sandals.
Isadora and her mother and her brother Raymond went about
Europe in sandals and fillets and Greek tunics
staying at the best hotels leading the Greek life of nature in a
flutter of unpaid bills.

Isadora's first solo recital was at a theater in Budapest;
after that she was the diva, had a loveaffair with a leading actor;
in Munich the students took the horses out of her carriage. Everything was flowers and hand-clapping and champagne suppers. In
Berlin she was the rage.

With the money she made on her German tour she took the Duncans all to Greece. They arrived on a fishingboat from Ithaca. They posed in the Parthenon for photographs and danced in the Theater of Dionysus and trained a crowd of urchins to sing the ancient chorus from the *Suppliants* and built a temple to live in on a hill overlooking the ruins of ancient Athens, but there was no water on the hill and their money ran out before the temple was finished

so they had to stay at the Hôtel d'Angleterre and run up a bill there. When credit gave out they took their chorus back to Berlin and put on the *Suppliants* in ancient Greek. Meeting Isadora in her peplum marching through the Tiergarten at the head of her Greek boys marching in order all in Greek tunics, the kaiserin's horse shied, and her highness was thrown.

Isadora was the vogue.

She arrived in St. Petersburg in time to see the night funeral of the marchers shot down in front of the Winter Palace in 1905. It hurt her. She was an American like Walt Whitman; the murdering rulers of the world were not her people; the marchers were her people; artists were not on the side of the machineguns; she was an American in a Greek tunic; she was for the people.

In St. Petersburg, still under the spell of the eighteenthcentury ballet of the court of the Sunking,

her dancing was considered dangerous by the authorities.

In Germany she founded a school with the help of her sister Elizabeth who did the organizing, and she had a baby by Gordon Craig.

She went to America in triumph as she'd always planned and harried the home philistines with a tour; her followers were all the time getting pinched for wearing Greek tunics; she found no freedom for Art in America.

Back in Paris it was the top of the world; Art meant Isadora. At the funeral of the Prince de Polignac she met the mythical millionaire (sewingmachine king) who was to be her backer and to finance her school. She went off with him in his yacht (whatever Isadora did was Art)

to dance in the Temple at Paestum

only for him,

but it rained and the musicians all got drenched. So they all got drunk instead.

Art was the millionaire life. Art was whatever Isadora did. She was carrying the millionaire's child to the great scandal of the old-lady clubwomen and spinster artlovers when she danced on her second American tour;

she took to drinking too much and stepping to the footlights and bawling out the boxholders.

Isadora was at the height of glory and scandal and power and wealth, her school going, her millionaire was about to build her a theater in Paris, the Duncans were the priests of a cult, (Art was whatever Isadora did),

when the car that was bringing her two children home from the other side of Paris stalled on a bridge across the Seine. Forgetting that he'd left the car in gear the chauffeur got out to crank the motor. The car started, knocked down the chauffeur, plunged off the bridge into the Seine.

The children and their nurse were drowned.

The rest of her life moved desperately on

in the clatter of scandalized tongues, among the kidding faces of reporters, the threatening of bailiffs, the expostulations of hotel-managers bringing overdue bills.

Isadora drank too much, she couldn't keep her hands off good-looking young men, she dyed her hair various shades of brightred, she never took the trouble to make up her face properly, was care-less about her dress, couldn't bother to keep her figure in shape, never could keep track of her money

but a great sense of health

filled the hall

when the pearshaped figure with the beautiful great arms tramped forward slowly from the back of the stage.

She was afraid of nothing; she was a great dancer.

In her own city of San Francisco the politicians wouldn't let her dance in the Greek Theater they'd built under her influence. Wherever she went she gave offense to the philistines. When the war broke out she danced to the *Marseillaise,* but it didn't seem quite respectable and she gave offense by refusing to give up Wagner or to show the proper respectable feelings

of satisfaction at the butchery.

On her South American tour

she picked up men everywhere,

a Spanish painter, a couple of prizefighters, a stoker on the boat, a Brazilian poet, brawled in tangohalls, bawled out the Argentines for niggers from the footlights, lushly triumphed in Montevideo and Brazil; but if she had money she couldn't help scandalously spending it on tangodancers, handouts, aftertheater suppers, the generous gesture, no, all on my bill. The managers gypped her. She was afraid of nothing, never ashamed in the public eye of the clatter of scandalized tongues, the headlines in the afternoon papers.

When October split the husk off the old world she remembered St. Petersburg, the coffins lurching through the silent streets, the white faces, the clenched fists that night in St. Petersburg, and danced the *Marche Slave*

and waved red cheesecloth under the noses of the Boston old ladies in Symphony Hall,

but when she went to Russia full of hope of a school and work and a new life in freedom, it was too enormous, it was too difficult: cold, vodka, lice, no service in the hotels, new and old still piled pellmell together, seedbed and scrapheap, she hadn't the patience, her life had been too easy;

she picked up a yellowhaired poet

and brought him back

to Europe and the grand hotels.

Yessenin smashed up a whole floor of the Adlon in Berlin in one drunken party, he ruined a suite at the Continental in Paris. When he went back to Russia he killed himself. It was too enormous, it was too difficult.

When it was impossible to raise any more money for Art, for the crowds eating and drinking in the hotel suites and the rent of Rolls-Royces and the board of her pupils and disciples,

Isadore went down to the Riviera to write her memoirs to scrape up some cash out of the American public that had awakened after the war to the crassness of materialism and the Greeks and scandal and Art, and still had dollars to spend.

She hired a studio in Nice, but she could never pay the rent. She'd quarrelled with her millionaire. Her jewels, the famous emerald, the ermine cloak, the works of art presented by the artists had all gone into the pawnshops or been seized by hotelkeepers. All she had was the old blue drapes that had seen her great triumphs, a redleather handbag, and an old furcoat that was split down the back.

She couldn't stop drinking or putting her arms round the neck of the nearest young man, if she got any cash she threw a party or gave it away.

She tried to drown herself but an English naval officer pulled her out of the moonlit Mediterranean.

One day at a little restaurant at Golfe Juan she picked up a goodlooking young wop who kept a garage and drove a little Bugatti racer.

Saying that she might want to buy the car, she made him go to her studio to take her out for a ride;

her friends didn't want her to go, said he was nothing but a mechanic, she insisted, she'd had a few drinks (there was nothing left she cared for in the world but a few drinks and a goodlooking young man);

she got in beside him and

she threw her heavilyfringed scarf round her neck with a big sweep she had and

turned back and said,

with the strong California accent her French never lost:

Adieu, mes amis, je vais à la gloire.

The mechanic put his car in gear and started.

The heavy trailing scarf caught in a wheel, wound tight. Her head was wrenched against the side of the car. The car stopped instantly; her neck was broken, her nose crushed, Isadora was dead

PEARL BUCK

****

NEW YORK

DEAR MR. BURNETT:

. . . As for Pearl Buck, it is quite true, as she wrote to you, that she cannot choose from her own writings. But I have done a good deal of homework myself, and have questioned her closely. . . .

She herself feels that she ought to be represented by fiction. But passages taken out of novels are never satisfactory, from her point of view. . . .

My own choice is quite definite. It is from Fighting Angel *which, while a biography, has the narrative qualities of fiction. The passage I suggest is pages 145-162.*

Sincerely yours,

RICHARD J. WALSH

P. S. I am quite willing to have this piece used.

PEARL S. BUCK

Thus—from Fighting Angel, *the biography of the author's father, an American who, Pearl Buck says, "wandered about China for more than half a century," a missionary, "with a sword-like single- ness of heart . . . a magnificent imperialism of the spirit. . . ."*

****

Fighting Angel

THOSE EIGHT YEARS before the Boxer Rebellion were the years of greatest danger in Andrew's mission. Since he never stayed in estab- lished places, but was always pushing out into the new and unknown he often found himself among hostile people. The Chinese were dis- trustful of foreigners, not only from other countries but even people of their own nation from other provinces or regions. This is perhaps because each village and town has maintained itself for centuries as a separate locality. There has been almost no government from above or outside, and the clan feeling is very strong. In some places it was

the usual custom to kill any stranger who came unexplained by bury-
ing him alive! It was the very common thing in a village, as it is
today, to set the savage half-wild dogs upon any newcomer. Andrew
went on, doing no more than carry a stout stick with which to beat off
the dogs. And the dogs, soon discovering him to be unafraid and
wary of their tricks at his heels, learned to leave him alone until he
pushed on into stranger places. They are cowards, those dogs!

No one will ever know exactly what dangers he endured, because
he never talked about them without a great deal of questioning and
drawing out. Then in a few sentences he might tell a story that
another would have made into a day's tale.

There was the time when he lay asleep upon the brick bed of an
inn and awoke, conscious of a light, to find the innkeeper standing
beside him, a bean-oil lamp flaming in his left hand and in his right
a meat-chopper from the inn's kitchen. Andrew, opening his eyes,
fixed them full upon the man's face and cried aloud to God.

"Deliver me, God!"

He spoke in English and the man grew afraid.

"What are you saying?" he asked.

"I am calling to my God," Andrew replied, never moving his
steady blue eyes from the man's face.

The man lifted the meat-chopper firmly and brandished it. "Are
you not afraid?" he shouted.

"No," said Andrew quietly. "Why should I be afraid? You can do
no more than kill my body, and my God will punish you."

"How?" asked the man, pausing again.

"You will live in torment," said Andrew with such calm certainty
that the man stared at him a while and went muttering away at last.

"What did you do then?" we asked Andrew, breathless.

"I turned over and went to sleep," he replied.

"He might have come back!" we breathed.

"There was a guard over me," he said simply.

Once he was pushed from a crowded ferry boat into a river by
a rough fellow who first cussed him, and finding him unmoved,
jostled him and tripped him over. But Andrew came up out of the
muddy water and caught hold of the junk's rudder and held on.
The crowd stared down at him, but not one offered him a hand. But
he did not ask for a hand. He clung on until the river bank came
under his feet and then he walked out, dripping wet, but imperturb-
able, to hunt for his box on the ferry boat. It was gone; the fellow
had taken it.

The crowd laughed. "It was full of silver dollars," they cried. "All foreigners travel with boxes of silver dollars!"

Andrew smiled and went on his way content. His few silver dollars were safely in his pocket and the box had been full of tracts and Gospel sheets. "God has ways for men," he said in telling of it, and was convinced that the man's soul would be saved.

More than once he was laid upon and beaten when he appeared unexpectedly in some strange town. They beat him, apparently, for no reason except that they had never seen anyone like him before, as dogs will set upon a strange dog they have not seen.

But the things he really minded the most were not these. He was a fastidious saint physically, and he came home often quite ill with sickness at what he had had to endure of filth. Once he came in green with horror.

"What is it?" cried his wife Carie.

"I have eaten serpent today," he said in a ghastly voice. "I ate it at an inn and did not know it until afterwards." And immediately he was sick with the thought.

The common custom of hawking and spitting he could not endure. He who was so infinitely patient with men's souls had no patience at all with their bodies. When the trains first began to run he rejoiced in the signs put up against spitting elsewhere than in the numerous spittoons provided. But no one paid any attention to the signs. The Chinese were accustomed to spit where they pleased. Most of them could not read, and those that could paid no heed. Physical convenience is the law of life in China. Andrew came home one summer evening looking very content.

"There was a great fat fellow on the train today," he said abruptly at the supper table.

We all looked at him, waiting.

"He had off his shirt and sat in his drawers and his belly was like a great frog's," he went on, disgust in his eyes. He wiped his mouth carefully. "He spat everywhere except in the spittoon. I could not bear it, and pointed to the sign."

"I hope it did some good," said Carie, skeptically.

"It did not and I told him what I thought of him," said Andrew. "What did you tell him?" we asked.

"I told him he was filthier than a beast," Andrew said gently.

"Father!" we cried.

"Oh, I told him very kindly and pleasantly," he replied, in the same mild voice, and could not understand why we laughed.

He had, of course, enemies. Most of them, it is true, were among
his fellow missionaries, but these he considered his natural enemies.
Missionaries and magistrates he put in the same class as his enemies,
that is, persons designed by the devil to thwart the will of God, or
what he, Andrew, wanted to do. Magistrates he was ruthless toward,
and he quite openly used every treaty right he had to force them to
allow him to rent property for chapels. For though he never opened
chapels unless there were those who wanted it, still there were always opposing groups who did not want the foreigner's religion in
their town. These Andrew disregarded completely. If there were one
soul who wanted to hear of God, it was that one's right to hear,
though there might be a hundred who did not want to hear. So
he went boldly to magistrates' courts, presenting himself again and
again, waiting hours upon their whims. Sometimes a magistrate, not
really meaning to see him at all, put him off from day to day with
one excuse and another. Day after day Andrew presented himself
at dawn to wait until night, only to come again, until everyone was
weary with him. Nor would he use the slightest touch of silver upon
the palms of the underlings. He knew very well that money would
have opened doors, but he had no money of his own and he would
not so use the church's money which he held to be for the preaching
of the Gospel alone. At last, if the magistrate proved obdurate,
Andrew would use force—that is, the force of the treaties made
after the Opium War by which Chinese citizens were to have the
right to be Christian if they liked and missionaries the right to
preach. If the magistrate were himself a doughty soul and would not
be awed by treaties even with the threat of gunboats behind them,
Andrew appealed to his own consul who, however he might curse
missionaries—and how many of them do curse missionaries and
groan, I suppose, very truly, that life would be simple without
them!—would nevertheless be compelled to send an official letter to
the magistrate. This letter, written upon official paper bearing the
large strange seal of the unknown United States, always did what
Andrew wanted. Grudgingly, in terms of carefully worded contempt,
the permission would be given. But Andrew cared nothing for man's
contempt. He went away to preach in triumph, being the stubborn-
est of the stubborn sons of God.

Well, all those years we at home scarcely saw Andrew, and to
his children he was a stranger, coming home very seldom, and when
he did, not as one who came home but as one who came only for a
night's rest before he went on again. Their lives were built without
him, their days filled with other presences than his. They were

fatherless because his life was dedicated to others, but they did not even know him well enough to miss him. He felt this vaguely, sometimes, when he came home and saw his son growing tall, and his daughter ceasing to be a little child, and the baby who had been born at the inn. But that one died when he was five, just before the last child, a girl, was born.

Sometimes he tried to enter into their lives. There were two times in the year when they remember him a little differently, not as a journeying angel who tarried with them a night, but as a man who shared the things they had to do. Of these two times one was Christmas and the other was when the boxes came from Montgomery Ward, and Christmas was really the less exciting.

For Christmas, of which Carie made so much for the children, was a somewhat doubtful occasion to Andrew. There had been no celebration of Christmas in his childhood home except going to church and having a dinner. There was no giving of gifts, no Santa Claus. His idea of gifts was strange, too. He could never think of things to give the children, except things he had wanted as a boy, and which they did not want. But if he did not know how to give gifts to his children, he knew less what to give Carie. Even the children felt the pain of an inadequate gift to her, and they knew enough to feel an ache in their hearts for her on Christmas morning when she opened a brown paper parcel and put it quietly aside without comment. But her eyes were shadowy. Yet we knew he meant nothing—only he never knew her, he did not know what she liked or what she wore or what she needed. The children, passionately adoring her, worked to give her what they could, spending weeks before Christmas to make "something pretty for Mother." They knew the secret craving of her heart for pretty things.

But of course Andrew, underneath all, could not bear the spending of money for anything that did not further the cause of his life. Money was the power to save souls—money to rent chapels, to open schools, to buy Bibles. He did not want anything for himself. So there was always a little ache about Christmas. And then he would murmur doubtfully, "No one knows the authentic date of Christ's birth. Besides, there is evidence that the festival is mixed with heathen traditions. We do not really know what we are celebrating—perhaps even the birthday of an ancient heathen god!"

"Fiddlesticks, Andrew," Carie exclaimed. "The point of it is to give the children a good time!"

But no one had ever troubled to give the child Andrew a good time, and he was more doubtful than ever. The truth is he was never free from the weight of his task. His happiness was measured by his success in that, and that alone. God had him.

But the Montgomery Ward boxes were another matter. They were necessities, ordered months before, paid for, and safely arrived. The children anticipated for weeks that morning when Andrew, looking up from the letters before him on the breakfast table, would say solemnly, "The boxes have come!" If he were not at home they could scarcely bear it, for Carie would not open them until he came. But he was nearly always there in the early winter. There was a regular routine to be followed, always exciting. Andrew must go down to the Customs office on the Bund and present the bill of lading and get the boxes through Customs. The children at home were waiting at the gate of the compound, if it were fair, climbing high so that they might catch the first glimpse of Andrew around the corner of the old Buddhist temple in the valley. If it were raining, they waited at the front door, their noses pressed white against the glass pane. Meanwhile Carie was preparing a place in the back hall for the boxes.

There was no greater ecstasy than the moment when Andrew appeared from behind the temple, followed by four or five coolies with boxes slung on ropes upon their carrying poles. The sound of their rhythmic step-keeping call floated up the hill and came nearer and nearer—"Heigh-ho—heigh-ho—" Soon, soon the boxes would be dropped in the hall, and the men clamoring about them in the dear confusion of the hour. Andrew would be waging a war over the tips the coolies were shouting for, slapping their sweaty breasts, pointing out the welts upon their horny shoulders.

"These foreign boxes are full of lead!" they would shout. "They are fit to kill us—and we came up the hill—and what is this mite upon my hand!" They would throw their coins down and spit upon them, and Carie would implore Andrew, "Give them a little more, Andrew—just this once!" And then very unwillingly he would give them a little more, and they would subside into grins and go away. And there were the boxes!

Some child always had the hammer and the big nail puller that Andrew had bought for such days, and breathless they watched while the strong iron teeth sank into the wood as Andrew pounded and clutched the nail head and the nail came up, screeching with reluctance.

Every board was saved as it came off, because the boxes were good American pine, dry as no wood in China was ever dry. All our bookcases and bureaus and the chests in the attic were made of the

Montgomery Ward boxes. Under the lid was strong brown paper. Carie pulled it away, and there were the things from America! It was our most real, most tangible touch with our own country.

Now, looking back, the things seem very simple, such things as the Americans order every day from their grocers and think nothing but necessities. But to us they were the dearest luxuries, things that could be bought nowhere around us, foods to be tasted and savored and enjoyed as precious, tools that seemed magic in complexity, garments made and ready to wear, marvels of fashion.

But really there were tins of coffee and bags of sugar, cakes of yeast and soap, a round keg of molasses for Carie's famous gingerbreads, and spices which perhaps had grown in the Orient and now were back again ready to be used. There were needles and pins, hairpins and threads, all the small things not to be found in Chinese stores—some ribbon in gay colors to be used to tie back little girls' curls on Sundays (dyed tape on other days) and there were other little luxuries—sassafras tea, which Andrew loved on a cold winter's night at supper, and a few pounds of hard peppermint candy, some packages of gelatin, jars for fruits that Carie put up against the winter. For clothing there were the necessities of long underwear for the damp Chinese winters in badly heated houses—Carie knitted our stockings and sweaters and little cuffs she called wristlets. And last there was always a little special thing that each child had chosen out of the fabulous catalogue. Oh, the lovely hours we all spent poring over the catalogue, searching for the one thing, costing not more than the dollar we were allowed, the heart-burning decisions as to whether it were better to have several small things costing less or the one beloved thing costing a full dollar! And the agony when the one beloved cost a dollar and nineteen cents! There was no use in going to Andrew—no child thought of it—but Carie, always too tender-hearted, could be persuaded, and when the bill was presented to Andrew's stern eyes, Carie could be trusted to speak up and say, "I told her she could, Andrew—I'll make it up out of something else, or take it out of the housekeeping!" So Andrew let it pass—although to do him full justice he sometimes let it pass anyway, if the work were going well and he was in a high humor.

Each child, then, had his little package, precious to receive, precious to unwrap and to look at and fondle and play with and put under the pillow at night. Yet the catalogue was a book of heart-burning, too. So many things cost much more than a dollar! There was one of Andrew's little girls, for instance, who yearned deeply over years for a certain large baby doll. To this day she has not forgotten that doll. The legend underneath read "life-size." That meant as big as a real baby. She remembers its round bisque face in a frilly lace bonnet, its chubby hands, its long dress and little knit jacket. But it cost three dollars and ninety-eight cents and was of course hopelessly out of possibility. She bought a little doll or two, but they were never the same. She prayed resolutely for years that some Christmas—but there never was such a Christmas. She had little cheap dolls, dressed exquisitely and completely by Carie's hands. But they were not life-size. Every Christmas Eve that child, having prayed hundreds of prayers, went to bed with her heart beating with hope. But the first glance at the stocking and at the tiny heap of packages swept the hope away again for another year. If Carie had realized, she would have somehow seen to it, by some prodigious slashing sacrifice, that the small heart had its desire. But she never knew, for the child never spoke, not dreaming that the fabulous sum was within her parents' possibility to give. Santa Claus—or God— might give it, but not Andrew who needed all the money. And Carie had no money of her own. So the doll remained upon the pages of the catalogue to dream over and at last to relinquish, except to this day that child, now long grown, cannot pass the doll counter in a toy shop—cannot have her fill, for that matter, of real babies.

But there were many little white children living in the heart of China to whom Montgomery Ward took place with Santa Claus and God. One child came home one day to say solemnly to her mother. "I feel sure Miss Nan and Mr. Rob are going to be married."

"How do you know?" the mother inquired.

"Because I saw them looking at a Montgomery Ward catalogue together," the child replied, astutely.

All this time a slow storm was rising out of the deeps of China. None of us realized it, certainly not I as a small child living in Andrew's house. Yet I remember being afraid in the night because of things I heard Andrew and Carie talk about. People were not as willing to hear Andrew preach as they had been, it seemed. He came home more often than he used to come, and very often he was dejected and downcast so that before he came Carie used to coax us to be especially good, to be affectionate with him and remember how tired he was.

"You children can't understand all the hard things he has to bear while you live safely here—" She paused, as though listening, wondering, perhaps, how safe the children were.

But they were warm-hearted little things and ran about doing things for Andrew's coming—picking flowers he never noticed, and putting his old leather slippers at the door for him to slip on when he came in—a thing he did notice and enjoy. There was a sort of symbolism in those large worn leather slippers, shaped to the angles of Andrew's feet. To a small child, carrying one in each hand, they seemed as enormous as a giant's shoes, and they had a sort of magic, too, because when Andrew put them on a different look came over his face. It was his home look—a desperate weariness of the body, a lightening of the heart, and a certain famishment in the eyes. But perhaps it was only eagerness for home and his own about him, an eagerness he was not able to put into words.

As the years went on which led to the Boxer Rebellion, he was more and more dejected when he came home. He spent hours sitting in his study, doing nothing, apparently. We used to see him sitting there in his old imitation leather armchair that he had picked up in a second-hand shop in Shanghai. It had, as long as I can remember, pieces of excelsior stuffing coming out of it, and spots where his body pressed upon it most hardly, especially in two spots where his elbows leaned when he prayed.

There was talk, too, because Andrew and Carie never hid the realities of their lives from their children. Andrew would say suddenly at the table, "I've had to close up three more chapels this last month. The landlords wouldn't let me keep them. I can't find another place—nobody will rent me a place to preach in now. Something's wrong."

Or he would say, "We're having meetings at the houses of different church members. We have to have them as the Christians did of old—at midnight, secretly, as we are able."

Many and many a night the children woke to hear the clang of the compound gate and to see the flicker of Andrew's big old kerosene oil lantern which he carried at night and kept spotlessly clean himself. It was one of his small fastidiousnesses—a clean lantern, or at home, the lamp clean and trimmed. For in those days we used oil lamps and American kerosene oil. When we saw the flicker of light upon the whitewashed wall, we knew that was Andrew coming home from a secret meeting of Christians.

The whole house came somehow to be filled not with fear but with a sort of solemn waiting. One by one the servants, on some pretext or another, left, until there were only the nurse and her son. And Andrew was at home more and more, his face growing daily more grim. He went several times to see the American consul and came back to say to Carie, "He can't do anything—they're all waiting."

And one night he never came home at all! It was nearly noon of the next day before he came in, and his wrists were bleeding where thongs had held him.

When Carie, frantic with anxiety, cried out, he answered soberly, "Be glad I am alive. I was at Lin Meng's administering communion to his old mother when soldiers came in. They took Lin away and tortured him until he died. But he remained true. They took his ten-year-old son, but let him go today, and he came back and told me and loosed me. I was left bound, and the woman died as I stood there, bound to a post." His face worked, and he sat down and groaned. Then he looked at us all strangely, his ice-colored eyes shining, his voice solemn and triumphant. "Lin Meng has entered into the presence of our Lord, a martyr, to stand among that glorified host!"

He got up quickly and went away into his study, to be alone a while.

So it was everywhere. For soon there began to come rumors of death. In one town in Shantung the small missionary community were all killed, including the children. Several times missionaries we had never seen before were brought to us by secret friends among the Chinese, ragged and starved and ill, and Carie cared for them and sent them on to Shanghai and safety. There were sometimes children of eight or ten with them, a very few, but never any little ones or any babies. These had died of dysentery, of fever, of hardships too dreadful to be told. The children of Carie never heard the rumors, but they saw Carie rock herself in weeping and anguish and fear for her own. So the storm mounted and mounted, until that day when the American flag raised at a point long agreed upon warned us to leave instantly, and Carie took the children and went. But Andrew stayed, alone.

It is not possible fully to know what was in Andrew's mind when he went back, the solitary white man in that whole countryside. Never, not then or after, did he leave his post when danger came. He went back quietly. On the way he was spat upon many times, and curses were shouted after him. But curses were common and he paid no heed to them. He entered the empty house, bathed and changed his clothing, and sat down to his supper. One young lad, the son of the children's faithful nurse, remained to serve him.

VAN WYCK BROOKS

****

For almost twenty years now I have been engaged in writing a literary history of the United States. This was planned to fill five volumes, and I expect the final volume will be published in 1951. In my earlier work I was more concerned with criticism in the proper sense. I look upon this, in fact, as my natural sphere, and I hope to return to it when my history is finished. But, occupied as I have been for so long with history, I have scarcely been able to do anything else, and therefore I have chosen, as an example of my work, a passage from one of my five historical volumes.

In this sketch of the poet Robinson, characterization and criticism are combined in a manner that is typical of my historical series. Robinson himself was the forerunner of the modern American movement in poetry, and I think it is generally acknowledged that his reputation has risen steadily since his death in 1935. While I suppose he will always remain a locally American figure, he is more than ever, in a literary sense, alive.

VAN WYCK BROOKS

****

Edwin Arlington Robinson

WITH HENRY ADAMS, the New England mind seemed to have come full circle. It had passed through its springtime, its summer and Indian summer, and Edwin Arlington Robinson was not the only Yankee who saw

> *A dreary, cold, unwholesome day,*
> *Racked overhead,*
> *As if the world were turning the wrong way,*
> *And the sun dead.*

Had Charles Francis Adams's "ice-age" reappeared in this vigorous region, which had produced such abundant fruits of the spirit? The fatalism of Henry Adams was surely ten times darker than Calvin's fatalism had ever been. Was the tale of the Adamses symbolic? One thought of old John Adams, under his apple-tree at Quincy, rejoicing in the prospects of his "Christian Sparta"; and one thought of his great-grandson invoking Nirvana under the sickly shoot of Buddha's bo-tree. How much had waxed and waned in these four generations! Brooks Adams had only to look homeward to find an illustration that seemed to prove the truth of his theory of cycles.

Edwin Arlington Robinson personified winter. Abandoning New England, he had carried to New York an aura of blight, desolation, decay and defeat. His view of the world was wintry,—so was his life,—and his style and his personality were bleak and bare. Had there ever been a poet who loved life less or found so little joy in the turning of the seasons? In the down-east phrase, Robinson was "master chilly." There was something starved and cold about him, as if his clothes were too scanty and his blood was too thin, as if the Maine wind had invaded his marrow. He was like the stranger in his *Tasker Norcross* who confessed that he had "never yet been warm." Taciturn, shy as an owl, diffident, lonely, he could only establish relations with others by drinking; yet everyone confided in him, for he was the most sympathetic of men, as winning as he was aloof, and completely unworldly. Helpless in practical matters, naturally forlorn, he had the will to write but not to live; and he suffered himself to be rescued again and again and reverted again and again to a life in the shadow. Abjuring the "octopus of superficial self-respect," he haunted mean streets and sordid houses, for the only success that he recognized was failure in the eyes of men, and he saw even this as distorted and thwarted. He had become vaguely known as the "poet in the subway," in days when few were aware that he wrote or existed; for he had a post, in New York, in the newly-built underground railway, checking the loads of material that were dumped at the mouths. There, all day, in his long black coat and broad-brimmed hat, he paced the damp dark tunnel, with its odour of gases. If he saw a light at the end of the tunnel, it was usually choked with mephitic mist: it was not so much a light as a murky glimmer. And this was like the light in Robinson's poems. He seemed to share at moments the old Emersonian faith, which he variously called the "gleam" and the "vision." But, in him, this faith was only a dim conjecture. More often he looked out upon "dark tideless floods of nothingness," where men escaped from their dungeons only to drown.

Robinson brought to the "Town Down the River" a view of life that was formed in "Tilbury Town." He saw New York as he had seen Gardiner, Maine, in his youth in this moribund port on the

Kennebec river. Gardiner, which had once been a thriving shipping-
centre, had gone the way of other New England towns, and Robinson, whose father had been a prosperous timber-merchant, had witnessed in his own household the decay of the region. The family
fortune, such as it was, had vanished, and Robinson's brothers had
fallen on evil days; and Gardiner abounded in men who had once
been important and who had no life any longer to shape to their
code. Their minds had been formed for a large way of living. They
had set the tone for their neighbours and headed their clans. But
they had no clans to lead now, and the making of laws was not for
them: they were left with the "dusty ruins of their fathers' dreams."
They had lost their confidence, as the years went by, and they crept
away into their houses and grew queerer and queerer. Eccentricities
multiplied on humbler levels also, and misery walked patch-clad
through the streets. There was never a more wintry world, as Robinson saw it. The sun rose dull there. Brown weeds grew through the
floors of houses. Torn curtains flapped in broken windows. The trees
were leafless, a ghostly band in cold array, and the thin leaves
skipped on the stones with a freezing whisper. The streets were
swept by an icy wind from the river, and the water was black under
the piles of the docks. Spring never came there. At best, a late
autumnal glimmer lingered by the river-side and warmed the bones
of aging men. There were Archibalds and Isaacs on some of the
farms, ripe and sweet as the cider they kept in their cellars; there
were good old uncles who were good old liars; there were admirable
doctors of billiards, "fallen from on high." But these were few beside
the lonely men who wandered through the scene, disconsolate shadows. There were outcasts, in broken shoes, sleeping in doorways on
Water Street, who had once driven their span of horses; there were
skirt-crazed old reprobates, misers and spendthrifts; there were men
who had been wrecked by kinks, horrors who had never lived, ruins
ridden by fear and killed by terror. There were creepers among catacombs, "whose occupation was to die," there were respected citizens
who blew their brains out; and one saw them straggling through the
town, stumbling over frozen ruts, in the cold white shine of a dreary
day. In short, this population was a whole *Spoon River Anthology,*
acting out its epitaphs in the world of the living.

Such was Robinson's picture of Gardiner, where he had seen his
future life as a "long and foggy voyage"; and through the cold fog,
wherever he went, he saw the old familiar faces. Sometimes the
derelicts of Gardiner appeared in New York, and "queer fellows"
drifted all over the city. But why were they derelicts? Why were

they queer?—and were they not, in any case, more interesting than men who were called successes? They interested Robinson more, as they interested many another young man who was living in New York at that moment and who found a spokesman in Robinson, then or later. Robinson was always drawn to them. Most of his Gardiner friends had been square pegs in round holes, a doctor, for example, who had lost his standing, a disreputable tinsmith, an outcast named Wash Benjamin who kept a mistress down the road. As long as the town did not respect them, they were likely to find a friend in him,—and not because he felt himself a failure. He had no interest in success; and he was quite content when a single suitcase contained all his possessions, including his books. Nor did his kindness explain it, kind as he was; he made an intimate friend of a lighthouse-keeper largely because he had had a foot wrenched off. He had, he said, a little of the hobo in him; and he sought, by a natural impulse, the despised and rejected, the lost, the maladjusted and the lonely because, in his time and his place, he was a poet. Who were the successful men, on the whole, in a world of business? One might have asked Sinclair Lewis, who was young just then, and who was so soon to reply with *Main Street* and *Babbitt*. Whether in New York, in Gardiner or in Gopher Prairie, the "bitch-goddess Success" repelled the young. It was noisome to the sensitive, as it had never been before: even for Horatio Alger it had lacked the glamour that failure as a symbol had for them. When Henry van Dyke was a great man and Veblen was a nobody, the Veblens had for the young an extraordinary charm; and one saw in every "queer fellow" a genius *in posse,* if not *in esse,*—one knew that if they were geniuses they had to be queer. To be adjusted to such a world, yet not to be a Babbitt, implied an all but unprecedented force of soul; and, as people had ceased to look for heroes and the young could scarcely believe they existed, they regarded maladjustment as a sign of grace. Five times out of ten, in fact, it was so. Most of Robinson's "lost" souls possessed some spirituality, and it was just for this reason that they were "lost." The people who were queer were the people who were real. Such was Robinson's message for an age of rebels.

Now, of course, there was nothing new in this. The founders of all the religions had known where to look for their apostles; and Hawthorne, in his *Feathertop,* had pictured the successful man who had not been able to pass through the eye of the needle. That successful men could not pass through it, neither Christ nor Hawthorne said; but a poet in a day like Robinson's could not dwell on exceptions. Poets had seldom dwelt on these exceptions, well knowing that successful men can look after themselves. In a day when success was the only visible goddess, a poet could only point out that it signified failure; and Robinson's successful men were Feathertops in every case, whited sepulchres full of dead men's bones. This, and its natural corollary, was the whole of his teaching. In all his long psychological poems, he stripped the emperors of their clothes,—what was false within always betrayed them; while he turned the tables on conventional opinion by showing goodness and genius walking in tatters. It was the Fernando Nashes and the Captain Craigs, the castaways who "went begging" that really "went giving"; and this, the oldest of morals for poets, had never ceased to be new. The novelty had always lain in the local application. Hawthorne had applied it, and Robinson applied it, each in his own place and time; and Robinson thus revealed a fact which Americans had almost forgotten, that poetry is always opportune. Emerson had restated this fact two generations before him, and only Emily Dickinson had revealed it since, in the line of the Yankee tradition; and Robinson carried on their line,—he was their natural heir,—just as he carried on the line of Hawthorne. If, moreover, the Yankee tradition seemed to be tapering off with him, this was characteristic of the moment. The scene that he pictured was moribund, and the Emersonian gleam that often appeared in his poems was shrouded and dim. He could not share the old assurance that life was part of a purposeful plan, much as he wished to share it and almost did so. A sad man in a withered world, he could not believe in the triumph of life, and the best of his real successes were scarred by their failure. They, too, all too often, were sterile fruit for the button-moulder, children of the abyss, impotent and vain.

In later years, after the first world-war, when poets talked of a "renaissance," Robinson was called its prime precursor. At a time when American poetry had reached its lowest ebb, he, in his obscurity, was real and vital; and the "irony and pity" with which he regarded his victims of fate struck the new note of the novelists as well as the poets. His probing, questioning, doubting mind was the mind of the new generation; and his portraits, even his sonnets, were novels in little. His longer psychological poems continued the line of Howells and James; and his technical development foreshadowed the poets that were coming. He had cast off early the influence of Aldrich, which dominated the magazine-verse of the moment, although, as if to train his hand, he had written his villanelles and ballades. He had reacted against this facile jingling. He had sought for the spoken phrase, for the neat and plain; and, if his style was too prosaic, if it was too bare and cold, it was hard, it was clear and it was honest. Here again Robinson was in the line of Emerson, who liked "dry light and hard clouds, hard expressions and hard manners." Robinson eschewed the nebulous, the blurred and the vague, as he abhorred the fatuous and the stereotyped. In short, in a poetical world of baker's bread and confectionery, Robinson brought forth real bread again.

It might have been foreseen that, after this return to nature, American poetry was destined for a liberation. The "renaissance" that soon occurred was the result of various causes, and Robinson was only one of these. But his austere integrity and his tragic feeling were more than a little influential and his style cleared the ground for other growths; and the time was approaching when no one who was concerned for poetry looked for this year's birds in last year's nests. Robinson, a traditional poet, carried on the New England tradition, together with the classical tradition that lay behind it; but "last year's nests" in poetry, as the new poets saw them, were the nests of the romantic mind in its hour of decay. Romanticism had given birth to a verbal fatty degeneration that revealed the degeneration of the life it sprang from, in a world whose actual deity was the goddess Success; and younger minds reacted against such phrases as "reverence for life" and "quest for beauty," because of their sense of the false and the hollow behind them. The older poets, in all good faith, had used these phrases because they meant them. They really reverenced life, they sought for beauty; while the recent poets, the magazine-poets, used them merely because the older poets had used them. They did not reverence life,—they only said so; and they sought for the pretty and the charming but not for beauty. The passions they claimed were not real passions; their heartbreaks never broke their hearts. They took in vain a language that had once been great. In short, they were "phonographs," as Amy Lowell presently said, or, as she might have said, ventriloquists, for their voice was not their own, it was alien to them, and they were either ordinary children of Mammon or wistful sentimentalists without strength. What had become of the great old life? What had become of the great old language? The bitch-goddess had them in her toils, and the "great words" had gone down with the great life-patterns. It was no use to talk to the young about "sacred" and "glorious" things, especially when the war had traduced them further; and the more sacred one felt they were, the more one felt it was obscene to use the words or even think about them. The younger writers, growing up in this dying phase of the old society, knew that Robinson was right. Success in this civilization was inevitably failure, although failure might be success. The more honest these younger writers were, the less they believed in the world they lived in,—they were all rebels at the outset,—and the better they expressed their minds, the surer they were to express them in terms for which Robinson had prepared the way. For just as he had swept the house for all that was truthful and loyal in living, he had swept it for plain speaking, veracity and candour. As for poetry, he had broken up the "roof of heaven,"—the cotton-batting roof it had become,—and the "new forms" followed as a matter of course. The free verse, the new rhythms, the imagism, the realism, the characteristic forms of the coming decades,—and especially the classicism that was salient also,—expressed new states of mind and new ideas of which Robinson was one of the prophets.

H. L. MENCKEN

****

"The Poetry of Christianity" seems to me to be a good new title for this extract. There is nothing to be said about my choice of it, save that I like it. Treatise on the Gods *is my own favorite among my books, and by long odds.*

H. L. MENCKEN

****

The Poetry of Christianity

CHRISTIANITY, as religions run in the world, is scarcely to be described as belonging to the first rank. It is full of vestiges of the barbaric cults that entered into it, and some of them are shocking to common sense, as to common decency. The old polytheism lingers on in the preposterous concept of the Trinity, defectively concealed by metaphysical swathings that are worse, if anything, than the idea itself. The Atonement is a reminder of blood sacrifice and the Eucharist of the pharmacology of cannibals. Judaism, in its theology, is far simpler and more plausible. So is Parseeism. A Parsee is not doomed to Hell for neglecting a sacrament, like a Catholic or a Baptist, nor is the Hell ahead of him, supposing he lands there on other counts, the savage and incredible chamber of horrors that Christians fear. He believes vaguely that his soul will go marching on after death, but he doesn't believe that it will go marching on forever; soon or late, he is taught, the whole cosmos must come to an end and start all over again. Buddhism leans the same way; it rejects immortality as not only unimaginable, but also as unendurable. Confucianism evades the question as unanswerable. It teaches that the dead survive, but doesn't pretend to say how long. On the ethical side it is much more rational than Christianity, and very much more humane, for its chief prophets and law-givers have not been ignorant fanatics but highly civilized men, some of them philosophers comparable to Plato or Aristotle. Even Moslemism, in this department, is superior to Christianity, if only because its ethical sys-

148

tem forms a connected and consistent whole. In Christianity the problem of evil, a serious difficulty in all religions that pretend to be logical, is enormously complicated by the plain conflict between the ethical teaching of the Old Testament and that of the New. Is God jealous or tolerant, vengeful or forgiving, a harsh and haughty monarch or a loving father? It is possible to answer these questions any way you choose, and to find revelation to support you. Christian theologians have been trying to dispose of them for nineteen centuries, but they still afflict every believer with any capacity, however slight, for anything reasonably describable as reflection.

But in one respect, at least, Christianity is vastly superior to every other religion in being today, and indeed, to all save one of the past: it is full of a lush and lovely poetry. The Bible is unquestionably the most beautiful book in the world. Allow everything you please for the barbaric history in the Old Testament and the silly Little Bethel theology in the New, and there remains a series of poems so overwhelmingly voluptuous and disarming that no other literature, old or new, can offer a match for it. Nearly all of it comes from the Jews, and their making of it constitutes one of the most astounding phenomena in human history. Save for a small minority of superior individuals, nearly unanimously agnostic, there is not much in their character, as the modern world knows them, to suggest a genius for exalted thinking. Even Ernest Renan, who was very friendly to them, once sneered at the *esprit sémitique* as *sans étendu, sans diversité,* and *sans philosophie.* As commonly encountered, they strike other peoples as predominantly unpleasant, and everywhere on earth they seem to be disliked. This dislike, despite their own belief to the contrary, has nothing to do with their religion: it is founded, rather, on their bad manners, their curious lack of tact. They have an extraordinary capacity for offending and alarming the *Goyim,* and not infrequently, from the earliest days down to our own time, it has engendered brutal wars upon them. Yet these same rude, unpopular and often unintelligent folk, from time almost immemorial, have been the chief dreamers of the Western world, and beyond all comparison its greatest poets. It was Jews who wrote the magnificent poems called the Psalms, the Song of Solomon, and the Books of Job and Ruth; it was Jews who set platitudes to deathless music in Proverbs; and it was Jews who gave us the Beatitudes, the Sermon on the Mount, the incomparable ballad of the Christ Child, and the twelfth chapter of Romans. I incline to believe that the scene recounted in John VIII, 3-11, is the most poignant drama ever written.

in the world, as the Song of Solomon is unquestionably the most
moving love song, and the Twenty-third Psalm the greatest of
hymns. All these transcendent riches Christianity inherits from a
little tribe of sedentary Bedouins, so obscure and unimportant that
secular history scarcely knows them. No heritage of modern man
is richer and none has made a more brilliant mark upon human
thought, not even the legacy of the Greeks.

All this, of course, may prove either one of two things: that the
Jews, in their heyday, were actually superior to all the great peoples
who disdained them, or that poetry is only an inferior art. My
private inclination is to embrace the latter hypothesis, but I do not
pause to argue the point. The main thing is that Christianity, alone
among the modern world religions, has inherited an opulent aesthetic
content, and is thus itself a work of art. Its external habiliments, of
course, are not unique. There are Buddhist temples that are quite
as glorious as the Gothic cathedrals, and in Shinto there is a dramatic liturgy that is at least as impressive as the Roman Mass. But
no other religion is so beautiful in its very substance—none other
can show anything to match the great strophes of flaming poetry
which enter into every Christian gesture of ceremonial and give an
august inner dignity to Christian sacred music. Nor does any other,
not even the parent Judaism, rest upon so noble a mythology. The
story of Jesus, as it is told in the Synoptic Gospels, and especially in
Luke, is touching beyond compare. It is, indeed, the most lovely
story that the human fancy has ever devised, and the fact that large
parts of it cannot be accepted as true surely does no violence to its
effectiveness, for it is of the very essence of poetry that it is not true:
its aim is not to record facts but to conjure up entrancing impos-
sibilities. The story of Jesus is the sempiternal Cinderella story, lifted
to cosmic dimensions. Beside it the best that you will find in the
sacred literature of Moslem and Brahman, Parsee and Buddhist,
seems flat, stale and unprofitable.

Moreover, it has the power, like all truly great myths, of throwing
off lesser ones, apparently in an endless stream. The innumerable
legends of the saints, many of them of great beauty, are mainly no
more than variations of one detail or another of the fable of Jesus,
and so are many of the stories that Christianity has concocted out of
what were, in the first place, pagan materials—for example, that of
Santa Claus. The human appeal of all this poetry is so extraordinarily potent that it promises to survive the decay of Christianity.
Everyone has observed how Jews and infidels succumb in Christendom to the spirit of Christmas. What is less noted is the fact that

among Christians themselves there is a growing tendency, when they throw off Christian theology, to salvage Christian poetry. This is plainly visible in the organized lovey-dovey that began with the Rotary movement and has since proliferated so enormously in the United States, with tentacles reaching out to not a few foreign lands. Robert S. and Helen M. Lynd tell us, in "Middletown," how, in the typical American community they describe, Rotary threatens to become a substitute for Christianity, to the grave damage of churches and clergy. It is not, of course, a theological system; it is simply a poetical system. Starting out in 1905 on a you-tickle-me-and-I'll-tickle-you basis, it quickly took on overtones of aspiration, and today its main purpose seems to be to convince emulous but unimaginative men that it offers a way to something resembling salvation on this earth—that its puerile mumbo-jumbo can convert stock-brokers, insurance agents and used-car dealers into passable imitations of Francis Xavier. The grandiose imbecility called Christian Science is tarred with the same stick. It is certainly not a science, not even in the lame sense that spiritualism and psychotherapy are, and no Christian theologian save a hopeless dipsomaniac would venture to call it Christianity. It is simply a kind of poetry—an organized and unquestioning belief in the palpably not true.

The thirst for such poetry, in the long run, may displace the old fear of the brutal and implacable gods. Something of the sort, in fact, was once envisaged by H. G. Wells, who proposed abandoning the Christian Scriptures in favor of a new Bible made up of extracts from Shakespeare, Shelley, Thomas Jefferson, Abraham Lincoln and Karl Marx—all of them poets, though some of them didn't know it. Upton Sinclair, the American Gnostic, went a step further: he undertook to write a sort of New Testament of his own, with incidental help from such thinkers as Frances E. Willard, Henry George, Dr. Albert Abrams, and Sacco and Vanzetti. The late Hitler had a somewhat similar scheme, and the lamented New Dealers played with one in which the Holy Saints were to be displaced by Roosevelt II, Eleanor Roosevelt and a host of lesser semi-divinities, including, I suppose, the go-getting Roosevelt boys. Such efforts to substitute poetry for theology may be expected to multiply in the near future, for the world is plainly entering upon a new stage of myth-making. The two things, indeed, are much alike, for both are based on the doctrine that it is better to believe what is false than to suffer what is true. That was undoubtedly a sound philosophy in the days when the great religions were born and the great poems were written; it may even be sound enough, at least for all save a small minority of men, today. But it is hard to imagine it continuing sound forever. That modern man still needs such consolations is no more than proof that the emancipation of the human mind has just begun—that he is yet much nearer to the ape than he is to the cherubim. Once he attains to anything approaching a genuine mastery of his environment that will become as irrational to him as the old belief in ghosts, witches and demoniacal possession. Religion, in fact, is already a burden to him. It sends fears to haunt him—fears which stalk upon him out of the shadows of the Ages of Faith, the Apostolic Age, the Age of the Great Migrations, the Stone Age. Its time-binding afflicts him with moral ideas born of the needs of primitive and long-forgotten peoples—ideas violently out of harmony with the new conditions of life that his own immense curiosity and ingenuity have set up. It is, in its very nature, a machine for scaring; it must needs fail and break down as man gains more and more knowledge, for knowledge is not only power; it is also courage.

It may be that, by thus moving away from religion man will be losing something. Perhaps the theologians are right when they argue that, whatever the falsity of their premises, they are at least more or less sound in their conclusions: that religion, taking it by and large, at least makes human beings happier. But that, after all, begs the question, for it is only a romantic delusion that makes happiness the one end of progress. It may be, for all we know, the *Übermensch* of the future will do without the boozy delusions of well being that we now call by that name. His prophet, Friedrich Nietzsche, has, in fact, hinted as much: his motto, says Nietzsche, will be, "Be hard!" To sentimentalists breathing Christian air this is revolting. They see in it only a counsel of brutality. But, as William James long ago pointed out, there is a hardness of the mind as well as a hardness of the fist, and we probably owe to it every advance that we have made away from the brutes—even the long, tortured advance toward kindness, charity, tolerance, tenderness, common decency. It has won for us, not only the concept of the immutability of natural laws, but also the concept of the mutability of all laws made by man. It has made us wary of our feelings at the same time that it has given us confidence in our growing store of fact. The truly civilized man, it seems to me, has already got away from the old puerile demand for a "meaning in life." It needs no esoteric significance to be interesting to him. His satisfactions come, not out of a childish confidence that some vague and gaseous god, hidden away in some impossible sky, made him for a lofty purpose and will preserve him to fulfill it, but out of a delight in the operations of the universe about him and of his own mind. It delights him to exercise that mind, regardless of the way it takes him, just as it delights the lower animals, including those of his own species, to exercise their muscles. If he really differs qualitatively from those lower animals, as all the theologians agree, then that is the proof of it. It is not a soul that he has acquired; it is a way of thinking, a way of looking at the universe, a way of facing the impenetrable dark that must engulf him in the end, as it engulfs the birds of the air and the protozoa in the sea ooze.

Thus he faces death the inexorable—not, perhaps, with complete serenity, but at least with dignity, calm, a gallant spirit. If he has not proved positively that religion is not true, then he has at least proved that it is not necessary. Men may live decently without it and they may die courageously without it. But not, of course, *all* men. The capacity for that proud imperturbability is still rare in the race—maybe as rare as the capacity for honor. For the rest there must be faith, as there must be morals. It is their fate to live absurdly, flogged by categorical imperatives of their own shallow imagining, and to die insanely, grasping for hands that are not there. Once, in my days as an active journalist, I attended one such poor fellow in his last moments. With the Seventh Commandment in mind, he had butchered his erring wife, and was now about to pay his debt to the Sixth. A devout Baptist, he was attended by a clergyman of his faith, and gave over his last hours to prayers to and praises of the Yahweh who had dealt with him so cruelly. When, finally the sheriff came to his cell and summoned him to the gallows he broke into a loud, confident recitation of the Twenty-third Psalm. Thus the last scene:

The march begins—first the sheriff, then the condemned with his arms bound, and then the clergyman.

THE CONDEMNED—(*Loudly*) The Lord is my shepherd; I shall not want. He maketh me to lie down in green pastures. (*They reach the foot of the gallows.*) He leadeth me beside the still waters. He restoreth my soul. (*They mount the steps.*) He leadeth me in the paths of righteousness for His name's sake. Yea, though I walk through the valley of the shadow of death (*The sheriff binds his legs*) I will fear no evil: for thou art with me; thy rod and thy staff they comfort me. (*The sheriff adjusts the noose.*) Thou preparest a table before me in the presence of mine enemies; thou anointest my head with oil; my cup runneth over. (*The sheriff signals to the hangman.*) Surely goodness and mercy shall follow me all the days of my life: and I will dwell in the house of ——

The drop falls.

As an American I naturally spend most of my time laughing, but that time I did not laugh.

WILLIAM FAULKNER

****

Many years after the literary world, or the best critics in it, hailed William Faulkner's odd, involved and tragic novel The Sound and the Fury *as a masterpiece, Mr. Faulkner wrote an appendix to the book for Malcolm Cowley's* The Portable Faulkner. *Of Dilsey, the central character in this scene, the author said merely that Dilsey "endured,"—and endured against the background of the decaying white Compsons in a doomed but tenacious civilization. This scene takes place in the old Compson place on a spring day in 1928 when the old governor's "doomed lost nameless seventeen-year-old great-greatgranddaughter" robbed her last remaining sane male relative (her uncle Jason IV) of his secret hoard of money and climbed down a rainpipe and ran off with a pitchman in a traveling street-show.*

****

Sunday Morning at the Compsons

The day dawned bleak and chill, a moving wall of gray light out of the northeast which, instead of dissolving into moisture, seemed to disintegrate into minute and venomous particles like dust that, when Dilsey opened the door of the cabin and emerged, needled laterally into her flesh, precipitating not so much a moisture as a substance partaking of the quality of thin, not quite congealed oil. She wore a stiff black straw hat perched upon her turban, and a maroon velvet cape with a border of mangy and anonymous fur above a dress of purple silk, and she stood in the door for a while with her myriad and sunken face lifted to the weather, and one gaunt hand flac-soled as the belly of a fish, then she moved the cape aside and examined the bosom of her gown.

The gown fell gauntly from her shoulders, across her fallen breasts, then tightened upon her paunch and fell again, ballooning a little above the nether garments which she would remove layer by layer as the spring accomplished and the warm days, in color regal

155

and moribund. She had been a big woman once but now her skeleton rose, draped loosely in unpadded skin that tightened again upon a paunch almost dropsical, as though muscle and tissue had been courage or fortitude which the days or the years had consumed until only the indomitable skeleton was left rising like a ruin or a landmark above the somnolent and impervious guts, and above that the collapsed face that gave the impression of the bones themselves being outside the flesh, lifted into the driving day with an expression at once fatalistic and of a child's astonished disappointment, until she turned and entered the house again and closed the door.

The earth immediately about the door was bare. It had a patina, as though from the soles of bare feet in generations, like old silver or the walls of Mexican houses which have been plastered by hand. Beside the house, shading it in summer, stood three mulberry trees, the fledged leaves that would later be broad and placed as the palms of hands steaming flatly undulant upon the driving air. A pair of jaybirds came up from nowhere, whirled up on the blast like gaudy scraps of cloth or paper and lodged in the mulberries, where they swung in raucous tilt and recover, screaming into the wind that ripped their harsh cries onward and away like scraps of paper or of cloth in turn. Then three more joined them and they swung and tilted in the wrung branches for a time, screaming. The door of the cabin opened and Dilsey emerged once more, this time in a man's felt hat and an army overcoat, beneath the frayed skirts of which her blue gingham dress fell in uneven balloonings, streaming too about her as she crossed the yard and mounted the steps to the kitchen door.

A moment later she emerged, carrying an open umbrella now, which she slanted ahead into the wind, and crossed to the woodpile and laid the umbrella down, still open. Immediately she caught at it and arrested it and held to it for a while, looking about her. Then she closed it and laid it down and stacked stovewood into her crooked arm, against her breast, and picked up the umbrella and got it open at last and returned to the steps and held the wood precariously balanced while she contrived to close the umbrella, which she propped in the corner just within the door. She dumped the wood into the box behind the stove. Then she removed the overcoat and hat and took a soiled apron down from the wall and put it on and built a fire in the stove. While she was doing so, rattling the grate bars and clattering the lids, Mrs. Compson began to call her from the head of the stairs.

She wore a dressing gown of quilted black satin, holding it close under her chin. In the other hand she held a red rubber hot water bottle and she stood at the head of the back stairway, calling, "Dilsey," at steady and inflectionless intervals into the quiet stairwell that descended into complete darkness, then opened again where a gray window fell across it. "Dilsey," she called, without inflection or emphasis or haste, as though she were not listening for a reply at all. "Dilsey."

Dilsey answered and ceased clattering the stove, but before she could cross the kitchen Mrs. Compson called her again, and before she crossed the dining room and brought her head into relief against the gray splash of the window, still again.

"All right," Dilsey said, "all right, here I is. I'll fill hit soon ez I git some hot water." She gathered up her skirts and mounted the stairs, wholly blotting the gray light. "Put hit down dar en g'awn back to bed."

"I couldn't understand what was the matter," Mrs. Compson said. "I've been lying awake for an hour at least, without hearing a sound from the kitchen."

"You put hit down and g'awn back to bed," Dilsey said. She toiled painfully up the steps, shapeless, breathing heavily. "I'll have de fire gwine in a minute, en de water hot in two mo'."

"I've been lying there for an hour, at least," Mrs. Compson said. "I thought maybe you were waiting for me to come down and start the fire."

Dilsey reach the top of the stairs and took the water bottle. "I'll fix hit in a minute," she said. "Luster overslep' dis mawnin, up half de night at dat show. I gwine build de fire myself. Go on now, so you won't wake de others twell I ready."

"If you permit Luster to do things that interfere with his work, you'll have to suffer for it yourself," Mrs. Compson said. "Jason won't like this if he hears about it. You know he won't."

"Twusn't none of Jason's money he went on," Dilsey said. "Dat's one thing sho." She went on down the stairs. Mrs. Compson returned to her room. As she got into bed again she could hear Dilsey yet descending the stairs with a sort of painful and terrific slowness that would have become maddening had it not presently ceased beyond the flapping diminishment of the pantry door.

She entered the kitchen and built up the fire and began to prepare breakfast. In the midst of this she ceased and went to the window and looked out toward her cabin, then she went to the door and opened it and shouted into the driving weather.

"Luster!" she shouted, standing to listen, tilting her face from the wind. "You, Luster?" She listened, then as she prepared to shout again Luster appeared around the corner of the kitchen.

"Ma'am?" he said innocently, so innocently that Dilsey looked down at him, for a moment motionless, with something more than mere surprise.

"Whar you at?" she said.

"Nowhere," he said. "Jes in de cellar."

"Whut you doin' in de cellar?" she said. "Don't stand dar in de rain, fool," she said.

"Ain't doin' nothin'," he said. He came up the steps.

"Don't you dare come in dis do' widout a armful of wood," she said. "Here I done had to tote yo wood en build yo fire bofe. Didn't I tole you not to leave dis place last night befo' dat woodbox was full to de top?"

"I did," Luster said. "I filled hit."

"Whar hit gone to, den?"

"I don't know'm. I ain't teched hit."

"Well, you git hit full up now," she said. "And git on up den en see 'bout Benjy."

She shut the door. Luster went to the woodpile. The five jaybirds whirled over the house, screaming, and into the mulberries again. He watched them. He picked up a rock and threw it. "Whoo," he said, "git on back to hell, whar you belong at. 'Tain't Monday yit."

He loaded himself mountainously with stove wood. He could not see over it, and he staggered to the steps and up them and blundered crashing against the door, shedding billets. Then Dilsey came and opened the door for him and he blundered across the kitchen. "You, Luster!" she shouted, but he had already hurled the wood into the box with a thunderous crash. "Hah!" he said.

"Is you tryin' to wake up de whole house?" Dilsey said. She hit him on the back of his head with the flat of her hand. "Go on up dar and git Benjy dressed, now."

"Yessum," he said. He went toward the outer door.

"Whar you gwine?" Dilsey said.

"I thought I better go round de house en in by de front, so I won't wake up Miss Cahline en dem."

"You go on up dem back stairs like I tole you en git Benjy's clothes on him," Dilsey said, "Go on, now."

"Yessum," Luster said. He returned and left by the dining-room door. After a while it ceased to flap. Dilsey prepared to make biscuit. As she ground the sifter steadily above the breadboard, she sang, to herself at first, something without particular tune or words, repetitive, mournful and plaintive, austere, as she ground a faint, steady snowing of flour onto the breadboard. The stove had begun to heat the room and to fill it with murmurous minors of the fire, and presently she was singing louder, as if her voice too had been thawed out by the growing warmth, and then Mrs. Compson called her name again from within the house. Dilsey raised her face as if her eyes could and did penetrate the walls and ceiling and saw the old woman in her quilted dressing gown at the head of the stairs, calling her name with machine-like regularity.

"Oh, Lawd," Dilsey said. She set the sifter down and swept up the hem of her apron and wiped her hands and caught up the bottle from the chair on which she had laid it and gathered her apron about the handle of the kettle which was now jetting faintly. "Jes a minute," she called. "De water jes dis minute got hot."

It was not the bottle which Mrs. Compson wanted, however, and clutching it by the neck like a dead hen Dilsey went to the foot of the stairs and looked upward.

"Ain't Luster up dar wid him?" she said.

"Luster hasn't been in the house. I've been lying here listening for him. I knew he would be late, but I did hope he'd come in time to keep Benjamin from disturbing Jason on Jason's one day in the week to sleep in the morning."

"I don't see how you expect anybody to sleep, wid you standin' in de hall, holl'in at folks fum de crack of dawn," Dilsey said. She began to mount the stairs, toiling heavily. "I sont dat boy up dar half hour ago."

Mrs. Compson watched her, holding the dressing gown under her chin. "What are you going to do?" she said.

"Gwine git Benjy dressed en bring him down to de kitchen, whar he won't wake Jason en Quentin," Dilsey said.

"Haven't you started breakfast yet?"

"I'll tend to dat too," Dilsey said. "You better git back in bed twell Luster make yo fire. Hit cold dis mawnin'."

"I know it," Mrs. Compson said. "My feet are like ice. They were so cold they waked me up." She watched Dilsey mount the stairs. It took her a long while. "You know how it frets Jason when breakfast is late," Mrs. Compson said.

"I can't do but one thing at a time," Dilsey said. "You git on back to bed, fo I has you on my hands dis mawnin' too."

"If you're going to drop everything to dress Benjamin, I'd better come down and get breakfast. You know as well as I do how Jason acts when it's late."

"En who gwine eat yo messin'?" Dilsey said. "Tell me dat. Go on now," she said, toiling upward. Mrs. Compson stood watching her as she mounted, steadying herself against the wall with one hand, holding her skirts up with the other.

"Are you going to wake him up just to dress him?" she said.

Dilsey stopped. With her foot lifted to the next step she stood there, her hand against the wall and the gray splash of the window behind her, motionless and shapeless she looked.

"He ain't awake den?" she said.

"He wasn't when I looked in," Mrs. Compson said. "But it's past his time. He never does sleep after half past seven. You know he doesn't."

Dilsey said nothing. She made no further move, but though she could not see her save as a blobby shape without depth, Mrs. Compson knew that she had lowered her face a little and that she stood now like a cow in the rain, as she held the empty water bottle by its neck.

"You're not the one who has to bear it," Mrs. Compson said. "It's not your responsibility. You can go away. You don't have to bear the brunt of it day in and day out. You owe nothing to them, to Mr. Compson's memory. I know you have never had any tenderness for Jason. You've never tried to conceal it."

Dilsey said nothing. She turned slowly and descended, lowering her body from step to step, as a small child does, her hand against the wall. "You go on and let him alone," she said. "Don't go in dar no mo', now. I'll send Luster up soon as I find him. Let him alone, now."

She returned to the kitchen. She looked into the stove, then she threw her apron over her head and donned the overcoat and opened the outer door and looked up and down the yard. The weather drove upon her flesh, harsh and minute, but the scene was empty of all else that moved. She descended the steps, gingerly, as if for silence, and went around the corner of the kitchen. As she did so Luster emerged quickly and innocently from the cellar door.

Dilsey stopped. "What you up to?" she said.

"Nothin'," Luster said. "Mr. Jason say fer me to find out whar dat water leak in de cellar fum."

"En when wus hit he say fer you to do dat?" Dilsey said. "Last New Year's day, wasn't hit?"

"I thought I jes be lookin whiles dey sleep," Luster said. Dilsey went to the cellar door. He stood aside and she peered down into the obscurity odorous of dank earth and mold and rubber.

"Huh," Dilsey said. She looked at Luster again. He met her gaze blandly, innocent and open. "I don't know what you up to, but you ain't got no business doin' hit. You jes trying me too dis mawnin cause de others is, ain't you? You git on up dar en see to Benjy, you hear?"

"Yessum," Luster said. He went on toward the kitchen steps, swiftly.

"Here," Dilsey said, "you git me another armful of wood while I got you."

"Yessum," he said. He passed her on the steps and went to the woodpile. When he blundered again at the door a moment later, again invisible and blind within and beyond his wooden avatar, Dilsey opened the door and guided him across the kitchen with a firm hand.

"Jes thow hit at dat box again," she said, "Jes thow hit."

"I got to," Luster said, panting, "I can't put hit down no other way."

"Den you stand dar en hold hit a while," Dilsey said. She unloaded him a stick at a time. "Whut got into you dis mawnin? Here I sont you fer wood en you ain't never brought mo'n six sticks at a time to save yo life twell today. Whut you fixin to ax me kin you do now? Ain't dat show left town yit?"

"Yessum. Hit done gone."

She put the last stick into the box. "Now you go on up dar wid Benjy, like I tole you befo," she said. "And I don't want nobody else yellin' down dem stairs at me twell I rings de bell. You hear me."

"Yessum," Luster said. He vanished through the swing door. Dilsey put some more wood in the stove and returned to the breadboard. Presently she began to sing again.

The room grew warmer. Soon Dilsey's skin had taken on a rich, lustrous quality as compared with that as of a faint dusting of wood ashes which both it and Luster's had worn, as she moved about the kitchen, gathering about her the raw materials of food, coordinating the meal. On the wall above a cupboard, invisible save at night, by lamplight and even then evincing an enigmatic profundity because it had but one hand, a cabinet clock ticked, then with a preliminary sound as if it had cleared its throat, struck five times.

"Eight o'clock," Dilsey said. She ceased and tilted her head upward, listening. But there was no sound save the clock and the fire. She opened the oven and looked at the pan of bread, then stooping she paused while someone descended the stair. She heard the feet cross the dining-room, then the swing door opened and Luster entered, followed by a big man who appeared to have been shaped of some substance whose particles would not or did not cohere to one another or to the frame which supported it. His skin was dead looking and hairless; dropsical too, he moved with a shambling gait like a trained bear. His hair was pale and fine. It had been brushed smoothly down upon his brow like that of children in daguerreotypes. His eyes were clear, of the pale sweet blue of cornflowers, his thick mouth hung open, drooling a little.

"Is he cold?" Dilsey said. She wiped her hands on her apron and touched his hand.

"Ef he ain't, I is," Luster said. "Always cold Easter. Ain't never seen hit fail. Miss Cahline say ef you ain't got time to fix her hot water bottle to never mind about hit."

"Oh, Lawd," Dilsey said. She drew a chair into the corner between the woodbox and the stove. The man went obediently and sat in it. "Look in de dinin' room and see whar I laid dat bottle down," Dilsey said. Luster fetched the bottle from the dining-room and Dilsey filled it and gave it to him. "Hurry up, now," she said. "See ef Jason 'wake now. Tell em hit's all ready."

Luster went out. Ben sat beside the stove. He sat loosely, utterly motionless save for his head, which made a continual bobbing sort of movement as he watched Dilsey with his sweet vague gaze as she moved about. Luster returned.

"He up," he said, "Miss Cahline say put hit on de table." He came to the stove and spread his hands palm down above the firebox. "He up, too," he said. "Gwine hit wid bofe feet dis mawnin."

"Whut's de matter now?" Dilsey said. "Git away fum dar. How kin I do anything wid you standing over de stove?"

"I cold," Luster said.

"You ought to thought about dat whiles you wus down dar in dat cellar," Dilsey said. "Whut de matter wid Jason?"

"Sayin' me en Benjy broke dat winder in his room."

"Is dey one broke?" Dilsey said.

"Dat's whut he sayin'," Luster said. "Say I broke hit."

"How could you, when he keep hit locked all day en night?"

"Say I broke hit chunkin' rocks at hit," Luster said.

"En did you?"

"Nome," Luster said.

"Don't lie to me, boy," Dilsey said.

"I never done hit," Luster said. "Ask Benjy ef I did. I ain't stud'in dat winder."

"Who could a broke hit, den?" Dilsey said. "He jes tryin hisself, to wake Quentin up," she said, taking the pan of biscuits out of the stove.

"Reckon so," Luster said. "Dese is funny folks. Glad I ain't none of em."

"Ain't none of who?" Dilsey said. "Lemme tell you somethin', nigger boy, you got jes as much Compson devilment in you es any of em. Is you right sho you never broke dat window?"

"Whut I want to break hit fur?"

"Whut you do any of yo devilment fur?" Dilsey said. "Watch him now, so he can't burn his hand again twell I git de table set."

She went to the dining-room, where they heard her moving about, then she returned and set a plate at the kitchen table and set food there. Ben watched her, slobbering, making a faint, eager sound.

"All right, honey," she said. "Here yo breakfast. Bring his chair, Luster." Luster moved the chair up and Ben sat down, whimpering and slobbering. Dilsey tied a cloth about his neck and wiped his mouth with the end of it. "And see kin you kep fum messin' up his clothes one time," she said, handing Luster a spoon.

Ben ceased whimpering. He watched the spoon as it rose to his mouth. It was as if even eagerness were muscle-bound in him too, and hunger itself inarticulate, not knowing it is hunger. Luster fed him with skill and detachment. Now and then his attention would return long enough to enable him to feint the spoon and cause Ben to close his mouth upon the empty air, but it was apparent that Luster's mind was elsewhere. His other hand lay on the back of the chair and upon that dead surface it moved tentatively, delicately, as if he were picking an inaudible tune out of the dead void, and once he even forgot to tease Ben with the spoon while his fingers teased out of the slain wood a soundless and involved arpeggio until Ben recalled him by whimpering again.

In the dining-room Dilsey moved back and forth. Presently she rang a small clear bell, then in the kitchen Luster heard Mrs. Compson and Jason descending, and Jason's voice, and he rolled his eyes whitely with listening.

"Sure, I know they didn't break it," Jason said. "Sure I know that. Maybe the change of weather broke it."

"I don't see how it could have," Mrs. Compson said. "Your room stays locked all day long, just as you leave it when you go to town. None of us ever go in there except Sunday, to clean it. I don't want you to think that I would go where I'm not wanted, or that I would permit anyone else to."

"I never said you broke it, did I?" Jason said.

"I don't want to go in your room," Mrs. Compson said. "I respect anybody's private affairs. I wouldn't put my foot over the threshold, even if I had a key."

"Yes," Jason said. "I know your keys won't fit. That's why I had the lock changed. What I want to know is, how that window got broken."

"Luster say he didn't do hit," Dilsey said.

"I knew that without asking him," Jason said, "Where's Quentin?" he said.

"Where she is ev'y Sunday mawnin," Dilsey said. "Whut got into you de last few days, anyhow?"

"Well, we're going to change all that," Jason said. "Go up and tell her breakfast is ready."

"You leave her alone now, Jason," Dilsey said. "She gits up fer breakfast ev'y week mawnin, en Cahline lets her stay in bed ev'y Sunday. You knows dat."

"I can't keep a kitchen full of niggers to wait on her pleasure, much as I'd like to," Jason said. "Go and tell her to come down to breakfast."

"Ain't nobody have to wait on her," Dilsey said, "I puts her breakfast in de warmer en she—"

"Did you hear me?" Jason said.

"I hears you," Dilsey said. "All I been hearin', when you in de house. Ef hit ain't Quentin er yo maw, hit's Luster en Benjy. Whut you let him go on dat way fer, Miss Cahline?"

"You'd better do as he says," Mrs. Compson said. "He's head of the house now. It's his right to require us to respect his wishes. I try to do it, and if I can, you can too."

"'Tain't no sense in him bein' so bad tempered he got to make Quentin git up jes to suit him," Dilsey said. "Maybe you think she broke dat window."

"She would, if she happened to think of it," Jason said. "You go and do what I told you."

"En I wouldn't blame her none ef she did," Dilsey said, going toward the stairs. "Wid you naggin' at her all de blessed time you in de house."

"Hush, Dilsey," Mrs. Compson said. "It's neither your place nor mine to tell Jason what to do. Sometimes I think he is wrong, but I try to obey his wishes for you all's sakes. If I'm strong enough to come to the table, Quentin can too."

Dilsey went out. They heard her mounting the stairs. They heard her a long while on the stairs.

"You've got a prize set of servants," Jason said. He helped his mother and himself to food. "Did you ever have one that was worth killing? You must have had some before I was big enough to remember."

"I have to humor them," Mrs. Compton said. "I have to depend on them so completely. It's not as if I were strong. I wish I were. I wish I could do all the housework myself. I could at least take that much off your shoulders."

"And a fine pigsty we'd live in, too," Jason said. "Hurry up, Dilsey," he shouted.

"I know you blame me," Mrs. Compson said, "for letting them off to go to church today."

"Go where?" Jason said. "Hasn't that damn show left yet?"

"To church," Mrs. Compson said. "The darkies are having a special Easter service. I promised Dilsey two weeks ago that they could get off."

"Which means we'll eat cold dinner," Jason said, "or none at all."

"I know it's my fault," Mrs. Compson said. "I know you blame me."

"For what?" Jason said. "You never resurrected Christ, did you?"

They heard Dilsey mount the final stair, then her slow feet overhead.

"Quentin," she said. When she called the first time Jason laid his knife and fork down and he and his mother appeared to wait across the table from one another, in identical attitudes; the one cold and shrewd, with close-thatched brown hair curled into two stubborn hooks, one on either side of his forehead like a bartender in caricature, and hazel eyes with black-ringed irises like marbles, the other cold and querulous, with perfectly white hair and eyes pouched and baffled and so dark as to appear to be all pupil or all iris.

"Quentin," Dilsey said, "get up, honey. Dey waitin' breakfast on you."

"I can't understand how that window got broken," Mrs. Compson said. "Are you sure it was done yesterday? It could have been like that a long time, with the warm weather. The upper sash, behind the shade like that."

"I've told you for the last time that it happened yesterday," Jason said. "Don't you reckon I know the room I live in? Do you reckon I could have lived in it a week with a hole in the window you could stick your hand—" his voice ceased, ebbed, left him staring at his mother with eyes that for an instant were quite empty of anything. It was as though his eyes were holding their breath, while his mother looked at him, her face flaccid and querulous, interminable, clairvoyant yet obtuse. As they sat so Dilsey said,

"Quentin. Don't play wid me, honey. Come on to breakfast, honey. Dey waitin' fer you."

"I can't understand it," Mrs. Compson said. "It's just as if somebody had tried to break into the house—" Jason sprang up. His chair crashed over backward. "What—" Mrs. Compson said, staring at him as he ran past her and went jumping up the stairs, where he met Dilsey. His face was now in shadow, and Dilsey said,

"She sullin. You ma ain't unlocked—" But Jason ran on past her and along the corridor to a door. He didn't call. He grasped the knob and tried it, then he stood with the knob in his hand and his head bent a little, as if he were listening to something much further away than the dimensioned room beyond the door, and which he already heard. His attitude was that of one who goes through the motions of listening in order to deceive himself as to what he already hears. Behind him Mrs. Compson mounted the stairs, calling his name. Then she saw Dilsey and she quit calling him and began to call Dilsey instead.

"I told you she ain't unlocked dat do' yit," Dilsey said.

When she spoke he turned and ran toward her, but his voice was quiet, matter of fact. "She carry the key with her?" he said. "Has she got it now, I mean, or will she have—"

"Dilsey," Mrs. Compson said on the stairs.

"Is which?" Dilsey said. "Whyn't you let—"

"The key," Jason said, "to that room. Does she carry it with her all the time, Mother." Then he saw Mrs. Compson and he went down the stairs and met her. "Give me the key," he said. He fell to pawing at the pockets of the rusty black dressing sacque she wore. She resisted.

"Jason," she said, "Jason! Are you and Dilsey trying to put me to bed again?" she said, trying to fend him off. "Can't you even let me have Sunday in peace?"

"The key," Jason said, pawing at her. "Give it here." He looked back at the door, as if he expected it to fly open before he could get back to it with the key he did not yet have.

"You, Dilsey!" Mrs. Compton said, clutching her sacque about her.

"Give me the key, you old fool!" Jason cried suddenly. From her pocket he tugged a huge bunch of rusted keys on an iron ring like a medieval jailer's and ran back up the hall with the two women behind him.

"You, Jason!" Mrs. Compson said. "He will never find the right one," she said. "You know I never let anyone take my keys, Dilsey," she said. She began to wail.

"Hush," Dilsey said. "He ain't gwine do nothin' to her. I ain't gwine let him."

"But on Sunday morning, in my own house," Mrs. Compson said. "When I've tried so hard to raise them Christians. Let me find the right key, Jason," she said. She put her hand on his arm. Then she began to struggle with him, but he flung her aside with a motion of his elbow and looked around at her for a moment, his eyes cold and harried, then he turned to the door again and the unwieldy keys.

"Hush," Dilsey said. "You, Jason!"

"Something terrible has happened," Mrs. Compson said, wailing again. "I know it has. You, Jason," she said, grasping at him again. "He won't even let me find the key to a room in my own house!"

"Now, now," Dilsey said, "whut kin happen? I right here. I ain't gwine let him hurt her. Quentin," she said, raising her voice, "don't you be skeered honey, I'se right here."

The door opened, swung inward. He stood in it for a moment, hiding the room, then he stepped aside. "Go in," he said in a thick light voice. They went in. It was not a girl's room. It was not anybody's room, and the faint scent of cheap cosmetics and the few feminine objects and the other evidences of crude and hopeless efforts to feminize it but added to its anonymity, giving it that dead and stereotyped transience of rooms in assignation houses. The bed had not been disturbed. On the floor lay a soiled undergarment of cheap silk a little too pink; from a half-open bureau drawer dangled a single stocking.

The window was open. A pear tree grew there, close against the house. It was in bloom and the branches scraped and rasped against the house and the myriad air, driving in the window, brought into the room the forlorn scent of the blossoms.

"Dar now," Dilsey said, "didn't I told you she all right?"

"All right?" Mrs. Compson said. Dilsey followed her into the room and touched her.

"You come on and lay down, now," she said. "I find her in ten minutes."

Mrs. Compson shook her off. "Find the note," she said. "Quentin left a note when she did it."

"All right," Dilsey said, "I'll find hit. You come on to you room, now."

"I knew the minute they named her Quentin this would happen,"

Mrs. Compson said. She went to the bureau and began to turn over the scattered objects there — scent bottles, a box of powder, a chewed pencil, a pair of scissors with one broken blade lying upon a darned scarf dusted with powder and stained with rouge. "Find the note," she said.

"I is," Dilsey said. "You come on, now. Me and Jason'll find hit. You come on to yo' room."

"Jason," Mrs. Compson said, "where is he?" She went to the door. Dilsey followed her on down the hall, to another door. It was closed. "Jason," she called through the door. There was no answer. She tried the knob, then she called him again. But there was still no answer for he was hurling things backward out of the closet; garments, shoes, a suitcase. Then he emerged carrying a sawn section of tongue-and-groove planking and laid it down and entered the closet again and emerged with a metal box. He set it on the bed and stood looking at the broken lock while he dug a key ring from his pocket and selected a key, and for a time he stood with the selected key in his hand, looking at the broken lock, then he put the keys back in his pocket and carefully tilted the contents of the box out upon the bed. Still carefully he sorted the papers, taking them up one at a time and shaking them. Then he upended the box and shook it too and slowly replaced the papers and stood again, looking at the broken lock, with the box in his hands and his head bent. Outside the window he heard some jaybirds swirl shrieking past, and away, their cries whipping away along the wind, and an automobile passed somewhere and died away also. His mother spoke his name again beyond the door, but he didn't move. He heard Dilsey lead her away up the hall, and then a door closed. Then he replaced the box in the closet and flung the garments back into it and went downstairs to the telephone. While he stood there with the receiver to his ear, waiting, Dilsey came down the stairs. She looked at him, without stopping, and went on.

The wire opened. "This is Jason Compson," he said, his voice so harsh and thick that he had to repeat himself. "Jason Compson," he said, controlling his voice. "Have a car ready, with a deputy, if you can't go, in ten minutes. I'll be there—What?—Robbery. My house. I know who it—Robbery, I say. Have a car read—What? Aren't you a paid law enforcement—Yes, I'll be there in five minutes. Have that car ready to leave at once. If you don't I'll report it to the governor."

He clapped the receiver back and crossed the dining-room, where the scarce-broken meal now lay cold on the table, and entered the kitchen. Dilsey was filling the hot water bottle. Ben sat, tranquil and empty. Beside him Luster looked like a fyce dog, brightly watchful. He was eating something. Jason went on across the kitchen.

"Ain't you going to eat no breakfast?" Dilsey said. He paid her no attention. "Go on and eat yo breakfast, Jason." He went on. The outer door banged behind him. Luster rose and went to the window and looked out.

"Whoo," he said, "whut happenin' up dar? He been beatin' Miss Quentin?"

"You hush yo mouf," Dilsey said. "You git Benjy started now en I beat yo head off. You keep him quiet es you kin twell I get back, now." She screwed the cap on the bottle and went out. They heard her go up the stairs, then they heard Jason pass the house in his car. Then there was no sound in the kitchen save the simmering murmur of the kettle and the clock.

"You know whut I bet?" Luster said. "I bet he beat her. I bet he knock her in de head en now he gone fer de doctor. Dat's whut I bet." The clock ticktocked, solemn and profound. It might have been the dry pulse of the decaying house itself; after a while it whirred and cleared its throat and struck six times. Ben looked up at it, then he looked at the bullet-like silhouette of Luster's head in the window and he began to bob his head again, drooling. He whimpered.

"Hush up, loony," Luster said without turning. "Look like we ain't gwine git to go to no church today." But Ben sat in the chair, his big soft hands dangling between his knees, moaning faintly. Suddenly he wept, a slow bellowing sound, meaningless and sustained. "Hush," Luster said. He turned and lifted his hand. "You want me to whup you?" But Ben looked at him, bellowing slowly with each expiration. Luster came and shook him. "You hush dis minute!" he shouted. "Here," he said. He hauled Ben out of the chair and dragged the chair around facing the stove and opened the door to the firebox and shoved Ben into the chair. They looked like a tug nudging at a clumsy tanker in a narrow dock. Ben sat down again facing the rosy door. He hushed. Then they heard the clock again, and Dilsey slow on the stairs. When she entered he began to whimper again. Then he lifted his voice.

"Whut you done to him?" Dilsey said. "Why can't you let him 'lone dis mawnin, of all times?"

"I ain't doin' nothin' to him," Luster said. "Mr. Jason skeered him, dats whut hit is. He ain't kilt Miss Quentin, is he?"

"Hush, Benjy," Dilsey said. He hushed. She went to the window and looked out. "Is it quit rainin'?" she said.

"Yessum," Luster said. "Quit long time ago."

"Den y'all go out do's awhile," she said. "I jes got Miss Cahline quiet now."

"Is we gwine to church?" Luster said.

"I let you know bout dat when de time come. You keep him away fum de house twell I calls you."

"Kin we go to de pastuh?" Luster said.

"All right. Only you keep him away fum de house. I done stood all I kin."

"Yessum," Luster said. "Whar Mr. Jason gone, mammy?"

"Dat some mo' of yo' business, ain't it?" Dilsey said. She began to clear the table. "Hush, Benjy. Luster gwine take you out to play."

"Whut he done to Miss Quentin, mammy?" Luster said.

"Ain't done nothin' to her. You all git outen here?"

"I bet she ain't here," Luster said.

Dilsey looked at him. "How you know she ain't here?"

"Me and Benjy seed her clamb out de window last night. Didn't us, Benjy?"

"You did?" Dilsey said, looking at him.

"We sees her doin' hit ev'y night," Luster said. "Clamb right down dat pear tree."

"Don't you lie to me, nigger boy," Dilsey said.

"I ain't lyin'. Ask Benjy ef I is."

"Whyn't you say somethin' about it, den?"

"'Twarn't none o' my business," Luster said. "I ain't gwine git mixed up in white folks business. Come on here, Benjy, les go out do's."

They went out. Dilsey stood for a while at the table, then she went and cleared the breakfast things from the dining-room and ate her breakfast and cleaned up the kitchen. Then she removed her apron and hung it up and went to the foot of the stairs and listened for a moment. There was no sound. She donned the overcoat and the hat and went across to her cabin.

The rain had stopped. The air now drove out of the southeast, broken overhead into blue patches. Upon the crest of a hill beyond the trees and roofs and spires of town sunlight lay like a pale scrap of cloth, was blotted away. Upon the air a bell came, then as if at a signal, other bells took up the sound and repeated it.

The cabin door opened and Dilsey emerged, again in the maroon cape and the purple gown, and wearing soiled white elbow-length gloves and minus her headcloth now. She came into the yard and called Luster. She waited a while, then she went to the house and around it to the cellar door, moving close to the wall, and looked into the door. Ben sat on the steps. Before him Luster squatted on the damp floor. He held a saw in his left hand, the blade sprung a little by pressure of his hand, and he was in the act of striking the blade with a worn wooden mallet with which she had been making beaten biscuit for more than thirty years. The saw gave forth a single sluggish twang that ceased with lifeless alacrity, leaving the blade in a thin clean curve between Luster's hand and the floor. Still, inscrutable, it bellied.

"Dat's de way he done hit," Luster said. "I jes ain't foun' de right thing to hit it wid."

"Dat's whut you doin', is it?" Dilsey said. "Bring me dat mallet," she said.

"I ain't hurt hit," Luster said.

"Bring hit here," Dilsey said. "Put dat saw whar you got hit first."

He put the saw away and brought the mallet to her. Then Ben wailed again, hopeless and prolonged. It was nothing. It might have been all time and injustice and sorrow become vocal for an instant by a conjunction of planets.

"Listen at him," Luster said. "He been gwine on dat way ev'y since you sont us outen de house. I don't know whut got into him dis mawnin."

"Bring him here," Dilsey said.

"Come on, Benjy," Luster said. He went back down the steps and took Ben's arm. He came obediently, wailing, that slow hoarse sound that ships make, that seems to begin before the sound itself has started, seems to cease before the sound itself had stopped.

"Run and git his cap," Dilsey said. "Don't make no noise Miss Cahline kin hear. Hurry, now. We already late."

"She gwine hear him anyhow, ef you don't stop him,," Luster said.

"He stop when we git off de place," Dilsey said. "He smellin' hit. Dat's whut hit is."

"Smell whut, mammy?" Luster said.

"You go git dat cap," Dilsey said. Luster went on. They stood in the cellar door, Ben one step below her. The sky was broken now into scudding patches that dragged their swift shadows up out of the shabby garden, over the broken fence and across the yard. Dilsey stroked Ben's head, slowly and steadily, smoothing the bang upon his brow. He wailed quietly, unhurriedly. "Hush," Dilsey said.

"Hush now. We be gone in a minute. Hush, now." He wailed quietly and steadily.

Luster returned, wearing a stiff new straw hat with a colored band and carrying a cloth cap. The hat seemed to isolate Luster's skull, in the beholder's eye as a spotlight would, in all its individual planes and angles. So peculiarly individual was its shape that at first glance the hat appeared to be on the head of someone standing immediately behind Luster. Dilsey looked at the hat.

"Whyn't you wear yo' old hat?" she said.

"Couldn't find hit," Luster said.

"I bet you couldn't. I bet you fixed hit last night so you couldn't find hit. You fixin' to ruin that un."

"Aw, mammy," Luster said, "hit ain't gwine rain."

"How you know? You go git dat old hat en put dat new un away."

"Aw, mammy."

"Den you go git de umbreller."

"Aw, mammy."

"Take yo choice," Dilsey said. "Git yo old hat, er de umbreller. I don't keer which."

Luster went to the cabin. Ben wailed quietly.

"Come on," Dilsey said, "dey kin ketch up wid us. We gwine to hear de singin'." They went around the house, toward the gate. "Hush," Dilsey said from time to time as they went down the drive. They reached the gate. Dilsey opened it. Luster was coming down the drive behind them, carrying the umbrella. A woman was with him. "Here dey come," Dilsey said. They passed out the gate. "Now, den," she said. Ben ceased. Luster and his mother overtook them. Frony wore a dress of bright blue silk and a flowered hat. She was a thin woman, with a flat, pleasant face.

"You got six weeks' work right dar on yo back," Dilsey said. "Whut you gwine do ef hit rain?"

"Git wet, I reckon," Frony said. "I ain't never stopped no rain yit."

"Mammy always talkin' bout hit gwine rain," Luster said.

"Ef I don't worry bout y'all, I don't know who is," Dilsey said. "Come on, we already late."

MAXWELL ANDERSON

****

The author of more than twenty-five plays, Maxwell Anderson has written from time to time penetrating essays about the theater and the relationship of the playwright to his medium and his material. The essay presented here was the title essay from Off Broadway, *retitled "A Faith in the Theater," and was delivered as a lecture at Rutgers University in 1942 as "The Basis of Artistic Creation in Literature." Mr. Anderson comes to the conclusion that the theater is an art with an almost religious importance and meaning to society. A practicing craftsman, but not bound by the demands of Broadway, he feels "those of us who fail to outlive the street on which we work will fail because we have accepted its valuations and measured our product by them."*

****

A Faith in the Theater

DURING THE SECOND WORLD WAR it seemed obvious that we were fighting to protect the earth and ourselves from men who believed that might makes right, that control of the sources of information makes truth, and that power makes justice. We believed violently enough to go to war about it that might is only sometimes right, that the sources of information should be at once open and uncontaminated, and that justice can only be arrived at by some kind of common consent which includes not only those to whom justice is to be applied but also those by whom it is carried out. When the war was over, the people of the democracies began to look hard and perhaps a little resentfully at these principles which had cost us so many billions, so many years, and so many lives. And for the first time in modern history it became apparent to us that we had emerged into an age of complete unfaith—an age in which everything by which we live is on trial and nothing is taken for granted.

It became apparent, too, that the fundamentals on which a civilization rests can never be proved. We take them for granted or we don't take them at all. But the fact that the necessity for our democracy has been questioned by men willing to give up their lives to make the challenge good has affected our thinking profoundly. Though the Nazis did not win they made us unsure of ourselves. And because we are a young nation, not much given to thought or to doubt, our present doubts rock us to the foundations of the republic. We are facing the ancient insoluble dilemma of mankind, but to us it is new and in the nature of a catastrophe. America has always been sure of itself. America unsure is almost another nation —a sleep-walking nation, feeling its way into the unknown.

This affects all of us—the businessman, the philosopher, the laborer, the investment banker, the boy and girl playing in the street. If you don't know what your work is for, or whether it can be justified, you know nothing about yourself or the meaning of your life— and your children are very soon aware that you don't know. The judges and the police and the school system very soon feel this uncertainty. The stores, the factories, the government bureaus, and the stock exchange all feel it. It slows them all down. It takes the edge off all effort and the imagination out of enterprise.

But the man most affected is the professional writer or artist. The professor of philosophy may state, and even feel, the question more urgently than the writer; on the other hand, he has no driving necessity for finding an immediately workable plan for living. He can talk the situation over with his students and take his time. But a practicing artist or a professional writer who uses ideas in his work is bound to conclude something, makeshift or profound, or shut up shop completely.

And a playwright, who must say something intelligible in every production, is driven more directly than any other writer or artist to make up his mind about his world or be silent until he can make up his mind. A man would be a fool who was certain that his vision of current events was the only right one, who believed that he had come upon the secret of the universe, or who thought he had penetrated, for certain, to the basis of things in literature or anywhere else. But if he is going to put plays on the stage he must have at least fragmentary convictions. Sometimes his convictions are subconscious; sometimes they are inherited. Sometimes the convictions that underlie the most modern and snappy of productions are simple-minded or old-fashioned. But dig for them and you will find them. A play can't be written without them—or, at least, it can't be a success—because no audience is satisfied with a play which doesn't take an attitude toward the world. Every artist is at a loss in a confused civilization, but the playwright is in the worst plight of all. For the best practice of his craft he needs a stable society within a stable congeries of nations. Our modern world has been the scene of vast mental and social confusion, and the theater has been shaken with every shift in the ideological weather. Those who have kept going as writers within it have done so because they could cling to inner beliefs not easily destroyed by exterior storm. Or because they believed in nothing and could simulate whatever belief happened to be popular.

Those who are old enough to remember the nineteen-twenties will recall one curious fallacy of that decade, a belief more extraordinary than the prosperity that accompanied it. The victory over Germany and the efflorescence of invention that went with and followed the war, staggered men's minds. They saw the earth and its creatures in a bright new scientific light in which the customs of our ancestors appeared to be based on inexplicable and ridiculous taboos. Religion was not only questioned but put aside. Social codes were scrutinized under microscopes, and scrapped along with the rules of Leviticus. There was a general belief that men were done with the foolishness of wars and conquest as a method of settling differences. On this side of the Atlantic at least, we thought men had learned better than to try again to grasp the steering wheel of the earth by violence. We closed our eyes to smoking volcanoes of malignity, wondering how men would adjust themselves to a life in which there was no more hell-fire. We believed that the war had been a mistake, that no war was worth fighting, even for the victor; that Gandhi was right, that non-resistance was more powerful than force, that the conqueror destroyed himself automatically, that good and evil came in unavoidable waves, that good would inevitably turn into evil and evil into good with the passage of years. We rejected the war between good and evil. We would fight it no more. Villains, we said, are made villains by circumstances, and we must fight the circumstances, not the poor individual wretches whose anti-social actions caused trouble. Peace conferences were held and humane agreements concerning the usages of war were made among the nations. Naval strength was adjusted by treaty, and battleships were sunk to limit the power of those who had too much. It was an era of reason and good feeling that seemed destined to last interminably. Having emerged into sunlight out of the darkness of history, we saw our way clearly. We saw clearly in those high-minded times that the race was not going to live by the Old or the New Testament. It was going to live in the light of scientific day, making its choices freely among the fruits of the new trees of knowledge. Crime was a disease, and curable. Poverty was a disease, and curable. God was to be replaced by a sort of higher expedience, arrived at by laboratory methods. There was no sin except that which made for inefficiency. Honor was a holdover from the past, retained mainly for business reasons. The need for sexual restraint was abolished by the discovery of contraceptives. Men were like trees, the race was like a forest. They needed nothing except proper conditions and free functioning to grow and prosper as never before. If there had been scarcities, if men had lacked and suffered, all lacks could be supplied by the multiplication of machinery. If there had been grim and terrible feuds over the love of a woman, the ownership of land or the conflicts of worship, they had become laughably unnecessary. Love should be free, land should bear beyond the capacity of the race to consume, religion was a laid ghost. We were to go forward and eat and drink and be merry, and right and wrong would dissolve into a series of realistic choices between that which was healthful and that which was poisonous.

Since every man's thinking is directed or deflected by that of his age, we all of us, in the nineteen-twenties, stared hard at this new and dazzling age which we were assured was just beyond the next elections. To most people it was not only acceptable but welcome as an inevitable step forward. What kind of environment it would make for us if it came none of us knew. What dangers lurked under its shiny blessings we could only guess. There was no precedent for the utopia of invention. Men were mainly concerned, then as always, with the problem of keeping some kind of place for themselves, philosophically and economically, on this whirling ball. It was no longer expected that the gods would help us. We knew no gods and honored no decalogue.

Yet it was in these godless nineteen-twenties that I stumbled upon the only religion I have. And I came upon it in the most unlikely and supposedly godless of places. I was a journalist, and I knew nothing about the theater except casually from the outside. But I wrote a verse tragedy, being bored with writing editorials, and a gallant producer put it on the stage—for no reason that I can see now. It failed quietly, as it deserved, but after its production the theater tugged at me, its rewards dazzled me—and I wrote other plays, some of them successful. However, from the very beginning the theater was to me, in some fundamental ways, an exasperating puzzle. Some plays succeeded, some did not, and why, nobody knew. Success on the stage seemed to be one of the ultimate mysteries.

Leaving aside the questions of acting and directing, the problems of theme, story, and writing appeared only more confused when discussed by the professors of playwriting. I developed a theory which still looks cogent to me—that a playwright's first success was always largely accidental. After that he could analyze what he had done, and begin to develop an intuition that would take him through the maze of difficulties and dangers his action and dialogues must thread. But intuition is an unreliable guide, and I was not as intuitive as some others. I needed a compass—or a pole star—or some theory of what the theater was about, and I had none.

However, I did discover that there were rules of playwriting which could not be broken. One by one I unearthed them for myself, or dug them out of the treatises of predecessors. And by and by some of them began to look like essentials. Let me cite a few of the first that came clear to me.

1. The story of a play must be the story of what happens within the mind or heart of a man or woman. It cannot deal primarily with external events. The external events are only symbolic of what goes on within.

2. The story of a play must be a conflict, and specifically, a conflict between the forces of good and evil within a single person. The good and evil to be defined, of course, as the audience wants to see them.

3. The protagonist of a play must represent the forces of good and must win, or, if he has been evil, must yield to the forces of the good, and know himself defeated.

4. The protagonist of a play cannot be a perfect person. If he were he could not improve, and he must come out at the end of the play a more admirable human being than he went in.

When I had once begun to make discoveries of this sort, they came thick and fast. And they applied not, as is natural to suppose, to extraordinary plays only—to Shakespeare and Jonson and the Greeks—but to all plays, and to those in our modern repertory as much as any others. I add a few more of the ancient and inescapable rules as they came to me.

5. The protagonist of a play must be an exceptional person. He or she cannot be run-of-the-mill. The man in the street simply will not do as the hero of a play. If a man be picked from the street to occupy the center of your stage, he must be so presented as to epitomize qualities which the audience can admire. Or he must indicate

how admirable human qualities can be wasted or perverted—must define an ideal by falling short of it, or become symbolic of a whole class of men who are blocked by circumstances from achieving excellence in their lives.

6. Excellence on the stage is always moral excellence. A struggle on the part of a hero to better his material circumstances is of no interest in a play unless his character is somehow tried in the fire, and unless he comes out of his trial a better man.

7. The moral atmosphere of a play must be healthy. An audience will not endure the triumph of evil on the stage.

8. There are human qualities for which the race has a special liking on the stage: in a man, positive character, strength of conviction not shaken by opposition; in a woman, fidelity, passionate faith. There are qualities which are especially disliked on the stage: in a man, cowardice, any refusal to fight for a belief; in a woman, an inclination toward the Cressid.

These are precepts, of course, only for the writing of a play. The presentation is quite as important, and hedged about with as many commandments; but since I am neither actor nor director I am aware of only a few. Let me indicate what some of them are. When you choose an actor to play the leading role in a play you try to find a man who is not only a good actor, but who can be looked upon with admiration by the people out in front. This may seem simple enough to do, but it is not. When you are casting a play you become acutely conscious of the mental, physical and moral shortcomings of the human race. If you will stand in the lobby of a theater as the patrons come in and examine them with the idea of finding a man or a woman who could take a leading part in the play, you will be disconcerted by the imperfection of mankind. So few, so lamentably few, would stand the test of the center of the stage, the concentrated lights and the concentrated scrutiny of a thousand fellow creatures insistent on perfection, or an approach to perfection. In that pool of light at the center of the stage all defects are magnified. Pick out the handsome, the attractive, the beautiful, the youthfully engaging and let the dissecting stares play on them one by one. Suppose you have chosen the best out of thousands. Suppose they are all attractive at first glance; but look again, for the audience will look again. Perhaps you find a too heavy jaw, slightly thin nostrils, an inadequate forehead, a shifty eye, faintly clumsy legs, an awkward pose, overeagerness, timidity, a slight indication of grossness, illness, hesitant speech. Physical defects are less disastrous than mental or spiritual faults. One in ten thousand will be worthy to stand in that blaze, and like as not that one, even if he be an actor, is a bad one, tied up emotionally, unable to pour his soul into words and emotional states not his own.

I list these technical difficulties because they began eventually to have one meaning for me. They mean that the purpose of the theater is to find, and hold up to our regard, what is admirable in the human race. The theatrical profession may protest as much as it likes, the theologians may protest, and the majority of those who see our plays would probably be amazed to hear it, but the theater is a religious institution devoted entirely to the exaltation of the spirit of man. It has no formal religion. It is a church without a creed, but there is no doubt in my mind that our theater, instead of being, as the evangelical ministers used to believe, the gateway to hell, is as much a worship as the theater of the Greeks, and has exactly the same meaning in our lives.

When I first wrote plays this statement would have seemed incredible to me. Broadway in the twenties, in the thirties, and now in the forties, has always worn an air of hard, garish, cheap professionalism. The lights, the chilly box-office men, the ornate and dirty buildings, the groups of actors lingering in drugstores and along side streets, these all proclaim clearly a place of entertainment for sale. The priest and priestesses of these temples are certainly unaware of the nature of their profession. But consider what they sell, and you face a different prospect. The plays that please most and run longest in these dusty alleys are representative of human loyalty, courage, love that purges the soul, grief that ennobles. Sometimes a simple tale like *Victoria Regina,* the story of a young girl faced suddenly with the responsibilities of an empire, unequal at first to the task, but developing and learning with the years, acquiring tolerance, wisdom and dignity, dying a great queen. Perhaps the story of Abraham Lincoln, a man with great endowments but afraid of life, forcing himself to face life, forcing himself to lead a nation in a war that sickened his soul, emerging at the end a great man. For those to whom this theory is novel, it will seem easy to refute. The case of *Rain* will come up, where the uncritical tolerance and good will of a prostitute are held better moral guides than the fanatical zeal of the missionary. They are better moral guides, no doubt of it. But the play does not praise the woman for being a prostitute. It finds virtue in her despite her vocation. It does not condemn the man for his religion, but the perversion of religion into an evil force. The case of *Tobacco Road* will come up, in which a poor white family struggles with a burden of poverty, ignorance, and adverse social conditions. There is no doubt that the run of the play was stimulated by a morbid curiosity concerning the unashamed sexual customs of the inhabitants of that mythical road through the tobacco fields, but if there had been no moral values in the piece nobody would have cared to see it. The sexual customs or lack of them wouldn't have drawn a nickel. There were heroic qualities in Jeeter Lester and his strange brood. They lacked many virtues. They were shiftless, dishonest, financially hopeless. But they were not afraid. They faced existence as it was handed out to them in a way that made them both pathetic and tragic. Nothing better is expected of any hero on the stage than this—that he take up what arms he has against what enemies assail him and come out of the battle with his morale intact. Jeeter Lester kept very little except his self-respect, but he did keep that, and those who saw him had a respect both for him and for the human spirit that cannot be quenched by squalor. I have witnessed several plays on Broadway that attempted to imitate *Tobacco Road* by duplicating the adverse conditions and the resultant twisted lives and depressed morals. But they were failures because they assumed that the public wanted only dirt. It wasn't the dirt of *Tobacco Road* that gave it a long run, but the accompanying, and to many invisible, gallantry of its people.

Perhaps I have made my point nauseatingly clear, but I should like to present a little more evidence. As everybody knows, the great plays of the world—those accepted by civilization as part of a great heritage and played for centuries—these are almost all concerned with the conduct of exceptional men or women in positions of great responsibility, men with tragic faults and weaknesses but with mind and strength enough to overcome, in the struggle with evil forces, both those within themselves and those without. This is *Hamlet, The Cid, Prometheus*. And it is also, please note, *Abe Lincoln in Illinois*. In such cases it is obvious that some kind of religious ritual is involved in reviving these symbols of national or cultural faith in a public performance. The *Oresteia* of Aeschylus is a ritual of crime and punishment, and ends by stating that Zeus himself must grow and learn and change if he is to avoid injustice. But here again we have a modern instance. *The Green Pastures* treats exactly the same theme, God's justice, and ends with exactly the same lesson, that God must learn and grow and change or his rigid justice will become an injustice in the end. I am fairly certain that Marc Connelly did not intentionally preach from the text of Aeschylus, but his play is no less a religious observance because it was presented in a plush-

chaired theater off our own gaudy Broadway. The worshipers pay
a fairly high rent for their pews in the theatrical Forties, and not
many of them realize that they are assisting in a worship, but they
sit in church nevertheless, and acquire virtue thereby according to
their understanding and the wisdom and skill of the functioning
playwright. *Oedipus Tyrannus* and *Macbeth* and *Little Eyolf* and
The Little Foxes teach one and all that an evil action revenges itself
upon the doer. *Antigone* and *Hamlet* and ten thousand modern
plays argue that injustice is a corrosive, and will eat the heart out
of him who practices it. Analyze any play you please which has survived the test of continued favor, and you will find a moral or a rule
of social conduct or a rule of thumb which the race has considered
valuable enough to learn and pass along. Take such seemingly meaningless escapades as *You Can't Take It with You* and *The Time of
Your Life*. The first says simply that money isn't everything, and the
second says, as plainly as the author can speak, that tolerance is the
great virtue. These are platitudes, of course. A play is not required
to make ethical discoveries. It is only required to have a meaning,
and a sound one—one, that is, which is accepted as sound by its
audience. Put on a play which sets out to prove that dishonesty is
the best policy and vice is triumphant in human affairs, and the
audience will refuse it coldly. They don't want to believe it and they
won't. You can poke farcical fun at homicide, as in *Arsenic and Old
Lace* or *The Playboy of the Western World* or *The Beggar's Opera*,
but you cannot seriously praise an unrepentant murderer. The race
—or the audiences—will not allow it. They will register disapproval
and they will stay away.

There have been critics who held that the theater was central
among the arts because it is a synthesis of all of them. Now I confess
that the theater appears to me to be the central art—but for a different reason. It does bring together all the arts, or a number of
them. But its distinction is that it brings them together in a communal religious service. Any other art, practiced separately, can be
either moral or amoral, religious or pagan, affirmative or despairing.
But when they come together in the theater they must affirm, they
cannot deny. It is as if poetry, music, narration, dancing, and the
mimetic arts were bits and pieces of theatrical art, stripped away
to function alone and rudderless without the moral compulsion of
the theater.

And now I must give a definition of what seems to me morally
sound. If morality depends on the existence of good and evil, then
the good and evil of the theater are those acceptable to the present

audience. The mores of the Greek theater are not at all points consistent with ours, though they come close to them. If good and evil
alter, the playwright must go along. To some artists the present good
may seem evil and the present evil good. That has happened often
in the case of a poet or a prophet. A playwright cannot run so far
ahead of his audience, for he must find a common denominator of
belief in his own generation, and even the greatest, the loftiest, must
say something which his age can understand. The heart of the
theater is a belief in democracy, a belief that the people must make
their own standards, must decide for themselves what to worship.

   In brief, I have found my religion in the theater, where I least
expected to find it, and where few will credit that it exists. But it is
there, and any man among you who tries to write plays will find
himself serving it, if only because he can succeed in no other way.
He will discover, if he works through his apprenticeship, that the
theater is the central artistic symbol of the struggle of good and evil
within men. Its teaching is that the struggle is eternal and unremitting, that the forces which tend to drag men down are always
present, always ready to attack, that the forces which make for good
cannot sleep through a night without danger. It denies the doctrine
of the nineteen-twenties emphatically. It denies that good and evil
are obverse and reverse of the same coin, denies that good can win
by waiting. It denies that wars are useless and that honor is without
meaning. It denies that we can live by the laboratory and without
virtue. It affirms that the good and evil in man are the good and
evil of evolution, that men have within themselves the beasts from
which they emerge and the god toward which they climb. It affirms
that evil is what takes man back toward the beast, that good is what
urges him up toward the god. It affirms that these struggles of the
spirit are enacted in the historic struggles of men—some representing evil, some good. It offers us criteria for deciding what is good
and what is evil. Set a man on the stage and you know instantly
where he stands morally with the race. Set Hitler on the stage and
loathing will rise from every seat in the house. Even in Germany,
had he been a character in a play, he would have been hated and
despised. You cannot be pitiless, merciless, ruthless, arrogant, and
without tolerance on the stage, and be considered a hero. That
which is considered despicable on the stage will be held despicable
in real life—not only evil but those who will not fight evil are rejected on both sides of the footlights. A man who accepts the wave
of the future and analyzes honor to a breath can be the comedian
to be laughed at but he cannot be the protagonist. According to

the worshipers of the good who sit in our theaters a hero may have his doubts and indecisions, for that's only human, but when it comes to the test he must be willing to take steel in his bosom or take lead through his intestines or he resigns his position as a man. The audiences, sitting in our theaters, make these rules and, in setting them, define the purposes and beliefs of homo sapiens. There is no comparable test that I know of for what is good in the human soul, what is most likely to lead to that distant and secret destination which the race has chosen for itself and will somehow find.

EDGAR LEE MASTERS

****

WOODLANDS,
RYDAL, PA.

DEAR MR. BURNETT:

Since my nomination for this collection probably came from the popularity of the two anthologies—the Spoon River Anthology *and the* New Spoon River, *both of which have come out in many foreign editions, I am selecting for your book two poems from the* New Spoon River *and three from* Spoon River Anthology.

EDGAR LEE MASTERS

****

Five From Spoon River

FIDDLER JONES

THE EARTH keeps some vibration going
There in your heart, and that is you.
And if the people find you can fiddle,
Why, fiddle you must, for all your life.
What do you see, a harvest of clover?
Or a meadow to walk through to the river?
The wind's in the corn; you rub your hands
For beeves hereafter ready for market;
Or else you hear the rustle of skirts
Like the girls when dancing at Little Grove.
To Cooney Potter a pillar of dust
Or whirling leaves meant ruinous drouth;
They looked to me like Red-Head Sammy
Stepping it off, to "Toor-a-Loor."
How could I till my forty acres
Not to speak of getting more,
With a medley of horns, bassoons and piccolos
Stirred in my brain by crows and robins

And the creak of a wind-mill—only these?
And I never started to plow in my life
That some one did not stop in the road
And take me away to a dance or picnic.
I ended up with forty acres;
I ended up with a broken fiddle—
And a broken laugh, and a thousand memories,
And not a single regret.

LUCINDA MATLOCK

I WENT to the dances at Chandlerville,
And played snap-out at Winchester.
One time we changed partners,
Driving home in the moonlight of middle June,
And then I found Davis.
We were married and lived together for seventy years,
Enjoying, working, raising the twelve children,
Eight of whom we lost
Ere I had reached the age of sixty.
I spun, I wove, I kept the house, I nursed the sick,
I made the garden, and for holiday
Rambled over the fields where sang the larks,
And by Spoon River gathering many a shell,
And many a flower and medicinal weed—
Shouting to the wooded hills, singing to the green valleys.
At ninety-six I had lived enough, that is all,
And passed to a sweet repose.
What is this I hear of sorrow and weariness,
Anger, discontent and drooping hopes?
Degenerate sons and daughters,
Life is too strong for you—
It takes life to love Life.

EMILY SPARKS

WHERE is my boy, my boy—
In what far part of the world?
The boy I loved best of all in the school?—
I, the teacher, the old maid, the virgin heart,
Who made them all my children.
Did I know my boy aright,
Thinking of him as spirit aflame,
Active, ever aspiring?
Oh, boy, boy, for whom I prayed and prayed
In many a watchful hour at night,
Do you remember the letter I wrote you
Of the beautiful love of Christ?
And whether you ever took it or not.
My boy, wherever you are,
Work for your soul's sake,
That all the clay of you, all of the dross of you,
May yield to the fire of you,
Till the fire is nothing but light! . . .
Nothing but light!

HOWARD LAMSON

ICE cannot shiver in the cold,
Nor stones shrink from the lapping flame.
Eyes that are sealed, no more have tears;
Ears that are stopped hear nothing ill;
Hearts turned to silt are strange to pain;
Tongues that are dumb report no loss;
Hands stiffened, well may idle be;
No sigh is from a breathless breast.
Beauty may fade, but closed eyes see not;
Sorrow may wail, but stopped ears hear not;
Work is, but folded hands need work not;
Nothing to say is for dumb tongues.
The rolling earth rolls on and on
With trees and stones and winding streams—
My dream is what the hill-side dreams!

CLEANTHUS TRILLING

THE URGE of the seed: the germ.
The urge of the germ: the stalk.
The urge of the stalk: leaves.
The urge of the leaves: the blossom.
The urge of the blossom: to scatter pollen.
The urge of the pollen: the imagined dream of life.
The urge of life: longing for tomorrow.
The urge of tomorrow: Pain.
The urge of Pain: God.

ARCHIBALD MacLEISH

****

Rather than discuss the poems selected for inclusion here, I should like to put down a few things which seem to me to be true about the condition of the art of poetry in our time. Specifically about its relation to our time.

The general opinion undoubtedly is that, whatever poetry may have been in the past, it is not now a matter of principal concern to a troubled and tragic generation. The truth I believe to be precisely the opposite.

The relation of poetry to life is the relation Aristotle described— the relation to which Wordsworth returned, though with a difference. Poetry, that is to say, is a means to knowledge of a certain kind: to Aristotle a means of revealing that coherence which life, in his world, possessed; to Wordsworth an instrument of intuitive apprehension, capable of carrying the truth, "not individual and local but general and operative . . . alive into the heart by passion." Poetry, until the psychologists make good their claims, is the one instrument by which a man as an individual, as a person, as a man alone, trusting and compelled to trust what he himself encounters, can know his experience and thus know himself. Religion, to those who possess it, may reveal reasons beyond the reasons, and ethics and philosophy may dictate their generalizations, but only poetry can admit the individual man as man directly into the individual and living experience of life.

The constant heart of the shifting crisis with us is the dilemma of the individual human being in an increasingly institutionalized world. In such a time the true importance of poetry necessarily increases. Increases at least to those who believe in, and hope for, the survival of a society based upon individual life—which is to say upon life, for there is no other. What is essential to the survival of such a society is the constant perception of the validity of that direct and personal relation to life and to experience—a man's own life, a man's own experience—upon which true individuality rests. Unless a man's perceptions are his own and are related to his experience of life, he cannot possess his life except at second hand. He cannot possess himself. He has no self.

188

*What is demanded of those who practise the art of poetry in a
time like ours is not that they write "political" poetry or attempt
to resolve in their poems the problems of their time. What is demanded of them is that they practise their art for the purposes of
their art and in the terms of their art realizing that it is through
their art that life and lives here touched each other in the past and
may again.*

ARCHIBALD MACLEISH

****

Poems

EPISTLE TO BE LEFT IN THE EARTH

... IT IS colder now
                    there are many stars
                                        we are drifting

North by the Great Bear
                    the leaves are falling

The water is stone in the scooped rocks
                                        to southward
Red sun grey air
                    the crows are

Slow on their crooked wings
                    the jays have left us

Long since we passed the flares of Orion
Each man believes in his heart he will die
Many have written last thoughts and last letters
None know if our deaths are now or forever
None know if this wandering earth will be found
We lie down and the snow covers our garments

I pray you
                    you (if any open this writing)
Make in your mouths the words that were our names

I will tell you all we have learned
I will tell you everything
The earth is round
there are springs under the orchards
The loam cuts with a blunt knife
beware of
Elms in thunder
the lights in the sky are stars
We think they do not see
we think also
The trees do not know nor the leaves of the grasses hear us
The birds too are ignorant

Do not listen
Do not stand at dark in the open windows
We before you have heard this
they are voices
They are not words at all but the wind rising ·
Also none among us has seen God
(... We have thought often
The flaws of sun in the late and driving weather
Pointed to one tree but it was not so)

As for the nights I warn you the nights are dangerous
The wind changes at night and the dreams come
It is very cold
there are strange stars near Arcturus
Voices are crying an unknown name in the sky

THE CAT IN THE WOOD

THE CAT in the wood cried farewell cried farewell
Farther and farther away and the leaves
Covered her over with sound of the leaves
And the sound of the wood O my love O my love
Farther and farther away and the sound
Of leaves overhead when I call to you
Leaves on the ground

WINTER IS ANOTHER COUNTRY

IF THE AUTUMN would
End! If the sweet season,
The late light in the tall trees would
End! If the fragrance, the odor of
Fallen apples, dust on the road,
Water somewhere near, the scent of
Water touching me; if this would end
I could endure the absence in the night,
The hands beyond the reach of hands, the name
Called out and never answered with my name:
The image seen but never seen with sight,
I could endure this all
If autumn ended and the cold light came.

YEARS OF THE DOG

BEFORE, though, Paris was wonderful. Wanderers
Talking in all tongues from every country.
Fame was what they wanted in that town.
Fame could be found there too—flushed like quail in the
Cool dawn—struck among statues
Naked in hawthorn in the silver light.
James Joyce found it. Dublin bore him.
Could have sung with McCormack! Could he? He could.
Did he? He didn't. He walked by the winding Seine.
And what did he eat? He ate orts: oddities:
Oh he was poor; obscure: no one had heard of him:
Rolled on the floor on the floor with the pain in his eyes.
And found fame? He did? Ulysses: Yule Book:
Published to every people even in Erse.
(Molly Molly why did you say so Molly!)
Or the lad in the Rue de Notre Dame des Champs
At the carpenter's loft on the left-hand side going down—
The lad with the supple look like a sleepy panther—
And what became of him? Fame became of him.
Veteran out of the wars before he was twenty:
Famous at twenty-five: thirty a master—
Whittled a style for his time from a walnut stick
In a carpenter's loft in a street of that April city.

Where do they hang out now, the young ones, the wanderers,
Following fame by the rumor of praise in a town?
Where is fame in the world now? Where are the lovers of
Beauty of Beauty that she moves along?

POEM IN PROSE

THIS POEM is for my wife
I have made it plainly and honestly
The mark is on it
Like the burl on the knife

I have not made it for praise
She has no more need for praise
Than summer has
Or the bright days

In all that becomes a woman
Her words and her ways are beautiful
Love's lovely duty
The well-swept room

Wherever she is there is sun
And time and a sweet air
Peace is there
Work done

There are always curtains and flowers
And candles and baked bread
And a cloth spread
And a clean house

Her voice when she sings is a voice
At dawn by a freshening sea
Where the wave leaps in the
Wind and rejoices

Wherever she is it is now
It is here where the apples are

Here in the stars
In the quick hour

The greatest and richest good—
My own life to live in—
This she has given me

If giver could

YOU, ANDREW MARVELL

AND HERE face down beneath the sun
And here upon earth's noonward height
To feel the always coming on
The always rising of the night

To feel creep up the curving east
The earthly chill of dusk and slow
Upon those under lands the vast
And ever climbing shadow grow

And strange at Ecbatan the trees
Take leaf by leaf the evening strange
The flooding dark about their knees
The mountains over Persia change

And now at Kermanshah the gate
Dark empty and the withered grass
And through the twilight now the late
Few travellers in the westward pass

And Baghdad darken and the bridge
Across the silent river gone
And through Arabia the edge
Of evening widen and steal on

And deepen on Palmyra's street
The wheel rut in the ruined stone
And Lebanon fade out and Crete
High through the clouds and overblown

And over Sicily the air
Still flashing with the landward gulls
And loom and slowly disappear
The sails above the shadowy hulls

And Spain go under and the shore
Of Africa the gilded sand
And evening vanish and no more
The low pale light across that land

Nor now the long light on the sea
And here face downward in the sun
To feel how swift how secretly
The shadow of the night comes on . . .

THE FLESH THAT ONCE SANG

THE FLESH that once sang
With the ardor of love
Is dumb and is mute
Where the dog stoops above
Where the dog with his jaws
In the charnel of leaves
Champs it with hate
But the flesh still believes.

The bone that once danced
In the intricate round
Of loving and giving
Is still and is bound.
The spider that stings
and the spider that weaves
Wind it with fear
But the bone still believes.

The flesh and the bone
That danced and that sang—
Fear with its web
And hate with its fang
Bind them in silence
And grind them and grieve

But the flesh and the bone
Still believe still believe.

Abandoned by the guardians and gods,
The great companion of the metaphor
Dead of the wars and wounds (O murdered dream!)

UPTON SINCLAIR

✳✳✳

The most widely quoted statement I have made in a long lifetime was that concerning The Jungle, *that "I aimed at the public's heart and by accident I hit it in the stomach." And here is the head of that arrow I shot,—the account of the pigs and their sad fate—which all the anthologists pick out and which apparently the public still wants to read. When it first came out, the deadly respectable* New York Evening Post *called the paragraph about God and the pigs "nauseous hogswash." See what you think of it!*

UPTON SINCLAIR

✳✳✳

The Hog Squeal of the Universe

"THEY don't waste anything here," said the guide, and then he laughed and added a witticism, which he was pleased that his unsophisticated friends should take to be his own: "They use everything about the hog except the squeal." In front of Brown's General Office building there grows a tiny plot of grass, and this, you may learn, is the only bit of green thing in Packingtown; likewise this jest about the hog and his squeal, the stock in trade of all the guides, is the one gleam of humor that you will find there.

After they had seen enough of the pens, the party went up the street, to the mass of buildings which occupy the centre of the yards. These buildings, made of brick and stained with innumerable layers of Packingtown smoke, were painted all over with advertising signs, from which the visitor realized suddenly that he had come to the home of many of the torments of his life. It was here that they made those products with the wonders of which they pestered him so—by placards that defaced the landscape when he travelled, and by staring advertisements in the newspapers and magazines—by silly little jingles that he could not get out of his mind, and gaudy pictures that lurked for him around every street corner. Here was where they made Brown's Imperial Hams and Bacon, Brown's Dressed Beef, Brown's Excelsior Sausages! Here was the headquarters of Durham's Pure Leaf Lard, of Durham's Breakfast Bacon, Durham's Canned Beef, Potted Ham, Devilled Chicken, Peerless Fertilizer!

Entering one of the Durham buildings, they found a number of other visitors waiting; and before long there came a guide, to escort them through the place. They made a great feature of showing strangers through the packing-plants, for it is a good advertisement. But ponas Jokubas whispered maliciously that the visitors did not see any more than the packers wanted them to.

They climbed a long series of stairways outside of the building, to the top of its five or six stories. Here was the chute, with its river of hogs, all patiently toiling upward; there was a place for them to rest to cool off, and then through another passageway they went into a room for which there is no returning for hogs.

It was a long, narrow room, with a gallery along it for visitors. At the head there was a great iron wheel, about twenty feet in circumference, with rings here and there along its edge. Upon both sides of this wheel there was a narrow space, into which came the hogs at the end of their journey; in the midst of them stood a great burly Negro, bare-armed and bare-chested. He was resting for the moment, for the wheel had stopped while men were cleaning up. In a minute or two, however, it began slowly to revolve, and then the men upon each side of it sprang to work. They had chains which they fastened about the leg of the nearest hog, and the other end of the chain they hooked into one of the rings upon the wheel. So, as the wheel turned, a hog was suddenly jerked off his feet and borne aloft.

At the same time the ear was assailed by a most terrifying shriek; the visitors started in alarm, the women turned pale and shrank back. The shriek was followed by another, louder and yet more agonizing—for once started upon that journey, the hog never came back; at the top of the wheel he was shunted off upon a trolley, and went sailing down the room. And meantime another was swung up, and then another, and another, until there was a double line of them, each dangling by a foot and kicking in frenzy—and squealing. The uproar was appalling, perilous to the ear-drums; one feared there was too much sound for the room to hold—that the walls must give way or the ceiling crack. There were high squeals and low squeals, grunts, and wails of agony; there would come a momentary lull, and then a fresh outburst, louder than ever, surging up to a deafening climax. It was too much for some of the visitors—the men would look at each other laughing nervously, and the women would stand with hands clenched, and the blood rushing to their faces, and the tears starting in their eyes.

Meantime, heedless of all these things, the men upon the floor were going about their work. Neither squeals of hogs nor tears of visitors made any difference to them; one by one they hooked up the hogs, and one by one with a swift stroke they slit their throats. There was a long line of hogs, with squeals and life-blood ebbing away together; until at last each started again, and vanished with a splash into a huge vat of boiling water.

It was all so very businesslike that one watched it fascinated. It was pork-making by machinery, pork-making by applied mathematics. And yet somehow the most matter-of-fact person could not help thinking of the hogs; they were so innocent, they came so very trustingly; and they were so very human in their protests—and so perfectly within their rights! They had done nothing to deserve it; and it was adding insult to injury, as the thing was done here, swinging them up in this cold-blooded, impersonal way, without a pretense of apology, without the homage of a tear. Now and then a visitor wept, to be sure; but this slaughtering-machine ran on, visitors or no visitors. It was like some horrible crime committed in a dungeon, all unseen and unheeded, buried out of sight and of memory.

One could not stand and watch very long without becoming philosophical, without beginning to deal in symbols and similes, and to hear the hog-squeal of the universe. Was it permitted to believe that there was nowhere upon the earth, or above the earth, a heaven for hogs, where they were requited for all this suffering? Each one of these hogs was a separate creature. Some were white hogs, some very black; some were brown, some were spotted; some were old, some were young; some were long and lean, some were monstrous. And each of them had an individuality of his own, a will of his own, a hope and a heart's desire; each was full of self-confidence, of self-importance, and a sense of dignity. And trusting and strong in faith he had gone about his business, the while a black shadow hung over him and a horrid Fate waited in his pathway. Now suddenly it had swooped upon him, and had seized him by the leg. Relentless, remorseless, it was; all his protests, his screams, were nothing to it— it did its cruel will with him, as if his wishes, his feelings, had simply no existence at all; it cut his throat and watched him gasp out his life. And now was one to believe that there was nowhere a god of hogs, to whom this hog-personality was precious, to whom these hog-squeals and agonies had a meaning? Who would take this hog into his arms and comfort him, reward him for his work well-done, and show him the meaning of his sacrifice? Perhaps some glimpse of all this was in the thoughts of our humble-minded Jurgis, as he turned to go on with the rest of the party, and muttered: "Dieve— but I'm glad I'm not a hog!"

The carcass hog was scooped out of the vat by machinery, and then it fell to the second floor, passing on the way through a wonderful machine with numerous scrapers, which adjusted themselves to the size and shape of the animal, and sent it out at the other end with nearly all of its bristles removed. It was then again strung up by machinery, and sent upon another trolley ride; this time passing between two lines of men, who sat upon a raised platform, each doing a certain single thing to the carcass as it came to him. One scraped the outside of a leg; another scraped the inside of the same leg. One with a swift stroke cut the throat; another with two swift strokes severed the head, which fell to the floor and vanished through a hole. Another made a slit down the body; a second opened the body wider; a third with a saw cut the breast-bone; a fourth loosened the entrails; a fifth pulled them out—and they also slid through a hole in the floor. There were men to scrape each side and men to scrape the back; there were men to clean the carcass inside, to trim it and wash it. Looking down this room, one saw, creeping slowly, a line of dangling hogs a hundred yards in length; and for every yard there was a man, working as if a demon were after him. At the end of this hog's progress every inch of the carcass had been gone over several times; and then it was rolled into the chilling-room, where it stayed for twenty-four hours, and where a stranger might lose himself in a forest of freezing hogs.

Before the carcass was admitted here, however, it had to pass a government inspector, who sat in the doorway and felt of the glands in the neck for tuberculosis. This government inspector did not have the manner of a man who was worked to death; he was apparently not haunted by a fear that the hog might get by him before he had finished his testing. If you were a sociable person, he was quite willing to enter into conversation with you, and to explain to you the deadly nature of the ptomaines which are to be found in tubercular pork; and while he was talking with you you could hardly be so ungrateful as to notice that a dozen carcasses were passing him untouched. This inspector wore an imposing silver badge, and he gave an atmosphere of authority to the scene, and, as it were, put the stamp of official approval upon the things which were done in Durham's.

Jurgis went down the line with the rest of the visitors, staring open-mouthed, lost in wonder. He had dressed hogs himself in the forest of Lithuania; but he had never expected to see one hog dressed by several hundred men. It was like a wonderful poem to him, and he took it all in guilelessly—even to the conspicuous signs demanding immaculate cleanliness of the employees. Jurgis was vexed when the cynical Jokubas translated these signs with sarcastic comments, offering to take them to the secret-rooms where the spoiled meats went to be doctored.

The party descended to the next floor, where the various waste materials were treated. Here came the entrails, to be scraped and washed clean for sausage-casings; men and women worked there in the midst of a sickening stench, which caused the visitors to hasten by, gasping. To another room came all the scraps to be "tanked," which meant boiling and pumping off the grease to make soap and lard; below they took out the refuse, and this, too, was a region in which the visitors did not linger. In still other places men were engaged in cutting up the carcasses that had been through the chilling-rooms. First there were the "splitters," the most expert workmen in the plant, who earned as high as fifty cents an hour, and did not a thing all day except chop hogs down the middle. Then there were "cleaver men," great giants with muscles of iron; each had two men to attend him—to slide the half carcass in front of him on the table; and hold it while he chopped it, and then turn each piece so that he might chop it once more. His cleaver had a blade about two feet long, and he never made but one cut; he made it so neatly, too, that his implement did not smite through and dull itself—there was just enough force for a perfect cut, and no more. So through various yawning holes there slipped to the floor below—to one room hams, to another forequarters, to another sides of pork. One might go down to this floor and see the pickling-rooms, where the hams were put into vats, and the great smoke-rooms, with their air-tight iron doors. In other rooms they prepared salt-pork—there were whole cellars full of it, built up in great towers to the ceiling. In yet other rooms they were putting up meat in boxes and barrels, and wrapping hams and bacon in oiled paper, sealing and labelling and sewing them. From the doors of these rooms went men with loaded trucks, to the platform where freight-cars were waiting to be filled; and one went out there and realized with a start that he had come at last to the ground floor of this enormous building.

Then the party went across the street to where they did the killing of the beef—where every hour they turned four or five hundred cattle into meat. Unlike the place they had left, all this work was done on one floor; and instead of there being one line of carcasses which moved to the workmen, there were fifteen or twenty lines, and the men moved from one to another of these. This made a scene of intense activity, a picture of human power wonderful to watch. It was all in one great room, like a circus ampitheatre, with a gallery for visitors running over the centre.

Along one side of the room ran a narrow gallery, a few feet from the floor; into which gallery the cattle were driven by men with goads which gave them electric shocks. Once crowded in here, the creatures were prisoned, each in a separate pen, by gates that shut, leaving them no room to turn around; and while they stood bellowing and plunging, over the top of the pen there leaned one of the "knockers," armed with a sledge-hammer, and watching for a chance to deal a blow. The room echoed with the thuds in quick succession, and the stamping and kicking of the steers. The instant the animal had fallen, the "knocker" passed on to another; while a second man raised a lever, and the side of the pen was raised, and the animal, still kicking and struggling, slid out to the "killing-bed." Here a man put shackles about one leg, and pressed another lever, and the body was jerked up into the air. There were fifteen or twenty such pens, and it was a matter of only a couple of minutes to knock fifteen or twenty cattle and roll them out. Then once more the gates were opened, and another lot rushed in; and so out of each pen there rolled a steady stream of carcasses, which the men upon the killing-beds had to get out of the way.

The manner in which they did this was something to be seen and never forgotten. They worked with furious intensity, literally upon the run—at a pace with which there is nothing to be compared except a football game. It was all highly specialized labor, each man having his task to do; generally this would consist of only two or three specific cuts, and he would pass down the line of fifteen or twenty carcasses, making these cuts upon each. First there came the "butcher," to bleed them; this meant one swift stroke, so swift that you could not see it—only the flash of the knife; and before you could realize it, the man had darted on to the next line, and a stream of bright red was pouring out upon the floor. This floor was half an inch deep with blood, in spite of the best efforts of men who kept shovelling it through holes; it must have made the floor slippery, but no one could have guessed this by watching the men at work.

The carcass hung for a few minutes to bleed; there was no time lost, however, for there were several hanging in each line, and one was always ready. It was let down to the ground, and there came the "headsmen," whose task it was to sever the head, with two or three swift strokes. Then came the "floorsman," to make the first cut in the skin; and then another to finish ripping the skin down the centre; and then half a dozen more in swift succession, to finish the skinning. After they were through, the carcass was again swung up; and while a man with a stick examined the skin, to make sure that it had not been cut, and another rolled it up and tumbled it through one of the inevitable holes in the floor, the beef proceeded on its journey. There were men to cut it, and men to split it, and men to gut it and scrape it clean inside. There were some with hose which threw jets of boiling water upon it, and others who removed the feet and added the final touches. In the end, as with the hogs, the finished beef was run into the chilling-room, to hang its appointed time.

The visitors were taken there and shown them, all neatly hung in rows, labelled conspicuously with the tags of the government inspectors—and some, which had been killed by a special process, marked with the sign of the "kosher" rabbi, certifying that it was fit for sale to the orthodox. And then the visitors were taken to the other parts of the building, to see what became of each particle of the waste material that had vanished through the floor; and to the pickling-rooms, and the salting-rooms, the canning-rooms, and the packing-rooms, where choice meat was prepared for shipping in refrigerator-cars, destined to be eaten in all the four corners of civilization. Afterward they went outside, wandering about among the mazes of buildings in which was done the work auxiliary to this great industry. There was scarcely a thing needed in the business that Durham and Company did not make for themselves. There was a great steam-power plant and an electricity plant. There was a barrel factory, and a boiler-repair shop. There was a building to which the grease was piped, and made into soap and lard; and then there was a factory for making lard cans, and another for making soap boxes. There was a building in which the bristles were cleaned and dried, for the making of hair cushions and such things; there was a building where the skins were dried and tanned, there was another where heads and feet were made into glue, and another where bones were made into fertilizer. No tiniest particle of organic matter was wasted in Durham's. Out of the horns of the cattle they made combs, buttons, hair-pins, and imitation ivory; out of the shin bones and other big bones they cut knife and tooth-brush handles, and mouth-pieces for pipes; out of the hoofs they cut hair-pins and buttons, before they had made the rest into glue. From such things as feet, knuckles, hide clippings, and sinews came such strange and unlikely products as gelatin, isinglass, and phosphorus, bone-black, shoe-blacking, and bone-oil. They had curled-hair works for the cattle-tails, and a "wool-pullery" for the sheep skins; they made pepsin from the stomachs of the pigs, and albumen from the blood, and violin strings from the ill-smelling entrails. When there was nothing else to be done with a thing, they first put it into a tank and got out of it all the tallow and grease, and then they made it into fertilizer. All these industries were gathered into buildings near by, connected by galleries and railroads with the main establishment; and it was estimated that they had handled nearly a quarter of a billion of animals since the founding of the plant by the elder Durham a generation or more before. If you counted with it the other big plants—and they were now really all one—it was, so Jokubas informed them, the greatest aggregation of labor and capital ever gathered in one place. It employed thirty thousand men; it supported directly two hundred and fifty thousand people in its neighborhood, and indirectly it supported half a million. It sent its products to every country in the civilized world, and it furnished the food for no less than thirty million people!

To all of these things our friends would listen open mouthed—it seemed to them impossible of belief that anything so stupendous could have been devised by mortal man. That was why to Jurgis it seemed almost profanity to speak about the place as did Jokubas, sceptically; it was a thing as tremendous as the universe—the laws and ways of its working no more than the universe to be questioned or understood. All that a mere man could do, it seemed to Jurgis, was to take a thing like this as he found it, and do as he was told; to be given a place in it and a share in its wonderful activities was a blessing to be grateful for, as one was grateful for the sunshine and the rain. Jurgis was even glad that he had not seen the place before meeting with his triumph, for he felt that the size of it would have overwhelmed him. But now he had been admitted—he was a part of it all! He had the feeling that this whole huge establishment had taken him under his protection, and had become responsible for his welfare. So guileless was he, and ignorant of the nature of business, that he did not even realize that he had become an employee of Brown's, and that Brown and Durham were supposed by all the world to be deadly rivals—were even required to be deadly rivals by the law of the land, and ordered to try to ruin each other under penalty of fine and imprisonment!

ROBERT SHERWOOD

****

"The playwright's chief stock in trade is feelings, not facts," wrote Robert E. Sherwood about one of his plays, the distinguished Abe Lincoln in Illinois. *In his representation in* THE WORLD'S BEST, *Mr. Sherwood is in the opposite camp, of facts, not feelings. . . . When Harry L. Hopkins died, leaving behind what was supposed to be an unfinished manuscript of a book about his assignments for the late President Roosevelt, Mr. Sherwood, who had been associated with both men during the war years, agreed to finish the task. He found later that no writing had been done on the book; but "the documentation was enormous," including forty filing cabinets packed with papers and a good many more in warehouses. The several years' job ending in* Roosevelt and Hopkins, An Intimate History, *is a contribution to American history during an international period of unparalleled significance, and the chapter on the conference at Teheran between Roosevelt, Churchill and Stalin is typical of the content of the book.*

****

The Titans Meet at Teheran

THERE WAS a meeting at Cairo of Roosevelt, Churchill and the Combined Chiefs of Staff, Hopkins being the only other civilian present, at which a general survey was made of future European operations in anticipation of the forthcoming discussions with Stalin at Teheran. Churchill gave a lengthy résumé of the general situation, reviewing the long series of Allied successes in the Mediterranean which, in recent weeks, had turned into a succession of disappointments on the Italian Front north of Naples and in the Dodecanese Islands. He urged that, despite the heavy German reinforcements that had been sent to the front in Italy, the Allied campaign there should be pushed more vigorously than ever with a view to capturing Rome at the earliest possible date—for "whoever holds Rome holds the title deeds of Italy." He placed particular emphasis on the assurance that he had in no way relaxed his zeal for OVERLORD but he recommended that this major operation should not be such a "tyrant" as to rule out every other activity in the Mediterranean. Among the various activities that he mentioned was the capture of the Island of Rhodes, which had been the ultimate objective of the recent, ill-fated Dodecanese campaign. He said that when the Allies had reached the Pisa-Rimini Line north of Rome, decisions could be taken as to whether the next move should be to the left (toward Southern France) or to the right (into the Balkans). The U.S. Chiefs of Staff had no doubt in their own minds as to just what all this signified. They felt certain that whenever the persistent Prime Minister started talking about Rhodes, or veering toward the "right" from Northern Italy, he was resuming the advocacy of strategic diversions into southeastern Europe and away from Northern France. They prepared themselves for battles at Teheran in which the Americans and the Russians would form a united front.

Roosevelt's party on the trip to Teheran numbered approximately seventy, including the indispensable Filipino mess men from Shangri-la. On the flight from Cairo of 1,310 miles the "Sacred Cow" flew over the Suez Canal, Jerusalem, Baghdad, the Euphrates and Tigris Rivers and the Iranian railroad which by now had become a vital link in the gigantic network of world supply lines.

At Teheran, Roosevelt, Hopkins, Leahy, Brown and Major John Boettiger (the President's son-in-law) at first occupied quarters in the American Legation as guests of the Minister, Louis G. Dreyfus. This Legation was at some distance from the compounds of the Russian and British Embassies which were close together. Harriman told Roosevelt of Stalin's concern over the strong possibility that there were many enemy agents in the city and the distinguished visitors might be subjected to what was described as "an unhappy incident"—a polite way, or course, of saying "assassination"—while driving back and forth between their separated residences.

On the day after his arrival at Teheran—this was Sunday, November 28—Roosevelt agreed to accept Stalin's invitation to move to a villa in the Russian Embassy compound where complete security could be enforced. It certainly was enforced, and the President and his party were never permitted to forget it, for the servants who made their beds and cleaned their rooms were all members of the highly efficient NKVD, the secret police, and expressive bulges were plainly discernable in the hip pockets under their neat, white coats. It was a nervous time for Michael F. Reilly and his own White

House secret service men, who were trained to suspect *everybody* and who did not like to admit into the President's presence anyone who was armed with as much as a gold toothpick.

Roosevelt arrived at his new quarters at three o'clock in the afternoon and fifteen minutes later Stalin came to call. This was the first meeting of the wartime leaders of the Soviet Union and the United States. Aside from the President and Marshal Stalin, the only two present at this meeting were the interpreters, Bohlen and Pavlov.

Roosevelt greeted Stalin with the statement, "I am glad to see you. I have tried for a long time to bring this about." Stalin, "after suitable expressions of pleasure at meeting the President, said that he was to blame for the delay in this meeting; that he had been very occupied because of military matters." Roosevelt asked Stalin how things were going on the Russian Front and Stalin gave a realistic picture of the situation which was somewhat less favorable at the moment than the information then available to the Western Allies had indicated. Roosevelt said that among the main topics for discussion at Teheran were measures which would bring about the removal of thirty or forty German divisions from the Eastern Front and Stalin agreed that such a transfer would be most helpful. Roosevelt then said that, by the end of the war, the American-British merchant fleet would have achieved such proportions that it would be more than two nations could possibly need and he felt that some of these ships should be made available to the Soviet Union. To this, Stalin replied that an adequate merchant fleet would be of great value, not only to the Soviet Union, but for the development of relations between the Soviet Union and the United States after the war, which he hoped would be greatly expanded. He said that if equipment were sent to the Soviet Union from the United States, a plentiful supply of the raw materials from that country could be made available to the United States.

There was considerable discussion of French affairs during which Stalin surprised the President by expressing the opinion that it was Pétain rather than de Gaulle who represented "the real physical France." There was no doubt in Roosevelt's mind on this and subsequent occasions that Stalin considered the collaborationists more important than the fighters of the resistance movement in expressing French sentiments.

Mention of Indo-China brought the conversation around to the Far East and Roosevelt told Stalin of his conversations with Chiang Kai-shek and the plans for offensive operations in Burma. Stalin expressed a low opinion of the fighting quality of Chinese troops but said that this was the fault of their leaders. Roosevelt referred to one of his favorite topics, which was the education of the peoples of the Far Eastern colonial areas, such as Indo-China, Burma, Malaya and the East Indies, in the arts of self-government; he pointed with pride to the American record in helping the people of the Philippines to prepare themselves for independence. He cautioned Stalin against bringing up the problems of India with Churchill, and Stalin agreed that this was undoubtedly a sore subject. Roosevelt said that reform in India should begin from the bottom and Stalin said that reform from the bottom would mean revolution.

This meeting lasted forty-five minutes but, like all conferences with the Russians most of the time was taken up in the arduous process of translation. At four o'clock, Churchill and the Combined Chiefs of Staff arrived for the First Plenary Session of the Teheran Conference, which bore the exultant code name, EUREKA. Also present at this first session were Hopkins, Eden and Molotov—and it should be noted that throughout the Teheran Conference Hopkins acted, in effect, as Secretary of State in relationship to the two Foreign Ministers. Stalin's only Chief of Staff was Marshal Voroshilov, and Leahy and King represented the U.S. Joint Chiefs. Marshall and Arnold were not present; they had misunderstood the time of the meeting and had gone off on a sightseeing tour around Teheran.

Stalin and Churchill agreed that the President should take the chair at this first meeting and he opened it by saying that he was glad to welcome the Russians as "new members of the family circle" and to assure them that these conferences were always conducted as gatherings of friends with complete frankness on all sides. He believed that the three nations represented would work together in close co-operation not only for the duration of the war but for generations to come. Churchill said that here was represented the greatest concentration of power that the world had ever seen and that in the hands of those present was the happy future of mankind; he prayed that they might be worthy of this God-given opportunity. Stalin said that this fraternal meeting did indeed represent a great opportunity and it was up to those present to use wisely the power which their respective peoples had given them.

Roosevelt then expressed the American point of view toward the war. He had the impression that Stalin knew very little about the progress of the war against Japan and he therefore dealt with that subject first. He said, according to the record, "that the United States was more directly affected by the war in the Pacific and that

the United States forces were bearing the chief burden in that area
with, of course, help from Australian and British forces; the greater
part of the U.S. naval establishment was in the Pacific and over a
million men were being maintained there. He pointed out as evidence of the immense distances in the Pacific that one supply ship
operating from the United States could make only three round trips
a year. The allied strategy in the Pacific was based on the doctrine
of attrition which was proving successful. We were sinking more
Japanese tonnage than the Japanese were able to replace. He said
that the allies were moving forward through the southern islands
and now through the islands to the east of Japan. On the north
little more could be done due to the distance between the Aleutian
and Kurile Islands. On the west our one great objective was to keep
China in the war, and for that purpose an expedition was in preparation to attack through North Burma and from Yunnan province.
In this operation Anglo-British forces would operate in North Burma
and Chinese forces from Yunnan. The entire operation would be
under the command of Lord Louis Mountbatten. In addition, am-
phibious operations were planned south of Burma to attack the important Japanese bases and lines of communication in the vicinity of
Bangkok. The President pointed out that although these operations
extended over vast expanses of territory the number of ships and
men allocated for the purpose was being held down to a minimum.
He summed up the aims of these operations as follows: (1) to open
the road to China and supply that country in order to keep it in the
war, and (2), by opening the road to China and through increased
use of transport planes to put ourselves in position to bomb Japan
proper.

"The President then said he would turn to the most important
theater of the war in Europe. He said he wished to emphasize that
for over one year and a half, in the last two or three conferences
which he had had with the Prime Minister, all military plans had
revolved around the question of relieving the German pressure on
the Soviet front; that largely because of the difficulties of sea transport it had not been possible until Quebec to set a date for the cross-
channel operations. He pointed out that the English Channel was a
disagreeable body of water and it was unsafe for military operations
prior to the month of May, and that the plan adopted at Quebec
involved an immense expedition and had been set at that time for
May 1, 1944."

At this point, Churchill interposed the remark that the British people had every reason in the past to be thankful that the English Channel was such a disagreeable body of water.

Roosevelt then went on to say that although he was not in favor of any secondary operations which might tend to delay the cross-Channel invasion, OVERLORD, he and the Prime Minister had been discussing possible future operations in Italy, the Adriatic and Aegean Seas, and from Turkey as a base in the event that the Turks might be induced to enter the war. The President also informed the Marshal of the plans for landings in Southern France.

Stalin then spoke of the war in the Pacific, making no bones of the fact that the Soviet Government welcomed all Anglo-American successes against the Japanese. He said that up to now the Russian forces had not been able to join in the war against Japan because of their heavy involvements with Germany. He explained that the Russian forces in Siberia were sufficient for purely defensive purposes but that they would have to be increased threefold before they could be strong enough to engage in offensive ground operations against the Japanese—and he added that when Germany was finally defeated the necessary Russian reinforcements could be sent to Eastern Siberia and then, he said, "We shall be able by our common front to beat Japan." (This was the first assurance given to Roosevelt or Churchill to that important effect.) Stalin gave a detailed analysis of German strength on the Russian Front and described the difficulties encountered by the Red Army in advancing over recaptured terrain where the Germans had systematically destroyed all possible facilities for communication and supply. Referring to the Italian campaign, he said that great benefit had resulted from the freeing of the Mediterranean to Allied shipping but he did not believe that further advances up the Peninsula would be of much avail, for the Alps presented "an almost insuperable barrier, as the famous Russian General Suvorov discovered in his time." He said the entry of Turkey into the war might be helpful in opening the way to the Balkans, but that the Balkans were far from the heart of Germany, and the only direct way of striking at that heart was through France.

Churchill gave assurance that both he and the President had long agreed as to the necessity of the cross-Channel operation and that it was now planned to put one million men on the continent of Europe in May, June and July, 1944. He said that the operations in North Africa and Italy had always been considered as secondary to OVERLORD. Stalin said that he had not meant to convey the impression that he considered these operations as secondary or to belittle their significance since they were of very real value.

Churchill said that the original force for OVERLORD would consist of nineteen American and sixteen British divisions, that being the maximum number that Britain could afford because of its manpower limitations. The additional divisions for the subsequent exploitation of OVERLORD would come in a steady stream from the United States. He said that there might be delays in the launching of OVERLORD—the great bottleneck at the moment being the shortage of landing craft—and that pending such delays the Allied forces should not remain idle. He then reverted to the desirability of getting Turkey into the war, as he did over and over again with a persistence that was both admirable and monotonous.

Roosevelt surprised and disturbed Hopkins by mentioning the possibility of an operation across the Adriatic for a drive, aided by Tito's Partisans, northeastward into Rumania to effect a junction with the Red Army advancing southward from the region of Odessa. Hopkins thereupon scribbled a note to Admiral King: "Who's promoting that Adriatic business that the President continually returns to?" To which King replied, "As far as I know it is his own idea." Certainly nothing could be farther from the plans of the U.S. Chiefs of Staff. Churchill was quick to associate himself with Roosevelt's suggestion, but Stalin asked if the continuation of operations in or from Italy would in any way affect the thirty-five divisions which he understood were earmarked for OVERLORD. Churchill replied at some length that they would not.

Stalin then expressed the opinion that it would be unwise to scatter forces in various operations throughout the Eastern Mediterranean. He said he thought that OVERLORD should be considered the basis for all operations in 1944 and that after the capture of Rome the forces used there should be sent into Southern France to provide a diversionary operation in support of OVERLORD. He even felt that it might be better to abandon the capture of Rome altogether, leaving ten divisions to hold the present line in Italy, and using the rest of the Allied force for the invasion of Southern France. He said it had been the experience of the Red Army that it was best to launch an offensive from two converging directions, forcing the enemy to move his reserves from one front to the other. Therefore, he favored simultaneous operations in Northern and Southern France, rather than the "scattering" of forces in the Eastern Mediterranean. He stated quite plainly and repeated it several times, his conviction that in any case Turkey would not agree to enter the war.

Churchill said that he could not believe the Turks would be so "mad" as to reject this opportunity to join with the United Nations under the most favorable circumstances, but Stalin observed that there were some people who apparently preferred to remain "mad."

Roosevelt said that if he were to meet with President Inonu of Turkey he would, of course, do everything possible to persuade him to enter the war, but that if he were in Inonu's place he would demand so heavy a price in airplanes, tanks and equipment that the granting of these requests would result in indefinite postponement of OVERLORD.

This first meeting ended at 7:20 P.M.—having lasted three hours and twenty minutes—and thereafter Roosevelt signed four more Congressional bills and a Proclamation and worked on his mail until dinnertime, 8:30, when he was host to Stalin, Molotov, Churchill, Eden, Sir Archibald Clark Kerr (British Ambassador in Moscow), Hopkins, Harriman and the three interpreters. This dinner represented a major achievement by the Filipino sailors who had moved only four hours previously into a strange kitchen, which, because of the haste with which the house had been made available, lacked most of the essential equipment, including a range. These deficiencies had been rapidly supplied and the dinner was served successfully.

Hopkins noted that Stalin was grayer than when he had seen him last in the summer of 1941 and also much dressier, now wearing a uniform with gold epaulettes each bearing a large, white star fastened with a red pin. Stalin doodled and smoked during the meetings. His voice was quiet—barely audible—and he seemed to expend no effort in placing emphasis on anything as he talked to the interpreter. Harriman has said that Stalin in greeting Hopkins at Teheran displayed more open and warm cordiality than he had been known to show to any foreigner; evidently the Marshal saw in Hopkins one who had made promises and done his level best to keep them.

At dinner on the first evening Roosevelt and Stalin discussed Fairbanks, Alaska, as a suitable spot for a later meeting. Stalin again expressed himself on the subject of France whose ruling class, he felt, was rotten to the core; he described the former Vichy Ambassador to Moscow, Bergery, as typical of the majority of French politicians. He did not consider that France could be trusted with

any strategic positions outside her own borders in the postwar
period. He still seemed to attach little importance to de Gaulle as a
real factor in political or other matters.

The conversation turned to the subject of postwar treatment of
Germany and the frontiers of Poland. Stalin said that Poland should
extend to the Oder and that the Russians would help the Poles to
establish their frontier thus far west, but he was not specific about
Poland's eastern frontier. According to the record: "The President
then said he would be interested in the question of assuring the approaches to the Baltic Sea and had in mind some form of trusteeship
with perhaps an international state in the vicinity of the Kiel Canal
to insure free navigation in both directions through the approaches.
Due to some error of the Soviet translator Marshal Stalin apparently thought that the President was referring to the question of the
Baltic States. On the basis of this understanding, he replied cate-
gorically that the Baltic States had by an expression of the will of
the people voted to join the Soviet Union and that this question
was not therefore one for discussion. Following the clearing up of
the misapprehension, he, however, expressed himself favorable in
regard to the question of insuring free navigation to and from the
Baltic Sea."

The following memorandum was written on Stalin's views concerning postwar Germany:

In regard to Germany, Marshal Stalin appeared to regard all
measures proposed by either the President or Churchill for the
subjugation and for the control of Germany as inadequate. He on
various occasions sought to induce the President or the Prime
Minister to go further in expressing their views as to the stringency of the measures which should be applied to Germany. He
appeared to have no faith in the possibility of the reform of the
German people and spoke bitterly of the attitude of the German
workers in the war against the Soviet Union. As evidence of the
fundamental German devotion to legality he cited the occasion in
1907 when he was in Leipzig when 200 German workers failed to
appear at an important mass meeting because there was no con-
troller at the station platform to punch their tickets which would
permit them to leave the station. He seemed to think that this
mentality of discipline and obedience could not be changed.

He said that Hitler was a very able man but not basically intelligent, lacking in culture and with a primitive approach to
political and other problems. He did not share the view of the

President that Hitler was mentally unbalanced and emphasized
that only a very able man could accomplish what Hitler had done
in solidifying the German people whatever we thought of the
methods. Although he did not specifically say so, it was apparent
from his remarks that he considered that Hitler through his stupidity in attacking the Soviet Union had thrown away all the
fruits of his previous victories.

As a war time measure Marshal Stalin questioned the advis-
ability of the unconditional surrender principle with no definition
of the exact terms which would be imposed upon Germany. He
felt that to leave the principle of unconditional surrender unclari-
fied merely served to unite the German people, whereas to draw
up specific terms, no matter how harsh, and tell the German
people that this was what they would have to accept, would, in
his opinion, hasten the day of German capitulation.

If Roosevelt made any comment on this expression of opinion on
the controversial question of unconditional surrender, it was not
recorded. But the subsequent record proves that he did not change
his mind.

The next morning, Monday, military staff talks were held at
which it was determined that it would be feasible to mount an
operation against Southern France with a two-division assault and
a ten-division follow-up to be launched simultaneously with OVER-
LORD D-Day or from two to three weeks preceding it. In the study
of personnel available in the Mediterranean theater made at this
meeting appeared the note, "Eisenhower states that 370,000 Italian
troops are now cooperating with Allied Forces," which seemed a remarkable number only ten weeks after Italy's surrender and with
two thirds of Italy still in German hands.

During these talks, Voroshilov asked a great many searching questions about innumerable details concerned with the actual preparations for OVERLORD. He was not interested in what the plans
were, or the "program" for production; he wanted to know what
was actually being *done*. He asked General Brooke point-blank if he
attached the same importance to OVERLORD that General Marshall did. Brooke replied in the affirmative but added that he knew
how strong the German defenses of Northern France were and that
under certain circumstances OVERLORD could fail. Voroshilov
said that the British and American forces had clearly demonstrated
their superiority over the Germans in the fighting on land in North
Africa and more particularly in the air over Europe and that if

the U.S. and British staffs really had the will and the desire to go through with OVERLORD it would be successful and would "go down in history as one of our greatest victories." He admitted the difficulties of a trans-Channel operation, as had Stalin, but said that the Russians had encountered comparable difficulties in the crossing of wide rivers and had overcome them because they "had the will to do it."

Marshall, whom both Stalin and Voroshilov obviously recognized as the supreme advocate of OVERLORD and therefore their friend, said that he wished to offer one comment: "The difference between a river crossing, however wide, and a landing from the ocean is that the failure of a river crossing is a reverse while the failure of a landing operation is a catastrophe." Marshall went on to say, "My military education and experience in the First World War has all been based on roads, rivers, and railroads. During the last two years, however, I have been acquiring an education based on oceans and I've had to learn all over again. Prior to the present war I never heard of any landing-craft except a rubber boat. Now I think about little else."

Voroshilov said admiringly to Marshall: "If you think about it, you will do it."

While this meeting was going on, Roosevelt attended to more mail. According to Harriman, Churchill sent over a message suggesting that he and the President have lunch together preparatory to the next Plenary Session that afternoon. But Roosevelt was too conscious of the presence of the NKVD men and did not want the report to be spread that he and the Prime Minister were hatching their own schemes. Harriman conveyed Roosevelt's regrets to Churchill who was not pleased by them and remarked that he could accept rebuffs as well as the next one—but, as Harriman told it, he said, "I shall insist on one thing: that I be host at dinner tomorrow evening. I think I have one or two claims to precedence. To begin with, I come first both in seniority and alphabetically. In the second place, I represent the longest established of the three governments. And, in the third place, tomorrow happens to be my birthday."

Roosevelt lunched quietly with his own household. His son Elliott had arrived that morning from Egypt, his plane having been delayed by engine trouble. After lunch the President had a short session with the Joint Chiefs of Staff, who reported their conclusions on ANVIL, the Southern France operation, and presented memoranda they had prepared for the President to discuss with Stalin for measures to be taken in anticipation of Russia's entry into the war against Japan. At 2:45 Stalin arrived. (The President's log book indicates that Molotov was also present, but the minutes of the meeting make no mention of his being there.) Roosevelt said he wished to lend Stalin a report from a U.S. Army officer who had been with Tito in Yugoslavia and had the highest respect for the work being done there by the Partisan forces. Stalin thanked the President and said he would read the report with interest and return it. Roosevelt then gave Stalin three memoranda:

(1) A request for permission for U.S. bombers from Britain to use Russian air bases for refueling, rearmament and emergency repair in the proposed "shuttle bombing" of Germany.

(2) A request that planning be started at once with a view to establishing bases for upwards of 1,000 U.S. heavy bombers in the Siberian Maritime Provinces for an air offensive against Japan.

(3) Requests for the exchange of information and for further preliminary planning for eventual operations against Japan. In this memorandum Roosevelt said:

> Specifically, I have in mind the following items:
>
> *a.* We would be glad to receive combat intelligence information concerning Japan.
>
> *b.* Considering that the ports for your Far Eastern submarine and destroyer force might be threatened seriously by land or air attack, do you feel it desirable that the United States should expand base facilities sufficiently to provide for these forces in U.S. bases?
>
> *c.* What direct or indirect assistance would you be able to give in the event of a U.S. attack against the northern Kuriles?
>
> *d.* Could you indicate what ports, if any, our forces could use, and could you furnish data on these ports in regard to their naval use as well as port capacities for dispatch of cargo?

Stalin promised to study these documents. (He later agreed to the shuttle bombing not only from bases in the United Kingdom but from Italy as well; he explained that he must defer consideration of the requests relative to the Far East until after his return to Moscow.)

Roosevelt then asked Stalin if he cared to discuss the future peace of the world and Stalin said there was nothing to prevent them from discussing anything they pleased. Whereupon, Roosevelt gave Stalin an outline of his concept of an organization, based on the United Nations, for the preservation of world peace. It was to consist of three main bodies:

First—an Assembly composed of all members of the United Nations which would meet in various places at stated times for the discussion of world problems and the making of recommendations for their solution. Stalin asked if this Assembly was to be world wide in scope, or merely European, and Roosevelt said it should be world wide.

Second—an Executive Committee which would consist of the U.S.S.R., the U.S., the U.K. and China, together with representatives of two European nations, one South American, one Middle Eastern, one Far Eastern and one British Dominion. This Executive Committee would deal with all nonmilitary questions—such as economy, food, health, etc.

Stalin asked whether this committee would have the right to make decisions which would be binding on all the nations. Roosevelt was indecisive in his answer to that one. He did not believe that the Congress would permit the United States to be bound by the decision of such a body. He said that the Committee could make recommendations for settling disputes with the hope that the nations concerned would be guided thereby.

The third body, as set forth by Roosevelt, was what he termed "The Four Policemen"—the U.S.S.R., U.S., U.K. and China. This as its name implied, would be the enforcing agency—with power to deal immediately with any threat to the peace or any sudden emergency. The President cited the Italian attack on Ethiopia in 1935 as an example of the failure of the League of Nations to deal promptly and forcibly with an act of aggression. He said that had the Four Policemen existed at that time it would have been possible to close the Suez Canal and thereby prevent Mussolini from attacking Ethiopia.

Stalin expressed the opinion that this proposal for the Four Policemen would not be favorably received by the small nations of Europe. For one thing he did not believe that China would be very powerful when the war ended—and, even if it were, European states would resent having China as an enforcement authority for themselves. He therefore suggested, as an alternative, that there be one committee for Europe and one for the Far East—the European committee to consist of Britain, Russia, the United States and possibly one other European nation. The President said that this suggestion was somewhat similar to one made by Churchill for regional committees—one for Europe, one for the Far East, and one for the Americas—and Roosevelt doubted that the Congress would agree to American participation in a purely European committee which might be able to compel the involvement of American troops. He said that only a crisis such as the present one could compel the Congress to agree to such a step—that it would not have been possible to send American troops to Europe in the present war had it not been for the Japanese attack on Pearl Harbor.

Stalin said that if the President's suggestion for a world organization were carried out—particularly the Four Policemen part of it—this might require the sending of American troops overseas. Roosevelt said that he had only foreseen the sending of American naval and air forces to Europe and that any land armies needed in the event of a future threat would have to be provided by Britain and the Soviet Union.

He saw two possible kinds of threat—one minor, and one major—to world peace. The minor threat might arise from a revolution or civil war in a small country, or the kind of Tacna-Arica dispute that sometimes arises between relatively small neighboring states. This could be met by application of the quarantine method, the closing of limited frontiers and the imposition of embargoes.

The major threat would be provided by a gesture of aggression on the part of a large power; in this case the Four Policemen would send an ultimatum to the threatening nation and, if the demands were not immediately met, they would subject that nation to bombardment and, if necessary, invasion. (There seems to be no evidence of any discussion of the possibility that the offending aggressor might be one of the Four Policemen.)

Stalin talked of the immediate problem of the future treatment of Germany. He said that he had discussed the question on the previous day with Churchill and considered that the Prime Minister was too hopeful in assuming that Germany could not rise again. It was Stalin's belief that Germany would be able to recover its power completely within fifteen or twenty years unless forcibly prevented from doing so, and that therefore there must be more certain safeguards than those provided by the type of organization which the President had proposed.

Stalin said that, to provide insurance against another career of aggression by Germany, the United Nations must gain and maintain control of physical strong points not only within Germany and along the borders of Germany, but also at strategic bases outside Germany. He mentioned Dakar specifically as one of such bases. He applied the same rules to the future containment of Japan, naming the islands in the vicinity of Japan as essential bases for the prevention of future aggression.

Stalin said that any organization or committee that might be set up for the preservation of peace must have the power not only to make decisions in times of emergency but to have continued military occupation of the necessary bases against Germany and Japan.

Roosevelt said that his agreement with Marshal Stalin on this was one hundred per cent. He said that although he was fully cognizant of the present weakness of China, he had insisted that the Chinese must participate in the four-power declaration at Moscow because he was thinking far into the future and believed that it was better to have the 400 million people of China as friends rather than as possible enemies.

There was then some discussion of the ability of the Germans to convert apparently peaceable industries secretly to wartime purposes. Stalin said that the Germans had shown great skill in such deception, but Roosevelt expressed confidence that if the world organization were sufficiently strong and effective it could prevent repetition of Germany's secret rearmament.

It was now 3:30, and Stalin and Roosevelt moved over to the large conference room of the Russian Embassy where Churchill, acting on behalf of King George VI, presented to the Marshal the "Sword of Stalingrad." Following this impressive ceremony, the twenty-eight participants in the conference sat down at the large round table and went to work on the Second Plenary Session. It started with a review of the morning staff session by Brooke, Marshall and Voroshilov, and then Stalin fired the big question:

"Who will command OVERLORD?"

Roosevelt replied that this had not yet been decided. Stalin thereupon made it clear that until a supreme commander were named he could not believe in the reality of the operation. Roosevelt must have been sorely tempted at that moment to name General Marshall as supreme commander and have done with it, but he did not do so, for reasons known only to himself. He said that the decisions taken at this Conference would affect the choice of the particular officer, and this probably meant that he would appoint Marshall only if the command involved *all* of Western and Southern Europe instead of OVERLORD alone.

Churchill then launched forth on a lengthy statement along familiar lines. He ranged from the Channel to Southern France to Italy to Yugoslavia to Rhodes and so to Turkey, dwelling for some time on that favorite subject. The record states that the Prime Minister "summed up the tasks before the conference as (1) to survey the whole field of the Mediterranean, and (2) how to relieve Russia, and (3) how to help OVERLORD."

Stalin said, "If we are here in order to discuss military matters, among all the military questions for discussion, we, the U.S.S.R., consider OVERLORD the most important and decisive." He said that, from the Russian point of view, Turkey, Rhodes, Yugoslavia and even the capture of Rome were not important. He recommended that a directive be given to the military staffs as follows:

"(1) In order that Russian help might be given from the East to the execution of OVERLORD, a date should be set and the Operation should not be postponed. (2) If possible the attack in Southern France should precede OVERLORD by two months, but if that is impossible, then it should be launched simultaneously with or even a little after OVERLORD. This would be an operation in direct support of OVERLORD as contrasted with diversionary operations in Italy or the Balkans. (3) The Commander-in-Chief for OVERLORD should be appointed as soon as possible. Until that is done, OVERLORD cannot be considered as really in progress." Stalin added that the appointment of the Commander-in-Chief was the business of the President and Mr. Churchill but that it would be advantageous to have the appointment made here in Teheran.

Churchill made a final and, one must say, gallant attempt in behalf of Rhodes and Turkey as strategic points, but Roosevelt said that it seemed that he and the Prime Minister and the Marshal were agreed on the main directive to the Chiefs of Staff which was to go ahead on the assumption that OVERLORD was the dominating operation and, while the Staffs might make recommendations for subsidiary operations in the Mediterranean area, they must be careful to consider nothing that could possibly cause a delay in OVERLORD.

Stalin thereupon said to Churchill that he would like to ask him a rather indiscreet question: did the British really believe in OVERLORD or were they expressing their approval of it merely as a means of reassuring the Russians? The record is not quite clear at this point but it would seem that Churchill now accepted the inevitable and said that Britain would hurl every ounce of her strength across the Channel at the Germans. Tension still existed, however, so Roosevelt observed that within an hour a very good dinner would be awaiting all of them, with Marshal Stalin as their host, and that he for one would have a large appetite for it. He suggested that the

Combined Chiefs of Staff meet again in the morning and settle the matter of OVERLORD once and for all. The meeting then ended.

The official records of these meetings were written with so much circumspection that the inherent drama was largely obscured; but it was far too big to be totally disguised. One cannot read these deliberately dry and guarded accounts without the feeling that here were Titans determining the future course of an entire planet. This was indeed the Big Three, Churchill employed all the debater's arts, the brilliant locutions and circumlocutions, of which he was a master, and Stalin wielded his bludgeon with relentless indifference to all the dodges and feints of his practiced adversary; while Roosevelt sat in the middle, by common consent the moderator, arbitrator and final authority. His contributions to the conversations were infrequent and sometimes annoyingly irrelevant, but it appears time and again—at Teheran and at Yalta—that it was he who spoke the last word.

Sometime during the Teheran Conference Roosevelt drew three circles, which represented his conception of the basis of the United Nations Organization. The center circle was marked "Executive Committee," the one on the right was marked "4 Policemen" and the one on the left "40 United Nations" (The General Assembly) under which came "I.L.O.-Health-Agriculture-Food." This, so far as I know, was the first crude outline of the U.N. structure put down by Roosevelt who, unlike Hopkins, loved to draw charts.

The dinner on Monday evening was marked by a great deal of "teasing" of Churchill by Stalin; I am not qualified to say whether it was intended or accepted in a spirit of good-humored raillery, but it was evidently unremitting throughout the evening. At one point, when the question of postwar control of strategic bases was being discussed, Churchill stated that Britain did not desire to acquire any new territory but intended to hold on to what she had and to reclaim what had been taken from her—specifically Singapore and Hong Kong—and that while she might eventually release portions of the Empire of her own free will, she could not be compelled to give up anything without a war. Stalin commented on this that Britain had fought well in the war and that he personally favored increases in the British Empire, particularly in the area around Gibraltar which was presently the property of Franco's Spain. When Churchill asked what territorial interests Russia might have in the future, Stalin was quoted as having replied, "There is no need to speak at the present time about any Soviet desires—but when the time comes, we will speak."

JOHN GUNTHER

****

My son John Gunther Jr., a student at Deerfield Academy, Massachusetts, became ill of a brain tumor in the spring of 1946, when he was sixteen. He had to leave school of course, underwent a series of formidable operations, and for a year struggled with marvelous courage against the creeping, implacable ravages of an incurable disease. Death Be Not Proud *describes in some detail the story of as gallant and spirited a fight for life and a whole mind as anybody ever made. Johnny, though frightfully ill, managed to keep up with his studies; he passed his examinations and in some fields went far beyond the normal curriculum for a boy of that age. All during the illness, as medical ordeal followed ordeal, his detachment, good humor, intense discriminating interest in everything about him, and above all his courage far beyond the line where any courage could be reasonably called for, made him a hero to his friends.*

The passage that follows tells of his return to Deerfield for the ceremony of commencement. More than a year had passed since he had fallen out. "Frances" is of course Johnny's mother, and Mr. Boyden is the headmaster. The quip about Hartford has to do with a book I was working on at the time.

Johnny died on June 30, 1947, a month after the events described. His last words were to ask whether or not Harvard would let him in.

JOHN GUNTHER

****

Death Be Not Proud: The Graduation

WE DROVE to Deerfield on May 27, and Johnny graduated on June 4, though he had not been to school for fourteen months. The days passed in a proud procession, and I think probably it was the happiest week of his life.

It seemed chilly when we started, and Johnny, as always extract-

221

ing compensation out of any ill fortune, said, "Well, at least we
don't have a heat wave." We passed through Hartford and he
asked, "Were you here when you did your research?—I wouldn't
dream of asking how long you stayed, probably half an hour." I was
full of nerves as we got near Deerfield with its stiff old houses and
great fanlike elms, and impatiently I asked him if I had overshot
the side road and did he recognize any landmarks. He replied
gently, "You know I don't see well out of my left eye."

Then without the slightest self-consciousness he took his place in
his class. He sat between old friends in the dining hall (the instructors had warned them) and Frances whispered that they should inconspicuously cut his meat if necessary. The boys stared at him for
a second as if he were a ghost—of course his hair had not grown
back fully after the last operation and he wore a white turban—
and then accepted his appearance without question.

Every evening after dinner an informal ceremony takes place at
Deerfield which is one of the distinguishing marks of this magnificent school; each boy from Freshman to Senior meets with Mr.
Boyden, and the roll of the entire school is called. The boys are
heaped together on the floor. Usually there is a casualty or two—
some youngsters hurt in a football game—for whom there are big
leather chairs. Johnny eased himself into one of these, and his name
was called in the roll exactly as if he had never been absent for a
moment. Then he limped slowly and proudly to the Senior Dorm
where he would have been living this past year, and looked at what
should have been his room with a piercing yearning. Boys were
moving back and forth in the orderly bustle that precedes commencement. Johnny had the attitude of one who is both a partici-
pant in and a spectator of a great event. Mr. Boyden crept up to us
and asked if we were sure he would not get too tired. Then he
joined calmly in a bull session.

It was decided that he should sleep in the infirmary—a building
he knew only too exasperatingly well. The next morning we came
to pick him up at what we thought was a reasonable hour. But he
had left the building before eight, alone, and was at that moment
taking the final exam in chemistry! He passed at B Minus—though
he had never taken a regular chemistry course in his life.

Later that day I bumped into him accidentally on the bright sunlit grass as he dragged himself from behind a hedge in shadow. His
left shoulder sagged; his arm hung almost useless; his mouth was
twisted with effort; the left side of his lip sank down; his eyes were
filmy; he was happy. "Oh, pardon me, sir," Johnny said. He had

not recognized me, and thought that I was some master he did not know.

Everybody tried hard to keep him from being too active. But he said, "Walking around this way helps the wound heal." Frances told him to sit around in the sun—how they both loved the sun!—and get brown and he answered, "All you are interested in, Mother, is my color!" When he had trouble with knife and fork one evening, he told her in exquisite parody of what she often said, "Be patient. Believe in calmness and Nirvana." It was a lovely day the next day and Johnny spent an hour learning some calculus from a fellow student. He worked out the equations on the bottom of a paper plate during a picnic lunch in the soft grass. Frances remonstrated that he might be getting tired. He replied briefly, "There's no future to just sitting."

The day before graduation was strenuous, with a lunch for the parents at noon and then a baseball game which Johnny watched with serious interest for about four innings. The dress-up banquet that night, to celebrate among other things Mr. Boyden's forty-fifth year as headmaster, lasted three hours. Johnny did not miss a minute of it. He tramped across the lawn afterward, with his classmate Henry Eisner holding his hand, for the off-the-record talk Mr. Boyden gives each graduating class. Then the class, standing under the trees in a night grown chilly, serenaded the Boydens on the front porch. Johnny, on the outskirts of the massed pack of boys, looked suddenly exhausted, and I slipped away from the adults to join him inconspicuously, standing just behind him. He did not mind, though as a rule he loathed having us anywhere near him at school. I was afraid he might fall. Then I heard his light, silvery tenor chime in with the other voices. The song floated across the lawn and echoed back. We hiked to the infirmary and Johnny ran into a classmate who had won an award. "Congratulations!" he snapped briskly.

The next morning the boys assembled early for the quarter-mile walk to the white-frame Deerfield church, arranging themselves four abreast in order of their height. I did not think Johnny could manage such a march. He shook us off and disappeared. The procedure is that the boys, reaching the church, line up behind the pews, and then walk one by one down the center aisle, as each name is called. Mr. Flynt, the president of the board of trustees, then shakes hands with each boy, giving him his diploma in the left hand. We explained that Johnny might not be able to grasp the smooth roll of diploma with his left fingers, and asked Mr. Flynt to try to slip it into the right hand instead. The boys began to

march in slowly, and though Johnny should have been conspicuous
with his white bandage, we did not see him and I was in an agony
fearing that he had fallen out. Mr. Boyden, sweeping the assembly
with his all-embracing sharp affectionate glance, caught Frances's
eye and nodded to her reassuringly. One by one the names were
called out, and each boy disassociated himself from the solid group
and marched forward alone. The call was alphabetical, and by the
time the G's were reached we were limp with suspense, since we
did not know for sure that Johnny had even got into the church.
As each boy passed down the aisle, there was applause, perfunctory
for some, pronounced for others. Gaines, Gillespie, Goodwin, Grif-
fin, Gunther. Slowly, very slowly, Johnny stepped out of the mass
of his fellows and trod by us, carefully keeping in the exact center
of the long aisle, looking neither to the left nor the right, but straight
ahead, fixedly, with the white bandage flashing in the light through
the high windows, his chin up, carefully, not faltering, steady, but
slowly, so very slowly. The applause began and then rose and the
applause became a storm, as every single person in that old church
became whipped up, tight and tense, to see if he would make it.
The applause became a thunder, it rose and soared and banged,
when Johnny finally reached the pulpit. Mr. Flynt carefully tried
to put the diploma in his right hand, as planned. Firmly Johnny
took it from right hand to left, as was proper, and while the whole
audience rocked now with release from tension, and was still wildly,
thunderously applauding, he passed around to the side and, not
seeing us, reached his place among his friends.

That evening we talked of Harvard. Some of the boys were getting their admission notices, and Johnny, now that he had actually
been graduated, wondered when his would come. He was impatient. He had a great sense of the passage of time.

Everything that Johnny suffered was in a sense repaid by the few
heroic moments of that walk down the center aisle of that church.
This was his triumph and indomitable summation. Nobody who saw
it will ever forget it, or be able to forget the sublime strength of will
and character it took.

WILLIAM ROSE BENÉT

****

PIGEON COVE,
CAPE ANN, MASS.

*I have selected four short poems from a great many written in my
lifetime. I have chosen "Fire and Glass" because it seems to me one
of my best earlier lyrics, as well as being one not usually preferred.
The two sonnets from* The Dust Which Is God *are complete in
themselves. I have merely given them a title and conforming punc-
tuation. "Harmony" and the sonnet, "Wound in Secret," from* The
Stairway of Surprise, *seem to me, perhaps, to convey something out
of universal experience.*

WILLIAM ROSE BENÉT

****

Four Poems

FIRE AND GLASS

THE THISTLY YELLOW FLAME flows up like water,
    The dusk brick glows.
Fashion the ropelike glass; your lip can blow it
    To a vase like a rose,
To a goblet curved like a wave, with a stem like a lily.
    Glass can be spun
To frailer lace than the cobweb brown old spiders
    Weave in the sun.

Not pure gold ingots nor all the renown of iron
    Nor the blushing brand,
Nor crackling cataracts of molten metal
    Kissing the sand,
So praise this cleanly and bewildered fury
    Potent to shape
Emerging contours scintillant as diamond,
    Smooth as the grape.

225

O self-consuming sun, the dew-on-the-gossamer's
          Delicate glint,
What symmetries petaled and pearled and fragile as flowers
          Take form and tint
From this fierce unslakable thirst and famine of fire
          Cold stars control!
Even thus, O love, through the blood's rebuked rebellion—
          Thus my soul—!

WHERE ALL IS GLACIER

For a similitude I give you this:
the mountaineer upon the high plateau
where the ice-daggered wind swirls on the snow
that blinds with glare, a white necropolis
of solitude. Far down through the abyss
the red sun welters in a furnace-glow.
Then higher and higher doth the darkness go
till only the summit of Mount Blanc is his,
a lost island of light. Then that is gone.
With blackness and the stiffening cold alone
terror hisses in ears. As hard as stone
the frozen bread. Aeons away the dawn.
Yet still, upon the membrane of the eye,
magnificence, climbing against the sky . . .

None knows, none knows! . . . But why should any know
the place where all is glacier, all is rock?
Or rather say: can any ward the shock
decreeing sojourn in that waste of snow
where the huge avalanche hurls to chasms below
the fortress crag, the rooted granite block—
where the crevasse of echoes will only mock
with mimic groans all facile human woe?
Think of Saussure, who at the very last
above a chaos of white and towering peaks
watched the sun coruscate on glasslike streaks
that were fardown ravines, in torment passed—
and looking up, through darker bluer skies
saw in broad daylight the stars of heaven rise!

HARMONY

MASTER OF MUSIC, wring again the strings,
wound the wide air with eddying chord on chord!
Something within me sings
and I would be delivered of a word,
word of creation,
word of wind and flame,
whereby am I its centre everywhere,
whence the hot clotted worlds from chaos came
to glitter like diamond on blue night air..

Melodic archer, bend the infinite bow
missiled with golden tones of rhythmic fire
like battle arrows with heads of blazing tow
arcing the dark rampire!
Twang the bow string, the harp string! Of what whole
my part, none knows—music not mine in breath
or sinew—yet this harmony my soul summoneth . . .

The harp frame racked from pedestal to crown,
vibrating life in pity and pain unending,
with great dim hands of shadow sweeping down,
some great vague visage bending . . .

WOUND IN SECRET

How ARE they divorced, cloven apart by war,
The heart and brain, that generous giant of flame
And that gray ingenious clerk in the pallid core
Of nerves and cells! For nothing is the same
When will says kill, love stares in a black abysm,
And conscious cortex is set like a murder mine,
With duty damnation, and blood for the only chrism,
Till the spirit shrieks, like the mandrakes of Leah's line,
Torn from its rooted flesh. The soul is forced
By Amnon Death, till shuddering silence falls
And glare is ghastly on indrawing walls . .
Of the obsessive. O how are they divorced, · · ·
The heart and brain, till the inwardly bleeding and maimed
Grope toward love again, in a dark world crumbled and shamed!

CARL VAN DOREN

✱✱

Since my Benjamin Franklin *has been more widely translated than any other of my books, I suppose that a passage from it is the natural choice for this collection. This account of the philosopher and the ladies he knew best while he lived at Passy presents him at the peak of his career and in his most charming aspect.*

CARL VAN DOREN

✱✱

Franklin and French Ladies

FRANKLIN'S CLOSEST FRIENDS in France were for the most part his nearest neighbours. He was on good terms with the parish priest and the village tradesmen. He and the Chaumont family, in the Hôtel Valentinois, saw each other almost daily. Franklin teasingly called the daughter Sophie his wife, which delighted her. Passy was then famous for its mineral springs, down the slope near the river. Louis Le Veillard, who managed the drinking, bottling, and bathing at the Eaux and became in 1789 the first mayor of the town, lived there, like Franklin, all the year round, and he and his wife and daughter were Franklin's friends for life. Across the street from Franklin was the Château de Passy, which belonged to the Comte de Boulainvilliers. His daughter was another of Franklin's favorites. When she became engaged to the Comte de Clermont-Tonnerre, all Passy said that Franklin's lightning rod (*paratonnerre*) had not been able to protect her. William Alexander, a Scot whom Franklin had known in Edinburgh and London, now lived with his family at Saint-Germain. His daughter Marianne was married in 1779 to Franklin's grand-nephew Jonathan Williams.

Franklin, John Adams disapprovingly said, "at the age of seventy-odd had neither lost his love of beauty nor his taste for it." But there is no support for the tradition which insists that the philosopher was a lively lecher in France. "You mention the kindness of the French ladies to me," he wrote to his Boston step-niece Elizabeth Partridge on 11 October 1779. "I must explain that matter. This is the civilest nation upon earth. Your first acquaintances endeavour to find out what you like, and they tell others. If 'tis understood that you like mutton, dine where you will you find mutton. Somebody, it seems, gave it out that I loved ladies; and then everybody presented me their ladies (or the ladies presented themselves) to be embraced; that is, have their necks kissed. For as to the kissing of lips or cheeks it is not the mode here; the first is reckoned rude, and the other may rub off the paint. The French ladies have, however, a thousand other ways of rendering themselves agreeable; by their various attentions and civilities and their sensible conversation."

Some of the attentions paid him were in the elaborate, Arcadian mode of the old regime which was so near its downfall. Madame Campan, companion of Marie Antoinette, later remembered a ceremonial occasion—of no given time or place—when the most beautiful of three hundred women placed a crown of laurel on Franklin's white head and kissed both his cheeks. In April 1781 he was the hero of a *fête champêtre* arranged by the Comtesse d'Houdetot (the Sophie of Rousseau's *Confessions*) at her house at Sannois, ten miles from Passy. She and her party came on foot half a mile to meet his carriage, and she welcomed him with verses she had composed herself. Liberty, the verses sighed, was far off, but here was a mortal who had made happy citizens. Hosts and guests (the gouty philosopher too?) walked to the château and dinner. At each glass of wine there was another stanza to be sung or spoken. There would be altars in America for Benjamin, the chorus said; let Sannois drink to his renown. He freed men by enlightening them, said a stanza, and virtue took its very countenance from him. William Tell was brave, but savage; our dear Benjamin, shaping the destiny of America, could laugh at this civilized table. Long live Philadelphia, sang the comtesse; its independence so tempted her that she would like to live there, though it had no balls or comedies.

Silent, smiling, Franklin went through these literary rites, too much pleased by the affectionate honours shown him to laugh at the artificial forms they took. But his close friendships with women were easier and more humorous. There was Madame Brillon, wife of a treasury official who was much older than she and less imaginative. She seems to have been in her thirties when she met Franklin soon after he arrived in Paris. From the first she loved the philosopher. He told her how the savages in America sometimes adopted their prisoners, in the place of kinsmen who had died. She adopted

Franklin to succeed her father whom she had loved and still missed. "Oh, my Papa," she wrote in November 1778, "I beg for your friendship, your healthy philosophy; my heart listens, and submits to you. . . . Never call me anything but 'my daughter.' Yesterday you called me 'Madame,' and my heart shrank." She confided to him, as she might have to her father, her difficulties with her husband, her jealousy of her daughters' governess, the ingratitude she had to bear. Franklin sent her, in his own French, the fatherly advice she asked for. Bad as ingratitude was, she must not try to pay it back. "If they have done you injuries, reflect that although they may formerly have been your equals they have by those means put themselves beneath you. If you avenge yourself and punish them in kind, you restore them to the state of equality which they have lost. But if you pardon them without any punishment, you will fix them in the low state to which they have fallen and from which they can never rise without true repentance and full reparation." Poor Richard had said almost the same thing in his almanac for 1749.

Still, Franklin and Madame Brillon were not father and daughter, and there was the spice of gallantry in their friendship. "People have the audacity," she wrote him, "to criticize my pleasant habit of sitting on your knee, and yours of always asking me for what I always refuse." She decided to be more discreet in the future.

One evening, while she sat in her covered bath, he and some friend, possibly her husband, got so absorbed in a game of chess they were playing in the room that it was eleven when Franklin reached home, and he was distressed for fear they had inconvenienced her by keeping her in the bath for so long.

Twice a week during the summer (usually Wednesday and Saturday) he came with Temple to her house after dinner, to idle on the terrace in the sun, with chess and tea, or to listen indoors to her and her daughters at their music. After Saratoga Madame Brillon composed for Franklin a *March of the Insurgents*. Sometimes he played on the harmonica. These concerts he called his opera, for he rarely went to the opera in Paris. The family gatherings were discreet enough. But during the winter when she was in Paris, and between their regular days of the week in summer, letters went back and forth between them in which he often urged his claim to be more than father, and she as often rejected it—without ever choosing to end the piquant debate.

"How am I going to spend the Wednesdays and Saturdays?" she asked after she had left Passy in November 1779. Perhaps another life might be better than this, with its enforced separations. "In paradise we shall be reunited, never to leave each other again. We shall there live on roast apples only; the music will be made up of Scotch airs; all parties will be given over to chess . . . everyone will speak the same language; the English will be neither unjust nor wicked there; the women will not be coquettes, the men will be neither jealous nor too gallant. . . . We shall never suffer from gout there nor from our nerves. . . . Ambition, envy, pretensions, jealousy, prejudices, all these will vanish at the sound of the trumpet. . . . Every day we shall love one another in order that we may love one another still more the day after; in a word, we shall be completely happy. In the meantime, let us get all the good we can out of this poor world of ours."

Franklin in reply said he had been thinking about how the two of them would manage their affairs in paradise. In the course of nature he would die forty years before her and have to wait that long till she came. He could not without scruple think of asking her to desert her husband, who was good and generous and loved them as they did him. "However, the idea of an eternity in which I shall be favoured with no more than permission to kiss your hands, or sometimes your cheeks, and to pass two or three hours in your sweet society on Wednesdays and Saturdays, is frightful." But he would leave it for her to decide in paradise. "If you reject me, perhaps I shall address myself to Madame d'Hardancourt (her mother), and she may be willing to live with me; then I shall pass my hours at home agreeably with her. . . . In forty years I shall have time to practise on the harmonica, and perhaps I shall play well enough to be worthy to accompany you on your pianoforte. From time to time we shall have little concerts." All their friends from Passy would be the audience. Her daughters and certain young angels would sing. "And we shall pity those who are not dead."

Madame Brillon relented—for the future. "I give you my word of honour that I will become your wife in paradise, on condition, however, that you do not make too many conquests among the heavenly maidens while you are waiting for me. I want a faithful husband when I take one for eternity." She would tell her mother of his "good intentions" towards her, but it might cause jealousy between the two women, devoted as they were to one another. He must not apologize for his French. If it was not very pure, it was at least very clear. As she said in another letter, it was "always very good French to say: *Je vous aime*." Leave grammar to the academicians.

The game of love and kisses ran through their correspondence, but their friendship included more than gallantry. In April 1781 Franklin formally proposed his grandson—whom the Brillons called Franklinet—as husband of their eldest daughter. The philosopher, believing he might not outlive the war and would have to remain in France, hoped to make his friends his family there. Temple might be given some diplomatic post in Europe, and would not have to take his wife away to America. . . . Madame Brillon, for herself and her husband, affectionately declined the offer. Temple, they were sure, belonged to America, and they required a husband for their daughter who could assume, as Temple was too young to do, the responsibilities which Brillon wished to give up to a successor in his post. . . .

Their affection and their letters continued to the end of his life, whether he was in Passy or in remote Philadelphia, after her husband died and her fortune was reduced and the French Revolution overturned her captivating world.

And there was Madame Helvétius, widow of the rich farmer-general who had been a philosopher and had given brilliant Tuesday dinners for philosophers. Since his death in 1771 his widow had lived with her two daughters at Auteuil, the village next to Passy. On the edge of the Bois de Boulogne, in a little park planted with hortensias and rhododendrons and swarming with cats, dogs (Temple Franklin brought a bulldog from England), chickens, pigeons, canaries, and wild birds from the Bois, Madame Helvétius kept up her spirited salon. When Voltaire came to call she met him at the gate, like a king. After Turgot had brought Franklin for his first visit she regretted that she had not shown him the same honour. He may have come, as he went to Madame du Deffand's, to win an influential woman to the side of America. But he and Madame Helvétius became instantly and permanently friends. She had been so beautiful that Fontenelle, who lived to be a hundred, was said to have paid her one of the most famous compliments of the age: "Ah, Madame, if I were only eighty again!" And at sixty she was still so pleasing that Franklin paid her, it is said, another which became as famous. There are different versions of the story, told of different women and different situations. The classic account is that Madame Helvétius accused Franklin of having put off a visit she expected. "Madame, I am waiting till the nights are longer."

Abigail Adams, arriving from Boston by way of congenial London in August 1784 and asked to dinner at Franklin's house with Madame Helvétius, thought her untidy, noisy, and brazen. She called

Dr. Franklin merely Franklin, kissed his cheeks and forehead when she greeted him, and sat beside him at dinner sometimes holding his hand and sometimes carelessly throwing her arm around his neck (her other arm now and then on the back of John Adams' chair). "I should have been greatly astonished at this conduct if the good Doctor had not told me that in this lady I should see a genuine Frenchwoman, wholly free from affectation or stiffness of behaviour, and one of the best women in the world. For this I must take the Doctor's word; but I should have set her down for a very bad one." Taught from her childhood to venerate the great Franklin, the Puritan lady was shocked to find that Madame Helvétius was bold with him and that he liked it.

Franklin could hardly have made clear to his American admirer why he enjoyed his French friend. But he explained it to Madame Helvétius. "I see that statesmen, philosophers, historians, poets, and men of learning of all sorts are drawn around you, and seem as willing to attach themselves to you as straws about a fine piece of amber. . . . I would not attempt to explain it by the story of the ancient who, being asked why philosophers sought the acquaintance of kings and kings not that of philosophers, replied that philosophers knew what they wanted, which was not always the case with kings. Yet thus far the comparison may go: that we find in your sweet society that charming benevolence, that amiable attention to oblige, that disposition to please and be pleased, which we do not always find in the society of one another. It springs from you; it has its influence on us all; and in your company we are not only pleased with you but better pleased with one another and with ourselves.". . .

Yet the casual records which are all that survive of the friendship of Franklin and Madame Helvétius seldom even mention the other great men who visited her. Franklin gave Madame Helvétius the name she had in their circle: Notre Dame d'Auteuil. He named her daughters the Étoiles, from the story of the mother who told her children that old moons were cut up to make new stars.

Franklin's devotion to Madame Helvétius was frank and open, and he wrote about it to Cabanis in the full assurance that she would be shown the letters. "As he has already given her many of his days," he wrote on 19 September 1779, in the third person and in French, "although he has so few of them left to give, it seems ungrateful in her that she has never given him a single one of her nights." And again to Cabanis: "M. Franklin being up, bathed, shaved, combed, beautified as best he could, all dressed, and on the point of going out, with his head full of the four Helvétius ladies and the sweet kisses he intends to steal from them, is much mortified to find the possibility of this happiness put off to next Sunday. He will be as patient as he can, hoping to see one of these ladies at M. de Chaumont's on Wednesday. He will be there early, to see her enter with that grace and that dignity which have charmed him for seven weeks at the same place. He even plans to capture her and keep her with him for life. The three others left at Auteuil ought to be enough for the canaries and the abbés."

Just when Franklin proposed marriage to Madame Helvétius and how seriously he meant it are neither of them certain. A letter to La Roche on 7 December 1778 refers to an "exercise" which Franklin was sending for the abbé to correct, "en forme de billet à Notre Dame d'Auteuil." This has been commonly thought to be *À Madame Helvétius,* the most graceful and felicitous of all his bagatelles. But the bagatelle itself speaks of Franklin as having been married long enough to bring the date to January 1780. In any case, he seems to have proposed, and she to have said that she had resolved to be faithful to the memory of her husband. (She had said the same thing to Turgot, her oldest friend, who had proposed to her after Helvétius died.) Franklin, according to his humorous account, went home mortified and dreamed that night that he was in the Elysian Fields, where he met Helvétius.

"He received me with much courtesy, having known me by reputation, he said, for some time. He asked me many things about the war and about the present state of religion, liberty, and government in France. 'You ask nothing then,' I said to him, 'about your dear friend Madame Helvétius; and yet she still loves you to excess; I was with her less than an hour ago.' 'Ah!' he said, 'you remind me of my former happiness. But we must forget if we are to be happy here. For several years at first I thought of nothing but her. At last I am consoled. I have taken another wife; the most like her I could find. She is not, it is true, altogether so beautiful, but she has as much good sense and plenty of wit, and she loves me infinitely. She studies continually to please me, and she has just now gone out to search for the best nectar and ambrosia to regale me with this evening. Stay with me and you will see her.' 'I perceive,' I said, 'that your former friend is more faithful than you; she has had several good offers and has refused them all. I confess to you that I have loved her, to madness; but she was cruel to me and absolutely rejected me for love of you.' 'I pity you,' he said, 'in your misfortune; for she is indeed a good and beautiful woman, and very amiable.' " Here Helvétius, Franklin said, advised him to make use of the abbés in his courtship. Morellet might argue in favour of her suitor, La Roche against him; both would be of service. Then "the new Madame Helvétius came in with the nectar; immediately I recognized her as Madame Franklin, my former friend. I claimed her again, but she said coldly: 'I was a good wife to you for forty-nine years and four months, almost half a century. Be content with that. I have formed a new connexion here which will last for eternity.'

"Indignant at this refusal from my Eurydice, I at once resolved to quit those ungrateful shades, return to this good world, and see again the sun and you. Here I am. Let us avenge ourselves."

Madame Helvétius, partly on the advice of Turgot, persisted in her resolution. Franklin had never been a tragic lover and was not one now. Whatever frustration or mortification he may have felt, he kept the affair on the most engaging level and teased her with a devotion at which he smiled himself. . . . His proposal and her refusal had no effect on their friendship. During his last four years in France he seems to have spent more time with her than with Madame Brillon, but the two women were not jealous of each other. (Madame Brillon wrote to him one Saturday morning that she could not see him at tea that afternoon and he might give the day to her amiable rival. Madame Helvétius pretended to be jealous of Madame de Forbach, Dowager Duchess of Deux-Ponts, who gave Franklin his crab-tree cane.) On his trying journey to the ship which was to take him home Franklin wrote twice to Madame Helvétius. "It seems to me that things are badly arranged in this world, when I see that two beings so made to be happy together are obliged to separate." "Often in my dreams," he wrote to her from Philadelphia three years later, "I have breakfast with you, I sit beside you on one of your hundred sofas, I walk with you in your beautiful garden." She wrote him scrawling, misspelled letters, sent news through her abbés, inquired about his grandsons, shopped for his daughter in Paris, and added presents to what she had bought. She had always loved him and always would. Though they would never see each other again in this world, perhaps in the next "we shall meet again, with all those who have loved us, I a husband and you a wife—but I believe you have been a rogue and will find more than one."

If in France there were new women whom Franklin loved and who loved him, he lost none of his old friends. In spite of the British he kept up an intermittent correspondence with Catharine Greene, whose husband was now governor of Rhode Island and who delighted the French officers who met her and told her about Frank-

lin. Letters still found their way back and forth between him and
Polly Hewson and Georgiana Shipley in England. The long life of
all his affectionate friendships helps to define them. Without the
brevity of ordinary lust, or the perseverance of obsession, they had a
general warmth which, while no doubt sexual in origin, made them
strong, tender, imaginative, and humorous beyond the reach of mere
desire, with its hard, impersonal appetite. Always a person himself,
Franklin treated every woman as if she were a person too, and made
her feel more truly one than ever. Because he loved, valued, and
studied women, they were no mystery to him, and he had no instinctive fear of them. Statesman and scientist, profoundly masculine, he took women into account as well as any other force of
nature.

Even in his political or moral writings, the sexes might furnish
him with images or examples. "What would you think of a proposition if I should make it," he wrote to David Hartley on 16 October 1783, "of a family compact between England, France, and
America? America would be as happy as the Sabine girls, if she
could be the means of uniting in perpetual peace her father and
her husband." And to Priestley on 7 June 1782: "Men I find to be
a sort of beings very badly constructed, as they are generally more
easily provoked than reconciled, more disposed to do mischief to
each other than to make reparation, much more easily deceived
than undeceived, and having more pride and even pleasure in
killing than in begetting one another; for without a blush they
assemble in great armies at noonday to destroy, and when they have
killed as many as they can, they exaggerate the number to augment
the fancied glory; but they creep into corners, or cover themselves
with the darkness of night, when they mean to beget, as being
ashamed of a virtuous action. A virtuous one it would be, and a
vicious one the killing of them, if the species were really worth producing or preserving; but of this I begin to doubt."

ERSKINE CALDWELL

****

TUCSON, ARIZ.

DEAR WHIT:

You make me feel good like an editor himself when you ask me to propose one of my own stories for your volume.

With the normal amount of doubts I have decided upon "Yellow Girl" as being representative.

Sincerely,

ERSKINE

****

Yellow Girl

NELL stood at the kitchen window packing the basket of eggs. She arranged eleven white eggs carefully, placing the cottonseed hulls between them and under them so that none would be broken. The last one to be put into the basket was large and brown and a little soiled. She dipped it into the pan of soap and warm water and wiped it dry with a fresh dishtowel. Even then she was not pleased with the way it looked, because it was brown; all the other eggs in the basket were as white as September cotton bolls.

Behind her in the room, Myrtie was scouring the two frying-pans with soapy water and a cloth dipped in sand. Nell laid down the brown egg and called Myrtie.

"Here's another of those big brown eggs, Myrtie," she said, pointing at the egg. "Do you have any idea where they come from? Have you seen any strange hens in the yard? There must be a visiting hen laying eggs in the chicken house."

Myrtie laid down the frying-pan and came over to the little table by the window. She picked up the large brown egg and looked at it. The egg no longer looked brown. Nell looked at the egg again, wondering why in Myrtie's hands it had apparently changed color.

"Where do these brown eggs come from, Myrtie?" she asked.

237

"There was one last week, and now today there's this. It was in the basket Mr. Willis brought in from the chicken house, but he said he forgot to notice which nest he took it from."

Myrtie turned the egg over in her hands, feeling the weight of it and measuring its enormous circumference with her fingers.

"Don't ask me, Miss Nell," Myrtie said, staring at the egg. "I've never seen a flock of Leghorns yet, though, that didn't lay a few brown eggs, sometime or other. Looks like it just can't be helped."

"What do you mean, Myrtie? What on earth are you talking about? Of course, Leghorns lay white eggs; this is a brown egg."

"I'm not saying the Leghorns lay them, Miss Nell, and I'm not saying they don't. Those old Buff Orpingtons and Plymouth Rocks and Domineckers lay funny-looking eggs, too, sometimes. I wouldn't take-on so much about finding one measly brown egg, though. I've never seen anybody yet, white or colored, who knew how such things happen. But I wouldn't worry about it, Miss Nell. Brown eggs are just as good as white eggs, to my way of tasting."

Nell turned her back on Myrtie and looked out the window until the girl had returned to the other side of the kitchen. Nell disliked to talk to Myrtie, because Myrtie pretended never to know the truth about anything. Even if she did know, she would invariably evade a straightforward answer. Myrtie would begin talking, and talk about everything under the sun from morning to night, but she would never answer a question that she could evade. Nell always forgave her, though; she knew Myrtie was not consciously evading the truth.

While the girl was scouring the pans, Nell picked up the egg again and looked at it closely. Mrs. Farrington had a flock of Dominique chickens, and she gathered in her chicken house eggs of all sizes, shapes, and colors. But that was to be expected, Mrs. Farrington had said, because she had two old roosters that were of no known name or breed. Nell had told Mrs. Farrington that some of her Dominiques were mixed-bred, and consequently they produced eggs of varying sizes, shapes, and colors; but Mrs. Farrington continued to lay all the blame on her two roosters, because, she said, they were a mixture of all breeds.

Once more Nell dipped the brown egg into the pan of water and wiped it with the fresh dishtowel, but the egg remained as brown as it was at first. The egg was clean by then, but soap and water would not alter its size or change its color. It was a brown egg, and it would remain brown. Nell gave up, finally; she realized that she could never change it in any way. If she had had another egg to put into the basket in its place, she would have laid it aside and substituted a white one; but she only had a dozen, counting the brown one, and she wished to have enough to make an even exchange with Mrs. Farrington when she went over after some green garden peas.

Before she finally placed the egg in the basket with the others she glanced out the window to see where Willis was. He was sitting in the crib door shelling red seed corn into an old wooden lard pail.

"I'm going over to Mrs. Farrington's now to exchange these eggs for some peas," she told Myrtie. "Keep the fire going good, and put on a pan of water to boil. I'll be back in a little while."

She turned around and looked at Myrtie.

"Suppose you mash the potatoes today, for a change, Myrtie. Mr. Willis likes them that way."

"Are you going to take that big egg, Miss Nell?" Myrtie asked, looking down at it in the basket with the eleven white Leghorns.

"Certainly," she said. "Why?"

"Mrs. Farrington will be surprised to see it in with all those white ones, won't she, Miss Nell?"

"Well, what if she does see it?" Nell asked impatiently.

"Nothing, Miss Nell," Myrtie said. "But she might want to know where it came from. She knows we've got Leghorn hens, and she might think one of her Domineckers laid it."

"I can't help that," Nell said, turning away. "And, besides, she should keep her Dominiques at home if she doesn't want them to lay eggs in somebody else's chicken house."

"That's right, Miss Nell," Myrtie said. "She sure ought to do that. She ought to keep her Domineckers at home."

Nell was annoyed by the girl's comments. It was none of Myrtie's business, anyway. Myrtie was getting to be impertinent, and she was forgetting that she was a hired servant in the house. Nell left the kitchen determined to treat Myrtie more coldly after that. She could not allow a colored cook to tell her what to do and what not to do.

Willis was sitting in the crib door shelling the red seed corn. He glanced up when Nell came down the back steps, and looked at her. He stopped shelling corn for a moment to wipe away the white flakes of husk that clung to his eyes.

"I'm going over to Mrs. Farrington's now and exchange a basket of eggs for some green peas, Willis," she said. "I'll not be gone long."

"Maybe she won't swap with you today," Willis said. He stopped and looked up at her through the thin cloud of flying husk that hovered around him. "How do you know she will want to take eggs for peas today, Nell?"

"Don't be foolish, Willis," she said, smiling at him; "why wouldn't she take eggs in exchange today?"

"She might get to wondering where the big brown egg came from," he said, laughing. "She might think it is an egg one of her hens laid."

Nell stopped, but she did not turn around. She waited, looking towards the house.

"You're as bad as Myrtie, Willis."

"In which way is that?"

The moment he spoke, she turned quickly and looked at him. He was bending over to pick up an ear of seed corn.

"I didn't mean to say that, Willis. Please forget what I said. I didn't mean anything like that."

"Like what?"

"Nothing," she said, relieved. "It wasn't anything; I've even forgotten what it was I said. Good-by."

"Good-by," he said, looking after her, wondering.

Nell turned and walked quickly out of the yard and went around the corner of the house towards the road. The Farrington house was half a mile away, but by taking the path through the cotton field it was two or three hundred yards nearer. She crossed the road and entered the field, walking quickly along the path with the basket of eggs on her arm.

Halfway to the Farringtons' Nell turned around and looked back to see if Willis was still sitting in the crib door shelling seed corn. She did not know why she stopped and looked back, but even though she could not see him there or anywhere else in the yard, she went on towards the Farringtons' without thinking of Willis again.

Mrs. Farrington was sitting on the back porch peeling turnips when Nell turned the corner of the house and walked across the yard. There was a bucket of turnips beside Mrs. Farrington's rockingchair, and long purple peelings were lying scattered on the porch floor around her, twisted into shapes like apple peelings when they were tossed over the shoulder. Nell ran up the steps and picked up the longest peeling she could find; she picked up the peeling even before she spoke to Mrs. Farrington.

"Sakes alive, Nell," Mrs. Farrington said; "why are you throwing turnip peelings over your shoulder? Doesn't that good-for-nothing husband of yours love you any more?"

Nell dropped the turnip peeling, and, picking it up again, tore it into short pieces and threw them into the bucket. She blushed and sat down in the chair beside Mrs. Farrington.

"Of course he loves me," Nell said. "I suppose I did that so many time when I was a little girl that I still have the habit."

"You mean it's because you haven't grown up yet, Nell," the woman said, chuckling to herself. "I used to be just like that myself; but, sakes alive, it doesn't last always, girl."

Both of them laughed, and looked away, one from the other. Over across the cotton field a cloud of white dust hung close to the earth. Mr. Farrington and the colored men were planting cotton, and the earth was so dry it rose up in the air when it was disturbed by the mules' hooves and the cotton planters. There was no wind to carry the dust away, and it hung over the men and mules, hiding them from sight.

Presently Mrs. Farrington dropped a peeled turnip into the pan and folded her hands in her lap. She looked at Nell, noting her neatly combed hair and her clean gingham frock and white hands. Mrs. Farrington turned away again after that and gazed once more at the cloud of dust where her husband was at work.

"Maybe you and Willis will always be like that," she said. "Seems like you and Willis are still in love with each other. As long as he stays at home where he belongs and doesn't run off at night, it's a pretty sure sign he isn't getting ready to chase after another woman. Sakes alive, men can't always be depended upon to stay at home at night, though; they go riding off when you are least looking for them to."

Nell sat up, startled by what Mrs. Farrington had said, terrified by the directness of her comments.

"Of course, Willis wouldn't do a thing like that," she said confidently. "I know he wouldn't. Willis wouldn't do a thing like that. That's impossible, Mrs. Farrington."

Mrs. Farrington glanced at Nell, and then once more she looked across the field where the planting was being done. The cloud of white dust followed the men and mules, covering them.

"Seems like men are always saying something about being compelled to go to Macon on business, and even up to Atlanta sometimes," she said, ignoring Nell. "And then there are the times when they say they have to go to town at night. Seems like they are always going off to town at night."

Several Dominique hens came from under the porch and stopped in the yard to scratch the hard white sand. They scratched listlessly;

they went through the motions of scratching as if they knew of
nothing else to do. They bent their long necks and looked down at
the chicken-scrawls they had made with their claws, and they
walked away aimlessly, neither surprised nor angry at not having
unearthed a worm to devour. One of them began singing in the
heat, drooping her wings until the tips of them dragged on the sand.
The other hens paid no attention to her, strolling away without
interest in the doleful music.

"You have pretty chickens, Mrs. Farrington," Nell said, watching
the Dominiques stroll across the yard and sit down in the shaded
dust holes as though they were nests.

"They're nothing but Domineckers," she said; "sakes alive, a body
can't call them much of a breed, but they do get around to laying
an egg or two once in a while."

Nell glanced down at the basket of eggs in her lap, covering the
brown egg with her hand. She looked quickly at Mrs. Farrington to
see if she had noticed what she had done.

"How are your Leghorns laying now, Nell?" she asked.

"Very well. Willis gathered sixteen eggs yesterday."

"My Domineckers seem to be taking a spell of resting. I only
gathered two eggs yesterday, and that's not enough for a hungry
man and a yard full of blacks. Sakes alive, we were saying only last
night that we wished you would bring over some eggs in a day or
two. And now, here you are with them. Half an hour's prayer
couldn't have done better."

"I thought you might let me have some green peas for dinner,"
Nell said, lifting the basket and setting it on the floor. "Willis likes
green peas at this time of year, and ours haven't begun to bear yet."

"You're welcome to as many as you want," Mrs. Farrington said.
"Just walk into the kitchen, Nell, and look on the big table and
you'll find a bushel basket of them. Help yourself to all you think
you and Willis will want. We've got more than we can use. Sakes
alive, there'll be another bushel ready for picking tomorrow morning, too."

Nell went into the kitchen and placed the eleven Leghorn eggs
and the big brown one in a pan. She filled the basket with green
peas and came back to the porch, closing the screen noiselessly
behind her.

"Sit down, Nell," Mrs. Farrington said, "and tell me what's been
happening. Sakes alive, I sit here all day and never hear a word of
what's going on."

"Why, I haven't heard of anything new," Nell said.

"What's Willis doing now?"

"He's getting ready to plant corn. He was shelling the seed when I left home. He should be ready to begin planting this afternoon. The planter broke down yesterday, and he had to send to Macon for a new spoke-chain. It should be here in the mail today."

"Myrtie is still there to help you with the house, isn't she?"

"Yes, Myrtie is still there."

The hens lying in the dust holes in the shade of the sycamore tree stood up and flapped their wings violently, beating the dust from their feathers. They stretched, one leg after the other, and flapped their wings a second time. One of them spread her legs, bending her knees as if she were getting ready to squat on the ground, and scratched the hard white sand five or tix times in quick succession. The other hens stood and watched her while she stretched her long neck and looked down at the marks she had made; and then, wiping her beak on her legs as one whets a knife-blade, she turned and waddled back across the yard and under the porch out of sight. The other hens followed her, singing in the heat.

"Couldn't you find a black woman to help you with the house?" Mrs. Farrington asked.

"A black woman?" Nell said. "Why, Myrtie is colored."

"She's colored all right," Mrs. Farrington said; "but sakes alive, Nell, she isn't black. Myrtie is yellow."

"Well, that's all right, isn't it?" Nell asked. "Myrtie is yellow, and she is a fairly good cook. I don't know where I could find a better one for the pay."

"I reckon I'd heap rather have a black girl and a poor cook, than to have a yellow girl and the finest cook in the whole country."

Nell glanced quickly at Mrs. Farrington, but her head was turned, and she did not look at Nell.

There was a long silence between them until finally Nell felt that she must know what Mrs. Farrington was talking about.

One of the Dominiques suddenly appeared on the bottom step. She came hopping up to the porch, a step at a time. When she reached the last one, Mrs. Farrington said, "Shoo!" The hen flew to the yard and went back under the porch.

"You don't mean——"

Mrs. Farrington began rocking slowly, backward and forward. She gazed steadily across the field where her husband was planting cotton with the colored men.

"You don't mean Willis and——"

One of the roosters strutted across the yard, his eye first upon the hens under the porch and next upon the two women, and stopped midway in the yard to stand and fix his eye upon Mrs. Farrington and Nell. He stood jerking his head from side to side, his hanging scarlet comb blinding his left eye, while he listened to the squeaking of Mrs. Farrington's chair. After a while he continued across the yard and went out of sight behind the smokehouse.

"Mrs. Farrington, Willis wouldn't do anything like that!" Nell said indignantly.

"Like what?" Mrs. Farrington asked. "Sakes alive, Nell, I didn't say he would do anything."

"I know you didn't say it, Mrs. Farrington, but I thought you said it. I couldn't help thinking that you did say it."

"Well, that's different," she replied, much relieved. "I wouldn't want you to go telling Willis I did say it. Menfolks never understand what a woman means, anyway, and when they are told that a woman says something about them, they sometimes fly off the handle something awful."

Nell got up and stood beside the chair. She wished she could run down the steps and along the path towards home without another second's delay, but she knew she could not jump up and leave Mrs. Farrington like that, after what had been said. She would have to pretend that she was not in a such a great hurry to get home.

"You're not going so soon, are you, Nell? Why, sakes alive, it seems like you only got here two or three minutes ago, Nell."

"I know," she said, "But it's getting late, and I've got to go home and get these peas ready for dinner. I'll be back to see you soon."

She walked carelessly down the steps. Mrs. Farrington got up and followed her across the hard yard. When they reached the beginning of the path that led across the field, Mrs. Farrington stopped. She never went any farther than that.

"I'm afraid I must hurry home now and hull the peas in time for dinner," Nell said, backing down the path. "I'll be back again in a few days, Mrs. Farrington. Thank you so much for the peas. Willis has wanted some for the past week or longer."

"It's as fair an exchange as I can offer for the Leghorn eggs," she said, laughing. "Because if there's anything I like better than those white Leghorn eggs, I don't know what it is. I get so tired of eating my old Domineckers' brown eggs I sometimes say I hope I may never see another one. Maybe I'll be asking you for a setting of them some day soon."

"Good-by," Nell said, backing farther and farther away. She

turned and walked several steps. "I'll bring you another basket soon, Mrs. Farrington."

It seemed as if she would never reach the house, even though it was only half a mile away. She could not run, because Mrs. Farrington was in the yard behind her watching, and she could not walk slowly, because she had to get home as soon as possible. She walked with her eyes on the path in front of her, forcing herself to keep from looking up at the house. She knew that if she did raise her eyes and look at it, she would never be able to keep herself from running. If she did that, Mrs. Farrington would see her.

It was not until she had at last reached the end of the path that she was able to look backward. Mrs. Farrington had left her yard, and Nell ran across the road and around to the back of the house.

Willis was nowhere within sight. She looked first at the crib where she had hoped she would find him, but he was not there, and the crib door was closed and locked. She looked down at the barn, but he was not there, either. When she glanced hastily over the fields, she was still unable to see him anywhere.

She stopped at the bottom step on the back porch. There was no sound within the house that she could hear, and not even the sound of Myrtie's footsteps reached her ears. The place seemed to be entirely deserted, and yet she knew that could not be, because only half an hour before when she left to go to Mrs. Farrington's to exchange eggs, Willis was sitting in the crib door shelling seed corn, and Myrtie was in the kitchen scouring the two frying-pans.

Nell's hands went out and searched for the railing that led up the porch steps. Her hands could not find it, and her eyes would not let her see it.

The thought of Mrs. Farrington came back to her again and again. Mrs. Farrington, sitting on her own back porch, talking. Mrs. Farrington, sitting in her rockingchair, looking. Mrs. Farrington, peeling purple-top turnips, talking about yellow girls.

Nell felt deathly sick. She felt as if she had been stricken with an illness that squeezed the core of her body. Deep down within herself, she was deathly ill. A pain that began by piercing her skull struck downward and downward until it became motionless in her stomach. It remained there, gnawing and biting, eating the organs of her body and drinking the flow of her blood. She sank limp and helpless upon the back porch steps. Although she did not know where she was, she could still see Mrs. Farrington. Mrs. Farrington, in her rockingchair, looking. Mrs. Farrington, peeling purple-top turnips, talking about yellow girls.

Nell did not know how much later it was when she opened her eyes. The day was the color of the red seed corn Willis had been shelling when she last saw him sitting in the crib door, and it swam in a sea so wide that she almost cried out in fear when she saw it. Slowly she remembered how she had come to be where she was. She got to her feet weakly, holding to the railing for support.

Stumbling up the steps and across the porch, she flung open the screen door and went into the kitchen. Myrtie was standing beside the table mashing the boiled Irish potatoes with a long fork that had seven tines. Myrtie looked up when Nell ran in, but she did not have an opportunity to speak. Nell ran headlong through the dining room and on into the front room. Myrtie looked surprised to see her running.

Nell paused a moment in the doorway, looking at Willis, at the room, at the daybed, at the floor, at the rugs, at the open door that led into their room. She stood looking at everything she could see. She looked at the pillows on the daybed, at the rugs on the floor, at the chairs against the wall, at the counterpane on their bed. Remembering, she looked at the carpet in their room. Willis sat in front of her reading *The Macon Telegraph* that had just come in the mail, and he was calmly smoking his pipe. She glanced once more at the daybed, at the pillows arranged upon it, and at the rug in front of it. Running, she went to their room and ran her hands over the counterpane of the bed. She picked up the pillows, feeling them, and laid them down again. She ran back into the other room where Willis was.

Willis looked up at her.

Nell ran and fell on her knees in front of him, forcing her body between his legs and locking her arms around him. She pressed her feverish face against his cool checks and closed her eyes tightly. She forced herself tightly to him, holding him with all her might.

"Did Mrs. Farrington exchange with you?" he asked. "I'll bet a pretty that she had something to say about that big brown egg in a basketful of Leghorns."

Nell felt her body shake convulsively, as if she were shivering with cold. She knew she had no control over herself now.

"Look here," he said, throwing aside *The Telegraph* and lifting her head and looking into her eyes. "I know where that brown egg came from now. I remember all about it. There was one of Mrs. Farrington's old Dominecker hens over here yesterday morning. I saw her scratching in the yard, and she acted like she didn't give a cuss whether she clawed up a worm or not. She would scratch a while and then walk off without even looking to see if she had turned up a worm."

Nell felt herself shaking again, but she did not attempt to control herself. If she could only lie there close to Willis with her arms around him, she did not care how much she shivered. As long as she was there, she had Willis; when she got up and walked out of the room, she would never again be that certain.

ROBINSON JEFFERS

****

*I have just now considered my shorter poems of the past quarter
century, trying to choose a few lines for this collection, and the conclusion is that I am quite unfit to be an anthologist, at least of my
own work. But perhaps it would be equally unpleasant to read any
other person's rapidly en masse for a purpose. It is like chewing
pebbles.*

*However, here are the three brief poems that I least dislike at
present; and that seem to represent the prevailing winds of my
thought in poetry. The first is about thirteen years old, the two
others recent.*

ROBINSON JEFFERS

****

Three Poems

LIFE FROM THE LIFELESS

SPIRITS and illusions have died,
The naked mind lives
On the beauty of inanimate things.

Flowers wither, grass fades, trees wilt,
The forest is burnt;
The rock is not burnt.

The deer starve, the winter birds
Die on their twigs and lie
In the blue dawns in the snow.

Men suffer want and become
Curiously ignoble; as prosperity
Made them curiously vile.

But look how noble the world is,
The lonely-flowing waters, the secret—
Keeping stones, the flowing sky.

CASSANDRA

THE MAD GIRL with the staring eyes and long white fingers
Hooked in the stones of the wall,
The storm-wrack hair and the screeching mouth: does it matter,
    Cassandra,
Whether the people believe
Your bitter fountain? Truly men hate the truth, they'd rather
Meet a tiger on the road.
Therefore the poets honey their truth with lying; but religion—
Venders and political men
Pour from the barrel, new lies on the old, and are praised for kindly
Wisdom. Poor bitch, be wise.
No: you'll still mumble in a corner a crust of truth, to men
And gods disgusting. —You and I, Cassandra.

THEIR BEAUTY HAS MORE MEANING

YESTERDAY MORNING enormous the moon hung low on the ocean,
Round and yellow-rose in the glow of dawn,
And the night-herons flapping home from the west looked golden.
    To-day
Black is the ocean, black and sulphur the sky,
And white seas leap. I honestly do not know which day is more
    beautiful.
I know that tomorrow or next year or in twenty years
I shall not see these things:—and it does not matter, it does not
    hurt;
They will be here. And when the whole human race
Has been like me rubbed out, they will still be here; storms, moon
    and ocean,
Dawn and the birds. And I say this: Their beauty has more
    meaning
Than the whole human race and the race of birds.

JAMES THURBER

DEAR WHIT BURNETT:

. . . It might be much simpler for you to use "More Alarms At Night" from My Life and Hard Times. *This has been considered by Fadiman and Gibbs and others the funniest of my stories and it is probably right for your purpose although I agree with White* that the word "Best" acts as a barrier, but I guess I can live it down.*

If you don't like "More Alarms At Night" you could use another from that book as this one has rarely, if ever, been published in anthologies.

Sincerely yours,

JAMES THURBER

*E. B. White, one of the editors of The New Yorker.

More Alarms at Night

ONE of the incidents that I always think of first when I cast back over my youth is what happened the night that my father "threatened to get Buck." This, as you will see, is not precisely a fair or accurate description of what actually occurred, but it is the way in which I and the other members of my family invariably allude to the occasion. We were living at the time in an old house at 77 Lexington Avenue, in Columbus, Ohio. In the early years of the nineteenth century, Columbus won out, as state capital, by only one vote over Lancaster, and ever since then has had the hallucination that it is being followed, a curious municipal state of mind which affects, in some way or other, all those who live there. Columbus is a town in which almost anything is likely to happen and in which almost everything has.

My father was sleeping in the front room on the second floor next to that of my brother Roy, who was then about sixteen. Father was usually in bed by nine-thirty and up again by ten-thirty to protest bitterly against a Victrola record we three boys were in the habit of playing over and over, namely, "No News, or What Killed the Dog," a recitation by Nat Wills. The record had been played so many times that its grooves were deeply cut and the needle often kept revolving in the same groove, repeating over and over the same words. Thus: "ate some burnt hoss flesh, ate some burnt hoss flesh, ate some burnt hoss flesh." It was this reiteration that generally got father out of bed.

On the night in question, however, we had all gone to bed at about the same time, without much fuss. Roy, as a matter of fact, had been in bed all day with a kind of mild fever. It wasn't severe enough to cause delirium and my brother was the last person in the world to give way to delirium. Nevertheless he had warned father when father went to bed, that he *might* become delirious.

About three o'clock in the morning, Roy, who was wakeful, decided to pretend that delirium was on him, in order to have, as he later explained it, some "fun." He got out of bed and going to my father's room, shook him and said, "Buck, your time has come!" My father's name was not Buck but Charles, nor had he ever been called Buck. He was a tall, mildly nervous, peaceable gentleman, given to quiet pleasures, and eager that everything should run smoothly. "Hmm?" he said, with drowsy bewilderment. "Get up, Buck," said my brother, coldly, but with a certain gleam in his eyes. My father leaped out of bed, on the side away from his son, rushed from the room, locked the door behind him, and shouted us all up.

We were naturally reluctant to believe that Roy, who was quiet and self-contained, had threatened his father with any such abracadabra as father said he had. My older brother, Herman, went back to bed without any comment. "You've had a bad dream," my mother said. This vexed my father. "I tell you he called me Buck and told me my time had come," he said. We went to the door of his room, unlocked it, and tiptoed through it to Roy's room. He lay in his bed, breathing easily, as if he were fast asleep. It was apparent at a glance that he did not have a high fever. My mother gave my father a look. "I tell you he did," whispered father.

Our presence in the room finally seemed to awaken Roy and he was (or rather, as we found out long afterward, pretended to be) astonished and bewildered. "What's the matter?" he asked. "Nothing," said my mother. "Just your father had a nightmare." "I did not have a nightmare," said father, slowly and firmly. He wore an old-fashioned, "side-slit" nightgown which looked rather odd on his tall, spare figure. The situation, before we let it drop and everybody went back to bed again, became, as such situations in our family usually did, rather more complicated than ironed out. Roy demanded to know what had happened, and my mother told him, in considerably garbled fashion, what father had told her. At this a light dawned in Roy's eyes. "Dad's got it backward," he said. He then explained that he had heard father get out of bed and had called to him. "I'll handle this," his father had answered. "Buck is downstairs." "Who is this Buck?" my mother demanded of father. "I don't know any Buck and I never said that," father contended, irritably. None of us (except Roy, of course) believed him. "You had a dream," said mother. "People have these dreams." "I did not have a dream," father said. He was pretty well nettled by this time, and he stood in front of a bureau mirror, brushing his hair with a pair of military brushes; it always seemed to calm father to brush his hair. My mother declared that it was "a sin and a shame" for a grown man to wake up a sick boy simply because he (the grown man: father) had got on his back and had a bad dream. My father, as a matter of fact, *had* been known to have nightmares, usually about Lillian Russell and President Cleveland, who chased him.

We argued the thing for perhaps another half-hour, after which mother made father sleep in her room. "You're all safe now, boys," she said, firmly, as she shut her door. I could hear father grumbling for a long time, with an occasional monosyllable of doubt from mother.

It was some six months after this that father went through a similar experience with me. He was at that time sleeping in the room next to mine. I had been trying all afternoon, in vain, to think of the name Perth Amboy. It seems now like a very simple name to recall and yet on the day in question I thought of every other town in the country, as well as such words and names and phrases as terra cotta, Walla-Walla, bill of lading, vice versa, hoity-toity, Pall Mall, Bodley Head, Schumann-Heink, etc., without even coming close to Perth Amboy. I suppose terra cotta was the closest I came, although it was not very close.

Long after I had gone to bed, I was struggling with the problem. I began to indulge in the wildest fancies as I lay there in the dark, such as that there was no such town, and even that there was no such state as New Jersey. I fell to repeating the word "Jersey" over and over again, until it became idiotic and meaningless. If you have ever lain awake at night and repeated one word over and over, thousands and millions and hundreds of thousands of millions of times, you know the disturbing mental state you can get into. I got to thinking that there was nobody else in the world but me, and various other wild imaginings of that nature. Eventually, lying there thinking these outlandish thoughts, I grew slightly alarmed. I began to suspect that one might lose one's mind over some such trivial mental tic as a futile search for terra firma Piggly Wiggly Gorgonzola Prester John Arc de Triomphe Holy Moses Lares and Penates. I began to feel the imperative necessity of human contact. This silly and alarming tangle of thought and fancy had gone far enough. I might get into some kind of mental aberrancy unless I found out the name of that Jersey town and could go to sleep. Therefore, I got out of bed, walked into the room where father was sleeping, and shook him. "Um!" he mumbled. I shook him more fiercely and he finally woke up, with a glaze of dream and apprehension in his eyes. "What's matter?" he asked, thickly. I must, indeed, have been rather wild of eye, and my hair, which is unruly, becomes monstrously tousled and snarled at night. "Wha's it?" said my father, sitting up, in readiness to spring out of bed on the far side. The thought must have been going through his mind that all his sons were crazy, or on the verge of going crazy. I see that now, but I didn't then, for I had forgotten the Buck incident and did not realize how similar my appearance must have been to Roy's the night he called father Buck and told him his time had come. "Listen," I said. "Name some towns in New Jersey quick!" It must have been around three in the morning. Father got up, keeping the bed between him and me, and started to pull his trousers on. "Don't bother about dressing," I said. "Just name some towns in New Jersey." While he hastily pulled on his clothes—I remember he left his socks off and put his shoes on his bare feet—father began to name, in a shaky voice various New Jersey cities. I can still see him reaching for his coat without taking his eyes off me. "Newark," he said, "Jersey City, Atlantic City, Elizabeth, Paterson, Passaic, Trenton, Jersey City, Trenton, Paterson—" "It has two names," I snapped. "Elizabeth and Paterson," he said. "No, no!" I told him, irritably. "This is one town with one name, but there are two words in it, like helter-skelter." "Helter-skelter," said my father, moving slowly toward the bedroom door and smiling in a faint, strained way which I understand now—but didn't then—was meant to humor me. When he was within a few paces of the door, he fairly leaped for it and ran out into the hall, his coat-tails and shoelaces flying. The exit stunned me. I had no notion that he thought I had gone out of my senses; I could only believe that he had gone out of *his* or that, only partially awake, he was engaged in some form of running in his sleep. I ran after him and I caught him at the door of mother's room and grabbed him, in order to reason with him. I shook him a little, thinking to wake him completely. "Mary! Roy! Herman!" he shouted. I, too, began to shout for my brothers and my mother. My mother opened her door instantly, and there we were at 3:30 in the morning grappling and shouting, father partly dressed, but without socks or shirt, and I in pajamas.

"*Now,* what?" demanded my mother, grimly, pulling us apart. She was capable, fortunately, of handling any two of us and she never in her life was alarmed by the words or actions of any one of us.

"Look out for Jamie!" said father. (He always called me Jamie when excited.) My mother looked at me.

"What's the matter with your father?" she demanded. I said I didn't know; I said he had got up suddenly and dressed and ran out of the room.

"Where did you think you were going?" mother asked him, coolly. He looked at me. We looked at each other, breathing hard, but somewhat calmer.

"He was babbling about New Jersey at this infernal hour of the night," said father. "He came to my room and asked me to name towns in New Jersey." Mother looked at me.

"I just asked him," I said. "I was trying to think of one and couldn't sleep."

"You see?" said father, triumphantly. Mother didn't look at him.

"Get to bed, both of you," she said. "I don't want to hear any more out of you tonight. Dressing and tearing up and down the hall at this hour in the morning!" She went back into the room and shut her door. Father and I went back to bed. "Are you all right?" he called to me. "Are you?" I asked. "Well, good night," he said. "Good night," I said.

Mother would not let the rest of us discuss the affair next morning at breakfast. Herman asked what the hell had been the matter. "We'll go on to something more elevating," said mother.

DOROTHY CANFIELD FISHER

****

I believe that a short story of mine, in Hillsboro People, *called "A Drop in the Bucket" would be as representative of my attitude towards life, and of my work as any other short selection.*

DOROTHY CANFIELD FISHER

****

A Drop in the Bucket

IF YOU HAVE READ, as most of us have, conventional New England dialect stories you do not need to be told about the central figure of this tale. Years ago, when I was young, she was the sole inhabitant of our Vermont village who came up to the expectations of our visiting city friends, on the lookout for Yankee characters. Italians used in those days, knowing what tourists wanted to see, always to take their foreign friends to see their one remaining bit of dilapidated Roman wall, or the windowless room which had been a mediaeval torture chamber, never to look at the new water-works, or the modern hospital. Just so, we always used to take visitors to Hillsboro to see Cousin Tryphena.

On the way to her tiny, three-roomed house, we had a set cicerone talk to give them; we told them that she lived without working and by unimaginable thrift kept up a social position on three hundred and forty-two dollars a year (this was a long time ago, remember), and that she had never been farther from home than to the next village. We suggested that they ask her—this always pleased her— about her one household treasure, the fine Sheraton sideboard, which had belonged to her great-grandfather, old Priest Perkins. And when, after an hour spent in the orderly, empty house full of somnolent, unprofitable respectability, we walked away, we knew that our friends from the city would exclaim, "How picturesque! Isn't she delicious!"

In our village nearly everyone owns his own roof. But next door to Cousin Tryphena's minute, white cottage is one of the few places

for rent. A forlorn old brown shed of a place, it had stood idle for
years, visibly tumbling to pieces. Then one day, years ago, a burly
white-bearded tramp stopped, looked at it reflectively, laid down his
stick and bundle and went to inquire at a neighbor's if the place
were for rent. He paid a month in advance and moved in. In his
bundle was a primitive outfit for cobbling shoes. He cut a large
wooden boot out of an old board, painted it black with axle-grease
and soot, hung it over the door as a sign, and settled down to stay.

We were all rather glad to have this dirty, but useful addition to
our community, all except Cousin Tryphena, who was sure, for
months afterward, that he would cut her throat some night and
steal away her Sheraton sideboard. It was an open secret that
Putnam, the antique furniture dealer in Troy, had offered her six
hundred dollars for it. The other women of the village, however, not
living alone as she did nor so near to the stranger, thought his long
white beard looked reassuring, and noticed that he was kind to little
children.

Although, from his name, as from his strong accent, it was evident
that old Jombatiste belonged, by birth, to our French-Canadian
colony, he never associated himself with that easy-going, devoutly
Catholic, law-abiding, and let-well-enough-alone group of our citizens. He made no secret of being an out-and-out radical—a Socialist. This in the days when to be a Socialist was to be a Red.

The central article of Jombatiste's passionately held creed seemed
to be that everything was exactly wrong, and that, while the Socialist party was not nearly sweeping enough in its ideas, it was, as
yet, the best means for accomplishing the inevitable, righteous transformation of society. Accordingly, he worked incessantly, not only
at his cobbling, but at any odd job he could find, went in rags, ate
mainly crackers and milk, and sent every penny he could save to the
Socialist Headquarters. We knew this not only through his own
trumpeting about the pattern of his life, but because Phil Latimer,
the postmaster, is cousin to all of us and often mentioned the old
man's money-orders, so large that they must have represented almost
all his earnings.

Yet he was never willing to join in any of our many local charit-
able and social welfare enterprises. It was evident that his ardent
old heart was as tender as it was hot. But he wanted no palliatives,
as he said "no ulcers hidden under clean poultices, when what they
need is lancing and draining and healing." Yet he himself could not
resist an occasional palliative. Nothing threw him into such bellowing fury as cruelty. He became the terror of all Hillsboro boys who

trapped rabbits, and, indeed, by his whirlwind descents upon them, and his illegal destruction of their traps, he practically made that boyish pastime a thing of the past. The boys talked mightily about how they'd have the law on dirty old Jombatiste, but somehow nobody got around to try it.

The Hillsboro tradition is strongly for letting people alone s'long as they pay their taxes, even if they are very queer. And also Jombatiste had on tap a red-hot flow of vituperation, astonishingly polysyllabic for a man who had evidently had little book-learning. Perhaps it came, we sometimes thought, from his incessant reading of what seemed to Hillsboro rather incendiary literature.

He took two Socialist newspapers and nobody ever numbered how many inflammatory little magazines. From them he read aloud selections to anyone at hand. Of course we all soon acquired a technique of varied reasons for having to move on to other errands. This was not so easy for his next-door neighbor, who hardly ever left home. Cousin Tryphena seemed to him, probably, an audience sent by Providence.

He was wrong. She was the worst possible audience for him. What she did not know about the world outside her kitchen, bedroom, living-room and front yard would have made a complete treatise on modern civilization. She never in her life had subscribed to a newspaper. At the time when she was acquiring her code, women didn't read newspapers. When once in a while she borrowed from a neighbor the weekly local sheet, it was solely to read the news-items from Greenford, where she had a second cousin. Sometimes a woman's magazine was loaned to her. But she looked only at the pictures and recipes. Like many another well-brought up complacent woman of her generation, who wrote a flowing Spencerian hand, spelled to perfection, and kept her house, her underwear and her hair immaculately clean, she was, as far as political or social realities went, as ignorant as any Digger Indian.

When therefore Jombatiste read loudly to her statements which seemed to him conclusive reasons for reaching for a bomb—as that ninety per cent of the money of this country is in the hands of two per cent of the population, Cousin Tryphena counted her tatting stitches and was glad that she no longer had to go to school and "do percentage" in arithmetic class, because she had never been able to make anything out of mathematics beyond the multiplication table. When he shouted that the franchise was a farce because the government was controlled by a Wall Street clique, she remained calm because she had never heard voting called the franchise and had no idea what he was talking about. When Jombatiste, choking with wrath over the iniquities of the profit system, shouted that any man who worked hard but could not earn enough for his family's health, had a right to shoot a millionaire's son on sight (or words to that effect) she did not believe a word he said. Here was something she had a real opinion about. She had never seen a millionaire or his son, but she knew from living for fifty-five years in Hillsboro what made people poor. It was shiftlessness. There was plenty of work to be had on the farms, on the railroad, in the stores, in the woods, at the brush-back factory, for any man who had the back-bone to keep at it. If they *would* stop work in deer-week to go hunting, or go on a spree Election Day, or run away from a good job for a week to go fishing, she'd like to know what business they had blaming millionaires and their sons because they lost their jobs.

She did not expound these opinions to Jombatiste because, in the first place she thought him a dirty Canuck, and secondly because opinions were "just talk-talk-talk" to her, of no consequence to sensible people. The important matters were to make your starch clear and to pay your taxes in time to get the discount.

People who are mostly silent are often credited with more wisdom than they have. Cousin Tryphena unconsciously profited in the estimation of her neighbor by this fact. Old Jombatiste had thundered his per cents of the distribution of capital in relation to the population for many months before he discovered that he was on the wrong track.

He found this out one winter day when Cousin Tryphena was hanging out her washing. Waving his favorite magazine, he ran over to read aloud to her, following her up and down the clothes-line, as she shook out and pinned up the wet clothes. Occasionally for emphasis striking the paper with his horny, blackened, shoemaker's hand, he came to a climax with—

"And thus it is definitely proved— any court of law would accept the evidence—that Senator Burlingame *was* in the pay of J. P. Darby, when he held up the Rouse Labor Bill in the Senate Committee. . . ." He stopped and glanced triumphantly at his old neighbor.

Cousin Tryphena was more than usually annoyed with him that day, for his lack of decent tact in following her about while she hung up garments associated in her mind with closed doors and lowered window-shades. As a matter of fact she left her wet night-gown in the bottom of the basket, sooner than flaunt it in the face of a strange man. Folding this together, tightly, and taking a clothespin out of her mouth, she asked, with whole-hearted indifference to his news, "Well what of it? Why shouldn't Senator what's-his-name pay anybody he wants to? It's his money, isn't it?"

She carried the basket back into the kitchen, and shut the door. Jombatiste stood there, stock-still, as if stunned. Then, coming to himself, he resolutely followed her in. Ignoring his presence, she began to put together her meager midday meal. To his urgent, almost imploring questioning, she returned brief answers, obviously truthful. "No." "I never heard of it." "I don't see that it's anybody's business if they do." "What of it?"

Leaning giddily over the abyss of her ignorance of political action, sociology and industrialism, the old Socialist dropped one exploring plummet after another into the depths of her mind, only to find nothing there. Silenced, for once, he went shakily back to his own house.

He was silenced for a long, long time. We began to think that he must be coming down with some sickness. He sewed on the harness he was mending, he tapped on the shoes he was half-soling, without lifting his shaggy white head. He did not even read. When he was not working he sat motionless in his chair, looking fixedly at nothing.

We knew afterwards that what he had been doing was to think more intently about old Cousin Tryphena and her mind than anyone ever had before, or ever will again. Presently he gathered together again three or four of his badly printed little magazines and went again to visit his self-satisfied Yankee neighbor.

But he did not begin, this time, by saying solemnly "Wealth comes from labor alone." He had begun to think that Miss Tryphena did not know what "wealth" meant. Nor did he mention "industrial slavery." He laid his little magazines down on her elegantly proportioned Sheraton sideboard and settled himself in a chair. Cousin Tryphena reached for her tatting, her eyes glazed and her lips began to move as she silently counted her stitches.

Jombatiste read aloud what we would now call "case histories," about human suffering in a society which still talked about the dangers of pampering the poor. He read the story of a wage-earner in the city who left a widow and three young children. These tried to earn their livings by making artificial flowers at home. (This was long before the Socialistic measure of outlawing sweat-shops.) All of them, working together, could earn about half of what they needed to live. When the last dollar of the dead father's savings were gone, and there was talk (this was before the socially radical measure of Mother's Aid) of putting the children in an asylum, the mother drowned the three little ones and herself after them. Cousin Tryphena dropped her tatting, her country-bred mind reeling, "For the Lord's sake, why didn't her folk help her out?"

Jombatiste explained that her folks, if she had any, were in Poland. Striking one fist inside his palm, he cried out, "and this in a country that produces three times the food it consumes." For the first time, a statistical statement awoke an echo in Cousin Tryphena's atrophied brain.

Old Jombatiste read on, this time about a girl of seventeen, left by her parents' death in charge of a small brother. She too had tried to earn their living by handwork, but twelve hours a day had not brought in enough. Seeing her little brother grow white and strengthless from lack of food, she had, in desperation, taken to the streets and had almost at once vanished, engulfed by the maelstrom of organized vice. The little brother had been taken to an orphan asylum, where he had since twice tried to commit suicide.

Cousin Tryphena sat rigid, her tatting fallen to the floor, breathing hard. It is probably impossible for us to average moderns, calloused as we are by promiscuous reading, to conceive the effect made upon the blankness of her mind by this attack from the printed page. She not only did not dream (as we might) that these stories were perhaps not true, they seemed as real to her as though she had seen the people. There was not a particle of blood in her haggard face.

Jombatiste read on . . . the story of a decent, ambitious man, employed in a wretched shop, who contracted tuberculosis from the foul air and slowly died, dragging down with him to the depths of misery, a wife and two children. He was now dead, and his wife was living in a corner of a dark and damp basement, their only heat what fire the mother could make out of rubbish picked up on the streets.

Cousin Tryphena's horrified eyes fell on her well-blacked stove, sending out the aromatic breath of burning white birch sticks. She recoiled from it with a shudder.

Jombatiste read on, the story of the woman who, when her three sons died in an accident due to negligence on their employer's part . . . he read no more that day, for Cousin Tryphena put her gray head down on the center table and wept such tears as she had never known. Jombatiste rose softly and tiptoed out of the room.

The tap-tap-tap of his hammer rang loud and fast the rest of that day. He was exulting over having aroused a bourgeois from greasy complacency. He had made a convert. To his pennilessness, Cousin Tryphena's tiny assured income seemed a fortune. We know from what happened next, that he had a golden dream of persuading her to join him in his weekly contributions to the sacred funds!

Early the next morning, his neighbor came to his door, white, hollow-eyed, a sleepless night evidently back of her, and asked for the papers he had read from. Jombatiste gave them to her in a tactful silence. She put out a shaking hand for them, and went back through the snow to her own house.

By noon that day, everyone in the village had heard the startling news that Miss Tryphena had gone over to Graham's store, asked to use the long-distance telephone and had telephoned to Putnam, the antique man, to come and get her sideboard. Hanging up the receiver, she had passed Albert Graham, standing amazed back of his counter, with so distraught a look that even he had not ventured to ask her any questions. But he naturally mentioned the matter to everyone who happened to come into the store; and by noon every family in Hillsboro was discussing over its mid-day pie the well-known queer streak which had sent several of Cousin Tryphena's ancestors to the asylum.

I did not reach her house that afternoon till nearly four; and I was almost the last to arrive. Cousin Tryphena was silent, her usually pale face deeply flushed, surrounded by a group of expostulating neighbors. They began, all talking at once, to tell me what had happened. . . . "Trypheny's crazy . . . she'd ought to have a guardeen . . . that Canuck shoemaker has addled her brains . . . there ought to be a law against that kind of newspaper he takes . . . Trypheny is actin' like her great-aunt Lucilly . . ."

I appealed to Cousin Tryphena. "What's the trouble?" I asked her.

"There ain't any trouble's I know of," she answered, in a hoarse unsteady voice. "I just happened to hear about a widow-woman, down in the city, who's bringin' up her two children in the corner of a basement where the green mold stands out on the wall, and I'm goin' down to fetch her an' the children up here to live with me . . . them an' a little orphan boy that don't like the 'sylum where they've put him—"

Somebody broke in on her, "Why, Trypheny, you old simpleton, that's four people! Where you goin' to put 'em in this little tucked-up place?"

Cousin Tryphena answered pointedly, "Your own grandmother,

Rebecca Mason, brought up a family of seven in a house no bigger than this, and no cellar either."

"But how . . ." another voice exclaimed, "are you goin' to get enough for 'em to eat? You ain't got but barely enough for yourself!"

Cousin Tryphena's flush paled, "I'm a good sewer, I could make money sewing . . . I could do washings for city-folks, summertimes. I could take care of their children and wash their dishes. They pay real good." Her set mouth told what a price she paid for this voluntary abandonment of her social standing. She turned on us, hotly, "You all act as though I was doin' it to amuse myself. I don't *want* to! When I think of my things I've kept so nice always, I'm *wild* . . . but how can I help it, now I know about 'em! I didn't sleep a wink last night. I saw those three children and one of them a baby, fighting the water and their mother a-holdin' on 'em down, and then jumpin' in herself—Why, I give enough milk to the *cat* to keep a baby . . . what else can I do?"

We all were touched by her defenselessness against this first vision of life, the vision which had been spared her so long, only to burst upon her like a forest-fire. It was as though she had awakened after half a century of ignorant sleep.

"Dear Cousin Tryphena," I said admiring my own gentleness and patience, "you haven't, you see, had a very wide experience of modern industrial or urban conditions. There are certainly some phases of this matter which you don't take into consideration." Then I brought out just as you would, probably, the traditional, reasonable arguments we use to dull the knife-thrust of self-questioning— how little any one person could do, and anyhow that it was very likely that the editor of that newspaper had invented, or at least greatly exaggerated those stories, and that she would find on investigation that there was no such poor family.

"I don't see how that lets me out of trying to find out if there *is*," said Cousin Tryphena, in a low tone.

"Well, at least," I told her "don't be in such a hurry about it! Take time to think it over. Wait till—"

"*Wait!*" cried Cousin Tryphena, her voice like a trumpet, "Why, another one may be jumpin' in the river this minute! If I'd ha' had the money, I'd ha' gone on the noon train!"

At this point, two men from Putnam's antique shop came to carry away the Sheraton sideboard. Cousin Tryphena bore herself like a self-contained martyr at the stake. She watched with dry eyes, the departure of her one certificate to gentle birth. She received with a casual gesture the crisp bills of a denomination most of us had never seen before.

"You won't need all that money just to go down to the city once," I remonstrated.

She turned her anguished eyes to me. "They'll likely be needing clothes and things," she explained with dignity.

I gave up.

It was time for us to go home to prepare our several suppers and we went our different ways, shaking our heads over Tryphena's queerness. I stopped a moment before the cobbler's open door, watched him briskly sewing a broken halter and telling a story to some children. When he finished, I said with as much acerbity as I could get into my voice, "Well, Jombatiste, I hope you're satisfied with what you've done to poor old Miss Tryphena . . . spoiling her life for her!"

"Such a life, Madame," said Jombatiste, "ought to be spoiled. The sooner the better."

"She's going to start for the city tomorrow," I said. I supposed of course that he had heard the news.

Jombatiste looked up quickly, very much surprised. "For what goes she to the city?"

"Why . . . she's gone daft over those bogie-stories of yours . . . she's looked the list over and picked out the survivors, the widow of the man who died of tuberculosis, and so on, and she's going to bring them back here to share her luxurious life."

Jombatiste bounded into the air, scattering his tools and the children, rushing past me out of the house, across the trampled snow of his side yard toward Cousin Tryphena's. As he ran, he did what I have never seen anyone do, out of a book; he tore at his bushy hair and scattered handfuls in the air. It seemed to me that a madness had struck our dull little village. I ran after him to protect Cousin Tryphena.

He battered at her door. She opened it and he burst out at her, "How dare you take what I tell you and use it to betray your fellow-man! How do you *dare* stand there, mealy-mouthed, and face me, when you are planning cowardly to make yourself feel better by— what would you think of a mother who covered up a skin disease her child had and hid it from the doctor because it did not look pretty? What else are *you* planning to do, you with your plan to put court-plaster over one pustule in ten million? Don't you see the patient will die if he isn't *healed*. Oh, idiot, idiot—!" he beat his hands on the door-jambs, ". . . if you had the money of forty millionaires,

you couldn't do anything yourself. We must *all*—how many people
do you think to help . . . two, three . . . maybe four! But there are
hundreds of others . . . why, I could read you a thousand stories of
worse—"

Cousin Tryphena's limit had been reached. She advanced upon
the intruder with a face as flaming as his own. . . . "Jombatiste
Ramotte, if you ever dare to read me another such story, I'll go right
out and jump in the Necronsett River!"

The mania of earlier generations of her family looked out horridly
from her eyes.

Goose-flesh contracted the skin on my arms. I was scared. Even
Jombatiste's blood was chilled. He stood silent.

Cousin Tryphena slammed the door in his face so that all the
house-walls shook.

He turned to me, his mouth slackly open in bewilderment. "Did
you hear . . . what sort of logic do you call—"

"Jombatiste," I counseled him, "stop talking about logic—for
heavens' sake, *logic!* And leave Miss Tryphena alone."

It was the very next morning, on the six-thirty train that Cousin
Tryphena started her crack-brained plan. Looking out sleepily, I
saw her trudging past our house in the bleak gray of our mountain
dawn, the inadequate little, yellow flame of her old-fashioned lantern
like a glowworm at her side.

A week passed before we heard from her. We had begun really
to fear that while she was among strangers, her unsettled mind
might have taken some new fancy which would be the end of her.

That week Jombatiste shut the door to his house. The children
reported that he would not let them in, and that they could see him
through the window stitching away in silence, muttering to himself.

Eight days after Cousin Tryphena had gone away, I had a telegram from her, "Please build fires in both my stoves tomorrow afternoon. Key under kitchen window shutter."

Dark comes early in the mountains in mid-winter and so, although I daresay there was not a house in the village where people
did not look out after the late evening train came up, none of us
saw anything but our usual December blackness. At least, I told
myself, Cousin Tryphena had taken her absurd old lantern and gone
forth through that darkness.

The next morning I set off for the other end of the street. Cousin
Tryphena saw me coming and opened the door. She did not smile,
and she was still pale, but I saw that she had regained her self-control. "Come right in," she said, in rather a tense voice, and, as I

entered she added, in our old rustic phrase for introduction, "Make you 'quainted with my friend, Mrs. Lindstrom. She's come up from the city to stay with me. And this is her little boy, Sigurd, and this is the baby."

I shook hands with a tall, thin, stoop-shouldered woman, in a new, ready-made dress that did not fit. Her abundant yellow hair was drawn back from a pale, sad face. She was holding a very clean baby, asleep, its long golden lashes lying on cheeks as white and sunken as her own. Over the baby she gave me a timid glance, shrinking from my eyes. A sturdily built boy of about six lay on the floor, playing with the cat. He looked at me shyly, hanging down his head.

Cousin Tryphena was evidently afraid that I would not take her cue, for she went on hastily, "Mrs. Lindstrom has been real sick and kind o' worried over the baby, so's she's feeling kind of nervous. I tell her Hillsboro air is thought very good for nerves. Lots of city folks come here in summer time, just for that. Don't you think Sigurd is a real big boy for only six and a half? He knows his letters too! He's goin' to school as soon as we get settled down. I want you should bring over those alphabet blocks that your Peggy doesn't use any more—"

The other woman began to cry, clinging to my old cousin's hand and holding it against her cheek as she sobbed.

Cousin Tryphena patted her hair awkwardly, but kept on talking, looking at me sternly as though defying me to show, by look or word, that there was anything unusual in the situation. "I see it snowed some while I was away," she said. We fell at once, she and I, into talking about the incidents of her trip on the train. Matt Bowen's boy was brakeman, now, she informed me.

When I came away, half an hour later, Cousin Tryphena put a shawl over her head and came down the front walk with me. I was affected, almost to the tears I would not dare to shed, by the sudden ending of the old woman's barren loneliness. I saw her as the Happy Fool of old folk-lore, the character who, through his very lack of worldly wisdom, attains without effort all that self-seeking people try for in vain. The happy outcome of her adventure filled me with a cheerful wonder at the ways of Providence. "Why Cousin Tryphena, it's like something in a story book! You're going to *enjoy* having those people. The woman is as nice as she can be, and her her little boy's as smart as a whip."

Cousin Tryphena's manner was still odd and tense. She sighed and said, "I don't sleep much better nights now I've done it!" Then facing me, "*I* hadn't ought to have brought them up here! I just did it to please myself! Once I saw 'em . . . I wanted 'em!"

This seemed to me the wildest possible display of the instinct for self-condemnation. I was really vexed with her.

But when I began to tell her so, she stopped me with a look and gesture Dante might have had, "You ain't seen what I've seen."

"Was it really as bad as that paper said?" I asked.

"Child, it was nothing like what the paper said . . . it was so much worse!"

I was half-frightened by her expression. She went on "I was five days looking for her . . . they'd moved from the address the paper give. And, in those five days, I saw so many others . . . *so many others* . . ." She put one lean old hand before her eyes.

The exclamation which next burst from her made me ashamed of the cheerfulness of my notion that her adventure had been picturesque. "Jombatiste is right!" she cried fiercely, "Everything is wrong! Everything *is* wrong! If there's anything I can do, I'd ought to do it to help them as want to smash up what kills folks, and start over again, to try to have things decent. What good does it do for me to bring up here just these three out of all I saw . . .?"

Her voice broke into self-excusing quavers, "but honestly when I saw them . . . the baby's so thin . . . and little Sigurd is so cunning . . . he took to me right away. This morning he wouldn't pick up his new rubbers off the floor for his mother, but, when I asked him, he did, right off. You ought to have seen what he had on, rags . . . such dirt . . . 'Twarn't her fault! She's . . . why she's like *any*body . . . like a person's cousin they never happened to see before . . . why, they were all *folks!*" she cried out.

"You didn't find the little boy that had been sent to—?" I asked.

"He was dead before I got to the asylum," she answered.

"Oh . . .!" I said, "Had he . . .?"

"I don't know whether he had or not. I didn't ask. I didn't want to know. I know too much now!"

She looked up fixedly at the mountain line, high and keen against the winter sky, "Jombatiste is right," she said unsparingly, "*I* hadn't ought to be enjoying them . . . their father ought to be alive and with them. He was willing to work all he could, and yet he . . . here I've lived for fifty-five years and never airned my salt a single day. What was I livin' on? The stuff these folks ought to ha' had to eat . . . them and the Lord only knows how many more besides! Jombatiste is right . . . what I'm doin' now is only a drop in the bucket!"

A child's wail came from the house . . . "That's Sigurd . . . I *knew*
that cat would scratch him!" she told me as though the skies were
falling, and ran stiffly back. I went back too and watched her bind
up with awkward old fingers the little scratched hand, watched the
frightened boy sob himself quiet on her old knees that had never
before known a child's weight, saw the expression in her eyes as she
looked down at the sleeping baby and gazed about the untidy room,
which had always been so orderly and so empty.

She lifted the little boy up so that his tousled yellow hair rested
against her bosom. He put an arm around her neck and she flushed
with pleasure; but, although she held him close to her, there was in
her eyes an austerity which forbade sentimentalizing.

"But, Cousin Tryphena," I urged, "it *is* a drop in the bucket, you
know, and that's something!"

She looked down at the child on her knee, she laid her wrinkled
cheek against his bright hair, she told me with self-accusing harsh-
ness, " 'Tain't right for me to be here alive enjoying that dead man's
little boy."

. . . .

That was long, long ago. Mrs. Lindstrom died of consumption;
but the two children were soon strong and hearty, not to be distinguished from their Yankee playmates at school. They grew up sound
as nuts, devotedly attached to their Aunt Tryphena, ruling her as
despotically as though she were their mother.

And so we lived along, like a symbol of the great world, bewildered Cousin Tryphena toiling lovingly for her adopted children, the
memory of her descent into hell darkening her eyes; Jombatiste
clothing his old body in rags and his soul in flaming indignation as
he battered hopefully at the ramparts of entrenched unrighteousness
. . . and the rest of us doing nothing at all.

JAMES BRANCH CABELL

****

I suggest that you consider "Is of Southern Ladies," in my latest literary offence, Let Me Lie. I do this impersonally upon the ground that it by long odds has been the most widely liked of all the brief articles I ever published. There is today, I believe, no elderly gentlewoman of Southern descent anywhere in the United States who has not written to me about this article. Moreover, it is first hand material and shows the better side of my nature. I am becoming, in my senescence, I find, a prey to the more noble emotions.

JAMES BRANCH CABELL

****

Is of Southern Ladies

1

THAT, without any fear of succeeding, the intrepid native Virginian will dauntlessly attempt to conceal his superiority to everybody else, remains a tribal virtue which has not escaped the comment of anthropologists. He treads among the commonalty of other commonwealths, it has been remarked, with the meticulous and maddening courtesy of M. le Duc upon a casual visit to the peasantry of this or the other of his minor estates. And yet not really for this Virginian version of politeness is any living Virginian who, let us say, can remember when Grover Cleveland occupied the White House at all blameworthy. Rather is this an enforced trait which has been developed in the man's nature by two circumstances such as through no precautions could he have avoided.

The one circumstance is that throughout the first years of his life (during which his character was taking form, irretrievably) he was reared as a godling who could not, not even in the false teeth of parental reproof, be wrong as to anything. The second circumstance is that he knows there has been reserved for him in heaven a very special place.

In short, he once had a mammy.

2

WITH A FORLORN SENSE of impotence, one pauses here to reflect that, nowadays, in no household anywhere does one find an authentic mammy; so that whosoever speaks as to this vanished subdivision of fauna needs to depend upon a scant number of sexagenarians to divine exactly what he may be talking about.—For the mammy, the true mammy, the mammy *au vieille roche,* is now extinct, along with the passenger pigeon and the bison and the hack driver; but in Richmond of the 1880's a mammy still ruled over every household in which there were children.

So in no part of Richmond were mammies infrequent; but it was in Monroe Park that you noted them, upon clear afternoons, in full panoply. To every bench there would be two or three mammies; alongside most of the benches sprawled a baby carriage formed of rotund and elaborately betwisted wicker-work, of which the occupant was screened by a vividly blue veil; and whatever it was that mammies talked about, for some two hours, with a serene and oriental indolence, between their slow outbursts of sedate Olympian chuckles, you did not ever hear, because you were playing, in common with a select number of yet other children, under the uncompromising surveillance of all these mammies. Any one of them, at any instant, might direct toward you the attention of Sister Nelson with an acerb shrillness.

And besides that, when you played in Monroe Park, you had to be careful not ever, upon any imaginable pretext, to get your nice clean linen suit messed up; because, otherwise, you became just the most aggravating child that ever was.

3

THESE LADIES wore white caps and large white aprons, befrilled proudly. They ran, rather, to stoutness; and to steel-rimmed spectacles they accorded a perceptible vogue. Each one of them was— legally, at any rate—a Negress. Each one of them some twenty years earlier had been a slave; but now they were tyrants. Not for one quarter-instant would I suggest that their despotism was often, or indeed ever, unkindly. I mean merely that none dared to assail the authority of the mammies of Richmond within the borders of their several kingdoms; and that this was especially true of the parents who paid to each one of them ten dollars a month.

I grant that in every household—in order, it is my theory, to cajole into self-complacence the cook and the house girl—the children's mammy was ranked, through a jocose flight of fancy, as being one of the servants.—For that, most precisely, is what a mammy was at no time whatever, except only upon the courteous principle by which a monarch elects, in state papers or in formal proclamations, to describe himself as being the servant of his people.

In brief, the mammy was a Virginian institution which, under the encroachments of democracy, has vanished; she survives only in the heart's core of her fosterlings; and she is not comprehensible any longer except by those who have need to remember her forever. The children of Virginia, so nearly as I can understand their unhappy estate, are looked after nowadays, more or less, by a visitant duchess, more or less Negroid, who stays with them for as long as the job contents her; and who passes on by-and-by to another nursery somewhere else. Her place is then filled, for a month or it may be for two months, by some other nomad; and later, by yet another. Thus Amurath to Amurath succeeds, barbarically. It must be, for these luckless children, rather like living in a world which every once in a while shoots off into space and finds an alien sun about which to revolve. It is, at any rate, a state of affairs which does not bear thinking about, by us who once had a mammy.

4

AND SO, while in theory I would like for a fair number of these children to be dealt with competently, by Mrs. Louisa Nelson, yet to the other side, Mrs. Nelson was my mammy; and she was by me regarded with an affection which, during some sixty years of research work, I have not found any other person to merit. Were she alive today, I with an incivic stoicism would observe every brat upon earth in transit toward a state reformatory rather than permit Mrs. Nelson to leave me.—For she was my mammy once, now, and forever afterward; so that I must decline, even in thought, to be severed from her by the dictates of altruism.

—Although, of course, she had not always been Mrs. Nelson. In fact, at the beginning, which was about 1820, she was just Louisa, when she belonged to Miss Patsy Brander. She was Miss Patsy's own colored girl; and every night she used to sleep in old Miss Patsy's room, in a trundle bed which enduring the day you stuck under Miss Patsy's big bed. That was so you could wait on Miss Patsy Brander, in case she wanted something, or if Miss Patsy got took sick in the night. She did, right often. And so Miss Patsy had a little stepladder to get in and out of bed with.

All this was sort of before Mammy had married up with Mr.

Cornelius Winston, who belonged to Miss Patsy too; and he was mighty handsome. He was always pleasant spoken. He toted fair with the high and the low. He was a fine good man. Mr. Winston was just the finest man that anybody ever knew. So he and Mammy were real happy together, in those bad old slavery times; and their daughter was named Kizzy. But Miss Patsy Brander up and died; and when her ownings got settled, Mr. Cornelius Winston was sold off to be the head butler for a white gentleman, that fancied him a heap, out West.

That was why Mammy did not ever see Mr. Winston again until after The War. He came back to her then, to find out how she and Kizzy were getting along; and he and Mr. Solomon Simms liked each other very much.

Mr. Solomon Simms was the other gentleman that Mammy was married to by this time. And Mr. Winston had married up too, to a colored lady in Kentucky; so he brought her picture along with him, and a picture of both the children, to let Mammy see what his family looked like. Mr. Winston was always mighty thoughtful. They were nice enough children; they took after Mr. Winston, you could tell that right off. The boy was his very living spit and image. But if you wanted an honest and true to God opinion, the fat, greasy-mouthed colored woman was kind of ornery-looking. Anyhow, Mr. Winston and Mr. Simms got along fine; and Mr. Winston stayed with them, out on the farm over in Powhatan County, for about two weeks.

After Mr. Winston went away, he sent back some presents for Kizzy, and along with them came a necklace of real coral beads for little Julia Simms, so as to keep her from having croup. Julia was Mammy's other daughter. You could always count on Mr. Winston to act handsome. And that was the last that Mammy ever heard about him. She most surely would have liked to find out what did become of Mr. Winston, when she had his street address out in Kentucky too, where he was setting up at catering and waiting on white people's parties; but then she and Mr. Winston never could get around to learning just how to read and write, what with all the other things they had to do.

And presently Mr. Simms, that nebulous and, as one somehow felt, that rather shiftless farmer—concerning whom, to the best of your recollection, you at no time heard anything quite definite, except only his delight in being honored with a visit by Mr. Winston, his all-gifted predecessor—Mr. Solomon Simms of Powhatan took

sick and died. That was how Mammy came to marry Mr. Jeremiah
Nelson, who was just as smart as you make them. He was right dark-
complected, though.

Mr. Nelson was a city gentleman. He was born and brought up
in Richmond. He had rooms upon St. James Street. He worked for
the *Richmond Evening State*. He packed papers.

One imagines, nowadays, this must mean that Mr. Jeremiah Nelson used to tie up, with very shaggy brown twine, and to deposit
within the *State's* delivery wagons, those oblong bundles of printed
matter which, later, at about five o'clock in the afternoon, when
people were watering their front yards, and Mammy was wheeling
John's baby carriage back home from Monroe Park, and you and
Robert were walking alongside her, were flung out upon the red
brick sidewalk, with an unforgettable massive slumping noise, and
came pretty close to you sometimes, so that you held on to Mammy's
skirts, while the enormous Percheron horse which drew the white-
and-blue covered wagon continued its unhurried trotting toward
wherever it was going.

One is not certain. One does not even know upon what principle
those big bundles of newspapers were flung out upon the pavement,
or who took charge of them afterward. One knows only that Mr.
Nelson packed papers for the *Richmond Evening State* until the
final 1870's, which was when Mr. Jeremiah Nelson died.

And to the very last, let it be observed, Mr. Nelson acted with
more force of character than was displayed by Mr. Solomon Simms
—who, so far as it can be remembered, did not even die of anything
in particular. But Mr. Jeremiah Nelson died of pneumonia, just like
that, and almost before you could snap your fingers, along about
three days after he caught a bad cold in a snow storm; and it
showed how careful you ought to be about not forgetting your rubbers.

That was why Mr. Nelson's widow kind of thought she might try
working out, for a sort of change. She retained the rooms upon St.
James Street. But she came to my parents when their first child was
a month old, and when she was fifty-two, and she remained with us
for the rest of her life.

5

IT IS a trait to be dwelt upon, the fact that after some threescore
years of existence, Mrs. Nelson came to us when she was fifty-two,
because never during the time that one knew her did her age vary.
She was fifty-two. If pressed as to this point, through any ignoble

considerations of arithmetic, or if reminded, with an unmannerly precision, as to the unusual number of years throughout which she had stayed fifty-two, she would so far yield as to concede that anyhow she was about fifty-two. Beyond that, there was no budging her, not even in her most lenient moments.

Now, technically, Mrs. Louisa Nelson was a Negress; but it is not conceivable that anybody ever said so in her presence, not even after she had become very deaf. She elected instead to rank as a colored person; and her color, to be precise, was the just not golden yellow of peanut butter. As to her parents it is not remembered that Mrs. Nelson ever spoke, but her features were unmistakably Indian; her eyes had the alert black gleam of undried ink; her nose hooked slightly; her lips were thin. She too was thin; and until she had passed eighty, a ramrod would have seemed, in comparison with Mrs. Nelson, to be liquescent. Upon her flat left breast, except only when she visited Monroe Park, or during yet more stately occasions which called for an appearance in her black silk dress, she wore two or three needles with thread in them; she had wholly beautiful white crinkly hair; and she smelled very pleasantly with the indefinable odor which I can but describe as that of musk flavored with cloth.

She must have had Negro blood, but in her exterior there was not any trace of it. She most certainly had a great deal of Caucasian blood; and one imagines that every drop of it was aristocratic. Mrs. Nelson, in any case, was.

She likewise was that patron saint who performed miracles for your comfort tirelessly; and who served as an efficient mediator between you and powers which (in academic theory) were stronger than Mrs. Nelson, such as unfamiliar policemen and God and large dogs and your parents. Parents were well enough in their place, and you loved both of them; but, relatively, their place was remote; and in it they now and then were engaged, with an irresponsible graveness, by grown-up affairs in which you were not interested.

Mrs. Nelson had no such frivolous avocations. To her children (a heading under which she did not include Julia and Kizzy, or any of Kizzy's descendants, but restricted to your two brothers and you) she devoted twenty-four hours of each day—excluding only her Sunday afternoons and her Thursday evenings out. She went then to her rooms upon St. James Street. She was Head of the Subobinate Department of the Tents of Ham and the Daughters of David; and upon St. James Street the members of this organization were accustomed to confer with Sister Nelson as to matters which she could not talk to you about because they were Lodge secrets.

You did not mind the Sunday afternoons, when company came in or else you went out with your parents somewhere, and were allowed to be company yourself, and to let people see your raising, just as Mrs. Nelson had told you to do. But Thursday evenings were lonesome, after you had gone to bed, and the gas jet out in the hall had been turned down, and when both your brothers were asleep. Robert talked in his sleep a great deal, but that was not any help. As you remembered it afterward, there was always a soft-coal fire in the room upon those long Thursday evenings; and this made the shadow of the mantelpiece, upon the wall above it, jump every which way, like a big black chained-up Something, such as might be a Carpet-bagger, that was trying to get loose with no friendly intentions.

So you did not ever quite fall asleep until after Mrs. Nelson came in at twenty minutes after eleven. She said that you ought to have been asleep long ago. She asked if you children had been good children, and not kept everything in a swivet the first minute her back was turned. She brought you a glass of water, because you said you were sort of thirsty. That was so you could touch her. Then she got into her bed, which was next to your bed; and you went to sleep in less than no time, because everything was all right now that Mammy was back.

6

So LONG as Mrs. Nelson stayed near you, all matters tended to straighten themselves out satisfactorily. Even when you were sick-in-bed (for until you were at least ten years old you thought of this condition as being one word) she saw to it that you were not very sick, and had a plenty of boiled custard, and in fact, rather enjoyed yourself. But she remained rigid. She was not touched to he quick, nor did she condole, when you were sick-in-bed. It was her official attitude upon all such occasions that you were just upsetting the house from top to bottom by being sick-in-bed. —For there was not anywhere one minim of tenderness in Mrs. Nelson's nature, nor any reasonableness either, but only an unlimited devotion to her children.

So did it follow that at all times her ideas as to corporal punishment stayed sound and unshakable. To begin with, she did not ever concede that in any circumstances any one of her children had been bad; at utmost, the small accused might have been, it was allowed fair-mindedly, sort of mischeevous, but then, good Lord, what child would not be, when folks started in to upset him like that without attending to their own business? Through this dashing gambit, any parentally discussed punishment, instead of figuring as the result of a misdemeanor, was left unmasked as the true cause of it.

The child had been mischeevous because folks who were more than twice as big, and who did not know how to keep their temper, had started in to spank him, and what child, what child anywhere upon this earth, would not be? That, and that alone, was just simply what the indignant dark lawyer for the defence wanted to ask of Dr. Cabell and Miss Annie; and did ask, freezingly.

Moreover, should the incriminated parent remain deaf to remorse, then promptly the exposed rear of the condemned was shielded by both of Mrs. Nelson's lean and wiry, and peanut-butter-colored hands. Nor from this strategic position was she detachable. So the foiled parent, or it might be both parents, withdrew. And Mrs. Nelson, triumphant but still icily offended, began to speak as to the convenience and the accessibility of her rooms upon St. James Street.

7

THROUGHOUT twenty-five years these rooms remained the weapon which made her always, at the last pinch, invincible. —For Mrs. Nelson did not have to stay where folks did not like her ways. She did not intend to go on slaving where people were not satisfied. And so, about once every month, we learned that she was going back home, the very first thing tomorrow morning, to live in her rooms over on St. James Street without being stormed at and fussed with enough to run anybody clean crazy.

I do not think that at any time she had the least intention of doing this. But the knowledge that she, after all, was free to desert us for those rooms upon St. James Street kept every one of her dependents in a proper state of subjection throughout the quarter of a century. —For Mrs. Nelson, of course, like all other authentic mammies, after her children had become too old to require a nurse, retained an anonymous ranking as a general assistant in our household affairs—and, at need, as their autocrat.

In title, to be sure, she remained Mammy. But so far as went her indoor pursuits, she merely swept, and dusted, and sewed, and excelled in darning, and delighted to wait at table in her black silk dress whensoever we had company. She tended the ill; she now and then cooked meals, but only when a creative urge to cook was upon her; and she "laundered"—if that verb be still in current usage—with a perfection which to the present age is unknown. In fine, Mrs.

Nelson, after her actual retirement as a mammy, did everything; but always, it must be recorded, upon her own terms.

—Which reminds me to record likewise that Mrs. Nelson, what with all the other things she had to do, still did not ever quite get around to learning just how to read and write. So she remained unfamiliar with novels as to the South of yesterday, and she did not ever hear about any mammies who termed their children "my precious lamb," or "my own baby," or "honey chile," or yet something else of a nature no less affectionate and revolting. I am rather glad of this fact: for in Mrs. Nelson's eyes, these graceless if not actively immoral women would have ceased to figure as colored ladies; and in a brief philippic they would have been dismissed, I am wholly certain, as niggers who were just plumb idiots.

8

So THEN did the fourth part of a century pass by without forcing us to conceive of a life without Mrs. Nelson, or to face the notion of any existence thus maimed and bone-bare. Nor did we, until her death, when she was about eighty-five, had left us no choice; and for my part, it is a notion to which, after forty-and-some years of deliberation, I have not as yet become reconciled.

It should be recorded that upon the last day of her life, she told the attendant physician she was fifty-two; as well as that, upon this same heart-breaking Sunday, when she was not permitted to leave her bed, she assured me that, the very first moment she got over this sort of sinking spell, she meant to go straight spang back to her rooms, over on St. James Street, and not be a bother to us, when once she was out of this bed, praise the Lord.

—Because it was getting right far past the time for her little biddy bed to be pushed back under Miss Patsy's big bed. That was why she was trying to get up, Mrs. Nelson explained. So please be good kind folks and let her get out of bed.

She, who had been indomitable, now spoke half timidly. She did not know any one of us. In her last thoughts we figured as unfamiliar, and it might be cruel, white persons who were interfering with the proper duties of Miss Patsy Brander's own colored girl, under the presidency of Andrew Jackson, now that Mrs. Nelson had put out of mind those twenty-five years of tyrannic devotion which she had given to us, "her children," and of which no mortal that ever lived could hope to be worthy. She had forgotten about Julia, and about Kizzy, and about her three husbands, even Mr. Cornelius

Winston. With a child's fitful and half-hushed persistence, she repeated that Miss Patsy Brander wanted to have her room kept right enduring the day time; and it was in this way that Mrs. Nelson left us, in an attempt to wait upon her first mistress, who had been buried for somewhat more than sixty years.

9

ALMOST at random I have set down these recollections, as to an illiterate and hard-headed and great-hearted Negress, just as I thought about them, and without any re-arrangement or recoloring, because to my judgment Mrs. Nelson explains several generations of not humble-minded Virginians. Every one of these Virginians once had his mammy; by her he was taught, from infancy onward, to regard himself as an all-superior person; by her he was spoiled, completely and forever; and by her, as he very well foreknows, he by-and-by is going to be put in his right heavenly place, not unseverely, with an injunction, for the good Lord's sake, to behave himself now, and to let people see his raising.

In view of these circumstances, I submit, the aforesaid Virginian should not, in common reason, be required to affect any mock modesty. He is of the elect; he willy-nilly has been made a sophomore seraph; and for him to deny the fact would be a sacrilege.

—For do you but consider the plight of my own generation. It is wholly certain that all those mammies who once forgathered in Monroe Park are now assembled on an eternally clear afternoon somewhere in heaven. It is just such a partly Hebraic and partly Baptist heaven as they expected, because God, if that were necessary, will have rebuilded it especially so as to prevent their being disappointed. But they will not be seated upon thrones unsociably. Instead, there will have been provided an infinity of broad benches, with room upon every one of them for three persons inclining toward stoutness; these benches will be molded of bright gold, I imagine; and they will be decorated suitably with all the gems which St. John mentions.

Nor will any one of these dark angels wear a long white robe such as, to a respectable colored person, could not but indecorously suggest nightgear. They instead will all wear black silk dresses of the very best quality, as well as befrilled caps and large aprons, and extra-large, loose golden slippers. And everywhere about them, but always under their uncompromising surveillance, will be frolicking obediently a throng of deceased Virginian lawyers and bankers and physicians and tobacconists and clergymen and, I daresay, a few convicts. —For the fact has been explained to Jehovah, quite firmly, that while upon earth all these Virginians, at their very worst, were just sort of mischeevous.

So then do the mammies of the 1880's as yet talk lazily together forever and ever, between their slow benignant chuckles, while these blessed spirits await the complete return of their children. And eventually, some one or the other of them will be inquiring—without, I am afraid, any special enthusiasm,—

"Ain't that your Jeemes, Sis' Nelson?"

Everything will be all right then.

JOHN P. MARQUAND

****

NEW YORK,
APRIL 22 1950

A single chapter selected from a novel and impaled in an anthology among other asserted literary specimens seldom presents a fair impression of an author or his work. A novel at its best is a picture of life and people as seen through the eyes of an individual writer. No one reader can remember all its pages. He can recall only his experience in reading them and this experience can only be gained by living vicariously for a while among fictional personalities and situations. Such an experience, if it is to be at all lasting, obviously demands both time and space. This chapter from my novel, H. M. Pulham, Esquire, *was never designed to stand by itself. It is like a brick taken from an arch. It is possible to examine the size and consistency of the brick but it offers few clues to the general structure of which it was a part.*

As a brick this single fragment may not have enough straw or exterior decoration to make it a solid or cohesive art form. If it has not, I can only ask any reader for sympathy and forbearance, but I can offer no apology. According to my own judgment, which may not coincide with that of others, H. M. Pulham, Esquire *is an integrated novel. It seems to me to achieve many, though not all, of the results I hoped it would, but no part of it can have the elements of its final unity.*

JOHN P. MARQUAND

****

Yoicks — and Away

IT WAS a busy time as it always was—getting ready to go away. It was the time when one came most in contact with those people whom we called the "natives." Since North Harbor had been a summer resort for almost two generations the natives now lived off all the rest of us in many different ways. Father had always made it a point and so had I, to be friendly with them and to make that friendship a part of the summer life. When it came time to go away, I had to have a number of talks with Mr. Alfred Boost, who was our general contractor. Everyone used to say that Mr. Boost was a fine Down East character who could turn his hand to everything, and this was true if you personally checked everything to which he turned his hand. It was necessary to show Mr. Boost all the valves for turning off the water. Then I found myself climbing up to the roof with him to show him about new flashings and how to get the dead leaves out of the gutter. Then Mr. Boost brought in Mr. Meigs, the painter, who called me "Harry" because he used to know me as a boy.

Mr. Meigs told me that he had once read in a trade magazine that it was the duty of a good house painter to tell his clients frankly just what work needed to be done; and so Mr. Meigs told me frankly that the whole exterior of the house should be repainted for three hundred and fifty dollars if I wanted to save any of it. He knew that it was a lot of money, but it was better than having the whole house rot away. When I pointed out to him that he had painted the whole outside of the house two years before, Mr. Meigs said that no matter what quality of paint was used the salt air would peel it. I could see for myself how it was peeling already.

Mr. Boost said that Mr. Meigs was perfectly right about the salt air. If you lived by the sea you had to pay for it. In Mr. Boost's opinion all the chimneys should be repointed and it was about time to put on a whole new roof. Of course the present roof could be patched up, but we would always run the risk—Mr. Boost usually got down to the collective pronoun—of having ugly inside leaks, and then where would we be? I knew what had happened to Mr. Frear's house last winter, didn't I? Now, Mr. Frear was a fine man and he wouldn't say anything against him, but I knew and he knew that Mr. Frear was tight with his money. As a result Mr. Frear had lost two ceilings and a wall, although Mr. Boost had warned him. Now Mr. Boost knew very well that Mrs. Pulham and I were not that kind of people. We were the kind of people who wanted our house tight and shipshape. He and Mr. Meigs had been having a talk about it. Mr. Boost hadn't wanted to say that we needed a new roof, because he was afraid that I would think he was looking for business. Mr. Meigs told Mr. Boost that it was only friendly to tell me about it and he wanted to be friends with the summer people. New roofing would cost five hundred dollars.

Then Mr. Mack who ran the nursery came around. Mr. Mack said that he loved trees and that he knew I loved them. He had looked after our trees so long that they were like friends. Only God, he said, could make a tree, and he often thought that trees were God's most perfect work. Mr. Mack wasn't much on religion, but he felt that he was helping Our Creator when he and his boys were up in the trees getting parasites out of the bark, and it made him feel good always, on long winter evenings, when he knew that the trees, his trees, were storing up health and energy out of a good dose of patented fertilizer inserted around their roots, and he knew I felt the same way about it, because the Pulhams loved their trees. He and the boys weren't very busy now and they could fix every tree on the place for four hundred and fifty dollars. I may not have noticed the lawn either, Mr. Mack said; the sea air was awfully hard on turf. What the lawn needed was a good hand weeding and a fine lot of leaf mold rolled into it. Mr. Mack and the boys could do that too since they weren't busy for only a hundred-dollar bill.

Then Mr. Boost took me aside, about another matter that he wanted to discuss in private, not in front of Mrs. Pulham. He had noticed that the toilet in the downstairs lavatory was getting noisy. He knew the way it was. He had children himself and children were hard on toilets. A whole new outfit installed by him and decorated by Mr. Meigs would only cost me two hundred and seventy-five dollars and now was the time to do it before it was too late. This all meant a long period of discussion since Kay wanted it one way and I wanted it another and Mr. Boost and Mr. Meigs and Mr. Mack had ideas of their own. As usual, Kay and I would start arguing in front of them and sometimes Mr. Mack took her side and Mr. Boost took mine and then before I knew it they would all shift around.

Then Kay and Ellen began getting together the essential articles which would have to go in the car when I drove it down, piling them up in the front hall. I pointed out that Jerry was bringing down a truck and Kay pointed out that there were some things that were too delicate to go in a truck and I said what I had often said—that the Packard was not a truck. Then Ellen brought out the ice-cream freezer. We had been dealing with the ice-cream freezer for the past five years. Kay said it was getting pretty rickety and Jerry would break it if he put it in the truck. I said it couldn't go in the Packard with the children and the cook and the dog. I said we ought to have two freezers and if we didn't have one in town that I would buy one. Kay said she was trying to save me money, that we weren't millionaires, and at least we could save on an ice-cream freezer. I said it wasn't any saving if the car was wrecked and Kay told me that we would have to start saving somewhere.

It was all building up to the sort of climax with which I was familiar. When Kay and Ellen left to open the house in town there was a lull, but it was like a lull before a storm. There was no place to sit, there was nothing to do when Kay was gone. A day seemed like a week and another day seemed like a month. I called her up each evening to ask how everything was going. The first evening Kay said that it was all right and dictated me a list of things to do. The second evening Ellen answered the telephone and said that Kay was out.

I found myself trying to interpret Kay to Gladys and George, so that I seemed to be two people.

"Your mother wouldn't want you to take those dungarees to town," I told them.

Then George and Gladys would interpret Kay to me. It seemed that Kay had distinctly told them that they were to bring all the odds and ends in the house.

"You don't understand," George would say. "Mother distinctly told me."

"Well, your mother isn't here now," I told George. "You'll do what I say."

"All right," George said. "Just don't blame me. That's all. I can't help it, can I, if Mother distinctly told me?"

The cook and the other maid and Mrs. Meigs and her daughter began wrapping the furniture in sheets on the last day, and rolling up the rugs and wrapping the andirons in newspapers and Jerry began loading the truck and I began loading the Packard. Kay had given me a list of what to leave out if it was absolutely necessary. Even when I added a good deal more to the list there was no room for the cook, so I arranged with a taxi to take her to the Junction for the evening train. George and Gladys and the dog and I would leave early in the morning—I told them so at supper. We were each having a chop and a glass of milk and a baked potato. That was all the food there was left in the house except a little something for breakfast.

"Now, listen," I said, "we're going to do this right tomorrow morning. You, George, and you, Gladys, are both old enough to pack your own suitcases without bothering anyone. We're all going to turn out at six. We're going to get through before there's any traffic. Remember, six in the morning."

They looked at me blankly.

"Mother distinctly said that she didn't want us to come too early," George told me. "Six o'clock is awful early."

"It will do you good," I said. "Now, don't argue."

"Where are we going to have lunch?" Gladys asked.

"I don't know," I told her, "somewhere. You always get car-sick if you eat too much."

"Gee, boss," George said, "not six o'clock in the morning! Mother distinctly said—"

"Don't argue," I told him.

"Gee, boss," George said, "there isn't any reason to be sore."

"I'm not sore," I said. "I'm just telling you."

"Well, it isn't my fault," George said.

That had been a favorite phrase of George's for some time. I told him it was not anybody's fault; it was just life. I told him I didn't enjoy moving any more than he did, but sometime when he grew up he would have to do the same thing, provided there was any money left when he grew up. I told George and Gladys that they were pretty lucky, that lots of children were starving to death, and here they were going for a nice ride tomorrow to the city! It ought to be fun for them, it used to be fun for me when I was a kid. Then I wondered to myself if it had been.

When the children went to bed, I walked through the pantry and the kitchen, looking for an alarm clock. A tap on the laundry tubs was leaking, but it made no difference now, since Mr. Boost would turn off the water in the morning. I found a clock on the top of the icebox and brought it upstairs to my room and I brought Bitsey up with me too and let him sleep on the foot of Kay's bed. I turned on the radio while I was packing, but pretty soon I turned it off because the news was terrible. Then I opened the window and looked out. It was getting cloudy and a breeze was coming up from the northeast.

Then I got into bed and started in on *The Education of Henry Adams.* Instead of finishing it on my vacation as I had intended, what with one thing or another I had only done about twenty pages. Kay always seemed to interrupt me just when I was in the middle of a paragraph and now, without her, I seemed to expect I would be interrupted. I was wondering whether I had actually been weak with Mr. Boost in letting him rip out all the plumbing in the downstairs lavatory. Although it was all very well to give work to the natives in hard times, it occurred to me that Mr. Boost went down to Daytona Beach every winter with his wife and mother-in-law and two daughters, which was more than I ever did. I suddenly found, while I was thinking, that I had read five pages of *Henry Adams*

without knowing what it was about. When I tried to begin again
I was too sleepy to get on with it.

When I finally went to sleep, it was a sort of rest which did not
do much good. In the back of my mind there must have been a feeling that tomorrow would be a trying day, that Gladys would stand
more than an even chance of being overcome with nausea. The
trouble with Gladys was that she would never say anything about it
until it was too late. It would be up to me to watch her while I was
driving the car, but maybe George could do it. All the other times
that I had moved from North Harbor, from childhood on, gathered
cloudily about me in a queer dreamlike confusion. I remembered
the things Father had said when the lid of a trunk went down on his
fingers and how Hugh had sat down hard when a trunk strap had
broken. And when I went to sleep, the ice-cream freezer came into
it. I dreamed that Kay was walking to Boston, carrying the ice-
cream freezer on her head and saying that it was all right, that it
was really economical.

Then the alarm clock was ringing. It was one of those clocks that
started with a whisper and ended with what its maker called "a
cheerful good-morning shout." I had put it somewhere across the
room so that I would be sure to get up to turn it off when it rang,
and now I stumbled about trying to control it. It was dusky and
cold and it was raining. I went into the hall and began knocking
on the children's doors. Gladys was up and dressed already with
her hat and coat on. Her bag was closed and she was holding a
candy box with holes punched in the top.

"What have you got in there?" I asked.

"Spiders," Gladys said.

"Well, let them out," I said. "We've got enough to bother with
without a lot of spiders."

Gladys looked as though she were about to cry.

"It's part of my Natural History," she said.

I wished that Kay were there.

"All right," I said, "but don't tell your mother."

I never knew a boy who could sleep like George. I had to shake
him and half pull him out of bed and then he began to complain.
He said it was raining. I told him I didn't give a damn if it was—
he ought to get used to taking it. I told him it was like the war; it
always rained in the war.

"But we're not going to the war," George said. "We're going to
Boston."

"Never mind," I said. "It's like the war to me."

I had always believed in assuming that a motor trip with the children would be pretty bad, but actually that trip was worse. I was stopped by a state trooper outside of Portland and then Gladys was sick. I picked up a nail outside of Saco and had to get out and change the tire. I tried to be nice to the children, but they began to wear me down. They began playing alphabet games and picking letters off the signs; then, when Gladys went to sleep, George began telling of his social triumphs among his own contemporaries. I tried to be as nice as I could about it. The one thing I wanted was to get to Boston and to get a hot bath and a drink, but I kept telling myself that I was fond of the children.

"When are we going to have lunch?" Gladys kept asking.

"Yes," George kept saying, "when are we going to get lunch? There's a Dixie stand. . . . There's a Tootsie stand. . . . Let's have lunch at Joe's Place. . . . Let's have lunch at Daddy and Ann's. . . . Let's have some fried clams. Say, boss, don't you want some nice fried clams?"

In the slightly fetid air of the closed car, the thought of fried clams made me ill.

"We'll be at home in time for you to get something there," I said.

"Oh, gosh almighty," George shouted, "we don't want to eat at home."

"Don't yell at me," I shouted back. "You'll eat at home and like it."

We got home at half past twelve, still in the driving rain. I was wet from changing the tire and I was tired. The first thing to do was to get the children inside, then to unload the car. I found my keys and opened the front door, and when I did so, I felt a great sense of peace. I seemed to have been through a good deal and now life could begin again, the steady, sensible life of autumn and winter. Tomorrow I would be back at the office and I could start in again with squash. The house was fresh and clean, solid and comfortable. Ellen hurried into the hall.

"Why, Mr. Pulham," she said, "we didn't expect you till evening."

"We started early," I said. "It's a great idea to get it over with."

Gladys was running upstairs quickly with her spiders before any-one could see them. I was telling George to take Bitsey around the corner. Ellen was saying there wasn't any food in the house. Then I heard Kay calling down the stairs.

"Harry," she called, "why on earth did you come so early? Why didn't you call up?"

Her voice was sharp. I suppose I should have called her up.

When I hurried upstairs, Kay was in the hall in front of the living room.

"I had a hell of a time," I said. "We picked up a nail outside of Saco and then Gladys was sick."

"Well, you might have telephoned," Kay said. "Bill's here."

"What?" I said.

"Bill's here," Kay said. "He was just going to take me to the Ritz."

Then Bill came out of the parlor, and I was awfully glad to see him.

"Why, Bill," I said, "where did you drop from?"

Bill smiled.

"I'm indispensable," he said. "When the boys need me, I just drop everything. Harvard—rah-rah—Harvard!"

"What are you talking about?" I asked.

"The Play Committee," Bill said. "The Twenty-fifth Reunion. Our old friend Bo-jo Brown, he got me."

"Bo-jo?" I repeated. "Bo-jo said he didn't want you."

"Maybe he didn't," Bill said, "but he wants me now."

Then Kay was speaking.

"It's pretty nice of Bill to come away up for that," she said.

"Why, yes," I said, "it's wonderful. It's mighty good of you, Bill, to give them the time."

"Somebody had to do it," Bill said. "Who else could they get? What are you laughing about?"

"And you always said the Class gave you a pain!" I said. Just seeing Bill there had made me laugh.

"Harry," Kay said, "Bill and I were going out to lunch. It's sort of mean of us running away, but you didn't telephone."

"Oh, that's all right," I said. "You go ahead and I'll take the kids out somewhere and then we can all have dinner, can't we?"

"Harry," Kay said, "what *are* you laughing at?"

"I just can't get over it," I said, "Bill's getting himself roped into the Reunion!"

I stopped, because Kay looked at me. It was one of those looks that meant that she would take up what I said sometime later and would ask me how I could possibly have been so rude and stupid. I stopped, though I could not see what on earth I had said that was disturbing, except that I may have sounded a little forced and flat, because I was overtired and wet. Nevertheless, when I looked at Bill, I knew that I had certainly put my foot in it. I had always thought that Bill was able to stand a lot of good-natured give and take, and I had never minded—indeed, I had rather liked it—when Bill used to put me over the jumps in front of Kay. Yet Bill had a peculiar expression, not exactly annoyed, but as though he were really worried about what I might say next, when all I had done was to intimate that Bill was not particularly loyal to his Class. I still could not see what was wrong with it, since Bill had gone out of his way for nearly twenty years to make gibes at class spirit and at all our classmates who tried to do their part in making things go when we got together. It all made me feel confused, as though I had not come into my house at all, but into someone else's.

"What have I done now?" I asked.

Then Bill laughed, as though he had seen the joke for the first time.

"All you've done is get home in time for lunch," he said. "You're coming with us, aren't you?"

It was all right as soon as Bill began to laugh.

"No, no," I said, "you go ahead. Somebody's got to feed the kids and I've got to get the things out of the car. I'll take them somewhere down the street. No, no, you and Kay go ahead."

"You don't think it's mean of us, do you?" Kay asked.

Making so much of going out to lunch began to make me a little impatient. I did not see why Bill and Kay seemed to be underlining everything, as though we weren't old friends.

"Of course it isn't mean of you, Kay," I said. "Now let's not bother about it. By the way, I brought the ice-cream freezer. It's tied on in back."

"What ice-cream freezer?" Kay asked.

It surprised me that she seemed to have forgotten all about the ice-cream freezer, when we had been all over it only three days before.

"What ice-cream freezer?" I repeated. "Why, *the* ice-cream freezer, that one we argue about every year. You don't mean to say you've forgotten all about it?"

"Oh!" Kay said, and she looked as though she remembered. "That was awfully sweet of you, darling. Did you all have a good time while I was away?"

"No," I said. "Come back pretty soon, won't you? The kids are sort of getting in my hair. I don't see how women stand it."

"You're sure you don't mind?" Bill said.

"Mind?" I repeated. "Haven't I been telling you, Bill, I don't mind? I think it's swell! You can have the car as soon as I take the things out—and give Kay a good lunch. She deserves it."

"I'll help you unload the car," Bill said.

It was nice of him to offer to do it, because Bill had never cared much about useful manual labor and he had on a navy blue pin-striped suit all nicely pressed.

"Oh, no," I said, "this isn't your funeral. You're not married."

Then I knew I'd said something else that was dull. I had completely forgotten that Elsie was out at Reno and I hadn't meant it that way.

"Boy," Bill told me, "that's the truest thing you ever said. I am less and less married every minute."

"I didn't mean it that way, Bill," I said, and then I saw Kay watching me again.

"Harry," Kay said, "I wish you wouldn't always bear down on everything. Bill, you don't have to help him really. He'll get everything out of the car in just a minute, and Harry knows where everything belongs. Harry loves to pack and unpack cars."

That was what Kay always said when someone else was around. She always said that Harry would love to do it. She was always telling Mrs. Jones or somebody not to let the hired man carry down the trunk or not to let the maid pick up the broken pieces of the goldfish bowl—that Harry would love to do it. She told me once that it was all unconscious on her part, that she only wanted people to see how nice I was. I went downstairs and opened the front door.

"Ellen," I called, "where's Master George?"

She didn't know. He had gone away somewhere, which was not strange, because George always faded out when there was any work. I asked her where the chore-man was, but he was not around anywhere either. I had never known him to be, when anything really had to be done—but after all, I had not telephoned.

I put on my raincoat and my hat and went out to the car. First I unlocked the luggage compartment and hauled out all the suitcases, finally getting into the rhythm of walking from the car and up and down the steps. I piled the suitcases in the hall and then I barked my knuckles on the ice-cream freezer. Then I hauled out a box of assorted canned goods, most of which we had brought up with us five months before, because Kay always wanted to have something in the house in case people dropped in unexpectedly. Then I lifted out a cardboard box, filled with half-empty tins of baking powder and spices and condiments which had been cleaned off the kitchen shelves. I had suggested to Kay that it might be just as well to leave them for Mrs. Meigs, but Kay had said we could use them ourselves—that we ought to try to save money. Halfway across the sidewalk, the bottom fell out of the box, and I had to spend several minutes gathering tins up in my arms. Even when I had finished, the sidewalk was covered with salt and cloves and cocktail wafers. Then I got out my account books and Kay's box of jewelry and George's radio and Gladys' microscope and Bitsey's rubber bone and comb and brush, two boxes of candles, an enema bag, a motion-picture projector, one rubber, a sneaker and three bars of Old Lavender toilet soap. George came up from somewhere down cellar.

"Where in thunder have you been?" I asked. "Why didn't you help me unload the car?"

"Oh," George said, "were you unloading the car, boss? I didn't know it."

"Just who did you think was going to do it?" I asked. "What have you been doing?"

"I was just down trying to find my electric train," George said. "Say, boss, can we go somewhere to get hamburgers?"

I did not answer his question. Instead, I called up the stairs.

"Kay," I called, "the car's all ready now."

Kay came down, in a new coat, with fur around the edge, carrying a brand-new handbag. She looked very pretty and not tired at all. I was surprised that she had found time to do any shopping. Bill followed her. He might have been coming out of a club car after the porter had brushed him.

"Fast work, boy!" Bill said. "You certainly brought everything except the kitchen stove."

"Harry," Kay said, "what have you done to your face?"

"What's the matter with my face?" I asked her.

"It's all grease and black," Kay said. "You've been rubbing your face with your hands."

Bill laughed.

"Spit on your handkerchief and take it off," he said.

"Say, Mother," George said, "when do we eat?"

"Your father will take you out in just a minute, dear," Kay said, "and Uncle Bill and I will be back pretty soon. We won't be gone long, Harry," and then they were gone.

"Hey, boss," George said, "when do we eat?"

"When we get cleaned up," I told him. "Now go upstairs and get washed and tell Gladys to get washed."

Now that I had arrived, with the car unpacked, North Harbor and the summer were slipping out of focus and blending in with all the summers I had known, and the reality of winter picked me up bodily in its arms. I had a comfortable sense that everything in the hall was in its place. The mirror, the table and the chairs were all fresh and clean, and exactly where they should be. Ellen was already arranging the silver on the sideboard in the dining room— Mother's teaset in the center, ornate and overdecorated, on either side the two enormous *bonbonnières* that used to be on the dining room table in Marlborough Street, and in the back the candelabra and the two knifecases. The decanters were on the low serving table beneath the portrait of Kay's grandfather, old Colonel Motford who fought in the Civil War, and between them was the silver pheasant. I was glad to see that the landscape by Henry Inman, which my grandfather had bought, was back from the gallery, freshly cleaned and varnished. Kay used to say that it was about the most stuffy dining room that anyone could find, that it was like living in someone else's shell; and this was why she had bought the Chinese screen and had put in light curtains, to try and brighten it up. I saw it all in a single glance, the way you see rooms that you know.

The stair carpet was very badly worn. It was one of those furnishings which we were going to change when the children grew up, but I was glad to see that it was all tacked tight. Up in the second-floor hall, the wall paper was dingy. No matter how often Kay and I had told George and Gladys, they always rubbed their hands over it. But the parlor looked splendid. Kay call it our only successful room, for somehow all the possessions we had bought and inherited fitted together. The Persian rug, which came from Kay's mother, was not too large for it and it went well with the Motford armchairs.

The Inness was over the fireplace, a restful canvas of hazy, rolling country. As long as I could remember, Mother and Father had talked about the Inness and it was the only item from the house in Marlborough Street over which Mary and I had argued. We finally had agreed to match for it, three times out of five. The brasses in the fireplace were all freshly shined. The secretary desk that came from the Motfords was waxed and so was Kay's piano, a baby grand. Neither of us was musical, but Kay always said that no room looked well without a piano—so there it was, for Gladys to practise on at two in the afternoon.

There were fresh flowers in the boxes by the windows—cyclamen, ferns and begonias. It was really Kay's room more than mine. Even with Kay out of it, I thought of her walking back and forth in it arranging this and that. The cushions on the chairs and sofas were all neatly plumped out and dusted, except for the sofa near the fireplace, where Kay and Bill must have been sitting when I arrived.

One of the pillows had fallen on the floor and there were some cigarette ashes on the carpet. The other pillows were all bashed in.

The library had been cleaned too. As always happened when the cleaning women got at the books, Thackeray was mixed in with Jane Austen and my college textbooks were in with the histories. I would have to straighten them out as soon as I had time, perhaps that afternoon. The flat-topped desk, which Kay had bought me once in England, was covered with all the second-class mail which had accumulated during the summer, mostly charity appeals—for Spanish orphans and blind children and Chinese victims of Japanese aggression and Jewish victims of German aggression and homeless waifs and fallen women and cancer clinics and epileptic clinics. There was never any way to escape from the background of misery, all packed into neat envelopes.

I actually just walked through the parlor and through the library, only a hasty detour on my way upstairs. Our bedroom was in the front of the house, a large room with comfortable twin beds and a chaise lounge which nobody ever used, because Kay hated resting, and a highboy that had come from the Motfords and the bureau that had been my father's and the dressing table that I had given Kay. All our tastes were mingled there into a sort of compromise. I was the one who had picked out the water carafe on the table between the beds and I had insisted on having two Currier and Ives prints of early locomotives. Kay was the one who had wanted two pastels of flowers in vases and the flowered chintz window curtains that went with the spread.

Like all the rest of the house, the room was fresh and spotless, silently waiting for Kay and me, although Kay must have slept there. Yet as I looked around, I knew she had not. It was all just as the cleaning women had left it, without any of the little things that Kay always brought with her to change that look. Her silver traveling clock was not on the bedside table. Not even her combs and brushes were on the dressing table. The bag she had taken from North Harbor, the little overnight case I had given her for Christmas the year before last, was not on the chaise lounge where she would have tossed it. At first I was only aware of a sterile sort of vacancy. In fact, I did not notice any of this until I had begun to change my clothes. It was just as though someone had played a bar of music that was off key. There was no untidiness—her slippers were not in the closet and her wrapper and dressing gown were not hanging on the hook on the bathroom door. The bathroom was just as impersonal as our bedroom, no toothbrush, no bath salts, no tooth paste. When I knotted my tie in front of the shaving mirror on my bureau I was sure of it. I was the first to come in the room. Kay had not been there.

The radio was playing in the library and George and Gladys were waiting.

"And now you can hear for yourself," a voice was saying, "how Aunt Mamie makes those fluffy cookies that are all full of good rich crunchiness."

"Turn that thing off," I said. "We're going to lunch."

"Well, it's about time," George said.

"Can I have a quarter?" Gladys asked.

"And what do you want a quarter for?" I asked her.

"She wants to buy doll's didies," George said.

"No, I don't," Gladys said. "Shut up!"

Both of them were getting cross and I did not blame them.

"Everybody stop," I said. "Come on."

I was getting cross myself. It was after two o'clock. Ellen was still working in the dining room.

"Ellen," I said, "wasn't Mrs. Pulham here last night?"

Ellen rubbed her hands on her apron.

"No," Ellen said, "she wasn't here, Mr. Pulham. There was so much cleaning going on. She has been spending the nights out in Brookline."

"In Brookline?" I said. "Oh, that's it—she must have been staying with Mr. Guy."

The children were standing behind me with their coats on.

"Come on," I said, "let's go!"

I was glad that Kay had been staying with Guy. She would have been lonely by herself, with only Ellen in the house. Then, as I was opening the door, I saw Kay's suitcase with its canvas cover and with her initials, C. M. P. She had left it under the hall table that morning and had not had time to bring it upstairs. Kay had been awfully busy.

The only place available for luncheon in our neighborhood was the Bob Cratchit Tea Roome and Coffee House, an establishment run by a group of dour-looking ladies who also sold cakes and cookies at the change desk—tea thirty-five cents, luncheon fifty-five cents and dinner seventy-five cents. On the whole, it always seemed to me that the Bob Cratchit Tea Roome was a sensible, nice place, patronized by people who did not care to pay any more for simple wholesome food, and by people like me who were driven there when there was no food at home. In the years since Kay and I had bought our house in town I may have been there four or five times— especially just after George and Gladys had been born—when the house was so filled with trained nurses that either the cook must leave or I must; and once Kay and I had gone there when the boiler at home had exploded. Every time we went, we always remarked that the blue and orange tables were most attractive and that the food was tremendously good, but we never became regular customers.

The girl who took our order said that they were out of beets and out of spinach, that the chicken pie was out, and that the luncheon hour was pretty well over. This was obvious enough, since George and Gladys and I were the only customers, with the exception of a mouse-colored man, who was reading a book on *The Measurements of the Great Pyramid*, and he got up and left by the time our beef stew appeared.

"Gee," George said, "this food is worse than school!"

Gladys did not say anything, but she did not eat much. I told George that it was time for him to cultivate a few thoughtful manners. This was one of the days, I told him, when we all were out of luck. When he grew older, I said, he would find there were lots and lots of times when things did not go right, when you must take them in your stride, making the best of them cheerfully, without griping and bellyaching. I asked him what he would have thought of me and what his mother and everyone else in the house would have thought, if I had begun whining and complaining when I had to unload the car and could not go to the Ritz with Mother and Uncle Bill, because I had to take two little brats out to lunch instead. I thought this example might hold them for a while, but Gladys asked:

"Why couldn't we all have gone to the Ritz?"

For some reason, this was hard to answer, but soon I began to think of a great many very good reasons why we couldn't have, and I pointed them out to Gladys and George while the waitress brought me a pot of stale coffee and brought each of the children a glass of milk flavored with chocolate. In the first place, I said, we could not have gone to the Ritz because Uncle Bill had asked Mother and had not asked us.

"Why didn't he ask us?" George said. "We were all there before they went out, weren't we?"

"He didn't ask us," I said, "because grown people like to be together sometimes and because he didn't want to have lunch with a lot of little brats who make noises with their soup."

"You make noises with your soup. Mother says so," Gladys said.

George began to laugh so loudly and immoderately that the ladies behind the cake counter frowned.

"Listen to the boss," George said. "He's making noises with his stew!"

I told George to shut up and behave himself, but Gladys had not lost her train of thought.

"Why couldn't you have taken us to the Ritz?" she asked.

"Oh!" I said. "Why couldn't *I* have taken you to the Ritz?"

Then I explained to them that it was time for them to learn that most people can not afford to do silly, extravagant things. This lunch here would cost fifty-five cents, whereas lunch at the Ritz would cost two dollars and fifty cents apiece and there would be no large tip here for the service, either, because gratuities were not allowed in the Bob Cratchit Tea Roome. I told them they might as well get it into their heads now as any other time that neither their mother nor I was made of money. We were doing the best we could to keep them dressed and to give them the advantages of an expensive education and this meant that their mother and I had to do without a great many things which we really wanted. They did not seem interested; they ate their stew slowly, but I kept on telling them. I told them they might not know it, but that they were mighty lucky—luckier than ninety-four out of a hundred other children. Here they were, with a comfortable home and comfortable beds, eating a good meal of wholesome stew with lots of fresh milk and bread and butter, when lots of other children right here in town were cold and hungry. Lots of other parents were on the WPA because they could not get a job. They were lucky and instead of knowing it, they wanted to go to the Ritz.

"Why don't you believe in the WPA?" George asked.

It surprised me sometimes, that George was old enough to read the papers.

"Whether I do or not," I said, "the WPA is here, and never mind about it!"

Gladys stared at us with wide, dreamy eyes.

"I thought you didn't like Mr. Roosevelt," she said.

"A lot of people don't like Mr. Roosevelt," I answered, "for a lot of different reasons, but Mr. Roosevelt's here, like the WPA."

"If I wrote Mr. Roosevelt, would he write me?" Gladys asked.

The conversation was making me confused, and convincing me that I had been with George and Gladys for altogether too long a time.

"You write him," I said. "You write him and tell him you're a big girl who still collects spiders, and misspell it, the way you've been taught to misspell at your school, and either Mr. Roosevelt will answer it or Mrs. Roosevelt will. Now both of you shut up! I want to eat."

George and Gladys did not shut up, but they changed the subject. They began to play what is known among progressive educators as "a game of the imagination." It had been amusing when they were younger, but now they were too old for it. Gladys was Mrs. Brown and George was Mr. Brown, and Mrs. Brown was telling Mr. Brown how to pack things in the car and Mr. Brown was complaining. It was a clumsy and humorless parody of Kay and me which made me wonder whether we really appeared that way through our children's eyes. It made me see that they did not know what we were like at all. I could hear their voices going on around me while I sat and ate, and my mind moved away from them.

Since the war had started all over again, I was more conscious than I had ever been of the misery around us. Yet most people I know were removed from it, insulated from all understanding of it, like figures under glass. The awful thing was that there did not seem to be anything much that a person like me could do. I had a feeling, which I had known when I was younger, that I had never really seen the world. I was closer to it there with George and Gladys than I was at the office. It occurred to me that I had been leading two lives—my business life and my private life, which I suppose must be true with everyone. Your business life, your activities and Clubs were what you talked about and put down in a Harvard Class Report.

[After leaving Harvard, I was employed by the firm of Smith and Wilding. At the conclusion of the war, I spent a year in New York in the advertising agency of J. T. Bullard. I then returned, rejoined the firm of Smith and Wilding, where I stayed until shortly before its dissolution in 1933. I then formed, with an associate, my own investment counsel service, where I am today.]

What was really important were the human contacts I had made. There was my life with Kay and the children, and what did it amount to? As I finished my vanilla ice cream with maple walnut sauce over it and listened to the rain lashing against the windows of Bob Cratchit's Tea Roome, I could not give a very encouraging answer. I began thinking about Dickens' *Christmas Carol*. That work of fiction was read annually to Mary and me from the time we were old enough to listen—and now I had been reading it ever since George and Gladys could listen. I would read it again this Christmas, as a duty, like writing checks for charity appeals, but I could not say that I had ever really appreciated the Cratchit family and Tiny Tim's thin voice joining in the chorus—"God bless us every one." The way the world was going now, Tiny Tim should have been saying, "God help us, every one!"

"Say, boss," George said, "do we have to sit here all afternoon?"

"No," I said. "Let's go."

JOHN HERSEY

****

The narrator of this passage from The Wall *is Noach Levinson, an imaginary historian of the Warsaw ghetto who is supposed to have gathered an archive documenting the fate of the Jews there between 1939 and 1943, and who is pictured in the novel as a studious, somewhat timorous, and indefatigably prying recorder of the lives and deaths of those around him. The passage describes a so-called selection, in which Jews from a given sector of the ghetto are designated, either for "resettlement in the East"—which in fact means extermination in the gas chambers of Treblinka—or for survival, for a time, within the ghetto. This chapter, which comes about halfway through the book, serves as a kind of fulcrum in the novel, for it squarely confronts the narrator (and therefore the reader) for the first time with the vindictive yet careless—almost frivolous— Fate which decides the life or death of the novel's protagonists. Before this point, existence in the ghetto has been a downward slope into mortal degradation; after it, the characters begin an upward climb toward unity of purpose, love of life, and a final episode of faith, their uprising of April, 1943.*

The "family" to which Levinson refers in these lines is the group of friends with whom he has been living. The character named Felix is a cautious, rather weak-willed functionary of the Judenrat, the German-sponsored Jewish Council, where Levinson also works. The two share an office and have been constant companions for many months.

****

Moment of Judgment

EVENTS AUGUST 25, 1942. ENTRY AUGUST 26, 1942—Noach Levinson. I feel better. I have faced a fifty-fifty chance of dying, and although I was terrified by the ordeal, I know now that it is possible to face this terror and neither go mad nor collapse—two possibilities that had frightened me, in anticipation, almost more

297

than the thought of death itself. It is curious that my innate
timidity, making me shamefully servile in the face of any authority,
even that which I hate, did not show itself in this moment of judgment. I was even rather bold.

At about ten o'clock yesterday morning, I was sitting at my desk
at the *Judenrat* more or less daydreaming. As a matter of fact, I
was thinking about the "family," wondering whether they were
safe. I recalled the way they had tiptoed out of the apartment, in
groups of three or four, in the middle of the night before; and
how despite all their efforts to get out without waking Wladislaw,
the boy had suddenly jumped up from the living room floor, leaping in one instant from sound asleep into vociferous wakefulness.
He demanded in a loud voice to know what was going on, and of
course, in order to avoid having the whole scheme given away by
his trumpeting, the others ended by taking him along. I had lain
alone for the rest of the night, trying to guess where they had hidden
themselves. Provident Berson! I had got away to the office before
anything had happened at the apartment, and now I sat at my
desk, feeling love and sorrow for my dear friends—at the very moment when I myself could have used just those feelings from others.
For we at the *Judenrat* were about to suffer our own selection.

It was in the midst of my reverie that a sudden racket broke
out in the courtyard of our building. This noise was soon dominated by the bellowing German voice in one of the corridors:

———*Alle Juden 'raus, 'Raus, 'raus! Hinunter! Alle Juden hinunter!* All Jews out. Out, out! Downstairs! All Jews downstairs!

Felix Mandeltort at his desk and I at mine both jumped to our
feet, and with a quickly exchanged glance we each saw that the
other knew what was happening. We walked out of our office and
down into the courtyard. There we found a disordered scene. At
one side of the courtyard, against the north wing of the building,
a portable desk had been set up. There a group of *S.D.* officers and
men was centered; a commanding officer was spreading out papers.
In the rest of the courtyard, Jews were milling frantically, seeking
relatives and friends, asking frightened questions, talking excitedly.
A large number of Jews not connected with the *Judenrat* had been
brought in from neighboring buildings. A gang of Ukrainian and
Lithuanian cadets was trying, with a great hubbub and occasional
roughness, to drive this agitated mass into a line, starting at the
desk, running across the courtyard, and doubling back around one
side.

Beside the desk and with the Germans stood Engineer Gross-

mann, our Chairman, and behind him were the Chief of the Jewish
Police and the Chairman's secretary. I could see that these high
officials were being besieged by influence-seekers, and were waving
them off impatiently. Schpunt was standing beside the dignitaries.
Schpunt is not so much official as officious these days: he goes
around to all the selections, as a kind of jester at the Germans'
feast of death, maintaining a prattle of abuse of both Jews and
Germans. The Germans, who are greatly amused by him, tolerate
and even encourage this behavior on his part.

Gradually the tumult in the courtyard abated.

Directly in front of Felix and me in the line were a man and
wife, arguing. They were not *Judenrat* people; they were quite
poor, to judge by their clothing. He wore a greasy black cap, a
heavy, patched, dirty shirt, and shiny cloth trousers; she had on a
torn and spot-stained black dress. They had become abusive toward each other in this their peril. The husband accused the wife
of slatternly habits; she said he was lazy. He said he had never
loved her—that the marriage broker had cheated him in the first
place and never since then had he loved her. She accused him of
having kept his earnings from her and the children, and then he
said she had made "*nebich* animals" of the children. An unnatural
hatred blazed between the two; it seemed that the sudden con-
frontation with death had made these poor people turn on each
other and say things to each other that they had always buried,
that they had never said before, and that may even have been untrue now. The woman seemed to sustain a physical blow every
time the man said he had never loved her; he perceived this, and
said it again and again.

The selection commenced. At the desk the officer began to pronounce the simple reprieves and sentences: *right* or *left*, according to the evidence of working cards, appearances, the officer's
judgment, the moment's sheer whim, or Chairman Grossmann's
opinion. Indeed, so far as the *Judenrat* personnel was concerned, it
can be said that this selection was conducted by Engineer Grossmann, for it was his intervention, or the lack of it, that decided
who should be sent to the left and who to the right.

The couple in front of us continued their bitter reproaches to
each other, hissing now in undertones: they seemed to want to
destroy each other before the inexorable German destroyed them
both. Ahead of them, in the line, was a big workman carrying a
suitcase. And ahead of him stood a young woman, holding a long
disused compact, powdering her face, applying rouge and lipstick,

combing her stringy hair, in hopes, evidently, that she might make herself appear attractive and above all *healthy* to the German: healthy enough to be a worker and survive. Felix seemed to stand rather apathetically beside me.

———Right . . . left . . . left . . . left. . . .

I thought once more of the "family." I wondered whether any of us would ever see each other again. I quieted my fears and for a few moments felt rather comfortable imagining their mourning me, in case they survived and I did not.

———Left . . . left . . . death . . . death. . . .

Some of the Jews tried to argue, some to beg; many were crying, men as well as women. I suppose everyone knew about Treblinka by this time. Each person tried, I dare say, to persuade himself that Treblinka does not exist; but each had to admit the possibility that it does. If any Jews who had been sent to the *left* caused delays, Junaks stepped in and bodily lifted them to the group headed for the *Umschlagplatz*. Some who were doomed bit, clawed, and fought back. Others were dull and passive.

———Left. . . .

Now it was the turn of the girl who had primped herself. She had no papers to offer. Her name was checked on the tenants' list of the near-by apartment from which she had been brought. The commanding officer looked up at her and smiled. In automatic response to the smile, in an awkward gesture that seemed to arise from a vague memory of a feeling as long disused as the girl's battered compact, she put a hand to her hair and preened it around the back. A cracked voice—I saw that it came from the grotesque mouth of Fischel Schpunt—said, in what evidently seemed to the Germans a comical Yiddish-twisted German:

———Oi, she's for a party dressed already.

The officer's smile, benign, almost urbane, widened, and the other Germans laughed.

———Left.

The girl walked without a moment's hesitation to the group designated for the *Umschlagplatz*.

The man with the suitcase stepped forward. He offered some papers. They seemed to be valid. The officer said:

———Right. (Then he asked:) What's in the suitcase?

———Personal possessions. The regulations permit fifteen kilograms to be taken, in case of resettlement. I thought perhaps . . .

———Correct. Fifteen kilograms are permitted. . . . Mittendorf, examine the suitcase

————But you said I could go to the right.

The officer merely looked up at the workman, as if to say: *Speak when spoken to*. The noncom addressed as Mittendorf took the suitcase from the workman, let it down on the cobblestones, flopped it onto one side, dropped on one knee, and opened the suitcase. Clothing seemed to be crammed into it. The noncom pulled the top pieces out. Underneath there was something larger. The noncom tore out the contents of the suitcase. Mainly there was a bundle, from which the noncom peeled off layers of shirting and articles of clothing. Inside was a baby. It was perhaps a year old. It was alive. Its mouth had been bound with strips of cloth. Its thin, old-looking face was bluish, but it struggled in the hands of the noncom, who seemed not to know how to hold the squirming body. The workman stood looking at the ground.

The German officer, expressing neither surprise nor anger:———— For the little stranger, left.

The noncom, Mittendorf, carried the baby to the group for the *Umschlagplatz* and put the infant in the arms of the girl who had prettied herself. The workman stood still, watching. The officer said to him:

————For you, right.

Slowly the workman walked to the group on the right, of those who were spared.

Now the man and wife who had just discovered that they had never loved each other came forward. The man presented papers; the woman had none. The officer held out the papers for the husband to take back, and said the man could go to the right. Then he looked at the woman and with a jerk of his head sent her to the left. The woman turned away from her husband without even looking at him and went to the group for the *Umschlagplatz*. The husband looked after her for a moment, then, with an unearthly sob, went after her and, showing no affection or surrender, stood beside her in the group designated for death.

Felix stepped forward. Grossmann condemned him. Felix went left. Felix!

It was my turn. My boldness, to which I have referred, consisted in the fact that when I approached the Germans' desk, I ignored the Germans entirely; I looked Engineer Grossmann squarely in the eye. I have never been close to him, as I think I was to Sokolczyk: it has always been necessary for me to make appointments to see Grossmann, whereas I was on a walk-in basis with his predecessor. I have sometimes had the feeling that Grossmann has actually disliked me. He is a "practical" man, one of those "realists" who like to fancy that they never let sentiment carry any weight with them, and I believe he considers me to be highly emotional and therefore highly suspect. He regards emotionalism and radicalism as synonymous: anyone who weeps easily is probably a Communist and certainly a Socialist. I regard myself as inwardly sensitive and perhaps even sentimental but on the surface fairly dry (actually the Drifter used to accuse me of being enigmatical—he blamed it partly on my eye-glasses); but these judgments as between men are usually founded upon inadequate evidence, and Engineer Grossmann judges me, I suppose, on the basis of a couple of displays of temper in *Judenrat* conferences.

At any rate, I came up to Grossmann, with my life wholly in his hands, thinking these thoughts, and I stared at him as coldly and scornfully as I could. I had seen him, a few moments before, press his lips together and shrug as Felix Mandeltort came up to the desk, and in the instant when the German harshly said, *Left!* I saw a momentary flicker of torment in Grossmann's eye. Indeed, what a horrible responsibility, to have to send some of his colleagues and subordinates to Treblinka! When I saw that blink of misery, I had an idea that I might be able to save myself by outcountenancing Grossmann. I tried to make my look at him say: *I hate you. You are practically a Nazi. Even if you send me to my death, I don't care, because I know that you will die a thousand deaths of guilt and regret and self-reproach. I hate you. Everyone hates you.* That is what my eyes said, and I think his eyes received that message; anyhow they soon dropped and looked then toward the German.

Grossmann:——This man keeps all my records. I can't function without him.

And the German sent me to the right.

Of course I cannot say whether my boldness had any influence upon this outcome. The Chairman might have said the same thing had I avoided his eye altogether. But at least my defiance made me feel better.

I stood in the group at the right, not daring to look across at those on the other side, for fear that now my eyes might meet those of my old friend Felix Mandeltort.

RICHARD WRIGHT

****

The fragment which follows, American Hunger, *tells in part a story lived often by Negroes in America. We Negroes are, because of historical circumstances, a migratory people, forever on the move, leaving one spot to seek for Freedom in another. We do this because we are Americans—and indigenous Americans, at that!—and we haunt the American landscape for our place, trying, as Americans, to feel at home in a land that spawned us but rejects us. Sometimes we find what we are seeking; most times we do not.*

Why are we Negroes so restless? It is because we are Americans and are acting upon the impulses which spur all Americans; but we soon find that our land contains no means through which we can realize these impulses. Our illusions fade, but in fading new ones come to take their place and we find ourselves pushing on, still with hope, into new areas, areas even beyond the boundaries of our country.

When I was a kid I had in me the urge to write; it was a dim and vague urge but still there. I left the South and went to Chicago. No matter what others may say, I think I had a truly modest aspiration; at least such aspirations make demands upon no one save him who holds them. . . .

In Chicago my mind and consciousness met and touched many segments of American life, books, people, ideas, feelings. . . . And out of those things, for good or ill, I was partly formed. It was a process of becoming, of changing, of shedding old emotions and absorbing new ones.

And it was not the last time that I was to do that, to leave and seek life elsewhere. New York came next, then Mexico, then Canada. Now, while in Paris, my eyes are turning toward Africa, India, and the Far East. And I've begun to suspect that this seeking is not merely a Negro's seeking, but a human one, the human condition, the main situation of our time for white as well as for black. So be it!

RICHARD WRIGHT

****

American Hunger[*]

MY FIRST GLIMPSE of the flat black stretches of Chicago depressed and dismayed me, mocked all my fantasies. Chicago seemed an unreal city whose mythical houses were built of slabs of black coal wreathed in palls of gray smoke, houses whose foundations were sinking slowly into the dank prairie. Flashes of steam showed intermittently on the wide horizon, gleaming translucently in the winter sun. The din of the city entered my consciousness, entered to remain for years to come. The year was 1927.[**]

What would happen to me here? Would I survive? My expectations were modest. I wanted only a job. Hunger had long been my daily companion. Diversion and recreation, with the exception of reading, were unknown. In all my life—though surrounded by many people—I had not had a single satisfying, sustained relationship with another human being and, not having had any, I did not miss it. I made no demands whatever upon others.

The train rolled into the depot. Aunt Maggie and I got off and walked slowly through the crowds into the station. I looked about to see if there were signs saying: FOR WHITE—FOR COLORED. I saw none. Black people and white people moved about, each seemingly intent upon his private mission. There was no racial fear. Indeed, each person acted as though no one existed but himself. It was strange to pause before a crowded newsstand and buy a newspaper without having to wait until a white man was served. And yet, because everything was so new, I began to grow tense again, although it was a different sort of tension than I had known before. I knew that this machine-city was governed by strange laws and I wondered if I would ever learn them.

As we waited for a streetcar to take us to Aunt Cleo's home for temporary lodging, I looked northward at towering buildings of steel and stone. There were no curves here, no trees; only angles, lines, squares, bricks and copper wires. Occasionally the ground beneath my feet shook from some faraway pounding and I felt that this world, despite its massiveness, was somehow dangerously fragile. Streetcars screeched past over steel tracks. Cars honked their horns. Clipped speech sounded about me. As I stood in the icy wind I wanted to talk to Aunt Maggie, to ask her questions, but her tight

[*] *The selection made by Richard Wright represents a continuance of his autobiography* Black Boy. *It appeared in the September, 1945 issue of the Magazine* Mademoiselle *and has not been used hitherto in book form.*
[**] *Wright was then 19 years old.*

face made me hold my tongue. I was learning already from the frantic light in her eyes the strain that the city imposed upon its people. I was seized by doubt. Should I have come here? But going back was impossible. I had fled a known terror, and perhaps I could cope with this unknown terror that lay ahead.

After an idle week, I got a job as a dishwasher in a North Side café that had just opened. My boss, a white woman, directed me in unpacking barrels of dishes, setting up new tables, painting and so on. I had charge of serving breakfast; in the late afternoons I carted trays of food to patrons in the hotel who did not want to come down to eat. My wages were fifteen dollars a week; the hours were long, but I ate my meals on the job.

Though I had fled the pressure of the South, my outward conduct had not changed. I had been schooled to present an unalteringly smiling face and I continued to do so despite the fact that my environment allowed more open expression. I hid my feelings and avoided all relationships with whites that might cause me to reveal them.

One afternoon the boss lady entered the kitchen and found me sitting on a box reading a copy of *The American Mercury*.

"What on earth are you reading?" she demanded.

I was at once on guard, though I knew I did not have to be.

"Oh, just a magazine," I said.

"Where did you get it?" she asked.

"Oh, I just found it," I lied; I had bought it.

"Do you understand it?" she asked.

"Yes, ma'am."

"Well," she exclaimed, "the colored dishwasher reads *The American Mercury!*"

She walked away, shaking her head. My feelings were mixed—I was glad that she had learned that I was not completely dumb, yet I felt a little angry because she seemed to think it odd for dishwashers to read magazines. Thereafter I kept my books and magazines wrapped in newspaper so that no one would see them, reading them at home and on the street car to and from work.

At night I read Stein's *Three Lives,* Crane's *The Red Badge of Courage,* and Dostoevsky's *The Possessed,* all of which revealed new realms of feeling. But the most important discoveries came when I veered from fiction proper into the fields of psychology and sociology. I ran through volumes that bore upon the causes of my conduct and the conduct of my people. I studied tables of figures relating population density to insanity, relating housing to disease, relating school and recreational opportunities to crime, relating various forms of neurotic behavior to environment, relating racial insecurities to the conflicts between whites and blacks. . . .

I still had no friends, casual or intimate, and felt the need for none. I had developed a self-sufficiency that kept me distant from others, emotionally and psychologically. Occasionally I went to house-rent parties, parties given by working-class families to raise money to pay the landlord, the admission to which was a quarter or a half dollar. At these affairs I drank home-brewed beer, ate spaghetti and chitterlings, laughed and talked with black, Southern-born girls who worked as domestic servants in white middle-class homes. But with none of them did my relations rest upon my deepest feelings. I discussed what I read with no one, and to none did I confide. Emotionally, I was withdrawn from the objective world; my desires floated loosely within the walls of my consciousness, contained and controlled.

As a protective mechanism I developed a terse, cynical mode of speech that rebuffed those who sought to get too close to me. Conversation was my way of avoiding expression; my words were reserved for those times when I sat down alone to write. My face was always a deadpan or a mask of general friendliness; no word or event could jar me into a gesture of enthusiasm or despair. A slowly, hesitantly spoken "yeah" was my general verbal reaction to almost everything I heard. "That's pretty good," said with a slow nod of the head, was my approval. "Aw, naw," muttered with a cold smile, was my rejection. Even though I reacted deeply, my true feelings raced along underground, hidden.

I did not act in this fashion deliberately; I did not prefer this kind of relationship with people. I wanted a life in which there was a constant oneness of feeling with others, in which the basic emotions of life were shared, in which common memory formed a common past, in which collective hope reflected a national future. But I knew that no such thing was possible in my environment. The only ways in which I felt that my feelings could go outward without fear of rude rebuff or searing reprisal were in writing or reading, and to me they were ways of living.

Aunt Maggie had now rented an apartment in which I shared a rear room. My mother and brother came and all three of us slept in that one room; there was no window, just four walls and a door. My excessive reading puzzled Aunt Maggie; she sensed my fiercely indrawn nature and she did not like it. Being of an open, talkative disposition, she declared that I was going about the business of living wrongly, that reading books would not help me at all. But nothing she said had any effect. I had long ago hardened myself to criticism.

"Boy, are you reading for law?" my aunt would demand.

"No."

"Then why are you reading all the time?"

"I like to."

"But what do you get out of it?"

"I get a great deal out of it."

And I knew that my words sounded wild and foolish in my environment, where reading was almost unknown, where the highest item of value was a dime or a dollar, an apartment or a job; where, if one aspired at all, it was to be a doctor or a lawyer, a shopkeeper or a politician. The most valued pleasure of the people I knew was a car, the most cherished experience a bottle of whisky, the most sought-after prize somebody else's wife. I had no sense of being inferior or superior to the people about me; I merely felt that they had had no chance to learn to live differently. I never criticized them or praised them, yet they felt in my neutrality a deeper rejection of them than if I had cursed them.

Repeatedly I took stabs at writing, but the results were so poor that I would tear up the sheets. I was striving for a level of expression that matched those of the novels I read. But I always somehow failed to get onto the page what I thought and felt. Failing at sustained narrative, I compromised by playing with single sentences and phrases. Under the influence of Stein's *Three Lives*, I spent hours and days pounding out disconnected sentences for the sheer love of words.

I would write: "The soft melting hunk of butter trickled in gold down the stringy grooves of the split yam."

Or: "The child's clumsy fingers fumbled in sleep, feeling vainly for the wish of its dream." "The old man huddled in the dark doorway, his bony face lit by the burning yellow in the windows of distant skyscrapers."

My purpose was to capture a physical state of movement that carried a strong subjective impression, an acomplishment which seemed supremely worth struggling for. If I could fasten the mind of the reader upon words so firmly that he would forget words and be conscious only of his response, I felt that I would be in sight of knowing how to write narrative. I strove to master words, to make them disappear, to make them important by making them new, to make them melt into a rising spiral of emotional stimuli.

I read Proust's *Remembrance of Things Past,* admiring the lucid, subtle but strong prose, stupefied by its dazzling magic, awed by the vast, delicate, intricate and psychological structure of the Frenchman's epic of death and decadence. But it crushed me with hopelessness, for I wanted to write of the people in my environment with an equal thoroughness, and the burning example before my eyes made me feel that I never could.

My ability to endure tension had now grown amazingly. From the accidental pain of Southern years, from anxiety that I had sought to avoid, from fear that had been too painful to bear, I had learned to like my unintermittent burden of feeling, had become habituated to acting with all of my being, had learned to seek those areas of life, those situations, where I knew that events would complement my own inner mood. I was conscious of what was happening to me; I knew that my attitude of watchful wonder had usurped all other feelings, had become the meaning of my life, an integral part of my personality; that I was striving to live and measure all things by it. Having no claims upon others, I bent the way the wind blew, rendering unto my environment that which was my environment's, and rendering unto myself that which I felt was mine.

It was a dangerous way to live, far more dangerous than violating laws or ethical codes of conduct; but the danger was for me and me alone. Had I not been conscious of what I was doing, I could have easily lost my way in the fogbound regions of compelling fantasy. Even so, I foundered, staggered; but somehow I always groped my way back to that path where I felt a tinge of warmth from an unseen light.

Hungry for insight into my own life and the lives about me, knowing my indrawn nature, I sought to fulfill more than my share of all obligations and responsibilities, as though offering libations of forgiveness to my environment. Indeed, the more my emotions claimed my attention, the sharper—as though in ultimate self-defense—became my desire to measure accurately the reality of the objective world so that I might more than meet its demands. At twenty years of age the mold of my life was set, was hardening into a pattern, a pattern that was neither good nor evil, neither right nor wrong.

VINCENT SHEEAN

****

This, which I wrote for the New Republic *about Winston Churchill when he lost the election in 1945, is about the best and most characteristic short piece of mine I can think of in just these years.*

VINCENT SHEEAN

****

Valediction to Churchill

THERE IS a tendency to draw back under the eaves, standing vaguely at attention, and salute as the valiant old gentleman makes his way back into that honorable shadow from which the war called him forth. He was not adjudged safe or sound enough for the responsibilities of government during the ten years before 1939, and there is little likelihood that his talents will again be needed in the arduous but unheroic years ahead, whatever the modifications of general opinion. He will thus have made his distinct contribution on the highest dramatic plane, that is to say in a crisis so great and sustained that his country's history affords no precedent for it; and those who feel most warmly toward him must hope that he will be content. From the purely aesthetic point of view the composition is already marred by his insistence upon contesting an election as Tory party leader, after he had led all parties with such unequalled vigor in the nation's years of trial. If he had left the partisan squabble to others, and retired upon his age and honor—to write a book, perhaps: and what a book it might be!—we should have been inclined to forget those events which, since the landings at Salerno in September, 1943, have successively darkened our view of this exceptional man in the affairs of Italy, Spain, Greece and India. But we know of old, however much we may regret it, that men who reach the supreme power seem incapable of surrendering it in good time, but must be dragged protesting from their places not when, but *after* the objective situation has made it imperative.

In the case of Mr. Churchill the hour came when he decided, tasting the delayed fruits of an intoxicating success, that the war had become "less ideological." How much of his work in the Mediterranean, inspired by this extraordinary personal concept, can be undone by more astute and perceptive contemporary minds is now to be seen. So far from being "less ideological" in essence, the war has been so consistently ideological right through to the end that the British Army, which was most concerned in obeying Mr. Churchill's orders in Italy and Greece, has been most legally active in getting him out of office. Mr. Churchill inhabits such a curiously antiquated mental geography, full of strong points and plains for battle, where every inequality in the ground becomes an escarpment and every flat space invites a cavalry charge, that he has had little opportunity to guess at the unheroic, empirical and in fact rather scientific mind of the ordinary modern soldier. When he talks about modern soldiers in his semi-Elizabethan vein, he reminds us of that speech he made about iceboxes early in the spring of 1944, when, to prove how tenderly the Tory party made plans for the returning warrior, he went into a maze of architectural and culinary detail about the prefabricated houses he was going to build, and succeeded in convincing us of only one simple truth: that Mr. Churchill had never been inside a kitchen in his life except during election campaigns, and that food arriving on his table has always been, and always will be, a supreme miracle worthy of his inexhaustible eloquence.

This attitude of sublime ignorance toward the gross, ordinary details of life is, of course, the result of social and economic conditions which, in England, are much more closely intertwined than they are in America. Mr. Churchill is not a rich man but he has always lived in the social style or manner of the privileged order, which, among other things, involves systematic ignorance of innumerable details farmed out among domestic servants. The attitude was an element of strength during the cruel days of 1940 and 1941: Churchill could quite easily concentrate upon the great, simple things of life and death for the nation, partly because the crisis called out all his simplicity and greatness, but partly also because he never had to worry about the little things in good times or bad. Mr. Churchill called upon the people to be worthy of their ancestry and traditions but he never called upon them to share out their cabbages and leeks, to stay off the railroad trains, to furnish milk to an agricultural pool or to make over last year's shoes for this year. All those duties were assumed by the British people—and how they were assumed has been the admiration of the world—at the request of lesser men fitted to lesser preoccupations, but taken all together they had a great deal to do with the endurance which helped to win the war.

Churchill's own lifelong aristocratic disregard for the small difficulties and arrangements which take up most ordinary people's time enabled him to get through the whole war without seeming to descend from that eminence on which he will now be symbolically fixed forever, cavalry sabre in one chubby hand and an expiring cigar in the other. "'Ow 'e do talk," Bert would say admiringly, listening to him in the corner by the vestigial fire at the Pig and Whistle, and then trudge out into the cold night on air raid warden's duty, feeling vaguely happier because of the stout words that stirred an echo in every English heart. And Mary would rip up all the children's sweaters to make them over again for another year, adding a little wool from an old scarf of her own, and combining the colors in such a way that even the keenest observer would never know that war, and not simple taste, had dictated their choice; and greasy Joan would keel the pot; and thus with one thing and another, the winter and spring of dreary news and privation and danger went by, and then the war between Russia and Germany began and there was no longer any possibility of defeat, especially after America came in in December, although the number of things to do with and to do without never seemed to grow less, and the last year was not much easier than the first. Through it all there was Winston's voice on the radio, admonishing, exhorting or explaining, a kind of quintessentially English voice which had its moment of speaking for all, and upon which with the passage of time there were accumulated the overtones of the recent, the incredible past, so that even tonight's speech would carry some echo of the day when he said "We shall never surrender."

But the trouble was that you couldn't be sure of just what all that would mean in peace time; and as events piled up in countries where the British could have their own way, it seemed clearer and clearer that the old sport of empire-building, the pride and joy of the Tory party, had come back as strong as ever—had come back, indeed, on the very continent of Europe, from which its energies had been tacitly barred for a century and a half. Moreover it was made plain that the Tory party did not intend to keep up the social and economic controls which had made it possible to win the war. Bert and Mary and all the rest of them felt a disquiet which was increased by every letter from the soldier son, brother, husband, overseas; and the sense of 1940-1941, that if this awful crisis were surmounted there would be another England in the future, was mocked at by the official blandness of 1945: the only thing to do was to vote plainly for the party which announced its awareness of the need for change and aid.

In a large number of ways, Mr. Churchill for two full years had been driving millions of people who were not hitherto socialists and have never belonged to the Labor Party into a frame of mind in which that party was the only hope. When, for example, Mr. Churchill on his visit to Rome took special care to demonstrate his monarchical and anti-populist prejudices, or when he went out of his way to say kind words to the last openly Fascist dictator, Franco, or when he lost his temper about Greece and lashed about him with wild words in the House of Commons and wilder shells in the hills of Attica—well, those were the times when he threw the votes at Labor with lavish generosity. All who knew anything of Mr. Churchill know that he has always been a true Tory and a true imperialist, whose patriotism for the native island rose above every other consideration at the time of greatest crisis, but could never supplant those articles of firm belief upon which he has built his life; but no argument against him, or in favor of alternative views of society and economy, could possibly have made the impression he made himself, with his sense of drama and his pomp of words, on such questions as Italy and Spain, Greece and India, the "Gestapo" of the British Labor Party, and—glory be!—Professor Harold Laski. The grandiose runs one peril from which commonplace men and ideas are happily exempt: it is always on the very brink of being ridiculous.

The common sense of the English people has now come to Mr. Churchill's rescue and saved him, but only just, from the final excesses of his temperament. In so doing it has removed what had become a toothache from the head of the world, and given those with any sense of the future more reason for a modicum of confidence than would have seemed possible a few months ago. The Labor Party's majority is so great that there is virtually no end to what it can do under the flexible limits of the British Constitution. It is obsessed by gradualism and hamstrung by the economic difficulties of a highly industrialized state which has for generations lived by empire; within its own membership there is a wide range of belief; opportunists have flocked to it in recent years; it would be stupid to look for too much change too quickly. But the *motives* are now different; it will no longer be necessary to connect every village argument in the Balkans with some eighteenth-century concept of the "defense of India," and we can stop worrying about those kings and marshals who were excavated every second Tuesday to plague the peoples.

The relation of this tremendous struggle to the future of men and women all over the world will at least be a living object of contemplation to the minds which rule in Whitehall.

As for Mr. Churchill himself, as he passes from history into literature, one's sense of fitness leads to the hope that some special honorific distinction will mark the event. In the old days it was possible for the nation to bestow a "purse," a great sum of money or huge pension awards, on those who had served it exceptionally well. That is how the Nelsons and Wellingtons and Marlboroughs were able to weigh the nation's gratitude. The fashion has changed and this may no longer be possible; if it were, there are many nations which should contribute heavily to that "purse." But one traditional expression remains which suits Mr. Churchill's habit of mind and life: he can be a duke. For my part, if I had the doing of it, I would have him called both marshal and king, since those words are so powerful an object of his respect: but owing to the fact that they still have functioning attributes in England the notion is not practical. Duke, therefore, let it be: but not merely duke of London or of any other geographical entity, however considerable. The exuberant Italians had a way, at the end of the last war, of making their great men dukes of the elements—"Duke of the Sea," for instance. For Mr. Churchill nothing less would be wholly appropriate: he could be Duke of the Channel which he made freedom's frontier for those twelve long months, or he could be duke of the burning deck, or duke of the air. Whatever he calls himself, he will always be the duke of the dark days, and since there are not likely to be any more winners or wearers of such a title, he might as well assume it in memory of June, 1940. Where the truth lies let the name lie also.

WILLIAM L. SHIRER

****

This piece, like most entries in a diary, was written in the mood of the moment and probably has many of the faults and—it may be —some of the virtues of anything that is composed under such circumstances. That cold, dismal day amidst the debris of Nuremberg, November 20, 1945, was, as I wrote, a climax. Justice did seem to have caught up with these evil little men who had tried to enslave or destroy our world.

Since I had watched them in their barbarous pursuits, noted closely how they had behaved in their moment of monstrous power and vain glory and had sometimes despaired that they might get away with their hideous crimes, I felt a certain emotion when I saw them in the dock for the first time. This feeling, I suppose, colors my description of the scene.

I also felt that this was a rather important and dramatic moment in contemporary history. The trial, as Lord Justice Lawrence, who presided over it, observed, was unique in the history of jurisprudence. One felt a certain excitement at being present, especially when one had lived through so many of the events which had finally led to this court-room and to what was about to take place in it.

The interest in this excerpt, if any there be, lies, I should think, in its being a recording of an historic scene by one who happened to be present. It was scribbled hastily and under the particular feelings which gripped me that day. Other observers no doubt saw it differently—a Nazi German, for instance.

The editor has asked whether after nearly five years my feelings toward the trial, the defendants and the fate they met have changed. I cannot honestly say they have. It is fashionable now to discredit the Nuremberg trial. Some even consider it to have been a beastly crime against the Germans. My own considered opinion is that justice, for once, was not badly served.

WILLIAM L. SHIRER

****

314

The Prisoners at Nuremberg

This, then, is the climax! This is the moment you have been waiting for all these black, despairing years! To see Justice catch up with Evil. To see it overtake these barbaric little men who almost destroyed our world. This, really, is the end of the long night, of the hideous nightmare.

And how the mighty have fallen! Shorn of the power and the glory and the glittering trappings of Nazidom, how little and mean and mediocre they look—the twenty defendants in the dock this day! How was it possible, you ask yourself in amazement, that these nondescript-looking individuals, fidgeting nervously in their rather shabby clothes, wielded, when last you saw them, only five years ago, such monstrous power? How could *they*, so measly of countenance as they slump in their seats, have conquered a great nation and almost the world? Their metamorphosis staggers you. Were *these* the conquerors, the strutting leaders of the Master Race? Why, the sudden loss of power seems to have stripped them clean of the arrogance, the insolence, the truculence that was their very being in all the years I knew them. How quickly they have become broken, miserable little men!

They are already seated in the prisoners' dock when I enter the courtroom at nine forty a. m. The first sight of them is indescribable.

There is Göring. He sits in the first seat in the first of the two rows that compose the dock. It is the number-one place and it strikes you that at last he has achieved his long ambition of being Number One in the Nazi hierarchy, though not precisely as he had once dreamed. At first glance I scarcely recognize him. He has lost much weight—eighty pounds, a U.S. Army doctor whispers to me. The fat, pouchy face I knew is much thinner now. He looks younger and healthier, with his excess weight gone and his drug habit cured —an achievement of our army medical corps. His faded air-force uniform, shorn of the insignia and of the medals he loved so childishly, hangs loosely on him. He could hardly strut in it now. And gone is his burliness, the old arrogance, the flamboyant air. Indeed, he sits through the five-and-a-half-hour opening session of court quite subdued, though attentive and alert to the proceedings. Often he reaches for his earphones and with a gesture that is almost meek, almost humble, cl ps them over his head so that he can listen to

the simultaneous German translation of something that is being said
in English or French or Russian. At such moments, I cannot help
thinking, he looks more like a genial radio operator on a ship at sea
than the former tyrant I had heard so often thundering his threats
against the world. It is wonderful how a twist of fate can reduce a
man to normal size.

Next to Göring sits Rudolf Hess, the number-three man of the
Third Reich until his ridiculous flight to England. How on earth,
you ask again, could *that* man have been one of the top leaders of
a great nation? Here is really a broken man, his face so emaciated
it looks like a skeleton, his mouth twitching nervously, his once
bright eyes staring vacantly and stupidly around the courtroom. It
is the first time I have ever seen Hess out of uniform. In the black
coat of the SS he always seemed a strapping fellow. Today in a
threadbare civilian suit he looks small and wizened. Unlike the
others, he pays little attention to what is going on and sits for most
of the time reading a novel balanced on his knees. We know that he
claims to have lost his memory, but he seems to me to behave
normally enough. He was never very bright and he certainly does
not appear bright today. It is his deterioration that startles you.
Here is the wreck of a man whom Hitler not so long ago wanted
to succeed him as dictator of Germany.

Next in line is the insufferable mountebank Joachim von Ribbentrop, Hitler's former Foreign Minister. How often in the grim years
have I sat in the Foreign Office in the Wilhelmstrasse and watched
this arrogant nincompoop strut in to a press conference to announce
in a snarling voice that another innocent, decent land had "provoked" Germany into attacking it! He was an evil, pompous little
ignoramus, this former champagne-salesman who had married the
boss's (the German champagne king, Henkell's) daughter, and only
in the underworld of the Nazi gangsters could such a creature attain
prominence. Even among most of them his vanity and arrogance
were too much, but Hitler, for some reason, liked him and kept him
on as his errand-boy at the Foreign Office until the very end. One
glance today shows that the turn of events has shattered this scheming little worm too. Ah, now he is bent and beaten and aged beyond
belief. During a recess he shuffles past me as two guards escort him
to the toilet. His body is stooped, his face pale, his eyes vacant—a
defeated, broken man. . . .

In the dock on Ribbentrop's left sits Wilhelm Keitel in an army
officer's faded uniform stripped of all markings. He had been some-

thing of a jaunty Prussian, this former field marshal and chief of
the Supreme Command. I had last seen him at close quarters at
Compiègne when he, on Hitler's behalf, dictated armistice terms to
France in the sad June days of 1940. I remember how cocky he was
then, like all Germans when they are on top, always prancing when
he walked and wearing his cap at a rakish angle. There is nothing
prancing or jaunty about the old field marshal today. He too is
subdued, though he is not a broken man as are most of the others.
The massacre of so many souls does not seem to weigh on him
unduly. His appetite obviously is still good. He keeps munching
crackers—from an American Army K-ration kit.

On his left squats Alfred Rosenberg, the phony "philosopher" and
once the mentor of Hitler and the Nazi movement. He too has lost
weight, the puffiness on the sallow, square face is gone, and he
looks younger and healthier than when I saw him last. Dressed in a
dark-brown suit, this dull, confused, but dangerous Balt who contributed so much to the Nazis' race hatreds, who superintended
the loot of art objects from the conquered lands, and who finally
helped direct the dreadful extermination of the Slav people in the
conquered Russian territories, is nervous in the dock, lurching forward to catch every word, his hands shaking.

Next is a real barbarian in captivity for you! Hans Frank, the
lawyer, who as Governor General of occupied Poland decimated the
Polish people and wiped out millions of Jews. He strikes you immediately as the type of refined murderer who, like Himmler, could
kill and kill without getting excited about it or even appearing,
personally, as particularly brutal. Today he is easily the most self-
assured man in the dock. He keeps his back half-turned on the
prosecutors as they read the lengthy indictment of his crimes.

At his side farther down is Wilhelm Frick, a cold and ruthless
man behind his rather modest exterior. He was one of Hitler's chief
henchmen, but toward the end of the regime became somewhat forgotten. Today he seems a forlorn figure in his checkered sport coat.
But one could not forget his brutality as Hitler's first Minister
of Interior and, in the end, as the "Protector" of Bohemia and
Moravia.

It is difficult to recognize the next man in the dock, Julius
Streicher. The former undisputed master of this town, who strode
through the ancient streets of Nuremberg brandishing a whip and
waxed fat on pornography and Jew-baiting, has rather wilted away.
He sits there, an obscene, bald, decrepit old man, perspiring pro-

fusely. Occasionally the old scowl comes back as he glares at the judges. The guards tell me Streicher is convinced they are all Jews. It fortifies your belief in ultimate justice to see this repulsive German at last brought to judgment.

Walther Funk, who shouldered Schacht out of the presidency of the Reichsbank and of the ministership of Economics, comes next. He merely looks like a more aged toad than before, still coarse, greasy, and shifty-eyed. Next to him, and the last one in the first row, is a man who would not speak to him for ten years until today—the inimitable Dr. Hjalmar Horace Greeley Schacht. It is evident from the very start that the wily banker, who did more than any other individual in Germany to bring Hitler to power, is furious at having to stand trial with men he now—conveniently—considers as thugs. Sitting erect, his head separated from the rest of his body by his high choker, he folds his arms defiantly across his chest. Knowing English, he follows the reading of the indictment without earphones and with rapt attention. Occasionally he deigns to turn to Funk, whom he despises, to exchange a word. I am told Schacht is sure he will be acquitted.

We can dispose of the second row of accused more quickly. The first two gentlemen are the two Grand Admirals, Karl Doenitz and Erich Raeder. Doenitz, an able naval officer who worked out the wolf-pack technique for German submarines before he succeeded Raeder as commander-in-chief of the navy, sits erect in a civilian suit and looks for all the world like a grocery clerk. Hard to imagine him as the successor of Hitler, which he was—for a brief moment. Raeder, still in uniform, still clinging to his high upturned collar, has aged beyond his already considerable years. The spark that enabled him to build up the German Navy after World War I has gone out of him completely. He is a bewildered old man today.

Beside him is the most personable-looking and the youngest of the defendants, Baldur von Schirach, leader of the Hitler Youth and, during the war, the hated *Gauleiter* of Vienna. He looks more American than German, his parents having been American, I believe, and one of his grandfathers a soldier in the Union Army during the American Civil War. Young Schirach actually believed in the Nazi nonsense, serving Hitler with fanatical loyalty and great ruthlessness, particularly in corrupting the youth of Germany with the poison of Nazism. Today he seems a bit dazed at finding himself in this place.

Fritz Sauckel, next to him, the boss of slave labor, looks like a pig, with his narrow little slit-eyes. If Germany had been a normal land, he would have found his place in life behind the counter in a butcher shop, for he looks like a small-town butcher. He is nervous today and sways to and fro. The stiff back of the man next to him, Alfred Jodl, does not sway. He sits gravely in his faded army uniform, this tight-lipped Bavarian who became the most powerful general in the German Army and the closest to Hitler. Like Keitel, he could never say no to Hitler, which was probably the principal reason for his advancement, as it was of Keitel's.

And next comes old Franz von Papen, incredibly aged, the eyes sunk in, the skin taut over the wizened face, the shoulders stooped, but still looking the part of the old fox. He has had many narrow escapes in his life, but here at last justice seems to have nailed him. He does not like it at all, you can see. Arthur Seyss-Inquart, the Austrian traitor and, during the war, the brutal oppressor of the Dutch, and Albert Speer, Hitler's Minister of Armament and Munitions, are next in line and show little emotion of any kind.

Next to the last is Baron Konstantin von Neurath, the typical career diplomat, without convictions and without integrity. Hitler had used him for a time as Foreign Minister and then as a front man for his butchery in Prague, where Neurath was the first "Protector." He sits in the dock today, a broken old man, apparently dazed by the discovery that one can come to the end of the road to compromise. He hardly knows how to stand up and be counted, for this forlorn remnant of a conservative old German family has never stood for anything in his life except serving whoever was his master. Last in the dock is the most unimportant, one Hans Fritzsche, whose voice on the radio was so like his master's, Goebbels's, that it was often difficult to tell them apart. He is here, I take it, as a sort of substitute for Goebbels and appears to be taken aback by the importance attached to him.

Promptly at ten a. m. the bailiff, whose manner and voice make plain he could only have been imported from an English law court, bawls to the occupants of the courtroom to come to attention and rise. The prisoners, quick to respond to any orders, leap to their feet. The judges file in.

They are an interesting lot. Lord Justice Lawrence, who will preside, is a fine old chunk of Britain with an ample Gladstonian forehead and the restrained self-assurance of all eminent British judges. He looks like a cross between Gladstone and Stanley Baldwin. Within a moment's passing he has stamped his dominance of the courtroom on all present, including the prisoners, you feel. He will be firm, unemotional, and fair. His alternate is Sir Norman Birkett, probably the keenest legal mind in the room, a thin, gangling fellow whom I had often seen at court in my younger days in London, where he was among the two or three greatest trial lawyers of the time.

Francis Biddle, our former Attorney General, is a bit self-conscious, almost tripping on his robe as he mounts the bench. At his side is Judge John J. Parker, a homespun North Carolinian, whom an irate Senate once kept out of the Supreme Court. Europe and especially the insane Nazi world are a bit strange to him, you feel, but he takes them in his even stride. The French judge, Donnedieu de Vabres, resembles Clemenceau one minute and Petain the next. His alternate, Robert Falco, looks like any French lawyer one used to see crowding the halls of the Palais de Justice in Paris. He seems to have a tendency to drool.

All these judges wear black, judicial robes, but the Russian judge, Major General Iona Timofeevich Nikitchenko, vice-president of the Supreme Court of the U.S.S.R., and his alternate, Lieutenant Colonel Alexander Fedorovich Volchkov, are in military uniform, resplendent with decorations.

Without ado, Justice Lawrence raps for order and proceeds to read an opening statement. "The trial," he says, "which is now about to begin is unique in the history of jurisprudence of the world, and it is of supreme importance to millions of people all over the globe. For these reasons, there is laid upon everybody who takes part in this trial a solemn responsibility to discharge their duties without fear or favor in accordance with the sacred principles of law and justice. . . . It is the duty of all concerned to see that the trial in no way departs from those principles and traditions which alone give justice its authority and the place it ought to occupy in the affairs of all civilized states."

He warns that the Tribunal "will insist upon the complete maintenance of order and decorum, and will take the strictest measures to enforce it."

Whereupon, getting down to business with dispatch, he directs the reading of the indictment. Everyone in the courtroom knows it almost by heart, but this is a trial by due process and it must be read. Justice Jackson picks his first assistant, Sidney S. Alderman, to begin the tedious task of reading, and later the British, French, and Russian attorneys pitch in to carry on with it. "The United

States of America," Alderman intones, "the French Republic, the United Kingdom of Great Britain and Northern Ireland, and the Union of Soviet Socialist Republics *against* Hermann Wilhelm Göring, Rudolf Hess, etc., defendants. . . ."

One by one the four counts are read: count one, the charge of conspiracy to commit crimes against peace, war crimes, and crimes against humanity; count two, the detailed charge of crimes against peace; count three, war crimes; count four, crimes against humanity. All the obscene atrocities, to which we seem to have become hardened, are described and enumerated. The prisoners are bored. So is everyone else.

One's eyes wander over this strange, unprecedented scene. On the right, as I look from the press box, the raised bench of the tribunal. Directly across the room, facing the judges, is the prisoners' dock. Back of the defendants, who sit on hard, bare, wooden benches, are eight American M.P.'s, in neat GI uniforms, white belts, and helmets, carrying night-sticks and side arms. They are on the alert to see that no materials for suicide pass between the prisoners and their lawyers, who are crowded at small tables immediately in front of them. Directly before us sit the prosecutors of the four nations. And at the opposite end are the interpreters, behind glass partitions, jabbering away into microphones in English, French, German, and Russian. You can adjust your earphone to whichever language you please. This setup, installed by the U.S. Navy, should save years of time, since it does away with the tedious business of waiting for every word spoken here to be translated into three other languages. Now the translation is simultaneous. Judge Lawrence, for example, poses a question in English to a German lawyer who understands only his own tongue. The question comes over his earphones in German. He answers in German and simultaneously the judge gets the answer in English. Thus international trials in our day, with the awful barriers of language practically wiped out.

Over the main entrance to the courtroom, one notices there is some rather bad German art work representing, I take it, eternal justice with the sword. The miserable little men in the dock and the system they built up had denied justice to all who stood in their way. Perhaps, in a rough sense, it was eternal, a durable thing you could not forever do away with despite your strength and your tyranny. Had it not, quietly and decently, returned to this little room today, as sure as death itself?

THE SENTENCES handed down by the International Military Tribunal in Nuremberg on Oct. 1, 1946:

DEATH BY HANGING: Goering, Ribbentrop, Kaltenbrunner, Keitel, Rosenberg, Frank, Frick, Streicher, Sauckel, Jodl, Seyss-Inquart, Borman.

LIFE IMPRISONMENT: Hess, Funk, Raeder.

Schirach and Speer got twenty years, Neurath fifteen years, Doenitz ten years. Schacht, Von Papen and Fritzsche were acquitted.

Borman, who was tried *in absentia,* was never found. Goering committed suicide by swallowing potassium cyanide in his cell two hours before his scheduled execution. The other ten who were condemned to death died on the gallows in the Nuremberg prison gymnasium on the morning of October 16, 1946.

MAZO DE LA ROCHE

****

*Adeline Whiteoak, Irish by birth, came from India to Canada in
1852, with her husband, Captain Philip Whiteoak, an ex-officer of
Hussars and here she lived till her death in 1926. Here she and her
family proudly cherished the customs which were their tradition.*

*It had been her ambition to live to be a hundred and she achieved
this, with a year added. I have chosen this scene of her death because it was very characteristic of her living. Also because in my
play—Whiteoaks—which had more than eight hundred performances in London and a successful run in New York, this scene was
so admirably played by Miss Nancy Price and Miss Ethel Barrymore.*

*Here we see Adeline surrounded by her family—her daughter,
Augusta, her sons Nicholas and Ernest, her four grandsons and her
grand-daughter, Meg, children of her dead son, Philip. Meg is
married to Maurice Vaughan whose illegitimate daughter, Pheasant
was an unwelcome addition to the family when she married Meg's
brother, Piers.*

*Young Finch and Adeline have a secret between them. He has
been going to her room, late at night, finding in his aged grandmother the sympathy he so greatly needed.*

MAZO DE LA ROCHE

****

Death of a Centenarian

OLD ADELINE was being dressed for tea by Augusta. That is, she
was having her hair tidied, her best cap with the purple ribbon
rosettes put on, and her box of rings displayed before her. She had
felt a little tired when she waked from her afternoon nap, so she
had had Augusta put a peppermint drop into her mouth, and she
mumbled this as she looked over her rings. She chose them with
especial care, selecting those of brilliant contrasting stones, for the
rector was to be present, and she knew that he disapproved of such
a show of jewels on such ancient hands, or indeed on any hands.

Augusta stood patiently holding the box, looking down her long nose at her mother's still longer one curved in pleasurable speculation. Adeline chose a ring—a fine ruby, set round with smaller ones. She was a long time finding the finger on which she wore it, and putting it on. The box trembled slightly in Augusta's hand. Her mother bent forward, fumbled, discovered her emerald ring, and put it on. Again she bent forward, dribbling a little from the peppermint on to the velvet lining of the box.

"Mamma," said Augusta, "must you do that?"

"Do what?"

"Dribble on the velvet."

"I'm not dribbling. Let me be." But she fumbled for her handkerchief and wiped her lips.

She put on six rings, a cameo bracelet, and a brooch containing her Philip's hair. She turned then to the mirror, adjusted her cap, and scrutinized her face with one eyebrow cocked.

"You look nice and bright this afternoon, Mamma," said Augusta.

The old lady shot an upward glance at her. "I wish I could say the same for you," she returned.

Augusta drew back her head with an offended air and surveyed her own reflection. Really, Mamma was very short with one! It took a lot of patience. . . .

Adeline stretched out her ringed hand and took the velvet-framed photograph of her Philip from the dresser. She looked at it for some moments, kissed it, and set it in its place.

"What a handsome man Papa was!" said Augusta, and surreptitiously wiped the picture with her handkerchief.

"He was. Put the picture down."

"Indeed, all our men are good-looking!"

"Aye, we're a shapely lot. I'm ready. Fetch Nick and Ernest."

Her sons were soon at her side, Nicholas walking less heavily than usual because his gout was not troubling him. They almost lifted her from her chair. She took an arm of each and said over her shoulder to Augusta, "Bring the bird along! Poor Boney, he's dull today."

The little procession moved along the hall so slowly that it seemed to Augusta, carrying the bird on his perch, that they were only marking time. But they were really moving, and at last had shuffled their way to where the light fell full upon them through the colored glass window.

"Rest here a bit," said their mother. "I'm tired." She was tall, but looked a short woman between her sons, she was so bent.

She glanced up at the window. "I like to see the light coming through there," she observed. "It's very pretty."

They were in the drawing-room, and she was established in her own chair, with Boney on his perch beside her. Mr. Fennel rose, but he gave her time to recover her breath before coming forward to take her hand and inquire after her health.

"I'm quite well," she said. "Don't know what it is to have any pain, except a little wind on the stomach. But Boney's dull. He hasn't spoken a word for weeks. D'ye think he's getting old?"

Mr. Fennel replied guardedly, "Well, he may be getting a little old."

Nicholas said, "He's moulting. He drops his feathers all over the place."

She asked Mr. Fennel about a number of his parishioners, but she had difficulty in remembering their names. Augusta, who had begun to pour tea, said in an undertone to Ernest, "I seem to notice a difference in Mamma. Her memory . . . and what a long time she was coming down the hall! Do you notice anything?"

Ernest looked toward his mother anxiously. "She did seem to lean heavily. Perhaps a little more than usual. But she ate a very good dinner. A very good dinner indeed."

Finch had come up behind them. He overheard the words, and thought he knew the reason why his grandmother showed a certain languor in the daytime. It would be strange if she did not, he thought, remembering her vigor, her clear-headedness of the night before. He had a guilty feeling that he was perhaps sapping her vitality by his midnight visits. . . . He came to his aunt's side.

Augusta handed him a cup of tea. "Take this to my mother," she said, "and then come back for the crumpets and honey."

Crumpets and honey! Finch's mouth watered. He wondered if he should ever get over this feeling of being ravenous. And yet he was so thin! He felt discouraged about himself. He wished his aunt would not send him about with tea. He invariably slopped it.

Old Adeline watched him with pursed mouth as he drew an occasional table to her side and set her tea on it. Her greed equaled his own Her hands, trembling a little, poured what tea had slopped into the saucer back into the cup, raised the cup to her lips, and drank gustily. The rings flashed on her shapely hands. Mr. Fennel marked them with disapproval.

His voice came muffled through his curly brown beard. "Well, Finch, and how goes the practising?"

"Very well, thank you, sir," mumbled Finch.

"The other night I was in my garden quite late. About eleven o'clock. I was surprised to hear the organ. You are quite welcome to use it in the daytime, you know." Gentle reproof was in his tone.

"I rather like the practising at night, sir, if you don't mind."

His eyes moved from Mr. Fennel's beard to his grandmother's face. They exchanged a look of deep complicity like two conspirators. Her gaze was clear. The tea had revived her.

She said, setting down the empty cup, "I like the boy to practise at night. Night's the time for music—for love. . . . Afternoon's the time for tea—sociability. . . . Morning's the time for—er—tea. Another cup, Finch. Is there nothing to eat?"

Pheasant appeared with tea for Mr. Fennel, and Piers with the crumpets and honey. He was in white flannels.

"Ah," observed the rector, "it is nice to see you looking cool, Piers! You looked pretty hot the last time I saw you."

"Yes, that was a hot spell. Things are easing off now. Late August, you know. The crops are in. Small fruit over. Apples not begun."

"But there is always the stock, eh?"

"Yes, always the stock. I don't get much time for loafing. But this is Pheasant's birthday, and I'm celebrating it by a day off and a clean suit."

"Her birthday, is it?" said Mr. Fennel. "I wish I had known! I would have brought some offering, if only a nosegay."

Grandmother blinked rapidly; she smacked the honey on her lips. "Pheasant's birthday, eh? Why wasn't I told? Why was it kept from me? I like birthdays. I'd have given her a present." She turned toward Meg, Maurice, and Renny, who had just come into the room. "Did you know, my dears, that we're having a birthday party? It's Pheasant's birthday, and we're all dressed up for it. Look at the rector! Look at Piers! Look at me. Aren't we trig?" She was all alive. She grinned at them, with the malicious and flashing grin for which the Courts had been famous.

Meg approached her and dropped a kiss on her forehead. "I had heard nothing of any birthday," she said coldly.

"Maurice," exclaimed Grandmother, "haven't you brought a birthday present for your daughter? Are you going to neglect old Baby just because new Baby's on the scene?"

Adeline kept on wagging her head at Renny, but now with reproof. "Too old to be nursed," she said.

"I know," replied Renny, "but he will clamber over me." He pushed Wakefield from his knee.

"'Poor darling! He looks like a young robin pushed from the nest! Tell me, did you pray for me last night?"

"Yes, my grandmother."

She looked triumphantly about her. "He never misses a night! And what did you pray?"

Wakefield drew up his eyebrows. "I prayed—let's see—I prayed" —his eyes lit on Pheasant's hand—"that you would give a present today, and—get one!"

She struck the arm of her chair with her palm. "Ha! Listen to that! A present! Now who would give me a present? No, no, I must do all the giving. Till the last. Then you can make me a present of a fine funeral. Ha!"

Nicholas growled to Ernest, "I shall have to cuff that young rascal before he'll stop this mischief of praying."

"It's very depressing for Mamma," said Ernest, gloomily. "It must be stopped."

"A game of backgammon will divert her."

Ernest looked dubious. "The last time I played with her she wasn't very clear about it."

"Never mind. She must be diverted. She's in the mood to give presents all around. I don't know what has come over her."

He found the backgammon board, and the velvet bag containing the dice and dice boxes. He said to Wakefield, hovering near, "Ask your Grandmamma and the parson if they will play backgammon. Place the small table between them. I shall cuff you if you persist in this praying business."

"Yes, Uncle Nick."

The little boy flew away, held whispered conversations, flew back. "Uncle Nick!"

"Yes."

"I've placed the table, and the parson, and Gran. They said they were nothing loath."

Finch said, "He made that last up. They didn't put it in those fool words."

"You are odious, Finch," retorted Wake. He adored his Aunt Augusta's vocabulary and had no self-consciousness in employing it.

The opponents faced each other. Bearded, untidy Mr. Fennel; gorgeous, ancient Adeline.

"I'm black," she said.

Very well, he was white. The men were placed on the tables. The dice were thrown.

"Deuce!" from the parson.

"Trey!" from Grandmother.

They made their moves. The dice rattled. The emeralds on her left hand winked.

"Doublets!"

"Quatre!" She pronounced it "cater."

The dice were shaken; the players pondered; the men were moved.

"Deuce!"

"Trey!"

"Cinq!"

"Ace!"

The game proceeded. Her head was as clear as ever it had been. Her eyes were bright. She fascinated Finch. He stood behind Mr. Fennel's chair watching her. Sometimes their eyes met, and always there was that flash between them, that complicity of conspirators. "Afraid of life!" her eyes said. "A Court afraid? Watch me!"

He watched her. He could not look away. Across the chasm of more than eighty years their souls met, touched fingers, touched lips.

One by one she got her men home. One by one she took them from the board. She had won the first game!

"A hit!" she cried, striking her hands together. "A hit!"

Two groups had formed in the room, away from the players and Finch, who stood behind the rector, and Wakefield perched on the arm of his grandmother's chair. One of these groups consisted of Meg, Nicholas, Ernest, and Augusta, who in undertones discussed what portent the gift of the ring might have. The other group was composed of Piers, Pheasant, Maurice, and Renny, who talked rather loudly, in an effort to appear unconscious that there was trouble in the air. As Grandmother cried, "A hit!" the faces of the members of both groups turned toward her, and they clapped their hands, applauding her.

"Well played, my grandmother!" cried Wakefield, patting her on the back.

Finch's eyes sought hers, found them, held them. She felt suddenly tired. She was very tired, but very happy.

"You have me badly beaten," said Mr. Fennel, stroking his beard.

"Ah, yes. I'm in good form to-day," she mumbled. "Very good form—to-night."

Boney shuffled on his perch, shook himself, gaped. Two bright feathers were loosened, and sank slowly to the floor.

Mr. Fennel stared at him.

"He doesn't talk now, eh?"

"No," she answered, craning her neck so as to see the bird. "He doesn't talk at all. Poor Boney! Poor old Boney! Doesn't talk at all. Doesn't say curse words. Doesn't say love words. Silent as the grave, hey, Boney?"

"Shall we have another game?" asked Mr. Fennel.

The two groups had resumed their preoccupations. Renny's laugh broke out sharply.

"Another game? Yes, I'd like another game. I'm white!"

Mr. Fennel and Wakefield exchanged glances.

"But, Gran," cried Wakefield, "you were black before!"

"Black! Not a bit of it, I'm white."

Mr. Fennel changed the men, giving her the white ones.

The men were placed. The dice shaken. The game proceeded.

"Deuce!"

"Cinq!"

"The Doublet!"

But her head was no longer clear. She fumbled for her men, and could not have got through the game had not Wakefield, leaning on her shoulder, helped her with the play.

She was beaten, but she did not know it.

"A double game!" she said, trimphantly. "A double game! Gammon!"

The rector smiled indulgently.

Finch felt himself sinking beneath a cloud.

"But, my grandmother," cried Wakefield, "you're beaten! Don't you know when you're beaten?"

"Me beaten? Not a bit of it. I won't have it! I've won." She was staring straight ahead of her into Finch's eyes. "Gammon!"

Mr. Fennel began gathering up the men.

"Another game?" he asked. "You may make it backgammon, this time."

She did not answer.

Wakefield nudged her shoulder. "Another game, Gran?"

"I'm afraid she's a little tired," said Mr. Fennel.

But she was still smiling, looking straight into Finch's eyes. Her eyes were saying to him, "A Court afraid? A Court afraid of death? Gammon!"

Again Boney shook himself, and another feather fluttered to the floor.

Nicholas had risen to his feet, and was looking across the room. Suddenly he shouted, "Mother!"

They were all on their feet, except Wakefield, who still hung on her shoulder, realizing nothing.

Her head sank.

Finch watched them as they gathered about her, raising her head, holding smelling salts to her long nose, forcing brandy between her blanched lips, wringing their hands, being frightened, half-demented. He had seen her spirit, staunch and stubborn, leave the body. He knew it was futile to try to recall it.

MORLEY CALLAGHAN

****

TORONTO, CANADA
FEB. 2, 1950

Rigmarole, the story, had an odd little history. When I first wrote it it couldn't be sold anywhere and so it found a haven in Story Magazine. *Most of my favorite editors seemed to think it was an elusive piece. But when it appeared in my book of stories,* Now That April's Here, *a number of critics singled it out as having a special interest. Then some years passed and it was suddenly translated into a number of European languages, and finally it was reprinted all over again in one of the big circulation magazines. In the beginning, when I wrote it I was surprised when no one seemed enthusiastic about it because I thought I had got down something I saw happening under my eyes again and again. So the story had to make its own way.*

MORLEY CALLAGHAN

****

Rigmarole

AFTER they had come in from the party, Jeff Hilton, the advertising man, looked up and saw his young wife, Mathilde, standing there beaming at him. She seemed to him to be glowing from the memory of many whispered conversations with young men who had been anxious to touch her hand or her arm; she smiled and went on dreaming and her wide dark eyes grew soft with tenderness. She began to hum as she walked over to the window and stood there looking down at the street in the early winter night; and as Jeff went on watching her he kept resenting that she should have had such a good time at a party that he had found so dull. She had left him alone a lot, but he had always remained aware of the admiration she aroused in the young men around her. And now she turned, all warm and glowing, and burst out, "Didn't you like the party, Jeff?"

333

"It was a lousy party," he said vindictively, "I'm fed up with that crowd. No one ever has anything new or bright to say. They've all gone a little stale."

Mathilde tried to stop smiling, but her dark, ardent face still glowed with warmth as she stood there with her hands clasped in front of her. Though Jeff went on talking with a kind of good-humored disgust his earnest face began to show such a desolate loneliness that she suddenly felt guilty; she longed to offer up to him all the tenderness, all the delight it had been so enchanting to have in her since the party. "I had an awfully good time," she said. "But I kept my eye on you. I know who you were with. Were you watching me, Jeff?" and she rushed over to him and threw herself on his lap and began to kiss him and rub her hand through his hair, laughing all the time like a little girl. "Did you think I was flirting? Did you think I laughed and whispered too much? Don't you love people to think I'm pretty?"

But Jeff, who had such a dull time, felt only that she was trying to console him and make him feel good; so he said irritably, "You don't need to feel you neglected me. Don't feel guilty. Nobody ever has to worry about me trailing you around. You can feel free."

"Jeff," she said very softly, "I don't want to feel free. I don't feel free now."

"Sure you do. You'd be the first to complain if you didn't."

"Didn't you worry a little about me once tonight, Jeff?"

"Listen here, Mathilde," he said shortly, "jealous men are the greatest bores in the world."

"Jeff, put your arms around me."

"What's the matter with you? You don't need to mollify me or feel guilty because you had a good time. Surely we've got beyond that."

"I wasn't trying to mollify you," she said, looking quite lost, and she began to show in her face much of that curious discontent he had felt growing in her the last three months. She was pouting like a child and she had the shame of one whose innocent gift has been rejected curtly, and then she went away from him awkwardly and curled herself up on the couch, almost crouching, her eyes hardening as she stared at him.

After a while he said, "You're childish, Mathilde. Why are you sitting there as if you hate me?" But he began to feel helpless against her silent, unreasonable and secret anger. "These last few months you've become about as unreasonable as a sick woman. What on earth is the matter with you?" he said. And he got up and paced up and down and his voice rose as he went on questioning her, but every time he passed the couch where she was crouching he became more disturbed by the passionate restlessness he felt in her.

So he tried to laugh and he said, "This is a lot of nonsense, Mathilde," and he sat down beside her. In a rough, good-natured way he tried to pull her against him. When she pushed him away he stared at her for a long time till at last he began to desire her, and again he put his arm around her, and again she pushed him away. Then he lost his temper; he threw his arms around her and held her down while he tried to caress her. "Stop it, stop it, Jeff!" she cried. "Haven't you got any sense at all? Doesn't it mean anything to you that you didn't want me near you a few minutes ago? What do you think I am?" As she pulled away roughly she was really pleading with him to see that she was struggling to hold on to something he had been destroying carelessly month after month. "Doesn't it mean anything?" she asked.

"There you go," he said. "Why can't you be direct about things instead of sentimental?"

"Because I don't want things that way," she said. And then she cried passionately, "You can't touch me whenever you like. You can't do that to me just when you feel like it," and her eyes were full of tears as if at last she had touched the true source of all her disappointment.

But he grabbed hold of her, held her a moment to show he could possess her, then pushed her away. "I'm not a little boy playing that old game," he shouted. "We've been married three years. Why all the rigmarole?" and he expressed the rage that was growing in him by banging her on the knee with his fist.

"Oh, you've hurt me," she said, holding the spot. "Why did you do that?" and she began to cry a little. "That ends it. You'll never hit me again," she said.

"Damn it all, I didn't hit you."

"You did. Oh, dear, you did! That settles it. I'll not stay around here! I'll not stay another night! I'm going now!"

"Go ahead. Do what you want to."

"Don't worry. I'll soon be gone," she said, and with tears streaming from her eyes she ran into the bedroom. He stood gloomily at the door with his arms folded across his chest. He watched her pull out drawers, toss dresses into a suit case, sweep silver at random from the top of the dresser. Sometimes she stopped to press her fists against her eyes. He began to feel so distressed, watching, that he shouted at last, "I won't stand for this stupid exhibition!" and he jumped at her and flung his arms around her and squeezed her as though he would crush forever the unreasonable revolt in her soul. Then he grew ashamed and said, "I won't stop you, and I won't stay and watch this stupid performance either. I'm going out." And when he left her she was still pulling out dresser drawers.

As soon as Jeff walked along the street from the apartment house on that early winter night he began to feel that he really had not left that room at all, that wherever he walked, wherever he went, he would still be pulled back there to the room to watch her, and when he went into the corner tavern to have a glass of beer he sat there mopping his forehead and thinking, "Not just when I want, not just when I feel like it! I can't go on with that stuff when we're so used to each other. I'd feel stupid."

In the crowded tavern men and women leaned close together and whispered and while he listened Jeff kept hearing her voice beneath the murmuring voices and the clink of glasses and seeing her face in the smoke of the tavern, and as he looked around a dreadful fear kept growing in him that whatever was warm and vital among people was being pushed out of his reach; and then he couldn't stop himself from getting up and hurrying back to the apartment house.

He saw her coming out wearing her brown coat, and her felt hat was pulled down over her eyes. She was carrying her bag. A taxi was waiting. In a foolish way, to hide his eagerness, he smiled and said, "May I take the bag for you, madam?" He even made a little bow.

"No, thanks," she said, and she swayed the bag away from his outstretched hand, looking at him in that shy pleading way.

"Are you sure you wouldn't like me to take it?"

"Quite sure," she said.

"All right," he said politely, and he stood there trying to smile while she got into the cab, and when the cab actually moved off along the street, he stood there, worried and unbelieving, feeling there was no place to go.

But he went into the apartment and as he wandered aimlessly into the bedroom and looked at the empty dresser drawers his loneliness deepened, and he thought, "I tried to use some common sense anyway. She'll come back. If I went on struggling with her like that all the time I'd never be able to hold my job. I'll bet a million dollars she'll be back."

And he waited and was desolate remembering the shy pleading

look in her eyes as she swayed the bag away from him on the sidewalk, and he listened for every small sound from the street, the stairs and the door; and when at last he heard the key turning in the lock he jumped up triumphantly and rushed to meet her.

She came in quietly with a timid, apologetic smile, and as she pulled off her hat she said in a bantering tone, "What were you doing, Jeff? What was keeping you up till this hour?"

"Waiting for you, of course."

"You mean you missed me?"

"Sure I missed you. You know I did, too," he said. He helped her off with her coat, begged her to sit down, rushed to the icebox to get a snack for them and his face kept showing all of his childish triumph. She was delighted to be waited on in this different way. Every time the broad smile came on his face she asked, "What are you laughing at Jeff?"

"How does it feel to be free?" was all he said.

But when they were going to bed and she had buried her dark head in the pillow she began to cry brokenly, and no matter how he coaxed her, or how gently he spoke she would not be quiet. "Aren't we happy now, Mathilde? Isn't it all over now," he kept on saying.

"No, I'm not happy. I can't bear it," she said.

"You can't bear what?"

"The way you let me go. No matter what happened I didn't think you'd ever let me go. You wouldn't have done it two years ago."

"But you wanted to go, Mathilde, and if I thought you wanted to . . ."

"Two years ago you would have made me come back. You would have been afraid of losing me."

"I knew you'd come back like a homing pigeon."

"Yes, you were so sure of it. You were so very sure," she said, and then she put her hands over her face and she turned her head away, mumbling, "I'm silly. I guess I sound silly. I guess I don't know what I want," and he could only see the back of her neck and her hand moving over her cheek.

As he walked around the bed, looking at her, he thought, "Why didn't I stop her? Why can't she see that knowing we love each other is better than worrying that we don't," but he began to feel terribly afraid. "Nobody loves insecurity," he said, knowing his words sounded weak and apologetic. For a while he watched her, then went to speak, but he found himself shyly fumbling what seemed to be old words; so he stood there, silent, with his love becoming an ache, for it seemed a terrible thing that such words should sound strange just because they had grown used to each other. Then he knew that his fear had been that he would never be able to express all the feeling he had for her. And all he said was, "I had a glass of beer at the corner and I began to feel terrible."

"Did you?" she said without looking up.

"I think I know what you've been missing," he said.

"Yes," she said.

"I couldn't stay away from here," he said. "I felt you'd be pulled back too."

She looked up at him timidly for though the words he used were neither new, nor warm, nor strange, she began to feel his awkward shyness, she began almost to hear him thinking. "What happens that you can't keep showing your love when it's so strong in you?" She just waited there and grew shy too, and the feeling between them at that moment seemed so much deeper than any earlier time of impulse and sudden joy.

MARIANO AZUELA

****

MEXICO CITY

In my novel Los de Abajo, *are found the most direct and intensely alive experiences of the lower class of Mexico. I belong to the middle class and perhaps due to this fact middle class types have attracted me less. In order to write most of my novels I have been able to have direct contact with the common people, which revealed their manners, customs and feelings. I have never succeeded better with my material than in* Los de Abajo, *since revolutions have the characteristic of stripping individuals no matter from what class they come.*

MARIANO AZUELA

[*The excerpt Mr. Azuela has chosen shows the day-to-day fighting between the two factions in the Mexican Revolution. Azuela as a doctor in 1914 and 1915 accompanied the fighting forces on the side of the "under dogs" who for four centuries lived a life of servitude. The novel was published in Mexico and after a few years was suddenly translated into many languages and had a world-wide sale.*]

****

The Under Dogs

On the day General Natera began his advance against the town of Zacatecas, Demetrio with a hundred men went to meet him at Fresnillo.

The leader received him cordially.

"I know who you are and the sort of men you bring. I heard about the beatings you gave the Federals from Tepic to Durango."

Natera shook hands with Demetrio effusively while Luis Cervantes said:

"With men like General Natera and Colonel Demetrio Macias, we'll cover our country with glory."

Demetrio understood the purpose of those words, after Natera had repeatedly addressed him as "Colonel."

Wine and beer were served; Demetrio and Natera drank many a toast. Luis Cervantes proposed: "The triumph of our cause, which is the sublime triumph of Justice, because our ideal—to free the noble long-suffering people of Mexico—is about to be realized and because those men who have watered the earth with their blood and tears will reap the harvest which is rightfully theirs."

Natera fixed his cruel gaze on the orator, then turned his back on him to talk to Demetrio. Presently, one of Natera's officers, a young man with a frank open face, drew up to the table and stared insistently at Cervantes.

"Are you Luis Cervantes?"

"Yes. You're Solís, eh?"

"The moment you entered I thought I recognized you. Well, well, even now I can hardly believe my eyes!"

"It's true though!"

"Well, but. . . . Look here, let's have a drink, come along." Then: "Hm," Solís went on, offering Cervantes a chair, "since when have you turned rebel?"

"I've been a rebel the last two months!"

"Oh, I see! That's why you speak with such faith and enthusiasm about things we all felt when we joined the revolution."

"Have you lost your faith or enthusiasm?"

"Look here, man, don't be surprised if I confide in you right off. I am so anxious to find some one intelligent among this crowd, that as soon as I get hold of a man like you I clutch at him as eagerly as I would at a glass of water, after walking mile after mile through a parched desert. But frankly, I think you should do the explaining first. I can't understand how a man who was Correspondent of a Government newspaper during the Madero régime, and later editorial writer on a Conservative journal, who denounced us as bandits in the most fiery articles, is now fighting on our side."

"I tell you honestly: I have been converted," Cervantes answered.

"Are you absolutely convinced?"

Solís sighed, filled the glasses; they drank.

"What about you? Are you tired of the revolution?" asked Cervantes sharply.

"Tired? My dear fellow, I'm twenty-five years old and I'm fit as a fiddle! But am I disappointed? Perhaps!"

"You must have sound reasons for feeling that way."

"I hoped to find a meadow at the end of the road, I found a

swamp. Facts are bitter; so are men. That bitterness eats your heart out; it is poison, dry-rot. Enthusiasm, hope, ideals, happiness—vain dreams, vain dreams. . . . When that's over, you have a choice. Either you turn bandit, like the rest, or the time-servers will swamp you. . . ."

Cervantes writhed at his friend's words; his argument was quite out of place . . . painful. . . . To avoid being forced to take issue, he invited Solís to cite the circumstances that had destroyed his illusions.

"Circumstances? No—it's far less important than that. It's a host of silly, insignificant things that no one notices except yourself . . . a change of expression, eyes shining—lips curled in a sneer—the deep import of a phrase that is lost! Yet take these things together and they compose the mask of our race . . . terrible . . . grotesque . . . a race that awaits redemption!"

He drained another glass. After a long pause, he continued:

"You ask my why I am still a rebel? Well, the revolution is like a hurricane: if you're in it, you're not a man . . . you're a leaf, a dead leaf, blown by the wind."

Demetrio reappeared. Seeing him, Solís relapsed in silence.

"Come along," Demetrio said to Cervantes. "Come with me."

Unctuously, Solís congratulated Demetrio on the feats that had won him fame and the notice of Pancho Villa's Northern division.

Demetrio warmed to his praise. Gratefully, he heard his prowess vaunted, though at times he found it difficult to believe he was the hero of the exploits the other narrated. But Solís' story proved so charming, so convincing, that before long he found himself repeating it as gospel truth.

"Natera is a genius!" Luis Cervantes said when they had returned to the hotel. "But Captain Solís is a nobody . . . a time-server."

Demetrio Macías was too elated to listen to him.

"I'm a Colonel, my lad! And you're my secretary!"

Demetrio's men made many acquaintances that evening; much liquor flowed to celebrate new friendships. Of course men are not necessarily even-tempered, nor is alcohol a good counselor; quarrels naturally ensued. Yet many differences that occurred were smoothed out in a friendly spirit, outside the saloons, restaurants or brothels.

On the morrow, casualties were reported. Always a few dead. An old prostitute was found with a bullet through her stomach; two of Colonel Macías' new men lay in the gutter, slit from ear to ear.

Anastasio Montáñez carried an account of the events to his chief. Demetrio shrugged his shoulders.

"Bury them!" he said.

"They're coming back!"

It was with amazement that the inhabitants of Fresnillo learned that the Rebel attack on Zacatecas had failed completely.

"They're coming back!"

The rebels were a maddened mob, sunburnt, filthy, naked. Their high wide-brimmed straw hats hid their faces. The "high hats" came back as happily as they marched forth a few days before, pillaging every hamlet along the road, every ranch, even the poorest hut.

"Who'll buy this thing?" one of them asked. He had carried his spoils long: he was tired. The sheen of the nickel on the typewriter, a new machine, attracted every glance. Five times that morning the Oliver had changed hands. The first sale netted the owner ten pesos; presently it had sold for eight; each time it changed hands, it was two pesos cheaper. To be sure, it was a heavy burden; nobody could carry it for more than a half-hour.

"I'll give you a quarter for it!" Quail said.

"Yours!" cried the owner, handing it over quickly, as though he feared Quail might change his mind. Thus for the sum of twenty-five cents, Quail was afforded the pleasure of taking it in his hands and throwing it with all his might against the wall.

It struck with a crash. This gave the signal to all who carried any cumbersome objects to get rid of them by smashing them against the rocks. Objects of all sorts, crystal, china, faïence, porcelain, flew through the air. Heavy, plated mirrors, brass candlesticks, fragile delicate statues, Chinese vases, any object not readily convertible into cash fell by the wayside in fragments.

Demetrio did not share the untoward exaltation. After all, they were retreating defeated. He called Montáñez and Pancracio aside and said:

"These fellows have no guts. It's not so hard to take a town. It's like this. First, you open up, this way. . . ." He sketched a vast gesture, spreading his powerful arms. "Then you get close to them, like this. . . ." He brought his arms together, slowly. "Then slam! bang! whack! crash!" He beat his hands against his chest.

Anastasio and Pancracio, convinced by this simple, lucid explanation answered:

"That's God's truth! They've got no guts! That's the trouble with them!"

Demetrio's men camped in a corral.

"Do you remember Camilla?" Demetrio asked with a sigh as he settled on his back on the manure pile where the rest were already stretched out.

"Camilla? What girl do you mean, Demetrio?"

"The girl that used to feed me up there at the ranch!"

Anastasio made a gesture implying: "I don't care a damn about the women . . . Camilla or anyone else. . . ."

"I've not forgotten," Demetrio went on, drawing on his cigarette. "Yes, I was feeling like hell! I'd just finished drinking a glass of water. God, but it was cool . . . 'Don't you want any more?' she asked me. I was half-dead with fever . . . and all the time I saw that glass of water, blue . . . so blue . . . and I heard her little voice, 'Don't you want any more?' That voice tinkled in my ears like a silver hurdy-gurdy! Well, Pancracio, what about it? Shall we go back to the ranch?"

"Demetrio, we're friends, aren't we? Well then, listen. You may not believe it, but I've had a lot of experience with women. Women! Christ, they're all right for a while, granted! Though even that's going pretty far. Demetrio, you should see the scars they've given me . . . all over my body, not to speak of my soul! To hell with women: They're the devil, that's what they are! You may have noticed I steer clear of them. You know why. And don't think I don't know what I'm talking about. I've had a hell of a lot of experience and that's no lie!"

"What do you say, Pancracio? When are we going back to the ranch?" Demetrio insisted, blowing gray clouds of tobacco smoke into the air.

"Say the day, I'm game. You know I left my woman there too!"

"Your woman, hell!" Quail said, disgruntled and sleepy.

"All right, then, our woman! It's a good thing you're kind-hearted so we all can enjoy her when you bring her over," Manteca murmured.

"That's right, Pancracio, bring one-eyed Maria Antonia. We're all getting pretty cold around here," Meco shouted from a distance.

The crowd broke into peals of laughter. Pancracio and Manteca vied with each other in calling forth oaths and obscenity.

"Villa is coming!"

The news spread like lightning. Villa—the magic word! The

Great Man, the salient profile, the unconquerable warrior who, even at a distance, exerts the fascination of a reptile, a boa-constrictor.

"Our Mexican Napoleon!" exclaimed Luis Cervantes.

"Yes! The Aztec Eagle! He buried his beak of steel in the head of Huerta the serpent!" Solís, Natera's Chief of Staff, remarked somewhat ironically, adding: "At least, that's how I expressed it in a speech I made at Ciudad Juárez!"

The two sat at the bar of the saloon, drinking beer. The "high hats" wearing mufflers around their necks and thick rough leather shoes on their feet, ate and drank endlessly. Their gnarled hands loomed across table, across bar. All their talk was of Villa and his men. The tales Natera's followers related won gasps of astonishment from Demetrio's men. Villa! Villa's battles! Ciudad Juárez . . . Tierra Blanca . . . Chihuahua . . . Torreon. . . .

The bare facts, the mere citing of observation and experience meant nothing. But the real story, with its extraordinary contrasts of high exploits and abysmal cruelties was quite different. Villa, indomitable Lord of the Sierra, the eternal victim of all Governments. . . . Villa tracked, hunted down like a wild beast . . . Villa the reincarnation of the old legend; Villa as Providence, the bandit, that passes through the world armed with the blazing torch of an ideal: to rob the rich and give to the poor. It was the poor who built up and imposed a legend about him which Time itself was to increase and embellish as a shining example from generation to generation.

"Look here, friend," one of Natera's men told Anastasio, "if General Villa takes a fancy to you, he'll give you a ranch on the spot. But if he doesn't, he'll shoot you down like a dog! God! You ought to see Villa's troops! They're all northerners and dressed like lords! You ought to see their wide-brimmed Texas hats and their brand-new outfits and their four dollar shoes, imported from the U.S.A."

As they retailed the wonders of Villa and his men, Natera's men gazed at one another ruefully, aware that their own hats were rotten from sunlight and moisture, that their own shirts and trousers were tattered and barely fit to cover their grimy, lousy bodies.

"There's no such thing as hunger up there. They carry box cars full of oxen, sheep, cows! They've got cars full of clothing, trains full of guns, ammunition, food enough to make a man burst!"

Then they spoke of Villa's aeroplanes.

"Christ, those planes! You know when they're close to you, be

damned if you know what the hell they are! They look like small
boats, you know, or tiny rafts . . . and then pretty soon they begin
to rise, making a hell of a row. Something like an automobile going
sixty miles an hour. Then they're like great big birds that don't
even seem to move sometimes. But there's a Joker! The god-damn
things have got some American fellow inside with hand-grenades
by the thousand. Now you try and figure what that means! The
fight is on, see? You know how a farmer feeds corn to his chickens,
huh? Well, the American throws his lead bombs at the enemy just
like that. Pretty soon the whole damn field is nothing but a grave-
yard . . . dead men all over the dump . . . dead men here . . . dead
men there . . . dead men everywhere!"

Anastasio Montáñez questioned the speaker more particularly. It
was not long before he realized that all this high praise was hearsay
and that not a single man in Natera's army had ever laid eyes on
Villa.

"Well, when you get down to it, I guess it doesn't mean so much!
No man's got much more guts than any other man, if you ask me.
All you need to be a good fighter is pride, that's all. I'm not a professional soldier even though I'm dressed like hell, but let me tell
you. I'm not forced to do this kind of bloody job, because I
own . . ."

"Because I own over twenty oxen, whether you believe it or not!"
Quail said, mocking Anastasio.

The firing lessened, then slowly died out. Luis Cervantes, who
had been hiding amid a heap of ruins at the fortification on the
crest of the hill, made bold to show his face. How he had managed
to hang on, he did not know. Nor did he know when Demetrio and
his men had disappeared. Suddenly he had found himself alone;
then, hurled back by an avalanche of infantry, he fell from his
saddle; a host of men trampled over him until he rose from the
ground and a man on horseback hoisted him up behind him. After
a few moments, both horse and riders fell. Left without rifle, revolver or arm of any kind, Cervantes found himself lost in the midst
of white smoke and whistling bullets. A hole amid a débris of
crumbling stone offered a refuge of safety.

"Hello, partner!"

"Luis, how are you!"

"The horse threw me. They fell upon me. Then they took my
gun away. You see, they thought I was dead. There was nothing
I could do!" Luis Cervantes explained apologetically. Then:

"Nobody threw me down," Solís said. "I'm here because I like
to play safe."

The irony in Solís' voice brought a blush to Cervantes' cheek.

"By God, that chief of yours is a man!" Solís said. "What daring,
what assurance! He left me gasping—and a hell of a lot of other
men with more experience than me, too!"

Luis Cervantes vouchsafed no answer.

"What! Weren't you there? Oh, I see! You found a nice place
for yourself at the right time. Come here, Luis, I'll explain; let's go
behind that rock. From this meadow to the foot of the hill, there's
no road save this path below. To the right, the incline is too sharp;
you can't do anything there. And it's worse to the left; the ascent
is so dangerous that a second's hesitation means a fall down those
rocks and a broken neck at the end of it. All right! A number of
men from Moya's brigade who went down to the meadow decided
to attack the enemy's trenches the first chance they got. The
bullets whizzed about us, the battle raged on all sides. For a time
they stopped firing, so we thought they were being attacked from
behind. We stormed their trenches—look, partner, look at that
meadow! It's thick with corpses! Their machine guns did for us.
They mowed us down like wheat; only a handful escaped. Those
god-damned officers went white as a sheet; even though we had
're-enforcements they were afraid to order a new charge. That was
when Demetrio Macías plunged in. Did he wait for orders. Not he!
He just shouted:

" 'Come on, boys! Let's go for them!'

" 'Damn fool!' I thought. 'What the hell does he think he's
doing!'

"The officers, surprised, said nothing. Demetrio's horse seemed
to wear eagle's claws instead of hoofs, it soared so swiftly over the
rocks. 'Come on! Come on!' his men shouted, following him like
wild deer, horses and men welded into a mad stampede. Only one
young fellow stepped wild and fell headlong into the pit. In a few
seconds the others appeared at the top of the hill, storming the
trenches and killing the Federals by the thousands. With his rope,
Demetrio lassoed the machine guns and carried them off, like a
bull herd throwing a steer. Yet his success could not last much
longer, for the Federals were far stronger in numbers and could
easily have destroyed Demetrio and his men. But we took advantage of their confusion, we rushed upon them and they soon cleared
out of their position. That chief of yours is a wonderful soldier!"

Standing on the crest of the hill, they could easily sight one side of the Bufa peak. Its highest crag spread out like the feathered head of a proud Aztec king. The three hundred foot slope was literally covered with dead, their hair matted, their clothes clotted with grime and blood. A host of ragged women, vultures of prey, ranged over the tepid bodies of the dead, stripping one man bare, despoiling another, robbing from a third his dearest possession.

Amid clouds of white rifle smoke and the dense black vapors of flaming buildings, houses, with wide doors and windows bolted, shone in the sunlight: The streets seemed to be piled upon one another, or wound picturesquely about fantastic corners, or set to scale the hills nearby. Above the graceful cluster of houses, rose the lithe columns of a warehouse and the towers and cupola of the church.

"How beautiful the revolution! Even in its most barbarous aspect it is beautiful," Solís said with deep feeling. Then a vague melancholy seized him, and speaking low:

"A pity what remains to do won't be as beautiful! We must wait a while, until there are no men left to fight on either side, until no sound of shot rings through the air save from the mob as carrion-like it falls upon the booty; we must wait until the psychology of our race, condensed into two words, shines clear and luminous as a drop of water: *Robbery! Murder!* What a colossal failure we would make of it, friend, if we, who offer our enthusiasm and lives to crush a wretched tyrant, became the builders of a monstrous edifice holding one hundred or two hundred thousand monsters of exactly the same sort. People without ideals! A tyrant folk! Vain bloodshed!"

Large groups of Federals pushed up the hill, fleeing from the "high hats." A bullet whistled past them, singing as it sped. After his speech, Alberto Solís stood lost in thought, his arms crossed. Suddenly, he took fright.

"I'll be damned if I like those plaguey mosquitoes!" he said, "Let's get away from here!"

So scornfully Luis Cervantes smiled that Solís sat down on a rock quite calm, bewildered. He smiled. His gaze roved as he watched the spirals of smoke from the rifles, the dust of roofs crumbling from houses as they fell before the artillery. He believed he discerned the symbol of the revolution in these clouds of dust and smoke that climbed upwards together, met at the crest of the hill and, a moment after, were lost. . . .

"By heaven, now I see what it all means!"

He sketched a vast gesture, pointing to the station. Locomotives

belched huge clouds of black dense smoke rising in columns; the
trains were overloaded with fugitives who had barely managed to
escape from the capture town.

Suddenly he felt a sharp blow in the stomach. As though his legs
were putty, he rolled off the rock. His ears buzzed. . . . Then darkness . . . silence. . . . Eternity. . . .

GABRIELA MISTRAL

****

The poems of Gabriela Mistral, selected by herself, are presented here in their first translation into English. The style of this South American winner of the Nobel Prize for Literature has been considered difficult to carry over in its fullness from the Spanish she uses as a Chilean. "I could not reproduce exactly the meter and rhyme of Gabriela Mistral's poetry and remain faithful to the vigor and vitality of her poems," says her translator, Frances P. Mousseau. "I have chosen instead to translate in free verse and retain the meaning and vigorous expression in the poems as near to the original as possible."

****

Three Poems

INTIMATE

Do NOT PRESS my hands.
The everlasting time of rest will come
with dust and darkness
in my intertwined fingers.

And you would say: "I cannot
love her because her fingers shatter
like ripe wheat.

Do not kiss my mouth.
The full instant will come
in waning light, when I, fleshless,
without lips shall lie in damp earth.

And you would say:—"I loved her
but I cannot love her longer,
for now she breathes not
the fragrance of my kiss."

349

And it will distress me hearing you,
and you will speak madly and blindly,
and my hand will be on your forehead
when my fingers wither,
and my breath will descend over
your anguished face.

Don't touch me, therefore. I would lie
in saying that I deliver to you my love
in these extended arms,
on this mouth, in this throat of mine
and you, believing that you drank it all,
would be deceived like a blind child.

Because my love is not alone
this stubborn and tired grain sheaf of my body,
that trembles totally with the haircloth friction
and falls from me in full wind.

It is in the kiss, and it is not the mouth;
it hoarsens the voice and it is not the breast:
it is a breath of God, that passes through me
cleaving the torn branch of my flesh, in flight!

THE FOOTPRINT*

To Eduardo Mallea

OF THE fugitive man
I have only the footprint,
the weight of his body
and the wind that carries it.
Neither address nor name,
nor country nor hamlet;
only the humid shell
of his footprint;
only this syllable
silent in sandprint
and the earth image whisper
in tones indistinct!

* Fugitives from the war and escapists from xenophobia in Europe and
elsewhere.

Only the anguish
that hastens his step:
the pounding pulse,
the gleaming sweat,
the panting gust,
the teeth-edged longing
and the wind dry and hard,
which lashes his back!

And the brambles he leaps,
the swamp that he flies,
the thicket that hides him,
and the sun that reveals him,
the dune that aids him,
another that stays him,
and the pine which fells him,
and God who erects him!

And his lifestream, his blood,
which cries out behind him:
the footprint, merciful God,
the scarlet footprint:
the voiceless cry,
the streaked footprint!

May the holy sands
consume his footprint.
May the dogs of mist
conceal his footprint.
May the coming night
remove at once
his mark of man
sweet and tremendous,
alive and delivered
free as the doe!

I see, I count
the infinite footprints.
I go running, running
over the ancient Earth,
breaking with mine
your poor footprint!

Either I stop
and my mad braids erase it,
or face downward my mouth
touches the footprint!

But the white Earth becomes
totally eternal;
it stretches endlessly
chainlike and immortal;
it lengthens rope-fashion
which God transcendental
preserves without break!
And your footprint continues
to the end of the world!

POEM OF THE SON

To Alfonsina Storni

I

A SON, a son, a son! I wanted a son of yours
and mine, in those days of ardent ecstasy,
when my very bones trembled at your murmur
and my face burned with a broad radiance.

I would say, "a son," as the tree sighs
with Spring and stretches its branches skyward.
A son with large and Christlike eyes,
and wide-eyed expression and eager lips!

Your arms, a garland around my neck entwined;
the fertile river of my life descending to him,
and my innermost being, like spilling perfume,
anointing in its path the hills of the world.

On passing a pregnant woman, we look at her
with twisted lips and prayerful eyes,
when, consumed with love, we pass among the multitude.
And there we were dazzled by a child with sweet eyes!

In those nights, wakeful with joy and dreams,
the fire of lust did not visit my bed.

For him who would be born clothed in song,
I stretched out my arms, I hollowed my breast.

The sun seemed not too intense for bathing;
I looked at my knees and hated their roughness;
my confused heart trembled at the immense gift;
and humble weeping watered my cheeks!

And I feared not death, foul destroyer;
the eyes of the little one would free yours from nothingness,
and by brilliant morning or at twilight
I would have passed under that shadowed death glance.

II

Now I am thirty, and the precocious ashes
of death sprinkle my temples. During my days now
bitterness drops with slow tear, salty and cold,
like the eternal rain of the earth's poles.

While the flame of the pine burns, quietly,
looking within I think what a son of mine
would have been, an infant with my tired mouth,
my bitter heart and my conquered voice.

And with your heart, the fruit of poison,
and your lips that would have denied again.
Forty moons might pass ere he slept on my breast,
and only because of you might he have forsaken me.

And in what gardens in flower, next to what running waters
might he wash, in Spring, his blood of my sorrow,
if I went sadly into merciful lands,
and in one whole mystic afternoon it would speak in his veins.

And the horror that one day with mouth burning
with rancor, he might say to me what I said to my father:
"Why has your sobbing flesh been fertile
and filled the breasts of my mother with nectar?"

I feel a bitter pleasure that you sleep below
in your earthen bed, and my hand does not rock a son,

for I sleep also without labors and without remorse,
under a fierce bramble of thorns.

Because I might no longer close my lids,
and madly I might hear across death,
and it would pierce me through, knees melted, mouth twisted,
If I should see him pass with my fever in his face.

And the truce of God might not descend to me:
in innocent flesh the wicked ones might wound me,
and through eternity my veins might speak aloud
in my sons with eyes and face enraptured.

Blessed be my breast in which I submerge my people
and blessed be my belly in which my race dies!
The face of my mother no longer will cross the world,
Nor her voice, borne on the wind, be permuted in miserere!

The forest become ashen will resound a hundred times
and it will fall a hundred times, mature, under the axe.
I shall fall once not to arise again in the month of harvest;
with me enter all mine into the everlasting night.

And if I should pay the debt of a race,
sorrows pierce my breast like a beehive.
I live an entire life in each hour that passes;
like the river toward the sea, my veins flow bitterness.

My poor dead ones look at the sun and the west winds,
with tremendous anguish, because now in me they grow blind,
my lips become tired of fervent prayers
which, before I am silent, emerge through my song.

I did not sow for my granary, I did not teach to make
for myself a loving arm for the final hour,
when my broken body no longer will sustain me
and my hand measures thoughtfully the thin sheet.

I taught the children nearby,
I heaped the granary with divine wheat,
and I only await you, Our Father who art in Heaven!
Receive your entreating servant, if in this night I die!

—Translated by Frances P. Mousseau

PABLO NERUDA

****

SANTIAGO, CHILE

Among my works, I have chosen a poem I am including, Alturas
de Macchu Picchu* *which I estimate the most representative of
my last production. It has not yet been included in any of my books.
First appeared in* Expressión *(1947), a literary magazine of Buenos
Aires, and then published in* Confluences *(1947), a literary magazine of Paris (translated into French by Roger Callois); is almost
an unknown piece of my work among a big portion of my readers.
This poem represents a tendency in my literary development to con-
fine and devote my efforts to my continent, America, its land, people
and culture. This tendency is visible in all of my poems which have
appeared in several Latin American periodicals lately. Part of them
are ready to be printed by Editorial Losada of Buenos Aires, this
year, under the name of* Canto General.

PABLO NERUDA

[*The following translation, specially prepared for* THE WORLD'S
BEST, *is the first English rendering of* Alturas de Macchu Picchu.]

****

* Translator's Note: *The ancient fortress city of Macchu Picchu, cradle
of the Inca Empire, is located more than 12,000 feet above sea-level in
the most inaccessible corner of the Peruvian Andes. Built some 3000 years
B. C., this oldest American city was lost for many centuries before it was
uncovered and excavated by Hiram Bingham in 1912. Although the roofs,
which were made of thatch, are gone, the city is still almost intact: a
terraced city of narrow streets, rock-hewn stairways (over a hundred of
them, some of more than 150 steps), walls (some of them curved) of
granite blocks, beautifully fitted together, a temple with sundial, mono-
lithic lintels, windows, hanging gardens. From the excavations of Macchu
Picchu the silver rings, bronze knives, bone needles, exquisite terra cotta
and pieces of pottery with complex decorations bear eloquent testimony to
the advanced techniques and aesthetic expressions of this early Inca civilization. Further details are given in Hiram Bingham's articles in* The
National Geographic Magazine *April 1913, February 1915 and May 1916,
and in his book* Lost City of the Incas *(1948).*
*In Neruda's long quest for the essence of America, it is fitting that he
should be inspired by these ruins. After the philosophical introduction,
the poet climbs up to Macchu Picchu (Stanza VI) and contemplates the
geology, geography and history of the Inca city, and reflects upon man's
cruelty to man and the meaning of "eternal" verities.*

Summits of Macchu Picchu

I

FROM AIR to air, like an empty net,
between the streets and the atmosphere, I arrived and bade
    farewell,
with the advent of autumn, to the lengthened coin
of the leaves, and, between the spring and the tassels,
to that which the greatest love, as if within a glove,
delivers us in falling like a long moon.

(Days of splendor I live in the elements
of bodies: steel reduced
to the silence of acid:
evenings ravelled unto the ultimate flour:
assaulted stamens of the nuptial fatherland.)
Someone awaiting me among the violins
discovered a world like a buried tower
sinking its spiral deeper than all
the leaves the color of acrid sulphur:
deeper still, into the gold of geology,
like a sword wrapped in meteors,
I sank my hand sweet and turbulent,
into the inmost terrestrial genital.
I placed my forehead amid the waves
deep,
descended like a drop into the sulphurous peace,
and, like a blindman, returned to the jasmine
of the spent human spring.

II

If the flower to the flower delivers the lofty germ
and the rock retains its disseminated flower
within its battered gown of diamond and sand,
man crumples the petal of the light which gathers
in certain nautical springs
and pierces the throbbing metal in his hands.
And then, amid the clothes and the smoke, on the sunken table,
like a shuffled quantity, there remains the soul:
quartz and sleeplessness, tears in the ocean

like pools of cold: nevertheless
slay it and torture it with paper and with hate,
immerse it in the quotidian carpet, rend it
on the hostile clothing of the wire.

No: along corridors, air, sea, or roads,
who can guard without a poignard (like incarnadine
poppies) his blood? Fury has wasted
the sad merchandise of the seller of souls,
and, from the height of the plum tree, the dew
of a thousand years leaves its clear letter
upon the same branch that awaits it, oh heart, oh forehead crushed
between the cavities of autumn!
How many times in wintry city streets or in
a bus or a boat in the twilight, or in the thickest of
solitudes, that of a party, under the sound
of shadows and bells, in the very grotto of human pleasure,
have I longed to stop to seek the fathomless eternal vein
which once I felt in the stone, or in the lightning loosed by a kiss.

(That which in the cereal like a story yellow
with small pregnant breasts goes on reiterating a number
which ceaselessly is tenderness in germinal layers
and which, forever identical, is threshed into ivory,
and that which in the water is transparent fatherland, bell
from the isolated snow unto the bloody waves.)

I could hold but a cluster of faces or fleeting masks,
like a ring of empty gold,
like the clothes of an angry autumn's daughters scattered
in shaking the miserable tree of terrified races.

I had no place to rest my hand,
a place which, gushing like water from a dammed-up spring,
or hard like a grume of anthracite or crystal,
would have returned the cold or the warmth of my outstretched
      hand.
What was man? In what part of his conversation begun
amid shops and whistles, in which one of his metallic movements
dwelt the indestructible, the imperishable, life?

III

Like an ear of corn man was threshed in the endless
granary of lost deeds, of squalid
events, from one to seven, to eight,
and not one death but many deaths came to each one:
each day a little death, dust, worm, lamp
which is extinguished in the mud of the slums, a little death with
    fat wings
penetrated each man like a short lance:
and man was hounded by bread or by knife:
cattleman, son of the ports, obscure captain of the plough
or gnawer of thick streets,
each one fainted awaiting his death, his brief daily death,
and their dread affliction of every day
was like a black cup from which they drank trembling.

IV

Powerful death has many times invited me:

it was like the salt invisible in the waves,
and the emanations from its invisible savor
were half like sinkings and half like height
or vast constructions of wind and snowdrift.

I came to the ferrous edge, to the narrows
of the air, to the winding sheet of stone and agriculture,
to the stellar emptiness of the last steps,
and to the vertiginous spiral road:
but broad sea, oh death! you do not come wave on wave,
but like a burst of evening brightness,
or like the total numbers of the night.

Never have you rummaged in my pocket, never
possible your visit without raiment of red:
without auroral carpet encircled in silence:
or high or buried legacies of tears.

I could not love in every man a tree
that bore within itself its little autumn (the death of a thousand
    leaves),
all the false deaths and the resurrections
without earth, without abyss:

I wanted to swim in the broadest lives,
in the freest river-mouths,
and when little by little men rejected me
and barred my step and my door lest with my gushing hands
I touch their wounded non-existence,
then I went along street and street and river and river
and city and city and bed and bed,
and my salty mask traversed the desert,
until in the last humiliated hovel, without lamp, without fire,
without bread, without stone, without silence, alone,
I rolled over dying my own death.

V

It was not you, grave death, iron-feathered bird,
not you the wretched heir of the rooms
bore between quick repasts, beneath his empty skin:
it was something, a poor petal of disintegrated rope:
an atom of his breast which did not join the combat
or of acrid dew which did not fall upon his temple.
It was that which could not be reborn, a particle
of little death with neither peace nor territory:
a bone, a bell dying within him.
I lifted the iodine bandages, put my hands
into the poor sorrows that were murdering death,
and I found in the wound but a cold draft
pervading the vague interstices of the soul.

VI

Then up the ladder of the world I climbed,
past the terrible tangle of the lost forests,

unto you, Macchu Picchu.

Lofty city of laddered stones,
ultimate abode of him whom the earthly
did not hide in robes of sleep.
In you as in two parallel lines
the cradle of the lightning and of man
rocked in a wind of thorns.
Mother of stone, foam of the Condors.

Lofty reef of the human dawn.

Shovel lost in the first sand.

This was the home, this is the site:
here the broad kernels of corn ascended
and descended again in the form of red hail.

Here the gold thread came from the vicuña
to dress the loves, the tombs, the mothers,
the king, the prayers, the warriors.
Here at night man rested his feet
beside the feet of the eagle, in lofty
carnivorous lairs, and at dawn
trampled with feet of thunder the rarefied mist,
feeling the ground and the stones
unto recognition by night or in death.
I see the garments and the hands,
the vestige of the water in the echoing chasm,
the wall rubbed smooth by the touch of a countenance
who watched with my eyes the terrestrial lamps,
who oiled with my hands the vanished
wood: for everything, clothes, furs, pots,
.words, wine, bread,
is gone, crumbled to the ground.
And the air came in with fingers
of orange blossoms upon all the sleeping ones,
a thousand years of air, months, weeks of air,
of blue wind, of ferrous mountain range,
like gentle, stepping hurricanes
polishing the lonely site of the stone.

VII

Dead men of a single abyss, shadows of one ravine,
the deep one, was it to contain
your magnitude
that there came such a veritable, such a blistering
death that from the perforated rocks,
from the scarlet capitals of the columns,
from the laddered aqueducts,
you fell, as if in an autumn,
in simultaneous death?

Today the empty air no longer weeps,
no longer knows your feet of clay,
forgotten already your jugs which once filtered the sky
pierced by the knives of the lightning,
and the powerful tree was consumed
by the mist, and felled by the gale.

Hands uplifted dropped abruptly
from the summit to the end of time.
Now you exist not, hands of spider, fragile
threads, entangled cloth,
whatever you were has collapsed: customs, wornout
syllables, masks of dazzling light.

But a permanence of stone and of word:
the city like a cup was raised in the hands
of all, the living, the dead, the silent, sustained
by so much death, a wall, by so much life a blow
of stone petals: the permanent rose, the domicile:
this Andean reef of glacial colonies.

When the clay-colored hand
turned to clay, and when the small eyelids,
filled with rough walls, peopled with castles, closed,
and when the whole man became enmeshed in his burrow,
there remained aloft exactitude:
the lofty site of the human dawn:
the loftiest vessel holding silence:
a life of stone after so many lives.

VIII

Climb up with me, American love.

Kiss with me the secret stones.

The torrential plant of the Urubamba
flings its pollen to its yellow cup.
Flung is the emptiness of the clinging vine,
the stony plant, the petrified garland,
over the silence of the rocky gorge.

Come, tiny life, between the wings
of the earth, while—crystal and cold, battered air—
past combated emeralds,
oh savage water, you descend from the snow.
Love, love, unto the sudden night,
from the sonorous Andean flint
to red-kneed dawn,
behold the blind son of the snow.

Oh Wilkamayu of sonorous threads,
when you shatter your lineal thunders
in white foam, like wounded snow,
when your steep gale
singing and lashing awakens the sky,
what language do you bring to the ear barely
torn from your Andean foam?

Who captured the lightning of the cold
and left it enchained on the summit,
dispersed in glacial tears,
shaken its rapid swords,
stricken its martial stamens,
borne on its warrior's bed
prostrate to its rocky finale?

What is it your troubled waters are saying?
Did once your secret mutinous lightning
travel populated with words?
Who is it that goes by shattering frozen syllables,
black languages, gold banners,
fathomless mouths, muffled shouts,
in your thin arterial waters?

Who is it that goes by clipping the floral eyelids
which come out of the earth to see?
Who speeds the dead branches
which cascade down your hands
to thresh their night threshed
in the carbon of geology?

Who flings down the cluster of ties?
Who buries again the farewells?

Love, love, do not touch the frontier,
do not adore the sunken head:
let time fulfill its stature
in its parlor of broken brooks,
and, between the swift water and the walls,
gather the air of the gorge,
the parallel sheets of the wind,
the blind canal of the mountain ranges,
the acrid salute of the dew,
and climb, flower by flower, through the thickness,
trampling the fallen serpent.

In craggy zone of stone and forest,
dust of green stars, clear woods,
Mantur bursts like a living lake
or like a new floor of the silence.

Come to my own being, to my very dawn,
unto solitudes enthroned.

The dead kingdom still lives.

And across the clock the sanguinary shadow
of the Condor passes like a black bird.

IX

Sidereal eagle, vine of mist.
Lost bastion, blind scimitar.
Starry belt, solemn bread.
Torrential ladder, vast eyelid.
Triangular tunic, pollen of stone.
Mineral serpent, rose of stone.
Buried ship, brook of stone.
Horse of moon, light of stone.
Equinoctial T-square, steamboat of stone.
Final geometry, book of stone.
Iceberg wrought by the gales.
Madrepore of sunken time.
Wall by fingers softened.
Roofs by feathers assailed.
Clusters of mirrors, foundations of tempest.
Thrones overturned by the clinging vine.

Reign of the pitiless claw.
Whirlwind suspended on the slope.
Motionless cataract of torquoise.
Patriarchal bell of the sleeping.
Shackle of subjugated snows.
Iron lying upon its statues.
Inaccessible barred tempest.
Hands of puma, sanguinary rock.
Lofty tower, discussion of snow.
Night upraised in fingers and roots.
Window of the mists, petrified dove.
Nocturnal plant, statue of thunders.
Essential mountain range, nautical roof.
Architecture of lost eagles.
Twine of the sky, bee of the heights.
Bloody level, constructed star.
Mineral bubble, quartz moon.
Andean serpent, amaranth forehead.
Dome of silence, pure fatherland.
Beloved of the sea, tree of cathedrals.
Cluster of salt, cherry tree of black wings.
Snowy teeth, cold thunder.
Scratched moon, threatening stone.
Mane of the cold, action of the air.
Volcano of hands, dark cataract.
Wave of silver, direction of time.

X

Stone within the stone, man, where was he?
Air within the air, man, where was he?
Time within time, man, where was he?
Were you too the broken fragment
of uncompleted man, of empty eagle
who through the streets of today, through the footprints,
through the leaves of the dead autumn,
grinds the soul unto the grave?
Poor hand, foot, poor life . . .
Luminous days wasted
in you like rain
on the pennants of the fiesta,
did they give petal by petal of their dark nourishment
unto your empty mouth?

Hunger, man's coral,
hunger, secret plant, woodcutters' root,
hunger, did your reef-frontier extend
to these lofty landslid towers?

I ask you, salt of the roads,
show me the spoon, allow me, architecture,
to know with a stick the stamens of stone,
to mount the steps of the air to the void,
to probe the entrail till I touch the man.
Macchu Picchu, did you put
stone upon stone and, at the base, a rag?
coal upon coal and, at the bottom, a tear?
fire in the gold and, within it, trembling,
the great red drop of blood?
return unto me the slave you buried!
Shake from the ground the hard bread
of the wretched, show me the clothes
of the serf and his window.
Tell me how he slept when he was alive.
Tell me if his sleep was
raucous, half open, like a black hole
bored by fatigue in the wall.
The wall, the wall! Tell me if upon his sleep
there weighed every floor of stone, and if he fell beneath it
as beneath a moon, with sleep!

XI

Across the confused splendor,
across the night of stone, let me plunge my hand
and let throb within me, like a bird imprisoned for a thousand
    years,
the ancient heart of the forgotten one!
Let me now forget this joy which is broader than the sea,
for man is broader than the sea and its islands,
and one must fall into him as into a pool
to emerge with a spray of secret water and sunken truths.
Let me forget, broad stone, the mighty proportions,
the transcendental measurement, the stones of the honeycomb,
and from the T-square let now my hand
slide down the hypotenuse of acrid blood and haircloth.

When, like a horseshoe of red elytra, the frantic Condor
strikes my temples in its flight
and the gale of bloodthirsty feathers whirls the sombre dust
of the sloping perron, I do not see the swift beast,
I do not see the blind cycle of its claws,
I see the ancient human being, the serf, the sleeper
in the fields, I see a body, a thousand bodies, a man, a thousand
      women.

Under the black blast,
with your heavy statue of stone,
blackened by the rain and by the night—
John Stonecutter, son of Wiracocha,
John Coldeater, son of the green star,
John Barefoot, grandson of the torquoise—
come with me, brother, to be born.

XII

Come with me, brother, to be born.
Extend me your hand from the deep
zone of your transmitted anguish.
Never will you come back from the depths of the rocks.
Never will you come back from subterranean time.
Never will your petrified voice come back.
Never will your perforated eyes come back.
Behold me from the depths of the earth,
plowman, weaver, silent shepherd:
tamer of the tutelary guanacos:
hewer of the challenged scaffolding:
waterer of the Andean tears:
jeweler of the bruised fingers:
sower trembling in the seed:
potter poured into your clay:
bring unto the cup of this new life
your ancient buried sorrows.
Show me your blood and your furrow.
Tell me: here I was punished
because the gem did not shine or the earth
deliver in time the stone or the grain:
Point out to me the stone upon which you fell
and the wood upon which you were crucified.
Set afire for me the ancient flints,

the ancient lamps, the whips stuck fast
in your wounds through the centuries
and the axes shining with blood.
I come to speak through your dead mouth.
From across the world gather all
the silent lips dispersed,
and from out of the depths talk to me all this long night through
as if I were there with you anchored.
Tell me everything, chain by chain,
link by link, and step by step,
sharpen the knives you used to keep,
place them on my breast and on my hand,
like a river of yellow sparks,
like a river of buried tigers,
and let me weep, hours, days, years,
blind ages, stellar centuries.

Give me the struggle, the volcanoes, the iron.

Affix your bodies unto mine, like magnets.

Enter my veins and my mouth.

Speak through my words and my blood.

—Translated by Angel Flores

EDUARDO MALLEA

****

*I am forty-six years old. I have written seventeen books. I have
destroyed three. I have had to begin my literary apprenticeship
anew each day. I have received more kindness than I thought I
deserved, and I have obtained the relative success which can be
hoped for by an author who writes in Spanish and who was born
near a bay of the South Atlantic, far from great centers of literature where literary values are determined. I have learned things
with pain and forgotten them with ease. I have sacrificed many
comforts for literary work. I have always written with suffering. It
has grieved me a great deal that I have not yet achieved the degree of skill and broadness that I wished for my production. I do
not like to discuss literature with my friends, and I always felt a
secret kinship for the Portuguese writer Eça de Queiroz, who lived
for many years in England. His friends, whom he always treated
with a gracious and consummate politeness, found out only after
his death that that pleasant and unassuming man was in addition
a writer, one of the greatest that Portugal had known. And in his
country, when they would look for him in order to praise him, he
would say with the great elegance of a well-bred person: "I am
only a simple man from Povoa de Varzim."*

*Perhaps at times I could wish that I had not found in my life
the hard and terrible fate of creating. But since it has been thrust
upon me, I have accepted it willingly and even with enthusiasm.
I have often allowed myself to be guided by the illusion that every
authentic poetic idea is a stimulus for the human heart; and that
by writing, I, although such an insignificant person, might do something for the benefit of mankind, even though my readers be few
and my message so imperfect and insufficient.*

*I have written a good deal about the men of my country, about
their lands, their illusions and their dreams. I have traveled through
other countries and other literatures. And in that way my indebtedness was becoming so great that I thought I would not rest until
I finished, in the chapters of the vast letter of my books, a sort of
fervent epistle or long story, told to all my friends in the world,
without raising my voice, by the side of a fire or near the shore of
a river, in which would be gathered the histories of certain beings*

whose destiny seemed to me admirable, or whose dreams I shared,
or whose tragedies caused me to think, or whose sleeplessness or
whose dramas held for me a mysterious and strange significance. I
am in the midst of that long narration. And I hope to tell it until
my strength gives out and the characters appear to be moving far-
ther away, like the spirit of the sad heroes in an ancient tragedy.

EDUARDO MALLEA

****

Pillars of Society*

SUDDENLY, unexpectedly, as at a magical word of command, the
lights flashed on, flooding the drawing-room with what was almost
a lunar radiance. The fleshy yellowish portait of Cardinal Wolsey,
so moribund among the shadows, became transformed into something brilliant and alive. Every corner of the room was illuminated,
bathed gloriously in light. The innumerable prisms of the Louis
Seize chandelier shivered with it, it was caught and tossed back by
the shining black tile of the floor. Mrs. Rague's treasures were
dazzlingly displayed, with such ostentation, indeed, such regal
splendor that the scene might have been laid for a court reception
instead of an ordinary private party.

Between all these fine objects, so haphazardly collected, so alien
to each other, a sort of *entente* had been established. They seemed,
in a way, to speak together as do guests who meet in the same home
and derive from the unity of their background a certain communal
understanding, a fleeting but genuine warmth. There were singular
and yet effective conversational units: the freesias strewn, like a
thousand starry faces, over the length of a carved Greek bench
with a *Dolorosa* made of jade; while, from the wall near-by, the
effigy—attributed to Hieronymus Bosch—of a Knight Templar,
fiery and tortured, seemed to appeal, with bloodstained mouth and
an anguished gesture, to the cool white flowers for surcease. Another
dialogue, of marked though discreet tone, obtained between three
small coffers of the Ming Dynasty and a pure cone of Aztec gold.

It was nine o'clock. Dignified, severely smiling, Mrs. Rague came
down the stairs, ready to take her position by the door. The shadow
of a great white orchid lay over her bare, freckled, and somewhat

*From Fiesta in November.

sunken chest. With a slight motion of eyes and chin she beckoned to her husband, who was following her down at a meditative and unhurried pace, It was, as he well knew, a minatory gesture and he hastened to get into place beside her, imitating at the same time her formal smile, like one who takes part in a ceremonial rite.

At this moment the doorman came up to Mrs. Rague for last-minute instructions. Having received them, he bowed and turned on his heels, but she checked him with her dry and acrimonious voice: 'Have you understood?' The servant's glance shied away from those icy eyes. He nodded timidly and went back to his post.

Mrs. Rague embarked on a low-toned and desultory conversation with her husband. Fulano had said he would come, Mengano that he would not. It would have been preferable to have Mengano rather than Fulano. Nevertheless, though the latter was unquestionably an idiot, it was important to have him see the three famous knockers of Saint George and those choir seats she wanted to dispose of.

From the winter garden next to the dining-room came the broken yet harmonious sound made by plucking a stringed instrument. The members of the orchestra were tuning up, the delicate 'ping' of the plucked strings giving way occasionally to a more full-bodied tone as the bow was swept across them. The pianist was leaning over the keyboard. He had a hungry face paled by powder and he scanned the score anxiously with his myopic eyes.

Like a vaudeville number which must be punctually timed, the first six guests made their entrance together: four women of various ages, all smelling of the same fashionable perfume, their heads sleek and shining with brilliantine, and two elderly diplomats. One of them had lyric hair, curling thickly and parted in the middle in the Southern style. The other's features were lean and unhealthy; he looked like an Erasmus devoured from within by doubt and worry but not unmindful of worldly pomp.

'Jílgoles!' Without paying any attention to protocol, Mr. Rague clasped in both his own the milky white hand, like an abbot's, of the curly-haired diplomat. The other he greeted with greater reserve, feeling almost instinctively that, at a certain time of life, one has already taken sides, chosen one's friendships according to a private system of values.

Mrs. Rague, meanwhile, touched lightly the hands of the four women, giving each the same regimented smile, the same lift, crinkling the high forehead, of her brows. She was far less influenced by personal predilections than her husband, but she knew that there were unfailing ways to limit a too confidential approach or cut short an excess of temperament. An opportune hoarseness, a calculated distraction, and everything was under control again.

'I thought I was going to be late,' one of the women was babbling. 'I was so absorbed, one of those quite unexpected enthusiasms. Ruskin, you know. He's too delicious, I couldn't stop reading.' She gurgled lusciously and went on without stopping for breath: 'I suppose I'm awfully impressionable. Things come home to me so . . . Oh, it isn't just books. A flower might do it, a lovely animal, the configuration of a cloud. All I know is that suddenly I'm caught by a sort of enchantment, almost paralyzed. It's just the way a cobra . . .' Her voice faltered, trailed off under Mrs. Rague's unvarying stare. She laughed abruptly: 'How silly I am!' A purplish stain dyed her cheeks, the brilliant sensual eyes shifted uneasily. The other women looked at her with barely concealed curiosity.

A brazen clangor sounded from the winter garden, where some metallic instrument had fallen to the floor. The women jumped. But Mrs. Rague showed no sign of disturbance; she merely stepped forward a little to greet newly arriving guests. Meanwhile, her husband ended his conversation with Jílgoles and proceeded to devote himself to his duties. The old diplomat followed the four women into the interior of the drawing-room, embracing them lightly with his greedy connoisseur's glance.

'You were talking about Ruskin,' he purred pleasantly. 'Certainly, he is always the modern, the eternal modern, I might say.'

Lucrecia Batros derived no comfort from this recruit to an enthusiasm hours old and already stale, an enthusiasm, moreover, which had caused her to suffer embarrassment. Emitting the pretty coquettish shriek of the overcivilized female, she pounced upon a beautiful crystal sphere which stood in elegant solitude upon a table near-by. Jílgoles smiled at her like one who understands all. 'As Gongora remarked,' he said, 'a serpent lurks in rock crystal.' The other man, the one with the meager intolerant Erasmian face, was obviously annoyed by this literary ostentation. He took his wife's arm and led her to another part of the room, to that point, exactly, where the effigy of the Knight Templar hung on the wall and sent its tortured appeal into space.

Marta came downstairs spiritlessly. She had put on a very light dress which harmonized with the freshness of her coppery body and with the expression, at once inhibited and savagely desperate, in her great gray eyes. (One would believe her won and suddenly

those eyes revolted, became desperate . . .) Her straight short
shining hair was brushed back smoothly from the temples. It was
still very wet; she had not felt like drying it after her bath. Before
hurrying downstairs, she stopped before a mirror in the hall, stared
at herself, and gave a quick pat to her hair. Then, almost precipi-
tately, but with her mind far away, she made her descent.

What, after all, did that sea of faces mean to her, that sea into
which in another moment she would plunge? Faces, minds, souls—
could one dare to expect that, hidden in one of them, there might
be a human message, some trace, not corrupted but pure, of an
instinct beyond dull cupidity and the desire for an easy and sheltered life? No, that was asking too much. Animals react with a
quick candor which resembles intelligence, they leave no doubt of
what they like or detest. But these people were always on guard,
mannered, egotistical, ready to put on a show. Their outward fervor
was accompanied by an inner apathy which was comparable only
with death.

She shrugged, herself indifferent. Two years ago, when she had
first begun to see through them, they had filled her with loathing.
That feeling was gone now, replaced by a sort of passive contempt,
a dry hard pity which it was hardly worth while indulging since
what caused it was so fundamentally inert. It was enough that she
had been able to rid herself of the slow and deadly poison which
had filtrated into her from years of contact with that species of
mind. Now she was immune to it, even having them beside her,
even exchanging with them the arid and conventional words which
formed the acknowledged code of their kind.

She entered the drawing-room. Immediately there was a buzz
around her and three young men approached her with demonstra-
tive enthusiasm. The youngest of them, who stammered, held his
cocktail glass high in greeting. Soon all those obliging male hands
were offering her other glasses and Marta took one without looking
to see from whom it came. Her lips were dry with thirst. The mixed
odor of lemon and gin was as revivifying as smelling-salts, and she
breathed it in before drinking. Glass in hand, she went on greeting
people, giving each a smile, a word, glancing now and then at a
rose, at the freesias, the native jasmine.

That quick and sidelong glance did not fail to take in, meanwhile, a general picture of the elegant creatures who crowded the
room. Isolated at one end it was a little group of visitors linked
to each other by the noble affinity of birth, bearers of illustrious
names: the Pieláride, the Muniagurri, the Ugué; at the other end

were the diplomats, from the Ambassador himself to the discreet
secretary of the chancellery; in between—listening to Mr. Rague,
who was at that moment involved in an enthusiastic but rather
vague description of a vase which he claimed had been saved from
the ruins during the notorious massacre on Saint Bartholomew's
Eve—were the opulent bourgeoisie. The worst of them were dressed
by the best tailors, plump painted ladies who were expiatory victims
of Patou and Coco Chanel, and men who seemed too large for their
brief frock coats, none of them, however, despised by Eugenia
Rague.

'Marta! My treasure!' Mr. Rague, with the air of a victim,
appealed to his daughter for assistance in these ceremonial duties.

'Isn't everybody here?' people were murmuring. It was time to
go in to dinner. 'We'll wait awhile longer,' Mr. Rague muttered.
His worried eyes wandered from the door to the place where his
wife was standing. If Ráices shouldn't come, he thought, but his
lips were saying something entirely different: '. . . of course, politics require one to look at things from a radical point of view, radical in the sense that it goes to the heart of the matter, leaving no
doubt. The moment a man hesitates he has stopped being a politician . . .' His face, greenish by now, was nevertheless perfectly
composed; nobody could have denied that, at the moment, he was
the very incarnation of prudence and good sense, even of sagacity.
He felt a slight moisture on his forehead, his upper lip, and wiped
it off with the white linen handkerchief.

'In conclusion . . .' One of the blue-blood contingent was holding
forth, with measured sententiousness, to an audience composed of
three young girls and two serious-looking men. Behind his head, a
quite accidental background, hung a tapestry depicting the *Descent
from the Cross.* 'The only action worthy of these times is extermination. Sweep out, purify . . .' He paused, took a swallow of gin and
tonic. 'The world belongs to the *élite.* To become better it should
belong altogether to those races which have been purified by their
history and their private tradition. We should apply—indeed, we
are backward if we do not—the excellent solution of the Tarpeian
Rock: whoever does not carry his letters patent in his blood must
pay for his bad luck. Destiny is not made, one is born with it.
Everyone not born to lead is born to be exterminated. *A bon
entendeur . . .*'

Marta rolled her eyes and saw Drabble near-by, standing alone
and drinking with concentration. She remembered the night, three

months ago, when a poor unfortunate woman had tried to kill
herself outside the night club. They had struggled with her heroically, she and Drabble, and had finally brought her to her senses.
Seen in the light of that fugitive episode, Drabble seemed to her
a man of honest mind, sane and mature. She would have liked to
join him now, but, before she had finished collecting her thoughts,
she was again surrounded by garrulous idiots, laughing with them
over some stupid anecdote.

Black shining heads and blond ones, perfumed and waved.
Springy waists, gracious lips, teeth dazzling white under the lights.
Men who argued, women who laughed, girls of a disturbing restless
charm. Old protruding bellies adorned with linked chains and the
two inevitable pearl studs. Insidious faces, faces of frigid women,
glances that went hunting through the room with a kind of desperate reserve. The waxed black floor had almost disappeared, lost
in the continuous movement of black trousers and trailing silken
skirts.

Phrases, bits of phrases, isolated words. Marta kept hearing them
as she moved through the room, her ears tuned unwillingly to that
absurd siren song. It brought to mind so many familiar things—
books, art, endless talk—and it roused the familiar feelings of boredom, of uselessness and pain. All her life now seemed to her a dull
and trivial sacrifice to what was essentially a stereotype, one, moreover, which had no chance of survival. The thought of it pounded
in her brain like a discordant and increasingly strident march,
chords swelling and breaking and incessantly beginning again. A
great march of doom, grimly sonorous and at the same time cloy-
ingly, ineffably sweet. Childhood and youth, perhaps even old age;
the sticky sweetness held her fast, she was caught in it as a fly is
caught in fly paper. With anguished effort it may lift a foot, but
the attempt to free itself is useless, body and wings remain glued to
the paper, and finally the foot drops back again, the fly is finally
conquered by the thick sweet force of the molasses.

She saw her father run and throw his arms joyously around
Ráices. Good! they could go in to dinner at last; it would mean a
little less contact with all these people. She remembered how,
when she was a little girl, her mother had made her sit, dumb and
solemn, at the dining-table and how she had thought longingly of
the children playing outside in the street, the flowers, the fish in
the pond, the rustle of leaves in the afternoon wind. The whole

world outside was alive and free. There were the passions: fear, pleasure, true pain; the cities and people; fire, water, earth, and air; there was experience in all its fullness.

Now, with the glass in her hand, brooding and silent among the lights and rich draperies, the garrulous laughing throng of people, she thought again of that other world 'outside,' of the universe which was not molasses, not just pretentious decay. The stupidity of her days, past, present, and future, seemed to her appalling; it aroused in the unfree intimate center of her being a curious obsessive rage.

Marta lifted her glass and drained it to the last drop. A tall man in a frock coat with faded receding hair asked to be presented to her. He stood before her stiff as a Prussian, smiled suddenly, then as suddenly became serious again. Taking out his cigarette case, he offered it around, lit a cigarette himself, and, without saying anything, looked at her fixedly, as though waiting for her to speak.

At this moment, Mr. Rague lifted his right hand and gestured in the general direction of the dining-room. With the other, he still clutched tightly the bent thin arm of Ráices. The guests who were sitting down rose with almost automatic precision and joined in the march toward the table. The next act, thought Marta, feeling on her own cold arm the arm of the man whose name was beside hers on the place cards.

The penetrating odor of lavender, of perfumes and naphtha, seemed to grow stronger as they moved. Filing into the dining-room, the serried rows of frock coats and light dresses had somewhat the air of a wedding procession, with the erect skeleton-like figure of Mrs. Rague in first place. Her small steely eyes ranged quickly over the table, inspected the servants who were standing at attention. She was as pleased and exalted by this party of hers as the Admiral, her revered and beloved Nelson, must have been before Trafalgar.

He practically burst into the house. Tossing his hat down in the cloakroom, he rushed through the first gap of doors, questioned the servants, walked only a little less hurriedly through the drawing-room, and then, with a sensation of relief, shoved in among the guests who were beginning to take their seats at the table. He had no time to greet Mr. Rague, he was himself already in the dining-room, swept on by that confused tide of men and women. He paused for a moment, nodding to this side and that in courteous salutation.

He had damp shining hair, irregularly parted, and an extraordinarily mobile face. The veins on his forehead were rather swollen. ('Ah, we'll have to use the electric needle on those,' Doctor Islas had told him, and he had answered: 'Another kind of life would do the trick even better. Less worry, less probing of the soul, not so many confusing questions and answers.') He glanced quickly up and down the length of the enormous table, hunting for his place; at last he found it and breathed deeply, 'Aah,' noting with pleasure that his neighbors were not yet in theirs.

Other people were sitting down, pulling out their chairs with the monotonous sound of wood scraping against wood. It seemed to him that the eyes of all these strangers were concentrated upon his forehead, focusing on the very spot where he could feel the pounding of his acclerated heart-beats. (How could that doctor cure him who had no weapons except a little science and a curious Spinozistic twist to his mind? His science wouldn't work, nor his way of saying, 'Pleasure is obviously never bad, but good; grief, on the other hand, is obviously bad.')

He was always late everywhere. Certain profound proclivities were simply not subject to modification. Nevertheless, in this case— the splendid-looking woman at his left; not so splendid the one at the right, stout and too ripe, she looked like the wife of a mayor— nevertheless, in this case, he should really have made a greater effort to be on time. With a smile curving her moist and charming lips, the young lady on the left offered him her hand. There were two rows of magnificent pearls around her powdered white throat. Julia Carves, the place card read. Yes, his effort should have been greater since the unexpected invitation from Mrs. Rague assumed, on her part, an attitude of good will toward him and his work.

Maybe it was just a capricious gesture; more probably, she had been impressed by what the English Ambassador had said to him a week ago, in reference to that painting of his in the Exposition: 'Such delicacy of design; your way of painting the crossed hands can be compared only to Giotto's. And that magnificent force of expression is very like van der Weyden.' Mrs. Rague, to judge from her surprised and enchanted air, must have taken these comparisons literally. She had come up to him at once and looked at him with a certain almost insolent greed. 'Do you admit a genuine kindred with the men of the Renaissance? What is your idea of the relation between painting and life? Should one be subordinate to the other —or is art completely independent?' She had kept on looking at him voraciously, like a district attorney who expects the poor fish at the bar to condemn himself out of his own mouth. He had laughed, good-naturedly, and replied with skillful and evasive urbanity: 'Madam, all I see is the form and color of things, the form and color of creation. I won't deny, however, that the way I see forms and colors may sometimes be affected by my private contradictions and exaltations.' It was, while tending to the didactic, a rather neat answer and it brought a friendly smile to Mrs. Rague's fleshless cheeks—a rare concession, indeed. The smile seemed to be compounded half and half of pride in her own question and approval for him. Such was the happy circumstance responsible for the invitation to this dinner at which he had arrived, as usual, late and out of breath.

The stout and mayoral lady favored him with an amiable smile. Miss Carves, at his left, was talking to her other neighbor. Quite serene now, he lifted the cup of consommé and studied the entire aspect of the table. This spectacle in which he was not only an actor but of which he was at the moment the only, though still somewhat absent-minded witness, this show of sumptuous bosoms, of smiling eyes and laughing exclamations, of heads inclining now toward this side, now toward that, seemed to him full of reticence and mysterious ingenuity.

His wandering eyes were suddenly arrested, meeting in perfect coincidence another pair of eyes, still and gray, cool in their transparency, singularly alone. They belonged to a woman sitting obliquely across the table from him, a woman with delicate high shoulders and a lovely coppery throat, superbly elegant, but with a touch of youthful solemnity about her, grave and silent as a child between the garrulous men who besieged her on either side. Not just for a second, but for perceptible moments they looked, they looked at each other, and it was his glance which was withdrawn first. The withdrawal was the result of an injunction from within; his lively pride did not permit him to deviate from his own reflective simplicity by seeming to ape the arrogant and falsely aristocratic manner affected by certain of the bourgeoisie. If he was here at all, it was out of politeness and perhaps because of the demands of an art which had to be passed around to achieve its purpose and sold like other merchandise.

This necessity had always infuriated him and he refused even to recognize it except in his darkest moments when everything seemed finished, anyway, and he was resigned to see himself as merely a single cell, without excessive importance in the collective organism. . . . He turned away his eyes and lifted the cup of consommé to his

lips. It was glutinous, pleasantly chilled. He drank, taking no part
in the conversation going on around him, not amused any longer
but innerly bound—and aware of it—because of the influence, the
near presence of that marvelous woman sitting almost across the
table from him. She was laughing now, no longer abstracted in
spirit but gay, the whole upper part of her body turned toward the
animated fashion plate at her left. He had a lean dark sensual face;
throwing back his head in convulsive rapture, he would shout,
'Splendid! Quite splendid!' at some point she brought up and then
return to the monotonous tone of his ordinary speech.

. . . He lifted his eyes again, this time without deliberate intention, merely as a natural reaction to the movement of the waiter
who was setting a fresh plate before him. The young woman's
guard was down; she seemed unconscious of her surroundings,
staring ahead into space. For a moment, and it was like a kind of
possession, he felt, full on his forehead, the impact of that gaze—
weary, distraught, and sad.

Replete, their faces glowing, the guests scattered about the garden
and the drawing-room. Time to dance! The orchestra was ready,
the violins nostalgically prepared to reconquer lost ground as a
Strauss waltz took the place of the syncopated symphonies. Standing near the open door which led to the garden, the conductor
lifted his baton and smiled, a smile enthusiastic, almost triumphant,
as though he were leading, not this small phalanx of musicians with
whose debts, miseries, and squabbles he was so wearisomely familiar,
but a brilliant and tightly packed ensemble, the aristocracy of
music, figures genuinely potent beneath their apparent obsequiousness.

The garden was enormous and lit only along the borders of the
lawns by small delicately swaying lanterns. But, on the open platform where five or six couples were already dancing, a powerful
spotlight threw its spectral rays. . . . Lintas remained in the drawing-room, sipping his coffee. His table companions had been
snatched away by their jealous husbands and he stood by himself,
solitary in all that luxurious stir, next to a tall column holding a
Greek statuette. He knew that Marta was dancing outside in the
garden, but he preferred to wait for her here, patiently, like a contemplative stranger who hardly expects, amid so much gaiety, a
response to his own essential loneliness. What difference did it
make? His case, as far as it concerned the rest of the world, was
already lost. He asked for no concession from the benevolence of

others; he would have been content, indeed, if they had forgotten him entirely. Was it not the way to reach that enjoyment known only by those who have nothing—or everything? He always remembered those lines of Thomas Hardy's in which the author remarks that one may have the air of a monarch, though one has neither possessions nor hearts over which to rule, though one has apparently lost both the one and the other. Hardy was right. To have lost both the one and the other. To have been left behind by both the one and the other. Or, rather, to have taken another road, slower, less secure, less open, a secretly more ambitious road. . . .

People were clapping, enthusiastically. They wanted, and received, a repetition of the waltz. The conductor's delight was boundless; it seemed about to burst open his red and swollen face. He lifted his arms and, before beginning the music again, paused a moment as though he were making a promise, as though he wanted this promise to be felt: 'You shall be as gods.' It was true; the offer of the serpent had—so cheaply!—become reality. Now, after the good food and the wine, light-hearted and a little dizzy, turning and turning in the dance, they all felt like small triumphant gods. Like gods!

Lintas turned around quickly—but no, it was just the waiter with the tray. He put his cup down on the shining silver surface, thinking how, every day, one's last despairing hope in mankind was taken away, empty, like that little cup. Yes, and the next day there would be other men and other hopes. Human credulity was endless, it was never really crushed, never quite beaten down. Hope gone inevitably returned, a constant tide in an inconstant ocean. 'Excuse me,' muttered a timid little man, pushing past him to get to the waiter with the *fines,* ancient cognac in huge belled glasses. . . . Let him pass, one had to let everybody pass, no matter how trifling the reason for their haste!

And now, at last, there was Marta, coming in from the garden with her table companion, the man with the yellowish dissipated face. They looked at each other again, a strange look, at once challenging and reticent. Then Marta tore away her eyes, walking erect and dignified toward the sofa. Lintas's glance followed her. She seemed overcome by the heat, which was far more stifling outside than here in the great hall. And yet, even here, it was close; there were too many people, drinking, talking, laughing, bodies curved back in laughter or swaying toward each other in an uncompleted caress.

Lintas did not hesitate, his instinct did not hesitate. Perhaps it

was not quite the right moment; the orchestra had stopped playing
and people were migrating indoors. Moreover, he had no idea of
what to say or what to do. But he did not hesitate, he walked
straight over to her; in a moment he was standing before those eyes
and their quick light questioning scrutiny. He spoke out of some
extreme of violence and bitterness in himself; he said harshly, 'I'm
Lintas'—just his name, nothing more. She kept on looking at him
without a change in her expression, without any apparent reaction,
coldly almost, completely disinterested, like one who counters a
gesture too vehement with the indifferent serenity of centuries, a
proud and sovereign calm. 'Yes,' she said. 'Yes, yes . . .' hardly
acknowledging to herself the faint resonance with which the artist's
name rang in her memory, not interested now in the fierce per-
suasiveness of this man whom she had stared at with such uneasy
curiosity during the dinner and who was now offering her his hand.
'Yes,' she said. 'I know your name.' She presented her companion,
who rose and bowed ungraciously.

Neither of them, not he nor she, was willing to give in. They
were both shy natures, fundamentally reserved. He had come to her,
hating himself for what seemed an abdication from his preferred
and haughty loneliness, indeed for seeking her out at all. As for her,
she would have hated herself if she had not opposed this stranger's
overt claim upon her with an attitude corresponding to it, a glacial
lack of response. They were the sort of persons whose loneliness
becomes deeper in crowds, who find it almost impossible to overcome their own distrust. Salt of the earth though they are, they live
silent, suspicious, withdrawn. What civilization will finally release
these hermetically sealed beings, allow these clear but secret lives
to flow freely into the great human sea? None, perhaps. . . .

The orchestra saved the situation, rescued them from the embarrassing silence into which they had plunged. The instruments
crashed out in their tremendous delirium at the very moment when
to speak at all began to seem to Lintas both foolish and inopppor-
tune. He asked her to dance and she rose. The gray eyes were only
inches away; holding her close to him, he felt the softness of her
dark skin, the firm delicacy of her breasts. And, as they danced,
he realized with a sense of strangeness that that hard, healthy, sen-
sitized, and vibrating flesh had no weight, that the whole shy and
lovely body was utterly alive in his arms. He felt himself invaded by
its fragrance, the touch of its skin, fenced in by a living wall; yes,
the body which he was holding so closely held and embraced him.
They danced without speaking, seriously, listening to the deep

monotonous murmur of the singer whose voice, carrying the melody, blended with the instruments.

Mrs. Rague looked around and saw Lintas sitting abstractedly on one of the carved walnut benches near-by, his virile head outlined against the black silk of an old Mongolian shawl. Ah, her prize! That was going to be the prize of her evening; from him would issue the word which she wanted spoken, the precise and categorical opinion on those precious canvases of whose presence in the house many people were unaware and whose real value was not known even to the man in the modest gallery at Antwerp who had sold them to her agent. She hoped for a great success from this transaction, a quite immeasurable yield. No expert appraisal was necessary—one had merely to use one's taste, the sensory delicacy of the true amateur—in order to see the quality of those three paintings, not much bigger, any of them, than an ordinary book. What she had bought for a few thousands she could sell for many more— and with renown, moreover. Not in vain does one discover—thanks to a sure instinct—behind the rather miserable mask of dirty crusted varnish the miracle of an authentic Titian!

But this Lintas, this man with the slow steady voice and the naturally elegant gestures—far too infrequent among the bourgeoisie —this man to whom she had so recently and casually been presented, did he know enough to make a discriminating verdict in such a difficult and delicate matter? She was inclined to think so. She had boasted more than once that she never made a mistake about men; and, a week ago, when she met Lintas at the exhibition, she had decided that his culture and discernment in artistic matters were beyond criticism. Now, having settled the question in her own mind, she walked down the steps and approached him with dignity.

Lintas was, at the moment, absorbed in minute scrutiny of a dancer's foot, carved out of black diorite, which stood on an otherwise bare wooden table. It was an oddly graceful piece, but firm, with a certain refractory hardness in all its contours. To pass from this hardness to another hardness, from the stone foot to the stony determination behind Eugenia Rague's smile, was a transition which could be made without difficulty or astonishment. Thinking these thoughts, he clasped ceremoniously the freckled hand which was extended to him. A superb emerald bracelet dangled from its bony wrist.

'I'm so glad you came,' Mrs. Rague said. 'Quite apart from the personal pleasure it gives me, I have another, less disinterested, reason for welcoming you. I'd like very much to have your opinion on my most recent acquisition, three small canvases . . .' Without really interrupting herself, merely by a backward motion of her arm, she stopped in their tracks Jílgoles and a lady to whom he was talking. 'I want you to meet Mr. Lintas,' she said.

She continued making introductions with the native efficiency of a cowherd calling in his flock. In a short time she had gathered around them a considerable number of people, whose presence in the circle had all the air of being motivated by a purely spontaneous curiosity. As a matter of fact, there *was* a kind of vague expectancy noticeable in these men and women so skillfully conscripted into the group. Among them, listening intently, with his great nose in the air, his mouth half open and his eyes heavy with lack of comprehension, was Senator Velarde, a man who had displayed some capacity in the halls of Parliament, but was pretty stupid outside it. There, too, was Miss Cisneros, the daughter of a well-known buyer of paintings.

Mrs. Rague was enjoying herself. One of her greatest pleasures lay in displaying her dilettante's virtuosity to an attentive audience, and she reveled in the belief that that particular corner of the great room had something about it both more intimate and more distinguished than any of the others. . . . Watching her, Lintas wondered to himself: What is my social obligation at this point? Shall I express approval, corroboration, or surprise? He decided, for the moment, on simple acquiescence.

'One afternoon,' Mrs. Rague launched into her speech, 'I was sitting on the terrace of a café on the Cannebière, when a very well-dressed and rather ducal-looking gentleman came up to my table. "Madam," he said to me, "I'd like to ask for a few minutes of your precious attention." Before I had time to consent, he was already sitting down opposite me. I found out soon enough that he considered himself a sort of executor, not of material properties, but of a theory which had been entrusted to him by a professor of languages who had died some years before. The theory—which he expounded in quite tiresome detail—was that the greater part of all social evils resulted from an improper use of words. "I'll give you a rough example," he said. "When we mean 'squash' we say 'watermelon' and when we mean 'watermelon' we say 'squash.' That's the way things go in the world." '

Mrs. Rague looked around at her guests and smiled, as though inviting them to share her enjoyment. 'I maintained a discreet composure,' she said. 'Of course, the theory was quite absurd; if there's injustice in the world today, it's due only to the bitter envy with which the poor regard the fortunes of the rich, and things will improve only when this failing of theirs is torn out by its roots, its moral roots.'

Nobody ventured to challenge her statement and she went on serenely: 'You know, in spite of his absurdity, I can't help thinking of that gentleman sometimes, whenever, for instance, I find the power to apply critical sanctions to myself weakening in me. Heaven knows, it may have been that casual conversation which taught me to prefer even the bare skeleton of truth to the richest combination of words. All my life I've been preoccupied with truth, truth before anything else. Perhaps I've had no other real passion. You know that, don't you, Berta Steligmann? You've traveled over two continents with me and you know how I am. Everything I see, everything I hear, smell, or touch, must be indisputably authentic; I won't permit even a shadow of doubt to exist.'

She fastened her cold eyes on Lintas. 'This is where you come in, Mr. Lintas,' she said. 'I haven't been speaking capriciously, I mean what I say. Will you, who are such an excellent artist, show yourself a generous spirit, too?'

He nodded in agreement and awaited developments. The circle of eyes took possession of him, surveyed him with a sort of animal-like distrust. Who was he, anyway?

'I need your unbiased judgment,' Mrs. Rague declared, 'a judgment as strict and uncompromising as the eye of a vulture. Yes, that's exactly what I mean—like the eye of a vulture. . . . I've got those three little things upstairs,' she said. 'I haven't wanted to bring them down until they'd been—well, shall we say "christened"? I'm counting on you to tell me if they are what they seem. . . . Shall we go up?'

Lintas followed her and all the others followed him. Mrs. Rague had pronounced 'Shall we go up?' in a tone loud enough to be heard in various parts of the drawing-room. So it happened that a good-sized crowd started trooping up the wide carved staircase, a noisy and impertinent caravan, highly amused curious people who did not even stop to wonder what they were curious about. The ladies' bracelets jangled metallically against hands which rested lightly on the broad baroque banisters; the gentlemen's shoes struck the rods holding down the thick carpet. At the head of this motley laughing throng, Mrs. Rague walked with her dignified air, serious and silent.

They reached the great covered gallery on the first floor. The lighting here was somber, almost shadowy. Three large easels, separated from each other but meticulously aligned, held Mrs. Rague's most recent acquisitions. She passed in front of the first, pointing at it wordlessly with her lorgnette, then came to a decided stance before the one in the middle. Lintas stepped forward. 'It's impossible to see in this light,' he said. With a brusque gesture, Mrs. Rague opened a path through the dense crowd and turned a switch on the wall. A strong white light flooded the gallery.

The canvas was a small detail from Titian's 'Perseus and Andromeda,' showing Andromeda's head and part of her manacled arm. It evoked at once the entire painting, the clotted sky and tempestuous ocean of the original painting. Lintas had seen it, years ago, at Hertford House. . . . The face, a little fleshy but dominated by the strength of the great black eyes, was turned toward the left in an attitude of expectancy.

Lintas scrutinized the small painting for some time. Then, followed by the entire group, except for a few people whose independent curiosity had already led them to the same place, he walked over to the one on the left, a little later to the one on the right. He bent over all three to examine them more closely. Then he stepped back, his brows lifted in a stare.

'Well . . .?' Mrs. Rague was coyly inquisitive.

Lintas looked at her without answering. He shoved his hands into his trousers-pockets and turned back to the canvases, as though trying to include all three in a single act of judgment. 'What did they tell you about these pictures?' he asked.

'Well,' said Mrs. Rague, like one unfortunately compelled to explain what is already obvious, 'the one you looked at first is a preliminary study of the "Perseus and Andromeda." The others are unknown primitives, dating from the fifteenth century or, possibly, the beginning of the sixteenth. It's of course superfluous to tell you that I acquired with them a certificate of authenticity.'

There was a long pause.

'I'm afraid you've been cheated,' Lintas said at last. 'I'm very much afraid of it.' He relapsed into silence again, glancing with slight interest into his hostess's eyes. There was an angry glitter in them, a lightning flash of furious opposition, and then they became calm again, as composed as before.

The silence was heavy. Marta came up and joined the group without being noticed. She looked over the shoulders of two women who sat listening, arm in arm.

Lintas felt the rebellious blood pounding in his head. A secret fury was in him, he could no longer withhold his protest against all this foolishness, this coarse indignity. 'You asked me for the truth, madam,' he said, hardly bothering to restrain his cynical and insolent tone. 'Now it annoys and irritates you. That seems to me far more indicative of a state of mind than what seems to you indicative of an age. Do you want me to believe that you prefer a comfortable falsehood to a harsh truth? What did you expect from me anyway? A polite willingness to play my rôle in the comedy, no doubt. But— forgive me—it's impossible to breathe in the air of such comedy, it's simply unbearable; one ends up by hating oneself for putting up with it at all.'

'What do you mean by "such comedy"?'

'What can I mean—except precisely that? I've just heard that the world is a paradise because, by virtue of knowing the Pandects, certain people are permitted to enjoy the exquisite dishes served at the Tour d'Argent. I've just learned—or, rather, I'm learning it to my cost—that *you've* decided, at all costs, to believe that you've acquired some authentic examples of classical painting. At all costs. *Malgré n'importe qui, quoi.* I should, of course, have enrolled in the circle and said "yes" to everything, added my confirmation in order not to interrupt the game. Instead, I'm guilty of a conflict, of having created a conflict. And there's no way to settle it. It's as though I'd opened the door and let in a draft which makes everybody uncomfortable. Somebody will have to get up and close the door, but it won't be I. I'm much more inclined to open it farther. If one had the courage to open more doors and windows, a great wind would sweep through the world. It might kill the frequenters of the Tour d'Argent but so much the worse for them. Or so much the better, because only a few are lucky enough to die in full enjoyment of what they've coveted most.'

'I consider that extremely impertinent!' Jarcelín said. Something innately cruel lurked in his eyes and around his peevish mouth.

'Nothing is impertinent. What *could* be now that we've heard your point of view?' Lintas's sardonic smile became broader. 'The proof that it's pertinent is your belief that it isn't. Of course, you're alarmed, you're one of those who fear the wind.'

Jarcelín's lips moved, but he said nothing. He plucked angrily at the white camellia in his buttonhole.

Lintas surveyed him coolly. 'Your gesture is not quite clear, my dear sir,' he said. 'I don't know whether it signifies "yes" or "no" . . . As a matter of fact, gestures are most untrustworthy things. We indulge in them far too much, we'd be better off without them.

It's no longer a question of "words, words, words," as Hamlet complained; on the contrary, nowadays people pick their words carefully in order not to betray their gestures. I don't mean simply
external movements. The really terrible gestures are the ones which
we make within our souls.' He paused a moment, then went on
thoughtfully: 'You see, sir, you're one of the exceptions—you
honestly like the food at the Tour d'Argent. Most people of your
sort don't give a damn about the magnificent food served there.
What pleases them is to be able to make the gesture of eating it.
The same tendency is present in other and far more important
fields. Even empires are gained by means of gestures today.'

Mrs. Rague cut in smoothly. 'All that sounds very well,' she said.
'But it doesn't seem to me particularly opportune.' Her neck arched
back. The low-hanging branch of a laurel bush almost touched her
stately head.

'Quite possibly it's not,' Lintas agreed. His features were relaxed,
he had an air of great candor and serenity. 'I didn't bring it up because I thought it was. The opportune is usually deadly. It kills off
what is genuine. I don't want to be opportune; I want only to be
honest with you, with everybody, including myself. I'm sorry that
I have to speak harshly about your comedy—which, by the way,
is mine, too, I'm thoroughly involved—but, if I didn't, I'd go to
bed uncomfortable. I might even suffer from insomnia. So I challenge your gestures with my gesture which is impertinent and rude
and perhaps rather savage. In this way, I can remain at peace with
myself instead of adding my little lie to all the other little lies.'

Nobody answered him; the whole elegant group appeared both
shocked and irritated.

He smiled and went on: 'We'll all go to bed more peacefully
now—*you* believing that I'm hopelessly ill-bred, *I* that I've made
you see with me how disagreeable is this spectacle of wasted words
and gestures. Such a lovely spring night deserves something better,
something more real. Moreover, I'm deluded enough to believe that,
when you wake up at dawn—each of you in his own bed, safely
shut up in his own room—you'll still feel that unpleasant sensation,
as of a draft, upon your skin. You'll get up to close the door and
it won't do any good because the draft—that mortal wind!—is inside you, it blows upon you from within . . . Yes, though you're
afraid of that health-giving wind, though you feel it as a mortal
danger, it's coming, it has to come.

'For more than four hundred years, the world has been shut up
in a heated stifling room. We've so perfected our system of mutual

deceptions that we're oppressed by each other, unable to breathe, unable to escape from the prison of lies which we ourselves have made. I'm quite aware that this doesn't seem particularly atrocious to you. To me it does. I wish I knew where the door was so I could open it wide. But I don't know yet and I don't want to open the wrong door, one that might lead only into another suffocating room. The door I want to open leads to the fresh air, to the natural freedom of things . . .'

'A figure of speech!' said one of the men. He spoke with a sort of sluggish hatred. His white-cuffed hand flicked the ash from his cigar, a thick dark fragrant Danneman.

'A figure of speech!' Lintas repeated. He looked at the man deliberately. 'When a horse is described to an ass, the latter says scornfully, "Figure of speech!" '

Two of the others broke into spasmodic laughter. The man with the cigar said, slowly, without moving, 'You'll have to explain that to me later.'

'I'd never be able to explain it to you because you could never understand it . . . Every now and then the world divides into two factions, into what seems, because of irrelevant circumstances, a profoundly social bifurcation. Actually the division is eternal, and much simpler, and the tragedy of most people is, not that they suffer or lose in the battle, but that they've been fighting on the wrong side. There are just men who league themselves tacitly on the side of the sinners and sinners who fight for the just. Men know little about themselves and, when they find out, it's usually too late, they're too thoroughly committed to change. . . .

'The eternal division is between those who are capable of governing their passions and appetites and those who are not. That alone is fundamental. We all come into the world the same dirty little creatures who have to be washed the first thing. But, once that outward cleanliness is achieved, our paths separate. Some of us have a basic tendency to injure anything alive and sensitive; others want only to keep it as it is, to warm and nourish it. The former are the impure, the latter the pure among humanity. What confounds these two real factions in life, what helps to divide them badly, putting them into the wrong category, is the derisive comedy of gestures, the artificial manners which obscure the truth. Because of it, humanity is three or four centuries in arrears. Only a few desperate passions have survived out of this prolonged lethargy of mankind, a few admirable outbursts—some cries of Rimbaud, some paintings by El Greco, a Ninth Symphony, some Masses by Bach. . .'

Mrs. Rague lifted her hand to her hair, calmly smoothed its flat waves, and fixed him with her piercing glance, 'Also,' she said maliciously, 'some rather lengthy sermons.'

'Yes,' Lintas agreed. 'I'm a man of quite disgusting candor.'

'Candor?' It was Jarcelín's high and sarcastic voice.

'And how!' laughed the man with the Danneman cigar.

Everybody began to laugh. White teeth and insolent red lips gleamed in the darkness. Lintas's eyes were somber, icy, contemptuous, his mouth bitterly awry. He reached for a cigarette with trembling hands. (But there was always a slight tremor in those thin, almost fleshless fingers; this nervousness was nothing new.) He lit the cigarette and looked again at the row of faces, glancing unhurriedly from one to the other.

'There's a third sort of fate,' he said, stabbing the words home, 'which I forgot to mention before. It belongs to those who've not yet succeeded in breaking through the foetal membrane.'

The collective gasp was clearly audible. But Mrs. Rague still had a gesture in reserve, a gesture elegantly condescending and of the utmost refinement. Waving away the servant who was approaching with a trayful of glasses, she rose and clapped her hands, graciously, as though to say, 'What *does* it all matter?' (The hands were long and white, they had no other function than to smooth the dry blond hair every morning and slap cream into the flabby skin at night.) 'We're spoiling our party!' she cried. 'That's unpardonable. Come now—no more soliloquies!'

The group broke up, laughing and talking. Lintas walked alone toward the terrace found himself face to face with Marta.

She looked at him silently, shaken anew by his nearness, but fighting against the strange emotion he roused in her as she so often fought against her own deepest inclination. He said, 'Good night' to her harshly and stepped around her as though she were merely some obstacle in his path. The voice with which she called after him 'Are you going already?' had in it a rare and quite perceptible quiver.

He stopped and turned around. His eyes, still heavy with anger, looked at the woman who came up to him. And it seemed to him that she was worthy of regard. There was something so unquestionably magnificent about her!

Staring into those eyes, Marta knew he was wounded and irremediably. 'Come with me,' she blurted out. 'I'll drive you home.'

Lintas protested. He preferred to walk, he said. He was accustomed to taking a long walk before going to bed.

'No,' she said, 'I'll drive you.'

He felt, deep in himself, an indignation toward this whole family, this whole world, this whole conspiracy of lies. He protested again with all the rudeness of which he was capable. But that other honest glance did not waver; it met his staunchly, almost hard in its resolute courtesy. There was in it a fund of truth against which no subterfuge could prevail . . . .

The door of the car slammed shut. To Marta's interrogative 'Where?' he gave the name of a station. Yes, he lived outside the city, in one of its suburbs, about a twenty-five-minute ride on the train. 'It's such a splendid night for driving,' she said. 'Suppose you let me take you all the way home. Then I can drive back slowly and get here after everybody else has left.'

He asked himself what on earth he was going to do with this woman. His thoughts, on that hot night, beneath that low and heavy sky, seemed to have an edge on them, they were at once rusty and sharp. He felt unbearably bad-tempered, wrathful rather than perplexed. . . . They swept into the dizzy center of the city, all lights and glaring white walls. Huge knife-like beams cut across the black lake of asphalt.

Lintas felt a need to wound, to say something hard and offensive, spattering with his contempt all that way of life in which he found himself still involved, from which he could not free himself. It was represented at this moment by the woman beside him, steering so skillfully through the hazards of the traffic, her coppery throat revealing its strong full tendons as she twisted it from left to right.

'You know, it's very odd,' she said. 'Your character seems so strong, and—well, secure, and yet you attach so much importance to the idotic whims of a frivolous world.'

'Importance?' he said. 'Not at all.'

'Importance,' she insisted, and repeated it monotonously: 'Importance. Importance.'

The sad unchangeable echo of the city came to them clearly, its mingled noises blending into the night like one noise, one continuous distant explosion. They had left behind them the theater district and the lordly streets of the wealthy, and now, at last, they were outside the city altogether, speeding down one of the broad suburban avenues.

—Translated by Alis De Sola

II

****

THE BRITISH ISLES

** *** ****************

ENGLAND · 393

SCOTLAND · 587

IRELAND · 592

T. S. ELIOT

****

Burnt Norton *is the initial section of Mr. T. S. Eliot's long poem,*
Four Quartets. *But in spite of its intimate integration in the com-*
plete poem with the three later sections, its publication apart from
them is in a way justified by its original conception. In 1935 when
Eliot's publishers proposed a volume of his collected poems, he felt,
as he has said, that it would be good to have an unpublished poem
in it. With this in view and with no conscious intention of develop-
ing the themes and imagery contained in it into a longer poem, he
wrote Burnt Norton. *It was only through the writing of his play*
Family Reunion, *published in 1939, that the idea of a further de-*
velopment of the approach of Burnt Norton *was suggested to him.*
The second Quartet, East Coker, *did not make its appearance until*
April 1940, more than four years after Burnt Norton.

Again, it is true that Eliot's poems, as Miss Marianne Moore has
phrased it, "are so consistently intricated that one rests on another
and is involved with what is earlier." There are no breaks in Eliot's
work—no unnecessary repetitions. Each of his poems in a sense may
be said to be an integral part of a long poem which he is still
writing. Nevertheless we can distinguish certain changes of emphasis,
particularly in his mode of expression, marking certain broad periods
of Eliot's work. For example, in Eliot's poetry, antecedent to and
culminating in The Waste Land *of 1922, we find a cryptic, oracular*
avoidance of direct statement: an emphasis on allusion, abrupt con-
trasts. With the Hollow Men *in 1925 came a more intensified in-*
terest in the ecclesiastical side of religion: allusion became more
narrowly focused towards this interest but the cryptic, oracular char-
acter of the expression persevered while a litanic repetition began
to dominate the concise, condensed earlier expression; finally, with
the second of the Quartets, East Coker, *in spite of the frankly philo-*
sophical emphases of the longer poem of which it makes a part,
Eliot's style has grown relatively diffuse, repetitive and inclining
towards the familiar. In the meanwhile he has been to school to an
audience in his efforts, in Family Reunion, *to write verse drama,*
and has been seeking that clarity of surface meaning essential to
drama, which must be taken in by ear no matter what the depth
may be.

393

Burnt Norton, *on the other hand, may be fairly said to represent at once the maturity of Eliot's interests in the period of which* Hollow Men *was the first fruit and the opening note of the latter phase. Independently it serves as a key to the wide appreciation of Eliot's work of the last twenty-five years. And read against the background of* The Waste Land *is a key to the complete poetic creation of its author.*

As a poem in its own right it has the structural authority that has marked all the Four Quartets, *a tighter unity than* The Waste Land *afforded, a more assured architectonic craftsmanship. It has a rounded clarity of expression, which though it does not realize "the flat direct style" of the later* Little Gidding, *is an anticipation of the direction Eliot's work in the theatre has since given him. Its introduction to Section II:*

> "Garlic and sapphires in the mud
>   Clot the bedded axle-tree——"

and Section IV:

> "Time and the bell have buried the day,
>   The black cloud carries the sun away——"

are two of the richest and, at the same time, most concentrated lyrics of Eliot. And finally it is the foundation from which the fabric of the Four Quartets *has sprung up and which supports it.*

JAMES JOHNSON SWEENEY

****

Burnt Norton

I

TIME present and time past
Are both perhaps present in time future,
And time future contained in time past.
If all time is eternally present
All time is unredeemable.
What might have been is an abstraction
Remaining a perpetual possibility
Only in a world of speculation.
What might have been and what has been
Point to one end, which is always present.

Footfalls echo in the memory
Down the passage which we did not take
Towards the door we never opened
Into the rose-garden. My words echo
Thus, in your mind.
                    But to what purpose
Disturbing the dust on a bowl of rose-leaves
I do not know.
                    Other echoes
Inhabit the garden. Shall we follow?
Quick, said the bird, find them, find them;
Round the corner. Through the first gate,
Into our first world, shall we follow
The deception of the thrush? Into our first world.
There they were, dignified, invisible,
Moving without pressure, over the dead leaves,
In the autumn heat, through the vibrant air,
And the bird called, in response to
The unheard music hidden in the shrubbery,
And the unseen eyebeam crossed, for the roses
Had the look of flowers that are looked at.
There they were as our guests, accepted and accepting.
So we moved, and they, in a formal pattern,
Along the empty alley, into the box circle,
To look down into the drained pool.
Dry the pool, dry concrete, brown edged,
And the pool was filled with water out of sunlight,
And the lotos rose, quietly, quietly,
The surface glittered out of heart of light,
And they were behind us, reflected in the pool.
Then a cloud passed, and the pool was empty.
Go, said the bird, for the leaves were full of children,
Hidden excitedly, containing laughter.
Go, go, go, said the bird: human kind
Cannot bear very much reality.
Time past and time future
What might have been and what has been
Point to one end, which is always present.

II

Garlic and sapphires in the mud
Clot the bedded axle-tree.

The trilling wire in the blood
Sings below inveterate scars
And reconciles forgotten wars.
The dance along the artery
The circulation of the lymph
Are figured in the drift of stars
Ascend to summer in the tree
We move above the moving tree
In light upon the figured leaf
And hear upon the sodden floor
Below, the boarhound and the boar
Pursue their pattern as before
But reconciled among the stars.

At the still point of the turning world. Neither flesh nor fleshless;
Neither from nor towards; at the still point, there the dance is,
But neither arrest nor movement. And do not call it fixity.
Where past and future are gathered. Neither movement from nor
                    towards,
Neither ascent nor decline. Except for the point, the still point,
There would be no dance, and there is only the dance.
I can only say, there we have been: but I cannot say where.
And I cannot say, how long, for that is to place it in time.

The inner freedom from the practical desire,
The release from action and suffering, release from the inner
And the outer compulsion, yet surrounded
By a grace of sense, a white light still and moving,
Erhebung without motion, concentration
Without elimination, both a new world
And the old made explicit, understood
In the completion of its partial ecstasy,
The resolution of its partial horror.
Yet the enchainment of past and future
Woven in the weakness of the changing body,
Protects mankind from heaven and damnation
Which flesh cannot endure.
                              Time past and time future
Allow but a little consciousness.
To be conscious is not to be in time
But only in time can the moment in the rose-garden,
The moment in the arbour where the rain beat,

The moment in the draughty church at smoke-fall
Be remembered; involved with past and future.
Only through time time is conquered.

III

Here is a place of disaffection
Time before and time after
In a dim light: neither daylight
Investing form with lucid stillness
Turning shadow into transient beauty
With slow rotation suggesting permanence
Nor darkness to purify the soul
Emptying the sensual with deprivation
Cleansing affection from the temporal.
Neither plenitude nor vacancy. Only a flicker
Over the strained time-ridden faces
Distracted from distraction by distraction
Filled with fancies and empty of meaning
Tumid apathy with no concentration
Men and bits of paper, whirled by the cold wind
That blows before and after time,
Wind in and out of unwholesome lungs
Time before and time after.
Eructation of unhealthy souls
Into the faded air, the torpid
Driven on the wind that sweeps the gloomy hills of London,
Hampstead and Clerkenwell, Campden and Putney,
Highgate, Primrose and Ludgate. Not here
Not here the darkness, in this twittering world.

Descend lower, descend only
Into the world of perpetual solitude,
World not world, but that which is not world,
Internal darkness, deprivation
And destitution of all property,
Dessication of the world of sense,
Evacuation of the world of fancy,
Inoperancy of the world of spirit;
This is the one way, and the other
Is the same, not in movement
But abstention from movement; while the world moves

In appetency, on its metalled ways
Of time past and time future.

IV

Time and the bell have buried the day,
The black cloud carries the sun away.
Will the sunflower turn to us, will the clematis
Stray down, bend to us; tendril and spray
Clutch and cling?
Chill
Fingers of yew be curled
Down on us? After the kingfisher's wing
Has answered light to light, and is silent, the light is still
At the still point of turning world.

V

Words move, music moves
Only in time; but that which is only living
Can only die. Words, after speech, reach
into silence. Only by the form, the pattern,
Can words or music reach
The stillness, as a Chinese jar still
Moves perpetually in its stillness.
Not the stillness of the violin, while the note lasts,
Not that only, but the co-existence,
Or say that the end precedes the beginning,
And the end and the beginning were always there
Before the beginning and after the end.
And all is always now. Words strain,
Crack and sometimes break, under the burden,
Under the tension, slip, slide, perish,
Decay with imprecision, will not stay in place,
Will not stay still. Shrieking voices
Scolding, mocking or merely chattering,
Always assail them. The Word in the desert
Is most attacked by voices of temptation,
The crying shadow in the funeral dance,
The loud lament of the disconsolate chimera.

The detail of the pattern is movement,

As in the figure of the ten stairs.
Desire itself is movement
Not in itself desirable;
Love is itself unmoving,
Only the cause and end of movement,
Timeless, and undesiring
Except in the aspect of time
Caught in the form of limitation
Between un-being and being.
Sudden in a shaft of sunlight
Even while the dust moves
There rises the hidden laughter
Of children in the foliage
Quick now, here, now, always—
Ridiculous the waste sad time
Stretching before and after.

ALDOUS HUXLEY

****

LOS ANGELES, CALIF.
APRIL 1, 1950

*Short only in relation to a full-length novel, the best of my stories
are far too long to be included in this anthology. Of the absolutely
short ones this "Tillotson Banquet" is probably as good as any. It
was written nearly thirty years ago and is therefore an "early work."
Indeed all my short stories are "early works"; for it is more than
twenty years since I felt the urge to write any piece of fiction briefer
than a novel.*

*Re-reading "The Tillotson Banquet," I am reminded nostalgically
of that remote Inter-Cataclysmic Period between the end of the
First World War and the beginning of the Depression. It was an
exciting time. Modern Art was still genuinely modern and not, as
now, a stale academic tradition. One could still believe in the
League of Nations and feel hopeful about the Russian Revolution.
"Bliss was it in that dawn to be alive." Every adolescent's emergence
into adult life and contemporary culture is a blissful dawn. But at
certain moments of history—moments of rapid disintegration and
renewal—the bliss of adolescence and youth is more than ordinarily
intense. In his earliest manhood, Wordsworth lived through such a
moment of history. And so did those of us who were young in the
twenties of the present century. But every dawn, whether personal or
historical, is followed by morning and afternoon, by evening and
finally night. The exhilaration of the Inter-Cataclysmic Period wore
off and was succeeded by an awareness, during the thirties and
forties, that the human situation was, in Waughian phraseology,
"madly ungay."*

*The Tillotson of my story had no precise counterpart in real life.
His predicament was suggested by that of Philip James Bailey who
published* Festus *at twenty-three, was hailed on both sides of the
Atlantic as a major philosophical poet, and died almost seventy
years later, in 1906, universally unknown and totally forgotten. And
in the background of the story hovers the ghost of Benjamin Robert
Haydon. That unhappy painter, who possessed all the characteristics
of a great genius except talent, has haunted my imagination ever*

since, as a boy, I first read his Journals. A modern version of him
appears as Lypiatt in the novel, Antic Hay, *which was written a year*
or two after "The Tillotson Banquet."

ALDOUS HUXLEY

****

The Tillotson Banquet

I

YOUNG SPODE was not a snob; he was too intelligent for that, too
fundamentally decent. Not a snob; but all the same he could not
help feeling very well pleased at the thought that he was dining,
alone and intimately, with Lord Badgery. It was a definite event in
his life, a step forward, he felt, towards that final success, social,
material, and literary, which he had come to London with the fixed
intention of making. The conquest and capture of Badgery was an
almost essential strategical move in the campaign.

Edmund, forty-seventh Baron Badgery, was a lineal descendant
of that Edmund, surnamed Le Blayreau, who landed on English
soil in the train of William the Conqueror. Ennobled by William
Rufus, the Badgerys had been one of the very few baronial families to survive the Wars of the Roses and all the other changes and
chances of English history. They were a sensible and philoprogen-
itive race. No Badgery had ever fought in any war, no Badgery
had ever engaged in any kind of politics. They had been content
to live and quietly to propagate their species in a huge machic-
olated Norman castle, surrounded by a triple moat, only sallying
forth to cultivate their property and to collect their rents. In the
eighteenth century, when life had become relatively secure, the
Badgerys began to venture forth into civilised society. From boorish
squires they blossomed into *grands seigneurs,* patrons of the arts,
virtuosi. Their property was large, they were rich; and with the
growth of industrialism their riches also grew. Villages on their
estate turned into manufacturing towns, unsuspected coal was discovered beneath the surface of their barren moorlands. By the middle of the nineteenth century the Badgerys were among the richest
of English noble families. The forty-seventh baron disposed of an
income of at least two hundred thousand pounds a year. Following

the great Badgery tradition, he had refused to have anything to do with politics or war. He occupied himself by collecting pictures; he took an interest in theatrical productions; he was the friend and patron of men of letters, of painters, and musicians. A personage, in a word, of considerable consequence in that particular world in which young Spode had elected to make his success.

Spode had only recently left the university. Simon Gollamy, the editor of the *World's Review* (the "Best of all possible Worlds"), had got to know him—he was always on the look out for youthful talent—had seen possibilities in the young man, and appointed him art critic of his paper. Gollamy liked to have young and teachable people about him. The possession of disciples flattered his vanity, and he found it easier, moreover, to run his paper with docile collaborators than with men grown obstinate and case-hardened with age. Spode had not done badly at his new job. At any rate, his articles had been intelligent enough to arouse the interest of Lord Badgery. It was, ultimately, to them that he owed the honour of sitting tonight in the dining-room of Badgery House.

Fortified by several varieties of wine and a glass of aged brandy, Spode felt more confident and at ease than he had done the whole evening. Badgery was rather a disquieting host. He had an alarming habit of changing the subject of any conversation that had lasted for more than two minutes. Spode had found it, for example, horribly mortifying when his host cutting across what was, he prided himself, a particularly subtle and illuminating disquisition on baroque art, had turned a wandering eye about the room and asked him abruptly whether he liked parrots. He had flushed and glanced suspiciously towards him, fancying that the man was trying to be offensive. But no, Badgery's white, fleshy, Hanoverian face wore an expression of perfect good faith. There was no malice in his small greenish eyes. He evidently did genuinely want to know if Spode liked parrots. The young man swallowed his irritation and replied that he did. Badgery then told a good story about parrots. Spode was on the point of capping it with a better story, when his host began to talk about Beethoven. And so the game went on. Spode cut his conversation to suit his host's requirements. In the course of ten minutes he had made a more or less witty epigram on Benvenuto Cellini, Queen Victoria, sport, God, Stephen Phillips, and Moorish architecture. Lord Badgery thought him the most charming young man, and so intelligent.

"If you've quite finished your coffee," he said, rising to his feet as he spoke, "We'll go and look at the pictures."

Spode jumped up with alacrity, and only then realised that he had drunk just ever so little too much. He would have to be careful, talk deliberately, plant his feet consciously, one after the other.

"This house is quite cluttered up with pictures," Lord Badgery complained. "I had a whole wagon-load taken away to the country last week; but there are still far too many. My ancestors would have their portraits painted by Romney. Such a shocking artist, don't you think? Why couldn't they have chosen Gainsborough, or even Reynolds? I've had all the Romneys hung in the servants' hall now. It's such a comfort to know that one can never possibly see them again. I suppose you know all about the ancient Hittites?"

"Well . . ." the young man replied, with befitting modesty.

"Look at that, then." He indicated a large stone head which stood in a case near the dining-room door. "It's not Greek, or Egyptian, or Persian, or anything else; so if it isn't ancient Hittite, I don't know what it is. And that reminds me of that story about Lord George Sanger, the Circus King . . ." and, without giving Spode time to examine the Hittite relic, he led the way up the huge staircase, pausing every now and then in his anecdote to point out some new object of curiosity or beauty.

"I suppose you know Deburau's pantomimes?" Spode rapped out as soon as the story was over. He was in an itch to let out his information about Deburau. Badgery had given him a perfect opening with his ridiculous Sanger. "What a perfect man, isn't he? He used to . . ."

"This is my main gallery," said Lord Badgery, throwing open one leaf of a tall folding door. "I must apologise for it. It looks like a roller-skating rink." He fumbled with the electric switches and there was suddenly light—light that revealed an enormous gallery, duly receding into distance according to all the laws of perspective. "I dare say you've heard of my poor father," Lord Badgery continued. "A little insane, you know; sort of mechanical genius with a screw loose. He used to have a toy railway in this room. No end of fun he had, crawling about the floor after his trains. And all the pictures were stacked in the cellars. I can't tell you what they were like when I found them: mushrooms growing out of the Botticellis. Now I'm rather proud of this Poussin; he painted it for Scarron."

"Exquisite!" Spode exclaimed, making with his hand a gesture as though he were modelling a pure form in the air. "How splendid the onrush of those trees and leaning figures is! And the way they're caught up, as it were, and stemmed by that single godlike form opposing them with his contrary movement! And the draperies . . ."

But Lord Badgery had moved on, and was standing in front of a little fifteenth-century Virgin of carved wood.

"School of Rheims," he explained.

They "did" the gallery at high speed. Badgery never permitted his guest to halt for more than forty seconds before any work of art. Spode would have liked to spend a few moments of recollection and tranquillity in front of some of these lovely things. But it was not permitted.

The gallery done, they passed into a little room leading out of it. At the sight of what the lights revealed, Spode gasped.

"It's like something out of Balzac," he exclaimed. *"Un de ces salons dorés où se déploie un luxe insolent.* You know."

"My nineteenth-century chamber," Badgery explained. "The best thing of its kind, I flatter myself, outside the State Apartments at Windsor."

Spode tiptoed round the room, peering with astonishment at all the objects in glass, in gilded bronze, in china, in feathers, in embroidered and painted silk, in beads, in wax, objects of the most fantastic shapes and colours, all the queer products of a decadent tradition, with which the room was crowded. There were paintings on the walls—a Martin, a Wilkie, an early Landseer, several Ettys, a big Haydon, a slight pretty water-colour of a girl by Wainewright, the pupil of Blake and arsenic poisoner, and a score of others. But the picture which arrested Spode's attention was a medium-sized canvas representing Troilus riding into Troy among the flowers and plaudits of an admiring crowd, and oblivious (you could see from his expression) of everything but the eyes of Cressida, who looked down at him from a window, with Pandarus smiling over her shoulder.

"What an absurd and enchanting picture!" Spode exclaimed.

"Ah, you've spotted my Troilus." Lord Badgery was pleased.

"What bright harmonious colours! Like Etty's only stronger, not so obviously pretty. And there's an energy about it that reminds one of Haydon. Only Haydon could never have done anything so impeccable in taste. Who is it by?" Spode turned to his host inquiringly.

"You were right in detecting Haydon," Lord Badgery answered. "It's by his pupil, Tillotson. I wish I could get hold of more of his work. But nobody seems to know anything about him. And he seems to have done so little."

This time it was the younger man who interrupted.

"Tillotson, Tillotson . . ." He put his hand to his forehead. A

frown incongruously distorted his round, floridly curved face. "No
. . . yes, I have it." He looked up triumphantly with serene and
childish brows. "Tillotson, Walter Tillotson—the man's still alive."

Badgery smiled. "This picture was painted in 1846, you know."

"Well, that's all right. Say he was born in 1820, painted his masterpiece when he was twenty-six, and it's 1913 now; that's to say
he's only ninety-three. Not as old as Titian yet."

"But he's not been heard of since 1860," Lord Badgery protested.

"Precisely. Your mention of his name reminded me of the discovery I made the other day when I was looking through the obituary notices in the archives of the *World's Review.* (One has to
bring them up to date every year or so for fear of being caught
napping if one of these old birds chooses to shuffle off suddenly.)
Well there, among them—I remembered my astonishment at the
time—there I found Walter Tillotson's biography. Pretty full to
1860, and then a blank, except for a pencil note in the early nineteen hundreds to the effect that he had returned from the East. The
obituary has never been used or added to. I draw the obvious conclusion: the old chap isn't dead yet. He's just been overlooked
somehow."

"But this is extraordinary," Lord Badgery exclaimed. "You must
find him, Spode—you must find him. I'll commission him to paint
frescoes round this room. It's just what I've always vainly longed
for—a real nineteenth-century artist to decorate this place for me.
Oh, we must find him at once—at once."

Lord Badgery strode up and down in a state of great excitement.

" I can see how this room could be made quite perfect," he went
on. "We'd clear away all these cases and have the whole of that
wall filled by a heroic fresco of Hector and Andromache, or 'Dis-
training for Rent,' or Fanny Kemble as Belvidera in 'Venice Preserved'—anything like that, provided it's in the grand manner of
the 'thirties and 'forties. And here I'd have a landscape with lovely
receding perspectives, or else something architectural and grand in
the style of Belshazzar's feast. Then we'll have this Adam fireplace
taken down and replaced by something Mauro-Gothic. And on
these walls I'll have mirrors, or no! let me see . . ."

He sank into meditative silence, from which he finally roused
himself to shout:

"The old man, the old man! Spode, we must find this astonishing
old creature. And don't breathe a word to anybody. Tillotson shall
be our secret. Oh, it's too perfect, it's incredible! Think of the
frescoes."

Lord Badgery's face had become positively animated. He had talked of a single subject for nearly a quarter of an hour.

II

THREE WEEKS LATER Lord Badgery was aroused from his usual after-luncheon somnolence by the arrival of a telegram. The message was a short one. "Found.—Spode." A look of pleasure and intelligence made human Lord Badgery's clayey face of surfeit. "No answer,'" he said. The footman padded away on noiseless feet.

Lord Badgery closed his eyes and began to contemplate. Found! What a room he would have! There would be nothing like it in the world. The frescoes, the fireplace, the mirrors, the ceiling . . . And a small, shrivelled old man clambering about the scaffolding, agile and quick like one of those whiskered little monkeys at the Zoo, painting away, painting away . . . Fanny Kemble as Beividera, Hector and Andromache, or why not the Duke of Clarence in the Butt, the Duke of Malmsey, the Butt of Clarence . . . Lord Badgery was asleep.

Spode did not lag long behind his telegram. He was at Badgery House by six o'clock. His lordship was in the nineteenth-century chamber, engaged in clearing away with his own hands the bric-à-brac. Spode found him looking hot and out of breath.

"Ah, there you are," said Lord Badgery. "You see me already preparing for the great man's coming. Now you must tell me all about him."

"He's older than I thought," said Spode. "He's ninty-seven this year. Born in 1816. Incredible, isn't it! There, I'm beginning at the wrong end."

"Begin where you like," said Badgery genially.

"I won't tell you all the incidents of the hunt. You've no idea what a job I had to run him to earth. It was like a Sherlock Holmes story, immensely elaborate, too elaborate. I shall write a book about it some day. At any rate, I found him at last."

"Where?"

"In a sort of respectable slum in Holloway, older and poorer and lonelier than you could have believed possible. I found out how it was he came to be forgotten, how he came to drop out of life in the way he did. He took it into his head, somewhere about the 'sixties, to go to Palestine to get local colour for his religious pictures— scapegoats and things, you know. Well, he went to Jerusalem and then on to Mount Lebanon and on and on, and then, somewhere in the middle of Asia Minor, he got stuck. He got stuck for about forty years."

"But what did he do all that time?"

"Oh, he painted, and started a mission, and converted three Turks, and taught the local Pashas the rudiments of English, Latin, and perspective, and God knows what else. Then, in about 1904, it seems to have occurred to him that he was getting rather old and had been away from home for rather a long time. So he made his way back to England, only to find that everyone he had known was dead, that the dealers had never heard of him and wouldn't buy his pictures, that he was simply a ridiculous old figure of fun. So he got a job as a drawing-master in a girls' school in Holloway, and there he's been ever since, growing older and older, and feebler and feebler, and blinder and deafer, and generally more gaga, until finally the school has given him the sack. He had about ten pounds in the world when I found him. He lives in a kind of black hole in a basement full of beetles. When his ten pounds are spent, I suppose he'll just quietly die there."

Badgery held up a white hand. "No more, no more. I find literature quite depressing enough. I insist that life at least shall be a little gayer. Did you tell him I wanted him to paint my room?"

"But he can't paint. He's too blind and palsied."

"Can't paint?" Badgery exclaimed in horror. "Then what's the good of the old creature?"

"Well, if you put it like that . . ." Spode began.

"I shall never have my frescoes. Ring the bell, will you?"

Spode rang.

"What right has Tillotson to go on existing if he can't paint?" went on Lord Badgery petulantly. "After all, that was his only justification for occupying a place in the sun."

"He doesn't have much sun in his basement."

The footman appeared at the door.

"Get someone to put all these things back in their places," Lord Badgery commanded, indicating with a wave of the hand the ravaged cases, the confusion of glass and china with which he had littered the floor, the pictures unhooked. "We'll go to the library, Spode; it's more comfortable there."

He led the way through the long gallery and down the stairs.

"I'm sorry old Tillotson has been such a disappointment," said Spode sympathetically.

"Let us talk about something else; he ceases to interest me."

"But don't you think we ought to do something about him? He's

only got ten pounds between him and the workhouse. And if you'd
seen the blackbeetles in his basement!"

"Enough—enough. I'll do everything you think fitting."

"I thought we might get up a subscription amongst lovers of the
arts."

"There aren't any," said Badgery.

"No; but there are plenty of people who will subscribe out of
snobbism."

"Not unless you give them something for their money."

"That's true. I hadn't thought of that." Spode was silent for a
moment. "We might have a dinner in his honour. The great Tillotson Banquet. Doyen of British Art. A Link with the Past. Can't you
see it in the papers? I'd make a stunt of it in the *World's Review*.
That ought to bring in the snobs."

"And we'll invite a lot of artists and critics—all the ones who
can't stand one another. It will be fun to see them squabbling."
Badgery laughed. Then his face darkened once again. "Still," he
added, "it'll be a very poor second best to my frescoes. You'll stay
to dinner, of course."

"Well, since you suggest it. Thanks very much."

III

THE TILLOTSON BANQUET was fixed to take place about three
weeks later. Spode, who had charge of the arrangements, proved
himself an excellent organizer. He secured the big banqueting-room
at the Café Bomba, and was successful in bullying and cajoling the
manager into giving fifty persons dinner at twelve shillings a head,
including wine. He sent out invitations and collected subscriptions.
He wrote an article on Tillotson in the *World's Review*—one of
those charming, witty articles, couched in the tone of amused patronage and contempt with which one speaks of the great men of
1840. Nor did he neglect Tillotson himself. He used to go to Holloway almost every day to listen to the old man's endless stories
about Asia Minor and the Great Exhibition of '51 and Benjamin
Robert Haydon. He was sincerely sorry for this relic of another age.

Mr. Tillotson's room was about ten feet below the level of the soil
of South Holloway. A little grey light percolated through the area
bars, forced a difficult passage through panes opaque with dirt, and
spent itself, like a drop of milk that falls into an inkpot, among the
inveterate shadows of the dungeon. The place was haunted by the
sour smell of damp plaster and of woodwork that has begun to

moulder secretly at the heart. A little miscellaneous furniture, including a bed, a washstand and chest of drawers, a table and one or two chairs, lurked in the obscure corners of the den or ventured furtively out into the open. Hither Spode now came almost every day, bringing the old man news of the progress of the banquet scheme. Every day he found Mr. Tillotson sitting in the same place under the window, bathing, as it were, in his tiny puddle of light. "The oldest man that ever wore grey hairs," Spode reflected as he looked at him. Only there were very few hairs left on that bald, unpolished head. At the sound of the visitor's knock Mr. Tillotson would turn in his chair, stare in the direction of the door with blinking, uncertain eyes. He was always full of apologies for being so slow in recognising who was there.

"No discourtesy meant," he would say, after asking. "It's not as if I had forgotten who you were. Only it's so dark and my sight isn't what it was."

After that he never failed to give a little laugh, and, pointing out of the window at the area railings, would say:

"Ah, this is the place for somebody with good sight. It's the place for looking at ankles. It's the grand stand."

It was the day before the great event. Spode came as usual, and Mr. Tillotson punctually made his little joke about the ankles, and Spode as punctually laughed.

"Well, Mr. Tillotson," he said, after the reverberation of the joke had died away, "to-morrow you make your re-entry into the world of art and fashion. You'll find some changes."

"I've always had such extraordinary luck," said Mr. Tillotson, and Spode could see by his expression that he genuinely believed it, that he had forgotten the black hole and the blackbeetles and the almost exhausted ten pounds that stood between him and the workhouse. "What an amazing piece of good fortune, for instance, that you should have found me just when you did. Now, this dinner will bring me back to my place in the world. I shall have money, and in a little while—who knows?—I shall be able to see well enough to paint again. I believe my eyes are getting better, you know. Ah, the future is very rosy."

Mr. Tillotson looked up, his face puckered into a smile, and nodded his head in affirmation of his words.

"You believe in the life to come?" said Spode, and immediately flushed for shame at the cruelty of the words.

"Life to come," he repeated. "No, I don't believe in any of that stuff—not since 1859. The 'Origin of Species' changed my views, you know. No life to come for me, thank you! You don't remember the excitement, of course. You're very young, Mr. Spode."

"Well, I'm not so old as I was," Spode replied. "You know how middle-aged one is as a schoolboy and undergraduate. Now I'm old enough to know I'm young."

Spode was about to develop this little paradox further, but he noticed that Mr. Tillotson had not been listening. He made a note of the gambit for use in companies that were more appreciative of the subtleties.

"You were talking about the 'Origin of Species,'" he said.

"Was I?" said Mr. Tillotson, waking from reverie.

"About its effect on your faith, Mr. Tillotson."

"To be sure, yes. It shattered my faith. But I remember a fine thing by the Poet Laureate, something about there being more faith in honest doubt, believe me, than in all the . . . all the . . . I forget exactly what; but you see the train of thought. Oh, it was a bad time for religion. I am glad my master Haydon never lived to see it. He was a man of fervour. I remember him pacing up and down his studio in Lisson Grove, singing and shouting and praying all at once. It used almost to frighten me. Oh, but he was a wonderful man, a great man. Take him for all in all, we shall not look upon his like again. As usual, the Bard is right. But it was all very long ago, before your time, Mr. Spode."

"Well, I'm not as old as I was," said Spode, in the hope of having his paradox appreciated this time. But Mr. Tillotson went on without noticing the interruption.

"It's a very, very long time. And yet, when I look back on it, it all seems but a day or two ago. Strange that each day should seem so long and that many days added together should be less than an hour. How clearly I can see old Haydon pacing up and down! Much more clearly, indeed, than I see you, Mr. Spode. The eyes of memory don't grow dim. But my sight is improving, I assure you; it's improving daily. I shall soon be able to see those ankles." He laughed, like a cracked bell—one of those little old bells Spode fancied, that ring, with much rattling of wires, in the far-off servants' quarters of ancient houses. "And very soon," Mr. Tillotson went on, "I shall be painting again. Ah, Mr. Spode, my luck is extraordinary. I believe in it, I trust it. And after all, what is luck? Simply another name for Providence, in spite of the 'Origin of Species' and the rest of it. How right the Laureate was when he said that there was more faith in honest doubt, believe me, than in all the . . . er, the . . . er . . . well, you know. I regard you, Mr.

Spode, as the emissary of Providence. Your coming marked a turning-point in my life, and the beginning, for me, of happier days. Do
you know, one of the first things I shall do when my fortunes are
restored will be to buy a hedgehog."

"A hedgehog, Mr. Tillotson?"

"For the blackbeetles. There's nothing like a hedgehog for beetles.
It will eat blackbeetles till it's sick, till it dies of surfeit. That reminds me of the time when I told my poor great master Haydon—
in joke, of course—that he ought to send in a cartoon of King John
dying of a surfeit of lampreys for the frescoes in the new Houses
of Parliament. As I told him, it's a most notable event in the annals
of British liberty—the providential and exemplary removal of a
tyrant."

Mr. Tillotson laughed again—the little bell in the deserted house;
a ghostly hand pulling the cord in the drawing-room, and phantom
footmen responding to the thin, flawed note.

"I remember he laughed, laughed like a bull in his old grand
manner. But oh, it was a terrible blow when they rejected his designs, a terrible blow! It was the first and fundamental cause of his
suicide."

Mr. Tillotson paused. There was a long silence. Spode felt
strangely moved, he hardly knew why, in the presence of this man,
so frail, so ancient, in body three parts dead, in the spirit so full of
life and hopeful patience. He felt ashamed. What was the use of his
own youth and cleverness? He saw himself suddenly as a boy with
a rattle scaring birds—rattling his noisy cleverness, waving his arms
in ceaseless and futile activity, never resting in his efforts to scare
away the birds that were always trying to settle in his mind. And
what birds! wide-winged and beautiful, all those serene thoughts
and faiths and emotions that only visit minds that have humbled
themselves to quiet. Those gracious visitants he was for ever using
all his energies to drive away. But this old man, with his hedgehogs
and his honest doubts and all the rest of it—his mind was like a
field made beautiful by the free coming and going, the unafraid
alightings of a multitude of white, bright-winged creatures. He felt
ashamed. But then, was it possible to alter one's life? Wasn't it a
little absurd to risk a conversion? Spode shrugged his shoulders.

"I'll get you a hedgehog at once," he said. "They're sure to have
some at Whiteley's."

Before he left that evening Spode made an alarming discovery.
Mr. Tillotson did not possess a dress-suit. It was hopeless to think

of getting one made at this short notice, and, besides, what an unnecessary expense!

"We shall have to borrow a suit, Mr. Tillotson. I ought to have
thought of that before."

"Dear me, dear me." Mr. Tillotson was a little chagrined by this
unlucky discovery. "Borrow a suit?"

Spode hurried away for counsel to Badgery House. Lord Badgery
surprisingly rose to the occasion. "Ask Boreham to come and see
me," he told the footman who answered his ring.

Boreham was one of those immemorial butlers who lingered on,
generation after generation, in the houses of the great. He was over
eighty now, bent, dried up, shrivelled with age.

"All old men are about the same size," said Lord Badgery. It was
a comforting theory. "Ah, here he is. Have you got a spare suit of
evening clothes, Boreham?"

"I have an old suit, my lord, that I stopped wearing in—let me
see—was it nineteen seven or eight?"

"That's the very thing. I should be most grateful, Boreham, if
you could lend it to me for Mr. Spode here for a day."

The old man went out, and soon reappeared carrying over his
arm a very old black suit. He held up the coat and trousers for inspection. In the light of the day they were deplorable.

"You've no idea, sir," said Boreham deprecatingly to Spode—
"you've no idea how easy things get stained with grease and gravy
and what not. However careful you are, sir—however careful."

"I should imagine so." Spode was sympathetic.

"However careful, sir."

"But in artificial light they'll look all right."

"Perfectly all right," Lord Badgery repeated. "Thank you, Boreham; you shall have them back on Thursday."

"You're welcome, my Lord, I'm sure," and the old man bowed
and disappeared.

On the afternoon of the great day Spode carried up to Holloway
a parcel containing Boreham's retired evening-suit and all the necessary appurtenances in the way of shirts and collars. Owing to the
darkness and his own feeble sight Mr. Tillotson was happily unaware of the defects in the suit. He was in a state of extreme nervous agitation. It was with some difficulty that Spode could prevent
him, although it was only three o'clock, from starting his toilet on
the spot.

"Take it easy, Mr. Tillotson, take it easy. We needn't start till
half-past seven, you know."

Spode left an hour later, and as soon as he was safely out of the room Mr. Tillotson began to prepare himself for the banquet. He lighted the gas and a couple of candles, and, blinking myopically at the image that fronted him in the tiny looking-glass that stood on his chest of drawers, he set to work, with all the ardour of a young girl preparing for her first ball. At six o'clock, when the last touches had been given, he was not unsatisfied.

He marched up and down his cellar, humming to himself the gay song which had been so popular in his middle years:

"Oh, oh, Anna Maria Jones!
Queen of the tambourine, the cymbals, and the bones!"

Spode arrived an hour later in Lord Badgery's second Rolls-Royce. Opening the door of the old man's dungeon, he stood for a moment, wide-eyed with astonishment, on the threshold. Mr. Tillotson was standing by the empty grate, one elbow resting on the mantelpiece, one leg crossed over the other in a jaunty and gentlemanly attitude. The effect of the candlelight shining on his face was to deepen every line and wrinkle with intense black shadow; he looked immeasurably old. It was a noble and pathetic head. On the other hand, Boreham's outworn evening-suit was simply buffoonish. The coat was too long in the sleeves and the tail; the trousers bagged in elephantine creases about his ankles. Some of the grease-spots were visible even in candlelight. The white tie over which Mr. Tillotson had taken infinite pains and which he believed in his purblindness to be perfect, was fantastically lop-sided. He had buttoned up his waistcoat in such a fashion that one button was widowed of its hole and one hole of its button. Across his chest front lay the broad green ribbon of some unknown Order.

"Queen of the tambourine, the cymbals, and the bones," Mr. Tillotson concluded in a gnat-like voice before welcoming his visitor.

"Well, Spode, here you are. I'm dressed already, you see. The suit, I flatter myself, fits very well, almost as though it had been made for me. I am all gratitude to the gentleman who was kind enough to lend it to me; I shall take the greatest care of it. It's a dangerous thing to lend clothes. For loan oft loseth both itself and friend. The Bard is always right."

"Just one thing," Spode said. "A touch to your waistcoat." He unbuttoned the dissipated garment and did it up again more symmetrically.

Mr. Tillotson was a little piqued at being found so absurdly in the wrong. "Thanks, thanks," he said protestingly, trying to edge away from his valet. "It's all right, you know; I can do it myself. Foolish oversight. I flatter myself the suit fits very well."

"And perhaps the tie might . . ." Spode began tentatively. But the old man would not hear of it.

"No, no. The tie's all right. I can tie a tie, Mr. Spode. The tie's all right. Leave it as it is, I beg."

"I like your Order."

Mr. Tillotson looked down complacently at his shirt front. "Ah, you've noticed my Order. It's a long time since I wore that. It was given me by the Grand Porte, you know, for services rendered in the Russo-Turkish War. It's the Order of Chastity, the second class. They only give the first class to crowned heads, you know—crowned heads and ambassadors. And only Pashas of the highest rank get the second. Mine's the second. They only give the first class to crowned heads . . ."

"Of course, of course," said Spode.

"Do you think I look all right, Mr. Spode?" Mr. Tillotson asked, a little anxiously.

"Splendid, Mr. Tillotson—splendid. The Order's magnificent."

The old man's face brightened once more. "I flatter myself," he said, "that this borrowed suit fits me very well. But I don't like borrowing clothes. For loan oft loseth both itself and friend, you know. And the Bard is always right."

"Ugh, there's one of those horrible beetles!" Spode exclaimed.

Mr. Tillotson bent down and stared at the floor. "I see it," he said, and stamped on a small piece of coal, which crunched to powder under his foot. "I shall certainly buy a hedgehog."

It was time for them to start. A crowd of little boys and girls had collected round Lord Badgery's enormous car. The chauffeur, who felt that honour and dignity were at stake, pretended not to notice the children, but sat gazing, like a statue, into eternity. At the sight of Spode and Mr. Tillotson emerging from the house a yell of mingled awe and derision went up. It subsided to an astonished silence as they climbed into the car. "Bomba's," Spode directed. The Rolls-Royce gave a faintly stertorous sigh and began to move. The children yelled again, and ran along beside the car, waving their arms in a frenzy of excitement. It was then that Mr. Tillotson, with an incomparably noble gesture, leaned forward and tossed among the seething crowd of urchins his three last coppers.

IV

IN BOMBA'S BIG ROOM the company was assembling. The long gilt-edged mirrors reflected a singular collection of people. Middle-aged Academicians shot suspicious glances at youths whom they suspected, only too correctly, of being iconoclasts, organisers of Post-Impressionist Exhibitions. Rival art critics, brought suddenly face to face, quivered with restrained hatred. Mrs. Nobes, Mrs. Cayman and Mrs. Mandragore, those indefatigable hunters of artistic big game, came on one another all unawares in this well-stored managerie, where each had expected to hunt alone, and were filled with rage. Through this crowd of mutually repellent vanities Lord Badgery moved with a suavity that seemed unconscious of all the feuds and hatreds. He was enjoying himself immensely. Behind the heavy waxen mask of his face, ambushed behind the Hanoverian nose, the little lustreless pig's eyes, the pale thick lips, there lurked a small devil of happy malice that rocked with laughter.

"So nice of you to have come, Mrs. Mandragore, to do honour to England's artistic past. And I'm so glad to see you've brought dear Mrs. Cayman. And is that Mrs. Nobes, too? So it is! I hadn't noticed her before. How delightful! I knew we could depend on your love of art."

And he hurried away to seize the opportunity of introducing that eminent sculptor, Sir Herbert Herne, to the bright young critic who had called him, in the public prints, a monumental mason.

A moment later the Maître d'Hôtel came to the door of the gilded saloon and announced, loudly and impressively, "Mr. Walter Tillotson." Guided from behind by young Spode, Mr. Tillotson came into the room slowly and hesitatingly. In the glare of the lights his eyelids beat heavily, painfully, like the wings of an imprisoned moth, over his filmy eyes. Once inside the door he halted and drew himself up with a conscious assumption of dignity. Lord Badgery hurried forward and seized his hand.

"Welcome, Mr. Tillotson—welcome in the name of English art!"

Mr. Tillotson inclined his head in silence. He was too full of emotion to be able to reply.

"I should like to introduce you to a few of your younger colleagues, who have assembled here to do you honour."

Lord Badgery presented everyone in the room to the old painter, who bowed, shook hands, made little noises in his throat, but still found himself unable to speak. Mrs. Nobes, Mrs. Cayman, and Mrs. Mandragore all said charming things.

Dinner was served; the party took their places. Lord Badgery sat at the head of the table, with Mr. Tillotson on his right hand and Sir Herbert Herne on his left. Confronted with Bomba's succulent cooking and Bomba's wines, Mr. Tillotson ate and drank a good deal. He had the appetite of one who has lived on greens and potatoes for ten years among the blackbeetles. After the second glass of wine he began to talk, suddenly and in a flood, as though a sluice had been pulled up.

"In Asia Minor," he began, "it is the custom, when one goes to dinner, to hiccough as a sign of appreciative fullness, *Eructavit cor meum**, as the Psalmist has it; he was an Oriental himself."

Spode had arranged to sit next to Mrs. Cayman; he had designs upon her. She was an impossible woman, of course, but rich and useful; he wanted to bamboozle her into buying some of his young friends' pictures.

"In a cellar?" Mrs. Cayman was saying, "with blackbeetles? Oh, how dreadful! Poor old man! And he's ninety-seven, didn't you say? Isn't that shocking! I only hope the subscription will be a large one. Of course, one wishes one could have given more oneself. But then, you know, one has so many expenses, and things are so difficult now."

"I know, I know," said Spode, with feeling.

"It's all because of Labour," Mrs. Cayman explained. "Of course, I should simply love to have him in to dinner sometimes. But, then, I feel he's really too old, too *farouche* and *gâteux;* it would not be doing a kindness to him, would it? And so you are working with Mr. Gollamy now? What a charming man, so talented, such conversation . . ."

"*Eructavit cor meum,*" said Mr. Tillotson for the third time. Lord Badgery tried to head him off the subject of Turkish etiquette, but in vain.

By half-past nine a kinder vinolent atmosphere had put to sleep the hatreds and suspicions of before dinner. Sir Herbert Herne had discovered that the young Cubist sitting next him was not insane and actually knew a surprising amount about the Old Masters. For their part these young men had realised that their elders were not all malignant; they were just very stupid and pathetic. It was only in the bosoms of Mrs. Nobes, Mrs. Cayman, and Mrs. Mandragore that hatred still reigned undiminished. Being ladies and old-fashioned, they had drunk almost no wine.

The moment for speech-making arrived. Lord Badgery rose to

---

* *My heart hath uttered: beginning Psalm XLIV of the Vulgate.*

his feet, said what was expected of him, and called upon Sir Herbert to propose the toast of the evening. Sir Herbert coughed, smiled, and began. In the course of a speech that lasted twenty minutes he told anecdotes of Mr. Gladstone, Lord Leighton, Sir Alma Tadema, and the late Bishop of Bombay; he made three puns, he quoted Shakespeare and Whittier, he was playful, he was eloquent, he was grave . . . At the end of his harangue Sir Herbert handed to Mr. Tillotson a silk purchase containing fifty-eight pounds ten shillings, the total amount of the subscription. The old man's health was drunk with acclamation.

Mr. Tillotson rose with difficulty to his feet. The dry, snakelike skin of his face was flushed; his tie was more crooked than ever; the green ribbon of the Order of Chastity of the second class had somehow climbed up his crumpled and maculate shirt-front.

"My lords, ladies, and gentlemen," he began in a choking voice, and then broke down completely. It was a very painful and pathetic spectacle. A feeling of intense discomfort afflicted the minds of all who looked upon that trembling relic of a man, as he stood there weeping and stammering. It was as though a breath of the wind of death had blown suddenly through the room, lifting the vapours of wine and tobacco-smoke, quenching the laughter and the candle flames. Eyes floated uneasily, not knowing where to look. Lord Badgery, with great presence of mind, offered the old man a glass of wine. Mr. Tillotson began to recover. The guests heard him murmur a few disconnected words.

"This great honour . . . overwhelmed with kindness . . . this magnificent banquet . . . not used to it . . . in Asia Minor . . . *eructavit cor meum.*"

At this point Lord Badgery plucked sharply at one of his long coat tails. Mr. Tillotson paused, took another sip of wine, and then went on with a newly won coherence and energy.

"The life of the artist is a hard one. His work is unlike other men's work, which may be done mechanically, by rote and almost, as it were, in sleep. It demands from him a constant expense of spirit. He gives continually of his best life, and in return he receives much joy, it is true—much fame, it may be—but of material blessings, very few. It is eighty years since first I devoted my life to the service of art; eighty years, and almost every one of those years has brought me fresh and painful proof of what I have been saying: the artist's life is a hard one."

This unexpected deviation into sense increased the general feeling of discomfort. It became necessary to take the old man seriously, to regard him as a human being. Up till then he had been no more than an object of curiosity, a mummy in an absurd suit of evening clothes with a green ribbon across the shirt-front. People could not help wishing that they had subscribed a little more. Fifty-eight pounds ten—it wasn't enormous. But happily for the peace of mind of the company, Mr. Tillotson paused again, took another sip of wine, and began to live up to his proper character by talking absurdly.

"When I consider the life of that great man, Benjamin Robert Haydon, one of the greatest men England has ever produced . . ." The audience heaved a sigh of relief; this was all as it should be. There was a burst of loud bravoing and clapping. Mr. Tillotson turned his dim eyes round the room, and smiled gratefully at the misty figures he beheld. "That great man, Benjamin Robert Haydon," he continued, "whom I am proud to call my master and who, it rejoices my heart to see, still lives in your memory and esteem,—that great man, one of the greatest that England has ever produced, led a life so deplorable that I cannot think of it without a tear."

And with infinite repetitions and divagations, Mr. Tillotson related the history of B. R. Haydon, his imprisonment for debt, his battle with the Academy, his triumphs, his failures, his despair, his suicide. Half-past ten struck. Mr. Tillotson was declaiming against the stupid and prejudiced judges who had rejected Haydon's designs for the decoration of the new Houses of Parliament in favour of the paltriest German scribblings.

"That great man, one of the greatest England has ever produced, that great Benjamin Robert Haydon, whom I am proud to call my master and who, it rejoices me to see, still lives on in your memory and esteem—at that affront his great heart burst; it was the unkindest cut of all. He who had worked all his life for the recognition of the artist by the State, he who had petitioned every Prime Minister, including the Duke of Wellington, for thirty years, begging them to employ artists to decorate public buildings, he to whom the scheme for decorating the Houses of Parliament was undeniably due . . ." Mr. Tillotson lost a grip on his syntax and began a new sentence. "It was the unkindest cut of all, it was the last straw. The artist's life is a hard one."

At eleven Mr. Tillotson was talking about the pre-Raphaelites. At a quarter-past he had begun to tell the story of B. R. Haydon all over again. At twenty-five minutes to twelve he collapsed quite speechless into his chair. Most of the guests had already gone away;

the few who remained made haste to depart. Lord Badgery led the old man to the door and packed him into the second Rolls-Royce. The Tillotson Banquet was over; it had been a pleasant evening, but a little too long.

Spode walked back to his rooms in Bloomsbury, whistling as he went. The arc lamps of Oxford Street reflected in the polished surface of the road: canals of dark bronze. He would have to bring that into an article some time. The Cayman woman had been very successfully nobbled. *"Voi che sapete,"* he whistled—somewhat out of tune, but he could not hear that.

When Mr. Tillotson's landlady came in to call him on the following morning, she found the old man lying fully dressed on his bed. He looked very ill and very, very old; Boreham's dress-suit was in a terrible state, and the green ribbon of the Order of Chastity was ruined. Mr. Tillotson lay very still, but he was not asleep. Hearing the sound of footsteps, he opened his eyes a little and faintly groaned. His landlady looked down at him menacingly.

"Disgusting!" she said; "disgusting, I call it. At your age."

Mr. Tillotson groaned again. Making a great effort, he drew out of his trouser pocket a large silk purse, opened it, and extracted a sovereign.

"The artist's life is a hard one, Mrs. Green," he said, handing her the coin. "Would you mind sending for the doctor? I don't feel very well. And oh, what shall I do about these clothes? What shall I say to the gentleman who was kind enough to lend them to me? Loan oft loseth both itself and friend. The Bard is always right."

W. SOMERSET MAUGHAM

****

*Mr. Maugham, so famous for his novels and short stories, agreed
to the use of part of* The Summing Up *in* THE WORLD'S BEST. *However, he thought selecting a fragment "would mean a considerable
amount of work which I am not prepared to do. If Whit Burnett
would like to choose a bit for himself I can see no reason why he
shouldn't do so."*

*It seems to Whit Burnett that no finer summary of three great
values has been written than the summary concluding the volume
from which "Truth, Beauty and Goodness" is taken. The editor
would also like to quote two paragraphs from the section which
immediately precedes this selection.*

I have always lived so much in the future that now though the future is so short, I cannot get out of the habit and my mind looks
forward with a certain complacency to the completion within an
indefinite number of years of the pattern that I have tried to make.
There are moments when I have so palpitating an eagerness for
death that I could fly to it as to the arms of a lover. It gives me the
same passionate thrill as years ago was given me by life. I am drunk
with the thought of it. It seems to me then to offer me the final
and absolute freedom. Notwithstanding, I am willing enough to go
on living so long as the doctors can keep me in tolerable health; I
enjoy the spectacle of the world and it interests me to see what is
going to happen. The consummation of many lives that have run
their course parallel with my own gives me continual food for reflection and sometimes for the confirmation of theories that I
formed long ago. I shall be sorry to part from my friends, I cannot
be indifferent to the welfare of some whom I have guided and protected, but it is well that after depending on me so long they should
enjoy their liberty whithersoever it leads them. Having held a certain place in the world for a long time I am content that others
soon should occupy it. After all the point of a pattern is that it
should be completed. When nothing can be added without spoiling
the design the artist leaves it.

But now if anyone should ask me what is the use or sense of this
pattern I should have to answer, none. It is merely something I have

imposed on the senselessness of life because I am a novelist. For my own satisfaction, for my amusement and to gratify what feels to me like an organic need, I have shaped my life in accordance with a certain design, with a beginning, a middle and an end, as from people I have met here and there I have constructed a play, a novel or a short story. We are the product of our natures and our environment. I have not made the pattern I thought best, or even the pattern I should have liked to make, but merely that which seemed feasible. There are better patterns than mine. I do not believe that I am influenced only by an illusion natural to the man of letters to think that the best pattern of all is the husbandman's who ploughs his land and reaps his crop, who enjoys his toil and enjoys his leisure, loves, marries, begets children and dies. When I have observed the peasantry in those favoured lands in which the earth produces her plenty without excessive labour, where the pleasures and pains of the individual are those incidental to the human race, it has seemed to me that there the perfect life was perfectly realized. There life, like a good story, pursues its way from beginning to end in a firm and unbroken line.

****

Truth, Beauty and Goodness

THE EGOISM of man makes him unwilling to accept the meaninglessness of life and when he has unhappily found himself no longer able to believe in a higher power whose ends he could flatter himself that he subserved he has sought to give it significance by constructing certain values beyond those that seem to further his immediate welfare. The wisdom of the ages has chosen three of these as most worthy. To aim at them for their own sake has seemed to give life some kind of sense. Though it can hardly be doubted that they too have a biologic utility, they have superficially an appearance of disinterestedness which gives man the illusion that through them he escapes from human bondage. Their nobility strengthens his wavering sense of his spiritual significance and, whatever the result, the pursuit of them appears to justify his efforts. Oases in the vast desert of existence, since he knows no other end to his journey, man persuades himself that they at all events are worth reaching and that there he will find rest and the answer to his question. These three values are Truth, Beauty and Goodness.

I have a notion that Truth finds a place in this list for rhetorical reasons. Man invests it with ethical qualities, such as courage, honour and independence of spirit, which indeed are often shown by his insistence on truth, but which in effect have nothing whatever to do with it. Finding in it so great an occasion for his own self-assertion he will be indifferent to any sacrifice that it entails. But then his interest is in himself and not in the truth. If truth is a value it is because it is true and not because it is brave to speak it. But truth is a character of judgments and so one would suppose that its value lay in the judgments it characterizes rather than in itself. A bridge that joined two great cities would be more important than a bridge that led from one barren field to another. And if truth is one of the ultimate values, it seems strange that no one seems quite to know what it is. Philosophers still quarrel about its meaning and the upholders of rival doctrines say many sarcastic things of one another. In these circumstances the plain man must leave them to it and content himself with the plain man's truth. This is a very modest affair and merely asserts something about particular existents. It is a bare statement of the facts. If this is a value one must admit that none is more neglected. The books on ethics give long lists of occasions on which it may be legitimately withheld; their authors might have saved themselves the trouble. The wisdom of the ages has long since decided that *toutes vérités ne sont pas bonnes à dire*. Man has always sacrificed truth to his vanity, comfort and advantage. He lives not by truth but by make-believe, and his idealism, it has sometimes seemed to me, is merely his effort to attach the prestige of truth to the fictions he has invented to satisfy his self-conceit.

Beauty stands in a better case. For many years I thought that it was beauty alone that gave significance to life and that the only purpose that could be assigned to the teeming generations that succeed one another on the face of the earth was to produce now and then an artist. The work of art, I decided, was the crowning product of human activity, and the final justification for all the misery, the endless toil and the frustrated strivings of humanity. So that Michelangelo might paint certain figures on the ceiling of the Sistine Chapel, so that Shakespeare might write certain speeches and Keats his odes, it seemed to me worth while that untold millions should have lived and suffered and died. And though I modified this extravagance later by including the beautiful life among the works of art that alone gave a meaning to life, it was still beauty that I valued. All these notions I have long since abandoned.

In the first place I discovered that beauty was a full stop. When I considered beautiful things I found that there was nothing for me to do but to gaze and admire. The emotion they gave me was exquisite, but I could not preserve it, nor could I indefinitely repeat it; the most beautiful things in the world finished by boring me. I noticed that I got a more lasting satisfaction from works of a more tentative character. Because they had not achieved complete success they gave more scope for the activity of my imagination. In the greatest of all works of art everything had been realized, I could give nothing, and my restless mind tired of passive contemplation. It seemed to me that beauty was like the summit of a mountain peak; when you had reached it there was nothing to do but to come down again. Perfection is a trifle dull. It is not the least of life's ironies that this, which we all aim at, is better not quite achieved.

I suppose that we mean by beauty that object, spiritual or material, more often material, which satisfies our æsthetic sense. That, however, tells you just about as much as you would know about water if you were told that it was wet. I have read a good many books to discover what the authorities had to say that made the matter a little plainer. I have known intimately a great many persons who were absorbed in the arts. I am afraid that neither from them nor from books have I learnt much that greatly profited me. One of the most curious things that has forced itself on my notice is that there is no permanence in the judgment of beauty. The museums are full of objects which the most cultivated taste of a period considered beautiful, but which seem to us now worthless; and in my own lifetime I have seen the beauty evaporate from poems and pictures, exquisite not so long ago, like hoar frost before the morning sun. Vain as we may be we can hardly think our own judgment ultimate: what we think beautiful will doubtless be scorned in another generation, and what we have despised may be raised to honour. The only conclusion is that beauty is relative to the needs of a particular generation, and that to examine the things we consider beautiful for qualities of absolute beauty is futile. If beauty is one of the values that give life significance it is something that is constantly changing and thus cannot be analyzed, for we can as little feel the beauty our ancestors felt as we can smell the roses they smelt.

I have tried to find out from the writers on æsthetics what it is in human nature that makes it possible for us to get the emotion of beauty and what exactly this emotion is. It is usual enough to talk of the æsthetic instinct: the term seems to give it a place among the mainsprings of the human being, like hunger and sex, and at the same time to endow it with a specific quality that flatters the philosophic craving for unity. So æsthetics have been derived from an instinct of expression, an exuberance of vitality, a mystical sense of the absolute and I know not what. For my part I should have said it was not an instinct at all, but a state of the body-mind, founded in part on certain powerful instincts, but combined with human characteristics, which are the result of the evolutionary progress, and with the common circumstances of life. That it has a great deal to do with the sexual instinct seems to be shown by the fact, commonly admitted, that those who possess an æsthetic sense of unusual delicacy diverge sexually from the norm to an extreme and often pathological degree. There may be in the constitution of the body-mind something that renders certain tones, certain rhythms and certain colours peculiarly attractive to man, so that there may be a physiological reason for the elements of what we consider beautiful. But we also find things beautiful because they remind us of objects, people or places, that we have loved or to which the passage of time has lent a sentimental value. We find things beautiful because we recognize them and contrariwise we find things beautiful because their novelty surprises us. All this means that association, by likeness or contrast, enters largely into the æsthetic emotion. It is only association that can explain the æsthetic value of the ugly. I do not know that anyone has studied the effect of time on the creation of beauty. It is not only that we grow to see the beauty of things as we know them better; it is rather that the delight, that succeeding ages take in them somehow adds to their beauty. That, I suppose, is why certain works whose beauty now seems manifest should, when first given to the world, have attracted no great attention. I have a notion that the odes of Keats are more beautiful than when he wrote them. They are enriched by the emotion of all who have found solace and strength in their loveliness. Far then from thinking the æsthetic emotion a specific, simple affair, I think it is a very complicated one, which is made up of various, often discordant elements. It is no good for the æstheticians to say that you ought not to be moved by a picture or a symphony because it fills you with erotic excitement or melts you to tears by reminding you of some long-forgotten scene, or through its associations exalts you to mystic rapture. It does; and these sides of it are just as much part and parcel of the æsthetic emotion as the disinterested satisfaction in balance and composition.

What exactly is one's reaction to a great work of art? What does one feel when for instance one looks at Titian's Entombment in the Louvre or listens to the quintet in the *Meistersinger?* I know what mine is. It is an excitement that gives me a sense of exhilaration, intellectual but suffused with sensuality, a feeling of well-being in which I seem to discern a sense of power and of liberation from human ties; at the same time I feel in myself a tenderness which is rich with human sympathy; I feel rested, at peace and yet spiritually aloof. Indeed on occasion, looking at certain pictures or statues, listening to certain music, I have had an emotion so strong that I could only describe it in the same words as those the mystics use to describe the union with God. That is why I have thought that this sense of communion with a larger reality is not only the privilege of the religious, but may be reached by other paths than prayer and fasting. But I have asked myself what was the use of this emotion. Of course it is delightful and pleasure in itself is good, but what is there in it that makes it superior to any other pleasure, so superior that to speak of it as pleasure at all means to depreciate it? Was Jeremy Bentham so foolish after all when he said that one sort of happiness was as good as another, and if the amount of pleasure was equal pushpin as good as poetry? The answer the mystics gave to this question was unequivocal. They said that rapture was worthless unless it strengthened the character and rendered man more capable of right action. The value of it lay in works.

It has been my lot to live much among persons of æsthetic sensibility. I am not speaking now of the creators: to my mind there is a great difference between those who create art and those who enjoy it; the creators produce because of that urge within them that forces them to exteriorize their personality. It is an accident if what they produce has beauty; that is seldom their special aim. Their aim is to disembarrass their souls of the burdens that oppress them and they use the means, their pen, their paints or their clay, for which they have by nature a facility. I am speaking now of those to whom the contemplation and appreciation of art is the main business of life. I have found little to admire in them. They are vain and self-complacent. Inapt for the practical affairs of life, they disdain those who with humility perform the modest offices to which their destiny has constrained them. Because they have read a great many books or seen a great many pictures they think themselves superior to other men. They use art to escape the realities of life and in their imbecile contempt for common things deny value to the essential activities of humanity. They are no better really than drug-fiends; worse rather, for the drug-fiend at all events does not set himself on a pedestal from which to look down on his fellow men. The value of art, like the value of the Mystic Way, lies in its effects. If it can only give pleasure, however spiritual that pleasure may be, it is of no great consequence or at least of no more consequence than a dozen oysters and a pint of Montrachet. If it is a solace, that is well enough; the world is full of inevitable evils and it is good that man should have some heritage to which from time to time he may withdraw himself; but not to escape them, rather to gather fresh strength to face them. For art, if it is to be reckoned as one of the great values of life, must teach men humility, tolerance, wisdom and magnanimity. The value of art is not beauty, but right action.

If beauty is one of the great values of life, then it seems hard to believe that the æsthetic sense which enables men to appreciate it should be the privilege only of a class. It is not possible to maintain that a form of sensibility that is shared but by the elect can be a necessity of human life. Yet that is what the æsthetics claim. I must confess that in my foolish youth when I considered that art (in which I included the beauties of nature, for I was very much of opinion, as indeed I still am, that their beauty was constructed by men as definitely as they constructed pictures or symphonies) was the crown of human endeavour and the justification of man's existence, it gave me a peculiar satisfaction to think that it could be appreciated only by the chosen few. But this notion has long stuck in my gizzard. I cannot believe that beauty is the appanage of a set and I am inclined to think that a manifestation of art that has a meaning only to persons who have undergone a peculiar training is as inconsiderable as the set to which it appeals. An art is only great and significant if it is one that all may enjoy. The art of a clique is but a plaything. I do not know why distinctions are made between ancient art and modern art. There is nothing but art. Art is living. To attempt to give an object of art life by dwelling on its historical, cultural or archæological associations is senseless. It does not matter whether a statue was hewn by an archaic Greek or a modern Frenchman. Its only importance is that it should give us here and now the aesthetic thrill and that this æsthetic thrill should move us to works. If it is to be anything more than a self-indulgence and an occasion of self-complacency, it must strengthen your character and make it more fitted for right action. And little as I like

the deduction, I cannot but accept it; and this is that the work of
art must be judged by its fruits, and if these are not good it is valueless. It is an odd fact, which must be accepted as in the nature of
things and for which I know no explanation, that the artist achieves
this effect only when he does not intend it. His sermon is most
efficacious if he has no notion that he is preaching one. The bee
produces wax for her own purposes and is unaware that man will
put it to diverse uses.

It appears then impossible to say that either truth or beauty has
intrinsic value. What about goodness? But before I speak of goodness I would speak of love; for there are philosophers who, thinking
that it embraced every other, have accepted it as the highest of
human values. Platonism and Christianity have combined to give it
a mystic significance. The associations of the word lend it an emotion that makes it more exciting than plain goodness. Goodness in
comparison is a trifle dull. But love has two meanings, love pure
and simple, sexual love, namely; and loving-kindness. I do not think
that even Plato distinguished them with exactness. He seems to me
to ascribe the exultation, the sense of power, the feeling of heightened vitality which accompany sexual love to that other love which
he calls the heavenly love and which I should prefer to call loving-
kindness; and by doing so infects it with the ineradicable vice of
earthly love. For love passes. Love dies. The great tragedy of life
is not that men perish, but that they cease to love. Not the least of
the evils of life, and one for which there is small help, is that someone whom you love no longer loves you; when La Rochefoucauld
discovered that between two lovers there is one who loves and
one who lets himself be loved he put in an epigram the discord that
must ever prevent men from achieving in love perfect happiness.
However much people may resent the fact and however angrily
deny it, there can surely be no doubt that love depends on certain
secretions of the sexual glands. In the immense majority these do
not continue indefinitely to be excited by the same object and with
advancing years they atrophy. People are very hypocritical in this
matter and will not face the truth. They so deceive themselves that
they can accept it with complacency when their love dwindles into
what they describe as a solid and enduring affection. As if affection
had anything to do with love! Affection is created by habit, community of interests, convenience and the desire of companionship. It
is a comfort rather than an exhilaration. We are creatures of change,
change is the atmosphere we breathe, and is it likely that the strong-

est but one of all our instincts should be free from the law? We are
not the same persons this year as last; nor are those we love. It is a
happy choice if we, changing, continue to love a changed person.
Mostly, different ourselves, we make a desperate, pathetic effort to
love in a different person the person we once loved. It is only because the power of love when it seizes us seems so mighty that we
persuade ourselves that it will last forever. When it subsides we are
ashamed, and, duped, blame ourselves for our weakness, whereas we
should accept our change of heart as a natural effect of our humanity. The experience of mankind has led them to regard love with
mingled feelings. They have been suspicious of it. They have as
often cursed as praised it. The soul of man, struggling to be free,
has except for brief moments looked upon the self-surrender that it
claims as a fall from grace. The happiness it brings may be the
greatest of which man is capable, but it is seldom unalloyed. It
writes a story that generally has a sad ending. Many have resented
its power and angrily prayed to be delivered from its burden. They
have hugged their chains, but knowing they were chains hated them
too. Love is not always blind and there are few things that cause
greater wretchedness than to love with all your heart someone who
you know is unworthy of love.

But loving-kindness is not coloured with that transitoriness which
is the irremediable defect of love. It is true that it is not entirely devoid of the sexual element. It is like dancing; one dances for the
pleasure of the rhythmic movement, and it is not necessary that one
should wish to go to bed with one's partner; but it is a pleasant exercise only if to do so would not be disgusting. In loving-kindness
the sexual instinct is sublimated, but it lends the emotion something
of its own warm and vitalizing energy. Loving-kindness is the better part of goodness. It lends grace to the sterner qualities of which
this consists and makes it a little less difficult to practise those minor
virtues of self-control and self-restraint, patience, discipline and
tolerance, which are the passive and not very exhilarating elements
of goodness. Goodness is the only value that seems in this world of
appearances to have any claim to be an end in itself. Virtue is its
own reward. I am ashamed to have reached so commonplace a conclusion. With my instinct for effect I should have liked to end my
book with some startling and paradoxical announcement or with a
cynicism that my readers would have recognized with a chuckle as
characteristic. It seems I have little more to say than can be read
in any copybook or heard from any pulpit. I have gone a long way
round to discover what everyone knew already.

I have little sense of reverence. There is a great deal too much of it in the world. It is claimed for many objects that do not deserve it. It is often no more than the conventional homage we pay to things in which we are not willing to take an active interest. The best homage we can pay to the great figures of the past, Dante, Titian, Shakespeare, Spinoza, is to treat them not with reverence, but with the familiarity we should exercise if they were our contemporaries. Thus we pay them the highest compliment we can; our familiarity acknowledges that they are alive for us. But when now and then I have come across real goodness I have found reverence rise naturally in my heart. It has not seemed to matter then that its rare possessors were perhaps sometimes a trifle less intelligent than I should have liked them to be. When I was a small boy and unhappy I used to dream night after night that my life at school was all a dream and that I should wake to find myself at home again with my mother. Her death was a wound that fifty years have not entirely healed. I have long ceased to have that dream; but I have never quite lost the sense that my living life was a mirage in which I did this and that because that was how it fell out, but which, even while I was playing my part in it, I could look at from a distance and know for the mirage it was. When I look back on my life, with its successes and its failures, its endless errors, its deceptions and its fulfilments, its joys and miseries, it seems to me strangely lacking in reality. It is shadowy and unsubstantial. It may be that my heart, having found rest nowhere, had some deep ancestral craving for God and immortality which my reason would have no truck with. In default of anything better it has seemed to me sometimes that I might pretend to myself that the goodness I have not so seldom after all come across in many of those I have encountered on my way had reality. It may be that in goodness we may see, not a reason for life nor an explanation of it, but an extenuation. In this indifferent universe, with its inevitable evils that surround us from the cradle to the grave, it may serve not as a challenge or a reply, but as an affirmation of our own independence. It is the retort that humour makes to the tragic absurdity of fate. Unlike beauty, it can be perfect without being tedious, and, greater than love, time does not wither its delight. But goodness is shown in right action and who can tell in this meaningless world what right action is? It is not action that aims at happiness; it is a happy chance if happiness results. Plato, as we know, enjoined upon his wise man to abandon the serene life of contemplation for the turmoil of practical affairs and thereby set the claim of duty above the desire for happiness; and we have all of us, I suppose, on occasion adopted a course because we thought it right though we well knew that it could bring us happiness neither then nor in the future. What then is right action? For my own part the best answer I know is that given by Fray Luis de Leon. To follow it does not look so difficult that human weakness quails before it as beyond its strength. With it I can end my book. The beauty of life, he says, is nothing but this, that each should act in conformity with his nature and his business.

JOHN MASEFIELD

****

The poet laureate of England, who had been for some time gravely ill, was not disposed to write anything about his selections, but chose for the volume the tale in verse "The Rider at the Gate," the two sonnets "On Growing Old" and the early lyric "Sea-fever."

****

Three Poems

THE RIDER AT THE GATE

A WINDY NIGHT was blowing on Rome.
The cressets guttered on Caesar's home.
The fish-boats, moored at the bridge, were breaking
The rush of the river to yellow foam.

The hinges whined to the shutters shaking,
When clip-clop-clep came a horse-hoofs raking
The stones of the road at Caesar's gate;
The spear-butts jarred at the guard's awaking.

"Who goes there?" said the guard at the gate.
"What is the news, that you ride so late?"
"News most pressing, that must be spoken
To Caesar alone, and that cannot wait."

"The Caesar sleeps; you must show a token
That the news suffice that he be awoken.
What is the news, and whence do you come?
For no light cause may his sleep be broken."

"Out of the dark of the sands I come,
From the dark of death, with news from Rome,
A word so fell that it must be uttered
Though it strike the soul of the Caesar dumb."

431

Caesar turned in his bed and muttered,
With a struggle for breath the lamp-flame guttered;
Calpurnia heard her husband moan:
                    "The house is falling,
The beaten men come into their own."

"Speak your word," said the guard at the gate;
"Yes, but bear it to Caesar straight,
Say 'Your murderer's knives are honing,
Your killer's gang is lying in wait.'

"Out of the wind that is blowing and moaning,
Through the city palace and the country loaning,
I cry, 'For the world's sake, Caesar, beware,
And take this warning as my atoning.

" 'Beware of the Court, of the palace stair,
Of the downcast friend who speaks so fair,
Keep from the Senate, for Death is going
On many men's feet to meet you there.'

"I who am dead, have ways of knowing
Of the crop of death that the quick are sowing.
I, who was Pompey, cry it aloud
From the dark of death, from the wind blowing.

"I, who was Pompey, once was proud,
Now I lie in the sand without a shroud;
I cry to Caesar out of my pain,
'Caesar, beware, your death is vowed.' "

The light grew grey on the window-pane,
The windcocks swung in a burst of rain,
The window of Caesar flung unshuttered,
The horse-hoofs died into wind again.

Caesar turned in his bed and muttered,
With a struggle for breath the lamp-flame guttered;
Calpurnia heard her husband moan:
                    "The house is falling,
The beaten men come into their own."

SEA-FEVER

I must down to the seas again, to the lonely sea and the sky,
And all I ask is a tall ship and a star to steer her by,
And the wheel's kick and the wind's song and the white sail's
 shaking,
And a grey mist on the sea's face and a grey dawn breaking.

I must down to the seas again, for the call of the running tide
Is a wild call and a clear call that may not be denied;
And all I ask is a windy day with the white clouds flying,
And the flung spray and the blown spume, and the sea-gulls crying.

I must down to the seas again to the vagrant gypsy life,
To the gull's way and the whale's way where the wind's like a
 whetted knife;
And all I ask is a merry yarn from a laughing fellow-rover,
And quiet sleep and a sweet dream when the long trick's over.

ON GROWING OLD

Be with me, Beauty, for the fire is dying;
My dog and I are old, too old for roving.
Man, whose young passion sets the spindrift flying,
Is soon too lame to march, too cold for loving.
I take the book and gather to the fire,
Turning old yellow leaves; minute by minute
The clock ticks to my heart. A withered wire,
Moves a thin ghost of music in the spinet.
I cannot sail your seas, I cannot wander
Your cornland, nor your hill-land, nor your valleys
Ever again, nor share the battle yonder
Where the young knight the broken square rallies.
Only stay quiet while my mind remembers
The beauty of fire from the beauty of embers.

Beauty, have pity! for the strong have power,
The rich their wealth, the beautiful their grace,
Summer of man its sunlight and its flower,

Spring-time of man all April in a face.
Only, as in the jostling in the Strand,
Where the mob thrusts or loiters or is loud,
The beggar with the saucer in his hand
Asks only a penny from the passing crowd,
So, from this glittering world with all its fashion,
Its fire, and play of men, its stir, its march,
Let me have wisdom, Beauty, wisdom and passion,
Bread to the soul, rain where the summers parch.
Give me but these, and, though the darkness close
Even the night will blossom as the rose.

E. M. FORSTER

****

Mr. E. M. Forster, on his recent visit to America, agreed to a representation from his most famous novel, A Passage to India. *This piece is a scene in a court room in India, where the young English woman, who had gone to India to visit her fiance, undertakes to testify against the native who in her bewilderment, she feels had (or had not) attempted an offence against her in the darkness of a cave on a tourist visit to the Marabar Hills.*

****

The Trial

THE COURT was crowded and of course very hot, and the first person Adela noticed in it was the humblest of all who were present, a person who had no bearing officially upon the trial; the man who pulled the punkah. Almost naked, and splendidly formed, he sat on a raised platform near the back, in the middle of the central gangway, and he caught her attention as she came in, and he seemed to control the proceedings. He had the strength and beauty that sometimes come to flower in Indians of low birth. When that strange race nears the dust and is condemned as untouchable, then nature remembers the physical perfection that she accomplished elsewhere, and throws out a god—not many, but one here and there, to prove to society how little its categories impress her. This man would have been notable anywhere: among the thin-hammed, flat-chested mediocrities of Chandrapore he stood out as divine, yet he was of the city, its garbage had nourished him, he would end on its rubbish heaps. Pulling the rope towards him, relaxing it rhythmically, sending swirls of air over others, receiving none himself, he seemed apart from human destinies, a male fate, a winnower of souls. Opposite him, also on a platform, sat the little assistant magistrate, cultivated, self-conscious, and conscientious. The punkah wallah was none of these things: he scarcely knew that he

435

existed and did not understand why the Court was fuller than usual, indeed he did not know that it was fuller than usual, didn't even know he worked a fan, though he thought he pulled a rope. Something in his aloofness impressed the girl from middle-class England, and rebuked the narrowness of her suffering. In virtue of what had she collected this roomful of people together? Her particular brand of opinions, and the suburban Jehovah who sanctified them—by what right did they claim so much importance in the world and assume the title of civilization? Mrs. Moore—she looked round, but Mrs. Moore was far away on the sea; it was the kind of question they might have discussed on the voyage out before the old lady had turned disagreeable and queer.

While thinking of Mrs. Moore she heard sounds, which gradually grew more distinct. The epoch-making trial had started, and the Superintendent of Police was opening the case for the prosecution.

Mr. McBryde was not at pains to be an interesting speaker; he left eloquence to the defence, who would require it. His attitude was, "Everyone knows the man's guilty, and I am obliged to say so in public before he goes to the Andamans." He made no moral or emotional appeal, and it was only by degrees that the studied negligence of his manner made itself felt, and lashed part of the audience to fury. Laboriously did he describe the genesis of the picnic. The prisoner had met Miss Quested at an entertainment given by the Principal of Government College, and had there conceived his intentions concerning her: prisoner was a man of loose life, as documents found upon him at his arrest would testify, also his fellow-assistant, Dr. Panna Lal, was in a position to throw light on his character, and Major Callendar himself would speak. Here Mr. McBryde paused. He wanted to keep the proceedings as clean as possible, but Oriental Pathology, his favourite theme, lay around him, and he could not resist it. Taking off his spectacles, as was his habit before enunciating a general truth, he looked into them sadly, and remarked that the darker races are physically attracted by the fairer, but not *vice versa*—not a matter for bitterness this, not a matter for abuse, but just a fact which any scientific observer will confirm.

"Even when the lady is so uglier than the gentleman?"

The comment fell from nowhere, from the ceiling perhaps. It was the first interruption, and the Magistrate felt bound to censure it. "Turn that man out," he said. One of the native policemen took hold of a man who had said nothing, and turned him out roughly. Mr. McBryde resumed his spectacles and proceeded. But the comment had upset Miss Quested. Her body resented being called ugly and trembled.

"Do you feel faint, Adela?" asked Miss Derek, who tended her with loving indignation.

"I never feel anything else, Nancy. I shall get through, but it's awful, awful."

This led to the first of a series of scenes. Her friends began to fuss around her, and the Major called out, "I must have better arrangements than this made for my patient; why isn't she given a seat on the platform? She gets no air."

Mr. Das looked annoyed and said: "I shall be happy to accommodate Miss Quested with a chair up here in view of the particular circumstances of her health." The chuprassies passed up not one chair but several, and the entire party followed Adela on to the platform, Mr. Fielding being the only European who remained in the body of the hall.

"That's better," remarked Mrs. Turton, as she settled herself.

"Thoroughly desirable change for several reasons," replied the Major.

The Magistrate knew that he ought to censure this remark, but did not dare to. Callendar saw that he was afraid, and called out authoritatively, "Right, McBryde, go ahead now; sorry to have interrupted you."

"Are you all right yourselves?" asked the Superintendent.

"We shall do, we shall do."

"Go on, Mr. Das, we are not here to disturb you," said the Collector patronizingly. Indeed, they had not so much disturbed the trial as taken charge of it.

While the prosecution continued, Miss Quested examined the hall —timidly at first, as though it would scorch her eyes. She observed to left and right of the punkah man many a half-known face. Beneath her were gathered all the wreckage of her silly attempts to see India—the people she had met at the Bridge Party, the man and his wife who hadn't sent their carriage, the old man who would lend his car, various servants, villagers, officials, and the prisoner himself. There he sat—strong, neat little Indian with very black hair, and pliant hands. She viewed him without special emotion. Since they last met, she had elevated him into a principle of evil, but now he seemed to be what he had always been—a slight acquaintance. He was negligible, devoid of significance, dry like a bone, and though he was "guilty" no atmosphere of sin surrounded him. "I suppose he *is* guilty. Can I possibly have made a mistake?"

she thought. For this question still occurred to her intellect, though since Mrs. Moore's departure it had ceased to trouble her conscience.

Pleader Mahmoud Ali now arose, and asked with ponderous and ill-judged irony whether his client could be accommodated on the platform too: even Indians felt unwell sometimes, though naturally Major Callendar did not think so, being in charge of a Government Hospital. "Another example of their exquisite sense of humour," sang Miss Derek. Ronny looked at Mr. Das to see how he would handle the difficulty, and Mr. Das became agitated, and snubbed Pleader Mahmoud Ali severely.

"Excuse me——" It was the turn of the eminent barrister from Calcutta. He was a fine-looking man large and bony, with grey closely cropped hair. "We object to the presence of so many European ladies and gentlemen upon the platform," he said in an Oxford voice. "They will have the effect of intimidating our witnesses. Their place is with the rest of the public in the body of the hall. We have no objection to Miss Quested remaining on the platform, since she has been unwell; we shall extend every courtesy to her throughout, despite the scientific truths revealed to us by the District Superintendent of Police; but we do object to the others."

"Oh, cut the cackle and let's have the verdict," the Major growled.

The distinguished visitor gazed at the Magistrate respectfully.

"I agree to that," said Mr. Das, hiding his face desperately in some papers. "It was only to Miss Quested that I gave permission to sit up here. Her friends should be so excessively kind as to climb down."

"Well done, Das, quite sound," said Ronny with devastating honesty.

"Climb down, indeed, what incredible impertinence!" Mrs. Turton cried.

"Do come quietly, Mary," murmured her husband.

"Hi! my patient can't be left unattended."

"Do you object to the Civil Surgeon remaining, Mr. Amritrao?"

"I should object. A platform confers authority."

"Even when it's one foot high; so come along all," said the Collector, trying to laugh.

"Thank you very much, sir," said Mr. Das, greatly relieved. "Thank you, Mr. Heaslop; thank you, ladies all."

And the party, including Miss Quested, descended from its rash eminence. The news of their humiliation spread quickly, and people jeered outside. Their special chairs followed them. Mahmoud Ali (who was quite silly and useless with hatred) objected even to these; by whose authority had special chairs been introduced, why had the Nawab Bahadur not been given one? etc. People began to talk all over the room, about chairs ordinary and special, strips of carpet, platforms one foot high.

But the little excursion had a good effect on Miss Quested's nerves. She felt easier now that she had seen all the people who were in the room. It was like knowing the worst. She was sure now that she should come through "all right"—that is to say, without spiritual disgrace, and she passed the good news on to Ronny and Mrs. Turton. They were too much agitated with the defeat to British prestige to be interested. From where she sat, she could see the renegade Mr. Fielding. She had had a better view of him from the platform, and knew that an Indian child perched on his knee. He was watching her. When their eyes met, he turned his away, as if direct intercourse was of no interest to him.

The Magistrate was also happier. He had won the battle of the platform, and gained confidence. Intelligent and impartial, he continued to listen to the evidence, and tried to forget that later on he should have to pronounce a verdict in accordance with it. The Superintendent trundled steadily forward: he had expected these outbursts of insolence—they are the natural gestures of an inferior race, and he betrayed no hatred of Aziz, merely an abysmal contempt.

The speech dealt at length with the "prisoner's dupes," as they were called—Fielding, the servant Antony, the Nawab Bahadur. This aspect of the case had always seemed dubious to Miss Quested, and she had asked the police not to develop it. But they were playing for a heavy sentence, and wanted to prove that the assault was premeditated. And in order to illustrate the strategy, they produced a plan of the Marbar Hills, showing the route that the party had taken, and the "Tank of the Dagger" where they had camped.

The Magistrate displayed interest in archaeology.

An elevation of a specimen cave was produced; it was lettered "Buddhist Cave."

"Not Buddhist, I think, a Jain. . . ."

"In which cave is the offence alleged, the Buddhist or the Jain?" asked Mahmoud Ali, with the air of unmasking a conspiracy.

"All the Marabar caves are Jain."

"Yes, sir; then in which Jain cave?"

"You will have an opportunity of putting such questions later."

Mr. McBryde smiled faintly at their fatuity. Indians invariably collapse over some such point as this. He knew that the defence had some wild hope of establishing an alibi, that they had tried (unsuccessfully) to identify the guide, and that Fielding and Hamidullah had gone out to the Kawa Dol and paced and measured all one moonlit night. "Mr. Lesley says they're Buddhist, and he ought to know if anyone does. But may I call attention to the shape?" And he described what had occurred there. Then he spoke of Miss Derek's arrival, of the scramble down the gully, of the return of the two ladies to Chandrapore, and of the document Miss Quested signed on her arrival, in which mention was made of the field glasses. And then came the culminating evidence: the discovery of the field glasses on the prisoner. "I have nothing to add at present," he concluded, removing his spectacles. "I will now call my witnesses. The facts will speak for themselves. The prisoner is one of those individuals who have led a double life. I dare say his degeneracy gained upon him gradually. He has been very cunning at concealing, as is usual with the type, and pretending to be a respectable member of society, getting a Government position even. He is now entirely vicious and beyond redemption, I am afraid. He behaved most cruelly, most brutally, to another of his guests, another English lady. In order to get rid of her, and leave him free for his crime, he crushed her into a cave among his servants. However, that is by the way."

But his last words brought on another storm, and suddenly a new name, Mrs. Moore, burst on the court like a whirlwind. Mahmoud Ali had been enraged, his nerves snapped; he shrieked like a maniac, and asked whether his client was charged with murder as well as rape, and who was this second English lady.

"I don't propose to call her."

"You don't because you can't, you have smuggled her out of the country; she is Mrs. Moore, she would have proved his innocence, she was on our side, she was poor Indians' friend."

"You could have called her yourself," cried the Magistrate. "Neither side called her, neither must quote her as evidence."

"She was kept from us until too late—I learn too late—this is English justice, here is your British Raj. Give us back Mrs. Moore for five minutes only, and she will save my friend, she will save the name of his sons; don't rule her out, Mr. Das; take back those words as you yourself are a father; tell me where they have put her; oh, Mrs. Moore. . . ."

"If the point is of any interest, my mother should have reached

Aden," said Ronny dryly; he ought not to have intervened, but the onslaught startled him.

"Imprisoned by you there because she knew the truth." He was almost out of his mind, and could be heard saying above the tumult: "I ruin my career, no matter; we are all to be ruined one by one."

"This is no way to defend your case," counselled the Magistrate.

"I am not defending a case, nor are you trying one. We are both of us slaves."

"Mr. Mahmoud Ali, I have already warned you, and unless you sit down I shall exercise my authority."

"Do so; this trial is a farce, I am going." And he handed his papers to Amritrao and left, calling from the door histrionically yet with intense passion. "Aziz, Aziz—farewell for ever." The tumult increased, the invocation of Mrs. Moore continued, and people who did not know what the syllables meant repeated them like a charm. They became Indianized into Esmiss Esmoor, they were taken up in the street outside. In vain the Magistrate threatened and expelled. Until the magic exhausted itself, he was powerless.

"Unexpected," remarked Mr. Turton.

Ronny furnished the explanation. Before she sailed, his mother had taken to talk about the Marabar in her sleep, especially in the afternoon when servants were on the verandah, and her disjointed remarks on Aziz had doubtless been sold to Mahmoud Ali for a few annas: that kind of thing never ceases in the East.

"I thought they'd try something of the sort. Ingenious." He looked into their wide-open mouths. "They get just like that over their religion," he added calmly. "Start and can't stop. I'm sorry for your old Das, he's not getting much of a show."

"Mr. Heaslop, how disgraceful dragging in your dear mother," said Miss Derek, bending forward.

"It's just a trick, and they happened to pull it off. Now one sees why they had Mahmoud Ali—just to make a scene on the chance. It is his specialty." But he disliked it more than he showed. It was revolting to hear his mother travestied into Esmiss Esmoor, a Hindu goddess.

> "Esmiss Esmoor
> Esmiss Esmoor
> Esmiss Esmoor
> Esmiss Esmoor. . . ."

"Ronny——"

"Yes, old girl?"

"Isn't it all queer?"

"I'm afraid it's very upsetting for you."

"Not the least, I don't mind it."

"Well, that's good."

She had spoken more naturally and healthily than usual. Bending into the middle of her friends, she said: "Don't worry about me, I'm much better than I was; I don't feel the least faint; I shall be all right, and thank you all, thank you, thank you for your kindness." She had to shout her gratitude, for the chant, Esmiss Esmoor, went on.

Suddenly it stopped. It was as if the prayer had been heard, and the relics exhibited. "I apologize for my colleague," said Mr. Amritrao, rather to everyone's surprise. "He is an intimate friend of our client, and his feelings have carried him away."

"Mr. Mahmoud Ali will have to apologize in person," the Magistrate said.

"Exactly, sir, he must. But we have just learnt that Mrs. Moore had important evidence which she desired to give. She was hurried out of the country by her son before she could give it; and this unhinged Mr. Mahmoud Ali—coming as it does upon an attempt to intimidate our only other European witness, Mr. Fielding. Mr. Mahmoud Ali would have said nothing had not Mrs. Moore been claimed as a witness by the police." He sat down.

"An extraneous element is being introduced into the case," said the Magistrate. "I must repeat that as a witness Mrs. Moore does not exist. Neither you, Mr. Amritrao, nor, Mr. McBryde, you, have have any right to surmise what that lady would have said. She is not here, and consequently she can say nothing."

"Well, I withdraw my reference," said the Superintendent wearily. "I would have done so fifteen minutes ago if I had been given the chance. She is not of the least importance to me."

"I have already withdrawn it for the defence." He added with forensic humour: "Perhaps you can persuade the gentlemen outside to withdraw it too," for the refrain in the street continued.

"I am afraid my powers do not extend so far," said Das smiling.

So peace was restored, and when Adela came to give her evidence, the atmosphere was quieter than it had been since the beginning of the trial. Experts were not surprised. There is no stay in your native. He blazes up over a minor point, and has nothing left for the crisis. What he seeks is a grievance, and this he had found in the supposed abduction of an old lady. He would now be less aggrieved when Aziz was deported.

But the crisis was still to come.

Adela had always meant to tell the truth and nothing but the truth, and she had rehearsed this as a difficult task—difficult because her disaster in the cave was connected, though by a thread, with another part of her life, her engagement to Ronny. She had thought of love just before she went in, and had innocently asked Aziz what marriage was like, and she supposed that her question had aroused evil in him. To recount this would have been incredibly painful, it was the one point she wanted to keep obscure; she was willing to give details that would have distressed other girls, but this story of her private failure she dared not allude to, and she dreaded being examined in public in case something came out. But as soon as she rose to reply, and heard the sound of her own voice, she feared not even that. A new and unknown sensation protected her, like magnificent armour. She didn't think what had happened or even remember in the ordinary way of memory, but she returned to the Marabar Hills, spoke from them across a sort of darkness to Mr. McBryde. The fatal day recurred, in every detail, but now she was of it and not of it at the same time, and this double relation gave it indescribable splendour. Why had she thought the expedition "dull?" Now the sun rose again, the elephant waited, the pale masses of the rock flowed round her and presented the first cave; she entered, and a match was reflected in the polished walls—all beautiful and significant, though she had been blind to it at the time. Questions were asked, and to each she found the exact reply; yes, she had noticed the "Tank of the Dagger," but not known its name; yes, Mrs. Moore had been tired after the first cave and sat in the shadow of the great rock, near the dried-up mud. Smoothly the voice in the distance proceeded, leading along the paths of truth, and the airs from the punkah behind her wafted her on. . . .

". . . the prisoner and the guide took you on to the Kawa Dol, no one else being present?"

"The most wonderfully shaped of those hills. Yes." As she spoke, she created the Kawa Dol, saw the niches up the curve of the stone, and felt the heat strike her face. And something caused her to add: "No one else was present to my knowledge. We appeared to be alone."

"Very well, there is a ledge half-way up the hill, or broken ground rather, with caves scattered near the beginning of a nullah."

"I know where you mean."

"You went alone into one of those caves?"

"That is quite correct."

"And the prisoner followed you."

"Now we've got 'im," from the Major.

She was silent. The court, the place of question, awaited her reply. But she could not give it until Aziz entered the place of answer.

"The prisoner followed you, didn't he?" he repeated in the monotonous tones that they both used; they were employing agreed words throughout, so that this part of the proceeding held no surprises.

"May I have half a minute before I reply to that, Mr. McBryde?"

"Certainly."

Her vision was of several caves. She saw herself in one, and she was also outside it, watching its entrance, for Aziz to pass in. She failed to locate him. It was the doubt that often visited her, but solid and attractive, like the hills, "I am not—" Speech was more difficult than vision. "I am not quite sure."

"I beg your pardon?" said the Superintendent of Police.

"I cannot be sure . . ."

"I didn't catch that answer." He looked scared, his mouth shut with a snap. "You are on that landing, or whatever we term it, and you have entered a cave. I suggest to you that the prisoner followed you."

She shook her head.

"What do you mean, please?"

"No," she said in a flat, unattractive voice. Slight noises began in various parts of the room, but no one yet understood what was occurring except Fielding. He saw that she was going to have a nervous breakdown and that his friend was saved.

"What is that, what are you saying? Speak up, please." The Magistrate bent forward.

"I'm afraid I have made a mistake."

"What nature of mistake?"

"Dr. Aziz never followed me into the cave."

The Superintendent slammed down his papers, then picked them up and said calmly: "Now, Miss Quested, let us go on. I will read you the words of the deposition which you signed two hours later in my bungalow."

"Excuse me, Mr. McBryde, you cannot go on. I am speaking to the witness myself. And the public will be silent. If it continues to talk, I'll have the court cleared. Miss Quested, address your remarks

to me, who am the Magistrate in charge of the case, and realize
their extreme gravity. Remember you speak on oath, Miss Quested."

"Dr. Aziz never—"

"I stop these proceedings on medical grounds," cried the Major
on a word from Turton, and all the English rose from their chairs
at once, large white figures behind which the little magistrate was
hidden. The Indians rose too, hundreds of things went on at once,
so that afterwards each person gave a different account of the
catastrophe.

"You withdraw the charge? Answer me," shrieked the representative of Justice.

Something that she did not understand took hold of the girl and
pulled her through. Though the vision was over, and she had returned to the insipidity of the world, she remembered what she had
learnt. Atonement and confession—they could wait. It was in hard
prosaic tones that she said, "I withdraw everything."

"Enough—sit down. Mr. McBryde, do you wish to continue in
the face of this?"

The Superintendent gazed at his witness as if she was a broken
machine, and said, "Are you mad?"

"Don't question her, sir; you have no longer the right."

"Give me time to consider——"

"Sahib, you will have to withdraw; this becomes a scandal,"
boomed the Nawab Bahadur suddenly from the back of the court.

"He shall not," shouted Mrs. Turton against the gathering tumult.
"Call the other witnesses; we're none of us safe——" Ronny tried
to check her, and she gave him an irritable blow, then screamed
insults at Adela.

The Superintendent moved to support his friends, saying non-
chalantly to the Magistrate as he did so, "Right, I withdraw."

Mr. Das rose, nearly dead with the strain. He had controlled the
case, just controlled it. He had shown that an Indian can preside.
To those who could hear him he said, "The prisoner is released
without one stain on his character; the question of costs will be decided elsewhere."

And then the flimsy framework of the court broke up, the shouts
of derision and rage culminated, people screamed and cursed, kissed
one another, wept passionately. Here were the English, whom their
servants protected, there Aziz fainted in Hamidullah's arms. Victory
on this side, defeat on that—complete for one moment was the antithesis. Then life returned to its complexities, person after person
struggled out of the room to their various purposes, and before long

no one remained on the scene of the fantasy but the beautiful naked god. Unaware that anything unusual had occurred, he continued to pull the cord of his punkah, to gaze at the empty dais and the overturned special chairs and rhythmically to agitate the clouds of descending dust.

BERTRAND RUSSELL

****

LONDON

I have selected this chapter because reverence for human individuality and mental initiative are, in my opinion, of the utmost importance, and are increasingly threatened in our highly organized and centralized societies.

BERTRAND RUSSELL

****

Education

No POLITICAL THEORY is adequate unless it is applicable to children as well as to men and women. Theorists are mostly childless, or, if they have children, they are carefully screened from the disturbances which would be caused by youthful turmoil. Some of them have written books on education, but without, as a rule, having any actual children present to their minds while they wrote. Those educational theorists who have had a knowledge of children, such as the inventors of Kindergarten and the Montessori system, have not always had enough realization of the ultimate goal of education to be able to deal successfully with advanced instruction. I have not the knowledge either of children or of education which would enable me to supply whatever defects there may be in the writings of others. But some questions, concerning education as a political institution, are involved in any hope of social reconstruction, and are not usually considered by writers on educational theory. It is these questions that I wish to discuss.

The power of education in forming character and opinion is very great and very generally recognized. The genuine beliefs, though not usually the professed precepts, of parents and teachers are almost unconsciously acquired by most children; and even if they depart from these beliefs in later life, something of them remains deeply implanted, ready to emerge in a time of stress or crisis. Education is, as a rule, the strongest force on the side of what exists

447

and against fundamental change: threatened institutions, while they are still powerful, possess themselves of the educational machine, and instil a respect for their own excellence into the malleable minds of the young. Reformers retort by trying to oust their opponents from their position of vantage. The children themselves are not considered by either party; they are merely so much material, to be recruited into one army or the other. If the children themselves were considered, education would not aim at making them belong to this party or that, but at enabling them to choose intelligently between the parties; it would aim at making them able to think, not at making them think what their teachers think. Education as a political weapon could not exist if we respected the rights of children. If we respected the rights of children, we should educate them so as to give them the knowledge and the mental habits required for forming independent opinions; but education as a political institution endeavors to form habits and to circumscribe knowledge in such a way as to make one set of opinions inevitable.

The two principles of *justice* and *liberty*, which cover a very great deal of the social reconstruction required, are not by themselves sufficient where education is concerned. Justice, in the literal sense of equal rights, is obviously not wholly possible as regards children. And as for liberty, it is, to begin with, essentially negative: it condemns all avoidable interference with freedom, without giving a positive principle of construction. But education is essentially constructive, and requires some positive conception of what constitutes a good life. And although liberty is to be respected in education as much as is compatible with instruction, and although a very great deal more liberty than is customary can be allowed without loss to instruction, yet it is clear that some departure from complete liberty is unavoidable if children are to be taught anything, except in the case of unusually intelligent children who are kept isolated from more normal companions. This is one reason for the great responsibility which rests upon teachers: the children must, necessarily, be more or less at the mercy of their elders, and cannot make themselves the guardians of their own interests. Authority in education is to some extent unavoidable, and those who educate have to find a way of exercising authority in accordance with the *spirit* of liberty.

Where authority is unavoidable, what is needed is *reverence*. A man who is to educate really well, and is to make the young grow and develop into their full stature, must be filled through and through with the spirit of reverence. It is reverence towards others that is lacking in those who advocate machine-made cast-iron systems: militarism, capitalism, Fabian scientific organization, and all the other prisons into which reformers and reactionaries try to force the human spirit. In education, with its codes of rules emanating from a Government office, its large classes and fixed curriculum and overworked teachers, its determination to produce a dead level of glib mediocrity, the lack of reverence for the child is all but universal. Reverence requires imagination and vital warmth; it requires most imagination in respect of those who have least actual achievement or power. The child is weak and superficially foolish, the teacher is strong, and in an every-day sense wiser than the child. The teacher without reverence, or the bureaucrat without reverence, easily despises the child for these outward inferiorities. He thinks it is his duty to "mold" the child: in imagination he is the potter with the clay. And so he gives to the child some unnatural shape, which hardens with age, producing strains and spiritual dissatisfactions, out of which grow cruelty and envy, and the belief that others must be compelled to undergo the same distortions.

The man who has reverence will not think it his duty to "mold" the young. He feels in all that lives, but especially in human beings, and most of all in children, something sacred, indefinable, unlimited, something individual and strangely precious, the growing principle of life, an embodied fragment of the dumb striving of the world. In the presence of a child he feels an unaccountable humility—a humility not easily defensible on any rational ground, and yet somehow nearer to wisdom than the easy self-confidence of many parents and teachers. The outward helplessness of the child and the appeal of dependence make him conscious of the responsibility of a trust. His imagination shows him what the child may become, for good or evil, how its impulses may be developed or thwarted, how its hopes must be dimmed and the life in it grow less living, how its trust will be bruised and its quick desires replaced by brooding will. All this gives him a longing to help the child in its own battle; he would equip and strengthen it, not for some outside end proposed by the State or by any other impersonal authority, but for the ends which the child's own spirit is obscurely seeking. The man who feels this can wield the authority of an educator without infringing the principle of liberty.

It is not in a spirit of reverence that education is conducted by

States and Churches and the great institutions that are subservient
to them. What is considered in education is hardly ever the boy or
girl, the young man or young woman, but almost always, in some
form, the maintenance of the existing order. When the individual is
considered, it is almost exclusively with a view to worldly success—
making money or achieving a good position. To be ordinary, and
to acquire the art of getting on, is the ideal which is set before the
youthful mind, except by a few rare teachers who have enough energy of belief to break through the system within which they are expected to work. Almost all education has a political motive: it aims
at strengthening some group, national or religious or even social,
in the competition with other groups. It is this motive, in the main,
which determines the subjects taught, the knowledge offered and
the knowledge withheld, and also decides what mental habits the
pupils are expected to acquire. Hardly anything is done to foster the
inward growth of mind and spirit; in fact, those who have had most
education are very often atrophied in their mental and spiritual life,
devoid of impulse, and possessing only certain mechanical apti-
tudes which take the place of living thought.

Some of the things which education achieves at present must
continue to be achieved by education in any civilized country. All
children must continue to be taught how to read and write, and
some must continue to acquire the knowledge needed for such pro-
fessions as medicine or law or engineering. The higher education
required for the sciences and the arts is necessary for those to whom
it is suited. Except in history and religion and kindred matters, the
actual instruction is only inadequate, not positively harmful. The
instruction might be given in a more liberal spirit, with more attempt to show its ultimate uses; and of course much of it is traditional and dead. But in the main it is necessary, and would have
to form a part of any educational system.

It is in history and religion and other controversial subjects that
the actual instruction is positively harmful. These subjects touch
the interests by which schools are maintained; and the interests
maintain the schools in order that certain views on these subjects
may be instilled. History, in every country, is so taught as to mag-
nify that country: children learn to believe that their own country
has always been in the right and almost always victorious, that it
has produced almost all the great men, and that it is in all respects
superior to all other countries. Since these beliefs are flattering, they
are easily absorbed, and hardly ever dislodged from instinct by later
knowledge.

The false ideas as to the history of the world which are taught in the various countries are of a kind which encourages strife and serves to keep alive a bigoted nationalism. If good relations between States were desired, one of the first steps ought to be to submit all teaching of history to an international commission, which should produce neutral textbooks free from the patriotic bias which is now demanded everywhere.

Exactly the same thing applies to religion. Elementary schools are practically always in the hands either of some religious body or of a State which has a certain attitude towards religion.

The result: . . . free inquiry is checked, and on the most important matter in the world the child is met with dogma or with stony silence.

It is not only in elementary education that these evils exist. In more advanced education they take subtler forms, and there is more attempt to conceal them, but they are still present. Eton and Oxford set a certain stamp upon a man's mind, just as a Jesuit College does. It can hardly be said that Eton and Oxford have a *conscious* purpose, but they have a purpose which is none the less strong and effective for not being formulated. In almost all who have been through them they produce a worship of "good form," which is as destructive to life and thought as the medieval Church. "Good form" is quite compatible with superficial open-mindedness, a readiness to hear all sides, and a certain urbanity towards opponents. But it is not compatible with fundamental open-mindedness, or with any inward readiness to give weight to the other side. Its essence is the assumption that what is most important is a certain kind of behavior, a behavior which minimizes friction between equals and delicately impresses inferiors with a conviction of their own crudity. As a political weapon for preserving the privileges of the rich in a snobbish democracy it is unsurpassable. As a means of producing an agreeable social *milieu* for those who have money with no strong beliefs or unusual desires it has some merit. In every other respect it is abominable.

The evils of "good form" arise from two sources: its perfect assurance of its own rightness, and its belief that correct manners are more to be desired than intellect, or artistic creation, or vital energy, or any of the other sources of progress in the world. Perfect assurance, by itself, is enough to destroy all mental progress in those who have it. And when it is combined with contempt for the angularities and awkwardnesses that are almost invariably associated with great mental power, it becomes a source of destruction to all who come in contact with it. "Good form" is itself dead and incapable of growth; and by its attitude to those who are without it it spreads its own death to many who might otherwise have life. The harm which it has done to well-to-do Englishmen, and to men whose abilities have led the well-to-do to notice them, is incalculable.

The prevention of free inquiry is unavoidable so long as the purpose of education is to produce belief rather than thought, to compel the young to hold positive opinions on doubtful matters rather than to let them see the doubtfulness and be encouraged to independence of mind. Education ought to foster the wish for truth, not the conviction that some particular creed is the truth. But it is creeds that hold men together in fighting organizations: Churches, States, political parties. It is intensity of belief in a creed that produces efficiency in fighting: victory comes to those who feel the strongest certainty about matters on which doubt is the only rational attitude. To produce this intensity of belief and this efficiency in fighting, the child's nature is warped, and its free outlook is cramped, by cultivating inhibitions as a check to the growth of new ideas. In those whose minds are not very active the result is the omnipotence of prejudice; while the few whose thought cannot be wholly killed become cynical, intellectually hopeless, destructively critical, able to make all that is living seem foolish, unable themselves to supply the creative impulses which they destroy in others.

The success in fighting which is achieved by suppressing freedom of thought is brief and very worthless. In the long run mental vigor is as essential to success as it is to a good life. The conception of education as a form of drill, a means of producing unanimity through slavishness, is very common, and is defended chiefly on the ground that it leads to victory. Those who enjoy parallels from ancient history will point to the victory of Sparta over Athens to enforce their moral. But it is Athens that has had power over men's thoughts and imaginations, not Sparta: any one of us, if we could be born again into some past epoch, would rather be born an Athenian than a Spartan. And in the modern world so much intellect is required in practical affairs that even the external victory is more likely to be won by intelligence than by docility. Education in credulity leads by quick stages to mental decay; it is only by keeping alive the spirit of free inquiry that the indispensable minimum of progress can be achieved.

Certain mental habits are commonly instilled by those who are engaged in educating: obedience and discipline, ruthlessness in the struggle for worldly success, contempt towards opposing groups, and an unquestioning credulity, a passive acceptance of the teacher's wisdom. All these habits are against life. Instead of obedience and discipline, we ought to aim at preserving independence and impulse. Instead of ruthlessness, education should try to develop justice in thought. Instead of contempt, it ought to instil reverence, and the attempt at understanding; towards the opinions of others it ought to produce, not necessarily acquiescence, but only such opposition as is combined with imaginative apprehension and a clear realization of the grounds for opposition. Instead of credulity, the object should be to stimulate constructive doubt, the love of mental adventure, the sense of worlds to conquer by enterprise and boldness in thought. Contentment with the *status quo,* and subordination of the individual pupil to political aims, owing to the indifference to the things of the mind, are the immediate causes of these evils; but beneath these causes there is one more fundamental, the fact that education is treated as a means of acquiring power over the pupil, not as a means of nourishing his own growth. It is in this that lack of reverence shows itself; and it is only by more reverence that a fundamental reform can be effected.

Obedience and discipline are supposed to be indispensable if order is to be kept in a class, and if any instruction is to be given. To some extent this is true; but the extent is much less than it is thought to be by those who regard obedience and discipline as in themselves desirable. Obedience, the yielding of one's will to outside direction, is the counterpart of authority. Both may be necessary in certain cases. Refractory children, lunatics, and criminals may require authority, and may need to be forced to obey. But in so far as this is necessary it is a misfortune: what is to be desired is the free choice of ends with which it is not necessary to interfere. . . .

If we took education seriously, and thought it as important to keep alive the minds of children as to secure victory in war, we should conduct education quite differently: we should make sure of achieving the end, even if the expense were a hundredfold greater than it is.

Discipline, as it exists in schools, is very largely an evil. There is a kind of discipline which is necessary to almost all achievement, and which perhaps is not sufficiently valued by those who react against the purely external discipline of traditional methods. The desirable kind of discipline is the kind that comes from within, which consists in the power of pursuing a distant object steadily, foregoing and suffering many things on the way. This involves the subordination of impulse to will, the power of a directing action by large creative desires even at moments when they are not vividly alive. Without this, no serious ambition, good or bad, can be realized, no consistent purpose can dominate. This kind of discipline is very necessary, but can only result from strong desires for ends not immediately attainable, and can only be produced by education if education fosters such desires, which it seldom does at present. Such discipline springs from one's own will, not from outside authority. It is not this kind which is sought in most schools, and it is not this kind which seems to me an evil.

Ruthlessness in the economic struggle will almost unavoidably be taught in schools so long as the economic structure of society remains unchanged. This must be particularly the case in middle-class schools, which depend for their numbers upon the good opinion of parents, and secure the good opinion of parents by advertising the successes of pupils. This is one of many ways in which the competitive organization of the State is harmful. Spontaneous and disinterested desire for knowledge is not at all uncommon in the young, and might be easily aroused in many in whom it remains latent. But it is remorselessly checked by teachers who think only of examinations, diplomas, and degrees.

Passive acceptance of the teacher's wisdom is easy to most boys and girls. It involves no effort of independent thought, and seems rational because the teacher knows more than his pupils; it is moreover the way to win the favor of the teacher unless he is a very exceptional man. Yet the habit of passive acceptance is a disastrous one in later life. It causes men to seek a leader and to accept as a leader whoever is established in that position. It makes the power of Churches, Governments, party caucuses, and all the other organizations by which plain men are misled into supporting old systems which are harmful to the nation and to themselves. It is possible that there would not be much independence of thought even if education did everything to promote it; but there would certainly be more than there is at present. If the object were to make pupils think, rather than to make them accept certain conclusions, education would be conducted quite differently: there would be less rapidity of instruction and more discussion, more occasions when pupils were encouraged to express themselves, more attempt to make education concern itself with matters in which the pupils felt some interest.

Above all, there would be an endeavor to rouse and stimulate the love of mental adventure. . . .

It will be said that the joy of mental adventure must be rare, that there are few who can appreciate it, and that ordinary education can take no account of so aristocratic a good. I do not believe this. The joy of mental adventure is far commoner in the young than in grown men and women. Among children it is very common, and grows naturally out of the period of make-believe and fancy. It is rare in later life because everything is done to kill it during education. Men fear thought as they fear nothing else on earth—more than ruin, more even than death. Thought is subversive and revolutionary, destructive and terrible; thought is merciless to privilege, established institutions, and comfortable habits; thought is anarchic and lawless, indifferent to authority, careless of the well-tried wisdom of the ages. Thought looks into the pit of hell and is not afraid. It sees man, a feeble speck, surrounded by unfathomable depths of silence; yet it bears itself proudly, as unmoved as if it were lord of the universe. Thought is great and swift and free, the light of the world, and the chief glory of man.

But if thought is to become the possession of many, not the privilege of the few, we must have done with fear. It is fear that holds men back—fear lest their cherished beliefs should prove delusions, fear lest the institutions by which they live should prove harmful, fear lest they themselves should prove less worthy of respect than they have supposed themselves to be. "Should the working man think freely about property? Then what will become of us, the rich? Should young men and young women think freely about sex? Then what will become of morality? Should soldiers think freely about war? Then what will become of military discipline? Away with thought! Back into the shades of prejudice, lest property, morals, and war should be endangered! Better men should be stupid, slothful, and oppressive than that their thoughts should be free. For if their thoughts were free they might not think as we do. And at all costs this disaster must be averted." So the opponents of thought argue in the unconscious depths of their souls. And so they act in their churches, their schools, and their universities.

No institution inspired by fear can further life. Hope, not fear, is the creative principle in human affairs. All that has made man great has sprung from the attempt to secure what is good, not from the struggle to avert what was thought evil. It is because modern education is so seldom inspired by a great hope that it so seldom achieves a great result. The wish to preserve the past rather than the hope of creating the future dominates the minds of those who control the teaching of the young. Education should not aim at a passive awareness of dead facts, but at an activity directed towards the world that our efforts are to create. It should be inspired, not by a regretful hankering after the extinct beauties of Greece and the Renaissance, but by a shining vision of the society that is to be, of the triumphs that thought will achieve in the time to come, and of the ever-widening horizon of man's survey over the universe. Those who are taught in this spirit will be filled with life and hope and joy, able to bear their part in bringing to mankind a future less somber than the past, with faith in the glory that human effort can create.

WALTER DE LA MARE

****

*The illness of Walter de la Mare prevented his writing any com-
mentary on his poems, and he asked his son-in-law Rupert S.
Thompson, to record his choices,* Dreams, *and* Fare Well.

****

Two Poems

DREAMS

Ev'n ONE who has little travelled in
This world of ample land and sea;
Whose Arctic, Orient, tropics have been—
Like Phoenix, siren, jinn, and *Sidhe*—
But of his thoughts' anatomy—
Each day makes measureless journeys twain:
From wake to dream; to wake again.

At night he climbs a quiet stair,
Secure within its pictured wall;
His clothes, his hands, the light, the air,
Familiar objects one and all—
Accustomed, plain, and natural.
He lays him down: and, ages deep,
Flow over him the floods of sleep.

457

Lapped in this influence alien
To aught save sorcery could devise,
Heedless of *Sesame* or *Amen,*
He is at once the denizen
Of realms till then beyond surmise;
Grotesque, irrational, and sans
All law and order known as Man's.

Though drowsy sentries at the gate
Of eye and ear dim watch maintain,
And, at his absence all elate,
His body's artisans sustain,
Their toil in sinew, nerve, and brain:
Nothing recks he; he roves afar,
Past compass, chart, and calendar.

Nor is he the poor serf who shares
One self alone where'er he range,
Since in the seven-league Boots he wears
He may, in scores of guises, change
His daily ego—simple or strange;
Stand passive looker-on; or be
A paragon of energy.

Regions of beauty, wonder, peace
By waking eyes unscanned, unknown.
Waters and hills whose loveliness,
Past mortal sense, are his alone.
There flow'rs by the shallows of Lethe sown
Distil their nectar, drowsy and sweet,
And drench the air with news of it.

Or lost, betrayed, forlorn, alas!
Gaunt terror leads him by the hand
Through demon-infested rank morass;
O'er wind-bleached wilderness of sand;
Where cataracts rave; or bleak sea-strand
Shouts at the night with spouted spume;
Or locks him to rot in soundless tomb.

Here, too, the House of Folly is,
With gates ajar, and windows lit,
Wherein with foul buffooneries
A spectral host carousing sit.
'Hail, thou!' they yelp. 'Come, taste and eat!'
And so, poor zany, sup must he
The nightmare dregs of idiocy.

All this in vain? Nay, thus abased,
Made vile in the dark's incontinence,
Though even the anguish of death he taste,
The murderer's woe—his penitence,
And pangs of the damned experience—
Will he God's mercy less esteem
When day spring prove them only a dream?

What bliss to clutch, when thus beset,
The folded linen of his sheet;
Or hear, without, more welcome yet,
A footfall in the dawnlit street;
The whist of the wind; or, far and sweet,
Some small bird's daybreak rhapsody,
That bids him put all such figments by.

Oh, when, at morning up, his eyes
Open to earth again, then, lo!
An end to all dream's enterprise!—
It melts away like April snow.
What night made false now true doth show;
What day discloses night disdained;
And who shall winnow real from feigned?

But men of learning little heed
Problems that simple folk perplex;
And some there are who have decreed
Dreams the insidious wiles of sex;
That slumber's plain is wake's complex;
And, plumbing their own minds, profess
Them quagmires of unconsciousness.

Sad fate it is, like one who is dead,
To lie inert the dark night through,
And never by dream's sweet fantasy led
To lave tired eyes in heavenly dew!
But worse—the prey of a gross taboo
And sport of a Censor—to squat and make
Pies of a mud forbidd'n the awake.

Nay, is that Prince of the Dust—a man,
But a tissue of parts, dissectable?
Lancet, balances, callipers—can
The least of his actions by human skill
Be measured as so much Sex, Want, Will?—
Fables so dull would the sweeter be
With extract of humour for company!

Once was a god whose lovely face,
Wan as the poppy and arched in wings,
So haunted a votary with his grace
And the still wonder that worship brings,
That, having sipped of Helicon's springs,
He cast his beauty in bronze. And now
Eternal slumber bedims his brow—

Hypnos: and Dream was his dear son.
Not ours these follies. We haunt instead
Tropical jungles drear and dun,
And see in some fetish of fear and dread
Our symbol of dream—that brooding head!
And deem the wellspring of genius hid
In a dark morass that is dubbed the Id.

Sacred of old was the dyed baboon.
Though least, of the monkeys, like man is he,
Yet, rank the bones of his skeleton
With *homo sapiens'*: will they be
Void of design, form, symmetry?
To each his calling. Albeit we know
Apes father no Michelangelo!

In truth, a destiny undivined
Haunts every cell of bone and brain;
They share, to time and space resigned,
All passions that to earth pertain,
And twist man's thoughts to boon or bane;
Yet, be he master, need we ban
What the amoeba's made of man?

Who of his thoughts can reach the source?
Who in his life-blood's secret share?
By knowledge, artifice, or force
Compel the self within declare
What fiat bade it earthward fare?
Or proof expound this journey is
Else than a tissue of fantasies?

See, now, this butterfly, its wing
A dazzling play of patterned hues;
Far from the radiance of Spring,
From every faltering flower it choose
'Twill dip to sip autumnal dews:
So flit man's happiest moments by,
Daydreams of selfless transiency.

Was it by cunning the curious fly
That preys in a sunbeam schooled her wings
To ride her in air all motionlessly,
Poised on their myriad winnowings?
Where conned the blackbird the song he sings?
Was Job the instructor of the ant?
Go bees for nectar to Hume and Kant?

Who bade the scallop devise her shell?
Who tutored the daisy at cool of eve
To tent her pollen in floreted cell?
What dominie taught the dove to grieve;
The mole to delve; the worm to weave?
Does not the rather their life-craft seem
A tranced obedience to a dream?

Thus tranced, too, body and mind, will sit
A winter's dawn to dark, alone,
Heedless of how the cold moments flit,
The worker in words, or wood, or stone:
So far his waking desires have flown
Into a realm where his sole delight
Is to bring the dreamed-of to mortal sight.

Dumb in its wax may the music sleep—
In a breath conceived—that, with ardent care,
Note by note, in a reverie deep,
Mozart penned, for the world to share.
Waken it, needle! And then declare
How, invoked by the tiny tang,
Sound such strains as the Sirens sang!

Voyager dauntless on Newton's sea,
Year after year still brooding on
His algebraical formulae,
The genius of William Hamilton
Sought the square root of *minus* one;
In vain; till—all thought of it leagues away—
The problem flowered from a dream one day.

Our restless senses leap and say,
'How marvellous this!—How ugly that!'
And, at a breath, will slip away
The very thing they marvel at.
Time is the tyrant of their fate;
And frail the instant which must be
Our all of actuality.

If then to Solomon the Wise
Some curious priest stooped low and said,
'Thou! with thy lidded, sleep-sealed eyes,
This riddle solve from out thy bed:
Art thou—am I—by phantoms led?
Where is the real? In dream? Or wake?'
I know the answer the King might make!

And teeming Shakespeare: would he avow
The creatures of his heart and brain,
Whom, Prospero-like, he could endow
With all that mortal souls contain,
Mere copies that a fool can feign
Out of the tangible and seen?—
This the sole range of his demesne?

Ask not the Dreamer! See him run,
Listening a shrill and gentle neigh,
Foot into stirrup, he is up, he has won
Enchanted foothills far away.
Somewhere? Nowhere? Who need say?
So be it in secrecy of his mind
He some rare delectation find.

Ay, once I dreamed of an age-wide sea
Whereo'er three moons stood leper-bright;
And once—from agony set free—
I scanned within the womb of night,
A hollow inwoven orb of light,
Thrilling with beauty no tongue could tell,
And knew it for Life's citadel.

And—parable as strange—once, I
Was lured to a city whose every stone,
And harpy human hastening by
Were spawn and sport of fear alone—
By soulless horror enthralled, driven on:
Even the water that, ebon-clear,
Coursed through its dark, raved only of *Fear!*

Enigmas these; but not the face,
Fashioned of sleep, which, still at gaze
Of daybreak eyes, I yet could trace,
Made lovelier in the sun's first rays;
Nor that wild voice which in amaze,
Wide-wok'n, I listened singing on—
All memory of the singer gone.

O Poesy, of wellspring clear,
Let no sad Science thee suborn,
Who art thyself its planisphere!
All knowledge is foredoomed, forlorn—
Of inmost truth and wisdom shorn—
Unless imagination brings
It skies wherein to use its wings.

Two worlds have we: without; within;
But all that sense can mete and span,
Until it confirmation win
From heart and soul, is death to man.
Of grace divine his life began;
And—Eden empty proved—in deep
Communion with his spirit in sleep

The Lord Jehovah of a dream
Bade him, past all desire, conceive
What should his solitude redeem;
And, to his sunlit eyes, brought Eve.
Would that my day-wide mind could weave
Faint concept of the scene from whence
She awoke to Eden's innocence!

Starven with cares, like tares in wheat,
Wildered with knowledge, chilled with doubt,
The timeless self in vain must beat
Against its walls to hasten out
Whither the living waters fount;
And—evil and good no more at strife—
Seek love beneath the tree of life.

When then in memory I look back
To childhood's visioned hours I see
What now my anxious soul doth lack
Is energy in peace to be
At one with nature's mystery:
And Conscience less my mind indicts
For idle days than dreamless nights.

FARE WELL

WHEN I LIE where shades of darkness
Shall no more assail mine eyes,
Nor the rain make lamentation
    When the wind sighs;
How will fare the world whose wonder
Was the very proof of me?
Memory fades, must the remembered
    Perishing be?

Oh, when this my dust surrenders
Hand, foot, lip, to dust again,
May these loved and loving faces
    Please other men!

May the rustling harvest hedgerow
Still the Traveller's Joy entwine,
And as happy children gather
    Posies once mine.

Look thy last on all things lovely,
Every hour. Let no night
Seal thy sense in deathly slumber
    Till to delight
Thou have paid thy utmost blessing;
Since that all things thou wouldst praise
Beauty took from those who loved them
    In other days.

V. SACKVILLE-WEST

****

DEAR MR. BURNETT:

I have not got a copy of the American edition of The Edwardians *so am unable to give you page references . . . but I would suggest the scene of the Duchess dressing for dinner.*

Yours sincerely,

V. SACKVILLE-WEST

****

The Duchess Dresses for Dinner

ON LEAVING LADY ROEHAMPTON, Lucy went to her own room: the great house was quiet; all the guests were safely shut into their rooms till dinner; no one was about, except a housemaid beating up the cushions or a footman emptying the waste-paper basket. Along the passages, the windows were open, for it was a warm July evening, and the pigeons cooing on the battlements made the silence murmurous as though the grey stone of the walls had itself become vocal. Lucy hurried through the empty rooms. She detested solitude, even for half an hour; the habit of constant company—it could scarcely be called companionship—had unfitted her for her own society, and now she sagged and felt forlorn. She ought to look into the schoolroom, she thought, and say good-night to Viola, who, in dressing-gown and pigtails would be eating her supper, but the idea, no sooner than conceived, filled her with boredom. She decided to summon her favourite Sebastian instead. Reaching her room, where her maid, Button, was laying out her dress, she said, "Send word to his Grace, Button, that I should like to see him here for a few minutes."

Oh, the weariness of life, she thought, sitting down at her dressing-table; and then she remembered how Leonard Anquetil had looked at her when she had shown him the garden after tea, and a slight zest for life revived. She sat with lowered eyes, smiling a downward smile, while her thoughts dawdled over Leonard An-

quetil and her fingers played with the jewels laid out on the dressing-table. She had recently had the family jewels reset by Cartier,
preferring the fashion of the day to the heavy gold settings of Victoria's time. The top of the dressing-table was of looking-glass, so
that the gems were duplicated; rubies to-night, she thought idly,
picking up a brooch and setting it down again; last night she had
worn the emeralds, and her depression returned as she reflected that
some day she would have to give up the jewels to Sebastian's wife.
She did not want to become either a dowager or a grandmother;
she did not want to renounce her position as mistress of Chevron.
Its luxury and splendour were very pleasant to her. Perhaps she
would end, by marrying Sir Adam after all, before Sebastian and his
bride could turn her out; it would be a come-down to marry a Jew,
and physically Sir Adam was not appetising, but then his millions
were fabulous, and she could make him buy a place quite as imposing as Chevron. Not as beautiful, perhaps, but quite as imposing.
Her hands strayed over the rubies; yes, and he would buy jewels for
her too; her own, this time; no question of heirlooms. Besides Sir
Adam could do whatever he liked with the King. If only Sir Adam
were not physically in love with her, she might really consider it.

Sebastian came in, and Lucy became brisk again.

"Give me a wrap, Button. You can start doing my hair. Sebastian, give me the plan of the dinner-table. On the table there. No,
silly boy. Button, give it to his Grace. Now, Sebastian, read it out to
me while I have my hair done. Oh, George Roehampton takes me
in, does he? *Must* he? Such a bore that man is. And Sir Adam the
other side. Don't pull my hair like that, Button; really, I never knew
such a clumsy woman; now you have given me a headache for the
rest of the evening. Do be more careful. Well, I am not going to
enjoy myself very much, I can see: Sir Adam and George Roehampton. However, it's inevitable. Or no, let me see for myself.
That Miss Wace is such a fool that she may quite well have made
a muddle of the whole thing. Come and hold the plan for me to see,
Sebastian. Button! you pulled my hair again. How many times must
I tell you to be careful? Once more, and I give you notice, I declare
I will. Tilt it up, Sebastian; I can't see."

Sebastian stood beside his mother holding the red leather pad,
with slits into which cards bearing the names of the guests were inserted. As he stood holding it, he watched his mother's reflection in
the mirror. With her fair hair and lively little crumpled face, she
looked extraordinarily young for her age as a rule, but now she was
busy applying cream and wiping the cosmetics from her face with

a handkerchief, at the same time as Button removed the pads from under her hair and laid them on the dressing-table. 'Rats,' her children called them. They were unappetising objects, like last year's birdsnests, hot and stuffy to the head, but they could not be dispensed with, since they provided the foundation on which the coiffure was to be swathed and piled, and into which the innumerable hairpins were to be stuck. It was always a source of great preoccupation with the ladies that no bit of the pad should show through the natural hair. Often they put up a tentative hand to feel, even in the midst of the most absorbing conversation; and then their faces wore the expression which is seen only on the faces of women whose fingers investigate the back of their heads. Sebastian had watched this hair-dressing process a hundred times, but now seeing it take place in the mirror, he observed it with a new eye. He stared at his mother's reflection, with the pool of rubies in the foreground, and the uncomely 'rats,' as though she were a stranger to him, realising that behind the glitter and animation in which they lived he had absolutely no knowledge of her. If he had been asked to describe his mother, he must have said, "She is a famous hostess, with a talent for mimicry and a genius for making parties a success. She is charming and vivacious. In private life she is often irritable and sometimes unkind. She likes bridge and racing. She never opens a book, and she cannot bear to be alone. I have not the faintest idea of what she is really like." He would not have added, because he did not know, that she was ruthless and predatory.

"Why are you staring like that, Sebastian? You make me quite shy." Her hair was about her shoulders now, and Button was busy with the curling-tongs. She heated them first on the spirit lamp, and then held them carefully to her own cheek to feel if they were hot enough. "Bless the boy, one would think he had never watched me dress before. Now about that dinner-table, yes, it's all wrong; I thought it would be. She has clean forgotten the ambassador. Button, you must call Miss Wace—no, Sebastian, you fetch her. No, ring the bell; I don't want you to go away. Why on earth can't people do their own jobs properly? What do I pay Wacey a hundred and fifty a year for, I should like to know? Oh dear, and look at the time; I shall be late for dinner. I declare the trouble of entertaining is enough to spoil all one's pleasure. It's a little hard, I do think, that one should never have any undiluted pleasure in life. Who's that at the door? Button, go and see. And Miss Wace must come at once."

"Lady Viola would like to know if she may come and say good night to your Grace."

"Oh, bother the child—well, yes, I suppose she must if she wants to. Now, Button, haven't you nearly finished? Don't drag my hair back like that, woman. Give me the tail comb. Don't you see, it wants more fullness at the side. Really, Button, I thought you were supposed to be an expert hairdresser. You may think yourself lucky, Sebastian, that you were born a boy. This eternal hair, these eternal clothes! they wear a woman out before her time. Oh, there you are, Miss Wace. This plan is all wrong—perfectly hopeless. I don't go in with Lord Roehampton at all. What about the ambassador? You must alter it. Do it in here, as quick as you can. Sebastian will help you. And Viola. Come in, Viola; don't look so scared, child; I can't bear people who look scared. Now I must leave you all while I wash. No, I don't want you now, Button; you get on my nerves. I'll call you when I want you. Get my dress ready. Children, help Miss Wace—yes, you too, Viola; it's high time you took a little trouble to help your poor mother—and do, all three of you, try to show a little intelligence."

The duchess retired into her dressing-room, from where she kept up a flow of comments.

"Viola, you must really take a little more trouble about your appearance. You looked a perfect fright at luncheon to-day; I was ashamed of you. And you really must talk more, instead of sitting there like a stuffed doll. You had that nice Mr. Anquetil, who is perfectly easy to get on with. You might be ten, instead of seventeen. I have a good mind to start you coming down to dinner, except that you would cast a blight over everything. Girls are such a bore —poor things, they can't help it, but really they are a problem. They ruin conversation; one has to be so careful. Women ought to be married, or at any rate widowed. I don't mean you, of course, Wacey. I'm ready for you, Button."

Button vanished into the dressing-room, and for a while there was silence, broken only by irritable exclamations from within. These inner mysteries of his mother's toilet were unknown to Sebastian, but Viola knew well enough what was going on: her mother was seated, poking at her hair meanwhile with fretful but experienced fingers, while Button knelt before her, carefully drawing the silk stockings on to her feet and smoothing them nicely up the leg. Then her mother would rise, and, standing in her chemise, would allow the maid to fit the long stays of pink coutil, heavily boned, round her hips and slender figure, fastening the busk down the front, after many adjustments; then the suspenders would be clipped to the stockings; then the lacing would follow, beginning at the waist and travelling gradually up and down, until the necessary proportions had been achieved. The silk laces and their tags would fly out, under the maid's deft fingers, with the flick of a skilled worker mending a net. Then the pads of pink satin would be brought, and fastened into place on the hips and under the arms, still further to accentuate the smallness of the waist. Then the drawers; and then the petticoat would be spread into a ring on the floor, and Lucy would step into it on her high-heeled shoes, allowing Button to draw it up and tie the tapes. Then Button would throw the dressing-gown round her shoulders again—Viola had followed the progress well, for here the door opened, and the duchess emerged. "Well, have you done that table? Read it out. Louder. I can't hear. Yes, that's better. I'm sorry, Sebastian, you'll have to take in old Octavia Hull again. Nonsense, she's very amusing when she's not too fuddled with drugs. She'll be all right tonight because she'll be afraid of losing too much money to Sir Adam after dinner. Now, Wacey, off you go and rearrange the cards on the table. And you too, Viola. There are too many people in this room. Oh, all right, you can stop till I'm dressed if you like. Button, I'm ready for my dress. Now be careful. Don't catch the hooks in my hair. Sebastian, you must turn round while I take off my dressing-gown. Now, Button."

Button, gathering up the lovely mass of taffeta and tulle, held the bodice open while the duchess flung off her wrap and dived gingerly into the billows of her dress. Viola watched enraptured the sudden gleam of her mother's white arms and shoulders. Button breathed a sigh of relief as she began doing up the innumerable hooks at the back. But Lucy could not stand still for a moment, and strayed all over the room with Button in pursuit, hooking. "Haven't you finished *yet*, Button? Nonsense, it isn't tight. You'll say next that I'm getting fat." Lucy was proud of her waist, which indeed was tiny, and had changed since her girlish days only from eighteen to twenty inches. "Only when your Grace stoops," said Button apologetically, for Lucy at the moment was bending forward and peering into her mirror as she puffed the roll of her hair into a rounder shape. "*There*, then," said the duchess, straightening herself, but reaching down stiffly for the largest of her rubies, which she tried first against her shoulder, but finally pinned into a knot at her waist. Then she encircled her throat with the high dog-collar of rubies and diamonds, tied with a large bow of white tulle at the back. "You must choose a wife who will do credit to the jewels, Sebastian," she said as she slipped an ear-ring into its place, "because, of course, the day will come when your poor old mother has to give up everything to her daughter-in-law, and we shan't like that—eh, Button?"—for she was in a better humour now, again completely adorned and clothed—"but we'll put up with it for the joy of seeing a bride brought to Chevron—eh, Button, eh, Wacey? oh, no, of course Wacey has gone to do the table—and you and I, Button, will retire to the Dower House and live humbly for the rest of our lives, and perhaps his Grace will ask us to the garden-party— eh, Sebastian, you rogue?—will you, if your wife allows it?" Lucy was herself again, adjusting her frock, clasping her bracelets, dusting her throat with powder—for she was one of those who used powder, to the disapproval of her elders—and everybody except Sebastian was radiant with responsive smiles. She flicked her handkerchief across Sebastian's lips. "Sulky boy! but Sylvia Roehampton says you are even more attractive when you sulk than when you are amiable, so I suppose I must believe her. Now Viola, my darling, I must run. Kiss me good-night. Go straight to bed. Do I look nice?"

"Oh, mother, you look too lovely!"

"That's all right." Lucy liked as much admiration as she could get. "Now you'll run away to bed, won't you? Dear me, I quite envy you the quiet of the schoolroom instead of that noisy dinner. Don't you, Sebastian? Good-night, my darling. Come along, Sebastian. I shall want you to wait up for me, Button, of course. You go in front, Sebastian, and open the doors. Dear, dear, how late you children have made me. Sebastian, you must apologise to old Octavia at dinner, and tell her it was all your fault. My fan, Button! good heavens, woman, what are you there for? One has to think of everything for oneself."

HILAIRE BELLOC

****

OCTOBER
LONDON

*Mr. Belloc is honoured to learn that his name is among the first 50
living writers chosen in your ballot and for your inclusion of some
part of his work in your volume, he begs you to excuse him from
making the selection himself. He is really too retiring to do it, I
assure you, and will be quite content to leave the choice to your
own taste and judgment.*

*Personally I consider the task very difficult! For Mr. Belloc's
range is so wide, but I may tell you privately that in his own opinion
his poetry is worth more than his prose.*

RONALD RICHINGS, *Secretary*

DECEMBER
LONDON

*It is useless for me to ask Mr. Belloc to write a paragraph for you
about the choice of· the poem. He invariably refuses any such request! But I can tell you privately that he himself rates it* much
higher than the poems that are included in most anthologies. "Symbol of The Free!" remember!*

RONALD RICHINGS

****

Heroic Poem in Praise of Wine

To Duff Cooper

To EXALT, enthrone, establish and defend,
To welcome home mankind's mysterious friend:
Wine, true begetter of all arts that be;

**Heroic Poem in Praise of Wine*

472

Wine, privilege of the completely free;
Wine the recorder; wine the sagely strong;
Wine, bright avenger of sly-dealing wrong,
Awake, Ausonian Muse, and sing the vineyard song!

Sing how the Charioteer from Asia came,
And on his front the little dancing flame
Which marked the God-head. Sing the Panther-team,
The gilded Thyrsus twirling, and the gleam
Of cymbals through the darkness. Sing the drums.
He comes: the young renewer of Hellas comes!
The Seas await him. Those Aegean Seas
Roll from the dawning, ponderous, ill at ease,
In lifts of lead, whose cresting hardly breaks
To ghostly foam, when suddenly there awakes
A mountain glory inland. All the skies
Are luminous; and amid the sea bird cries
The mariner hears a morning breeze arise.
Then goes the Pageant forward. The sea-way
Silvers the feet of that august array
Trailing above the waters, through the airs;
And as they pass a wind before them bears
The quickening word, the influence magical.
The Islands have received it, marble-tall;
The long shores of the mainland. Something fills
The warm Euboean combes, the sacred hills
Of Aulis and of Argos. Still they move
Touching the City walls, the Temple grove,
Till, far upon the horizon-glint, a gleam
Of light, of trembling light, revealed they seem
Turned to a cloud, but to a cloud that shines,
And everywhere as they pass, the Vines! The Vines!
The Vines, the conquering Vines! And the Vine breathes
Her savour through the upland, empty heaths
Of treeless wastes; the Vines have come to where
The dark Pelasgian steep defends the lair
Of the wolf's hiding; to the empty fields
By Aufidus, the dry campaign that yields
No harvest for the husbandman, but now
Shall bear a nobler foison than the plough;

To where, festooned along the tall elm trees,
Tendrils are mirrored in Tyrrhenian seas;
To where the South awaits them; even to where
Stark, African, informed of burning air,
Upturned to Heaven the broad Hipponian plain
Extends luxurious and invites the main.
Guelma's a mother: barren Thapsa breeds;
And northward in the valleys, next the meads
That sleep by misty river banks, the Vines
Have struck to spread below the solemn pines.
The Vines are on the roof-trees. All the Shrines
And Homes of men are consecrate with Vines.

And now the task of that triumphant day
Has reached to victory. In the reddening ray
With all his train, from hard Iberian lands
Fulfilled, apparent, that Creator stands
Halted on Atlas. Far beneath him, far,
The strength of Ocean darkening and the star
Beyond all shores. There is a silence made.
It glorifies: and the gigantic shade
Of Hercules adores him from the West.
Dead Lucre: burnt Ambition: Wine is best.

But what are these that from the outer murk
Of dense mephitic vapours creeping lurk
To breathe foul airs from that corrupted well
Which oozes slime along the floor of Hell?
These are the stricken palsied brood of sin
In whose vile veins, poor, poisonous and thin,
Decoctions of embittered ha_reds crawl:
These are the Water-Drinkers, cursed all!
On what gin-sodden Hags, what flaccid sires
Bred these White Slugs from what exhaust desires?
In what close prison's horror were their wiles
Watched by what tyrant power with evil smiles;
Or in what caverns, blocked from grace and air
Received they, then, the mandates of despair?
What! Must our race, our tragic race, that roam
All exiled from our first, and final, home:
That in one moment of temptation lost

Our heritage, and now wander, hunger-tost
Beyond the Gates (still speaking with our eyes
For ever of remembered Paradise),
Must we with every gift accepted, still,
With every joy, receive attendant ill?
Must some lewd evil follow all our good
And muttering dog our brief beatitude?
A primal doom, inexorable, wise,
Permitted, ordered, even these to rise.
Even in the shadow of so bright a Lord
Must swarm and propagate the filthy horde
Debased, accursed I say, abhorrent and abhorred.
Accursed and curse-bestowing. For whosoe'er
Shall suffer their contagion, everywhere
Falls from the estate of man and finds his end
To the mere beverage of the beast condemned.
For such as these in vain the Rhine has rolled
Imperial centuries by hills of gold;
For such as these the flashing Rhone shall rage
In vain its lightning through the Hermitage
Or level-browed divine Touraine receive
The tribute of her vintages at eve.
For such as these Burgundian heats in vain
Swell the rich slope or load the empurpled plain.
Bootless for such as these the mighty task
Of bottling God the Father in a flask
And leading all Creation down distilled
To one small ardent sphere immensely filled.
With memories empty, with experience null,
With vapid eye-balls meaningless and dull
They pass unblest through the unfruitful light;
And when we open the bronze doors of Night,
When we in high carousal, we, reclined,
Spur up to Heaven the still ascending mind,
Pass with the all inspiring, to and fro,
The torch of genius and the Muse's glow,
They, lifeless, stare at vacancy alone
Or plan mean traffic, or repeat their moan.
We, when repose demands us, welcomed are
In young white arms, like our great Exemplar

Who, wearied with creation, takes his rest
And sinks to sleep on Ariadne's breast.
They through the darkness into darkness press
Despised, abandoned and companionless.
And when the course of either's sleep has run
We leap to life like heralds of the sun;
We from the couch in roseate mornings gay
Salute as equals the exultant day
While they, the unworthy, unrewarded, they
The dank despisers of the Vine, arise
To watch grey dawns and mourn indifferent skies.

Forget them! Form the Dionysian ring
And pulse the ground, and Io, Io, sing.

Father Lenaean, to whom our strength belongs,
Our loves, our wars, our laughter and our songs,
Remember our inheritance, who praise
Your glory in these last unhappy days
When beauty sickens and a muddied robe
Of baseness fouls the universal globe.
Though all the Gods indignant and their train
Abandon ruined man, do thou remain!
By thee the vesture of our life was made,
The Embattled Gate, the lordly Colonnade,
The woven fabric's gracious hues, the sound
Of trumpets, and the quivering fountain-round,
And, indestructible, the Arch, and, high,
The Shaft of Stone that stands against the sky,
And, last, the guardian-genius of them, Rhyme,
Come from beyond the world to conquer time:
All these are thine, Lenaean.

By thee do seers the inward light discern;
By thee the statue lives, the Gods return;
By thee the thunder and the falling foam
Of loud Acquoria's torrent call to Rome;
Alba rejoices in a thousand springs,
Gensano laughs, and Orvieto sings . . .
But, Ah! With Orvieto, with that name

Of dark, Eturian, subterranean flame
The years dissolve. I am standing in that hour
Of majesty Septembral, and the power
Which swells the clusters when the nights are still
With autumn stars on Orvieto hill.

Had these been mine, Ausonian Muse, to know
The large contented oxen heaving slow;
To count my sheaves at harvest; so to spend
Perfected days in peace until the end;
With every evening's dust of gold to hear
The bells upon the pasture height, the clear
Full horn of herdsmen gathering in the kine
To ancient byres in hamlets Appenine,
And crown abundant age with generous ease:
Had these, Ausonian Muse, had these, had these . . . .

But since I would not, since I could not stay,
Let me remember even in this my day
How, when the ephemeral vision's lure is past
All, all, must face their Passion at the last

Was there not one that did to Heaven complain
How, driving through the midnight and the rain,
He struck, the Atlantic seethe and surge before,
Wrecked in the North along a lonely shore
To make the lights of home and hear his name no more.
Was there not one that from a desperate field
Rode with no guerdon but a rifted shield;
A name disinherited; a broken sword;
Wounds unrenowned; battle beneath no Lord;
Strong blows, but on the void, and toil without reward.

When from the waste of such long labour done
I too must leave the grape-ennobling sun
And like the vineyard worker take my way
Down the long shadows of declining day,
Bend on the sombre plain my clouded sight
And leave the mountain to the advancing night,
Come to the term of all that was mine own

With nothingness before me, and alone;
Then to what hope of answer shall I turn?
Comrade-Commander whom I dared not earn,
What said You then to trembling friends and few?
"A moment, and I drink it with you new:
But in my Father's Kingdom." So, my Friend,
Let not Your cup desert me in the end.
But when the hour of mine adventure's near
Just and benignant, let my youth appear
Bearing a Chalice, open, golden, wide,
With benediction graven on its side.
So touch my dying lip: so bridge that deep:
So pledge my waking from the gift of sleep,
And, sacramental, raise me the Divine:
Strong brother in God and last companion, Wine.

W. H. AUDEN

****

For the Time Being, a Christmas Oratorio, is one of W. H. Auden's book-length poems and by many is considered the finest work accomplished by its author. One poet has described it as the most "minute dissection of the spiritual illness of our day" (Louise Bogan). It was characterized by a critic in Time Magazine *as "simultaneously an intense declaration of the poet's new found religious faith and a rejection of the more self-centered aspects of his brilliant past." In connection with the excerpting of* The Massacre of the Innocents, *the closing section of the Oratorio, Mr. Auden did not feel he had anything to say about it. "You might point out," he added, "that it is far harder to pick a representative piece in poetry than it is in prose."*

****

The Massacre of the Innocents

I

HEROD

BECAUSE I am bewildered, because I must decide, because my decision must be in conformity with Nature and Necessity, let me honour those through whom my nature is by necessity what it is.

To Fortune—that I have become Tetrarch, that I have escaped assassination, that at sixty my head is clear and my digestion sound.

To my Father—for the means to gratify my love of travel and study.

To my Mother—for a straight nose.

To Eva, my coloured nurse—for regular habits.

To my brother, Sandy, who married a trapeze-artist and died of drink—for so refuting the position of the Hedonists.

479

To Mr. Stewart, nicknamed The Carp, who instructed me in the elements of geometry through which I came to perceive the errors of the tragic poets.

To Professor Lighthouse—for his lectures on The Peloponnesian War.

To the stranger on the boat to Sicily—for recommending to me Brown on Resolution.

To my secretary, Miss Button—for admitting that my speeches were inaudible.

There is no visible disorder. No crime—what could be more innocent than the birth of an artisan's child? Today has been one of those perfect winter days, cold, brilliant, and utterly still, when the bark of a shepherd's dog carries for miles, and the great wild mountains come up quite close to the city walls, and the mind feels intensely awake, and this evening as I stand at this window high up in the citadel there is nothing in the whole magnificent panorama of plain and mountains to indicate that the Empire is threatened by a danger more dreadful than any invasion of Tartars on racing camels or conspiracy of the Praetorian Guard.

Barges are unloading soil fertiliser at the river wharves. Soft drinks and sandwiches may be had in the inns at reasonable prices. Allotment gardening has become popular. The highway to the coast goes straight up over the mountains and the truck-drivers no longer carry guns. Things are beginning to take shape. It is a long time since anyone stole the park benches or murdered the swans. There are children in this province who have never seen a louse, shopkeepers who have never handled a counterfeit coin, women of forty who have never hidden in a ditch except for fun. Yes, in twenty years I have managed to do a little. Not enough, of course. There are villages only a few miles from here where they still believe in witches. There isn't a single town where a good bookshop would pay. One could count on the fingers of one hand the people capable of solving the problem of Achilles and the Tortoise. Still it is a beginning. In twenty years the darkness has been pushed back a few inches. And what, after all, is the whole Empire, with its few thousand square miles on which it is possible to lead the Rational Life, but a tiny patch of light compared with those immense areas of barbaric night that surround it on all sides, that incoherent wilderness of rage and terror, where Mongolian idiots are regarded as sacred and mothers who give birth to twins are instantly put to death, where malaria is treated by yelling, where warriors of superb courage obey the commands of hysterical female impersonators, where the best cuts of meat are reserved for the dead, where, if a white blackbird has been seen, no more work may be done that day, where it is firmly believed that the world was created by a giant with three heads or that the motions of the stars are controlled from the liver of a rogue elephant?

Yet even inside this little civilised patch itself, where, at the cost of heaven knows how much grief and bloodshed, it has been made unnecessary for anyone over the age of twelve to believe in fairies or that First Causes reside in mortal and finite objects, so many are still homesick for that disorder wherein every passion formerly enjoyed a frantic licence. Caesar flies to his hunting lodge pursued by ennui; in the faubourgs of the Capital, Society grows savage, corrupted by silks and scents, softened by sugar and hot water, made insolent by theatres and attractive slaves; and everywhere, including this province, new prophets spring up every day to sound the old barbaric note.

I have tried everything. I have prohibited the sale of crystals and ouija-boards; I have slapped a heavy tax on playing cards; the courts are empowered to sentence alchemists to hard labor in the mines; it is a statutory offence to turn tables or feel bumps. But nothing is really effective. How can I expect the masses to be sensible when, for instance, to my certain knowledge, the captain of my own guard wears an amulet against the Evil Eye, and the richest merchant in the city consults a medium over every important transaction?

Legislation is helpless against the wild prayer of longing that rises, day in, day out, from all these households under my protection: "O God, put away justice and truth for we cannot understand them and do not want them. Eternity would bore us dreadfully. Leave Thy heavens and come down to our earth of waterclocks and hedges. Become our uncle. Look after Baby, amuse Grandfather, escort Madam to the Opera, help Willy with his home-work, introduce Muriel to a handsome naval officer. Be interesting and weak like us, and we will love you as we love ourselves."

Reason is helpless, and now even the Poetic Compromise no longer works, all those lovely fairy tales in which Zeus, disguising himself as a swan or a bull or a shower of rain or what-have-you, lay with some beautiful woman and begot a hero. For the Public has grown too sophisticated. Under all the charming metaphors and symbols, it detects the stern command, "Be and act heroically"; behind the myth of divine origin, it senses the real human excellence that is a reproach to its own baseness. So, with a bellow of rage, it kicks Poetry downstairs and sends for Prophecy. "Your sister has just insulted me. I asked for a God who should be as like me as possible. What use to me is a God whose divinity consists in doing difficult things that I cannot do or saying clever things that I cannot understand? The God I want and intend to get must be someone I can recognise immediately without having to wait and see what he says or does. There must be nothing in the least extraordinary about him. Produce him at once, please. I'm sick of waiting."

Today, apparently, judging by the trio who came to see me this morning with an ecstatic grin on their scholarly faces, the job has been done. "God has been born," they cried, "we have seen him ourselves. The World is saved. Nothing else matters."

One needn't be much of a psychologist to realise that if this rumour is not stamped out now, in a few years it is capable of diseasing the whole Empire, and one doesn't have to be a prophet to predict the consequences if it should.

Reason will be replaced by Revelation. Instead of Rational Law, objective truths perceptible to any who will undergo the necessary intellectual discipline, and the same for all, Knowledge will degenerate into a riot of subjective visions—feelings in the solar plexus induced by undernourishment, angelic images generated by fevers or drugs, dream warnings inspired by the sound of falling water. Whole cosmogonies will be created out of some forgotten personal resentment, complete epics written in private languages, the daubs of school children ranked above the greatest masterpieces.

Idealism will be replaced by Materialism. Priapus will only have to move to a good address and call himself Eros to become the darling of middle-aged women. Life after death will be an eternal dinner party where all the guests are twenty years old. Diverted from its normal and wholesome outlet in patriotism and civic or family pride, the need of the materialistic Masses for some visible Idol to worship will be driven into totally unsocial channels where no education can reach it. Divine honours will be paid to silver teapots, shallow depressions in the earth, names on maps, domestic pets, ruined windmills, even in extreme cases, which will become increasingly common, to headaches, or malignant tumours, or four o'clock in the afternoon.

Justice will be replaced by Pity as the cardinal human virtue, and all fear of retribution will vanish. Every cornerboy will congratulate himself: "I'm such a sinner that God had to come down in person to save me. I must be a devil of a fellow." Every crook will argue:

"I like committing crimes. God likes forgiving them. Really the world is admirably arranged." And the ambition of every young cop will be to secure a death-bed repentance. The New Aristocracy will consist exclusively of hermits, bums, and permanent invalids. The Rough Diamond, the Consumptive Whore, the bandit who is good to his mother, the epileptic girl who has a way with animals will be the heroes and heroines of the New Tragedy when the general, the statesman, and the philosopher have become the butt of every farce and satire.

Naturally this cannot be allowed to happen. Civilisation must be saved even if this means sending for the military, as I suppose it does. How dreary. Why is it that in the end civilisation always has to call in these professional tidiers to whom it is all one whether it be Pythagoras or a homicidal lunatic that they are instructed to exterminate. O dear, Why couldn't this wretched infant be born somewhere else? Why can't people be sensible? I don't want to be horrid. Why can't they see that the notion of a finite God is absurd? Because it is. And suppose, just for the sake of argument, that it isn't, that this story is true, that this child is in some inexplicable manner both God and Man, that he grows up, lives, and dies, without committing a single sin? Would that make life any better? On the contrary it would make it far, far worse. For it could only mean this; that once having shown them how, God would expect every man, whatever his fortune, to lead a sinless life in the flesh and on earth. Then indeed would the human race be plunged into madness and despair. And for me personally at this moment it would mean that God had given me the power to destroy Himself. I refuse to be taken in. He could not play such a horrible practical joke. Why should He dislike me so? I've worked like a slave. Ask anyone you like. I read all official dispatches without skipping. I've taken elocution lessons. I've hardly ever taken bribes. How dare He allow me to decide? I've tried to be good. I brush my teeth every night. I haven't had sex for a month. I object. I'm a liberal. I want everyone to be happy. I wish I had never been born.

II

SOLDIERS

WHEN THE SEX WAR ended with the slaughter of the
    Grandmothers,
They found a bachelor's baby suffocating under them;

Somebody called him George and that was the end of it:
  They hitched him up to the Army.
  George, you old debutante,
  How did you get in the Army?

In the Retreat from Reason he deserted on his rocking-horse
And lived on a fairy's kindness till he tired of kicking her;
He smashed her spectacles and stole her check-book
    and mackintosh
  Then cruised his way back to the Army.
  George, you old numero,
  How did you get in the Army?

Before the Diet of Sugar he was using razor-blades
And exited soon after with an allergy to maidenheads;
He discovered a cure of his own, but no one would patent it,
  So he showed up again in the Army.
  George, you old flybynight,
  How did you get in the Army?

When the Vice Crusades were over he was hired by some
    Muscovites
Prospecting for deodorants among the Eskimos;
He was caught by a common cold and condemned to the
    whiskey mines,
  But schemozzled back to the Army.
  George, you old Emperor,
  How did you get in the Army?

Since Peace was signed with Honour he's been minding
    his business;
But, whoops, here comes His Idleness, buttoning
    his uniform;
Just in tidy time to massacre the Innocents;
  He's come home to roost in the Army.
  George, you old matador,
  Welcome back to the Army.

III
RACHEL

On the Left are grinning dogs, peering down into a solitude too
deep to fill with roses.

On the Right are sensible sheep, gazing up at a pride where no
dream can grow.

Somewhere in these unending wastes of delirium is a lost child,
speaking of Long Ago in the language of wounds.

Tomorrow, perhaps, he will come to himself in Heaven.

But here Grief turns her silence, neither in this direction, nor in
that, nor for any reason.

And her coldness now is on the earth forever.

THE FLIGHT INTO EGYPT

I
JOSEPH

Mirror, let us through the glass
No authority can pass.

MARY

Echo, if the strong should come,
Tell a white lie or be dumb.

VOICES OF THE DESERT

It was visitors' day at the vinegar works
In Tenderloin Town where I tore my time;
A sorrowful snapshot was my sinful wage:
Was that why you left me, elusive bones?
 Come to our bracing desert
 Where eternity is eventful,
  For the weather-glass
  Is set at Alas,
 The thermometer at Resentful.

MARY

The Kingdom of the Robbers lies
Between Time and our memories;

JOSEPH

Fugitives from Space must cross
The waste of the Anonymous.

VOICES OF THE DESERT

How should he figure my fear of the dark?
The moment he can he'll remember me,
The silly, he locked in the cellar for fun,
And his dear little doggie shall die in his arms,
  Come to our old-world desert
  Where everyone goes to pieces;
    You can pick up tears
    For souvenirs
  Or genuine diseases.

JOSEPH

Geysers and volcanoes give
Sudden comical relief;

MARY

And the vulture is a boon
On a dull hot afternoon.

VOICES OF THE DESERT

All Father's nightingales knew their place,
The gardens were loyal: look at them now.
The roads are so careless, the rivers so rude,
My studs have been stolen; I must speak to the sea.
  Come to our well-run desert
  Where anguish arrives by cable,
    And the deadly sins
    May be bought in tins
  With instructions on the label.

MARY

Skulls recurring every mile
Direct the thirsty to the Nile;

JOSEPH

And the jackal's eye at night
Forces Error to keep right.

VOICES OF THE DESERT

In a land of lilies I lost my wits,
Nude as a number all night I ran
With a ghost for a guest along green canals;
By the waters of waking I wept for the weeds.
  Come to our jolly desert
  Where even the dolls go whoring;
    Where cigarette-ends
    Become intimate friends,
  And it's always three in the morning.

JOSEPH AND MARY

Safe in Egypt we shall sigh
For lost insecurity;
For lost insecurity;
Only when her terrors come
Does our flesh feel quite at home.

II

RECITATIVE

Fly, Holy Family, from our immediate rage,
That our future may be freed from our past; retrace
  The footsteps of law-giving
  Moses, back through the sterile waste,

Down to the rotten kingdom of Egypt, the damp
Tired delta where in her season of glory our
  Forefathers sighed in bondage;
  Abscond with the Child to the place

That their children dare not revisit, to the time
They do not care to remember; hide from our pride
  In our humiliation;
  Fly from our death with our new life.

III

NARRATOR

Well, so that is that. Now we must dismantle the tree,
Putting the decorations back into their cardboard boxes—
Some have got broken—and carrying them up to the attic.
The holly and the mistletoe must be taken down and burnt,
And the children got ready for school. There are enough

Left-overs to do, warmed-up, for the rest of the week—
Not that we have much appetite, having drunk such a lot,
Stayed up so late, attempted—quite unsuccessfully—
To love all of our relatives, and in general
Grossly overestimated our powers. Once again
As in previous years we have seen the actual Vision and failed
To do more than entertain it as an agreeable
Possibility, once again we have sent Him away,
Begging though to remain His disobedient servant,
The promising child who cannot keep His word for long.
The Christmas Feast is already a fading memory,
And already the mind begins to be vaguely aware
Of an unpleasant whiff of apprehension at the thought
Of Lent and Good Friday which cannot, after all, now
Be very far off. But, for the time being, here we all are,
Back in the moderate Aristotelian city
Of darning and the Eight-Fifteen, where Euclid's geometry
And Newton's mechanics would account for our experience,
And the kitchen table exists because I scrub it.
It seems to have shrunk during the holidays. The streets
Are much narrower than we remembered; we had forgotten
The office was as depressing as this. To those who have seen
The Child, however dimly, however incredulously,
The Time Being is, in a sense, the most trying time of all.
For the innocent children who whispered so excitedly
Outside the locked door where they knew the presents to be
Grew up when it opened. Now, recollecting that moment
We can repress the joy, but the guilt remains conscious;
Remembering the stable where for once in our lives
Everything became a You and nothing was an It.
And craving the sensation but ignoring the cause,
We look round for something, no matter what, to inhibit
Our self-reflection, and the obvious thing for that purpose
Would be some great suffering. So, once we have met the Son,
We are tempted ever after to pray to the Father;
"Lead us into temptation and evil for our sake."
They will come, all right, don't worry; probably in a form
That we do not expect, and certainly with a force
More dreadful than we can imagine. In the meantime
There are bills to be paid, machines to keep in repair,
Irregular verbs to learn, the Time Being to redeem
From insignificance. The happy morning is over,

The night of agony still to come; the time is noon:
When the Spirit must practise his scales of rejoicing
Without even a hostile audience, and the Soul endure
A silence that is neither for nor against her faith
That God's Will will be done, that, in spite of her prayers,
God will cheat no one, not even the world of its triumph.

IV

CHORUS

He is the Way.
Follow Him through the Land of Unlikeness;
You will see rare beasts, and have unique adventures.

He is the Truth.
Seek Him in the Kingdom of Anxiety;
You will come to a great city that has expected your return
    for years.

He is the Life.
Love Him in the World of the Flesh;
And at your marriage all its occasions shall dance for joy.

JULIAN HUXLEY

****

I have chosen my "Uniqueness of Man" because I consider that it illustrates better than any other of my writings my central preoccupation with scientific humanism, which seeks to combine a rigorously scientific approach with a recognition of the many-sidedness of human nature.

J U L I A N   H U X L E Y

****

The Uniqueness of Man

MAN'S OPINION of his own position in relation to the rest of the animals has swung pendulum-wise between too great or too little a conceit of himself, fixing now too large a gap between himself and the animals, now too small. The gap, of course, can be diminished or increased at either the animal or the human end. One can, like Descartes, make animals too mechanical, or, like most unsophisticated people, humanize them too much. Or one can work at the human end of the gap, and then either dehumanize one's own kind into an animal species like any other, or superhumanize it into beings a little lower than the angels.

After Darwin, man could no longer avoid considering himself as an animal; but he is beginning to see himself as a very peculiar and in many ways a unique animal. The analysis of man's biological uniqueness is as yet incomplete. This essay is an attempt to review its present position.

The first and most obviously unique characteristic of man is his capacity for conceptual thought; if you prefer objective terms, you will say his employment of true speech, but that is only another way of saying the same thing.

This basic human property has had many consequences. The most important was the development of a cumulative tradition. The beginnings of tradition, by which experience is transmitted from one generation to the next, are to be seen in many higher animals. But in no case is the tradition cumulative. Offspring learn from parents, but they learn the same kind and quantity of lessons as they, in turn, impart; the transmission of experience never bridges more than one generation. In man, however, tradition is an independent and potentially permanent activity, capable of indefinite improvement in quality and increase in quantity. It constitutes a new accessory process of heredity in evolution, running side by side with the biological process, heredity of experience to supplement the universal heredity of living substance.

The existence of a cumulative tradition has as its chief consequence—or if you prefer, its chief objective manifestation—the progressive improvement of human tools and machinery. Many animals employ tools; but they are always crude tools employed in a crude way. Elaborate tools and skilled technique can develop only with the aid of speech and tradition.

In the perspective of evolution, tradition and tools are the characters which have given man his dominant position among organisms. This biological dominance is, at present, another of man's unique properties. Since the early Pleistocene, widespread extinction has diminished the previously dominant group of placental mammals, and man has not merely multiplied, but has evolved, extended his range, and increased the variety of his modes of life.

Biology thus reinstates man in a position analogous to that conferred on him as Lord of Creation by theology. There are, however, differences, and differences of some importance for our general outlook. In the biological view, the other animals have not been created to serve man's needs, but man has evolved in such a way that he has been able to eliminate some competing types, to enslave others by domestication, and to modify physical and biological conditions over the larger part of the earth's land area. The theological view was not true in detail or in many of its implications; but it had a solid biological basis.

Speech, tradition, and tools have led to many other unique properties of man. These are, for the most part, obvious and well known, and I propose to leave them aside until I have dealt with some less familiar human characteristics. For the human species, considered as a species, is unique in certain purely biological attributes; and these have not received the attention they deserve, either from the zoological or the sociological standpoint.

In the first place, man is by far the most variable wild species known. Domesticated species like dog, horse, or fowl may rival or exceed him in this particular, but their variability has obvious reasons, and is irrelevant to our inquiry.

In correlation with his wide variability, man has a far wider range than any other animal species, with the possible exception of some of his parasites. Man is also unique as a dominant type. All other dominant types have evolved into many hundreds or thousands of separate species, grouped in numerous genera, families, and larger classificatory groups. The human type has maintained its dominance without splitting: man's variety has been achieved within the limits of a single species.

Finally, man is unique among higher animals in the method of his evolution. Whereas, in general, animal evolution is divergent, human evolution is reticulate. By this is meant that in animals, evolution occurs by the isolation of groups which then become progressively more different in their genetic characteristics, so that the course of evolution can be represented as a divergent radiation of separate lines, some of which become extinct, others continue unbranched, and still others divergently branch again. Whereas in man, after incipient divergence, the branches have come together again, and have generated new diversity from their Mendelian recombinations, this process being repeated until the course of human descent is like a network.

Let us remind ourselves that superposed upon this purely biological or genetic variability is the even greater amount of variability due to differences of upbringing, profession, and personal tastes. The final result is a degree of variation that would be staggering if it were not so familiar. It would be fair to say that, in respect to mind and outlook, individual human beings are separated by differences as profound as those which distinguish the major groups of the animal kingdom. This enormous range of individual variation in human minds often leads to misunderstanding and even mutual incomprehensibility; but it also provides the necessary basis for fruitful division of labour in human society.

Another biological peculiarity of man is the uniqueness of his evolutionary history. Writers have indulged their speculative fancy by imagining other organisms endowed with speech and conceptual thought—talking rats, rational ants, philosophic dogs, and the like. But closer analysis shows that these fantasies are impossible. A brain capable of conceptual thought could not have been developed elsewhere than in a human body.

Evolution consists of an enormous number of blind alleys, with a very occasional path of progress. It is like a maze in which almost all turnings are wrong turnings. The goal of the evolutionary maze, however, is not a central chamber, but a road which will lead indefinitely onwards.

If now we look back upon the past history of life, we shall see that the avenues of progress have been steadily reduced in number, until by the Pleistocene period, or even earlier, only one was left. Let us remember that we can and must judge early progress in the light of its latest steps. The most recent step has been the acquisition of conceptual thought, which has enabled man to dethrone the non-human mammals from their previous position of dominance. It is a biological fact that conceptual thought could never have arisen save in a mammal.

Most mammalian lines, however, cut themselves off from indefinite progress by one-sided evolution, turning their limbs and jaws into specialized and therefore limited instruments. And, for the most part, they relied mainly on the crude sense of smell, which cannot present as differentiated a pattern of detailed knowledge as can sight. Finally, the majority continued to produce their young several at a time, in litters. As J. B. S. Haldane has pointed out, this gives rise to an acute struggle for existence in the prenatal period, a considerable percentage of embryos being aborted or resorbed. Such intra-uterine selection will put a premium upon rapidity of growth and differentiation, since the devil takes the hindmost; and this rapidity of development will tend automatically to be carried on into postnatal growth.

As everyone knows, man is characterized by a rate of development which is abnormally slow as compared with that of any other mammal. The period from birth to the first onset of sexual maturity comprises nearly a quarter of the normal span of his life, instead of an eighth, a tenth or twelfth, as in some other animals. This again is in one sense a unique characteristic of man, although from the evolutionary point of view it represents merely the exaggeration of a tendency which is operative in other Primates. In any case, it is a necessary condition for the evolution and proper utilization of rational thought. If men and women were, like mice, confronted with the problems of adult life and parenthood after a few weeks, or even, like whales, after a couple of years, they could never acquire the skills of body and mind that they now absorb from and contribute to the social heritage of the species.

This slowing (or "foetalization," as Bolk has called it, since it prolongs the foetal characteristics of earlier ancestral forms into postnatal development and even into adult life) has had other important by-products for man. Here I will mention but one—his nakedness. The distribution of hair on man is extremely similar to that on a late foetus of a chimpanzee, and there can be little doubt that it represents an extension of this temporary anthropoid phase into permanence. Hairlessness of body is not a unique biological characteristic of man; but it is unique among terrestrial mammals, save for a few desert creatures, and some others which have compensated for loss of hair by developing a pachydermatous skin. In any case, it has important biological consequences, since it must have encouraged the comparatively defenceless human creatures in their efforts to protect themselves against animal enemies and the elements, and so has been a spur to the improvement of intelligence.

Now, foetalization could never have occurred in a mammal producing many young at a time, since intra-uterine competition would have encouraged the opposing tendency. Thus we may conclude that conceptual thought could develop only in a mammalian stock which normally brings forth but one young at a birth. Such a stock is provided in the Primates—lemurs, monkeys, and apes.

The Primates also have another characteristic which was necessary for the ancestor of a rational animal—they are arboreal. It may seem curious that living in trees is a prerequisite of conceptual thought. But Elliot Smith's analysis has abundantly shown that only in an arboreal mammal could the forelimb become a true hand, and sight become dominant over smell. Hands obtain an elaborate tactile pattern of what they handle, eyes an elaborate visual pattern of what they see. The combination of the two kinds of pattern, with the aid of binocular vision, in the higher centres of the brain allowed the Primate to acquire a wholly new richness of knowledge about objects, a wholly new possibility of manipulating them. Tree life laid the foundation both for the fuller definition of objects by conceptual thought and for the fuller control of them by tools and machines.

Higher Primates have yet another prerequisite of human intelligence—they are all gregarious. Speech, it is obvious, could never have been evolved in a solitary type. And speech is as much the physical basis of conceptual thought as is protoplasm the physical basis of life.

For the passage, however, of the critical point between subhuman and human, between the biological subordination and the biological primacy of intelligence, between a limited and a potentially unlimited tradition—for this it was necessary for the arboreal animal to descend to the ground again. Only in a terrestrial creature could fully erect posture be acquired; and this was essential for the final conversion of the arms from locomotor limbs into manipulative hands. Furthermore, just as land life, ages previously, had demanded and developed a greater variety of response than had been required in the water, so now it did the same in relation to what had been required in the trees. An arboreal animal could never have evolved the skill of the hunting savage, nor ever have proceeded to the domestication of other animals or to agriculture.

We are now in a position to define the uniqueness of human evolution. The essential character of man as a dominant organism is conceptual thought. And conceptual thought could have arisen only in a multicellular animal, an animal with bilateral symmetry, head and blood system, a vertebrate as against a mollusc or an arthropod, a land vertebrate among vertebrates, a mammal among land vertebrates. Finally, it could have arisen only in a mammalian line which was gregarious, which produced one young at a birth instead of several, and which had recently become terrestrial after a long period of arboreal life.

There is only one group of animals which fulfills these conditions —a terrestrial offshoot of the higher Primates. Thus not merely has conceptual thought been evolved only in man: it could not have been evolved except in man. There is but one path of unlimited progress through the evolutionary maze. The course of human evolution is as unique as its result. It is unique not in the trivial sense of being a different course from that of any other organism, but in the profounder sense of being the only path that could have achieved the essential characters of man. Conceptual thought on this planet is inevitably associated with a particular type of Primate body and Primate brain.

A further property of man in which he is unique among higher animals concerns his sexual life. Man is prepared to mate at any time: animals are not.

Another of the purely biological characters in which man is unique is his reproductive variability. In a given species of animals, the maximum litter-size may, on occasions, reach perhaps double the minimum, according to circumstances of food and temperature, or even perhaps threefold. But during a period of years, these variations will be largely equalized within a range of perhaps fifty per cent, either way from the average, and the percentage of wholly infertile adults is very low. In man, on the other hand, the range of positive fertility is enormous—from one to over a dozen, and in

exceptional cases to over twenty; and the number of wholly infertile adults is considerable. This fact, in addition to providing a
great diversity of patterns of family life, has important bearings on
evolution. It means that in the human species differential fertility
is more important as a basis for selection than is differential mortality; and it provides the possibility of much more rapid selective
change than that found in wild animal species. Such rapidity of
evolution would, of course, be effectively realized only if the stocks
with large families possessed a markedly different hereditary constitution from those with few children; but the high differential
fertility of unskilled workers as against the professional classes in
England, or of the French Canadians against the rest of the inhabitants of Canada, demonstrates how rapidly populations may
change by this means.

Still another point in which man is biologically unique is the
length and relative importance of his period of what we may call
"post-maturity." If we consider the female sex, in which the transition from reproductive maturity to non-reproductive post-maturity
is more sharply defined than in the male, we find, in the first place,
that in animals a comparatively small percentage of the population
survives beyond the period of reproduction; in the second place,
that such individuals rarely survive long, and so far as known never
for a period equal to or greater than the period during which reproduction was possible; and thirdly, that such individuals are
rarely of importance in the life of the species. The same is true of
the male sex, provided we do not take the incapacity to produce
fertile gametes as the criterion of post-maturity, but rather the appearance of signs of age, such as the beginnings of loss of vigour
and weight, decreased sexual activity, or greying hair.

But in civilized man the average expectation of life now includes
over ten post-mature years, and about a sixth of the population
enjoys a longer post-maturity than maturity. What is more, in all
advanced human societies, a large proportion of the leaders of the
community are always post-mature. All the members of the British
War Cabinet were in their post-maturity.

This is truly a remarkable phenomenon. Through the new social
mechanisms made possible by speech and tradition, man has been
able to utilize for the benefit of the species a period of life which in
almost all other creatures is a mere superfluity. We know that the
dominance of the old can be overemphasized; but it is equally obvious that society cannot do without the post-mature. To act on the
slogan "Too old at forty"—or even at forty-five—would be to rob

man of one of his unique characteristics, whereby he utilizes tradition to best advantage.

We have now dealt in a broad way with the unique properties of man both from the comparative and the evolutionary point of view. Now we can return to the present and the particular and discuss these properties and their consequence a little more in detail. First, let us remind ourselves that the gap between human and animal thought is much greater than is usually supposed. The tendency to project familiar human qualities into animals is very strong, and colours the ideas of nearly all people who have not special familiarity both with animal behaviour and scientific method.

Man is more intelligent than the animals because his brain mechanism is more plastic. This fact also gives him, of course, the opportunity of being more nonsensical and perverse: but its primary effects have been more analytical knowledge and more varied control.

This increase of flexibility has also had other psychological consequences which rational philosophers are apt to forget: and in some of these, too, man is unique. It has led, for instance, to the fact that man is the only organism normally and inevitably subject to psychological conflict. You can give a dog neurosis, as Pavlov did, by a complicated laboratory experiment: you can find cases of brief emotional conflict in the lives of wild birds and animals. But, for the most part, psychological conflict is shirked by the simple expedient of arranging that now one and now another instinct should dominate the animal's behaviour.

When we reach the human level, there are new complications; for, as we have seen, one of the peculiarities of man is the abandonment of any rigidity of instinct, and the provision of association-mechanisms by which any activity of the mind, whether in the spheres of knowing, feeling, or willing, can be brought into relation with any other. It is through this that man has acquired the possibility of a unified mental life. But, by the same token, the door is opened to the forces of disruption, which may destroy any such unity and even prevent him from enjoying the efficiency of behaviour attained by animals.

I need not pursue the subject further. Here I am only concerned to show that the great biological advantages conferred on man by the unification of mind have inevitably brought with them certain counterbalancing defects. The freedom of association between all aspects and processes of the mind has provided the basis for conceptual thought and tradition; but it has also provided potential antagonists, which in lower organisms were carefully kept apart, with the opportunity of meeting face to face, and has thus made some degree of conflict unavoidable.

In rather similar fashion, man's upright posture has brought with it certain consequential disadvantages in regard to the functioning of his internal organs and his proneness to rupture. Thus man's unique characteristics are by no means wholly beneficial.

In close correlation with our subjection to conflict is our proneness to laughter. So characteristic of our species is laughter that man has been defined as the laughing animal. It is true that, like so much else of man's uniqueness, it has its roots among the animals, where it reveals itself as an expression of a certain kind of general pleasure—and thus in truth perhaps more of a smile than a laugh. And in a few animals—ravens, for example—there are traces of a malicious sense of humour. Laughter in man, however, is much more than this. There are many theories of laughter, most of them containing partial truth. But biologically the important feature of human laughter seems to lie in its providing a release for conflict, a resolution of troublesome situations.

Those of man's unique characteristics which may better be called psychological and social than narrowly biological spring from one or other of three characteristics. The first is his capacity for abstract and general thought: the second is the relative unification of his mental processes, as against the much more rigid compartmentalization of animal mind and behaviour: the third is the existence of social units, such as tribe, nation, party, and church, with a continuity of their own, based on organized tradition and culture.

There are various by-products of the change from pre-human to the human type of mind which are, of course, also unique biologically. Let us enumerate a few: pure mathematics; musical gifts; artistic appreciation and creation; religion; romantic love.

Mathematical ability appears, almost inevitably, as something mysterious. Yet the attainment of speech, abstraction, and logical thought, bring it into potential being. It may remain in a very rudimentary state of development; but even the simplest arithmetical calculations are a manifestation of its existence. Like any other human activity, it requires proper tools and machinery. Arabic numerals, algebraic conventions, logarithms, the differential calculus, are such tools: each one unlocks new possibilities of mathematical achievement. But just as there is no essential difference between man's conscious use of a chipped flint as an implement and his design of the most elaborate machine, so there is none between such simple operations as numeration or addition and the comprehensive flights of higher mathematics. Again, some people are by nature more gifted than others in this field; yet no normal human being is unable to perform some mathematical operations. Thus the capacity for mathematics is, as I have said, a by-product of the human type of mind.

We have seen, however, that the human type of mind is distinguished by two somewhat opposed attributes. One is the capacity for abstraction, the other for synthesis. Mathematics is one of the extreme by-products of our capacity for abstraction. Arithmetic abstracts objects of all qualities save their enumerability; the symbol π abstracts in a single Greek letter a complicated relation between the parts of all circles. Art, on the other hand, is an extreme by-product of our capacity for synthesis. In one unique production, the painter can bring together form, colour, arrangement, associations of memory, emotion, and idea. Dim adumbrations of art are to be found in a few creatures such as bower-birds; but nothing is found to which the word can rightly be applied until man's mind gave the possibility of freely mingling observations, emotions, memories, and ideas, and subjecting the mixture to deliberate control.

But it is not enough here to enumerate a few special activities. In point of fact, the great majority of man's activities and characteristics are by-products of his primary distinctive characteristics, and therefore, like them, biologically unique.

On the one hand, conversation, organized games, education, sport, paid work, gardening, the theatre; on the other, conscience, duty, sin, humiliation, vice, penitence—these are all such unique by-products. The trouble, indeed, is to find any human activities which are not unique. Even the fundamental biological attributes such as eating, sleeping, and mating have been tricked out by man with all kinds of unique frills and peculiarities.

There may be other by-products of man's basic uniqueness which have not yet been exploited. For let us remember that such by-products may remain almost wholly latent until demand stimulates invention and invention facilitates development. It is asserted that there exist human tribes who cannot count above two; certainly some savages stop at ten. Here the mathematical faculty is restricted to numeration, and stops short at a very rudimentary stage of this rudimentary process. Similarly, there are human societies in which art has never been developed beyond the stage of personal

decoration. It is probable that during the first half of the Pleistocene period, none of the human race had developed either their
mathematical or their artistic potentialities beyond such a rudimentary stage.

It is perfectly possible that today man's so-called super-normal or
extra-sensory faculties are in the same case as were his mathematical faculties during the first or second glaciations of the Ice Age—
barely more than a potentiality, with no technique for eliciting and
developing them, no tradition behind them to give them continuity and intellectual respectability. Even such simple performances as
multiplying two three-figure numbers would have appeared entirely
magical to early Stone Age men.

It is only exceptionally that men have dared to uphold their
uniqueness and to be proud of their human superiority to the im-
personality of the rest of the universe. It is time now, in the light
of our knowledge, to be brave and face the fact and the consequences of our uniqueness. That is the view of Dr. Everett of the
University of California, as it was also that of T. H. Huxley in his
famous Romanes lecture. I agree with them; but I would suggest
that the antimony between man and the universe is not quite so
sharp as they have made out. Man represents the culmination of
that process of organic evolution which has been proceeding on this
planet for over a thousand million years. That process, however
wasteful and cruel it may be, and into however many blind alleys it
may have been diverted, is also in one aspect progressive. Man has
now become the sole representative of life in that progressive aspect
and its sole trustee for any progress in the future.

Meanwhile it is true that the appearance of the human type of
mind, the latest step in evolutionary progress, has introduced both
new methods and new standards. By means of his conscious reason
and its chief offspring, science, man has the power of substituting
less dilatory, less wasteful, and less cruel methods of effective progressive change than those of natural selection, which alone are
available to lower organisms. And by means of his conscious purpose and his set of values, he has the power of substituting new
and higher standards for change than those of mere survival and
adaptation to immediate circumstances, which alone are inherent
in pre-human evolution. To put the matter in another way, progress
has hitherto been a rare and fitful by-product of evolution. Man
has the possibility of making it the main feature of his own future

evolution, and of guiding its course in relation to a deliberate aim.

But he must not be afraid of his uniqueness. There may be other beings in this vast universe endowed with reason, purpose, and aspiration: but we know nothing of them. So far as our knowledge goes, human mind and personality are unique and constitute the highest product yet achieved by the cosmos. Let us not put off our responsibilities on to the shoulders of mythical gods or philosophical absolutes, but shoulder them in the hopefulness of tempered pride. In the perspective of biology, our business in the world is seen to be the imposition of the best and most enduring of our human standards upon ourselves and our planet. The enjoyment of beauty and interest, the achievement of goodness and efficiency, the enhancement of life and its variety—these are the harvest which our human uniqueness should be called upon to yield.

EDITH SITWELL

****

Edith Sitwell, who has shown a lifelong aversion to being included in anthologies, made an exception in the case of THE WORLD'S BEST *but regretted her inability to furnish a comment on her choices. "I am very unwell," she wrote, "and the doctor has ordered me a complete rest and to make notes about these poems would be an arduous task. If it were possible, I would indeed do so."*

****

Five Poems

STILL FALLS THE RAIN

The Raids, 1940   *Night and Dawn*
Still falls the Rain—
Dark as the world of man, black as our loss—
Blind as the nineteen hundred and forty nails
Upon the Cross.

Still falls the Rain
With a sound like the pulse of the heart that is changed to the
        hammer-beat
In the Potter's Field, and the sound of the impious feet
On the Tomb:
                Still falls the Rain
In the Field of Blood where the small hopes breed and the human
        brain
Nurtures its greed, that worm with the brow of Cain.

Still falls the Rain
At the feet of the Starved Man hung upon the Cross.
Christ that each day, each night, nails there, have mercy on us—
On Dives and on Lazarus:
Under the Rain the sore and the gold are as one.

Still falls the Rain—
Still falls the Blood from the Starved Man's wounded Side:
He bears in His Heart all wounds—those of the light that died,
The last faint spark
In the self-murdered heart, the wounds of the sad uncomprehending
      dark,
The wounds of the baited bear—
The blind and weeping bear whom the keepers beat
On his helpless flesh . . . the tears of the hunted hare.

Still falls the Rain—
Then—O Ile leape up to my God: who pulles me doune—
See, see where Christ's blood streames in the firmament:
It flows from the Brow we nailed upon the tree
Deep to the dying, to the thirsting heart
That holds the fires of the world—dark-smirched with pain
As Caesar's laurel crown.

Then sounds the voice of One who like the heart of man
Was once a child who among beasts has lain—
'Still do I love, still shed my innocent light, my Blood, for thee.'

HEART AND MIND

Said the Lion to the Lioness—'When you are amber dust—
No more a raging fire like the heat of the Sun
(No liking but all lust)—
Remember still the flowering of the amber blood and bone,
The rippling of bright muscles like a sea,
Remember the rose-prickles of bright paws,
Though we shall mate no more
Till the fire of that sun the heart and the moon-cold bone are one.'

Said the Skeleton lying upon the sands of Time—
'The great gold planet that is the mourning heat of the Sun
Is greater than all gold, more powerful
Than the tawny body of a Lion that fire consumes
Like all that grows or leaps . . . so is the heart
More powerful than all dust. Once I was Hercules
Or Samson, strong as the pillars of the seas:
But the flames of the heart consumed me, and the mind
Is but a foolish wind.'

Said the Sun to the Moon—'When you are but a lonely white crone,
And I, a dead King in my golden armor somewhere in a dark wood,
Remember only this of our hopeless love:
That never till Time is done
Will the fire of the heart and the fire of the mind be one.'

THE BEE ORACLES

I. THE BEE-KEEPER

to Denys and Elizabeth Kilham Roberts

In the plain of the world's dust like a great Sea,
The golden thunders of the Lion and the Honey-Bee
In the Spirit, held with the Sun a Colloquy

Where an old woman stood—thick Earthiness—
Half Sun, half Clod,
A plant alive from the root, still blind with earth
And all the weight of Death and Birth.

She, in her primitive dress
Of clay, bent to her hives
And heard her sisters of the barren lives

Begin to stir . . . the Priestesses of the Gold Comb
Shaped by Darkness, and the Prophetesses
Who from a wingless pupa, spark of gold

In the Dark, rose with gold bodies bright as the Lion,
And the trace of the Hand of God on ephemeral wings
To sing the great Hymn of Being to the Lost:

'This Earth is the honey of all Beings, and all Beings
Are the honey of this Earth . . . O bright immortal Lover
That is incarnate in the body's earth—
O bright immortal Lover who is All!'

'This Water is the honey of all Beings, and all Beings
Are the honey of this Water . . . O bright immortal Lover
That is in water and that is the seed
Of Life . . . O bright immortal Lover who is All!'

'This Fire is the honey of all Beings, and all Beings
Are the honey of this Fire . . . O bright immortal Lover
That is in fire and shines in mortal speech—
O bright immortal Lover who is All!'

'This Air is the honey of all Beings, and all Beings
Are the honey of this Air . . . O bright immortal Lover
That is in air and is our Being's breath—
O bright immortal Lover who is all!'

'This Sun is the honey of all Beings, and all Beings
Are the honey of this Sun . . . O bright immortal Lover
That is in the sun and is our Being's sight—
O bright immortal Lover who is all!'

'This Thunder is the honey of all Beings, and all Beings
Are the honey of this Thunder . . . O bright immortal Lover
That is in thunder and all voices—the beasts' roar—
Thunder of rising saps—the voice of Man!
O bright immortal Lover who is All!'

This was the song that came from the small span
Of thin gold bodies shaped by the holy Dark.
And the old woman in her mortal dress of clay
(That plant alive from the root, still thick with earth)
Felt all the saps of Day.

And in the plain of dust like a great Sea
The Lion in the Spirit cried, 'Destroy—destroy
The old and wrinkled Darkness.' But the Sun—
That great gold simpleton—laughed like a boy
And kissed the old woman's cheek and blessed her clay.

The great Sun laughed, and, dancing over Chaos,
Shouts to the dust, 'O mortal Lover! Think what wonders
May be born of our love—what golden heroes!'
The bee in the Spirit said, 'The gold combs lay
In the cold rock, and the slain Lion, amid spent golden thunders.'

THE COAT OF FIRE

Amid the thunders of the falling Dark
In the Tartarean darkness of the fog
I walk, a Pillar of Fire,
On pavements of black marble, hard
And wide as the long boulevard
Of Hell . . . I, in whose veins the Furies wave
Their long fires, move where purgatories, heavens, hells, and worlds
Wrought by illusion hide in the human breast
And tear the enclosing heart. . . . And the snow fell
(Thin flakes of ash from Gomorrah) on blind faces
Turned to the heedless sky. . . . A dress has the sound
Of Reality, reverberates like thunder.
And ghosts of aeons and of equinoxes
(Of moments that seemed aeons, and long partings)
Take on the forms of fashionable women
With veils that hide a new Catastrophe, and under
Is the fall of a world that was a heart. Some doomed to descend
Through all the hells and change into the Dog
Without its faithfulness, the Crocodile
Without its watchfulness, and then to Pampean mud.
In the circles of the city's hells beneath the fog
These bear, to light them, in the human breast,
The yellow dull light from the raging human dust,
The dull blue light from the brutes, light red as rust
Of blood from eyeless weeping ghosts, light black as smoke
From hell. And those breasts bear
No other light. . . . They circle in the snow
Where in the dust the apterous
Fates turned insects whisper, 'Now abandon
Man the annelida. Let all be wingless
That hang between the abyss and Abaddon.
The Catastrophes with veils and trains drift by,
And I to my heart, disastrous Comet, cry,
'Red heart, my Lucifer, how fallen art thou,
And lightless, I!'
The dresses sweep the dust of mortality
And roll the burden of Atlas' woe, changed to a stone,

Up to the benches where the beggars sway—
Their souls alone as on the Judgment Day—
In their Valley of the myriad Dry Bones under world-tall houses.
Then with a noise as if in the thunders of the Dark
All sins, griefs, aberrations of the world rolled to confess,
Those myriad Dry Bones rose to testify:

'See her, the Pillar of Fire!
    The aeons of Cold
And all the deaths that Adam has endured
Since the first death cannot outfreeze our night!'
And where is the fire of love that will warm our hands?
There is only this conflagration
Of all the sins of the world! To the dust's busyness
She speaks of the annihilation
Of every form of dust, burned down to Nothingness!
To the small lovers, of a kiss that seems the red
Lightning of Comets firing worlds—and of a Night
That shall outburn all nights that lovers know—
The last red Night before the Judgment Day!
O Pillar of Flame, that drifts across the world to Nowhere!
The eyes are seas of fire! All forms, all sights,
And all sensations are on fire! The storms
Of blood, a whirlpool of the flame! The ears, all sounds
Of all the world, a universe of fire! All smells, a ravening
Raging cyclone of wild fire! The nose, burned quite away!
The tongue is on fire, all tastes on fire, the mind
Is red as noon upon the Judgment Day!
The tears are rolling, falling worlds of fire!
With what are these on fire? With passion, hate,
Infatuation, and old age, and death,
With sorrow, longing, and with laboring breath,
And with despair and life are these on fire!
With the illusions of the world, the flames of lust,
And raging red desire!
A Pillar of Fire is she in the empty dust,
And will not change those fires into warmth for our hands,
Said the beggars, lolling and rocking
The heedless world upon a heaving shoulder.

THE CANTICLE OF THE ROSE

to Geoffrey Gorer

The Rose upon the wall
Cries—'I am the voice of Fire:
And in me grows
The pomegranate splendor of Death, the ruby garnet almandine
Dews: Christ's Wounds in me shine!

I rise upon my stem—
The Flower, the whole Plant-being, produced by Light
With all Plant-systems and formations. . . . As in Fire
All elements dissolve, so in one bright
Ineffable essence all Plant-being dissolves to make the Flower.

My stem rises bright—
Organic water polarized to the dark
Earth-center, and to Light.'

Below that wall, in Famine Street,
There is nothing left but the heart to eat

And the Shade of Man. . . . Buyers and sellers cry:
'Speak not the name of Light—
Her name is Madness now. . . . Though we are black beneath
              her kiss,
As if she were the Sun, her name is Night:
She has condemned us, and decreed that Man must die.'

There was a woman combing her long hair
To the rhythm of the river flowing. . . .
She sang, 'All things will end—
Like the sound of Time in my veins growing:
The hump on the dwarf, the mountain on the plain,
The fixed red of the rose and the rainbow's red,
The fires of the heart, the wandering planet's pain—
All loss, all gain—
Yet will the world remain!'

The song died in the Ray. . . . Where is she now?
Dissolved and gone—
And only her red shadow stains the unremembering stone.

A dress for the Bride?
(But all the molds of generation died '
Beneath that Ray.)

      'Or a winding-sheet?'
(Outworn. . . . The Dead have nothing left to hide.)

'Then buy,' said the Fury arisen from Hell—
That Fate of rags and patches—
'A box of matches!
For the machine that generated warmth
Beneath your breast is dead. . . . You need a fire
To warm what lies upon your bone. . . .
Not all the ashes of your brother Men
Will kindle that again—
Nor all the world's incendiaries!
Who buys—Who buys—?
Come, give me pence to lay upon my staring lidless eyes!'

But high upon the wall
The Rose where the Wounds of Christ are red
Cries to the Light—
'See how I rise upon my stem, ineffable bright
Effluence of bright essence. . . . From my little span
I cry of Christ, Who is the ultimate Fire
Who will burn away the cold in the heart of Man.
Springs come, springs go. . . .
"I was reddere on Rode than the Rose in the rayne . . ."
"This smel is Crist, clepid the plantynge of the Rose in Jerico."'

NOEL COWARD

****

Noel Coward chose first as the work he wanted to have appear in THE WORLD'S BEST *a wartime poem entitled* Lie In The Dark and Listen, *a work written during an English bomb raid and reflective of his preoccupation with the survival of England and of himself in the last war; but he conceded that perhaps poetry was not what he was best known for and in cooperation with his Editor at Doubleday and Company, Ken McCormick, a second choice was made available in the one-act play* Hands Across The Sea. *Mr. Coward has written four kinds of plays—the serious drama, the musical play, the patriotic pageant and the flippant society comedy—of which* Hands Across The Sea *is an excellent one-act example.*

****

Hands Across The Sea

CHARACTERS

LADY MAUREEN GILPIN (Piggie)
COMMANDER PETER GILPIN, R.N., her husband
THE HON. CLARE WEDDERBURN
LIEUT. COMMANDER ALASTAIR CORBETT, R.N.
MAJOR GOSLING (Bogey)
MR. WADHURST
MRS. WADHURST
MR. BURNHAM
WALTERS

The action of the play takes place in the drawing-room of the Gilpins' flat in London.

Time: Present Day.

The Scene is the drawing-room of the GILPINS' *flat in London. The room is nicely furnished and rather untidy. There is a portable gramophone on one small table and a tray of cocktail things on another; apart from these, the furnishings can be left to the discretion of the producer.*

When the Curtain rises the telephone is ringing. WALTERS, *a neat parlourmaid, enters and answers it. The time is about six p.m.*

WALTERS (*at telephone*). Hallo—yes—no, her ladyship's not back yet—she said she'd be in at five, so she ought to be here at any minute now—what name, please?—Rawlingson—Mr. and Mrs. Rawlingson—— (*She scribbles on the pad.*) Yes—I'll tell her—— *She hangs up the receiver and goes out. There is the sound of voices in the hall and* LADY MAUREEN GILPIN *enters, followed at a more leisurely pace by her husband,* PETER GILPIN. MAUREEN, *nicknamed* PIGGIE *by her intimates, is a smart, attractive woman in the thirties.* PETER *is tall and sunburned and reeks of the Navy.*

PIGGIE (*as she comes in*). —and you can send the car back for me at eleven-thirty—it's quite simple, darling, I wish you wouldn't be so awfully complicated about everything——

PETER. What happens if my damned dinner goes on longer than that and I get stuck?

PIGGIE. You just get stuck, darling, and then you get unstuck and get a taxi——

PETER (*grumbling*). I shall be in uniform, clinking with medals——

PIGGIE. If you take my advice you'll faint dead away at eleven o'clock and then you can come home in the car and change and have time for everything——

PETER. I can't faint dead away under the nose of the C.-in-C.

PIGGIE. You can feel a little poorly, can't you—anybody has the right to feel a little poorly—— (*She sees the telephone pad.*) My God!

PETER. What is it?

PIGGIE. The Rawlingsons.

PETER. Who the hell are they?

PIGGIE. I'd forgotten all about them—I must get Maud at once —— (*She sits at the telephone and dials a number.*)

PETER. Who are the Rawlingsons?

PIGGIE. Maud and I stayed with them in Samolo, I told you about it, that time when we had to make a forced landing—they practically saved our lives—— (*At telephone.*) Hullo—Maud—darling, the Rawlingsons are on us—what—the RAWLINGSONS—yes— I asked them to-day and forgot all about it—you must come at once—but, darling, you *must*—Oh, dear—no, no, that was the

Frobishers, these are the ones we stayed with—mother and father and daughter—you must remember—pretty girl with bad legs——No—they didn't have a son—we swore we'd give them a lovely time when they came home on leave—I know they didn't have a son, that was those other people in Penang—— Oh, all right—you'll have to do something about them, though—let me ask them to lunch with you to-morrow—all right—one-thirty—I'll tell them—— (*She hangs up.*)—she can't come——

PETER. You might have warned me that a lot of Colonial strangers were coming trumpeting into the house——

PIGGIE. I tell you I'd forgotten——

PETER. That world trip was a grave mistake——

PIGGIE. Who can I get that's celebrated—to give them a thrill?

PETER. Why do they have to have a thrill?

PIGGIE. I'll get Clare, anyway—— (*She dials another number.*)

PETER. She'll frighten them to death.

PIGGIE. Couldn't you change early and come in your uniform? That would be better than nothing——

PETER. Perhaps they'd like to watch me having my bath!

PIGGIE (*at telephone*). I want to speak to Mrs. Wedderburn, please—yes—— (*To* PETER.) I do wish you'd be a little helpful—— (*At telephone.*) Clare?—this is Piggie—I want you to come round at once and help me with the Rawlingsons—no, I know you haven't, but that doesn't matter—— Mother, father and daughter—very sweet—they were divine to us in the East—I'm repaying hospitality—Maud's having them to lunch to-morrow and Peter's going to take them round the dockyard——

PETER. I'm not going to do any such thing——

PIGGIE. Shut up, I just thought of that and it's a *very* good idea —— (*At telephone.*) All right, darling—as soon as you can—— (*She hangs up.*)—I must go and change——

PETER. You know perfectly well I haven't time to take mothers and fathers and daughters with bad legs round the dockyard——

PIGGIE. It wouldn't take a minute, they took us all over their rubber plantation.

PETER. It probably served you right.

PIGGIE. You're so disobliging, darling, you really should try to conquer it—it's something to do with being English, I think—as a race I'm ashamed of us—no sense of hospitality—the least we can do when people are kind to us in far-off places is to be a little gracious in return.

PETER. They weren't kind to me in far-off places.

PIGGIE. You know there's a certain grudging, sullen streak in your character—I've been very worried about it lately—it's spreading like a forest fire——

PETER. Why don't you have them down for the week-end?

PIGGIE. Don't be so idiotic, how can I possibly? There's no room to start with and even if there were they'd be utterly wretched——

PETER. I don't see why.

PIGGIE. They wouldn't know anybody—they probably wouldn't have the right clothes—they'd keep on huddling about in uneasy little groups——

PETER. The amount of uneasy little groups that three people can huddle about in is negligible.

ALASTAIR CORBETT *saunters into the room. He is good-looking and also distinctly Naval in tone.*

ALLY. Hallo, chaps.

PIGGIE. Ally, darling—how lovely—we're in trouble—Peter'll tell you all about it——

The telephone rings and she goes to it. The following conversations occur simultaneously.

ALLY. What trouble?

PETER. More of Piggie's beach friends.

ALLY. Let's have a drink.

PETER. Cocktail?

ALLY. No, a long one, whisky and soda.

PETER (*going to drink table*). All right.

ALLY. What beach friends?

PETER. People Maud and Piggie picked up in the East.

PIGGIE (*at 'phone*). Hullo!—Yes—Robert, dear—how lovely! (*To others.*) It's Robert.

ALLY. Piggie ought to stay at home more.

PIGGIE (*on 'phone*). Where are you?

PETER. That's what I say!

PIGGIE (*on 'phone*). Oh, what a shame!—No—Peter's going to sea on Thursday—I'm going down on Saturday.

ALLY. Rubber, I expect—everybody in the East's rubber.

PIGGIE (*on 'phone*). No—nobody particular—just Clare and Bogey and I think Pops; but he thinks he's got an ulcer or something and might not be able to come.

PETER. We thought you might be a real friend and take them over the dockyard.

ALLY. What on earth for?

PETER. Give them a thrill.

PIGGIE (*on 'phone*). All right—I'll expect you—no, I don't think it can be a very big one—he looks as bright as a button.

ALLY. Why don't you take them over the dockyard?

PETER. I shall be at sea, Thursday onwards—exercises!

PIGGIE (*on 'phone*). No, darling, what is the use of having her—she only depresses you—oh—all right! (*Hangs up.*) Oh, dear——

PETER. It's quite easy for you—you can give them lunch on board.

ALLY. We're in dry dock.

PETER. They won't mind. (*To* PIGGIE.) What is it?

PIGGIE. Robert—plunged in gloom—he's got to do a course at Greenwich—he ran into a tram in Devonport—and he's had a row with Molly—he wants me to have her for the week-end so that they can make it up all over everybody. Have you told Ally about the Rawlingsons?

PETER. Yes, he's taking them over the dockyard, lunching them on board and then he's going to show them a submarine——

PIGGIE. Marvellous! You're an angel, Ally—I must take off these clothes, I'm going mad—— .

She goes out of the room at a run.

There is the sound of the front-door bell.

PETER. Let's go into my room—I can show you the plans——

ALLY. Already? They've been pretty quick with them.

PETER. I made a few alterations—there wasn't enough deck space—she ought to be ready by October, I shall have her sent straight out to Malta——

ALLY. Come on, we shall be caught——

They go off on the left as WALTERS *ushers in* MR. *and* MRS. WADHURST *on the right.*

The WADHURSTS *are pleasant, middle-aged people, their manner is a trifle timorous.*

WALTERS. Her ladyship is changing, I'll tell her you are here.

MRS. WADHURST. Thank you.

MR. WADHURST. Thank you very much.

WALTERS *goes out.*

The WADHURSTS *look round the room.*

MRS. WADHURST. It's a very nice flat.

MR. WADHURST. Yes—yes, it is.

MRS. WADHURST (*scrutinizing a photograph*). That must be him.

MR. WADHURST. Who?

MRS. WADHURST. The Commander.

MR. WADHURST. Yes—I expect it is.

Mrs. Wadhurst. Sailors always have such nice open faces, don't they?

Mr. Wadhurst. Yes, I suppose so.

Mrs. Wadhurst. Clean-cut and look you straight in the eye—I like men who look you straight in the eye.

Mr. Wadhurst. Yes, it's very nice.

Mrs. Wadhurst (*at another photograph*). This must be her sister—I recognise her from the *Tatler*—look—she was Lady Hurstley, you know, then she was Lady Macfadden and I don't know who she is now.

Mrs. Wadhurst. Neither do I.

Mrs. Wadhurst. What a dear little boy—such a sturdy little fellow—look at the way he's holding his engine.

Mr. Wadhurst. Is that his engine?

Mrs. Wadhurst. He has rather a look of Donald Hotchkiss, don't you think?

Mr. Wadhurst. Yes, dear.

Mrs. Wadhurst. I must say they have very nice things—oh, dear, how lovely to be well off—I must write to the Brostows by the next mail and tell them all about it

Mr. Wadhurst. Yes, you must.

Mrs. Wadhurst. Don't you think we'd better sit down?

Mr. Wadhurst. Why not?

Mrs. Wadhurst. You sit in that chair and I'll sit on the sofa. *She sits on the sofa. He sits on the chair.*

Mr. Wadhurst. Yes, dear.

Mrs. Wadhurst. I wish you wouldn't look quite so uncomfortable, Fred, there's nothing to be uncomfortable about.

Mr. Wadhurst. She does expect us, doesn't she?

Mrs. Wadhurst. Of course, I talked to her myself on the telephone last Wednesday, she was perfectly charming and said that we were to come without fail and that it would be divine.

Mr. Wadhurst. I still feel we should have telephoned again just to remind her. People are always awfully busy in London.

Mrs. Wadhurst. I do hope Lady Dalborough will be here, too —I should like to see her again—she was so nice.

Mr. Wadhurst. She was the other one, wasn't she?

Mrs. Wadhurst (*irritably*).What do you mean, the other one?

Mr. Wadhurst. I mean not this one.

Mrs. Wadhurst. She's the niece of the Duke of Frensham, her mother was Lady Merrit, she was a great traveller too—I believe she went right across the Sahara dressed as an Arab. In those days that was a very dangerous thing to do.

MR. WADHURST. I shouldn't think it was any too safe now.

WALTERS *enters and ushers in* MR. BURNHAM, *a nondescript young man carrying a longish roll of cardboard.*

WALTERS. I'll tell the Commander you're here.

MR. BURNHAM. Thanks—thanks very much.

WALTERS *goes out.*

MRS. WADHURST (*after a slightly awkward silence*). How do you do?

MR. BURNHAM. How do you do?

MRS. WADHURST (*with poise*). This is my husband.

MR. BURNHAM. How do you do?

MR. WADHURST. How do you do?

They shake hands.

MRS. WADHURST (*vivaciously*). Isn't this a charming room— so—so lived in.

MR. BURNHAM. Yes.

MR. WADHURST. Are you in the Navy, too?

MR. BURNHAM. No.

MRS. WADHURST (*persevering*). It's so nice to be home again— we come from Malaya, you know.

MR. BURNHAM. Oh—Malaya.

MRS. WADHURST. Yes, Lady Maureen and Lady Dalborough visited us there—my husband has a rubber plantation up-country —there's been a terrible slump, of course, but we're trying to keep our heads above water—aren't we, Fred?

MR. WADHURST. Yes, dear, we certainly are.

MRS. WADHURST. Have you ever been to the East?

MR. BURNHAM. No.

MRS. WADHURST. It's very interesting really, although the climate's rather trying until you get used to it, and of course the one thing we do miss is the theatre——

MR. BURNHAM. Yes—of course.

MRS. WADHURST. There's nothing my husband and I enjoy so much as a good play, is there, Fred?

MR. WADHURST. Nothing.

MRS. WADHURST. And all we get is films, and they're generally pretty old by the time they come out to us—— (*She laughs gaily.*)

MR. WADHURST. Do you get to the theatre much?

MR. BURNHAM. No.

There is a silence which is broken by the telephone ringing. Everybody jumps.

MRS. WADHURST. Oh, dear—do you think we ought to answer it?

MR. WADHURST. I don't know.

The telephone continues to ring. CLARE WEDDERBURN *comes in. She is middle-aged, well-dressed and rather gruff. She is followed by "*BOGEY*"* GOSLING, *a Major in the Marines, a good-looking man in the thirties.*

CLARE. Hallo—where's the old girl?

MRS. WADHURST (*nervously*). I—er, I'm afraid I——

CLARE (*going to the telephone*). Mix a cocktail, Bogey—I'm a stretcher case——(*At telephone.*) Hallo—no, it's me—Clare—— God knows, dear—shall I tell her to call you back?—all right—no, it was bloody, darling—a gloomy dinner at the Embassy, then the worst play I've ever sat through and then the Café de Paris and that awful man who does things with a duck—I've already seen him six times, darling—oh, you know, he pinches its behind and it quacks Land of Hope and Glory—I don't know whether it hurts it or not—I minded at first but I'm past caring now, after all, it's not like performing dogs, I mind about performing dogs terribly —all right—good-bye—— (*She hangs up and turns to* MRS. WADHURST.) Ducks are pretty bloody anyway, don't you think?

MRS. WADHURST. I don't know very much about them.

CLARE. The man swears it's genuine talent, but I think it's the little nip that does it.

MRS. WADHURST. It sounds rather cruel.

CLARE. It's a gloomy form of entertainment anyhow, particularly as I've always hated Land of Hope and Glory——

BOGEY. Cocktail?

CLARE (*taking off her hat*). Thank God!

BOGEY *hands round cocktails, the* WADHURSTS *and* MR. BURNHAM *accept them and sip them in silence.*

BOGEY. I suppose Piggie's in the bath.

CLARE. Go and rout her out.

BOGEY. Wait till I've had a drink.

CLARE (*to* MRS. WADHURST). Is Peter home or is he still darting about the Solent?

MRS. WADHURST I'm afraid I couldn't say—you see——

BOGEY. I saw him last night with Janet——

CLARE. Hasn't she had her baby yet?

BOGEY. She hadn't last night.

CLARE. That damned baby's been hanging over us all for months.
*The telephone rings—*CLARE *answers it.*

(*At telephone.*) Hallo—yes—hallo, darling—no, it's Clare—yes,
he's here—— No, I really couldn't face it—yes, if I were likely to
go to India I'd come, but I'm not likely to go to India—— I think
Rajahs bumble up a house-party so terribly—yes, I know *he's* different, but the other one's awful—Angela had an agonising time
with him—all the dining-room chairs had to be changed because
they were leather and his religion prevented him sitting on them—
all the dogs had to be kept out of the house because they were un-
clean, which God knows was true of the Bedlington, but the other
ones were clean as whistles—and then to round everything off he
took Laura Merstham in his car and made passes at her all the way
to Newmarket—all right, darling—here he is——(*To* BOGEY.) It's
Nina, she wants to talk to you——

She hands the telephone to BOGEY, *who reaches for it and lifts
the wire so that it just misses* MRS. WADHURST'S *hat. It isn't quite
long enough so he has to bend down to speak with his face practically touching her.*

BOGEY (*at telephone*). Hallo, Nin—— I can't on Wednesday, I've
got a Guest Night—it's a hell of a long way, it'd take hours——

PIGGIE *comes in with a rush.*

PIGGIE. I am so sorry——

CLARE. Shhh!

BOGEY. Shut up, I can't hear——

PIGGIE (*in a shrill whisper*). Who is it?

CLARE. Nina.

BOGEY (*at telephone*). Well, you can tell George to leave it for
me—and I can pick it up.

PIGGIE. How lovely to see you again!

BOGEY (*at telephone*). No, I shan't be leaving till about ten, so
if he leaves it by nine-thirty I'll get it all right——

PIGGIE. My husband will be here in a minute—he has to go to
sea on Thursday, but he's arranged for you to be taken over the
dockyard at Portsmouth——

BOGEY (*at telephone*). Give the old boy a crack on the jaw.

PIGGIE. It's the most thrilling thing in the world. You see how
the torpedoes are made—millions of little wheels inside, all clicking away like mad—and they cost thousands of pounds each——

BOGEY (*at telephone*). No, I saw her last night—not yet, but at
any moment now—I should think—— All right—— Call me at

Chatham—if I can get away I shall have to bring Mickey, too——

PIGGIE. How much do torpedoes cost each, Clare?

CLARE. God knows, darling—something fantastic—ask Bogey——

PIGGIE. Bogey——

BOGEY. What?

PIGGIE. How much do torpedoes cost each?

BOGEY. What?—(*At telephone.*)—wait a minute, Piggie's yelling at me——

PIGGIE. Torpedoes—— (*She makes a descriptive gesture.*)

BOGEY. Oh, thousands and thousands—terribly expensive things—ask Peter—— (*At telephone.*)—If I do bring him you'll have to be frightfully nice to him, he's been on the verge of suicide for weeks——

PIGGIE. Don't let her go, I must talk to her——

BOGEY (*at telephone*). Hold on a minute, Piggie wants to talk to you—all right—I'll let you know—here she is——

PIGGIE *leans over the sofa and takes the telephone from* BOGEY, *who steps over the wire and stumbles over* MRS. WADHURST.

BOGEY. I'm most awfully sorry——

MRS. WADHURST. Not at all——

PIGGIE (*to* MRS. WADHURST). It's so lovely you being in England——(*At telephone.*) Darling—what was the meaning of that sinister little invitation you sent me?

BOGEY. You know what Mickey is.

PIGGIE (*at telephone*). No, dear, I really can't—I always get so agitated——

CLARE. Why does he go on like that? It's so tiresome.

PIGGIE (*at telephone*). I'll come if Clare will—— (*To* CLARE.) Are you going to Nina's Indian ding-dong?

CLARE. Not without an anæsthetic.

PIGGIE (*at telephone*). She's moaning a bit, but I'll persuade her—what happens after dinner?—the man with the duck from the Café de Paris—— (*To the room in general.*) She's got that sweet duck from the Café de Paris——

CLARE. Give me another cocktail, Bogey, I want to get so drunk that I just can't hear any more——

PIGGIE (*at telephone*). But, darling, do you think it's quite *wise*—I mean Maharajahs are terribly touchy and there's probably something in their religion about ducks being mortal sin or something—you know how difficult they are about cows and pigs—just a minute— (*To the* WADHURSTS.) You can tell us, of course——

MR. WADHURST. I beg your pardon?

PIGGIE. Do Indians mind ducks?

MR. WADHURST. I—I don't think so——

BOGEY. Do you come from India?

MRS. WADHURST. No. Malaya.

PIGGIE. It's the same sort of thing, though, isn't it?—if they don't mind them in Malaya it's unlikely that they'd mind them in India —— (*At telephone.*) It'll probably be all right, but you'd better get Douglas Byng as a standby.

CLARE. There might be something in their religion about Douglas Byng.

PIGGIE. Shh! (*At telephone.*) Everyone's making such a noise! The room's full of the most frightful people. Darling, it definitely *is* Waterloo Station—— No, I'm almost sure he can't—he's going to sea on Thursday—don't be silly, dear, you can't be in the Navy without going to sea *sometimes*——

PETER *enters, followed by* ALLY.

(*At telephone.*) Here he is now, you can ask him yourself—— (*To* PETER.) Peter, it's Nina, she wants to talk to you—— (*To the* WADHURSTS.) This is my husband and Commander Corbett—he's been longing to meet you and thank you for being so sweet to us— I told him all about your heavenly house and the plantation——

MRS. WADHURST (*bridling—to* ALLY). It was most delightful, I assure you, to have Lady Maureen with us——.

PIGGIE. Not him, him—that's the wrong one——

MRS. WADHURST. Oh, I'm sorry——

PETER (*shaking hands with* MRS. WADHURST). It was so kind of you—my wife has talked of nothing else——

PIGGIE (*grabbing him*). Here—Nina's yelling like a banshee——

PETER. Excuse me. (*He takes the telephone.*) Hallo, Nin—what for?——No, I can't but Piggie probably can——(*To* PIGGIE.) Can you go to Nina's party for the Rajahs?

PIGGIE. We've been through all that——

PETER. All right—I didn't know——(*At telephone.*) No, I shall be at sea for about three days—it isn't tiresome at all, I like it——

PIGGIE (*to* MRS. WADHURST). How's your daughter?

MRS. WADHURST (*surprised*). She's a little better, thank you.

PIGGIE. Oh, has she been ill? I'm so sorry.

MR. WADHURST (*gently*). She's been ill for five years.

PIGGIE (*puzzled*). How dreadful for you—are you happy with that cocktail, or would you rather have tea?

MRS. WADHURST. This is delicious, thank you.

PETER (*at telephone*). I honestly can't do anything about that,

Nina, you might be able to find out from the Admiral—well, if his mother was mad too that is an extenuating circumstance—he'll probably be sent home—— (*To* CLARE.) Did you know that Freda Bathurst had once been in an asylum?

CLARE. No, but it explains a lot.

PIGGIE. Why?

PETER. Her son went mad in Hong Kong.

CLARE. What did he do?

PETER. I don't know, but Nina's in a state about it.

PIGGIE. I don't see what it's got to do with Nina——

PETER. He's a relation of some sort—— (*At telephone.*) What did he do, Nina?—— Oh—— Oh, I see—— Oh—well, he'll certainly be sent home and a good job too, we can't have that sort of thing in the Service—— If I were you I'd keep well out of it—all right —— Good-bye. (*He hangs up.*)

PIGGIE. What was it?

PETER. I couldn't possibly tell you.

PIGGIE. Poor boy, I expect the climate had something to do with it—the climate's awful in Hong Kong—look at poor old Wally Smythe——

ALLY (*to the* WADHURSTS). Did you ever know Wally Smythe?

MRS. WADHURST. No, I'm afraid not.

CLARE. You didn't miss much.

PIGGIE. I adored Wally, he was a darling.

CLARE. He kept on having fights all the time—I do hate people hitting people—— (*To* MRS. WADHURST.) Don't you?

MRS. WADHURST. Yes.

There is suddenly complete silence—PIGGIE *breaks it with an effort.*

PIGGIE (*vivaciously to the* WADHURSTS). Maud was so frightfully sorry that she couldn't come to-day—she's pining to see you again and she asked me to ask you if you'd lunch there to-morrow?

MRS. WADHURST. How very kind of her.

PIGGIE She's got a divine little house hidden away in a mews, it's frightfully difficult to find—— (*The telephone rings.*) I've got millions of questions I want to ask you, what happened to that darling old native who did a dance with a sword—— (*At telephone.*) Hallo— (*Continuing to everyone in general.*) It was the most exciting thing I've ever seen, all the villagers sat round in torchlight and they beat—— (*At telephone.*) Hallo—yes, speaking—— (*Continuing*) beat drums and the——(*At telephone.*) hallo—darling, I'd no idea you were back——(*To everybody*) and the old man tore himself to shreds in the middle, it was marvellous—— (*At telephone.*)

I can't believe it, where are you speaking from?—•— My dear, you're *not!*—— (*To everybody.*) It's Boodie, she got back last night and she's staying with Norman——

CLARE. Is Phyllis there?

PIGGIE (*at telephone*). Is Phyllis there?—— She's away?—— (*To* CLARE.) She's away.

PETER (*to* MRS. WADHURST). That's the best joke I ever heard.

CLARE. It's made my entire season that's all, it's just made it.

PIGGIE (*at telephone*). You'd better come and dine to-night—I'm on a diet, so there's only spinach, but we can talk—— Yes, she's here—absolutely worn out—we all are—— Oh yes, it was pretty grim, it started all right and everything was going beautifully when Vera arrived, unasked, my dear, and more determined than Hitler— of course there was the most awful scene—Alice flounced upstairs with tears cascading down her face and locked herself in the cook's bedroom—— Clare tried to save the situation by dragging Lady Borrowdale on to the terrace——

CLARE (*sibilantly*). That was *afterwards!*——

PIGGIE (*at telephone*). Anyhow hell broke loose—you can imagine —Janet was there, of course, and we were all worried about her— no, it hasn't arrived yet, but the odds are mounting—— (*To everybody.*) She hasn't had it yet, has she, Peter?

PETER. If she has it was born in the gramophone department at Harrods—I left her there at four-thirty——

PIGGIE (*at telephone*). No, it's still what's known as on the way— I'll expect you about eight-thirty—I've got to do my feet and then I'm going to relax—all right—yes, she's here—— (*To* CLARE.) Here, Clare, she wants to talk to you——

CLARE *in order to reach the telephone comfortably has to kneel on the sofa.*

CLARE. Excuse me.

MRS. WADHURST. I'm so sorry.

CLARE (*at telephone*). Darling I'm dead with surprise——

PIGGIE (*to* MRS. WADHURST). Now you must tell me some more—

MRS. WADHURST. Well, really, I don't——

CLARE. Shhh!—I can't hear a word—— (*At telephone.*) He what?—When?——He must be raving——

PIGGIE (*in a harsh whisper*). Have you still got that sweet dog?

MRS. WADHURST (*also whispering*). Yes, we've still got Rudolph.

PIGGIE (*to everybody*). Rudolph's an angel, I can never tell you how divine he was—he used to come in every morning with my breakfast tray and jump on to the bed——

MRS. WADHURST (*horrified*). Oh, you never told me that, how very naughty of him—he's very seldom allowed in the house at all——

PIGGIE (*puzzled*). But—but——

MR. WADHURST. Perhaps you're thinking of some other dog, Lady Maureen—Rudolph is a Great Dane——

PIGGIE (*bewildered*). Oh, yes, of course, how idiotic of me——

CLARE (*at telephone*). —Well, all I can say is she ought to be deported—you can't go about making scenes like that, it's so lacking in everything—all right, darling—call me in the morning—I've got a hairdresser in the afternoon, why don't you make an appointment at the same time?—lovely——Good-bye. (*She hangs up.*)

PIGGIE. Do sit down, Clare, and stop climbing about over everybody. (*To* MRS. WADHURST.) You must forgive me—this is a madhouse—it's always like this—I can't think why——

CLARE (*in a whisper to* PETER, *having noticed* MR. BURNHAM). Why's that man got a roll of music, is he going to sing?

PETER (*also in a whisper*). I don't know—he ought by rights to be a lovely girl of sixteen——

MRS. WADHURST. Have you been in London for the whole season?

PIGGIE. Yes, it's been absolutely frightful, but my husband is getting leave soon, so we shall be able to pop off somewhere——

ALLY (*to* MR. WADHURST). I suppose you've never run across a chap in Burma called Beckwith?

MR. WADHURST. No, I've never been to Burma.

ALLY. He's in rubber too, I believe—or tea—he's very amusing.

MRS. WADHURST (*to* PIGGIE).We did hope you'd come and lunch with us one day—but I expect you're terribly busy——

PIGGIE. My dear, I'd worship it—— (*The telephone rings.*) Oh really, this telephone never stops for one minute—— (*At telephone*). Hallo—yes, speaking—— Who?—Mrs. Rawlingson—— Oh, yes, yes, yes—— (*She hands the telephone to* MRS. WADHURST). Here—it's for you——

MRS. WADHURST (*astonished*). For me? How very curious——

PIGGIE. Give me a cocktail. Bogey—I haven't had one at all yet and I'm exhausted——

MRS. WADHURST (*at telephone*). Hallo—what—who?—I'm afraid I don't quite understand——

BOGEY (*giving* PIGGIE *a cocktail*). Here you are—it's a bit weak——

MRS. WADHURST (*still floundering*). —I think there must be

some mistake—just a moment—— (*To* PIGGIE.) It's for you, Lady Maureen—a Mrs. Rawlingson——

PIGGIE (*laughing*). Now isn't that the most extraordinary coincidence—— (*She takes the telephone.*) —Hallo—yes—speaking —— (*She listens and her face changes.*)—Oh yes, of course, how stupid of me—— (*She looks hurriedly at the* WADHURSTS, *then at* PETER.) I'm so awfully sorry, I only just came in—— Oh, what a shame—no, no, no, it doesn't matter a bit—— No—indeed you must call me up the first moment he gets over it—— Yes—I expect it was—yes—— Good-bye.

She slowly hangs up the receiver, looking at the WADHURSTS *in complete bewilderment. She makes a sign to* PETER *over* MRS. WADHURST'S *shoulder, but he only shakes his head.*

PIGGIE (*brightly, but with intense meaning*). That was Mrs. Rawlingson.

PETER. Good God!

PIGGIE (*with purpose, sitting next to* MRS. WADHURST). Did you ever meet the Rawlingsons out East?

MRS. WADHURST. No—I don't know them.

PIGGIE. Maud and I stayed with them too, you know.

MRS. WADHURST. Where?

PIGGIE. It was in Malaya somewhere, I think—I do get so muddled.

MRS. WADHURST. I think we should have heard of them if they lived in Malaya.

PETER *meanwhile has gone to the piano and started to strum idly —he begins to hum lightly at the same time.*

PETER (*humming to a waltz refrain, slightly indistinctly, but clearly enough for* PIGGIE *to hear*). If these are not them, who are they? Who are they? Who are they?

PIGGIE *rises and saunters over to the piano.*

PIGGIE. Play the other bit, dear, out of the second act—— (*She hums.*)—you know—"I haven't the faintest idea—— Oh no—I haven't the faintest idea."

PETER (*changing tempo*). "Under the light of the moon, dear— you'd better find out pretty soon, dear."

CLARE. What on earth's that out of?

PIGGIE. Don't be *silly*, Clare—all I ask is that you shouldn't be *silly!*

CLARE (*understanding*). Oh, yes—I see.

There is silence except for PETER'S *playing—everyone looks covertly at the* WADHURSTS. PIGGIE *goes over to* MR. WADHURST.

PIGGIE (*with determination*). What ship did you come home in?

MR. WADHURST. The *Naldera*.

ALLY. P & O?

MRS. WADHURST. Yes.

PIGGIE. I suppose you got on at Singapore?

MR. WADHURST. No, Penang.

PIGGIE (*the light breaking*). Penang! Of course, Penang.

MRS. WADHURST. Yes, we have some friends there, so we went by train from Singapore and stayed with them for a couple of days before catching the boat.

PIGGIE (*sunk again*). Oh yes—yes, I see.

PETER (*at piano, humming to march time*). When you hear those drums rat-a-plan—rat-a-plan—find out the name of the place if you can—la la la la la la la la——

PIGGIE (*persevering*). How far is your house from the sea? Maud and I were arguing about it for hours the other day——

MRS. WADHURST. It's right on the sea.

PIGGIE. That's exactly what I said, but you know Maud's so vague —she never remembers a thing——

CLARE. I suppose it's hell hot all the year round where you are?

MRS. WADHURST. Yes, the climate is a little trying, but one gets used to it.

BOGEY. Are you far from Kuala Lumpur?

MRS. WADHURST. Yes, a long way.

BOGEY. Oh, I knew some people in Kuala Lumpur once.

MR. WADHURST. What were their names?

BOGEY. Damn it, I've forgotten—something like Harrison——

PIGGIE (*helpfully*). Morrison?

ALLY. Williamson?

PETER. Lightfoot?

BOGEY. No, it's gone—

PIGGIE (*irritably*). Never mind—it couldn't matter less really, could it?

MRS. WADHURST (*rising*). I'm afraid we must really go now, Lady Maureen——

PIGGIE. Oh no—please——

MRS. WADHURST. We have to dress because we're dining and going to the theatre—that's the one thing we do miss dreadfully in Pendarla—the theatre——

CLARE. We miss it a good deal here, too.

PIGGIE (*remembering everything*). Pendarla—oh dear, what a long way it seems—dear Mrs. Wadhurst—(*She shoots a triumphant glance at* PETER.)—it's been so lovely having this little peep at you—you and Mr. Wadhurst must come and dine quietly one night and we'll go to another theatre——

MRS. WADHURST. That would be delightful—Fred——

MR. WADHURST. Good-bye.

PIGGIE. Peter—come and say good-bye to Mr. and Mrs. Wadhurst.

PETER (*coming over and shaking hands*). Good-bye—I can never tell you how grateful I am to you for having been so kind and hospitable to my wife——

MRS. WADHURST. Next time, I hope you'll come and call on us too.

PETER. I should love to.

MRS. WADHURST. Good-bye.

CLARE. Good-bye——

Everybody says good-bye and shakes hands, PETER *opens the door for the* WADHURSTS *and they go out on a wave of popularity. He goes out into the hall with them closing the door after him.* PIGGIE *collapses on to the sofa.*

PIGGIE (*hysterically*). Oh, my God, that was the most awful half an hour I've ever spent——

CLARE. I thought it all went down like a dinner.

PIGGIE. I remember it all now, we stayed one night with them on our way from Siam—a man in Bangkok had wired to them or something——

ALLY. That was a nice bit you did about the old native dancing with a sword——

PIGGIE. Oh dear, they must have thought I was drunk.

PETER *re-enters.*

PETER. Next time you travel, my darling, I suggest you keep a diary.

PIGGIE. Wasn't it frightful—poor angels—I must ring up Maud ——(*She dials a number.*) I think they had a heavenly time though, don't you—I mean they couldn't have noticed a thing——

PETER. Oh no, the whole affair was managed with the utmost subtlety—I congratulate you——

PIGGIE. Don't be sour—Peter—— (*At telephone.*) Hallo—Maud? —darling, it's not the Rawlingsons at all, it's the Wadhursts—— (*To everybody.*) Good heavens, I never gave them Maud's address. (*At telephone.*) I forgot to give them your address—how can you be so unkind, Maud, you ought to be ashamed of yourself—they're absolute pets, both of them——

PETER. Come on, Ally, I've got to dress——

ALLY. All right——

CLARE. Shall I see you on Sunday?

ALLY. Yes—I'll be over——

PIGGIE (*at telephone*). —they had a lovely time and everybody was divine to them——

CLARE. Come on, Bogey, we must go, too—

PIGGIE. Wait a minute, don't leave me—I've got to do my feet ——(*At telephone.*) —no, I was talking to Clare—— My dear, I know, she rang me up too—she's staying with Norman—Phyllis will be as sour as a quince——

PETER *and* ALLY *go off talking.*

CLARE. Darling, I really *must* go——

PIGGIE (*at telephone*). —all right—I'll try to get hold of them in the morning and put them off—I do think it's horrid of you though, after all, they were frightfully sweet to us—I've done all I can— well, there's no need to get into a rage, I'm the one to get into a rage—yes, you are, I can hear you—your teeth are chattering like dice in a box—— Oh, all right! (*She hangs up.*) Maud's impossible——

CLARE. Listen, Piggie——

PIGGIE. Wait just one minute, I've got to get the things to do my feet——

She rushes out of the room.

CLARE. I really don't see why we should all wait about—— (*She suddenly sees* MR. BURNHAM.) Oh—hallo.

MR. BURNHAM (*nervously*). Hallo.

CLARE. I thought you'd left with your mother and father.

MR. BURNHAM. They weren't my mother and father—I'm from Freeman's. I've brought the designs for the Commander's speed boat—Mr. Driscoll couldn't come——

CLARE. Well, you'd better wait—he'll be back soon——

MR. BURNHAM. I'm afraid I can't wait much longer—I have to get back to the shop——

CLARE. You should have piped up before——

BOGEY. Listen, Clare, we must push off——

CLARE. All right.

MR. BURNHAM *retires again into the shadows as* PIGGIE *returns with several bottles, a towel and a pair of scissors. She sits on the sofa and takes her shoes and stockings off.*

PIGGIE. The trouble with Maud is, she's too insular——

CLARE. Are you driving down on Saturday?

PIGGIE. Yes—I promised to stop off at Godalming and have a cutlet with Freda on the way—do you want to come?

CLARE. You know perfectly well I hate Freda's guts.

PIGGIE (*beginning on her feet*). All right, darling—I'll expect you in the afternoon.

The telephone rings—PIGGIE *reaches for it with one hand and goes on painting her toe nails with the other*—*at telephone:* Hallo—yes. Oh, David, I'm *so* sorry—I completely forgot——

CLARE *and* BOGEY *hiss good-bye at her, she waves to them, and they go out.*

I couldn't help it, I had to be sweet to some people that Maud and I stayed with in Malaya—— Oh! David darling, don't be so soured-up—yes, of course I do, don't be so silly—— No, I'm quite alone doing my feet—well, I can't help that, I happen to *like* them red—well, after all they are my feet, I suppose I can paint them blue if I want to——

MR. BURNHAM *begins to tiptoe out of the room, he leaves his roll of designs on the table.* PIGGIE *catches sight of him just as he is gingerly opening the door.*

(*To* MR. BURNHAM.) Oh, good-bye—it's been absolutely lovely, you're the sweetest family I've ever met in my life——

CURTAIN

SIEGFRIED SASSOON

****

*I choose this because it is a sensitive and highly finished piece of
writing which represents my characteristic feeling for the past and
gives a good picture of English country life as it was before 1914.
W. is an evocation of my youthful self which seems to me to have
the delicacy, warmth and depth at which I aim in my prose writing.*

SIEGFRIED SASSOON

****

The Weald of Youth

DURING THESE GENTLE REVISITATIONS of the days that are no more
I sometimes enliven my imagination by resorting to an Ordnance
Survey map of those parts of Kent and Sussex with which I am
concerned. The Survey was made in 1866 and brought up to date
and the map re-engraved in 1893; so it enables me to lose sight of
the arterial road makings and other tyrannies of mechanized traf-
ficry which have since altered the character of so much of the
countryside. Far back in the '90's my mother had acquired it for
finding her way to distant meets of the hounds; and in later years
I myself never failed to unfold it after a day's hunting. It is therefore an old and valued friend, and no map could be more imbued
with memorial associations and finger-marks.

My most recent porings over it have been for the purpose of
measuring a few of the distances I drove with friends at whose
houses I stayed for balls, in the days before motor-cars were much
in use. For I was an enthusiastic dancer, though I can't claim ever
to have been to more than about half-a-dozen important ones in a
twelve-month. An earnest rather than volatile performer with my
patent-leather pumps, I never "sat out" anything—not even "The
Lancers"—and I was hard at it until the band had played its final
bar—unless some beckoning and unevadable chaperon decreed that
her party must leave before the finish. "Such a long way home for

the horses" was the reason given for our reluctant departure—including the customary concession of "Well, just *one* more, Marjorie, and that really must be the last." And ten miles home on frosty roads frequently justified it.

"Do you reverse?" . . . How those words bring my silly self back to me, with my inability to make my white ties look as effortless as other young men's and my white gloves which always would split in at least one place before the "supper extras" emptied the floor for some really strenuous waltzing. I was particularly proud of my reversing, but I suspect that the young ladies found it a somewhat left-handed experience. One just went resolutely round the other way and made sketchy movements with the feet. "The music seems to be playing specially for us, doesn't it?" murmured some light-footed partner, while we swayed to the soul-transporting strains of *Songe d'Automne.* And in my white simplicity I agreed with her, unaware that the remark was an artless variation of that traditional suggestion "the world seems to have been made specially for us two!" I remember one unromantic evening in a ballroom of Italianate design which contained a picture by Burne-Jones called *The Hours.* The room was overcrowded, and while I bumped into people and apologized I was seldom unmindful of those languid and sedentary Preraphaelite ladies who were presiding over our exertions—"wall-flowers" they were, every one of them, like the shyly stoical girls whose programmes were so depressingly full of blanks.

The Hours were six in number—just about the duration of the dance—and I have mentioned them because it now seems so peculiar that I should have been revolving beneath them for so many hours on end, and that I should now be putting their presence in my past on paper. One might be excused for moralizing about it. But the implications of the picture are obvious—many of the dancers and most—if not all—of the sedately watchful dowagers having since then asked for their carriages and departed for some destination beyond the reach of gilt-edged invitation cards. Would one willingly invite them back, to be as they then were in the world darkness of today? I cannot think so. And I remember—with a sigh—how more than once I have thought that it was well for my old friends that they went when they did.

Meanwhile I am still overhearing the muffled thrum and throb of music from ballrooms thirty years ago—overhearing, perhaps, that "Blue Hungarian Band" which we all thought so wonderful. And I get a glimpse of myself, waiting impatiently for an overdue partner in some empty ante-room of mirrors that reflect my flushed and callow countenance. But the gaiety and the sentiment of what then was—do not these forbid me to make further game of old dancing days, reminding me, not of laborious toe-treading couples, but of those who took the floor triumphally and carried the music along with them in their controlled and graceful career—exemplifying, for older eyes that watched them, the momentary conquest of youth and the pathos of its unawareness?

Anyhow, here I am, with the dear old map yet again unfolded— quite in the mood to revisit one of those Queen Anne country houses where I awoke on the morning after a dance and drowsily observed the discreet man-servant putting a hot-water can into the hip-bath, wondering whether he was expecting me to give him half-a-sovereign or whether five bob would be decent, until he'd creaked away along the passage and I was up and looking out at frosted lawns and the sun just breaking through mist beyond the elm avenue. Revisiting some such house I should go there in summer—preferably on a dozy July morning. I should find myself in an upstairs room, leaning out of the tall sash-window from a sun-warmed window-seat. It is an unfrequented room, seeming to contain vibrations of vanished life. A summer room, too, where the cushions along the window-seat have had the colour faded out of them by many a morning such as this. Year after year the sunlight has come past half-drawn curtains to slant idly along the oak floor and up the panelled wall, at certain seasons creeping across the portrait above the fireplace—a girl in eighteenth-century dress with a little posy in her hands. "The past is over and gone," the sunlight seems to be saying, "but the present is only that mottled butterfly fluttering dryly against the ceiling, and the old white pony pulling the mowing-machine to and fro on the lawn." Down in the drawing-room the young lady of the house if practising Greig's *Schmetterling* with rippling rapidity and a proper appreciation of its lyrical tenderness. And "The past ought always to be like this," I tell myself. "Music with a heart-ache of happiness in it, overheard from the upstairs room of one's acquiescent mind, where the present is only waiting to become the past and be laid up in lavender for commemorative renewal." But I must be getting back to realities again—or to such realities as I can muster-up from my obsolete Ordnance Map.

Meanwhile I will ask to be allowed to do it affectionately, taking my own time. Leaning on the sun-blistered white paint of the window-ledge, I must enjoy my final stare at the garden; listen to the stable clock striking twelve; hear the clink of a bucket as the stable-boy finishes washing the carriage-wheels, and then one of the horses neighing and snorting while the coachman goes to the corn bin with his sieve. From somewhere beyond a yew hedge comes a murmur of voices, talking contentedly as people do while sitting out of doors on a fine summer day—talking, I like to think, about the new standard roses which have done so well this year; with an afterword that perhaps it *would* be as well to have iced-coffee besides claret-cup for the small tennis party this afternoon. . . . And now I emerge from the upstairs room—a half-ghost, soundless from the shades of the future. Down the wide and slippery oak stairs I go, as I used to do when dressed and button-holed for a ball; and across the lofty panelled hall with its bland periwigged portraits and great open fireplace where huge smouldering logs sent out their pungent wood-smoke smell—that hall where I had danced Sir Roger de Coverley on stormy winter nights when I was only an awkward excited little boy. Then out by the big double doors, and away under the whispering trees, pausing near the homely farm buildings for a last look at the gracious red brick front of the house. Here it all is on my map; a name, and a few marks and dots; and just beyond the farm, the tiny river Bewlt joining the tiny river Teise.

For on the map they are both awarded the rank of River, though the youthful Bewlt in its five-mile wanderings had never been more than a brook; while the stripling Teise, which had yet another ten miles to travel before merging itself in the Medway at Yalding, was content to saunter past orchards, copses, pastures, and hop-gardens without achieving the dignity of working a water-mill or even earning a rent for its fishing-rights. I had never seen much of the Bewlt; but the windings of the Teise were well known to me, with the added interest that, for some seven miles before it met its tiny tributary, this pleasant alder-shaded stream formed the boundary between Kent and Sussex. The bit of it which I knew best was in Squire Morland's park at Lamberhurst, for it flowed past the fourth green of the nine-hole golf course, and many a time I had almost been into it with my second shot after topping my drive. And since the Teise was never more than a few miles from my home, I had always looked upon it as our local river, and as such had wished it well where it gurgled under little bridges.

Meanwhile I feel inclined to compare it—not only to this dallying digression—but also to the whole narrative thread of this discursive chapter. For I began my chapter with an unparticularized intention of amusing myself by memories of the adolescence of the

auto-car; but I am already well away from the main roads, and glad
of any excuse for continuing my journey by field paths and bridle
tracks. "For most, I know, thou lov'st retirèd ground" . . . I could
quote several stanzas of *The Scholar Gipsy* in support of my propensity for meditative ramblings in the by-ways of my mind. I have
never liked following the telegraph-poles on the straightest road to
a populous destination. Give me the manor-farmstead that can only
be reached after opening half-a-dozen gates, and the unassuming
stream which never tells you what parish it intends to pass through
next.

Squire Morland's park, which I mentioned not far back, provides
yet another excuse for dawdling a bit longer in the vicinity of the
River Teise. Some of my readers will recognize the scene, since I
have described it—more briefly than it deserved—in an earlier volume of Memoirs. But that was fully a dozen years ago, so I may
be forgiven this renewed retrospection of a place which I was fond
of, and have always enjoyed thinking about. Let me add that although the course wasn't at all a good one I must have played many
more rounds there than on any other. The worst thing about Lamberhurst golf was that it provided very poor practice for playing
anywhere else. In fact one could almost say that it was "a game of
its own." For one thing, you were perpetually hoicking the ball out
of tussocky lies; and for another, the greens had justifiably been
compared to the proverbial postage-stamp. If you pitched adroitly
on to a green, it was more than likely that you wouldn't remain
there. If, on the other hand, your ball fell short, you stopped where
you were, which was in the rough grass. And the otherwise almost
hazardless charm of our local links didn't always atone for these
disadvantages, especially when one happened to be playing a medal-
round at the Spring or Autumn Meeting. During the summer
months the course got completely out of control and nobody bothered to play there except Squire Morland himself, and he had seldom done the nine holes in under fifty at the best of times. Go there
on a fine April day, however, and there was nothing to complain of,
provided that one gave the idyllic pastoral surroundings their due
and didn't worry about the quality of the golf. I say "pastoral" because the place was much frequented by sheep, and I cannot visua-
lize it without an accompaniment of bells and baa-ings.

Standing near the quiet-flowing tree-shaded river at the foot of
the park, one watches a pottering little group of golfers moving deliberately down the south-westerly slope. It is one of those after-
luncheon foursomes in which the Squire delighted; and there he is,

playing an approach-shot to the third hole in that cautious, angular, and automatic style of his. The surly black retriever is at his heels, and his golf-bag has a prop to it, so as to save him stooping to pick it up, and also to keep his clubs dry. The clock on the village school strikes three, and one is aware of the odour of beer-making from the Brewery. The long hole to the farthest corner of the park is known as "the Brewery Hole." And now they are all on the green, and gallant old General Fitzhugh, who had conspicuously distinguished himself in the Afghanistan campaign some thirty years before, is taking tremendous pains over his putt. The General has quite lately acquired one of those new Schenectady putters, mallet-shaped and made of aluminum, and popularized by Walter Travis, the first American who ever reached and won the Final of the Amateur Championship in England; and the non-success of his stroke is duly notified when he brandishes the weapon distractedly above his head. I now identify the stocky upright figure of my old friend Captain Ruxton, who evidently has "that for it," and sinks the ball with airy unconcern; whereupon the Squire, I can safely assume, ejaculates "My word, that's a hot 'un, Farmer!" in his customary clipped and idiomatic manner.

The fourth member of the party, I observe—unless one includes a diminutive boy from the village who staggers under the General's bristling armoury of clubs—is Mr. Watson, a tall, spectacled Scotsman, still in the prime of life, whose game is a good deal above Lamberhurst standards. Watson is a man well liked by everyone—without his ever saying much, possibly because he can't think of anything to say. My mother once remarked that when Mr. Watson ran out of small talk at a tea-party he told her that he always gave his hens salad-oil for the good of their health. But his favourite conversational opening was "Have you been to Macrihanish?"—Macrihanish being an admirable but rather un-get-at-able golf course within easy reach of the Mull of Kintyre. A person of strict principles, he had never been heard to utter the mildest of expletives, even when he found one of his finest drives reposing in the footprint of a sheep. After making a bad shot he used to relieve his feelings, while marching briskly toward his ball, with a snatch of cheerful song. "Trol-de-rol-de-rol" went Mr. Watson. But one had to have been to Macrihanish if one wanted to get much out of him in the way of conversation.

The friendly foursome is now well on toward the fourth green, where—in my mind's eye—I am standing by the tin flag, which requires repainting and has been there ever since the Club was founded. Following the flight of their tee-shots, I have remembered with amusement that Squire Morland occupies what might be called a duplicated position in the realms of print. His name appears, of course, in Burke's *Landed Gentry* and similar publications of lesser importance. But it also figures in *The Golfing Annual* as "green-keeper to the Lamberhurst Golf Club." (Nine holes. Subscription 21/- per annum.) The Squire's assumption of this sinecure appointment is due to the fact that by so doing he cannily obtains for himself and his cronies all the golf balls that he needs, at wholesale price. It is just conceivable that he does pull the light roller up and down about once a year; but I never heard of him doing so, though I myself had put in an hour's voluntary worm-cast sweeping now and again—the green-man being rather apt to neglect his duties.

In the meantime the foursome has another fourteen holes to play before it adjourns to the House for tea and a stroll in the garden to admire daffodils. And while those kindly ghosts gather round me on the green I can do no more than wish that I could be greeting them there again, on some warm April afternoon, with the sheep munching unconcernedly and the course—as the Squire used to say —" in awful good condition." But as the scene withdraws and grows dim I hear a blackbird warbling from the orchard on the other side of the river; and I know that his song on the springtime air is making even elderly country gentlemen say to themselves that one is only as old as one feels, especially when there is nothing forbidding about the foreground of the future—into which they are now, with leisurely solemnity, making ready to smite the ball.

J. B. PRIESTLEY

****

. . . as I write plays (probably my best work), novels and essays of many kinds, no single specimen can well represent me. After some thought I have decided that the description of the Grand Canyon in Midnight in the Desert *will do as well as anything. The passage begins in the second paragraph of Chapter XIV. The passage is a favorite one with many readers, and has the advantage, from your point of view, of describing an American scene.*

J. B. PRIESTLEY

****

The Grand Canyon

THIS WAS NOT our first visit to the Grand Canyon. . . . I plunged farther into recollection, and arrived at that first visit. We had planned "a stop-over" of a few hours. Your coach leaves the main west-bound train at Williams, Arizona, wanders up the sixty-four miles to the station at the Southern Rim of the Canyon, doing this during the night when you are fast asleep, and when you wake in the morning—there you are. That is the theory of this "side trip." It did not work well for me in practice. The night that had seemed very convenient and comfortable in the railway time-table was actually most unpleasant. First there were giant shuntings and bangings that made sleep impossible. By the time I had adapted myself to these shuntings and bangings, they stopped, and the train was left paralyzed in an uneasy silence and stillness, a doomed train that whispered, "Sleep no more." In the end I must have slept a little, for I remember waking to find that we were somewhere very high and it was snowing. Heavy and hot about the eyes, I put on some clothes, then went blinking and shuffling out into the cold blue morning, a peevish passenger.

The little station looked dreary. The young man waiting with the hotel bus did not look dreary, but he looked all wrong, for he wore a ten-gallon hat and an embroidered cowboy coat with English riding-breeches and long boots, like a cowboy in a musical comedy.

The bus turned two corners and landed us at the front door of an hotel that was so tremendously Western that it might have been created by a German scene-designer who had never been farther west than Hamburg. I felt grumpy about all this. A lot of nonsense. The interior of the hotel took my breath away, not because it was very beautiful, but because it was overheated and seven thousand feet above sea-level. I continued to disapprove of everything, but condescended to eat a large breakfast. After breakfast it was still snowing a little and there was nothing to be seen through the hotel windows but snowflakes and mist. I went panting up and down-stairs several times, a man in a temper with a large breakfast getting at him, and then very soon it stopped snowing, so I went out. A few paces in front of the hotel there were some seats, a low wall, and then nothing. The world did not extend beyond that wall. Appar-ently it was a flat world, after all, and here was the edge. I stared over these battlements and saw a few last snowflakes fall into misty space. I walked a few paces through the slush, moving parallel with the wall, and it was wet and raw and there was nothing more to see. I might have been standing on the Thames Embankment on a foggy morning, except that the misty nothing over the edge here had a vaguely illimitable look about it. I decided that I had had enough of this. I threw a last glance over the wall, and then, down there somewhere, there was a swirling, a lifting, a hint of some early creative effort in the mist of Time. The next moment what breath I had left was clean gone. I was looking into the Grand Canyon.

Once I had made sure it really was like that, I hurried back to the hotel, shouted the good news, arranged to stay on, and canceled the seats we had booked in the next train. There was to be no thought of trains. Even this one misty glimpse told me that a mir-acle had happened. At last, in all my travels, I had arrived and there had been no anticlimax, and my imagination, after weeks or months of expectant dreaming, had not cried, "Is that all?" Reality, stung by my many jeers at its poverty, had gone to work to show me a thing or two. I thought I could imagine a better Grand Can-yon, Did I? Well, cried Reality, take a look at this—and—oh boy! —you ain't seen nothing yet.

It juggled with all kinds of weather for us during that first short stay. We saw snow falling into that vast gulf, saw clouds stream below us, looked down on thunderstorms, stared at Nineveh and Thebes, rusty in the sunlight, coming through the mists, and watched rainbows arch and brighten and fade over the Painted Desert. We seemed to be witnessing, within a few hours, all the mad prodigality of Nature. One stupendous effect was piled on another; veils of mist and broken rainbows were caught in forests hanging in midair; the sunlight far below fell on ruined red cities; and to one hand, across the gulf, was a vertical Egypt, and to the other a perpendicular Assyria. There was in this immensity, although the weathers of four seasons and several climates seemed to chase one another down there, a silence so profound that soon all the noises from the life about us on the Rim were lost in it, as if our ears had been captured forever, drowned in these deeps of quiet. We had only to walk a few hundred yards to find ourselves staring at new gigantic vistas, more forests hanging in the mists, more temples crumbling in the sunlight, more rosy peaks, green chasms, and cloud shadows like wandering stains. But it is useless to try to describe the Grand Canyon. Those who have not seen it will not believe any possible description; and those who have seen it know that it cannot be painted in either pigments or words.

I have heard rumors of visitors who were disappointed. The same people will be disappointed at the Day of Judgment. In fact, the Grand Canyon is a sort of landscape Day of Judgment. It is not a show place, a beauty spot, but a revelation. The Colorado River, which is powerful, turbulent, and so thick with silt that it is like a saw, made it with the help of the erosive forces of rain, frost, and wind, and some strange geological accidents; and all these together have been hard at work on it for the last seven or eight million years. It is the largest of the eighteen canyons of the Colorado River, is over two hundred miles long, has an average width of twelve miles, and is a good mile deep. It is the world's supreme example of erosion. But this is not what it really is. It is, I repeat, a revelation. The Colorado River made it, but you feel when you are there that God gave the Colorado River its instructions. It is all Beethoven's nine symphonies in stone and magic light. Even to remember that it is still there lifts up the heart. If I were an American, I should make my remembrance of it the final test of men, art, and policies. I should ask myself: Is this good enough to exist in the same country as the Canyon? How would I feel about this man, this kind of art, these political measures, if I were near that Rim? Every member or officer of the Federal Government ought to remind himself, with triumphant pride, that he is on the staff of the Grand Canyon.

This incredible pageantry of sunlight and chasm, I thought, is our nearest approach to fourth-dimensional scenery. The three dimensions are on such a scale that some of the fourth has been

WINSTON CHURCHILL

****

Brought back into the Government May 14, 1940 to form the War Cabinet and going to the British people with his first speech offering them nothing but "blood, toil, tears and sweat" in defining his policy to wage war against Germany, Winston Churchill made his second speech in the House on May 28th with the announcement of the Belgian army's withdrawal from the war. On June 4th, he went before the House of Commons with his Dunkirk speech after the British Expeditionary Force had been successfully evacuated from Flanders. (This selection from the "literature of eloquence" was made for this volume by Dr. Houston Peterson, an authority in the field, Mr. Churchill having written the editor he was not in a position to make a choice of his own writings.)

****

Dunkirk: The Miracle of the Evacuation

Speech delivered in the House of Commons on June 4, 1940, after the British Expeditionary Force had been successfully evacuated from Flanders.

FROM THE MOMENT the French defences at Sedan and on the Meuse were broken at the end of the second week of May, only a rapid retreat to Amiens and the south could have saved the British and French armies who had entered Belgium at the appeal of the Belgian King, but this strategic fact was not immediately realized. The French High Command first thought that they would be able to close the gap and the armies of the north were under their orders. Moreover, retirement then would have involved almost certainly destruction of the fine Belgian army of over 20 divisions and abandonment of the whole of Belgium.

Therefore, when the force and scope of the German penetration were realized and when the new French Generalissimo, General Weygand, assumed command in the place of General Gamelin, an

541

effort was made by the French and British armies in Belgium to keep on holding the right hand of the Belgians and to give their own right hand to the new army which was to have an advance guard on the Somme in great strength to clasp it.

However, German irruption swept to the right and rear of the armies of the north.

Eight or nine armoured divisions, each of about 400 armoured vehicles of different kinds, were employed. This force cut off all communications between us and the main French armies.

It severed our own communications for food and ammunition which reached first through Amiens and afterwards through Abbeville, and it swept off to the coast to Boulogne and Calais and almost to Dunkirk.

The Rifle Brigade, the 60th Rifles and the Queen Victoria Rifles, with a battalion of British tanks and 1,000 Frenchmen, in all about 4,000 strong, defended Calais to the last.

The British brigadier was given an hour to surrender. He spurned the offer and four days of intense street fighting passed before silence reigned over Calais, which marked the end of a memorable resistance.

Only 30 unwounded survivors were brought off by the Navy and we do not know the fate of their comrades. Their sacrifice, however, is not in vain. At least two armoured divisions which otherwise would have been turned against the B.E.F. had to be sent for to overcome them.

They have added another page to the glorious history of the Light Division and time was gained to enable the water-line as far as Gravelines to be opened and to be held by the French troops. Thus it was that the port of Dunkirk was kept open. When it was found impossible for the armies in the north to reopen communications through Amiens with the main French armies, only one choice remained. It seemed indeed forlorn. The British, French and Belgian armies were almost surrounded. Their sole line of retreat was to a single port and its neighbouring beaches. They were pressed on every side by heavy attacks and far outnumbered in men.

Suddenly, without prior consultation, without the least possible notice, without the advice of his Ministers, upon his own personal act, King Leopold sent a plenipotentiary to the German Command to surrender his army and exposed our whole flank and means of security. I asked the House a week ago to suspend its judgment because the facts were not clear but I do not feel any reason now exists why we should not form our own opinion upon this pitiful episode. The surrender of the Belgian Army compelled the British at the shortest notice to cover a flank of more than 30 miles in length. Otherwise all would have been cut off and all would have shared the fate to which King Leopold had condemned the finest army his country had ever formed.

In closing this flank, contact was lost inevitably between the British and two of the three corps forming the first French Army who were still farther from the coast than we and it seemed impossible that a large number of the Allied troops could reach the coast. The enemy attacked on all sides in great strength and fury and their main power—the power of their far more numerous air force—was thrown into the battle or was concentrated upon Dunkirk and the beaches.

Pressing in upon the narrow exits both from the east and from the west, the enemy began to fire with cannon upon the beaches by which alone shipping could approach or depart. They sowed magnetic mines in the Channel and the sea. They sent repeated waves of hostile aircraft, sometimes more than a hundred strong in one formation, to cast their bombs upon a single pier that remained and upon the sand dunes amid which troops as they arrived sought shelter. Their U-boats, one of which was sunk, and their motor launches took toll of the vast traffic which now began. For four or five days an intense struggle raged. All armoured divisions or what was left of them, together with great masses of German infantry and artillery, hurled themselves in vain upon the ever narrowing and contracting appendix within which the British and French armies fought.

Meanwhile, the Royal Navy, with the willing help of countless merchant seamen and a host of volunteers, strained every nerve to embark British and Allied troops.

Over 220 light warships and more than 650 other vessels were engaged. They had to operate upon a difficult coast, often in adverse weather, under an almost ceaseless hell of bombs and an increasing concentration of artillery fire.

Nor were the seas themselves free from mines and torpedoes. It was in conditions such as these that our men carried on with little or no rest for days and nights on end, making trip after trip across the dangerous waters, bringing with them always men whom they had rescued. The numbers brought back are a measure of their devotion and their courage.

Now, suddenly, the scene has cleared. The crack of thunder has for the moment, but only for the moment, died away. The miracle of deliverance achieved by valour, by perseverance, by perfect discipline, by dauntless service, by resource, by skill, by unconquerable fidelity, is manifest to us all.

The enemy was hurled back by the retreating French and British troops. He was so roughly handled that he did not dare molest their departure seriously. The Air Force decisively defeated the main strength of the German air force and inflicted upon them losses of at least four to one. And the navy, using nearly 1,000 ships of all kinds, carried over 335,000 men—French and British—out of the jaws of death and brought them back to their native land and to the tasks which lie immediately ahead.

We must be very careful not to assign to this deliverance attributes of victory. Wars are not won by evacuations. But there is victory inside this deliverance which should be noted, and it was gained by the Air Force. Many of our soldiers coming back had not seen the Air Force at work. They only saw the bombers which escaped their protective attack. They underrate its achievement. We have heard much talk of that, and that is why I go out of my way to tell the House about it. This was a great trial of strength between the British and German air forces.

Can you conceive a greater objective for the power of Germany in the air than to make all evacuation from these beaches impossible and to sink all the ships which were displayed, almost to the number of a thousand? Could there have been an objective of greater military importance or greater military significance for the whole purposes of the war than this?

They tried hard and they were beaten back. They were frustrated in their attacks. We got the army away and they paid fourfold for any losses they inflicted upon us.

Very large formations of German airplanes—and we know this is a very brave race—have turned on several occasions from the attack of a quarter of their number of R.A.F. machines and dispersed.

I return to the Army. In the long series of very fierce battles now on this front, now on that, fighting on three fronts at once, battles fought by two or three divisions against an equal or somewhat larger number of the enemy, and fought very fiercely on the old ground that so many of us know so well, our losses in men have exceeded 30,000 killed, wounded or missing.

Our losses in material are enormous. We have perhaps lost one-third of the men we lost in the opening days of the battle of March 21, 1918, but we have lost nearly as many guns, nearly 1,000 guns and all our transport and all the armoured vehicles that were with the army in the north. This loss will impose a further delay on the expansion of our military strength. That expansion had not been proceeding as we had hoped. The best of all we had to give had gone to the B.E.F. Although they had not the numbers of tanks and some articles of equipment that were desirable, they were a very well and finely equipped army.

They had the first fruits that our industry had to give. That has gone and now here is this further delay. How long will it be, how long will it last, will depend on the exertions made in these Islands. An effort, the like of which has never been seen in our records, is now being made. Work is proceeding everywhere night and day, on Sundays and weekdays.

Capital and labour have cast aside their interests, rights and customs and put them into the common stock. Already the flow of munitions has leapt forward.

There is no reason why we should not in a few months overtake the sudden and serious loss that has come upon us, without retarding the development of our general programme.

Nevertheless, our thankfulness at the escape of our army and so many men whose loved ones have passed through an agonising time must not blind us to the fact that what has happened in France and Belgium is a colossal military disaster. The French army has been weakened, the Belgian army lost. A large part of those fortified lines whereupon so much faith had been reposed is gone. Many valuable mining districts and factories have passed into the enemy's possession.

The whole of the Channel Ports are in his hands with all the strategic consequences that follow from that, and we must expect another blow to be struck almost immediately at us or at France. We are told that Hitler has a plan for invading the British Isles. This has often been thought of before. The whole question of home defence against invasion is, of course, powerfully affected by the fact that we have for the time being in this Island incomparably more powerful military forces than we have had at any moment of this war or the last. This will not continue. We shall not be content with a defensive war. We have our duty to our Allies. We have to reconstitute and build up the B.E.F. once again under the gallant Commander-in-Chief, Lord Gort.

All this is in train and in the interval we must put our defences of these islands into such a high state of organization that the fewest

possible number will be required to give effective security and that
the largest possible potential of offensive effort may be released. On
this we are now engaged.

We found it necessary to take measures of increasing stringency
not only against enemy aliens and suspicious characters of other nationalities but also against British subjects, who may become a danger or a nuisance should war be transported to the United Kingdom. I know there are a great many people affected by the orders
we have made who are passionate enemies of Nazi Germany. I am
very sorry for them, but we cannot at the present time and under
the present circumstances draw all the distinctions we should like.

If parachute landings were attempted and fierce fighting contingent upon them followed, these unfortunate people would be far
better out of the war for their own sake as well as ours.

There is another class with whom I do not feel the slightest sympathy. Parliament has given us the power to put down Fifth Column activities with a strong hand. We shall use those powers, subject to the supervision and correction of the House, without the
slightest hesitation until we are satisfied, and more than satisfied,
that this malignancy in our midst has been effectively stamped out.

Turning once again this time more generally to the question of
an invasion, I would observe that there never has been a period in
all these long centuries of which we boast that an absolute guaran-
tee against invasion, and still less against serious air-raids, could
have been given to our people. In the days of Napoleon the same
wind which would have carried his transports across the Channel
might have stood in the way of the blockading fleet.

I think that no idea is so outlandish that it should not be considered and viewed with a watchful but steady eye. One must never
forget the solid assurances of seapower and those which belong to
airpower if it can be locally exercised.

I feel confident that if all do their duty and nothing is neglected
and the best arrangements are made, as they are being made, we
shall prove ourselves once again able to defend our island home and
ride out the storm of war and outlive the menace of tyranny, if
necessary for years and if necessary alone.

That is what we are going to try to do, and that is the resolve of
His Majesty's Government, every man of them. That is the will of
Parliament and the nation.

Even though large tracts of Europe and many old famous States
have fallen or may fall into the grip of the Gestapo and all the

odious apparatus of Nazi rule, we shall not flag or fail. We shall go on to the end.

We shall fight in France; we shall fight on the seas and oceans; we shall fight with growing confidence and strength in the air; we shall defend our island whatever the cost may be; we shall fight on the beaches; we shall fight on landing grounds; we shall fight in fields, in streets and in hills. We shall never surrender and even if—which I do not for a moment believe—this island or a large part of it was subjected and starving, then our Empire beyond the seas, armed and guarded by the British Fleet, will carry on the struggle until in God's good time, a new world with all its power and might steps forth to the liberation and rescue of the old.

REBECCA WEST

Rebecca West, who has been called by her contemporaries "the best reporter in the world" and one who has elevated journalism to a literary art, chose for her presentation in THE WORLD'S BEST *the essay she wrote for* Harper's Magazine, *entitled "The Meaning of Treason" which later, in more condensed form, she used as the epilogue of the book of the same title which told the story of England's traitors in the "underworld of modern war." This selection is the full, unabridged version of her essay.*

****

The Meaning of Treason

FROM TIME TO TIME during my career as a journalist I have reported notable law cases, and I know that it is not only morbidity which makes the public enjoy following the trial of a serious crime. It is very difficult for those who study life to find a story that comes to its end under their eyes. When we select an individual whose course we want to trace, it is as likely as not that he covers his tracks with secrecy, or moves to a field outside our view, or delays his end until we ourselves have ended. That is why classical history is a valuable study; we can see the whole story, the beginning, the middle, and the end of Greece and Rome, Egypt and Persia. That is why the lives of great men in the past teach us more than knowledge of great men in the present; we know their remoter consequences. The dock brings a like illumination.

Here an individual story comes to its end in a collision with the community. Every case has its unique intellectual and spiritual significance. The appearance of the accused person, the changes in his face and voice, his agreement with society as disclosed by the witnesses who approve of him, his conflict with society as disclosed by the witnesses who disapprove of him, his relation to the crime of which he is truly or falsely accused, always reveal a special case. But the crime which he committed, if he was justly accused, or the other crime which was committed by the representatives of society if he was falsely accused, has always the same cause; refusal to respect the individuality of another or others. A world in which each man respected the soul of all other men, no matter how little they seemed to merit respect, would be crimeless.

There is an obvious political implication to be drawn from this. The authoritarian state is *ipso facto* criminal. When I covered the trial of William Joyce ("Lord Haw-Haw") for the *New Yorker* I saw a man in the dock who was doubly criminal. He had committed crimes against the law out of his desire to substitute a criminal state for a state which, if not completely innocent, aimed at the innocence of freedom. It was obviously doubtful if he would ever have been guilty of any offense had he not been tainted by this political guilt. But when his actual offense against the law was examined it was seen that he had acted in a manner which had long been extolled by many who were in theory pure of that guilt and firmly opposed to the authoritarian state.

Almost all contemporary left-wing writers of this generation and the last attacked the idea of nationalism. It was true that many of these attacks were made under the delusion that the words nationalism and imperialism mean the same thing, whereas nationalism— which means simply a special devotion of a people to its own material and spiritual achievements—implies no desire for the annexation of other territories and enslavement of other peoples. But a great many of these attacks were made under no such apprehension. It was genuinely felt that it was pure superstition which required a man to feel any warmer emotion about his own land, race, and people than about any other. Why then should any man feel a lump in his throat when he saw his flag or the statue at the harbor gate of his native land, or feel that in a dispute between his people and another he must obey the will of his kin and not aid their enemy?

I watched the trial of William Joyce, and of all traitors who were charged in courts which I could conveniently attend. They had all cleared their throats of that lump, they had all made that transit of frontiers recommended by the nationalists; and this had landed them in the service of the persecutors of reason, the fanatical believers in frontiers as the demarcation lines between the saved and the damned. But as their lives were unfolded it appeared that none of them had cast off their nationalist prejudice because of their strength, but had been divested of it by maladjusted ambition, by madness, by cowardice, by weakness. It seemed as if contemporary rationalists had been wrong, and I remembered that the trouble about man is twofold. He cannot learn truths which are too complicated; he forgets truths which are too simple. After I had seen twenty traitors tried it seemed to me that the reason why they were in the dock, why intellectuals preach against nationalism, is that we have forgotten certain simple truths.

We have forgotten that we live outward from the center of a circle and that what is nearest to the center is most real to us. If a man cut his hand, it hurts him more than if he cuts some other man's hand; therefore he is more careful to guard his own. Even if he spend his whole life in teaching himself that we are all of one body, and that therefore his neighbor's pain is his also, he will still suffer more when his own hand is hurt, for the message then runs straight from his palm and fingers to his brain, traveling at a speed faster than light or sound, which bear the news of others' accidents. Throughout his life it remains true that what is nearest to his body is of greatest interest to his mind. When a baby is given food and held warmly by a certain woman, he grows up to feel a closer concern for her than for other women of her generation, and at her death will feel greatly disturbed. Should he be institution-bred and have no woman as his particular slave and tyrant, grievance will sour him till his last day.

If in his maturity he should live with a woman for any considerable period of time, he and she are apt, unless they are overtaken by certain obviously disagreeable circumstances, to behave as though there were a complete community of interest between them. There must have been some instinctive liking between them or they would never have been drawn together in the first place; they became involved in each other's prosperity; experience has taught each how the other will behave in most eventualities. Therefore they do better by one another than strangers would. Should he have children by this or any other woman, they will have great power over him, while other children will have little or none. He will know so much more about them. The veiled moment of their conception is his secret, and resemblances to him, to a familiar woman, or to his kin enable him to trace their inner lives, disguised though they be first by their inarticulateness and then by their articulateness. He can read them by the light of his own nature, and read his own nature by their light, and will have a sense of fusion between himself and those who are so inextricably tangled with that self.

If that man live in a house during the days of his childhood, he will know it better than any house he lives in later, though it shelter him forty years longer; and though the staircase wind as deviously as any in the world he will find his way down it in the darkness as surely as if it were straight. All his life long, when he hears talk of woods, he shall see beechwoods, if he come from a Buckinghamshire village, and a castle to him shall stand on Castle Rock, if Edinburgh was his home, and in the one case he shall know Southern English country folk, and in the other Lowland Scottish townsfolk, better than other Britons. Born and bred in England, he will find it easier to understand the English than the rest of men, not for any mystical reason, but because their language is his, because he is fully acquainted with their customs, and because he is the product of their common history. So also each continent enjoys a vague unity of self-comprehension, and is divided from the others by a sharp disunity; and even those who profess the closest familiarity with the next world speak with more robust certainty of this world and seem not to want to leave it.

This is not to say that a man loves what is nearest to him. He may hate his parents, his wife, and his children. Millions have done so. On the tables of the Law it was written "Honor thy father and thy mother, as the Lord God hath commanded thee; that thy days may be prolonged, and that it may go well with thee in the land which the Lord thy God giveth thee," and it is advice of almost gross practicality aimed at preventing the faithful from abandoning themselves to their natural impulses and wasting all their force on family rows. St. Paul, that great artist who perpetually betrayed his art because he was also a great man of action, and constantly abandoned the search for truth to seek instead a myth to inspire vigorous action, tried to gild the bondage of man to the familiar. "So ought men to love their own wives as their own body," he says. "He that loveth his wife loveth himself. For no man ever yet hated his own flesh, but nourished it and cherisheth it, even as the Lord the Church." But countless men have hated their own flesh. Everywhere and at all times men have carried such hatred to the point of slaying it, and still more have persecuted it by abstinence and mortification and debauchery. It has a value to them far above their loathing or their liking. It is their own flesh and they can have no direct experience of any other. Not with all the gold in the world or by incessant prayer can we obtain another instrument-case, packed with these our only instruments, the five senses, by which alone we can irradiate the universe that is a black void around us, and build a small irradiated platform in that darkness. A wife is someone who has stood on that irradiated platform long enough to be fully examined and to add the testimony of her own sense as to the nature of that encircling mystery. She may be loved or hated, or loved and hated, and serve in that research.

A child knows that what is near is easier for him to handle than what is far. All men took it for granted till recent times, when it was challenged, together with some other traditional assumptions, not because they had proved unsound, but because a number of urbanized populations from which the intellectual classes were largely drawn had lost their sense of spiritual as well as material process. They had lost their sense of material process owing to the development of the machine; goods which had formerly been produced by simple and comprehensible processes, often carried on where they could be witnessed by the consumer, were now produced by elaborate processes, not to be grasped by people without mechanical training, and carried on in the privacy of the large factories.

The reason for their ignorance of spiritual process was the urban lack of the long memory and the omniscient gossip enjoyed by the village. The townsman is surrounded by people whose circumstances he does not know and whose heredities are the secrets of other districts; and he is apt to take their dissimulating faces and their clothed bodies as the sum of them. People began to think of each other in a new way; as simple with a simplicity in fact unknown in organic life. They ignored the metabolism of human nature, by which experiences are absorbed into the mind and magically converted into personality, which rejects much of the material life brings to it and handles the rest to serve the interests of love or hate, good or evil, life or death, according to an inhabiting daemon, whose reasons are never given. Man conceived himself as living reasonably under the instruction of the five senses, which tell him to seek pleasure and avoid pain.

The first effect of this rational conception of life was cheerful vulgarity; and there are worse things than that. Man might well have felt this view of his destiny as a relief after the Christian philosophy, which abased his origin to criminality, and started him so low only to elevate him to the height, most disagreeable to most people, of company with godhead, after dragging him through all sorts of unpalatable experiences, including participation in a violent and apparently unnecessary death. In so far as a man adopted the new and rationalist philosophy he could be compared to an actor who, after spending a lifetime playing Hamlet and Othello and King Lear, retires to keep a country pub. All was thenceforward to go at a peaceable jog-trot. Children were to grow up straight strip-lings of light, undeformed by repression, unscarred by conflicts, because their parents would hand them over in their earliest years to the care of pedagogic experts. Divorce was not to be reckoned as a disgrace nor as tragedy nor even as a failure, but as a pleasurable extension of experience, like travel. Furthermore—and this was considered as the sanest adjustment of all—the ardors of patriotism were to be abandoned, and replaced by a cool resolution to place one's country on a level with all others in one's affections, and to hand it over without concern to the dominion of any other power which could offer it greater material benefits. It was not out of cynicism that the benefits demanded were material: it was believed that the material automatically produced the intellectual and the spiritual. These reasonable steps having been taken, there was to follow harmony. The only peril was that it might become too sweet.

But the five senses had evidently not been rightly understood. Such children as were surrendered by their parents to expert treatment, complained against that surrender as if it had been any other kind of abandonment. They quarreled with the pedagogues as much as they would have quarreled with their parents; but, the bond of the flesh being absent, there was something sapless in their quarrels, and there was less energy engendered. Sexual life was not noticeably smoother than it had been. The epic love of marriage and the lyric love-song of the encounter both lost much by the pretense that they were the same. Nor, as patriotism was discredited, did peace come nearer. Indeed, the certainty of war now arched over the earth like a second sky, inimical to the first. If harmony had been our peril, we were preserved from it, both within and without. For it was plain that, as Christian philosophy had so harshly averred, the world was a stage on which an extraordinary drama, not yet fully comprehended by the intellect, was being performed; and its action was now an agony. But, owing to the adoption of the rationalist philosophy, some of the actors filling the most important parts were now incapable of speaking their lines. It appeared that *Hamlet* and *Othello* and *King Lear* would be no longer cathartic tragedies but repellent and distressing farces if the leading characters had, in the climactic scenes, been overtaken by the delusion that they had retired and were keeping country pubs.

So the evil moment came and was clear: not surpassed in evil since the days of the barbarian invasions. The devil of nationalism had been driven out of man, but he had not become the headquarters of the dove. Instead there had entered into him the seven devils of internationalism, and he was torn by their frenzies. Then what is against all devils came to his aid. The achievement (which, as yet, is unfinished, since peace does not reign) was accomplished by a continuance of the drama in spite of the difficulties created by the rationalist philosophy. Since the actors cast to play the leading parts would not speak, the action was carried on by the peoples who used to walk to and fro at the back of the scene, softly laughing or softly weeping, or simply quietly being. Now these people streamed across the continents, inscribing their beliefs on the surface of the earth by the course of their flights, and on the sites of their martyrdoms. They defeated fascism by not being fascist. They showed the contrast between fascism and nonfascism so clearly that the world, wishing to live, defended their side because it could be seen that they were the representatives of life. As they exorcised the devils from the body of Europe they seemed to affirm certain values. It was perhaps true that the origin of man was in criminality, for once a community refused to make the effort of seeking the company of godhead it certainly became criminal. It was perhaps true that hedonism is an impotent gospel, for now it could be seen that pleasure means nothing to many men. As fast as those who ran to save their lives ran those who ran to slay them, even if their pursuit, pressed too hard, might change them into fugitives, whose own lives were in danger. Now the scorned bonds of the flesh asserted their validity. It was the final and unbearable misery of these flights that husbands were separated from their wives, and parents lost sight of their children. The men who performed the cruelest surgery on these families, who threw the husband and wife into the gas chamber while the children traveled by train to an unkown destination, had themselves been brought up to condemn their own ties of blood. The anguish of the divided was obviously holy. The contentment of those who felt no reluctance to divide was plainly damned.

In this day of exposition those who made the other sacrifice of the near for the far, and preferred other countries to their own, proved also to be unholy. The relationship between a man and a fatherland is always disturbed by conflict, if either man or fatherland is highly developed. A man's demands for liberty must at some point challenge the limitations the state imposes on the individual for the sake of the mass. If he is to carry on the national tradition he must wrestle with those who, speaking in its name, desire to crystallize it at the point reached by the previous generation. In any case national life itself must frequently exasperate him, because it is the medium in which he is expressing himself, and every craftsman or artist is repelled by the resistance of his medium to his will. All men should have a drop or two of treason in their veins, if the nations are not to go soft like so many sleepy pears.

Yet to be a traitor is most miserable. All the men I saw in the prisoner's dock were sad as they stood their trials, not only because they were going to be punished. They would have been sad even if they had never been brought to justice. They had forsaken the familiar medium; they had trusted themselves to the mercies of those who had no reason to care for them; knowing their custodians' indifference they had lived for long in fear; and they were aware that they had thrown away their claim on those who might naturally have felt affection for them. Strangers, as King Solomon put it, were filled with their wealth, and their labors were in the house of a stranger, and they mourned at the last when their flesh and body were consumed. As a divorce sharply recalls what a happy marriage should be, so the treachery of these men recalled what a nation should be; a shelter where all talents are generously recognized, all forgivable oddities forgiven, all viciousness quietly frustrated, and those who lack talent honored for equivalent contributions of graciousness. Each of these men was as dependent on the good opinion of others as one is oneself; they needed a nation which was also a hearth, and their capacity for suffering made it tragic that they had gone out from their own hearth to suffer among strangers, because the intellectual leaders of their time had professed a philosophy which was scarcely more than a lapse of memory, and had forgotten, that a hearth gives out warmth.

C. E. M. JOAD

****

LONDON
JANUARY, 1950

DEAR MR. BURNETT:

.... *Excluding books of mine on technical philosophy,* Decadence *is, I think, a book reasonably representative of my later writings and I would as lief see a selection from that book as from any other in your anthology.*

I would suggest two passages, the first beginning on page 29, line 1 "Yet while our mastery of means . . . p. 34 (bottom) need for the vulgarisateur *arises." And page 251, "The universe as I have suggested . . . page 255, to "peters out altogether."*

As for the paragraph on what I mean by the phrase "the dropping of the object," the phrase refers to a tendency which pervades modern thinking, to translate statements about "things" and "objects" into statements about the person or persons making the statement. Thus, when confronted with an aesthetic object, we translate "This picture is beautiful" into "This human being is experiencing certain sensations or emotions when he experiences the picture," on the ground that "beauty is in the eye of the beholder." When confronted with an ethical object we translate the judgment "this is right," into "so-and-so is experiencing certain emotions of approval in regard to this," on the ground that "nothing is right or wrong but thinking makes it so."

Again, under the influence of psychology, when a person expresses an opinion or a judgment of any question, instead of considering whether the opinion or judgment is true—which, after all, is what matters—we enquire "what are the considerations in his personal life and history which led him to entertain the opinion or to pass the judgment?" Thus in a variety of ways we "drop the object" by so analyzing and interpreting thought as to make it refer, not to that to which it purports to refer, namely the outside world, but to the mind or personality of the thinker.

C. E. M. JOAD

****

Decadence

THE FUNCTION OF PHILOSOPHY

WHILE OUR MASTERY of means grows apace, our knowledge of ends remains stationary or even diminishes. It is probable that men today know less of the art of life, its values, its duties and its pleasures, than the average male citizen of Renaissance Italy or of fifth-century B.C. Athens. Yet almost all of us are today educated to the point of being able to read. Hence arises, as it seems to me, a challenge to essay the task which philosophy has traditionally tried to perform, that of giving such information and guidance as the wisdom of the past may have to offer as to the meaning of life and the way it should be lived. This function contemporary philosophers largely disavow. They accept no duty of trying to enlighten the mind, to guide the opinions or correct the values of the public. Rather, confronted by the stresses of our time, they withdraw from the vulgarity of contacts which would, they feel, cheapen themselves and their work. The results of this withdrawal I venture to put in the words of the late Professor Collingwood:

'Since one must not seek it from thinkers or from ideals or from principles, one must look (for guidance) to people who were not thinkers (but fools), to processes that were not thinking (but passion), to aims that were not ideals (but caprices), and to rules that were not principles (but rules of expediency). If philosophers had wanted to train up a generation of Englishmen and Englishwomen expressly as the potential dupes of every adventurer in morals or politics, commerce or religion who should appeal to their emotions and promise them private gains which he neither could procure them nor even meant to procure them, no better way of doing it could have been discovered.'

A second reason for the special need of philosophy in our time is in part derived from the first. For the gulf between theory and practice, between ends and means, which science has accentuated is far from being the only reason for the metaphysical and moral agnosticism of the age. A second is to be found in the fact that for the first time in the history of civilized man most people grow to maturity without a creed to focus their aspirations or a code to guide their steps. Millions today hold no belief of any kind either about the way in which the universe is ordered, or about the way in which life ought to be lived. For the lack of a creed is only too often responsible for the abandonment of a code. A large part of morality has in all ages sprung from a desire to please God, a desire which the prospect of the respective consequences of His pleasure and displeasure, consequences which most religions have painted in the liveliest colours, has done much to intensify. When heavenly rewards and hellish punishments are no longer operative to attract and to deter, the incentive to observe the traditional restraints is correspondingly diminished. A number of other factors contribute to the same result, of which the most important is the international situation. The nightmare fear of war has for years operated like a shutter cutting off the prospect of the future and investing with a remote and somewhat academic air the injunction to adopt what may be described as a long-term attitude to life with all that it implies in the way of discipline and training in the present in the interests of character-building for the future. The fear of the atomic bomb and of what it holds in store for our civilization takes pride of place in any estimate of prospects for the future. 'Let us eat and drink for tomorrow the atomic bomb falls,' is an understandable creed in a situation in which to postpone the fruition of the more obvious desires seems tantamount to forgoing them altogether.

The more intellectually sophisticated embrace a miscellany of different creeds and cults, turning from one to another with the changing waves of intellectual fashion. Reflecting upon the contemporary scene one is impressed with the terrifying topicality of Plato's picture of the democratic man in the eighth book of the Republic.

Plato proceeds to point out that sooner or later the democratic way of life is found unsatisfying. Sooner or later a single tyrant desire will dominate the others, or men will submit themselves to the tyranny of an external authority in order to escape the tyranny of their own passions. This has already happened on the continent of Europe. In England young people have for years past been accumulating a fund of unexpended seriousness which only awaits a suitable channel through which to pour. It is in the existence in all the countries of Western civilization of masses of disillusioned young men with energies untapped, minds unextended, and loyalties unawakened that lie civilization's danger and the philosopher's opportunity. It was a precisely similar opportunity that Socrates, Plato and Aristotle were anxious to seize, holding it to be part of the function of philosophy both to prescribe ends for conduct and rules for their attainment. Plato, in particular, sought to make the Academy a school of political planning from which statesmen and legislators might issue to put into practice for the guidance of mankind the lessons which philosophy had taught. No parallel anxiety is shown, no parallel endeavour made by contemporary philosophers.

The predicament of the contemporary individual is largely reflected in that of his society. For it, too, lacks any agreed assurance as to the ends to which its overwhelmingly powerful means should be directed. In so far as it entertains any conscious doctrine of ends, it tends to identify them with the maximum production and equal distribution of commodities. The mastery of matter places in our hands unprecedented powers of destruction, yet we show ourselves no wiser than our predecessors in regard to the use we make of them. Hence, it is not sufficient to show that those who direct our societies are not morally worse or intellectually more stupid than the rulers and statesmen of the past; nor, indeed, are they. It is necessary to point to the obligation which is laid upon them to be better and wiser, precisely because the powers they wield are greater. Hence arises a third challenge to philosophy to perform its traditional function by indicating ends and prescribing values. If the philosopher assures us in his modesty that he has no wisdom of his own to offer, he should at least remember that he is the official repository of the philosophical wisdom of the past and that it is his duty to transmit and interpret it for the guidance of a distracted present.

I emphasize the words 'the philosophical wisdom of the past' because they enable me to disclaim the suggestion that I have any of my own to offer. I am not proposing in this book to lay bare some new revelation, for none has been vouchsafed to me. Nor do I claim a wisdom superior to that of scientists or of men of affairs. I claim only to have some acquaintance with the thought both of Greece and Christianity which constitute at once the main sources and the dominant strands of the intellectual tradition of Western Europe. I think that we neglect this tradition at our peril. It is the tradition of a liberal and humane civilization which values personal freedom and is willing, at least in theory, to treat the individual as an end in himself and not merely as a means to ends other than his own. For the past fifty years the soul of liberal civilization in Europe has been dying and with the decay of the informing spirit, the body also has begun to collapse. Unless the spirit can be restored to it, the civilization of Europe will fall. Either it will succumb to the social and political chaos resulting from years of internecine warfare or it will be borne down by alien traditions deriving from different sources.

I think that the threat from the totalitarian States, when seen in its true perspective, may well reveal itself as the contemporary version of the secular pattern of history, whereby the barbarians break into and disrupt older and by comparison effete civilizations. The threat offered by the Nazis has been successfully averted, but it still exists in a different form in the growing power of totalitarian Russia. It is in this situation that, as I conceive, the philosopher is called upon to perform what I have called his traditional function and to interpret in the light of the Graeco-Christian tradition the accumulating factual knowledge of the twentieth century which is at once so bewildering and so unassimilable.

More precisely, it is assimilated in bits since those who have mastered one department of it are increasingly ignorant of what lies outside their special sphere. I deduce that one of the needs of our time is the need for synopsis followed by synthesis on the part of those who, because they have viewed synoptically, have viewed also in perspective. It is only in the light of a perspective that the relative values of different ends can be graded and assessed. If the perspective is provided by the synoptic view, the assessment should be in terms of the scale of values established by the Graeco-Christian tradition and embodied in the *philosophia perennis* which, beginning with Plato and continuing through Plotinus, comes down to us through the scholastic philosophers of the early Christian centuries, forms part of the Catholic philosophy of the Christian Church, was reaffirmed in England in the seventeenth and eighteenth centuries by the Cambridge Platonists and which, though except by Catholics comparatively neglected today, may still rank as the dominant tradition in our philosophy.

The task of the philosopher is, then, I conceive, first to endeavour to see as a whole and so to obtain a perspective for valuation; then, in the light of his concept of values, to grade and assess; thirdly, to make plain his results for the benefit of others, seeking both to present his perspective and to convey the valuations which he has made within it. This, the work of the *vulgarisateur*—there is no exact English equivalent for the man who spreads with clarity, vividness, force and accuracy, the knowledge obtained by and the wisdom derived from others—seems to me to be the work which philosophers are particularly fitted by their training and tradition to undertake.

This precisely was the task which, over four centuries ago, Erasmus set himself to perform in a time of similar chaos at the end of the fifteenth and the beginning of the sixteenth centuries. Himself a learned man, he was one of the first to set the task of communicating knowledge above that of increasing it. As H. A. L. Fisher says of him in his *History of Europe:* 'he was a citizen of the world, interested in conduct above all things, and quite as much concerned with popularizing knowledge as with extending it.' And the knowledge which he sought to popularize was precisely that tradition of classical and Christian culture which was then and which is still the common possession of Western and Central Europe and of which the world today stands desperately in need.

Erasmus's primary concerns were that the Scriptures should be translated into every language and that the teachings both of Plato and of Christ be disinterred from the deposits of centuries of theological and academic disputation under which they had been buried. A similar task has been undertaken in our own time by H. G. Wells who has done more than any other of his contemporaries to educate adult men and women. While his main concern has been the elucidation of the relation of science to human affairs, he has also in his *Outline of History* provided a perspective within which the course of those affairs can be viewed as a whole. Thus, instead of seeing history as a number of little lighted patches environed by an enormous darkness, many of us were for the first time enabled to survey man's past as a continuous process. I believe that a similar task awaits philosophy today; I do not, of course, mean that I think this to be its only task, but I think that it is an important one and that it is not performed.

The Adult Education movement performs something of this office for those whose education has been cut short at fourteen and, taking all knowledge for its province, seeks to make working men and women free of the cultural inheritance of our civilization and to acquaint them with what great men have thought and said memorably about life. But for the so-called educated no provision of a similar kind is made.

At the Universities diminishing numbers pursue the humane studies, while oppressed by the growing departmentalization of knowledge, scientists, administrators and executives have no time to travel outside the spheres of the specialized techniques in which they are instructed. As a result, they go through life without that perspective of principle and value in the light of which educated men have in the past sought to regulate conduct and view the universe.

Immersed in the studies of their special departments, they simply do not know what the great philosophers and teachers of mankind have said about man's life and how it should be lived, or about man's communities and how they should be run. I do not wish to suggest that civilization depends upon men's willingness to devote at least a proportion of their time to making themselves acquainted with and pondering upon the wisdom which men have distilled through the long centuries from monasteries and cells, from libraries and studies, even from habitations in the desert; yet, one is sometimes tempted to think, our civilization cannot survive in its continued absence. It is from these considerations that the need for the *vulgarisateur* arises.

THE CULTURE OF THE MANY

THE UNIVERSE, as I have suggested, consists of different orders or levels of being. One such order or level of being is deity. Deity is manifested in what we know as values. The most eminent of the values, as they are the most easily apprehensible by us, are goodness, truth and beauty. Deity and the values in which deity manifests itself constitute the order of being which I call reality; the spatio-temporal world which common sense knows and science explores constitutes another order of being to which, precisely because it is always changing is, that is to say, in a state of flux, Plato gave the title of 'becoming.' The world of becoming is, by the standard of reality, semi-real.

Human beings, by reason of the fact that they have bodies, belong in part to the world of becoming. They have, however, also minds; they are also, I should add, spirits. For it seems to me that the traditional division of the human being into the three categories of body, mind and spirit, which belongs to the central tradition of that *philosophia perennis* which takes its rise in Plato and runs through the scholastic philosophy of the Middle Ages down to our own time, covers more of the facts than either the dualist division into mind and body, or the psychological division into the faculties of reason, emotion, instincts, appetites, sentiments, and so on. In virtue of our being or possessing spirits, we are in some sense members of the world of reality.

I think that the mind is largely, though not wholly, determined by the body but that the spirit is, at least in part, free of the body and is a witness to the manifestation in us of another order of reality or, to put it theologically—and this after all is, I suspect, the best way to put it—a witness to the presence in us of a spark of the divine. I have chosen the words 'largely,' 'in part,' and 'in some sense' deliberately, in order to indicate the impossibility of introducing clear-cut lines of division. There is, for example, no clear-cut line between mind and spirit, and mind, therefore, is not wholly determined by body, nor spirit wholly free of body; nor is it true to say without qualification that the spirit is the immanence of the divine. It is, however, I believe substantially correct to think of man as a member of two orders of being; of the sensory world to which his body belongs, which he experiences through his senses and knows with his mind, and of the real world in which he participates by virtue of his spirit. The real world is primarily revealed to us in the knowledge of values, in moral experience, in the appreciation of beauty and in the recognition of truth. But this knowledge is not merely an activity of the mind, but is itself infused with spirit. In other words, it is because we are ourselves participators in reality that we are enabled to know it.

I further believe that it is natural to man to endeavour to increase in respect of his participation in and knowledge of reality. As the poets and mystics have put it, he seeks for permanence amid change and decay, for perfection amid imperfections or, more simply, for God. As I have put it in this book, he aspires after truth, goodness and beauty, which in their degree are made manifest to him in his present condition. He seeks, therefore, to know, to become a better man and to appreciate beauty. It is chiefly by reason of this attribute that he is differentiated from the beasts, is, in fact, a being set apart. Beauty, truth, and goodness in all the different modes of their manifestation, in art and literature, in nature, in science, in scholarship and in learning, in good actions, fine characters and just institutions are all, in their different ways, included within the meaning of the term, the 'object.' Thus, in seeking to know the 'object,' in striving after it and in communing with it, man is fulfilling the demands of his spirit, and aspiring after reality. I have also maintained that value belongs to the 'object' but not, except derivatively, to the mind that knows it, the relation of the mind to value being that of knowing, of appreciating, of striving after, but not that of embodying. But I have excepted from this generalization the indwelling of value as goodness in the human personality.

A decadent age is one in which the 'object' is lost or in which its character of independence is denied, with the result that value, instead of being recognized in the object known, is appropriated by the knowing mind and so becomes identified with the experience of the knower. This identification is chiefly met with at the higher aesthetic and intellectual level, that is to say, in the minds of those who mould the thought and set the standards of the community, the level of the artists, novelists, thinkers, scholars, scientists and political leaders. At lower levels, at, for example, the level of ordinary folk who are not and never have been conscious strivers after the good, the beautiful and the true, the symptoms are different. It would not, for example, be true to say of them that they 'dropped' an 'object' which they never consciously apprehended; or that they tend consciously to adopt a subjectivist analysis of judgment or deliberately to concentrate upon experience as an end in itself. The many, in short, are not philosophers. For them at nearly all times and, indeed, for all of us at most times, the 'object' is food, drink, money, games, amusement, desirable positions, houses, sport, the other sex. All these 'objects' belong to the spatio-temporal order, nor have we any temptation to analyse them on subjectivist lines as merely modes of our own experience. At this level what I have called the 'dropping of the object' exhibits itself in an extreme concentration upon material things and material values, in an indifference to beauty, a semi-contemptuous patronage of art, a depreciation of knowledge for its own sake combined with a purely utilitarian attitude to education, in a decline in respect of the practice of the specifically Christian virtues, notably compassion, gentleness, humility and mercy—above all, in an indifference to or contempt of religion which expresses itself in an aggressive scepticism combined with an absence of religious experience and a disinclination to concern oneself one way or the other with the matters which belong traditionally to religion's sphere.

In so far as this attitude receives conscious expression in the formulation of doctrine, it may be recognized in such phrases as 'beauty is in the eye of the beholder,' 'I don't know anything about art but I do know what I like,' one man's taste is as good as another's,' 'there's nothing good or bad but thinking makes it so,' 'religion is wish fulfilment' or 'the opium of the people.' I want to consider how far these symptoms may be discerned in our own age.

I shall draw my examples chiefly from these two spheres and for two reasons. Art and literature are, if I am right, among the responses of the human spirit to reality manifested as value. Now this is not a religious age and, so far as that direct response to reality which mystics and others have made is concerned, the spirit of Western man sleeps. We are, in other words, poor in respect of religious experience. (With the response of the human mind to the value of truth I have, by implication, been engaged and am, indeed, still engaged. In philosophy the 'dropping of the object' expresses itself in a refusal to apply the philosophical method to its traditional subject matter, that is to say, to a consideration of the nature of the universe as a whole, or to the problems and distresses of our times and the mode of their alleviation. My attempt is a modest one to bring philosophy back to what I take to be its traditional function.)

Since religion remains a closed preserve for most of us, the spirit of contemporary man is moved chiefly by beauty. Beauty in art, music and nature is, indeed, the chief spiritual food of our generation; beauty is, as it were, the stop gap which keeps us spiritually alive until either religion comes once more into its own, or the flickering spirit peters out altogether.

GRAHAM GREENE

****

A literary craftsman whose novels have brought him a distinguished reputation, Graham Greene selected for this volume one of the nineteen short stories which, over a period of years, he has written between his longer works. The short story, Mr. Greene concedes, "is an exacting form. . . ." In this odd story of a 10-year-old who would not betray the Host even for a bribe of his heart's desire is a characteristic example of Mr. Greene's style and particularly of his insight into the mind and fears of a child.

****

The Hint of an Explanation

A LONG TRAIN JOURNEY on a late December evening, in this new version of peace, is a dreary experience. I suppose that my fellow traveller and I could consider ourselves lucky to have a compartment to ourselves, even though the heating apparatus was not working, even though the lights went out entirely in the frequent Pennine tunnels and were too dim anyway for us to read our books without straining our eyes, and though there was no restaurant car to give at least a change of scene. It was when we were trying simultaneously to chew the same kind of dry bun bought at the same station buffet that my companion and I came together. Before that we had sat at opposite ends of the carriage, both muffled to the chin in overcoats, both bent low over type we could barely make out, but as I threw the remains of my cake under the seat our eyes met, and he laid his book down.

By the time we were half-way to Bedwell Junction we had found an enormous range of subjects for discussion; starting with buns and the weather, we had gone on to politics, the government, foreign affairs, the atom bomb, and, by an inevitable progression, God. We had not, however, become either shrill or acid. My companion, who now sat opposite me, leaning a little forward, so that our knees nearly touched, gave such an impression of serenity that it would have been impossible to quarrel with him, however much our views differed, and differ they did profoundly.

I had soon realized I was speaking to a Catholic, to someone who believed—how do they put it?—in an omnipotent and omniscient Deity, while I was what is loosely called an Agnostic. I have a certain intuition (which I do not trust, founded as it may well be on childish experiences and needs) that a God exists, and I am surprised occasionally into belief by the extraordinary coincidences that beset our path like the traps set for leopards in the jungle, but intellectually I am revolted at the whole notion of such a God who can so abandon his creatures to the enormities of Free Will. I found myself expressing this view to my companion, who listened quietly and with respect. He made no attempt to interrupt: he showed none of the impatience or the intellectual arrogance I have grown to expect from Catholics; when the lights of a wayside station flashed across his face that had escaped hitherto the rays of the one globe working in the compartment, I caught a glimpse suddenly of—what? I stopped speaking, so strong was the impression. I was carried back ten years, to the other side of the great useless conflict, to a small town, Gisors in Normandy. I was again, for a moment, walking on the ancient battlements and looking down across the grey roofs, until my eyes for some reason lit on one grey stony "back" out of the many, where the face of a middle-aged man was pressed against a windowpane (I suppose that face has ceased to exist now, just as I believe the whole town with its medieval memories has been reduced to rubble). I remembered saying to myself with astonishment, "That man is happy—completely happy." I looked across the compartment at my fellow traveller, but his face was already again in shadow. I said weakly, "When you think what God—if there is a God—allows. It's not merely the physical agonies, but think of the corruption, even of children. . . ."

He said, "Our view is so limited," and I was disappointed at the conventionality of his reply. He must have been aware of my disappointment (it was as though our thoughts were huddled as closely as ourselves for warmth), for he went on, "Of course there is no answer here. We catch hints . . ." and then the train roared into another tunnel and the lights again went out. It was the longest tunnel yet; we went rocking down it, and the cold seemed to become more intense with the darkness like an icy fog (perhaps when one sense—of sight—is robbed of sensation, the others grow more sensitive). When we emerged into the mere grey of night and the globe lit up once more, I could see that my companion was leaning back on his seat.

I repeated his last words as a question, "Hints?"

"Oh, they mean very little in cold print—or cold speech," he said, shivering in his overcoat. "And they mean nothing at all to a human being other than the man who catches them. They are not scientific evidence—or evidence at all for that matter. Events that don't, somehow, turn out as they were intended—by the human actors I mean, or by the thing behind the human actors."

"The thing?"

"The word Satan is so anthropomorphic."

I had to lean forward now: I wanted to hear what he had to say. I am—I really am, God knows—open to conviction.

He said, "One's words are so crude, but I sometimes feel pity for that thing. It is so continually finding the right weapon to use against its Enemy and the weapon breaks in its own breast. It sometimes seems to me so—powerless. You said something just now about the corruption of children. It reminded me of something in my own childhood. You are the first person—except for one—that I have thought of telling it to, perhaps because you are anonymous. It's not a very long story, and in a way it's relevant."

I said, "I'd like to hear it."

"You mustn't expect too much meaning. But to me there seems to be a hint. That's all. A hint."

He went slowly on, turning his face to the pane, though he could have seen nothing real in the whirling world outside except an occasional signal lamp, a light in a window, a small country station torn backwards by our rush, picking his words with precision. He said, "When I was a child they taught me to serve at Mass. The church was a small one, for there were very few Catholics where I lived. It was a market town in East Anglia, surrounded by flat, chalky fields and ditches—so many ditches. I don't suppose there were fifty Catholics all told, and for some reason there was a tradition of hostility to us. Perhaps it went back to the burning of a Protestant martyr in the sixteenth century—there was a stone marking the place near where the meat stalls stood on Wednesdays. I was only half aware of the enmity, though I knew that my school nickname of Popey Martin had something to do with my religion, and I had heard that my father was nearly excluded from the Constitutional Club when he first came to the town.

"Every Sunday I had to dress up in my surplice and serve Mass.

I hated it—I have always hated dressing up in any way (which is funny when you come to think of it), and I never ceased to be afraid of losing my place in the service and doing something which would put me to ridicule. Our services were at a different hour from the Anglican, and as our small, far-from-select band trudged out of the hideous chapel the whole of the townsfolk seemed to be on the way past to the proper church—I always thought of it as the proper church. We had to pass the parade of their eyes, indifferent, supercilious, mocking; you can't imagine how seriously religion can be taken in a small town, if only for social reasons.

"There was one man in particular; he was one of the two bakers in the town, the one my family did not patronize. I don't think any of the Catholics patronized him because he was called a free-thinker —an odd title, for, poor man, no one's thoughts were less free than his. He was hemmed in by his hatred—his hatred of us. He was very ugly to look at, with one wall-eye and a head the shape of a turnip, with the hair gone on the crown, and he was unmarried. He had no interests, apparently, but his baking and his hatred, though now that I am older I begin to see other sides to his nature —it did contain, perhaps, a certain furtive love. One would come across him suddenly sometimes on a country walk, especially if one were alone and it was Sunday. It was as if he rose from the ditches, and the smear of chalk on his clothes reminded one of the flour on his working overalls. He would have a stick in his hand and stab at the hedges, and if his mood were very black he would call out after one strange abrupt words like a foreign tongue—I know the mean-ing of those words, of course, now. Once the police went to his house because of what a boy said he'd seen, but nothing came of it except that the hate shackled him closer. His name was Blacker and he terrified me.

"I think he had a particular hatred of my father—I don't know why. My father was manager of the Midland Bank, and it's possible that at some time Blacker may have had unsatisfactory dealings with the bank; my father was a very cautious man who suffered all his life from anxiety about money—his own and other people's. If I try and picture Blacker now I see him walking along a narrowing path between high windowless walls, and at the end of the path stands a small boy of ten—me. I don't know whether it's a symbolic picture or the memory of one of our encounters—our encounters somehow got more and more frequent. You talked just now about the corruption of children. That poor man was preparing to revenge

himself on everything he hated—my father, the Catholics, the God
whom people persisted in crediting—and that by corrupting me.
He had evolved a horrible and ingenious plan.

"I remember the first time I had a friendly word from him. I was
passing his shop as rapidly as I could when I heard his voice call
out with a kind of sly subservience as though he were an under
servant. 'Master David,' he called, 'Master David,' and I hurried
on. But the next time I passed that way he was at his door (he
must have seen me coming) with one of those curly cakes in his
hand that we called Chelsea buns. I didn't want to take it, but he
made me, and then I couldn't be other than polite when he asked
me to come into his parlour behind the shop and see something
very special.

"It was a small electric railway—a rare sight in those days, and
he insisted on showing me how it worked. He made me turn the
switches and stop and start it, and he told me that I could come
in any morning and have a game with it. He used the word 'game'
as though it were something secret, and it's true that I never told
my family of this invitation and of how, perhaps twice a week those
holidays, the desire to control that little railway become overpowering, and looking up and down the street to see if I were observed,
I would dive into the shop."

Our larger, dirtier, adult train drove into a tunnel and the light
went out. We sat in darkness and silence, with the noise of the train
blocking our ears like wax. When we were though we didn't speak
at once and I had to prick him into continuing. "An elaborate
seduction," I said.

"Don't think his plans were as simple as that," my companion
said, "or as crude. There was much more hate than love, poor man,
in his make-up. Can you hate something you don't believe in? And
yet he called himself a free-thinker. What an impossible paradox,
to be free and to be so obsessed. Day by day all through those holidays his obsession must have grown, but he kept a grip; he bided
his time. Perhaps that thing I spoke of gave him the strength and
the wisdom. It was only a week from the end of the holidays that
he spoke to me on what concerned him so deeply.

"I heard him behind me as I knelt on the floor, coupling two
coaches. He said, 'You won't be able to do this, Master David, when
school starts.' It wasn't a sentence that needed any comment from
me any more than the one that followed. 'You ought to have it for
your own, you ought,' but how skilfully and unemphatically he had
sowed the longing, the idea of a possibility. . . . I was coming to

his parlour every day now; you see, I had to cram every opportunity
in before the hated term started again, and I suppose I was becoming accustomed to Blacker, to that wall-eye, that turnip head, that
nauseating subservience. The Pope, you know, describes himself as
'the servant of the servants of God,' and Blacker—I sometimes think
that Blacker was 'the servant of the servants of . . . ,' well, let it be.

"The very next day, standing in the doorway watching me play,
he began to talk to me about religion. He said, with what untruth
even I recognized, how much he admired the Catholics; he wished
he could believe like that, but how could a baker believe? He ac-
cented 'a baker' as one might say a biologist, and the tiny train
spun round the gauge 0 track. He said, 'I can bake the things you
eat just as well as any Catholic can,' and disappeared into his shop.
I hadn't the faintest idea what he meant. Presently he emerged
again, holding in his hand a little wafer. 'Here,' he said, 'eat that
and tell me. . . .' When I put it in my mouth I could tell that it
was made in the same way as our wafers for communion—he had
got the shape a little wrong, that was all—and I felt guilty and
irrationally scared. 'Tell me,' he said, 'what's the difference?'

" 'Difference?' I asked.

" 'Isn't that just the same as you eat in church?'

"I said smugly, 'It hasn't been consecrated.'

"He said, 'Do you think, if I put the two of them under a microscope, you could tell the difference?'

"But even at ten I had the answer to that question. 'No,' I said,
'the—accidents don't change,' stumbling a little on the word 'accidents' which had suddenly conveyed to me the idea of death and
wounds.

"Blacker said with sudden intensity, 'How I'd like to get one of
your ones in my mouth—just to see. . . .'

"It may seem odd to you, but this was the first time that the idea
of transsubstantiation really lodged in my mind. I had learned it all
by rote; I had grown up with the idea. The Mass was as lifeless to
me as the sentences in *De Bello Gallico;* communion a routine like
drill in the school-yard, but here suddenly I was in the presence of
a man who took it seriously, as seriously as the priest whom naturally one didn't count—it was his job. I felt more scared than ever.

"He said, 'It's all nonsense, but I'd just like to have it in my
mouth.'

" 'You could if you were a Catholic,' I said naïvely.

"He gazed at me with his one good eye, like a Cyclops. He said,
'You serve at Mass, don't you? It would be easy for you to get at

one of those things. I tell you what I'd do—I'd swap this electric
train for one of your wafers—consecrated, mind. It's got to be
consecrated.'

" 'I could get you one out of the box,' I said. I think I still
imagined that his interest was a baker's interest—to see how they
were made.

" 'Oh, no,' he said, 'I want to see what your God tastes like.'

" 'I couldn't do that.'

" 'Not for a whole electric train, just for yourself? You wouldn't
have any trouble at home. I'd pack it up and put a label inside that
your dad could see: "For my bank manager's little boy from a
grateful client." He'd be pleased as punch with that.'

"Now that we are grown men it seems a trivial temptation,
doesn't it? But try to think back to your own childhood. There was
a whole circuit of rails there on the floor at our feet, straight rails
and curved, and a little station with porters and passengers, a
tunnel, a foot-bridge, a level crossing, two signals, buffers, of course
—and, above all, a turntable. The tears of longing came into my
eyes when I looked at the turntable. It was my favorite piece—it
looked so ugly and practical and true. I said weakly, 'I wouldn't
know how.'

"How carefully he had been studying the ground! He must have
slipped several times into Mass at the back of the church. It would
have been no good, you understand, in a little town like that, presenting himself for communion. Everybody there knew him for what
he was. He said to me, 'When you've been given communion you
could just put it under your tongue a moment. He serves you and
the other boy first, and I saw you once go out behind the curtain
straight afterwards. You'd forgotten one of those little bottles.'

" 'The cruet,' I said.

" 'Pepper and salt.' He grinned at me jovially, and I—well, I
looked at the little railway which I could no longer come and play
with when term started. I said, 'You'd just swallow it, wouldn't
you?'

" 'Oh, yes,' he said. 'I'd just swallow it.'

"Somehow I didn't want to play with the train any more that
day. I got up and made for the door, but he detained me, gripping
my lapel. He said, 'This will be a secret between you and me.
Tomorrow's Sunday. You come along here in the afternoon. Put
it in an envelope and post it me. Monday morning the train will
be delivered bright and early.'

" 'Not tomorrow,' I implored him.

" 'I'm not interested in any other Sunday,' he said. 'It's your only chance.' He shook me gently backwards and forwards. 'It will always have to be a secret between you and me,' he said. 'Why, if anyone knew they'd take away the train and there'd be me to reckon with. I'd bleed you something awful. You know how I'm always about on Sunday walks. You can't avoid a man like me. I crop up. You wouldn't ever be safe in your own house. I know ways to get into houses when people are asleep.' He pulled me into the shop after him and opened a drawer. In the drawer was an odd looking key and a cut-throat razor. He said, 'That's a master key that opens all locks and that—that's what I bleed people with.' Then he patted my cheek with his plump floury fingers and said, 'Forget it. You and me are friends.'

"That Sunday Mass stays in my head, every detail of it, as though it had happened only a week ago. From the moment of the Confession to the moment of Consecration it had a terrible importance; only one other Mass has ever been so important to me—perhaps not even one, for this was a solitary Mass which would never happen again. It seemed as final as the last Sacrament when the priest bent down and put the wafer in my mouth where I knelt before the altar with my fellow server.

"I suppose I had made up my mind to commit this awful act— for, you know, to us it must always seem an awful act—from the moment when I saw Blacker watching from the back of the church. He had put on his best black Sunday clothes and, as though he could never quite escape the smear of his profession, he had a dab of dried talcum on his cheek, which he had presumably applied after using that cut-throat of his. He was watching me closely all the time, and I think it was fear—fear of that terrible undefined thing called bleeding—as much as covetousness that drove me to carry out my instructions.

"My fellow server got briskly up and, taking the paten, preceded Father Carey to the altar rail where the other communicants knelt. I had the Host lodged under my tongue: it felt like a blister. I got up and made for the curtain to get the cruet that I had purposely left in the sacristy. When I was there I looked quickly round for a hiding place and saw an old copy of the *Universe* lying on a chair. I took the Host from my mouth and inserted it between two sheets —a little damp mess of pulp. Then I thought: perhaps Father Carey has put out the paper for a particular purpose and he will find the Host before I have time to remove it, and the enormity of my act began to come home to me when I tried to imagine what punishment I should incur. Murder is sufficiently trivial to have its appropriate punishment, but for this act the mind boggled at the thought of any retribution at all. I tried to remove the Host, but it stuck clammily between the pages, and in desperation I tore out a piece of the newspaper and, screwing the whole thing up, stuck it in my trousers pocket. When I came back through the curtain carrying the cruet my eyes met Blacker's. He gave me a grin of encouragement and unhappiness—yes, I am sure, unhappiness. Was it perhaps that the poor man was all the time seeking something incorruptible?

"I can remember little more of that day. I think my mind was shocked and stunned, and I was caught up too in the family bustle of Sunday. Sunday in a provincial town is the day for relations. All the family are at home, and unfamiliar cousins and uncles are apt to arrive, packed in the back seats of other people's cars. I remember that some crowd of the kind descended on us and pushed Blacker temporarily out of the foreground of my mind. There was somebody called Aunt Lucy, with a loud hollow laugh that filled the house with mechanical merriment like the sound of recorded laughter from inside a hall of mirrors, and I had no opportunity to go out alone even if I had wished to. When six o'clock came and Aunt Lucy and the cousins departed and peace returned, it was too late to go to Blacker's, and at eight it was my own bed-time.

"I think I had half forgotten what I had in my pocket. As I emptied my pocket the little screw of newspaper brought quickly back the Mass, the priest bending over me, Blacker's grin. I laid the packet on the chair by my bed and tried to go to sleep, but I was haunted by the shadows on the wall where the curtains blew, the squeak of furniture, the rustle in the chimney, haunted by the presence of God there on the chair. The Host had always been to me—well, the Host. I knew theoretically, as I have said, what I had to believe, but suddenly, as someone whistled in the road outside, whistled secretively, knowingly, to me, I knew that this which I had beside my bed was something of infinite value—something a man would pay for with his whole peace of mind, something that was so hated one could love it as one loves an outcast or a bullied child. These are adult words, and it was a child of ten who lay scared in bed, listening to the whistle from the road, Blacker's whistle, but I think he felt fairly clearly what I am describing now. That is what I meant when I said this Thing, whatever it is, that seizes every possible weapon against God, is always, everywhere, disappointed at the moment of success. It must have felt as certain of me as Blacker did. It must have felt certain too of Blacker. But I wonder, if one knew what happened later to that poor man, whether one would not find again that the weapon had been turned against its own breast.

"At last I couldn't bear that whistle any more and got out of bed. I opened the curtains a little way, and there right under my window, the moonlight on his face, was Blacker. If I had stretched my hand down, his fingers reaching up could almost have touched mine. He looked up at me, flashing the one good eye, with hunger— I realize now that near-success must have developed his obsession almost to the point of madness. Desperation had driven him to the house. He whispered up at me. 'David, where is it?'

"I jerked my head back at the room. 'Give it me,' he said. 'Quick. You shall have the train in the morning.'

"I shook my head. He said, 'I've got the bleeder here, and the key. You'd better toss it down.'

" 'Go away,' I said, but I could hardly speak for fear.

" 'I'll bleed you first and then I'll have it just the same.'

" 'Oh, no, you won't,' I said. I went to the chair and picked it— Him—up. There was only one place where He was safe. I couldn't separate the Host from the paper, so I swallowed both. The newsprint stuck like a prune skin to the back of my throat, but I rinsed it down with water from the ewer. Then I went back to the window and looked down at Blacker. He began to wheedle me. 'What have you done with it, David? What's the fuss? It's only a bit of bread,' looking so longingly and pleadingly up at me that even as a child I wondered whether he could really think that, and yet desire it so much.

" 'I swallowed it,' I said.

" 'Swallowed it?'

" 'Yes,' I said. 'Go away.'

"Then something happened which seems to me now more terrible than his desire to corrupt or my thoughtless act: he began to weep —the tears ran lopsidedly out of the one good eye and his shoulders shook. I only saw his face for a moment before he bent his head and strode off, the bald turnip head shaking, into the dark. When I think of it now, it's almost as if I had seen that Thing weeping for its inevitable defeat. It had tried to use me as a weapon, and now I had broken in its hands and it wept its hopeless tears through one of Blacker's eyes."

The black furnaces of Bedwell Junction gathered around the line. The points switched and we were tossed from one set of rails to

another. A spray of sparks, a signal light changing to red, tall chimneys jetting into the grey night sky, the fumes of steam from stationary engines—half the cold journey was over, and now remained
the long wait for the slow cross-country train. I said, "It's an interesting story. I think I should have given Blacker what he wanted.
I wonder what he would have done with it."

"I really believe," my companion said, "that he would first of all
have put it under his microscope—before he did all the other things
I expect he had planned."

"And the hints," I said. "I don't quite see what you mean by
that."

"Oh, well," he said vaguely, "you know for me it was an odd
beginning, that affair, when you come to think of it," but I never
should have known what he meant had not his coat, when he rose
to take his bag from the rack, come open and disclosed the collar
of a priest.

I said, "I suppose you think you owe a lot to Blacker."

"Yes," he said, "you see, I am a very happy man."

ARNOLD J. TOYNBEE

****

THE ROYAL INSTITUTE OF INTERNATIONAL AFFAIRS,
10 ST. JAMES SQUARE
LONDON S. W. I.

I should be quite glad to see Chapter 8 of Civilization On Trial *republished although, alternatively, you might care to republish the chapter on history which I contributed to* The Legacy of Greece, *an Oxford book. This second suggestion is not so topical as the other, but it is a more serious piece of work which contains more of my underlying ideas.*

ARNOLD J. TOYNBEE

****

Civilization on Trial

OUR PRESENT WESTERN OUTLOOK on history is an extraordinarily contradictory one. While our historical horizon has been expanding vastly in both the space dimension and the time dimension, our historical vision—what we actually do see, in contrast to what we now could see if we chose—has been contracting rapidly to the narrow field of what a horse sees between its blinkers or what a U-boat commander sees through his periscope.

This is certainly extraordinary; yet it is only one of a number of contradictions of this kind that seem to be characteristic of the times in which we are living. There are other examples that probably loom larger in the minds of most of us. For instance, our world has risen to an unprecedented degree of humanitarian feeling. There is now a recognition of the human rights of people of all classes, nations, and races; yet at the same time we have sunk to perhaps unheard-of depths of class warfare, nationalism, and racialism. These bad passions find vent in cold-blooded, scientifically planned cruelties; and the two incompatible states of mind and standards of conduct are to be seen to-day, side by side, not merely in the same

577

world, but sometimes in the same country and even in the same soul.

Again, we now have an unprecedented power of production side by side with unprecedented shortages. We have invented machines to work for us, but have less spare labour than ever before for human service—even for such an essential and elementary service as helping mothers to look after their babies. We have persistent alternations of widespread unemployment with famines of manpower. Undoubtedly, the contrast between our expanding historical horizon and our contracting historical vision is something characteristic of our age. Yet, looked at in itself, what an astonishing contradiction it is!

Let us remind ourselves first of the recent expansion of our horizon. In space, our Western field of vision has expanded to take in the whole of mankind over all the habitable and traversable surface of this planet, and the whole stellar universe in which this planet is an infinitesimally small speck of dust. In time, our Western field of vision has expanded to take in all the civilizations that have risen and fallen during these last 6000 years; the previous history of the human race back to its genesis between 600,000 and a million years ago; the history of life on this planet back to perhaps 800 millions years ago. What a marvellous widening of our historical horizon! Yet, at the same time, our field of historical vision has been contracting; it has been tending to shrink within the narrow limits in time and space of the particular republic or kingdom of which each of us happens to be a citizen. The oldest surviving Western states— say France or England—have so far had no more than a thousand years of continuous political existence; the largest existing Western state—say Brazil or the United States—embraces only a very small fraction of the total inhabited surface of the Earth.

Before the widening of our horizon began—before our Western seamen circumnavigated the globe, and before our Western cosmogonists and geologists pushed out the bounds of our universe in both time and space—our pre-nationalist mediaeval ancestors had a broader and juster historical vision than we have to-day. For them, history did not mean the history of one's own parochial community; it meant the history of Israel, Greece, and Rome. And, even if they were mistaken in believing that the world was created in 4004 B.C., it is at any rate better to look as far back as 4004 B.C. than to look back no farther than the Declaration of Independence or the voyages of the *Mayflower* or Columbus or Hengist and Horsa. (As a matter of fact, 4004 B.C. happens, though our ancestors did not know this, to be a quite important date: it approximately marks the first appearance of representatives of the species of human society called civilizations.)

Again, for our ancestors, Rome and Jerusalem meant much more than their own home towns. When our Anglo-Saxon ancestors were converted to Roman Christianity at the end of the sixth century of the Christian era, they learned Latin, studied the treasures of sacred and profane literature to which a knowledge of the Latin language gives access, and went on pilgrimages to Rome and Jerusalem—and this in an age of difficulties and dangers of travelling. . . . Our ancestors seem to have been big-minded, and this is a great intellectual virtue as well as a great moral one, for national histories are unintelligible within their own time limits and space limits.

II

IN THE TIME DIMENSION, you cannot understand the history of England if you begin only at the coming of the English to Britain, any better than you can understand the history of the United States if you begin only at the coming of the English to North America. In the space dimension, likewise, you cannot understand the history of a country if you cut its outlines out of the map of the world and rule out of consideration anything that has originated outside that particular country's frontiers.

What are the epoch-making events in the national histories of the United States and the United Kingdom? Working back from the present towards the past, I should say they were the two world wars, the Industrial Revolution, the Reformation, the Western voyages of discovery, the Renaissance, the conversion to Christianity. Now I defy anyone to tell the history of either the United States or the United Kingdom without making these events the cardinal ones, or to explain these events as local American or local English affairs. To explain these major events in the history of any Western country, the smallest unit that one can take into account is the whole of Western Christendom. By Western Christendom I mean the Roman Catholic and Protestant world—the adherents of the Patriarchate of Rome who have maintained their allegiance to the Papacy, together with the former adherents who have repudiated it.

But the history of Western Christendom, too, is unintelligible within its own time limits and space limits. While Western Christendom is a much better unit that the United States or the United Kingdom or France for a historian to operate with, it too turns out, on inspection to be inadequate. In the time dimension, it goes back only to the close of the Dark Ages following the collapse of the western part of the Roman Empire; that is, it goes back less than 1300 years, and 1300 years is less than a quarter of the 6000 years during which the species of society represented by Western Christendom has been in existence. Western Christendom is a civilization belonging to the third of the three generations of civilizations that there have been so far.

In the space dimension, the narrowness of the limits of Western Christendom is still more striking. If you look at the physical map of the world as a whole, you will see that the small part of it which is dry land consists of a single continent—Asia—which has a number of peninsulas and off-lying islands. Now, what are the farthest limits to which Western Christendom has managed to expand? You will find them at Alaska and Chile on the west and at Finland and Dalmatia on the east. What lies between those four points is Western Christendom's domain at its widest. And what does that domain amount to? Just the tip of Asia's European peninsula, together with a couple of large islands. (By these two large islands, I mean, of course, North and South America.) Even if you add in the outlying and precarious footholds of the Western world in South Africa, Australia, and New Zealand, its total habitable present area amounts to only a very minor part of the total habitable area of the surface of the planet. And you cannot understand the history of Western Christendom within its own geographical limits.

Western Christendom is a product of Christianity, but Christianity did not arise in the Western world; it arose outside the bounds of Western Christendom, in a district that lies today within the domain of a different civilization: Islam. We Western Christians did once try to capture from the Muslims the cradle of our religion in Palestine. If the Crusades had succeeded, Western Christendom would have slightly broadened its footing on the all-important Asiatic mainland. But the Crusades ended in failure.

Western Christendom is merely one of five civilizations that survive in the world to-day; and these are merely five out of about nineteen that one can identify as having come into existence since the first appearance of representatives of this species of society about 6000 years ago.

III

To TAKE the four other surviving civilizations first: if the firmness of a civilization's foothold on the continent—by which I mean the solid land-mass of Asia—may be taken as giving a rough indication of that civilization's relative expectation of life, then the other four surviving civilizations are 'better lives'—in the jargon of the life insurance business—than our own Western Christendom.

Our sister civilization, Orthodox Christendom, straddles the continent from the Baltic to the Pacific and from the Mediterranean to the Arctic Ocean: it occupies the northern half of Asia and the eastern half of Asia's European peninsula. Russia overlooks the back doors of all the other civilizations; from White Russia and North-Eastern Siberia she overlooks the Polish and Alaskan back doors of our own Western world; from the Caucasus and Central Asia she overlooks the back doors of the Islamic and Hindu worlds; from Central and Eastern Siberia she overlooks the back door of the Far Eastern world.

Our half-sister civilization, Islam, also has a firm footing on the continent. The domain of Islam stretches from the heart of the Asiatic continent in North-Western China all the way to the west coast of Asia's African peninsula. At Dakar, the Islamic world commands the continental approaches to the straits that divide Asia's African peninsula from the island of South America. Islam also has a firm footing in Asia's Indian peninsula.

As for the Hindu society and the Far Eastern society, it needs no demonstration to show that the 400 million Hindus and the 400 or 500 million Chinese have a firm foothold on the continent.

But we must not exaggerate the importance of any of these surviving civilizations just because, at this moment, they happen to be survivors. If, instead of thinking in terms of 'expectation of life,' we think in terms of achievement, a rough indication of relative achievement may be found in the giving of birth to individual souls that have conferred lasting blessings on the human race.

Now who are the individuals who are the greatest benefactors of the living generation of mankind? I should say: Confucius and Lao-tse; the Buddha; the Prophets of Israel and Judah: Zoroaster, Jesus, and Muhammad; and Socrates. And not one of these lasting benefactors of mankind happens to be a child of any of the five living civilizations. Confucius and Lao-tse were children of a now extinct Far Eastern civilization of an earlier generation; the Buddha was the child of a now extinct Indian civilization of an earlier generation. Hosea, Zoroaster, Jesus and Muhammad were children of a now extinct Syrian civilization. Socrates was the child of a now extinct Greek civilization.

Within the last 400 years, all the five surviving civilizations have

been brought into contact with each other as a result of the enterprise of two of them: the expansion of Western Christendom from
the tip of Asia's European peninsula over the ocean, and the expansion of Orthodox Christendom overland across the whole breadth
of the Asiatic continent.

The expansion of Western Christendom displays two special features: being oceanic, it is the only expansion of a civilization to date
that has been literally world-wide in the sense of extending over the
whole habitable portion of the Earth's surface; and, owing to the
'conquest of space and time' by modern mechanical means, the
spread of the network of Western material civilization has brought
the different parts of the world into far closer physical contact than
ever before. But, even in these points, the expansion of the Western
civilization differs in degree only, and not in kind, from the contemporary overland expansion of Russian Orthodox Christendom,
and from similar expansions of other civilizations at earlier dates.

There are earlier expansions that have made important contributions towards the present unification of mankind—with its corollary, the unification of our vision of human history. The now extinct Syrian civilization was propagated to the Atlantic coasts of
Asia's European and African peninsulas westward by the Phoeni-
cians, to the tip of Asia's Indian peninsula south-eastwards by the
Himyarites and Nestorians, and to the Pacific north-eastwards by
the Manichaeans and Nestorians. It expanded in two directions
overseas and in a third direction overland. Any visitor to Peking
will have seen a striking monument of the Syrian civilization's
overland cultural conquests. In the trilingual inscriptions of the
Manchu Dynasty of China at Peking, the Manchu and Mongol
texts are inscribed in the Syriac form of our alphabet, not in Chinese characters.

Other examples of the expansion of now extinct civilizations are
the propagation of the Greek civilization overseas westwards to
Marseilles by the Greeks themselves, overland northwards to the
Rhine and Danube by the Romans, and overland eastwards to the
interiors of India and China by the Macedonians; and the expansion of the Sumerian civilization in all directions overland from its
cradle in Iraq.

IV

As a result of these successive expansions of particular civilizations, the whole habitable world has now been unified into a single
great society. The movement through which this process has been

finally consummated is the modern expansion of Western Christendom. But we have to bear in mind, first, that this expansion of Western Christendom has merely completed the unification of the world and has not been the agency that has produced more than the last stage of the process; and, second, that, though the unification of the world has been finally achieved within a Western framework, the present Western ascendency in the world is certain not to last.

In a unified world, the eighteen non-Western civilizations—four of them living, fourteen of them extinct—will assuredly reassert their influence. And as, in the course of generations and centuries, a unified world gradually works its way toward an equilibrium between its diverse component cultures, the Western component will gradually be relegated to the modest place which is all that it can expect to retain in virtue of its intrinsic worth by comparison with those other cultures—surviving and extinct—which the Western society, through its modern expansion, has brought into association with itself and with one another.

History, seen in this perspective, makes, I feel the following call upon historians of our generation and of the generations that will come after ours. If we are to perform the full service that we have the power to perform for our fellow human beings—the important service of helping them to find their bearings in a unified world—we must make the necessary effort of imagination and effort of will to break our way out of the prison walls of the local and short-lived histories of our own countries and our own cultures, and we must accustom ourselves to taking a synoptic view of history as a whole.

Our first task is to perceive, and to present to other people, the history of all the known civilizations, surviving and extinct, as a unity. There are, I believe, two ways in which this can be done.

One way is to study the encounters between civilizations, of which I have mentioned four outstanding examples. These encounters between civilizations are historically illuminating, not only because they bring a number of civilizations into a single focus of vision, but also because, out of encounters between civilizations, the higher religions have been born—the worship, perhaps originally Sumerian, of the Great Mother and her Son who suffers and dies and rises again; Judaism and Zoroastrianism, which sprang from an encounter between the Syrian and Babylonian civilization; Christianity and Islam, which sprang from an encounter between the Syrian and Greek civilizations; the Mahayana form of Buddhism and Hinduism, which sprang from an encounter between the Indian and Greek civilizations. The future of mankind in this world—if mankind is going to have a future in this world—lies, I believe, with these higher religions that have appeared within the last 4000 years (and all but the first within the last 3000 years), and not with the civilizations whose encounters have provided opportunities for the higher religions to come to birth.

A second way of studying the history of all the known civilizations as a unity is to make a comparative study of their individual histories, looking at them as so many representatives of one particular species of the genus Human Society. If we map out the principal phases in the histories of civilizations—their birth, growths, breakdowns, and declines—we can compare their experiences phase by phase; and by this method of study we shall perhaps be able to sort out their common experiences, which are specific, from their unique experiences, which are individual. In this way we may be able to work out a morphology of the species of society called civilizations.

If, by the use of these two methods of study, we can arrive at a unified vision of history, we shall probably find that we need to make very far-going adjustments of the perspective in which the histories of divers civilizations and peoples appear when looked at through our peculiar present-day Western spectacles.

In setting out to adjust our perspective, we shall be wise, I suggest, to proceed simultaneously on two alternative assumptions. One of these alternatives is that the future of mankind may not, after all, be going to be catastrophic and that, even if the Second World War prove not to have been the last, we shall survive the rest of this batch of world wars as we survived the first two bouts, and shall eventually win our way out into calmer waters. The other possibility is that these first two world wars may be merely overtures to some supreme catastrophe that we are going to bring on ourselves.

This second, more unpleasant, alternative has been made a very practical possibility by mankind's unfortunately having discovered how to tap atomic energy before we have succeeded in abolishing the institution of war. Those contradictions and paradoxes in the life of the world in our time, which I took as my starting point, also look like symptoms of serious social and spiritual sickness, and their existence—which is one of the portentous features in the landscape of contemporary history—is another indication that we ought to take the more unpleasant of our alternatives as a serious possibility, and not just as a bad joke.

On either alternative, I suggest that we historians ought to concentrate our own attention—and direct the attention of our listeners and readers—upon the histories of those civilizations and peoples which, in the light of their past performances, seem likely, in a unified world, to come to the front in the long run in one or other of the alternative futures that may be lying in wait for mankind.

V

IF THE FUTURE of mankind in a unified world is going to be on the whole a happy one, then I would prophesy that there is a future in the Old World for the Chinese, and in the island of North America for the *Canadiens*. Whatever the future of mankind in North America, I feel pretty confident that these French-speaking Canadians, at any rate, will be there at the end of the story.

On the assumption that the future of mankind is to be very catastrophic, I should have prophesied, even as lately as a few years ago, that whatever future we might be going to have would lie with the Tibetans and the Eskimos, because each of these peoples occupied, till quite lately, an unusually sheltered position. 'Sheltered' means, of course, sheltered from the dangers arising from human folly and wickedness, not sheltered from the rigors of the physical environment. Mankind has been master of its physical environment, sufficiently for practical purposes, since the middle palaeolithic age; since that time, man's only dangers—but these have been deadly dangers—have come from man himself. But the homes of the Tibetans and the Eskimos are sheltered no longer, because we are on the point of managing to fly over the North Pole and over the Himalayas, and both Northern Canada and Tibet would (I think) be likely to be theatres of a future Russo-American war.

If mankind is going to run amok with atom bombs, I personally should look to the Negrito Pygmies of Central Africa to salvage some fraction of the present heritage of mankind. (Their eastern cousins in the Philippines and in the Malay Peninsula would probably perish with the rest of us, as they both live in what have now come to be dangerously exposed positions.)

The African Negritos are said by our anthropologists to have an unexpectedly pure and lofty conception of the nature of God and of God's relation to man. They might be able to give mankind a fresh start; and, though we should then have lost the achievements of the last 6000 to 10,000 years, what are 10,000 years compared to the 600,000 or a million years for which the human race has already been in existence?

The extreme possibility of catastrophe is that we might succeed in exterminating the whole human race, African Negritos and all.

On the evidence of the past history of life on this planet, even that is not entirely unlikely. After all, the reign of man on the Earth, if we are right in thinking that man established his present ascendency in the middle palaeolithic age, is so far only about 100,-000 years old, and what is that compared to the 500 million or 800 million years during which life has been in existence on the surface of this planet? In the past, other forms of life have enjoyed reigns which have lasted for almost inconceivably longer periods—and which yet at last have come to an end. There was a reign of the giant armoured reptiles which may have lasted about 80 million years; say from about the year 130 million to the year 50 million before the present day. But the reptiles' reign came to an end. Long before that—perhaps 300 million years ago—there was a reign of giant armoured fishes—creatures that had already accomplished the tremendous achievement of growing a movable lower jaw. But the reign of the fishes came to an end.

The winged insects are believed to have come into existence about 250 million years ago. Perhaps the higher winged insects— the social insects that have anticipated mankind in creating an in-stitutional life—are still waiting for their reign on Earth to come. If the ants and bees were one day to acquire even that glimmer of intellectual understanding that man has possessed in his day, and if they were then to make their own shot at seeing history in perspec-tive, they might see the advent of the mammals, and the brief reign of the human mammal, as almost irrelevant episodes, 'full of sound and fury, signifying nothing.'

The challenge to us, in our generation, is to see to it that this interpretation of history shall not become the true one.

A. J. CRONIN

****

I have chosen this because I think it illustrates fairly well a quality of sincerity which, if anything, characterizes my work. It has been said that the medical profession proves the best training ground for a novelist since there it is possible to see people with their masks off. Certainly, in my writing, I have drawn largely upon my experience as a doctor, and for this reason also I submit to you the enclosed fragment, since it deals with something which actually took place.

A. J. CRONIN

****

Birth

THOUGH IT WAS nearly midnight when Andrew reached Bryngower, he found Joe Morgan waiting on him, walking up and down with short steps between the closed surgery and the entrance to the house. At the sight of him the burly driller's face expressed relief.

"Eh, Doctor, I'm glad to see you. I been back and forward here this last hour. The missus wants ye—before time, too."

Andrew, abruptly recalled from the contemplation of his own affairs, told Morgan to wait. He went into the house for his bag, then together they set out for Number 12 Blaina Terrace. The night air was cool and deep with quiet mystery. Usually so perceptive, Andrew now felt dull and listless. He had no premonition that this night call would prove unusual, still less that it would influence his whole future in Blaenelly.

The two men walked in silence until they reached the door of Number 12, then Joe drew up short.

"I'll not come in," he said, and his voice showed signs of strain. "But, man, I know ye'll do well for us."

Inside, a narrow stair led up to a small bedroom, clean but poorly furnished, and lit only by an oil lamp. Here Mrs. Morgan's mother, a tall grey-haired woman of nearly seventy, and the stout elderly

587

midwife waited beside the patient, watching Andrew's expression as he moved about the room.

"Let me make you a cup of tea, Doctor, bach," said the former quickly, after a few moments.

Andrew smiled faintly. He saw that the old woman, wise in experience, realized there must be a period of waiting, that she was afraid he would leave the case, saying he would return later.

"Don't fret, Mother. I'll not run away."

Down in the kitchen he drank the tea which she gave him. Overwrought as he was, he knew he could not snatch even an hour's sleep if he went home. He knew, too, that the case here would demand all his attention. A queer lethargy of spirit came upon him. He decided to remain until everything was over.

An hour later he went upstairs again, noted the progress made, came down once more, sat by the kitchen fire. It was still, except for the rustle of a cinder in the grate and the slow tick-tock of the wall clock. No, there was another sound—the beat of Morgan's footsteps as he paced in the street outside. The old woman opposite him sat in her black dress, quite motionless, her eyes strangely alive and wise, probing, never leaving his face.

His thoughts were heavy, muddled. The episode he had witnessed at Cardiff station still obsessed him morbidly. He thought of Bramwell, foolishly devoted to a woman who deceived him sordidly, of Edward Page, bound to the shrewish Blodwen, of Denny, living unhappily, apart from his wife. His reason told him that all these marriages were dismal failures. It was a conclusion which, in his present state, made him wince. He wished to consider marriage as an idyllic state; yes, he could not otherwise consider it with the image of Christine before him. Her eyes, shining towards him, admitted no other conclusion. It was the conflict between his level, doubting mind and his overflowing heart which left him resentful and confused. He let his chin sink upon his chest, stretched out his legs, stared broodingly into the fire. He remained like this so long, and his thoughts were so filled with Christine, that he started when the old woman opposite suddenly addressed him. Her meditation had pursued a different course.

"Susan said not to give her the chloroform if it would harm the baby. She's awful set upon this child, Doctor, bach." Her old eyes warmed at a sudden thought. She added in a low tone: "Ay, we all are, I fancy."

He collected himself with an effort.

"It won't do any harm, the anaesthetic," he said kindly. "They'll be all right."

Here the nurse's voice was heard calling from the top landing. Andrew glanced at the clock, which now showed half-past three. He rose and went up to the bedroom. He perceived that he might now begin his work.

An hour elapsed. It was a long, harsh struggle. Then, as the first streaks of dawn strayed past the broken edges of the blind, the child was born, lifeless.

As he gazed at the still form a shiver of horror passed over Andrew. After all that he had promised! His face, heated with his own exertions, chilled suddenly. He hesitated, torn between his desire to attempt to resuscitate the child, and his obligation towards the mother, who was herself in a desperate state. The dilemma was so urgent he did not solve it consciously. Blindly, instinctively, he gave the child to the nurse and turned his attention to Susan Morgan who now lay collapsed, almost pulseless, and not yet out of the ether, upon her side. His haste was desperate, a frantic race against her ebbing strength. It took him only an instant to smash a glass ampule and inject pituitrin. Then he flung down the hypodermic syringe and worked unsparingly to restore the flaccid woman. After a few minutes of feverish effort, her heart strengthened; he saw that he might safely leave her. He swung round, in his shirt sleeves, his hair sticking to his damp brow.

"Where's the child?"

The midwife made a frightened gesture. She had placed it beneath the bed.

In a flash Andrew knelt down. Fishing amongst the sodden newspapers below the bed, he pulled out the child. A boy, perfectly formed. The limp warm body was white and soft as tallow. The cord, hastily slashed, lay like a broken stem. The skin was of a lovely texture, smooth and tender. The head lolled on the thin neck. The limbs seemed boneless.

Still kneeling, Andrew stared at the child with a haggard frown. The whiteness meant only one thing: asphyxia pallida, and his mind, unnaturally tense, raced back to a case he once had seen in the Samaritan, to the treatment that had been used. Instantly he was on his feet.

"Get me hot water and cold water," he threw out to the nurse. "And basins too. Quick! Quick!"

"But, Doctor—" she faltered, her eyes on the pallid body of the child.

"Quick!" he shouted.

Snatching a blanket he laid the child upon it and began the special method of respiration. The basins arrived, the ewer, the big iron kettle. Frantically he splashed cold water into one basin; into the other he mixed water as hot as his hand could bear. Then, like some crazy juggler, he hurried the child between the two, now plunging it into the icy, now into the steaming bath.

Fifteen minutes passed. Sweat was now running into Andrew's eyes, blinding him. One of his sleeves hung down, dripping. His breath came pantingly. But no breath came from the lax body of the child.

A desperate sense of defeat pressed on him, a raging hopelessness. He felt the midwife watching him in stark consternation, while there, pressed back against the wall where she had all the time remained,—her hand pressed to her throat, uttering no sound, her eyes burning upon him,—was the old woman. He remembered her longing for a grandchild, as great as had been her daughter's longing for this child. All dashed away now; futile, beyond remedy . . .

The floor was now a draggled mess. Stumbling over a sopping towel, Andrew almost dropped the child, which was now wet and slippery in his hands, like a strange white fish.

"For mercy's sake, Doctor," whimpered the midwife. "It's stillborn."

Andrew did not heed her. Beaten, despairing, having laboured in vain for half an hour, he still persisted in one last effort, rubbing the child with a rough towel, crushing and releasing the little chest with both his hands, trying to get breath into that limp body.

And then, as by a miracle, the pigmy chest, which his hands enclosed, gave a short convulsive heave. Another . . . And another . . . Andrew turned giddy. The sense of life, springing beneath his fingers after all that unavailing striving, was so exquisite it almost made him faint. He redoubled his efforts feverishly. The child was gasping now, deeper and deeper. A bubble of mucus came from one tiny nostril, a joyful iridescent bubble. The limbs were no longer boneless. The head no longer lay back spinelessly. The blanched skin was slowly turning pink. Then, exquisitely, came the child's cry.

"Dear Father in Heaven," the nurse sobbed hysterically, "It's come—it's come alive."

Andrew handed her the child. He felt weak and dazed. About him the room lay in a shuddering litter; blankets, towels, basins, soiled instruments, the hypodermic syringe impaled by its point in the linoleum, the ewer knocked over, the kettle on its side in a puddle of water. Upon the huddled bed the mother still dreamed her way quietly through the anaesthetic. The old woman still stood against the wall. But her hands were together, her lips moved without sound. She was praying.

Mechanically Andrew wrung out his sleeve, pulled on his jacket. "I'll fetch my bag later, Nurse."

He went downstairs, through the kitchen into the scullery. His lips were dry. At the scullery he took a long drink of water. He reached for his hat and coat.

Outside he found Joe standing on the pavement with a tense, expectant face.

"All right, Joe," he said thickly. "Both all right."

It was quite light. Nearly five o'clock. A few miners were already in the streets: the first of the night shift moving out. As Andrew walked with them, spent and slow, his footfalls echoing with the others under the morning sky, he kept thinking blindly, oblivious to all other work he had done in Blaenelly: "I've done something; oh, God! I've done something real at last."

LORD DUNSANY

****

DUBLIN

By all means print that chapter about business and call it "Business in Ireland" as you suggest. That would be better than the one about the moon, because the first I wrote myself, and the other is an actual letter to me from somebody else, repeating the words of a countryman.

LORD DUNSANY

****

Business in Ireland

"Are you coming out tomorrow?" said a friend to me, for the hounds were to be within five miles of me.

"No," I said. "I am writing a book about Ireland, and want to get on with it."

"About Ireland," he said. "What are you telling them?"

"Oh, sport," I said, "and poetry and history, and of course politics. But not much history, for the book is to be in one volume and that volume is to be lifted with one hand."

"Another reason why much history would be out of place in a book about Ireland," he said, "is that they none of them know any of it."

"I thought it was one of the things the people are fondest of," I said.

"They are," said he, "but in the schools, where they learn it, it is only used as missiles to throw at England, so that it gets rather tattered. It is very exciting of course, but you couldn't any longer call it history, after it has been the round of a few schools."

"Well, I don't know very much about it myself," I said.

"No, nobody does," he replied. "But you're right to give them sport; and I think there's some poetry in all of them."

"Their talk is full of it," I answered, "and all their legends."

"Yes," he said. "But what are you doing about politics?"

And then I told him about Old Mickey, and how there was one thing that everybody would want to know and Old Mickey was going to tell it me.

"Yes, you'll have to tell them that," he said. "But what about business? You should say something of that."

"Oh, yes," I said, "I suppose I should."

But the remark rather bothered me, we haven't very much business in County Meath. We used to sell fat cattle before the treaty and got £35 a head. We still sell fat cattle; but, as we only get from £12 to £14 a head for them, one can hardly call that business.

"What business is there?" I asked.

"Well, there's Guinness," he said. "And there's bound to be some more somewhere, if only you look for it. Anyway you'll have to have something about it in your book."

We were both agreed about that. And I decided to make further inquiries, and with the help of them to study the matter locally.

And by good luck I met next day just the kind of man that I wanted, a man whose kindness had helped me to get many a teal; for he had not only showed me a reedy pond to which the teal came, but many a time he had driven them for me, telling me just where to hide myself and seeming to know exactly the line that the teal would fly. He was an old friend of mine, who had known a good deal of prison in his youth; and the imprisonment, while gaining him the respect of all his neighbors, had never impaired his cheerfulness. Now that the words will soon be in cold print I begin to realize that to know the flight of teal is not in itself sufficient qualification for knowledge about business, and that there may even be amongst my readers some that will hold that before venturing to address them upon this matter I should have found an adviser with better qualifications. That may be so; indeed it is incontrovertible; and I should certainly have done so. On the other hand I was not at once able to find a man with the better qualifications, and I was undoubtedly hindered in my search for one by a certain charm that there was in Stephen O'Lara, who now stood before me, and who would, I believe, have exerted the same misleading charm on the most critical of my readers; but that, of course, I cannot prove. I had found him a good deal occupied watching a river. It was a bright morning, and he was leaning over a bridge and did not recognize me till I spoke to him. Then he jumped up, all smiles.

"I was watching the river," he said, "and didn't see you."

"It's a fine day to be doing it," said I.

"Begob," he said, "it must take a long time to get to the sea, the pace it's going now."

"It gets there all right," I said.

"I was wondering did it ever get there," he answered.

"How is the country doing?" I asked.

"Sure, it's doing grand," he said.

"And how is business doing?" I asked.

"Business is it?" said he.

"Well, yes," I said. "I rather wanted to make a study of it."

"Sure it's doing grand too," said O'Lara. "They are after opening a great new bank over at Bohermeen."

"At Bohermeen?" I said.

"Aye," he said, "to the west of the road."

It was the kind of thing that I wanted to know.

"That's the road to Fahan," I asked, so as to make no mistake.

"Aye, three or four hundred yards from the crossroads," he said.

"When did they build it?" I asked.

"They're just after finishing it," he said.

"Who is the manager?"

"The honestest man in all Ireland," he said.

And then he told me this rather interesting story.

"Pat had a bit of an army of young lads down in the West, no more nor about half a dozen. He wasn't the general himself, but there was another lad over him. And one day he went into the big bank that there is down there, and asked to see the manager. And the manager came out of his office, all business and buttons, and said: 'What can I do for you?'

"And the young lads put up their pistols, and Pat said: 'I want £4000.'

"And the manager said: 'I haven't got it.'

"And Pat said: 'Then you've not long to live.'

"And the manager said: 'I might scrape it together.'

"And he did.

" 'Can I put it into some bags for you?' said the manager.

" 'You need not,' said Pat. 'Do you think I am going about with all that money on me? Sure, I wouldn't be able to walk.'

" 'I thought you wanted to take it away,' said the manager.

" 'Have more sense,' said Pat.

" 'Then what do you want to do with it?' he asked.

" 'Sure, I'll bank it,' said Pat.

" 'Where?' said the manager.

" 'With you. Why not?' said Pat. 'You can put it to my account.'

" 'I'll want a specimen of your signature,' said the manager.

" 'There'll be no difficulty about that,' said Pat. For they had learned him to write. So he wrote down his signature, and they all walked away; and Pat turned his head round, as he was going out, in the doorway, and said: 'Is there a priest handy?'

"And the manager said: 'There is.'

" 'Because, said Pat, 'if ever I come here for the money and don't find it, you'll want him in a great hurry.'

"With that he went away, and there was £4000 to his credit in the bank. Am I tiring you?"

"You are not," I said. "What happened?"

"Well, a few weeks went by and then the general that I told you about, who was over Pat, died one night from the prod of a cow's horn. I knew the doctor who attended him, and he told me that that was what he died of. It went through the whole length of his body. 'It must have been a very long horn,' said the doctor to me, 'and a very thin one. But that was not my affair.' Well, when Pat heard the general was dead, and being a queer fellow and the honestest man in Ireland, what's he do but go back to the manager of the bank and give him back his £4000. Yes, he done that. He did indeed. And when they wanted an honest man to run a bank, what did they do only get Pat? And where could they have got a better? For he knew a little about banking, through having had an account of his own, and he was dead honest. And it's a true story I'm telling you."

"I want nothing but the truth," I said, "for I'm writing a book about Ireland."

"It's God's truth," he said.

And then I left him to look at the river, while I went home to write about business.

But when I got home I decided that I had best first go and see Bohermeen, and have a talk with the manager of the new bank.

So when my gamekeeper came to see me next morning to ask me where I would shoot, I told him that I couldn't shoot that day, as I had some business to attend to and wanted to see the manager of the bank at Bohermeen.

"I never heard of a bank at Bohermeen," he said.

"No. It's a new one," said I.

"But it would be a grand place for snipe," he said, "and there's none of the men with rights in the bog who will object to your going there."

"Well, I'll take my gun," I said, "and we'll bring the dog, and I might get some shooting when I've finished the business I have to do."

But I said no more of the bank; for, though I valued his opinion on sport, I did not think that he had sufficiently accurate knowledge of business to justify me in basing upon his opinion on banking the information about business in Ireland that I desire to give to my reader. And soon we were off, with dog and gun in the car, to Bohermeen, which lies northwest from Tara. One cannot see from the famous hill the low levels to which I went, but very clearly one can see the Hill of Fahan, against whose feet laps the heather of Bohermeen. I have seen the Hill of Fahan from Tara at evening, with its wood on top turning ruby, till the gap that there is in the wood becomes like a gateway of Fairyland. The low steep hill in the plain is one of the principal landmarks of the country. We came to Klimessan hill, where the land dips to the west, and we saw Meath and Westmeath lying blue before us. We crossed the Boyne, and went through lands of green pastures, till we came to little fields of coarser grass, which very soon ceased altogether, and we came to the lower levels of the bog, that men have plundered but not yet tamed. A few young birches stood there, that men had planted in rows along ditches that they had dug, and some turf-stacks stood there drying; but there was nothing else on those levels that told of the work of man. A road ran very lonely over the bog, looking almost shy of its own sophistication amongst ancient primitive nature. And then another road ran away to the right. So narrow was this one that it seemed almost to slink over the bog, like a man in patent-leather boots, tall hat and frock coat going on tiptoe through an encampment of gypsies, knowing he had no business there. This was the road we followed, till I came to the exact spot of which O'Lara had told me. The low levels of the cut-away bog had ended before I came there and the long black cliff lay before us at the edge of the high bog, its outline jagged by the turf-cutters. It was two hundred yards past this that O'Lara had told me I should come on the new bank. I stopped the car, and the distance seemed about right and I should have been standing just about at the doorway. But no bank was there nothing but pale brown grasses, with patches of heather amongst them, and a view over bog unbroken but for one dark row of pines to the left hand side of the view and a small wood to the right, and some mountains that are in Westmeath rising beyond it. Behind me on the other side of the road lay the lower levels with patches of whitish grass and patches of moss, and square pools shining; I saw a loose donkey there, and one in a cart, and two men standing by turf-stacks. I looked again over the bog, and away to those mountains in Westmeath, but the only sign of sophistication I saw was one broken bottle, that had been thrown to the bog from the road; but certainly no bank. Had I been content to write about the Ireland I know, instead of wishing to instruct my reader about whatever business may be done in the country, I should not have been out on this wild-goose-chase. Let the metaphor pass: I know of no more unsuitable one by which to describe a search for a bank; but let it pass.

"We'd better shoot snipe," I said to my keeper. And that is what we did.

I was rather annoyed with O'Lara for sending me off on this absurd quest, when it was solid information I wanted; so I went a little out of my way, coming back, so as to find O'Lara. And I found him, where I usually find him, not far from the Boyne; and he seemed as pleased as ever to see me, and seemed to know, too, where I was coming from, and looked as though he were happy to have provided me with just the information I wanted. I seemed to see all that in his smile. But all I said to him by way of greeting was:

"There is no bank at Bohermeen."

"Ah," he replied, "perhaps it was a turf-bank I meant."

"You told me," I said, though my annoyance was melting before his smiling face as I spoke, "that there was a particularly honest man as manager there, and I went all the way to have a talk with him."

"Sure, everything I told you about him was true," said O'Lara. "Doesn't the whole country know it? And what for do you want his right address? Wouldn't the story about him be just as true whatever address I gave you? Begob, it would. And maybe the wrong address might be better. But, sure, I'll find him for you and bring him to see you."

"It doesn't matter," I said.

"What was it you wanted him for?" said O'Lara.

"I wanted to have a talk with him about business," I said. "I'm writing a book about Ireland, and they'll want to know what business the country does."

"Haven't we Guinness?" said he. "And what do we want with any more business than that? Don't they pay millions in taxes?"

And then a troubled look came over his face.

"Begob," he said, "I've nearly given up drinking it."

"Why's that?" I gasped.

"Because of a dream I had," said O'Lara, "after drinking no more nor a bottle. And then I went to bed and I had the dream."

"What was the dream?" I asked.

"Begob," said he, "it was terrible. I dreamed that I walked down to the shore of the sea one evening; I don't know what I was doing there, but I walked down to the shore; and it was somewhere near Dublin, for I could see the Wicklow mountains. And it wasn't night, for there was still some light in the sky; but it was getting late. And the shore was crowded with people all looking out to the sea. And I said, 'What's the matter, boys?' And one or two of them answered, 'It is the end,' and went on looking out to sea. So I looked too, in my dream. And I saw the horizon all dark with the smoke of ships, and the people staring at them as though the end of the world were there. Begob, I said to myself, it's the English fleet, and those great big shells will be coming soon.

"For the smoke was tearing up and the sky was black as thunder.

" 'Is it the English fleet?' I said.

"But they had all gone silent, and wouldn't speak any more.

"And then I saw that the ships were nearer than they looked in the evening. They weren't far away at all, and were quite small. And I took a man by the arm who was standing quite near me and I shook him, and said, 'Those little boats can't hurt us; sure, they're no bigger than Guinness' boats that do be on the Liffy.'

"And the man gave a great sigh and said, 'It is what they are.'

"And I cried out then, 'Ah, boys, is it Guinness's going?'

"And I knew from the awful stillness that this was so.

"And I daren't have a sup of porter before going to bed any more, for fear would I get that dream."

"Oh, I wouldn't bother," I said. "It was only a dream."

For he looked so doleful, I had to say something to try to cheer him.

"It isn't the dream I mind," he said, "but all the truth that there is in it."

SEAN O'CASEY

✳✳

*Judged by most critics as the greatest living Irish playwright, "Shaw
aside," as George Jean Nathan says, Sean O'Casey has chosen the
second act, the famous pub scene, from one of his finest plays,* The
Plough And The Stars, *the play which caused a riot at the opening
night in 1926 (and which was quelled by the poet Yeats).* The
Plough and The Stars *is a tragedy of the Easter Rebellion of 1916 in
Dublin, and the pub scene involves a few of the lesser characters
while an orator outside is addressing a crowd. Mr. O'Casey's comment on this act from his play is reticent in the extreme. "He says
that all his work is representative of work done and work in progress
and he is very busy. He therefore cannot give any further reasons."*

✳✳

The Plough and the Stars

ACT II: THE PUB

THE TIME: November 1915.

SCENE.—*A Dublin Public-house at the corner of the street in
which the meeting is being addressed from Platform No. 1. One end
of the house is visible to the audience. On the counter are glasses,
beer-pulls, and a carafe filled with water. Behind the counter, on the
back wall, are shelves containing bottles of wine, whisky and beer.
At back center is a wide, high, plateglass window. Under the window is a seat to hold three or four persons seated. Left are the wide
swing-doors. At wall, right, is a seat to hold two persons. A few
gaudy-colored show-cards on the walls.*

A band is heard outside playing "The Soldiers' Song," before the
CURTAIN *rises, and for a few moments afterwards, accompanied by
the sounds of marching men.*

The BARMAN *is seen wiping the part of the counter which is in
view.* ROSIE REDMOND *is standing at the counter toying with what
remains of a half of whisky in a wine-glass. She is a sturdy, well-*

*shaped girl of 20; pretty and pert in manner. She is wearing a
cream blouse, with an obviously suggestive glad neck; a grey tweed
dress, brown stockings and shoes. The blouse and most of the dress
are hidden by a black shawl. She has no hat, and in her hair is
jauntily set a cheap, glittering, jewelled ornament.*

BARMAN *(wiping counter)*. Nothin' much doin' in your line tonight, Rosie?

ROSIE. Curse o' God on th' haporth, hardly, Tom. There isn't
much notice taken of a pretty petticoat of a night like this. . . .
They're all in a holy mood. Th' solemn-lookin' dials on th' whole o'
them an' they marchin' to th' meetin'. You'd think they were th'
glorious company of th' saints, an' th' noble army of martyrs
thrampin' through th' sthreets of Paradise. They're all thinkin' of
higher things than a girl's garther. . . . It's a tremendous meetin';
four platforms they have—there's one o' them just outside opposite
th' window.

BARMAN. Oh, ay; sure when th' speaker comes *(motioning with
his hand)* to th' near end, here, you can see him plain, an' hear
nearly everythin' he's spoutin' out of him.

ROSIE. It's no joke thryin' to make up fifty-five shillin's a week
for your keep an' laundhry, an' then taxin' you a quid for your own
room if you bring home a friend for th' night. . . . If I could only
put by a couple of quid for a swankier outfit, everythin' in th' garden ud look lovely—

*(In the window, back, appears the figure of a tall man, who, stand-
ing on a platform, is addressing a crowd outside. The figure is
almost like a silhouette. The* BARMAN *comes to left end of counter
to listen, and* ROSIE *moves center to see and listen too.)*

BARMAN *(to* ROSIE). Whisht, till we hear what he's sayin'.

THE VOICE OF THE MAN. It is a glorious thing to see arms in the
hands of Irishmen. We must accustom ourselves to the thought of
arms, we must accustom ourselves to the sight of arms, we must accustom ourselves to the use of arms. . . . Bloodshed is a cleansing
and sanctifying thing, and the nation that regards it as the final horror has lost its manhood. . . . There are many things more horrible
than bloodshed, and slavery is one of them!

(The figure passes the window, and is lost to sight and hearing. The
BARMAN *goes back to wiping off the counter.* ROSIE *remains
looking out of the window.)*

Rosie. It's th' sacred thruth, mind you, what that man's afther sayin'.

Barman. If I was only a little younger, I'd be plungin' mad into th' middle of it!

Rosie (*who is still looking out of the window*). Oh, here's th' two gems runnin' over again for their oil!

(*The doors swing open, and* Fluther, *a carpenter of forty, and* Peter, *a laborer, enter tumultuously. They are hot and hasty with the things they have seen and heard. They hurry across to the counter,* Peter *leading the way.* Rosie, *after looking at them listlessly for a moment, retires to the seat under the window, sits down, takes a cigarette from her pocket, lights it and smokes.*)

Peter (*splutteringly to the* Barman). Two halves . . . (*To* Fluther.) A meetin' like this always makes me feel as if I could dhrink Loch Erinn dhry!

Fluther. You couldn't feel anyway else at a time like this when th' spirit of a man is pulsin' to be out fightin' for th' thruth with his feet thremblin' on th' way, maybe to th' gallows, an' his ears tinglin' with th' faint, far-away sound of burstin' rifle-shots that'll maybe whip th' last little shock o' life out of him that's left lingerin' in his body!

Peter. I felt a burnin' lump in me throat when I heard th' band playin' "The Soldiers' Song," rememberin' last hearin' it marchin' in military formation, with th' people starin' on both sides at us, carryin' with us th' pride an' resolution o' Dublin to th' grave of Wolfe Tone.

Fluther. Get th' Dublin men goin' an' they'll go on full force for anything that's thryin' to bar them away from what they're wantin', where th' slim thinkin' counthry boyo ud limp away from th' first faintest touch of compromization!

Peter (*hurriedly to the* Barman). Two more, Tom! . . . (*To* Fluther.) Th' memory of all th' things that was done, an' all th' things that was suffered be th' people, was boomin' in me brain. . . . Every nerve in me body was quiverin' to do somethin' desperate!

Fluther. Jammed as I was in th' crowd, I listened to th' speeches pattherin' on th' people's head, like rain fallin' on th' corn; every derogatory thought went out o' me mind, an' I said to meself, "You can die now, Fluther, for you've seen th' shadow-dhreams of th' past leppin' to life in th' bodies of livin' men that show, if we were without a titther o' courage for centuries, we're vice versa now!" Looka here. (*He stretches out his arm under* PETER's *face and rolls up his sleeve.*) The blood was *boilin'* in me veins!

(*The silhouette of the tall figure again moves into the frame of the window, speaking to the people.*)

PETER (*unaware, in his enthusiasm, of the speaker's appearance, to* FLUTHER). I was burnin' to dhraw me sword, an' wave it over me——

FLUTHER (*overwhelming* PETER). Will you stop your blatherin' for a minute, man, an' let us hear what he's sayin'!

(*The* BARMAN *comes to aft end of the counter to look at the figure in the window:* ROSIE *rises from the seat, stands and looks.* FLUTHER *and* PETER *move to see and listen.*)

THE VOICE OF THE MAN. Comrade soldiers of the Irish Volunteers and of the Citizen Army, we rejoice in this terrible war. The old heart of the earth needed to be warmed with the red wine of the battlefields. . . . Such august homage was never offered to God as this: the homage of millions of lives given gladly for love of country. And we must be ready to pour out the same red wine in the same glorious sacrifice, for without shedding of blood there is no redemption!

(*The figure moves out of sight and hearing.*)

(FLUTHER *runs back to the counter and gulps down the drink remaining in his glass;* PETER *does the same, less rapidly; the* BARMAN *leaves the end of the counter;* ROSIE *sits on the seat again.*)

FLUTHER (*finishing drink, to* PETER). Come on, man; this is too good to be missed!

(FLUTHER *rushes across out the doors.* PETER *wipes his mouth and hurries after* FLUTHER. *The doors swing open, and the* COVEY, *a thin lad of 25, enters. He collides with* PETER. PETER *stiffens his body, like a cock, and, with a look of hatred on his face, marches stiffly out. The* COVEY [*a fitter*] *looks scornfully after* PETER, *and then crosses to the counter.* ROSIE *sees possibilities in the* COVEY, *gets up and comes to the counter.*)

THE COVEY (*to* BARMAN). Give us a glass o' malt, for God's sake, till I stimulate meself from the shock of seeing the sight that's afther goin' out.

ROSIE (*slyly, to the* BARMAN). Another one for me, Tommy; the young gentleman's ordherin' it in the corner of his eye.

(*The* BARMAN *gets a drink for the* COVEY, *leaves it on the counter;* ROSIE *whips it up. The* BARMAN *catches* ROSIE'S *arm, and takes glass from her, putting it down beside the* COVEY.)

BARMAN (*taking the glass from* ROSIE). Eh. houl' on there, houl' on there, Rosie.

ROSIE (*angrily, to the* BARMAN). What are you houldin' on out o' you for? Didn't you hear th' young gentleman say that he couldn't refuse anything to a nice little bird? (*To the* COVEY.) Isn't that right, Jiggs? (*The* COVEY *says nothing.*) Didn't I know, Tommy, it would be all right? It takes Rosie to size a young man up, an' tell th' thoughts that are thremblin' in his mind. Isn't that right, Jiggs?

(*The* COVEY *stirs uneasily, moves a little farther away, and pulls his cap over his eyes.*)

(*Moving after him.*) Great meetin' that's gettin' held outside. Well, it's up to us all, anyway, to fight for our freedom.

THE COVEY (*to the* BARMAN). Two more, please. (*To* ROSIE.) Freedom! What's th' use o' freedom, if it's not economic freedom?

ROSIE (*emphasizing with extended arm and moving finger*). I used them very words just before you come in. "A lot o' thricksters," says I, "that wouldn't know what freedom was if they got it from their mother." . . . (*To the* BARMAN.) Didn't I, Tommy?

BARMAN. I disremember.

ROSIE (*to the* BARMAN). No, you don't disremember. Remember you said, yourself, it was all "only a flash in th' pan." Well, "flash in th' pan, or no flash in th' pan," says I, "they're not goin' to get Rosie Redmond," says I, "to fight for freedom that wouldn't be worth winnin' in a raffle!"

THE COVEY (*contemptuously*). There's only one freedom for th' workin' man: conthrol o' th' means o' production, rates of exchange an' th' means of disthribution. (*Tapping* ROSIE *on the shoulder.*)

Look here, comrade, I'll leave here to-morrow night for you a copy of Jenersky's *Thesis on the Origin, Development an' Consolidation of the Evolutionary Idea of th' Proletariat.*

ROSIE (*throwing off her shawl on to the counter, an showing an exemplified glad neck, which reveals a good deal of a white bosom*). If y'ass Rosie, it's heartbreakin' to see a young fella thinkin' of anything, or admirin' anything, but silk thransparent stockin's showin' off the shape of a little lassie's legs!

(*The* COVEY *is frightened, and moves away from* ROSIE *along the counter.* ROSIE *follows, gliding after him in a seductive way.*)

(*Following him.*) Out in th' park in th' shade of a warm summery evenin', with your little darlin' bridie to be, kissin' an' cuddlin' (*she tries to put her arm around his neck*), kissin' an' cuddlin', ay?

THE COVEY (*frightened*). Ay, what are you doin'? None o' that now; none o' that. I've something else to do besides shinannickin' afther Judies!

(*The* COVEY *turns and moves slowly away from* ROSIE; *she turns with him, keeping him facing her, holding his arm.*)

ROSIE. Oh, little duckey, oh, shy little duckey! Never held a mot's hand, an' wouldn't know how to tittle a little Judy! (*She clips him under the chin.*) Tittle him undher th' chin, tittle him undher th' chin!

THE COVEY (*breaking away and running out*). Aye go on, now; I don't want to have any meddlin' with a lassie like you!

ROSIE (*enraged—returning to the seat at the window*). Jasus, it's in a monasthery some of us ought to be, spendin' our holidays kneelin' on our adorers, tellin' our beads an' knockin' hell out of our buzzums!

(*The voice of the* COVEY *is heard outside doors calling in a scale of notes,* "Cuckoo-ooooo." *Then the swing-doors open, and* PETER *and* FLUTHER, *followed by* MRS. GOGAN, *a middle-aged charwoman, come in.* MRS. GOGAN *carries a baby in her arms.*)

PETER (*in plaintive anger, looking towards the door*). It's terrible that young Covey can't let me pass without proddin' at me! Did you hear him murmurin' "cuckoo" when he were passin'?

FLUTHER (*irritably—to* PETER). I wouldn't be everlastin' cockin' me ear to hear every little whisper that was floatin' around about me! It's my rule never to lose me temper till it would be dethromental to keep it. There's nothin' derogatory in th' use o' th' word "cuckoo," is there?

(Mrs. Gogan, *followed by* Peter, *go up to the seat under the window and sit down,* Peter *to the right of* Mrs. Gogan. Rosie, *after a look at those who've come in, goes out by doors, left.*)

Peter (*tearfully*). It's not the word, it's the way he says it! He never says it straight out, but murmurs it with curious quiverin' ripples, like variations on a flute.

Fluther (*standing in front of the seat*). A' what odds if he gave it with variations on a thrombone? (*To* Mrs. Gogan.) What's yours goin' to be, maam?

Mrs. Gogan. Ah, half a malt, Fluther.

(Fluther *goes from the seat over to the counter.*)

Fluther (*to the* Barman). Three halves, Tommy.

(*The* Barman *gets the drinks, leaves them on the counter.* Fluther *pays the* Barman; *takes drinks to the seat under the window; gives one to* Mrs. Gogan, *one to* Peter, *and keeps the third for himself. He then sits on the seat to the left of* Mrs. Gogan.)

Mrs. Gogan (*drinking, and looking admiringly at* Peter's *costume*). The Foresthers' is a gorgeous dhress! I don't think I've seen nicer, mind you, in a pantomime. . . . Th' loveliest part of th' dhress, I think, is th' osthrichess plume. . . . When yous are goin' along, an' I see them wavin' an' noddin' an' waggin', I seem to be lookin' at each of yous hangin' at th' end of a rope, your eyes bulgin' an your legs twistin' an' jerkin', gaspin' an' gaspin' for breath while yous are thryin' to die for Ireland!

Fluther (*scornfully*). If any o' them is ever hangin' at the end of a rope, it won't be for Ireland!

Peter. Are you goin' to start th' young Covey's game o' proddin' an' twartin' a man? There's not many that's talkin' can say that for twenty-five years he never missed a pilgrimage to Bodenstown!

Fluther (*looking angrily at* Peter). You're always blowin' about goin' to Bodenstown. D'ye think no one but yourself ever went to *Bodenstown?*

Peter (*plaintively*). I'm not blowin' about it; but there's not a year that I go there but I pluck a leaf off Tone's grave, an' this very day me prayer-book is nearly full of them.

Fluther (*scornfully*). Then Fluther has a vice-versa opinion of them that put ivy leaves into their prayer-books, scabbin' it on th' clergy, an' thryin' to out-do th' haloes o' th' saints be lookin' as if he was wearin' around his head a glittherin' aroree boree allis! (*Fiercely.*) Sure, I don't care a damn if you slep' in *Bodenstown*! You can take your breakfast, dinner an' tea on th' grave, in Bodenstown, if you like, for Fluther!

MRS. GOGAN. Oh, don't start a fight, boys, for God's sake; I was only sayin' what a nice costume it is—nicer than th' kilts, for, God forgive me, I always think th' kilts is hardly decent.

FLUTHER (*laughing scornfully*). Ah, sure, when you'd look at him, you'd wondher whether th' man was makin' fun o' th' costume, or th' costume was makin' fun o' th' man!

BARMAN (*over to them*). Now, then, thry to speak asy, will yous? We don't want no shoutin' here.

(*The swing-doors open and the* COVEY, *followed by* BESSIE BURGESS, *40, a street fruit-vendor, come in. They go over and stand at the counter. Passing,* BESSIE *gives a scornful look at those seated near the window.* BESSIE *and the* COVEY *talk together, but frequently eye the group at the window.*)

COVEY (*to the* BARMAN). Two glasses o' malt.

(*The* BARMAN *gets the drinks; leaves them on the counter. The* COVEY *puts one beside* BESSIE *and keeps the other. He pays the* BARMAN.)

PETER (*plaintively*). There he is now—I knew he wouldn't be long till he folleyed me in.

BESSIE (*speaking to the* COVEY, *but really at the other party*). I can't for th' life o' me undherstand how they can call themselves Catholics, when they won't lift a finger to help poor little Catholic Belgium.

MRS. GOGAN (*raising her voice*). What about poor little Catholic Ireland?

BESSIE (*over to* MRS. GOGAN). You mind your own business, maam, an' stupify your foolishness be gettin' dhrunk.

PETER (*anxiously—to* MRS. GOGAN). Take no notice of her; pay no attention to her. She's just tormentin' herself towards havin' a row with somebody.

BESSIE (*in quiet anger*). There's a storm of anger tossin' in me heart, thinkin' of all th' poor Tommies, an' with them me own son, dhrenched in water an' soaked in blood, gropin' their way to a shattherin' death, in a shower of shells! Young men with th' sunny lust o' life beamin' in them, layin' down their white bodies, shredded into torn an' bloody pieces, on th' althar that God Himself has built for th' sacrifice of heroes!

MRS. GOGAN (*indignantly*). Isn't it a nice thing to have to be listenin' to a lassie an' hangin' our heads in a dead silence, knowin' that some persons think more of a ball of malt than they do of th' blessed saints.

FLUTHER (*deprecatingly*). Whisht; she's always dangerous an' derogatory when she's well oiled. Th' safest way to hindher her from havin' any enjoyment out of her spite, is to dip our thoughts into the fact of her bein' a female person that has moved out of th' sight of ordinary sensible people.

BESSIE (*over to* MRS. GOGAN, *viciously*). To look at some o' th' women that's knockin' about, now, is a thing to make a body sigh. . . . A woman on her own, dhrinkin' with a bevy o' men is hardly an example to her sex. . . . A woman dhrinkin' with a woman is one thing, an' a woman dhrinkin' with herself is still a woman— flappers may be put in another category altogether—but a middle-aged married woman makin' herself th' centre of a circle of men is as a woman that is loud an' stubborn, whose feet abideth not in her own house.

THE COVEY (*to* BESSIE—*with a scornful look at* PETER). When I think of all th' problems in front o' th' workers, it makes me sick to be lookin' at oul' codgers goin' about dhressed up like green-accoutered figures gone asthray out of a toyshop!

PETER (*angrily*). Gracious God, give me patience to be listenin' to that blasted young Covey proddin' at me from over at th' other end of th' shop!

MRS. GOGAN (*dipping her finger in the whisky, and moistening with it the lips of her baby*). Cissie Gogan's a woman livin' for nigh on twenty-five years in her own room, an' beyond biddin' th' time o' day to her neighbours, never yet as much as nodded her head in th' direction of other people's business, while she knows some (*with a look at* BESSIE) as are never content unless they're standin' senthry over other people's doin's!

(*Again the figure appears, like a silhouette, in the window, back, and all hear the voice of the speaker declaiming passionately to the gathering outside.* FLUTHER, PETER *and* MRS. GOGAN *stand up, turn, and look towards the window. The* BARMAN *comes to the end of the counter;* BESSIE *and the* COVEY *stop talking, and look towards the window.*)

THE VOICE OF THE SPEAKER. The last sixteen months have been

the most glorious in the history of Europe. Heroism has come back to the earth. War is a terrible thing, but war is not an evil thing. People in Ireland dread war because they do not know it. Ireland has not known the exhilaration of war for over a hundred years. When war comes to Ireland she must welcome it as she would welcome the Angel of God!

(*The figure passes out of sight and hearing.*)

THE COVEY (*towards all present*). Dope, dope. There's only one war worth havin': th' war for th' economic emancipation of th' proletariat.

BESSIE (*referring to* MRS. GOGAN). They may crow away out o' them; but it ud be fitther for some o' them to mend their ways, an' cease from havin' scouts out watchin' for th' comin' of th' Saint Vincent de Paul man, for fear they'd be nailed lowerin' a pint of beer, mockin' th' man with an angel face, shinin' with th' glamour of deceit an' lies!

MRS. GOGAN (*over to* BESSIE). An' a certain lassie standin' stiff behind her own door with her ears cocked listenin' to what's being said, stuffed till she's sthrained with envy of a neighbour thryin' for a few little things that may be got be hard sthrivin' to keep up to th' letther an' th' law, an' th' practices of th' Church!

PETER (*to* MRS. GOGAN). If I was you, Mrs. Gogan, I'd parry her jabbin' remarks be a powerful silence that'll keep her tantalizin' words from penethratin' into your feelin's. It's always betther to leave these people to th' vengeance o' God!

BESSIE (*at the counter*). Bessie Burgess doesn't put up to know much, never havin' a swaggerin' mind, thanks be to God, but goin' on packin' up knowledge accordin' to her conscience: precept upon precept, line upon line; here a little, an' there a little.

(BESSIE, *with a vigorous swing of her shawl, turns, and with a quick movement, faces* MRS. GOGAN.)

(*Furiously.*) But, thanks be to Christ, she knows when she was got, where she was got, an' how she was got; while there's some she knows, decoratin' their finger with a well-polished weddin' ring, would be hard put to it if they were assed to show their weddin' lines!

(MRS. GOGAN *springs from the seat and bounces up to face* BESSIE BURGESS. MRS. GOGAN *is wild with anger.*)

MRS. GOGAN (*with hysterical rage*). Y' oul' rip of a blasted liar, me weddin' ring's been well earned be twenty years be th' side o' me husband, now takin' his rest in heaven, married to me be Father Dempsey, in th' Chapel o' Saint Jude's, in th' Christmas Week of eighteen hundhred an' ninety-five; an' any kid, livin' or dead, that Jinnie Gogan's had since, was got between th' bordhers of th' Ten Commandments! . . .

BESSIE (*bringing the palms of her hands together in sharp claps to emphasize her remarks*). Liar to you, too, maam, y'oul' hardened thresspasser on other people's good nature, wizenin' up your soul in th' arts o' dodgeries, till every dhrop of respectability in a female is dhried up in her, lookin' at your ready-made manœuverin' with th' menkind!

BARMAN (*anxiously leaning over the counter*). Here, there; here, there; speak asy there. No rowin' here, no rowin' here, now.

(FLUTHER *comes from the seat, gets in front of* MRS. GOGAN, *and tries to pacify her;* PETER *leaves the seat, and tries to do the same with* BESSIE, *holding her back from* MRS. GOGAN. BARMAN *behind the counter, leaning forward;* MRS. GOGAN, *with baby in her arms. The* COVEY *remains leaning on the counter, looking on.*)

FLUTHER (*trying to calm* MRS. GOGAN). Now, Jinnie, Jinnie, it's a derogatory thing to be smirchin' a night like this with a row; it's rompin' with th' feelin's of hope we ought to be, instead o' bein' vice versa!

PETER (*trying to quiet* BESSIE). I'm terrible dawny, Mrs. Burgess, an' a fight leaves me weak for a long time aftherwards. . . . Please, Mrs. Burgess, before there's damage done, thry to have a little respect for yourself.

BESSIE (*with a push of her hand that sends* PETER *tottering to the end of the counter*). G'way, you little sermonizing, little yella-faced, little consequential, little pudgy, little bum, you!

MRS. GOGAN (*screaming and struggling*). Fluther, leggo! I'm not goin' to keep an unresistin' silence, an' her scatherin' her festher-in' words in me face, stirrin' up every dhrop of decency in a respect-able female, with her restless rally o' lies that would make a saint say his prayer backwards!

BESSIE (*shouting*). Ah, everybody knows well that th' best charity that can be shown to you is to hide th' thruth as much as our thrue worship of God Almighty will allow us!

MRS. GOGAN (*frantically*). Here, houl' th' kid, one o' yous; houl' th' kid for a minute! There's nothin' for it but to show this lassie a lesson or two. . . . (*To* PETER.) Here, houl' th' kid, you.

(MRS. GOGAN *suddenly rushes over to* PETER, *standing, trembling with fear, between the end of the counter and the seat under the window. Bewildered, and before he's aware of it,* MRS. GOGAN *has put the baby in his arms.* MRS. GOGAN *rushes to put herself in a fighting attitude in front of* BESSIE.)

(*To* BESSIE, *standing before her in a fighting attitude.*) Come on, now, me loyal lassie, dyin' with grief for little Catholic Belgium! When Jinnie Gogan's done with you, you'll have a little leisure lyin' down to think an' pray for your king an' counthry!

BARMAN (*coming from behind the counter, getting between the women, and proceeding to push* BESSIE *towards the door*). Here, now, since yous can't have a little friendly argument quietly, yous'll get out o' this place in quick time. Go on, an' settle your differences somewhere else—I don't want to have another endorsement on me licence.

(*The* BARMAN *pushes* BESSIE *towards the doors,* MRS. GOGAN *following.*)

PETER (*anxiously calling to* MRS. GOGAN). Here, take your kid back ower this. How nicely I was picked now for it to be plumped into my arms!

THE COVEY (*meaningly*). She knew who she was givin' it to, maybe.

(PETER *goes over near to the* COVEY *at the counter to retort indignantly, as the* BARMAN *pushes* BESSIE *out the doors and gets hold of* MRS. GOGAN *to put her out too.*)

PETER (*hotly to the* Covey), Now, I'm givin' you fair warnin', me young Covey, to quit firin' your jibes an' jeers at me. . . . For one o' these days, I'll run out in front o' God Almighty an' take your sacred life!

BARMAN (*pushing* MRS. GOGAN *out after* BESSIE). Go on, now; out you go.

PETER (*leaving the baby down on the floor*). Ay, be Jasus, wait there, till I give her back her youngster!

(PETER *runs to the door, opens it, and calls out after* MRS. GOGAN.)

PETER (*calling at the door*). Eh, there, eh! What about the kid? (*He runs back in, and looks at* FLUTHER *and the* COVEY.) There, she's afther goin' without her kid—what are we goin' to do with it now?

THE COVEY (*jeering*). What are *you* goin' to do with it? Bring it outside an' show everybody what you're afther findin'.

PETER (*in a panic—to* FLUTHER). Pick it up, you, Fluther, an' run afther her with it, will you?

FLUTHER (*with a long look at* PETER). What d'ye take Fluther for? You must think Fluther's a right gom. D'ye think Fluther's like yourself, destitute of a titther of undherstandin'?

BARMAN (*imperatively to* PETER). Take it up, man, an' run out afther her with it, before she's gone too far. You're not goin' to leave th' bloody thing there, are you?

PETER (*plaintively, as he lifts up the baby*). Well, God Almighty, give me patience with all th' scorners, tormentors, an' twarters that are always an' ever thryin' to goad me into prayin' for their blindin' an' blastin' an' burnin' in th' world to come!

(PETER, *with the baby, goes out of the door.* FLUTHER *comes from the front of the window to the counter and stands there, beside the* COVEY.)

FLUTHER (*with an air of relief*). God, its a relief to get rid o' that crowd. Women is terrible when they start to fight. There's no holdin' them back. (*To the* COVEY.) Are you goin' to have anything?

THE COVEY. Ah, I don't mind if I have another half.

FLUTHER (*to the* BARMAN). Two more, Tommy, me son.

(*The* BARMAN *gets the drinks,* FLUTHER *pays.*)

FLUTHER (*to the* COVEY). You know there's no conthrollin' a woman when she loses her head.

(ROSIE *appears at the doors. She looks over at the counter, sees the two men, then crosses over to the end of the counter, where she stands, with a suggestive look towards* FLUTHER.)

ROSIE (*to the* BARMAN). Divil a use o' havin' a thrim little leg on a night like this; things was never worse. . . . Give us a half till to-morrow, Tom, duckey.

BARMAN (*coldly*). No more to-night, Rosie; you owe me for three already.

ROSIE (*combatively*). You'll be paid, won't you?

BARMAN. I hope so.

ROSIE. You hope so! Is that th' way with you, now?

FLUTHER (*with a long glance at* ROSIE, *to the* BARMAN). Give her one—it'll be all right.

(*The* BARMAN *gets a drink, and puts it on the counter before* ROSIE; FLUTHER *pays for it.*)

ROSIE (*clapping* FLUTHER *on the back*). Oul' sport!

FLUTHER (*to* COVEY). Th' meetin' should be soon over, now.

THE COVEY (*in a superior way*). Th' sooner th' betther. It's all a lot o' blasted nonsense, comrade.

FLUTHER. Oh, I wouldn't say it was all nonsense. Afther all, Fluther can remember th' time, an' him only a dawny chiselur, bein' taught at his mother's knee to be faithful to th' Shan Vok Vok!

THE COVEY. That's all dope, comrade; th' sort o' thing that workers are fed on be th' Boorzwawzee.

FLUTHER (*a little sharply*). What's all dope? Though I'm sayin' it that shouldn't: (*catching his cheek with his hand, and pulling down the flesh from the eye*) d'ye see that mark there, undher me eye? . . . A sabre slice from a dragoon in O'Connell Street! (*Thrusting his head forward towards* ROSIE.) Feel that dint in th' middle o' me nut!

ROSIE (*rubbing* FLUTHER'S *head, and winking at the* COVEY). My God, there's a holla!

FLUTHER (*putting on his hat with quiet pride*). A skelp from a bobby's baton at a Labour meetin' in th' Phœnix Park!

THE COVEY (*sarcastically*). He must ha' hitten you in mistake. I don't know what you ever done for th' Labour movement.

FLUTHER (*loudly*). D'ye not? Maybe, then, I done as much, an' know as much about th' Labour movement as th' chancers that are blowin' about it!

BARMAN (*over the counter*). Speak easy, Fluther, thry to speak easy.

THE COVEY (*quietly*). There's no necessity to get excited about it, comrade.

FLUTHER (*more loudly*). Excited? Who's gettin' excited? There's no one gettin' excited! It would take something more than a thing like you to flutther a feather o' Fluther. Blatherin', an', when all is said, you know as much as th' rest in th' wind up!

THE COVEY (*emphatically*). Well, let us put it to th' test, then, an' see what you know about th' Labour movement: what's the mechanism of exchange?

FLUTHER (*roaring, because he feels he is beaten*). How th' hell do I know what it is? There's nothin' about that in th' rules of our Thrades Union!

BARMAN (*protestingly*). For God's sake, thry to speak easy, Fluther.

THE COVEY. What does Karl Marx say about th' Relation of Value to th' Cost o' Production?

FLUTHER (*angrily*). What th' hell do I care what he says? I'm Irishman enough not to lose me head be follyin' foreigners!

BARMAN. Speak easy, Fluther.

THE COVEY (*contemptuously*). It's only waste o' time talkin' to you, comrade.

FLUTHER. Don't be comradin' me, mate. I'd be on me last legs if I wanted you for a comrade.

ROSIE (*to the* COVEY, *taking* FLUTHER'S *part*). It seems a highly rediculous thing to hear a thing that's only an inch or two away from a kid, swingin' heavy words about he doesn't know th' meanin' of, an' uppishly thryin' to down a man like Misther Fluther here, that's well flavoured in th' knowledge of th' world he's livin' in.

THE COVEY (*bending over the counter—savagely to* ROSIE). Nobody's askin' you to be buttin' in with your prate. . . . I have you well taped, me lassie. . . . Just you keep your opinions for your own place. . . . It'll be a long time before th' Covey takes any insthructions or reprimandin' from a prostitute!

(ROSIE, *wild with humiliation, bounds from the end of the counter and with eyes blazing, faces towards the* COVEY.)

ROSIE. You louse, you louse, you! . . . You're no man. . . . You're no man . . . I'm a woman, anyhow, an' if I'm a prostitute aself, I have me feelin's. . . . Thryin' to put his arm around me a minute ago, an' givin' me th' glad eye, th' little wrigglin' lump o' desolation turns on me now, because he saw there was nothin' doin'. . . . You louse, you! If I was a man, or you were a woman, I'd bate th' puss o' you!

BARMAN. Ay, Rosie, ay! You'll have to shut your mouth altogether, if you can't learn to speak easy!

(FLUTHER, *with a dignified walk, goes over to* ROSIE *and puts a hand on her shoulder.*)

FLUTHER (*to* ROSIE). Houl' on there, Rosie; houl' on, there. There's no necessity to flutther yourself when you're with Fluther. . . . Any lady that's in th' company of Fluther is goin' to get a fair hunt. . . . This is outside your province. . . . I'm not goin' to let you demean yourself be talking to a tittherin' chancer. . . . Leave this to Fluther—this is a man's job. . . . (*He turns from* ROSIE, *comes back, crosses the* COVEY, *then turns and faces him. To the* COVEY.) Now, if you've anything to say, say it to Fluther; an' let me tell you, you're not goin' to be pass-remarkable to any lady in my company.

THE COVEY. Sure I don't care if you were runnin' all night afther your Mary o' th' Curlin' Hair, but, when you start tellin' luscious lies about what you done for th' Labour movement, it's nearly time to show y'up!

FLUTHER (*fiercely*). Is it you show Fluther up? G'way, man, I'd beat two o' you before me breakfast!

THE COVEY (*contemptuously*). Tell us where you bury your dead, will you?

FLUTHER (*with his face stuck into the face of the* COVEY). Sing a little less on th' high note, or, when I'm done with you, you'll put a Christianable consthruction on things, I'm tellin' you!

THE COVEY. You're a big fella, you are.

FLUTHER (*tapping the* COVEY *threateningly on the shoulder*). Now, you're temptin' Providence when you're temptin' Fluther!

THE COVEY (*losing his temper, knocking* FLUTHER'S *hands away, and bawling*). Easy with them hands, there, easy with them hands! You're startin' to take a little risk when you commence to paw the Covey!

(FLUTHER *suddenly springs into the center of the shop, flings his hat into the corner, whips off his coat, and begins to paw the air like a pugilist.*)

FLUTHER (*roaring*). Come on, come on, you lowser; put your mits up now, if there's a man's blood in you! Be God, in a few minutes you'll see some snots flyin' around, I'm tellin' you. . . . When Fluther's done with you, you'll have a vice-versa opinion of him! Come on, now, come on!

(*The* COVEY *squares up to* FLUTHER.)

BARMAN (*running from behind the counter and catching hold of the* COVEY). Here, out you go, me little bowsey. Because you got a couple o' halves you think you can act as you like. (*He pushes the* COVEY *to the doors.*) Fluther's a friend o' mine, an' I'll not have him insulted.

THE COVEY (*struggling with the* BARMAN). Ay, leggo, leggo there; fair hunt, give a man a fair hunt! One minute with him is all I ask; one minute alone with him, while you're runnin' for th' priest an' th' doctor!

FLUTHER (*to the* BARMAN). Let him go, let him go, Tom: let him open th' door to sudden death if he wants to!

BARMAN (*grappling with the* COVEY). Go on, out you go an' do th' bowsey somewhere else.

(*The* BARMAN *pushes the* COVEY *out, and goes back behind the counter.* FLUTHER *assumes a proud air of victory.* ROSIE *gets his coat, and helps him to put it on; she then gets his hat and puts it on his head.*)

ROSIE (*helping* FLUTHER *with his coat*). Be God, you put th' fear o' God in his heart that time! I thought you'd have to be dug out of him. . . . Th' way you lepped out without any of your fancy side-steppin'! "Men like Fluther," says I to meself, "is gettin' scarce nowadays."

FLUTHER (*with proud complacency*). I wasn't goin' to let meself be malignified by a chancer. . . . He got a little bit too derogatory for Fluther. . . . Be God, to think of a cur like that comin' to talk to a man like me!

ROSIE (*fixing on his hat*). Did j'ever!

FLUTHER. He's lucky he got off safe. I hit a man last week, Rosie, an' he's fallin' yet!

ROSIE. Sure, you'd ha' broken him in two if you'd ha' hitten him one clatther!

FLUTHER (*amorously, putting his arm around* ROSIE). Come on into th' snug, me little darlin', an' we'll have a few dhrinks before I see you home.

ROSIE. Oh, Fluther, I'm afraid you're a terrible man for th' women.

(FLUTHER *leads* ROSIE *to the seat with the round table in front. She sits down on the seat. He goes to the counter.*)

FLUTHER (*to the* BARMAN). Two, full ones, Tommy.

(BARMAN *gets the drinks.* FLUTHER *brings them over to seat, leaves them on the table, and sits down beside* ROSIE. *The swing-doors open and* CAPTAIN BRENNAN, *a young man, a chicken butcher—of the Irish Volunteers,* COMMANDANT CLITHEROE, *a bricklayer—Commandant in the Irish Citizens Army, and* LIEUTENANT LANGON, *a civil servant of the Irish Volunteers, enter, and cross quickly to the counter.* CAPT. BRENNAN *carries the banner of The*

Plough and the Stars, and LIEUT. LANGON *a green, white and orange Tri-colour. They are in a state of emotional excitement. Their faces are flushed and their eyes sparkle; they speak rapidly, as if unaware of the meaning of what they say. They have been mesmerized by the fervency of the speeches.*)

CLITHEROE (*almost pantingly to the* BARMAN). Three glasses o' port!

(*The* BARMAN *brings the drinks,* CLITHEROE *pays.*)

CAPT. BRENNAN. We won't have long to wait now.

LIEUT. LANGON. Th' time is rotten ripe for revolution.

CLITHEROE (*to* LIEUT. LANGON). You have a mother, Langon.

LIEUT. LANGON. Ireland is greater than a mother.

CAPT. BRENNAN (*to* CLITHEROE). You have a wife, Clitheroe.

CLITHEROE. Ireland is greater than a wife.

LIEUT. LANGON. Th' time for Ireland's battle is now—th' place for Ireland's battle is here.

(*The tall, dark figure again appears in the window. The three men stiffen to attention. They stand out from the counter,* BRENNAN *nearest counter, then* CLITHEROE, *then* LIEUT. LANGON. FLUTHER *and* ROSIE, *busy with each other, take no notice.*)

THE VOICE OF THE MAN. Our foes are strong, but strong as they are, they cannot undo the miracles of God, who ripens in the heart of young men the seeds sown by the young men of a former generation. They think they have pacified Ireland; think they have foreseen everything; think they have provided against everything; but the fools, the fools, the fools!—they have left us our Fenian dead, and, while Ireland holds these graves, Ireland, unfree, shall never be at peace!

CAPT. BRENNAN (*lifting up the Plough and the Stars*). Imprisonment for th' Independence of Ireland!

LIEUT. LANGON (*lifting up the Tri-colour*). Wounds for th' Independence of Ireland!

CLITHEROE. Death for th' Independence of Ireland!

THE THREE (*together*). So help us God!

(*They lift their glasses and drink together. The "Assembly" is heard on a bugle outside. They leave their glasses on the counter, and hurry out by doors. A pause. Then* FLUTHER *and* ROSIE *rise from the seat, and start to go.* ROSIE *is linking* FLUTHER, *who is a little drunk. Both are in a merry mood.*)

Rosie. Are you afraid or what? Are you goin' to come home, or are you not?

Fluther. Of course I'm goin' home. What ud ail me that I wouldn't go?

Rosie (*lovingly*). Come on, then, oul' sport.

Officer's Voice (*giving command outside*). Irish Volunteers, by th' right, quick march!

Rosie (*putting her arm round* Fluther *and singing to the air* "*Twenty-four Strings to my Bow*"). I once had a lover, a tailor, but he could do nothin' for me,
An' then I fell in with a sailor as strong an' as wild as th' sea.
We cuddled an' kissed with devotion, till th' night from th' mornin' had fled;
An' there, to our joy, a bright bouncin' boy
Was dancin' a jig in th' bed!

Dancin' a jig in th' bed, an' bawlin' for butther an' bread.
An' there, to our joy, a bright bouncin' boy
Was dancin' a jig in th' bed!

(*They go out with their arms round each other.*)

Clitheroe's Voice (*in command outside*). Dublin Battalion of the Irish Citizen Army, by th' right, quick march!

CURTAIN

PADRAIC COLUM

****

DEAR WHIT BURNETT,

I am not sure what sort of comment I am expected to make on these poems; I suppose it should be about the influences that went to shaping them. I was already, in my twenties, connected with the Irish Theatre (the embryonic Irish Theatre) when I began to write the poems that are in my first book, Wild Earth. *This gave them a dramatic cast; my early verse took the form of dramatic lyrics. I was a very enthusiastic member of the Gaelic League whose object was the re-creation of a native culture. This gave me a bent towards folk-song, the language and rhythm of which (I am speaking now of the songs in English) I tried to reproduce. Learning Irish I was fascinated by the wonderful examples of West of Ireland folk-songs in Gaelic given in Douglas Hyde's* Love Songs of Connacht. *These are simple poems that nevertheless are as finely wrought and as poignant as any in the world's great literature. They gave me an idea of the directness and simplicity one might get into poetry. One of the poems given here, "I Shall Not Die For Thee" is translated from one in the Connacht Songs. It is not a folk-song, however, but a poem made by an aristocrat working in the bardic tradition and influenced as many Irish aristocratic poets of the fifteenth century as did the French poetry of the Courts of Love.*

PADRAIC COLUM

****

Five Poems

WHAT THE SHUILER SAID AS SHE LAY BY THE FIRE IN THE FARMER'S HOUSE

I'M GLAD to lie on a sack of leaves
By a wasted fire and take my ease.
For the wind would strip me bare as a tree—
The wind would blow old age upon me.
And I'm dazed with the wind, the rain, and the cold.
   If I had only the good red gold
To buy me the comfort of a roof,
And under the thatch the brown of the smoke!
   I'd lie up in my painted room
Until my hired girl would come;
And when the sun had warmed my walls
I'd rise up in my silks and shawls,
And break my fast before the fire.
And I'd watch them that had to sweat
And shiver for shelter and what they ate.
The farmer digging in the fields;
The beggars going from gate to gate;
The horses striving with their loads,
And all the sights upon the roads.

I'd live my lone without clan or care,
And none about me to crave a share.
The young have mocking, impudent ways,
And I'd never let them a-nigh my place.
And a child has often a pitiful face.
   I'd give the rambling fiddler rest,
And for me he would play his best.
And he'd have something to tell of me
From the Moat of Granard down to the sea!
And, though I'd keep distant, I'd let in
Old women who would card and spin
And clash with me, and I'd hear it said,
   "Mór who used to carry her head
As if she was a lady bred—

619

Has little enough in her house, they say—
And such-a-one's child I saw on the way
Scaring crows from a crop, and glad to get,
In a warmer house, the bit to eat.
O! none are safe, and none secure,
And it's well for some whose bit is sure!"

I'd never grudge them the weight of their lands
If I had only the good red gold
To huggle between my breast and hands!

SCANDERBEG

SHE SAT on the wall and dangled her silk-stockinged legs,
Saying, "I'll not have them stung for any old man who is dead,"
So I went where nettles were rank and came on a stone that read.—
'Matthew de Rienzi,
Knight, born in Germany.
Descended from George Castriot, alias Scanderbeg,
Who fifty-two battles broke with conquest against the Great Turk.'
More: the Knight de Rienzi,
Learned in Irish, composed for it a Dictionary,
Corresponded with men of state upon affairs,
And died here; fifty seven his years.
Peace be with Matthew!
Then I looked where she sat on the wall dangling her silk stockinged
      legs,
Which she would not have stung for any old man who was dead,
As she said—
Not even, I supposed, for a descendant of Scanderbeg!
But I heard a curlew
Over the river beside me, the Shannon it was,
And saw from that to the Danube, and it was crossed
By turbaned men under whose stallions' hoofs the grass
Never grew again;
And that battlefield the Plain of the Blackbirds, Kassoro,
And the Sultan Murad slain,
And the breach in Constantinople's wall, and Belgrade,
Buda and Vienna under great cannonade,
And the sweep of the Pashas onwards until Hungary, Poland, the
      Germanies were all dismayed,
And that historyless man, George Castriot, holding at bay

Byzantium's conquerors in the mountains of Albania;
Then battles along the Rhine,
And Dutchmen and English, Frenchmen and Irish forcing or
    holding this line,
And the Shannon crossed and Aughrim lost to our own overthrow!
Two hundred years' battling in Europe at the name of Scanderbeg
Spun through my mind as a curlew cried overhead!

FOLDING HOUR

THEN COMES the lad with hazel,
And the folding star's in the rack—
"Night's a good herd," to the cattle
He sings, "she brings all things back."

But the bondwoman there by the boorie
Sings with a heart grown wild,
How a hundred rivers are flowing
Between herself and her child—

"The geese, even they, trudge homeward
That have their wings and the waste;
Let your thoughts be on Night the Herder,
And be quiet for a space—

See! The Moon cradle's rocking and rocking,
Where a cloud and a cloud go by,
Silently rocking and rocking,
The moon-cradle out in the sky!"

I SHALL NOT DIE FOR THEE

O WOMAN shapely as the swan,
On your account I shall not die:
The men you've slain, a trivial clan,
Were less than I!

I ask me shall I die for these—
For blossom teeth and scarlet lips,
And shall that delicate swan shape,
Bring me eclipse?

Well-shaped the breasts and smooth the skin,
The cheeks are fair, the tresses free,
And yet I shall not suffer death,
God over me!

Those even brows, that hair like gold,
Those langrous tones, that virgin way,
The flowing limbs, the rounded heel
Slight men betray!

Thy spirit keen through radiant mien,
Thy shining throat and smiling eye,
Thy little palm, thy side like foam—
I cannot die!

O woman shapely as the swan,
In a cunning house hard reared was I,
O bosom white, O well-shaped palm,
I shall not die!

                              —*Translated from the Irish*

THE SEER

"BELOW there are white-faced throngs,
  Their march is a tide coming nigher;
Below there are white-faced throngs,
  Their faith is a banner flung higher;
Below there are white-faced throngs,
  White swords they have yet, but red songs;
Place and lot they have lost—hear you not?
For a dream you once dreamed and forgot."

"But a dream has a life of its own,
  The wizard seas it can cross;
A dream has a life of its own,
  It comes like the albatross.
A dream has a life of its own;
From my feet to your feet it has flown,
And you, you victorious,
  That wild live thing will lose."

ELIZABETH BOWEN

****

*I think this story arose from my wondering what becomes, after-
wards, of children who are for a short time in the limelight in some
"ugly" case. The completely normal child would, no doubt, throw
the thing off; but on the narcissistic or at all exhibitionistic child,
I imagine that some unfortunate imprint might be left. The little
girl in this story stands for the latter case. I have treated—I must
confess—as comedy a tale which might have tragic implications.
I cannot help seeing funniness in the total inadequacy of Eunice
and Isabelle Evers. Kindliness, idealism and "clean fun" are excellent things—but not, alas, the antidote to all human ills.*

ELIZABETH BOWEN

****

The Easter Egg Party

THEIR OBJECT was to restore her childhood to her. They were
simple and zealous women, of an integrity rooted in flawless sentiment; they bowed to nothing but their own noble ideas and flinched
from nothing but abandoning these. They issued the invitation on
an impulse but awaited the answer with no drop in morale. They
did not shrink from facts, for they attended committees for the good
of the world—most facts, however, got to West Wallows a little bit
watered down: such things did happen, but not to people one knew.
So that when their eye was drawn—they were unmarried sisters,
with everything in common, and had, in regard to some things, one
eye between them—when their eye was drawn by a once-quite-
familiar name to an obscure paragraph in their daily paper, their
hearts (or their heart) stopped. The case was given in outline, with
unusual reticence. When they saw what had either happened or
nearly happened—they were not quite clear which—to the little
girl of a friend they had known as a little girl, shyness and horror
drove a wedge between them; they became two people whose looks

623

could not quite meet. Across the breakfast-table of their large cottage, in the half-acre of garden already gladey and glittering with the first greens of spring, they failed to discuss the matter. After a day of solitary side-by-side reflection it came up with them in its happier practical aspect: 'Could one *do* anything, now? . . . Is there any way one could help?'

Eunice and Isabelle Evers were both just over fifty: their un-perplexed lives showed in their faces, lined only by humour, and in their frank high foreheads. They were Amazons in homespuns, Amazons, without a touch of deprivation or pathos; their lives had been one long vigorous country walk. Like successful nuns, they both had a slightly married air. An unusual number of people in Gloucestershire knew and respected them, and they cut ice in the village of West Wallows. They thought the world of children, of any children; and children, in consequence, thought the world of them: they were past mistresses at blowing that bubble world that is blown for children by children-loving grown-ups—perhaps, also, the dearest of their own pleasures lay there. If they had any fantasies, these centred round ponies and bread-and-jam on the beach, and they still received intimations of immortality.

Therefore, any unspeakable thing happening to any child was more upsetting to them than if they had been mothers. It was against their natures to judge Dorothea (the friend they had known as a little girl) in any way. All the same, across what line, into what world had she wandered in these years since her marriage, since they had lost sight of her, that *her* little girl should be exposed to such things as this? Dorothea's marriage had failed. Must one own she failed as a mother? They knew, vaguely, Dorothea was 'on the stage'—though one never saw her name on the programme of any play.

Dorothea's answer to their invitation took so long in coming that they had begun to fear she was out of reach. But when she did answer, Dorothea accepted with alacrity. She said that it really was truly sweet of them, and she only hoped they would find Hermione good. 'She's really as good as gold, but she's always rather reserved. I am sure it might do her good to be away from me for a bit; you see, I am really very upset these days. I suppose that's only natural; my nerves have always been awful, and now *this* coming, on top of everything else. It's nearly killed me, of course. I suppose one will get over it. Well, it really is dear of you; you always were such dears. *Oh,* how far away all those happy days seem now! . . . I will send Hermione down on 12th April. Yes, I think she's fond of animals; at all events you could try. Of course she's never had any, poor little soul.'

So they began to prepare for Hermione.

West Wallows was more than a village: it was a neighbourhood. From the wide street branched roads that led past the white gates of many homes. The rector was tactful and energetic, the squire unusually cultivated; there were a number of moderate-sized dwellings—some antique, some quite recently built. Inexpensive sociability, liberal politics, shapely antique family furniture, 'interests,' enlightened charity set the note of the place. No one was very rich; nobody was eccentric, and, though few people hunted, nobody wrote letters against blood sports. The local families harmonized with the pleasant retired people who had settled here. Probably few neighbourhoods in England have such a nice atmosphere as West Wallows. In the holidays all the children had a jolly time. . . . The Easter holidays were in progress now, and this created a slight predicament: how much should Hermione be with other children?

The Misses Evers decided to wait and see.

They decided to wait for grace and see what line things took. They hinted at nothing to anyone. In the week before Hermione came, the tortoiseshell cat Barbara was persuaded to wean her two patchy kittens, who learnt to lap prettily from an Umbrian saucer. The honeysuckle up the south front of the cottage unfolded the last of its green shoots, and in the garden and in the strip of orchard the other side of the brook daffodils blew their trumpets.

The first afternoon was windy. Every time a sucker of honeysuckle swung loose and tapped the window Hermione jumped. This was the only sign she gave of having grown-up nerves. She was not quite a pretty child; her face was a long, plump oval; her large dark-grey eyes were set rather close together, which gave her an urgent air. Her naturally curly dark hair had grown too long for a bob and swung just clear of her shoulders. She sat in the dark glass dome of her own inside world, just too composedly eating bread and honey. Now and then she glanced, with mysterious satisfaction, at the bangles on one or the other of her wrists.

'This is honey from our own bees, Hermione.'

'Goodness.'

'It tastes quite different from other honey, *we* think.'

'Yes; Mummy said you kept bees. Do you keep doves too?'

Eunice glanced at the white forms that whirled rather frighten-

ingly over the wind-teased garden. 'Those are the next-door pigeons;
they keep on flying over, so we have the fun of them.'

'The next-door cat in London keeps getting into our larder. I do
hate cats.'

'Oh, but you must like Barbara—and she's got two kittens.'

'Cats always do that, don't they?'

After tea Eunice took her up to what was to be her room, the
spare-room over the porch, snug as a ship's cabin and frilly with
sprigged stuff. She showed her the sampler worked by another little
girl of eleven, just a hundred years ago, and some framed photographs of Italy. 'That's Assisi, where St. Francis lived.'

'Goodness,' said Hermione, biting her thumb vaguely. She looked
through the loops of dotted muslin curtain at the tops of the apple
trees. 'It's just like on a calendar,' she said. She sat on the bed, with
her tongue feeling round one cheek, while Eunice unpacked her
two suit-cases for her. 'Oh, what pretty clothes and things,' said
Eunice deprecatingly. 'But I don't think you'll have a chance to
wear most of them here. You'll want to wear old clothes and simply
tumble about.'

'I haven't got any old clothes. Mummy gives them away.'

In her tweed skirt, with her knotted oak walking-stick, lifting her
forehead to the sweet spring air Isabelle, next morning, swung down
the village street, and Hermione walked beside her, changing step
now and then with a queer little dancing hop. In her raspberry
woollen dress, her turned-up hat with the Donald Duck clip and
her long, white, carefully pulled-up socks, the child looked like a
stage child half-way through a tour: nothing would tone her down.
Isabelle pointed out the village pond with its white ducks, the
saddleback church tower, the Beacon on the top of the steep, green
nursery-rhyme hill, the quaint old sign of the Spotted Cow, which
made all children laugh—Hermione did not smile. A street is a
street, and the point of a street is, people: looking boldly up, she
challenged whoever passed with her dusky, gelatinous dark-grey
eyes. It was their attention she wanted; she collected attention like
twists of silver paper or small white pebbles. Her search for attention was so arduous that she gave less than half her mind to whatever Isabelle said. Whenever Isabelle turned into a shop, Hermione
would ferret along the counter. In the chemist's she said she would
like to buy that green celluloid box to keep her toothbrush in.

'Have you brought your pocket-money?' said Isabelle brightly.

'Oh—but I haven't any.'

'Then I'm afraid the green box will have to wait,' said Isabelle still more brightly, with an inspiring smile. She did not approve of buying hearts with small gifts: besides, one must teach Hermione not to 'hint.' Hermione gave the green box a last look, the first fully human look she had spent on anything since she came to West Wallows. She slowly dragged her eyes from it and followed Isabelle out of the chemist's shop.

'This afternoon,' said Isabelle, 'we'll go primrosing.'

'I think those lambs are pretty,' said Hermione, suddenly pointing over a wall. 'I should like a pet lamb of my own; I should call it Percy.'

'Well, perhaps you can make a friend of one of these lambs. If you go every day very quietly into the field——'

'But I want it to be my own; I want to call it Percy.'

'Well, let's *call* "Percy," and see which of them comes. . . . Percy, Percy, Percy!' called Isabelle, leaning over the wall. None of the lambs took any notice: one of the sheep gave her a long, reproving look. Hermione, meanwhile, had frigidly walked away.

Eunice and Isabelle took it in turns to what they called take Hermione out of herself. They did not confess how unnerved they sometimes were by their sense of intense attention being focused on nothing. They took her in to see the neighbour who kept the pigeons; Eunice taught her to climb the safe apple trees; Isabelle took her out in a pair of bloomers and dared her to jump the brook. Hermione jumped in and was pulled out patient and very wet. They borrowed a donkey for her, and the run of a paddock, but she fell off the donkey three times. This child stayed alone the whole time and yet was never alone: their benevolent spying on her, down the orchard or through windows, always showed them the same thing— Hermione twirling round her silver bangles at some unseen person, or else tossing her hair. They took her primrosing three times; then they took her bird's-nesting in the Hall grounds. In the great hollow beech hedges, in the dense ivy, the secret nests excited her: she stood up on tiptoes; her cheeks flamed. But all this waned when she might not touch the eggs. She could not understand why. The glossy blues, the faint greens, the waxy buff-pinks, the freckles seemed to her to be for nothing: while the sisters, breathless, held apart the branches she now looked only glumly into the nests. When they found a brood of fledglings she ran six yards back and said: *'Ugh! Fancy leaving eggs just for that!'*

'But they're alive, dear. Next spring they'll be singing away, like all the birds we hear now, or laying eggs of their own.'

'Well, I don't see why.'

The sisters bound each other to silence with quick glances.

Hermione said: 'I'd sooner have sugar eggs.'

It was from this rather baffling afternoon that the idea of the Easter egg party arose.

Hermione ought now, they felt, if ever, to be fit for younger society. Perhaps she might find friends—how they doubted this! At all events, one must see. And since she was to meet children, why should she not meet all the West Wallows children at once? About a quite large party there should be something kind and ambiguous: if she failed to hit it off with Maisie or Emmeline, she might hit it off with Harriet or Joanne. (The fact was, they felt, in a way they rather dreaded to face, that in a large party she would stand out less.) The Misses Evers were well known for their juvenile parties, but up to now these had always been held at Christmas, when guessing games could be played, or at Midsummer, when they got permission for their young guests to help to make someone's hay. An Easter party was quite a new idea and looked like running them in for more expense—they did not jib at this, but they dreaded the ostentation. Isabelle bicycled into Market Chopping and bought three dozen sweet eggs—a little reduced in price, as Easter was just over. Some were chocolate, wrapped in brilliant metallic paper; some were marzipan, with the most naturalistic freckles; some were cardboard, containing very small toys. That same afternoon Eunice, at her bureau, wrote out invitations to the fourteen young guests, ranging in age from fourteen down to six. As she addressed each envelope she would pause, to give Hermione, entrancedly doing nothing on the sofa beside her, a biography of each possible child.

The afternoon of the party was, happily, very fine. From three o'clock on the garden gate clicked incessantly: unaccompanied by grown-ups the guests in their coloured jerseys or very clean blouses came up the path—to be mustered by Eunice and Isabelle on the patch of lawn by the sundial. They were already tanned or freckled by the spring sun, and all wore an air of stolid elation. 'Now, finding *ought* to be keeping,' said Isabelle, 'but we think that if any one of you people finds more than three, he or she might hand the rest back, to go at the end to some other person who may not have been so clever.'

Eunice put in: 'And we shall be giving a prize: this Easter rabbit' (she held up a china ornament) 'to whoever hands in most eggs by the end of the afternoon.'

Isabelle took up: 'They are hidden about the garden and in the orchard the other side of the stream. To make things just a little easier we have tied a piece of pink wool *somewhere near* every place where an egg is. And whoever finds each egg must untie the pink wool, please, or it will be so difficult. Now, are we all here? Oh, no: we are still waiting for Poppy. The moment she's here I'm going to blow this whistle, then—off with you all! At five o'clock I shall blow the whistle for tea.'

At this moment the late-comer bolted in at the gate, whereupon Isabelle blew the whistle piercingly. The children—the boys were small, the girls larger-sized, some of them quite lumpy—glanced at each other, tittered and moved off. For some distance they stayed in compact formation, like explorers advancing in dangerous territory; though all the time their sharp eyes were glancing left and right. Then, in the glittering sunshine of the garden, shreds of pink wool began to be discerned. One by one children bounded off from the others, glancing jealously round to see that no one was on their tracks.

Hermione had lagged a little behind the party that moved off. She had been introduced to all the children by name, but after the how-d'you-do's no one had spoken to her. She had secured by the wrist the only other child that tagged behind the party, a small, dumb little boy: she gripped this child by the wrist as though he were not human—he appeared in some way to give her countenance. From the beginning she had been difficult: she had been reluctant to come down from her room at all: from the lawn below Eunice had called and waved; Hermione had answered but not come. Ghostly just inside her shut bedroom window, or like a paper figure pasted against the glass, she had watched strange children invade the garden she knew. She had gone on like a kitten that somehow gets up a tree, panics, and cannot be got down again—till Eunice ran up to dislodge her with some well-chosen words. But alas, once one had got her onto the lawn, her up-a-tree air only became more noticeable. She shook hands with a rigid arm, on which all the bracelets jumped. She looked straight at everyone, but from a moody height: what was evident was not just fear or shyness but a desperate, cut-off haughtiness. In her eyes existed a world of alien experience. The jolly tallish girls with their chubbed hair, the straddling little boys with their bare knees, apt to frown at the grass between their sandshoes, rebounded from that imperious

stare. Either she cared too much or she did not care a fig for them—
and in either case they did not know how to meet her.

Sloping south to the brook, the garden was made devious by
swastika hedges: it was all grots and plots. Japanese plums caught
light in their ethereal petals; flowering currants set out their sweet,
hot smell. The waving shreds of pink wool made round themselves
centres of magnetic attraction, in which children hummed and
jostled, like the bees round the currants. The garden, the orchard
became tense with the search: now and then yelps of triumphs
struck their silence like sharp bells. By the end of a half-hour everyone seemed to have found at least one egg. Children met to compare their spoils, then pounced jealously off again.

Only Hermione and the doomed little boy that she would not let
go of had not yet found an egg. She sometime shifted her grip on
his hot wrist. In her haze of self-consciousness, weighted by that
deep-down preoccupation, she moved too slowly, dragging the little
boy. Once or twice she did see pink wool, but when she got to the
spot it was always being untied by the child who had found the egg.
Disgraced by their failure, she and the little boy said not a word to
each other; they moved about in a silence of deeping animosity.
Now they stood on the bridge, between the garden and orchard:
Hermione looked from one shore to the other with eyes that held
incredulity and despair. She had not found *any* egg.

Without warning the little boy went rigid all over, braced himself
against the rail of the bridge, threw open his cave of mouth and
yelled: 'Oh, *Mais-see*, I wanner go with you!'

A girl bustling contently through the orchard, three bright eggs
shining on the palm of her hand, stopped and lifted her nose like a
mother dog. Then she approached the bridge. 'I say,' she said to
Hermione, 'would you mind letting my little brother go? He'd like
to look by himself.'

'He and I are looking together.'

'Oh. How many have you each found?'

'Somebody else always finds the ones we are looking for.'

'Good gracious,' said Maisie, 'then haven't you found *any*? Someone says that Harriet's got six, and everyone else here has found at
least two. Do you mean to say poor Simon hasn't got *any*? . . .
Never mind, Simon; come and look with me. *We'll* soon find some.'

'I don't see why he should. Why should I be the only person left
who hasn't got any egg?'

'Well, I can't help that, can I? You'd better look more properly.
. . . Come along, Simon.'

Hermione let him go.

When she found herself quite alone on the bridge she shaded her eyes (because the sun was descending) to peer at the round white object under one apple tree. It was a panama hat, last seen on the girl Harriet: now it sat on the grass. As though something inside her answered a magnet, Hermione left the bridge and ran to that apple tree. The general search had ebbed back to the garden: in the orchard no one shouted; no one swished through the long grass— the place was deserted suddenly. Hermione knelt down, cautiously raised the hat, and saw the clutch of six supernatural eggs—two gold, one red, one silver and two blue. They lay tilted together in their nest in the grass. Trembling with satisfaction, she regarded them steadily. Then she made a pouch of her skirt and gathered the eggs up into it. Clumsily, cautiously rising, she made off at a trot for the hedge that cut off the orchard from Church Lane.

She was not missed till the five o'clock whistle sounded and the children trooped in through the French window for tea. Then Eunice and Isabelle combined to pass the contretemps over as smoothly as possible. While Eunice poured out, and kept the chatter going, Isabelle, with the whistle, slipped out for a thorough look. Sadly, sadly, she saw some trampled daffodils—the nicer the set of children, the larger their feet. When she got to the end of the orchard she saw the gap forced through the hedge, and her heart sank.

The big scandal only broke at the end of tea-time, when Eunice began to check up the eggs found. Throughout tea the outraged Harriet had not suffered in silence: there had been a good deal of mumbling at her end of the table, but Eunice did not know what the matter was. When the loss came out Eunice put two and two together with disheartening rapidity—so did everyone else. Speaking looks were cast by the West Wallows children at the place where Hermione did not sit. There was nothing for it but to present the china rabbit to Harriet with as much haste, and still as much pomp, as possible and to suggest we should now all play prisoners' base on the lawn.

Seven strokes from the church clock fell on the sad, clear evening. The Easter egg party guests had been sent home an hour ago; the sisters had returned from their desperate search, up and down the village, in the fields, in the near woods. Something made Eunice go up to Hermione's room—there *was* Hermione, sitting on the bed. She must have slipped back while nobody was about. In the deep dusk she was sitting across her bed, legs stuck out and back stuck to the wall, in the attitude in which one props up a doll. She was, presumably, waiting: the moment the door opened, she said, without looking up: 'I want to go home now.'

'But, Hermione——'

'Mummy said I needn't stay if I didn't like it. She said I could come straight home.'

'Dear, this isn't because you think *we* are . . . upset about anything.'

'I can't help *what* you are,' said Hermione, quite dispassionate. 'Couldn't you get some other girl to stay with you? There's nothing for me to do here; I mean, I can't do anything. And all those girls were awful to me today; nobody cared if I found an egg or not. That girl Maisie wouldn't let me play with her brother. No one has ever been so awful to me as they all were; they took all the eggs, and I never found even one. And you never let me talk, all the time, and you never let me touch anything. You keep on making me take an interest in things, and you never take the slightest interest in me. Mummy said you were interested in me, but now I don't believe her. I feel just as if I was dead, and I do want to go home. Oh, and *I* took those six old eggs.'

'Well, hush now, dear: we're all tired. Hop into bed, like a good girl, and I'll bring you some biscuits and milk. Would you like me to bring up one of the kittens too?'

'No, thank you; your kittens scratch. Well, can I go home tomorrow?'

'We'll see about that tomorrow.'

Eunice sighed and went downstairs. She filled a beaker with milk and put out a plate of biscuits, then she looked into the parlour for a word with Isabelle. The lamps were lit, but the curtains were not drawn yet: outside there was a dark twitter of birds. Isabelle, reading the look on her sister's face, came round the table, saying: 'Oh, Eunice . . .'

'I know,' Eunice said. 'It apparently can't be helped. Her mind's set now on going home. I wonder whether she'd better. . .'

'Eunice, that's *not* like you!' cried Isabelle, with a burst of their old heroic energy.

'I know,' said Eunice, putting down the biscuits. Absently, she began to sip the milk. 'But you see, *this* is really not like anything else. There are times when being like one's self, however much one's self, does not seem much help. Well, there it is, Isabelle. We've always known life was difficult, but I must confess, till today I'd never really believed it. I don't see quite where we failed: she *is* a child, after all.'

'I suppose, once a child has been the centre of things . . .'

'Oh, look—I'm drinking this milk. It really was for Hermione.'

Hermione left next day: perhaps it was for the best. They never speak of her to the children at West Wallows, and the West Wallows children do not ask about her. The sisters seldom speak of her even between themselves; she has left a sort of scar, like a flattened grave, in their hearts. It rained the day she left, but cleared up again at sunset. When Isabelle, in her gum-boots, walking in the orchard, found the six Easter eggs under the original apple tree, the chocolate under the paper had gone to a pulp, and the gold and colours of the paper had run.

LIAM O'FLAHERTY

****

Bellicose is the word for the roaring fighters in The Challenge *by Liam O'Flaherty, typical of his humorous and lyrical understanding of a certain kind of Irishman. His old friend, Sean O'Faolain, has said of O'Flaherty: "Wonder is his weapon and folly is his enemy . . . one feels that O'Flaherty writes in a kind of fury." In his short story the fury is reflected in his characters, as well as quite a lot of sound.*

****

The Challenge

THE FAIR was almost over. The street cleaners were already at work on the western end of the great square. Down there the ground looked like the surface of a flooded bog after the heavy rain that had fallen almost constantly during the afternoon. The slush rose in a thick brown wave before the massive brooms of the sweepers.

Some horses still remained unsold on the high ground at the northeastern corner. There was a little group of men around each horse. They had the collars of their greatcoats turned up about their ears, as protection against the cold east wind. Jobbers walked briskly from group to group.

A long row of red-wheeled carts stood before the taverns, from which the sound of drunken singing issued in ever-changing volume. Women sat patiently in the carts, waiting until their men were ready to quit drinking and go home. Here and there, a man could be seen lying on his back in a cart, one arm thrown limply across his face. A party of four civic guards stood outside the door of the farthest tavern, trying to pacify two men who had been quarreling.

In the space between the horses and the carts, a large crowd faced the gable end of the little house in which pigs are weighed. They stood in a wide half circle, watching the antics of a tinker couple. The tinker's wife sat on an orange box against the wall of the house. She had a leash to which a white hound was attached in her right hand. She brandished a short stick that she held in her left hand at the people. Five asses, with their heads tied close together and their snouts to the ground, stood facing the gable end to her left. Now and then she struck at the nearest one of them with her stick. Her husband stood a short distance out from the gable end, with his legs spread wide and his clenched fists close to his hips, challenging the people to fight him.

He was yelling at them arrogantly in a hoarse voice. "If there is a cocky man among you," he cried, "e'er a boastful fellow that fancies himself, let him come out here to me on this clear ground. I'll tear the living heart out of him!"

He was a handsome man, even though he was middle-aged and ravaged by debauch. He had no more belly than a hound. His body widened out gradually from waist to shoulder. Like a bull, it was about his upper chest and the base of his neck that he had most muscle. His jaws were heavy and square. His nose was short and thick. His complexion and what remained of his hair were dark. His small blue eyes lay far back in his skull. A piece of his right ear was missing. He wore a black jacket and gray trousers. Both garments were in tatters. The jacket had no buttons in front. He wore only a flimsy cotton shirt beneath it. The shirt also was in rags. It was pulled up from the trousers in front. The thick black growth of hair on his chest was visible between the strips of blue cotton. The peak of his gray cap was turned to the rear.

"What ails the lot of you?" he yelled, as he stamped with one foot and then with the other. "Does the very sight of me strike terror into you?"

The people watched him with amused interest, just as if he were putting on a spectacle for their entertainment. Nobody spoke.

"Come on out here," the tinker yelled. "Let that boastful fellow that has all the talk come on out here, so I can tear the heart out of him. I'll wipe him off the face of the earth."

His wife jumped to her feet, threw her shawl to the ground and swung the stick about her head. "I could lick the whole fair for a shilling," she cried.

She walked back and forth a few steps, brandishing the stick, in the way a boxer acknowledges the salutations of the audience on coming into the ring. Then she stamped on the ground before her orange box.

"I could lick every man Jack here present for one lousy shilling," she cried.

She was very tall and slender. She had scarcely any breasts. Her thin bony face was without color. She had large green eyes like a cat. Her brown hair hung down in disorder about her cheeks. She was much younger than her husband. Her blue skirt, her heavy Kashmir shawl of blue and orange color, her gray bodice and the red kerchief that she wore as a band around the top of her skull were all new and spotless. Only her shoes were filthy and ragged. There were no laces in them and the tongues protruded.

"Don't waste your breath, darling," her husband said to her. "You could lick any man here with one hand tied behind your back."

The wife picked up her shawl, threw it casually about her shoulders and sat down on her box. Then she struck the ass nearest to her a violent blow on the side with her stick.

"For one lousy shilling," she yelled, " I could lick the whole bloody fair without any bother at all!"

The husband walked around the inner rim of the half circle, looking insolently into the eyes of the people. He now held his fists out in front of him. He did not speak until he had returned to his former position before the gable end. Then he yelled ferociously, "There isn't a man from here to Ballyvaughan that I couldn't crucify," he shouted. "I could make mince meat of all the rowdies that were ever pupped in Castlegar. There isn't a gouger in the whole of Connemara that I wouldn't floor with one blow. As for the pampootie men from the Aran Islands, I could send all them cowardly scissorbills off the face of this holy earth with the back of my hand. Come on out now if you have any spunk in you! Come on, you Connemara gougers! I'm the man to tame the lot of you."

Then he turned suddenly and struck one of the asses a mighty blow in the side with his right fist. "I'm the best man in the whole county of Galway," he shouted.

His wife yelled and rapped the ground with her stick. "True for you, treasure," she cried. "You're the best man and I'm the second best. Barring the two of us, treasure, there isn't the makings of a middling man here present. There isn't even the makings of a man among the lousy lot of them."

A young man spoke in the center of the crowd. "Make way for me, good people," he cried.

He shouldered the people to right and left and made his way to the center of the half circle. There he stood arrogantly on widespread legs, with his arms folded across his chest and his back to the tinkers. He was no more than a stripling, of slight build, tall and very handsome. Indeed, his face looked rather effeminate owing to the expression of girlish conceit in his large blue eyes. He had full rosy cheeks. A large mop of curly black hair showed between the top of his forehead and the peak of his gray cap. He wore a new serge suit, a knitted white jumper and elegant English shoes with pointed toes.

"I heard some man here talking about Connemara gougers," he cried, with his head thrown back to one side in conceited fashion. "That's an insulting word. As I happen to be a Connemara man myself, I'll stand here to see will that man repeat it. If he does there will be a fight. I'm a quiet, well-behaved lad. I never pick a quarrel with any man. Neither do I run from a fight, though. Where I am, I stand."

There was silence for a little while. Then the tinker's wife jumped to her feet and swung her stick about her head. "I could lick all the bloody gougers in Connemara," she cried.

The tinker leaped clean off the ground and struck his buttocks with his heels while in the air. He struck the ground on descending with the flat of both feet simultaneously. Then he yelled mightily and threw off his jacket in haste. He took the wretched garment by the end of one sleeve and let it trail upon the ground behind him. Then he walked briskly around the young man from Connemara. "I double dare any man to put a foot on my coat," he cried, as he walked around. "Who dares to face me puts his foot on my coat."

When he had returned to his former position, he threw down the jacket. "There it is," he cried. "Let the man that has courage put a foot on it."

The young man took off his own jacket slowly. He folded it neatly and laid it down on a dry part of the square out in front of him. Then he resumed his former position and folded his arms across the breast of his knitted white jumper. "If any man puts a foot on my jacket," he said, "there will be a fight. I never start a fight, but I never funk a challenge. Where I am, I stand!"

The tinker's wife ran over to the young man's jacket. She stooped and held her stick over it, within a few inches of the cloth. Then she spat very deliberately on the ground at four points around it. "That's what I think of the Connemara gougers," she cried as she straightened herself. "I spit on the lot of them."

She went back to the gable and struck the nearest ass a sharp blow on the side with her stick. Then she sat down on her orange box. "I spit on the whole of Connemara," she cried. "There isn't the makings of a man in the whole bloody place."

The young man shrugged his shoulders contemptuously and said to the people, "It's a cowardly man that sends his wife to offer a challenge."

The tinker leaped into the air once more clean from the ground and struck his buttocks with his heels. Then he rushed around in all directions shadow-boxing, with his teeth clenched and growling in his throat like a dog. Finally he went to one of the asses and struck the animal in the side several times. "That for the gougers of Connemara," he cried as he struck the poor beast. "I challenge the whole of Connemara from Leenane to Rosmuc."

He ran out to the young man's coat and leaped over it, back and forth, as if he were executing a sword dance. He spat on the ground at each jump. When he had finished, he raised his fists high above his head and struck them together. "I challenge the whole of Connemara from Maam to Clifden," he yelled. "I challenge all the gougers that were ever pupped in Lettermullen, Letterfrack and Carraroe!"

The young man walked over very deliberately to the tattered garment of his opponent. He leaped over it, back and forth, spitting on the ground with each jump. Then he returned to his former position and struck his clenched fists together high above his head. "I challenge all the tinkers from here to County Wicklow," he cried. "There isn't a tinker now living that I couldn't crucify!"

The tinker screamed and began to tear the strips of his cotton shirt from his bosom. His wife rushed to him and caught him by the arms. "Give me a hand with him, neighbors," she cried in a tone of agonized entreaty. "If he isn't held, he'll murder the young lad!"

Several people from the audience came to her aid. They laid hands on the tinker, who made a pretence of struggling violently to escape from their grasp.

"Let me at that gouger," roared the tinker, as he struggled with mock violence. "I'll tear the living heart out of him! I'll put murder on my soul because of him!"

The young man suddenly gave rein to simulated rage on his own account. He yelled with startling force and began to remove his knitted white jumper. "I'll crucify that tinker," he shouted. "I'll make a pancake of him!"

A group of people came from the crowd and seized the young man by the arms. With his jumper half removed, he struggled to free himself from their grasp, while he continued to insult his opponent in a loud voice. "Neighbors," he implored, "for the love and honor of God let me at him. I'll drink that dirty man's blood before the sun goes down."

Suddenly there was an interruption. Voices were raised demanding passage for a horse.

"Make way for a horse," the voices cried. "Make way, there."

The crowd parted to make way for a yellow pony that was being put through his paces. A very tall and bony man dressed in a black frieze coat that came to his heels led the pony by a halter. The animal was so tiny compared to the giant size of the man who led him that he had to trot at full speed in order to keep pace with the man's enormous strides. The man kept yelling at the minute pony and striking him on the haunches with an ash plant as he paced him. "Twous, you devil," the man cried. "Go on now!"

The yellow trotting pony and the striding frieze-coated man went between the challengers, who were still struggling to bridge the gap of five yards that separated them. The pony and the man went to the gable end of the little house. Then they turned back and passed once more between the yelling, struggling challengers. "Twous, twous, you devil," the frieze-coated man yelled at the pony, without even glancing at the challengers. "Go on there now."

When the man and the pony had passed, the challengers increased the pretended frenzy of their efforts to break loose. Those who held each man now joined in the challenging. They shouted insults at those opposite. The crowd pressed forward on all sides, so that it became impossible to determine who were the chief actors in the spectacle. Dogs began to bark.

Suddenly there was another interruption, at the very moment when a general encounter seemed on the point of beginning.

"The guards!" somebody cried. "Here come the guards."

Silence fell on the crowd almost at once, as four civic guards pressed forward to the center of the throng. The people drifted away quickly to a short distance. The tinker couple and the young man from Connemara were left alone once more in the center of the arena.

"What's going on here?" said the sergeant in charge of the guards.

He towered over all present. He was of enormous girth. In spite of the flesh that weighed down his body on all sides, there was no doubt about his fighting qualities. He had a hard face and he protruded from the ground like a rock.

"Holy God!" said the tinker woman. "It's bloody Sergeant Heffernan himself."

"The very same," said the sergeant, glaring at the woman, "and may I tell you that he's spoiling for a fight." The sergeant held out his two great hands in front of his chest and added, "There's nothing Sergeant Heffernan would rather do at this very moment than take a couple of tinkers, one in each hand, like this . . ." He pretended to pluck two tinkers out of the air with his hands, which he then struck together. "I'll make mince meat out of the two of you," he yelled suddenly, "unless you get out of here at once. Be off now."

The tinker and his wife turned away without saying a word. They went to collect their hound and their asses.

"You run along, too, sonny," the sergeant said to the young man from Connemara. "It's time for you to go home to your mother."

The young man from Connemara had already put on his jumper and his jacket. He was standing with his arms folded on his chest and his head thrown back in conceited fashion.

"Where I am, I stay," he said insolently to the sergeant.

Without seeming effort, the sergeant took him by the back of the neck and walked off with him to the nearest cart. He carried the youth in the way a puppy is carried. He threw him onto the cart.

"Get out of my sight," he said, "before I lose my temper with you."

The lad lay down on the bottom of the cart and said nothing.

"Move on now, the lot of you," the sergeant said, as he walked back to the little house where the pigs are weighed. "I don't want any trouble with anybody. I'm not in a good humor. I wouldn't be responsible for myself if anybody crossed me."

The tinker and his wife glanced at the sergeant as they moved west along the square. The man went in front leading the five asses by a single halter. The woman brought up the rear, leading the white hound by a leash. They took courage again when they reached the western end, where the cleaners were at work with their massive brooms. They began to shout insults at the people.

"I could crucify any man in County Galway," the tinker shouted. "I'm a terrible man! I don't know my own strength."

The woman began to flog the asses in the hindquarters with her stick, while she insulted the people.

"I could lick the whole fair," she cried, "without any trouble at

all and I wouldn't ask any more than one lousy shilling for doing
it."

The cleaners never even raised their heads to look at the passing
tinkers, as they drove the mire before their massive brooms in a
thick brown wave.

III

****

EUROPE

****

FRANCE · 645

GERMANY · 757

SWITZERLAND · 830

NORWAY · 841

DENMARK · 862

FINLAND · 889

ICELAND · 898

ITALY · 912

SPAIN · 936

HOLLAND · 965

GREECE · 971

HUNGARY · 977

RUSSIA · 1008

ANDRÉ GIDE

****

Ill and disinclined to make any selection of his own for this anthology, M. Gide is represented by fragments from two books out of his fifteen volumes of criticism, essays, dramatic and novel writing, much of which has not yet been translated into English. The editor owes his thanks to Justin O'Brien for the suggestion that a representative quality of the French Nobel Prize winner might be found in selections from The Fruits of the Earth *and* The New Fruits, *the first of which was published in 1897 and again in 1927, and the second book of which was issued in 1935 and re-issued in 1949. Justin O'Brien is contributor to the Columbia Dictionary of Modern Literature and Professor of Contemporary French Literature at Columbia University, and translator of* The Journals of André Gide.

****

Fruits of the Earth and New Fruits

Do NOT HOPE, Nathaniel, to find God *here* or *there*—but everywhere.

Every creature points to God, none reveals Him.

Every creature we let our eyes dwell on distracts us **from God.**

While other people were publishing or working, I, on the contrary, devoted three years of travel to forgetting all that I had learned with my head. This unlearning was slow and difficult; it was of more use to me than all the learning imposed by men, and was really the beginning of an education.

You will never know the efforts it cost us to become interested in life; but now that life does interest us, it will be like everything else —passionately.

I chastised my flesh gladly, taking more pleasure in the chastisement than in the fault—so intoxicating was the pride I took in not sinning simply.

Suppress in yourself the idea of *merit*—one of the mind's great stumbling-blocks.

. . . All our life long we have been tormented by the uncertainty of our paths. How can I put it? All choice, when one comes to think of it, is terrifying: liberty when there is no duty to guide it, terrifying. The path that has to be chosen lies through a wholly un-explored country, where each one makes *his own* discoveries, and —note this—for himself alone; so that the vaguest track in the darkest Africa is more easily distinguishable. . . . Shady groves al-lure us, and the mirage of perennial springs. Or rather, springs will flow where our desires bid them; for the country only comes into existence as our approach gives it form, and the landscape about us gradually falls into shape as we advance; we cannot see as far as the horizon; and even the foreground is nothing but a successive and changeable appearance.

But why comparisons when the matter is so serious? We all be-lieve we shall eventually discover God. In the meantime, alas, where are we to address our prayers? At last we end by saying that He— the Unfindable—is everywhere, anywhere, and kneel down at hap-hazard.

And so, Nathaniel, you are like the man who should follow as his guide the light he holds in his own hand.

Wherever you go, you will never meet with anything but God. "God," said Menalcas, "is what lies ahead of us."

Nathaniel, look at everything as you pass on your way, but stay nowhere. Remember that it is only God who is not transitory.

Let the *importance* lie in your look, not in the thing you look at.

All your gathered knowledge of what is *outside* you will remain outside you to all eternity. Why do you attach so much importance to it?

There is profit in desires, and profit in the satisfaction of desires —for so they are increased. And indeed, Nathaniel, each one of my desires has enriched me more than the always deceitful possession of the object of my desire.

Many are the delicious things, Nathaniel, for which I have been consumed with love. Their splendor came from my ceaseless burning for them. I never wearied. All fervor consumed me with love—consumed me deliciously.

A heretic among heretics, I was constantly drawn to the most opposite opinions, the most devious thoughts, the extremest divergences. Nothing interested me in a mind but what made it different from others. I went so far as to forbid myself sympathy, which seemed to me the mere recognition of a common emotion.

No, not sympathy, Nathaniel—love.

Act without *judging* whether the action is right or wrong. Love without caring whether what you love is good or bad.

Nathaniel, I will teach you fervor.

A harrowing life, Nathaniel, rather than a quiet one. Let me have no rest but the sleep of death. I am afraid that every desire, every energy I have not satisfied during my life may survive to torment me. I hope that after I have expressed on this earth all that was in me waiting to be expressed—I *hope* that I may die satisfied and utterly *hopeless.*

No, not sympathy, Nathaniel, love. Surely you understand they are not the same. It was the fear of losing love that made me sometimes sympathize with sorrows, troubles, sufferings that else I could hardly have borne. Leave to each one the care of his own life.

II

There are extravagant illnesses
   Which consist in wanting what one hasn't got.
   "We too," they said, "we too have known the lamentable sickness of the soul!" In the cave of Adullam, David, you longed for water of the well of Bethlehem. "Oh, who will bring me," you sighed, "the cool water that gushes from the foot of the walls of Bethlehem? As a child I quenched my thirst at it; but now it runs captive, that water my fever pants for."

Never long, Nathaniel, to taste the waters of the past.

Never seek, Nathaniel, to find again the past in the future. Seize from every moment its unique novelty and do not prepare your joys—or else believe that in its prepared place *another* joy will surprise you.

Why have you not understood that all happiness is a chance encounter and at every moment presents itself to you like a beggar by the roadside? Woe betide you if you say your happiness is dead because you had not imagined it in *that* form—and because you

will only accept a happiness in conformity with your principles and
wishes.

Your dream of tomorrow is a delight, but the delight of tomorrow is another, and nothing fortunately resembles the dream we
have dreamed of it, for each thing has a *different* value.

I don't like you to say to me: Come, I have prepared such or
such a joy for you. I only care now for the joys met by chance and
for those that spring at my bidding from the rocks; thus they flow
for us fresh and strong, like new wine when it gushes from the press.

I don't want my joy to be dressed up for me, nor the Shulamite
to come to me through palace halls; I kissed her without wiping
the stains of grape juice from my lips; after my kisses I drank
sweet wine without rinsing my mouth; and I ate honey from the
hive with its comb.

Nathaniel, never prepare your joys.

ENVOI

AND NOW, Nathaniel, throw away my book. Shake yourself free of
it. Leave me. Leave me; now you are in my way; you hamper me;
I have exaggerated my love for you and it occupies me too much.
I am tired of pretending I can educate anyone. When have I said
that I wanted you to be like me? It is because you differ from me
that I love you; the only thing I love in you is what differs from
me. Educate! Whom should I educate but myself? Nathaniel, shall
I tell you? I have educated myself interminably. And I have not
done yet. I only esteem myself for my possibilities.

Nathaniel, throw away my book; do not let it satisfy you. Do not
think *your* truth can be found by anyone else; be ashamed of nothing more than of that. If I found your food for you, you would have
no appetite for it; if I made your bed, you would not be able to
sleep in it.

Throw away my book; say to yourself that it is *only one* of the
thousand possible postures in life. Look for your own. Do not do
what someone else could do as well as you. Do not say, do not
write, what someone else could say, could write, as well as you.
Care for nothing in yourself but what you feel exists nowhere else,
and out of yourself create, impatiently or patiently, ah, Nathaniel,
the most irreplaceable of beings.

THE NEW FRUITS

All nature teaches that man is born for happiness.

AN ALL-PERVADING joy suffuses the earth, and the earth exudes it at the sun's call. It is joy that thrills the atmosphere in which the elements come to life and, still submissive, make their escape from the primal rigor. . . . Lovely complexities are born from the interweaving of the laws of nature—the seasons, the movement of the tides, the vapors that are drawn up and showered down again in streams, the tranquil alternation of the days, the periodic recurrence of the winds—everything, as it comes into being, sways to and fro in a harmonious rhythm. Everything is prepared for the organization of joy, and soon joy is born; it flutters unwittingly in the leaf, it takes name and diversity, becomes fragrance in the flower, flavor in the fruit, a conscious voice in the bird. So that the return, the informing, and then the disappearance of life imitate the circuitous passage of water, which evaporates in the sunshine and then re-gathers again to fall in the shower.

Each animal is nothing but a parcel of joy.

Everything is glad to be and every being rejoices. You call it fruit when joy becomes succulence, bird when it is turned into song.

All nature indeed teaches that man is born for happiness. It is the effort after pleasure that makes the plant germinate, fills the hive with honey, and the human heart with love.

II

FROM the day that I succeeded in persuading myself that I had no need to be happy, happiness began to dwell in me; yes, from the day I persuaded myself that I needed nothing in order to be happy. After I had struck my pick at the roots of selfishness, I felt that a fountain of joy had sprung up from my heart so abundant that I should be able to quench everybody else's thirst with it. I understood that the best teaching was example. I took up my happiness as a vocation.

What! I thought then, if my soul must dissolve at the same time as my body, let me realize my joy as quickly as possible. If by chance my soul is immortal, shall I not have eternity to spend on what can be of no interest to my sense? Am I to disdain this beautiful country through which I am passing, to refuse its delights, because they will soon be taken from me? The swifter my passage, the more eager

let my eyes be; the more precipitate my flight, the more immediate be my embrace! Why, lover of a moment, should I clasp less
fondly what I know I cannot keep? Inconstant soul, hasten! Remember that the loveliest flower is the one that soonest fades.
Breathe its perfume quickly. The everlasting has no scent.

Soul born for joy, fear nothing but what may dim the brightness
of your song.

But now I understand that God, permanently present in all that
passes, dwells not in the object but in love; and now I know how
to enjoy the quiet of eternity in the fleeting moment.

If you feel that you cannot remain in this state of joy, do not
make too great an effort to attain it.

> Greet me as I awake,
> Dazzling and lovely light!
> I claim no immaterial
> Delight.

> As Ariel winged and free,
> I love you, cloudless sky,
> But even in heaven's blue,
> If caught, I die.

> Can anything be more
> Substantial than this?
> To listen is to hear—
> To hear and not to miss.

> Haste then, oh, let me haste
> Those honeyed sweets to taste.

This morning I am like the man who knows that his pen is a
little too full of ink and, for fear of making a blot, traces a garland
of words.

III

EVERY AFFIRMATION is accomplished in abnegation. Everything you
resign within you will come to life. All affirmation of self is self-

destroying; all self-denial is self-affirming. Perfect possession is only to be proved by the perfect gift. It is you who are possessed by all you will not give. Without sacrifice there is no resurrection. Nothing grows and blooms save by giving. All you try to save in yourself wastes and perishes.

How do you know the fruit is ripe? Because it leaves the bough. All things ripen for the giving's sake and in the giving are consummated.

O luscious fruit wrapped round with delight, I know that in order to germinate you must sacrifice yourself. Let it die then, let it die, that delicious envelope! Let it die, that sweet and juicy flesh, for it belongs to the earth. Let it die that you may live. I know that "except it die, it abideth alone."

O Lord! grant me not to wait for death in order to die.

It is renunciation that brings all virtue to perfection. The extreme succulence of the fruit is its effort toward germination.

True eloquence renounces eloquence; the individual is never so self-expressive as in self-forgetfulness. The thought of self is a hindrance to self. I never admire beauty so much as when it is unconscious of being beautiful. That line is most touching that is least assertive. Christ in truth becomes God by renouncing his divinity. And conversely, God by renouncing himself in Christ becomes God.

IV

You needn't pretend to be so clever. You have seen people die; there's nothing very funny about it. You try to joke so as to hide your fear; but your voice trembles and your sham poem is frightful.

Perhaps. . . . Yes, I have seen people die. In most cases it seemed to me that just before death and once the crisis was past the sharpness of the sting was in a way blunted. Death puts on velvet gloves to take us. He does not strangle us without first lulling us to sleep, and the things he robs us of have already lost their distinctness, their presence, and, as it were, their reality. The universe becomes so colorless that it is no longer very difficult to leave it, and nothing is left to regret.

So I say to myself that it can't be so difficult to die since, as a matter of fact, everybody manages it. And, after all, it would perhaps be nothing but a habit to fall into if only one died more than once.

But death is dreadful to those who have not filled their lives. In

their case it is only too easy for religion to say: "Never mind! It's in the other world that things begin; you'll get your reward there."
It is *now* and in *this* world that we must live.

Comrade, believe in nothing—accept nothing without proof. Never anything was proved by the blood of martyrs. No religion, however mad, that has not had its own, none that has failed to rouse passionate convictions. It is in the name of faith that men die; and it is in the name of faith that they kill. The desire for knowledge springs from doubt. Stop believing and begin learning. It is only when proofs are lacking that people try to impose their opinions. Do not let yourself be credulous. Do not let yourself be imposed on.

√

IF THEN I CALL nature God, it is for simplicity's sake and because it irritates the theologians. For you may have noticed that such people shut their eyes to nature, or if they happen to glance at it, they are incapable of observing it.

Instead of trying to get instruction from men, let your teaching come from God. Man has grown crooked; his history is simply that of his false pretenses and his sham excuses. "A market gardener's cart," I once wrote, "carries with it more truths than Cicero's finest periods." There is man's history and the history so rightly called *natural*. In *Natural History* you must listen to the voice of God. And don't be satisfied with listening to it vaguely; put definite questions to God and insist on his answering you definitely. Don't be satisfied with gazing—observe.

You will notice then that everything that is young is tender. In how many sheaths is not every bud wrapped round! But all that at first protected the tender germ, when once germination is accomplished, hinders it; and no growth is possible unless it burst the sheaths in which at first it was swaddled.

Mankind clings to its swaddling-clothes, but it will never grow unless it succeeds in getting rid of them. The child that has been weaned is not ungrateful if it pushes away its mother's breast. It is no longer milk that it needs. Comrade, you must refuse henceforth to seek your nourishment in the milk of tradition, man-distilled and man-filtered. You have teeth now with which to bite and chew and you must find your food in what is real. Stand up erect, naked and valiant; burst your wrappings, push aside your props; to grow straight you need nothing now but the urge of your sap and the sun's call.

You will notice that every plant casts its seeds to a distance; either the seeds have a delicious covering that tempts the bird's appetite, so that they are carried to places they could not otherwise reach; or else, equipped with spirals or feathers, they trust themselves to the wandering breezes. For if it nourishes the same kind of plant too long, the soil becomes impoverished and poisonous, and the new generation cannot find its food in the same place as the preceding one. Do not try to eat again what your fathers before you have already digested. Look at the winged seeds of the plane or the sycamore flying off as if they understood that the paternal shade can offer them nothing but a dwindling and atrophied existence.

And you will notice too that the rush of the sap goes preferably to swell the buds at the extreme tips of the branches, those that are farthest from the trunk. Understand this rightly and put the longest possible distance between you and the past.

Understand rightly the Greek fable. It teaches us that Achilles was invulnerable except in that spot of his body which had been made soft by the remembrance of his mother's touch.

O you for whom I write—whom in other days I called by a name that seems to me now too plaintive—Nathaniel—whom today I call comrade—rid your heart henceforth of all that is plaintive.

Obtain from yourself all that makes complaining useless. No longer implore from others what you yourself can obtain.

I have lived; it is your turn now. It is in you that my youth will be prolonged. I pass you my powers. If I feel that you are my successor, I shall resign myself more easily to dying. I hand on my hopes to you.

The knowledge that you are brave and strong enables me to leave life without regret. Take my joy. Let your happiness be to increase that of others. Work and strive and accept no evil that you might change. Keep saying to yourself: "It lies with me." One cannot resign oneself to the evils that come from men without baseness. Cease believing, if you ever believed it, that wisdom consists in resignation; or else cease laying claim to wisdom.

Comrade, do not accept the life that is offered you by men. Never cease to be convinced that life might be better—your own and others'; not a future life that might console us for the present one and help us to accept its misery, but this one of ours. Do not accept. As soon as you begin to understand that it is not God but man who is responsible for nearly all the ills of life, from that moment you will no longer resign yourself to bearing them.

Do not sacrifice to idols.

—Translated by Dorothy Bussy

JULES ROMAINS

✶✶✶

PARIS

I have selected this piece: 1) because it comes from my main work,
Men of Good Will; *2) because it presents, facing each other, two of
my principal characters, Jerphanion and Paris; 3) because some of
the important topics of my work are indicated there.*

JULES ROMAINS

✶✶✶

On the College Roof

"Let's go along here. I don't know whether it's the best way; but
it's one way."

"We're not going to break our necks, eh?"

"No. I gather that nobody ever has broken his neck, as far back
as the records go. There must be a special dispensation of Providence for us—considering what a lot of Collegers, like myself, are
just clumsy clodhoppers and no acrobats. I told you I believed in
the God of Voltaire and Victor Hugo, didn't I? This window is
blasted hard to open. A Deist—that's what I am. In other words,
the kind of fellow a 'thala' regards as the worst of errors. I've
marked down an attic not far from here, carefully locked up, where
the Pot keeps his stock of classical books. We ought to be able to
get into it without much trouble through a window. I'll see about
that."

"Tell me," demanded Jerphanion. "A grammarian like you—"

"I?" Caulet made a gesture of protest, which cocked up the skirt
of his cape solemnly.

"Still—"

"Don't you get wrong ideas into your head. I've chosen grammar
because they say that the grammar fellowship is the easiest. If there
were an alphabet fellowship, I should have chosen the alphabet fellowship."

655

"Anyway, so far as you are a grammarian, doesn't it shock you that, in College slang, Pot should mean two things which, after all, are quite different?"

"For that matter, it means three. Yes, three: any meal in particular; feeding in general; and the Bursar, because among his other low-down jobs, he looks after the feeding."

"Doesn't this poverty of vocabulary give you a pain?"

"I'm told there's a Chinese word, also a monosyllable, which means, just as you like, the Evening Star, the river which flows through the Seventeenth Province, the tax-collector, and a girl's first periods. And that's been going on for three thousand years. You see how wide the gutter is. I may tell you that I came along this way yesterday; and if I'm doing it again, you may take it the danger is practically negligible. My ancestors left me a horror of danger."

"Doesn't that cape of yours get in your way?"

"No. Hullo!—good recovery that, wasn't it? Give me your hand and I'll hoist you up. I'm holding on to this pediment. I've brought my cape because it's cold up here. I'm subject to colds. Here comes the winter, slayer of the poor. Don't get alarmed—that's the only quotation from modern poetry I feel like making; that, and two or three lines of Heredia's. 'Like a flight of falcons out of their natal charnel-house.' And that thingummy that ends with 'the bleeding Emperor.' I've found that answers to all the circumstances of life. Haven't we just come out of that attic 'like a flight of falcons'? Just like one. And Sidre, on the ridge of the roof there, against the red sky of November—if you feel you want to compare him with something, what could you have better than a bleeding emperor? That always fits."

Caulet was walking along carefully in the very middle of the gutter. Every three paces he found the cornice of an attic ready to his left hand. He took advantage of it to make sure of his equilibrium. From one attic to the next he felt time drag a little. His arms, under his cape, went through the wary motions of a tight-wire walker's pole.

"Not so bad after all, is it?"

Jerphanion had played on village roofs, climbed over falls of rock, run barefoot over goat-tracks along the edge of precipices; and it was only for a moment that he let himself be daunted by this Parisian gutter. Besides, the College roof presented more majesty than danger. Before discovering Paris to you, it made you measure the quadrilateral of buildings in all their internal amplitude. With your feet in the gutter, you could admire the noble se-

quence of attics, the symmetry of the chimneys. Away down there
you could see a deep courtyard, almost regal in its air, with a round
pond hemmed by a strip of grass.

A wind which people on sidewalks never know began to get you
under the shoulders. For, between the wind shut up in the streets
and the wind that lords it over a city, the difference is not so much
in its force as in that way it has of surrounding you on all sides and
pressing you as closely as it can.

But these imposing roofs, not lacking in steep slopes, which at
first sight repelled the pedestrian because they struck him as so in-
congruous, really seemed, once you knew the secret of their structure, to be made for foot-faring. At the end of the gutter, on the
corner of the building, little filigree steps, of a metal heavier than
brass, awaited you, airily attached to the ramp of the roof. You had
only to follow them to reach the ridge of the roof itself, which consisted, for the whole length of the building, in a kind of lintel, a
foot wide and striated with tiny traverses which stuck out.

This pathway, sprightly and risky as a foot-bridge over a torrent,
gave the mind the sense of excitement, the exhilaration, that you
get on a high terrace; but it refused the body any ease of attitude,
any abandon in its movments. There was no obvious danger. There
was nothing even that demanded any dexterity. But you had to keep
the idea of a false step out of your mind. Without threatening you
in the least, the slope and the precipice kept up with you all the
time, like those wild beasts in certain countries which, so they say,
escort the traveller and never attack him, but only wait for his horse
to stumble. You had to hold the mount of your muscles well in
hand, and ride it with a short rein. It was enough to scare off weak-
lings and old men, or nervous women. One would not even have
ventured to recommend this passage to Pascal's philosopher who
was seized with vertigo on his plank between the two towers of
Notre-Dame. In short, it was a place for the insolence of youth. A
fine spot, too, to take your ambitious dreams for a walk.

"Will you have a Valda pastille?" said Caulet. "They're essential
if you want to avoid a sore throat. One can imagine Valda as a goddess clad in white, extracting the sap from the mistletoe around an
oak. Or as a Russian girl student, or, more exactly, a Moldo-Wallachian one. Which reminds me—I give you fair warning—watch
out, at lectures at the Sorbonne, for the Moldo-Wallachian students.
They flock to France in droves, trying to get married. Like a flight
of falcons. They are quite satisfied with a Sorbonnard, who makes
a tasty enough morsel for them. But they regard a Colleger as a prey

de luxe. I'm hard-boiled, and I don't run any risk. But innocents like you—There'll be some victims. Poor French families!

"To get along here, if you funk it, you can hold on to the chimney. The freshness of these pastilles makes me quite drunk. It must be like that when you become an opium addict. For years I had a passion for liquorice pastilles. It was frightful. From morning to night I was dribbling liquorice, belching liquorice. I got a stomach, I can tell you, like those cauldrons of tar those fellows use when they're repairing the sidewalks.

"But, of course, you're not familiar with Parisian civilization. Have the Lyons people discovered the use of tar for sidewalks yet? Don't suppose they have. As for Puy-en-Velay, I can just imagine that: big cobblestones; streams running down the middle of the streets; and the footsteps of the watchman sounding after curfew. . . . Do you see that tower?"

"Yes."

"That's the Tour Saint-Jacques."

"Oh, is it?"

"No, it isn't, old man. I really can't impose on your innocence. That's the tower of Lycée Henri IV—my own tower. I lived for three years in its shadow. As you see, I haven't got away from it yet. The Tour Saint-Jacques is somewhere over there—much farther away. No, it must be down in that hollow, behind the Panthéon. Doesn't it look enormous from here, the Panthéon? Simply crushes us. It must be the Panthéon too, I imagine, that hides the Sacré-Coeur and the Butte from us. Because there really isn't much mist; and the Sacré-Coeur is so white!"

"And what's that dome, quite close to us?"

"That's the Invalides, where sleeps Napoleon, the bleeding Emperor. No, old man, I haven't the heart to fool you. It's too easy. That dome belongs to Val-de-Grâce. I've never seen Rome, but all this strikes me as violently Roman—Val-de-Grâce even more so than the Panthéon. I haven't a trace of artistic instinct; but there are some things that do move me. Though I never read anything but the authors in the lecture-course, and as little as possible of them, I've happened by chance to dip into old tomes with engravings in them. In some of them you could see a dome like that, and other monuments, all around a great square in which there wasn't a soul stirring, or at most an almost imperceptible little priest. I don't know why, but it struck me as so wistful and so impressive. Little though I'm given to romantic nostalgia, I felt that I'd like to live there—live in a city like the one in the engravings and have my place in it. I was born to have an ecclesiastical dignity, a benefice, a canon's stall. (Only up to the age of seventy-eight; and then— sudden death.) While you chant your stuff, with your hands locked across your belly, you can think about the dinner that's waiting for you. . . ."

"And about the serving-maid. . . ."

"Of course. And about your penitents. As I'm too shy by nature, I can't imagine bawdiness except in certain conditions of respectable mystery—and complete security. That sky really is fine. Just look at that red! I must show you some monkeys at the zoo that have the skin of their buttocks exactly that color. But the backside of monkeys is less veiled, I'll grant you that—less indefinite."

Jerphanion contemplated the horizon with a mixture of restraint and eagerness. It was the first time that he had seen Paris from a high place. Until now Jallez had dissuaded him. "You wouldn't make anything of it yet. You'd be carried away by the lighting effects. Keep that in reserve; you've plenty of time." They had even put off until later the excursion to the top of the hill of Montmartre that Jerphanion wanted to make.

But the College roof did not flatter itself that it dominated Paris. It merely put you on a level with her. You emerged from the depths of a ship, and you found the sea all around you. The wind spread its cloth quite horizontally. You had the remoteness, the circular background, of the reddish mist. Paris glided past you. Despite its monuments and all their magnificence when you were close up to them, this city had no spectacular air about it. It had, much more, that of a difficult element, which navigators surveyed, and whose agitation obsessed them, leaving them unable to look as far as they should or discern the origin of the forces which stirred it.

Jerphanion had never seen the sea, but he felt himself at home with the feelings of a sailor. This narrow strip along which he made his way—he could easily imagine it aboard some hull swayed by the sea. A path for a sailor. For the supple stride of the sailor, who had no right to lose his footing either.

"Shall we go down again?" said Caulet. "I'm feeling a bit cold."

"Are you? . . . I'd like to stay a little longer."

"But can you find your way back?"

"Of course I can."

"Suppose you break your neck. I should feel it was my fault."

"You said nobody ever broke his neck."

"Anyway, try to keep still until you see me in safety. The noise of your falling might make me lose my balance. I don't mind being told about accidents, afterwards. In fact, I rather like it. But I hate being present at them."

Caulet made his way back, with his head cocked a little on one side. He walked quite slack. He did not use his arms as a balancing-pole any more. With his right hand he stroked his moustache. He had all the air of a promenader who is thinking about something else, but keeps to the edge of the sidewalk automatically.

Jerphanion went and leant against a chimney-stack. He had the Panthéon behind his back; in front of him, Val-de-Grâce; and far-ther away, some swellings with a vaguely sexual appeal about them, which might be, though he was not sure, the cupolas of the Ob-servatory.

"Greatness. That's the thing that goes to my head—greatness. Caulet, for all the airs he puts on, is by no means to be despised. I'd rather have him than a lot of those poor devils grinding away at their studies. Just like respectable clerks. Improving works on their bookshelves. Pindar and Lucretius, out of whom they can make mottoes, fit their hearts just like a pair of shoes. Their pre-decessors swore loyalty to the Second Empire; and, alas! without any mental reservation. They cut Hugo to pieces in the rhetoric classes. Hugo, far away across the sea! This sky—it's his kind of sky, A red, marine, Guernsey November.

"What am I going to be in ten years' time? I'm not going to ac-cept being a failure. What was that Jallez said, the first day we went for a walk? I won't put up with anything but real greatness. Not just playing the grand; I know all about myself. I must talk to Jallez about Spinoza. He ought to like him. *Life of Spinoza,* by Colerus. 'Sometimes he went down to his landlord's and smoked a pipe of tobacco.' I've no gift for philosophy. I'll never make a great writer, either.

"Where am I going to find it, this greatness of mine? It's rather as though I had to go and look for it right in front of me; as though it were down there somewhere, in this jumble between me and the horizon. It's an idea I've always had, that reality is full of oracles. It's an urge I've always had, to turn toward it for an-swers. Toward it rather than toward myself. I'm no man of action, if that means a beast of burden: ready to shove himself between a pair of shafts and to pull harder than anybody else, without really knowing what for or where to. Sooner dreaming than that. But I'm the kind of man whose dreams aren't destined to end inside his own mind. Or on paper, for that matter.

"I wonder whether Sidre has noticed me? That's a queer head he has. He's upsetting. Hardened criminals have an expression like that of his.

"I haven't got much standing here, because I passed in low down the list, and I'm a raw provincial, and I'm not a brilliant talker. Still, Jallez took to me. He keeps on preferring me to anybody else, quite obviously. And Jallez takes a lot of beating. What can the rest of them put up against him? Passed in with honors; a real Parisian; dazzling in his talk, when he likes; with a range of culture that knocks them all over, though you can never tell where he gets it from even, if you can guess all that lies behind it, which he keeps to himself so carefully. Disdaining to shove himself forward.

"I'd never dare to talk to him about myself and all these dreams of greatness of mine. I shouldn't like to see that little wrinkling around his eyes, even if he followed it up by saying something friendly and indulgent. I'm afraid of that irony of his. Not that he uses it very often, and he scarcely ever abuses it, and for my part I haven't received—at least, I don't think so—the least little scratch from it; but you can still feel it in its sheath, as it were, always whetted and perfect and terrible. . . .

"One thing's certain, and that is that society is going to change—and during our lifetime. What I have before my eyes here isn't exactly society, of course. It's less; and—as Jallez would say—it's more. No matter. It's inside there that the change is coming.

"The idea of justice is irresistible. A mere drop suffices. From the day when societies accept one drop of justice, you can foresee there isn't going to be any more rest until that drop has wrought everything over again, transformed everything, brought everything to a state of justice.

"For my part, I feel that passionately. I can well imagine myself in front of a crowd. I believe I'm eloquent, or that I could be. Real eloquence. Not that lamentable facility of elocution of Leroux's, yesterday, when he was delivering his lecture; just like a mechanical piano. Enough to give you a taste for stammering.

"I should begin by failing to find my words: a kind of weight, a stoppage between the temples. Even a complete void. While my thoughts were mobilizing, every one in its own corner, putting on their equipment, making sure of everything, trying not to forget anything, their place of assembly would remain empty. But excitement would come, little by little. Like Mirabeau's early speeches. The mere idea of a crowd makes me feel bigger, gives me a sense of ascendancy. I lean on such an idea.

"I have a voice that's fit for anything. When I shouted, they

could hear me clearly on the other side of the valley. My accent? I
haven't got much. Though it's difficult to tell, oneself. You don't
listen to yourself. A stranger to your own voice. Since mirrors were
invented, our faces are no longer strange to us. Besides, there are
photos. You can do a lot of thinking in front of your own photo.
Some day, perhaps, we shall use a phonograph as we now use a
mirror. . . .

"Normally, you ought not to be able to find a trace of accent in
yourself. Our own way of speaking is the very presence of words in
us. Their absolute sound. Language imposing itself on us like something definite. Still, every time I don't pronounce a word or syllable just like Jallez, I have a distinct feeling that I'm talking with
an accent.

"But in front of a great crowd, especially a crowd of ordinary
people, I'm sure that a trace of accent does not count. Unless, of
course, the intonation strikes you as silly and ridiculous. All prejudice apart, there are accents which simply tickle your diaphragm.
It's irresistible. The one I have isn't comic; at the most it calls up
the stolidity of the peasant, the space of the mountains; and it has
something of a southern gilding about it. In any case, it's docile; it
can be made to veer fast enough. My uncle, for example—who
could tell now where he comes from? His accent has simply saved
him from that vile suburban pronunciation which gives me the horrors. Jallez will never give me a liking for that. . . . At Lyons, in less
than three years, my own accent changed. But then there was the
father of that pal of mine who came from the Aveyron, I think—
an official in Lyons for twenty years; and people still had to bite
their lips for fear of laughing at him. . . .

"It's getting a bit chilly. I always feel the cold in my feet. Bad
circulation. . . .

"It isn't in front of a constituted assembly, a parliament, that I
see myself, for choice. I've a horror of compromising and jobbery.
No vocation for individual attentions, manoeuvres *ad hominem,*
whispered conversations in the lobby. No desire, either, to know
the names of everybody in the place. I want something more anonymous, something more heroic. 'O soldiers of the year II, O wars,
O epics!' "

Among the monuments which the red evening still enveloped, he
watched the intermediate mass of Paris darken. It was not of an
epic of war and of soldiers that he dreamed. He interrogated the
expanse around him, at once fluid and solid. Breaks and shelvings
of roofs, valleys and plains of road—metal, chimneys, blocks of new

masonry, a tower, a steeple, a marsh of mist. Despite a difference in scale, in order of greatness, able to make one dizzy, the action of one man upon this immensity was not inconceivable.

Jerphanion vaguely imagined something issuing out of him, going and insinuating itself in the distance into some fissure, some crack, and getting a leverage there. Great fragments of the city rose up. The whole crust of stone and men split. His vision was accompanied by the sense of an enormous expenditure of energy.

But what counted most in this vision of his was not strength. Nor was it appetite for power. It was the direction of the effort. The times were gone when an adventurer could carve out an empire for his own pleasure, for his own pride, or purely and simply to ease himself of his genius. Jerphanion did, indeed, think of the financiers, the captains of industry, who, even today, conquered vast regions of society, with nothing more than selfish ends in view. But he lacked experience for estimating their power; and he was inclined to believe it less profound than people said.

In any case, he wanted to feel sure that his own enthusiasm had no relationship with their covetousness. If one of them, at his age, had found himself in his place, on this roof, would he have had exactly the same kind of inner impulses? Would he have felt himself starting to go through the same imaginary motions? Jerphanion could not bring himself to think so. An attitude of lying in expectant ambush, a look of greedy penetration, a motion of craft and capture, a daring gesture of clutching towards himself things farther and still farther away. . . . Surely that was what there would have been in the day-dreams of such a man—not that vision of a gigantic lever on which you leant with all your strength, not thinking about yourself, but thinking only, like a workman, about the job to be done, the thing to be moved.

"Those fellows—what can their maxim of life be? To utilize the arrangement of things to their own best advantage. That means the present arrangement. Accordingly, they labour to maintain it. Without any special conviction. Just as a gambler would object to anybody changing the value of the cards in the middle of a game. As to altering it, as to creating a new world, they don't even think of it. And it's just as well they don't. Because it takes more than a lot of strength, with all the skill you like in addition, to create a new world."

Jerphanion failed to recognize the power of automatic transformation which industry and finance exercised upon society, in proportion as they developed, became concentrated, or linked up with one another. He was not ignorant of Marx's theories; but, in default of any vital sympathy with them, he could rather appreciate the originality of their dialectic than feel any virtue of explanation in them.

What you needed, if you would dare to dream about changing society, what no strength could replace, that old word "ideal" hinted at. But in so hackneyed, so conventional a way that you felt as though your mouth were munching some dead phrase for the sake of chattering. As to the thing itself, Jerphanion represented it to himself forcibly. Somewhere there was a man; a man with a head on his shoulders; and in that head ideas, which you might find more or less in other heads, but not grouped in the same way, or kept so warm, or outlined with the same phosphorescence. Ideas, moreover, which were as little mortified and extinct as possible, as intense and active as possible. Instead of remaining innocuous for outside purposes, and confining itself to doing a little duty inside, as was the case in ordinary heads, this load of ideas left nothing whatever at peace around it. In the sphere of humanity, in which it was immersed, in which it moved about, it set up a zone of vibrant thought, of life restless and disturbed.

Jerphanion imagined that, through the expanse of stone and red mist which lay before him, he could see this load of ideas advancing, carried by a man. The strength of the man served to break a way, to overcome difficult obstacles, to attain the vital points. (The same strength that leant on the crow-bar, in the vision of the lever.)

But it was the ideas themselves that did the rest. In proportion as they moved, and in the course of their radiation, a transformation began and spread. Under their impact, in the old mental constructions of the multitude, there took place a series of disturbances of equilibrium, which ended by extending to the whole of the social world.

It was essential, too, that the old equilibrium should be on the point of breaking down; and that among the new combinations which might succeed it the ideal of this man should be one of the most probable, or even the most probable of all. (For there could be no question of destroying without setting something up afterwards.)

So far was this true that Jerphanion asked himself sometimes whether the whole rôle of a great man was not simply precipitating transformations that would have taken place later, not in the least spontaneously, but in response to the urge of much smaller causes, which owed to their very smallness the fact that they were frequent and, in the long run, inevitable. This was not the same thing, however, as denying the importance of great men, or believing that the march of events would be the same in any case.

For one thing, two transformations, very different from each other, might be equally probable; and then it was the intervention of the great man that decided between them. For another thing, the date of a change, like that of a harvest, might have its influence upon the kind of fruit you got. It was not the same thing to shake the tree, or to wait for the berries to fall by themselves. There might be over-ripening and rottenness, for lack of a great man to give the shake at the right moment. Not to speak of the fact that you could never be sure that the worrying of little commonplace causes would end by taking the place of the shock administered by the one and great and single cause. Jerphanion had done enough mathematics to know that the expression: "inevitable in the long run," does not exclude an element of doubt. In any case, he found in these considerations a way of distinguishing, for his own private use, between the ambitious man and the careerist.

With a strictness which was perhaps rather narrow, he reserved the name of ambitious men to those who dreamed of acting upon society, by supplying it with the intellectual "loads" which it needed to start its transformation; while the careerist was the gentleman who coveted the best possible place in the established order. These definitions enabled him to range himself on the right side.

It was certainly true that he possessed no material greed. Poverty seemed to him inseparable from a heroic life. An iron bedstead in a whitewashed room: such was one of the inner images which fortified him most surely. (His quarters in the College pleased him very much from this point of view. The only objection he had to his cell was that it was not properly sealed. A partition which did not reach the ceiling outraged every man's right to solitude.)

He was perhaps a little less detached where honors were concerned. When he compared himself with his less fortunate comrades, whom the examination had definitely rejected, he was hard put to it to defend himself against pride in being a Colleger: and he was also hard put to it to defend himself against a sense of the relative humiliation of having passed low down on the list.

If society had suddenly offered him a position, poorly paid but prominent, it would perhaps have gained for the cause of established order one man more. He had told himself so once or twice, in moments of bitter clear-sightedness. But, at bottom, he was not so

sure. If he had not been born to be grasping, neither had he been
born merely to be replete. The prominent position would not have
kept him quiet for long. He would soon have made use of it to start
the attack upon the unjust social order from higher up. This, at
least, was the conclusion to which he had come.

Whatever he had of vanity in him would always find a means of
satisfying itself in the very victories which his ideas won. For the
purest of victories brings with it a train of meaner satisfactions, in
which the lower parts of ourselves can find meat and drink. So this
danger was not one that worried him much.

Another scruple embarrassed him more, and it had taken him
some time to clear it up. "I have admitted," he said to himself,
"that the great man of action has it as his rôle to provoke the transformation, or one of the two or three social transformations which
is most probable at any given moment; if you like, one of the two
or three which the period demands more or less equally. But the
'load of ideas' whose bearer he is, and which constitutes his strength,
may have come to him in two very different ways. First possible
origin: an inner necessity. These ideas are truth as he sees it. A
truth which his mind has recognized, and to which he bears witness,
and for which he would fight even if it turned its back on the period; even if, apart from his own mind, there was nothing in its
favor. He finds that it coincides with an expectation, a desire on the
part of society. But he has not sought this coincidence. He may even
not realize it until afterwards—when society begins to 'respond.'

"On the other hand, one can imagine a man who is in himself
neutral, unattached. There is nothing personal, one might even say
nothing exceptional, about him but his aptitude as a vehicle for an
important 'load of ideas.' He studies the society of his time. He
scents it. He asks himself what its aspirations are. He senses which
ideas have the best chance of provoking and guiding a transformation. And he proceeds to *adopt* them. Isn't that a bit chilling? His
cold-bloodedness, his freedom of choice—don't they come pretty
near lack of sincerity? This great man whom I imagine—isn't he
just a kind of advocate, ready to espouse any cause at all?"

Jerphanion added, of course, that, in reality, the opposition is
never so clear-cut as all that. A body of ideas, political and social,
does not come to you by a simple process of illumination. You must
have reflected about society in general, and then interrogated yourself in particular about what it demands or expects. To recognize
that a thing is true and just in the eyes of your solitary reason, and

to recognize that it is, as a matter of fact, a deep desire on the part of society, are often one and the same task.

This attitude becomes displeasing only in the cold-blooded man of ambition, who believes in nothing and has no passion for anything, and in whose eyes all the aspirations of humanity are chimeras equally valueless. (Just as a mercenary captain agrees to fight for national causes at which he mocks.) It becomes positively odious if by chance the man of ambition is convinced that society is making a mistake, and if he cunningly helps it to fall into the abyss, because the abyss is what it wants, and what he wants is to keep himself busy.

But Jerphanion found it difficult to picture such attitudes in any vivid way. He supposed them to be possible, because he had done some reading, and also because, two or three times, he had come into contact with people who seemed to conceal some secret of the kind. For his own part, he could not conceive either scepticism or, still less, lack of enthusiasm for a truth which you have recognized.

He could much more easily understand—without being inclined in that direction in the very least—what a satanic joy you might experience in propagating an error which you knew to be fatal for society. You might have an act of vengeance to accomplish: the equivalent of the Anarchist's bomb. Society had committed so many crimes against the mind. The mind might deal out to it this slow punishment.

But these were thoughts remote from his heart, and he did not linger over them. As for himself, to round off his own reassurance, he had to tell himself that the ideas which he could feel becoming his own, little by little, were dictated by his temperament and his experience as well as endorsed by his reason—that nothing could now prevent him from having them.

"Son of a village schoolmaster. Grandson and nephew of peasants. A strong, pure race. The healthiest you could find in the country. Neither the tired vices of the big cities, nor plebian envy. Nothing of that implication of being embittered, of being staled, of being soiled, which is evoked, alas, by the word 'proletariat.' (That dear proletariat, all the same. My poor brother! . . .) No need of revenge. A steady gaze which bends itself upon injustice. Wrath comes only after judgment and is far from dictating it.

"And my experience—for I have some experience, though it makes old people smile when one talks to them about such a thing, at my age. I have seen the common people from close up, and from

inside. I know what they do, where they live, how much they earn,
what they think. Short time though it is that I've been in Paris, I
have already—because I have the key, the passwords, the guide-
posts—fastened upon many details of the condition of the people.
My uncle's house; the streets; the talk in shops; the silent people
in the omnibus and standing up in the subway. I know ten times
more about it than the Saint-Papoul boys, born and bred here.
Much more than the son of any well-meaning member of the middle classes. Not more than Jallez, of course. Because there's nothing,
except peasant life, that Jallez doesn't know better than I do. But
Jallez hasn't made of it, so far, the same kind of fervor. His fervor
is of another nature, it seems to me. . . .

"I know injustice, not in bulk—like the middle-class young man
who 'has a bent' for social questions—but in its ins and outs. In its
ins and outs, all reeking of day-to-day suffering. Even Jallez is just a
bit middle-class. (It's not very nice of me to be thinking like this
about him.) Oh, only just a bit, of course. Simply because it's very
difficult, in a city like Paris, not to become somewhat middle-class,
once you give up belonging strictly to the people. . . ."

Still, Jerphanion ventured to ask himself this question: "Suppose
I were profoundly convinced that social evolution was turning away
from my ideas, and that they had the future against them? Would
I go on keeping them? Would I resign myself to defending a cause
lost in advance?"

He had to confess to himself that he would not. But, stern though
he was tempted to be towards himself—Catholic by birth and by
maternal education, he had inhaled in his mountains a trace of
Protestant strictness—he could not feel that he had any right to im-
pute to base motives this repugnance in principle of his for lost
causes.

"I have nothing of idolatry of success about me. Quite the contrary. Howl with the wolves? Rush to the help of victory? Nothing
could be further from me. I have more of the spirit of contradiction. I come of nonconformist ancestors. To belong to a militant
minority, even a persecuted minority—I can't imagine any situation
which would excite me more. I wouldn't mind even being quite
alone in my way of thinking, and fighting all alone; but it must be
for a cause that will win some day. Let the future, if needs must,
be my sole comrade. But I must have it on my side.

"I'm not enough of a dilettante to put up with wasting my time.
Devotion to lost causes? Oh yes, I know—all very chivalrous and
fashionable. But, fundamentally, how sceptical it all is! I'd sooner

be taken for a fool. For, obviously, it's folly to believe that the best causes can depend inevitably on the future. But that folly is the mainspring that has kept the world going so far. Yes, it belongs to the same order as faith in progress. Rather elementary, so we're told. So much the worse for the clever people and the tired people! I have faith in progress."

He thought it somewhat eloquently, somewhat provocatively, as though he were face to face with an adversary or haranguing a crowd. But underneath this polemical tone of his he had the deeper feeling that the individual cannot go on being in the right indefinitely against humanity. The most he can hope is that he will prove to be in the right sooner than it will.

While Jerphanion stood meditating on the College roof, perhaps Wazemmes, exploring on Haverkamp's behalf the little streets of some out-of-the-way neighborhood, but rubbing himself up on his own account against the diverse peculiarities of life, was interrogating himself once more about the point of view of "people." The two young fellows, who belonged to the same age of humanity, thus seemed, each in his own way, to bow down before collective wisdom.

But their two ways of doing so were very different; and they tended towards practical conclusions which were quite opposed. What Wazemmes asked of "people" was advice, or even "tips," about the individual art of living; whereas for Jerphanion the problem was to find out how, through the strength of an ideal, a man might deliver society of the future with which it was pregnant.

—Translated by Warre B. Wells

ANDRÉ MAUROIS

****

As to my own work, I believe that the most representative chapter would be the first and last of I Remember, I Remember.

ANDRÉ MAUROIS

****

The Kingdom of God

The Kingdom of God is within you

LUKE xvii:20

I AM FINISHING this book high up in a tower overlooking Manhattan. This morning in the violet haze of dawn I seem to see an Italian city at my feet, bristling with churches and fortresses. In the distance the blue lake in Central Park, surrounded by pale foliage and wrapped in mist, recalls those tiny scenes almost lost in luminous confusion in the background of the paintings of the Primitives. Innumerable cars, yellow, gray and black, glide by even at this early hour, obediently following, on the checker board of the streets, their precise ballet to the rhythm of the red and green lights. The pedestrians, seen from above, are no more than dark or brighter spots. Isolated on this peak I sometimes have the illusion of escaping like a lonely hermit on his column from the vanity and uproar of the city. These heights are favorable to contemplation. Let us take our bearings.

"Here below we are like spectators in a theater," wrote Chateaubriand, "if we turn our heads away for a moment, a whistle shrills, the enchanted palaces vanish and when we bring our eyes back to the stage we find nothing but deserts and unfamiliar actors. . . ." For a long time on the stage of my own life I had seen a familiar settting which I thought was permanent. "A view that cannot be taken away," the architect had said when I bought my house in Neuilly. In this setting of the Bois, of Paris, of France, players whose lines and ability I knew had been enacting for twenty years a drama whose vicissitudes and dénouement I believed I had foreseen. The whistle of Destiny shrills. The view that "could not be taken away" disappears. The Bois de Boulogne ascends into the flies; the Arc de Triomphe fades; the scene shifters bestir themselves in the shadows. When the footlights come up again the spectator discovers a backdrop that represents Rockefeller Center, the Empire State building, and on the stage are characters that had no part in the preceding scene and who do not even speak the same language.

"My life is like a story from *The Thousand and One Nights*," I said to myself during my days of good fortune, "in which the magician comes to seek a cobbler in his workshop and make him a caliph. My life," I said, "is a fairy tale. One morning I am living in a sorry province admiring from a distance great men whom I despair of ever meeting; that evening I have left my sorry province and those whom I idolized without hope have become my friends." I forgot that often in *The Thousand and One Nights,* on the last page, the magician turns the caliph back into a cobbler again. This also is the ending of the strange story that I call my life. . . . Friends, fortune, honors, home, I have had them all, lost them all, and now nothing remains except my workshop of public scrivener. More than ever my life is a fairy tale, but one in which the bad fairies have had the last word.

Let us take our bearings. As in the photograph of an infant we find, to our surprise, the outlines of an old man's face, so in the heart of the man still burn the passions of the boy. The desperate need of devotion that I felt at eight when seated in the forked lilac tree in Normandy I read *The Young Russian Soldiers,* is the need which today still dictates for me a course of conduct that is so far from easy. The happiness I found in a well-turned phrase at the time when I was discovering the classics at college, remains one of my greatest pleasures, and the first dollars I earned in this country went to collect around me once more Pascal and Bossuet, Retz and Saint-Simon. These scholarly virtues, this thirst for knowledge, this desire to teach, they were what made possible last summer those delightful weeks at Mills College.

Among the characters of fiction I find brothers who help me to understand myself. One is Tolstoy's Prince André; the other is the Dr. Antoine Thibault of Roger Martin du Gard, both curiously moral without knowing why, through simple need of personal integrity. The Ethic of Loyalty, I believe that is the definition of the personal code that controls my actions. It seems to me that in an indifferent universe man cannot rely either on nature, whose laws ignore our feelings, nor on the masses of humanity, whose actions are still natural phenomena, but that he must be able to rely on himself and on like-minded companions. The Kingdom of God can only be in the hearts of the "faithful." I have attempted all my life, by instinct rather than by deliberate choice, to be faithful to agreements, to the persons I love, to my country. Sometimes contradictory loyalties have made the choice difficult, almost impossible. I have done my best, not without anguish, awkwardness and mistakes.

I say: "faithful to my country, to persons," not to a doctrine nor to a sect. Few men are less partisan in spirit than I. I do not like systems and I do not believe in them. I do not concern myself with factional disputes except, as Montesquieu said, "to bewail them." I will accept tomorrow any form of government the French freely choose for themselves provided it assures their union, their independence and their security. But if in effort and in action I conform to the most exact disciplines, I cling tenaciously to liberty of mind. The scrupulous scholars who taught me physics, chemistry and history made me singularly exacting when it comes to determining facts. It is not enough for me that an event should support my thesis for me to believe in its reality. I listen to an adversary with the dangerous desire to understand him. I have difficulty in imagining bad faith, deliberate ill will, Machiavellianism. Hence a naïve trust, countless imprudent actions, and the vain hope of converting fanatics by proving to them that they are wrong. That is to forget that they want to be wrong.

Are the fanatics mistaken? I believe so. But I know that others whom I admire hold the contrary view that these bitter and furious minds are the salt of the earth. "You lack aggressiveness," Lucien Romier used to say to me; and it is true that the moderation which is natural to me robs the mind of its mordancy. "Truth is excessive," our Alain used to teach, "and one must go beyond, well beyond, the point of moderation if one wishes to understand even the simplest thing." And Blake: "The road of excess leads to the palace of wisdom." I see clearly what they all mean by this, but excess is a climate in which I cannot live and in which I do not think wounded France has any chance of regaining her strength. Perhaps all sorts are necessary to make a world: the fanatics to shake the masses out of their lethargy and impartial minds devoid of bitterness, to appease, when dawn appears, the Furies, daughters of the Night.

Misfortune which throws some souls into revolt has cured me of certain prejudices. Because I began life in the camp of those who command, for a long time I had difficulty in understanding the grievances of those who are commanded. I would gladly have said with Goethe: "I prefer an injustice to disorder." Through my misfortunes I was to acquire, I hope, more tolerance, patience and pity. For a long time I believed, too, that every woman whose beauty enchanted me was intelligent, modest and good. Experience has not confirmed this agreeable belief and the cure has been painful. But another fundamental truth that misfortune has taught me is that sacrifice, when it is unmixed with pride, gives man incomparable joys. In fact, the greatest happiness of my life, the brief moments of ecstasy and rapture, have been those when I was delivered through love or charity from vain consideration of myself. To forget oneself is wonderful and in humility, if it be complete and freely accepted, there is immense security. According to the beautiful words of Sygne in Claudel's *Hostage:* "I am then seated in the lowest place, I can no longer be deposed."

Night is falling. Shadows envelop the city while myriads of lights spring up. A long string of rubies mark our Park Avenue; then suddenly they are replaced by a long string of emeralds. In the direction of the East River the earth is more thickly sown with lights than the sky of Périgord was with stars. The nearest ones are fixed; those on the horizon twinkle in the trembling mist, outlining unknown constellations. To the south towers and steeples glow. Illuminated by the white radiance of flood lights, pitted with dark holes, the giant figure of Radio City resembles a Brobdingnagian honeycomb raised against a stormy sky. The lines of the other buildings retreat and are lost in the night, but their bright windows rising skyward to the stars are like the stained glass of an immense cathedral, huge as the city. From these millions of faithful what prayer ascends?

Ah, I know very well what they would ask if they were wise, or rather what they would swear to keep. It is what they have. It is this liberty, this tolerance, these relatively gentle ways. Happy America, remember our mistakes and our anguish; do not believe that the future can be founded upon contempt for the past; reform and preserve; work, do not destroy. What have these many catastrophes taught us? That there is no justice without discipline. I was and I remain a liberal; that is to say, I believe men are happier and better if they enjoy the essential liberties. But I know today that there is no liberty without security, no security without unity. I know that if France wishes to remain a great country after this war she must fill in "the bloody ditch" and reconcile the French.

Last summer when my students at Mills College brought to life
some of my heroes I was struck by the predominance in my books
of the theme of Reconciliation. *Colonel Bramble* was an effort to
make the French understand the English soul; the English the
French soul; *Bernard Quesnay* was an effort to show that good
faith is to be found on the employers' side as well as on that of the
workers; *Atmosphere* was an effort to present fairly the woman's
point of view and the man's point of view in a marriage. *The Family Circle* was an effort to reconcile the generations. Always I have
believed that words rather than facts pit men against one another
and that in silence or in action understanding becomes easier. Even
today in this chaos in which a civilization is dying I search anxiously
for opportunities of conciliation, and frequent failures have not
killed in me the persistent and perhaps absurd hope of seeing love
triumph over hate.

Lack of realism? Not entirely, for love is a reality. But no one
can bring it about that men shall be devoid of passions. The problem is to have them live under such institutions that these passions
themselves will unite and reinforce society. I do not think this is
impossible. More than once in the course of history a happy equilibrium has obtained. Never doubt that after this war a new equilibrium will be found. For a decade or a century it will seem stable.
Then once more the fragile edifice will begin to tremble. "What are
the best laws?" Solon was asked. "For what people and at what
period?" he replied. Nations, like individuals, through all their lives
ascend a steep slope, flanked by precipices, on which they are never
permitted to rest. Each minute is a departure, each day a battle.
Life is a game from which no one can withdraw with his winnings
at any time.

News of the world still comes to me in my tower. A young man
asks to see me. He has arrived from Elbeuf and shows me little
photographs in which one can see, reduced to powder, the houses
that were the setting of my first years and the ruin of the fine quais
of Rouen that I used to admire each morning with never-failing
pleasure as I crossed the Boïeldieu Bridge. I question him and discover he is the great-nephew of the fire chief with the copper hel-
ment and the red plume who is my earliest memory.

"And what became of the Captain?"

"I only knew him," he says, "as an old family legend. . . . His
son, my uncle, became a Colonel and died several years ago."

A telephone message informs me that the former headmaster of the Lycée of Rouen has come as a refugee to his daughter's home in New York. I go to see him and am pleased to find an old and charming French scholar who in the time of disaster still wisely quotes the classics.

"How fine it was," he says, "that Court of Honor, the Corneille of David d'Angers and the noble chapel of the Jesuits in front of which I was going to restore the statue of Loyola. . . ."

The mail brings me a letter from Gabriel Hanotaux. Despite his eight-eight years he remains courageous and brilliant. "Everything," he writes, "is going as well as anything can when all goes ill." A letter from Louis Gillet, excellent and heroic as befits that great-hearted man. A letter from André Gide, grave and affectionate; one from Anne Desjardins who is in Algeria and is bravely trying to supply my children with food, for France is famished and food occupies a pathetically large place in our correspondence. Gérald has found a position and is at work; he has lost twenty pounds. Olivier is in a school in the mountains. Of my daughter and my mother I have no news except through the Family Journal which my mother-in-law edits for us at Essendiéras and which will be for our great grandchildren a precious chronicle of this frightful epoch. From these wounded envelopes, bandaged by the censor's stickers, there escapes an air of sadness. One dreams, one longs to see again those whom one loves and to say to them those things which letters must omit.

But it is time to get back to work. Already in the neighboring room can be heard the clicking of my wife's typewriter. Occupied simultaneously by this book, by the lectures that must be prepared, by the war charities that are at present so difficult to support, we live almost alone and never have a moment's boredom. A happy marriage is a long conversation that always seems too short. Sometimes in the evening when the news from France has been better, when we have been satisfed by the day's work, when the lights of the city in the calm of night afford a sublime spectacle, we experience a fugitive, a culpable, a foolhardy feeling of assurance.

"Alas!" Simone says shivering. . . . "What more is going to happen?"

She knows now, as I do, that happiness like the pink and white anemones of my childhood is a flower that must not be picked.

Is she right? Will the whistle blast of Destiny in a few seconds put an end to this setting as it once caused the trees of the Bois to vanish? Will Rockefeller Center and the Empire State ascend into the flies? Will the fragile and precarious existence that we have

so painfully constructed during this year collapse like the one that
formerly seemed to us so substantial? And what shall we see when
the footlights come up again, if ever they do come up? No one
knows. But timidly, anxiously, ardently we hope that it may be noble
and lovely Périgord, a long valley lined with poplars, the red roofs
of the farm at Brouillac lighted by the setting sun, and when the
night shall come, in a French sky above the plane trees and the
cedars, familiar constellations which French voices will call by name
in the most beautiful of languages.

                                      —*Translated by Denver and Jane Lindley*

ANDRÉ MALRAUX

****

. . . as for the lines which you ask explaining "Why have you chosen this piece?" the answer is:

Because the essential problems which face us today appear in this fragment which was written more than ten years ago.

ANDRÉ MALRAUX

****

The Essential Problems

A THIN, BENT FIGURE, alone in the midst of the vast staircase, Guernico had come to the War Ministry to enlist official support for the ambulance corps he was trying to reorganize. As the tide of war drew nearer to Madrid, the ambulance corps he had built up in the Toledo days was losing its efficiency. On the ground floor of the Ministry was a display of armour, and in the gathering dusk the Catholic writer with the tall, spare form and the fair complexion we find in so many of Velasquez' portraits, looked as if he might have stepped out of one of those historic coats of mail, pledged to return to it before the break of day. Garcia, who had not met him for the last three weeks, was wont to describe Guernico as the only one of his friends in whom intelligence took the form of charity. And, for all the gulf that yawned between them, Guernico was perhaps the only man for whom Garcia had a real affection.

The two set out together for the Plaza Mayor.

Shadows glided along drawn shutters and bare walls, shadows parallel and bending forward, like haulers towing a boat upstream. Tawny smoke-clouds from the suburbs were rolling over the city. "The exodus," Garcia thought—but then he saw that none of the passers-by carried bundles. All were walking very fast in the same direction.

"It has pluck," he said, "our city of Madrid."

A blind man, his begging-bowl before him, was playing the *Inter-*

677

national. In their lightless houses, the fascists, a hundred thousand strong, were waiting for the next day's battle.

"There's not a sound," Guernico said.

Only a sound of footsteps. The street was throbbing like a vein. The Moors were at the south and western gates, but the wind was blowing away from the city. Not a rifle-shot could be heard, not even the boom of cannon. Only the constant rustle of the moving crowd, like an army of moles digging their tunnels underground. And the accordion.

They walked towards the Puerta del Sol, in the same direction as the reddish smoke that drifted overhead and the unseen river bearing the crowd on its futile way towards the plaza—as though the Carabanchel barricades had been erected there.

"Supposing we stop them here. . . ."

A woman plucked Guernico's sleeve and addressed him in French. "Do you think I ought to leave?"

"She's a German comrade," Guernico explained to Garcia, but did not answer her.

"He says I ought to go," the woman went on. "He says he can't fight properly when I'm around."

"And I'm quite sure he's right," Garcia said.

"But I just can't *live* if I know he's fighting here and I don't even hear what's happening."

Another accordion playing the *International* droned an accompaniment to the words; a second blind man, begging-bowl on lap, was carrying on the tune from the point where the first had dropped it.

The women are all alike, Garcia mused. If that one goes, she'll take it hard at first, but she'll see it through; whereas, if she stays, he'll be killed. He could not see her face; she was much shorter than he and her face was screened by shadows of the passers-by.

"Why do you want to stay?" Guernico's voice was gentle.

"I don't mind dying, but food's the trouble; I've got to eat my fill, and now that won't be possible. . . . I'm pregnant."

Garcia did not hear Guernico's reply. The woman drifted away on another stream of shadows.

"What can one do . . . ?" Guernico murmured.

Some *milicianos* in overalls caught them up and passed them. Paving-stones had been pulled up and phantom figures were building a barricade across the street.

"When are you leaving?" Garcia asked.

"I'm not leaving."

Guernico would be among the first for the firing-squad when the fascists entered the city. Though Garcia did not turn towards his friend, he visualized him now, as he walked beside him, with his little fair moustache, his tousled hair and long, lean arm. The defencelessness of that body touched him in the way that children always stirred his pity, for it ruled out all ideas of fighting. No, Guernico would not fight; he would be killed.

Neither mentioned the Madrid ambulance section, for neither really believed it would materialize.

"So long as one can serve the revolution, it's up to us to do so. But getting oneself killed doesn't help in the least, my dear fellow. The Republic's not a matter of geography and its fate isn't sealed just because one town more or less gets captured."

"I was at the Puerta del Sol on the day of the Montana affair, when the crowd was being fired on from every window. The people in the street lay flat; the whole square was a mass of prostrate bodies, on which the enemy were firing. On the next day but one, when I went to the Ministry I found a long queue of women outside it; they had come to offer their blood for transfusion. Twice I've *seen* the Spanish people. This war is the people's war, whatever the outcome; and I'll stand by it wherever it is. There are two hundred thousand workers here and *they* haven't any cars to take them to Valencia."

Obviously nothing Garcia might say could have weighed with Guernico as the lives of his wife and children must have weighed with him. And Garcia could not bear the thought that if they were never to meet again their last conversation should have ended on a sort of wrangle.

Guernico made a spacious gesture with his long, slender hand. "After all," he said, "perhaps I'll leave at the last moment." But Garcia felt sure that he was lying.

A thud of heavy foosteps echoed down the street, seeming to precede the body of men who now emerged into the light. "It's the diggers," Garcia said. They were off to the front just behind Carabanchel for trench-digging and laying mines. In front, another company of shadows, dim in the mist, were building another barricade.

"They're staying right enough, you see," Guernico said.

"At a pinch they've a retreat open by the Guadalajara road. But your rooms and the Association premises are positive deathtraps."

Guernico made the same gesture of uncertain fatalism. Another blind beggar; still the *International*. The only tune blind men played just now. And more shadowy forms, building more barricades.

"Perhaps," Guernico said, "more duties are imposed on us, as Christian writers, than on other people." They were passing the Alcalá Church. Guernico pointed vaguely towards it. By his tone Garcia guessed that his lips were twisted in a bitter smile, as he continued. "After a sermon by a fascist preacher in French Catalonia— the text was: 'Be ye not unequally yoked together with unbelievers' —I saw Father Sarazola go up to the preacher. After the preacher had gone away Sarazola said to me: 'Once to have known Christ leaves its mark. Of all the fascists I've seen here, he's the first to be ashamed of it.'"

A lorry passed, laden with a serried mass of *milicianos* squatting on the floor, the muzzles of their obsolete machine-guns swaying above them. When Guernico spoke again, his voice was lower.

"Only, you know, when I see the way they're behaving now, it's I who feel ashamed."

Garcia was about to reply when a little weasel-faced *miliciano* suddenly gripped his arm.

"They'll be right here tomorrow!" he said.

"Who's that fellow?" Guernico asked in an undertone.

"He used to work in Magnin's squadron, as a clerk."

"This Government—there's not a bloody thing to be done with it," said the weasel-faced man. "Why, ten days ago I brought them a plan, worked out in detail, mind you, for the large-scale culture of typhoid germs. Fifteen years' research, and I didn't ask a sou for it, just to down the fascists. They wouldn't do a thing about it. Turned it down, like they turned down my bomb. Well, the fascists will be here tomorrow."

"Oh, shut your mouth, you!" Garcia exclaimed.

But already the little man had bobbed back like a jack-in-the-box into the stream of passing shadows; the *International* had accompanied his appearance and eclipse.

"Come across many of his type?" Guernico inquired.

"At first, yes. . . . The sort of volunteer we got at first was usually a bit of a lunatic or a bit of a hero. Sometimes, both at once."

On the Alcalá, as on all the narrow streets, brooded the feverish expectancy of nights when history is in the making. And here, too, there was no sound of guns, only the throbbing of accordions. Suddenly at the far end of the street a machine-gun loosed off a strip— a gunner opening fire on ghosts.

More barricades were being hastily thrown together. Garcia had no great faith in the utility of barricades; these, however, looked business-like enough. Everywhere in the dim light spectral forms were flitting to and fro, with here and there a stationary wraith that, after a brief gesture, resumed its immobility—a man directing operations. The mist was steadily thickening. Men and women carrying building materials sped through the gloom, and workers from the various building unions were carrying out the tasks of supervision assigned them by their foremen. Experts from the Fifth Regiment had trained these foremen in two strenuous days. And in this silent phantasmagoria the Old Madrid was passing away; for the first time, behind the drama of private lives, of personal dreams and aspirations, beyond the lesser hopes and fears that urged these people on their diverse ways, a will commensurate with the collective soul of New Madrid was developing in the fogbound dusk of the beleaguered city.

The lamps along the avenue were dwindling to dismal, ineffectual blurs of light under the prehistorically monstrous forms of the intricate skyscrapers. And Garcia recalled what his friend had said: "More duties are imposed on us, as Christian writers, than on other people."

"What the devil can you expect from them—things being as they are?" he asked, jerking his pipe in the direction of another church.

They were under a street-lamp. On Guernico's face was the pensive smile that so often gave him the look of an ailing child.

"Don't forget I'm one of those people who believe in an eternity." He took Garcia's arm. "I suspect that what's happening here just now—even the burning of churches in Catalonia—may do far more for my Church than the last hundred years of Spanish Catholicism have done for it. For twenty years I've watched the priests officiating here and in Andalusia. Well, in all those twenty years, I've never had a glimpse of a truly Catholic Spain. Only rites and ceremonies, and in the people's hearts as on the face of nature—a wasteland!"

At the Puerta del Sol all the doors of the State Building were open. Just before the rebellion an exhibition of sculpture was being held in the vestibule, and statues of all kinds—nudes, groups and animals—were awaiting the coming of the Moors in the vast empty hall. Only the click of a distant typewriter fretted the silence; evidently the building was not completely abandoned.

And in all the streets radiating from the square, ubiquitous as the mist, similar wraiths were building similar barricades.

"Is it a fact that Caballero asked your advice about reopening the churches?"

"Yes."

"What did you say?"

" 'No,' of course."

"You told him not to open them?"

"Obviously. That may surprise you, but it doesn't surprise Catholics at all. If I'm shot tomorrow, I'll have the usual fears for myself, like any other man; but not one on that score. I'm neither a heretic nor a Protestant; I'm a Spanish Catholic. If theology were in your line, I'd tell you I'm appealing to the soul of the Church against its body; but that's another story. Faith doesn't imply a lack of love. And hope doesn't imply a world that would justify itself by making people worship once again, like a fetish, that crucifix at Seville which they call 'The Rich Man's Christ.' (Simony, not heresy's the trouble with our Church.) Nor is it looking forward to a Spanish empire as the be-all and the end-all of the world; a régime in which no sound is heard because those who suffer must hide themselves to weep. 'Order'—you find that in a convict prison, too. Even the best of the fascists hasn't a single hope that isn't founded on pride. But what has Christ to do with such a world?"

Garcia tripped over a large dog and nearly fell. There were numbers of magnificent dogs—abandoned by owners who had fled—straying in Madrid. With the blind men they had taken possession of the city, pending the issue between Republicans and Moors.

"Those priests of Navarre," Guernico continued, "who permit men to be shot for the glory of the Holy Virgin, what have they to do with 'charity'? No, it's the Basque priests who stand for charity; those priests who till the fascists killed them went on administering the benediction, in the cellars of Irun, to the anarchists who'd burned their churches. I'm not anxious, Garcia. I recognize the Church of Spain, but—all the faith I've in me bears me out—I'm against it in the name of the three major virtues of our creed: Faith, Hope and Charity."

"Where will you find the church that answers to your faith?"

Guernico stroked back his hair, which was falling on his forehead. Almost soundlessly the crowd was flowing to and fro between the arcades and hoardings which all but blocked the Plaza Mayor. The earthwork going on in the square had been held up, and it was littered with heaps of stone and paving-blocks; over these the moving stream of shadows skipped or glided in a tragic nocturnal ballet, against a background of haggard pinnacles resembling those of the

Escorial. Madrid tonight seemed so thickly covered with barricades that in the whole city not one open space remained.

"Look!" Guernico exclaimed. "In those squalid houses, and in the hospitals, there are priests at this very moment, dressed up in waistcoats like Parisian waiters, and collarless—and they're hearing confessions, giving extreme unction, perhaps baptising children. I said to you that for twenty years I've not heard Christ's word in Spain. But those priests are being heard now. Yes, they're being listened to, and nobody, nobody will listen to the men who turn out tomorrow in the cassocks they've fetched out of hiding, to bless Franco. How many priests are carrying on their ministry just now? Fifty, perhaps a hundred. Napoleon once walked under these arcades; in those days the Church of Spain shielded its flock; but since then I doubt that there's been a single night, till these last few nights, when Christ's words were *living* in our midst. Yes, tonight His Gospel is a living presence."

His foot caught on a displaced paving-block and his hair sagged forward again.

"A living presence," he repeated. "There aren't many places in the world of which one can say: 'His Word was present here.' But soon it will be known that here, in Madrid, during these recent nights, His Word was among us all. In this land something is dawning for my Church, something which may well be its renaissance. I saw the last sacrament administered to a Belgian *miliciano* yesterday at San Carlos Hospital, do you know it?"

"Yes, when we were running that armoured train, I had some casualties treated there."

The enormous, musty rooms came back to Garcia's mind, the foliage sprouting through the narrow windows. How far away all that seemed!

"It was a ward for arm cases. When the priest said, *Requiem aeternam dona ei Domine,* several voices made the response: *Et lux perpetual luceat.* . . . Four or five voices, just behind me."

"Do you remember Manuel's *Tantum Ergo*?"

Five months earlier several of Garcia's friends, including Manuel and Guernico, had spent with him the last night before he started out on a journey; at daybreak they had all gone together to the hills overlooking Madrid. As the pale, mauve forms of the buildings loomed slowly forth against the shadows and the dark mass of the Escorial woods, Manuel had sung some Asturian folksongs and the others joined in the strains. Then he had said, "Now, for Guernico's benefit, I'm going to sing the *Tantum Ergo*." All had been educated by priests and all had joined in the last verse, singing the parts in Latin. As those half-forgotten Latin phrases had come back to his friend that morning, charged with a certain amiable irony, so to the wounded revolutionaries in the San Carlos Hospital had recurred the Latin of the death-bed.

"The priest said to me," Guernico went on: " 'When I came in, they all took off their hats; they knew that I was bringing them consolation in the hour of death.' He was wrong. They took off their hats because the priest who'd entered might have been their enemy, but was not."

He stumbled against another loose stone; uprooted paving-stones lay everywhere as if the square had been through a bombardment. His voice was different when he spoke again.

"Oh, I know our 'realists' are out to make us see all that from a new angle. The Son of God came down on earth merely to talk a lot of idle nonsense; His sufferings must have turned His head a little—considering the time he was hanging on the Cross, of course. . . .

"God alone knows the trials He is about to impose on the priesthood; but I think that the priest's vocation *should* become a hard task once again." He paused for a moment, then added: "As indeed every Christian life is hard."

Garcia watched their twisted shadows gliding in front of them along the iron-shuttered shopfronts and remembered the twelve bombs of the thirtieth of October.

"What's hardest," Guernico continued in a low tone, "is the problem of the women and children. Anyhow, I've that much luck, my family's not here."

Garcia turned to see his friend's face, but could make out little of his features. There was still no sign of battle; yet somehow, like a presence in a darkened room, the crescent of the fascist army made itself felt closing in upon the city. Garcia recalled his last meeting with Caballero, and how the words "eldest son" had cropped up in their conversation. He was aware that Caballero's eldest boy was held prisoner by the fascists at Segovia and would be shot. That had been in September; they had sat at the table facing each other; Caballero in dungarees, Garcia in a *mono*. Through a window open on the autumn sun a grasshopper had blundered in and fallen upside down on the table between them. Half-stunned, the insect tried to keep from moving, but its brittle legs were quivering and, as Garcia watched him, both men had kept silent.

—Translated by Stuart Gilbert and Alastair MacDonald

JACQUES MARITAIN

****

I do not know whether this excerpt from Art *and* Scholasticism *represents the manner of the author in an adequate fashion. I chose it because it is perhaps likely to have meaning for the common reader, and because its subject-matter is especially significant, at least to my mind. I am more interested in the subject-matter than in the author.*

JACQUES MARITAIN

****

Art and Beauty

St. Thomas, who was as simple as he was wise, defined the beautiful as what gives pleasure on sight, *id quod visum placet.** The four words say all that is necessary: a vision, that is to say an *intuitive knowledge,* and a *joy.* The beautiful is what gives joy, not all joy, but joy in knowledge; not the joy peculiar to the act of knowing, but a joy super-abounding and overflowing from such an act because of the object known. If a thing exalts and delights the soul by the bare fact of its being given to the intuition of the soul, it is good to apprehend, it is beautiful.

Beauty is essentially the object of *intelligence,* for what *knows* in the full meaning of the word is the mind, which alone is open to the infinity of being. The natural site of beauty is the intelligible world: thence it descends. But it also falls in a way within the grasp of the senses, since the senses in the case of man serve the mind and can themselves rejoice in knowing "the beautiful relates only to sight and hearing of all the senses, because these two are *maxime cognoscitivi.*" The part played by the senses in the perception of beauty becomes in our case enormous and well-nigh indispensable, because our mind is not intuitive like the angelic mind: it can perceive, no doubt, but only on condition of abstracting and discoursing. In man only knowledge derived through the senses possesses fully the intu-

* Summa Theologica, *i.q. 5, a. 4,* ad *1.*

ivity necessary for the perception of the beautiful. So also man can
certainly enjoy purely intelligible beauty, but the beautiful which is
connatural to man is that which comes to delight the mind through
the senses and their intuition. Such also is the peculiar beauty of
our art, which works upon a sensible matter for the joy of the spirit.
It would fain so persuade itself that paradise is not lost. It has the
savour of the terrestrial paradise, because it restores for a brief moment the simultaneous peace and delight of the mind and the senses.

If beauty delights the mind, it is because beauty is essentially a
certain excellence or perfection in the proportion of things to the
mind. Hence the three conditions assigned to it by St. Thomas:
integrity, because the mind likes being; proportion, because the
mind likes order and likes unity; lastly and above all brightness or
clarity, because the mind likes light and intelligibility. A certain
splendour is indeed according to all the Ancients the essential character of beauty,—*claritas est de ratione pulchritudinis, lux pulchri-
ficat, quia sine luce omnia sunt turpia,*—but it is a splendour of
intelligibility: *splendor veri,* said the Platonists, *splendor ordinis,*
said St. Augustine, adding that "unity is the form of all beauty,"
splendor formae, said St. Thomas with a metaphysician's precision
of language: for *form,* that is to say the principle determining the
peculiar perfection of everything which is, constituting and completing things in their essence and their qualities, the ontological secret,
so to speak, of their innermost being, their spiritual essence, their
operative mystery, is above all the peculiar principle of intelligibility,
the peculiar *clarity* of every thing. Every form, moreover, is a remnant or a ray of the creative Mind impressed upon the heart of the
being created. All order and proportion, on the other hand, are the
work of the mind. So, to say with the Schoolmen that beauty is the
splendour of form shining on the proportioned parts of matter is to
say that it is a lightning of mind on a matter intelligently arranged.
The mind rejoices in the beautiful because in the beautiful it finds
itself again: recognizes itself, and comes into contact with its very
own light. This is so true that they especially perceive and particularly relish the beauty of things who, like St. Francis of Assisi, for
example, know that they emanate from a mind and refer them to
their Author.

Every sensible beauty, no doubt, implies a certain delight of the
eye or the ear or the imagination: but there can be no beauty unless
the mind also is in some way rejoiced. A beautiful colour "washes
the eye" as a powerful scent dilates the nostrils: but of these two

"forms" or qualities only colour is called "beautiful," because being received, as opposed to the perfume, in a sense capable of disinterested knowledge, it can be, even through its purely sensible brilliance, an object of joy to the mind. Again, the more highly developed a man's culture becomes, the more spiritual grows the brilliance of the form which ravishes him.

It is important, however, to observe that in the beauty which has been termed connatural to man and is peculiar to human art this brilliance of form, however purely intelligible it may be in itself, is apprehended *in the sensible and by the sensible,* and not separately from it. The intuition of artistic beauty so stands at the opposite pole from the abstraction of scientific truth. For in the former case it is precisely through the apprehension of sense that the light of being penetrates to the mind.

The mind then, spared the least effort of abstraction, rejoices without labour and without discussion. It is excused its customary task, it has not to extricate something intelligible from the matter in which it is buried and then step by step go through its various attributes; like the stag at the spring of running water, it has nothing to do but drink, and it drinks the clarity of being. Firmly fixed in the intuition of sense, it is irradiated by an intelligible light granted to it of a sudden in the very sensible in which it glitters; and it apprehends this light not *sub ratione veri,* but rather *sub ratione delectabilis,* by the happy exercise it procures for it and the succeeding joy in appetite, which leaps out to every good of the soul as its own peculiar object. Only afterwards will it more or less successfully analyse in reflection the causes of such joy.

So, although the beautiful is in close dependence upon what is metaphysically true, in the sense that every splendour of intelligibility in things presupposes some degree of conformity with that Intelligence which is the cause of things, the beautiful nevertheless is not a kind of truth, but a kind of good. The perception of the beautiful is related to knowledge, but by way of addition, "as its bloom is an addition to youth"; it is not so much a kind of knowledge as a kind of delight.

The beautiful is essentially delightful. Therefore by its very nature, by its very beauty, it stirs desire and produces love, whereas truth as such only illuminates. *"Omnibus igitur est pulchrum et bonum desiderabile et amabile et diligibile."* It is for its beauty that Wisdom is loved. And it is for its own sake that every form of beauty is loved at first, even if later the too frail flesh is caught in the snare. Love in its turn produces ecstasy, that is to say, makes the lover beside himself: an ecstasy of which the soul experiences a lesser form when it is gripped by the beauty of a work of art, and the fullness when it is absorbed, like dew, by the beauty of God.

And of God Himself, according to Denys the Areopagite, one must be bold enough to say that He suffers as it were an ecstasy of love, because of the abundance of His goodness which makes Him give all things a share of His magnificence. But His love causes the beauty of what He loves, whereas our love is caused by the beauty of what we love.

The speculations of the Ancients concerning the nature of the beautiful must be taken in the most formal sense and their thought should not be materialised in any too narrow specification. The idea of *integrity* or perfection or complete execution can be realised not in one way only but in a thousand or ten thousand different ways. The lack of a head or an arm is a considerable defect in a woman but of much less account in a statue—whatever disappointment M. Ravaisson may have felt at being unable to *complete* the Venus of Melos. The slightest sketch of Leonardo's or even Rodin's is nearer to perfection than the most finished Bouguereau. And if it pleases a futurist to paint a lady with only one eye, or a quarter of an eye, nobody denies him such a right: all one is entitled to require —and here is the whole problem—is that the quarter eye is all the lady needs *in the given case*.

It is the same with proportion, fitness and harmony. They differ with the object and the end aimed at. Proportions good in a man are not good in a child. Figures constructed according to the Greek or the Egyptian canon are perfectly proportioned in their kind: but Rouault's yokels are also as perfectly proportioned in their kind. Integrity and proportion have no absolute significance and must be understood solely *in relation* to the end of the work, which is to make a form shine on the matter.

Last and most important: this very brilliance of form, the essence of beauty, shines on matter in an infinite variety of ways.

At one time it is the sensible brilliance of colour or tone, at another the intelligible clarity of an arabesque, a rhythm or an harmonious balance, an activity or a movement, or again the reflection upon things of some human or divine thought, but above all it is the profound splendour of the soul shining through, of the soul which is the principle of life and animal energy or the principle of spiritual life, of pain and passion. There is also a more exalted splendour, the splendour of Grace, which the Greeks never knew.

Beauty therefore does not consist in conformity to a certain ideal and unchanging type, in the sense understood by those who, confusing the true and the beautiful, knowledge and delight, insist that to perceive beauty man shall discover "by the vision of ideas," "through the material envelope," "the invisible essence of things" and their "necessary type." St. Thomas was as far removed from this pseudo-Platonism as from the idealist fancy fair of Winckelman and David. Beauty for him begins to exist as soon as the radiation of any form over a suitably proportioned matter succeeds in pleasing the mind, and he is careful to warn us that beauty is in a manner *relative*,—not to the dispositions of the subject in the sense in which relativity is understood nowadays, but to the peculiar nature and end of the thing and to the formal conditions in which it is involved. *"Pulchritudo quodammodo dicitur per respectum ad aliquid. . . ." "Alia enim est pulchritudo spiritus et alia corporis, atque alia hujus et illius corporis."* And however beautiful a created thing may be, it may appear beautiful to some and not to others, because it is beautiful only under certain aspects which some discover and others do not see: it is therefore "beautiful in one place and not beautiful in another."

If this be so, it is because the beautiful belongs to the order of *transcendentals*—that is to say, of concepts which surpass all limits of kind of category and will not suffer themselves to be confined in any class, because they absorb everything and are to be found everywhere. Like the one, the true and the good, it is *being* itself considered from a certain aspect, it is a property of being: it is not an accident super-added to being, it adds to being merely a relation of reason, it is being considered as delighting, by the mere intuition of it, an intellectual nature. So everything is beautiful as everything is good, at least in a certain relation. And as being is everywhere present and everywhere various, the beautiful likewise is scattered everywhere and everywhere various. Like being and the other transcendentals, it is essentially *analogous*, that is to say it is predicated for divers reasons, *sub diversa ratione*, of the divers subjects of which it is predicated: each kind of being *is* in its own way, is *good* in its own way, is *beautiful* in its own way.

Analogous concepts are properly predicable only of God, in whom the perfection they describe exists in a "formal-eminent" manner, in a pure and infinite state. God is their "sovereign analogue" and they are to be found in things only as a scattered and prismatised reflection of the face of God. So Beauty is one of the divine attributes.

God is beautiful. He is the most beautiful of beings, because, as Denys the Areopagite and St. Thomas explain, His beauty is without alteration or vicissitude, without increase or diminution: and because it is not like the beauty of things, which have all a particularised beauty, *particulatam pulchritudinem, sicut et particulatam naturam,* He is beautiful by Himself and in Himself, absolutely beautiful.

He is exceedingly beautiful (*superpulcher*), because there is preexistent in a super-excellent way in the perfectly simple unity of His nature the fountain of all beauty.

He is beauty itself, because He imparts beauty to all created beings, according to the peculiar nature of each, and because He is the cause of all harmony and brightness. Every form indeed, that is to say every light, is "a certain irradiation proceeding from the first brightness," "a participation in the divine brightness." And every consonance or harmony, every concord, every friendship and union of whatever sort between creatures, proceeds from the divine beauty, the primitive, super-eminent type of all consonance, which gathers all things together and calls them to itself, well deserving on that account "the name of καλός, which derives from calling." Thus "the beauty of the creature is nothing but a similitude of the divine beauty shared among things," and on the other hand, every form being a principle of being and every consonance or harmony being a preservation of being, the divine beauty must be said to be the cause of being in everything which is. *Ex divina pulchritudine esse omnium derivatur.*

In the Trinity, St. Thomas goes on to say, the title Beauty is specially appropriated to the Son. As for integrity or perfection, He has truly and perfectly in Himself, without the least diminution, the nature of the Father. As for due proportion or consonance, He is the express image of the Father, a perfect likeness; and it is proportion which befits the picture as such. As for brilliance, He is the Word, the light and splendour of the mind, "perfect Word, lacking nothing and, so to speak, art of the Almighty God."

Beauty therefore belongs to the transcendental and metaphysical

order. For this reason it tends of itself to carry the soul beyond creation. Of the instinct for beauty, the *accursed poet** to whom modern
art owes the recovery of the consciousness of the theological quality
and the tyrannical spirituality of beauty, says, "it is that immortal
instinct for the beautiful which makes us consider the world and its
pageants as a glimpse of, a *correspondence* with, Heaven. The in-
satiable thirst for everything beyond, which life reveals, is the liveliest proof of our immortality. It is at once by poetry and *through*
poetry, by music and *through* music that the soul perceives what
splendours shine behind the tomb; and when an exquisite poem
brings tears to the eyes, such tears do not argue an excess of enjoyment but rather attest an irritation of melancholy, some peremptory
need of the nerves, a nature exiled in the imperfect which would
fain possess immediately, even on this earth, a paradise revealed."

Once we touch a transcendental, we touch being itself, a likeness
of God, an absolute, all that ennobles and makes the joy of life:
we enter the realm of the spirit. It is remarkable that the only real
means of communication between human creatures is through being
or some one of the properties of being. This is their only means of
escape from the individuality in which they are enclosed by matter.
If they remain on the plane of their sensible needs and their sentimental selves they tell their stories to one another in vain; they
cannot understand each other. They watch each other and cannot
see, each infinitely alone, however closely work or the pleasure of
love may bind them together. But once touch the good and Love,
like the Saints, or the true, like an Aristotle, or the beautiful, like
a Dante, a Bach or a Giotto, then contact is established and souls
communicate. Men are only really united by the spirit: light alone
gathers them together, *intellectualia et rationalia omnia congregans,
et indestructibilia faciens.*

Art in general tends to make a work. But certain arts tend to
make a work of *beauty* and thereby differ essentially from all the
rest. The work which involves the labour of all the other arts is itself
ordered to the service of man and is therefore a mere means: it is
completely enclosed in a definite material *genus* or kind. The work
which involves the labour of the Fine Arts is ordered to beauty: in

---

* *Baudelaire*, L'Art Romantique. *Baudelaire is here reproducing an extract
from the preface to his own translation,* Nouvelles Histoires Extraordinaires,
an extract inspired by a translation of a passage in a lecture by Poe,
The Poetic Principle.

so far as it is beautiful it is an end, an absolute, self-sufficient; and if, as work to be done, it is material and enclosed in a kind, as beautiful it belongs to the realm of the spirit and dives deep into the transcendence and the infinity of being.

The Fine Arts therefore stand out in the *genus* art as man stands out in the *genus* animal. And like man himself they are like a horizon where matter comes into contact with spirit. They have a spiritual soul. Therefore they have many distinctive properties. Their association with the beautiful modifies in their case certain characteristics of art in general, notably, as I shall endeavour to show, all that concerns the rules of art. On the other hand it emphasises and carries to a kind of excess other generic characteristics of the artistic virtue, above all its intellectual character and its resemblance to the speculative virtues.

There is a curious analogy between the Fine Arts and wisdom. Like wisdom, they are ordered to an object transcending man and of value in itself, whose fullness is without limit, for beauty is as infinite as being. They are disinterested, pursued for their own sake, truly noble because their work considered in itself is not made to be used as a means, but to be enjoyed as an end, being a true fruit, *aliquid ultimum et delectabile*. Their whole value is spiritual and their manner of being is contemplation. For if contemplation is not their activity, as it is the activity of wisdom, their object is nevertheless to produce an intellectual delight, that is to say a kind of contemplation, and they also pre-suppose in the artist a kind of contemplation, whence the beauty of the work ought to overflow. For this reason there may be applied to them, due allowance being made, the comparison drawn by St. Thomas between wisdom and games: "The contemplation of wisdom is rightly compared with games for two things to be found in games. The first is that games give pleasure and the contemplation of wisdom gives the very greatest pleasure, according to what Wisdom says of itself in Ecclesiasticus: *My spirit is sweet above honey*. The second is that the movements in games are not contrived to serve another end but are pursued for their own sake. It is the same with the delights of wisdom. . . . Hence divine Wisdom compares its delight to games: *I was with him forming all things and was delighted every day playing before him at all times: playing in the world*."

But Art remains always essentially in the sphere of Making and it is by drudgery upon some matter that it aims at rejoicing the spirit. Hence for the artist a strange and pathetic condition, the very image of man's condition in the world, where he is condemned to wear himself out among bodies and live with minds. Although he reproaches the old poets for making the Divinity jealous, Aristotle admits that they were right in saying that to the Divinity alone is reserved the possession of wisdom as His true property: "The possession of it is beyond human power, for human nature in many ways is in bondage." So the production of beauty belongs to God alone as His true property. And if the condition of the artist is more human and less exalted than that of the wise man, it is also more discordant and painful, because his activity is not wholly confined within the pure immanence of spiritual operations and does not consist in itself of contemplating, but of making. Unable to enjoy the substance and the peace of wisdom, he is caught by the harsh exigencies of the mind and the speculative life and condemned to every servile misery of temporal practice and production.

"Dear brother Leo, God's little beast, if a minor friar were to speak the language of the angels and raise to life a man already four days dead, write it well that even in so doing perfect joy is not to be found . . ."

Even if the artist were to compass in his work all the light of the sky and all the grace of the first garden, he would not have perfect joy, because he is on the tracks of wisdom and running upon the scent of its perfumes, but never possesses it. Even if the philosopher were to know every reason susceptible of comprehension and every virtue of being, he would not have perfect joy, because his wisdom is human. Even if the theologian were to know every analogy of the divine processions and every motive of Christ's actions, he would not have perfect joy, because his wisdom, though it has a divine origin, is of a human fashion and speaks with a human voice.

Sweet voices, die, . . . dying indeed you are!

The Poor and the Peaceful alone have perfect joy because they have wisdom and contemplation *par excellence,* in the silence of created things and in the voice of Love: united without intermediary to subsisting Truth, they know "the sweetness God gives and the delicious taste of the Holy Ghost." Hence the exclamation of St. Thomas, shortly before his death, with reference to his unfinished *Summa Theologica:* "What rubbish it is! *mihi videtur ut palea.*" And the Parthenon and Our Lady of Chartres, the Sistine Chapel and the Mass in B minor are also rubbish, destined to be burned on the Last Day. "Created things have no savour."

The Middle Ages knew such order. The Renaissance shattered it. After three centuries of infidelity, Art, the prodigal, would fain have become the ultimate end of man, his Bread and Wine, the consubstantial mirror of beatific Beauty. In reality it has only squandered its substance. And the poet hungering for beatitude who asked of Art the mystic fullness which God alone can give could find his only outlet in *Sigê l'abîme*. Rimbaud's *silence* denotes perhaps the end of an age-old apostasy. At all events it clearly indicates that it is folly to try to find in art the words of eternal life and rest for the human heart: and that the artist, if he is not to shatter his art or his soul, must simply be, as artist, what art would have him be—a good workman.

But now the modern world, which had promised the artist all things, will soon scarcely leave him even the bare means of subsistence. Founded upon the two *unnatural* principles of the *fecundity of money* and the *finality of the useful,* multiplying its needs and servitudes without any possibility of there ever being a limit, ruining the leisure of the soul, withdrawing the material *factible* from the control which proportioned it to the ends of the human being, imposing on man its puffing machinery and its speeding up of matter, the modern world is shaping human activity in a properly inhuman way, in a properly devilish direction, for the ultimate end of all this frenzy is to prevent man from remembering God,

> *dum nil perenne cogitat,*
> *seseque culpis illigat.*

He must consequently, if he is to be logical, regard as useless, and therefore despicable, everything which for any reason bears the mark of the spirit.

"An aristocracy in the order of deeds, but a truly democratic barbarism of the mind, is the portion of the time to come; the dreamer, the man of speculative mind, will be able to maintain his place only at the expense of his security and comfort; jobs, success, or glory will reward the versatility of the mountebank: more than ever, to a degree unknown in the iron age, the hero and the saint will pay for their pride in poverty and loneliness."

Persecuted like the wise man and almost like the Saint, the artist will perhaps recognise his brethren at last and find his vocation once again: for in a way he is not of this world, being, from the

moment he begins working for beauty, on the road which leads
upright souls to God and makes invisible things clear to them by
visible. However few they may then be who will disdain to gratify
the Beast and turn with the wind, in them, for the simple reason
that they will be exercising a *disinterested* activity, the human race
will live.

—Translated by J. F. Scanlan

FRANÇOIS MAURIAC

✸✸✸

EDITORIAL DEPARTMENT
EYRE & SPOTTISWOODE
LONDON

As you will know from the book, Thérèse, A Portrait in Four Parts, *the two sections, "Thérèse and the Doctor" and "Thérèse at the Hotel,"* are taken from a volume of short stories called Plongées *which M. Mauriac published in 1938, and which had not previously been included in the narrative of the story of Thérèse Desqueyroux. They seem to me to be exceptionally interesting for a variety of reasons. First, they are technically superior in handling, I think, to either of the novels, i. e., they mark an increasing maturity in the writer's craftsmanship, and secondly because they throw a light on the buried portions of Thérèse's life, which have always excited the reader and which for many years seem to have troubled the author himself. You may remember that he inserted a fugitive incident in which Thérèse makes a brief appearance, in his novel,* Ce qui etait Perdu, *before these two stories were written.*

*It is impossible to read the story of Thérèse as it appears in the two novels only, without wondering what sort of use this strange creature made of her freedom [after her trial and acquittal for the attempted poisoning of her husband and his recovery and taking her to Paris to live by herself—*ED.*]; whether her impulse to destroy ever reappeared and whether she ever found the love for which, in a contorted form, she seems always to have sought.*

In addition to its light on the character and story of Thérèse herself, the episode of Thérèse and the Doctor, which I personally think superior to the other, includes two other first-class portraits, that of the psychiatrist himself, half charlatan, half self-deceiver, and that of his wife. Only a master of the novel could have thrown such vivid light on the past and characters of three such different people in a few thousand words. . . .

It is quite difficult to get M. Mauriac to talk about his writing but I hope the foregoing notes will be of some interest to you.

RUBY HILLAR

✸✸✸

Thérèse and the Doctor

I HAVE already told you that the doctor will not be doing any more work this evening. You can go as soon as you like."

No sooner had Dr. Elisée Schwartz heard Catherine's words through the wall than he opened the door of his consulting room. Without so much as a glance at his wife, he said to his secretary:

"I will call you in a moment. Please remember that in this house it is I who give orders."

Catherine Schwartz did not quail beneath Mademoiselle Parpin's insolent stare. Instead, she smiled, took up a book, and walked over to the French window. The shutters had not been closed. The rain was pelting down on the balcony of their sixth-floor flat. The ceiling light in the doctor's consulting room illuminated the gleaming flagstones. For a moment Catherine followed with her eyes the distant vista of a street in Grenelle dwindling away between the shadowed mass of sleeping factories. Elisée, she thought, had yielded, as so often before during the last twenty years, to the pleasure of contradicting and humiliating her. But already, no doubt, he was paying the penalty. What was there, this evening, for him to dictate to Mademoiselle Parpin? . . . Three or four pages, perhaps. . . . His study of the *Sexual Life of Blaise Pascal* was making very slow progress. Ever since the great psychiatrist had indulged the whim of annotating a chapter in the history of literature he had become more and more bogged down in the difficulties of the undertaking.

The secretary had remained standing. Her eyes, fixed on the door of her employer's room, were those of a faithful dog. Catherine opened her book and tried to read. The lamp was set on a very low modern table, and, though the couch, too, was low, she had to sit on the floor in order to catch the light. The sound of the little girl upstairs practicing her piano in no wise drowned the noise of the radio next door. The "Death of Isolde" was suddenly cut short. In its place came the strains of a French music-hall song. The young couple in the apartment below were quarreling. A door slammed.

Maybe Catherine was dreaming of the silence that used to envelop her parents' big house in the Rue de Babylone, with its courtyard on one side and its garden on the other. By marrying, just before the war, a young, half-Jewish doctor from Alsace, Catherine de Borresch had not merely been yielding to the fascination of an intelligence in which, at that time, she could find no blemish, nor even to that physical appeal, that dominating force of character before which so many patients still felt themselves to be helpless. The truth of the matter was that between 1910 and 1913 the Baron de Borresch's daughter had reacted violently against her family. She had hated her awful-looking father, whose ugliness was almost a crime against society, the clockwork figure whom Dr. Elisée Schwartz came twice or three times a week to wind up. Her contempt for her mother's narrow existence was hardly less acute. In those days it was a pretty daring thing for a young woman of her social position to read for a degree and attend lectures at the Sorbonne. Her acquaintance with Schwartz had been limited to a few glances exchanged at hurried lunches, and to the sound of his voice booming away at the far end of the table when he was asked to formal dinner parties. But in her eyes he stood for progress and the sacred integrity of science. She had built up their marriage into a sort of wall between herself and that world from which she had fought free. As a matter of fact, this man who had already attained some degree of eminence, and was Secretary to the League of the Rights of Man, was only too glad to have the freedom of the great front door of the Borresch house. He would have liked dearly to make his peace with the family, and had almost succeeded in doing so. He had already placed his batteries in position for the final assault, and gave up the attempt only when he realized that his betrothed had fathomed his intentions. Their life together had begun in insincerity. Beneath Catherine's eagle eye, Schwartz had had to swallow his snobbish instincts and resume his role of the advanced and emancipated man of science.

He had taken his revenge by treating her, especially when other people were present, with an extraordinary lack of consideration. His language, when he addressed her, was carefully designed to wound. After twenty years, he had got so much into the habit of humiliating her on every possible occasion that he did so now, as on the evening with which we are concerned, quite automatically and without any deliberate intention.

He was fifty, and there was a look of nobility about his head with its shock of gray hair. His dark, tanned face, in which the blood showed warm, was of the type that stands up well to the ravages of time. He still had the supple skin of a young man, and his mouth told of health unimpaired. This it was, thought the world, that kept Catherine faithful to him (for the people from whom she had set herself to escape had gradually drifted back, attracted now by those

very same Left Wing ideas which had once alienated them). It was
said, too, that she enjoyed being "knocked about." But those who
had known the Baroness were of the opinion that her daughter, for
all her airs of emancipation, and though she probably did not know
it, was remarkably like her mother. She had the same absent-
minded ways, alternating with periods of excessive friendliness and,
in spite of changing fashions, the same severe taste in clothes.

Nothing could have been less in the tone of her general "style"
than to sit on the floor as she was doing this evening. Her short
hair, touched with gray, left the back of her neck uncovered. Her
face was small, and the way in which she wrinkled her brow gave
her the appearance of a pug dog. Her lips lacked fullness and
she suffered from a nervous tic which made people believe, quite
wrongly, that she looked at the world with a mocking grin.

Mademoiselle Parpin, still on her feet, was turning over a pile
of illustrated papers which lay on a side table. Their pages showed
the finger marks of the doctor's patients. She was a shortish woman
running to fat. She would have been well advised to wear stays. The
telephone bell in the hall started to ring. She went to answer it,
pointedly closing the door behind her as a hint to Madame Schwartz
that she had no right to listen to what was being said. The precaution, however, was quite useless, because everything that happened
in one room could be heard in the others, even when the piano upstairs and the radio next door were going full blast. Besides, the secretary's voice grew louder and louder as the conversation proceeded.

"Would you like me to make an appointment for you, Madame?
. . . You want to see the doctor now, at once? . . . Quite out of the
question. . . . It's really no good insisting. . . . I can't believe he
ever promised any such thing. . . . You must have made a mistake,
Madame: Dr. Elisée Schwartz is not in the habit of frequenting
night clubs. . . . I can't stop you from coming, of course . . . but I
warn you, you'll merely be wasting your time. . . ."

Mademoiselle Parpin entered the doctor's consulting room by a
door which gave directly onto the hall. Catherine could hear every
word without having to strain her ears.

"It was some mad creature, sir, who says that you promised to
see her at any hour of the day or night she might like to come.
. . . She says she met you two years ago in some bar or other . . . it
sounded like *Gerlis* or *Gernis* . . . I couldn't quite hear."

"And I suppose you put her off, eh?" fumed the doctor. "Who
gave you the right to make decisions for me? . . . I wish to goodness you'd mind your own business."

She stammered that it was after ten o'clock . . . that it had never occurred to her that he would consent to see a patient at that hour . . . to all of which he replied in a loud voice that he didn't care a damn what she thought. He knew all about the patient in question —a remarkably interesting case. . . . Another opportunity missed through her blundering idiocy. . . .

"But she said she'd be here in less than half an hour, sir."

"So she *is* coming, after all?"

He seemed to be both excited and put out. After a brief hesitation, he said:

"Show her in as soon as she turns up, and then you can go and catch your train."

At this moment Catherine entered the room. The doctor, who had resumed his seat at the table, half rose, and asked her roughly what she wanted.

"Elis, you're *not* going to see this woman?" She remained standing there in front of him, her body encased in a dark-red stockinet dress, angular, narrow hipped, holding her head high. Her eyes were devoid of lashes, and she blinked them in the glare that beat down from the ceiling. Her long, well-formed right hand was motionless at her throat, the fingers clutching at her coral necklace.

"So you've taken to listening at keyholes, have you?"

She smiled, as she might have done had he indulged in a joke.

"Short of having the door padded, the wall and the floor and the ceiling lined with felt . . . I must say you've chosen the oddest sort of place in which to hear the intimate confessions of the poor wretches who come to see you. . . ."

"All right . . . all right . . . and now let me get on with my work."

A bus came charging noisily down the Rue de Boulainvilliers. Catherine, her hand on the latch, turned towards him.

"Mademoiselle Parpin will tell this woman, of course, that you can't see her?"

He took a few steps towards her, his hands stuffed in his pockets, swaying his heavy shoulders: a great, hulking figure of a man. Was she, he inquired, often taken that way? Lighting a Caporal cigarette, he went on to say:

"I don't suppose you've got the slightest idea what's at issue, have you?"

Catherine, leaning against the radiator, replied that she knew perfectly well.

"I remember the evening clearly. It was in February or March three years ago, at a time when you were going about a good deal.

You told me all about it when you came home—about the woman with an obsession who had made you promise . . ."

He was looking, now, at the floor. There was something slightly furtive in the expression of his face. Catherine sat down on the leather-covered couch which Elisée called his "Confessional." Stretched upon it, as thousands of poor sufferers had stammered out the stories of their lives, lying, hesitating, and striving to reveal secrets which they pretended not to know. . . . On the radio a juicy and aggressively stupid voice was recommending furniture bearing the label "Levikhan." There was an uninterrupted noise of cars sounding their horns at the street crossing below. Silence would set in only at midnight, and not even then if somebody in the block was giving a party. The doctor raised his eyes and saw Mademoiselle Parpin waiting by the little table on which the typewriter stood. He told her to go into the hall and stay there until the lady arrived. When she had left the room, Catherine said dryly:

"You won't let her come in?"

"We'll see about that."

"You won't let her come in because she's dangerous. . . ."

"It would be nearer the truth to say that you are jealous. . . ."

There was an unexpected spontaneity about the laugh with which she greeted this statement.

"Oh, come now . . . my poor dear . . . *I*, jealous?" For a brief moment she seemed to be thinking nostalgically of the time when she might have been jealous. Then, suddenly:

"You're not, presumably, any more attracted than I am by the idea of stopping a revolver bullet. . . . Such things don't happen, you say? . . . How about Pozzi? . . . You think I don't know her, have never set eyes on her? I could repeat, word for word, what you told me that evening. . . . I've got a frighteningly good memory where you are concerned. Nothing that you say in my hearing is ever lost—not a syllable. I may not actually have seen her, but I'm pretty sure I should recognize her at once: a woman with a Tartar face, the only one among all your naked little friends who was wearing a tailor-made suit, the only one with a hat pulled down over her eyes. . . . Later in the evening she took it off, revealing a superb forehead. . . . You were a bit drunk, you know, when you told me all that. Do you remember how you kept on saying, 'A marvelous forehead, like a tower.'. . . You can't have forgotten how you went on and on about it? And then you said, 'One can't be too careful with women of that Kalmuck type.' You're a bit frightened of her even now; you can't deny it. . . . You're longing to show her the

door. If you do see her, it'll be only because you're ashamed not
to. . . ."

Elisée made no attempt to insult her. Since there was no stranger
present, he did not see any point in feigning heroism. He contented
himself with saying in a low voice, "I gave her my word."

They both fell silent, listening with strained attention to a rumbling sound in the belly of the building which indicated that someone
had started the elevator. The doctor muttered: "That can't be her
—she said half an hour. . . ." Both husband and wife were busy
with their secret thoughts, shut away from one another, remembering, perhaps, the time when he was trailing along after the notorious
Zizi Bilaudel. It had been necessary to keep from the world what
was really in the wind. Every day Catherine said, "People are laughing at you." Unknown to her, he had started taking private lessons
in the tango. At the various night clubs haunted by Zizi and her
faithful followers the youngsters laughed themselves sick at the sight
of this great lump of a man dancing with a strained and concentrated look. He sweated like a pig, and was forever going to the
lavatory to change his collar. At that time the painter Bilaudel had
not yet married Zizi, though she already bore his name. She was
not exactly "received," but had managed to pick up a number of
acquaintances among the less fastidious members of the fashionable
world. The plump, golden-haired creature, who passed for being so
"*terribly* Renoir," thoroughly deserved her reputation for intelligence. She was one of those women who can live a life of the wildest debauchery without showing the slightest sign of it, and had
amassed an amount of varied experience which would have brought
ruin to anyone less skillful in her technique of exploration. But
from what particular gutter she had collected the rag, tag, and bob-
tail who trailed behind her no one knew. Catherine let it be known
that they furnished the doctor with admirable subjects for study,
implying that he was getting a great deal of material out of this
affair which would be useful to him in his scientific work. The lie
was generally believed. As a matter of fact, it was perfectly true
that one woman of the group *did* interest him to an exceptional
degree. She alone could distract his attention when Zizi Bilaudel
danced with younger men. This woman it was who had just telephoned: who, in a few minutes, would be actually in the flat.

The doctor was making a pretense of reading. Catherine went
across and laid a hand on his shoulder.

"Listen to me. Do you remember what it was she told you that

evening when you promised that you would see her whenever she
liked to come?—that ever since she had tried to poison her husband she had been hagridden by the desire to commit murder . . .
that she had to fight tooth and nail against the temptation? . . .
That's the woman with whom you propose to shut yourself in a
room at eleven o'clock at night!"

"If that had been the truth she would never have told it to me.
She was putting on an act. But even supposing there *were* a risk,
what do you take me for?"

Her eyes were as honest as the day. She spoke again in the same
low, level tones:

"You're afraid, Elis: look at your hands."

He thrust them into his pockets, hunched his shoulders, and made
a short, sharp gesture with his head towards the right-hand side of
the room.

"Off with you—and don't let me set eyes on you again till tomorrow morning."

Very calmly she opened the door which led into the hall. The
secretary was sitting on a bench. He called to her to show the lady
in as soon as she arrived, and then to clear out.

On the other side of the closed door Catherine and Mademoiselle
Parpin remained for a moment or two in darkness. Then the secretary switched on the light.

"Madame!"

Catherine, already halfway up the stairs leading to the bedrooms,
turned her head and noticed that the plump young woman's cheeks
were wet with tears.

"Madame, you won't be far off, will you?" Her voice had lost all
hint of insolence. She spoke as one asking a favor.

"It is important that this woman should realize that she's being
watched. She must be made to feel that there's somebody next door.
Hadn't I better stay? It would be better if there were two of us. . . .
But, no, I can't do that . . . he's forbidden it."

"He need never know."

The secretary shook her head. "I daren't do it!" she whispered.
She suspected a trick to get her fired. Madame Schwartz would
give her away. The doctor would never forgive the least movement
of disobedience. For a moment or two neither woman spoke. This
time there could be no doubt about it: the elevator really was coming up. In a low voice Catherine said:

"Show her in, and then go home. You can sleep in peace. I

promise that nothing shall happen to the doctor tonight. I was his guardian angel for twenty years—long before you came on the scene, Mademoiselle."

She vanished up the dark staircase. But no sooner had she reached the landing than she turned and came a little way down again. She stood leaning on the banisters.

The gate of the elevator clanged. There was a quick ring at the bell. . . . It was impossible to see the visitor's face as Mademoiselle Parpin stood aside to let her pass. A quiet voice asked whether this was where Dr. Schwartz lived. The secretary took her dripping umbrella, and would have relieved her of her bag. But to that she clung fast.

Mademoiselle joined Catherine where she was sitting on the stairs. She whispered nervously that the stranger smelt of whisky. . . . They strained their ears, but could hear nothing beyond the booming of the doctor's voice. Catherine asked how the woman was dressed. She had on a dark coat, said the other, with a rather shabby chinchilla collar.

"It's the bag that worries me, Madame. She kept it tight under her arm. . . . We *must* try to get it from her. . . . She may have a revolver in it. . . ."

There was a burst of laughter from the stranger, followed by the sound of the doctor speaking again. Catherine told Mademoiselle Parpin not to get rattled, but to keep her head. The secretary seized her hand with a sudden little display of emotion, and could not keep herself from murmuring "Thank you"—though she realized how absurd the phrase must sound almost as soon as she had spoken it. From her post of vantage at the top of the stairs, Catherine, quite unmoved, watched the girl arranging her hat before the glass, and powdering her flushed cheeks. At last she went.

Once more Catherine squatted on the stairs. The sound of the two voices, her husband's and the woman's, reached her. They seemed to be talking very quietly. There were no sudden bursts of louder words. How odd it seemed to be listening to Elis unseen by him! She could have sworn that it was another man he had in there with him, some good-natured friend whom she did not know. She realized why it was that his patients so often said: "He's perfectly charming—so kind, so gentle."

The woman's voice was too high pitched for Catherine's taste. Maybe she had been drinking and was in an excited mood. Her rather unbalanced laugh reawakened the watching wife's anxiety.

She tiptoed down the stairs, slipped into the drawing room and, without switching on the light, sat down.

In front of her, through the muslin curtains, she could see the rain-drenched balcony shining like a lake. Beyond, the lights of Grenelle showed as scattered points of fire in the wet darkness. The doctor, in easy, conversational tones, was talking of Zizi Bilaudel, and asking what had happened to the "gang."

"Blown to the four winds, Doctor. . . . I'm beginning to know something about 'happy bands of brothers' . . . they have a way of breaking up pretty quickly. I've seen a goodish few in my time. Bilaudel and I are the only two left of the particular one in which you were caught up for a few weeks, Doctor. Palaisy—you remember him?—a fine figure of a man who drank like a fish (and the stuff just made him gayer and gayer)—well, he broke up altogether, and went off to live with his parents in Languedoc. Then there was the fierce little surrealist, the one who tried to scare us, like children who try to frighten each other by tying handkerchiefs round their heads and pretending to be brigands (he had a way of scowling and never brushing his hair, and generally doing all he could to seem like an escaped convict—but somehow, whatever he did, he always looked like an angel). . . . We used to ask him whether his suicide was timed for the next morning . . . though personally I never treated it as a joke, because heroin's not like other drugs—it always ends up badly. . . . Yes, it happened last month, over the telephone. . . . Azévédo rang him up one night, just for fun— didn't let on who it was, but just said that Dora was playing fast and loose with Raymond . . . he meant it as a legpull, because he knew perfectly well that it was a lie. . . . He heard a quiet voice at the other end of the line saying, 'You're sure of that?' . . . and then a dull thud. . . ."

The unknown visitor was talking fast and rather breathlessly. Catherine was so intent on listening to the doctor's grave, kindly tone (which he never used to her) that she did not fully grasp the purport of his reply. There, in the dark drawing room, her face turned towards the streaming panes, the drowned roof tops, the dwindling perspective of street lights, she sat brooding over the thought that only to her did this man make a deliberate display of brutality . . . only to her.

"Oh,"—a note of insistence had crept into the woman's voice— "please don't feel embarrassed. I don't in the least mind talking about Azévédo. . . . I can afford to laugh at all that now. . . . No, that's not quite true. . . . Love doesn't ever die altogether. I ought

to hate him, but he still exercises a spell over my imagination, if
for no other reason than that he hurt me so abominably. I know
exactly what manner of man he is—the sort who can make money
on the stock exchange on a rising market—but that doesn't alter
the fact that he succeeded in dragging from my body every scrap
of pain of which it was capable. No matter how petty a man may
be, he can always attain a certain greatness by the sheer power of
destruction. Because of his meanness I have sunk an inch or two
deeper into the mud, have plunged farther into the mire, have
reached the last door of all. . . ."

In honeyed tones the doctor said:

"But at least, dear lady, he has cured you of love, has he not?"

Catherine trembled. The peal of laughter with which the unknown greeted these words (it was like the sound of rending calico)
must, she felt sure, have penetrated down through all seven floors of
the building until it was audible even in the cellar.

"Should I be here at eleven o'clock at night? . . . Haven't you
noticed that ever since I entered this room I have been on fire?
What's the use of all your fine knowledge?"

He replied, in high good humor, that he did not claim to be a
wizard.

"I take no notice of what you tell me. I am just a pair of ears—
nothing more. . . . All I do is help you straighten your own tangled
skein. . . ."

"One gives away only what one wants to. . . ."

"That is where you are profoundly wrong, Madame. . . . In this
room people let the light in on what they most want to conceal. Let
me correct what I said just now. I *do* take notice, but only of what
they try to hide, of what leaks out in spite of themselves. It's my
job to hold it out for their inspection. I give the little gnawing creature its true name . . . and then they are no longer afraid of it. . . ."

"The mistake you make is in believing what we say. . . . Love can
turn us into terrible liars. For instance, when I broke with Azévédo,
he sent me back all my letters. I spent one whole evening just sitting with the bundle in front of me. It seemed so light! I had always
fondly imagined that I should need a suitcase, that nothing less
would suffice to hold that vast mass of correspondence. But here it
all was, just a few sheets that would go comfortably into an envelope. I laid them out on the table. When I thought of all the pain
those letters contained—you'll think me an awful fool—I was filled
with a feeling of respect and terror (that's made you laugh; I knew
it would!) . . . So strong was the feeling that I couldn't pluck up

courage to read a single one of them. And then, at last, I forced myself to open the most frightening of the whole collection. I remembered the agonies I had gone through when I wrote it, one day in August, at Cap Ferrat. It was mere chance that I had not killed myself then and there . . . and now, three years later, with all love dead in my heart, my hand still trembled at the touch of that piece of paper. Yet, would you believe it? when I did bring myself to look it over it seemed so mild, so harmless, that for a moment I thought I must have picked on the wrong one. . . . But no, there couldn't be any doubt about it. Those were the very lines I had scribbled within touching distance of death. They revealed nothing but a pitiful attempt at flippancy, nothing but my eagerness to hide the appalling pain I was suffering, as I might have concealed a physical wound—from a sense of shame, from a fear that the sight of it might disgust the man I loved, or move him to a show of pity. . . . Don't you think there's something rather comic, Doctor, about tricks like that which never, somehow, come off? I had believed, poor fool, that if I assumed an attitude of indifference, I might succeed in making Azévédo jealous. . . . The rest of the letters were all of the same kind. Nothing can well be less natural, less spontaneous, than love's double-dealing. . . . But I'm not telling you anything you don't know already. It's your job, and you know it better than anyone else. When I'm in love I'm forever plotting, planning, anticipating, but with a constant clumsiness which ought to touch the heart of him I love, instead of irritating him, as it always does. . . ."

Catherine Schwartz, sitting in the darkness, heard every word. The woman was talking in an odd, jerky way. Her phrases followed no ordinary speech rhythm. It was as though her voice had suddenly got out of control. Why had she come to Elis?—why chosen him, of all men, as the repository of her confidences? Catherine felt a sudden desire to fling open the door of the consulting room, to cry to the unknown woman within, "He has nothing to give you: all he can do is tread you still deeper into the mud. I don't know to whom you ought to go, but certainly not to him—no, certainly not to him!"

"I wouldn't mind betting, dear lady, that you couldn't talk so eloquently of love if you hadn't let yourself be caught a second time. . . . I'm right, am I not?"

There was something paternal, gentle, calm, kindly, in the way he spoke. But the tone in which the visitor broke in upon his words was vulgar, almost coarse.

"Of course I have—any fool could see that. . . . You don't have to work hard to make me talk—why else do you think I have come here? If you leave the room I shall still go on talking—to the leg of the table, if need be, or the wall."

It was borne in sharply on Catherine how atrociously she was behaving—a doctor's wife listening at doors and overhearing the secrets confided to her husband. . . . Her cheeks felt on fire. She got up, went into the hall and up the short flight of stairs to her own room, which was brilliantly illuminated by a single hanging light. She crossed to the mirror and looked long and hard at the unattractive face which must be her constant companion through life. The light, the familiar objects, all reassured her. Why had she been frightened? What danger was there? Besides, that woman down there was no casual stranger. . . .

At that moment a sound of raised voices set her trembling. The door of the room was only half closed. She pushed it open and went part way down the stairs—though not far enough to enable her to hear what the visitor was shouting (for shouting she was). A few steps farther and she would hear everything. The secret of the Confessional . . . yes, but perhaps Elis's life was at stake. . . . Once again she yielded to temptation, and sat down on the couch in the hall. For a moment the noise of the elevator prevented her from hearing. Then:

"You do understand, don't you, Doctor? . . . I had spent the whole summer away from Phili. I have never needed anyone, not even Azévédo, as I need Phili. When he's not there I feel as though I am suffocating. He had been avoiding me—oh, on all sorts of pretexts—business, visits. . . . What was really happening was that he was hunting for a rich wife . . . but that's not so easy to find these days . . . besides, he's already been divorced once, even though he is only twenty-four. . . . I just couldn't stay still anywhere. I can't begin to describe the kind of life I was leading. I wanted only one thing—letters. In every town where I stopped only one object held any interest for me—the counter of general delivery. That's what traveling always means to me, general delivery."

Catherine knew perfectly well that she was not listening now merely from a sense of duty. She was no longer concerned to help her husband in case of attack. No, she was a prey to irresistible curiosity—she, who had always been so scrupulously discreet that discretion had become almost a mania with her. This unknown voice fascinated her. But even while she felt the lure of it, she could not bear to think of the disappointment lying in wait for its wretched owner. Elis was quite incapable of understanding her, even of feeling compassion for her. All he would do, as he had done with other victims, was to urge her to find relief—to free her emotions through the gratification of the body. That was what his method amounted to. The same filthy key served him whether it was heroism, crime, sanctity, or renunciation that he had to interpret. . . . These thoughts passed confusedly through her mind, though they did not prevent her from hearing all that was going on in the consulting room.

". . . Imagine my surprise when I began to notice that Phili's letters were getting longer and longer, that he seemed to be writing them with considerable care, that he seemed to want to console me, to make me happy. They became increasingly frequent as the summer wore away, until at last they were coming daily.

"It all happened during the week I was spending, as I do every year, with my daughter. She's eleven now. Her governess takes her to some place that I have fixed on in advance, somewhere that must always be at least five hundred kilometers from Bordeaux— my husband insists on that. It's always a terrible time for me. You see, I don't know whether the child knows of the horrible charge hanging over me, and, in any case, she is frightened of me. The governess always arranges things so that I never pour out her drinking water. I'm the sort of woman, you see, who would stop at nothing—which is what my husband said the evening of the day on which my case was dismissed. (I can still hear that country drawl of his: 'You don't really think I'd leave the child to your tender mercies. She, too, must be kept at a safe distance from your drugs. If I'm poisoned, the estate will go to her when she's twenty-one . . . first the father, then the child! You wouldn't hesitate two seconds about liquidating her!') All the same, he lets me have her for one week in every year. I take her to restaurants, the circus . . . but that's all by the way. . . . As I've told you, Phili's letters had made me happy. I wasn't suffering any more. He couldn't wait to see me. He was more impatient even than I was. I was happy and at peace. It must have shown in my face. Marie was less frightened of me than usual. One evening at Versailles, on a bench near the Petit Trianon, I stroked her hair. . . . Poor fool!—I was thinking, hoping . . . I had reached a stage at which I even felt gratitude to God. I was ready to bless life. . . ."

Once more Catherine got up and started to climb the stairs that led to her room. Her cheeks were aflame. Listening there, behind the door, she had felt like a criminal engaged in a particularly low form of theft. What was Elis going to do with that poor creature emptying her heart of all its secrets at his feet? No sooner had she sat down than she got up again, and a moment later was at her post of observation on the stairs. The unknown was still talking:

"He was waiting for me at the station exit. It was seven o'clock in the morning. I was in Heaven, as you can imagine. I saw his poor, worn, hunted face. There always comes one brief moment, when one sees the man one loves for the first time after a long absence, in which he stands before us as he really is and not as our infatuation has painted him. Don't you agree, Doctor?—one tiny second in which we can take the squalid tricks of passion unaware. But we are too much in love with suffering to seize such opportunities to the full. He took me along to the Café d'Orsay. We chatted casually of this and that, joining up loose ends. . . . He asked me about the resin, the trees, the pit props (at that time I was still getting an income from my property). I laughed and told him that we should have to tighten our belts. The bottom had fallen out of the resin market. The Americans had found a substitute for turpentine. It was quite impossible to sell timber. The Argelouse sawmills were working on imported lumber from Poland, and the pines growing at their very doors were left to rot where they stood. I was faced with ruin . . . like everybody else. . . . I rattled on, and Phili grew paler and paler. He kept on asking whether the trees couldn't be sold even at a loss, and when I protested that to take such a step would be to court disaster, I could feel that his attention was beginning to wander. Whatever value I had for him diminished in strict ratio with that of my Argelouse property. You do understand what I'm talking about, don't you, Doctor? I didn't cry. I actually laughed— laughed at myself, as no doubt you realize. And all the time he was utterly withdrawn from me: he might have been a thousand miles away. He no longer even saw me. Only those who have suffered as I did then can possibly know what such an experience is like. Not so much as to exist in the eyes of the man who is the only living creature in one's world. I would have done anything, no matter how mad, to recapture his attention. . . . But you'll never guess what I did do."

"The puzzle is not insoluble. . . . You told him about your past, about the crime with which you had been charged. . . ."

"How on earth did you know that? . . . Yes, that is precisely what I did do. . . . I didn't know then that there was someone who had a hold over Phili, someone who was blackmailing him and could

have had him arrested (but I won't go into all that). I just told
him about my own troubles. . . ."

"And he was interested?"

"You'd never guess how much. He listened with a terrible sort
of concentration. In a vague kind of way I was frightened. I began
to feel that I had been a fool to give myself away so completely. Oh
yes, he was interested now all right, much *too* interested, if you
see what I mean. At first I thought that he was planning to use
what I had said to get something out of me. But it wasn't that. . . .
Besides, he couldn't. . . . That particular danger, so far as I was concerned, had long passed. My case had been shelved. No: his mind
was working along quite different lines. . . . He thought I might be
able to help him."

"Help him—but how?"

"Aren't you being a bit slow, Doctor?—help him, of course, to
commit a deed from which his conscience recoiled. He swore that
once it was all over he would marry me, that we should be irretrievably bound to one another, because I should have a hold on
him and he on me. He had got a plan all worked out. He gave me
his word that I should run no risk whatever. What I had done once
I could do again. . . . I must tell you that his enemy, the man who
held his life in his hands, lived in the country. He was a small
landowner, scarcely better than a peasant, somewhere in the Southwest—a vine grower. I had been to see him once with the idea of
buying some of his wine. Nowadays, you know, there is no job a
woman can't take on, even to selling on commission. I had put
through one or two deals for him, quite successfully. He showed me
round his cellars; we sampled his vintages. . . . Do you see what I'm
getting at? We drank out of the same glass. He was known to be
a tippler . . . and had already had more than one stroke, though
nothing very serious. . . . It wouldn't cause the slightest surprise . . .
and, you know, they don't go in for post-mortems in the country.
. . . The chances of anything ever coming out were nil. . . ."

She broke off. The doctor said nothing. Catherine, in the darkness of the staircase, felt her heart thumping. Then the woman's
voice began again, but a change had come into it.

"Save me, Doctor! . . . He gives me no peace. . . . I shall end
by doing what he wants. He looks as innocent as a child, I know,
but there's something about him that terrifies me. . . . What is this
awful power that you sometimes find in people with angel faces?
One feels it was only yesterday that they were schoolboys. . . . Do

you believe in a Devil, Doctor? Do you think that Evil can take on human form?"

Catherine could not bear the sound of her husband's laughter. She shut the door of her room behind her, sank to her knees beside the bed, put her fingers in her ears, and so remained for a long while, utterly prostrated, shattered, thinking of nothing. . . . And then, suddenly, she heard her name cried aloud on a note of terror. She rushed downstairs and burst into the consulting room. At first she could not see her husband and thought he must be dead. But a moment later she heard him.

"She's got nothing against *you* . . . but be careful all the same. . . . Quick! get it away from her! . . . She's armed!" She realized then that he was crouching behind his desk. The stranger was leaning against the wall. Her right hand was concealed in her half-open bag, and she was staring fixedly in front of her. Quite calmly, Catherine took hold of her wrist. The woman made no attempt to resist. She let her bag fall to the ground. Her hand had closed about something, but it was not a revolver. The doctor had emerged now. He was pale, and took no trouble to conceal the fact that his hands, as he leaned forward on the desk, were trembling. Catherine, still holding the other's wrist, forced her to loosen her grasp. A packet wrapped in white paper dropped to the carpet.

The unknown looked at Catherine. She took off her close-fitting hat and revealed her forehead. It was much too massive. Her drab, sparse hair was going gray. There was neither rouge nor powder on her thin face, her roughened lips, her cheekbones. The yellow skin was marked with blotches of purple beneath the eyes.

She did nothing to prevent Catherine from picking up the packet and reading what was written on the label—an ordinary chemist's label. She opened the door, still holding her hat. In the hall she said that she had an umbrella. Catherine spoke gently to her.

"Would you like me to ring for a cab? It's raining hard."

The woman shook her small head. Catherine led the way to the stairs, switching on the self-extinguishing light as she went.

"Aren't you going to put on your hat?"

Getting no answer, she herself put the hat upon the stranger's head, buttoned her coat for her, turned up the chinchilla collar. She wanted to smile, to lay a comforting hand on her shoulder. . . . She watched her disappear down the staircase, hesitated a moment, and then went back into the apartment.

The doctor was standing in the middle of the room, his hands in his pockets. He did not look at Catherine.

"You were quite right—the most dangerous kind of lunatic. In future I shall be more careful. She pretended she'd got a revolver. . . . Anyone would have been taken in. . . . Let me tell you what happened. It was like this. After she'd told me her wretched story she said I'd got to cure her. . . . It was when I explained that I'd already done more than enough by letting her sort out her troubles that she lost her temper. I pointed out that she'd be able to see her way more clearly now, that she would be mistress of the situation, that she'd manage to get all she wanted from this man without falling in with his plans. . . . Didn't you hear her scream? She said I was a thief. . . . 'You pretend you want to cure the soul,' she shouted 'and all the time you don't believe in the soul. Psychiatrist . . . that means a soul doctor, but you say there's no such thing as the soul. . . .' The same old story, of course . . . a familiar tendency to indulge in the crudest form of superstition. . . . She'd been bad enough earlier on, but nothing to what she was then. . . . Why are you laughing, Catherine? Have I said anything comic?"

He looked at his wife in amazement. Never before had he seen such a glow of happiness on her face. She stood there, her arms hanging at her sides, her hands held slightly away from her skirt.

"It's taken twenty years. . . . But it's all over now . . . I'm a free woman at last. You see, Elis, I realize now that I don't love you any more."

—Translated by Gerard Hopkins

JEAN COCTEAU

✱✱

Jean Cocteau called attention to his latest book of essays La Difficulté D'Etre *as representative of his work, and the book which he most prefers. The following, which contains material from that book, appeared in* Vogue, *August 15th, 1949 and is reprinted with the cooperation of the author and the magazine.*

✱✱

Proust and Laughter

IT IS RARE not to find in a man's work all that is valid in his conversation, but decanted and elevated in the same way that Picasso, picking up everything that he comes across, elevates it to the dignity of service. Can one call conversation that genius with which Picasso grumbles and sets up barbed wire between the world and what he thinks of the world? He kills stupidity every time he opens his mouth, even if he insists on contradicting himself. Picasso's speech is a sort of massacre which leaves nothing standing but the hard, the solid, and the valid.

Of the three or four people whose conversation dazzled me, Marcel Proust was really astonishing. Proust would arrive at impossible hours (if he went out), stammer, laugh, and gradually this accumulation of moaned parentheses became so beautiful that people who had started to leave did not leave at all.

Marcel Proust lived in a universe into which very few people succeeded in penetrating. His best-known conversation is epistolary. He wrote innumerable letters in which his ink spoke. It is impossible for me to read Marcel Proust without hearing his voice. His voice and the voice of Apollinaire will reman forever in my ear, or, to be more exact, in the auricles—the ears of my heart.

Nothing is stranger than the witchery of certain voices. It is probable that these voices are translated into the works of the men to whom they belong, are transported into them by I know not what mysterious vehicle, and affect even people who have never known

714

the writer. I am almost certain that the works of Pushkin conserve intact the charm of his voice. Otherwise he would be translatable. But he is untranslatable into any language.

At Marcel Proust's apartment on the Boulevard Haussmann, one could see the cork sentry-box behind the brass bed, the table covered with bottles, a theatrophone (for listening to certain theatres), a pile of school notebooks, and, as on all the other furniture, a fur of dust that was never dusted on the chandelier wrapped in cloth. On the ebony table in a dark corner, an accumulation of photographs of cocottes, duchesses, dukes, and footmen of the great houses; the chimney with its lifeless mirror, and slip covers, slip covers everywhere, and that dust, and that odour of anti-asthmatic powder, that sepulchral odour—the whole Jules Verne room was a Nautilus where it was fatal to see appear, in person, Captain Nemo: Marcel Proust, thin, bloodless, with the beard of the dead Carnot.

That black caliph's beard—Proust put it on and took it off as quickly as those amateur impersonators in the provinces imitating politicians and orchestra conductors. We knew him with a beard, we knew him beardless as Jacques-Émile Blanche has painted him, with an orchid in his buttonhole and a face like an egg.

Proust used to receive us on his bed fully dressed with collar and tie and gloves, in terror of a perfume, a breath of air, a half-open window, a ray of sunlight. "Dear Jean," he would say, "are you sure you haven't held a lady's hand which might have touched a rose?" "No, Marcel." "Are you positive?" and half serious, half laughing he would explain that the phrase in *Pelléas* where the wind has passed over the sea, was enough to start an attack of asthma.

Lying stiff and oblique, not among oyster shells like the sequestered woman of Poitiers, but in a sarcophagus full of the débris of souls, of landscapes, of everything in Balbec, Chambray, Méséglise, in the Comtesse de Chevigné, the Comte Greffulhe, Haas and Robert de Montesquiou that he could not use, in short, just as later for the last time we admired his remains beside the pile of notebooks containing his work which still continued, lived on at his left hand like the wrist watches of dead soldiers, every evening Marcel Proust would read to us from *Swann's Way.*

These sessions added to the pestilential disorder of the room a chaos of perspectives, for Proust would start reading any place at all, make a mistake, mistake a page, jump one, begin again, interrupt himself to explain that the tip of a hat in the first chapter would be understood in the last volume, and he would splutter with laughter behind his gloved hand, a smile he seemed to be stirring into his beard and cheeks. "It's too silly," he kept repeating. "No, I won't read any more. It's too silly." His voice became again an endless far-away wail, a tearful music of excuses, of civilities, of remorse. It was too silly. He was ashamed of making us listen to such silly stuff. It was his fault. And besides he could never re-read himself. He should never have begun.

And when we had finally persuaded him to go on, he would stretch out his arm, pick up the first sheet of his conjurer's book his hand lighted on, and we would find ourselves, without preamble, plumped down at the Guermanteses' or the Verdurins'. After fifty lines, his tricks began again. He would groan, explode, excuse himself for reading so badly. Sometimes he would get up, take off his short jacket, run his hand through his inky hair which he cut himself and which straggled over his stiff collar. He would go into a dressing room whose livid light designed an oblong on the wall. There we could see him standing in his shirt sleeves and violet vest that covered the torso of a mechanical toy, a plate in one hand and a fork in the other, eating noodles.

Don't expect me to follow Proust through all his nocturnal prowlings and relate them for you. You must know that they took place in a hired carriage belonging to Albaret, Céleste's husband, a perfect nocturnal cab of *Fantomas*. From these prowlings, from which he would return at dawn wrapping his fur-lined coat about him, livid, with dark circles under his eyes, a bottle of Evian sticking out of his pocket, his black bang limp over his forehead, one of his boots unbuttoned and holding his derby in his hand like the ghost of Sacher Masoch, Proust would bring back all those figures and calculations that made it possible for him to build a cathedral in his room and to grow eglantines.

Albaret's cab took on a really lugubrious aspect by day. Proust's daytime excursions occurred once or twice a year. I went with him on one of them. It was to see the Gustave Moreau paintings at Madame Ayem's, and then to the Louvre to look at the "San Sebastian" of Mantegna and the "Turkish Bath" of Ingres.

But to get back to his computations. I linger over the description of Proust because he illustrates my thesis. What do they resemble, his writings in those schoolboy notebooks that all the members of the *Nouvelle Revue Française* consolidated, cut, pasted, tried to figure out at Rue Madame? Figures, as the expression suggests.

By dint of adding, multiplying, dividing in time and space, Proust ends his work by the simplest of proofs by nine. He comes back to the figures of the operation with which his work begins. And it is because of this that he pleases me.

For his intrigues have lost their charm, the Verdurins their humour, Charlus his tragic appeal, the duchesses the prestige of Madame de Maufrigneuse and Madame d'Espars. But the edifice of his computations remains intact. They intertwine, free of anecdote. They become the work itself. They are the scaffolding that hides the monument.

Swann, Odette, Gilberte, Albertine, Oriane, Vinteuil, Elstir, Françoise, Madame de Villeparisis, Charlus, the Queen of Naples, the Verdurins, Cottard, Morel, Rachel, Saint-Loup, la Berma, what are all these marionettes to me? I touch the skeleton that links them together, the joints of their contacts, the fine lacework of their courses. I am more struck by the convolutions of organs than of sentiments, by the tortuosity of veins than by the flesh. I have the eye of a carpenter on the king's scaffold. The boards interest me more than the execution.

Now all these convolutions, this whole scaffolding of which I speak, are the absolutely exact image of Proust's voice and his way of tangling his sentences, drawing them out, superposing them, of losing them and picking them up again after seeming to have lost the thread.

How I used to laugh with Proust! There is no perfect conversation without bursts of uncontrollable laughter. For I do not rank as conversation the professorial faculty of developments. First and foremost, a man who converses must not appear to be delivering a lecture, nor to be teaching anything to anybody.

The gift of belly laughter is a proof of an excellent soul. I distrust people who avoid laughter and refuse its overtures. They are afraid to shake the tree, miserly as they are, of its fruits and birds, afraid that people will notice that none fall from their branches. I know people who go off into fits of laughter with me, while other persons present only laugh with their faces, fail to understand, and sometimes imagine that they are being laughed at.

The automatism of laughter is implacable. It often happens that we are overcome by a desire to laugh at funerals from which laughter is officially excluded.

Bergson attributes the cruel laughter that greets a fall to the rupture of equilibrium which dehumanizes a man and changes him into a puppet. Other philosophers disagree with this thesis. They insist that, on the contrary, man, accustomed to his artificial mechanism, is de-puppetized by the fall, and suddenly reveals himself as he really is. It is, they say, this brutal discovery of man by man that excites laughter.

What I regret in all of them is that they fail to apply their methods to the study of the laughter caused by works of art. The surprise caused by new works provokes a rupture between the mind's habits and the novelty presented to it, and the public stumbles. There will consequently follow fall and laughter. That is perhaps the explanation of the laughter of crowds which, except for tears and insults, has no other way of expressing itself.

I like farce, but long and realistic. If I make up names, places, and events, I want them to be credible and have real weight. I feel true gratification in playing this game with skillful players. If a third person knowing the rules intervenes and is off key—in short, if the person seems to take it as a joke—I freeze and want to stop the game. For playing is not joking, and risqué stories do not make me laugh. They are valid only if they take their place naturally in a conversation. Nothing is more rare than a gathering that enjoys itself without confusing fancy and frivolity.

Ordinarily people jump about to the right and to the left, and up and down. Everyone adds to the confusion, talks at the same time. That is why I limit myself to the circle I am used to and which uses the same terms I do.

One lives most of the time with one's head under one's wing. One is loath to admit the extent of the lack of culture and the mental disorder in which people flounder. Out of caution, one makes it a practice to go among them with a slightly myopic eye and deaf ear.

Stupidity dismays and gives one no desire to laugh. It saddens us rather, and makes us stupid by contagion. We only open up and are at our best with people who return our serve. I like to talk, I like to listen. I like to be talked to and to be listened to. I like laughter from which sparks fly at the shock.

I remember one summer at Trie-Château at Madame Casimir Périer's (Mme. Simone) with Péguy, Casimir Périer, and Alain Fournier, who was writing *Le Grand Meaulnes*. We laughed until we were sore, and when we started upstairs to bed, a word rekindled our laughter and we threw ourselves on the stairs leading up to our rooms. It nailed us there by the belly until the small hours of the morning.

I am a very good audience. At the theatre, at the movies, I cry or I laugh without my critical sense being involved. Nothing disgusts me if some force shakes me, pins me to the mat, forces me to let myself go.

On the other hand, my critical sense comes into play for works that claim to affect zones in me which are neither those of laughter nor tears, and which bring tears to the eyes through the privilege of beauty alone.

Our knowledge is lightened by laughter. Its lightness consoles us for having such heavy soles to carry us to the scaffold. False gravity loathes laughter because it reveals the soul which it undresses like a thunderbolt. It has happened to me to overhear through a doorway the laugh of a person against whom there was nothing to warn me. This atrocious laugh revealed the true character of the person I was one day to unmask.

Laughter may also act inversely, and a soul that our soul has resisted may overcome our reserve by a burst of childlike laughter.

I know an interesting story concerning such involuntary laughter. In 1940, Germany sent its young people to the armament factories. A young man from Essen, employed by Krupp, was dismissed because he was subject to fits of uncontrollable laughter. He was sent to other factories. He was dismissed from all of them, because he laughed. He was not punished. There was nothing else against him. They sent him home with this official notice which I saw in 1946: *Incurable frivolity.*

To kill laughter in man is a crime. That is what happens when he gets mixed up in political problems which make him take himself seriously, and when he is consulted on things he knows nothing about. He can no longer laugh. He becomes pompous. The same thing happens when he is not consulted at all and is ruled with a rod of iron.

The painter, Pierre Roy, whom I consulted on his political opinions declared: *"I am a moderate anarchist."* I wonder if he hasn't found the right formula, and if all France is not committed to this doctrine.

—Translated by Louise Varèse

PAUL CLAUDEL

****

A great mystic poet and playwright whose plays are poems in drama, Paul Claudel is as much admired as a writer of great French prose, and is here represented with an essay from the first book which was published under his own name, The East I Know. *(His career as a writer was begun anonymously while he was in the French diplomatic service.) This and other essays in the book, translated by Teresa Frances and William Rose Benét, grew out of his years in the consular service in Shanghai, Hankow, Peking and other points in the East. Some years later, from 1921 to 1925, he was French ambassador to Japan. His preoccupation, in nearly all of his writing from the time of his conversion at the age of eighteen, has been with expressing his Catholic point of view in literature. In this essay he adds a commentary on Buddha and Nirvana.*

****

The East I Know: Here and There

IN THE STREET called Nihon Bashi, near the merchants of books and lanterns, of embroideries and bronzes, miniature gardens are sold: and, as a studious idler amid this fantastic display, I mentally compare these little fragments of the world. The artists have subtly shown themselves masters of the exquisite laws by which the lines of a landscape are composed, like those of a physiognomy. Instead of drawing nature they .reproduce it, constructing their counterfeits from the very elements of the original, which they borrow— as a rule is illustrated by an example. These images are usually exact and perfect replicas. All sorts and kinds of pines, for instance, are offered me to choose from; and their position in the jar, with their height as a scale, proportionately shows the dimensions of their original territory. Here is a rice-field in Springtime; in the distance is a hill fringed with trees (they are made of moss). Here is the sea, with its archipelago and its capes! By the artifice of two stones, one black, one red, and rather worn and porous, they have represented

720

two islands that appear to be joined together, whose difference in distance is shown only by their different colors, apparently due to the light of the setting sun. And even the many colored sunset is represented by this bed of motley pebbles covered with the contents of two carafes.

Now, to amplify my thought!

The European artist copies nature according to the sentiment that he has for it. The Japanese imitates it according to the materials with which it furnishes him. One expresses himself, the other expresses nature. One creates, the other mimics. One paints, the other constructs. One is a student; the other in a way, a master. One reproduces in its detail the spectacle that he surveys with a searching and subtle gaze; the other disengages its law with a flash of the eye, in the freedom of his fancy; and applies it with a scriptural conciseness.

Here the first inspiration of the artist is the material on which he exercises his hand. Good-humoredly, he consults its intrinsic properties, its tints; and, appropriating the soul of the brute thing, he constitutes himself its interpreter. Of all the things that he might say, he expresses only the essential and significant characteristics; and, merely making a few shy indications here and there, leaves to the paper the task of concealing all those infinite complexities which are implied freely because they are taken for granted. It is a frolic of certitude, it is caprice with restraint; and the underlying idea, snared by such a method of argument, imposes itself upon us with an insidious conviction.

Now, first of all, to speak of Color! We note that the Japanese artist has reduced his palette to a limited number of general and predetermined tones. He understands that the beauty of a color resides less in its intrinsic quality than in its implicit accord with contrasted tones. And because of the unmodified blending of two values laid on in equal quantities, he repairs the omission of the many intermediate shades by the vivacity that he gives to the juxtaposition of the essential notes; calmly indicating one repetition or two. He knows that the value of a tone results more from its position than from its intensity; master of keys, he transposes them as he will. Furthermore, as color is nothing less than the particular homage that all visible things render to the universal light, everything fitly takes its place within the frame through the power of color, in accord with the theme that the artist has chosen.

But now the roving eye remains fixed; and, instead of contemplating, it interrogates. Color is the passion of matter; it signalizes the participation of each object in the common course of glory. Design expresses the energy proper to each being; his action, his rhythm, his postures. The one makes manifest his relations to space, the other fixes his movement in time. One gives the form, the other gives the sense. And as the Japanese, careless of life, paints only by contour and mass, the chief characteristic of his design is a schematic stroke. While the tones are in contrast, the lines are in unity; and while the painting is a harmony, the design is an idea; and if the interpretation of this idea comes in a flash of recognition, complete and instantaneous, the design has a satisfactory abstract significance and expresses the idea in all its purity, just as well as might a word made of letters. Each form, each movement, each group furnishes its hieroglyph.

I understand this when I revel among these bundles of Japanese prints. At Shidzuoka, among the ex-votos of the temple, I have seen many admirable examples of this art. A warrior leaps from the vermilion wood like a frantic exclamation. This prancing or kicking thing is no longer the picture of a horse, but the symbol of his revolt against bondage; a sort of reversed figure 6, equipped with a mane and tail, represents his repose in the grass. Embraces, battles, landscapes, crowds, fitted into a small space, resemble the designs on seals. This man bursts into laughter; and, falling, he no longer seems a man, but immediately becomes his own character in writing.

With horrible and careless crudity, the French or English construct barbarous barracks; pitiless toward the earth they disfigure, concerned only with their expansion, seizing upon all possible space with their eyes, if not with their hands. They exploit a view as they would a waterfall. The Oriental knows enough to flee from vast landscapes, where multifold aspects and divergent lines do not lend themselves to that exquisite co-ordination between the eye and the view which alone makes a sojourn possible for him. His home is not open to all the winds. Choosing a retreat in some peaceful valley, his care is to achieve a perfect location where his view composes so harmonious a landscape that it is impossible to imagine seeing it other wise. His eyes furnish him with all the elements of happiness, and he replaces furniture with open windows. Inside, the art of the painter, ingeniously tracing his visions upon a fictitiously transparent window, multiplies the imaginary openings. In the ancient imperial palace that I visited, its magnificent and movable treasures had been carried away, and there remained only the pictorial decorations arranged in a black room—the familiar visions of its august inhabitant.

The paper dwelling is composed of successive apartments, divided by partitions which slide on moldings. A single theme of decoration has been chosen for each of the series, and it is introduced by screens similar to the wings of a theater. I can prolong or shorten my contemplation at will. I am less the spectator of the painter than his host; each subject is expressed by a choice in harmony with the tone of the paper, a color representing the opposite end of the gamut. It is so at Gosho. An indigo and cream motif suffices for the room called "Freshness and Purity," seeming all filled with sky and water. But at Nijo the imperial habitation is done in gold alone. Emerging from the matting-covered rafters, painted life-size, crowns of the pine tree extend their grotesque boughs along the sunlit walls. The Prince, upon his seat, saw only great bands of tawny fire; and his sensation was one of floating on the evening sky with awful sunset fires beneath him.

At Shidzuoka, at the time of Rinzaimji, I saw a landscape made of colored dust. They had put it under glass, for fear that a breath would blow it away.

Before the golden Buddha in the leaves, time is measured by the burning of a little candle; and in the depth of this ravine, by the dripping of a triple fountain.

Swept away, overthrown in the chaos and turmoil of the incomprehensible sea, lost in the churning abyss, mortal man with all his strength clutches at something that may prove solid in his grasp. That is why he accords with permanence of wood, metal, or stone to the human figure, and makes it the object of his devotion and his prayer. Besides their common names, he gives proper names to the forces of nature; and, by means of concrete image which symbolizes them like a syllable, still mysteriously conscious in his abasement of the superior authority of the Word, he calls upon it in his necessities. Thus, like a child who constructs the history of his doll from everything around him, humanity in its memories unites all that it discovers with all that it dreams, and so composes the romance of mythology.

Here beside me is this poor little old woman, who makes her salutation by striking her hands carefully together before a colossal female statue, in whose bosom an ancient prince, when led by a toothache and a dream to honor the skull of an ancestor, inserted the worn sphere after finding it wedged by the jawbone in the roots of a willow. At my right and at my left, all the length of the dark cavern, the three thousand golden Kwannon, each one resembling the others in the embellishment of arms that frame it, are aligned

in rows of a hundred, in ranks fifteen deep. A ray of sunlight flick-
ers over this barrier built of goddesses. Seeking the reason for uniformity in this multitude, and from what bulb all these identical
stalks have sprung, I find that the worshiper here doubtless wishes a
wider sounding-board for his prayers, and imagines that in multiplying the object of his entreaty he increases its efficacy.

But not for long did the sages rest their eyes on the eyes of these
crude likenesses. Having perceived the unity of all things, they found
the basis of their philosophy in that fact. Though each individual
were transitory and capricious, the richness of the common fund remained inexhaustible. No need that Man should apply his hatchet
to the tree, or his cleaver to the rock; in the grain of millet and the
egg, alike in the immobility and the convulsions of sun and sea, he
found the same principle of plastic energy; and the earth sufficed
for the construction of its own idols. Further, admitting that the
whole is formed of homogeneous parts; if, to better pursue their
analysis, the Sages turned it back upon themselves, they discovered
that the fugitive, blameworthy, unjustifiable thing in them was the
fact of their presence in the world,—and that the element in them
which was free of space and limitless of duration was the very conception they had formed of this contingent character.

If a diabolical fraud had not led them astray at that point, they
might have recognized in the harmony of this principle of independent existence (with its main idea common to all and its expression so varied) a faith similar to that in the Word, which implies a vow—the voluntary restitution of breath to its divine Source.
For every creature, born of the impression of Divine Unity upon
indeterminate matter, is the very acknowledgment that he makes
to his Creator, and the expression of the nothingness from which he
has been drawn. This is the living, breathing rhythm of the world;
where Man, dowered with consciousness and language, has been instituted their priest, to make dedication and offering of them,—and,
of his own nothingness united to essential grace, to make a filial gift
of himself, through love's most intimate choice.

But these blind eyes refused to recognize unconditional being; and
to him whom they call Buddha was it given to perfect the Pagan
blasphemy. To return to this comparison of the Word; from the
moment that they ignored the object of the discourse, its order and
sequence escaped them entirely, and nothing remained but the ravings of delirium. But a horror of that which is not the Absolute is
essential to man; and to escape the frightful circle of your vanity,
Buddha, you have not hesitated to embrace Nothingness! For in-

stead of explaining all things by their final end, he searched in himself for their intrinsic principle; and, finding there only nothingness, his doctrine teaches this monstrous communion.

This is the method; that the Sage,—having banished successively from his mind the ideas of form and of space, and the very idea of an idea,—arrives finally at Nothingness, and so enters into Nirvana. And people are awed by this revelation! As for me, I find that to the idea of Nothingness they have added that of Enjoyment. This seems to me the last and most Satanic mystery; the silence of a creature intrenched in its final refusal, the incestuous quietude of a soul seated on its integral difference!

—Translated by Teresa Frances and William Rose Benét

JEAN-PAUL SARTRE

****

The following selection on prose has been taken from the significant and provocative analysis of writing, What Is Literature?, *by the philosopher, playwright and novelist, Jean-Paul Sartre. The book is a literary manifesto, and an appeal for writers to "engage" themselves in the social meaning of their times, and to accept the responsibility of their rôles.*

****

The Art of Prose

THE ART of prose is employed in discourse; its substance is by nature significative; that is, the words are first of all not objects but designations for objects; it is not first of all a matter of knowing whether they please or displease in themselves, but whether they correctly indicate a certain thing or a certain notion. Thus, it often happens that we find ourselves possessing a certain idea that someone has taught us by means of words without being able to recall a single one of the words which have transmitted it to us.

Prose is first of all an attitude of mind. As Valéry would say, there is prose when the word passes across our gaze as the glass across the sun. When one is in danger or in difficulty he grabs any instrument. When the danger is past, he does not even remember whether it was a hammer or a stick; moreover, he never knew; all he needed was a prolongation of his body, a means of extending his hand to the highest branch. It was a sixth finger, a third leg, in short, a pure function which he assimilated. Thus, regarding language, it is our shell and our antennae; it protects us against others and informs us about them; it is a prolongation of our senses, a third eye which is going to look into our neighbor's heart. We are within language as within our body. We *feel* it spontaneously while going beyond it toward other ends, as we feel our hands and our feet; we perceive it when it is the other who is using it, as we perceive the limbs of others. There is the word which is lived and the word which is met.

But in both cases it is in the course of an undertaking, either of me acting upon others, or the other upon me. The word is a certain particular moment of action and has no meaning outside of it. In certain cases of aphasia, the possibilities of acting, of understanding situations, and of having normal relations with the other sex, are lost.

At the heart of this apraxia the destruction of language appears only as the collapse of one of the structures, the finest and the most apparent. And if prose is never anything but the privileged instrument of a certain undertaking, if it is only the poet's business to contemplate words in a disinterested fashion, then one has the right to ask the prose-writer from the very start, "What is your aim in writing? What undertakings are you engaged in, and why does it require you to have recourse to writing?" In any case this undertaking cannot have pure contemplation as an end. For, intuition is silence, and the end of language is to communicate. One can doubtless *pin down* the results of intuition, but in this case a few words hastily scrawled on paper will suffice; it will always be enough for the author to recognize what he had in mind. If the words are assembled into sentences, with a concern for clarity, a decision foreign to the intuition, to the language itself, must intervene, the decision of confiding to others the results obtained. In each case one must ask the reason for this decision. And the common sense which our pedants too readily forget never stops repeating it. Are we not in the habit of putting this basic question to young people who are thinking of writing: "Do you have anything to say?" Which means: something which is worth the trouble of being communicated. But what do we mean by something which is "worth the trouble" if it is not by recourse to a system of transcendent values?

Moreover, to consider only this secondary structure of the undertaking, which is what the *verbal moment* is, the serious error of pure stylists is to think that the word is a gentle breeze which plays lightly over the surface of things, which grazes them without altering them, and that the speaker is a pure *witness* who sums up with a word his harmless contemplation. To speak is to act; anything which one names is already no longer quite the same; it has lost its innocence.

If you name the behavior of an individual, you reveal it to him; he sees himself. And since you are at the same time naming it to all others, he knows that he is *seen* at the moment he *sees* himself. The furtive gesture which he forgot while making it, begins to exist beyond all measure, to exist for everybody; it is integrated into the objective mind; it takes on new dimensions; it is retrieved. After that, how can you expect him to act in the same way? Either he will persist in his behavior out of obstinacy and with full knowledge of what he is doing, or he will give it up. Thus, by speaking, I reveal the situation by my very intention of changing it; I reveal it to myself and to others *in order* to change it. I strike at its very heart, I transpierce it, and I display it in full view; at present I dispose of it; with every word I utter, I involve myself a little more in the world, and by the same token I emerge from it a little more, since I go beyond it toward the future.

Thus, the prose-writer is a man who has chosen a certain method of secondary action which we may call action by disclosure. It is therefore permissible to ask him this second question: "What aspect of the world do you want to disclose? What change do you want to bring into the world by this disclosure?" The "engaged" writer knows that words are action. He knows that to reveal is to change and that one can reveal only by planning to change. He has given up the impossible dream of giving an impartial picture of Society and the human condition. Man is the being toward whom no being can be impartial, not even God. For God, if He existed, would be, as certain mystics have seen Him, in a *situation* in relationship to man. And He is also the being Who can not even see a situation without changing it, for His gaze congeals, destroys, or sculpts, or, as does eternity, changes the object in itself. It is in love, in hate, in anger, in fear, in joy, in indignation, in admiration, in hope, in despair, that man and the world reveal themselves *in their truth.* Doubtless, the engaged writer can be mediocre; he can even be conscious of being so; but as one can not write without the intention of succeeding perfectly, the modesty with which he envisages his work should not divert him from constructing it *as if* it were to have the greatest celebrity. He should never say to himself "Bah! I'll be lucky if I have three thousand readers," but rather, "What would happen if everybody read what I wrote?" He remembers what Mosca said beside the coach which carried Fabrizio and Sanseverina away, "If the word Love comes up between them, I'm lost." He knows that he is the man who names what has not yet been named or what dares not tell its name. He knows that he makes the word "love" and the word "hate" *surge up* and with them love and hate between men who had not yet decided upon their feelings. He knows that words, as Brice-Parrain says, are "loaded pistols." If he speaks, he fires. He may be silent, but since he has chosen to fire, he must do it like a man, by aiming at targets, and not like a child, at random, by shutting his eyes and firing merely for the pleasure of hearing the shot go off.

From this point on we may conclude that the writer has chosen to reveal the world and particularly to reveal man to other men so that the latter may assume full responsibility before the object which has been thus laid bare. It is assumed that no one is ignorant of the law because there is a code and because the law is written down; thereafter, you are free to violate it, but you know the risks you run. Similarly, the function of the writer is to act in such a way that nobody can be ignorant of the world and that nobody may say that he is innocent of what it's all about. And since he has once engaged himself in the universe of language, he can never again pretend that he can not speak. Once you enter the universe of significations, there is nothing you can do to get out of it. Let words organize themselves freely and they will make sentences, and each sentence contains language in its entirety and refers back to the whole universe. Silence itself is defined in relationship to words, as the pause in music receives its meaning from the group of notes around it. This silence is a moment of language; being silent is not being dumb; it is to refuse to speak, and therefore to keep on speaking. Thus, if a writer has chosen to remain silent on any aspect whatever of the world, or, according to an expression which says just what it means, to *pass over* it in silence, one has the right to ask him a third question: "Why have you spoken of this rather than that, and—since you speak in order to bring about change—why do you want to change this rather than that?"

All this does not prevent there being a manner of writing. One is not a writer for having chosen to say certain things, but for having chosen to say them in a certain way. And, to be sure, the style makes the value of the prose. But it should pass unnoticed. Since words are transparent and since the gaze looks through them, it would be absurd to slip in among them some panes of rough glass. Beauty is in this case only a gentle and imperceptible force. In a painting it shines forth at the very first sight; in a book it hides itself; it acts by persuasion like the charm of a voice or a face. It does not coerce; it inclines a person without his suspecting it, and he thinks that he is yielding to arguments when he is really being solicited by a charm that he does not see. The ceremonial of the mass is not faith; it disposes the harmony of words; their beauty, the balance of the phrases, *dispose* the passions of the reader without his being aware and order them like the mass, like music, like the dance. If he happens to consider them by themselves, he loses the meaning; there remains only a boring seesaw of phrases.

In prose the aesthetic pleasure is pure only if it is thrown into the bargain. I blush at recalling such simple ideas, but it seems that to-day they have been forgotten. If that were not the case, would we be told that we are planning the murder of literature, or, more simply, that engagement is harmful to the art of writing? If the contamination of a certain kind of prose by poetry had not confused the ideas of our critics, would they dream of attacking us on the matter of form, when we have never spoken of anything but the content? There is nothing to be said about form in advance, and we have said nothing. Everyone invents his own, and one judges it afterward. It is true that the subjects suggest the style, but they do not order it. There are no styles ranged a priori outside of the literary art. What is more engaged, what is more boring than the idea of attacking the Jesuits? Yet, out of this Pascal made his *Provincial Letters*. In short, it is a matter of knowing what one wants to write about, whether butterflies or the condition of the Jews. And when one knows, then it remains to decide how one will write about it.

Often the two choices are only one, but among good writers the second choice never precedes the first. I know that Giraudoux has said that "the only concern is finding the style; the idea comes afterwards"; but he was wrong. The idea did not come. On the contrary, if one considers subjects as problems which are always open, as solicitations, as expectations, it will be easily understood that art loses nothing in engagement. On the contrary, just as physics submits to mathematicians new problems which require them to produce a new symbolism, in like manner the always new requirements of the social and the metaphysical engage the artist in finding a new language and new techniques. If we no longer write as they did in the eighteenth century, it is because the language of Racine and Saint-Evremond does not lend itself to talking about locomotives or the proletariat. After that, the purists will perhaps forbid us to write about locomotives. But art has never been on the side of the purists.

—*Translated by Bernard Frechtman*

ST. JOHN PERSE

****

"I believe the poetry of Perse," Archibald MacLeish wrote* *a few years ago, "which has been a powerful influence in the minds of many men who could not remember what it was that so deeply moved them but only that they were moved as a man might be moved by a fragrance he could not remember—that this poetry, like all true poetry, will take its place outside literature and all doctrine, in the desert sunlight where the stone survives."*

The poet, who is now living in America, told the editor, "as to the choice of material, I have no wishes in the matter, you may choose what you will. Snows might be suitable."

****

The Snows

To Françoise-Renée Saint-Léger Léger

1

AND THEN the snows came, the first snows of absence, on the great linens of dream and reality interwoven; and, with all their affliction remitted unto men of memory, there was a freshness of linen-cloths about our temples. And it was at morning, beneath the grey salt of dawn, a little before the sixth hour, as in a fortuitous haven, a place of grace and of mercy for releasing the swarms of the great odes of silence.

And all night long, unknown to us, under this lofty feat of feathers, bearing aloft the souls' vestiges, the souls' burden, lofty pumice stone cities bored through by luminous insects had not ceased growing, transcendent, forgetful of their weight. And those alone knew something of it, whose memories are uncertain, whose stories aberrant. What part the mind played in these notable things, that we know not.

* *In an introduction to* Éloges, *by St. John Perse.*

731

None has come upon, none has known, at the highest stone frontal, the first alighting of this silken hour, the first light touch of this thing, agile and so trifling, like a fluttering of eyelashes. On bronze revetments and on leaping chromium steel, on rubble of heavy porcelain and on thick glass tiles, on rocket of black marble and on white metal spur, none has come upon, none has tarnished

that mist of breath at its birth like the first shiver of a sword bared. . . . It snowed, and behold, we shall tell the wonder of it: how dawn silent in its feathers, like a great fabulous owl under the breath of the spirit, swelled out in its white dahlia body. And from all sides there came upon us marvel and festival. And let there be salutation upon the surface of the terraces, where the Architect, that summer, showed us the eggs of night-hawks!

2

I know that ships in distress in this wide, pale oyster-spat thrust their lowing of deaf beasts against the blindness of men and gods; and the whole world's wretchedness calls the pilot off the estuaries. I know of strange alliances between sky and water at the waterfalls of the great rivers: white nuptials of noctuids, white festivals of may-flies. And on the vast railway-stations smoky with dawn like palm-groves under glass, the milky night begets a mistletoe feast.

And there is that siren from the factories too, a little before the sixth hour and the day-shift, above there in the great lake country, where the shipyards lit up all night stretch a long sidereal trellis across the espalier of the sky: a thousand lamps fondled by the raw-silk things of snow. . . . Great pearl-fields widening, great flawless pearls, are they meditating their reply at the deepest depths of the waters?—O all things there to be reborn, O you entire reply! And the vision at last without fault or flaw! . . .

It is snowing on the gods of alloy and on the steelworks lashed by short liturgies; on the slag and the sweepings and the embankment grasses: it is snowing on the fever and implements of men—snow finer than the coriander seed in the dessert, snow fresher than the first milk of young creatures in April. . . . It is snowing away down there towards the West, on the silos and the ranches and the vast, unhistorical plains marched over by pylons; on the layout of unborn cities and on the dead ashes where the camps were;

on the high unbroken soil, poisoned with acids, and on the hordes of black fir-trees entangled with barbed eagles, like war trophies. . . . What had you to say, trapper and your two hands on leave

of absence? And what disquieting gentleness has laid its cheek tonight upon the pioneer's axe? . . . It is snowing outside Christendom
on the youngest bramble and on the tenderest creature. Spouse of
the world, my presence! . . . And somewhere in the world where
silence illuminates a larch-tree's dream, sadness raises its servant
mask.

3

IT WAS NOT enough that so many seas, it was not enough that so
many lands had scattered the ways of our life. On the new shore,
where we are hauling in the net of our routes, a growing burden,
had there to be, also, all this plain-chant of the snows to rob us of
the trace of our footsteps? . . . Are you stretching over the roads of
the wide world the meaning and measurement of our years, snows
prodigal of absence, snows cruel to the heart of women where hope
wastes away?

And She whom I think of among all the women of my race, from
the depths of her old age raises to her God her face of gentleness.
And it is a pure lineage that her grace keeps in me. "Let us be left,
the two of us, to this speech without words which is yours to speak,
O you all presence, O you all patience! And like a great *Ave* of
grace on our path, there sings low the pure song of our race. And
for so long a time this agony of sweetness has kept vigil in me. . . .

A Lady of high lineage was your silent soul in the shadow of your
crosses; but a poor woman's flesh in her old age was your living
heart of a woman put to death in all women. . . . In the heart of
the beautiful captive country where we shall burn the thorn, it is
indeed a great pity for the women of every age whose men's arms
have failed them. And who is it will lead you, in this greater widow-
hood, to your Churches underground, where the lamp is frugal and
the bee divine?

. . . And all this time of my silence in a far country, I have
watched on the pale bramble roses your worn eyes become paler.
And you alone were spared that speechlessness that is like a black
stone in the heart of man. . . . For our years are lands in tenure
which no one holds in fief, but like a great *Ave* of grace on our
path, there follows us afar the song of pure lineage; and for so long
a time this agony of sweetness has kept vigil in us. . . .

Did it snow, this night, on that side of the world where you join
your hands? . . . Here, there is great noise of chains in the streets
where men go running towards their shadow. And it was not known
that there were still so many chains in the world for the equipment

of wheels in flight towards the day. And there is also a great noise
of spades at our doors, O vigils! The hireling negroes move upon
the scurf of the earth like people of the Salt Excise. A lamp
survives the cancer of the night. And a bird of pink ash, which
was a burning ember all summer, suddenly lights up the crypts of
winter, like the Phasis Bird in the Hour Books of the Year One
Thousand. . . . Spouse of the world, my presence, spouse of the
world, my vigil! May the fresh wind of falsehood ravish us once
more! . . . And in men is the sadness of men, but also that
strength which is nameless and, at moments, that grace at which
they surely must have smiled."

4

I, ONLY ACCOUNTANT, from the height of this corner room surrounded by an Ocean of snows.—Precarious guest of the moment,
man without proof or witness, shall I unmoor my low bed like a
canoe from its cove? . . . Those who, each day, pitch camp further
off from their birthplace, those who, each day, haul in their boat on
other banks, know better, day by day, the course of illegible things;
and tracing the rivers towards their source, between the green appearances they are caught up suddenly into that harsh glare in
which all language loses its power.

Thus man, half naked on the Ocean of the snows, suddenly
breaking asunder the vast libration, follows a singular design in
which words cease to take hold. Spouse of the world, my presence,
spouse of the world, my prudence! . . . And turning with the day
towards the primal waters, like the traveller at new moon whose
direction is uncertain and his gait aberrant, it is my design, now, to
wander among the oldest layers of speech, among the farthest pho-
netic strata: as far as the most far-off languages, as far as the most
whole and most parsimonious languages,

like those Dravidian languages which had no distinct words for
"yesterday" and "to-day." . . . Come and follow us, who have no
words to say: ascending that pure unwritten delight where runs the
ancient human phrase, we move about among clear elisions, the
residues of old prefixes that have lost their initial, and, forestalling
the master works in linguistics, we hack out our new pathways to
those unheard-of locutions where the aspiration withdraws behind
its vowels and the modulation of the breath spreads out, under the
sway of certain half-voiced labials, in search of pure vocalic finals.

And it was at morning, beneath the purest of word-forms, a beautiful country without hatred or meanness, a place of grace and of mercy for the ascension of the unfailing presages of the mind; and like a great *Ave* of grace on our path, the great white rose-gardens of all the snows all around. . . . Freshness of umbels, of corymbs, freshness of aril under the bean, ah! so many wafers still on the lips of the wanderer! . . . What new flora, in a freer place, absolves us from the flower and from the fruit? What bone shuttle in the hands of very old women, what ivory almond in the hands of very young women will weave us fresher linen for the burns of the living? . . . Spouse of the world, our patience, spouse of the world, our vigil! . . . Ah! all the dwarf-elder of dream against our faces! And ravish us once again, O world! your fresh wind of falsehood! . . . There where the rivers are still fordable, there where the snows are still fordable, we shall pass on, this night, an unfordable soul. . . . And beyond are the great linens of dream and all that fungible wealth in which man involves his fate. . . .

*

Henceforth this page on which no more is written.

New York, 1944

—Translated by Denis Devlin

ALBERT CAMUS

****

*One of the newest stars in the field of French literature is Albert
Camus, who left the choice of his material to the editor. The following is the final chapter in his short novel* The Stranger. *The novel
is the tragic chronicle of an enigmatic though average-placed young
man living in Algiers, with a job, his girl, his few bachelor friends
and one day his inexplicable killing of an Arab, an act which, as he
says, was "pure chance." Tried and sentenced to death largely on
the basis of his "callousness" a short time earlier at the death of his
mother in a home for the poor, the young man is found in the last
chapter awaiting the guillotine.*

****

Sentence of Death

I HAVE JUST REFUSED, for the third time, to see the prison chaplain.
I have nothing to say to him, don't feel like talking—and shall be
seeing him quite soon enough, anyway. The only thing that interests me now is the problem of circumventing the machine, learning
if the inevitable admits a loophole.

They have moved me to another cell. In this one, lying on my
back, I can see the sky, and there is nothing else to see. All my time
is spent in watching the slowly changing colors of the sky, as day
moves on to night. I put my hands behind my head, gaze up, and
wait.

This problem of a loophole obsesses me; I am always wondering
if there have been cases of condemned prisoners' escaping from the
implacable machinery of justice at the last moment, breaking
through the police cordon, vanishing in the nick of time before the
guillotine falls. Often and often I blame myself for not having given
more attention to accounts of public executions. One should always
take an interest in such matters. There's never any knowing what
one may come to. Like everyone else I'd read descriptions of execu-

tions in the papers. But technical books dealing with this subject must certainly exist; only I'd never felt sufficiently interested to look them up. And in these books I might have found escape stories. Surely they'd have told me that in one case, anyhow, the wheels had stopped; that once, if only once, in that inexorable march of events, chance or luck had played a happy part. Just once! In a way I think that single instance would have satisfied me. My emotion would have done the rest. The papers often talk of "a debt owed to society"—a debt which, according to them, must be paid by the offender. But talk of that sort doesn't touch the imagination. No, the one thing that counted for me was the possibility of making a dash for it and defeating their bloodthirsty rite; of a mad stampede to freedom that would anyhow give me a moment's hope, the gambler's last throw. Naturally, all that "hope" could come to was to be knocked down at the corner of a street or picked off by a bullet in my back. But, all things considered, even this luxury was forbidden me; I was caught in the rattrap irrevocably.

Try as I might, I couldn't stomach this brutal certitude. For really, when one came to think of it, there was a disproportion between the judgment on which it was based and the unalterable sequence of events starting from the moment when that judgment was delivered. The fact that the verdict was read out at eight P.M. rather than at five, the fact that it might have been quite different, that it was given by men who change their underclothes, and was credited to so vague an entity as the "French people"—for that matter, why not to the Chinese or the German people?—all these facts seemed to deprive the court's decision of much of its gravity. Yet I could but recognize that, from the moment the verdict was given, its effects became as cogent, as tangible, as, for example, this wall against which I was lying, pressing my back to it.

When such thoughts crossed my mind, I remembered a story Mother used to tell me about my father. I never set eyes on him. Perhaps the only things I really knew about him were what Mother had told me. One of these was that he'd gone to see a murderer executed. The mere thought of it turned his stomach. But he'd seen it through and, on coming home, was violently sick. At the time, I found my father's conduct rather disgusting. But now I understood; it was so natural. How had I failed to recognize that nothing was more important than an execution; that, viewed from one angle, it's the only thing that can genuinely interest a man? And I decided that, if ever I got out of jail, I'd attend every execution that took

place. I was unwise, no doubt, even to consider this possibility. For,
the moment I'd pictured myself in freedom, standing behind a
double rank of policemen—on the right side of the line, so to
speak—the mere thought of being an onlooker who comes to see
the show, and can go home and vomit afterward, flooded my mind
with a wild, absurd exultation. It was a stupid thing to let my
imagination run away with me like that; a moment later I had a
shivering fit and had to wrap myself closely in my blanket. But my
teeth went on chattering; nothing would stop them.

Still, obviously, one can't be sensible all the time. Another
equally ridiculous fancy of mine was to frame new laws, altering
the penalties. What was wanted, to my mind, was to give the
criminal a chance, if only a dog's chance; say, one chance in a
thousand. There might be some drug, or combination of drugs,
which would kill the patient (I thought of him as "the patient")
nine hundred and ninety times in a thousand. That he should know
this was, of course, essential. For after taking much thought, calmly,
I came to the conclusion that what was wrong about the guillotine
was that the condemned man had no chance at all, absolutely none.
In fact, the patient's death had been ordained irrevocably. It was a
foregone conclusion. If by some fluke the knife didn't do its job,
they started again. So it came to this, that—against the grain, no
doubt—the condemned man had to hope the apparatus was in
good working order! This, I thought, was a flaw in the system; and,
on the face of it, my view was sound enough. On the other hand,
I had to admit it proved the efficiency of the system. It came to
this; the man under sentence was obliged to collaborate mentally,
it was in his interest that all should go off without a hitch.

Another thing I had to recognize was that, until now, I'd had
wrong ideas on the subject. For some reason I'd always supposed
that one had to go up steps and climb on to a scaffold, to be guillotined. Probably that was because of the 1789 Revolution; I mean,
what I'd learned about it at school, and the pictures I had seen.
Then one morning I remembered a photograph the newspapers had
featured on the occasion of the execution of a famous criminal.
Actually the apparatus stood on the ground: there was nothing
very impressing about it, and it was much narrower than I'd
imagined. It struck me as rather odd that picture had escaped
my memory until now. What had struck me at the time was the
neat appearance of the guillotine; its shining surfaces and finish
reminded me of some laboratory instrument. One always has ex-

aggerated ideas about what one doesn't know. Now I had to admit it seemed a very simple process, getting guillotined; the machine is on the same level as the man, and he walks toward it as he steps forward to meet somebody he knows. In a sense, that, too, was disappointing. The business of climbing a scaffold, leaving the world below, so to speak, gave me something for a man's imagination to get hold of. But, as it was, the machine dominated everything; they killed you discreetly, with a hint of shame and much efficiency.

There were two other things about which I was always thinking: the dawn and my appeal. However, I did my best to keep my mind off these thoughts. I lay down, looked up at the sky, and forced myself to study it. When the light began to turn green I knew that night was coming. Another thing I did to deflect the course of my thoughts was to listen to my heart. I couldn't imagine that this faint throbbing which had been with me for so long would ever cease. Imagination has never been one of my strong points. Still, I tried to picture a moment when the beating of my heart no longer echoed in my head. But, in vain. The dawn and my appeal were still there. And I ended by believing it was a silly thing to try to force one's thoughts out of their natural groove.

They always came for one at dawn; that much I knew. So, really, all my nights were spent in waiting for that dawn. I have never liked being taken by surprise. When something happens to me I want to be ready for it. That's why I got into the habit of sleeping off and on in the daytime and watching through the night for the first hint of daybreak in the dark dome above. The worst period of the night was that vague hour when, I knew, they usually come; once it was after midnight I waited, listening intently. Never before had my ears perceived so many noises, such tiny sounds. Still, I must say I was lucky in one respect; never during any of those periods did I hear footsteps. Mother used to say that however miserable one is, there's always something to be thankful for. And each morning, when the sky brightened and light began to flood my cell, I agreed with her. Because I might just as well have heard footsteps, and felt my heart shattered into bits. Even though the faintest rustle sent me hurrying to the door and, pressing an ear to the rough, cold wood, I listened so intently that I could hear my breathing, quick and hoarse like a dog's panting—even so there was an end; my heart hadn't split, and I knew I had another twenty-four hours' respite.

Then all day there was my appeal to think about. I made the most of this idea, studying my effects so as to squeeze out the maximum of consolation. Thus, I always began by assuming the worst; my appeal was dismissed. That meant, of course, I was to die. Sooner than others, obviously. "But," I reminded myself, "it's common knowledge that life isn't worth living, anyhow." And, on a wide view, I could see that it makes little difference whether one dies at the age of thirty or threescore and ten—since, in either case, other men and women will continue living, the world will go on as before. Also, whether I died now or forty years hence, this business of dying had to be got through, inevitably. Still, somehow this line of thought wasn't as consoling as it should have been; the idea of all those years of life in hand was a galling reminder! However, I could argue myself out of it, by picturing what would have been my feelings when my term was up, and death had cornered me. Once you're up against it, the precise manner of your death has obviously small importance. Therefore—but it was hard not to lose the thread of the argument leading up to that "therefore"—I should be prepared to face the dismissal of my appeal.

At this stage, but only at this stage, I had, so to speak, the *right,* and accordingly I gave myself leave, to consider the other alternative; that my appeal was successful. And then the trouble was to calm down that sudden rush of joy racing through my body and even bringing tears to my eyes. But it was up to me to bring my nerves to heel and steady my mind; for, even in considering this possibility, I had to keep some order in my thoughts, so as to make my consolations, as regards the first alternative, more plausible. When I'd succeeded, I had earned a good hour's peace of mind; and that, anyhow, was something.

It was at one of these moments that I refused once again to see the chaplain. I was lying down and could mark the summer evening coming on by a soft golden glow spreading across the sky. I had just turned down my appeal, and felt my blood circulating with slow, steady throbs. No, I didn't want to see the chaplain. . . . Then I did something I hadn't done for quite a while; I fell to thinking about Marie. She hadn't written for ages; probably, I surmised, she had grown tired of being the mistress of a man sentenced to death. Or she might be ill, or dead. After all, such things happen. How could I have known about it, since, apart from our two bodies, separated now, there was no link between us, nothing to remind us of each other? Supposing she were dead, her memory would mean nothing; I couldn't feel an interest in a dead girl. This seemed to me quite normal; just as I realized people would soon forget me once I was dead. I couldn't even say that this was hard to stomach; really, there's no idea to which one doesn't get acclimatized in time.

My thoughts had reached this point when the chaplain walked in, unannounced. I couldn't help giving a start on seeing him. He noticed this evidently, as he promptly told me not to be alarmed. I reminded him that usually his visits were at another hour, and for a pretty grim occasion. This, he replied, was just a friendly visit; it had no concern with my appeal, about which he knew nothing. Then he sat down on my bed, asking me to sit beside him. I refused—not because I had anything against him; he seemed a mild, amiable man.

He remained quite still at first, his arms resting on his knees, his eyes fixed on his hands. They were slender but sinewy hands, which made me think of two nimble little animals. Then he gently rubbed them together. He stayed so long in the same position that for a while I almost forgot that he was there.

All of a sudden he jerked his head up and looked me in the eyes.

"Why," he asked, "don't you let me come to see you?"

I explained that I didn't believe in God.

"Are you really so sure of that?"

I said I saw no point in troubling my head about the matter; whether I believed or didn't was, to my mind, a question of so little importance.

He then leaned back against the wall, laying his hands flat on his thighs. Almost without seeming to address me, he remarked that he'd often noticed one fancies one is quite sure about something, when in point of fact one isn't. When I said nothing, he looked at me again, and asked:

"Don't you agree?"

I said that seemed quite possible. But, though I mightn't be so sure about what interested me, I was absolutely sure about what didn't interest me. And the question he had raised didn't interest me at all.

He looked away and, without altering his posture, asked if it was because I felt utterly desperate that I spoke like this. I explained that it wasn't despair I felt, but fear—which was natural enough.

"In that case," he said firmly, "God can help you. All the men I've seen in your position turned to Him in their time of trouble."

Obviously, I replied, they were at liberty to do so, if they felt like it. I, however, didn't want to be helped, and I hadn't time to work up interest for something that didn't interest me.

He fluttered his hands fretfully; then, sitting up, smoothed out his cassock. When this was done he began talking again, addressing me as "my friend." It wasn't because I'd been condemned to death, he said, that he spoke to me in this way. In his opinion every man on the earth was under sentence of death.

There, I interrupted him; that wasn't the same thing, I pointed out, and, what's more, could be no consolation.

He nodded. "Maybe. Still, if you don't die soon, you'll die one day. And then the same question will arise. How will you face that terrible, final hour?"

I replied that I'd face it exactly as I was facing it now.

Thereat he stood up, and looked me straight in the eyes. It was a trick I knew well. I used to amuse myself trying it on Emmanuel and Céleste, and nine times out of ten they'd look away uncomfortably. I could see the chaplain was an old hand at it, as his gaze never faltered. And his voice was quite steady when he said: "Have you no hope at all? Do you really think that when you die you die outright, and nothing remains?"

I said: "Yes."

He dropped his eyes and sat down again. He was truly sorry for me, he said. It must make life unbearable for a man, to think as I did.

The priest was beginning to bore me, and, resting a shoulder on the wall, just beneath the little skylight, I looked away. Though I didn't trouble much to follow what he said, I gathered he was questioning me again. Presently his tone became agitated, urgent, and, as I realized that he was genuinely distressed, I began to pay more attention.

He said he felt convinced my appeal would succeed, but I was saddled with a load of guilt, of which I must get rid. In his view man's justice was a vain thing; only God's justice mattered. I pointed out that the former had condemned me. Yes, he agreed, but it hadn't absolved me from my sin. I told him that I wasn't conscious of any "sin"; all I knew was that I'd been guilty of a criminal offense. Well, I was paying the penalty of that offense, and no one had the right to expect anything more of me.

Just then he got up again, and it struck me that if he wanted to move in this tiny cell, almost the only choice lay between standing up and sitting down. I was staring at the floor. He took a single step toward me, and halted, as if he didn't dare to come nearer. Then he looked up through the bars at the sky.

"You're mistaken, my son," he said gravely. "There's more that might be required of you. And perhaps it *will* be required of you."

"What do you mean?"

"You might be asked to see . . ."

"To see what?"

Slowly the priest gazed round my cell, and I was struck by the sadness of his voice when he replied:

"These stone walls, I know it only too well, are steeped in human suffering. I've never been able to look at them without a shudder. And yet—believe me, I am speaking from the depths of my heart— I *know* that even the wretchedest amongst you have sometimes seen, taking form against that grayness, a divine face. It's that face you are asked to see."

This roused me a little. I informed him that I'd been staring at those walls for months; there was nobody, nothing in the world, I knew better than I knew them. And once upon a time, perhaps, I used to try to see a face. But it was a sun-gold face, lit up with desire—Marie's face. I had no luck; I'd never seen it, and now I'd given up trying. Indeed, I'd never seen anything "taking form," as he called it, against those gray walls.

The chaplain gazed at me with a sort of sadness. I now had my back to the wall and light was flowing over my forehead. He muttered some words I didn't catch; then abruptly asked if he might kiss me. I said, "No." Then he turned, came up to the wall, and slowly drew his hand along it.

"Do you really love these earthly things so very much?" he asked in a low voice.

I made no reply.

For quite a while he kept his eyes averted. His presence was getting more and more irksome, and I was on the point of telling him to go, and leave me in peace, when all of a sudden he swung round on me, and burst out passionately:

"No! No! I refuse to believe it. I'm sure you've often wished there was an afterlife."

Of course I had, I told him. Everybody has that wish at times. But that had no more importance than wishing to be rich, or to swim very fast, or to have a better-shaped mouth. It was in the same order of things. I was going on in the same vein, when he cut in with a question. How did I picture the life after the grave?

I fairly bawled out at him: "A life in which I can remember this life on earth. That's all I want of it." And in the same breath I told him I'd had enough of his company.

But, apparently, he had more to say on the subject of God. I went close up to him and made a last attempt to explain that I'd very little time left, and I wasn't going to waste it on God.

Then he tried to change the subject by asking me why I hadn't once addressed him as "Father," seeing that he was a priest. That irritated me still more, and I told him he wasn't my father; quite the contrary, he was on the others' side.

"No, no, my son," he said, laying his hand on my shoulder. "I'm on *your* side, though you don't realize it—because your heart is hardened. But I shall pray for you."

Then, I don't know how it was, but something seemed to break inside me, and I started yelling at the top of my voice. I hurled insults at him, I told him not to waste his rotten prayers on me; it was better to burn than to disappear. I'd taken him by the neckband of his cassock, and, in a sort of ecstasy of joy and rage, I poured out on him all the thoughts that had been simmering in my brain. He seemed so cocksure, you see. And yet none of his certainties was worth one strand of a woman's hair. Living, as he did, like a corpse, he couldn't even be sure of being alive. It might look as if my hands were empty. Actually, I was sure of myself, sure about everything, far surer than he; sure of my present life and of the death that was coming. That, no doubt, was all I had; but at least that certainty was something I could get my teeth into—just as it had got its teeth into me. I'd been right, I was still right, I was always right. I'd passed my life in a certain way, and I might have passed it in a different way, if I'd felt like it. I'd acted thus, and I hadn't acted otherwise; I hadn't done *x*, whereas I had done *y* or *z*. And what did that mean? That, all the time, I'd been waiting for this present moment, for that dawn, tomorrow's or another day's, which was to justify me. Nothing, nothing had the least importance, and I knew quite well why. He, too, knew why. From the dark horizon of my future a sort of slow, persistent breeze had been blowing toward me, all my life long, from the years that were to come. And on its way that breeze had leveled out all the ideas that people tried to foist on me in the equally unreal years I then was living through. What difference could they make to me, the deaths of others, or a mother's love, or his God; or the way a man decides to live, the fate he thinks he chooses, since one and the same fate was bound to "choose" not only me but thousands of millions of privileged people who, like him, called themselves my brothers. Surely, surely he must see that? Every man alive was privileged; there was only one class of men, the privileged class. All alike would be condemned to die one day; his turn, too, would come like the others'. And what difference could it make if, after being charged with murder, he were executed because he didn't weep at his mother's funeral, since it all came to the same thing in the end? The same thing for Salamano's wife and for Salamano's dog. That little robot woman was as "guilty" as the girl from Paris who had married Masson, or as Marie, who wanted me to marry her. What did it matter if Raymond was as much my pal as Céleste, who was a far worthier man? What did it matter if at this very moment Marie was kissing a new boy friend? As a condemned man himself, couldn't he grasp what I meant by that dark wind blowing from my future? . . .

I had been shouting so much that I'd lost my breath, and just then the jailers rushed in and started trying to release the chaplain from my grip. One of them made as if to strike me. The chaplain quietened them down, then gazed at me for a moment without speaking. I could see tears in his eyes. Then he turned and left the cell.

Once he'd gone, I felt calm again. But all this excitement had exhausted me and I dropped heavily on to my sleeping plank. I must have had a longish sleep, for, when I woke, the stars were shining down on my face. Sounds of the countryside came faintly in, and the cool night air, veined with smells of earth and salt, fanned my cheeks. The marvelous peace of the sleepbound summer night flooded through me like a tide. Then, just on the edge of daybreak, I heard a steamer's siren. People were starting on a voyage to a world which had ceased to concern me forever. Almost for the first time in many months I thought of my mother. And now, it seemed to me, I understood why at her life's end she had taken on a "fiancé"; why she'd played at making a fresh start. There, too, in that Home where lives were flickering out, the dusk came as a mournful solace. With death so near, Mother must have felt like someone on the brink of freedom, ready to start life all over again. No one, no one in the world had any right to weep for her. And I, too, felt ready to start life all over again. It was as if that great rush of anger had washed me clean, emptied me of hope, and, gazing up at the dark sky spangled with its signs and stars, for the first time, the first, I laid my heart open to the benign indifference of the universe. To feel it so like myself, indeed, so brotherly, made me realize that I'd been happy, and that I was happy still. For all to be accomplished, for me to feel less lonely, all that remained to hope was that on the day of my execution there should be a huge crowd of spectators and that they should greet me with howls of execration.

—*Translated by Stuart Gilbert*

COLETTE

A subtle psychologist, wise in the ways of women, children, and animals, Colette is represented by a self-commenting little essay from her childhood, her early reading, and her later writing. She is considered by many figures in contemporary French literature as one of the greatest stylists of our time. She says here she has never found French an easy language to write—although she has been writing it with great distinction for many years.

Reading and Writing

YOUTHFUL promise, early flickerings of the sacred flame, lisping in numbers, predestination? I find no trace of these within my memory. My career as a writer began with a footwarmer. . . . Soon, to be understood, I would need to describe this all but extinct household utensil. I open my dictionary to *footwarmer: a metal box to hold live coals, and on which one placed the feet to keep them warm.* Already the dictionary speaks in the past tense. . . . Well, it was a footwarmer that reigned over my intellectual or, I should say, scholastic beginnings. Within the glacial, barnlike houses of our countryside, the footwarmer was an article of prime necessity. In my parents' home, the cook had her footwarmer, so did the seamstress who came in by the day; my mother had hers, and lastly I had mine, which I carried to school, filled with poplar embers buried in ashes. . . . I was given the handsomest because it was the most solid; a magnificent object all of forged steel, indestructible, heavy as a packed valise. Has anyone an idea of how admirable a weapon, both defensive and offensive, a steel footwarmer can be at recess time? I carry the ineradicable evidence of a duel with footwarmers: a broken cartilage in my left ear. Shield, missile, stove —primitive luxury in a countryside with few comforts. Each little girl had her own, in the first class—the six- to eight-year-olds—of our poor barren school. Clouds of coal gas rose from all those braziers. The children dozed, half asphyxiated. . . .

My first winter in school was bitterly cold; I trudged through two walls of snow taller than I was. . . . What has happened to those severe winters of yesteryear, white, solid, lasting, with their deep snows, fantastic tales, fir trees and wolves? Are they as lost as my childhood? As lost as old Mlle Fanny, our wraithlike teacher, who kept alive on novels and hardships? Sometimes Mlle Fanny would whinny her way out of her romantic dream, and we would have a reading lesson. . . . Our textbook was the New Testament. Why the New Testament? Because it happened to be there, I think. And the phantom old maid would scan, to the beat of a ruler against her desk, the rhythm of the holy syllables, while we droned in chorus: "Then—said—Je—sus—un—to—His—dis—ci—ples. . . ." Every so often a baby pupil, who had been sitting on her footwarmer for extra heat, would utter a piercing cry, having just burned her little behind. Or a column of smoke would rise from the floor, spreading an aroma of chestnut, potato or winter pear, which one of us was trying to roast. . . . All around us was the winter, a silence disturbed by crows, the mewing wind, the click of sabots. The winter, and the belt of woods around our village. . . . Nothing else. Nothing more. A humble, a rustic image. . . .

But if by some harmless trick of magic, I could bring back all at once the aroma of foaming potato, charring chestnut, mingled with that of our old New Testament, dogeared, tattered, moldy, wherein Mlle Fanny had preserved dried tulips transparent as red onyx, the gray cadavers of violets, the spade-bearded faces of April violets, I believe, yes, that I would be truly content. I believe that somewhere in that strange fragrance I would find the key to the past, the key to the door that opens on childhood; and once again I would be the six-year-old who knew how to read but hated to learn how to write. No, I had no wish to write. When I could wander at will within the enchanted kingdom of reading, why learn to write? And yet this aversion which the act of writing aroused in me, might it not have been inspired by a providential instinctive wisdom? It is a little late to question myself on that. What is done is done. But in my youth I never, never wanted to write. No, I never got up furtively during the night to scribble verses on a shoebox cover. No, I never whispered my masterpieces to the west wind by moonlight. No, I never won a composition prize when I was twelve or fifteen. Because I felt, and every day more so, that I was created just *not* to write. I never sent a famous writer essays that showed a pretty amateur talent. . . . Yet, today, every one must be doing it, because I am forever receiving manuscripts. I conclude that I must have been unique of my kind, the only mortal put on earth not to write. What sweetness I tasted in such an absence of literary vocation. My childhood, my adolescence, both preserved from the worry of self-expression, were given over to the exposure of subtle antennae to all that could be watched, heard, felt and breathed. Fenced-in fields, free of perils; tracks, in the snow, of bird and hare; pools covered with ice or veiled in warm summer mist: assuredly you gave me as many jobs as I could hold. Should I call my school a school? No; it was a sort of rugged paradise with disheveled angels who chopped wood of a morning to get the fire started under the stove, and who ate, as their heavenly manna, thick sandwiches made of red beans cooked in wine sauce and spread on the gray bread kneaded by the farm women. . . . No railroad through my birthplace, no electricity, no near-by college, no big city. In my family no money, but plenty of books. No luxury, but freedom. There was no one to borrow the wind's voice to whisper coldly in my ear that I must write, and write more—and thus dim, as I wrote, my bounding or tranquil perception of a living universe. . . .

I had at first thought to make my readers laugh with this tale of a writer who never wished to write. And now, as I come to an end, I see that it has been a melancholy tale. Because, when I was seventeen and love entered my life, I still had no wish to write about it, to describe it, and I thought that love could get along very well without love letters, that a silent self-absorption was enough. Love, I thought, should find a sovereign presence more satisfactory than the writing of its own novel.

Nevertheless, my life has been spent in writing. . . . Born into a family without means, I was never taught a metier. I knew how to climb, whistle, run, but no one came along to offer me a job as a squirrel, a bird or a deer. The day when necessity put a pen into my hand, and in exchange for the pages I had written, I was given a little money, I understood that I must every day slowly, obediently, write; patiently fusing sound and cadence, getting up early by choice, going to bed late when work had to be finished. French is a terribly difficult language. It is only when you have been writing for forty-five years that you begin to realize it.

LOUIS ARAGON

Taken from various of the six volumes of poems Louis Aragon wrote during the Second World War, the four poems in this book are thought by many to be most representative of the French writer who more than any other is considered the poet who best recorded the feelings of his fellow Frenchmen during the war and the invasion of France.

Poems in War Time

THE LILACS AND THE ROSES

O MONTHS of blossoming, months of transfigurations,
May without cloud and June stabbed to the heart,
I shall not ever forget the lilacs or the roses
Nor those the spring has kept folded away apart.

I shall not ever forget the tragic sleight-of-hand,
The cavalcade, the cries, the crowd, the sun,
The lorries loaded with love, the Belgian gifts,
The road humming with bees, the atmosphere that spun,
The feckless triumphing before the battle,
The scarlet blood the scarlet kiss bespoke
And those about to die bolt upright in the turrets
Smothered in lilac by a drunken folk.

I shall not ever forget the flower gardens of France—
Illuminated scrolls from eras more than spent—
Nor forget the trouble of dusk, the sphinxlike silence,
The roses all along the way we went;

Flowers that gave the lie to soldiers passing
On wings of fear, a fear importunate as a breeze,
And gave the lie to the lunatic push-bikes and the ironic
Guns and the sorry rig of the refugees.

But what I do not know is why this whirl
Of memories always comes to the same point and drops
At Sainte-Marthe . . . a general . . . a black pattern,
A Norman villa where the forest stops;
All is quiet here, the enemy rests in the night
And Paris has surrendered, so we have just heard—
I shall never forget the lilacs nor the roses
Nor those two loves whose loss we have incurred:

Bouquets of the first day, lilacs, Flanders lilacs,
Soft cheeks of shadow rouged by death—and you,
Bouquets of the retreat, delicate roses, tinted
Like far-off conflagrations: roses of Anjou.

—Translated by Louis MacNeice

SONG FOR A BARREL ORGAN

THE REFUGEES the bombers stopped
Turned and came back in broad daylight
Touched in the head, so tired they dropped
   Turned and came back in broad daylight
   Under their loads the women bent
   The men were crazy with their plight

Under their loads the women bent
And children crying for lost toys
Looked without knowing what it meant
   And children crying for lost toys
   Opened their eyes too wide upon
   The shattered world of little boys
Opened their eyes too wide upon
The bakery at the corner burned
The crossroads with a Hotchkiss gun

At the corner where the bakery burned
Soldiers who count in an undertone
And a colonel looking unconcerned
The soldiers count in an undertone
Their dead and wounded one by one
From the schoolhouse comes a single groan
 The dead and wounded one by one
 Their girls at home, what will they do?
 Oh, sweetheart, if I were not gone

The girls at home, what will they do?
The men sleep with their photographs
The sky outlasts the swallows too
 The men sleep with their photographs
 On canvas stretchers head by head
 Each with a pictured girl who laughs
On canvas stretchers head by head
We'll take them away, the young men
Whose skin is gray, whose bellies red

 We'll take them away, the young men
 But who knows if it's worth our while
 Look, Sergeant, they'll be dead by then
And who knows if it's worth our while
Should they arrive at Saint-Omer
What will they find with every mile?
 Should they arrive at Saint-Omer
 The tanks have cut us from the sea
 They'll find the enemy is there

The tanks have cut us from the sea
We hear they've taken Abbeville
May all our sins forgiven be
 "We hear they've taken Abbeville"
 So said the gunners who passed by
 Seeing civilians at their heel
So said the gunners who passed by
Like painted ghosts, they were so pale
The wild head and the starting eye

Like painted ghosts they were so pale
A fellow who came into view
Laughed like a savage at their tale
A fellow who came into view
He was as dark as the mines
As dark as life itself in hue
   He was as dark as the mines
   This giant going home again
   To Méricourt or Sallaumines

This giant going home again
Cried, "We return, no matter what
If it is bombs or only rain"
   Cried, "We return no matter what
   Better by far die where you are
   With one or two shots in the gut
Better by far die where you are
Than go into a strange country
Better a hundred times in war

   Die than go to a strange country.
   We're turning back, we're going home
   The heart full, the stomach empty
We're turning back, we're going home
All hope we lack and tears and arms
We found we're not allowed to roam
   All hope we lack and tears and arms
   Little they care in safety there
   Those people chased us with gendarmes

Little they care in safety there
They sent us back beneath the bombs
'You can't get by,' they told us. 'Bear
   Your lot. Go back beneath the bombs'
   We're going while as yet we live
   No need for us to dig our tombs
We're going while as yet we live
Still with our children, with our wives
Thanks to no one. No thanks we give"

Still with their children, with their wives
Saint Christophers of the hard road
They walked the way that cut like knives
Back to the flames, the burnt abode
Saint Christophers of the hard road
Giants outlined as they went by
No staff in hand to help the load
Giants outlined as they went by
Against the white rage of the sky.*

NIGHT AT DUNKERQUE

FRANCE UNDERFOOT like a worn-out carpet spread
Has shrunk away beneath our constant tread

We bivouac, a hundred thousand where
The beach of Malo bridges sea and air

And dead men drift like seaweed. Yachts and lighters
Are overturned to look like bishops' mitres

Into the air where rotting horseflesh reeks
Rises a sound as of stampeding beasts

The crossing gate lifts crooked arms to the sky
Within our breasts we feel the hearts awry

A hundred thousand hearts of landless men
When will they utter cries of love again?

O Saint Sebastians pierced, in agony
How much you are like me, how much like me

Alone will understand me the ill-starred
Who value more the heart's wound than the heart

But I shall cry this anguish, this desire
As night makes visible the flowers of fire

---

* *Translated, except for the title, by Sally Wood. She says in a footnote:
"The title,* Complainte pour l'Orgue de la Nouvelle Barbarie, *cannot be
translated because we do not call a barrel organ an organ of* Barbarie,
which can also mean barbarity. A complainte *is a sad popular song."*

Shall cry aloud till sleepwalkers tumble down
From burning roofs all over the burning town

Shall cry my love like the man who used to screech
Knives, knives to grind, in the early-morning streets

Shall cry and cry, Where are you, eyes I love
Where have you flown, my lark, my mourning dove?

Louder than all the shells above me crying
Louder than drunkards, louder than the dying

Shall cry, Your lips are flagons where I find
The long draft of love that is like red wine

Your arms around me build a parapet
I cannot die. To die would be to forget

Seeing the eyes of the soldiers who embark
Who could forget his longing at Dunkerque?

Lying awake while star-shells flared and sank
Who could forget the potion that he drank?

Each soldier, having dug a life-size cave
Now sleeps as in the shadow of the grave

Faces like flint, demented attitudes
Over their slumber grim foreboding broods

Spring and its fragrance never haunt this land
Here May lies dying in the drifted sand.
    —*Translated by Rolfe Humphries and Malcolm Cowley*

CHRISTMAS ROSES

WHEN WE were the wineglass overturned,
Were the cherry tree of blossom shorn,
The broken crust, the plowland upchurned
And the drowned through Paris riverborne;
When we were the yellow trampled grass,

The pilfered granary, the loose shutter,
The song choked off, the sob from the mass,
The fallen horse that pants in the gutter;

When we were exiles in our own France
Who wandered the highroads begging alms,
To spectres holding in suppliance
The pitiful bareness of our palms,

Then, then was the moment they uprose,
If briefly, if in a day struck down—
In dead of winter blossomed the rose,
The gleam of swordblades was in their frown.

Noel, Noel! That faint sunrise
Gave back to you, men of little faith,
The love for which one willingly dies
And the future that relives his death.

Dare you take the road December went,
Bright Aprils beyond the years of dread,
Or dare recall the roses' deep scent
With the shepherds' planet overhead?

At morning will you forget the star
And the dawn forget at eventide,
Or sailing with godsent winds deplore
The altar on which the victims died?

And if, on the Easter daisy's wax,
Blood against pallor, a blush should rise,
Will you forget the always waiting axe?
Will you look back at them with absent eyes?

Spilt blood cannot forever be still.
Will you forget what nourished the grain,
And the grape-red lips against the soil
And the black taste the vintages retain?
                    —*Translated by Helen Burlin and Malcolm Cowley*

THOMAS MANN

****

THE WORLD'S BEST—*will these youthful pages, written by one who had barely turned twenty-five, toward the end of a work the autonomous aspiration to greatness of which far surpassed the original intentions of the author and had to be fulfilled by him in patient toil—will they do justice to the bold title of this book and will they be able to hold their own besides examples of mature literary mastery? Just between you and me, it was not I who selected the chapter. Confronted with a number of proposals, the editor decided on this piece. "So many people," he explained, "feel so warmly about this particular novel, and this is such a distinguished unit from it, that we consider it a very good and representative selection."* Habeant—*I was glad to be relieved of the decision what from among my writings should be counted among the "World's Best," or even only what is nearest to my own heart. Is it these humorous school tales which I wrote at a time when the experiences on which they are based were still fresh in my memory, half bitter and half comical? I hardly think so. Is it the figure of their sensitive hero, little Hanno, and his escape into music which so soon becomes an escape into death and indeed is nothing but a preliminary to it? Yes, that is much more likely. The sad figure of Hanno and his sufferings have remained near and dear to me, and it was not without a certain amount of autobiographical meditation that I gave my consent to the editor's choice.*

It is a significant bit of chance—and perhaps more than chance, in other words it may be what we call fate—to see a section of that melancholy work of my youth in which the bourgeois elements are dissolved in music, reappear within the framework of an anthology just at the moment when the Anglo-American edition of my most recent novel, a book vibrating with all the terror of our era and a late counterpart to the Buddenbrooks, goes to press. Written along the lines of the old German chap-book about Dr. Faustus the exorcist, the story treats the plight of music in our time as a paradigm for the crisis of art itself, of our culture in general. After fifty years of roaming through space and time, my road leads me back to the familiar German scene, to German cities of old and to German

757

music, and I become once more aware of that early effort of mine which for all its youthfulness is not without knowledge about many things and which has made its way in this world with all its humorous melancholia. I wonder why? Perhaps because—despite its artistic innocence (which did not preclude a good bit of precociously artful finesse)—it had given more than it was conscious of, more than it had ever aspired to giving. It had set out to describe the "decline of a family," of one individual Hanseatic north-German family, using the newly won technique of the naturalistic novel, a technique that had to be conquered while being applied; but it so happened that in the book's images, characters, moods and fates the European middle class as a whole recognized its own portrait, its own and that of the condition of its soul at the turn of the century, when barely a decade and a half separated it from the outbreak of the First World War, the beginning of the World Revolution and the end of the bourgeois era.

Buddenbrooks is a profoundly German book, and not only because of its setting; low-German humor and the kind of epic "motiv"-technique used by Richard Wagner were strangely fused in it. But however much it tended to please German sensitivities and to become a stand-by in the German home, just as strong is its tendency toward Europeanization and a literary cosmopolitanism which set it far afield from what at that time in German was called Heimatkunst (Homeland-art). The influences determining its artistic attitude reached it from everywhere: from France, England, Russia, the Scandinavian North—influences accepted eagerly by the young author who was glad to learn and who considered them indispensable for a work the most essential concern of which was psychology, and more specifically the psychology of fatiguing life, the spiritual refinements and the esthetic ecstasies which accompany biological decay.

I remember very well that the thing which I had originally at heart, was only the figure and the experiences of the sensitive scion Hanno—that is to say only the material contained in this chapter and set down in its own time from a fresh memory, from poetic introspection. Basically, this was what conformed to my youthful years as well as to German literary tradition which had rarely been concerned with social criticism. But since an epic instinct drove me to begin ab ovo and to include the entire preliminary history, I did not end up with writing an adolescent short story which would not have been very different from other contemporary German efforts, but rather a social novel, disguised as a family saga, which as such came much closer to the Western European type of novel than to the German one; a cultural portrait conceived under the shadow of the thought of decay, the critical attitude of which is expressed in humorous form, up to the moment when in characterizing the German high school of that time, it turns into accusing satire.

The editor of this volume added the following words in explaining his choice of the school chapter from my early novel: "This chapter shows young Buddenbrook in relation to his masters at the school, in such a light, that, it seems to me, it is representative of one phase of your thought and writing that has many times been presented, that is to say, the tyranny of the authoritarian over an individual less extroverted and more sensitive. It gives a picture of a German school, many years before this element in German life became violently clear to many outside of the country."—Very fine; but I have heard confessions from young, highly qualified and poetically endowed Englishmen about the sufferings of their school years—sufferings which were in no way less unforgettably bitter than those of Hanno Buddenbrooks; and there are literary descriptions of French boarding schools the critical, denunciatory rage of which by far exceeds the classroom scenes in Buddenbrooks. *The kind of public school in which I personally would have been happy and successful—I will frankly admit—remains to be invented! It does not exist and can never exist; and in writing my youthful criticism of the way the German high schools were run, I was tacitly conscious of the fact. This criticism is refracted in the very personal medium through which it passes: i.e. the experiences of Hanno, the little prince of decadence; and far too completely does school here take the place of* life *itself with its sardonic hardness and vulgarity, of life which strikes terror in the heart of its late offspring —so completely that no melioristic tendency could possibly be implied and that the satire could never consciously aim at school reform. Whenever life, reality and also human society are criticised in art—is it not always a little Hanno who does the criticising?*

This question contains the source of all the irony which the spirit aims at itself—and which, strangely enough, so little impairs either its pride or its secret feeling of superiority. Without the "less extroverted and more sensitive" type, without resentful weakness, its moral intolerance and suffering urge to criticise; without that exacting frailness which cannot bear reality as it is and as it pleases those equipped to face it—in a word: without little Hanno the decadent, neither humanity nor society would have advanced one single step since diluvial times. It is infirmity which intensifies life, because it is allied with the spirit.

The young author of Buddenbrooks *had learned the psychology of decay from Nietzsche. The thing he rejected or simply did not take seriously, was the impassioned vitalist's pronouncement that there was "no fixed basis outside of life from where it was possible to reflect upon life, no authority before which life could be ashamed." This may be a German thought, it is certainly not a European one—not the philosophy of European humanism of which I was a pupil at the age of twenty-five just as much as at that of seventy. This "fixed basis," this "authority" do exist, and they are inherent in man who with that part of him which is spiritual, stands outside of life and above it in a frail kind of human sensitivity, not accepting life as it is, but passing judgment on it in all liberty—even while going down before it.*

Besides, this human sensitivity goes under only in the naturalistic novel, and it may happen that life puts one over on biology. The "decline of a family" was a useful epic subject, but after the dissolution of our bourgeois status, we Buddenbrooks reached farther out into the world, and in the end gave more to life than was ever granted our respectable ancestors within their walls.

THOMAS MANN

****

The Masters of Buddenbrooks

THE ALARM-CLOCK went off with cruel alacrity. It was a hoarse rattling and clattering that it made, rather than a ringing, for it was old and worn out; but it kept on for a painfully long time, for it had been thoroughly wound up.

Hanno Buddenbrook was startled to his inmost depths. It was like this every morning. His very entrails rebelled, in rage, protest, and despair, at the onslaught of this at once cruel and faithful monitor standing on the bedside table close to his ear. However, he did not get up, or even change his position in the bed; he only wrenched himself away from some blurred dream of the early morning and opened his eyes.

It was perfectly dark in the wintry room. He could distinguish nothing, not even the hands on the clock. But he knew it was six o'clock, because last night he had set his alarm for six. Last night— And as he lay on his back, with his nerves rasped by the shock of waking, struggling for sufficient resolution to make a light and jump out of bed, everything that had filled his mind yesterday came gradually back into his consciousness.

It was Sunday evening; and after having been maltreated by Herr Brecht for several days on end, he had been taken as a reward to a performance of *Lohengrin*. He had looked forward for a whole week to this evening with a joy which absorbed his entire existence. Only, it was a pity that on such occasions the full pleasure of the anticipation had to be marred by disagreeable commonplaces that went on up to the very last minute. But at length Saturday came, school was over for the week, and Herr Brecht's little drill had bored and buzzed away in the mouth for the last time. Now everything was out of the way and done with—for he had obstinately put off his preparation for Monday until after the opera. What was Monday to him? Was it likely it would ever dawn? Who believes in Monday, when he is to hear *Lohengrin* on Sunday evening? He would get up early on Monday and get the wretched stuff done— and that was all there was to it. Thus he went about free from care, fondled the coming joy in his heart, dreamed at his piano, and forgot all unpleasantness to come.

And then the dream became reality. It came over him with all its enchantment and consecration, all its secret revelations and tremors, its sudden inner emotion, its extravagant, unquenchable intoxication. It was true that the music of the overture was rather too much for the cheap violins in the orchestra; and the fat conceited-looking Lohengrin with straw-coloured hair came in rather hind side foremost in his little boat. And his guardian, Herr Stephan Kistenmaker, had sat in the next box and grumbled about the boy's being taken away from his lessons and having his mind distracted like that. But the sweet, exalted splendour of the music had borne him away upon its wings.

The end had come at length. The singing, shimmering joy was quenched and silent. He had found himself back home in his room, with a burning head and the consciousness that only a few hours of sleep, there in his bed, separated him from dull everyday existence. And he had been overpowered by an attack of the complete despondency which was all too familiar an experience. Again he had learned that beauty can pierce one like a pain, and that it can sink profoundly into shame and a longing despair that utterly consume the courage and energy necessary to the life of every day. His despondency weighed him down like mountains, and once more he told himself, as he had done before, that this was more than his own individual burden of weaknesses that rested upon him: that his burden was one which he had borne upon his soul from the beginning of time, and must one day sink under at last.

He had wound the alarm-clock and gone to sleep—and slept that dead and heavy sleep that comes when one wishes never to awake again. And now Monday was here, and he had not prepared a single lesson.

He sat up and lighted the bedside candle. But his arms and shoulders felt so cold that he lay down again and pulled up the covers.

The hand pointed to ten minutes after six. Oh, it was absurd to get up now! He should hardly have time to make a beginning, for there was preparation in nearly every lesson. And the time he had fixed was already past. Was it as certain, then, as it had seemed to him yesterday that he would be called up in Latin and Chemistry? It was certainly to be expected—in all human probability it would happen. The names at the end of the alphabet had lately been called in the Ovid class, and presumably they would begin again at the beginning. But, after all, it wasn't so absolutely certain, beyond a peradventure—there were exceptions to every rule. Chance sometimes worked wonders, he knew. He sank deeper and deeper into these false and plausible speculations; his thoughts began to run in together—he was asleep.

The little schoolboy bedchamber, cold and bare, with the copper-plate of the Sistine Madonna over the bed, the extension-table in the middle, the untidy book-shelf, a stiff-legged mahogany desk, the harmonium, and the small wash-hand stand, lay silent in the flickering light of the candle. The window was covered with ice-crystals, and the blind was up in order that the light might come earlier. And Hanno slept, his cheek pressed into the pillow, his lips closed, the eyelashes lying close upon his cheek; he slept with an expression of the most utter abandonment to slumber, the soft, light-brown hair clustering about his temples. And slowly the candle-flame lost its reddish-yellow glow, as the pale, dun-coloured dawn stole into the room through the icy coating on the window-pane.

At seven he woke once more, with a start of fear. He must get up and take upon himself the burden of the day. There was no way out of it. Only a short hour now remained before school would begin. Time pressed; there was no thought of preparation now. And yet he continued to lie, full of exasperation and rebellion against this brutal compulsion that was upon him to forsake his warm bed in the frosty dawning and go out into the world, into contact with harsh and unfriendly people. "Oh, only two little tiny minutes more," he begged of his pillow, in overwhelming tenderness. And then he gave himself a full five minutes more, out of sheer bravado, and closed his eyes, opening one from time to time to stare despairingly at the clock, which went stupidly on in its insensate, accurate way.

Ten minutes after seven o'clock, he tore himself out of bed and began to move about the room with frantic haste. He let the candle burn, for the daylight was not enough by itself. He breathed upon a crystal and, looking out, saw a thick mist abroad.

He was unutterably cold, and a shiver sometimes shook his entire body. The ends of his fingers burned; they were so swollen that he could do nothing with the nail-brush. As he washed the upper parts of his body, his almost lifeless hand let fall the sponge, and he stood a moment stiff and helpless, steaming like a sweating horse.

At last he was dressed. Dull-eyed and breathless, he stood at the table, collected his despairing senses with a jerk, and began to put together the books he was likely to need to-day murmuring in an anguished voice: "Religion, Latin, chemistry," and shuffling together the wretched ink-spotted paper volumes.

Yes, he was already quite tall, was little Johann. He was more than fifteen years old, and no longer wore a sailor costume, but a light-brown jacket suit with a blue-and-white spotted cravat. Over his waistcoat he wore a long, thin gold chain that had belonged to his grandfather, and on the fourth finger of his broad but delicately articulated right hand was the old seal ring with the green stone. It was his now. He pulled on his heavy winter jacket, put on his hat, snatched his school-bag, extinguished the candle, and dashed down the stair to the ground floor, past the stuffed bear, and into the dining-room on the right.

Fräulein Clementine, his mother's new factotum, a thin girl with curls on her forehead, a pointed nose, and short-sighted eyes, already sat at the breakfast-table.

"How late is it, really?" he asked between his teeth, though he already knew with great precision.

"A quarter before eight," she answered pointing with a thin, red, rheumatic-looking hand at the clock on the wall. "You must get along, Hanno." She set a steaming cup of cocoa before him, and pushed the bread and butter, salt, and an egg-cup toward his place.

He said no more, clutched a roll, and began, standing, with his hat on and his bag under his arm, to swallow his cocoa. The hot drink hurt the back tooth which Herr Brecht had just been working at. He let half of it stand, pushed away the egg, and with a sound intended for an adieu ran out of the house.

It was ten minutes to eight when he left the garden and the little brick villa behind him and dashed along the wintry avenue. Ten, nine, eight minutes more. And it was a long way. He could scarcely see for the fog. He drew it in with his breath and breathed it out again, this thick, icy cold fog, with all the power of his narrow chest; he stopped his still throbbing tooth with his tongue, and did fearful violence to his leg muscles. He was bathed in perspiration; yet he felt frozen in every limb. He began to have a stitch in his side. The morsel of breakfast revolted in his stomach against this morning jaunt which it was taking; he felt nauseated, and his heart fluttered and trembled so that it took away his breath.

The Castle Gate—only the Castle Gate—and it was four minutes to eight! As he panted on through the streets, in an extremity of mingled pain, perspiration, and nausea, he looked on all sides for his fellow pupils. No, there was no one else; they were all on the spot—and now it was beginning to strike eight. Bells were ringing all over the town, and the chimes of St. Mary's were playing, in celebration of this moment, "now let us all thank God." They played half the notes falsely; they had no idea of rhythm, and they were badly in want of tuning. Thus Hanno, in the madness of despair. But what was that to him? He was late; there was no longer any room for doubt. The school clock was usually a little behind, but not enough to help him this time. He stared hopelessly into people's faces as they passed him. They were going to their offices or about their business; they were in no particular hurry; nothing was threatening them. Some of them looked at him and smiled at his distracted appearance and sulky looks. He was beside himself at these smiles. What were they smiling at, these comfortable, unhurried people? He wanted to shout after them and tell them their smiling was very uncivil. Perhaps *they* would just enjoy falling down dead in front of the closed entrance gate of the school!

The prolonged shrill ringing which was the signal for morning prayers struck on his ear while he was still twenty paces from the long red wall with the two cast-iron gates, which separated the court of the school-building from the street. He felt that his legs had no more power to advance; he simply let his body fall forward, the legs moved willy-nilly to prevent his stumbling, and thus he staggered on and arrived at the gate just as the bell had ceased ringing.

Herr Schlemiel, the porter, a heavy man with the face and rough beard of a labourer, was just about to close the gate. "Well!" he said, and let Buddenbrook slip through. Perhaps, perhaps, he might still be saved! What he had to do now was to slip unobserved into his classroom and wait there until the end of prayers, which were held in the drill-hall, and to act as if everything were in order. Panting, exhausted, in a cold perspiration, he slunk across the courtyard and through the folding doors with glass panes that divided it from the interior.

Everything in the establishment was now new, clean, and adequate. The time had been ripe; and the grey, crumbling walls of the ancient monastic school had been levelled to the ground to make room for the spacious, airy, and imposing new building. The style of the whole had been preserved, and corridors and cloisters were still spanned by the fine old Gothic vaulting. But the lighting and heating arrangements, the ventilation of the classrooms, the comfort of the masters' rooms, the equipment of the halls for the teaching of chemistry, physics and design, all this had been carried out on the most modern lines with respect to comfort and sanitation.

The exhausted Hanno stuck close to the wall and kept his eyes open as he stole along. Heaven be praised, the corridors were empty. He heard distantly the hubbub made by the hosts of masters and pupils going into the drill-hall, to receive there a little spiritual strengthening for the labours of the week. But here everything was empty and still, and his road up the broad linoleum-covered stairs lay free. He stole up cautiously on his tip-toes, holding his breath, straining his ears for sounds from above. His classroom, the lower second of the *Realschule,* was in the first storey, opposite the stairs, and the door was open. Crouched on the top step, he peered down the long corridor, on both sides of which were the entrances to the various classrooms, with porcelain signs above them. Three rapid, noiseless steps forward—and he was in his own room.

It was empty. The curtains of the three large windows were still drawn, and the gas was burning in the chandelier with a soft hissing noise. Green shades diffused the light over the three rows of desks. These desks each had room for two pupils; they were made of light-coloured wood, and opposite them, in remote and edifying austerity, stood the master's platform with a blackboard behind it. A yellow wainscoting ran round the lower part of the wall, and above it the bare white-washed surface was decorated with a few maps. A second blackboard stood on an easel by the master's chair.

Hanno went to his place, which was nearly in the centre of the room. He stuffed his bag into the desk, sank upon the hard seat, laid his arms on the sloping lid, and rested his head upon them. He had a sensation of unspeakable relief. The room was bare, hard, hateful, and ugly; and the burden of the whole threatening forenoon, with its numerous perils, lay before him. But for the moment he was safe; he had saved his skin, and could take things as they came. The first lesson, Herr Ballerstedt's class in religious instruction, was comparatively harmless. He could see, by the vibration of the little strips of paper over the ventilator next the ceiling, that warm air was streaming in, and the gas, too, did its share to heat the room. He could actually stretch out here and feel his stiffened limbs slowly thawing. The heat mounted to his head: it was very pleasant, but not quite healthful; it made his ears buzz and his eyes heavy.

A sudden noise behind him made him start and turn around. And behold, from behind the last bench rose the head and shoulders of Kai, Count Mölln. He crawled out, did this young man, got up, shook himself, slapped his hands together to get the dust off, and came up to Hanno with a beaming face.

"Oh, it's you, Hanno," he said. "And I crawled back there because I took you for a piece of the faculty when you came in."

His voice cracked as he spoke, because it was changing, which Hanno's had not yet begun to do. He had kept pace with Hanno in his growth, but his looks had not altered, and he still wore a dingy suit of no particular colour, with a button or so missing and a big patch in the seat. His hands, too, were not quite clean; narrow and aristocratic-looking though they were, with long, slender fingers and tapering nails. But his brow was still pure as alabaster beneath the carelessly parted reddish-yellow hair that fell over it, and the glance of the sparkling blue eyes was as keen and as profound as ever. In fact, the contrast was even more striking between his neglected toilette and the racial purity of his face, with its delicate bony structure, slightly aquiline nose, and short upper lip, upon which the down was beginning to show.

"Oh, Kai," said Hanno, with a wry face, putting his hand to his heart. "How can you frighten me like that? What are you doing up here? Why are you hiding? Did you come late too?"

"Dear me, no," Kai said. "I've been here a long time. Though one doesn't much look forward to getting back to the old place, when Monday morning comes round. *You* must know that yourself, old fellow. No, I only stopped up here to have a little game. The deep one seems to be able to reconcile it with his religion to hunt people down to prayers. Well, I get behind him, and I manage to keep close behind his back whichever way he turns, the old mystic! So in the end he goes off, and I can stop up here. But what about you?" he said sympathetically, sitting down beside Hanno on the bench. "You had to run, didn't you? Poor old chap! You look perfectly worn out. Your hair is sticking to your forehead." He took a ruler from the table and carefully combed little Johann's hair with it. "You overslept, didn't you? Look," he interrupted himself, "here I am sitting in the sacred seat of number one—Adolf Todtenhaupt's place! Well, it won't hurt me for once, I suppose. You overslept, didn't you?"

Hanno had put his head down on his arms again. "I was at the opera last night," he said, heaving a long sigh.

"Right—I'd forgotten that. Well, was it beautiful?"

He got no answer.

"You are a lucky fellow, after all," went on Kai perseveringly. "I've never been in the theatre, not a single time in my whole life, and there isn't the smallest prospect of my going—at least, not for years."

"If only one did not have to pay for it afterwards," said Hanno gloomily.

"The headache next morning—well, I know how that feels, anyhow." Kai stooped and picked up his friend's coat and hat, which lay on the floor beside the bench, and carried them quietly out into the corridor.

"Then I take for granted you haven't done the verses from the *Metamorphoses?*" he asked as he came back.

"No," said Hanno.

"Have you prepared for the geography test?"

"I haven't done anything, and I don't know anything," said Hanno.

"Not the chemistry nor the English, either? *Benissimo!* Then there's a pair of us—brothers-in-arms," said Kai, with obvious gratification. "I'm in exactly the same boat," he announced jauntily. "I did no work Saturday, because the next day was Sunday; and I did no work on Sunday, because it was Sunday! No, nonsense, it was mostly because I'd something better to do." He spoke with sudden earnestness, and a slight flush spread over his face. "Yes, perhaps it may be rather lively to-day, Hanno."

"If I get only one more bad mark, I shan't go up," said Johann; "and I'm sure to get it when I'm called up for Latin. The letter B comes next, Kai, so there's not much help for it."

"We shall see: What does Caesar say? 'Dangers may threaten me in the rear; but when they see the front of Caesar—' " But Kai did not finish. He was feeling rather out of sorts himself; he went to the platform and sat down in the master's chair, where he began to rock back and forth, scowling. Hanno still sat with his forehead resting on his arms. So they remained for a while in silence.

Then, somewhere in the distance, a dull humming was heard, which quickly swelled to a tumult of voices, approaching, imminent.

"The mob," said Kai, in an exasperated tone. "Goodness, how fast they got through. They haven't taken up ten minutes of the period!"

He got down from the platform and went to the door to mingle with the incoming stream. Hanno, for his part, lifted up his head for a minute, screwed up his mouth, and remained seated.

Stamping, shuffling, with a confusion of masculine voices, treble and falsetto, they flooded up the steps and over the corridor. The classroom suddenly became full of noise and movement. This was the lower second form of the *Realschule,* some twenty-five strong, comrades of Hanno and Kai. They loitered to their places with their hands in their pockets or dangling their arms, sat down, and opened their Bibles. Some of the faces were pleasant, strong, and healthy; others were doubtful or suspicious-looking. Here were tall, stout, lusty rascals who would soon go to sea or else begin a mercantile career, and who had no further interest in their school life; and small, ambitious lads, far ahead of their age, who were brilliant in subjects that could be got by heart. Adolph Todtenhaupt was the head boy. He knew everything. In all his school career he had never failed to answer a question. Part of his reputation was due to his silent, impassioned industry; but part was also due to the fact that the masters were careful not to ask him anything he might not know. It would have pained and mortified them and shaken their faith in human perfectibility to have Adolf Todtenhaupt fail to answer. He had a head full of remarkable bumps, to which his blond hair clung as smooth as glass; grey eyes with black rings beneath them, and long brown hands that stuck out beneath the too short sleeves of his neatly brushed jacket. He sat down next Hanno Buddenbrook with a mild, rather sly smile, and bade his neighbour good morning in the customary jargon, which reduced the greeting to a single careless monosyllable. Then he began to employ himself silently with the class register, holding his pen in a way that was incomparably correct, with the slender fingers outstretched; while about him people yawned, laughed, conned their lessons, and chattered half aloud.

After two minutes there were steps outside. The front rows of pupils rose, and some of those seated farther back followed their example. The rest scarcely interrupted what they were doing as Herr Ballerstedt came into the room, hung his hat on the door, and betook himself to the platform.

He was a man in the forties, with a pleasant *embonpoint,* a large bald spot, a short beard, a rosy complexion, and a mingled expression of unctuousness and sensuality on his humid lips. He took out his notebook and turned over the leaves in silence; but as the order in the classroom left much to be desired, he lifted his head, stretched out his arm over the desk, and waved his flabby white fist a few times powerlessly in the air. His face grew slowly red—such a dark red that his beard looked pale-yellow by contrast. He moved his lips and struggled spasmodically and fruitlessly for half a minute to speak, and finally brought out a single syllable, a short, suppressed grunt that sounded like "Well!" He still struggled after further expression, but in the end gave it up, returned to his notebook, calmed down, and became quite composed once more. This was Herr Ballerstedt's way.

He had intended to be a priest; but on account of his tendency to stutter and his leaning toward the good things of life he had become a pedagogue instead. He was a bachelor of some means, wore a small diamond on his finger, and was much given to eating and drinking. He was the head master who associated with his fellow masters only in working hours; and outside them he spent his time chiefly with the bachelor society of the town—yes, even with the officers of the garrison. He ate twice a day in the best hotel and was a member of the club. If he met any of his elder pupils in the streets, late at night or at two or three o'clock in the morning, he would puff up the way he did in the classroom, fetch out a "Good morning," and let the matter rest there, on both sides. From this master Hanno Buddenbrook had nothing to fear and was almost never called up by him. Herr Ballerstedt had been too often associated with Hanno's Uncle Christian in all too purely human affairs, to make him inclined to conflict with Johann in an official capacity.

"Well," he said, looked about him once more, waved his flabby fist with the diamond upon it, and glanced into his notebook. "Perlemann, the synopsis."

Somewhere in the class, up rose Perlemann. One could hardly see that he had risen; he was one of the small and forward ones. "The synopsis," he said, softly and politely, craning his neck forward with a nervous smile. "The Book of Job falls into three sections. First, the

condition of Job before he fell under the chastening of the Lord:
Chapter One, Verses one to six: second, the chastening itself, and
its consequences, Chapter—"

"Right, Perlemann," interrupted Herr Ballerstedt, touched by so
much modesty and obligingness. He put down a good mark in his
book. "Continue, Heinricy."

Heinricy was one of the tall rascals who gave themselves no
trouble over anything. He shoved the knife he had been playing
with into his pocket, and got up noisily, with his lower lip hanging,
and coughing in a gruff voice. Nobody was pleased to have him
called up after the gentle Perlemann. The pupils sat drowsing in
the warm room, some of them half asleep, soothed by the purring
sound of the gas. They were all tired after the holiday; they had all
crawled out of warm beds that morning with their teeth chattering,
groaning in spirit. And they would have preferred to have the gentle
Perlemann drone on for the remainder of the period. Heinricy was
almost sure to make trouble.

"I wasn't here when we had this," he said, none too respectfully.

Herr Ballerstedt puffed himself up, waved his fist, struggled to
speak, and stared young Heinricy in the face with his eyebrows
raised. His head shook with the effort he made; but he finally managed to bring out a "well!" and the spell was broken. He went on
with perfect fluency. "There is never any work to be got out of you,
and you always have an excuse ready, Heinricy. If you were ill the
last time, you could have had help in that part; besides, if the first
part dealt with the condition before the tribulation, and the second
part with the tribulation itself, you could have told by counting on
your fingers that the third part must deal with the condition after
the tribulation! But you have no application or interest whatever;
you are not only a poor creature, but you are always ready to excuse
and defend your mistakes. But so long as this is the case, Heinricy,
you cannot expect to make any improvement, and so I warn you.
Sit down, Heinricy. Go on, Wasservogel."

Heinricy, thick-skinned and defiant, sat down with much shuffling
and scraping, whispered some sort of saucy comment in his neighbour's ear, and took out his jack-knife again. Wasservogel stood up:
a boy with inflamed eyes, a snub nose, prominent ears, and bitten
finger-nails. He finished the summary in a rather whining voice, and
began to relate the story of Job, the man from the land of Uz, and
what happened to him. He had simply opened his Bible, behind the
back of the pupil ahead of him; and he read from it with an air
of utter innocence and concentration, staring then at a point on the

wall and translated what he read, coughing the while, into awkward and hesitating modern German. There was something positively repulsive about Wasservogel; but Herr Ballerstedt gave him a large meed of praise. Wasservogel had the knack of making the masters like him; and they praised him in order to show that they were incapable of being led away by his ugliness to blame him unjustly.

The lesson continued. Various pupils were called up to display their knowledge touching Job, the man from the land of Uz. Gottlob Kassbaum, son of the unfortunate merchant P. Phillipp Kassbaum, got an excellent mark, despite the late distressing circumstances of his family, because he knew that Job had seven thousand sheep, three thousand camels, five hundred yoke of oxen, five hundred asses, and a large number of servants.

Then the Bibles, which were already open, were permitted to be opened, and they went on reading. Wherever Herr Ballerstedt thought explanation necessary, he puffed himself up, said "Well!" and after these customary preliminaries made a little speech upon the point in question, interspersed with abstract moral observations. Not a soul listened. A slumberous peace reigned in the room. The heat, with the continuous influx of warm air and the still lighted gas burners, had become oppressive, and the air was well-nigh exhausted by these twenty-five breathing and steaming organisms. The warmth, the purring of the gas, and the drone of the reader's voice lulled them all to a point where they were more asleep than awake. Kai, Count Mölln, however, had a volume of Edgar Allan Poe's *Tales* inside his Bible, and read in it, supporting his head on his hand. Hanno Buddenbrook leaned back, sank down in his seat, and looked with relaxed mouth and hot, swimming eyes at the Book of Job, in which all the lines ran together into a black haze. Now and then, as the Grail *motif* or the Wedding March came into his mind, his lids drooped and he felt an inward soothing; and then he would wish that this safe and peaceful morning hour might go on for ever.

Yet it ended, as all things must end. The shrill sound of the bell, clanging and echoing through the corridor, shook the twenty-five brains out of their slumberous calm.

"That is all," said Herr Ballerstedt. The register was handed up to him and he signed his name in it, as evidence that he had performed his office.

Hanno Buddenbrook closed his Bible and stretched himself, yawning. It was a nervous yawn; and as he dropped his arms and relaxed his limbs he had to take a long, deep breath to bring his heart back to a steady pulsation, for it weakly refused its office for a

second. Latin came next. He cast a beseeching glance at Kai, who
still sat there reading and seemed not to have remarked the end of
the lesson. Then he drew out his Ovid, in stitched covers of marbled
paper, and opened it at the lines that were to have been learned by
heart for to-day. No, it was no use now trying to memorize any of
it: the regular lines, full of pencil marks, numbered by fives all the
way down the page, looked hopelessly unfamiliar. He barely understood the sense of them, let alone trying to say a single one of them
by heart. And of those in to-day's preparation he had not puzzled
out even the first sentence.

"What does that mean—'*deciderant, patula Jovis arbore glan-
des'?*" he asked in a despairing voice, turning to Adolf Todtenhaupt,
who sat beside him working on the register.

"What?" asked Todtenhaupt, continuing to write. "The acorns
from the tree of Jupiter—that is the oak; no, I don't quite know
myself—"

"Tell me a bit, Todtenhaupt, when it comes my turn, will you?"
begged Hanno, and pushed the book away. He scowled at the cool
and careless nod Todtenhaupt gave by way of reply; then he slid
sidewise off the bench and stood up.

The scene had changed. Herr Ballerstedt had left the room, and
his place was taken by a small, weak enervated little man who stood
straight and severe on the platform. He had a sparse white beard
and a thin red neck that rose out of a narrow turned-down collar.
He held his top hat upside down in front of him, clasped in two
small hands covered with white hair. His real name was Professor
Hückopp, but he was called "Spider" by the pupils. He was in
charge of classrooms and corridors during the recess. "Out with the
gas! Up with the blinds! Up with the windows!" he said, and gave
his voice as commanding a tone as possible, moving his little arm in
the air with an awkward, energetic gesture, as if he were turning
a crank. "Everybody downstairs, into the fresh air, as quick as possible!"

The gas went out, the blinds flew up, the sallow daylight filled
the room. The cold mist rushed in through the wide-open windows,
and the lower second crowded past Professor Hückopp to the exit.
Only the head boy might remain upstairs.

Hanno and Kai met at the door and went down the stairs together, and across the architecturally correct vestibule. They were
silent. Hanno looked pathetically unwell, and Kai was deep in
thought. They reached the courtyard and began to stroll up and

down across the wet red tiles, among school companions of all ages and sizes.

A youthful looking man with a blond pointed beard kept order down here: Dr. Goldener, the "dressy one." He kept a *pensionnat* for the sons of the rich landowners from Mecklenburg and Holstein, and dressed, on account of these aristocratic youths, with an elegance not apparent in the other masters. He wore silk cravats, a dandified coat, and pale-coloured trousers fastened down with straps under the soles of his boots, and used perfumed handkerchiefs with coloured borders. He came of rather simple people, and all this elegance was not very becoming—his huge feet, for example, looked absured in the pointed buttoned boots he wore. He was vain of his plump red hands, too, and kept rubbing them together, clasping them before him, and regarding them with every mark of admiration. He carried his head laid far back on one side, and constantly made faces by blinking, screwing up his nose, and half-opening his mouth, as though he were about to say: "What's the matter now?" But his refinement led him to overlook all sorts of small infractions of the rules. He overlooked this or that pupil who had brought a book with him into the courtyard to prepare a little at the eleventh hour; he overlooked the fact that one of his boarding-pupils handed money to the porter, Herr Schlemiel, and asked him to get some pastry; he overlooked a small trial of strength between two third-form pupils, which resulted in a beating of one by the other, and around which a ring of connoisseurs was quickly formed; and he overlooked certain sounds behind him which indicated that a pupil who had made himself unpopular by cheating, cowardice, or other weakness was being forcibly escorted to the pump.

It was a lusty, not too gentle race, that of these comrades of Hanno and Kai among whom they walked up and down. The ideals of the victorious, united fatherland were those of a somewhat rude masculinity; its youth talked in a jargon at once brisk and slovenly; the most despised vices were softness and dandyism, the most admired virtues those displayed by prowess in drinking and smoking, bodily strength and skill in athletics. Whoever went out with his coat-collar turned up incurred a visit to the pump; while he who let himself be seen in the streets with a walking-stick must expect a public and ignominious correction administered in the drill-hall.

Hanno's and Kai's conversation was in striking contrast to that which went on around them among their fellows. This friendship had been recognized in the school for a long time. The masters suffered it grudgingly, suspecting that it meant disaffection and future trouble. The pupils could not understand it, but had settled down to regarding it with a sort of embarrassed dislike, and to thinking of the two friends as outlaws and eccentrics who must be left to their own devices. They recognized, it is true, the wildness and insubordination of Kai, Count Mölln, and respected him accordingly. As for Hanno Buddenbrook, big Heinricy, who thrashed everybody, could not make up his mind to lay a finger on him by way of chastisement for dandyism or cowardice. He refrained out of an indefinite respect and awe for the softness of Hanno's hair, the delicacy of his limbs, and his sad, shy, cold glance.

"I'm scared," Hanno said to Kai. He leaned against the wall of the school, drawing his jacket closer about him, yawning and shivering. "I'm so scared, Kai, that it hurts me all over my body. Now just tell me this: is Herr Mantelsack the sort of person one ought to be afraid of? Tell me yourself! If this beastly Ovid lesson were only over! If I just had my bad mark, in peace, and stopped where I am, and everything was in order! I'm not afraid of that. It is the row that goes beforehand that I hate!"

Kai was still deep in thought. "This Roderick Usher is the most remarkable character ever conceived," he said suddenly and abruptly. "I have read the whole lesson-hour. If ever I could write a tale like that!"

Kai was absorbed in his writing. It was to this he had referred when he said that he had something better to do than his preparation, and Hanno understood him. Attempts at composition had developed out of his old propensity for inventing tales; and he had lately completed a composition in the form of a fantastic fairy tale, a narrative of symbolic adventure, which went forward in the depths of the earth among glowing metals and mysterious fires, and at the same time in the souls of men: a tale in which the primeval forces of nature and of the soul were interchanged and mingled, transformed and refined—the whole conceived and written in a vein of extravagant and even sentimental symbolism, fervid with passion and longing.

Hanno knew the tale well, and loved it; but he was not now in a frame of mind to think of Kai's work or of Edgar Allan Poe. He yawned again, and then sighed, humming to himself a *motif* he had lately composed on the piano. This was a habit with him. He would often give a long sigh, a deep indrawn breath, from the instinct to calm the fluctuating and irregular action of his heart; and he had accustomed himself to set the deep breathing to a musical theme of his own or some one else's invention.

"Look, there comes the Lord God," said Kai. "He is walking in his garden."

"Fine garden," said Hanno. He began to laugh nervously, and could not stop; putting his handkerchief to his mouth the while and looking across the courtyard at him whom Kai called the Lord God.

This was Director Wulicke, the head of the school, who had appeared in the courtyard: an extremely tall man with a slouch hat, a short heavy beard, a prominent abdomen, trousers that were far too short, and very dirty funnel-shaped cuffs. He strode across the flagstones with a face so angry in its expression that he seemed to be actually suffering, and pointed at the pump with outstretched arm. The water was running! A train of pupils ran before him and stumbled in their zeal to repair the damage. Then they stood about, looking first at the pump and then at the Director, their faces pictures of distress; and the Director, meanwhile, had turned to Dr. Goldener, who hurried up with a very red face and spoke to him in a deep hollow voice, fairly babbling with excitement between the words.

This Director Wulicke was a most formidable man. He had succeeded to the headship of the school after the death, soon after 1871, of the genial and benevolent old gentleman under whose guidance Hanno's father and uncle had pursued their studies. Dr. Wulicke was summoned from a professorship in a Prussian high school; and with his advent an entirely new spirit entered the school. In the old days the classical course had been thought of as an end in itself, to be pursued at one's ease, with a sense of joyous idealism. But now the leading conceptions were authority, duty, power, service, the career; "the categorical imperative of our philosopher Kant" was inscribed upon the banner which Dr. Wulicke in every official speech unfurled to the breeze. The school became a state within a state, in which not only the masters but the pupils regarded themselves as officials, whose main concern was the advancement they could make, and who must therefore take care to stand well with the authorities. Soon after the New Director was installed in his office the tearing down of the old school began, and the new one was built up on the most approved hygienic and aesthetic principles, and everything went swimmingly. But it remained an open question whether the old school, as an institution, with its smaller endowment of modern comfort and its larger share of gay good nature, courage, charm, and good feeling, had not been more blest and blessing than the new.

As for Dr. Wulicke himself personally, he had all the awful mystery, duplicity, obstinacy, and jealousy of the Old Testament God. He was as frightful in his smiles as in his anger. The result of the enormous authority that lay in his hands was that he grew more and more arbitrary and moody—he was even capable of making a joke and then visiting with his wrath anybody who dared to laugh. Not one of his trembling creatures knew how to act before him. They found it safest to honour him in the dust, and to protect themselves by a frantic abasement from the fate of being whirled up in the cloud of his wrath and crushed for ever under the weight of his righteous displeasure.

The name Kai had given Dr. Wulicke was known only to himself and Hanno, and they took the greatest pains not to let any of the others overhear it, for they could not possibly understand. No, there was not one single point on which those two stood on common ground with their schoolfellows. Even the methods of revenge, of "getting even," which obtained in the school were foreign to Hanno and Kai; and they utterly disdained the current nicknames, which did not in the least appeal to their more subtle sense of humour. It was so poor, it showed such a paucity of invention, to call thin Professor Hückopp "Spider" and Herr Ballerstedt "Cocky." It was such scant compensation for their compulsory service to the state! No, Kai, Count Mölln, flattered himself that he was not so feeble as that! He invented, for his own and Hanno's use, a method of alluding to all their masters by their actual names, with the simple prefix, thus: Herr Ballerstedt, Herr Hückopp. The irony of this, its chilly remoteness and mockery, pleased him very much. He liked to speak of the "teaching body"; and would amuse himself for whole recesses with imagining it as an actual creature, a sort of monster, with a repulsively fantastic form. And they spoke in general of the "Institution" as if it were similar to that which harboured Hanno's Uncle Christian.

Kai's mood improved at sight of the the Lord God, who still pervaded the playground and put everybody in a pallid fright by pointing, with fearful rumblings, to the wrapping papers from the luncheons which strewed the courtyard. The two lads went off to one of the gates, through which the masters in charge of the second period were now entering. Kai began to make bows of exaggerated respect before the red-eyed, pale, shabby-looking seminarists, who crossed over to go to their sixth and seventh form pupils in the back court. And when the grey-haired mathematics master, Herr Tietge, appeared, holding a bundle of books on his back with a shaking hand, bent, yellow, cross-eyed, spitting as he walked along, Kai said, "Good-morning, old dead man." He said this, in a loud voice and gazed straight up into the air with his bright, sharp gaze.

Then the bell clanged loudly, and the pupils began to stream through the entrances into the building. Hanno could not stop laughing. He was still laughing so hard on the stairs that his classmates looked at him and Kai with wonder and cold hostility, and even with a slight disgust at such frivolity.

There was a sudden hush in the classroom, and everybody stood up, as Herr Professor Mantelsack entered. He was the Professor *ordinarius,* for whom it was usual to show respect. He pulled the door to after him, bowed, craned his neck to see if all the class were standing up, hung his hat on its nail, and went quickly to the platform, moving his head rapidly up and down as he went. He took his place and stood for a while looking out the window and running his forefinger, with a large seal ring on it, around inside his collar. He was a man of medium size, with thin grey hair, a curled Olympian beard, and short-sighted prominent sapphire-blue eyes gleaming behind his spectacles. He was dressed in an open frock-coat of soft grey material, which he habitually settled at the waist with his short-fingered, wrinkled hand. His trousers were, like all the other masters', even the elegant Dr. Goldener's, far too short, and showed the legs of a pair of very broad and shiny boots.

He turned sharply away from the window and gave vent to a little good-natured sigh, smiling familiarly at several pupils. His mood was obviously good, and a wave of relief ran through the classroom. So much—everything, in fact—depended on whether Dr. Mantelsack was in a good mood! For the whole form was aware that he gave way to the feeling of the moment, whatever that might happen to be, without the slightest restraint. He was most extraordinarily, boundlessly, naïvely unjust, and his favour was as inconstant as that of fortune herself. He had always a few favourites —two or three—whom he called by their given names, and these lived in paradise. They might say almost anything they liked; and after the lesson Dr. Mantelsack would talk with them just like a human being. But a day would come—perhaps after the holidays —when for no apparent reason they were dethroned, cast out, rejected, and others elevated to their place. The mistakes of these favourites would be passed over with neat, careful corrections, so that their work retained a respectable appearance, no matter how bad it was; whereas he would attack the other copy-books with heavy, ruthless pen, and fairly flood them with red ink, so that their appearance was shocking indeed. And as he never troubled to count the mistakes, but distributed bad marks in proportion to the red ink he had expended, his favourites always emerged with great credit from these exercises. He was not even aware of the rank injustice of this conduct. And if anybody had ever had the temerity to call his attention to it, that person would have been for ever deprived of even the chance of becoming a favourite and being called by his first name. There was nobody who was willing to let slip the chance.

Now, Dr. Mantelsack crossed his legs, still standing, and began to turn over the leaves of his notebook. Hanno Buddenbrook wrung his hands under the desk. B, the letter B, came next. Now he would hear his name, he would get up, he would not know a line, and there would be a row, a loud frightful catastrophe—no matter how good a mood Dr. Mantelsack might be in. The seconds dragged out, each a martyrdom. "Buddenbrook"— Now he would say "Buddenbrook." "Edgar," said Dr. Mantelsack, closing his notebook with his finger in it. He sat down, as if all were in the best of order.

What? Who? Edgar? That was Lüders, the fat Lüders boy over there by the window. Letter L, which was not next at all! No! Was it possible? Dr. Mantelsack's mood was so good that he simply selected one of his favourites, without troubling in the least about whose turn it was.

Lüders stood up. He had a face like a pug dog, and dull brown eyes. He had an advantageous seat, and could easily have read it off, but he was too lazy. He felt too secure in his paradise, and answered simply, "I had a headache yesterday, and couldn't study."

"Oh, so you are leaving me in the lurch, Edgar," said Dr. Mantelsack with tender reproach. "You cannot say the lines on the Golden Age? What a shocking pity, my friend! You had a headache? It seems to me you should have told me before the lesson began, instead of waiting till I called you up. Didn't you have a headache just lately, Edgar? You should do something for them, for otherwise there is danger of your not passing. Timm, will you take his place?"

Lüders sat down. At this moment he was the object of universal hatred. It was plain that the master's mood had altered for the worse, and that Lüders, perhaps in the very next lesson, would be called by his last name. Timm stood up in one of the back seats. He was a blond country-looking lad with a light-brown jacket and short, broad fingers. He held his mouth open in a funnel shape, and hastily found the place, looking straight ahead the while with the most idiotic expression. Then he put down his head and began to read, in long-drawn-out, monotonous, hesitating accents, like a child with a first lesson-book: *"Aurea prima sata est ætas!"*

It was plain that Dr. Mantelsack was calling up quite at random, without reference to the alphabet. And thus it was no longer so imminently likely that Hanno would be called on, though this might happen through unlucky chance. He exchanged a joyful glance with Kai and began to relax somewhat.

But now Timm's reading was interrupted. Whether Dr. Mantelsack could not hear him, or whether he stood in need of exercise, is not to be known. But he left his platform and walked slowly down through the room. He paused near Timm, with his book in his hand; Timm meanwhile had succeeded in getting his own book out of sight, but was now entirely helpless. His funnel-shaped mouth emitted a gasp, he looked at the *Ordinarius* with honest, troubled blue eyes, and could not fetch out another syllable.

"Well, Timm," said Dr. Mantelsack. "Can't you get on?"

Timm clutched his brow, rolled up his eyes, sighed windily, and said with a dazed smile: "I get all mixed up, Herr Doctor, when you stand so close to me."

Dr. Mantelsack smiled too. He smiled in a very flattered way and said, "Well, pull yourself together and get on." And he strolled back to his place.

And Timm pulled himself together. He drew out and opened his book again, all the time apparently wrestling to recover his self-control and staring about the room. Then he dropped his head and was himself again.

"Very good," said the master, when he had finished. "It is clear that you have studied to some purpose. But you sacrifice the rhythm too much, Timm. You seem to understand the elisions; yet you have not been really reading hexameters at all. I have an impression as if you had learned the whole thing by heart, like prose. But, as I say, you have been diligent, you have done your best—and whoever does his best—; you may sit down."

Timm sat down, proud and beaming, and Dr. Mantelsack gave him a good mark in his book. And the extraordinary thing was that at this moment not only the master, but also Timm himself and all his classmates, sincerely felt that Timm was a good industrious pupil who had fully deserved the mark he got. Hanno Buddenbrook, even, thought the same, though something within him re-

volted against the thought. He listened with strained attention to
the next name.

"Mumme," said Dr. Mantelsack. "Again: *aurea prima—*"

Mumme! Well! Thank Heaven! Hanno was now in probable
safety. The lines would hardly be asked for a third time, and in the
sight-reading the letter B had just been called up.

Mumme got up. He was tall and pale, with trembling hands and
extraordinarily large round glasses. He had trouble with his eyes,
and was so short-sighted that he could not possibly read standing up
from a book on the desk before him. He had to learn, and he
had learned. But to-day he had not expected to be called up; he
was, besides, painfully ungifted; and he stuck after the first few
words. Dr. Mantelsack helped him, he helped him again in a
sharper tone, and for the third time with intense irritation. But
when Mumme came to a final stop, the *Ordinarius* was mastered by
indignation.

"This is entirely insufficient, Mumme. Sit down. You cut a disgraceful figure, let me tell you, sir. A *cretin!* Stupid and lazy both
—it is really too much."

Mumme was overwhelmed. He looked the child of calamity, and
at this moment everybody in the room despised him. A sort of disgust, almost like nausea, mounted again in Hanno Buddenbrook's
throat; but at the same time he observed with horrid clarity all
that was going forward. Dr. Mantelsack made a mark of sinister
meaning after Mumme's name, and then looked through his notebook with frowning brows. He went over, in his disgust, to the
order of the day, and looked to see whose turn it really was. There
was no doubt that this was the case: and just as Hanno was overpowered by this knowledge, he heard his name—as if in a bad
dream.

"Buddenbrook!" Dr. Mantelsack had said "Buddenbrook." The
scale was in the air again. Hanno could not believe his senses. There
was a buzzing in his ears. He sat still.

"Herr Buddenbrook!" said Dr. Mantelsack, and stared at him
sharply through his glasses with his prominent sapphire-blue eyes.
"Will you have the goodness?"

Very well, then. It was to be. It had to come. It had come differently from his expectations, but still, here it was, and he was none
the less lost. But he was calm. Would it be a very big row? He rose
in his place and was about to utter some forlorn and absurd excuse
to the effect that he had "forgotten" to study the lines, when he

became aware that the boy ahead of him was offering him his open book.

This boy, Hans Hermann Kilian, was a small brown lad with oily hair and broad shoulders. He had set his heart on becoming an officer, and was so possessed by an ideal of comradeship that he would not leave in the lurch even little Buddenbrook, whom he did not like. He pointed with his finger to the place.

Hanno gazed down upon it and began to read. With trembling voice, his face working, he read of the Golden Age, when truth and justice flourished of their own free will, without laws or compulsions. "Punishment and fear did not exist," he said, in Latin. "No threats were graven upon the bronze tablets, nor did those who came to petition fear the countenance of the judges. . . ." He read in fear and trembling, read with design badly and disjointedly, purposely omitted some of the elisions that were marked with pencil in Kilian's book, made mistakes in the lines, progressed with apparent difficulty, and constantly expected the master to discover the fraud and pounce upon him. The guilty satisfaction of seeing the open book in front of him gave him a pricking sensation in his skin; but at the same time he had such a feeling of disgust that he intentionally deceived as badly as possible, simply to make the deceit seem less vulgar to himself. He came to the end, and a pause ensued, during which he did not dare to look up. He felt convinced that Dr. Mantelsack had seen all, and his lips were perfectly white. But at length the master sighed and said:

"Oh, Buddenbrook! *Si tacuisses!* You will permit me the classical thou, for this once. Do you know what you have done? You have conducted yourself like a vandal, a barbarian. You are a humourist, Buddenbrook; I can see that by your face. If I ask myself whether you have been coughing or whether you have been reciting this noble verse, I should incline to the former. Timm showed small feeling for rhythm, but compared to you he is a genius, a rhapsodist! Sit down, unhappy wretch! You have studied the lines, I cannot deny it, and I am constrained to give you a good mark. You have probably done your best. But tell me—have I not been told that you are musical, that you play the piano? How is it possible? Well, very well, sit down. You have worked hard—that must suffice."

He put a good mark down in his book, and Hanno Buddenbrook took his seat. He felt as Timm, the rhapsodist had felt before him—that he really deserved the praise which Dr. Mantelsack gave him.

Yes, at the moment he was of the opinion that he was, if rather a dull, yet an industrious pupil, who had come off with honour, comparatively speaking. He was conscious that all his schoolmates, not excepting Hans Hermann Kilian, had the same view. Yet he felt at the same time somewhat nauseated. Pale, trembling, too exhausted to think about what had happened, he closed his eyes and sank back in lethargy.

Dr. Mantelsack, however, went on with the lesson. He came to the verses that were to have been prepared for to-day, and called up Petersen. Petersen rose, fresh, lively, sanguine, in a stout attitude, ready for the fray. Yet to-day, even to-day, was destined to see his fall. Yes, the lesson hour was not to pass without a catastrophe far worse than that which had befallen the hapless, short-sighted Mumme.

Petersen translated, glancing now and then at the other page of his book, which should have had nothing on it. He did it quite cleverly: he acted as though something there distracted him—a speck of dust, perhaps, which he brushed with his hand or tried to blow away. And yet—there followed the catastrophe.

Dr. Mantelsack made a sudden violent movement, which was responded to on Petersen's part by a similar movement. And in the same moment the master left his seat, dashed headlong down from his platform, and approached Petersen with long, impetuous strides.

"You have a crib in your book," he said as he came up.

"A crib—I—no," stammered Petersen. He was a charming lad, with a great wave of blond hair on his forehead and lovely blue eyes which now flickered in a frightened way.

"You have no crib in your book?"

"A crib, Herr Doctor? No, really, I haven't. You are mistaken. You are accusing me falsely." Petersen betrayed himself by the unnatural correctness of his language, which he used in order to intimidate the master. "I am not deceiving you," he repeated, in the greatness of his need. "I have always been honourable, my whole life long."

But Dr. Mantelsack was all too certain of the painful fact.

"Give me your book," he said coldly.

Petersen clung to his book; he raised it up in both hands and went on protesting. He stammered, his tongue grew thick. "Believe me, Herr Doctor. There is nothing in the book—I have no crib— I have not deceived you—I have always been honourable—"

"Give me your book," repeated the master, stamping his foot.

Then Petersen collapsed, and his face grew grey.

"Very well, said he, and delivered up his book. "Here it is. Yes, there is a crib in it. You can see for yourself; there it is. But I haven't used it," he suddenly shrieked, quite at random.

Dr. Mantelsack ignored this idiotic lie, which was rooted in despair. He drew out the crib, looked at it with an expression of extreme disgust, as if it were a piece of decaying offal, thrust it into his pocket, and threw the volume of Ovid contemptuously back on Petersen's desk.

"Give me the class register," he said in a hollow voice.

Adolf Todtenhaupt dutifully fetched it, and Petersen received a mark for dishonesty which effectually demolished his chances of being sent up at Easter. "You are the shame of the class," said Dr. Mantelsack.

Petersen sat down. He was condemned. His neighbour avoided contact with him. Every one looked at him with a mixture of pity, aversion, and disgust. He had fallen, utterly and completely, because he had been found out. There was but one opinion as to Petersen, and that was that he was, in very truth, the shame of the class. They recognized and accepted his fall, as they had the rise of Timm and Buddenbrook and the unhappy Mumme's mischance. And Petersen did too.

Thus most of this class of twenty-five young folk, being of sound and strong constitution, armed and prepared to wage the battle of life as it is, took things just as they found them, and did not at this moment feel any offence or uneasiness. Everything seemed to them to be quite in order. But one pair of eyes, little Johann's, which stared gloomily at a point on Hans Hermann Kilian's broad back, were filled, in the blue-shadowed depths, with abhorrence, fear, and revulsion. The lesson went on. Dr. Mantelsack called on somebody, anybody—he had lost all desire to test any one. And after Adolf Todtenhaupt, another pupil, who was but moderately prepared, and did not even know what *"patula Jovis abore"* meant, had been called on, Buddenbrook had to say it. He said it in a low voice, without looking up, because Dr. Mantelsack asked him, and he received a nod of the head for the answer.

And now that the performance of the pupils was over, the lesson had lost all interest. Dr. Mantelsack had one of the best scholars read at his own sweet will, and listened just as little as the twenty-four others, who began to get ready for the next class. This one was finished, in effect. No one could be marked on it, nor his interest or industry judged. And the bell would soon ring. It did ring.

It rang for Hanno, and he had received a nod of approbation. Thus it was.

"Well!" said Kai to Hanno, as they walked down the Gothic corridor with their classmates, to go to the chemistry class, "what do you say now about the brow of Caesar? You had wonderful luck!"

"I feel sick, Kai," said little Johann, "I don't like that kind of luck. It makes me sick." Kai knew he would have felt the same in Hanno's place.

The chemistry hall was a vaulted chamber like an amphitheatre with benches rising in tiers, a long table for the experiments, and two glass cases of phials. The air in the classroom had grown very hot and heavy again; but here it was saturated with an odour of sulphuretted hydrogen from a just-completed experiment, and smelled abominable. Kai flung up the window and then stole Adolf Todtenhaupt's copy-book and began in great haste to copy down the lesson for the day. Hanno and several others did the same. This occupied the entire pause till the bell rang, and Dr. Marotzke came in.

This was the "deep one," as Kai and Hanno called him. He was a medium-sized dark man with a very yellow skin, two large lumps on his brow, a stiff smeary beard, and hair of the same kind. He always looked unwashed and unkempt but his appearance probably belied him. He taught the natural sciences, but his own field was mathematics, in which subject he had the reputation of being an original thinker. He liked to hold forth on the subject of metaphysical passages from the Bible; and when in a good-natured or discursive mood, he would entertain the boys of the first and second forms with marvellous interpretations of mysterious passages. He was, besides all this, a reserve officer, and very enthusiastic over the service. As an official who was also in the army, he stood very well with Director Wulicke. He set more store by discipline than any of the other masters: he would review the ranks of sturdy youngsters with a professional eye, and he insisted on short, brisk answers to questions. This mixture of mysticism and severity was not, on the whole, attractive.

The copy-books were shown, and Dr. Marotzke went around and touched one with his finger. Some of the pupils who had not done theirs at all, put down other books or turned this one back to an old lesson; but he never noticed.

Then the lesson began, and the twenty-five boys had to display their industry and interest with respect to boric acid, and chlorine, and strontium, as in the previous period they had displayed it with respect to Ovid. Hans Hermann Kilian was commended because he knew that $BaSO_4$, or barytes, was the metal most commonly used in counterfeiting. He was the best in the class, anyhow, because of his desire to be an officer. Kai and Hanno knew nothing at all, and fared very badly in Dr. Marotzke's notebook.

And when the tests, recitation, and marking were over, the interest in chemistry was about exhausted too. Dr. Marotzke began to make a few experiments; there were a few pops, a few coloured gases, but that was only to fill out the hour. He dictated the next lesson; and then the third period, too, was a thing of the past.

Everybody was in good spirits now—even Petersen, despite the blow he had received. For the next hour was likely to be a jolly one. Not a soul felt any qualms before it, and it even promised occasion for entertainment and mischief. This was English, with Candidate Modersohn, a young philologian who had been for a few weeks on trial in the faculty—or, as Kai, Count Mölln, put it, he was filling a limited engagement with the company. There was little prospect, however, of his being re-engaged. His classes were much too entertaining.

Some of the form remained in the chemistry hall, others went up to the classroom; nobody needed to go down and freeze in the courtyard, because Herr Modersohn was in charge up in the corridors, and he never dared send any one down. Moreover, there were preparations to be made for his reception.

The room did not become in the least quieter when it rang for the fourth hour. Everybody chattered and laughed and prepared to see some fun. Count Mölln, his head in his hands, went on reading Roderick Usher. Hanno was audience. Some of the boys imitated the voices of animals; there was the shrill crowing of a cock; and Wasservogel, in the back row, grunted like a pig without anybody's being able to see that the noise came from his inside. On the blackboard was a huge chalk drawing, a caricature, with squinting eyes, drawn by Timm the rhapsodist. And when Herr Modersohn entered he could not shut the door, even with the most violent efforts, because there was a thick fir-cone in the crack; Adolph Todtenhaupt had to take it away.

Candidate Modersohn was an undersized, insignificant looking man. His face was always contorted with a sour, peevish expression, and he walked with one shoulder thrust forward. He was frightfully self-conscious, blinked, drew in his breath, and kept opening his mouth as if he wanted to say something if he could only think of it.

Three steps from the door he trod on a cracker of such exceptional quality that it made a noise like dynamite. He jumped violently; then, in these straits, he smiled exactly as though nothing had happened and took his place before the middle row of benches, stooping sideways, in his customary attitude, and resting one palm on the desk in front of him. But this posture of his was familiar to everybody; somebody had put some ink on the right spot, and Herr Modersohn's small clumsy hand got all inky. He acted as though he had not noticed, laid his wet black hand on his back, blinked, and said in a soft, weak voice: "The order in the classroom leaves something to be desired."

Hanno Buddenbrook loved him in that moment, sat quite still, and looked up into his worried, helpless face. But Wasservogel grunted louder than ever, and a handful of peas went rattling against the window and bounced back into the room.

"It's hailing," somebody said, quite loudly. Herr Modersohn appeared to believe this, for he went without more ado to the platform and asked for the register. He needed it to call the names from, for, though he had been teaching the class for five or six weeks, he hardly knew any of them by name.

"Feddermann," he said, "will you please recite the poem?"

"Absent," shouted a chorus of voices. And there sat Feddermann, large as life, in his place, shooting peas with great skill and accuracy.

Herr Modersohn blinked again and selected a new name. "Wasservogel," he said.

"Dead," shouted Petersen, attacked by a grim humour. And the chorus, grunting, crowing, and with shouts of derision, asseverated that Wasservogel was dead.

Herr Modersohn blinked afresh. He looked about him, drew down his mouth, and put his finger on another name in the register. "Perlemann," he said, without much confidence.

"Unfortunately, gone mad," uttered Kai, Count Mölln, with great clarity and precision. And this also was confirmed by the chorus amid an ever-increasing tumult.

Then Herr Modersohn stood up and shouted in to the hub-bub: "Buddenbrook, you will do me a hundred lines imposition. If you laugh again, I shall be obliged to mark you."

Then he sat down again. It was true that Hanno had laughed. He had been seized by a quiet but violent spasm of laughter, and went on because he could not stop. He had found Kai's joke so good—the "unfortunately" had especially appealed to him. But he became quiet when Herr Modersohn attacked him, and sat looking

solemnly into the Candidate's face. He observed at that moment
every detail of the man's appearance; saw every pathetic little hair
in his scanty beard, which showed the skin through it; saw his
brown, empty, disconsolate eyes; saw that he had on what appeared
to be two pairs of cuffs, because the sleeves of his shirt came down
so long; saw the whole pathetic, inadequate figure he made. He saw
more: he saw into the man's inner self. Hanno Buddenbrook was
almost the only pupil whom Herr Modersohn knew by name, and
he availed himself of the knowledge to call him constantly to order,
give him impositions, and tyrannize over him. He had distinguished
Buddenbrook from the others simply because of his quieter behaviour—and of this he took advantage to make him feel his authority,
an authority he did not dare exert upon the real offenders. Hanno
looked at him and reflected that Herr Modersohn's lack of fine
feeling made it almost impossible even to pity him! "I don't bully
you," he addressed the Candidate, in his thoughts: "I don't share
in the general tormenting like the others—and how do you repay
me? But so it is, and so will it be, always and everywhere," he
thought; and fear, and that sensation almost amounting to physical
nausea, rose again in him. "And the most dreadful thing is that I
can't help seeing through you with such disgusting clearness!"

At last Herr Modersohn found some one who was neither dead
nor crazy, and who would take it upon himself to repeat the English
verse. This was a poem called "The Monkey," a poor childish composition, required to be committeed to memory by these growing
lads whose thoughts were already mostly bent on business, on the
sea, on the coming conflicts of actual life.

> "Monkey, little, merry fellow,
> Thou art nature's punchinello . . ."

There were endless verses—Kassbaum read them, quite simply,
out of his book. Nobody needed to trouble himself about what Herr
Modersohn thought. The noise grew worse and worse, the feet
shuffled and scraped on the dusty floor, the cock crowed, the pig
grunted, peas filled the air. The five-and-twenty were drunk with
disorder. And the unregulated instincts of their years awoke. They
drew obscene pictures on pieces of paper, passed them about, and
laughed at them greedily.

All at once everything was still. The pupil who was then reciting
interrupted himself; even Herr Modersohn got up and listened.
They heard something charming: a pure, bell-like sound, coming
from the bottom of the room and flowing sweetly, sensuously, with

indescribably tender effect, on the sudden silence. It was a music-box which somebody had brought, playing *"Du, du, liegst mir am Herzen"* in the middle of the English lesson. But precisely at that moment when the little melody died away, something frightful en-sued. It broke like a sudden storm over the heads of the class, un-expected, cruel, overwhelming, paralyzing.

Without anybody's having knocked, the door opened wide with a great shove, and a presence came in, high and huge, growled, and stood with a single stride in front of the benches. It was the Lord God.

Herr Modersohn grew ashy pale and dragged down the chair from the platform, dusting it with his handkerchief. The pupils had sprung up like one man. They pressed their arms to their sides, stood on their tip-toes, bent their heads, and bit their tongues in the fervour of their devotion. The deepest silence reigned. Somebody gasped with the effort he made—then all was still again.

Director Wulicke measured the saluting columns for a while with his eye. He lifted his arm with its dirty funnel-shaped cuff, and let it fall with the fingers spread out, as if he were attacking a key-board. "Sit down," he said in his double-bass voice.

The pupils sank back into their seats. Herr Modersohn pulled up the chair with trembling hands, and the Director sat down beside the dais. "Please proceed," he said. That was all, but it sounded as frightful as if the words he uttered had been "Now we shall see, and woe to him who—"

The reason for his coming was clear. Herr Modersohn was to give evidence of his ability to teach, to show what the lower second had learned in the six or seven hours he had been with them. It was a question of Herr Modersohn's existence and future. The Candidate was a sorry figure as he stood on the platform and called again on somebody to recite "The Monkey." Up to now it had been only the pupils who were examined, but now it was the master as well. Alas, it went badly on both sides! Herr Director Wulicke's appearance was entirely unexpected, and only two or three of the pupils were prepared. It was impossible for Herr Modersohn to call up Adolf Todtenhaupt for the whole hour on end; after "The Monkey" had been recited once, it could not be asked for again, and so things were in a bad way. When the reading from *Ivanhoe* began, young Count Mölln was the only person who could translate it at all, he having a personal interest in the novel. The others hemmed and hawed, stuttered, and got hopelessly stuck. Hanno Buddenbrook was called up and could not do a line. Director Wulicke gave utterance to a sound that was as though the lowest string of his double-bass had been violently plucked, and Herr Modersohn wrung his small, clumsy, inky hands repeating plaintively over and over. "And it went so well—it always went so well!"

He was still saying it, half to the pupils and half to the Director, when the bell rang. But the Lord God stood erect with folded arms before his chair and stared in front of him over the heads of the class. Then he commanded that the register be brought, and slowly marked down for laziness all those pupils whose performances of the morning had been deficient—or entirely lacking—six or seven marks at one fell swoop. He could not put down a mark for Herr Modersohn, but he was much worse than the others. He stood there with a face like chalk, broken, done for. Hanno Buddenbrook was among those marked down. And Director Wulicke said besides, "I will spoil all your careers for you." Then he went.

The bell rang; class was over. It was always like that. When you expected trouble it did not come. When you thought all was well— then, the catastrophe. It was now impossible for Hanno to go up at Easter. He rose from his seat and went drearily out of the room, seeking the aching back tooth with his tongue.

Kai came up to him and put his arm across his shoulders. Together they walked down to the courtyard, among the crowd of excited comrades, all of whom were discussing the extraordinary event. He looked with loving anxiety into Hanno's face and said, "Please forgive, Hanno, for translating. It would have been better to keep still and get a mark. It's so cheap—"

"Didn't I say what *'patula Jovis arbore'* meant?" answered Hanno. "Don't mind, Kai. That doesn't matter. One just mustn't mind."

"I suppose that's true. Well, the Lord God is going to ruin your career. You may as well resign yourself, Hanno, because if it is His inscrutable will—. Career—what a lovely word 'career' is! Herr Modersohn's career is spoilt too. He will never get to be a master, poor chap! There are assistant masters, you may know, and there are head masters; but never by any chance a plain master. This is a mystery not to be revealed to youthful minds; it is only intended for grown-ups and persons of mature experience. An ordinary intelligence might say that either one is a master or one is not. I might go up to the Lord God or Herr Marotzke and explain this to him. But what would be the result? They would consider it an insult, and I should be punished for insubordination—all for having discovered for them a much higher significance in their calling than they themselves were aware of! No, let's not talk about them—they're all thick-skinned brutes!"

They walked about the court; Kai made jokes to help Hanno forget his bad mark, and Hanno listened and enjoyed.

"Look, here is a door, an outer door. It is open, and outside there is the street. How would it be if we were to go out and take a little walk? It is recess, and we have still six minutes. We could easily be back in time. But it is perfectly impossible. You see what I mean? Here is the door. It is open, there is no grating, there is nothing, nothing whatever to prevent us. And yet it is impossible for us to step outside for even a second—it is even impossible for us to think of doing so. Well, let's not think of it, then. Let's take another example: we don't say, for instance, that it is nearly half-past twelve. No, we say, 'It's nearly time for the geography period'! You see? Now, I ask, is this any sort of a life to lead? Everything is wrong. Oh, Lord, if the institution would just once let us out of her loving embrace!"

"Well, and what then? No, Kai, we should just have to do something then; here, at least we are taken care of. Since my Father died Herr Stephan Kistenmaker and Pastor Pringsheim have taken over the business of asking me every day what I want to be. I don't know. I can't answer. I can't be anything. I'm afraid of everything—"

"How can anybody talk so dismally? What about your music?"

"What about my music, Kai? There is nothing to it. Shall I travel round and give concerts? In the first place, they wouldn't let me; and in the second place, I should never really know enough. I can play very little. I can only improvise a little when I am alone. And then, the travelling about must be dreadful, I imagine. It is different with you. You have more courage. You go about laughing at it all—you have something to set against it. You want to write, to tell wonderful stories. Well, that *is* something. You will surely become famous, you are so clever. The thing is, you are so much livelier. Sometimes in class we look at each other, the way we did when Petersen got marked because he read out of a crib, when all the rest of us did the same. The same thought is in both our minds— but you know how to make a face and let it pass. I can't. I get so tired of things. I'd like to sleep and never wake up. I'd like to die, Kai! No, I am no good. I can't want anything. I don't even want to be famous. I'm afraid of it, just as much as if it were a wrong thing to do. Nothing can come of me, that is perfectly sure. One day, after confirmation-class, I heard Pastor Pringsheim tell somebody that one must just give me up, because I come of a decayed family."

"Did he say that?" Kai asked with deep interest.

"Yes; he meant my Uncle Christian, in the institution in Hamburg. One must just give me up—oh, I'd be so happy if they would! I have so many worries; everything is so hard for me. If I give myself a little cut or bruise anywhere, and make a wound that would heal in a week with anybody else, it takes a month with me. It gets inflamed and infected and makes me all sorts of trouble. Herr Brecht told me lately that all my teeth are in a dreadful condition—not to mention the ones that have been pulled already. If they are like that now, what will they be when I am thirty or forty years old? I am completely discouraged."

"Oh, come," Kai said, and struck a livelier gait. "Now you must tell me something about your playing. I want to write something marvellous—perhaps I'll begin it to-day, in drawing period. Will you play this afternoon?"

Hanno was silent a moment. A flush came upon his face, and a painful, confused look.

"Yes, I'll play—I suppose—though I ought not. I ought to practise my sonatas and études and then stop. But I suppose I'll play; I cannot help it, though it only makes everything worse."

"Worse?"

Hanno was silent.

"I know what you mean," said Kai after a bit, and then neither of the lads spoke again.

They were both at the same difficult age. Kai's face burned, and he cast down his eyes. Hanno looked pale and serious; his eyes had clouded over, and he kept giving sideways glances.

Then the bell rang, and they went up.

The geography period came next, and an important test on the kingdom of Hesse-Nassau. A man with a red beard and brown tailcoat came in. His face was pale, and his hands were very full of pores, but without a single hair. This was "the clever one," Dr. Mühsam. He suffered from occasional haemorrhages, and always spoke in an ironic tone, because it was his pose to be considered as witty as he was ailing. He possessed a Heine collection, a quantity of papers and objects connected with that cynical and sickly poet. He proceeded to mark the boundaries of Hesse-Nassau on the map that hung on the wall, and then asked, with a melancholy, mocking smile, if the gentlemen would indicate in their books the important features of the country. It was as though he meant to make game of the class and of Hesse-Nassau as well; yet this was an important test, and much dreaded by the entire form.

Hanno Buddenbrook knew next to nothing about Hesse-Nassau. He tried to look on Adolf Todtenhaupt's book; but Heinrich Heine, who had a penetrating observation despite his suffering, melancholy air, pounced on him at once and said: "Herr Buddenbrook, I am tempted to ask you to close your book, but that I suspect you would be glad to have me do so. Go on with your work."

The remark contained two witticisms. First, that Dr. Mühsam addressed Hanno as Herr Buddenbrook, and, second, that about the copy-book. Hanno continued to brood over his book, and handed it in almost empty when he went out with Kai.

The difficulties were now over with for the day. The fortunate ones who had come through without marks, had light and easy consciences, and life seemed like play to them as they betook themselves to the large well-lighted room where they might sit and draw under the supervision of Herr Drägemüller. Plaster casts from the antique stood about the room, and there was a great cupboard containing divers pieces of wood and doll-furniture which served as models. Herr Drägemüller was a thick-set man with a full round beard and a smooth, cheap brown wig which stood out in the back of the neck and betrayed itself. He possessed two wigs, one with longer hair, the other with shorter; if he had had his beard cut he would don the shorter wig as well. He was a man with some droll peculiarities of speech. For instance, he called a lead pencil a "lead." He gave out an oily-alcoholic odour; and it was said of him that he drank petroleum. It always delighted him to have an opportunity to take a class in something besides drawing. On such occasions he would lecture on the policy of Bismarck, accompanying himself with impressive spiral gestures from his nose to his shoulder. Social democracy was his bugbear—he spoke of it with fear and loathing. "We must keep together," he used to say to refractory pupils, pinching them on the arm. "Social democracy is at the door!" He was possessed by a sort of spasmodic activity: would sit down next a pupil, exhaling a strong spirituous odour, tap him on the forehead with his seal ring, shoot out certain isolated words and phrases like "Perspective! Light and shade! The Lead! Social democracy! Stick together!"— and then dash off again.

Kai worked at his new literary project during this period, and Hanno occupied himself with conducting, in fancy, an overture with full orchestra. Then school was over, they fetched down their things, the gate was opened, they were free to pass, and they went home.

Hanno and Kai went the same road together as far as the little red villa, their books under their arms. Young Count Mölln had a good distance farther to go alone before he reached the paternal dwelling. He never wore an overcoat.

The morning's fog had turned to snow, which came down in great white flocks and rapidly became slush. They parted at the Buddenbrook gate; but when Hanno was half-way up the garden Kai came back to put his arm about his neck. "Don't give up— better not play!" he said gently. Then his slender, careless figure disappeared in the whirling snow.

Hanno put down his books on the bear's tray in the corridor and went into the living room to see his mother. She sat on the sofa reading a book with a yellow paper cover, and looked up as he crossed the room. She gazed at him with her brown, close-set, blue-shadowed eyes; as he stood before her, she took his head in both her hands and kissed him on the brow.

He went upstairs, where Fräulein Clementine had some luncheon ready for him, washed, and ate. When he was done he took out of his desk a packet of little biting Russian cigarettes and began to smoke. He was no stranger to their use by now. Then he sat down at the harmonium and played something from Bach: something very severe and difficult, in fugue form. At length he clasped his hands behind his head and looked out the window at the snow noiselessly tumbling down. Nothing else was to be seen; for there was no longer a charming little garden with a plashing fountain beneath his window. The view was cut off by the grey side-wall of the neighbouring villa.

Dinner was at four o'clock, and Hanno, his mother, and Fräulein Clementine sat down to it. Afterward Hanno saw that there were preparations for music in the salon, and awaited his mother at the piano. They played the Sonata Opus 24 of Beethoven. In the adagio the violin sang like an angel; but Gerda took the instrument from her chin with a dissatisfied air, looked at it in irritation, and said it was not in tune. She played no more, but went up to rest.

Hanno remained in the salon. He went to the glass door that led out on the small verandah and looked into the drenched garden. But suddenly he took a step back and jerked the cream-coloured curtains across the door, so that the room lay in a soft yellow twilight. Then he went to the piano. He stood for a while, and his gaze, directed fixed and unseeing upon a distant point, altered slowly, grew blurred and vague and shadowy. He sat down at the instrument and began to improvise.

It was a simple *motif* which he employed—a mere trifle, an unfinished fragment of melody in one bar and a half. He brought it
out first, with unsuspected power, in the bass, as a single voice:
indicating it as the source and fount of all that was to come, and
announcing it, with a commanding entry, by a burst of trumpets.
It was not quite easy to grasp his intention; but when he repeated
and harmonized it in the treble, with a timbre like dull silver, it
proved to consist essentially of a single resolution, a yearning and
painful melting of one tone into another—a short-winded, pitiful
invention, which nevertheless gained a strange, mysterious, and significant value precisely by means of the meticulous and solemn precision with which it was defined and produced. And now there
began more lively passages, a restless coming and going of syncopated sound, seeking, wandering, torn by shrieks like a soul in unrest
and tormented by some knowledge it possesses and cannot conceal,
but must repeat in ever different harmonies, questioning, complaining, protesting, demanding, dying away. The syncopation increased,
grew more pronounced, driven hither and thither by scampering
triplets; the shrieks of fear recurred, they took form and became
melody. There was a moment when they dominated, in a mounting,
imploring chorus of wind-instruments that conquered the endlessly
thronging, welling, wandering, vanishing harmonies, and swelled
out in unmistakable simple rhythms—a crushed, childlike, imposing, imploring chorale. This concluded with a sort of ecclesiastical
cadence. A *fermate* followed, a silence. And then, quite softly, in a
timbre of dull silver, there came the first *motif* again, the paltry invention, a figure either tiresome or obscure, a sweet, sentimental
dying-away of one tone into another. This was followed by a tremendous uproar, a wild activity, punctuated by notes like fanfares,
expressive of violent resolve. What was coming? Then came horns
again, sounding the march; there was an assembling, a concentrat-
ing, firm, consolidated rhythms; and a new figure began, a bold
improvisation, a sort of lively, stormy hunting song. There was no
joy in this hunting song; its note was one of defiant despair. Signals
sounded through it; yet they were not only signals but cries of fear;
while throughout, winding through it all, through all the writhen,
bizarre harmonies, came again that mysterious first *motif,* wandering in despair, torturingly sweet. And now began a ceaseless hurry
of events whose sense and meaning could not be guessed, a restless
flood of sound-adventures, rhythms, harmonies, welling up uncontrolled from the keyboard, as they shaped themselves under Hanno's
labouring fingers. He experienced them, as it were; he did not know

them beforehand. He sat a little bent over the keys, with parted lips and deep, far gaze, his brown hair covering his forehead with its soft curls. What was the meaning of what he played? Were these images of fearful difficulties surmounted flames passed through and torrents swum, castles stormed and dragons slain? But always—now like a yelling laugh, now like an ineffably sweet promise—the original *motif* wound through it all, the pitiful phrase with its notes melting into one another! Now the music seemed to rouse itself to new and gigantic efforts: wild runs in octaves followed, sounding like shrieks; an irresistible mounting, a chromatic upward struggle, a wild relentless longing, abruptly broken by startling, arresting pianissimi which gave a sensation as if the ground were disappearing from beneath one's feet, or like a sudden abandonment and sinking into a gulf of desire. Once, far off and softly warning, sounded the first chords of the imploring prayer; but the flood of rising cacophonies overwhelmed them with their rolling, streaming, clinging, sinking, and struggling up again, as they fought on toward the end that must come, must come this very moment, at the height of this fearful climax—for the pressure of longing had become intolerable. And it came; it could no longer be kept back—those spasms of yearning could not be prolonged. And it came as though curtains were rent apart, doors sprang open, thorn-hedges parted of themselves, walls of flame sank down. The resolution, the redemption, the complete fulfilment—a chorus of jubilation burst forth, and everything resolved itself in a harmony—and the harmony, in sweet *ritardando,* at once sank into another. It was the *motif,* the *first motif!* And now began a festival, a triumph, an unbounded orgy of this very figure, which now displayed a wealth of dynamic colour which passed through every octave, wept and shivered in tremolo, sang, rejoiced, and sobbed in exultation, triumphantly adorned with all the bursting, tinkling, foaming, purling resources of orchestral pomp. The fanatical worship of this worthless trifle, this scrap of melody, this brief, childish harmonic invention only a bar and a half in length, had about it something stupid and gross, and at the same time something ascetic and religious—something that contained the essence of faith and renunciation. There was a quality of the perverse in the insatiability with which it was produced and revelled in: there was a sort of cynical despair; there was a longing for joy, a yielding to desire, in the way the last drop of sweetness was, as it were, extracted from the melody, till exhaustion, disgust, and satiety supervened. Then, at last; at last, in the weariness after excess, a long, soft arpeggio in the minor trickled through, mounted

a tone, resolved itself in the major, and died in mournful lingering
away.

Hanno sat still a moment, his chin on his breast, his hands in his
lap. Then he got up and closed the instrument. He was very pale,
there was no strength in his knees, and his eyes were burning. He
went into the next room, stretched himself on the chaise-lounge, and
remained for a long time motionless.

Later there was supper, and he played a game of chess with his
mother, at which neither side won. But until after midnight he still
sat in his room, before his harmonium, and played—played in
thought only, for he must make no noise. He did this despite his
firm intention to get up the next morning at half-past five, to do
some most necessary preparation.

This was one day in the life of little Johann.

—*Translated by H. T. Lowe-Porter*

ERICH REMARQUE

****

Taken from Arch of Triumph, *the closing scenes of that novel by Erich Maria Remarque depict Paris on the verge of its catastrophe, the outbreak of the war which caused its occupation by the Nazis. Dr. Ravic, a refugee German surgeon, the central character of the novel, is watching the lights go out in Paris and the darkness enfold him and other refugees about to be shipped off to concentration camps by the French police. Mr. Remarque debated writing a comment on this excerpt but finally gave it up, saying that "in spite of all my efforts to write you a few introductory lines, I am just not made for it."*

****

Darkness in Paris

THE HOSPITAL was a cheerful place in comparison with the Catacombs. Here too was pain, sickness, and misery; but here at least it had some kind of logic and sense. One knew why it was this way and what was to be done and what not. These were facts: one could see them and one could try to do something about them.

At the hospital Dr. Veber was sitting in his examination room, reading a newspaper. Ravic looked over his shoulder. "Fine state of affairs, isn't it?"

Veber threw the paper onto the floor. "That corrupt gang! Fifty per cent of our politicians should be hanged!"

"Ninety," Ravic declared. "Did you get more news about the woman in Durant's hospital?"

"She is all right." Veber nervously reached for a cigar. "It's simple for you, Ravic. But I am a Frenchman."

"I am nothing at all. But I only wish Germany were just as corrupt as France."

Veber glanced up. "I am talking nonsense. I'm sorry." He forgot to light his cigar. "There can't be war, Ravic. It simply can't be!

It's all barking and threatening. Something will happen at the last moment!"

He remained silent for a while. The self-assurance he had had before was gone. "After all, we still have the Maginot Line," he said then, almost entreatingly.

"Naturally," Ravic replied without conviction. He had heard that a thousand times. Discussions with Frenchmen usually ended with this statement.

Veber wiped his forehead. "Durant has transferred his fortune to America. His secretary told me."

"Typical."

Veber looked at Ravic with weary eyes. "He isn't the only one. My brother-in-law exchanged his French bonds for American securities. Gaston Nerée has his money in dollars in a safe. And Dupont is supposed to have hidden a few sacks of gold in his garden." He rose. "I can't talk about it. I refuse. It is impossible. It is impossible that France could be betrayed and sold out. When danger threatens all will unite. All."

"All," Ravic said without smiling. "Even the industrialists and politicians who are doing business with Germany now."

Veber controlled himself. "Ravic—we'd better talk about something else."

"All right. I'm taking Kate Hegstroem to Cherbourg. I'll be back at midnight."

Veber breathed heavily. "What—what have you arranged for yourself, Ravic?"

"Nothing. We'll be sent to a French concentration camp. It'll be better than a German one."

"Impossible. France won't lock up any refugees."

"Let's wait and see. It's a matter of course and one can't say anything against it."

"Ravic—"

"All right. Let's wait and see. Let's hope you're right. Do you know that the Louvre is being emptied? They are sending the best paintings to central France."

"No. Who told you?"

"I was there this afternoon. The blue windows of the cathedral in Chartres have been packed up, too. I was there yesterday. A sentimental journey. Wanted to see them once more. They had already been removed. There is an airfield too close. New windows had been put in. Just as they did last year at the time of the Munich conference."

"You see!" Veber instantly seized upon this. "Nothing happened then. Great excitement, and then came Chamberlain with the umbrella of peace."

"Yes. The umbrella of peace is still in London, and the goddess of victory is still standing in the Louvre—without a head. It will stay there. Too heavy to move. I must go. Kate Hegstroem is waiting."

The *Normandie* was lying at the quay, blazing in the night with a thousand lights. The wind came from the water, cool and salty. Kate Hegstroem drew her fur closer to her. She was very thin. Her face was almost all bone over which the skin was stretched, with frighteningly large eyes like dark pools.

"I'd rather stay here," she said. "Suddenly it's so difficult to leave."

Ravic stared at her. There lay the mighty ship, the gangway was brightly lighted, people streamed inside, many of them hurrying as if they were afraid of arriving too late at the last moment. There lay the shimmering palace, and its name was no longer *Normandie,* its name was Escape, Flight, Salvation; in a thousand cities and rooms and dirty hotels and cellars of Europe it was life's unattainable fata morgana for ten thousand people, and here beside him someone at whose vitals death was gnawing said in a thin and lovely voice, "I'd rather stay here."

All this made no sense. For the refugees in the Hotel International, for the thousand Internationals throughout Europe, for all the harassed, the tortured, the fleeing, the trapped, this would have been the Land of Promise; they would have broken down sobbing and kissed the gangway and would have believed in miracles if they had held the ticket that fluttered in the tired hand beside him, the ticket of a human being who in any case was traveling into death and who said indifferently, "I'd rather stay here."

A group of Americans arrived. Deliberate, jovial, noisy. They had all the time in the world. The consulate had urged them to leave. They discussed it. It was really a pity. It would have been fun to look on longer. What could happen to them, after all? The ambassador! They were neutral! It was really a pity!

The fragrance of perfume. Jewels. The sparkling of diamonds. A few hours ago they were still sitting in Maxim's, ridiculously cheap in dollars, with a Corton '29, a Pol Roger '28 as the climax— now on ship they would sit in the bar playing backgammon, drinking whisky—

and in front of the consulate the long lines of hopeless people, the smell of mortal dread like a cloud above them, a few over-worked employees, the court of last resort, an assistant secretary shaking his head again and again, "No, no visa, no, impossible," the silent condemnation of silent innocence; Ravic stared at the ship which was not a ship any more, which was an ark, the last ark about to glide off before the deluge, the deluge which one had once escaped and which now was about to overtake one.

"It's time to go, Kate."

"Is it? Adieu, Ravic."

"Adieu, Kate."

"We don't need to lie to each other, eh?"

"No."

"Follow me soon—"

"Certainly, Kate, soon—"

"Adieu, Ravic. Thanks for everything. I'll go now. I'll go up there and wave to you. Stay here until the ship sails and wave to me."

"All right, Kate."

Slowly she went up the gangway. Her body swayed ever so slightly. Her figure, slimmer than all the others beside her, clear in its structure, almost without flesh, had the black elegance of certain death. Her face was bold as the head of an Egyptian bronze cat—only contour, breath, and eyes.

The last passengers. A Jew, streaming with sweat, a fur coat over his arm, almost hysterical, with two porters, yelling, running. The last Americans. Then the gangway slowly being drawn up. A strange feeling. Drawn up, irrevocably. The end. A narrow strip of water. The frontier. Two meters of water only—but already the frontier between Europe and America. Between rescue and destruction.

Ravic looked for Kate Hegstroem. He soon found her. She was standing at the railing, waving. He waved back.

The ship did not seem to move. The land seemed to withdraw. Only a little. Hardly perceptible. And suddenly the blazing ship was free. It floated upon the dark water, against the dark sky, unat-tainable. Kate Hegstroem was no longer to be recognized, no one was to be recognized any longer, and those left behind looked at each other silently, embarrassed or with false gaiety, and then hurriedly or hesitatingly they went their ways.

He drove the car back through the night to Paris. The hedges and orchards of Normandy flew past him. The moon hung oval and large in the misty sky. The ship was forgotten. Only the landscape remained. The landscape, the smell of hay and ripe apples, the silence and the deep peace of the inevitable.

The car ran almost noiselessly. It ran as if gravity had no power over it. Houses glided past, churches, villages, the golden spots of the estaminets and bistros, a gleaming river, a mill, and then again the even contour of the plain, the sky arching above it like the inside of a huge shell in whose milky nacre shimmered the pearl of the moon.

It was like an end and a fulfillment. Ravic had felt this several times before; but now it had become entire, very strong and unescapable, it penetrated him and there was no longer any resistance.

Everything was floating and without weight. Future and past met and both were without desire or pain. No one thing was more important and stronger than anything else. The horizons were in equilibrium and for one strange moment the scales of his existence were even. Fate was never stronger than the serene courage with which one faced it. If one could no longer stand it, one could kill oneself. This was good to know, but it was also good to know that one was never completely lost so long as one was alive.

Ravic knew the danger; he knew whither he was going and he also knew that tomorrow he would resist again—but suddenly in this night, in this hour of his return from a lost Ararat into the blood-smell of coming destruction, everything became nameless. Danger was danger and not danger; fate was at the same time a sacrifice and the deity to whom one sacrificed. And tomorrow was an unknown world.

Everything was all right. That which had been and that which was still to come. It was enough. If it were the end, it was all right so. He had loved somebody and lost her. He had hated another and killed him. Both had freed him. One had brought his feelings to life again; the other had eradicated his past. Nothing remained behind unfulfilled. No desire was left; no hatred, nor any lament. If this were a new beginning, then that was what it was. One would start without expectation, prepared for many things, with the simple strength of experience which had strengthened and not torn asunder. The ashes had been cleared away. Paralyzed places were alive again. Cynicism had turned into strength. It was all right.

Beyond Caen came the horses. Long columns in the night, horses,

horses, shadowy in the moonlight. And then men, four deep, with bundles, cardboard boxes, packages. The beginning of the mobilization.

One could hardly hear them. No one sang. Hardly anyone spoke. They moved silently through the night. Columns of shadows on the right side of the road to leave space for the cars.

Ravic passed one after the other. Horses, he thought, horses. Like 1914. No tanks. Horses.

He stopped near a gasoline station and had the car refilled. There were still some lights in the windows of the village, but it had become almost silent. One of the columns was moving through it. People stared after it; they did not wave.

"I've got to go tomorrow," the man at the gasoline station said. He had a brown, clear-cut, peasant face. "My father was killed in the last war. My grandfather in 1870. I go tomorrow. It's always the same. We have been doing this now for a couple of hundred years. And it doesn't help; we have to go again."

His look embraced the shabby pump, the small house next to it, and the woman standing silently beside him. "Twenty-eight francs thirty, sir."

Again the landscape. The moon. Lisieux. Evreux. Columns. Horses. Silence. Ravic stopped before a small restaurant. Outside were two tables. The proprietress declared she had nothing left to eat. A dinner was a dinner, and in France an omelette and cheese were not a dinner. But finally she was persuaded and even provided salad and coffee and a carafe of vin ordinaire.

Ravic sat alone in front of the pink house and ate. Mist drifted over the meadows. A few frogs croaked. It was very quiet. But from the top floor of the house came the sounds of a loud-speaker. A voice. The usual voice, comforting, confident, hopeless, and completely superfluous. Everyone listened and no one believed.

He paid. "Paris will be blacked out," the proprietress said. "They have just announced it over the radio."

"Really?"

"Yes. Against air raids. As a precaution. They say on the radio everything is only a precaution. There will be no war. They are about to negotiate. What do you say?"

"I don't think there will be a war." Ravic did not know what else he could say.

"God grant it. But what's the use? The Germans will take Poland. And then they will demand Alsace-Lorraine. Then the colonies.

Then something else. And always more until we give up or have to make war. And so it's better to do it right away."

The proprietress went slowly back into the house. A new column came down the road.

The red reflection of Paris against the horizon. Blacked out; Paris would be blacked out. It was natural; but it sounded strange: Paris blacked out. Paris. As if the light of the world were to be blacked out.

The suburbs. The Seine. The bustle of the small streets. Swinging into the avenue which led directly to the Arc de Triomphe, rising faint but still illumined in the misty light of the Etoile, and behind it, still shimmering, in full brilliance the Champs Elysées.

Ravic drove down the avenue. He drove on through the city and then he suddenly saw: the darkness had already begun to descend upon it. Like mangy spots on a shiny fur, areas of sick dimness appeared here and there. The multicolored play of the electric signs was eaten up by long shadows which crouched threateningly between bits of anxious red and white and blue and green. Some streets lay dead already, as if black worms had crept in and smothered all brightness. The Avenue George V no longer had any light; on the Avenue Montaigne it was just dying out. Buildings which had thrown nightly cascades of light toward the stars, stared now with bare dark fronts. One half of the Avenue Victor-Emanuel III was blacked out, the other half still lighted, like a paralyzed body in agony, half dead and half alive. The sickness spread everywhere and when Ravic came back to the Place de la Concorde, its spacious circle too had died meanwhile.

The ministries lay pale and colorless, the garlands of light had gone out, the dancing Tritons and Nereids of the white nights of foam had stiffened to gray shapeless lumps on their dolphins, the fountains were laid waste, the flowing water obscured, the once brilliant obelisk rose leadenly like a mighty threatening finger of eternity in the darkened sky, and everywhere, like microbes, crept out the small, dim blue, hardly visible electric bulbs of the air-raid alarm, and with a dirty glimmer spread like cosmic tuberculosis over the silently collapsing city.

The streets were full of people. They stood in clusters in front of the big running electric bulletins of the newspapers. Ravic drove to the Jardin de Luxembourg. He wanted to be alone for a few hours before he was arrested.

The garden was empty. It lay in the warm light of the late summer afternoon. The trees showed a first premonition of fall, not of the fall that withers, but of the fall that matures. The light was golden, and the blue was a last silk flag of summer.

Ravic sat there for a long time. He saw the light change and the shadows grow longer. He knew they were the last hours in which he would be free. The proprietress of the International could no longer shield anyone once war was declared. He thought of Rolande. Not Rolande either. No one. If he made an attempt to continue his flight now he would be suspected of being a spy.

He sat there until evening. He was not sad. Faces drifted past him. Faces and years. And then the last unmoving face.

At seven he departed. He was leaving the last remnant of peace, the darkening park, and he knew it. A few steps farther up the street, he saw the extra editions of the newspapers. War had been declared.

He ate in a bistro that had no radio. Then he walked back to the hospital. Veber met him. "Will you perform a Caesarean? Someone has just been brought in."

"Of course."

He went to change. On his way he met Eugénie. She was taken aback at seeing him. "Didn't you expect me any more?" he asked.

"No," she replied and passed him quickly.

The child squealed. It was being washed. Ravic looked at its red screaming face and the tiny fingers. We don't come into the world with a smile, he thought. He handed the child to the assistant nurse. It was a boy. "Who knows what sort of war he's in time for," he said.

He washed. Veber was washing at his side. "If it should turn out that you are arrested, Ravic, will you let me know right away where you are?"

"Why do you want to get into difficulties? It is better now not to know people of my type."

"Why? Because you were a German? You are a refugee."

Ravic smiled sadly. "Don't you know that refugees are always as stones between stones? To their native country they are traitors. And abroad they are still citizens of their native country."

"That makes no difference to me. But I want you to get out as quickly as possible. Will you give me as a reference?"

"If you want me to." Ravic knew that he would not do it.

"It is an abominable thought. What would you do there?"

"For a doctor there is something to do everywhere." Ravic dried his hands.

It was dark. A truck was standing in front of the hotel. "Ravic," Morosow said, coming out from a house entrance near the hotel.

"Boris?" Ravic stopped.

"The police are in the place."

"I thought so."

"I have Ivan Kluge's *carte d'identité* here. You know, the dead Russian. Still valid for eighteen months. Come with me to the Scheherazade. We'll change the photos. Then you can stay at another hotel as a Russian refugee."

Ravic shook his head. "Too risky, Boris. One oughtn't to have forged papers in wartime. Better none at all."

"Then what will you do?"

"I'll go into the hotel."

"Have you thought it over carefully, Ravic?" Morosow asked.

"Yes, carefully."

"Damn it! Who knows where they will put you."

"At any rate, they won't deport me to Germany. That's over. They won't even deport me to Switzerland." Ravic smiled. "For the first time in seven years the police will want to keep us, Boris. It took a war to get that far."

"It's rumored they're going to set up a concentration camp at Longchamp." Morosow pulled at his beard. "For this you had to flee a German concentration camp—to get into a French one now."

"Maybe they'll set us free again soon."

Morosow did not answer. "Boris," Ravic said. "Don't worry about me. Doctors are needed in time of war."

"What name will you give them when they arrest you?"

"My own. I have only made use of it once here—five years ago." Ravic was silent for a while. "Boris," he said then. "Joan is dead. Shot by a man. She is lying in Veber's hospital. She must be buried. Veber has promised to take care of it, but I don't know whether he'll be called up before that. Will you look after it? Don't ask me any questions, say yes and be done with it."

"Yes," Morosow said.

"All right. Adieu, Boris. Take any of my belongings you can use. And move into my room. You always wanted my bathroom anyway. I'll go now. So long."

"*Merde!*" Morosow said.

"All right. I'll meet you after the war at Fouquet's."

"Which side? Champs Elysées or George V?"

"George V. We are idiots. Heroic snotty idiots. So long, Boris."

"*Merde!*" Morosow said. "We don't even dare to say goodbye decently. Come here, idiot."

He kissed Ravic on the right and left cheek. Ravic felt his beard and the smell of pipe tobacco. It was not pleasant. He walked to the hotel.

The refugees were standing in the Catacombs. Like the first Christians, Ravic thought. The first Europeans. A plain-clothes man was sitting at a desk under the artificial palm, writing down the particulars about each person. Two policemen guarded the doors through which no one had any intention of fleeing.

"Passport?" the man in plain clothes asked Ravic.

"No."

"Other papers?"

"No."

"Illegally here?"

"Yes."

"Why?"

"I fled from Germany. It was impossible to obtain papers'

"Your name?"

"Fresenburg."

"First name?"

"Ludwig."

"Jew?"

"No."

"Profession?"

"Doctor."

The man was writing. "Doctor?" he said and held a slip of paper toward him. "Do you know a doctor who calls himself Ravic?"

"No."

"He is supposed to live here. We received a denunciation of him."

Ravic looked at him. Eugénie, he thought. She had asked him if he was going to return to his hotel, and she had been so surprised to see him still free.

"I told you that no one of that name lives here," declared the proprietress, who was standing by the door leading to the kitchen.

"Be quiet," the man said ill-humouredly. "You'll be punished anyway because you did not report these people."

"I'm proud of it. If humaneness is to be punished, then go ahead!"

The man looked as if he wanted to answer; but he stopped himself with a gesture of dismissal. The proprietress stared at him challengingly. She had protection and was not afraid.

"Pack your things," the man said to Ravic. "Take your underwear with you and something to eat, enough for a day. Also a blanket, if you have one."

A policeman came upstairs with him. The doors to most rooms stood open. Ravic took his suitcase and blanket.

"Nothing else?" the policeman asked.

"Nothing else."

"You are leaving the other things here?"

"I'm leaving the other things here."

"This too?" The policeman pointed to the little wooden Madonna that Joan had sent him at the International after they had first met.

"That too."

They went downstairs. Clarisse, the Alsatian maid, handed Ravic a package. Ravic noticed that the others had similar packages. "Something to eat," declared the proprietress. "So that you won't go hungry. I'm convinced there will be no preparations made where you're going."

She stared at the plain-clothes man. "Don't talk so much," he said angrily. "I didn't declare war."

"Nor did these people."

"Leave me alone." He looked at the policeman. "Ready? Take them away."

The dark crowd began to move. Ravic noticed the man with the woman who had seen the cockroaches. The man supported her with his free arm. Under the other he had a suitcase, and he held another in his hand. The boy also was dragging a suitcase. The man looked at Ravic beseechingly. Ravic nodded. "I have instruments and medicine with me," he said. "Don't be afraid."

They climbed into the truck. The motor roared. The car moved off. The proprietress stood in the doorway and waved. "Where are we going?" someone asked a policeman.

"I don't know."

Ravic stood beside Rosenfeld and the false Aaron Goldberg. Rosenfeld carried a roll under his arm. The Cézanne and Gaugin were in it. His face worked. "The Spanish visa," he said. "Expired before I—" He broke off. "The Bird of Death has gone," he said then. "Markus Meyer, yesterday to America."

The truck shook. They all stood tightly pressed against one another. Hardly anyone spoke. They drove around a corner. Ravic noticed the fatalist Seidenbaum. He stood pressed into a corner. "Here we are again," he said.

Ravic searched for a cigarette. He found none. But he remembered he had packed enough in his bag. "Yes," he said. "Human beings can stand a great deal."

The car drove along the Avenue Wagram and turned into the Place de l'Etoile. There was no light anywhere. The square was nothing but darkness. It was so dark that one could not even see the Arc de Triomphe.

—Translated by Walter Sorell and Denver Lindley

ALBERT SCHWEITZER

****

*To some persons Dr. Albert Schweitzer's autobiographical writing
seems the least satisfactory of all. They feel it doesn't tell enough
about him. And they are avid to know about him.*

*This unsatisfied desire perhaps results from two very pronounced
Schweitzerian traits. He is a man of most incisive and unfailing
directness and meticulous detail in many things. But in others he
seems, to some who do not know him well, bafflingly indirect, even
circuitous and persistently vague. It is usually this latter trait which
predominates when he is writing or speaking of the* him *about which
many people want to know.*

*The following section of Dr. Schweitzer's writings chosen by Mr.
Burnett and the publishers well illustrates this point, as does, in fact,
the whole book from which it is taken.* Out of My Life and Thought
*is perhaps as much of an autobiography as we shall get from
Schweitzer. But to the knowing its very title is warning. It is* not
My Life and Thought. *It is* Out of *My Life and Thought. It is a,
if, for his own unannounced but to be revealed ends, he purposes
to select bits here and there from mind and life not, indeed, primarily to reveal either mind or life—not to reveal him—but to illustrate rather the why of what happened, the stimuli and matrix involved in getting his principal philosophical writings started, and
their objective.*

*The selection herewith does that very well indeed. But the ques-
tions that are left unanswered! Internment? Food? Mail? Others
involved? Indignities? Hatred? Desire to escape? A score of questions. And no answers at all.*

The one thing that stands fully but indirectly revealed about the
him *is that the day he and Mrs. Schweitzer were barred from their
hospital work, he took pen and paper to begin another work that is
already, though unfinished, a great intellectual and spiritual contribution to man's treasure.*

*A few pages beyond the present selection he and his wife are seen
on a smallish ship being taken, prisoners, to an internment camp in
Europe. They are confined to a cabin except when a steward "at
certain appointed hours took us on deck. Since writing was impos-*

*sible, I filled up my time with learning by heart some of Bach's
fugues, and Widor's Sixth Organ Symphony." Was there a piano?
Quite unlikely, but no word. Then how? To those who have seen
him memorizing music and practicing it—mind, hands and feet—
with no instrument at all, the explanation is unforgettable and
amazing. But to his readers, not a word. One just knows again that
misfortune was opportunity, and opportunity meant progress.*

*To one who reads in some such fashion the selection below and
others of Schweitzer's "autobiographical" writings, the him and how
may seem unhappily veiled. But the why and whither which these
writings reveal will reveal also the realities that are Schweitzer.*

DR. EMORY ROSS

****

Out of my Life and Thought

MY WIFE and I had now completed our second dry season in Africa,
and were beginning to sketch out plans for going home at the opening of the third, when on August 5th, 1914, the news came that war
had broken out in Europe. On the evening of that very day we
were informed that we must consider ourselves to be prisoners of
war; we might, indeed, for the present remain in our own house,
but we must stop all intercourse with either white people or natives,
and obey unconditionally the regulations of the black soldiers who
were assigned us as guards. One of the missionaries and his wife,
who like ourselves were Alsatians, were also interned at the Lambaréné mission-station.

The only thing about the war which the natives understood at
first was that it was all over with the timber trade, and that all
commodities had become dearer. It was only later, when many of
them were transported to Cameroon to serve as carriers for the
active forces, that they began to understand what the war really
meant.

As soon as it became known that of the white men who used to
live on the Ogowe ten had already fallen, an old savage remarked:
"What, so many men killed already in this war! Why don't their
tribes meet to talk out the palaver? How can they ever pay for all
these dead men?" For in native warfare those who fall, whether
among the conquerors or the conquered, have to be paid for by the

opposite side. This same savage expressed the criticism that Europeans kill each other merely out of cruelty, because of course they don't want to eat the dead.

That white people were making prisoners of other whites and putting them under the authority of black soldiers was something incomprehensible to the natives. What a torrent of abuse my black guards came in for from the people of the neighbouring villages because they thought they were "the Doctor's masters."

When I was forbidden to work in the Hospital, I thought at first that I would proceed to the completion of my book on St. Paul. But another subject at once forced itself upon me, one which I had had in my mind for years, and which the war was now making a real live issue: the problem of our civilization. So on the second day of my internment, still quite amazed at being able to sit down at my writing-table early in the morning as in the days before I took up medicine, I set to work on the Philosophy of Civilization.

My first incitement to take up this subject I had received in the summer of 1899 at the house of the Curtius family in Berlin. Hermann Grimm and others were conversing there one evening about a sitting of the Academy from which they had just come, when suddenly one of them—I forget which it was—came out with: "Why, we are all of us just nothing but 'Epigoni'!"* It struck home with me, like a flash of lightning, because it put into words what I myself felt.

As early as my first years at the University I had begun to feel misgivings about the opinon that mankind is constantly developing in the direction of progress. My impression was that the fire of its ideals was burning low without anyone noticing it or troubling about it. On a number of occasions I had to acknowledge that public opinion did not reject with indignation inhumane ideas which were publicly disseminated, but accepted them, and that it approved of, as opportune, inhumane courses of action taken by governments and nations. Even for what was just and expedient as well there seemed to me to be only a luke-warm zeal available. From a number of signs I had to infer the growth of a peculiar intellectual and spiritual fatigue in this generation which is so proud of what it has accomplished. It seemed as if I heard its members arguing to each other that their previous hopes for the future of mankind had

---

* *A Latin word used of the generation following those who lived in a great age; inheritors of a great past. The contemporaries of James I may be called Epigoni of the great Elizabethans*—TRANSLATOR'S NOTE.

been pitched too high, and that it was becoming necessary to limit oneself to striving for what was attainable. The slogan which was given out for all countries, *Realpolitik,* meant the approbation of a short-sighted nationalism, and compromises with forces and tendencies which had been resisted hitherto as hostile to progress. One of the clearest indications of decline for me was the fact that superstition, which had hitherto been banished from educated circles, was again thought fit for admission to society.

When about the end of the century men began to take a retrospective review of every field of human activity in order to determine and fix the value of their achievements, this was done with an optimism which to me was incomprehensible. It seemed to be assumed everywhere not only that we had made progress in inventions and knowledge, but also that in the intellectual and ethical spheres we lived and moved at a height which we had never before reached, and from which we should never decline. My own impression was that in our mental and spiritual life we were not only below the level of past generations, but were in many respects only living on their achievements . . . and that not a little of this heritage was beginning to melt away in our hands.

And now—here was someone giving expression to the criticism which I myself had silently and half unconsciously passed upon our age! After that evening at Professor Curtius's house I was always, along with my other work, inwardly occupied with another book, which I entitled *Wir Epigonen* ("We Inheritors of a Past"). I often put before friends the thoughts contained in it, but they usually took them as just interesting paradoxes and manifestations of a *fin-de-siècle* pessimism. After that I kept my ideas strictly to myself, and only in sermons allowed my doubts about our civilization and our spirituality to find expression.

And now war was raging as a result of the downfall of civilization.

"We Inheritors of a Past," then, had in reality no longer any meaning. The book had been conceived as a criticism of civilization. It was meant to demonstrate its decline and to draw attention to the accompanying dangers. But if the catastrophe had already come about, what good was deliberation about the causes, which were now patent to everyone?

The book which had thus become out of date I thought of writing for my own sake. Could I be certain that the pages would not be taken from a prisoner of war? And was there any prospect of my seeing Europe again?

In this attitude of entire detachment I began the work and went on with it when I was again allowed to go about and devote myself to the sick. For at the end of November we were released from our internment, thanks to Widor's exertions, as I afterwards learnt. Even before that the order which kept me away from the sick had proved incapable of enforcement. White and black alike had protested against being deprived without any perceivable reason of the services of the only doctor for hundreds of miles around. The District Commandant had consequently found himself compelled to give now to one, now to another, a note for my guards, telling them to let the bearer see me because he needed my help.

But when I resumed my medical activities in comparative freedom, I still found time to occupy myself with the book on civilization. Many a night did I sit at it, thinking and writing with deepest emotion as I thought of those who were lying in the trenches.

At the beginning of the summer of 1915 I awoke from a sort of stupor. Why only criticism of civilization? Why content myself with analysing ourselves as *Epigoni*? Why not go on to something constructive?

So now I began a search for the knowledge and convictions to which we must refer the will to civilization and the power to realize it. "We Inheritors of a Past" expanded into a work dealing with the restoration of civilization.

As I worked I became clear about the connexion between civilization and the world-view (*Weltanschauung*), and I recognized that the catastrophe of civilization started from a catastrophe of world-view.

The ideals of true civilization had become powerless, because the idealistic world-view in which they are rooted has been gradually lost to us. All the happenings which come about within nations and within mankind as a whole arise out of spiritual causes which are contained in the prevailing world-view.

But what is civilization?

We may take as the essential element in civilization the ethical perfecting of the individual and of society as well. But at the same time, every spiritual and every material step in advance has a significance for civilization. The will to civilization is then the universal will to progress which is conscious of the ethical as the highest value for all. In spite of the great importance we attach to the triumphs of knowledge and achievement, it is nevertheless obvious that only a humanity which is striving after ethical ends can in full measure share in the blessings brought by material progress and become master of the dangers which accompany it. To the generation which had adopted a belief in an immanent power of progress realizing itself, in some measure, naturally and automatically, and which thought that it no longer needed any ethical ideals but could advance to its goal by means of knowledge and achievement alone, terrible proof was being given by its present position of the error into which it had sunk.

The only possible way out of the present chaos is for us to adopt a world-view which will bring us once more under the control of the ideals of true civilization which are contained in it.

But what is the nature of the world-view on which the universal will to progress and the ethical alike are founded and in which they are linked together each with the other?

It consists in an ethical affirmation of the world and of life.

What is world- and life-affirmation?

To us Europeans and to people of European descent everywhere the will to progress is something so natural and so much a matter of course that it never occurs to us to recognize that it is rooted in a world-view, and springs from an act of the spirit. But if we look about us in the world, we see at once that what is to us such a matter of course is in reality anything but that. To Indian thought all effort directed to triumphs in knowledge and power and to the improvement of man's outer life and of society as a whole is mere folly. It teaches that the only sensible line of conduct for a man is to withdraw entirely into himself and to concern himself solely with the deepening of his inner life. He has nothing to do with what may become of human society and of mankind. The deepening of one's inner life, as Indian thought interprets it, means that a man surrenders himself to the thought of "no more will to live," and by abstention from action and by every sort of life denial reduces his earthly existence to a condition of being which has no content beyond a waiting for the cessation of being.

It is interesting to trace the origin of this idea, so contrary to nature, of world and life denial. It had at first nothing whatever to do with any world-view, but was a magical conception of the Indian priests of early times. These believed that by detachment from the world and from life they could become in some measure supernatural beings, and obtain power over the gods. In accordance with this idea arises the custom that the Brahmin, after living part of his life in the normal way and founding a family, terminates his life in complete renunciation of the world.

In the course of time this world- and life-negation which originally formed the Brahmin's privilege was developed into a world-view which claimed to be valid for men as such.

It depends on the world-view, then, whether there is any will-to-progress or not. The world-view of world- and life-negation excludes it; that of world- and life-affirmation demands it. Among primitive and half-primitive peoples too, whose unformed world-view has not yet reached the problem of world affirmation or negation, there is no will to progress. Their ideal is the simplest life with the least possible trouble.

Even we Europeans have only in the course of time and through a change in our world-view arrived at our will to progress. In antiquity and in the Middle Ages there was nothing more than attempts at it. Greek thinking does try to reach a world-view of world- and life-affirmation, but it fails in the attempt and ends in resignation. The world-view of the Middle Ages is determined by the ideas of primitive Christianity as brought into harmony with Greek metaphysics. It is fundamentally world and life negating because the interest of that stage of Christianity was concentrated on a supersensible world. All that in the Middle Ages made itself felt as world- and life-affirmation is a fruit of the active ethic contained in the preaching of Jesus and of the creative forces of the fresh and unspoilt new peoples on whom Christianity had imposed a world-view which was in contradiction to their nature.

Then little by little the world- and life-affirmation that was already germinating among the peoples formed as a result of the *Völkerwanderung* (the Great Migration) begins to manifest itself. The Renaissance proclaims its rejection of the world and life negating world-view of the Middle Ages. And an ethical character is given to this new world- and life-affirmation by its taking over from Christianity the ethic of love taught by Jesus. This, as an ethic of activity, is strong enough to throw off the world-view of life- and world-negation in which it arose, to unite itself with the new world- and life-affirmation, and thereby to reach the ideal of realizing a spiritual and ethical world within the natural world.

The striving for material and spiritual progress, then, which characterizes the peoples of modern Europe, has its source in the world-view to which these peoples have come. As a result of the Renaissance and the spiritual and religious movements bound up with it, men have entered on a new relation to themselves and to the world, and this has aroused in them a need to create by their own activities spiritual and material values which shall help to a higher development of individuals and of mankind. It is not the case that the man of modern Europe is enthusiastic for progress because he may hope to get some personal advantage from it. He is less concerned about his own condition than about the happiness which he hopes will be the lot of coming generations. Enthusiasm for progress has taken possession of him. Impressed by his great experience of finding the world revealed to him as constituted and maintained by forces which carry out a definite design, he himself wills to become an active, purposeful force in the world. He looks with confidence towards new and better times which shall dawn for mankind, and learns by experience that the ideals which are held and acted upon by the mass of people do win power over circumstances and remould them.

It is on his will to material progress, acting in union with the will to ethical progress, that the foundations of modern civilization are being laid.

There is an essential relationship between the modern European world-view of ethical world- and life-affirmation and those of Zarathustra and of Chinese thought, as the latter meets us in the writings of Kungtse (Confucius), Mengtse (Mencius), Mitse (Nicius), and the other great ethical thinkers of China. In each of these we can see the striving to remould the circumstances of peoples and of mankind with the intention of progress, even if the efforts are not so powerful as those of modern Europe. Within the region influenced by the religion of Zarathustra and in China, there were actually established, as in Europe, civilizations which met the demands of an ethical world- and life-affirmation. But each met with a tragic end. The neo-Persian civilization of the Zarathustran world-view was blotted out by Islam. Chinese civilization is hampered in its natural development and threatened with decay by the pressure exerted upon it by European ideas and problems, and by confusion wrought in the country's political and economic condition.

In modern European thought there is being enacted a tragedy, in that by a slow but irresistible process the bonds originally existing between world- and life-affirmation and the ethical are becoming slack and are finally being severed. The result that we are coming to is that European humanity is being guided by a will-to-progress that has become merely external and has lost its bearings.

World- and life-affirmation can produce of itself only a partial and imperfect civilization. Only if it becomes inward and ethical can the will-to-progress which results from it possess the requisite insight to distinguish the valuable from the less valuable and strive after a civilization which does not consist only in achievements of knowledge and power, but before all else will make men, both individually and collectively, more spiritual and more ethical.

But how could it come about that the modern world-view of world- and life-affirmation, ethical as it was originally, changed and became non-ethical?

The only possible explanation is that it was not really founded on thought. The thought out of which it arose was noble and enthusiastic but not deep. The intimate connexion of the ethical with world- and life-affirmation was for it a matter of feeling and experience rather than of proof. It took the side of world- and life-affirmation and of the ethical, without having penetrated their inner nature and their inward connexion.

This noble and valuable world-view, then, being rooted in belief rather than in thought which penetrated to the real nature of things, was bound to wither and lose its power over the minds of men. All subsequent thinking about the problems of ethics and of the relation of man to this world could not but expose the weak points in this world-view, and thereby help to hasten its decay. Its activity took effect in this direction even when its intention was to give support, for it never succeeded in replacing the inadequate foundation by one that was adequate. Again and again the new foundations and the underpinning masonry which it had taken in hand showed themselves too weak to support the building.

Thanks to my apparently abstract, yet absolutely practical thinking about the connexion of civilization with world-view, I had come to see the decay of civilization as a result of a growing impotence in the traditional modern world-view of ethical world- and life-affirmation, an impotence which there was no arresting. It had become clear to me that, like so many other people, I had clung to that world-view from inner necessity, without troubling at all about how far it could really be proved by thought.

I had got so far during the summer of 1915. But what was to come next?

Was the difficulty soluble which till now had seemed insoluble? Or had we to regard the world-view through which alone civilization is possible as an illusion within us which never ceases to stir our hearts yet never really gets dominion over us?

To continue holding it up to our generation as something to be believed seemed to me foolish and hopeless. Only if it offers itself to us as something desired from the depth of thought can it become spiritually our own.

At bottom I remained convinced that the mutual connexion between world- and life-affirmation and the ethical, declared to belong to that world-view which it had been found hitherto impossible to carry out fully, had come from a presentiment of truth. So it was necessary to undertake to grasp as a necessity of thought by fresh, simple, and sincere thinking the truth which had hitherto been only suspected and believed in although so often proclaimed as proved.

In undertaking this I seemed to myself to be like a man who has to build a new and better boat to replace a rotten one in which he can no longer venture to trust himself to the sea, and yet does not know how to begin.

For months on end I lived in a continual state of mental excitement. Without the least success I let my thought be concentrated, even all through my daily work at the hospital, on the real nature of world- and life-affirmation and of ethics, and on the question of what they have in common. I was wandering about in a thicket in which no path was to be found. I was leaning with all my might against an iron door which would not yield.

All that I had learnt from philosophy about ethics left me in the lurch. The conceptions of the Good which it had offered were all so lifeless, so unelemental, so narrow, and so destitute of content that it was quite impossible to bring them into union with world- and life-affirmation. Moreover philosophy could be said never to have concerned itself with the problem of the connexion between civilization and world-view. The modern world- and life-affirmation had become to it such a matter of course that it had felt no need for coming to clear ideas about it.

To my surprise I had also to establish the fact, that the central province of philosophy, into which meditation about civilization and world-view had led me, was practically unexplored land. Now from this point, now from that, I tried to penetrate to its interior, but again and again I had to give up the attempt. I was already exhausted and disheartened. I saw, indeed, the conception needed before me, but I could not grasp it and give it expression.

While in this mental condition I had to undertake a longish journey on the river. I was staying with my wife on the coast at Cape Lopez for the sake of her health—it was in September 1915—when I was summoned to visit Madame Pelot, the ailing wife of a missionary, at N'Gômô, about 160 miles upstream. The only means of conveyance I could find was a small steamer, towing an over-laden barge, which was on the point of starting. Except myself, there were only natives on board, but among them was Emil Ogouma, my friend from Lambaréné. Since I had been in too much of a hurry to provide myself with enough food for the journey, they let me share the contents of their cooking-pot. Slowly we crept upstream, laboriously feeling—it was the dry season—for the channels between the sandbanks. Lost in thought I sat on the deck of the barge, struggling to find the elementary and universal conception of the ethical which I had not discovered in any philosophy. Sheet after sheet I covered with disconnected sentences, merely to keep myself concentrated on the problem. Late on the third day, at the very moment when, at sunset, we were making our way through a herd of hippopotamuses, there flashed upon my mind, unforeseen and unsought, the phrase, "Reverence for Life." The iron door had yielded: the path in the thicket had become visible. Now I had found my way to the idea in which world- and life-affirmation and ethics are contained side by side! Now I knew that the world-view of ethical world- and life-affirmation, together with its ideals of civilization, is founded in thought.

What is Reverence for Life, and how does it arise in us?

If man wishes to reach clear notions about himself and his relation to the world, he must ever again and again be looking away from the manifold, which is the product of his thought and knowledge, and reflect upon the first, the most immediate, and the continually given fact of his own consciousness. Only if he starts from this can he arrive at a thinking world-view.

Descartes makes thinking start from the sentence "I think; so I must exist" (*Cogito, ergo sum*), and with his beginning thus chosen he finds himself irretrievably on the road to the abstract. Out of this empty, artificial act of thinking there can result, of course, nothing which bears on the relation of man to himself, and to the universe. Yet in reality the most immediate act of consciousness has some content. To think means to think something. The most immediate fact of man's consciousness is the assertion: "I am life which wills to live, in the midst of life which wills to live," and it is as will-to-live in the midst of will-to-live that man conceives himself during every moment that he spends in meditating on himself and the world around him.

As in my will-to-live there is ardent desire for further life and for the mysterious exaltation of the will-to-live which we call pleasure, while there is fear of destruction and of that mysterious depreciation of the will-to-live which we call pain: so too are these in the will-to-live around me, whether it can express itself to me, or remains dumb.

Man has now to decide what his relation to his will-to-live shall be. He can deny it. But if he bids his will-to-live change into will-not-to-live, as is done in Indian and indeed in all pessimistic thought, he involves himself in self-contradiction. He raises to the position of his world and life view something unnatural, something which is in itself untrue, and which cannot be carried to completion. Indian thought, and Schopenhauer's also, is full of inconsistencies because it cannot help making concessions time after time to the will-to-live which persists in spite of all world and life denial, though it will not admit that the concessions are really such. Negation of the will-to-live is self-consistent only if it is really willing actually to put an end to physical existence.

If man affirms his will-to-live, he acts naturally and honestly. He confirms an act which has already been accomplished in his instinctive thought by repeating it in his conscious thought. The beginning of thought, a beginning which continually repeats itself, is that man does not simply accept his existence as something given, but experiences it as something unfathomably mysterious. Life-affirmation is the spiritual act in which he ceases to live unreflectively and begins to devote himself to his life with reverence, in order to raise it to its true value. To affirm life is to deepen, to make more inward, and to exalt the will-to-live.

At the same time the man who has become a thinking being feels a compulsion to give to every will-to-live the same reverence for life that he gives to his own. He experiences that other life in his own. He accepts as being good: to preserve life, to promote life, to raise to its highest value life which is capable of development; and as being evil: to destroy life, to injure life, to repress life which is capable of development. This is the absolute, fundamental principle of the moral, and it is a necessity of thought.

The great fault of all ethics hitherto has been that they believed themselves to have to deal only with the relations of man to man. In reality, however, the question is what is his attitude to the world and all life that comes within his reach. A man is ethical only when life, as such, is sacred to him, that of plants and animals as that of his fellow-men, and when he devotes himself helpfully to all life that is in need of help. Only the universal ethic of the feeling of responsibility in an ever-widening sphere for all that lives—only that ethic can be founded in thought. The ethic of the relation of man to man is not something apart by itself: it is only a particular relation which results from the universal one.

The ethic of Reverence for Life, therefore, comprehends within itself everything that can be described as love, devotion, and sympathy whether in suffering, joy, or effort.

The world, however, offers us the horrible drama of Will-to-Live divided against itself. One existence holds its own at the cost of another: one destroys another. Only in the thinking man has the Will-to-Live become conscious of other will-to-live, and desirous of solidarity with it. This solidarity, however, he cannot completely bring about, because man is subject to the puzzling and horrible law of being obliged to live at the cost of other life, and to incur again and again the guilt of destroying and injuring life. But as an ethical being he strives to escape whenever possible from this necessity, and as one who has become enlightened and merciful to put a stop to this disunion *(Selbstentzweiung)* of the Will-to-Live so far as the influence of his own existence reaches. He thirsts to be permitted to preserve his humanity, and to be able to bring to other existences release from their sufferings.

The Reverence for Life, therefore, which has arisen in the thinking Will-to-Live, contains world- and life-affirmation and the ethical fused together. Its aim is to create values, and to realize progress of different kinds which shall serve the material, spiritual, and ethical development of men and mankind. While the unthinking modern world- and life-affirmation stumbles about with its ideals of power won by discovery and invention, the thinking world- and life-affirmation sets up the spiritual and ethical perfecting of mankind as the highest ideal, and an ideal from which alone all other ideals of progress get their real value.

Through ethical world- and life-affirmation we reach a power of reflection which enables us to distinguish between what is essential in civilization and what is not. The stupid arrogance of thinking ourselves civilized loses its power over us. We venture to face the truth that with so much progress in knowledge and power true civilization has become not easier but harder. The problem of the mutual relationship between the spiritual and the material dawns upon us. We know that we all have to struggle with circumstances to preserve our humanity, and that we must be anxiously concerned to turn once more towards hope of victory the almost hopeless struggle which many carry on to preserve their humanity amid unfavourable social circumstances.

A deepened, ethical will to progress which springs from thought will lead us back, then, out of uncivilization and its misery to true civilization. Sooner or later there must dawn the true and final Renaissance which will bring peace to the world.

Now there stood out clearly before my mind the plan of the whole Philosophy of Civilization. It divided itself as if automatically into four parts: (1) On the present lack of civilization and its causes; (2) a discussion of the idea of Reverence for Life in connexion with the attempts made in the past by European philosophy to provide foundations for the world-view of ethical world- and life-affirmation; (3) exposition of the world-view of Reverence for Life; (4) concerning the civilized state.

The writing of the second part, the description of European philosophy's tragic struggle for ethical world- and life-affirmation, was forced upon me by the inward necessity I felt for getting to know the problem I was dealing with in its historical development, and of comprehending the solution I offered as the synthesis of all previous ones. That I once more succumbed to this temptation I have never regretted. Through my coming to an understanding of other thought, my own became clearer.

Some of the philosophical works needed for this historical task I had by me. What others I needed were sent to me by J. Strohl, Professor of Zoology at Zürich, and his wife. And the well-known Bach singer, Robert Kaufmann of Zürich, whom I had so often accompanied on the organ, made it his business, with the help of the Office des Internés Civils at Geneva, to keep me, as well as might be, in touch with the world.

Without haste I put on paper, one after another, rough drafts in which I collected and sifted the material without reference to the structure of the treatise already planned. Along with that I began to write out single sections in full. I felt it every day to be a great mercy that while others had to be killing, I could not only save life but even work as well to bring nearer the coming of the Era of Peace.

Fortunately my supply of drugs and bandages did not give out, for by one of the last boats which arrived before the outbreak of war I had received a big supply of all necessary things.

The rainy season of 1916–17 we spent on the coast, because my wife's health had suffered from the sultry air of Lambaréné. A timber merchant placed at our disposal a house at Chienga near

Cape Lopez at the mouth of one of the branches of the Ogowe. It was the home of the man who looked after his timber-rafts, but as a consequence of the war it now stood empty. In return for his kindness I joined those of his native labourers who were still on the spot in the work of rolling on to dry land the many okoume logs which had been already tied together in rafts, so that during the long interval which might elapse before cargoes could again be shipped to Europe they should not fall victims to the bore-worm *(Teredo navalis)*. This heavy work—we often needed hours to roll up on to the shore one of these logs weighing from two to three tons—was only possible at high tide. When the tide was out, I sat at my Philosophy of Civilization, so far as my time was not claimed by patients.

—Translated by C. T. Campion

ALBERT EINSTEIN

****

The four excerpts which follow were taken from Dr. Albert Einstein's latest collection of essays which appeared early in 1950: Out of My Later Years. *The distinguished physicist thought they needed no personal introduction.*

****

Science and Life

I. SOLITUDE

OF WHAT IS SIGNIFICANT in one's own existence one is hardly aware, and it certainly should not bother the other fellow. What does a fish know about the water in which he swims all his life?

The bitter and the sweet come from the outside, the hard from within, from one's own efforts. For the most part I do the thing which my own nature drives me to do. It is shameful to earn so much respect and love for it. Arrows of hate have been shot at me too; but they never hit me, because somehow they belonged to another world, with which I have no connection whatsoever.

I live in that solitude which is painful in youth, but delicious in the years of maturity.

II. TEN FATEFUL YEARS

READING ONCE AGAIN the lines I wrote* almost ten years ago, I receive two strangely contrasting impressions. What I wrote then still seems essentially as true as ever; yet, it all seems curiously remote and strange. How can that be? Has the world changed so profoundly in ten years, or is it merely that I have grown ten years older, and my eyes see everything in a changed, dimmer light? What are ten years in the history of humanity? Must not all those forces that determine the life of man be regarded as constant compared

* *In a first volume of essays: these sections are taken from a second volume, published in 1950, embracing writings between 1934 and 194* '6

with such a trifling interval? Is my critical reason so susceptible that the physiological change in my body during those ten years has been able to influence my concept of life so deeply? It seems clear to me that such considerations cannot throw light upon a change in the emotional approach to the general problems of life. Nor may the reasons for this curious change be sought in my own external circumstances; for I know that these have always played a subordinate part in my thoughts and emotions.

No, something quite different is involved. In these ten years confidence in the stability, yes, even the very basis for existence, of human society has largely vanished. One senses not only a threat to man's cultural heritage, but also that a lower value is placed upon all that one would like to see defended at all costs.

Conscious man, to be sure, has at all times been keenly aware that life is an adventure, that life must, forever, be wrested from death. In part the dangers were external: one might fall downstairs and break one's neck, lose one's livelihood without fault, be condemned though innocent, or ruined by calumny. Life in human society meant dangers of all sorts; but these dangers were chaotic in nature, subject to chance. Human society, as a whole, seemed stable. Measured by the ideals of taste and morals it was decidedly imperfect. But, all in all, one felt at home with it and, apart from the many kinds of accidents, comparatively safe in it. One accepted its intrinsic qualities as a matter of course, as the air one breathed. Even standards of virtue, aspiration, and practical truth were taken for granted as an inviolable heritage, common to all civilized humanity.

To be sure, the World War had already shaken this feeling of security. The sanctity of life vanished and the individual was no longer able to do as he pleased and to go where he liked. The lie was raised to the dignity of a political instrument. The War was, however, widely regarded as an external event, hardly or not at all as the result of man's conscious planful action. It was thought of as an interruption of man's normal life from the outside, universally considered unfortunate and evil. The feeling of security in regard to human aims and values remained, for the main part, unshaken.

The subsequent development is sharply marked by political events that are not as far-reaching as the less easily grasped socio-psychological background. First a brief, promising step forward characterized by the creation of the League of Nations through the grandiose initiative of Wilson, and the establishment of a system of collective security among the nations. Then the formation of Fascist states, attended by a series of broken pacts and undisguised acts of violence against humanity and against weaker nations. The system of collective security collapsed like a house of cards—a collapse the consequences of which cannot be measured even today. It was a manifestation of weakness of character and lack of responsibility on the part of the leaders in the affected countries, and of shortsighted selfishness in the democracies—those that still remain outwardly intact—which prevented any vigorous counterattack.

Things grew even worse than a pessimist of the deepest dye would have dared prophesy. In Europe to the East of the Rhine free exercise of the intellect exists no longer, the population is terrorized by gangsters who have seized power, and youth is poisoned by systematic lies. The pseudo-success of political adventurers has dazzled the rest of the world; it becomes apparent everywhere that this generation lacks the strength and force which enabled previous generations to win, in painful struggle and at great sacrifice, the political and individual freedom of man.

Awareness of this state of affairs overshadows every hour of my present existence, while ten years ago it did not yet occupy my thoughts. It is this that I feel so strongly in re-reading the words written in the past.

And yet I know that, all in all, man changes but little, even though prevailing notions make him appear in a very different light at different times, and even though current trends like the present bring him unimaginable sorrow. Nothing of all that will remain but a few pitiful pages in the history books, briefly picturing to the youth of future generations the follies of its ancestors.

III. THE LAWS OF SCIENCE AND THE LAWS OF ETHICS

SCIENCE searches for relations which are thought to exist independently of the searching individual. This includes the case where man himself is the subject. Or the subject of scientific statements may be concepts created by ourselves, as in mathematics. Such concepts are not necessarily supposed to correspond to any objects in the outside world. However, all scientific statements and laws have one characteristic in common: they are "true or false" (adequate or inadequate). Roughly speaking, our reaction to them is "yes" or "no."

The scientific way of thinking has a further characteristic. The concepts which it uses to build up its coherent systems are not expressing emotions. For the scientist, there is only "being," but no wishing, no valuing, no good, no evil; no goal. As long as we remain within the realm of science proper, we can never meet with a sentence of the type: "Thou shalt not lie." There is something like a Puritan's restraint in the scientist who seeks truth: he keeps away from everything voluntaristic or emotional. Incidentally, this trait is the result of a slow development, peculiar to modern Western thought.

From this it might seem as if logical thinking were irrelevant for ethics. Scientific statements of facts and relations, indeed cannot produce ethical directives. However, ethical directives can be made rational and coherent by logical thinking and empirical knowledge. If we can agree on some fundamental ethical propositions, then other ethical propositions can be derived from them, provided that the original premises are stated with sufficient precision. Such ethical premises play a similar role in ethics, to that played by axioms in mathematics.

This is why we do not feel at all that it is meaningless to ask such questions as: "Why should we not lie?" We feel that such questions are meaningful because in all discussions of this kind some ethical premises are tacitly taken for granted. We then feel satisfied when we succeed in tracing back the ethical directive in question to these basic premises. In the case of lying this might perhaps be done in some way such as this: Lying destroys confidence in the statements of other people. Without such confidence, social cooperation is made impossible or at least difficult. Such cooperation, however, is essential to make human life possible and tolerable. This means that the rule "Thou shalt not lie" has been traced back to the demands: "Human life shall be preserved" and "Pain and sorrow shall be lessened as much as possible."

But what is the origin of such ethical axioms? Are they arbitrary? Are they based on mere authority? Do they stem from experiences of men and are they conditioned indirectly by such experiences?

For pure logic all axioms are arbitrary, including the axioms of ethics. But they are by no means arbitrary from a psychological and genetic point of view. They are derived from our inborn tendencies to avoid pain and annihilation, and from the accumulated emotional reaction of individuals to the behavior of their neighbors.

It is the privilege of man's moral genius, impersonated by inspired individuals, to advance ethical axioms which are so comprehensive and so well founded that men will accept them as grounded in the vast mass of their individual emotional experiences. Ethical axioms are found and tested not very differently from the axioms of science. Truth is what stands the test of experience.

IV. THE MENACE OF MASS DESTRUCTION

EVERYONE is aware of the difficult and menacing situation in which human society—shrunk into one community with a common fate—finds itself, but only a few act accordingly. Most people go on living their every-day life: half frightened, half indifferent, they behold the ghostly tragi-comedy that is being performed on the international stage before the eyes and ears of the world. But on that stage, on which the actors under the floodlights play their ordained parts, our fate of tomorrow, life or death of the nations, is being decided.

It would be different if the problem were not one of things made by Man himself, such as the atomic bomb and other means of mass destruction equally menacing all peoples. It would be different, for instance, if an epidemic of bubonic plague were threatening the entire world. In such a case conscientious and expert persons would be brought together and they would work out an intelligent plan to combat the plague. After having reached agreement upon the right ways and means, they would submit their plan to the governments. Those would hardly raise serious objections but rather agree speedily on the measures to be taken. They certainly would never think of trying to handle the matter in such a way that their own nation would be spared whereas the next one would be decimated.

But could not our situation be compared to one of a menacing epidemic? People are unable to view this situation in its true light, for their eyes are blinded by passion. General fear and anxiety create hatred and aggressiveness. The adaptation to warlike aims and activities has corrupted the mentality of man; as a result, intelligent, objective and humane thinking has hardly any effect and is even suspected and persecuted as unpatriotic.

There are, no doubt, in the opposite camps enough people of sound judgment and sense of justice who would be capable and eager to work out together a solution for the factual difficulties. But the efforts of such people are hampered by the fact that it is made impossible for them to come together for informal discussions. I am thinking of persons who are accustomed to the objective approach to a problem and who will not be confused by exaggerated nationalism or other passions. This forced separation of the people of both camps I consider one of the major obstacles for the achievement of an acceptable solution of the burning problem of international security.

As long as contact between the two camps is limited to the official negotiations I can see little prospect for an intelligent agreement being reached, especially since considerations of national prestige as well as the attempt to talk out of the window for the benefit of the masses are bound to make reasonable progress almost impossible. What one party suggests officially is for that reason alone suspected and even made unacceptable to the other. Also behind all official negotiations stands—though veiled—the threat of naked power. The official method can lead to success only after spade-work of an informal nature has prepared the ground; the conviction that a mutually satisfactory solution can be reached must be gained first; then the actual negotiations can get under way with a fair promise of success.

We scientists believe that what we and our fellow-men do or fail to do within the next few years will determine the fate of our civilization. And we consider it our task untiringly to explain this truth, to help people realize all that is at stake; and to work, not for appeasement, but for understanding and ultimate agreement between peoples and nations of different views.

HERMANN HESSE

✱✱✱

MONTAGNOLA, SWITZERLAND

I sent you back the ballot with my vote. If anything of my work should be published in THE WORLD'S BEST *I should propose* Innen und Aussen, *a story of 4,000 words, which I think to be a good representation of my kind of writing. . . . Up to now it has never been translated into English.*

H. HESSE

✱✱✱

Within and Without

THERE WAS ONCE a man by the name of Frederick; he devoted himself to intellectual pursuits and had a wide range of knowledge. But not all knowledge was the same to him, nor was any thought as good as any other: he loved a certain type of thinking, and disdained and abominated the others. What he loved and revered was logic—that so admirable method—and, in general, what he called "science."

"Twice two is four," he used to say. "This I believe; and man must do his thinking on the basis of this truth."

He was not unaware, to be sure, that there were other sorts of thinking and knowledge; but they were not "science," and he held a low opinion of them. Although a freethinker, he was not intolerant of religion. Religion was founded on a tacit agreement among scientists. For several centuries their science had embraced nearly everything that existed on earth and was worth knowing, with the exception of one single province: the human soul. It had become a sort of custom, as time went on, to leave this to religion, and to tolerate its speculations on the soul, though without taking them seriously. Thus Frederick too was tolerant toward religion; but everything that he recognized as superstition was profoundly odious and repugnant to him. Alien, uncultured, and retarded peoples might occupy themselves with it; in remote antiquity there might have been mystical or magical thinking; but since the birth of

science and logic there was no longer any sense in making use of
these outmoded and dubious tools.

So he said and so he thought; and when traces of superstition
came to his attention he became angry and felt as if he had been
touched by something hostile.

It angered him most of all, however, if he found such traces
among his own sort, among educated men who were conversant
with the principles of scientific thinking. And nothing was more
painful and intolerable to him than that scandalous notion which
lately he had sometimes heard expressed and discussed even by men
of great culture—that absurd idea that "scientific thinking" was
possibly not a supreme, timeless, eternal, foreordained, and unassailable mode of thought, but merely one of many, a transient way
of thinking, not impervious to change and downfall. This irreverent,
destructive, poisonous notion was abroad—even Frederick could
not deny it; it had cropped up here and there as a result of the
distress throughout the world brought about by war, revolution, and
hunger, like a warning, like a white hand's ghostly writing on a
white wall.

The more Frederick suffered from the fact that this idea existed
and could so deeply distress him, the more passionately he assailed
it and those whom he suspected of secretly believing in it. So far
only a very few from among the truly educated had openly and
frankly professed their belief in this new doctrine, a doctrine that
seemed destined, should it gain in circulation and power, to destroy
all spiritual values on earth and call forth chaos. Well, matters had
not reached that point yet, and the scattered individuals who openly
embraced the idea were still so few in number that they could be
considered oddities and crotchety, peculiar fellows. But a drop of
the poison, an emanation of that idea, could be perceived first on
this side, then on that. Among the people and the half-educated no
end of new doctrines could be found anyway, esoteric doctrines,
sects, and discipleships; the world was full of them; everywhere one
could scent out superstition, mysticism, spiritualistic cults, and other
mysterious forces, which it was really necessary to combat, but to
which science, as if from a private feeling of weakness, had for
the present given free rein.

One day Frederick went to the house of one of his friends, with
whom he had often studied. It so happened that he had not seen
this friend for some time. While he was climbing the stairs of the
house he tried to recall when and where it was that he had last
been in his friend's company; but much as he could pride himself

on his good memory for other things he could not remember. Because of this he fell imperceptibly into a certain vexation and ill humor, from which, as he stood before his friend's door, he was obliged forcibly to free himself.

Hardly had he greeted Erwin, his friend, when he noticed on his genial countenance a certain, as it were forbearing, smile, which it seemed to him he had never seen there before. And hardly had he seen this smile, which despite its friendliness he at once felt to be somehow mocking or hostile, when he immediately remembered what he had just been searching his memory for in vain—his last previous meeting with Erwin. He remembered that they had parted then without having quarreled, to be sure, but yet with a sense of inner discord and dissatisfaction, because Erwin, as it had seemed to him, had given far too little support to his attacks at that time on the realm of superstition.

It was strange. How could he have forgotten that entirely? And now he also knew that this was his only reason for not having sought out his friend for so long, merely this dissatisfaction, and that he had known this all the time, although he had invented for himself a host of other excuses for his repeated postponement of this visit.

Now they confronted one another; and it seemed to Frederick as if the little rift of that day had meantime tremendously widened. He felt that in this moment something was lacking between him and Erwin that had always been there before, an aura of solidarity, of spontaneous understanding—indeed, even of affection. Instead of these there was a vacuum. They greeted each other; spoke of the weather, their acquaintances, their health; and—God knows why! —with every word Frederick had the disquieting sensation that he was not quite understanding his friend, that his friend did not really know him, that his words were missing their mark, that they could find no common ground for a real conversation. Moreover Erwin still had that friendly smile on his face, which Frederick was beginning almost to hate.

During a pause in the laborious conversation Frederick looked about the studio he knew so well and saw, pinned loosely on the wall, a sheet of paper. This sight moved him strangely and awakened ancient memories; for he recalled that, long ago in their student years, this had been a habit of Erwin's, a way he sometimes chose of keeping a thinker's saying or a poet's verse fresh in his mind. He stood up and went to the wall to read the paper.

There, in Erwin's beautiful script, he read the words: "Nothing is without, nothing is within; for what is without is within."

Blanching, he stood motionless for a moment. There it was! There he stood face to face with what he feared! At another time he would have let this leaf of paper pass, would have tolerated it charitably as a whim, as a harmless foible to which anyone was entitled, perhaps as a trifling sentimentality calling for indulgence. But now it was different. He felt that these words had not been set down for the sake of a fleeting poetic mood; it was not a vagary that Erwin had returned after so many years to a practice of his youth. What stood written here, as an avowal of his friend's concern at the moment, was mysticism! Erwin was unfaithful.

Slowly he turned to face him, whose smile was again radiant.

"Explain this to me!" he demanded.

Erwin nodded, brimming with friendliness.

"Haven't you ever read this saying?"

"Certainly!" Frederick cried. "If course I know it. It's mysticism, it's Gnosticism. It may be poetic, but—Well, anyway, explain the saying to me, and why it's hanging on your wall."

"Gladly," Erwin said. "The saying is a first introduction to an epistemology that I've been going into lately, and which has already brought me much happiness."

Frederick restrained his temper. He asked, "A new epistemology? Is there such a thing? And what's it called?"

"Oh," Erwin answered, "it's only new to me. It's already very old and venerable. It's called magic."

The word had been uttered. Profoundly astonished and startled by so candid a confession, Frederick, with a shudder, felt that he was confronted eye to eye with the arch-enemy, in the person of his friend. He did not know whether he was nearer rage or tears; the bitter feeling of irreparable loss possessed him. For a long time he remained silent.

Then, with a pretended derision in his voice, he began, "So now you want to become a magician?"

"Yes," Erwin replied unhesitatingly.

"A sort of sorcerer's apprentice, eh?"

"Certainly."

A clock could be heard ticking in the adjoining room, it was so quiet.

Then Frederick said, "This means, you know, that you are abandoning all fellowship with serious science, and hence all fellowship with me."

"I hope that is not so," Erwin answered. "But if that's the way it has to be, what else can I do?"

"What else can you do?" Frederick burst out. "Why, break, break once and for all with this childishness, this wretched and contemptible belief in magic! That's what else you can do, if you want to keep my respect."

Erwin smiled a little, although he too no longer seemed cheerful.

"You speak as if," he said, so gently that through his quiet words Frederick's angry voice still seemed to be echoing about the room, "you speak as if that lay within my will, as if I had a choice, Frederick. That is not the case. I have no choice. It was not I that chose magic: magic chose me."

Frederick sighed deeply. "Then goodby," he said wearily, and stood up, without offering to shake hands.

"Not like that!" Erwin cried out. "No, you must not go from me like that. Pretend that one of us is lying on his deathbed—and that is so!—and that we must say farewell."

"But which of us, Erwin, is dying?"

"Today it is probably I, my friend. Whoever wishes to be born anew must be prepared to die."

Once more Frederick went up to the sheet of paper and read the saying about within and without.

"Very well," he said finally. "You are right, it won't do any good to part in anger. I'll do what you say; I'll pretend that one of us is lying on his deathbed. For that matter, I might be the one who is dying. Before I go I want to make a last request of you."

"I'm glad," Erwin said. "Tell me, what kindness can I show you on our leave-taking?"

"I repeat my first question, and this is also my request: explain this saying to me, as well as you can."

Erwin reflected a moment and then spoke:

"Nothing is without, nothing is within. You know the religious meaning of this: God is everywhere. He is in the spirit, and also in nature. All is divine, because God is all. Formerly this was called pantheism. Then the philosophic meaning: we are used to divorcing the within from the without in our thinking, but this is not necessary. Our spirit is capable of withdrawing behind the limits we have set for it, into the beyond. Beyond the pair of antitheses of which our world consists a new and different knowledge begins. . . . But, my dear friend, I must confess to you—since my thinking has changed there are no longer any unambiguous words and sayings for me: every word has tens and hundreds of meanings. And here what you fear begins—magic."

Frederick wrinkled his brow and was about to interrupt, but

Erwin looked at him disarmingly and continued, speaking more distinctly, "Let me give you an example. Take something of mine along with you, any object, and examine it a little from time to time. Soon the principle of the within and the without will reveal one of its many meanings to you."

He glanced about the room, took a small clay figurine from a wall shelf, and gave it to Frederick, saying:

"Take this with you as my parting gift. When this thing that I am now placing in your hands ceases to be outside you and is within you, come to me again! But if it remains outside you, the way it is now, forever, then this parting of yours from me shall also be forever!"

Frederick wanted to say a great deal more; but Erwin took his hand, pressed it, and bade him farewell with an expression that permitted no further conversation.

Frederick left; descended the stairs (how prodigiously long ago he had climbed them!); went through the streets to his home, the little earthen figure in his hand, perplexed and sick of heart. In front of his house he stopped, shook the fist fiercely for a moment in which he was clutching the figurine, and felt a great urge to smash the ridiculous thing to the ground. He did not do so; he bit his lip and entered the house. Never before had he been so agitated, so tormented by conflicting emotions.

He looked for a place for his friend's gift, and put the figure on the top of a bookcase. For the time being it stayed there.

Occasionally, as the days went by, he looked at it, brooding on it and on its origins, and pondering the meaning that this foolish thing was to have for him. It was a small figure of a man or a god or an idol, with two faces, like the Roman god Janus, modeled rather crudely of clay and covered with a burnt and somewhat cracked glaze. The little image looked coarse and insignificant; certainly it was not Roman or Greek workmanship; more likely it was the work of some backward, primitive race in Africa or the South Seas. The two faces, which were exactly alike, bore an apathetic, indolent, faintly grinning smile—it was downright ugly the way the little gnome squandered his stupid smile.

Frederick could not get used to the figure. It was totally unpleasant and offensive to him, it got in his way, it disturbed him. The very next day he took it down and put it on the stove, and a few days later moved it to a cupboard. Again and again it got in the path of his vision, as if it were forcing itself upon him; it laughed at him coldly and dull-wittedly, put on airs, demanded attention. After a few weeks he put it in the anteroom, between the photographs of Italy and the trivial little souvenirs which no one ever looked at. Now at least he saw the idol only when he was entering or leaving, and then he passed it quickly, without examining it more closely. But here too the thing still bothered him, though he did not admit this to himself.

With this shard, this two-faced monstrosity, vexation and torment had entered his life.

One day, months later, he returned from a short trip—he undertook such excursions now from time to time, as if something were driving him restlessly about; he entered his house, went through the anteroom, was greeted by the maid, and read the letters waiting for him. But he was ill at ease, as if he had forgotten something important; no book tempted him, no chair was comfortable. He began to rack his mind—what was the cause of this? Had he neglected something important? eaten something unsettling? In reflecting it occurred to him that this disturbing feeling had come over him as he had entered the apartment. He returned to the anteroom and involuntarily his first glance sought the clay figure.

A strange fright went through him when he did not see the idol. It had disappeared. It was missing. Had it walked away on its little crockery legs? Flown away? By magic?

Frederick pulled himself together, and smiled at his nervousness. Then he began quietly to search the whole room. When he found nothing he called the maid. She came, was embarrassed, and admitted at once that she had dropped the thing while cleaning up.

"Where is it?"

It was not there any more. It had seemed so solid, that little thing; she had often had it in her hands; and yet it had shattered to a hundred little pieces and splinters, and could not be fixed. She had taken the fragments to a glazier, who had simply laughed at her; and then she had thrown them away.

Frederick dismissed the maid. He smiled. That was perfectly all right with him. He did not feel bad about the idol, God knows. The abomination was gone; now he would have peace. If only he had knocked the thing to pieces that very first day! What he had suffered in all this time! How sluggishly, strangely, craftily, evilly, satanically that idol had smiled at him! Well, now that it was gone he could admit it to himself: he had feared it, truly and sincerely feared it, this earthen god. Was it not the emblem and symbol of everything that was repugnant and intolerable to him, everything that he had recognized all along as pernicious, inimical, and worthy of suppres-

sion—an emblem of all superstition, all darkness, all coercion of conscience and spirit? Did it not represent that ghastly power that one
sometimes felt raging in the bowels of the earth, that distant earthquake, that approaching extinction of culture, that looming chaos?
Had not this contemptible figure robbed him of his best friend—
nay, not merely robbed him, but made of the friend an enemy?
Well, now the thing was gone. Vanished. Smashed to pieces. Done
for. It was good so; it was much better than if he had destroyed
it himself.

So he thought, or said. And he went about his affairs as before.

But it was like a curse. Now, just when he had got more or less
used to that ridiculous figure, just when the sight of it in its usual
place on the anteroom table had gradually become a bit familiar
and unimportant to him, now its absence began to torment him!
Yes, he missed it every time he went through that room; all he
could see there was the empty spot where it had formerly stood, and
emptiness emanated from the spot and filled the room with strangeness.

Bad days and worse nights began for Frederick. He could no
longer go through the anteroom without thinking of the idol with
the two faces, missing it, and feeling that his thoughts were tethered
to it. This became an agonizing compulsion for him. And it was not
by any means simply on the occasions when he went through that
room that he was gripped by this compulsion—ah, no. Just as emptiness and desolation radiated from the now empty spot on the anteroom table, so this compulsive idea radiated within him, gradually
crowded all else aside, rankling and filling him with emptiness and
strangeness.

Again and again he pictured the figure with utmost distinctness,
just to make it clear to himself how preposterous it was to grieve its
loss. He could see it in all its stupid ugliness and barbarity, with its
vacuous yet crafty smile, with its two faces—indeed, as if under
duress, full of hatred and with his mouth drawn awry, he found
himself attempting to reproduce that smile. The question pestered
him whether the two faces were really exactly alike. Had not one of
them, perhaps only because of a little roughness or a crack in the
glaze, had a somewhat different expression? Something quizzical?
Something sphinxlike? And how peculiar the color of that glaze had
been! Green, and blue, and gray, but also red, were in it—a glaze
that he now kept finding often in other objects, in a window's reflection of the sun or in the mirrorings of a wet pavement.

He brooded a great deal on this glaze, at night too. It also struck him what a strange, foreign, ill-sounding, unfamiliar, almost malignant word "glaze" was. He analyzed the word, and once he even reversed the order of its letters. Then it read "ezalg." Now where the devil did this word get its sound from? He knew this word "ezalg," certainly he knew it; moreover, it was an unfriendly and bad word, a word with ugly and disturbing connotations. For a long while he tormented himself with this question. Finally he hit upon it: "ezalg" reminded him of a book that he had bought and read many years ago on a trip, and that had dismayed, plagued, and yet secretly fascinated him; it had been entitled *Princess Ezalka*. It was like a curse: everything connected with the figurine—the glaze, the blue, the green, the smile—signified hostility, tormenting and poisoning him. And how very peculiarly *he*, Erwin, his erstwhile friend, had smiled as he had given the idol into his hand! How very peculiarly, how very significantly, how very hostilely!

Frederick resisted manfully—and on many days not without success—the compulsive trend of his thoughts. He sensed the danger clearly: he did not want to go insane! No, it were better to die. Reason was necessary, life was not. And it occurred to him that perhaps *this* was magic, that Erwin, with the aid of that figure, had in some way enchanted him, and that he should fall as a sacrifice, as the defender of reason and science against these dismal powers. But if this were so, if he could even conceive of that as possible, then there *was* such a thing as magic, then there *was* sorcery. No, it were better to die!

A doctor recommended walks and baths; and sometimes in search of amusement, he spent an evening at an inn. But it helped very little. He cursed Erwin; he cursed himself.

One night, as he often did now, he retired early and lay restlessly awake in bed, unable to sleep. He felt unwell and uneasy. He wanted to meditate; he wanted to find solace, wanted to speak sentences of some sort to himself, good sentences, comforting, reassuring ones, something with the straightforward serenity and lucidity of the sentence, "Twice two is four." Nothing came to mind; but, in a state almost of lightheadedness, he mumbled sounds and syllables to himself. Gradually words formed on his lips, and several times, without being sensible of its meaning, he said the same short sentence to himself, which had somehow taken form in him. He muttered it to himself, as if it might stupefy him, as if he might grope his way along it, as along a parapet, to the sleep that eluded him, on the narrow, narrow path that skirted the abyss.

But suddenly, when he spoke somewhat louder, the words he was mumbling penetrated his consciousness. He knew them: they were, "Yes, now you are within me!" And instantly he knew. He knew what they meant—that they referred to the clay idol and that now, in this gray night hour, he had accurately and exactly fulfilled the prophecy Erwin had made on that unearthly day, that now the figure, which he had held contemptuously in his fingers then, was no longer outside him but within him! "For what is without is within."

Bounding up in a leap, he felt as if transfused with ice and fire. The world reeled about him, the planets stared at him insanely. He threw on some clothes, put on the light, left his house and ran in the middle of the night to Erwin's. There he saw a light burning in the studio window he knew so well; the door to the house was unlocked: everything seemed to be awaiting him. He rushed up the stairs. He walked unsteadily into Erwin's study, supported himself with trembling hands on the table. Erwin sat by the lamp, in its gentle light, contemplative, smiling.

Graciously Erwin arose. "You have come. That is good."

"Have you been expecting me?" Frederick whispered.

"I have been expecting you, as you know, from the moment you left here, taking my little gift with you. Has what I said then happened?"

"It has happened," Frederick said. "The idol is within me. I can't bear it any longer."

"Can I help you?" Erwin asked.

"I don't know. Do as you will. Tell me more of your magic! Tell me how the idol can get out of me again."

Erwin placed his hand on his friend's shoulder. He led him to an armchair and pressed him down in it. Then he spoke cordially to Frederick, smiling, in an almost brotherly tone of voice:

"The idol will come out of you again. Have trust in me. Have trust in yourself. You have learned to believe in it. Now learn to love it! It is within you, but it is still dead, it is still a phantom to you. Awaken it, speak to it, question it! For it is you yourself! Do not hate it any longer, do not fear it, do not torment it—how you have tormented this poor idol, who was yet you yourself! How you have tormented yourself!"

"Is this the way to magic?" Frederick asked. He sat deep in the chair, as if he had grown older, and his voice was low.

"This is the way," Erwin replied, "and perhaps you have already taken the most difficult step. You have found by experience: the without can become the within. You have been beyond the pair of antitheses. It seemed a hell to you; learn, my friend, it is heaven! For it is heaven that awaits you. Behold, this is magic: to interchange the without and the within, not by compulsion, not in anguish, as you have done it, but freely, voluntarily. Summon up the past, summon up the future: both are in you! Until today you have been the slave of the within. Learn to be its master. That is magic."

—*Translated by T. K. Brown, III*

SIGRID UNDSET

****

December 19, 1947
You asked me why I chose this* as representative of my writings:
"Because the book is less known than my historical novels, and
because it means much to me, and I think it is a piece of simple,
forward writing which cannot be interpreted otherwise than I did
intend."

SIGRID UNDSET

****

The Loss and the Healing

MAMMA came and told them one day that she had taken a house at Hvitsten for the rest of the summer vacation. Frida, her friend, had made them a present of the money for a stay in the country.

At the moment Ingvild was more shocked and ashamed than anything else. Accepting money from strangers was to her a thing unheard-of. Her mother must have seen it, for she said curtly: "Your father needs a change of air." So Ingvild shook off her feeling of repugnance as well as she could. Naturally she would like awfully to go into the country. Though she was concerned about her garden—how would it get on with no one to water it—?

Once more she enjoyed a time which was outside all other time. Looking back on it she thought of forest paths over which the smooth-worn roots of firs stretched their claws, and the pits between the roots were thick with old pine-needles. She remembered crevices running diagonally through rounded light-red rocks, in which grew scanty sun-scorched grass and flowers with silvery grey-green leaves reminding one of the sea. The paths ended in a scrap of shelly beach, and there they undressed and ran naked over the bare rocks, which burnt the soles of their feet. It was horrid to get entangled in the sea-weed which lay heaving, however calm the fjord might be—

---

* *From her autobiographical novel* The Longest Years. *Chosen before her death, June 10, 1949.*

841

but the spot was so secluded that they could bathe without wearing dresses. And that was so lovely, as you didn't even notice you were swimming—you could move about in the water just as naturally and unthinkingly as you could walk on dry land. They were in and out, sitting on the rocks and in again, all the morning.

The country looked so fine as one lay floating on one's back and looking towards the shore. The wooded hills seemed to suck in the sunlight with every crest of fir and spruce. The little houses, pearl-grey and white and red, looked so sweet and homelike from here, they tucked themselves away in the clefts round the curve of the bay, and the old foliage trees and orchards of dark-green cherry that people had planted about their homes contrasted strongly with the pine woods at the foot of the hills surrounding the little seaside place.

Their nearest neighbour, the Customs boatman, had many children, and they were cheerful and amusing, and there was one little girl of about Ingvild's age, so she could always find some fun all day long.

What the house they lived in looked like inside Ingvild had not the slightest recollection—it seemed as if she had scarcely been indoors the whole summer, except to sleep. There was a veranda where her father sat—they took most of their meals there. Then she and Marit sat on a couch covered with faded chintz; there was so little room that they kept pushing each other, and mamma told them to be quiet: "It annoys papa to hear you constantly quarrelling." He scarcely saw them except at meal-times.

Her mother used to send Ingvild to get things at the shop by the steamer-pier. Every step of the way was amusing. It was only a track that had been worn over the rocks and through little hollows among them—the houses were scattered irregularly up and down on both sides of the path. Farther down towards the pier were some larger houses, painted white with verandas in the Swiss style, standing in big orchards. They were inhabited by shipowners and people like that.

There was also a bathing-place by the pier, used by the summer visitors who lodged in the cottages round about with the fishermen and sailors' wives. Ingvild hardly saw them except in the shop and on the pier when they were waiting for the steamer. It was amusing to go down to the pier and watch the boat come and go. Her mother scolded her for making them anxious by staying away so long. But Ingvild was incorrigible in that way.

In the afternoon she went to fetch the letters. The post office was a little wooden house that stood high above the little place on a bare crag. In the evening sun people sat or lay on the rock outside, all those who had come to fetch their mail, while the postmaster was busy in his office sorting the contents of the bag that had come by the boat.

There was one girl that Ingvild couldn't keep her eyes off, she was so pretty. She wore one of those bright red felt hats that people use to call "ruffian hats," soft and untrimmed, with the brim turned straight up over the forehead. Underneath it the girl's curly mass of hair shone like bright gold in the sunlight. She had the kind of face that is boldly prominent, especially in profile, with large nose and mouth; and her complexion was peculiar, a dry white with pink roses on the high cheek-bones. Her bust too had something audacious about it; above a high leather belt her thin light-blue blouse fitted so tightly that you saw her breasts as two big, firm hemispheres standing far apart.—She was always the centre of a crowd of girls.

One evening Ingvild heard her say to the others in general—her voice too was uncommon, there was such a ring in it although it was a little hoarse, the hoarseness having the effect of a sort of dew upon the metallic sound of the voice:

"I know *that* very well—but I don't care. I don't give a hoot for what people say about *me!* When I know I'm going the same way as the others—"

Her friends murmured remonstrances, but in hushed and frightened tones.

"Don't I know that I shall die in my turn?" Her voice was arrogant, clear, with the strange dewy veil over it. "And I'm not afraid, I can assure you. When it's no use—"

There was a queer stillness around her. The people sitting on the rocks seemed to shrink and bowed their heads—some of them sighed and spoke to each other in shocked and horrified whispers. The girl stood enveloped by the fitful rays of the evening sun, so that her mass of hair under the fiery hat and the lines of her profile and bosom glimmered in the strong light.

Her father owned one of the finest houses right down on the shore and he had a cutter. She was the last survivor of several brother and sisters; the others had died of consumption. Ingvild never forgot her, as she stood that evening in the glory of the sunshine, saying she knew she was going to die.—What was her fate she never heard.

School had begun in town and most of the summer visitors had

left. But Anine decided that they were to stay a few weeks longer—
papa liked looking at the sea. The children rejoiced over every day
they thus saw pinched from their school term. And there were
masses of berries in the woods, and apples and pears cost next to
nothing now that the visitors had gone, so mamma could buy all
they were able to eat.

The lady from whom they rented the villa had a name for being
difficult to deal with; she was lively and amusing, but had a pretty
sharp tongue. Anine and she appeared to get on well. She lived in
a little cottage which stood by itself in a corner of her piece of
ground; it was really a studio. The young grown-up son she had
living with her was good-natured. He got hold of a boat and took
them for long rows inshore—to out-of-the-way coves where you
found a solitary house standing back and where tall pointed junipers
like the cypresses in pictures grew in lean meadows just beyond the
light sand of the beach. Ingvild thought it must be lovely to live in
a place like these—she had never before seen anything that looked
so solitary. She had never before tried to imagine what it would be
like to live in a lonely place, but she was sure she would like it, if it
was on the fjord. Then she would have a boat, and she would bathe
again in the evening, after the sun had gone down. Mamma generally went to bathe after papa had gone to bed; it must be particularly lovely on these autumn evenings when there was a moon. But
Ingvild was not allowed to bathe after sunset.

She hadn't the slightest desire to go back to school and town and
Observatory Street. But at last they had to go all the same

Then the same old routine began again—everything! The ground
under the trees in the Park was getting so light as she went to school
in the morning, she waded through drifts of fallen leaves. Smooth
brown horse-chestnuts lay gleaming among the leaves—Ingvild
picked them up and thought of all the different things she would
make of them, but when they had been lying for a day or two they
lost their juicy gloss and their shells got dry and dull and shrivelled.
And she was always getting bad marks at school for coming too late.

Then the mornings grew dark; black clouds and floods of cold
rain. Then came the fjord fog. Then came snow, and turned to
mud and slush. Ingvild thought of papa again.

Mamma sat at her sewing-machine in the dining-room; there
were so many things they all had to have for the winter. Papa sat
in his little bedroom, so that he might be spared the hum of the
sewing-machine, and it wasn't very comfortable either when the

table was littered with sewing. Ingvild was in his room, reading aloud. They had taken up the Icelandic sagas, but it was a Danish translation, and Danish was so ill suited to them. But she was not equal to reading them in Old Norse. Only now and then her father asked her to look up a section, a piece of dialogue or something of the sort that she had read in translation—he wanted to hear how it sounded in reality. The Old Norse editions were mostly old books printed on rough paper with uncut edges—they were lovely to turn over and the type was clear and handsome. All the saga editions were on the lowest shelves of the bookcase, so Ingvild lay face down on the carpet when she was reading sagas to papa, then she had only to reach out an arm to find the volumes he wanted.—Now and again mamma appeared in the doorway: "Can you come in for a moment, I want to try on—." Ingvild was to have a school dress of an entirely new material; mamma had bought a remnant at a sale, but Ingvild didn't like the brown colour.—She went back to papa and continued her reading about the Vatsdal people, but got confused over their mutual relationships. It was rather a long way between the interesting bits in that saga.

She longed impatiently—there was Christmas to look forward to and the Christmas holidays, and then it would not be long till the Fair; she looked forward to going to that. And to the days growing longer so that she wouldn't have to get up by lamplight and find the lamps burning when she reached school. Spring and the summer holidays she looked forward to in such a way that it positively hurt her to think of them. She never imagined any change—springs and summers, when she was always out of doors and thought of nothing but her own affairs, would alternate with autumns and winters, when she kept her father company and let her mind be fed by him—.

It never occurred to her that the end might come at any time. Perhaps the grown-ups did not know either that it was so near.

During some dull, dark days at the end of November he was so ill that he had to stay in bed all day. The doctor, his life-long friend, came to see him morning and evening. Five or six days went by, and then it looked as if he was regaining a little strength.

It was Saturday afternoon. Mamma had to do some shopping. "Ingvild, can you sit with papa while I am out—?"

Ingvild lay down on the floor by the bookcase: "Shall I go on reading to you, papa?" He turned his head slightly on the pillow as he lay in the darkness: "Thanks, will you—"

They were doing Haavard Isfjording's saga. Olav Haavardssön, whose blood was as warm as a bear's and who was so strong and brave, but handsome and kind—she imagined him as *her* Olav. It gave her a sharp pang when he was killed, but all that about how he was mourned was so beautiful, and she who was in love with him went away and no one ever heard what had become of her. When she came to the place where Olav's mother goes round to her brothers to bespeak the help of her nephews in avenging him, Ingvild looked at her father. She expected him to say that she was to read these passages again in Old Norse. But he said nothing. He must be very tired, she thought. She searched in the shelf—at any rate she would see for herself what the real words were. But she could not find any edition of Haavard Isfjording's saga in Icelandic.

Next day her mother sat with him all day long. In the course of the afternoon they had a visit from a maid who had been in their service. Which of them it was Ingvild did not remember afterwards. All she remembered was having a strange oppressive feeling that the visitor must not notice she had called inopportunely—she worked as hard as she could to keep a conversation going. Laboriously they dragged the words out of one another.—

When her mother came to the door, she *saw* it in her face before she had uttered a word. The visitor slipped away—and to Ingvild this was like a sign that now her old familiar life had slipped away from them. Her mother, as she had known her, was also gone—she was now another, quenched in tears. She took the children with her into the little room that they might see, their father lay in his bed and was dead.

Her memories of the time that followed were like images seen in the scattered fragments of a broken mirror.

The coffin stood in the drawing-room for several days, and they passed in and out every day. The yellowish waxen image of a man lying in those snow-white surroundings was so beautiful, but so strange that she only *knew* it to be papa—she could not *feel* it. All that had been between her and her father—she had shared with another than this.—But that he had such long eyelashes she had never noticed before. And it dawned on her that a man of forty is not an old man.

She was more oppressed than afraid or saddened by the strangeness and incomprehensibility of it all. When she touched the dead he was cold in a different way from all other cold things. Ever after she knew what nonsense it is when people speak of the dead being cold as a stone or ice or anything else. The coldness of death is like no other coldness. Nearest to it was the coldness of the thick white flowers—hyacinths and lilies of the valley—which lay strewed over the body. For a long time after she could not bear the smell of hyacinths; she traced the other smell, as of rancid wax, beneath the scent of the flowers.

Her mother too would be changed in the future, she knew that already.—Each time she had to make an effort, having so many practical details to attend to after the death and in preparation for the funeral, Ingvild felt that when once she had composed herself again after this shattering time she would in many ways be unlike mamma as the children remembered her. She would take up her life again; in a sense perhaps one might say she would be more herself.—The only person to whom she had voluntarily and intentionally adapted herself was gone.

And she never forgot that in the midst of all the rest she had been delighted with her new mourning dress. It was of fine light woollen material, quite in the fashion, with a yoke and trimmed with many rows of black mohair braid. The doctor's wife had asked to be allowed to see to this and had presented all three little girls with these fine mourning frocks.

The interior of the mortuary chapel was so dismal that it gave her a new sense of the horrors of death and burial. There was such a crowd of strangers at the funeral that she could not cry—all the black top-hats and veils made her feel it would be unbearable if she were to cry in the sight of strangers. If she had even had a veil which she could pull down, as mamma did. So she sat looking at the great mountain of pale wintry flowers and stiff green palm-branches. Long, broad silk streamers with words printed on them hung from it. Most of them were glaring white, but it was a relief to look at those that were coloured. Some were in the Norwegian and some in the Swedish and Danish colours, but there were other colours the meaning of which she did not know. Under this pile the coffin was hidden, and in the coffin lay her father, but she was unable to conceive it.

As they took their places behind the coffin when it was carried out of the chapel, she saw Herr Wilster. It was he who had played the organ, she knew. And now she began to cry after all, and it seemed not to matter because he was here.

The clergyman came to call on them. His name was Andreas Hansen. She thought him very kind; there was something about him which made it feel good to have him sitting in the room for an hour or so. Mamma thought the same. But Ingvild couldn't remember anything of what he said—the good was in himself.

They went to the cemetery every day during this first time. It snowed and the snow thawed again, the paths were muddy and the black trees hung with drops. The flowers on the grave were withered, nasty, and drenched with rain, the ribbons were limp and sodden. The grinning mound of yellow clay showed through more and more.

They went up there with a wreath which had arrived the day after the funeral. It was from Marit's godfather, papa's best friend in Denmark. It was of laurel-leaves without a single flower; that was fine. On the broad red and white ribbon were some runes and underneath in Danish: "Few better will come after."

Ingvild knew very well where that came from—it was the conclusion of the inscription on the Tryggevælde stone, and it was a wife who had raised it to her husband. And suddenly she seemed to *see* it all—men dying and dying, they had gone on dying through all the thousands of years, and among all those forgotten dead there had always been some whose loss their nearest and dearest thought irreparable and of whom they said: "Few better will come after." And then they went on living.

The whole of that winter was one long breaking-up.

Ingvild was aware that mamma did not know what they were going to live on. She would have to find some work. But it wasn't easy to say what that was to be. Even Ingvild guessed that, although her mother possessed a fund of varied knowledge and worked like a horse, for many reasons it would probably not be easy for her to find work among strangers.

In the first place they would have to look out for a small and cheap apartment and part with a great many of their things. The dining-room furniture was sold, a lot of the things from the drawing-room were sold to museums and antique-dealers. Other things their mother gave away to relations and friends.

Two young men who had been papa's pupils came day after day and catalogued his library, packing the books in boxes. *That* made the house look emptier than anything else, for there were book-cases along all the walls, and when they stood there gaping and grinning with nothing on their shelves they were a dismal kind of furniture. One day the boxes of books were gone. A second-hand-bookseller in Copenhagen had bought the whole lot.

One day mamma came and told Ingvild that she had been to see Fru Ragna Nielsen. Well, the fact was she couldn't afford to pay their school fees any longer, so she had given notice to withdraw the children and was going to send them to the Government school. But to that Fru Nielsen had replied that Seming's children should have education at her school gratis, all three of them, until they passed their matriculation. Seming had brought honour to the name of Norway in foreign countries; she was sure that his daughters would not disgrace their father's name.

Ingvild listened, red as fire. In other words, they were to be dead-heads at the school.—Her mother guessed what was in her mind: "You understand, Ingvild, don't you—what Fru Nielsen did not say and never will say is that she expects you three to do honour to the school for your part. You know that in a way her position is a mili-tant one, it is the new, radical principles that she champions, in some measure. And when your father and I sent you there it was because on the whole we believed in her principles and not in the ordinary old-fashioned girls' schools.—And you know that she has ambitions about her pupils. So from now on you will have to be *very industrious* at school. And you can very easily be that, if only you will take some trouble with those subjects which cost you a little effort. And which bore you."

There was nothing she could say to that. But she was not happy about it. True, she would rather go to Ragna Nielsen's school than to any other she had heard of. But even at Ragna Nielsen's school she wanted to have the right of being in opposition, and it was a heavy blow to be obliged in future to work hard at all those things that didn't amuse her.

There was nothing to be done about that. But even at that date she knew in her heart that she would never matriculate. She was now in the third middle. In the sixth middle they took their school diploma. And beyond that she would not go.

In any case there was no chance of taking up any study for which she had an inclination. Most girls who matriculated were destined to become teachers. In the Seventeenth of May procession there were always so many teachers in students' caps that it made you shudder to see them. And she would try to be independent as quickly as possible. Now that papa was dead there was no one on whom she cared to be dependent. Not even on mamma, any more than she could help—she saw this in a flash—.

This time it was no distance from the school to their new home. She was able to give mamma a good deal of help. The two younger ones were sent away to some friends.

She liked their new street the moment she saw it—yes, here she would feel at home! The house they were to live in was one of four big houses standing in a row—on the opposite side of the street there was only an old villa in a little garden, tucked away behind "Blaasen"—she would have Blaasen just outside the front door and it was only a few minutes' run to Lydersagen. She could sit at the drawing-room window looking on to the little mountain with its bushes and rocks and patches of grass. And from the kitchen and dining-room she looked out over fields she did not know—they had not yet been built over. The Bislet brook ran in a little valley and beyond it were the Idiot hills and far away the old villa gardens towards St. Hans' Hill. And it was April—and she had the whole of West Aker to roam over. This year she and Klara would be able to go to Frognersæter as they had talked of doing last year.

The four apartment-houses were not "fine" houses, she saw that at once; they were narrow and grey, without any ornaments or flourishes, the entrances were cramped and untidy. But after that horrible Observatory Street quarter where everything seemed designed to keep up a pretence of what wasn't there, gentility and prosperity on the outside, despondency and scandal behind, these houses had quite a comfortable look. There was a refreshing frankness about their poverty. Here one was free—.

The bedroom was overcrowded with two grown-up beds side by side—she was now to sleep in one of them—and two child's beds. But the window looked on to the street. The drawing-room was small, but could be made charming, she could see that already. And they would have a fire in the stove here every day all through the winter, as the rooms were so arranged that all the others could be warmed from this one. The dining-room was long and narrow; there was only just room for the old kitchen table in the middle, with four of the small drawing-room chairs round it. Papa's desk could just stand along one wall by the window, and at the other end of the room mamma had put one of the old bookcases, but now the shelves would be filled with things from the sideboard. It looked pretty and cheerful.

From a portfolio that Ingvild dropped on the floor a number of little watercolours fell out—some of those her mother had done when she went to the school of art. Ingvild found a box of drawing-pins and stuck them up on the narrow wall by the door in the dining-room. "Mamma—come and look!" Her mother came, shook her head, and laughed: "But, child, they're not the kind of thing to put on the walls—they're not much good." But she let them stay there, and she was not displeased.

Next morning she woke quite early, and outside she saw Blaasen with the morning sun on it, so that it shone with the pale yellow of last year's grass and the bare briers glistened. Above its top the sky was clear and blue and springlike. The sight made her so happy that it gave her heart a pang.

She had not felt so cheerful for ever so long—. And that was just what made her think of papa's death—and there was no one she had been so fond of as of him, and as she thought back over it there came such a smarting wish that she had been much kinder to him and much more faithful in keeping him company while she had him. But now it was too late, and she knew with a strange and bitter certainty that it could not have been otherwise—that there is a borderline which no one can remove between the life of those who are to die and of those who are to live. It seemed to her that she already knew so much that was evil in the world and so much that was boundlessly good that it was all beyond her—there was so much to shudder at and so much to rejoice in that for a moment she almost felt weary in advance.—The little mountain outside shining in the sun, the home that had drawn closer and was beginning to heal after its loss, the freedom which awaited her out in the fields— she was so happy in it all that she could hardly bear such happiness—.

—Translated by Arthur G. Chater

KNUT HAMSUN

****

From his Nobel Prize novel Growth of the Soil, *Knut Hamsun selected as representative of his work that chapter from his saga of
the northern soil in which Isak, the pioneer settler in the northern
wilderness, now a settled farmer, brings home from a distant village
not only a new horse, but a wonderful new machine.*

****

The Wonderful New Machine

Isak came back from the village with a horse.

Ay, it had come to that; he had bought the horse from the Lensmand's* assistant; the animal was for sale, as Lensmand Geissler
had said, but it cost two hundred and forty *Kroner*—that was sixty
Daler. The price of horseflesh had gone up beyond all bounds:
when Isak was a boy the best horse could be bought for fifty *Daler*.

But why had he never raised a horse himself? He had thought of
it, had imagined a nice little foal—that he had been waiting for
these two years past. That was a business for folk who could spare
the time from their land, could leave waste patches lying waste till
they got a horse to carry home the crop. The Lensmand's assistant
had said: "I don't care about paying for a horse's keep myself; I've
no more hay than my womenfolk can get in by themselves while
I'm away on duty."

The new horse was an old idea of Isak's, he had been thinking
of it for years; it was not Geissler who had put him up to it. And
he had also made preparations such as he could; a new stall, a new
rope for tethering it in the summer; as for carts, he had some
already, he must make some more for the autumn. Most important
of all was the fodder, and he had not forgotten that, of course; or
why should he have thought it so important to get that last patch
broken up last year if it hadn't been to save getting rid of one of

* *The Lensmand is a Sheriff's officer, in charge of a small district.*

the cows, and yet have enough keep for a new horse? It was sown for green fodder now; that was for the calving cows.

Ay, he had thought it all out. Well might Inger be astonished again, and clap her hands just as in the old days.

Isak brought news from the village; Breidablik was to be sold, there was a notice outside the church. The bit of crop, such as it was,—hay and potatoes,—to go with the rest. Perhaps the live stock, too; a few beasts only, nothing big.

"Is he going to sell up the home altogether and leave nothing?" cried his wife. "And where's he going to live?"

"In the village," he answered Inger. . . .

Isak had more news from the village: the Lensmand's lady had had a baby. Inger was suddenly interested at this: "Boy or girl?"

"Why, I didn't hear which," said Isak. . . .

Isak understood his work, his calling. He was a rich man now, with a big farm, but the heavy cash payments that had come to him by a lucky chance he used but poorly; he put the money aside. The land saved him. If he had lived down in the village, maybe the great world would have affected even him; so much gaiety, so many elegant manners and ways; he would have been buying useless trifles, and wearing a red Sunday shirt on weekdays. Here in the wilds he was sheltered from all immoderation; he lived in clear air, washed himself on Sunday mornings, and took a bath when he went up to the lake. Those thousand *Daler*—well, 'twas a gift from Heaven, to be kept intact. What else should he do? His ordinary outgoings were more than covered by the produce of his fields and stock.

Eleseus, of course, knew better; he had advised his father to put the money in the Bank. Well, perhaps that was the best, but Isak had put off doing it for the present—perhaps it would never be done at all. Not that Isak was above taking advice from his son; Eleseus was no fool, as he showed later on. Now, in the haymaking season, he had tried his hand with the scythe—but he was no master hand at that, no. He kept close to his younger brother Sivert, and had to get him to use the whetstone every time. But Eleseus had long arms and could pick up hay in first-rate fashion. And he and Sivert and their sister Leopoldine, and Jensine the servant-maid, they were all busy now in the fields with the first lot of hay that year. Eleseus did not spare himself either, but raked away till his hands were blistered and had to be wrapped in rags. He had lost his appetite for a week or so, but worked none the worse for it now. Something had come over the boy; it looked perhaps as if a certain unhappy love affair or something of the sort, a touch of never-to-be-forgotten sorrow and distress, had done him a world of good. And, look you, he had by now smoked the last of the tobacco he had brought with him from town; ordinarily, that would have been. enough to make a clerk go about banging doors and expressing himself emphatically upon many points; but no, Eleseus only grew the steadier for it; firmer and more upright; a man indeed. Even Sivert, the jester, could not put him out of countenance. Today the brothers were lying out on boulders in the river to drink, and Sivert imprudently offered to get some extra fine moss and dry it for tobacco—"unless you'd rather smoke it raw?" he said.

"I'll give you tobacco," said Eleseus, and reaching out, ducked Sivert head and shoulders in the water. Ho, one for him! His brother came back with his hair still dripping.

"Looks like Eleseus he's turning out for the good," thought Isak to himself, watching his son at work. And to Inger he said: "H'm—wonder if Eleseus he'll be staying home now for good?"

And she just as queerly cautious again: "'Tis more than I can say. No, I doubt if he will."

"Ho! Have you said a word of it to himself?"

"No—well, yes, I've talked a bit with him, maybe. But that's the way I think."

"Like to know, now—suppose he'd a bit of land of his own . . ."

"How do you mean?"

"If he'd work on a place of his own?"

"No."

"Well, have you said anything?"

"Said anything? Can't you see for yourself? No, I don't see anything in him Eleseus, that way."

"Don't sit there talking ill of him," said Isak impartially. "All I can see is, he's doing a good day's work down there."

"Ay, maybe," said Inger submissively.

"And I can't see what you've got to find fault with the lad," cried Isak, evidently displeased. "He does his work better and better every day, and what can you ask more?"

Inger murmured: "Ay, but he's not like he used to be. You try talking to him about waistcoats."

"About waistcoats? What d'you mean?"

"How he used to wear white waistcoats in summer when he was in town, so he says."

Isak pondered this a while; it was beyond him. "Well, can't he have a white waistcoat?" he said. Isak was out of his depth here; of course it was only women's nonsense; to his mind, the boy had a perfect right to a white waistcoat, if it pleased him; anyhow, he couldn't see what there was to make a fuss about, and was inclined to put the matter aside and go on.

"Well, what do you think, if he had Brede's bit of land to work on?"

"Who?" said Inger.

"Him Eleseus."

"Breidablik? Nay, 'tis more than's worth your while."

The fact was, she had already been talking over that very plan with Eleseus, she had heard it from Sivert, who could not keep the secret. And indeed, why should Sivert keep the matter secret when his father had surely told him of it on purpose to feel his way? It was not the first time he had used Sivert as a go-between. Well, but what had Eleseus answered? Just as before, as in his letters from town, that no, he would not throw away all he had learned, and be an insignificant nothing again. That was what he had said. Well, and then his mother had brought out all her good reasons, but Eleseus had said no to them all; he had other plans for his life. Young hearts have their unfathomable depths, and after what had happened, likely enough he did not care about staying on with Barbro as a neighbour. Who could say? He had put it loftily enough in talking to his mother; he could get a better position in town than the one he had; could go as clerk to one of the higher officials. He must get on, he must rise in the world. In a few years, perhaps, he might be a Lensmand, or perhaps a lighthouse keeper, or get into the Customs. There were so many roads open to a man with learning.

However it might be, his mother came round, was drawn over to his point of view. Oh, she was so little sure of herself yet; the world had not quite lost its hold on her. Last winter she had gone so far as to read occasionally a certain excellent devotional work which she had brought from Trondhjem, from the Institute; but now, Eleseus might be a Lensmand one day!

"And why not?" said Eleseus. "What's Lensmand Heyerdahl himself but a former clerk in the same department?"

Splendid prospects. His mother herself advised him not to give up his career and throw himself away. What was a man like that to do in the wilds?

But why should Eleseus then trouble to work hard and steadily as he was doing now on his father's land? Heaven knows, he had some reason, maybe. Something of inborn pride in him still, per-

haps; he would not be outdone by others; and besides, it would do
him no harm to be in his father's good books the day he went away.
To tell the truth, he had a number of little debts in town, and it
would be a good thing to be able to settle them at once—improve
his credit a lot. And it was not a question now of a mere hundred
Kroner, but something worth considering.

Eleseus was far from stupid, but on the contrary, a sly fellow in
his way. He had seen his father come home, and knew well enough
he was sitting there in the window at that moment, looking out.
No harm in putting his back into it then for a bit, working a little
harder for the moment—it would hurt no one, and might do himself
good.

Eleseus was somehow changed; whatever it might be, something
in him had been warped, and quietly spoiled; he was not bad, but
something blemished. Had he lacked a guiding hand those last few
years? What could his mother do to help him now? Only stand by
him and agree. She could let herself be dazzled by her son's bright
prospects for the future, and stand between him and his father, to
take his part—she could do that.

But Isak grew impatient at last over her opposition; to his mind,
the idea about Breidablik was by no means a bad one. Only that
very day, coming up, he had stopped the horse almost without thinking, to look out with a critical eye over the ill-tended land; ay, it
could be made a fine place in proper hands.

"Why not worth while?" he asked Inger now. "I've that much
feeling for Eleseus, anyway, that I'd help him to it."

"If you've any feeling for him, then say never a word of Breidablik again," she answered.

"Ho!"

"Ay, for he's greater thoughts in his head than the like of us."

Isak, too, is hardly sure of himself here, and it weakens him; but
he is by no means pleased at having shown his hand, and spoken
straight out about his plan. He is unwilling to give it up now.

"He shall do as I say," declares Isak suddenly. And he raises his
voice threateningly, in case Inger by any chance should be hard
of hearing. "Ay, you may look; I'll say no more. It's midway up,
with a schoolhouse by, and everything; what's the greater thoughts
he's got beyond that, I'd like to know? With a son like that I might
starve to death—is that any better, d'you think? And can you tell
me why my own flesh and blood should turn and go contrary to—
to my own flesh and blood?"

Isak stopped; he realized that the more he talked the worse it 'would be. He was on the point of changing his clothes, getting out of his best things he had put on to go down to the village in; but no, he altered his mind, he would stay as he was—whatever he meant by that. "You'd better say a word of it to Eleseus," he says then.

And Inger answers: "Best if you'd say it yourself. He won't do as I say."

Very well, then, Isak is head of the house, so he should think; now see if Eleseus dares to murmur! But, whether it were because he feared defeat, Isak draws back now, and says: "Ay, 'tis true, I might say a word of it myself. But by reason of having so many things to do, and busy with this and that, I've something else to think of."

"Well . . . ?" said Inger in surprise.

And Isak goes off again—not very far, only to the farther fields, but still, he goes off. He is full of mysteries, and must hide himself out of the way. The fact is this: he had brought back a third piece of news from the village today, and that was something more than the rest, something enormous; and he had hidden it at the edge of the wood. There it stands, wrapped up in sacking and paper; he uncovers it, and lo, a huge machine. Look! red and blue, wonderful to see, with a heap of teeth and a heap of knives, with joints and arms and screws and wheels—a mowing machine. No, Isak would not have gone down today for the new horse if it hadn't been for that machine.

He stands with a marvellously keen expression, going over in his mind from beginning to end the instructions for use that the store-keeper had read out; he sets a spring here, and shifts a bolt there, then he oils every hole and every crevice, then he looks over the whole thing once more. Isak had never known such an hour in his life. To pick up a pen and write one's mark on a paper, a document —ay, 'twas a perilous great thing that, no doubt. Likewise in the matter of a new harrow he had once brought up—there were many curiously twisted parts in that to be considered. Not to speak of the great circular saw that had to be set in its course to the nicety of a pencil line, never swaying east nor west, lest it should fly asunder. But this—this mowing-machine of his—'twas a crawling nest of steel springs and hooks and apparatus, and hundreds of screws— Inger's sewing-machine was a bookmarker compared with this!

Isak harnessed himself to the shafts and tried the thing. Here was the wonderful moment. And that was why he kept out of sight and was his own horse.

For—what if the machine had been wrongly put together and did not do its work, but went to pieces with a crash! No such calamity happened, however; the machine could cut grass. And so indeed it ought, after Isak had stood there, deep in study, for hours. The sun had gone down. Again he harnesses himself and tries it; ay, the thing cuts grass. And so indeed it ought!

When the dew began to fall close after the heat of the day, and the boys came out, each with his scythe to mow in readiness for next day, Isak came in sight close to the house and said:

"Put away scythes for tonight. Get out the new horse, you can, and bring him down to the edge of the wood."

And on that, instead of going indoors to his supper as the others had done already, he turned where he stood and went back the way he had come.

"D'you want the cart, then?" Sivert called after him.

"No," said his father, and walked on.

Swelling with mystery, full of pride; with a little lift and throw from the knee at every step, so emphatically did he walk. So a brave man might walk to death and destruction, carrying no weapon in his hand.

The boys came up with the horse, saw the machine, and stopped dead. It was the first mowing-machine in the wilds, the first in the village—red and blue, a thing of splendour to man's eyes. And the father, head of them all, called out, oh, in a careless tone, as if it were nothing uncommon: "Harness up to this machine here."

And they drove it; the father drove. Brrr! said the thing, and felled the grass in swathes. The boys walked behind, nothing in their hands, doing no work, smiling. The father stopped and looked back. H'm, not as clear as it might be. He screws up a nut here and there to bring the knives closer to the ground, and tries again. No, not right yet, all uneven; the frame with the cutters seems to be hopping a little. Father and sons discuss what it can be. Eleseus has found the instructions and is reading them. "Here, it says to sit up on the seat when you drive—then it runs steadier," he says.

"Ho!" says his father. "Ay, 'tis so, I know," he answers. "I've studied it all through." He gets up into the seat and starts off again; it goes steadily now. Suddenly the machine stops working—the knives are not cutting at all. *"Ptro!* What's wrong now?" Father down from his seat, no longer swelling with pride, but bending an anxious, questioning face down over the machine. Father and sons all stare at it; something must be wrong. Eleseus stands holding the instructions.

"Here's a bolt or something," says Sivert, picking up a thing from the grass.

"Ho, that's all right, then," says his father, as if that was all that was needed to set everything in order. "I was just looking for that bolt." But now they could not find the hole for it to fit in—where in the name of wonder could the hole be now?

And it was now that Eleseus could begin to feel himself a person of importance; he was the man to make out a printed paper of instructions. What would they do without him? He pointed unnecessarily long to the hole and explained: "According to the illustration, the bolt should fit in there."

"Ay, that's where she goes," said his father. " 'Twas there I had it before." And, by way of regaining lost prestige, he ordered Sivert to set about looking for more bolts in the grass. "There ought to be another," he said, looking very important, as if he carried the whole thing in his head. "Can't you find another? Well, well, it'll be in its hole then, all right."

Father starts off again.

"Wait a minute—this is wrong," cried Eleseus. Ho, Eleseus standing there with the drawing in his hand, with the Law in his hand; no getting away from him! "That spring there goes outside," he says to his father.

"Ay, what then?"

"Why, you've got it under, you've set it wrong. It's a steel spring, and you have to fix it outside, else the bolt jars out again and stops the knives. You can see in the picture here."

"I've left my spectacles behind, and can't see it quite," says his father, something meekly. "You can see better—you set it as it should go. I don't want to go up to the house for my spectacles now."

All in order now, and Isak gets up. Eleseus calls after him: "You must drive pretty fast, it cuts better that way—it says so here."

Isak drives and drives, and everything goes well, and Brrr! says the machine. There is a broad track of cut grass in his wake, neatly in line, ready to take up. Now they can see him from the house, and all the womenfolk come out; Inger carries little Rebecca on her arm, though little Rebecca has learned to walk by herself long since. But there they come—four womenfolk, big and small—hurrying with straining eyes down towards the miracle, flocking down to see. Oh, but now is Isak's hour. Now he is truly proud, a mighty man, sitting high aloft dressed in holiday clothes, in all his finery; in jacket and hat, though the sweat is pouring off him. He swings round in four big angles, goes over a good bit of ground, swings round, drives, cuts grass, passes along by where the women are standing; they are dumbfounded, it is all beyond them, and Brrr! says the machine.

Then Isak stops and gets down. Longing, no doubt, to hear what these folk on earth down there will say; what they will find to say about it all. He hears smothered cries; they fear to disturb him, these beings on earth, in his lordly work, but they turn to one another with awed questionings, and he hears what they say. And now, that he may be a kind and fatherly lord and ruler to them all, to encourage them, he says: "There, I'll just do this bit, and you can spread it tomorrow."

"Haven't you time to come in and have a bite of food?" says Inger, all overwhelmed.

"Nay, I've other things to do," he answers.

Then he oils the machine again; gives them to understand that he is occupied with scientific work. Drives off again, cutting more grass. And, at long last the womenfolk go back home.

Happy Isak—happy folk at Sellanraa!

Very soon the neighbours from below will be coming up. Axel Ström is interested in things, he may be up tomorrow. But Brede from Breidablik, he might be here that very evening. Isak would not be loth to show them his machine, explain it to them, tell them how it works, and all about it. He can point out how that no man with a scythe could ever cut so fine and clean. But it costs money, of course—oh, a red-and-blue machine like that is a terribly costly thing!

Happy Isak!

But as he stops for oil the third time, there! his spectacles fall from his pocket. And, worst of all, the two boys saw it. Was there a higher power behind that little happening—a warning against overweening pride? He had put on those spectacles time and again that day to study the instructions, without making out a word; Eleseus had to help him with that. Eyah, *Herregud,* 'twas a good thing, no doubt, to be book-learned. And, by way of humbling himself, Isak determines to give up his plan of making Eleseus a tiller of soil in the wilds; he will never say a word of it again.

Not that the boys made any great business about that matter of the spectacles; far from it. Sivert, the jester, had to say something, of course; it was too much for him. He plucked Eleseus by the sleeve and said: "Here, come along, we'll go back home and throw those scythes on the fire. Father's going to do all the mowing now with his machine." And that was a jest indeed.

—*Translated by W. W. Worster*

ISAK DINESEN

****

"The Pearls" is taken from one of her volumes of long short stories,
Winter's Tales, *by the Baronesse Karen Blixen, who writes under
the name of Isak Dinesen. It is representative of her distinguished
and interesting style and insight.*

****

The Pearls

ABOUT EIGHTY YEARS AGO a young officer in the guards, the youngest son of an old country family, married, in Copenhagen, the
daughter of a rich wool merchant whose father had been a peddler
and had come to town from Jutland. In those days such a marriage
was an unusual thing. There was much talk of it, and a song was
made about it, and sung in the streets.

The bride was twenty years old, and a beauty, a big girl with
black hair and a high colour, and a distinction about her as if she
were made from whole timber. She had two old unmarried aunts,
sisters of her grandfather the peddler, whom the growing fortune
of the family had stopped short in a career of hard work and thrift,
and made to sit in state in a parlour. When the elder of them first
heard rumours of her niece's engagement she went and paid her a
visit, and in the course of the conversation told her a story.

"When I was a child, my dear," she said, "young Baron Rosenkrantz became engaged to a wealthy goldsmith's daughter. Have
you heard such a thing? Your great-grandmother knew her. The
bridegroom had a twin sister, who was a lady at Court. She drove
to the goldsmith's house to see the bride. When she had left again,
the girl said to her lover: 'Your sister laughed at my frock, and
because, when she spoke French, I could not answer. She has a
hard heart, I saw that. If we are to be happy you must never see
her again, I could not bear it.' The young man, to comfort her,
promised that he would never see his sister again. Soon afterwards, on a Sunday, he took the girl to dine with his mother. As

862

he drove her home she said to him: 'Your mother had tears in her eyes, when she looked at me. She has hoped for another wife for you. If you love me, you must break with your mother.' Again the enamoured young man promised to do as she wished, although it cost him much, for his mother was a widow, and he was her only son. The same week he sent his valet with a bouquet to his bride. Next day she said to him: 'I cannot stand the mien your valet has when he looks at me. You must send him away at the first of the month.' 'Mademoiselle,' said Baron Rosenkrantz, 'I cannot have a wife who lets herself be affected by my valet's mien. Here is your ring. Farewell forever.' "

While the old woman spoke she kept her little glittering eyes upon her niece's face. She had an energetic nature and had long ago made up her mind to live for others, and she had established herself as the conscience of the family. But in reality she was, with no hopes or fears of her own, a vigorous old moral parasite on the whole clan, and particularly on the younger members of it. Jensine, the bride, was a full-blooded young person and a gratifying object to a parasite. Moreover, the young and the old maid had many qualities in common. Now the girl went on pouring out coffee with a quiet face, but behind it she was furious, and said to herself: "Aunt Maren shall be paid back for this." All the same, as was often the case, the aunt's admonition went deep into her, and she pondered it in her heart.

After the wedding, in the Cathedral of Copenhagen, on a fine June day, the newly married couple went away to Norway for their wedding trip. They sailed as far north as Hardanger. At that time a journey to Norway was a romantic undertaking, and Jensine's friends asked her why they did not go to Paris, but she herself was pleased to start her married life in the wilderness, and to be alone with her husband. She did not, she thought, need or want any further new impressions or experiences. And in her heart she added: God help me.

The gossips of Copenhagen would have it that the bridegroom had married for money, and the bride for a name, but they were all wrong. The match was a love affair, and the honeymoon, technically, an idyll. Jensine would never have married a man whom she did not love; she held the god of love in great respect, and had already for some years sent a little daily prayer to him: "Why dost thou tarry?" But now she reflected that he had perhaps granted her her prayer with a vengeance, and that her books had given her but little information as to the real nature of love.

The scenery of Norway, amongst which she had her first experience of the passion, contributed to the overpowering impression of it. They country was at its loveliest. The sky was blue, the
bird-cherry flowered everywhere and filled the air with sweet and
bitter fragrance, and the nights were so light that you could see
to read at midnight. Jensine, in a crinoline and with an alpen-
stock, climbed many steep paths on her husband's arm—or alone,
for she was strong and lightfooted. She stood upon the summits,
her clothes blown about her, and wondered and wondered. She
had lived in Denmark, and for a year in a pension in Lubeck, and
her idea of the earth was that it must spread out horizontally, flat
or undulating, before her feet. But in these mountains everything
seemed strangely to stand up vertically, like some great animal
that rises on its hind legs—and you know not whether to play, or
to crush you. She was higher than she had ever been, and the air
went to her head like wine. Also, wherever she looked there was
running water, rushing from the sky-high mountains into the lakes,
in silvery rivulets or in roaring falls, rainbow-adorned. It was as
if Nature itself was weeping, or laughing, aloud.

At first all this was so new to her that she felt her old ideas of
the world blown about in all directions, like her skirts and her
shawl. But soon the impressions converged into a sensation of the
deepest alarm, a panic such as she had never experienced.

She had been brought up in an atmosphere of prudence and
foresight. Her father was an honest tradesman, afraid both to lose
his own money, and to let down his customers. Sometimes this
double risk had thrown him into melancholia. Her mother had
been a God-fearing young woman, a member of a pietistic sect;
her two old aunts were persons of strict moral principle, with an
eye to the opinions of the world. At home Jensine had at times
believed herself a daring spirit, and had longed for adventure.
But in this wildly romantic landscape, and taken by surprise and
overwhelmed by wild, unknown, formidable forces within her own
heart, she looked round for support. Where was she to find it? Her
young husband who had brought her there, and with whom she was
all alone, could not help her. He was, on the contrary, the cause of
the turbulence in her, and he was also, in her eyes, pre-eminently
exposed to the dangers of the outward world. For very soon after
her marriage Jensine realized—as she had perhaps dimly known
from their first meeting—that he was a human being entirely
devoid, and incapable, of fear.

She had read in books of heroes, and had admired them with all her heart. But Alexander was not like the heroes of her books. He was not braving, or conquering, the dangers of this world, but he was unaware of their existence. To him the mountains were a playground, and all the phenomena of life, love itself included, were his playmates within it. "In a hundred years, my darling," he said to her, "it will all be one." She could not imagine how he had managed to live till now, but then she knew that his life had been, in every way, different from hers. Now she felt, with horror, that here she was, within a world of undreamt of heights and depths, delivered into the hands of a person totally ignorant of the law of gravitation. Under the circumstances her feelings for him intensified into both a deep moral indignation, as if he had deliberately betrayed her, and into an extreme tenderness, such as she would have felt towards an exposed, helpless child. These two passions were the strongest of which her nature was capable; they took speed with her, and developed into a possession. She recalled the fairy tale of the boy who is sent out in the world to learn to be afraid, and it seemed to her that for her own sake and his, in self-defense as well as in order to protect and save him, she must teach her husband to fear.

He knew nothing of what went on in her. He was in love with her, and he admired and respected her. She was innocent and pure; she sprang from a stock of people capable of making a fortune by their wits; she could speak French and German, and knew history and geography. For all these qualities he had a religious reverence. He was prepared for surprises in her, for their acquaintance was but slight, and they had not been alone together in a room more than three or four times before their wedding. Besides, he did not pretend to understand women, but held their incalculableness to be part of their grace. The moods and caprices of his young wife all confirmed in him the assurance, with which she had inspired him at their first meeting, that she was what he needed in life. But he wanted to make her his friend, and reflected that he had never had a real friend in his life. He did not talk to her of his love affairs of the past—indeed he could not have spoken of them to her if he had wanted to—but in other ways he told her as much as he could remember of himself and his life. One day he recounted how he had gambled in Baden-Baden, risked his last cent, and then won. He did not know that she thought, by his side: "He is really a thief, or if not that, a receiver of stolen goods, and no better than a thief." At other times he made fun of the debts he had had, and the trouble he had had to take to avoid meeting his tailor. This talk sounded really uncanny to Jensine's ears. For to her debts were an abomination, and that he should have lived on in the midst of them without anxiety, trusting to fortune to pay up for him, seemed against nature. Still, she reflected, she herself, the rich girl he married, had come along in time, as the willing tool of fortune, to justify his trust in the eyes of his tailor himself. He told her of a duel that he had fought with a German officer, and showed her a scar from it. As, at the end of it all, he took her in his arms, on the high hilltops, for all the skies to see them, in her heart she cried: "If it be possible, let this cup pass from me."

When Jensine set out to teach her husband to fear, she had the tale of Aunt Maren in her mind, and she made the vow that she would never cry quarter, but that this should be his part. As the relation between herself and him was to her the central factor of existence, it was natural that she should first try to scare him with the possibility of losing her. She was an unsophisticated girl, and resorted to simple measures.

From now on she became more reckless than he in their climbs. She would stand on the edge of a precipice, leaning on her parasol, and ask him how deep it was to the bottom. She balanced across narrow, brittled bridges, high above foaming streams, and chattered to him the while. She went out rowing in a small boat, on the lake, in a thunderstorm. At nights she dreamed about the perils of the days, and woke up with a shriek, so that he took her in his arms to comfort her. But her daring did her no good. Her husband was surprised and enchanted at the change of the demure maiden into a Valkyrie. He put it down to the influence of married life, and felt not a little proud. She herself, in the end, wondered whether she was not driven on in her exploits by his pride and praise as much as by her resolution to conquer him. Then she was angry with herself, and with all women, and she pitied him, and all men.

Sometimes Alexander would go out fishing. These were welcome opportunities to Jensine to be alone and collect her thoughts. So the young bride would wander about alone, in a tartan frock, a small figure in the hills. Once or twice, in these walks, she thought of her father, and the memory of his anxious concern for her brought tears to her eyes. But she sent him away again; she must be left alone to settle matters of which he could know nothing.

One day, when she sat and rested on a stone, a group of children, who were herding goats, approached and stared at her. She called them up and gave them sweets from her reticule. Jensine had adored her dolls, and as much as a modest girl of the period dared, she had longed for children of her own. Now she thought with sudden dismay: "I shall never have children! As long as I must strain myself against him in this way, we will never have a child." The idea distressed her so deeply that she got up and walked away.

On another of her lonely walks she came to think of a young man in her father's office who had loved her. His name was Peter Skov. He was a brilliant young man of business, and she had known him all her life. She now recalled how, when she had had the measles, he had sat and read to her every day, and how he had accompanied her when she went out skating, and had been distressed lest she should catch cold, or fall, or go through the ice. From where she stood she could see her husband's small figure in the distance. "Yes," she thought, "this is the best thing I can do. When I come back to Copenhagen, then, by my honour, which is still my own"—although she had doubts on this point—"Peter Skov shall be my lover."

On their wedding day Alexander had given his bride a string of pearls. It had belonged to his grandmother, who had come from Germany and who was a beauty and a *bel esprit*. She had left it to him to give to his future wife. Alexander had talked much to her of his grandmother. He did, he said, first fall in love with her because she was a little like his grandmama. He asked her to wear the pearls every day. Jensine had never had a string of pearls before, and she was proud of hers. Lately, when she had so often been in need of support, she had got into the habit of twisting the string, and pulling it with her lips. "If you go on doing that," Alexander said one day, "you will break the string." She looked at him. It was the first time that she had known him to foresee disaster. "He has loved his grandmother," she thought, "or is it that you must be dead to carry weight with this man?" Since then she often thought of the old woman. She, too, had come from her own milieu and had been a stranger in her husband's family and circle of friends. She had managed to get this string of pearls from Alexander's grandfather, and to be remembered by it down through the generations. Were the pearls, she wondered, a token of victory, or of submission? Jensine came to look upon Grandmama as her best friend in the family. She would have liked to pay her a grand-daughterly visit, and to consult her on her own troubles.

The honeymoon was nearing its end, and that strange warfare, the existence of which was known to one of the belligerents only, had come to no decision. Both the young people were sad to go away. Only now did Jensine fully realize the beauty of the land-

scape round her, for, after all, in the end she had made it her ally.
Up here, she reflected, the dangers of the world were obvious, ever
in sight. In Copenhagen life looked secure, but might prove to be
even more redoubtable. She thought of her pretty house, waiting
for her there, with lace curtains, chandeliers and linen cupboards.
She could not at all tell what life within it would be like.

The day before they were to sail they were staying in a small
village, from where it was six hours' drive in a cariole down to the
landing-place of the coast steamer. They had been out before breakfast. When Jensine sat down and loosened her bonnet, the string
of pearls caught in her bracelet, and the pearls sprang all over the
floor, as if she had burst into a rain of tears. Alexander got down
on his hands and knees, and, as he picked them up one by one,
placed them in her lap.

She sat in a kind of mild panic. She had broken the one thing
in the world that she had been afraid of breaking. What omen did
that have for them? "Do you know how many there were?" she
asked him. "Yes," he said from the floor, "Grandpapa gave Grandmama the string at their golden wedding, with a pearl for each
of their fifty years. But afterwards he added one every year, at
her birthday. There are fifty-two. It is easy to remember; it is
the number of cards in a pack." At last they got them all collected
and wrapped them up in his silk handkerchief. "Now I cannot
put them on till I get to Copenhagen," she said.

At that moment their landlady came in with the coffee. She observed the catastrophe and at once offered to assist them. The
shoemaker in the village, she said, could do up the pearls for them.
Two years ago an English lord and his lady, with a party, had
travelled in the mountains, and when the young lady broke her
string of pearls, in the same way, he had strung them for her to
her perfect satisfaction. He was an honest old man, although very
poor, and a cripple. As a young man he had got lost in a snowstorm
in the hills, and been found only two days later, and they had had
to cut off both his feet. Jensine said that she would take her pearls
to the shoemaker, and the landlady showed her the way to his
house.

She walked down alone, while her husband was strapping their
boxes, and found the shoemaker in his little dark workshop. He
was a small, thin, old man in a leather apron, with a shy, sly smile
in a face harassed by long suffering. She counted the pearls up
to him, and gravely confided them into his hands. He looked at

them, and promised to have them ready by next midday. After she had settled with him she kept sitting on a small chair, with her hands in her lap. To say something, she asked him the name of the English lady who had broken her string of pearls, but he did not remember it.

She looked round at the room. It was poor and bare, with a couple of religious pictures nailed on the wall. In a strange way it seemed to her that here she had come home. An honest man, hard tried by destiny, had passed his long years in this little room. It was a place where people worked, and bore troubles patiently, in anxiety for their daily bread. She was still so near to her school books that she remembered them all, and now she began to think of what she had read about deep-water fish, which have been so much used to bear the weight of many thousand fathoms of water, that if they are raised to the surface, they will burst. Was she herself, she wondered, such a deep-water fish that felt at home only under the pressure of existence? And her father, her grandfather and his people before him, had they been the same? What was a deep-water fish to do, she thought on, if she were married to one of those salmon which here she had seen springing in the water-falls? Or to a flying-fish? She said good-bye to the old shoemaker, and walked off.

As she was going home she caught sight, on the path in front of her, of a small stout man in a black hat and coat who walked on briskly. She remembered that she had seen him before; she even believed that he was staying in the same house as she. There was a seat by the path, from which one had a magnificent view. The man in black sat down, and Jensine, whose last day in the mountains it was, sat down on the other end of the seat. The stranger lifted his hat a little to her. She had believed him to be an elderly man, but now saw that he could not be much over thirty. He had an energetic face and clear, penetrating eyes. After a moment he spoke to her, with a little smile. "I saw you coming out from the shoe-maker's," he said. "You have not lost your sole in the mountains?" "No, I brought him some pearls," said Jensine. "You brought him pearls?" said the stranger humorously. "That is what I go to collect from him." She wondered if he were a bit deranged. "That old man," said he, "has got, in his hut, a big store of our old national treasures—pearls if you like—which I happen to be collecting just now. In case you want children's tales, there is not a man in Norway who can give you a better lot than our shoemaker. He once

dreamed of becoming a student, and a poet—do you know that?—
but he was hard hit by destiny, and had to take to a shoemaker's
trade."

After a pause he said: "I have been told that you and your
husband come from Denmark, on your wedding trip. That is an
unusual thing to do; these mountains are high and dangerous.
Who of you two was it who desired to come here? Was it you?"
"Yes," said she. "Yes," said the stranger. "I thought so. That he
might be the bird, which upward soars, and you the breeze, which
carries him along. Do you know that quotation? Does it tell you
anything?" "Yes," said she, somewhat bewildered. "Upwards,"
said he, and sat back, silent, with his hands upon his walking-
stick. After a little while he went on: "The summits! Who knows?
We two are pitying the shoemaker for his bad luck, that he had to
give up his dreams of being a poet, of fame and a great name.
How do we know but that he has had the best of luck? Greatness,
the applause of the masses! Indeed, my young lady, perhaps they
are better left alone. Perhaps in common trade they cannot reasonably purchase a shoemaker's sign board, and the knowledge of
soling. One may do well in getting rid of them at cost price. What
do you think, Madam?" "I think that you are right," she said
slowly. He gave her a sharp glance from a pair of ice-blue eyes.

"Indeed," said he. "Is that your advice, on this fair summer
day? Cobbler, stay by your last. One should do better, you think,
in making up pills and draughts for the sick human beings, and
cattle, of this world?" He chuckled a little. "It is a very good jest.
In a hundred years it will be written in a book: A little lady from
Denmark gave him the advice to stay by his last. Unfortunately,
he did not follow it. Good-bye, Madam, good-bye." With these
words he got up, and walked on. She saw his black figure grow
smaller amongst the hills. The landlady had come out to hear if
she had found the shoemaker. Jensine looked after the stranger.
"Who was that gentleman?" she asked. The woman shaded her
eyes with her hand. "Oh, indeed," said she. "He is a learned man,
a great man, he is here to collect old stories and songs. He was an
apothecary once. But he has had a theatre in Bergen, and written
plays for it, too. His name is Herr Ibsen."

In the morning news came up from the landing-place that
the boat would be in sooner than expected, and they had to start in
haste. The landlady sent her small son to the shoemaker to fetch
Jensine's pearls. When the travellers were already seated in the
cariole, he brought them, wrapped in a leaf from a book, with a

waxed string round them. Jensine undid them, and was about to count them, but thought better of it, and instead clasped the string round her throat. "Ought you not to count them?" Alexander asker her. She gave him a great glance. "No," she said. She was silent on the drive. His words rang in her ears: "Ought you not count them?" She sat by his side, a triumphator. Now she knew what a triumphator felt like.

Alexander and Jensine came back to Copenhagen at a time when most people were out of town and there were no great social functions. But she had many visits from the wives of his young military friends, and the young people went together to the Tivoli of Copenhagen in the summer evenings. Jensine was made much of by all of them.

Her house lay by one of the old canals of the town and looked over to the Thorwaldsen Museum. Sometimes she would stand by the window, gaze at the boats, and think of Hardanger. During all this time she had not taken off her pearls or counted them. She was sure that there would at least be one pearl missing. She imagined that she felt the weight, on her throat, different from before. What would it be, she thought, which she had sacrificed for her victory over her husband? A year, or two years, of their married life, before their golden wedding? This golden wedding seemed a long way off, but still each year was precious; and how was she to part with one of them?

In the last months of this summer people began to discuss the possibility of war. The Schleswig-Holstein question had become imminent. A Danish Royal Proclamation, of March, had repudiated all German claims upon Schleswig. Now in July a German note demanded, on pain of federal execution, the withdrawal of the Proclamation.

Jensine was an ardent patriot and loyal to the King, who had given the people its free constitution. The rumours put her into the highest agitation. She thought the young officers, Alexander's friends, frivolous in their light, boastful talk of the country's danger. If she wanted to debate the crisis seriously she had to go to her own people. With her husband she could not talk of it at all, but in her heart she knew that he was as convinced of Denmark's invincibility as of his own immortality.

She read the newpapers from beginning to end. One day in the *Berlingske Tidende* she came upon the following phrase: "The moment is grave to the nation. But we have trust in our just cause, and we are without fear."

It was, perhaps, the words "without fear" which now made her collect her courage. She sat down in her chair by the window, took off her pearls and put them in her lap. She sat for a moment with her hands folded upon them, as in prayer. Then she counted them. There were fifty-three pearls on her string. She could not believe her own eyes, and counted them over again; but there was no mistake, there were fifty-three pearls and the one in the middle was the biggest.

Jensine sat for a long time in her chair, quite giddy. Her mother, she knew, had believed in the Devil. At this moment the daughter did the same. She would not have been surprised had she heard laughter from behind the sofa. Had the powers of the universe, she thought, combined, here, to make fun of a poor girl?

When she could again collect her thoughts, she remembered that before she had been given the necklace, the old goldsmith of her husband's family had repaired the clasp of it. He would therefore know the pearls, and might tell her what to believe. But she was so thoroughly scared that she dared not go to him herself, and only a few days later she asked Peter Skov, who came to pay her a visit, to take the string to him.

Peter returned and told her that the goldsmith had put on his spectacles to examine the pearls, and then, in amazement, had declared that there was one more than when he had last seen them. "Yes, Alexander gave me that," Jensine interrupted him, blushing deeply at her own lie. Peter reflected, as the goldsmith had done, that it was a cheap generosity in a lieutenant to make the heiress he had married a rich present. But he repeated to her the old man's words. "Mr. Alexander," he had declared, "shows himself a rare judge of pearls. I shall not hesitate to pronounce this one pearl worth as much as all the others put together." Jensine, terrified but smiling, thanked Peter, but he went away sadly, for he felt as if he had annoyed or frightened her.

She had not been feeling well for some time, and when, in September, they had a spell of heavy, sultry weather in Copenhagen, it left her pale and sleepless. Her father and her two old aunts were upset about her and tried to make her come and stay at his villa on the Strandvej, outside town. But she would not leave her own house or her husband, nor would she, she thought, ever get well, until she had come to the bottom of the mystery of the pearls. After a week she made up her mind to write to the shoemaker at Odda. If, as Herr Ibsen had told her, he had been a student and a poet, he would be able to read, and would answer her letter. It seemed to her that in her present situation she had no friend in the world but this crippled old man. She wished that she could go back to his workshop, to the bare walls and the three-legged chair. She dreamed at night that she was there. He had smiled kindly at her; he knew many children's tales. He might know how to comfort her. Only for a moment she trembled at the idea that he might be dead, and that then she would never know.

Within the following weeks the shadow of the war grew deeper. Her father was worrying over the prospects and about King Frederik's health. Under these new circumstances the old merchant began to take pride in the fact that he had his daughter married to a soldier, which before had been far from his mind. He and her old aunts showed Alexander and Jensine great respect.

One day, half against her own will, Jensine asked Alexander straight out if he thought there would be war. "Yes," he answered quickly and confidently, "there will be war. It could not be avoided." He went on to whistle a bit of a soldier's song. The sight of her face made him stop. "Are you afrightened of it?" he asked. She considered it hopeless, and even unseemly, to explain to him her feelings about the war. "Are you frightened for my sake?" he asked her again. She turned her head away. "To be a hero's widow," he said, "would be just the part for you, my dear." Her eyes filled with tears, as much of anger as of woe. Alexander came and took her hand. "If I fall," he said, "it will be a consolation to me to remember that I have kissed you as often as you would let me." He did so now, once more, and added: "Will it be a consolation to you?" Jensine was an honest girl. When she was questioned she tried to find the truthful answer. Now she thought: Would it be a consolation to me? But she could not, in her heart, find the reply.

With all this Jensine had much to think of, so that she half forgot about the shoemaker, and, when one morning she found his letter on the breakfast table, she for a minute took it to be a mendicant's letter, of which she got many. The next moment she grew very pale. Her husband, opposite her, asked her what was the matter. She gave him no reply, but got up, went into her own small sitting-room, and opened the letter by the fireplace. The characters of it, carefully printed, recalled to her the old man's face, as if he had sent her his portrait.

"Dear young Danish Missus," the letter went.

"Yes, I put the pearl onto your necklace. I meant to give you a small surprise. You made such a fuss about your pearls, when you brought them to me, as if you were afraid that I should steal one of them from you. Old people, as well as young, must have a little fun at times. If I have frightened you, I beg that you will forgive me all the same. This pearl I got two years ago, when I strung the English lady's necklace. I forgot to put the one in, and only found it afterwards. It has been with me for two years, but I have no use for it. It is better that it should be with a young lady. I remember that you sat in my chair, quite young and pretty. I wish you good luck, and that something pleasant may happen to you on the very same day as you get this letter. And may you wear the pearl long, with a humble heart, a firm trust in the Lord God, and a friendly thought of me, who am old, here up at Odda. Good-bye.

"Your friend, Peiter Viken."

Jensine had been reading the letter with her elbows on the mantelpiece, to steady herself. As she looked up, she met the grave eyes of her own image in the looking-glass above it. They were severe; they might be saying: "You are really a thief, or if not that, a receiver of stolen goods, and no better than a thief." She stood for a long time, nailed to the spot. At last she thought: "It is all over. Now I know that I shall never conquer these people, who know neither care nor fear. It is as in the Bible; I shall bruise their heel, but they shall bruise my head. And Alexander, as far as he is concerned, ought to have married the English lady."

To her own deep surprise she found that she did not mind. Alexander himself had become a very small figure in the background of life; what he did or thought mattered not in the least. That she herself had been made a fool of did not matter. "In a hundred years," she thought, "it will all be one."

What mattered then? She tried to think of the war, but found that the war did not matter either. She felt a strange giddiness as if the room was sinking away round her, but not unpleasantly. "Was there," she thought, "nothing remarkable left under the visiting moon?" At the word of the visiting moon the eyes of the image in the looking-glass opened wide; the two young women stared at one another intensely. Something, she decided, was of great importance, which had come into the world now, and in a hundred years would still remain. The pearls. In a hundred years, she saw, a young man would hand them over to his wife and tell the young woman her own story about them, just as Alexander had given them to her, and had told her of his grandmother.

The thought of these two young people, in a hundred years' time, moved her to such tenderness that her eyes filled with tears, and made her happy, as if they had been old friends of hers, whom she had found again. "Not cry quarter?" she thought. "Why not? Yes, I shall cry as high as I can. I cannot, now, remember the reason why I would not cry."

The very small figure of Alexander, by the window in the other room said to her: "Here is the eldest of your aunts coming down the street with a big bouquet."

Slowly, slowly Jensine took her eyes off the looking-glass, and came back to the world of the present. She went to the window. "Yes," she said, "they are from Bella Vista," which was the name of her father's villa. From their window the husband and wife looked down into the street.

JOHANNES V. JENSEN

****

Forces which point back to lost elements in his origin, but whose tendency was influenced from elsewhere, directed Columbus onward in search of a world he was never to find.

Deep-lying Northern instincts were crossed and dominated by surface currents from the world that had shaped his consciousness, the Southerner's world, the local stamp, the stamp of his time; he behaved now as an Italian, now as a Spaniard, always as a Christian; an inner illusory world stood between him and Nature, which he still regarded with the prejudiced eyes of his day, several realities one within another, like the heavens of that age, and all of them fairly independent of experience, in conformity with the contemporary imago mundi—*and yet Columbus went clean through all imaginary realities and came out with a new one.*

Pure and monumental was that quality in him which made this possible: courage, a complete dauntlessness which he had received as a heritage from ancestors who were conquerors and colonists and to generations of whom uncertainty and playing for high stakes had become the very form of their existence. Courage and endurance, the sailor's daring, inflexibility of purpose, are the clean line which runs through Columbus' character as a discoverer. He was a sportsman, and he was a man of genius, his motives rose superior to his age; where he regarded his voyage as a mission the elements were at work within him, he pressed on as though the whole of human nature had been pressing upon him. . . .

Only he in whom the past is stowed is freighted for the future. Columbus grows with the bearing of his exploit; we see, however, looking backward, that history passed through his heart. As he stands, he bears a bridge which joins widely separated worlds and epochs. He sets up a boundary between illusion and reality, not by what he thought but by what he was and what his passion gave an impulse to.

J. V. J.

****

Columbus in the Trade Wind

THE SARGASSO SEA, hundreds of leagues from land; three little ships lost on the boundless ocean, and their crews in despair.

The worst of their fright over this threatening new phenomenon, the masses of seaweed floating mile after mile in the ocean, had subsided; but it had been a hard trial. The first floating island of weed was taken for firm ground, land; it looked like a very low stretch of meadow lying flush with the water, and for a moment the idea that it might be land raised a flicker of hope, which was only to give way to deep disappointment and uneasiness—if it was not land, what could it be?

Soon the islands became so numerous that they formed a continuous carpet of weed over the whole surface of the sea as far as the eye could reach, and the Admiral kept straight ahead, while the crew cried out, in God's holy name, and implored the helmsman to fall off. Too late, they were already in the midst of the green, and look! she could sail through it without losing so very much of her way—for the present. But supposing the masses of weed got denser and they ended by sticking fast in them? That it was a sort of seaweed the Admiral convinced them all by having some of it fished up; but not any known kind of weed, and how could it grow here, how did it come here, many many leagues from land?

They need not be too sure that they were so very far from land, suggested the Admiral, sanguine of course as usual, and putting on a bold face just when the others looked blackest. But where could this land be? At any rate it was not to be seen for miles ahead or on either side, only a boundless pale-green expanse of tufted water with a false promise of meadows—so deceptive indeed that many believed in them. Might it not be supposed that sunken countries or submarine realms lay underneath here, from which all this grass had come loose and floated up? In that case it was dangerous; there must be shoals, at any moment they might run aground, and stranding so far from any coast would mean death. The Admiral's only reply to these complaints was to have soundings taken, and the lead ran out for hundreds of fathoms, all the line they had, and no bottom! If the pastures they were talking about lay below, then he must say they were a long way down; and the Admiral was cruel enough to add that *now* nobody would be likely to expect a cow to stick its

head out of the sea from the meadows below or to see a church spire
jutting out. Loud cries of pain drowned his words; the men were
thrown from fright into terror. So deep! Why, there was no bottom
at all here! So they *were* outside the world now and over the inconceivable abyss of Ocean. They had to prop each other up at the
thought, and their eyes nearly dropped out of their heads. To be
wrecked here, to sink and sink and sink. . . . But the Admiral asked
them rather dryly if it wouldn't be all the same to them how much
water they drowned in, a fathom or a mile, if it had to be: a heart-
less thing to say, and incautious. They roared—one man threw his
cap at him. The Admiral turned his back on them, but came again
and pointed with a great sweep of the arm out over the sea of weed
that shone like gold in the dazzling rays of the sun: if they believed
that all this splendor came from impossible submarine islands, then
it was *his* belief that it was a presage of real islands, perhaps not so
very far off, where the golden fields extended just as far as the seaweed here—floors of gold far and wide! And then they made a fuss
like a pack of women over the trouble and risk of getting there—as
if the islands wouldn't have been discovered and occupied long ago
if there had been no danger in it!

Silence, not a sound; some of them were put to shame, others led
into a new train of thought—it sounded wonderful, that about the
gold. And the end of it was that they went on sailing; while bandy-
ing words they easily did a half-day's run. But the men stuck to their
opinion. They passed through the weed right enough, but all the
same it was an ominous sign that the sea was getting so thick. What
if it thickened still more? They might sail in gruel, but in porridge
any man would stick fast. And the Admiral's words had left a sting
behind them: if he had more learning, it didn't give him the right
to make fun of poor Christian men.

If, however, there were lamentations over the danger of getting
stuck in the sea of weed, it was not long before the fact of their slipping so easily through it gave uneasiness. What would be the end
of it? This everlasting breeze from the north-east! Why, it held for
weeks, they never touched the sails, which stood day and night on
the starboard tack, easy sailing, but what about it when they had to
go the other way? How would they come home again? What kind
of a wind was it anyhow? It had never been reported anywhere else
that the wind held so long from one quarter; it could scarcely be
interpreted otherwise than that there was a sucking from the opposite quarter, the one they were making for, like the wind that goes

over a waterfall; it was from the *Abyss* the sucking came, they were
in it now, and it was a desperate thing, it was tempting God and
throwing away one's fair wind, which was of the kind the Evil One
sends . . .

The Admiral shrugged his shoulders. Truth to tell, he did not understand himself why the wind held so long; it was a new thing in
his experience, and every day he scanned the clouds and all other
indications a seaman stores in his head and recognizes on later occasions; but these waters were strange to him, and nobody as yet
could know how it was with this wind. There was every reason to
be grateful for it though, if the crew had not been growing more
anxious every day and scarcely to be managed in the long run.

Then it happened one day, the 23rd of September, that the wind
changed, they had a head-sea, and the crew could no longer maintain that there were no other winds in these seas but from the north-
east; Columbus was saved for another space, and he it was who
clasped his hands that evening in deepest gratitude to the All-
bountiful, in spite of the fact that they had made no headway that
day.

In his private meditations, divided between the Bible and the log-
book, he could not help thinking that evening of Moses, who led
his refractory people through so many real dangers, but whose most
difficut task was to preserve them from their own imagination and
instinct of self-destruction.

But all the complaints returned with renewed force when the
wind changed again; once more every one could clearly see that all
the waves were hurrying to the west, the whole sea was flowing that
way, straight into the Abyss!

They now passed out of the Sargasso Sea, out into clear deep
waves again, and if lately they had eyed the hated weed with furtive
looks of woe, they now cast back inconsolable glances after it. For
all the signs of land the Admiral had fabricated with his ready
tongue while it was there, were vanished now. That seaweed showed
the proximity of a coast had sounded right enough; but now? That
crabs which they had found in the weed were a good sign, that birds
and fish they had seen, which found food in it, also pointed to the
nearness of land, of course—but now it was days ago, and still
there was no land!

The men's heads were beginning to get a little addled: they saw
sea monsters in every wave that curled, and huddled together in

groups at night, afraid of the dark; they wept over the increasing heat, which left no doubt that they were approaching the scorching regions in the immediate neighborhood of the sun, where nothing can live, except salamanders; they would not escape with being turned as dark as the blackamoors in Africa, they would be completely charred, scorched up like flies, the whole ship would blaze up—in the name of the most merciful God, man, turn about before it is too late!

Other voices made themselves heard, and those of the soberest men on board, the officers themselves. The bottom could be seen of the ship's provisions, in a literal sense; in several places they had gone down through the cargo to the bottom of the ship; if they were to count on food for the same number of days back as they had sailed out, they would have to turn pretty soon. To this Columbus said nothing. In his own mind he looked forward to the hour when they no longer *could* turn back, when their food was exhausted to that extent; then there would be no other way than straight ahead, but he didn't say this.

The other complaints he took up, rather glad to be able to keep them alive, so that they might overshadow thoughts of the provisions; he went through them again with the crew, as often and as long as they liked, talking and talking, hollow-eyed, stiff with fatigue but indefatigable. It ended in a sort of permanent ship's parliament on board, where all, even the ordinary seamen, had a voice, and where the tone grew sharper and sharper. During these discussions all the theoretical side of the voyage was probed deeper and deeper, a kind of cross-examination which the Admiral accepted in good part, and which he spun out with a certain warmth, keeping an inner eye on the log the whole time.

All that Columbus had adduced again and again for fourteen years, before a commission of scholars in Portugal, and before a learned commission at Salamanca, had to come up, and he had to listen to the same arguments against him and refute them again as well as he could. Now how did he think he would reach the Indies by this crazy route which took him farther and farther away from them every day he sailed?

To put it briefly, if the earth was round . . .

Yes, but the earth wasn't round! Everybody knew that, everybody could see it, and it was heresy to assert the contrary, high treason against the Church and against God. Juan de la Cosa, who was the owner of the vessel and accompanied the exposition in that capacity, here acted as spokesman and displayed no mean biblical knowledge.

Neither the Pentateuch nor the Prophets nor the Apostles said anything about the earth being a globe; besides, ordinary common sense told you it was an error; take the Deluge, for instance, how would it have been possible if the earth was not flat? all the water would have run off if it had been curved . . .

Storms of applause from the whole crew for Juan de la Cosa, who modestly withdrew into the crowd, and a malicious chorus of yelping at Columbus.

But now the Admiral took to both Latin and Greek against Juan de la Cosa, quoted utterances of St. Augustine and compared them with things Aristotle had said, Strabo, Seneca, Pythagoras, Eratosthenes . . .

Aristotle . . . Juan de la Cosa nodded manfully, he had heard the name before, and knew that it carried weight, but he was not sure of his ground and the Admiral was given a chance of quoting at length all the reasons that had induced the ancients to assume the spherical form of the earth, the shadow it cast on the moon in an eclipse, the weightiest of proofs, which passed over the heads of the crew like the wildest moonshine. Juan de la Cosa, however, had understood it and came forward with an objection:

How was it possible that the earth cast a shadow on the moon, *even* if it was round? In that case the sun would have to pass right round the earth, *under* it so to speak . . .

COLUMBUS: That is just what it does.

JUAN DE LA COSA: Oh, I see. But then the earth must rest upon something, whether it is flat or round, a foundation; how can a heavenly body pass under that?

COLUMBUS: The earth has no foundation; it is a globe hanging freely in space.

Sensation. Suppressed passion here and there. All eyes hung upon Juan de la Cosa, who was quite distressed and looked at the Admiral with genuine sorrow, as he asked in a faltering voice how . . . how . . . the earth, weighing many hundred thousand quintals . . . hang freely in space, how could that be?

What is impossible to Almighty God? answered the Admiral with force. He who has set the spheres in motion and keeps them going, with sun, moon and stars to give light and measure the day, should He not be able to keep the earth suspended in its place in space? *He* alone knows how!

Juan da la Cosa bowed his head and his forefinger went up to his breast, the sign of the cross made itself at the mention of the holy name of God. The crew followed his example, they felt as if they

were in church, and the threatening conflict of opinion was resolved
in a moment of solemn awe.

But the dispute blazed up again, and Juan de la Cosa obstinately
insisted, on behalf of all, that *even* if the earth was round, which it
was *not;* nay, even if hung freely in space, by the power of God,
whose name be praised, then it was neverthless an impossible thing
they were trying to do. A globe *might* be so big that to us men it
would appear to be flat in that part where one was situated,
granted, and that must necessarily be the upper part; but if one left
it, one would have to proceed along a slope which would get steeper
and steeper, vertical at last, and then turn inward on the under side,
always supposing that the spherical theory held, which, of course,
was sheer nonsense, for how could water hang on a globe all the
way round?

Applause. *Bravo! bravo!* they cried to Juan de la Cosa; and he
was really brave, he looked the Admiral straight in the face as, with
a bow to his superior, he resumed his place in the crowd.

The last question the Admiral left alone and seized on the first,
pounced on it like a hawk:

We are sailing *downward* at this moment!

Pause, until his meaning dawned on them, then violent excitement; several men shrieked aloud and ran to the bulwarks to look,
some instinctively laid hand on hilt. Juan de la Cosa turned pale,
but pulled himself together and asked:

And how did the Admiral think of sailing upward again?

Everybody grasped at once the bearing of Juan de la Cosa's
words, pictured the immense curve down which they were engaged
in sailing, saw the impossibility of ever coming up it again and stood
as though turned to stone . . .

In the midst of this consternation the Admiral was heard to laugh,
a perfectly careless laugh at such a serious moment; he was making
fun of them, the hell-hound, the cup was full, they wouldn't listen
to him any more . . .

We are sailing *upward* also at this moment, said the Admiral
mildly to Juan de la Cosa, and explained his meaning more precisely; if the earth was really round there could be neither up nor
down at any given point, except in the direction that passed through
the centre of the earth and the zenith . . . But Juan de la Cosa
shook his head, gave the Admiral an honest look and shook his
head, grieved for him, for his ship and for them all.

The Admiral then changed his tone, laughed with his cavernous
eyes, and made as though he accepted the others' view, since they

were in the majority; suppose they were right and the earth was flat. But in that case it could not be surrounded by an abyss down which the water plunged, for then the seas would long ago have run off the earth, the Deluge would have been impossible, as Juan de la Cosa very rightly pointed out. If on the other hand the Ocean lay about the earth in a ring, the common conception, it by no means precluded the idea of sailing westward to the Indies, round behind instead of straight ahead, not on a globe but on a circle, half-way round the earth's disc, if they preferred it that way . . .

Chorus of all hands that Juan de la Cosa was right, angry exclamation against the Admiral for evidently trying to obscure the heart of the matter and avoid Juan de la Cosa's direct question: how were you to sail up the curve of the earth again, when once you had had the mad idea of sailing down it? Out with it!

THE ADMIRAL: Now it was *they* who all believed that the earth was round.

Yells and bawling, cries of shame and general howls; and so the lesson came to an end.

In a succeeding one the Admiral had to produce all his reasons and proofs of the existence of land westward in the Ocean, apart from the cosmic ones; an argument they had heard before and that every man in Spain and Portugal had heard before, until they cried for help at the very sight of Columbus; an old trite lesson which he actually repeated for positively the last time, in fluent Spanish but with an accent that betrayed the Italian. In other circumstances than these, where their lives were at stake, they would have taken a wild delight in him, a glorious fool to have on board, all the more glorious as he was so big, so tall and so touched in the upper storey; had they not hated him as they did they might even have pitied him, alone against all, far out at sea, doubly alone as a stranger among strangers, this queer fish who was getting old and made himself a laughing-stock by repeating and repeating, explaining and dogmatizing about the same things over and over again—

Such as: From time immemorial ["Time immemorial . . ." Diego mimicked him, with Italian accent, discreet tone and all; aside, of course, but loud enough to amuse his neighbours]—from time immemorial there had been reports of a vanished land out in the Atlantic Ocean, Plato's Atlantis; opinions were divided as to whether it had been swallowed up by the sea or the way to it had been forgotten; the latter view was supported by rumours repeated through the ages of such lands or islands far to the west of Europe. Many were of the opinion that these were Paradise itself, the Lost Country, from which mankind had once been driven out and had never found the way back; the holy Brandanus had set out in search of them and had actually arrived at a happy isle in the Ocean, the abode of the Blest, as might be read in his legend; but since then the way had been lost again, it was eight hundred years since St. Brandan's voyage. The legend had afterwards been connected with the Canary Isles, wrongly of course; the islands must lie much farther out in the Ocean, at least twice as far as the Azores, which were also out of the question, and presumably more to the southward, possibly in the very direction in which they were now sailing.

Now it was to be remarked that in another, more recent view the legend of these mysterious islands or continents far far to the west might be regarded as obscure but substantially correct reports of the east coast of India, which extended so far around the earth that perhaps there had been contact with it now and then by the other way, straight across the Atlantic. It was known that very large islands lay off the coast of India, like Zipangu, of which Marco Polo had sufficiently trustworthy accounts; these must then be the same as the Antilia or the Island of Brazil which the latest geographers, in anticipation of their discovery, had already marked on their maps, as for example the most learned and famous Toscanelli [What kind of a fool was he?" from Diego], and as the distance between the west coast of Europe and the extremity of India was more or less known, the width of the Atlantic, that is, the distance to be deducted from the whole circumference of the earth, could be approximately determined; in the Admiral's opinion it was neither more nor less than the distance they had already sailed, so now the islands might appear any day [scornful snorts from Diego and the rest of the audience; how often they had heard this sanguine irresponsible tale!]

Well, well, if the geographical arguments were no more obvious to them than the cosmic, then they had the direct, tangible proofs, the missives to be taken up and felt which from time to time had been brought by the Atlantic and which must point to there being land on the other side. In the first place there were the reports of many people who had *seen* the islands, on very clear days, out in the ocean to the west of the Canary Isles ["Long-sighted people, I must say"—Diego]; that was as it might be. Personal evidence: Columbus himself many years before in Madeira had given shelter to a ship-wrecked man who disclosed to him on his deathbed that he had been driven by a storm twenty-eight days out into the

Atlantic on a voyage to England, and had there come upon islands the natives of which went about naked; afterwards he had got a fair wind back to Europe but was so worn out that he died in Madeira, the last of a crew of seventeen ["A nice story that! Why didn't he stay in the islands? Weren't they worth it?"]

There was Pedro Correa ["Oh, *that* fellow"] who was able to tell Columbus about a remarkable piece of driftwood that had come ashore at Porto Santo, curiously dark wood and, be it noted, carved, though apparently not with iron tools. Still more remarkable: some big reeds had drifted up on the same shore, like a sort of grass on an extraordinarily large scale, almost as though they came from a country where everything was of supernatural size. ["Let's see them!"] Columbus himself might have had a chance of seeing them washed up with his own eyes; he had spent three years in Porto Santo and had himself observed many things there which indirectly pointed to lands in the west, curious cloud formations and appearances of the sky, on which, however, he would not lay stress. The reeds, on the other hand, had been sent to the King of Portugal, and there he had *seen* them. Martin Vincenti, a seaman of worthy credit ["I'd like to have him here"—Diego], had also found carved driftwood far to the west of Cape St. Vincent.

But the most remarkable of all proofs was that reported from the Azores: there after westerly winds they had found boats washed up on the beach, hollowed out of a single trunk, evidently the craft of savages; and on Flores, one of the Azores, two corpses had been washed up, possibly these same savages; they were broad in face and did not resemble any known race of men. This one might almost call tangible proof of the existence of the Antipodes . . .

The Antipodes . . . here Juan de la Cosa coughed and ventured an observation. To a sober view the finding of the two corpses, if the account was to be relied upon, did not appear to him to convey any information about the Antipodes, since from what one knew about them they must have an entirely different appearance, scarcely confined to such a trifle as greater breadth of face. In the nature of things nothing definite could be known about the Antipodes, but it was obvious that beings who were to inhabit the under side of the earth, where the trees grew downward and the rain fell straight up in the air, must at any rate have suckers on their feet, like certain kinds of lizards, to stay where they were; in other respects also they were doubtless very different from Christians. It was not necessary indeed to go so far as the earth's poles or supports to find monsters; even in the heathen world, towards the outskirts of the earth, there was a great falling-off from the human form, if one might believe travellers and writings whose age entitled them to veneration. Not that he was himself a man of great reading, but still he had heard of the Arimaspians and of the Satyrs and knew that beyond Arabia there were people with only one leg, on which they hopped around, and that very swiftly; that there were Amazons and men without a head but with a face in their stomach was also known. From this it appeared that the farther one travelled from the Christian world, the more men ceased to be created in God's image, and there seemed to be good grounds for supposing that those who dwelt farthest down were created in the image of quite another Person, if indeed one might include the Devil in Creation; in which case they had wings and were to that extent capable of keeping on the under side of the earth. Instead of supposing Paradise to lie in that quarter it was more natural to imagine Hell there, even to an unenlightened view, since there was every reason to presume that the earth rested on fire or had fire in its depths, as could be seen by volcanoes; the fact that it grew hotter and hotter the farther one sailed to the south was an indication in the same direction, as all those present were in a position to confirm. Thus the two corpses at the Azores, in Juan de la Cosa's humble layman's opinion, did not tell them much about the Antipodes. The mention of them, on the other hand, suggested quite other and horrible ideas to the mind.

An uncanny silence fell upon the crew at Juan de la Cosa's rational words. Of course, the Admiral always made it appear to them that the only goal of their desires was to sight land, but it depended a good deal on what awaited them when they did reach land. Speechless resentment against the Admiral was reflected in their features at the thought of what Juan de la Cosa had pictured; they could not find words for their horror and abomination. Was it possible that he intended and had been intending all the time to sail them straight into Hell? Were they to lose their salvation as well as their lives? Had he sold their souls? Then let the Devil take him ... The oath stuck in their throats, for if he was the foul fiend himself ...

Ugly pause. Even Jorge, the wholly inarticulate, who sat on deck poking bits of salt pork into his mouth with his knife and audibly pulling the blade out again between his teeth, an old galley slave with scars on his ankles from the shackles and bare places on his scalp like an old horse chafed by the harness—even he gave an *Ouf!* and raised his pock-marked face, shaking a little with age, blinked and cocked his ear: What now, what made the men so quiet? Unwholesome air, he had always found, when abuse died away on men's lips! Could there be worse things in store for him than he had already gone through, in his long, precarious life?

But Jorge was quickly reassured and shoved in another mouthful that had been checked in the air on the point of his knife, for the Admiral was evidently saying things that restored the men's breath and gave them back the use of speech: the Admiral crossed himself so frankly and feelingly for his own part at the mention of the Evil One and his abode that only the most grudging could doubt his piety; assuredly *he* was not in league with the Prince of Fire, far less was he that personage himself, so much would have to be admitted.

A protracted exchange of opinions ensued on difficult theological problems. The Admiral did not hold the view that the Underworld was a place which could be reached by any known route, at any rate not by sea; that was out of the question, since water was an element hostile and opposed to fire; the way thither was inaccessible to man, while alive; for such as died without grace it was easy to find. Paradise, on the other hand, which was commonly placed in Heaven, without more precise indication . . . well, they had no priest on board, but even in the absence of one the holy articles of faith and the revelation of the Scriptures should remain entirely undisturbed; however, even the Scriptures gave nothing that one might call definite observation of the position of the Kingdom of Heaven; but as we were told that our first parents were driven from thence it was permissible to suppose that it had lain and still lay somewhere on earth. In contradistinction to the Underworld we had an example in Holy Writ that men might be taken up alive into Heaven, the prophet Elijah; although this happened a long time ago it could not therefore be regarded as absolutely impossible that it might take place again.

Shaking of heads among the Admiral's hearers, divided opinions and an uncomfortable feeling in their insides; as usual, the talk had an inconclusive, unsatisfied ending. To many whose sole unhappy thought was their abandonment in the midst of Ocean, the future appeared in a doubtful, hopeless light; in truth, with all the various prospects suggested by the officers, the cry of *Land* could not come soon enough!

When at last it came, however, it swept aside all other thoughts . . .

Land, land!

It was from Martin Alonzo Pinzon the blessed cry came. He had just closed the flagship in the *Pinta*, a comparison had been made of logs and charts, apparently of a disquieting nature, when Martin Alonzo noticed something like a low cloud or indication of land ahead to the westward, right in the sunset, a long way off, but with so unmistakably the character of a long, broken coast-line that Martin Alonzo was not in doubt for a moment:

Land, land!

They all saw it, the Admiral saw it and immediately fell on his knees on the quarter-deck and began to thank God with hands raised high. Immense sensation, all troubles forgotten, wild joy all over the ship at the sight of the distant blessed streak of land; the men ran up the masts and down again, fell into each other's arms, were quite beside themselves.

Ay, a mad scene of confusion, until the Admiral in a powerful, solemn voice which penetrated from one end of the ship to the other, ordered all hands to be called on deck for divine service

A gun was fired, and the *Niña* sailed up; the three ships sailed abreast in the falling darkness, and as the streak of land vanished in the great glow of the sunset, and the afterglow paled away and gave place to the first tiny twinkling stars, the hymn arose from the *Santa Maria*, from the *Pinta* and the *Niña*, three choirs of men's voices which united in one and cried out upon the sea and to the stars:

Salve Regina, Mater misericordiæ, vita, dulcedo, et spes nostra, salve.

Ad te clamamus exsules, filii Hevæ.

Ad te suspiramus, gementes, et flentes in hoc lacrymarum valle.

Eia ergo advocata nostra, illos tuos misericordes oculos ad nos converte.

Et Jesum benedictum fructum ventris tui, nobis post hoc exsilium ostende.

O clemens, o pia, o dulcis Virgo Maria.

—Translated by Arthur G. Chater

FRANS EEMIL SILLANPÄÄ

****

F. E. Sillanpää, Finnish Nobel Prize winner, considers "The Night of the Harvest Festival" from his novel, The Maid Silja, *representative of his work. This episode in the novel, translated from the Finnish by Alexander Matson, concerns the central character, Silja, daughter of a small farmer whose fortunes so deteriorated that, after his death, Silja has had to go from one farm to another as a serving girl.*

****

The Night of the Harvest Festival

So PASSED the early part of the summer. Night was at one time almost non-existent, a mere holding of the breath, as it were, by the heavens while evening gave way to morning. The young and happy needed sleep only as the slightest break in their days, and very little food either. For many young people, and older ones, it was the last beautiful summer. To be sure, there are always some living their last summer, but in the case of this summer there were special reasons. Everyone had his or her premonitions, but no one knew.

Midsummer too passed. The human mind still tried to imagine the nights were white. Here a girl sat by a window reading, as midnight drew nigh, the letter she had received that evening. She even took out her writing materials and set to work on her answer; it was still light enough for that, though July had begun. And so expressive was still the nocturnal light that the writer got no further in her intention than the opening phrase: "I am writing to you in the delicious summer night. . . ."—before she was lost in memories of her distant friend, fancying herself walking with him this same night there where they had once. . . .and the dawn was reddening the north-west. The young lady is on a holiday here and has hoped for more experiences than have come her way, by these hopes betraying her friend. But her hopes have remained unfulfilled, and now she tries to compose a pretty answer to her friend's letter. Only longing

889

disturbs her. Dawn comes glowing, a precious day and night of summer and youth has gone.

A week later, when she reads a new letter, the dusk surprises her and this time there can be no thought of writing an answer. The leaves have grown darker with the nights, bats fly around the old building.

Around Rantoo way the summer has been quiet and peaceful, and even from the middle of the parish come tidings of peace. On the small farms where the workers are old friends, the haymaking passes off easily. The master tries to be merrier than usual, as though by these means to lead his own thoughts and those of his men away from the burden of the times.

Ever further the summer progresses. The rye pales, and on southward slopes shocks begin to appear. The material for bread was safe, no small matter that summer. As the sickle swished into the ripened stalks life felt safer, warmer.

. . . Here and there young reapers, with the fire of those mysterious times* flaming in their eyes, refused to work a minute over the agreed time, although a quarter of an hour would have seen the rye all harvested. But on most of the reapers such behavior on a fine harvest-time evening in an ancient field made an unpleasant impression. . . .

The Kulmala kitchen is small and faces north, so that Sofia already has to use a lamp as she busies herself with coffee-making and other preparations one Sunday evening at harvest-time. In her field a merry reaping-bee is in progress. A girl comes every now and again from the field to confer with Sofia, anxious lest the musician should fail to appear. Someone sets off on a bicycle to seek him. There is not much space in the kitchen, the big coffee-pot is nearly in darkness on the range; but Sofia is able to judge its boiling so well that not a drop brims over, only the scent of coffee steals into this first lamplight of the autumn. One of the girls is helping by now to set the table, taking down the cups from a familiar shelf. Through the open window the voices of newcomers can be heard, among them the Professor's voice. Sofia glances out of the window and sees her cousin stopping out briskly beside the young gentleman from Rauhala. The old man has a wonderful red hat on his head.

"Are you a Turk or something?" Sofia asked as she met him outside the door.

* *1917: The year of the overthrow of the Czar in Russia.*

"Is there anything left to reap?" asked the Professor in turn and continued his way to the field, from which came the swish of sickles and shouted conversation, merged into familiar noise of a reaping-bee.

The Professor had not brought a sickle with him, but at the first expression of disbelief in his ability to cut rye he snatched the sickle from the hand of the nearest worker, and grunting with the intensity of his efforts began reaping swiftly and skilfully. Beautifully the first swathe grew along his path and he went on with the second until the others all began watching him, upon which he stopped. An old cottar, of the same age as the Professor, remarked, addressing the crowd: "We've reaped together, that man and I, in earnest and all day long—I'll bet the Professor remembers the time we worked in the Hillu fields, when he was still a young man." His surmise was confirmed, and the sickle went back to its younger owner.

"Do you fancy you know something too?" the Professor shouted to the young gentleman, who was neatly tying a sheaf, which he lifted with an easy motion into the middle of the plot, where the next shock was to stand. This too was no small marvel, for he was of gentle birth.

"When did that Silja manage to slip here?" the Professor went on almost at once, as the girl threw down beside him a sheaf she had just tied. The Professor had begun in earnest to build up the sheaves into shocks, as there did not seem to be anyone regularly on that job. The smile in the girl's eyes was all the answer he got. The atmosphere of the field was intense and happy. Here and there backs straightened and eyes sought the gate, where Eemeli Kukkola could already be seen with his accordion. Farther down the road the Professor's daughter was approaching with the young lady who was spending the summer at Rauhala. Sofia came from the yard towards the field, apparently with an invitation to coffee. Some of the reapers went, but others stayed, for the rye was nearly cut. "Don't go yet, it'll get dark if we start coffee drinking in between." But down on the house steps someone was testing the accordion's tone and the trills fired the minds of the young so strongly that many of them were too impatient to go on working. Finally Sofia alone remained in the field to glean fallen ears and straighten a hastily-made shock or two. In the house and beside the steps the voices of the coffee drinkers blended already in a steady murmur. As the widow drew nearer the house she heard a rhythmic thumping emerge from it in time to a trill-embellished valse. She looked once more behind her at the darkening field, at the rows of shocks that had arisen as in a twinkling, sighed deeply and entered the circle of din made by the reapers.

All the doors were open. The shyer lads stood about and sky-larked in the darkness of the porch, and to these Sofia uttered a merry exhortation. On the back bench of the living room the Professor was sitting with the owner of the neighbouring farm, who had arrived unobserved at the house. The young gentleman from Rauhala was dancing with Miss Laura: Sofia paused to watch them. Was there anything between the two, as people were whispering? If there was, it was something pretty much settled by now, for Sofia could not see them talk much or even exchange glances. Now the young gentleman was bowing to Silja. A beautiful girl, that Silja; her eyes looked so good, especially in the lamplight.

Indeed, she looked very lovely this evening; Silja herself felt it somehow. This was the highest harvest-festival of her life. No doubts about anything, she felt it anew from the arm that wound itself about her body and in winding seemed to be sensing the feel of her back and waist. This youth had recently been tying sheaves; chaff still clung to the lapel of his coat, and from his skin came a faint male scent. They danced well together; instinctively, in the darker parts of the room, they pressed closer together until each was aware of the existence of the girl's breasts. The music stopped, one could crowd through the door into the yard, still maintaining one's hold of one's partner.

The red full moon peered through an opening in the woods as though playfully spying on someone. When it first appeared it was impossibly big, only to shrink and turn paler as it rose in the sky. The dark green of the earth's surface could still add its own tinge to the moonlight; the atmosphere was warm and intimate. Silja Salmelus gazed out of her dark eyes, moonbeams entangled in her lashes and flashing reflections from her pupils.

The ale-barrel was broached, the crowd grew livelier, each member of it occupied solely with the person with whom his or her conversation was proceeding. It was easy for couples to vanish and appear again. The first rest was already over. The accordion-player had had his coffee and ale; taking up his instrument again he began a fine new valse.

The Professor's high spirits had risen higher. He listened to the tune for a while, then frowned, got up and went over to the musician. "Give it here, and I'll play," he said, and the next moment he had drawn the accordion to him as, earlier in the evening, he had seized a sickle.

"Now there's another tone in the old musical-box," chuckled the farmer beside whom the Professor had been sitting. The Professor played to the full extent of the bellows, and the young gentleman happening to dance past him just then with Silja, he winked at the youth and broke audibly into the words of a Swedish song.

The floor filled, everyone wishing to be in the dance when it was the Professor who played. By now the old man was singing loudly and infectiously; he went on while there was a single couple left out on the floor.

Silja and Armas did not exchange a word during the dance, but they clung to each other closer and longer than before.

"Let's go. . . ." whispered the youth's voice in the girl's ear.

No one was in the yard or on the steps when they went.

There was only the moon to stare and keep on staring. It was cooler now, a fine smell rose from the dry clay of the drive, something moved in the dim grass, a mouse or a disturbed grasshopper. The barn was on a hillside, behind a cluster of low bushes. They were quite certain no one had seen them come here. The Professor had apparently stopped playing, for a couple of laughing remarks in male voices were wafted from the steps over the yard. The men had girls with them, but these made no sound. They went off somewhere towards the brook, none of them remembering the existence of the barn.

It was a warm night, the sun had had time during the past few weeks to charge young people with the whole strength of summer, the blood throbbed through full veins, and with it awoke in every nerve all the instincts placed there by Nature, almost to pain and bliss simultaneously. The cooler night held in condensed form the relaxing fire of the day. Young betrothed people sought out each other, and those too, whose glances had recently been kindled, the one by the other, walked the silent by-paths, avoiding those who, so they believed, had never known anything like this and were therefore likely to envy them and spread base rumours; such were in particular, the oldest women, and men at the worst period of middle-age toil.

Hundreds and thousands of couples crept thus, nor were they aware of what they were doing. For in fulfilling the raw command of Nature their souls drank into a deep and pure childlike self-

sleep. During those decisive moments the rough and foul-mouthed
farmhand, who had at last succeeded in persuading the poultry-
maid from the manor to accompany him, lived through the same
experience as the pure gentle youth in whose embrace a noble and
innocent human flower emerged from its bud. None of them remembered at the moment what Nature's aim had been in guiding
them so far. To them it was Life, the finest perfume of young delightful life, up to the penultimate moment of its climax. After it
had happened, Nature drew as it were away, after-moments not
being its concern. The couple might doze in each other's arms for a
few moments, drawing a veil between what had been and the approaching everyday dawn.

"Let's go and dance again," Silja said, passionately clinging to her
lover's arm.

"Will there be anybody left there now?" the youth replied in a
slightly cooler tone.

They went into the yard.

Down the steps came a young reaper, too young yet for such
gatherings, his brain fuddled with ale, his face grey and uglily
contorted. The boy hurried off and vanished. Sofia came out too
and whispered to Silja and her companion where she had hidden
the ale, not wishing to keep it freely available after a few of those
lads had gone at it senselessly. She was giving them small beer now
—"But there's plenty left for you, just try."

They went, delighted to be going together on this little secret errand. Unconsciously Silja still clung to the young man's arm, as
though never more intending to withdraw her hand from it, and he
had not the heart to thrust it away, so deliciously it quivered there.
Indeed there was no one left to fear. The Professor and Laura and
the guests from Rauhala had already gone. While they were going
they had looked for Armas, but had then decided that he must have
left before them.

Silja drank the ale as though in defiance, her mood seemingly
still in the ascendant. Her glowing eyes sought those of her companion over the tankard with such power that the young man
seemed inwardly to shrink. A polka tune still burst from the house.
They went in to dance. In the dust the red of dawn was already dis-
cernible, the musician's fingers fumbled, the keys clapped more
loudly than before. A quite young farmhand, who had danced
hard all evening and not got drunk, was still dancing, though his
collar had stuck together into one limp band. He danced with all

of the women in turn, and politely begged for a dance with Sofia too. He did not forget Silja either. Armas watched them dancing and was strangely moved—what a perfect gentleman the boy was, so faultless his behaviour.

When Silja was free again, Armas motioned to her that he was going for another drink from a certain tankard, and Silja followed him. The girl's eyes glowed deep and unfathomable; the youth's white teeth broke into view as he licked his lips after drinking. Then they went back to the house, a good deal more warmed than they were a while back.

"And now, Kukkola, let's have the Professor's valse," the young gentleman shouted with a queer boldness.

The tune began, and everybody danced as before. A couple of middle-aged cattle-maids for whom there were no male partners left over, danced together. They were out on a spree merely by the act of keeping awake. For them it was experience enough to be able to go straight from this house, without a wink of sleep, to the morning milking in the cowyards and then, with the sun already flaming high, drive their cattle to familiar pastures, through a familiarly worn gate, past and over familiar cattle-tracks.

When the valse ended these same maids gave what turned out to be the signal to break up. They fetched their shawls and went in full view of all, the blameless young farmhands going with them as escort. There were no more dances after that. Eemeli Kukkola rolled his eyes a little and made ready to go. Sofia led him to the hidden ale before he left. The day was clear and bright, permitting thick folds of dust to be distinguished from the shining streaks of uncovered floor in the living-room.

Outside the daylight was still more clearly evident, or rather the early morning, which had almost a stronger individuality than the day. The time when the Professor, Miss Laura and the summer visitors from Rauhala were here seemed immensely distant. They were wholly unrelated to the life that now reigned, diminished in scale and intimate, around Kulmala. Armas was especially aware of this when he noted the growing boldness with which his girl clung to his arm.

Actually this was something both of them were experiencing for the first time. The young man had naturally danced with many girls before this, and many of them had taken his arm, but in it all there had been nothing like this. Silja had no thought whatever this night, but sped forward along the flower-bordered track of her life, speeding all the quicker for that she was now at its summit. Her soul was full of the glow of emotion, her body had, as well, known something unforeseen, miraculous, ecstatic, painful—something beyond which there was no going, beyond which one had no desire to go, nothing shameful, nothing to deny—so long as one could hold on to that arm, so long as one could trust as now, fully trust. . . .

It was still some hours to their usual getting-up time. Silja longed for an opportunity to rest together somewhere in peace, to sit closely-held, to approach each other. The new and miraculous she had experienced still drew her. It was unlike anything she had even imagined before, anything she had ever heard of during the many everyday hours of her life; not that she had ever stopped to ponder over the meaning of what she heard: such phrases had recoiled harmlessly from her. Thus her experience of the night had no connection in her consciousness with anything she had ever heard mentioned. It had no connection anywhere, neither with the past nor with the future; it was merely life on this blissful night, for which everything in the past had been, and from which onward the future was a blank even to the imagination.

"Let's go that way yet, there's such a beautiful rock there."

They passed quite close to a solitary sleeping farm. Silja knew the way. They followed the garden fence, climbed a rock mound, which gave excuses for helping each other, came to a smithy and went on through a lush pasture, until a belt of bushes thinned, showing a rock cliff that fell steeply before their eyes down to the shore. From the top of the cliff the crowns of the spruce growing along the shore could almost be touched. On the opposite side of the narrowish channel a long narrow bay opened out, at the end of which the sun was just rising. The sight joined together in strange fashion these two playthings of Fate. The place had been known to the girl, and here she had brought her lover in this dawn when her past life was in any case over, happen what would.

It was easy to feel that here was peace undisturbed, that not even chance could bring anyone here at this hour. Only the sun rose and saw. The young man and the girl—the young woman—knew already what would happen to them here. No uncertainty, no fear, nothing—only the miracle revealed by their now merged lives.

They were never to learn whether their arrival together was observed at Rauhala or Rantoo. Miss Laura, who did in fact see it, was too high-minded to disclose it to either of them.

But when the day began the atmosphere of Rantoo Villa, hitherto so fresh, seemed in some way to have become vitiated. Even the Professor's wings drooped a little, as he himself described his condition, adding his opinon that it was due to his staying up past midnight and then being unable to sleep at once owing to the ale he had drunk. At the breakfast-table, just as Silja was bringing in a dish from the kitchen, Miss Laura remarked in a careless drawling fashion that the young gentleman Armas—her own words—was said to be leaving by the day-steamer. The dish in Silja's hand shook a little, so slightly that it would have been impossible for any one to swear that it had trembled. Perhaps Silja's steps, as she went back into the kitchen, were quicker than usual, with an effect of acceleration, but the door did not close any more loudly than usual, and no sound came from the kitchen.

Most noticeable of all was perhaps the very fact that nothing was heard from the kitchen, although the serving would really have needed continued attention. When the bell rang for her, Silja came in as one asleep and empty-handed, although the signal was for her to bring in the next dish.

"Well, are you too dance-befuddled, like me?" growled the Professor.

"It wouldn't be surprising if she were, seeing that she came home at four," Silja heard Miss Laura answer.

"If this wasn't Silja's first dance, I might lose my temper but I'll let it pass," the Professor said.

Miss Laura made no reply—except by her silence.

HALLDÓR LAXNESS

****

*From Iceland, Halldór Laxness agreed to be represented by a sec-
tion from the saga of his native country,* Independent People. *This
section concerns Bjartur of Summerhouses, a small freeholder, who
having given eighteen years to a master in order to lay by the purchase price of a small mountain sheep farm, is now his own master
and at this point in the novel, as the Icelandic winter approaches, is
out in the moorland valleys attempting to find one of his lost sheep.*

****

An Icelandic Pioneer

BJARTUR OF SUMMERHOUSES knew better than most people all those
nooks and crannies of the far mountain pastures where sheep are
still to be found after the last of the round-ups. It was on the
eastern slopes of this extensive moorland plateau that he had spent
his childhood, on its western border that he had worked as a
shepherd all the years of his youth, and in one of its valleys that
he now lived as a freeholder, so he knew it from spring to the
end of winter, in fragrance and the song of birds, in frost and
silence, through innumerable journeys in search of the sheep that
bound him so closely to it. But the high heath had also a value for
this man other than the practical and the economic. It was his
spiritual mother, his church, his better world, as the ocean must
inevitably be to the seafarer. When he walked along over the moors
on the clear, frosty days of late autumn, when he ran his eyes over
the desert's pathless range and felt the cold clean breeze of the
mountains on his face, then he too would prove the substance of
patriotic song. He would feel himself exalted above the trivial, commonplace existence of the settlements and live in that wonderful
consciousness of freedom that can be likened to nothing except
perhaps the love of native land shown by sheep themselves, for
they would die on their own mountains were they not driven back
to the farmsteads by dogs. On such autumn journeys, when he

walked from watercourse to watercourse, from crest to crest of the undulating tableland, as if his path lay through infinity itself, there was nothing to trouble the proud eye of the poet. Nothing nurtures the poet's gift so much as solitude on long mountain journeys. He could chew over the same words for hours on end till he had succeeded in beating them into verse. Here there was nothing to distract the mind from poetry. Today when he once more greeted his old friend the moorland breeze, he allowed no sentimental twinges about his parting from Rosa to delay him longer from enjoying the true freedom of the wastes. Nothing is so alluring in the autumn as to make off into the wilderness, away, away, for then the Blue Mountains gleam with a greater fascination than at any other time. The winged summer visitors of the moors have most of them flown, but the grouse has not yet left for the farms and remains to skim the frozen peat in low flight, gurgling much, blinking an inquisitive eye. Most of the ducks have flown down to the seashore, or to the warmer lakes near the coast, for the moorland tarns are frozen over and the rivers edged with ice. Occasional ravens may be seen flapping round, croaking horribly, and this may often be an ominous sign that a sheep, dying or dead, lies somewhere in the neighbourhood. On this occasion there was still very little snow, but where the ground was bare of turf it was covered with little flat cakes of ice. In one place a fox darted behind a hummock, and an hour or two later he crossed the spoor of a number of reindeer in the snow.

Bjartur that day explored two valleys, in one of which he remembered sheltered slopes with ling on them, and in the other, evergreen swamps round a spring which kept the same temperature all the year round. But in neither place was there living creature to be seen, except a family of mallards in an open pool in the river flowing through the more southerly of the two valleys, just below the swamps. Evening was now falling and there was scarcely light enough left to search for sheep, so Bjartur headed for a place in the Blue Mountains where he knew of hospitable night quarters, intending also to search the mountains on the morrow, especially those to the south, where there are valleys in which the ground is warm and sheep have been known to live all through the winter without harm. Early in the evening the moon peeped over the horizon and swept first the moorland bluffs, then the valleys, with its blue light, making the dusty ice-flats shine like gold. The silence of the moors was perfect. In this silence, this light, this landscape, the man was perfect in his harmony with the soul within him.

Late in the evening he reached his lodging, a cave under Strut-fell formed of projecting rocks, and sitting down in the entrance, he ate facing the moon. When he had eaten he went into the cave, where a great flat block of stone, lying on some large pebbles, had served from time immemorial as a resting-place for travellers. On this Bjartur lay down to sleep using his bundle as a pillow. He was practically the only traveller who paid a regular yearly visit to the cave at this season, and as he had acquired the art of sleeping on the block without ill effect in any weather, he was very fond of the place. When he had slept for a good while, he woke up shivering. This shiver was a characteristic of the lodging, but it was unneces-sary to lose one's temper over it if one only knew the trick of get-ting rid of it. This trick consisted in getting up, gripping the block with both arms, and turning it round till one was warm again. Ac-cording to ancient custom it had to be turned around eighteen times, thrice a night. It would have been considered a most formid-able task in any other lodging, for the block weighed not less than a quarter of a ton, but Bjartur thought nothing more natural than to revolve it fifty-four times a night, for he enjoyed trying his strength on large stones. Each time that he had given the block eighteen turns, he felt warm enough to lie down again and go to sleep with his bundle under his head. But when he woke up the fourth time, he was well rested, and, indeed, dawn was in the sky. He set out at once up the mountain slopes and looked in several gullies. When he had warmed himself with walking, he sat down on a stone and ate some black pudding. After threading a pass in the mountains, he came about midday into the district of Reykjadalir. In the valleys here there are many places where the soil is warm and steam rises from the sands, but there are no open hot springs here; farther down are great tracts of ground stained red with iron-water, and descending towards them from the mountain slopes, strips of grass and ling where stray sheep are often to be found. On this occasion, however, there was nothing to be seen except a bird that Bjartur did not know; it rose from one of the warm spots and flew off, probably a hot-spring bird.

He decided now to make his way eastwards in order to search some gullies running down into Glacier River, then spend the night in a shepherds' hut near the river and on the eastern boundary of the moors, a far cry. There was not much frost, but the sky was overcast, and as day wore on, it began to snow quite heavily. His way lay along the western bank of Glacier River, for on the other side began the far pastures of another county, and as this was a major river, flowing deep and swift all the way from its source in Glacier, sheep had seldom been known to cross from one bank to the other. But on many of the curves of the river flats had been formed, with a fair growth of ling on them, and sheep often hid themselves there until well on into the winter. The river thundered past, dark and heavy in the drizzling snow, with a roar that could be heard for miles around. The nights had long been creeping in, but today the period of light was shortened further the thicker the drizzle grew; the snow fell to the earth in heavy flakes and in a short while it lay so deep underfoot that the going rapidly worsened. In the snow the ice-free Glacier River seemed to stream through its wilderness in redoubled coldness.

Bjartur now realized that there would be little point in trying to find any animal in this light, the snow growing heavier and heavier, the face of the desert wearing a sullen look. He was beginning also to feel anxious about his lambs, which were still out in the open at home, and in danger if it came to a blizzard. But in the circumstances the idea of making his way home now right over the plateau was not very tempting, since night was almost upon him, the weather was rapidly deteriorating, and he was not altogether fresh after the day's tramp; so he decided to make the best of it and hold to his original intention of heading eastward along Glacier River towards the shepherds' hut, there to spend the night.

But it is one of the peculiarities of life that the most unlikely accident, rather than the best-laid plan, may on occasion determine the place of a man's lodging; and thus it fared for Bjartur of Summerhouses now. Just as he was about to cross one of the many gullies that cleave the sides of the valley all the way down to the river, he saw some animals leap lightly down a watercourse not far ahead of him and come to a halt well out on the river bank. He saw immediately that they were reindeer, one bull and three cows. They tripped about on the bank for a little while, the bull next the river and the cows seeking shelter in his lee, all with their antlers in the weather and their hindquarters facing the man, for the wind was blowing from across the river.

Halting in the gully, Bjartur eyed the animals for some moments. They kept up a continual shifting about, but always so that they were turned away from him. They were fine beasts, probably just in their prime, so it was no wonder that it occurred to Bjartur that he was in luck's way tonight, for it would be no mean catch if he could trap only one of them even. The bull especially looked as if it would make an excellent carcass, judging by its size, and he had not forgotten that reindeer venison is one of the tastiest dishes that ever graced a nobleman's table. Bjartur felt that even if he did not find the ewe, the trip would have proved well worth while if he managed now to capture a reindeer. But supposing that he caught the bull, how was he to kill it so that its blood did not run to waste?—for from reindeer blood may be made really first-class sandwich meat. The best plan, if he could only manage it would be to take it back home alive, and with this intention in his mind he searched his pockets for those two articles which are most indispensable to a man on a journey, a knife and some string, and found both, a nice hank of string and his pocket-knife. He thought: "I'll make a rush at him now and get him down. Then I'll stick the point of my knife through his nose, thread the string through the hole, and make a lead of it. In that way I ought to be able to lead him most of the way over the moors, or at least till I come to some easily remembered spot where I can tether him and keep him till I go down to the farms and fetch men and materials." Summerhouses was, of course easily a day's journey for a man travelling on foot. When Bjartur had completed his plan of attack he stole half-bent down the gully hill he was opposite the reindeer, where they stood with their horns in the wind on the strip between the gully and the river. He stole cautiously over the runnels, crept silently up the bank, and, peeping over the edge, saw that he was no more than twelve feet from the buck. His muscles began to tauten with the thrill of the hunt and he felt a certain amount of palpitation. Inch by inch he pulled himself higher over the brink, until he was standing on the bank; slowly, very slowly he stole up to the bull, half a pace alongside—and the next instant had leaped at him and gripped him by one of the antlers, low down near the head. At the man's unexpected attack, the animals gave a sudden bound, flung up their heads, and pricked their ears, and the cows were off immediately, running lightly down the river through the drizzling snow. At first the bull had intended making off with Bjartur holding on to its head as if he made no difference at all, but Bjartur hung on and the bull could not get free, and though it tossed its head repeatedly, it was none the freer for it. But Bjartur soon found that his hold on the antler was uncertain, there being something on it like smooth bark that kept on slipping in his grip, and the creature too lively to allow a secure purchase anywhere else. He saw too, when it came to the point, that he would have to abandon his hope of getting under the animal's neck and gripping it with a wrestling hold, for its horns were of the sharpest and the prospect of having them plunged into his bowels not particularly attractive. For a while they continued their tug of war, the reindeer gradually gaining ground, till it had reached a tolerable speed and had dragged Bjartur quite a distance down the river. Then involuntarily there flashed across Bjartur's mind the trick he had been taught from childhood to use with wild horses: try to get alongside them, then jump on their backs. It succeeded. Next instant he was sitting astride the reindeer's back holding on to its antlers—and said later that though this animal species seemed light enough on its feet, a bull reindeer was as rough a ride as he had ever come across, and, indeed, it took him all his time to hang on. But the jaunt was not to be a long one. For when the bull had hopped a few lengths with this undesirable burden on his back without managing to shake it off, he saw quickly that desperate measures would have to be taken and, making a sudden leap at right angles to his previous course, shot straight into Glacier River and was immediately churning the water out of his depth.

Well, well. Bjartur had set out on a trip after sheep right enough, but this was becoming something more in the nature of a voyage. Here he was sitting neither more nor less than up to the waist in Glacier River, and that on no ordinary steed, but on the only steed that is considered suitable for the most renowned of adventures. But was Bjartur really proud of this romantic progress? No, far from it. He had at the moment no leisure to study either the distinctive features of his exploit or the rarity of its occurrence, for he had as much as he could do to hold his balance on the reindeer's back. Desperately he hung on to its horns, his legs glued to its flanks, gasping for breath, a black mist before his eyes. The rush of the water swept the animal down-stream for a while, and for a long time it seemed as if it intended making no effort to land. Across the river the banks, which rose high and steep out of the water, showed intermittently through the snow, but in spite of the nearness of land Bjartur felt himself as unhappily situated as a man out in mid-ocean in an oarless boat. Sometimes the cross-currents caught the bull, forcing it under, and then the water, so unbearably cold that it made his head reel, came up to the man's neck and he was not sure which would happen first, whether he would lose consciousness or the deer would take a dive that would be the end of him. In this fashion they were carried down Glacier River for some time.

At long last it began to look as if the bull was thinking of landing. Bjartur suddenly realized that they had neared the eastern bank of the river and were now not more than a yard or two from

the jagged fringe of ice that formed the only shore. They were carried downstream along by the ice for a while longer, but as the
banks rose everywhere with equal steepness from the ice edge, the
matter of effecting a landing remained a most unattractive project.
Bjartur nevertheless felt that his best course, if the bull neared the
land sufficiently, would be to seize the opportunity and throw himself overboard, then try to haul himself up on the ice, for this stay
in cold water was becoming more than he could stand. He realized,
of course, that it would be a death-jump that could only end in one
of two ways. Finally there came a time when the bull swam for a
few yards not more than half an arm's length from the ice, and
the man watched his chance, let go of the antlers, heaved himself
out of the water, and swung the upper part of his body on the ice;
and there Bjartur parted from the bull, never to set eyes on it again,
and with a permanent dislike for the whole of that animal species.

There occurred moments, both then and later, when it struck
Bjartur that the bull reindeer was no other than the devil Kolum-
killi in person.

The ice was thin and broke immediately under the man's weight,
so that he was near to being carried away with the fragments; but as
his days were not yet numbered he managed somehow to hang on
to the unbroken ice, and succeeded finally in wriggling his lower
limbs also out of the water. He was shaking from head to foot with
the cold, his teeth chattering, not a single dry stitch in all his
clothes. But he did not feel particularly safe on this narrow fringe
of ice and began now to tackle the ascent of the river bank. This in
itself was a sufficiently hazardous undertaking, for the bank was not
only precipitous, but also covered with icicles formed by the rising
of the river, and there could only be one end to a fall if hand or
foot should lose its grip. As he was fatigued after his exploit in the
water, it took him longer to work his way up to the top than it
would otherwise have done, but finally the moment arrived when
he was standing safe and sound on the eastern bank of Glacier River
—on the far pastures of another county. He took off his jacket and
wrung it out, then rolled about in the snow to dry himself, and
considered the snow warm in comparison with the glacier water.
At intervals he stood up and swung his arms vigorously to rid himself of his shivering. It was, of course, not long before he realized
to the full what a trick the bull had played on him by ferrying him
over Glacier River. In the first place he had cheated him of the
quarters he had proposed to use for the night, the shepherds' hut
on the western side of the river. But that actually was only a trifle.

Altogether more serious was to find himself suddenly switched to the eastern bank of Glacier River, for the river flowed north-east, whereas Bjartur's direction home lay a trifle west of north-west. To cross the river he would therefore be forced to make a detour in an opposite direction to Summerhouses, all the way down to the aerial ferry in the farming districts, and this was not less than a twenty hours' walk, even at a good speed, for the nearest farm in Glacierdale was at least fifteen hours away. Though he were to travel day and night this adventure of his would thus delay him almost forty-eight hours—and that in weather like this, and his lambs still out.

He was pretty well worn out, though loath to admit it to himself, and his wet clothes would be a poor protection if he decided to bury himself in the snow in this hardening frost. The snow-flakes grew smaller and keener; no sooner had they fallen than the wind lifted them again and chased them along the ground in a spuming, knee-deep smother. His underclothes remained unaffected by the frost as long as he was on the move, but his outer clothes were frozen hard and his eyelashes and beard stiff with ice. In his knapsack there remained one whole blood pudding, frozen hard as a stone, and half of another; he had lost his stick. The night was as black as pitch, and the darkness seemed solid enough to be cut with a knife. The wind blew from the east, sweeping the blizzard straight into the man's face. Time and time again he tumbled from another and yet another brink into another and yet another hollow where the powdery snow took him up to the groin and flew about him like ash. One consolation only there was: happen what might, he could not lose his way, for on his left he had Glacier River with its heavy, sullen roar.

He swore repeatedly; ever the more violently the unsteadier his legs became, but to steel his senses he kept his mind fixed persistently on the world-famous battles of the rhymes. He recited the most powerful passages one after another over and over again, dwelling especially on the description of the devilish heroes, Grimur Ægir and Andri. It was Grimur he was fighting now, he thought; Grimur, that least attractive of all fiends, that foul-mouthed demon in the form of a troll, who had been his antagonist all along; but now an end would be put to the deadly feud, for now the stage was set for the final struggle. In mental vision he pursued Grimur the length of his monstrous career, right from the moment when Groa the Sibyl found him on the foreshore, yellow and stuffed with treachery; and again and again he depicted the monster in the poet's words, bellowing, wading in the earth up to the thighs, filled with devilish hate and sorcery, fire spouting from his grinning mouth, by human strength more than invincible:

> The monster lived on moor or fen;
>   The sea was in his power.
> He'd shamelessly drink the blood of men,
>   The steaming flesh devour.

> The crags before him split apart,
>   The rivers ran in spate;
> He cleft the rocks by magic art,
>   His cunning was so great.

For this fiend there was not a shred of mercy in Bjartur. No matter how often he sprawled headlong down the gullies, he was up again undaunted and with redoubled fury making yet another attack, grinding his teeth and hurling curses at the demon's gnashing jaws, determined not to call a halt before Grimur's evil spirit had been hounded to the remotest corners of hell and the naked brand had pierced him through and his death-throes had begun in a ring-dance of land and sea.

Again and again he imagined that he had made an end of Grimur and sent him howling to hell in the poet's immortal words, but still the blizzard assailed him with undiminished fury when he reached the top of the next ridge, clawed at his eyes and the roots of his beard, howled vindictively in his ears, and tried to hurl him to the ground—the struggle was by no means over, he was still fighting at close quarters with the poison-spewing thanes of hell, who came storming over the earth in raging malice till the vault of heaven shook to the echo of their rush.

> His loathsome head aloft he reared,
>   With hellish hate he roared.
> His slavering lips with froth were smeared,
>   Vilely his curses poured.

And so on, over and over again.

Never, never did these thanes of hell escape their just deserts. No one ever heard of Harekur or Gongu-Hrolfur or Bernotus being worsted in the final struggle. In the same way no one will be able to say that Bjartur of Summerhouses ever got the worst of it in his world war with the country's spectres, no matter how often he might tumble over a precipice or roll head over heels down a gully— "while there's a breath left in my nostrils, it will never keep me down, however hard it blows." Finally he stood still, leaning against the blizzard as against a wall; and neither could push the other back. He then resolved to house himself in the snow and began looking for a sheltered spot in a deep gully. With his hands he scooped out a cave in a snowdrift, trying to arrange it so that he could sit inside on his haunches to pile up the snow at the mouth, but the snow, loose and airy, refused to stick together, and as the man was without implements, the cave simply fell in again. He had not rested long in the snowdrift before the cold began to penetrate him; a stiffness and a torpor crept up his limbs, all the way to his groin, but what was worse was the drowsiness that was threatening him, the seductive sleep of the snow, which makes it so pleasant to die in a blizzard; nothing is so important as to be able to strike aside this tempting hand which beckons so voluptuously into realms of warmth and rest. To keep the oblivion of the snow at bay it was his custom to recite or, preferably, sing at the top of his voice all the obscene verse he had picked up since childhood, but such surroundings were never very conducive to song and on this occasion his voice persisted in breaking; and the drowsiness continued to envelop his consciousness in its mists, till now there swam before his inner eye pictures of men and events, both from life and from the Ballads —horse-meat steaming on a great platter, flocks of sheep bleating in the fold, Bernotus Borneyarkappi in disguise, clergymen's wanton daughters wearing real silk stockings; and finally, by unsensed degrees, he assumed another personality and discovered himself in the character of Grimur the Noble, brother of Ulfar the Strong, when the visit was paid to his bedchamber. Matters stood thus, that the King, father of the brothers, had taken in marriage a young woman, who, since the King was well advanced in years, found a sad lack of entertainment in the marriage bed and became a prey to melancholy. But eventually her eyes fell on the King's son, Grimur the Noble, who far outshone all other men in that kingdom, and the young Queen fell so deeply in love with this princely figure that she could neither eat nor sleep and resolved finally to go to him at night in his chamber. Of the aged King, his father, she spoke in the most derisive of terms:

Of what use to red-blood maid
Sap of such a withered blade?
Or to one so sore in need,
Spine of such a broken reed?

Grimur, however, found this visit displeasing and relished even
less such shameless talk, but for some time he retreated in courtly
evasion of the issue. But

No refusals ought availed,
Words of reason here had failed.
All intent on lustful play
Softly on the bed she lay.

And before Grimur the Noble had time to marshal his defences,
there occurred the following:

In her arms she clasped him tight,
Warm with promise of delight;
Honey-seeming was her kiss,
All her movements soft with bliss.

But at this moment there dawned upon Grimur the Noble the
full iniquity of what was taking place, and springing to his feet in
a fury, he turned upon the shameless wanton:

Up the hero rose apace,
Smote her sharply on the face;
Scornful of such shameful deed,
Thrust her to the floor with speed.

Angrily the hero cried,
Whilst she lay, bereft of pride:
"Lustful art thou as a swine,
Little honour can be thine."

"To hell with me, then," cried Bjartur, who was now standing in
the snow after repulsing the seductive bed-blandishments of the
lecherous Queen. Did the heroes of the rhymes ever allow themselves to be beguiled into a life of adultery, debauchery, and that
cowardice in battle which characterizes those who are the greatest
heroes in a woman's embrace? Never should it be said of Bjartur of

Summerhouses that on the field of battle he turned his back on his foes to go and lie with a trollopy slut of a queen. He was in a passion now. He floundered madly about in the snow, thumping himself with all his might, and did not sit down again till he had overcome all those feelings of the body that cry for rest and comfort, everything that argues for surrender and hearkens to the persuasion of faint-hearted gods. When he had fought thus for some time, he stuck the frozen sausages inside his trousers and warmed them on his flesh, then gnawed them from his fist in the darkness of this relentless winter night and ate the driving snow as savoury.

This was rather a long night. Seldom had he recited so much poetry in any one night; he had recited all his father's poetry, all the ballads he could remember, all his own palindromes backwards and forwards in forty-eight different ways, whole processions of dirty poems, one hymn that he had learned from his mother, and all the lampoons that had been known in the Fourthing from time immemorial about bailiffs, merchants, and sheriffs. At intervals he struggled up out of the snow and thumped himself from top to toe till he was out of breath.

Finally his fear of frost-bite became so great that he felt it would be courting disaster to remain quietly in this spot any longer, and as it must also be wearing on towards morning and he did not relish the idea of spending a whole day without food in a snowdrift miles from any habitation, he now decided to forsake his shelter and leave the consequences to take care of themselves. He forced his way at first with lowered head against the storm, but when he reached the ridge above the gully, he could no longer make any headway in this fashion, so he slumped forward on to his hands and knees and made his way through the blizzard on all fours, crawling over stony slopes and ridges like an animal, rolling down the gullies like a peg; barehanded, without feeling.

On the following night, long after the people of Brun, the nearest farm of Glacierdale, had retired to bed—the storm had raged relentlessly now for a full twenty-four hours—it came to pass that the housewife was wakened from her sleep by a hubbub at the window, a groaning, even a hammering. She woke her husband, and they came to the conclusion that some creature gifted with the power of reasoning must surely be afoot and about the house, though on this lonely croft visitors were the last thing to be expected in such a storm—was it man or devil? They huddled on their most necessary garments and went to the door with a light. And when they had opened the door, there toppled in through the drift outside a creature resembling only in some ways a human being; he rolled in through the doorway armoured from head to foot in ice, nose and mouth encrusted, and came to rest in a squatting position with his back against the wall and his head sunk on his chest, as if the monstrous spectre, despairing of maltreating him further, had finally slung him through the door and up against the wall; the light of the house shone on this visitor. He panted heavily, his chest heaving and groaning, and made an effort to clear his throat and spit, and when the crofter asked him who he was and where he came from, he tried to get to his feet, like an animal trying to stand upon its hind legs, and gave his name—"Bjartur of Summerhouses."

The crofter's son had now risen also, and together he and his father made an attempt to help their visitor into the room, but he refused any such assistance. "I'll walk by myself," he said, "I'll follow the woman with the lamp." He laid himself across the son's bed and for a while made no answer to their questions, but mumbled like a drunkard, rumbled like a bull about to bellow. At last he said:

"I am thirsty."

The woman brought him a three-pint basin of milk, and he set it to his mouth and drank it off, and said as he passed her the basin: "Thanks for the drink, mother." With her warm hands she helped to thaw the clots of ice in his beard and eyebrows, then drew off his frozen clothes and felt with experienced fingers for frost-bite. Fingers and toes were without feeling, his skin smarting with frost, but otherwise he appeared to have taken no hurt. When the crust of ice had been thawed off, he stretched himself out naked in the son's warm bed and had seldom felt so comfortable in all his life. After the housewife had gone to prepare him some food, father and son sat down beside him, their eyes bewildered, as if they did not really believe this phenomenon and did not know quite what to say. In the end it was he who spoke, as he asked in a hoarse voice from under the coverlet:

"Were your lambs in?"

They replied that they were, and asked in turn how it had come about that he had landed here, on the eastern bank of Glacier River, in murderous weather that would kill any man.

"Any man?" he repeated querulously. "What do the men matter? I always thought it was the animals that came first."

They continued to question him.

"Oh, as a matter of fact I was just taking a little walk by myself," he vouchsafed. "I missed a ewe, you see, and took a stroll along the heights there just to soothe my mind."

For a while he was silent, then he added:

"It's been a trifle rough today."

"It wasn't any pleasanter last night either," they said, "a regular hurricane."

"Yes," agreed Bjartur, "it was just a trifle rough last night, too."

They wanted to know where he had put in the night, and he replied: "In the snow." They were particularly curious about how he had managed to cross Glacier River, but he would give no details. "It's a nice thing to have one's lambs out in this," he said mournfully.

They said that in his shoes they wouldn't trouble themselves about lambs tonight, but think themselves lucky to be where they were.

"It's easy to see," he replied, "that you people have found your feet. But I am fighting for my independence. I have worked eighteen years for the little livestock I have, and if they're under snow, it would be better for me to be under snow too."

But when the woman had brought him a meal in bed and he had eaten his fill, he lay down without further discourse and was asleep and snoring loudly.

—Translated by J. A. Thompson

BENEDETTO CROCE

****

The soliloquy of Italy's most famous living philosopher was written January, 1942, and speaks for itself. He placed it at the end of his latest collected volume of essays and it is a representation of his consistent and passionate belief in the liberty of the individual.

****

Soliloquy of an Old Philosopher

ANYONE who like myself was born and grew up in the early years of the unity and liberty of Italy must proclaim in every company and against all opponents, that he knows what it is to have lived the greater and best part of his life in a sublime spiritual atmosphere. He 'knows,' he does not merely 'feel' it; for these words of his are no mere effusion of a nostalgic sentiment for the past, or even an imaginative picture of it, but an affirmation of the very truth. And as an affirmation, in the strict sense, it claims to be distinguished from that sort of utopia projected into the past, which leads men to think that some golden age ever fleeted the time in 'blissful ignorance,' a phrase which is purely nonsensical. At the time of which I speak, as in every other, men lived a human, not a superhuman or heavenly life, a life marred by cares and griefs, sorrows, solitude, despair, sullied by reprehensible deeds. It could not even be called more moral or less moral than the life of earlier or later generations, for morality is an inner energy, whose quality cannot be measured, and whose external manifestations, which alone can be measured, are mere events, and as such neither moral nor immoral. A sophistical trick used to discredit the age of liberalism, and invented by the vulgar for the vulgar, is to air all the dirty linen of this period, the poverty, the blunders, the pride, the scandals, the crimes, of which it may have been guilty, in order to show that it was politically inferior and contemptible; as if a similar collection of anecdotes could not be made, and a similar picture as fairly painted of any other stage or period of history.

912

A historical period cannot be truly described or judged by accumulating scandalous stories, but only by pondering and enquiring whether it had a moral ideal governing and illuminating the minds of those members of human societies who are capable of ideals; capable of loving something above their own happiness or that of others on which it depends, that of sons, wives, friends; capable of something above the 'natural' or 'sensual' love (to use an old phrase of the Churchmen) for the persons or things with which, for all of us, the 'joy of life' and self-preservation is interwoven. There are historical periods in which the power of such moral ideals grows faint, and almost seems to disappear, and these are called ages of barbarism or decadence; while other periods are active and flourishing and signalise advances in civilisation, and the attainment of richer and deeper ideas, with corresponding progress in practical activity.

The period to which my thoughts and memories now recur rejoiced in the calm assurance of a secure, full, and fruitful expansion of energies, and a noble co-operation of man with man. It saw all men as possessed of equal rights, without slavery or despotism, all at liberty to express their thoughts and to further their policies, under the free judgment of public opinion, which, in spite of inevitable oscillations and mistakes, usually in the end supported truth and equity. At this period the development of the human spirit had attained in Italy and Europe a more reflective self-consciousness, coherence, and harmony than had ever before been reached by that dynamic tendency to liberty which gives history its positive progress. It was an exalted ideal of liberty that now shone forth as the rule and guide and ultimate criterion of every effort. Behind this new form could be recognised, illuminated by a new light, the stern ideal of the old Greek and Roman heroes of liberty, but also the more intense and continuous influence of a process, begun or quickened by Christianity, towards a humanity united in love and sorrow and sublime aspirations. The Christian ideal had been brought down from heaven to earth at the Renaissance; it seemed to be denied by the Enlightenment, which celebrated the cult of abstract reason but in fact by this very 'reason' worked towards the same ends, dissipating darkness and promoting liberty, equality, and fraternity. And now, in the time I am speaking of, Christianity, reconciled to the long, painful development of which it had been the seed, arose, one might say, refreshed by its contact with philosophy and history. The fact that, nevertheless, the Roman Church grew intolerant of liberation was due to the way in which she came to mould Christian minds in conformity with her political ends; but the close bond between the two was felt, not only by pure liberals, to whose lips religious phrases and metaphors so readily sprang, but also by liberal Catholics, who were the deepest thinkers and most generous spirits of their Church. We still have the proof of this bond today, a proof that liberalism is essentially Christian, when we see that those who hate and abuse it most are either inflamed by the passion for extolling and reviving distant epochs of pre-Christian history, such as paganism, or frankly profess the most crudely materialist, utilitarian, fratricidal conception of human life.

Certainly the ideal of liberty which flourished in the nineteenth century can and must be deepened, defined and widened; and this will be the business of the following periods, whose growth and progress will depend upon new experiences critically sifted and assimilated. But since its essential principle is moral, or rather is the development of morality itself, that principle can never be denied or replaced by any other; nor can we go back on its past history, or abandon the point it has reached; we can only advance further.

It is, of course, possible to 'deny' it by vocal articulations, signifying nothing, and to refute it or claim to refute it, and to cry up as the true ideal its opposite, and to triumph over its supposed death. But since this proclaimed opposite is self-contradictory and morally unacceptable, the idea of liberty remains after all invulnerable, and when the storm has blown over it blossoms freshly and renews its youthful prime.

'When the storm is over'? Is there something in the world which can resist and impede and delay and shatter, for however short a time, the practical influence of this high ideal? Most certainly; and we should not be surprised at it, nor be panic-stricken for the fate of the world, as if it were thereby irrevocably compromised or beyond hope ruined. Nor, on the other hand, is it for the enemies of the ideal to argue that therefore it is essentially invalid and inadequate, and that their substitute has a monopoly of power and permanence. The delays and breakdowns in the advance of liberty are in fact evident in past and present history, the history of which goes on within us. But the reason and justification of this fact are not far to seek, and though some through thoughtlessness seem not to see it, or to have forgotten it, a little reflection will bring it to their mind.

The obvious reason is that there can be no life or reality without differences and perpetual opposition or composition of forces, without war and peace, war which brings peace and peace which leads again to war. This is the plain truth, accepted by common sense no

less than by profound philosophy, but contested and denied by all
Utopians, pessimists and sceptics, ever seeking a good unconditioned
by evil, a life whose complement is not death; who, when they are
unable to find this good in reality, shudder, or prate about the inscrutable mystery of things. Seen in the dialectical conflicts which
are the law of history, man's moral action does not stand alone, an
abstraction in a world of abstractions, but, always in relation to that
which is at once its material and its instrument, its enemy and its
ally, the vital force, whose moving principle is the prime mover. It
is this force which continually contributes to the creation not only
of the earth with its 'lovely family of beasts and flowers,' its volcanoes and earthquakes, but also, by continual conflict, of ever-
changing conditions of life. And most directly it operates in that
sphere of human life* which is called 'the world of affairs,' that is
the world of business** and of practical politics, which is always en-
gendering new patterns of nations and of states.

It is the professed ideal of liberal statesmen, not to extinguish
economic and political rivalries, as some airy castle-builders might
desire, and thus dry up the very spring of all activity and advance,
but so to guide them that they may develop and give room for the
necessary changes and re-groupings. Hence the internal policy of
liberal states is to maintain with scrupulous firmness a respect for
general liberty, and hence also their vigilant precaution that the
powers of the government should not exceed its legitimate authority.
Hence too the anxiety of the leaders in such states, of the ruling
classes, and of all men of goodwill, however they may differ in other
opinions and policies, to preserve international peace and to substitute for physical combat diplomacy, compromise and treaties.
But all such action, whether internal or external, is itself a kind of
warfare, though as we have said, not fought with weapons, or at
least with different weapons, and, like other warfare, it has its turns
of victory and defeat.

When these defeats occur, liberal constitutions and the love of
peace are overcome and destroyed, and for a longer or shorter time,
in greater or lesser degrees, give place to their opponents, the savage
vital force. Such are the changes which succeed one another on
every page of history; and it is unthinkable that this rhythm of
victory and defeat should ever cease. The very idea of its cessation,
the idea of a liberty completely and finally achieved, settled and immutable, of a liberty without dangers, or with only those fictitious

* Spirito.
** Economia.

dangers, which can always be escaped or checked, is as self-contradictory and empty as the idea of an end of the world and of universal life and being. But being cannot be annihilated since not-
being is within its realm. Serious thinkers will never take the absurd
line of preaching and demanding the abolition of war, and the
establishment of perpetual peace and of static material equality.
Nor, when they see unleashed the violent wars and revolutions
which they have vainly tried to avert by defending peace and liberty
to their utmost, will they cherish the equally absurd design of sitting
in judgment on these mortal struggles and of arbitrating between
parties while passions are still high. Strife knows no law but strife;
its only arbiters are the actual results in which it will issue, and what
these are to be is no man's secret, for no man knows. It is 'God's
secret,' as the wise proverb says. And philosophy agrees with common sense in refusing to individuals, each of whom has to fight
his own battle in the universal warfare, the right to make himself
the judge and master in matters too high for him. Each must be
content to fulfil his individual duty, in his own situation and state of
life, as the voice of conscience bids him. Who, indeed, however sure
he felt of rare intellectual and political genius, however sublimely
self-confident, would accept at God's hand the task of deciding
human destiny? Who would presume to decide, by such criterion
as he might vainly seek in his own mind, what can only be decided
by the outcome?

But it is only in souls apt to despair and to lose their way, only
in minds apt to confusion, that the necessary rhythm of history,
with its recurring horrors of war and its recurrent back-slidings
from peace and liberty, can inspire the thought that liberty can
ever vanish even from a world which desires to be governed by a
different law. Is liberty then a by-product, which dies and is not
born again? Is it not the very activity of man, which is by definition
free, and which nobody has yet ventured to define as determined?*
It is within the realm of possiblities that the liberal period of the
nineteenth century, which men of my generation have seen, and to
which some of them are still loyal, splendid in its achievement,
proud of the mutual respect of its citizens, will one day be compared
with the great periods of philosophy and art, the Athens of Pericles,
the Italy of the Renaissance, the France of Descartes, Corneille and
Racine, the Germany of idealism and romance. Such periods open
rarely and quickly close, leaving admiration and regret behind them.
But though such marvellous seasons of blossoming pass, not for that
* Un essere che serve.

reason will art and philosophy be banished from the world; arts and philosophical genius will arise again in men as great as those of old, and, what is more, the search for truth and the worship of art will never fail to inspire love and longing in the heart of man, and to shine there with all their former splendour. So too liberty has fallen, and will again, on days of opposition, of indifference and of persecution, but none the less it lives in the hearts of its lovers, it lives and operates in the sphere of action, where by right it moves, and which it naturally enlarges. Liberty can settle its account clearly enough with everything that neglects it or opposes it, for whatever 'comes to pass' and comes under its thought and judgment has 'passed' into the conditions of its own activity. The functions of liberty are different in the church triumphant and the church militant, but it can never be condemned to impotence or death, or at least no man has the power to execute the sentence he pronounces.

I have now brought back my argument to its main point of moral duty; I have shown that duty alone can be the end of all our efforts and all our practical activity; I have shown that moral duty is not subservient to the traffic of the world, or to its violent deliriums, to its demands or their satisfaction and appeasement. For the world, as Campanella wrote with lyric admiration, is a 'great and perfect animal' which goes its own way and finds it own means from time to time of accomplishing the various stages.

And now I can conclude my argument by pointing out that our duty likewise has its own good and its own means. And one of its first demands is that we should refute the illusion, which these vital forces suffer or create in their activity, when they claim moral worth and the right to fix our standards. No doubt, in political and social struggles, banners are hoisted, slogans are shouted, idols of love and hate are fashioned; and men inspired or maddened by these symbols are ready to fight and die. But all this is quite different from the moral ideals or from the ideal of liberty which comprises them. Factions fight to keep what they have or to gain something for themselves and their own party, where one man's loss is another's gain. But the moral ideal of liberty is a message to universal man as man; it is no incitement to the pursuit of private interests or more or less general goods, it is an educative and redeeming revelation to the heart. Even when, as sometimes happens, the aims of parties are inspired by a moral spirit, that is the moral ideal entering into them and beginning this education, converting them and raising them above themselves. This can be seen in the word 'patriot' which at one time expressed the reverent pride, the loftiest feelings, and the noblest dreams of all who could claim it. Indeed it symbolised their devotion to the cause of humanity, a meaning exactly opposite to that of the word 'nationalist,' which came to be substituted for it, as was 'my nation' for 'my country,' as though it were a translation, though in fact it was the expression of dominating and predatory natures.

Political ideologies, and slogans bandied against slogans, have no doubt their necessary uses, they call to arms, unite the combatants to attack and defence and intoxicate them with the hope or joy of victory; but they leave empty the heart of man in his simple and essential humanity, which only finds itself at home in union with the universal. It seems as if there were two histories, and two ways of relating history, which run closely parallel but never meet, the political and the moral. But in truth they are two aspects or 'dialectical moments' of the one history, which is the constant creation of life and the perpetual elevation and sublimation of life in its dedication to the universal. A man whose mind is so religiously disposed gladly leaves the care of political history to the politicians and soldiers and economists. He fixes his thoughts on moral history where is unrolled the drama which also goes on in himself, and where throughout the centuries he meets his fathers and brothers, who loved liberty as he does, and like him knew how to work and suffer for her.

—*Translated by E. F. Carritt*

IGNAZIO SILONE

****

*The four fragments selected represent one of the typical aspects
of my work, because they contain a reversal of values which may
surprise the ordinary reader: things which the world despises are
shown to be precious, eccentricity is a protective cloak for honesty,
and law-breaking is only a homage to common sense. In* The Seed
Beneath the Snow, *the beggars seem kings in exile, and Crown
Prince Umberto, on his one appearance, is mistaken for a film-actor.*

*Simone and Faustina live on the margin of the community from
which they have voluntarily estranged themselves. Faustina is held
to be the mistress of an old musician in whose house she lives, and
she accepts this unfounded reputation because it is a means of
breaking off all connections with people whom she despises. Simone,
for analogous reasons, is reduced to living in a stable in the open
country. Pietro Spina, to evade the pursuit of the Fascist police, has
unexpectedly taken refuge with him in this stable.*

*Pietro and Faustina. Pietro, on the point of being captured by the
police, is saved by Faustina, and together they take refuge in a
mountain village. It is their first meeting since childhood, and in the
meantime both, quite independently of each other, have caused
scandal in their respective families.*

Pietro preaches pride. The moral landscape of The Seed Beneath
the Snow *is that of a society which has reached the extreme limits
of decadence. The resistance to tyranny has not succeeded in finding
political forms. Only the very poor remain outside the general corruption. It is towards them, therefore, that Pietro spontaneously
goes. It is not a question of spreading political slogans, but of
wakening the sense of man.*

IGNAZIO SILONE

****

The Seed Beneath the Snow

(Fragments from the novel hitherto unpublished in English)

SIMONE AND FAUSTINA

SIMONE mounted his donkey, lit his pipe, and made his way through the tortuous streets of Orta in the direction of Colle. As he passed the Spina house he saw Don Bastino standing at the top of the outside stairway, silent and alone, wrapped in a black overcoat and bareheaded despite the cold. Simone hesitated for a moment, then rode on without making any sign. As he passed the church of Sant'-Antonio he took off his hat and greeted the saint with a wave of his hand, like an old acquaintance. As he passed the house of Don Severino he was surprised to see light filtering through the shutters. Hadn't Don Severino stayed at Colle with Donna Maria Vincenza? Simone looked around suspiciously, got down and tied the donkey to a ring in the wall; then untied it again, went behind the house and tethered it to a tree in the garden, so as not to be seen from the street.

"Good evening," said Simone to a woman who opened the door. But the moment he took a step forward to enter the house, the door slammed violently, as though blown by a gust of wind, almost hitting him in the face. Simone shrugged his shoulders and moved away; then he turned back and knocked again lightly on the door. A window on the ground floor opened.

"Who is there?" called the angry voice of a woman.

"Good evening," Simone repeated, turning to the window. "If Don Severino isn't asleep yet and if I'm not disturbing him, I'd like to have a word with him. My name is Simone," he added in a lower voice, "they call me Simone the Polecat. I think he'll understand why I've come at this time of night."

The door opened at once.

"Oh, are you Simone?" asked Faustina in surprise and in a very friendly tone. "Come in, do excuse me, how was I to know? Has something serious happened?" She turned on the light in the hall. "Don Severino hasn't come back yet from Colle," she went on courteously and anxiously, "but he'll be here any moment. Has something serious happened? Please don't stand there on the doorstep, Simone, do come in, someone might see you."

She ushered him into a large room on the ground floor and turned on all the lights. A grand piano occupied half the room; in one corner there was a chimney-place with a fire burning, flanked by two very deep and comfortable leather armchairs. One entire wall was lined with bookshelves; the other walls were hung with an old red tapestry patterned with golden flowers, but the gold had almost completely faded, and nothing remained of the flowers but the thorns. The floor was entirely covered by a red and black carpet.

"Please come in, Simone," repeated Donna Faustina, smiling pleasantly. "You must really forgive me, how could I have known? I assure you, Severino will be glad to find you here. He has often talked to me about you lately; he admires you very much, indeed to tell the truth he envies you."

Simone blushed.

"Really?" he asked in embarrassment. "Really? I don't see why." Simone had remained standing, very shyly, near the door, perhaps afraid to spoil the carpet with his muddy boots. In the lighted room he actually looked like a beggar. His patched and shapeless trousers were covered with mud up to the knees; a piece of twine tied tightly around his waist held together both his trousers and his coat that was innocent of buttons; his coat-sleeves were short and frayed; his collar was turned up and fastened at the neck with a safety-pin. Simone looked around him curiously.

"It's quite nice here, Donna Faustina," he said flatteringly, "and it's warm, but at home there's more fresh air. I don't want to boast about it, but there's much more fresh air."

"Have you got a big house?" asked Donna Faustina. "Where do you live? Pardon my asking; no one would think that we came from the same village."

"In my house, if you want to light the fire, you don't, so to speak, have to stand there blowing on it," explained Simone with obvious pride. "The wind comes and does the job. Indeed, when I light the fire, I have to be careful that the wind doesn't spread it to the whole house."

"Oh," exclaimed Donna Faustina admiringly, "is your house so big that even the wind can live there?"

"Not only the wind," boasted Simone, losing all shame. "Not only the wind. The rain, too, and the snow in the raw season. And in the summer the sun during the daytime; and during the night the moon and the stars."

"It must be splendid," repeated Donna Faustina, suddenly enthusiastic. "It must be wonderful."

"However, it's more sheltered here," added Simone politely, not wanting to offend his hostess. "And for a girl it's certainly more suitable."

Donna Faustina went out by the garden gate to cover up the donkey with a woollen blanket, a magnificent hand-woven blanket of black and red wool. Simone was greatly surprised and touched by this unexpected gesture.

"No one ever does that, you know, Donna Faustina," he had barely time to say. "You cover up horses, but not donkeys. A donkey has a tough hide." But Donna Faustina was already in the garden, and Simone watched the scene from the window, excited and moved, hardly believing his own eyes.

"Now he looks just like a cardinal," he said in a grave tone to the girl when she came back. "Donna Faustina, I don't know if you realise what you have done."

"I realise it now that I see it has given you pleasure," she answered laughingly.

The two of them stood at the window looking out at the donkey thus strangely and sumptuously arrayed; but, to tell the truth, it did not seem in the least impressed, and its head dangled beside the tree with the greatest unconcern.

"Donna Faustina, please don't be offended," begged Simone, "please don't misunderstand my donkey's indifference. He's not stupid, I assure you, and he's not ungrateful; but as for luxury—I don't know if you, being a girl, can understand this—he's just not interested in luxury. He never wanted luxury, not even in his young days. Ah, how can I explain?"

Donna Faustina seemed highly amused.

"Yes, of course," she hastened to agree. "I should expect nothing else from a donkey of yours, Simone. Have you had him for a long time?"

"Donna Faustina," corrected Simone, "I don't want you to form too good an opinion of me, I don't want to deck myself with borrowed plumes. Cherub (that's the name of my donkey) was perfect even as a young thing, and to tell the truth, in all the years of our life together, it's not he that learned from me, but I that learned from him. I hope, Donna Faustina, that you are taking me literally, and don't think I'm joking."

Donna Faustina grew very serious.

"Simone," she said, "you mustn't expect me to grasp all at once the full significance of what you have just revealed to me. One thing I can assure you: I shall meditate on it at length, and perhaps in the end I shall get myself a donkey too. Or do you think it's too late? Please, Simone answer me frankly."

"For any other girl, it would be too late," answered Simone after some reflection. "But not for you. I don't say this to flatter you."

"Thank you," said Donna Faustina, blushing. "Please, Simone," she added in an affectionate voice, "don't stand there between the door and the window, come and sit at the fire. Severino won't be long now. You'll see how delighted he'll be to find you here."

Donna Faustina bent down in front of the hearth to put another log on the fire, then she moved a little brass coffee-pot close to the grate. Simone sat watching her, feeling by now as much at his ease as though he were at home. The girl's movements had a grace, a nimbleness, a charm that enchanted him. She must have been getting near thirty; peasant women already look old at that age, and donkeys of that age are old too, but she still looked a girl. Her hair, which she had let down for the night, was magnificent, thick and abundant; her complexion was still fresh and soft; her large eyes also, that flashed excitely and almost feverishly, and her mouth with its vividly painted lips, still had something of unripeness about them. In between the two armchairs she moved a little table with the coffee-cups and a sugar-bowl, and sat down opposite her guest. Simone's enormous shapeless muddy boots, laced with packing twine, were side by side with Donna Faustina's little crocodile shoes.

"I must undoubtedly have passed you on the road a great many times," she said after a long silence, "but I didn't know who you were. Of course, if I hadn't been stupid, I ought to have recognised you."

Donna Faustina rose to turn off the glare of the ceiling bulbs and light the candles of a branched candelabrum on the piano. The subdued light cloaked Simone's poverty and threw into relief the underlying quality of his features; the lean worn regular face, the straight finely-chiselled nose, the shrewd intelligent eyes, the courteous and ironic smile.

"No one would think that we were from the same village," he remarked laughingly.

"The fact is," she added, "as you know, Simone, I haven't had anything to do with these people for a long time. I stayed on here, but only as an outlaw."

"Me too, Donna Faustina," Simone hastened to explain. "In a sense I too have run away from the ranks of honest folk. I'm not saying this to boast or to compare myself to you, but I too have

been an outlaw from the society of good Christians this many a
long year. "

"We've played truant, both of us; that's true," admitted Donna
Faustina contentedly, "but you took one road and I took another.
That's why we never met until to-day. From the same village!
And such a little village too. It took the sheer accident of this eve-
ning to make us acquainted."

"It wasn't an accident," corrected Simone politely. "When two
outlaws meet, Donna Faustina, it's never due to accident, however
much it may seem so."

Donna Faustina agreed at once.

"That's just it," she said, "when two outlaws meet. You must
forgive me for being so stupid, Simone," she added humbly. "How
could I have thought there was anything accidental about a person like you?"

At this point Simone was filled with sudden compassion.

"It's hard for women to escape, to run away," he reflected sadly.
"I mean, on account of their skirts, Donna Faustina. When one
runs away, it's obviously much more practical to have trousers."

"The important thing is to save oneself," answered Donna
Faustina, in a decided voice. "In one way or another."

"The important thing is perhaps to lose oneself," corrected Simone, "but it comes to the same thing, it's just a question of words.
I was going to say, Donna Faustina, that it's very hard for women
to lose themselves. It's much more painful, I mean, on account of
the scandal and the gossip and all the rest of it. Now there's Don
Timoteo, for example, the parish priest of Cerchio. He was no coward in his young days, I knew him well, a fine lad he was; I don't
know if you've ever had anything to do with him, Donna Faustina;
but now he's a piece of trash like the rest of them, a capon like so
many of them. 'What's this?' I said the last time I met him; 'poor
devil! is this what the Gospel has done to you?' 'It's not the Gospel,'
he told me, 'it's having to wear a skirt. You see, Simone, I have to
be careful on account of the soutane, I obviously can't say or do
any of the things I'd really like to: there would be too much of a
scandal.' Maybe Dom Timoteo was right. What can you expect of
a man that wears a skirt?"

"All the same, Simone, scandals have got to happen," concluded
Donna Faustina, her face clouding.

She said "have got to" with an effort, clenching her fists. It was
a tone of her voice with which Simone was already familiar; the
tone she had used a little while ago at the window; the tone of her

encounters, fortunately less and less frequent, with the people of the village. Whenever Simone had had occasion to observe Donna Faustina, she had seemed to him a disdainful and irascible being, proud, impassioned and intimidated; never before in that part of the countryside had there been anyone so slandered, nor anyone whose head was held so high. One day when she came back to Colle to fetch her luggage and other personal belongings, she narrowly escaped being stoned by the village women; the two-horse phaeton on which she had laden her things was held up and surrounded in the middle of the square by a mob of dishevelled screaming aggressive women, and she had to cut her way through with blows of the whip. One of them hit Simone in the face, although he had hurried to join the crowd simply in order to help her. Another time Simone had witnessed a similar scene outside the door of the church where a funeral service was being held for the repose of the soul of Don Saverino: a few old sodality women stopped Donna Faustina from entering the church and she gave way in the end, probably so as not to disturb the sacred ceremony. Simone saw her turn away with a disconsolate face, tears pouring down her cheeks, and fearing perhaps that she intended some desperate piece of folly, he quickened his pace so as to catch up with her and accompany her back to Orta; but the moment Donna Faustina noticed she was being followed, she took to her heels like a madwoman, panic-stricken, and Simone let her go.

Said Donna Faustina:

"I hope it won't seem unpardonably careless, Simone, but Severino has told me about certain things. He is very much alone, you know, even Don Luca the curate has broken with him now, and we are vegetating here, where our families have lived for centuries, as if we were in a foreign and hostile country."

She got up to serve the coffee and spoke again:

"Severino is sorry not to have seen more of you; yes, that's the truth, Simone, I'm not trying to flatter you, and I'm convinced your company would have been a good thing for him."

Said Simone:

"I'm afraid I've got to be too much of a plebeian for his taste, too much one of the rabble, too earthy; making friends with me would cost him too much of an effort. And forgive me if I say that for me Don Severino is perhaps too fastidious, too aloof, too formal-mannered, too well-bred and so forth. But aside from these differences . . ."

Said Faustina:

"Of course, Simone, you are quite right, but these are only appearances. I'm convinced that in your hearts you both belong to the same race, which seems to be dying out."

Said Simone:

"Your coffee is excellent, Donna Faustina. It's a good sign, you know, I'm very glad to see it. I congratulate you. I shan't deny that I was a little worried, wondering if you would be able to make good coffee. Ah, you are right, Donna Faustina, these are bad times for our kind. But perhaps we shouldn't lose heart," he laughed. "Madmen there will always be."

"Always? You don't think they'll be commercialized out of existence?" asked Donna Faustina anxiously.

"Madmen, Donna Faustina," explained Simone with tranquil optimism, "are like the birds of the air and the lilies of the field. No one breeds them, no one tends them; yet there they are."

"Are you really sure?" asked Donna Faustina tremulously and dubiously. "You're not saying this just to console me? You know, Simone, I get Severino to explain these things to me, and he says every day now they think up a new way of making people stupider."

"I know, I know," agreed Simone laughingly. "But there's no doing away with madness from mankind, that's the main thing, and if it's banished from the streets it takes refuge in the convents, and if it's banished from the convents it takes refuge underground, and if it's banished from underground it takes refuge in schools or in barracks or heaven knows where; but as for madmen, believe me, there will always be some left."

"You know, Simone," said Donna Faustina, in high excitement and with tears of joy in her eyes, "Severino is a little mad too. What may seem to you indifference or aloofness in Severino is in reality, you know, just bashfulness, shyness, and also fear of ridicule. He sometimes has sudden spurts and impulses of generosity which make him almost unrecognizable even to me; but his fear of ridicule holds him back, he ponders them over, and rejects them. His enthusiasms are always like fireworks. For years he tried to make his life endurable by imitating others; maybe you too remember that time, Simone. And when that didn't work, he did his best to hide this inconvenient honesty of his behind a mask of eccentricity, because as we all know, eccentricity is now less of a scandal than virtue to these good Christian people, and what's more important, it's less ridiculous. In this way Severino has got into the habit of hiding his deepest feelings behind mannerisms and habits that are conventional and bizarre by turns. A couple of years ago he thought of going to America, and I with him; we used to talk about it every evening, we applied for passports, we looked around for someone to buy this house and the bit of land that Severino still possesses, we bought dictionaries and grammars and began to learn English; but by the time everything was ready, he had lost all interest in the journey. 'There's too much water to be crossed,' was the excuse he produced. 'The idea makes me sick.' But in reality a native of this village, who has been living in Philadelphia for the last twenty years, had written to him: 'If only you arrive here with plenty of money, you'll find it easy to make more, and you will be honoured and respected by everyone and surrounded with friends.' How I wish you could get to know Severino really well, Simone; I feel sure he would surprise you. He affects the rôle of a bear, a recluse, a pessimistic philosopher, and he quite enjoys having this reputation; and yet he would like so much to have company. And since we often endow strangers with the qualities we fail to find in those near to us (I can tell this secret to you, Simone), I know he sometimes goes out of the house in despair; he stays away the whole day on the strength of whatever pretext has come into his head, but I always know when he is telling fibs because he doesn't know how to lie. On these occasions he makes for remote cross-roads, and for taverns where he finds wagon-drivers, dealers and farmers coming back from the market, and he stays hours on end in their company. Then if he finds one more congenial than the rest, he goes part of the road along with him, talking to him and questioning him on the weather or the crops or his way of thinking about this or that."

Said Simone:

"Yes, I ran into him myself two or three times, a long way off from here, tearing along the country roads, like a poacher with the carabinieri after him. He always looked very annoyed at meeting me and barely acknowledged my greeting."

Said Donna Faustina:

"A wagon-driver from Lama, whom he had met on some such occasion, came here once with a present of game for him, a hare if I remember rightly, and in Severino's absence, not dreaming that he was betraying a secret, he told me the purpose of these frequent flights. You can't imagine, Simone, what ridiculous complicated childish pretexts the poor man is obliged to invent every time in order to justify, to casual acquaintances, his presence in such strange and out-of-the-way places. But in the long run even these escapades brought him only an illusory and passing satisfaction. They degraded friendship to the level of a stealthy adventure, whose meetings were as guarded by precautions and subterfuge as though they had been indecent and shameful acts. And he often takes up with people who make fun of him just so as to get him to buy them a drink."

Said Simone:

"If things keep going on at this rate, Donna Faustina, there will of course be a few simple and disinterested friendships left, but they will be considered as indecency and provocation, as an inadmissible outrage to propriety. And yet, life might be so pleasant if it were lived among friends. Of course there will always be troubles, coughs and deafness and lice, the pip for hens, hail and fire and death and so many other natural ills, how are we to do away with them? Alas, perhaps we shan't be able either to root out altogether the other and graver ills that have nested in men's hearts; but, Donna Faustina, just think how easy it would be to endure misfortune and even persecution if at least we could be together with our friends, vying with each other in helpfulness, each wanting the heaviest burden for himself so as to relieve his companion. If that could be, Donna Faustina, I think that even prison would become positively a pleasure resort."

From behind the piano came the noise of a mouse. The logs in the fireplace were breaking up and the embers smouldered. Simone bent down to poke the fire, got on his knees and took the logs in his hands without using the tongs.

"The house is old, so it's full of mice," said Donna Faustina. "Simone, couldn't you make me a present of a good cat?"

"Not a cat," apologized Simone, "but if you like I could give you more mice. I have several interesting breeds at home."

"The mice have been attacking Severino's manuscripts lately," complained Donna Faustino. "There's no way of protecting them."

"So Don Severino writes?" asked Simone. "What sort of things?"

"He has been writing for many years," Donna Faustina told him. "He began several novels and stories and a sort of confession, but he never finishes anything. If I'm to keep them safe I shall have to buy a mouse-trap," she wound up.

"A mouse-trap?" interrupted Simone. "Oh, Donna Faustina, please think it over. Pietro would be so sad to hear of it."

"Pietro?" repeated Donna Faustina. "Why?"

There was a long pause full of that name.

"I don't pretend to understand politics," said Donna Faustina at last. "And, to tell you the truth, Simone, they don't interest me either. I can understand risking one's life for a person; but for an idea? If I had lived at the time of the Catacombs, Simone, I too might have given up my life for Jesus; but for Christianity as it is to-day? What a pity it is, Simone," she added, lowering her voice, "that a man like Pietro Spina should have fallen a captive to political fanaticism!"

"I felt the same way, Donna Faustina, before good fortune brought him to my house," answered Simone with a smile. "If I were to tell you about it, it would seem a legend; if it had happened on Christmas Eve I should have thought it a grace bestowed by the angels; if it had happened at the Epiphany I should have thought it a present from the Magi Kings. I found him in my house like an impossible long-dreamed-of gift, that one finds in the chimney-place on waking up one morning. A miracle is the only admissible explanation of such things. I assure you, Donna Faustina, he has nothing to do with politics, that is to say with struggles or conspiracies or intrigues for power. Power is the secret dream of every slave, Donna Faustina, but he, as you know, was not born a slave. If he had wanted to command he need only have stayed at home. But he ran away too, that's the fact of the matter, he too wanted to lose himself, or, as you would say, save himself, he too wanted to play truant. Like you, like Don Severino, like me, and some others. Everyone in his own way. But he took the road that leads farthest, and he found the *cafoni**; indeed he found the raw material out of which the *cafoni* are made, that is to say earth and manure. Oh, it's easy to say that everyone knows the *cafoni*. The earth is swarming with them just as it swarms with donkeys and worms. I'm in their company every day, along the road and in the taverns, I know many of them by name, and there's nothing in my appearance to distinguish me from them. When Pietro began talking to me about the *cafoni*, I couldn't help laughing. I began thinking of the delusions and hallucinations of the humanitarian young gentlemen who descend to the common people. But then I realized that this was something entirely different. It's like this, Donna Faustina: he has lived underground and from there he has seen the world from the inside and this way of seeing things has never left him since. Now he sees everything permanently from the inside, without effort and quite naturally; he has only got to open his eyes. No, I assure you, Donna Faustina, he is no spinner of theories, no casuist, no hair-splitter. He is still a lad from this part of the world, a country lad, a bit of a dreamer, a bit absurd, and rather sentimental, but you

* *landless Italian peasants*

wouldn't even think he had been to college. Fate would have it that he should go down underground and see everything from the inside, so that appearances don't deceive him any more the way they deceive other people. He sees clearly that the things which the world adores and venerates are worth nothing at all, and so he scorns them instinctively and without effort; as for the things which the world mocks and abhors, he sees that on the contrary they are the only real and true things, and so it comes quite naturally to him to honor and respect them. But how can I explain, Donna Faustina? How can I make you understand what I really mean?"

"Oh, tell me, tell me," begged Donna Faustina, with tears in her eyes. Simone smiled, filled his pipe and lit it with a spill from the chimney-place. Donna Faustina moved another coffee-pot full of coffee over to the fire. Simone spent the rest of the night telling her.

PIETRO AND FAUSTINA

SAID FAUSTINA:

"Isn't human truth in the Cross, Pietro?"

Said Pietro:

"Yes, Faustina, but it is on the poor that the Cross weighs heaviest, on the factory-workers and *cafoni* and fellahs and coolies and peons, and on the poor homeless Jews, persecuted wherever they go. It was not for nothing, Faustina, that the poor were called the members of Jesus; not of the clerical Jesus, risen from the dead and triumphant, but of Jesus in His agony, Jesus crucified. In a country like ours, where the real workings of society are hidden away behind a skilfully camouflaged façade built by the collective efforts of Church and State, of Art and the Press, and above all, of course, by the driving force of all these institutions, namely immortal Eloquence, there's only one way left to find out how things really stand: one must go to the poor, live with them, if possible become like them. I don't labor under the illusion that the poor as individuals possess the truth. I am only too well aware that their spiritual poverty, carefully nurtured by those who derive a profit from it, is often as great as their material wretchedness; the pity of it is that they are often mean, brutal, superstitious, egoistical, and if they manage to scramble up one step in the social ladder, and get to own a little property, they become positively fierce. Nevertheless, I have known some exceptional people even among the poor. But whoever is possessed by the desire to understand, to become aware of things, should go and live among the poor, and there he will discover what lies hidden behind the classical shams of our ancient and famous civilization. Unfortunately it's not in the conscience of the poor that the truth is to be found, but in the very nature of their existence; they are immured, embedded in it from head to foot. Existence is reduced in them to its slenderest and barest essence; but in that small measure lies the cosmos, unmasked and unadorned."

Said Faustina:

"I too once met a man without a mask, a man with all the flesh burned away from his face. He must have been in the war, or in some fire or other. Except for a little skin around the eyes and ears, his face was that of a bleeding skull. He offered me his hand, but I ran away in horror—I was fifteen or sixteen years old at the time —I ran away without turning back; but in the act of escaping, suddenly—I don't know how—there came to me the idea that this unhappy creature was not just an ordinary poor wretch, a poor wretch only a little more unfortunate than the others, but that he was actually Christ Our Lord in person, and I turned back at once, as fast as I could run; but I didn't find him. I asked everyone I met on the road, but no one had seen him."

Said Pietro:

"I think Christ inhabits every poor wretch, Faustina. He Himself has told us as much. The priests have forgotten it, and those of them who do refer to it, interpret it in their own way, in a symbolical or in a rhetorical sense. But Christ was no rhetorician, He called bread bread and wine wine, and we have either got to reject His words or else accept them to the very letter."

Said Faustina:

"Ah, poor human life, what sadness and agony it is, if everything in it outside of suffering is falsehood. And how are we to look suffering in the face without being horror-stricken?"

Said Pietro:

"I had the same piece of luck as befell poor Don Giovanni De Benedictis. You remember? If I'm not mistaken, Faustina, he was a distant relative of yours. A fortunate man too."

Said Faustina:

"You mean the one who was buried in a cellar for two months after the earthquake, and had gone mad by the time they found him?"

Said Pietro:

"Did they get you to believe that story too, Faustina? He was not mad at all. His family had him locked up in a lunatic asylum because he wanted to marry the kitchenmaid; but I heard from Don Benedetto that he was anything but mad."

Said Faustina:

"They told me that even before the earthquake he wasn't altogether normal; it appears he used to spend his time collecting butterflies and the corks of champagne bottles."

Said Pietro:

"When the earthquake happened, Don Giovanni fell from the third floor, where he kept his collections, down to the cellar, in a corner stored with piles of onions, apples and potatoes, and as chance would have it, the kitchenmaid was there too. He escaped from the fall with a few harmless bruises. As the entire house had collapsed, no one dreamt that underneath the mountain of fallen masonry there could be this kind of saving grotto. The clearance work progressed slowly and for two months Don Giovanni learned to live on onions, apples and raw potatoes. He also got to know the kitchenmaid, he heard the story of her past life, the difficulties, misfortunes and joys of a kitchenmaid's existence, and when at last they dug down to his hideout, he didn't want to leave it, but begged them to let him stay in peace down there, where he was so comfortable. A similar piece of luck happened to me too, as you know, Faustina. As a result of that adventure I had, I too left my collection of butterflies and bottle-stoppers, and came back to everyday humanity. I found my parish again, the diocese of my soul, I appeased my leaning towards earth, my longing for earth, my need of earth. I cast down my roots, that were on the point of withering, into this hard barren rocky thorny earth for which they were intended and where they feel at home. Ah, I should die if I had to leave it now."

PIETRO PREACHES PRIDE

A PEASANT of Introdacqua, whom Pietro had met only two or three times some fifteen years earlier and had always remembered with affection, had died the month before Pietro returned. Pietro found his old mother, a sorrowful and spectral figure draped in black, in her silent house. Taking Pietro aside, she whispered in his ear: "Are you the one that was to come and that my poor boy waited for so long? Ah, why couldn't you have come at least a month ago? If you only knew what toils and tribulations he endured, how many bitter tears he swallowed in secret, that boy of mine! But now he is at rest, now he's in Paradise; there's nothing to be done about it there."

The dead man's brother invited Pietro to the tavern and insisted on offering him wine. Along the road he met other people and invited them to drink with him also, and his wife called to him from the window of their house:

"Do you too want to be ruined, like your brother? Why do you throw money away in the taverns when your children go barefoot and have nothing to eat?"

"There's no better way of spending money than drinking with one's friends," answered her husband laughingly. "Come and drink with me," he added, turning to the people around him.

Pietro drank a glass of wine, and as the tavern had become crowded with people he wanted to go. But the dead man's brother made him stay, and asked him, out in front of everyone:

"Aren't you the one that was to come and that my brother, poor soul, was waiting for? The things you would have told him—tell them to us."

Pietro drank another glass of wine and after a long silence he said to the people who were thronging the tavern and hanging on his words: "Sons and daughters of the poor, listen to me, I preach one thing to you: pride."

The ragged peasants listened to him with stupefaction. In a sudden outburst, he continued: "Poor ones, it is high time for you to be proud. I assure you that there is nothing nobler than you on the face of the earth. I have really nothing else to say to you beyond this: poor ones, be proud. Feeble-memoried Christians, must I remind you that God Himself, when he wished to take human form and come to live on earth, had to incarnate Himself in you? Have you forgotten that you are the members of the crucified Jesus? Mark well, this is no mere phrase: each one of you is really Jesus crucified; you, and not the princes of this world; you, and not the Pope or the cardinals. And if the earth has not yet rotted away, it is thanks to you alone. Therefore, poor ones, I preach you vanity. Be vain, hold your heads high, be proud. I believe that the world may soon have need of your pride. May your bones exult."

Amid the stupefaction of all present, Pietro managed to leave the tavern. On the outskirts of Introdacqua two men in uniform asked for his papers and, finding them in order, allowed him to proceed. He related the episode to Simone, with some excitement, and not

without a few blushes at this relapse into oratory; but Simone made
no comment. All he said was that it might end up badly, one day
or another.

PIETRO'S DEPARTURE FROM ACQUAVIVA

"Are you going?" asked Cesidio.

"Yes," answered Pietro, and he wanted to add something else,
but could not.

An embarrassing silence arose between the two.

"I've counted up the days you've worked for me," said Cesidio,
showing him a piece of paper.

"I'm sorry," answered Pietro, "but I haven't counted up all the
bread you've given to Infante and me."

"Bread?" exclaimed Cesidio stupefied. "But nobody counts bread,
for pity's sake. I don't understand why you want to offend me,
Pietro."

"Neither is my work for sale," declared Pietro resentfully. "Ah,
Cesidio, that has always been my dream: to work for nothing and
live on charity. I know, Cesidio, it's an ideal that can't be achieved
for the present, it's utopian. But let me have this, Cesidio, let me
have lived utopian days here with you, days of the Kingdom of
God, do me this favor."

"And why do you want to leave the Kingdom of God? Who's
driving you away?"

Pietro appeared deeply impressed by this exclamation of Cesidio's and he repeated several times over to himself: "Who's driving
me away? Eh, who's driving me away?"

Sor Quintino had prepared a little party in honor of the heroic
guest's departure, but when he saw him appear he did not dare
even to mention it. The guest sat at his table, alone, acknowledging
no greetings, absorbed, hostile, closed in on himself like a clenched
fist; what could he be hiding? A gold medal? A weapon, something
he had stolen? His appearance among the eminent gentlemen already at supper was that of an outsider on the stage while the actors
are playing. The eminent gentlemen crunched the bones of rickety
little birds, spread putrid cheese on their bread, licked their mous-
taches. On a small table there stood an antiquated gramophone,
with a dented blue horn.

"The radio has announced an event which will fill you with joy,"
said the mayor to the captain.

"The only items of news which fill me with joy are those announced by the radio as occasions of mourning," replied the captain.

"Excuse me, captain," observed the mayor, "but sometimes you go a little too far in what you say, I think."

"You are perfectly right, mayor," replied the captain. "I come from far away and I am going far also."

Sor Quintino arrived with the dishes to serve him; but he stood up, saluted those present, and went out.

The evening had a bitter-sweet fragrance of mown grass. He took the shortest way out of the village. He saw the windows lighting up in distant farms and hamlets; half-way up the other slope of the valley, he saw a train wind among the trees like a luminous caterpillar and then disappear into the hillside. He went down a path bordered with fruit trees; the tree-trunks were whitened with lime; he wandered at random among the vines, wrapped in his thoughts. Meanwhile the sky was coming alive with stars. He gazed at the sky and smiled. Had his grandmother already persuaded the Eternal Father to take him under His direct protection? A shudder ran through him. It would be terrible to fall into the hands of the Lord. He arrived at the bank of a mountain stream. The waters of the stream had swollen and grown tawny. Branches of trees, planks and kitchen utensils were swept all together in its onrush. There must have been a storm on the mountains; down in the hills nobody had noticed it.

"Praised be Jesus Christ," said an old woman passing by.

"Good evening," he replied.

"The flood has carried the bridge away," the old woman told him. "Give heed to me, turn back."

He turned back, wandering here and there, undecided.

He returned late to the inn and packed his bags.

—Translated by Darina Silone

GEORGE SANTAYANA

****

VIA SANTO STEFANO ROTONDO 6

ROME

DEAR MR. BURNETT:

I am pleased to hear of your proposed book, in which something of mine is to be included. You do not speak of the length that would be suitable. Some of the pieces you mention are of considerable length, and might prove heavy to the average reader. There is another which I, personally, prefer, namely, in Dialogues in Limbo, *the third Dialogue entitled "Normal Madness." I have rashly lent my copy to a friend, and have only the reprint in the Triton Edition, where it fills 15 pages. But it could be abridged to advantage, without touching the three themes that I think in depth and variety reveal my philosophy better than any other selection could in the same compass. The book has been out of print, but is to be re-issued soon by Scribners together with the three "new" Dialogues that have recently appeared in the* Atlantic Monthly. *In case you approve, I suggest in the enclosed the possible cuts.*

Yours sincerely,

G. SANTAYANA

****

Normal Madness

A DIALOGUE IN LIMBO

Persons in the Dialogue

The Shades of
> Democritus,
> Alcibiades,
> Aristippus,
> Dionysius the Younger.

The Spirit of one still living on earth, called
The Stranger.

DEMOCRITUS. You reappear in season, inquisitive Pilgrim, and today you must take a seat beside me. These young men are compelling my hoary philosophy to disclose the cause of all the follies that they perpetrated when alive. They still wear, as you see, their youthful and lusty aspect; for when we enter these gates Minos and Rhadamanthus restore to each of us the semblance of that age at which his spirit on earth had been most vivid and masterful and least bent bv tyrant circumstances out of its natural straightness. Therefore Alcibiades and Dionysius and Aristippus walk here in the flower of their youth and I sit crowned with all the snows and wisdoms of extreme old age; because their souls, though essentially noble, grew daily more distracted in the press of the world and more polluted, but mine by understanding the world grew daily purer and stronger. They are still ready for every folly, though luckily they lack the means; and the chronicle of vanity remains full of interest for them, because they are confident of shining in it. Yet the person whom this subject most nearly touches is you, since you are still living, and life is at once the quintessence and the sum of madness. Here our spirits can be mad only vicariously and at the second remove, as the verses in which Sophocles expresses the ravings of Ajax are themselves sanely composed, and a calm image of horror. But your thoughts, in the confusion and welter of existence, are still rebellious to metre; you cannot yet rehearse your alloted part, as we do here, with the pause and pomp of a posthumous self-knowledge. My discourse on madness, therefore, will not only celebrate your actions, but may open your eyes; and I assign to you on this occasion, the place of honour, as nearest of kin to the goddess Mania, who today presides over our games.

Those closed systems which the atoms often form by their cyclical motion are automatic; they complete and repeat themselves by an inward virtue whenever circumstances permit; yet even when circumstances do not permit, they madly endeavour to do so. This mad endeavour, when only partially defeated, may restore and propagate itself with but slight variations, and it is then called life. Of life madness is an inseparable and sometimes a predominant part: every living body is mad in so far as it is inwardly disposed to permanence when things about it are unstable, or is inwardly disposed to change when, the circumstances being stable, there is no occasion for changing. That which is virtue in season is madness out of season, as when an old man makes love; and Prometheus or Alexander attempting incredible feats is a miracle of sanity, if he attempts them at the right moment.

So much for madness in action, inevitable whenever the impulses of bodies run counter to opportunity. But life, both in its virtue and in its folly, is also expressed in fancy, creating the world of appearance. In the eye of nature all appearance is vain and a mere dream, since it adds something to substance which substance is not; and it is no less idle to think what is true than to think what is false.

That the intoxication of life is the first cause of appearance you have all observed and experienced when you have danced in a chorus, or performed your military exercises, stamping on the ground in unison and striking your swords together; ordered motion being naturally fertile in sound, in flashing light, and in gladness. Such appearances, in the safe and liberal life of a god, would not be deceptive, since a god need not be concerned about his own existence, which is secure, or that of other things, which is indifferent, and he is not tempted to assert falsely, as men do, that sound and splendour and gladness are the substance of those things or of himself. In him the intoxication of life in creating appearance would not create illusion, but only an innocent and divine joy. Accordingly, when the voice of a god traverses the air, the burden of it is neither true nor false; only the priest or the people, anxiously interpreting that oracle according to their fears and necessities, render false or true by their presumption such scraps of it as they may hear. The god, however, was not mindful of them but was singing to himself his own song. This divine simplicity of nature is ill understood by mortals, who address everything to their mean uses and vain advantage; whereby in the struggle to lengthen their days a little they fill them with distraction.

This is a third and most virulent form of madness, in which the dreams of the vegetative soul are turned into animal error and animal fury. For animals cannot wait for the slow ministrations of earth and air, but as you see in birds and kittens and young children, must be in a fidget to move; prying in all directions and touching and gobbling everything within reach. This is their only entertainment, for they have lost all finer inner sensibility, and their feelings and fancies arise only when their whole soul is addressed to external things of which they are necessarily ignorant—for what can a simpleton know of the streams of atoms actually coursing about him? His mind is furnished only with feelings and images generated within, but being distracted by the urgency of his lusts and fears, he takes those images and feelings for pleasant lures or fantastic and stalking enemies. Thus whereas locomotion by itself would be unconscious and fancy by itself would be innocent and free from error, fancy married with locomotion, as it must be in the strife of animals, begets false opinion and wraps the naked atoms in a veil of dreams.

Two protecting deities, indeed, like two sober friends supporting a drunkard, flank human folly and keep it within bounds. One of these deities is Punishment, and the other Agreement. The very mad man chokes, starves, runs into the sea, or having committed some fearful rape or murder is sentenced to death by the magistrates. Even if harmless, he is tied with a chain, and dies like a dog in his kennel. Punishment thus daily removes the maddest from the midst of mankind. The remnant, though their thoughts be in their homely way still dull or fantastic, then plod on in relative safety, while the unhappy souls whom Punishment has overtaken rest from their troubles. For no sooner has the system of atoms forming an animal body lost its equilibrium and been dispersed in death, than no pain or fancy or haggard hope subsists in that system any longer, and the peace of indifference and justice returns to the world; and if here or in the memory of men some echo of that life reverberates, it rings without anguish, the note once sounded repeating itself perpetually, pure and undisturbed. This is the good work which Punishment does daily, healing and harmonising the worst of follies.

Yet before dying in the arms of Punishment madness may be mitigated and tamed by Agreement, like a young colt broken in and trained to gallop in harness. The automatism of life, which is necessarily spontaneous and blind, may by adjustment with its occasions become a principle of health and genius, the parent of noble actions and beautiful works. Fancy, too, in creating images which have no originals in nature—since in nature there is nothing but atoms and the void—may by union with the times and order of natural events become the mother of names, pleasant and familiar, by which those events are called in the language of sense. Thus the most diverse imaginations in various species of animals may be rendered compatible with sagacity and with a prosperous life. Migratory fowl do not record their voyages in books, like human geographers, yet they have appointed dreams and secret sensations which warn them of the season for flight, and they are well informed about Egypt without consulting Herodotus. If omens were observed scientifically and not superstitiously interpreted, augury might be a true art of substitution, like language. There are many false tales told both by Greeks and barbarians which at times are useful to the state, because by an artful disposition of signs and sounds they dispose the inner parts of men favourably for breasting labour or war. Thus the most deep-dyed illusion, if it be interwoven with good habits, may flourish in long amity with things, naming and saluting them, as we do the stars, or the gods, without understanding their nature.

Such amity can the god Agreement establish even between aliens, but between brothers he weaves a subtler and a sweeter bond. For when kindred bodies have the same habitat and the same arts they also have the same illusions; and their common madness gives to each a perfect knowledge of the other's mind. Whereas the images in the eye or the thoughts of the heart can agree but loosely and, as it were, politically with material things, they may agree exactly with the images in another eye, and the thoughts of another heart. This free unanimity was called friendship by the Greeks, who alone of all nations have understood the nature of friendship. Barbarians of course may fight faithfully in bands, and may live in tribes and in cities, hugging their wives and children to their bosom; but such instinctive love, which all animals manifest, is not friendship. It moves in the realm of nature, and concerns only action and fate, whereas friendship is agreement in madness, when the same free thoughts and the same fraternal joys visit two kindred spirits. It was not for fighting loyally side by side that the Spartan phalanx or the Theban band were incomparable in the annals of war, but for fighting side by side for the sake of the beautiful, and in order that the liberal madness of their friendship might not end, unless it ended in death. All the glories of Greece are the fruits of this friendship and belong to the realm of madness tempered by Agreement; for out of the very fountain of madness Apollo and the Muses drew that intoxication which they taught to flow in the paths of health and of harmony. The Greeks in the intervals between their wars, instead of sinking into luxury and sloth, or into a vain industry, instituted games, in which peace was made keen and glorious by a beautiful image of war. Actual war is a conflict of matter with matter, as blind as it is inevitable; but the images which it breeds survive in peace, as we survive in these removed spaces after the battle of existence. So even the wisest when alive play with images and interests, and the glitter of many rival opinions hides the deep harmony with nature by which these opinions live. There is sweetness and quaint reason in these frail thoughts of our after-life, as in the wisdom of children. What could be madder than a ghost? Yet by the harmony which each of us has long since attained with himself, and by the freedom and peace which we gladly grant to one another, we immortalise the life of friendship and share it with the gods.

Let such, then, be my discourse upon madness. Philosophers are unjust to the madness of the vulgar, and the vulgar to that of mad-men and philosophers, not seeing how plausible a substitute it is for their own, because everybody thinks himself sane; wherein precisely shines his blinding illusion. I have wished in a manner to remove the mystery and the odium from this universal predicament of mortals, and to show it to be no anomaly. Madness is natural and, like all things natural, it loves itself, and often, by its innocence or by its signification, it lives in harmony with the rest of nature; other-wise, by the action it comports, it finds its quietus in punishment and death.

ALCIBIADES. Your discourse, indomitable Sage, has filled us with wonder, and left us without the wish to speak. The Stranger, if he had dared, should have broken this silence rather than I, for you tell us that madness comes of being alive, and very likely he thinks that such an opinion comes of being dead.

DEMOCRITUS. Very likely, but let him speak for himself.

THE STRANGER. I should not hesitate to do so if I had anything to object to so persuasive a discourse, but words on my part are super-fluous, since I recognise the truth of every part of it. To show you, however, that the living are not always unwilling to confess their plight, I will repeat an old story of the sort which we compose for children. It seems curiously to confirm all that the noble Democritus has taught us.

Once upon a time, so the story runs, the whole world was a gar-den in which a tender fair-haired child, whose name was Autologos, played and babbled alone. There was, indeed, an old woman who tended the garden, a goddess in disguise; but she lived in a cave and came out only at night when the child was asleep, for like the bat and the astronomer she could see better in the dark. She had a sharp pruning-hook on a very long pole, with which she silently pruned every tree and shrub in the garden, even the highest branches, cutting off the dead twigs and shaking down the yellow leaves in showers; and often, muttering surly words to herself which were not intelligible, she would cut off some flower or some bud as well, so that when the child awoke he missed them and could not imagine what had become of them. Now the child in his play gave names to everything that he liked or disliked; and the rose he called Beauty, and the jasmin Pleasure, and the hyacinth Sweetness, and the violet Sadness, and the thistle Pain, and the olive Merit, and the laurel Triumph, and the vine Inspiration. He was highly pleased with all these names, and they made those flowers and plants so much more interesting to him that he thought those names were their souls. But one day, having pricked himself with the thorns of a rose, he changed her name to Love; and this caused him to wonder why he had given those particular names to everything rather than quite different names; and the child began to feel older. As he sat brooding on this question, for he had stopped playing, a man in a black gown came into the garden who was a botanist, and said: "It matters little what names you give to flowers because they already have scientific names which indicate their true genera and species; the rose is only a rose, and is neither Beauty nor Love; and so with all the other flowers. They are flowers and plants merely, and they have no souls." Hearing this the child began to cry, very much to the botanist's annoyance, for being a busy man he disliked emotion. "After all," he added, "those names of yours will do no harm, and you may go on using them if you please; for they are prettier than those which truly describe the flowers, and much shorter; and if the word soul is particularly precious to you, you may even say that plants and flowers have souls: only, if you wish to be a man and not always a child, you must understand that the soul of each flower is only a name for its way of life, indicating how it spreads its petals in the morning and perhaps closes them at night, as you do your eyes. You must never suppose, because the flower has a soul, that this soul does anything but what you find the flower actually doing." But the child was not comforted, and when the wind had dried his tears, he answered: "If I cannot give beautiful names to the plants and flowers which shall be really their souls, and if I cannot tell myself true tales about them, I will not play in the garden any more. You may have it all to yourself and botanise in it, but I hate you." And the child went to sleep that night quite flushed and angry. Then, as silently as the creeping moonlight, the old woman came out of her cave and went directly to the place where the child was sleeping, and with a great stroke of her pruning-knife cut off his head; and she took him into her cave and buried him under the leaves which had fallen on that same night, which were many. When the botanist returned in the morning and found the child gone he was much perplexed. "To whom," said he to himself, "shall I now teach botany? There is nobody now to care for flowers, for I am only a professor, and if I can't teach anybody the right names of flowers, of what use are flowers to me?" This thought oppressed the poor man so much that he entirely collapsed, and as he was rather wizened to begin with, he was soon reduced to a few stiff tendons and bones, like the ribs of a dry leaf; and even these shreds soon crumbled, and he evaporated altogether. Only his black gown remained to delight the rag-picker. But the goddess in guise of that old woman went on pruning the garden, and it seemed to make no difference in her habits that the child and the botanist were dead.

I think we may surmise that the true name of this goddess must have been Dikè, the same that the wise Democritus was calling Punishment; and the botanist's name must have been Nomos, whom he was calling Agreement; and of course the child Autologos was that innocent illusion which was the theme of his whole discourse.

ARISTIPPUS. If this be the nature of madness, I propose that we immediately raise an altar to that deity, and worship him hereafter as the only beneficent god; and in order to avoid the protests of the vulgar, who think madness an evil, we will disguise our deity under the name of Autologos, borrowed from the Stranger's tale; and we will not identify him with the Furies or Harpies, but with Pan, Apollo, Orpheus and Dionysus.

DIONYSIUS. Agreed: and since my name is derived from that of Dionysus, who must have been my ancestor, I proclaim myself high priest of the new temple.

DEMOCRITUS. You pay my speech a great tribute. I have cele-brated the mad god so fitly that I have filled his votaries with a new frenzy of worship.

ALCIBIADES. Aristippus and Dionysius are enemies of science, and you, Democritus, are a believer in it. Being no judge in the matter, I will not pronounce between you, but I can conceive that a man who has spent his whole long life distilling herbs and grinding stones into powder should believe that he knows something of their substance. Nevertheless, intense study, too, is hypnotic, and might not the lucid theory of nature which you think partly awakens you out of the dream of life, be but a dream within a dream and the deepest of your illusions? My whole career seems a myth to me now in memory; yet when I interpret it in terms of your philosophy and imagine instead nothing but clouds of atoms drifting through a black sky, I seem to be descending into an even deeper cavern of reverie. Suppose I was dreaming of a chariot race, hearing the shouting crowds, blushing to be myself the victor, and reining in my quivering steeds to receive the crown, and suppose that suddenly my dream was transformed, and Olympia and the sunshine and myself and my horses and my joy and the praises of the Athenians turned to atoms fatally combined—I am afraid that, like the child in the Stranger's tale, I should burst into tears at that change of dreams.

DEMOCRITUS. Do you think I should blame you? Is the sublimity of truth impatient of error? I know well the shock that comes to innocence on discovering that the beautiful is unsubstantial. The soul, too, has her virginity and must bleed a little before bearing fruit. You misconceive my philosophy if you suppose that I deny the beautiful or would madly forbid it to appear. Has not my whole discourse been an apology for illusion and a proof of its necessity? When I discover that the substance of the beautiful is a certain rhythm and harmony in motion, as the atoms dance in circles through the void (and what else should the substance of the beautiful be if it has a substance at all?) far from destroying the beautiful in the realm of appearance my discovery raises its presence there to a double dignity; for its witchery, being a magic birth, is witchery indeed; and in it its parent nature, whose joy it is, proves her fertility. I deny nothing. Your Olympian victory and your trembling steeds, spattered with foam, and your strong lithe hand detaining them before the altar of Apollo, while you receive the crown—how should science delete these verses from the book of experience or prove that they were never sung? But where is their music now? What was it when passing? A waking dream. Yes, and grief also is a dream, which if it leaves a trace leaves not one of its own quality, but a transmuted and serene image of sorrow in this realm of memory and truth. As the grief of Priam in Homer and the grief of Achilles, springing from the dreadful madness of love and pride in their two bosoms, united in the divine ecstasy of the poet, so all the joys and griefs of illusion unite and become a strange ecstasy in a sane mind. What would you ask of philosophy? To feed you on sweets and lull you in your errors in the hope that death may overtake you before you understand anything? Ah, wisdom is sharper than death and only the brave can love her. When in the thick of passion the veil suddenly falls, it leaves us bereft of all we thought ours, smitten and consecrated to an unearthly revelation, walking dead among the living, not knowing what we seem to know, not loving what we seem to love, but already translated into an invisible paradise where none of these things are, but one only companion, smiling and silent, who by day and night stands beside us and shakes his head gently, bidding us to say Nay, nay, to all our madness. Did you think, because I would not spare you, that I never felt the cold steel? Has not my own heart been pierced? Shed your tears, my son, shed your tears. The young man who has not wept is a savage, and the old man who will not laugh is a fool.

JOSÉ ORTEGA Y GASSET

****

Taken from the Revolt of The Masses, *his most widely read book, in which the Spanish essayist and philosopher analyzed society as an inversion of values stemming from a crisis in European culture due to the preponderance of a mass mind, the opening chapter of that book is representative of the style and thinking of Ortega y Gasset. Although this book was published in Spain in 1930, much of its analysis has withstood almost a generation's test of time.*

****

The Coming of the Masses

THERE IS one fact which, whether for good or ill, is of utmost importance in the public life of Europe at the present moment. This fact is the accession of the masses to complete social power. As the masses, by definition, neither should nor can direct their own personal existence, and still less rule society in general, this fact means that actually Europe is suffering from the greatest crisis that can afflict peoples, nations, and civilisation. Such a crisis has occurred more than once in history. Its characteristics and its consequences are well known. So also is its name. It is called the rebellion of the masses. In order to understand this formidable fact, it is important from the start to avoid giving to the words "rebellion," "masses," and "social power" a meaning exclusively or primarily political. Public life is not solely political, but equally, and even primarily, intellectual, moral, economic, religious; it comprises all our collective habits, including our fashions both of dress and of amusement.

Perhaps the best line of approach to this historical phenomenon may be found by turning our attention to a visual experience, stressing one aspect of our epoch which is plain to our very eyes. This fact is quite simple to enunciate, though not so to analyse. I shall call it the fact of agglomeration, of "plentitude." Towns are full of people, houses full of tenants, hotels full of guests, trains full of travellers, cafés full of customers, parks full of promenaders, consul-

ting-rooms of famous doctors full of patients, theatres full of spectators, and beaches full of bathers. What previously was, in general,
no problem, now begins to be an everyday one, namely, to find
room.

That is all. Can there be any fact simpler, more patent, more
constant in actual life? Let us now pierce the plain surface of this
observation and we shall be surprised to see how there wells forth
an unexpected spring in which the white light of day, of our actual day, is broken up into its rich chromatic content. What is it
that we see, and the sight of which causes us so much surprise? We
see the multitude, as such, in possession of the places and the instruments created by civilisation. The slightest reflection will then
make us surprised at our own surprise. What about it? Is this not
the ideal state of things? The theatre has seats to be occupied—in
other words, so that the house may be full—and now they are overflowing; people anxious to use them are left standing outside.
Though the fact be quite logical and natural, we cannot but recognise that this did not happen before and that now it does; consequently, there has been a change, an innovation, which justifies, at
least for the first moment, our surprise.

To be surprised, to wonder, is to begin to understand. This is the
sport, the luxury, special to the intellectual man. The gesture characteristic of his tribe consists in looking at the world with eyes wide
open in wonder. Everything in the world is strange and marvellous
to well-open eyes. This faculty of wonder is the delight refused to
your football "fan," and, on the other hand, is the one which leads
the intellectual man through life in the perpetual ecstasy of the
visionary. His special attribute is the wonder of the eyes. Hence it
was that the ancients gave Minerva her owl, the bird with ever-
dazzled eyes.

Agglomeration, fullness, was not frequent before. Why then is it
now? The components of the multitudes around us have not sprung
from nothing. Approximately the same number of people existed
fifteen years ago. Indeed, after the war it might seem natural that
their number should be less. Nevertheless, it is here we come up
against the first important point. The individuals who made up
these multitudes existed, but not *qua* multitude. Scattered about the
world in small groups, or solitary, they lived a life, to all appearances, divergent, dissociate, apart. Each individual or small group
occupied a place, its own, in country, village, or quarter of the great
city. Now, suddenly, they appear as an agglomeration, and looking
in any direction our eyes meet with the multitudes. Not only in any

direction, but precisely in the best places, the relatively refined creation of human culture, previously reserved to lesser groups, in a word, to minorities. The multitude has suddenly become visible, installing itself in the preferential positions in society. Before, if it existed, it passed unnoticed, occupying the background of the social stage; now it has advanced to the footlights and is the principal character. There are no longer protagonists; there is only the chorus.

The concept of the multitude is quantitative and visual. Without changing its nature, let us translate it into terms of sociology. We then meet with the notion of the "social mass." Society is always a dynamic unity of two component factors: minorities and masses. The minorities are individuals or groups of individuals which are specially qualified. The mass is the assemblage of persons not specially qualified. By masses, then, is not to be understood, solely or mainly, "the working masses." The mass is the average man. In this way what was mere quantity—the multitude—is converted into a qualitative determination: it becomes the common social quality, man as undifferentiated from other men, but as repeating in himself a generic type. What have we gained by this conversion of quantity into quality? Simply this: by means of the latter we understand the genesis of the former. It is evident to the verge of platitude that the normal formation of a multitude implies the coincidence of desires, ideas, ways of life, in the individuals who constitute it. It will be objected that this is just what happens with every social group, however select it may strive to be. This is true; but there is an essential difference. In those groups which are characterised by not being multitude and mass, the effective coincidence of its members is based on some desire, idea, or ideal, which of itself excludes the great number. To form a minority, of whatever kind, it is necessary beforehand that each member separate himself from the multitude for special, relatively personal, reasons. Their coincidence with the others who form the minority is, then, secondary, posterior to their having each adopted an attitude of singularity, and is consequently, to a large extent, a coincidence in not coinciding. There are cases in which this singularising character of the group appears in the light of day: those English groups, which style themselves "nonconformists," where we have the grouping together of those who agree only in their disagreement in regard to the limitless multitude. This coming together of the minority precisely in order to separate themselves from the majority is a necessary ingredient in the formation of every minority. Speaking of the limited public which listened to a musician of refinement, Mallarmé wittily says that this public by its presence in small numbers stressed the absence of the multitude.

Strictly speaking, the mass, as a psychological fact, can be defined without waiting for individuals to appear in mass formation. In the presence of one individual we can decide whether he is "mass" or not. The mass is all that which sets no value on itself—good or ill—based on specific grounds, but which feels itself "just like everybody," and nevertheless is not concerned about it; is, in fact, quite happy to feel itself as one with everybody else. Imagine a humble-minded man who, having tried to estimate his own worth on specific grounds—asking himself if he has any talent for this or that, if he excels in any direction—realises that he possesses no quality of excellence. Such a man will feel that he is mediocre and common-place, ill-gifted, but will not feel himself "mass."

When one speaks of "select minorities" it is usual for the evil-minded to twist the sense of this expression, pretending to be unaware that the select man is not the petulant person who thinks himself superior to the rest, but the man who demands more of himself than the rest, even though he may not fulfil in his person those higher exigencies. For there is no doubt that the most radical division that it is possible to make of humanity is that which splits it into two classes of creatures: those who make great demands on themselves, piling up difficulties and duties; and those who demand nothing special of themselves, but for whom to live is to be every moment what they already are, without imposing on themselves any efforts towards perfection; mere buoys that float on the waves. This reminds me that orthodox Buddhism is composed of two distinct religions: one, more rigorous and difficult, the other easier and more trivial: the Mahayana—"great vehicle" or "great path"—and the Hinayana—"lesser vehicle" or "lesser path." The decisive matter is whether we attach our life to one or the other vehicle, to a maximum or a minimum of demands upon ourselves.

The division of society into masses and select minorities is, then, not a division into social classes, but into classes of men, and cannot coincide with the hierarchic separation of "upper" and "lower" classes. It is, of course, plain that in these "upper" classes, when and as long as they really are so, there is much more likelihood of finding men who adopt the "great vehicle," whereas the "lower" classes normally comprise individuals of minus quality. But, strictly speaking, within both these social classes, there are to be found mass and genuine minority. As we shall see, a characteristic of our times is the predominance, even in groups traditionally selective, of the mass and the vulgar. Thus, in the intellectual life, which of its essence requires and presupposes qualification, one can note the progressive triumph of the pseudo-intellectual, unqualified, unqualifiable, and, by their very mental texture, disqualified. Similarly, in the surviving groups of the "nobility," male and female. On the other hand, it is not rare to find to-day amongst working men, who before might be taken as the best example of what we are calling "mass," nobly disciplined minds.

There exist, then, in society, operations, activities, and functions of the most diverse order, which are of their very nature special, and which consequently cannot be properly carried out without special gifts. For example: certain pleasures of an artistic and refined character, or again the functions of government and of political judgment in public affairs. Previously these special activities were exercised by qualified minorities, or at least by those who claimed such qualification. The mass asserted no right to intervene in them; they realised that if they wished to intervene they would necessarily have to acquire those special qualities and cease being mere mass. They recognised their place in a healthy dynamic social system.

If we now revert to the facts indicated at the start, they will appear clearly as the heralds of a changed attitude in the mass. They all indicate that the mass has decided to advance to the foreground of social life, to occupy the places, to use the instruments and to enjoy the pleasures hitherto reserved to the few. It is evident, for example, that the places were never intended for the multitude, for their dimensions are too limited, and the crowd is continuously overflowing; thus manifesting to our eyes and in the clearest manner the new phenomenon: the mass, without ceasing to be mass, is supplanting the minorities.

No one, I believe, will regret that people are to-day enjoying themselves in greater measure and numbers than before, since they have now both the desire and the means of satisfying it. The evil lies in the fact that this decision taken by the masses to assume the activities proper to the minorities is not, and cannot be, manifested solely in the domain of pleasure, but that it is a general feature of our time. Thus—to anticipate what we shall see later—I believe that the political innovations of recent times signify nothing less than the political domination of the masses. The old democracy was tempered by a generous dose of liberalism and of enthusiasm for law. By serving these principles the individual bound himself to maintain a severe discipline over himself. Under the shelter of liberal prin-

ciples and the rule of law, minorities could live and act. Democracy
and law—life in common under the law—were synonymous. To-day
we are witnessing the triumphs of a hyperdemocracy in which the
mass acts directly, outside the law, imposing its aspirations and its
desires by means of material pressure. It is a false interpretation of
the new situation to say that the mass has grown tired of politics
and handed over the exercise of it to specialised persons. Quite the
contrary. That was what happened previously; that was democracy.
The mass took it for granted that after all, in spite of their defects
and weaknesses, the minorities understood a little more of public
problems than it did itself. Now, on the other hand, the mass believes that it has the right to impose and to give force of law to
notions born in the café. I doubt whether there have been other
periods of history in which the multitude has come to govern more
directly than in our own. That is why I speak of hyperdemocracy.

The same thing is happening in other orders, particularly in the
intellectual. I may be mistaken, but the present-day writer, when he
takes his pen in hand to treat a subject which he has studied deeply,
has to bear in mind that the average reader, who has never concerned himself with this subject, if he reads does so with the view,
not of learning something from the writer, but rather, of pronounc-
ing judgment on him when he is not in agreement with the commonplaces that the said reader carries in his head. If the individuals
who make up the mass believed themselves specially qualified, it
would be a case merely of personal error, not a sociological subver-
sion. *The characteristic of the hour is that the commonplace mind,
knowing itself to be commonplace, has the assurance to proclaim the
rights of the commonplace and to impose them wherever it will.* As
they say in the United States: "to be different is to be indecent."
The mass crushes beneath it everything that is different, everything
that is excellent, individual, qualified and select. Anybody who is
not like everybody, who does not think like everybody, runs the risk
of being eliminated. And it is clear, of course, that this "everybody"
is not "everybody." "Everybody" was normally the complex unity
of the mass and the divergent, specialised minorities. Nowadays,
"everybody" is the mass alone. Here we have the formidable fact of
our times, described without any concealment of the brutality of its
features.

SALVADOR DE MADARIAGA

****

OXFORD, ENGLAND

DEAR MR. BURNETT,

I need not waste your time explaining why your letter of September 26th has waited so long. Overwork is the word. For the same reason, I limit my answer to giving you two ideas about the work of mine that you could include in your anthology: one is any extract of any length you may wish from the enclosed lecture, Don Juan as a European Figure; *the other one is the chapter entitled "Dedicated to Women" (ch. Vi of part II) of my book* The World's Design *published in this country by George Allen and Unwin, and so far not published, nor likely to be published in the U.S.A. It is very likely to be available in the Library of Congress.*

Yours sincerely,

SALVADOR DE MADARIAGA

****

Dedicated to Women

THIS AGE of ours has brought in the fashion of warlike women. The Russian Revolution began it. Isolated cases there always were—women who, too spirited to be content with the possibilities of warfare which every healthy home affords, sallied forth in search of bellicose adventures. But this fashion of arraying hundreds and thousands of women in military uniform and teaching them how to shoot and destroy life—that life which they are meant to give—is new. And many women seem to like it.

Why is it so repellent? Why do we dislike the even less acute forms of the military tendency in women witnessed during the last War, when militant amazons went about hounding men of military age to the trenches and presenting white feathers to their countrymen at home, some of whom, for all they knew, might be more useful at home than thousands of soldiers in the field?

Let us dismiss all sentimentality about a subject which invites it

951

more, perhaps, than any other. Sentimentality in women is but a
fleeting state of mind, and even then, mostly to humour some specimen of the most sentimental animal there is—man. Women are
essentially practical and unsentimental. In normal times they are
equal to any difficult situation which may arise, and can handle it
coolly and without nonsense. In a tight corner they can be hard,
and even heroic. Child-birth, moreover, is no bed of roses. If, then,
we object so strongly to see women militarized, or even militant,
there must be a more substantial reason than a mere misunderstanding of them as soft, tender beings unable to stare facts in the face.

There is food for thought in this idea that mankind is housed for
the first nine months of its existence in the living body of its women.
Lope de Vega, for whom feminine nature had few secrets, used to
say that we owe respect and courtesy to women in return for that
generous hospitality. During those nine months they are engaged in
the most delicate work of construction which can be imagined. It is
on that divine creation that their physical—and probably much of
their sub-conscious—energies are concentrated; to it that their activities and pleasures are disciplined. For many women it is a time
of keen discomfort, a long never-ending period during which physical suffering of some kind is undergone almost hourly. For all of
them it is a period of subordination of the self to another self, a deep
experience, a living lesson in self-denial and devotion. And then,
the labour of child-birth, the gates of torture to the paradise of
maternity.

The child is there, alive, a source of joy, but a source of responsibility. The mother becomes a slave. Day or night, in health or in
sickness, all her time belongs to the new master, blissfully ignorant
of his egoism and privilege. Fears, cares, precautions, saving of food
and money for the child, rosaries of small, quiet sacrifices, a continuous attitude of self-denial, watchful attention over everything from
vehicles to microbes, always from the point of view of that precious
life. The school years. More expense. A wider area of dangers. A
deeper concern. Perhaps an illness or two. The terrible doubts on
the doctor's face. Sleepless nights of agony. Life like a black, blank
sphinx, cruelly silent. The world like a meaningless desert when that
precious life is imagined lost. The joy of recovery. The convales-
cence. More expense. More courage. More work. More patience.
More sacrifice. More years of silent drudgery and routine in the
backyard of life. And so that precious life is twenty. It took twenty
years of anxiety, labour, sacrifice and intelligence; but see, the

precious life is there. A joy to the eyes. A youth full of health, intelligence, force and beauty.

A stray bullet in one second strikes him dead.

It had taken twenty years to make him. It took one second to destroy him. It had taken love, labour, intelligence, perseverance, courage, sacrifice, all the virtues to make him. Hazard has no virtues, and needed none to destroy him.

Worst of all, this is no unlucky example, no oddity in the general pattern of life. This is a law of nature: *Construction is long and difficult. Destruction is immediate and easy.*

Consider the *Titanic*. A wonder of human creativeness. Imagine the numerous lines of ability and civilization which, along the several techniques, had converged towards the thought and the realization of that great ship—mathematics, metallography, siderurgy, naval engineering, thermo-dynamics, electricity, the social arts, the arts of wood, leather, glass, the arts of navigation and optics, the arts of decoration and good living, all cultivated in specific individuals, every one of whom had capitalized considerable national and human endeavours, every one of whom had devoted to that ship a valuable amount of his time—years of work implying toil, care, intelligence, and all the delicate dovetailing of so many multifarious activities. But at last, the glory is there and all this patience, attention, talent and co-operation sublimated into efficiency and beauty, sails the seas.

An iceberg, a thoughtless, indifferent, passive object of an iceberg, sinks it into nothingness in less than half an hour.

Think now of a picture, one of those pictures you love, a Titian or a Tintoretto. First, the artist had to be born—a gift from beyond, which comes when it comes, but cannot be produced at will. Not all the Academies and Art schools of the world will ever produce a Titian at will. Generations of quiet, pensive, open-eyed Venetians, looking vacantly on what lay before them, drinking in the lovely gold and green sunsets of their luminous country, had to live and die and bury their unmanifested visual dreams and joys in the recesses of the race, for a Titian or a Tintoretto to rise triumphantly, and give them back to the world in canvases which are a dream of joy.

Then Tintoretto or Titian had to conceive his plastic poem. And then live with it for days, weeks, months, nursing it with all the treasures of race and genius accumulated in his soul—and then, the painting; the wide, bold, yet sure lines of the first construction, the careful balancing of volumes and colours to reach that unforgettable harmony which is like a perfect musical chord. There, at last, is the picture, the fruit of long-prepared genius and of patient talent, for the world to enjoy.

But any fool can burn it in a few minutes.

Unfortunate mankind. Wherever it turns it finds the forces of destruction heavily favoured by nature. Whether it be to make a man, a tree, a boat, a picture, a building, an institution of any kind, men and women must give generously of their life, intelligence, attention, self-denial, heroic resistance at times—all the talents and all the virtues. But any one of their creations, even the most precious, even those which were most difficult to set up, nurse, develop and achieve—any and all are at the mercy of an accident, a distraction, a foolish act, a senseless reaction of the underman, the brute, the force of nature, the microbe, mere hazard, or that most impiously designated of irremediable disasters—an act of God.

And yet the world is there, a marvel of construction. So that in the end the forces of destruction do not win. This is now our problem: how is it that, terribly handicapped as it seems to be, construction wins over destruction? The answer is that *construction has a purpose and destruction has none.*

Construction works with an aim in view. Therefore it draws to itself and marshals many forces which lie in waiting and which separately are each worth no more than itself, but together multiply each other's values. Construction implies foresight, method, continuity, perseverance and co-operation, a formidable combination of creative moods; and, moreover, since construction implies a general plan within which the thing constructed must fit, it and all its works benefit from all that is already purposely made. A house-builder makes a house; but, precisely because it is a dwelling, the house fits into the dwelling system of the town, itself set into the dwelling system of the nation and the world. The house that is built is, therefore, not merely the outcome of the harmonious co-operation of all the mental and manual crafts that go to its making, but also a piece in a complicated machinery—or should we say organism—formed by all the networks of light, water, communications, sanitation, insurance and fire-saving appliances which were there awaiting it. For construction is a never-ending process towards more construction, order, health and peaceful life.

Destruction has no purpose. The absent-minded smoker who dropped the match which set fire to the house did not mean to do so much harm, in fact he meant to do no harm at all; the criminal incendiary who out of vengeance sets fire to the farm of his enemy is not particularly interested in fire, unless it be the fire that burns in his primeval heart; the lightning which strikes a tree and burns a dry forest has no aim whatever, within the scheme of human aims. And in any case, there is no alliance, no connected purpose linking together the several causes of destructive fire here and there in the world. Destruction is dispersive, disconnected. It proceeds not by controlled and directed efforts as those of construction, but by uncontrolled and anarchical outbursts of energy. Destruction is essentially unco-operative and aimless. This explains that, heavily favoured though it is in every individual case, it is easily defeated by construction when taken as a whole.

All this marvel of the civilized world, the towns, roads, railways, telegraphs and telephones and shipping lines, libraries, clubs, schools and universities, parliaments and ministries, all this ordered and co-operative activity which makes of mankind a unique experiment and a unique achievement in the universe, is the outcome of deliberate construction, local, general, national, universal. There runs through it all a steady purpose, an open-eyed spirit, a Great Design.

Yet how about the constructive value of destruction? Old houses are pulled down that new ones may be built. Institutions fall under the violence of revolutionary crowds, that new and juster ones may flourish: wars are fought and lives lost for liberty, for justice and for a better mankind. This is a favourite thought in all ages, and it has often been symbolized in the homely saying that "the chicken must break the egg." As if the egg were something in itself distinct from the chicken. The idea of the constructive value of destruction is merely the outcome of that human, all too human frailty— muddle-headedness.

Yes, the Bastille had to be taken; but only because it had been erected, or rather changed by tyrants from a constructive monument of stones into a destructive monument of oppression. An anti-error is not a truth. The architect who destroys an obsolete house is destroying nothing; he is performing the constructive act of clearing up a site occupied by a useless pile of worthless material. Wars, holy or otherwise, can be given as examples of nothing but the shortcomings of mankind. There is nothing constructive in them. They may help a part of mankind to scrape out of a bad situation into which it would not have strayed had it had more sense; but that does not confer on the war in question any special constructive value of its own. Wars are episodes on the stray paths of history into which mankind digresses from the royal road of progress. They may

at times bring lost tribes back to the true road, but they are not on
the true road. Revolutions belong to the same category of remedial
diseases, or rather, remedial phases in a disease. If a body-politic,
sick for generations with incompetence, corruption and oppression,
passes through a high fever in the process of getting rid of the
disease (or, what proves oftener to be the case, which remains after
the fever has abated) the fact does not make the fever either holy
or glorious. Destruction of destructive agents is a necessary evil, but
it is neither good in itself nor constructive.

No doubt, situations may arise when violence is inevitable. But
true strength dislikes violence enough to be content with patience to
the last. Till when? There is no general rule. There never is in
actual life. Not the letter of a precept, valid once and for all, but
the spirit of a living attitude, always adaptable though always sincere, is what is wanted; an attitude which, realizing the gravity of
violent solutions, tries every possible way of meeting difficulties
before having recourse to violence. It follows that war must never
be offered, nor must it be accepted unless with the full certainty that
it is inevitable. All this used to be common sense not long ago;
of late, particularly alas, amongst intellectuals, it has become a
paradox.

There is more than a mere distinction or shade of meaning in it.
Destruction is a negative state of the mind. If, owing to unfortunate
circumstances, this or that human being or nation has to perform
destruction, it is, whether they know it or not, a bad day for those
concerned. They become, for the time being, the dwelling of an evil
spirit, and are bound to remain infected by their deeds long after
they have committed them. Men may have to take on that painful
rôle. Good men do not like it. That is why true soldiers do not like
war, the glories of which are extolled by scribblers, bookish historians and frivolous princes, but not by those who actually do the
fighting. No human being whose spirit is healthy likes destruction
of any kind. A part of creation, he sides instinctively with the creative forces of the world.

If this be true of men, how could it not be true of women? Biologically they are the true modellers of the human race. Sociologi-
cally they are the promoters, and in many ways the creators, of all
the values of collective life—cleanliness, order, comfort, security,
beauty, good manners,—all the values which raise human communities above the pig-sty, the bee-hive, the cave. Women impersonate
the creative spirit in a particularly felicitous way. Less systematic
than men, they are more persevering; less logical, they are more

consistent; less busy, they are more active; less ambitious, they are more powerful; less scheming, they are more purposeful; less informed, they are more knowing; less sure of themselves, they are more sure of the world. Women are the favourite instruments of the Great Design.

That is why the sight of a woman in alliance with the forces of destruction is so repulsive. And of all the forces of destruction, those which are furthest removed from the true feminine spirit are those which aim at destroying human beings. A woman with a rifle in her hand is an abhorrent sight. A woman vociferating death, civil war, international war, is a monstrosity. The rôle of women should consist in removing causes of war, i.e., in working through peaceful ways to correct injustice; and in delaying by all the means in their power the time when, patience exhausted, violence breaks out. A woman inciting men to violence is a traitor to her sex, no matter the cause.

The Great War has cheapened human lives to an incredible extent. There have always been men with an inborn tendency to deal summarily with the lives of others. They are known as criminals. But in our day, human beings who believe themselves normal, think nothing of shooting a man dead because "he is a fascist" or because "he is a communist." A sudden release of sub-human bestiality is granted an intellectual or political dignity, purely superimposed, for it has, in fact, no connection whatever with the brutal destructive tendency which masquerades under it. Political divisions are mental; they have nothing whatever to do with the physical destruction of the adversary. Such at least was the case until Lenin and his three disciples, Stalin, Hitler and Mussolini, gave back to violence a political status which it was fast losing. Women have been caught on both sides of this tragic turmoil.

But, let there be no mistake about it, the remedy does not lie merely in the removal of violent schools of politics such as fascism and communism—a removal, by the way, which can only come about through a historical evolution bound to be slow. The active violence of fascism and communism is but the harvest of long years of passive violence during which privileged selfishness refused to move on towards justice and real peace. The rôle of women cannot be limited to a quiet opposition to active violence, but must also be an endeavour to remove the passive violence which breeds it. We may all be proud of having shed our ancestral cannibalism; but a man who achieves his aims at the cost of another man's life— whether he takes that life by active violence at one swift stroke, or

piecemeal by a passive violence which consumes it in slow misery—
that man is no better than a cannibal. If not the flesh, he devours
the spirit of his fellow men.

Nothing could be more contrary to true femininity than this kind
of spiritual cannibalism. Women are life-givers, not life-consumers.
And, as all life is one, women, by merely remaining true to their
life-giving genius, are sure to become the most efficient workers in
the Great Design.

PIO BAROJA

Novelist, critic, essayist, infusing a brilliant wit into all he writes, Pio Baroja left the selection of his work to the editor. Faced with a formidable task, the editor thought a fair representation of his style and point of view might be from a rather little-known volume of personalia, Youth and Egolatry, *translated from the Spanish by Jacob S. Fassett, Jr., and Frances L. Phillips for Knopf.*

Youth and Egolatry

ARCH-EUROPEAN

I AM a Basque, if not on all four sides, at least on three and a half. The remaining half, which is not Basque, is Lombard.

Four of my eight family names are Guipúzcoan, two of them are Navarrese, one Alavese, and the other Italian. I take it that family names are indicative of the countries where one's ancestors lived, and I take it also that there is great potency behind them, that the influence of each works upon the individual with a duly proportioned intensity. Assuming this to be the case, the resultant of the ancestral influences operative upon me would indicate that my geographical parallel lies somewhere between the Alps and the Pyrenees. Sometimes I am inclined to think that the Alps and the Pyrenees are all that is European in Europe. Beyond them I seem to see Asia; below them, Africa.

In the riparian Navarrese, as in the Catalans and the Genovese, one already notes the African; in the Gaul of central France, as well as in the Austrian, there is a suggestion of the Chinese.

Clutching the Pyrenees and grafted upon the Alps, I am conscious of being an Arch-European.

DIONYSIAN OR APOLLONIAN

FORMERLY, when I believed that I was both humble and a wanderer, I was convinced that I was a Dionysian. I was impelled toward turbulence, the dynamic, the theatric. Naturally, I was an anarchist. Am I today? I believe I still am. In those days I used to enthuse about the future, and I hated the past.

Little by little, this turbulence has calmed down—perhaps it was never very great. Little by little I have come to realize that if following Dionysus induces the will to bound and leap, devotion to Apollo has a tendency to throw the mind back until it rests upon the harmony of eternal form. There is great attraction in both gods.

EVIL AND ROUSSEAU'S CHINAMAN

I DO NOT believe in utter human depravity, nor have I any faith in great virtue, nor in the notion that the affairs of life may be removed beyond good and evil. We shall outgrow, we have already outgrown, the conception of sin, but we shall never pass beyond the idea of good and evil; that would be equivalent to skipping the cardinal points in geography. Nietzsche, an eminent poet and an extraordinary psychologist, convinced himself that he should be able to leap over good and evil with the help of a springboard of his manufacture.

Not with this springboard, nor with any other, shall we escape from the polar North and South of the moral life.

Nietzsche, a product of the fiercest pessimism, was at heart a good man, being in this respect the direct opposite of Rousseau, who, despite the fact that he is forever talking about virtue, about sensibility, the heart and the sublimity of the soul, was in reality, a low, sordid creature.

The philanthropist of Geneva shows the cloven hoof now and then. He asks: "If all that it were necessary for us to do in order to inherit the riches of a man whom we had never seen, of whom we had never even heard, and who lived in the furthermost confines of China, were to press a button and cause his death, what man living would not press that button?"

Rousseau is convinced that we should all press the button, and he is mistaken, because the majority of men who are civilized would do nothing of the kind. This, to my mind, is not to say that men are good; it is merely to say that Rousseau, in his enthusiasm for humanity, as well as in his aversion to it, is wide of the mark. The evil in man is not evil of this active sort, so theatrical, so self-interested; it is a passive, torpid evil which lies latent in the depths of the human animal, it is an evil which can scarcely be called evil.

SENSIBILITY

IN MY BOOKS, as in most that are modern, there is an indefinable resentment against life and against society.

Resentment against life is of far more ancient standing than resentment against society.

The former has always been a commonplace among philosophers.

Life is absurd, life is difficult of direction, life is a disease, the better part of the philosophers have told us.

When man turned his animosity against society, it became the fashion to exalt life. Life is good; man, naturally, is magnanimous, it was said. Society had made him bad.

I am convinced that life is neither good nor bad; it is like Nature, necessary. And society is neither good nor bad. It is bad for the man who is endowed with a sensibility which is excessive for his age; it is good for a man who finds himself in harmony with his surroundings.

A Negro will walk naked through a forest in which every drop of water is impregnated with millions of paludal germs, which teems with insects, the bites of which produce malignant abscesses, and where the temperature reaches fifty degrees Centigrade in the shade.

A European, accustomed to the sheltered life of the city, when brought face to face with such a tropical climate, without means of protection, would die.

Man needs to be endowed with a sensibility which is proper to his epoch and his environment; if he has less, his life will be merely that of a child; if he has just the right measure, it will be the life of an adult; if he has more, he will be an invalid.

LONGING FOR CHANGE

JUST AS the aim of politicians is to appear constant and consistent, artists and literary men aspire to change.

Would that the desire of one were as easy of attainment as that of the other!

To change! To develop! To acquire a second personality which shall be different from the first! This is given only to men of genius and to saints. Thus Caesar, Luther, and Saint Ignatius each lived two distinct lives; or, rather, perhaps, it was one life, with sides that were obverse and reverse.

The same thing occurs sometimes also among painters. The evolution of El Greco in painting upsets the whole theory of art.

There is no instance of a like tranformation either in ancient or modern literature. Some such change has been imputed to Goethe, but I see nothing more in this author than a short preliminary period of exalted feeling, followed by a lifetime dominated by study and the intellect.

Among other writers there is not even the suggestion of change. Shakespeare is alike in all his works; Calderón and Cervantes are always the same, and this is equally true of our modern authors. The first pages of Dickens, Tolstoi or of Zola could be inserted among the last, and nobody would be the wiser.

Even the erudite rhetorical poets, the Victor Hugos, the Gautiers, and our Spanish Zorillas, never get outside of their own rhetoric.

BAROJA, YOU WILL NEVER AMOUNT TO ANYTHING
(A Refrain)

"BAROJA does not amount to anything, and I presume that he will never amount to anything," Ortega y Gasset observes in the first issue of the *Spectator*.

I have a suspicion myself that I shall never amount to anything. Everybody who knows me has always thought the same.

When I first went to school in San Sebastian, at the age of four —and it has rained a great deal since that day—the teacher, Don Léon Sánchez y Calleja, who made a practice of thrashing us with a very stiff pointer (oh, these hallowed traditions of our ancestors!), looked me over and said:

"This boy will prove to be as sulky as his brother. He will never amount to anything."

I studied for a time in the Institute of Pamplona with Don Gregorio Pano, who taught us mathematics; and this old gentleman, who looked like the Commander in "Don Juan Tenorio," with his frozen face and his white beard, remarked to me in his sepulchral voice:

"You are not going to be an engineer like your father. You will never amount to anything."

When I took therapeutics under Don Benito Hernando in San Carlos, Don Benito planted himself in front of me and said:

"That smile of yours, that little smile . . . it is impertinent. Don't you come to me with any of your satirical smiles. You will never amount to anything, unless it is negative and useless."

I shrugged my shoulders.

Women who have known me always tell me: "You will never amount to anything."

And a friend who was leaving for America volunteered:

"When I return in twenty or thirty years, I shall find all my acquaintances situated differently; one will have become rich, another will have ruined himself, this fellow will have entered the cabinet, that one will have been swallowed up in a small town; but you will be exactly what you are today, you will live the same life and you will have just two pesetas in your pocket. That is as far as you will get."

The idea that I shall never amount to anything is now deeply rooted in my soul. It is evident that I shall never become a deputy, nor an academician, nor a Knight of Isabella the Catholic, nor a captain of industry, nor alderman, nor Member of the Council, nor a common cheat, nor shall I ever possess a good black suit.

And yet when a man has passed forty, when his belly begins to take on adipose tissue and he puffs out with ambition, he ought to do something, to sport a title, to wear a ribbon, to array himself in a black frock coat and a white waistcoat; but these ambitions are denied to me. The professors of my youth rise up before my eyes like the ghost of Banquo, and proclaim: "Baroja, you will never amount to anything."

When I go down to the seashore, the waves lap at my feet and murmur: "Baroja, you will never amount to anything." The wise owl that perches at night on our roof at Itzea calls to me: "Baroja, you will never amount to anything," and even the crows, winging their way across the sky, incessantly shout at me from above: "Baroja, you will never amount to anything."

And I am convinced that I shall never amount to anything.

THE PATRIOTISM OF DESIRE

I MAY NOT appear to be a very great patriot, but, nevertheless, I am. Yet I am unable to make my Spanish or Basque blood an exclusive criterion for judging the world. If I believe that a better orientation may be acquired by assuming an international point of view, I do not hold it improper to cease to feel, momentarily, as a Spaniard or a Basque.

In spite of this, a longing for the accomplishment of what shall be for the greatest good of my country, normally obsesses my mind, but I am wanting in the patriotism of lying.

I should like to have Spain the best place in the world, and the Basque country the best part of Spain.

The feeling is such a natural and common one that it seems scarcely worth while to explain it.

The climate of Touraine or of Tuscany, the Swiss lakes, the Rhine and its castles, whatever is best in Europe, I would root up, if I had my say, and set down here between the Pyrenees and the Straits of Gibraltar. At the same time, I should denationalize Shakespeare, Dickens, Tolstoi and Dostoievski, making them Spaniards. I should see that the best laws and the best customs were those of our country. But wholly apart from this patriotism of desire, lies the reality. What is to be gained by denying it? To my mind nothing is to be gained.

There are many to whom the only genuine patriotism is the patriotism of lying, which in fact is more of a matter of rhetoric than it is of feeling.

Our falsifying patriots are always engaged in furious combat with other equally falsifying internationalists.

"Nothing but what we have is of any account," cries one party.

"No, it is what the other fellow has," cries the other.

Patriotism is telling the truth as to one's country, in a sympathetic spirit which is guided and informed by a love of that which is best.

Now someone will say: "Your patriotism, then, is nothing but an extension of your ego; it is purely utilitarian."

Absolutely so. But how can there be any other kind of patriotism?

MY HOME LANDS

I HAVE two little countries, which are my homes—the Basque provinces, and Castile; and by Castile I mean old Castile. I have, further, two points of view from which I look out upon the world; one is my home on the Atlantic; the other is very like a home to me on the Mediterranean.

All my literary inspirations spring either from the Basque provinces or from Castile. I could never write a Gallegan or a Catalan novel.

I could wish that my readers were all Basque and Castilians.

Other Spaniards interest me less. Spaniards who live in America, or Americans, do not interest me at all.

PIERRE VAN PAASSEN

****

I am happy to send you some pages from Earth Could Be Fair *for* THE WORLD'S BEST. *These pages, as you will see no doubt, form a continuous story.*

PIERRE VAN PAASSEN

****

Uncle Kees Protests

THE FEAST of Saint Nicholas on December 6, with its brightly decorated shops and the children's procession through the streets, provided a brief respite from the monotony of the long winter months.
But Christmas Day did not. With us the commemoration of the
Saviour's birth was by no means a joyous celebration, or the occasion for mirth, conviviality, good cheer, and pleasant social gatherings, as it is in all other countries of Christendom, and in latter
years, I understand, in many places in Holland too. In my youth we
clung to the old Calvinist interpretation of Christmas as handed
down, I presume, from that gloomiest of men, John Calvin himself.
Christmas was a purely ecclesiastical function, a solemn observance
of the most awesome mystery of the ages: the Incarnation of God
Himself.

Others may look upon the birth in Bethlehem as a turning-point
in human history, as the dawn of a new era of grace and freedom,
and thus make it the occasion of rejoicing. Not so our spiritual
leaders. There are some out-of-the-way places in the highlands of
Scotland and in the Cévennes in France, among kirkmen and
Huguenots of the old stamp, where the same mournful and funereal
atmosphere prevails around Christmas. But I think we were unique
in this respect, that even the singing of carols was considered tantamount to blasphemy, that festive candles and gaily decorated fir
trees were deemed pagan abominations, while light talk or a specially elaborate meal on that day was a snare of Satan.

I do not recall the year—it may have been 1911, but it may also have been a year earlier or a year later—when an incident occurred that makes the memory of an old-fashioned Calvinist Christmas linger in my mind both with dread and amusement. It was bitter cold in the Great Church that morning. Worshipers pulled the collars of their overcoats up around their chins and sat with their hands in their pockets. Women wrapped their shawls tightly around their shoulders, for the vast nave and transept were unheated, except for little wooden boxes open on one side to hold a small earthen pot with charcoal. The heat escaping through five holes in the top of the box, or *stoof*, as it was called, was supposed to keep your feet warm.

These boxes were carried around in huge stacks by the ushers before the service. You could get one for the price of ten cents. Many men covered their heads with skullcaps such as the Jews wear in their synagogues, or they simply kept their hats on. That morning I had a muffler wrapped around my face and still my teeth chattered with the cold. When the congregation sang, their breath steamed up in faint white clouds toward the golden chandeliers.

The preacher that morning was a certain Dr. van Hoorn, a man of small stature with dark eyes and a coal-black beard. He was a representative of the ultraorthodox or confessional faction. Nobody in our family ever went to hear him. But that Christmas morning we made an exception.

For it so happened that on Christmas Eve, the organist Frans Pommard, had sent word to my Uncle Kees that he was too ill to fulfill his duties at the service on the morrow. Kees, happy over the opportunity to play the great organ, now sat in the loft peering down through the green-baize curtains on the congregation of about two thousand souls and on the pulpit, which stood fifteen feet high, a sculptured wooden tower, with its back to one of the pillars in the middle of the nave.

The organ, a towering structure, rested on two marble columns and stood in a niche on the west side of the church on the site where in pre-Reformation days had been the high altar. It reached upward a full hundred and twenty-five feet. Although quite old, it still had a superb tone. Its viola di gamba and its vox humana especially were renowned throughout the land and indeed in all Europe, having been deemed worthy of praise by four master organists as far apart in time as Constantine Huygens, Pieter Sweelinck, Widor, and Albert Schweitzer. All four had played on it.

It had three keyboards, one free-pedal, thirty-eight so-called "speaking voices," and forty-eight stops. The wind was provided by a man treading over a huge pedal consisting of twelve parallel beams. By stepping on those beams air was blown into the bellows. These beam pedals were located in a large inner room above the Consistory Chambers, that is, outside the church proper. A narrow passage between the pipes led from the organist's seat to the pedal room.

Uncle Kees took my brother and myself with him into the loft that morning. He chuckled softly as the minister in his opening prayer blessed the Almighty for having called "but one from a house and two from a city" to form with the other elect of all the ages "Thine own Israel in all eternity." But that was only the beginning. In his sermon Dr. van Hoorn soon struck an even more pessimistic note. Christmas, he said, signified the descent of God into the tomb of human flesh, "that charnel house of corruption and dead bones." He called it an inconceivable humiliation for the Divine Majesty to have left His glory in Heaven behind and to have entered the vile cesspool of time by clothing Himself with the mantle of our sordid humanity. He dwelt almost sadistically on our depravity, our utter worthlessness, the blackness of our hearts, tainted as we were from birth with original sin. We were worms, we were gall, we were abject, contemptible, and black as the night with sin.

Kees listened spellbound as the minister grew more dismal every minute. Christmas was God's descent into Hell, into torture unimaginable, eternity voluntarily submitting to the limitation of time. The assumption of the human estate was so at variance with the divine essence that it amounted to God's self-immolation. The dominie groaned and the men and women of the congregation bowed their heads in awful awareness of guilt for God's distress.

As the sermon progressed—sermons usually lasted a full two hours —Kees grew more and more restless. He scratched his head, pulled his hair back and forth onto his face, giving himself alternately a ludicrous and a sinister appearance. Then again he tugged at his mustache and goatee in a manner betraying extreme nervous tension and mental agitation. He could scarcely sit still for a minute. Now he rose from his seat to take a few steps in the narrow space in front of the organ bench only to sit down again and, with a rapid gesture, spreading apart the short curtains above the balustrade and cupping his head in his hands, to resume his fixed staring at the pulpit.

"Man, man," he muttered, shaking his head, "are these the good tidings, the simple glad message, that?" And turning to my brother and myself, he whispered fiercely: "That man smothers the hope of the world in the dustbin of theology!"

We sang a doleful psalm by way of interlude and the sermon, which had already lasted an hour and forty minutes, now moved toward its climax. It ended in so deep a note of despair that across the span of years I still feel a recurrence of the anguish I then experienced. It was quite well possible, nay, it was more than likely, the Doctor threw out by way of a parting shot that of his entire congregation not a single soul would enter the Kingdom of Heaven. Many were called, but few were chosen. The number and the identity of the elect was God's own secret, guarded from before the beginning of time, which we should not even try to unravel, for that would be pride and presumption. Man's eternal fate was settled, he said, and nothing, not good works or contrition, not piety or merit, not the most ardent prayers, could change by as much as one iota the immutability of the divine decree.

Kees shook with indignation as the minister concluded. He seated himself on the organ bench and began leafing through a volume of Bach's postludes. But after one glance he slammed the book shut.

For a moment I feared that he would not play any postlude at all and would walk off in a huff. I had known him to do rash things before in a fit of exasperation or impatience. Down below in the church Dr. van Hoorn could be seen lifting his hands for the benediction. Kees looked away from the scene and suddenly threw off his jacket, kicked off his shoes, and pulled out all the stops on the organ. From the nave, reverberating against the vaulted ceiling, came the unctuous voice of the Doctor. When he had finished speaking there followed a moment of intense silence.

Presently the minister put on his velvet cap and, holding up the skirts of his Geneva gown, began the descent of the spiral pulpit stair. Six of the Elders, dressed in frock coats, stood waiting for him at the foot of the steps. They formed a small procession, the Elders walking in pairs and the Pastor bringing up the rear. They went in the direction of the Consistory Chambers, the entrance to which lay through a door situated directly beneath the organ.

"Is he down?" asked Kees, who had just pulled the bell cord to give the signal to the organ attendant to begin working the bellows. He sat facing the keyboard with his back to the nave and could therefore not see what went on below.

"Yes," I said, "they are walking this way."

Kees waited one instant longer while we heard the air pour into the old instrument. His face was set and grim and he looked extremely pale. He was biting his mustache and I noticed that his chin trembled as my mother's chin trembled when she was overcome with emotion. Then, throwing his head back and opening his mouth as if he were going to shout, he brought his fingers down on the keyboard.

Hallelujah! Hallelujah! Hallelujah! Hallelujah!

The organ roared the tremendous finale of Händel's chorus from *The Messiah*. And again with an abrupt crashing effect, as if a million voices burst into song: Hallelujah! Hallelujah! Hallelujah! The music swelled and rolled with the boom of thunder against the vaulted dome, returning again and again with the hallelujah blast of praise like breakers bursting on the seashore.

It was a storm of music that Kees unleashed, a tornado of melody. Heaven and earth, the voices of men and angels, seemed joined in a hymn of praise to a God who did not doom and damn, but who so loved, loved, loved the world . . . Kees played on. Mountains leaped with joy. Icebergs melted. The hills and the seas clapped their hands in gladness.

The perspiration was rolling in big drops off his fine face. His eyes were blurred with tears. But his hands moved over the keyboard with speed and force. His stockinged feet flew over the pedal as if their owner were dashing in haste on a desperate errand. . . .

Now the vox humana softly intoned the tender, plaintive recital that comes just before the end. It was like the still small voice that followed the whirlwind of Elijah's vision in the wilderness. Kees beckoned to me with his head. I stepped nearer. "More air!" he called out. "Tell Leendert to give me more air!"

I ran back quickly behind the pipe cases into the bellows chamber, where the attendant, Leendert Bols, was stamping down the beams like a madman, transported by the music, waving his arms in the air.

"More air!" I shouted. "He wants more air!"

"Hallelujah!" Leendert shouted back. "Hallelujah!" The man grabbed me by the arm and together we fairly broke into a trot on the pedal beams.

Once more the organ's notes were swelling into that crescendo of hallelujahs which seems to reach forth to the end of time. Then the anthem came to a close.

But Kees was not through yet. He pushed in a few stops, and now the organ sang out sweetly what is the Dutch people's most-beloved evangelical song: "The Name above every Name, the Name of Jesus!" which is sung in Holland to a tune very similar to "Home, Sweet Home."

We sang it with all our hearts, Leendert, my brother, and I, and below in the church the congregation, on its way out, could be heard joining the chorus. Kees had triumphed.

His face was bathed in sweat. He wiped his forehead. I noticed that his handkerchief was wringing wet. In the subzero temperature the steam rose from his body. Leendert Bols came out of the bellows chamber and stood gazing at my uncle as if he beheld a phantom.

Kees had finished putting on his shoes and now he threw his Sunday cloak over his shoulders. He did not say a word as we clattered down the stone steps of the narrow staircase that ran from the organ loft into the nave. But as he flung open the iron door at the foot of the stairs we stood face to face with Dr. van Hoorn and the Elders. Crowding behind them were hundreds of members of the congregation, curiously craning their necks to witness the encounter between the Doctor and the organist.

"You?" exclaimed the Pastor even before we had closed the door behind us. "You? How did you get up there? Since when are you the organist? If I had known . . ." He did not finish the sentence, for Kees interrupted him by explaining the circumstances of Frans Pommard's illness.

"But why did you do that, play that?" Dr. van Hoorn in turn interrupted angrily.

"That," said Kees, "that was a protest against your sermon!"

"You have no right to protest!" fairly shouted the minister.

"I did protest, nevertheless," said Kees. "I protested because you dishonored man. You . . ." He got no further.

"*Ketter!*" screamed the minister, and his fanatical black eyes darted flames of wrath. "Heretic, madman, anarchist, that you are! Go away from God's house! Never," he yelled, "never, do you hear, will you play that tune again! Never will you . . ."

Kees threw his head back and burst into laughter. And then, bending forward, for he towered over the raging Pastor, my uncle said quietly: "You are wrong again, Doctor! I shall be playing that hymn, only much better, I trust, up there in Heaven on the day when you and millions and millions of the elect come marching in!"

With that he swept his hand from his cloak in a gesture that embraced the whole world.

ANGELOS SIKELIANOS

****

I suggest that you choose March of the Spirit *and* The Sacred Way.
*And I hope that you will take both of the poems and not one only,
because together they do represent somewhat the broad scope of the
writing of Angelos Sikelianos as no one of the single poems could do.*

EVA SIKELIANOS

****

Two Poems

MARCH OF THE SPIRIT

As I threw the last log on the hearth,
(log of my life locked in time),
on the hearth of your new Liberty, Greece,
my soul suddenly blazed as if space
were all copper, or as if I had
the sacred cell of Heraclitus around me,
where for years,
for eternity, he forged out his thoughts
and hung them as weapons
in the temple of Ephesus . . .

Gigantic thoughts,
like fiery clouds or red islands
in a fabulous sunset,
flamed in my mind,
for all at once my whole life was burning
in the care of your Liberty, Greece!
That is why I did not say:
This is the light of my funeral pyre . . .
I cried, I am the torch of your history!
And there, let my desolate carcass burn like a torch,
Empyrean vine-shoot,
with this torch

walking erect till the last hour,
to light at last all corners of the earth,
to pave a road into the soul,
into your mind, your body, Greece!
I spoke and I paced
bearing my enflamed liver
in your Caucasus,
and each step of mine
was my first and it was I believed my last,
for my bare feet waded in your blood,
for my bare feet stumbled among your corpses,
for my body, my face, my whole mind,
was mirrored as in a lake, in your blood!

There in such a red mirror, Greece,
a fathomless mirror, abysmal mirror
of your liberty and your thirst, I saw myself
heavy with red earth, moulded clay,
a new Adam of the newest creation
we will mould for you, Greece!
And I said:
I know, yes, I know, even your Olympian
Gods have now become a nether foundation,
for we buried them deep—deep so strangers will not find them,
And the whole foundation is doubly and triply fortified
with all the remains our enemies heaped upon it . . .
And I even know that for the libations and the vow
of the new Temple we dreamed for you, Greece,
days and nights, more comrades were slaughtered among them
than lambs were ever slain for Easter! . . .

Fate, and your fate my own to the very depths!
And through love, through great creative love
see how my soul has hardened, hardened and now
enters entire in your mud and your blood, to form
the new heart needed in your new struggle, Greece!
The new heart already locked in my breast,
and today I cry out with her to all comrades:

"Forward, help to lift the sun over Greece!
Forward, help to lift the sun over the world!
For see, his wheel is stuck deep in the mud,

and ah, see, his axle is buried deep in the blood!
Forward, boys, it isn't easy for the sun to rise alone,
push with knee and chest to get him out of the mud,
push with chest and knee to get him out of the blood,
See, we lean on him, we his blood brothers!
Forward brothers, he encircles us with his fire,
forward, forward, we are wrapped in his flame!

Forward creators! . . . Support your burden-bearing impulse
with head and foot, so the sun will not sink!
And help me too, brothers, not to sink with him . . .
For now he is over me, within and around me,
for now I spin in a sacred vertigo with him! . .

A thousand bulls' rumps support the base;
a two-headed eagle shakes its wings
over me and its flapping whirrs
beside my head and in my soul,
and the far and the near for me now are one! . . .
Newly heard, heavy harmonies encircle me! Forward, comrades
help him to rise, so the sun may become Spirit!

The new word is nearing that will dye all
in its new flame, mind and body, pure steel . . .
Our earth has fattened enough from human flesh . . .
Fat and fertile, let us not allow our earth
to harden from this deep blood-bath,
richer, deeper than any first rain!
Tomorrow each one of us must go out with twelve pairs of oxen,
to till this blood-drenched soil . . .
For the laurel to blossom on it and become a tree of life,
and our Vine to spread to the ends of the earth . . .

Forward boys, the sun cannot rise alone . . .
Push with knee and chest to get him out of the mud;
push with chest and knee, to get him out of the blood;
push with hand and head, for the sun to flash as Spirit!"

So, when I threw the last log on the hearth,
(log of my life locked in time),
on the hearth of your new Liberty, Greece,
my dread cry suddenly took new breath
as if space were all copper, or as if I had

the sacred cell of Heraclitus around me,
where for years,
for eternity, he forged out his thoughts
and hung them as weapons
in the Temple of Ephesus
as I called you comrades!

THE SACRED WAY

Through the new wound that fate opened in me
I felt the setting sun piercing my heart,
like the sudden surge of the wave
entering through a gash
in a ship rapidly sinking . . .
For at last that evening,
like a man long sick who first comes out
to milk life from the outside world,
I was a solitary walker on the road
that starts from Athens,
and has Eleusis as its sacred goal,
for this road always was for me
like the road of the soul . . . flowing
like a great manifest river:
wagons slowly drawn by oxen,
full of haystacks or logs, and other
carriages quickly passing
with the people inside them like shadows . . .
But farther on, as if the world were lost
and nature alone were left, little by little
a stillness settled . . . And the rock
I saw rooted at the edge,
appeared like a throne the centuries
had destined for me. And as I sat,
I crossed my hands around my knees, forgetting
whether I had started that day or whether I had taken
this same road centuries ago . . .

But see; from the nearest circle, in this quiet,
three shadows appeared.
One was a gypsy coming toward me,
and behind him, dragged by chains
followed two slow-moving bears.

And see; in a little while as they came near me
and the gypsy saw me, before I could look at him well,
he pulled his tambourine from his shoulder,
and, striking it with one hand,
with the other dragged the chains
violently. And then the two bears
rose up heavily on their hind legs . . . The one,
(clearly it was the mother), the large one,
her brow all adorned with a braid of blue beads
and over it a white amulet to ward off the evil eye,
suddenly raised herself with majesty,
as if she wore a wooden idol of the Great Goddess,
centuries old, of the eternal Mother,
of the same one who in sacred sorrow,
in the course of time, as she took human form,
here was named Demeter, pining for her daughter,
and there named Alcmene, or the Virgin,
pining for her son.
And the little bear beside her,
like a big toy, a small ignorant child,
raised itself also, obeying,
but not yet foreseeing
the length of its pain, and the bitterness
of the slavery his mother mirrored
looking at it with her two fiery eyes!

But being exhausted, she was slow
in starting to dance and the gypsy,
with an adroit pull of the chain
on the little one's nostril, still bleeding
from the metal that evidently had pierced it
a few days before, made the mother
groaning with pain, suddenly stand up,
bend her head towards her child,
and begin a wild dance . . .

And I, as I looked on, proceeded
out of time, far from time,
free from forms locked in time,
free from statues and icons;
I was outside, I was outside of time . . .
But before me, forced up by the violence

of the metal ring, and her yearning love,
I saw nothing else but the majestic bear,
with the blue beads on her head,
a monstrous symbol of martyrdom
of the whole world, present and past,
a monstrous symbol of martyrdom
of all ancient pain, whose tax of the soul
is still unpaid by the mortal centuries . . .
for the soul was and still is in Hell . . .
And I kept
my head continuously bent,
as I threw a drachma into the tambourine,
for I too was a slave of the world . . .
But at last, as
the gypsy went ahead, again
dragging the two slow-moving bears,
and was lost in the twilight, my heart
lifted me to take again the road
ending at the ruins
of the sanctuary of the soul of Eleusis.
And as I walked, my heart groaned:
"Will the hour never come,
when the soul of the bear and the gypsy,
and my soul, that I call initiate,
will feast together?"
And as I went on
and night fell, again through the same
wound that fate had opened in me I felt
the darkness surging into my heart
as the wave rushes suddenly through a gash
in a ship rapidly sinking . . .
And yet it was as if my heart thirsted
for such a flood when it sank
totally drowned in the darkness,
totally drowned in the darkness.
A murmur spread over me,
a murmur
and it seemed to say:
"The hour will come!"

—Translated by Rae Dalven

ARTHUR KOESTLER

****

This section* is mainly a dialogue between Rubashov, former People's Commissar arrested for oppositionary tendencies, and the investigating magistrate Ivanov. Just before the dialogue starts a former friend of Rubashov's has been led past his cell to execution, with the obvious intention of showing Rubashov the fate which is in store for him. I have selected this dialogue as it gives one essential aspect of the ethical problems underlying the book.

ARTHUR KOESTLER

****

Apage Satanas

RUBASHOV was lying on his bunk again, without knowing how he had got there. He still had the drumming in his ears, but the silence was now a true silence, empty and relaxed. No. 402 was presumably asleep. Bogrov, or what had remained of him, was presumably dead by now.

"Rubashov, Rubashov. . . ." That last cry was branded ineffaceably in his acoustic memory. The optic image was less sharp. It was still difficult for him to identify with Bogrov that doll-like figure with wet face and stiff, trailing legs, which had been dragged through his field of vision in those few seconds. Only now did the white hair occur to him. What had they done to Bogrov? What had they done to this sturdy sailor, to draw this childish whimpering from his throat? Had Arlova whimpered in the same way when she was dragged along the corridor?

Rubashov sat up and leant his forehead against the wall behind which No. 402 slept; he was afraid he was going to be sick again.

---

* *From* Darkness at Noon, *of which the author wrote:*
"The characters in this book are fictitious. The historical circumstances which determined their actions are real. The life of the man N. S. Rubashov is a synthesis of the lives of a number of men who were victims of the so-called Moscow Trials. Several of them were personally known to the author. This book is dedicated to their memory."

Up till now, he had never imagined Arlova's death in such detail. It had always been for him an abstract occurrence; it had left him with a feeling of strong uneasiness, but he had never doubted the logical rightness of his behaviour. Now, in the nausea which turned his stomach and drove the wet perspiration from his forehead, his past mode of thought seemed lunacy. The whimpering of Bogrov unbalanced the logical equation. Up till now Arlova had been a factor in this equation, a small factor compared to what was at stake. But the equation no longer stood. The vision of Arlova's legs in their high-heeled shoes trailing along the corridor upset the mathematical equilibrium. The unimportant factor had grown to the immeasurable, the absolute; Bogrov's whining, the inhuman sound of the voice which had called out his name, the hollow beat of the drumming, filled his ears; they smothered the thin voice of reason, covered it as the surf covers the gurgling of the drowning.

Exhausted, Rubashov fell asleep, sitting—his head leaning against the wall, the pince-nez before his shut eyes.

He groaned in his sleep; the dream of his first arrest had come back; his hand, hanging slackly from the bed, strained for the sleeve of his dressing-gown; he waited for the blow to hit him at last, but it did not come.

Instead, he woke up, because the electric light in his cell was turned on suddenly. A figure stood next to his bed, looking at him. Rubashov could hardly have slept a quarter of an hour, but after that dream he always needed several minutes to find himself again. He blinked in the bright light, his mind worked laboriously through the habitual hypotheses, as though he were carrying out an unconscious ritual. He was in a cell; but not in the enemy country—that was only dreamed. So he was free—but the colour-print of No. 1 hanging over his bed was lacking, and over there stood the bucket. Besides, Ivanov was standing at his bedside and blowing cigarette smoke into his face. Was that also dreamed? No, Ivanov was real, the bucket was real. He was in his own country, but it had become an enemy country; and Ivanov, who had been his friend, had now also become an enemy; and the whimpering of Arlova was not a dream either. But no, it had not been Arlova, but Bogrov, who had been dragged past like a wax-doll; Comrade Bogrov, faithful unto the grave; and he had called out his name; that was not dreamed. Arlova, on the other hand, had said: 'You can do whatever you like with me. . . .'

'Do you feel ill?' asked Ivanov.

Rubashov blinked at him, blinded by the light. 'Give me my dressing-gown,' he said.

Ivanov watched him. The right side of Rubashov's face was swollen. 'Would you like some brandy?' Ivanov asked. Without waiting for a reply, he hobbled to the spy-hole and called out something into the corridor. Rubashov's eyes followed him, blinking. His dazedness would not go. He was awake, but he saw, heard and thought in a mist.

'Have you been arrested too?' he asked.

'No,' said Ivanov quietly. 'I only came to visit you. I think you have a temperature.'

'Give me a cigarette,' said Rubashov. He inhaled deeply once or twice, and his gaze became clearer. He lay down again, smoking, and looked at the ceiling. The cell door opened; the warder brought a bottle of brandy and a glass. This time it was not the old man, but a lean youth in uniform, with steel-rimmed spectacles. He saluted Ivanov, handed the brandy and glass over to him and shut the door from outside. One heard his steps receding down the corridor.

Ivanov sat down on the edge of Rubashov's bunk and filled the glass. 'Drink,' he said. Rubashov emptied the glass. The mistiness in his head cleared, events and persons—his first and second imprisonment, Arlova, Bogrov, Ivanov—arranged themselves in time and space.

'Are you in pain?' asked Ivanov.

'No,' said Rubashov. The only thing he did not yet understand was what Ivanov was doing in his cell.

'Your cheek is badly swollen. Probably you also have a temperature.'

Rubashov stood up from the bunk, looked through the spy-hole into the corridor, which was empty, and walked up and down the cell once or twice until his head became quite clear. Then he stopped in front of Ivanov, who was sitting on the end of the bunk, patiently blowing smoke-rings.

'What are you doing here?' he asked.

'I want to talk to you,' Ivanov said. 'Lie down again and drink some more brandy.'

Rubashov blinked at him ironically through his pince-nez. 'Until now,' he said, 'I was tempted to believe you were acting in good faith. Now I see that you are a swine. Get out of here.'

Ivanov did not move. 'Be good enough to give the reasons for this assertion,' he said.

Rubashov leaned his back against the wall of No. 406 and looked down at Ivanov. Ivanov was smoking with equanimity.

'Point one,' said Rubashov. 'You knew of my friendship with Bogrov. Therefore you take care that Bogrov—or what was left of him—is taken past my cell on his last journey, as a reminder. To make sure that I do not miss this scene, Bogrov's execution is discreetly announced beforehand, on the assumption that this news will be tapped through to me by my neighbours, which, in fact, happens. A further finesse of the producer's is to inform Bogrov of my presence here, just before he is dragged off—on the further assumption that this final shock will draw from him some audible manifestation; which also happens. The whole thing is calculated to put me into a state of depression. In this darkest hour, Comrade Ivanov appears as a saviour, with a bottle of brandy under his arm. Follows a touching scene of reconciliation, we fall into each other's arms, exchange moving war memories and incidentally sign the statement with my confession. Whereupon the prisoner sinks into a gentle slumber; Comrade Ivanov leaves on the tip of his toes with the statement in his pocket, and is promoted a few days later. . . . Now have the goodness to get out of here.'

Ivanov did not move. He blew smoke into the air, smiled and showed his gold teeth. 'Do you really think I have such a primitive mind?' he asked. 'Or, to be more exact: do you really believe I am such a bad psychologist?'

Rubashov shrugged. 'Your tricks disgust me,' he said. 'I cannot throw you out. If you have a trace of decency left in you, you will now leave me alone. You can't imagine how you all disgust me.'

Ivanov lifted the glass from the floor, filled it and drank it. 'I propose the following agreement,' he said. 'You let me speak for five minutes without interrupting me, and listen with a clear head to what I am saying. If after that you still insist on my going—I will go.'

'I'm listening,' said Rubashov. He stood leaning against the wall opposite Ivanov and glanced at his watch.

'In the first place,' said Ivanov, 'in order to remove any possible doubts or illusions you may have: Bogrov has in fact been shot. Secondly, he has been in prison for several months, and at the end was tortured for several days. If you mention this during the public trial, or even so much as tap it through to your neighbours, I am done for. About the reasons for treating Bogrov like that, we will speak later. Thirdly, it was intentional that he was taken past your cell, and intentional that he was told of your presence here.

Fourthly, this filthy trick, as you call it, was not arranged by me, but by my colleague Gletkin, against my express instructions.'

He paused, Rubashov stood leaning against the wall and said nothing.

'I should never have made such a mistake,' Ivanov went on; 'not out of any regard for your feelings, but because it is contrary to my tactics and to my knowledge of your psychology. You have recently shown a tendency to humanitarian scruples and other sentimentalities of the sort. Besides, the story of Arlova still lies on your stomach. The scene with Bogrov must only intensify your depression and moralistic leanings—that could be foreseen; only a bungler in psychology like Gletkin could have made such a mistake. Gletkin has been dinning into my ears for the last ten days that we should use "hard methods" on you. For one thing, he doesn't like you because you showed him the holes in your socks; for another, he is used to dealing with peasants. . . . So much for the elucidation of the affair with Bogrov. The brandy, of course, I ordered because you were not in full possession of your wits when I came in. It is not in my interest to make you drunk. It is not in my interest to lay you open to mental shocks. All that only drives you further into your moral exaltation. I need you sober and logical. My only interest is that you should calmly think your case to a conclusion. For, when you have thought the whole thing to a conclusion—then, and only then, will you capitulate. . . .'

Rubashov shrugged his shoulders; but before he could say anything, Ivanov cut in:

'I know that you are convinced that you won't capitulate. Answer me only one thing: *if* you became convinced of the logical necessity and the objective rightness of capitulating—would you then do it?'

Rubashov did not answer at once. He felt dully that the conversation had taken a turn which he should not have allowed. The five minutes had passed, and he had not thrown out Ivanov. That alone, it seemed to him, was a betrayal of Bogrov—and of Arlova; and of Richard and Little Loewy.

'Go away,' he said to Ivanov. 'It's no use.' He noticed only now that he had for some time been walking up and down his cell in front of Ivanov.

Ivanov was sitting on the bunk. 'By your tone of voice, I notice,' he said, 'that you recognize your mistake concerning my part in the Bogrov affair. Why, then, do you want me to go? Why don't you answer the question I asked? . . .' He bent forward a little and looked Rubashov mockingly in the face; then he said slowly, emphasizing each word: *'Because you are afraid of me.* Because my way of thinking and of arguing is your own, and you are afraid of the echo in your own head. In a moment you will be calling out: Get thee behind me, Satan. . . .'

Rubashov did not answer. He was walking to and fro by the window, in front of Ivanov. He felt helpless and incapable of clear argument. His consciousness of guilt, which Ivanov called 'moral exaltation,' could not be expressed in logical formulæ—it lay in the realm of the 'grammatical fiction.' At the same time, every sentence spoken by Ivanov did in fact evoke an echo in him. He felt he ought never to have let himself be drawn into this discussion. He felt as if he were on a smooth, slanting plane, down which one slid irresistibly.

'Apage Satanas!' repeated Ivanov and poured himself out another glass of brandy. 'In old days, temptation was of carnal nature. Now it takes the form of pure reason. The values change. I would like to write a Passion play in which God and the Devil dispute for the soul of Saint Rubashov. After a life of sin, he has turned to God—to a God with the double chin of industrial liberalism and the charity of the Salvation Army soups. Satan, on the contrary, is thin, ascetic and a fanatical devotee of logic. He reads Machiavelli, Ignatius of Loyola, Marx and Hegel, he is cold and unmerciful to mankind, out of a kind of mathematical mercifulness. He is damned always to do that which is most repugnant to him: to become a slaughterer, in order to abolish slaughtering, to sacrifice lambs so that no more lambs may be slaughtered, to whip people with knouts so that they may learn not to let themselves be whipped, to strip himself of every scruple in the name of a higher scrupulousness, and to challenge the hatred of mankind because of his love for it—an abstract and geometric love. *Apage Satanas!* Comrade Rubashov prefers to become a martyr. The columnists of the liberal Press, who hated him during his lifetime, will sanctify him after his death. He has discovered a conscience, and a conscience renders one as unfit for the revolution as a double chin. Conscience eats through the brain like a cancer, until the whole of the grey matter is devoured. Satan is beaten and withdraws—but don't imagine that he grinds his teeth and spits fire in his fury. He shrugs his shoulders; he is thin and ascetic; he has seen many weaken and creep out of his ranks with pompous pretexts. . . .'

Ivanov paused and poured himself another glass of brandy. Rubashov walked up and down in front of the window. After a while he said:

'Why did you execute Bogrov?'

'Why? Because of the submarine question,' said Ivanov. 'It concerned the problem of tonnage—an old quarrel, the beginnings of which must be familiar to you.

'Bogrov advocated the construction of submarines of large tonnage and a long range of action. The Party is in favour of small submarines with a short range. You can build three times as many small submarines for your money as big ones. Both parties had valid technical arguments. The experts made a big display of technical sketches and algebraic formulæ; but the actual problem lay in quite a different sphere. Big submarines mean: a policy of aggression, to further world revolution. Small submarines mean: coastal defense—that is, self-defense and postponement of world revolution. The latter is the point of view of No. 1, and the Party.

'Bogrov had a strong following in the Admiralty and amongst the officers of the old guard. It would not have been enough to put him out of the way; he also had to be discredited. A trial was projected to unmask the partisans of big tonnage as *saboteurs* and traitors. We had already brought several little engineers to the point of being willing to confess publicly to whatever we liked. But Bogrov wouldn't play the game. He declaimed up to the very end of big tonnage and world revolution. He was two decades behind the times. He would not understand that the times are against us, that Europe is passing through a period of reaction, that we are in the hollow of a wave and must wait until we are lifted by the next. In a public trial he would only have created confusion amongst the people. There was no other way possible than to liquidate him administratively. Would not you have done the same thing in our position?'

Rubashov did not answer. He stopped walking, and again remained leaning against the wall of No. 406, next to the bucket. A cloud of sickening stench rose from it. He took off his pince-nez and looked at Ivanov out of red-rimmed, hunted eyes.

'You did not hear him whimpering,' he said.

Ivanov lit a new cigarette on the stump of the old one; he too found the stench of the bucket rather overpowering.

'No,' he said, 'I did not hear it. But I have heard and seen similar things. What of it?'

Rubashov was silent. It was no use to try and explain it. The whimpering and the muffled drumming again penetrated his ears, like an echo. One could not express that. Nor the curve of Arlova's breasts with its warm, steep points. One could express nothing. 'Die

in silence,' had been written on the message given him by the
barber.

'What of it?' repeated Ivanov. He stretched out his leg and
waited. As no answer came, he went on speaking:

'If I had a spark of pity for you,' he said, 'I would now leave you
alone. But I have not a spark of pity. I drink; for a time, as you
know, I drugged myself; but the vice of pity I have up till now
managed to avoid. The smallest dose of it, and you are lost. Weeping over humanity and bewailing oneself—you know our race's
pathological leaning to it. Our greatest poets destroyed themselves
by this poison. Up to forty, fifty, they were revolutionaries—then
they became consumed by pity and the world pronounced them
holy. You appear to have the same ambition, and to believe it to
be an individual process, personal to you, something unprecedented.
. . .' He spoke rather louder and puffed out a cloud of smoke. 'Beware of these ecstasies,' he said. 'Every bottle of spirits contains a
measurable amount of ecstasy. Unfortunately, only few people, particularly amongst our fellow countrymen, ever realize that the ecstasies of humility and suffering are as cheap as those induced chem-
ically. The time when I woke from the anæsthetic, and found that
my body stopped at the left knee, I also experienced a kind of absolute ecstasy of unhappiness. Do you remember the lectures you
gave me at the time?' he poured out another glass and emptied it.

'My point is this,' he said; 'one may not regard the world as a
sort of metaphysical brothel for emotions. That is the first commandment for us. Sympathy, conscience, disgust, despair, repentance, and atonement are for us repellent debauchery. To sit down
and let oneself be hypnotized by one's own navel, to turn up one's
eyes and humbly offer the back of one's neck to Gletkin's revolver—
that is an easy solution. The greatest temptation for the like of us
is: to renounce violence, to repent, to make peace with oneself.
Most great revolutionaries fell before this temptation, from Sparta-
cus to Danton and Dostoevsky; they are the classical form of betrayal of the cause. The temptations of God were always more dangerous for mankind than those of Satan. As long as chaos dominates
the world, God is an anachronism; and every compromise with one's
own conscience is perfidy. When the accursed inner voice speaks to
you, hold your hands over your ears. . . .'

He felt for the bottle behind him and poured out another glass.
Rubashov noticed that the bottle was already half empty. You also
could do with a little solace, he thought.

'The greatest criminals in history,' Ivanov went on, 'are not of the type Nero and Fouché, but of the type Gandhi and Tolstoy. Gandhi's inner voice has done more to prevent the liberation of India than the British guns. To sell oneself for thirty pieces of silver is an honest transaction; but to sell oneself to one's own conscience is to abandon mankind. History is *a priori* amoral; it has no conscience. To want to conduct history according to the maxims of the Sunday school means to leave everything as it is. You know that as well as I do. You know the stakes in this game, and here you come talking about Bogrov's whimpering. . . .'

He emptied his glass and added:

'Or with conscience pricks because of your fat Arlova.'

Rubashov knew from before that Ivanov could hold a lot; one did not notice any change in his behaviour, beyond a slightly more emphatic way of speaking than usual. You do need consolation, thought Rubashov again, perhaps more than I do. He sat down on the narrow stool opposite Ivanov and listened. All this was not new to him; he had defended the same point of view for years, with the same or similar words. The difference was that at that time he had known those inner processes of which Ivanov spoke so contemptuously, merely as an abstraction; but since then he had experienced the 'grammatical fiction' as a physical reality in his own body. But had these irrational processes become more admissible merely because he had a personal acquaintance with them now? Was it any the less necessary to fight the 'mystical intoxication' merely because one had oneself become intoxicated by it? When a year ago he had sent Arlova to her death, he had not had enough imagination to picture the details of an execution. Would he now behave differently merely because he now knew some of its aspects? Either it was right —or it was wrong to sacrifice Richard, Arlova and Little Loewy. But what had Richard's stutter, the shape of Arlova's breasts or Bogrov's whimpering to do with the objective rightness or wrongness of the measure itself?

Rubashov began again to walk up and down his cell. He felt that everything he had experienced since his imprisonment had been only a prelude; that his cogitations had led him to a dead end—on to the threshold of what Ivanov called the 'metaphysical brothel'— and that he must begin again from the beginning. But how much time was there left? He stopped, took the glass out of Ivanov's hand and drained it. Ivanov watched him.

'That's better,' he said with a fleeting smile. 'Monologues in the form of a dialogue are a useful institution. I hope I reproduced the voice of the tempter effectively. A pity that the opposite party is not represented. But that is part of its tricks, that it never lets itself be drawn into a rational discussion. It always attacks a man in defenceless moments, when he is alone and in some effective *mise en scène:* from burning thorn-bushes or cloud-covered mountain tops— and with a special preference for a sleeping victim. The methods of the great moralist are pretty unfair and theatrical. . . .'

Rubashov was no longer listening. Walking up and down, he was wondering whether to-day, if Arlova were still alive, he would sacrifice her again. This problem fascinated him; it seemed to contain the answer to all other questions. . . . He stopped in front of Ivanov and asked him:

'Do you remember "Raskolnikov"?'

Ivanov smiled at him with irony. 'It was to be expected that you would sooner or later come to that. *Crime and Punishment.* . . . You are really becoming childish or senile. . . .'

'Wait a bit. Wait a bit,' said Rubashov, walking up and down agitatedly. 'All this is just talk, but now we are getting nearer the point. As far as I remember, the problem is, whether the student Raskolnikov has the right to kill the old woman? He is young and talented; he has as it were an unredeemed pledge on life in his pocket; she is old and utterly useless to the world. But the equation does not stand. In the first place, circumstances oblige him to murder a second person; that is the unforeseeable and illogical consequence of an apparently simple and logical action. Secondly, the equation collapses in any case, because Raskolnikov discovers that twice two are not four when the mathematical units are human beings. . . .'

'Really,' said Ivanov. 'If you want to hear my opinion, every copy of the book should be burnt. Consider a moment what this humanitarian fog-philosophy would lead to, if we were to take it literally; if we were to stick to the precept that the individual is sacrosanct, and that we must not treat human lives according to the rules of arithmetic. That would mean that a battalion commander may not sacrifice a patrolling party to save the regiment. That we may not sacrifice fools like Bogrov, and must risk our coastal towns being shot to pieces in a couple of years. . . .'

Rubashov shook his head:

'Your examples are all drawn from war—that is, from abnormal circumstances.'

'Since the invention of the steam engine,' replied Ivanov, 'the world has been permanently in an abnormal state; the wars and revolutions are just the visible expressions of this state. Your Raskolnikov is, however, a fool and a criminal; not because he behaves logically in killing the old woman, but because he is doing it in his personal interest. The principle that the end justifies the means is and remains the only rule of political ethics; anything else is just vague chatter and melts away between one's fingers. . . . If Raskolnikov had bumped off the old woman at the command of the Party —for example, to increase strike funds or to instal an illegal Press— then the equation would stand, and the novel with its misleading problem would never have been written, and so much the better for humanity.'

Rubashov did not answer. He was still fascinated by the problem as to whether to-day, after the experiences of the last few months and days, he would again send Arlova to her death. He did not know. Logically, Ivanov was right in everything he said; the invisible opponent was silent, and only indicated its existence by a dull feeling of uneasiness. And in that, too, Ivanov was right, that this behaviour of the 'invisible opponent,' in never exposing itself to argument and only attacking people at defenceless moments, showed it in a very dubious light. . . .

'I don't approve of mixing ideologies,' Ivanov continued. 'There are only two conceptions of human ethics, and they are at opposite poles. One of them is Christian and humane, declares the individual to be sacrosanct, and asserts that the rules of arithmetic are not to be applied to human units. The others starts from the basic principle that a collective aim justifies all means, and not only allows, but demands, that the individual should in every way be subordinated and sacrificed to the community—which may dispose of it as an experimentation rabbit or a sacrificial lamb. The first conception could be called anti-vivisection morality, the second, vivisection morality. Humbugs and dilettantes have always tried to mix the two conceptions; in practice, it is impossible. Whoever is burdened with power and responsibility finds out on the first occasion that he has to choose; and he is fatally driven to the second alternative. Do you know, since the establishment of Christianity as a state religion, a single example of a state which really followed a Christian policy? You can't point out one. In times of need—and politics are chronically in a time of need—the rulers were always able to evoke "exceptional circumstances," which demanded exceptional measures of defence. Since the existence of nations and classes, they live in a permanent state of mutual self-defence, which forces them to defer to another time the putting into practice of humanism. . . .'

Rubashov looked through the window. The melted snow had

again frozen and sparkled, an irregular surface of yellow-white crystals. The sentinel on the wall marched up and down with shouldered rifle. The sky was clear but moonless; above the machine-gun turret shimmered the Milky Way.

Rubashov shrugged his shoulders. 'Admit,' he said, 'that humanism and politics, respect for the individual and social progress, are incompatible. Admit that Gandhi is a catastrophe for India; that chasteness in the choice of means leads to political impotence. In negatives we agree. But look where the other alternative has led us. . . .'

'Well,' asked Ivanov, 'where?'

Rubashov rubbed his pince-nez on his sleeve, and looked at him shortsightedly. 'What a mess,' he said, 'what a mess we have made of our golden age.'

Ivanov smiled. 'Maybe,' he said happily. 'Look at the Gracchi and Saint-Just and the Commune of Paris. Up to now, all revolutions have been made by moralizing dilettantes. They were always in good faith and perished because of their dilettantism. We for the first time are consequent. . . .'

'Yes,' said Rubashov. 'So consequent, that in the interests of a just distribution of land we deliberately let die of starvation about five million farmers and their families in one year. So consequent were we in the liberation of human beings from the shackles of industrial exploitation that we sent about ten million people to do forced labour in the Arctic regions and the jungles of the East, under conditions similar to those of antique galley slaves. So consequent that, to settle a difference of opinion, we know only one argument: death, whether it is a matter of submarines, manure, or the Party line to be followed in Indo-China. Our engineers work with the constant knowledge that an error in calculation may take them to prison or the scaffold; the higher officials in our administration ruin and destroy their subordinates, because they know that they will be held responsible for the slightest slip and be destroyed themselves; our poets settle discussions on questions of style by denunciations to the Secret Police, because the expressionists consider the naturalistic style counter-revolutionary, and *vice versa*. Acting consequentially in the interests of the coming generations, we have laid such terrible privations on the present one that its average length of life is shortened by a quarter. In order to defend the existence of the country, we have to take exceptional measures and make transition-stage laws, which are in every point contrary to the aims of the Revolution. The people's standard of life is lower than it was before the

Revolution; the labour conditions are harder, the discipline is more inhuman, the piecework drudgery worse than in colonial countries with native coolies; we have lowered the age limit for capital punishment down to twelve years; our sexual laws are more narrow-minded than those of England, our leader-worship more Byzantine than that of the reactionary dictatorships. Our Press and our schools cultivate Chauvinism, militarism, dogmatism, conformism and ignorance. The arbitrary power of the Government is unlimited, and unexampled in history; freedom of the Press, of opinion and of movement are as thoroughly exterminated as though the proclamation of the Rights of Man had never been. We have built up the most gigantic police apparatus, with informers made a national institution, and with the most refined scientific system of physical and mental torture. We whip the groaning masses of the country towards a theoretical future happiness, which only we can see. For the energies of this generation are exhausted; they were spent in the Revolution; for this generation is bled white and there is nothing left of it but a moaning, numbed, apathetic lump of sacrificial flesh. . . . Those are the consequences of our consequentialness. You called it vivisection morality. To me it sometimes seems as though the experimenters had torn the skin off the victim and left it standing with bared tissues, muscles and nerves. . . .'

'Well, and what of it?' said Ivanov happily. 'Don't you find it wonderful? Has anything more wonderful ever happened in history? We are tearing the old skin off mankind and giving it a new one. That is not an occupation for people with weak nerves; but there was once a time when it filled you with enthusiasm. What has so changed you that you are now as pernickety as an old maid?'

Rubashov wanted to answer: 'Since then I have heard Bogrov call out my name.' But he knew that this answer did not make sense. So he answered instead:

'To continue with the same metaphor: I see the flayed body of this generation: but I see no trace of the new skin. We all thought one could treat history like one experiments in physics. The difference is that in physics one can repeat the experiment a thousand times, but in history only once. Danton and Saint-Just can be sent to the scaffold only once; and if it should turn out that big submarines would after all have been the right thing. Comrade Bogrov will not come to life again.'

'And what follows?' asked Ivanov. 'Should we sit with idle hands because the consequences of an act are never quite to be foreseen, and hence all action is evil? We vouch for every act with our heads

—more cannot be expected of us. In the opposite camp they are not so scrupulous. Any old idiot of a general can experiment with thousands of living bodies; and if he makes a mistake, he will at most be retired. The forces of reaction and counter-revolution have no scruples or ethical problems. Imagine a Sulla, a Galliffet, a Koltschak reading Raskolnikov. Such peculiar birds as you are found only in the trees of revolution. For the others it is easier. . . .'

He looked at his watch. The cell window had turned a dirty grey; the newspaper which was stuck over the broken pane swelled and rustled in the morning breeze. On the rampart opposite, the sentry was still doing his hundred steps up and down.

'For a man with your past,' Ivanov went on, 'this sudden revulsion against experimenting is rather naïve. Every year several million people are killed quite pointlessly by epidemics and other natural catastrophes. And we should shrink from sacrificing a few hundred thousand for the most promising experiment in history? Not to mention the legions of those who died of undernourishment and tuberculosis in coal and quicksilver mines, rice-fields and cotton plantations. No one takes any notice of them; nobody asks why or what for; but if here we shoot a few thousand objectively harmful people, the humanitarians all over the world foam at the mouth. Yes, we liquidated the parasitic part of the peasantry and let it die of starvation. It was a surgical operation which had to be done once and for all; but in the good old days before the Revolution just as many died in any dry year—only senselessly and pointlessly. The victims of the Yellow River floods in China amount sometimes to hundreds of thousands. Nature is generous in her senseless experiments on mankind. Why should mankind not have the right to experiment on itself?'

He paused; Rubashov did not answer. He went on:

'Have you ever read brochures of an anti-vivisectionist society? They are shattering and heartbreaking; when one reads how some poor cur which has had its liver cut out, whines and licks its tormentor's hands, one is just as nauseated as you were tonight. But if these people had their say, we would have no serums against cholera, typhoid, or diphtheria. . . .'

He emptied the rest of the bottle, yawned, stretched and stood up. He limped over to Rubashov at the window, and looked out.

'It's getting light,' he said. 'Don't be a fool, Rubashov. Everything I brought up to-night is elementary knowledge, which you know as well as I. You were in a state of nervous depression, but now it is over.' He stood next to Rubashov at the window, with his arm round Rubashov's shoulders; his voice was nearly tender. 'Now go and sleep it off, old warhorse; to-morrow the time is up, and we will both need a clear head to concoct your deposition. Don't shrug your shoulders—you are yourself at least half convinced that you will sign. If you deny it, it's just moral cowardice. Moral cowardice has driven many to martyrdom.'

Rubashov looked out into the grey light. The sentry was just doing a right-about turn. Above the machine-gun turret the sky was pale grey, with a shade of red. 'I'll think it over again,' said Rubashov after a while.

When the door had closed behind his visitor, Rubashov knew that he had already half-surrendered. He threw himself on the bunk, exhausted and yet strangely relieved. He felt hollowed-out and sucked dry, and at the same time as if a weight had been lifted from him. Bogrov's pathetic appeal had in his memory lost some of its acoustic sharpness. Who could call it betrayal if, instead of the dead, one held faith with the living?

While Rubashov slept quietly and dreamlessly—the toothache had also quieted down—Ivanov, on the way to his room, paid a visit to Gletkin. Gletkin sat at his desk in full uniform, and was working through files. For years he had had the habit of working right through the night three or four times a week. When Ivanov entered the room, Gletkin stood up to attention.

'It is all right,' said Ivanov. 'To-morrow he will sign. But I had to sweat to repair your idiocy.'

Gletkin did not answer; he stood stiffly in front of his desk. Ivanov, who remembered the sharp scene he had had with Gletkin before his visit to Rubashov's cell and knew that Gletkin did not forget a rebuff so easily, shrugged his shoulders and blew cigarette smoke into Gletkin's face. 'Don't be a fool,' he said. 'You all still suffer from personal feelings. In his place, you would be even more stubborn.'

'I have a backbone, which he hasn't,' said Gletkin.

'But you're an idiot,' said Ivanov. 'For that answer you ought to be shot before him.'

He hobbled to the door and banged it from outside.

Gletkin sat down to his desk again. He did not believe Ivanov would succeed, and at the same time he was afraid of it. Ivanov's last sentence had sounded like a threat, and with him one never knew what was a joke and what serious. Perhaps he did not know himself—like all these intellectual cynics. . . .

Gletkin shrugged his shoulders, shoved his collar and crackling cuffs into place, and went on with his work on the pile of documents.

—Translated by Daphne Hardy

FERENC MOLNÁR

****

I wrote the concluding scenes of this play at an unhappy period of my life. While writing, I tried to give free rein to my feelings of pain and bitterness—the feelings of a deeply hurt young man of twenty-seven, transposed into terms of the theatre.

FERENC MOLNÁR

****

Liliom's Return

SCENE—*In the Beyond. A whitewashed courtroom. There is a green-topped table; behind it a bench. Back center is a door with a bell over it. Next to this door is a window through which can be seen a vista of rose-tinted clouds.*

Down right there is a grated iron door. Down left another door.

Two men are on the bench when the curtain rises. One is richly, the other poorly dressed.

From a great distance is heard a fanfare of trumpets playing the refrain of the thieves' song in slow, altered tempo.

Passing the window at back appear LILIOM *and the* TWO POLICE-MEN.

The bell rings.

An old guard enters at right. He is bald and has a long white beard. He wears the conventional police uniform.

He goes to the door at back, opens it, exchanges silent greetings with the TWO POLICEMEN *and closes the door again.*

LILIOM *looks wonderingly around.*

THE FIRST (*to the old* GUARD). Announce us.

(THE GUARD *exits at left.*)

LILIOM. Is this it?

THE SECOND. Yes, my son.

993

LILIOM. This is the police court?

THE SECOND. Yes, my son. The part for suicide cases.

LILIOM. And what happens here?

THE FIRST. Here justice is done. Sit down.

(LILIOM *sits next to the two men. The* TWO POLICEMEN *stand silent near the table.*)

THE RICHLY DRESSED MAN (*whispers*). Suicide, too?

LILIOM. Yes.

THE RICHLY DRESSED MAN (*points to* THE POORLY DRESSED MAN). So's he. (*Introducing himself*) My name is Reich.

THE POORLY DRESSED MAN (*whispers, too*). My name is Stephen Kadar.

(LILIOM *only looks at them.*)

THE POORLY DRESSED MAN. And you? What's your name?

LILIOM. None of your business.

(*Both move a bit away from him.*)

THE POORLY DRESSED MAN. I did it by jumping out of a window.

THE RICHLY DRESSED MAN. I did it with a pistol—and you?

LILIOM. With a knife.

(*They move a bit further away from him.*)

THE RICHLY DRESSED MAN. A pistol is cleaner.

LILIOM. If I had the price of a pistol——

THE SECOND. Silence!

(*The* POLICE MAGISTRATE *enters. He has a long white beard, is bald, but only in profile can be seen on his head a single tuft of snow-white hair. The* GUARD *reënters behind him and sits on the bench with the dead men. As the* MAGISTRATE *enters, all rise, except* LILIOM, *who remains surlily seated. When the* MAGISTRATE *sits down, so do the others.*)

THE GUARD. Yesterday's cases, your honor. The numbers are entered in the docket.

THE MAGISTRATE. Number 16,472.

THE FIRST (*looks in his notebook, beckons the* RICHLY DRESSED MAN). Stand up, please.

(*The* RICHLY DRESSED MAN *rises.*)

THE MAGISTRATE. Your name?

THE RICHLY DRESSED MAN. Doctor Reich.

THE MAGISTRATE. Age?

THE RICHLY DRESSED MAN. Forty-two, married, Jew.

THE MAGISTRATE (*with a gesture of dismissal*). Religion does not interest us here—why did you kill yourself?

THE RICHLY DRESSED MAN. On account of debts.

THE MAGISTRATE. What good did you do on earth?

THE RICHLY DRESSED MAN. I was a lawyer——

THE MAGISTRATE (*coughs significantly*). Yes—we'll discuss that later. For the present I shall only ask you: Would you like to go back to earth once more before sunrise? I advise you that you have the right to go if you choose. Do you understand?

THE RICHLY DRESSED MAN. Yes, sir.

THE MAGISTRATE. He who takes his life is apt, in his haste and his excitement, to forget something. Is there anything important down there you have left undone? Something to tell someone? Something to undo?

THE RICHLY DRESSED MAN. My debts——

THE MAGISTRATE. They do not matter here. Here we are concerned only with the affairs of the soul.

THE RICHLY DRESSED MAN. Then—if you please—when I left— the house—my youngest son, Oscar—was asleep. I didn't trust myself to wake him—and bid him good-bye. I would have liked—to kiss him good-bye.

THE MAGISTRATE (*to* THE SECOND). You will take Dr. Reich back and let him kiss his son Oscar.

THE SECOND. Come with me, please.

THE RICHLY DRESSED MAN (*to* THE MAGISTRATE). I thank you. (*He bows and exits at back with* THE SECOND.)

THE MAGISTRATE (*after making an entry in the docket*). Number 16,473.

THE FIRST (*looks in his notebook, then beckons* LILIOM). Stand up.

LILIOM. You said *please* to him. (*He rises.*)

THE MAGISTRATE. Your name?

LILIOM. Liliom.

THE MAGISTRATE. Isn't that your nickname?

LILIOM. Yes.

THE MAGISTRATE. What is your right name?

LILIOM. Andreas.

THE MAGISTRATE. And your last name?

LILIOM. Zavocki—after my mother.

THE MAGISTRATE. Your age?

LILIOM. Twenty-four.

THE MAGISTRATE. What good did *you* do on earth? (LILIOM *is silent*) Why did you take your life? (LILIOM *does not answer*. THE MAGISTRATE *addresses* THE FIRST) Take that knife away from him. (THE FIRST *does so*) It will be returned to you, if you go back to earth.

LILIOM. Do I go back to earth again?

THE MAGISTRATE. Just answer my questions.

LILIOM. I wasn't answering then, I was asking if——

THE MAGISTRATE. You don't ask questions here. You only answer. Only answer, Andreas Zavocki! I ask you whether there is anything on earth you neglected to accomplish? Anything down there you would like to do?

LILIOM. Yes.

THE MAGISTRATE. What is it?

LILIOM. I'd like to break Ficsur's head for him.

THE MAGISTRATE. Punishment is our office. Is there nothing else on earth you'd like to do?

LILIOM. I don't know—I guess, as long as I'm here, I'll not go back.

THE MAGISTRATE (*to* THE FIRST). Note that. He waives his right. (LILIOM *starts back to the bench*) Stay where you are. You are aware that you left your wife without food or shelter?

LILIOM. Yes.

THE MAGISTRATE. Don't you regret it?

LILIOM. No.

THE MAGISTRATE. You are aware that your wife is pregnant, and that in six months a child will be born?

LILIOM. I know.

THE MAGISTRATE. And that the child, too, will be without food or shelter? Do you regret that?

LILIOM. As long as I won't be there, what's it got to do with me?

THE MAGISTRATE. Don't try to deceive us, Andreas Zavocki. We see through you as through a pane of glass.

LILIOM. If you see so much, what do you want to ask me for? Why don't you let me rest—in peace?

THE MAGISTRATE. First you must earn your rest.

LILIOM. I want—only—to sleep.

THE MAGISTRATE. Your obstinacy won't help you. Here patience is endless as time. We can wait.

LILIOM. Can I ask something—I'd like to know—if Your Honor will tell me—whether the baby will be a boy or a girl.

THE MAGISTRATE. You shall see that for yourself.

LILIOM (*excitedly*). I'll see the baby?

THE MAGISTRATE. When you do it won't be a baby any more. But we haven't reached that question yet.

LILIOM. I'll see it?

THE MAGISTRATE. Again I ask you: Do you not regret that you deserted your wife and child; that you were a bad husband, a bad father?

LILIOM. A bad husband?

THE MAGISTRATE. Yes.

LILIOM. And a bad father?

THE MAGISTRATE. That, too.

LILIOM. I couldn't get work—and I couldn't bear to see Julie—all the time—all the time——

THE MAGISTRATE. Weeping! Why are you ashamed to say it? You couldn't bear to see her weeping. Why are you afraid of that word? And why are you ashamed that you loved her?

LILIOM (*shrugs his shoulders*). Who's ashamed? But I couldn't bear to see her—and that's why I was bad to her. You see, it wouldn't do to go back to the carousel—and Ficsur came along with his talk about—that other thing—and all of a sudden it happened, I don't know how. The police and the Jew with the pistol—and there I stood—and I'd lost the money playing cards—and I didn't want to be put in prison. (*Demanding justification*) Maybe I was wrong not to go out and steal when there was nothing to eat in the house? Should I have gone out to steal for Julie?

THE MAGISTRATE (*emphatically*). Yes.

LILIOM (*after an astounded pause*). The police down there never said that.

THE MAGISTRATE. You beat that poor, frail girl; you beat her because she loved you. How could you do that?

LILIOM. We argued with each other—she said this and I said that—and because she was right I couldn't answer her—and I got mad—and the anger rose up in me—until it reached here (*points to his throat*) and then I beat her.

THE MAGISTRATE. Are you sorry?

LILIOM (*shakes his head, but cannot utter the word "no"; continues softly*). When I touched her slender throat—then—if you like—you might say—— (*Falters, looks embarrassed at* THE MAGIS-TRATE.)

THE MAGISTRATE (*confidently expectant*). Are you sorry?

LILIOM (*with a stare*). I'm not sorry for anything.

THE MAGISTRATE. Liliom, Liliom, it will be difficult to help you.

LILIOM. I'm not asking any help.

THE MAGISTRATE. You were offered employment as a caretaker on Arader Street. (*To* THE FIRST) Where is that entered?

THE FIRST. In the small docket. (*Hands him the open book.* THE MAGISTRATE *looks in it.*)

THE MAGISTRATE. Rooms, kitchen, quarterly wages, the privilege of keeping poultry. Why didn't you accept it?

LILIOM. I'm not a caretaker. I'm no good at caretaking. To be a caretaker—you have to be a caretaker——

THE MAGISTRATE. If I said to you now: Liliom, go back on your stretcher. Tomorrow morning you will arise alive and well again. Would you be a caretaker then?

LILIOM. No.

THE MAGISTRATE. Why not?

LILIOM. Because—because that's just why I died.

THE MAGISTRATE. That is not true, my son. You died because you loved little Julie and the child she is bearing under her heart.

LILIOM. No.

THE MAGISTRATE. Look me in the eye.

LILIOM (*Looks him in the eye*). No.

THE MAGISTRATE (*stroking his beard*). Liliom, Liliom, if it were not for our Heavenly patience—— Go back to your seat. Number 16,474.

THE FIRST (*looks in his note book*). Stephan Kadar.

(THE POORLY DRESSED MAN *rises.*)

THE MAGISTRATE. You came out today?

THE POORLY DRESSED MAN. Today.

THE MAGISTRATE (*indicating the crimson sea of clouds*). How long were you in there?

THE POORLY DRESSED MAN. Thirteen years.

THE MAGISTRATE. Officer, you went to earth with him?

THE FIRST. Yes, sir.

THE MAGISTRATE. Stephan Kadar, after thirteen years of purification by fire you returned to earth to give proof that your soul had been burned clean. What good deed did you perform?

THE POORLY DRESSED MAN. When I came to the village and looked in the window of our cottage I saw my poor little orphans sleeping peacefully. But it was raining and the rain beat into the room through a hole in the roof. So I went and fixed the roof so it wouldn't rain in any more. My hammering woke them up and they were afraid. But their mother came in to them and comforted them. She said to them: "Don't cry! It's your poor, dear father hammering up there. He's come back from the other world to fix the roof for us."

THE MAGISTRATE. Officer?

THE FIRST. That's what happened.

THE MAGISTRATE. Stephan Kadar, you have done a good deed. What you did will be written in books to gladden the hearts of children who read them. (*Indicates the door at left*) The door is open to you. The eternal light awaits you. (THE FIRST *escorts* THE POORLY DRESSED MAN *out at left with great deference*) Liliom! (LILIOM *rises*) You have heard?

LILIOM. Yes.

THE MAGISTRATE. When this man first appeared before us he was as stubborn as you. But now he has purified himself and withstood the test. He has done a good deed.

LILIOM. What's he done, anyhow? Any roofer can fix a roof. It's much harder to be a barker in an amusement park.

THE MAGISTRATE. Liliom, you shall remain for sixteen years in the crimson fire until your child is full grown. By that time your pride and your stubbornness will have been burnt out of you. And when your daughter——

LILIOM. My daughter!

THE MAGISTRATE. When your daughter has reached the age of sixteen——

(LILIOM *bows his head, covers his eyes with his hands, and to keep from weeping laughs defiantly, sadly.*)

THE MAGISTRATE. When your daughter has reached the age of sixteen you will be sent for one day back to earth.

LILIOM. Me?

THE MAGISTRATE. Yes—just as you may have read in the legends of how the dead reappear on earth for a time.

LILIOM. I never believed them.

THE MAGISTRATE. Now you see they are true. You will go back to earth one day to show how far the purification of your soul has progressed.

LILIOM. Then I must show what I can do—like when you apply for a job—as a coachman?

THE MAGISTRATE. Yes—it is a test.

LILIOM. And will I be told what I have to do?

THE MAGISTRATE. No.

LILIOM. How will I know, then?

THE MAGISTRATE. You must decide that for yourself. That's what you burn sixteen years for. And if you do something good, something splendid for your child, then——

LILIOM (*laughs sadly*). Then? (*All stand up and bow their heads reverently. There is a pause*) Then?

THE MAGISTRATE. Now I'll bid you farewell, Liliom. Sixteen years and a day shall pass before I see you again. When you have returned from earth you will come up before me again. Take heed and think well of some good deed to do for your child. On that will depend which door shall be opened to you up here. Now go, Liliom. (*He exits at left.* THE GUARD *stands at attention. There is a pause.*)

THE FIRST (*approaches* LILIOM). Come along, my son. (*He goes to the door at right; pulls open the bolt and waits.*)

LILIOM (*to the old* GUARD, *softly*). Say officer.

THE GUARD. What do you want?

LILIOM. Please—can I get—have you got——?

THE GUARD. What?

LILIOM (*whispers*). A cigarette?

(*The old* GUARD *stares at him, goes a few paces to the left, shakes his head disapprovingly. Then his expression softens. He takes a cigarette from his pocket and, crossing to* LILIOM—*who has gone over to the door at right—gives him the cigarette.* THE FIRST *throws open the door. An intense rose-colored light streams in. The glow of it is so strong that it blinds* LILIOM *and he takes a step backward and bows his head and covers his eyes with his hand before he steps forward into the light.*)

THE CURTAIN FALLS

SCENE SEVEN

SCENE—*Sixteen years later. A small, tumble-down house on a bare, unenclosed plot of ground. Before the house is a tiny garden enclosed by a hip-high hedge.*

At back a wooden fence crosses the stage; in the center of it is a door large enough to admit a wagon. Beyond the fence is a view *of a suburban street which blends into a broad vista of tilled fields.*

It is a bright Sunday in Spring.

In the garden a table for two is laid.

JULIE, *her daughter* LOUISE, WOLF *and* MARIE *are discovered in the garden.* WOLF *is prosperously dressed,* MARIE *somewhat elaborately, with a huge hat.*

JULIE. You could stay for lunch.

MARIE. Impossible, dear. Since he became the proprietor of the Café Sorrento, Wolf simply has to be there all the time.

JULIE. But you needn't stay there all day, too.

MARIE. Oh, yes. I sit near the cashier's cage, read the papers, keep an eye on the waiters and drink in the bustle and excitement of the great city.

JULIE. And what about the children?

MARIE. You know what modern families are like. Parents scarcely ever see their children these days. The four girls are with their governess, the three boys with their tutor.

LOUISE. Auntie, dear, do stay and eat with us.

MARIE (*importantly*). Impossible today, dear child, impossible. Perhaps some other time. Come, Mr. Beifeld.

JULIE. Since when do you call your husband mister?

WOLF. I'd rather she did, dear lady. When we used to be very familiar we quarreled all the time. Now we are formal with each other and get along like society folk. I kiss your hand, dear lady.

JULIE. Good-bye, Wolf.

MARIE. Adieu, my dear. (*They embrace*) Adieu, my dear child.

LOUISE. Good-bye, Aunt Marie. Good-bye, Uncle Wolf.

(WOLF *and* MARIE *exit.*)

JULIE. You can get the soup now, Louise dear.

(LOUISE *goes into the house and re-enters with the soup. They sit at the table.*)

LOUISE. Mother, is it true we're not going to work at the jute factory any more?

JULIE. Yes, dear.

LOUISE. Where then?

JULIE. Uncle Wolf has gotten us a place in a big establishment where they make all kinds of fittings for cafés. We're to make big curtains, you know, the kind they hang in the windows, with lettering on them.

LOUISE. It'll be nicer there than at the jute factory.

JULIE. Yes, dear. The work isn't as dirty and pays better, too. A poor widow like your mother is lucky to get it. (*They eat.* LILIOM *and the two* HEAVENLY POLICEMEN *appear in the big doorway at back. The* POLICEMEN *pass slowly by.* LILIOM *stands there alone a moment, then comes slowly down and pauses at the opening of the hedge. He is dressed as he was on the day of his death. He is very pale, but otherwise unaltered.* JULIE, *at the table has her back to him.* LOUISE *sits facing the audience.*)

LILIOM. Good day.

LOUISE. Good day.

JULIE. Another beggar! What is it you want, my poor man?

LILIOM. Nothing.

JULIE. We have no money to give, but if you care for a plate of soup—— (LOUISE *goes into the house*) Have you come far today?

LILIOM. Yes—very far.

JULIE. Are you tired?

LILIOM. Very tired.

JULIE. Over there at the gate is a stone. Sit down and rest. My daughter is bringing you the soup.

(LOUISE *comes out of the house.*)

LILIOM. Is that your daughter?

JULIE. Yes.

LILIOM (*to* LOUISE). You are the daughter?

LOUISE. Yes, sir.

LILIOM. A fine healthy girl. (*Takes the soup plate from her with one hand, while with the other he touches her arm.* LOUISE *draws back quickly.*)

LOUISE (*crosses to* JULIE). Mother!

JULIE. What, my child?

LOUISE. The man tried to take me by the arm.

JULIE. Nonsense! You only imagined it, dear. The poor, hungry man has other things to think about than fooling with young girls. Sit down and eat your soup.

(*They eat.*)

LILIOM (*eats, too, but keeps looking at them*). You work at the factory, eh?

JULIE. Yes.

LILIOM. Your daughter, too?

LOUISE. Yes.

LILIOM. And your husband?

JULIE (*after a pause*). I have no husband. I'm a widow.

LILIOM. A widow?

JULIE. Yes.

LILIOM. Your husband—I suppose he's been dead a long time. (JULIE *does not answer*) I say—has your husband been dead a long time?

JULIE. A long time.

LILIOM. What did he die of?

(JULIE *is silent.*)

LOUISE. No one knows. He went to America to work and he died there—in the hospital. Poor father, I never knew him.

LILIOM. He went to America?

LOUISE. Yes, before I was born.

LILIOM. To America?

JULIE. Why do you ask so many questions? Did you know him, perhaps?

LILIOM (*puts the plate down*). Heaven knows! I've known so many people. Maybe I knew him, too.

JULIE. Well, if you knew him, leave him and us in peace with your questions. He went to America and died there. That's all there is to tell.

LILIOM. All right. All right. Don't be angry with me. I didn't mean any harm.

(*There is a pause.*)

LOUISE. My father was a very handsome man.

JULIE. Don't talk so much.

LOUISE. Did I say anything——?

LILIOM. Surely the little orphan can say that about her father.

LOUISE. My father could juggle so beautifully with three ivory balls that people used to advise him to go on the stage.

JULIE. Who told you that?

LOUISE. Uncle Wolf.

LILIOM. Who is that?

LOUISE. Mr. Wolf Beifeld, who owns the Café Sorrento.

LILIOM. The one who used to be a porter?

JULIE (*astonished*). Do you know him, too? It seems that you know all Budapest.

LILIOM. Wolf Beifeld is a long way from being all Budapest. But I do know a lot of people. Why shouldn't I know Wolf Beifeld?

LOUISE. He was a friend of my father.

JULIE. He was not his friend. No one was.

LILIOM. You speak of your husband so sternly.

JULIE. What's that to you? Doesn't it suit you? I can speak of my husband any way I like. It's nobody's business but mine.

LILIOM. Certainly, certainly—it's your own business. (*Takes up his soup plate again. All three eat.*)

LOUISE (*to* JULIE). Perhaps he knew father, too.

JULIE. Ask him, if you like.

LOUISE (*crosses to* LILIOM. *He stands up*). Did you know my father? (LILIOM *nods.* LOUISE *addresses her mother*) Yes, he knew him.

JULIE (*rises*). You knew Andreas Zavocki?

LILIOM. Liliom? Yes.

LOUISE. Was he really a very handsome man?

LILIOM. I wouldn't exactly say handsome.

LOUISE (*confidently*). But he was an awfully good man, wasn't he?

LILIOM. He wasn't so good, either. As far as I know he was what they called a clown, a barker in a carousel.

LOUISE (*pleased*). Did he tell funny jokes?

LILIOM. Lots of 'em. And he sang funny songs, too.

LOUISE. In the carousel?

LILIOM. Yes—but he was something of a bully, too. He'd fight anyone. He even hit your dear little mother.

JULIE. That's a lie.

LILIOM. It's true.

JULIE. Aren't you ashamed to tell the child such awful things about her father? Get out of here, you shameless liar. Eats our soup and our bread and has the impudence to slander our dead!

LILIOM. I didn't mean—I——

JULIE. What right have you to tell lies to the child? Take that plate, Louise, and let him be on his way. If he wasn't such a hungry-looking beggar, I'd put him out myself.

(LOUISE *takes the plate out of his hand.*)

LILIOM. So he didn't hit you?

JULIE. No, never. He was always good to me.

LOUISE (*whispers*). Did he tell funny stories, too?

LILIOM. Yes, and *such* funny ones.

JULIE. Don't speak to him any more. In God's name, go.

LOUISE. In God's name.

(JULIE *resumes her seat at the table and eats.*)

LILIOM. If you please, Miss—I have a pack of cards in my pocket. And if you like, I'll show you some tricks that'll make you split your sides laughing. (LOUISE *holds* LILIOM'S *plate in her left hand. With her right she reaches out and holds the garden gate shut*) Let me in, just a little way, Miss, and I'll do the tricks for you.

LOUISE. Go, in God's name, and let us be. Why are you making those ugly faces?

LILIOM. Don't chase me away, Miss; let me come in for just a minute—just for a minute—just long enough to let me show you something pretty, something wonderful. (*Opens the gate*) Miss. I've something to give you. (*Takes from his pocket a big red hand-kerchief in which is wrapped a glittering star from Heaven. He looks furtively about him to make sure that the* POLICE *are not watching.*)

LOUISE. What's that?

LILIOM. Pst! A star! (*With a gesture he indicates that he has stolen it out of the sky.*)

JULIE (*sternly*). Don't take anything from him. He's probably stolen it somewhere. (*To* LILIOM) In God's name, be off with you.

LOUISE. Yes, be off with you. Be off. (*She slams the gate.*)

LILIOM. Miss—please, Miss—I've got to do something good—or—do something good—a good deed——

LOUISE (*pointing with her right hand*). That's the way out.

LILIOM. Miss——

LOUISE. Get out!

LILIOM. Miss! (*Looks up at her suddenly and slaps her extended hand, so that the slap resounds loudly.*)

LOUISE. Mother! (*Looks dazedly at* LILIOM, *who bows his head dismayed, forlorn.* JULIE *rises and looks at* LILIOM *in astonishment. There is a long pause.*)

JULIE (*comes over to them slowly*). What's the matter here?

LOUISE (*bewildered, does not take her eyes off* LILIOM). Mother —the man—he hit me—on the hand—hard—I heard the sound of it—but it didn't hurt—mother—it didn't hurt—it was like a caress —as if he had just touched my hand tenderly. (*She hides behind* JULIE. LILIOM *sulkily raises his head and looks at* JULIE.)

JULIE (*softly*). Go, my child. Go into the house. Go.

LOUISE (*going*). But mother—I'm afraid—it sounded so loud— (*Weepingly*) And it didn't hurt at all—just as if he'd—kissed my hand instead—mother! (*She hides her face.*)

JULIE. Go in my child, go in. (LOUISE *goes slowly into the house.* JULIE *watches her until she has disappeared, then turns slowly to* LILIOM.)

JULIE. You struck my child.

LILIOM. Yes—I struck her.

JULIE. Is that what you came for, to strike my child?

LILIOM. No—I didn't come for that—but I did strike her—and now I'm going back.

JULIE. In the name of the Lord Jesus, who are you?

LILIOM (*simply*). A poor, tired beggar who came a long way and who was hungry. And I took your soup and bread and I struck your child. Are you angry with me?

JULIE (*her hand on her heart; fearfully, wonderingly*). Jesus protect me—I don't understand it—I'm *not* angry—not angry at all——

(LILIOM *goes to the doorway and leans against the doorpost, his back to the audience.* JULIE *goes to the table and sits.*)

JULIE. Louise! (LOUISE *comes out of the house*) Sit down, dear, we'll finish eating.

LOUISE. Has he gone?

JULIE. Yes. (*They are both seated at the table.* LOUISE, *her head in her hands, is staring into space*) Why don't you eat, dear?

LOUISE. What has happened, mother?

JULIE. Nothing, my child.

(*The* HEAVENLY POLICEMEN *appear outside.* LILIOM *walks slowly off at left. The* FIRST POLICEMAN *makes a deploring gesture. Both shake their heads deploringly and follow* LILIOM *slowly off at left.*)

LOUISE. Mother, dear, why won't you tell me?

JULIE. What is there to tell you, child? Nothing has happened. We were peacefully eating, and a beggar came who talked of by-gone days, and then I thought of your father.

LOUISE. My father?

JULIE. Your father—Liliom.

(*There is a pause.*)

LOUISE. Mother—tell me—has it ever happened to you—has anyone ever hit you—without hurting you in the least?

JULIE. Yes, my child. It has happened to me, too.

(*There is a pause.*)

LOUISE. Is it possible for someone to hit you—hard like that—real loud and hard—and not hurt you at all?

JULIE. It is possible, dear—that someone may beat you and beat you and beat you,—and not hurt you at all.——

(There is a pause. Nearby an organ-grinder has stopped. The music of his organ begins.)

THE CURTAIN FALLS

IVAN BUNIN

****

*Although the Russian Nobel prize-winning writer Ivan Bunin has
written several volumes of short stories since his memorable classic*
The Gentleman from San Francisco, *he preferred this work to
represent him in this volume. Asked for his present-day comment
on the story, Mr. Bunin who has been living in France since he left
Russia in 1919, replied that he was now eighty years old and did
not care to make any further comment.*

****

The Gentleman from San Francisco

> "Alas, alas, that great city Babylon, that mighty city!"—
> —*Revelation of St. John.*

THE GENTLEMAN from San Francisco—neither at Naples nor on
Capri could any one recall his name—with his wife and daughter,
was on his way to Europe, where he intended to stay for two whole
years, solely for the pleasure of it.

He was firmly convinced that he had a full right to a rest, enjoyment, a long comfortable trip, and what not. This conviction had a
two-fold reason: first, he was rich, and second, despite his fifty-
eight years, he was just about to enter the stream of life's pleasures.
Until now he had not really lived, but simply existed, to be sure—
fairly well, yet putting off his fondest hopes for the future. He toiled
unweariedly—the Chinese, whom he imported by thousands for his
works, knew full well what it meant,—and finally he saw that he
had made much, and that he had nearly come up to the level of
those whom he had once taken as a model, and he decided to catch
his breath. The class of people to which he belonged was in the
habit of beginning its enjoyment of life with a trip to Europe, India,
Egypt. He made up his mind to do the same. Of course, it was first
of all himself that he desired to reward for the years of toil, but he
was also glad for his wife and daughter's sake. His wife was never
distinguished by any extraordinary impressionability, but then, all

1008

elderly American women are ardent travelers. As for his daughter, a girl of marriageable age, and somewhat sickly,—travel was the very thing she needed. Not to speak of the benefit to her health, do not happy meetings occur during travels? Abroad, one may chance to sit at the same table with a prince, or examine frescoes side by side with a multi-millionaire.

The itinerary the Gentleman from San Francisco planned out was an extensive one. In December and January he expected to relish the sun of southern Italy, monuments of antiquity, the tarantella, serenades of wandering minstrels, and that which at his age is felt most keenly—the love, not entirely disinterested though, of young Neapolitan girls. The Carnival days he planned to spend at Nice and Monte Carlo, which at that time of the year is the meeting-place of the choicest society, the society upon which depend all the blessings of civilization: the cut of dress suits, the stability of thrones, the declaration of wars, the prosperity of hotels. Some of these people passionately give themselves over to automobile and boat races, others to roulette, others, again, busy themselves with what is called flirtation, and others shoot pigeons, which soar so beautifully from the dove-cote, hover a while over the emerald lawn, on the background of the forget-me-not colored sea, and then suddenly hit the ground, like little white lumps. Early March he wanted to devote to Florence, and at Easter, to hear the Miserere in Paris. His plans also included Venice, Paris, bull-baiting at Seville, bathing on the British Islands, also Athens, Constantinople, Palestine, Egypt, and even Japan, of course, on the way back. . . . And at first things went very well indeed.

It was the end of November, and all the way to Gibraltar the ship sailed across seas which were either clad by icy darkness or swept by storms carrying wet snow. But there were no accidents, and the vessel did not even roll. The passengers,—all people of consequence—were numerous, and the steamer, the famous "Atlantis," resembled the most expensive European hotel with all improvements; a night refreshment-bar, Oriental baths, even a newspaper of its own. The manner of living was a most aristocratic one; passengers rose early, awakened by the shrill voice of a bugle, filling the corridors at the gloomy hour when the day broke slowly and sulkily over the grayish-green watery desert, which rolled heavily in the fog. After putting on their flannel pajamas, they took coffee, chocolate, cocoa; they seated themselves in marble baths, went through their exercises, whetting their appetites and increasing their sense of well-being, dressed for the day, and had their breakfast.

Till eleven o'clock they were supposed to stroll on the deck, breathing in the chill freshness of the ocean, or they played table-tennis, or other games which arouse the appetite. At eleven o'clock a collation was served consisting of sandwiches and bouillon, after which people read their newspapers, quietly waiting for luncheon, which was more nourishing and varied than the breakfast. The next two hours were given to rest; all the decks were crowded then with steamer chairs, on which the passengers, wrapped in plaids, lay stretched, dozing lazily, or watching the cloudy sky and the foamy-fringed water hillocks flashing beyond the sides of the vessel. At five o'clock, refreshed and gay, they drank strong, fragrant tea; at seven the sound of the bugle announced a dinner of nine courses. . . . Then the Gentleman from San Francisco, rubbing his hands in an onrush of vital energy, hastened to his luxurious state-room to dress.

In the evening, all the decks of the "Atlantis" yawned in the darkness, shone with their innumerable fiery eyes, and a multitude of servants worked with increased feverishness in the kitchens, dish-washing compartments, and wine-cellars. The ocean, which heaved about the sides of the ship, was dreadful, but no one thought of it. All had faith in the controlling power of the captain, a red-headed giant, heavy and very sleepy, who, clad in a uniform with broad golden stripes, looked like a huge idol, and but rarely emerged, for the benefit of the public, from his mysterious retreat. On the fore-castle, the siren gloomily roared or screeched in a fit of mad rage, but few of the diners heard the siren: its hellish voice was covered by the sounds of an excellent string orchestra, which played ceaselessly and exquisitely in a vast hall, decorated with marble and spread with velvety carpets. The hall was flooded with torrents of light, radiated by crystal lustres and gilt chandeliers; it was filled with a throng of bejeweled ladies in low-necked dresses, of men in dinner-coats, graceful waiters, and deferential maîtres-d'hôtel. One of these,—who accepted wine orders exclusively—wore a chain on his neck like some lord-mayor. The evening dress, and the ideal linen made the Gentleman from San Francisco look very young. Dry-skinned, of average height, strongly, though irregularly built, glossy with thorough washing and cleaning, and moderately animated, he sat in the golden splendor of this palace. Near him stood a bottle of amber-colored Johannisberg, and goblets of most delicate glass and of varied sizes, surmounted by a frizzled bunch of fresh hyacinths. There was something Mongolian in his yellowish face with its trimmed silvery moustache; his large teeth glimmered with gold fillings, and his strong, bald head had a dull glow, like old ivory. His wife, a big, broad and placid woman, was dressed richly, but in keeping with her age. Complicated, but light, transparent, and innocently immodest was the dress of his daughter, tall and slender, with magnificent hair gracefully combed; her breath was sweet with violet-scented tablets, and she had a number of tiny and most delicate pink dimples near her lips and between her slightly-powdered shoulder blades. . . .

The dinner lasted two whole hours, and was followed by dances in the dancing hall, while the men—the Gentleman from San Francisco among them—made their way to the refreshment bar, where Negroes in red jackets and with eye-balls like shelled hard-boiled eggs, waited on them. There, with their feet on tables, smoking Havana cigars, and drinking themselves purple in the face, they settled the destinies of nations on the basis of the latest political and stock-exchange news. Outside, the ocean tossed up black mountains with a thud; and the snow-storm hissed furiously in the rigging grown heavy with slush; the ship trembled in every limb, struggling with the storm and ploughing with difficulty the shifting and seething mountainous masses that threw far and high their foaming tails; the siren groaned in agony, choked by storm and fog; the watchmen in their towers froze and almost went out of their minds under the superhuman stress of attention. Like the gloomy and sultry mass of the inferno, like its last, ninth circle, was the submersed womb of the steamer, where monstrous furnaces yawned with red-hot open jaws, and emitted deep, hooting sounds, and where the stokers, stripped to the waist, and purple with reflected flames, bathed in their own dirty, acid sweat. And here, in the refreshment-bar, care-free men, with their feet, encased in dancing shoes, on the table, sipped cognac and liqueurs, swam in waves of spiced smoke, and exchanged subtle remarks, while in the dancing-hall everything sparkled and radiated light, warmth and joy. The couples now turned around in a waltz, now swayed in the tango; and the music, sweetly shameless and sad, persisted in its ceaseless entreaties. . . . There were many persons of note in this magnificent crowd; an ambassador, a dry, modest old man; a great millionaire, shaved, tall, of an indefinite age, who, in his old-fashioned dress-coat, looked like a prelate; also a famous Spanish writer, and an international belle, already slightly faded and of dubious morals. There was also among them a loving pair, exquisite and refined, whom everybody watched with curiosity and who did not conceal their bliss; he danced only with her, sang—with great skill—only to her accompaniment, and they were so charming, so graceful. The captain

alone knew that they had been hired by the company at a good
salary to play at love, and that they had been sailing now on one,
now on another steamer, for quite a long time.

In Gibraltar everybody was gladdened by the sun, and by the
weather which was like early Spring. A new passenger appeared
aboard the "Atlantis" and aroused everybody's interest. It was the
crown-prince of an Asiatic state, who traveled incognito, a small
man, very nimble, though looking as if made of wood, broad-faced,
narrow-eyed, in gold-rimmed glasses, somewhat disagreeable because
of his long moustache, which was sparse like that of a corpse, but
otherwise—charming, plain, modest. In the Mediterranean the
breath of winter was again felt. The seas were heavy and motley
like a peacock's tail and the waves stirred up by the gay gusts of the
tramontane, tossed their white crests under a sparkling and perfectly
clear sky. Next morning, the sky grew paler and the skyline misty.
Land was near. Then Ischia and Capri came in sight, and one
could descry, through an opera-glass, Naples, looking like pieces of
sugar strewn at the foot of an indistinct dove-colored mass, and
above them, a snow-covered chain of distant mountains. The decks
were crowded, many ladies and gentlemen put on light fur-coats;
Chinese servants, bandy-legged youths—with pitch black braids
down to the heels and with girlish, thick eyelashes,—always quiet
and speaking in a whisper, were carrying to the foot of the staircases, plaid wraps, canes, and crocodile-leather valises and hand-
bags. The daughter of the Gentleman from San Francisco stood
near the prince, who, by a happy chance, had been introduced to
her the evening before, and feigned to be looking steadily at something far-off, which he was pointing out to her, while he was, at
the same time, explaining something, saying something rapidly and
quietly. He was so small that he looked like a boy among other men,
and he was not handsome at all. And then there was something
strange about him; his glasses, derby and coat were most commonplace, but there was something horse-like in the hair of his sparse
moustache, and the thin, tanned skin of his flat face looked as
though it were somewhat stretched and varnished. But the girl
listened to him, and so great was her excitement that she could
hardly grasp the meaning of his words, her heart palpitated with
incomprehensible rapture and with pride that he was standing and
speaking with her and nobody else. Everything about him was different: his dry hands, his clean skin, under which flowed ancient
kingly blood, even his light shoes and his European dress, plain,

but singularly tidy—everything hid an inexplicable fascination and engendered thoughts of love. And the Gentleman from San Francisco, himself, in a silk-hat, gray leggings, patent leather shoes, kept eyeing the famous beauty who was standing near him, a tall, stately blonde, with eyes painted according to the latest Parisian fashion, and a tiny, bent peeled-off pet-dog, to whom she addressed herself. And the daughter, in a kind of vague perplexity, tried not to notice him.

Like all wealthy Americans he was very liberal when traveling, and believed in the complete sincerity and good-will of those who so painstakingly fed him, served him day and night, anticipating his slightest desire, protected him from dirt and disturbance, hauled things for him, hailed carriers, and delivered his luggage to hotels. So it was everywhere, and it had to be so at Naples. Meanwhile, Naples grew and came nearer. The musicians, with their shining brass instruments had already formed a group on the deck, and all of a sudden deafened everybody with the triumphant sounds of a ragtime march. The giant captain, in his full uniform appeared on the bridge and like a gracious Pagan idol, waved his hands to the passengers,—and it seemed to the Gentleman from San Francisco,—as it did to all the rest,—that for him alone thundered the march, so greatly loved by proud America, and that him alone did the captain congratulate on the safe arrival. And when the "Atlantis" had finally entered the port and all its many-decked mass leaned against the quay, and the gang-plank began to rattle heavily,— what a crowd of porters, with their assistants, in caps with golden galloons, what a crowd of various boys and husky ragamuffins with pads of colored postal cards attacked the Gentleman from San Francisco, offering their services! With kindly contempt he grinned at these beggars, and, walking towards the automobile of the hotel where the prince might stop, muttered between his teeth, now in English, now in Italian—"Go away! *Via . . .*"

Immediately, life at Naples began to follow a set routine. Early in the morning breakfast was served in the gloomy dining-room, swept by a wet draught from the open windows looking upon a stony garden, while outside the sky was cloudy and cheerless, and a crowd of guides swarmed at the door of the vestibule. Then came the first smiles of the warm roseate sun, and from the high suspended balcony, a broad vista unfolded itself: Vesuvius, wrapped to its base in radiant morning vapors; the pearly ripple, touched to silver, of the bay, the delicate outline of Capri in the skyline; tiny

asses dragging two-wheeled buggies along the soft, sticky embankment, and detachments of little soldiers marching somewhere to the
tune of cheerful and defiant music.

Next on the day's program was a slow automobile ride along
crowded, narrow, and damp corridors of streets, between high,
many-windowed buildings. It was followed by visits to museums,
lifelessly clean and lighted evenly and pleasantly, but as though
with the dull light cast by snow;—then to churches, cold, smelling
of wax, always alike; a majestic entrance, closed by a ponderous,
leather curtain, and inside—a vast void, silence, quiet flames of
seven-branched candlesticks, sending forth a red glow from where
they stood at the farther end, on the bedecked altar,—a lonely, old
woman lost among the dark wooden benches, slippery gravestones
under the feet, and somebody's "Descent from the Cross," infallibly
famous. At one o'clock—luncheon, on the mountain of San-Mar-
tius, where at noon the choicest people gathered, and where the
daughter of the Gentleman from San Francisco once almost fainted
with joy, because it seemed to her that she saw the Prince in the
hall, although she had learned from the newspapers that he had
temporarily left for Rome. At five o'clock it was customary to take
tea at the hotel, in a smart *salon,* where it was far too warm because
of the carpets and the blazing fireplaces; and then came dinnertime—and again did the mighty, commanding voice of the gong
resound throughout the building, again did silk rustle and the mirrors reflect files of ladies in low-necked dresses ascending the staircases, and again the splendid palatial dining hall opened with broad
hospitality, and again the musicians' jackets formed red patches on
the estrade, and the black figures of the waiters swarmed around
the maître-d'hôtel, who, with extraordinary skill, poured a thick
pink soup into plates. . . . As everywhere, the dinner was the crown
of the day. People dressed for it as for a wedding, and so abundant
was it in food, wines, mineral waters, sweets and fruits, that about
eleven o'clock in the evening chambermaids would carry to all the
rooms hot-water bags.

That year, however, December did not happen to be a very propi-
tious one. The doormen were abashed when people spoke to them
about the weather, and shrugged their shoulders guiltily, mumbling
that they could not recollect such a year, although, to tell the truth,
that it was not the first year they mumbled those words, usually
adding that "things are terrible everywhere"; that unprecedented
showers and storms had broken out on the Riviera, that it was
snowing in Athens, that Aetna, too, was all blocked up with snow,

and glowed brightly at night, and that tourists were fleeing from Palermo to save themselves from the cold spell. . . .

That winter, the morning sun daily deceived Naples; toward noon the sky would invariably grow gray, and a light rain would begin to fall, growing thicker and duller. Then the palms at the hotel-porch glistened disagreeably like wet tin, the town appeared exceptionally dirty and congested, the museums too monotonous, the cigars of the drivers in their rubber raincoats, which flattened in the wind like wings, intolerably stinking, and the energetic flapping of their whips over their thin-necked nags—obviously false. The shoes of the signors, who cleaned the street-cars tracks, were in a frightful state, the women who splashed in the mud, with black hair unprotected from the rain, were ugly and short-legged, and the humidity mingled with the foul smell of rotting fish, that came from the foaming sea, was simply disheartening. And so, early-morning quarrels began to break out between the Gentleman from San Francisco and his wife; and their daughter now grew pale and suffered from headaches, and now became animated, enthusiastic over everything, and at such times was lovely and beautiful. Beautiful were the tender, complex feelings which her meeting with the ungainly man aroused in her,—the man in whose veins flowed unusual blood, for, after all, it does not matter what in particular stirs up a maiden's soul: money, or fame, or nobility of birth. . . . Everybody assured the tourists that it was quite different at Sorrento and on Capri, that lemon-trees were blossoming there, that is was warmer and sunnier there, the morals purer, and the wine less adulterated. And the family from San Francisco decided to set out with all their luggage for Capri. They planned to settle down at Sorrento, but first to visit the island, tread the stones where stood Tiberius' palaces, examine the fabulous wonders of the Blue Grotto, and listen to the bagpipes of Abruzzi, who roam about the island during the whole month preceding Christmas and sing the praises of the Madonna.

On the day of departure—a very memorable day for the family from San Francisco—the sun did not appear even in the morning. A heavy winter fog covered Vesuvius down to its very base and hung like a gray curtain low over the leaden surge of the sea, hiding it completely at a distance of half a mile. Capri was completely out of sight, as though it had never existed on this earth. And the little steamboat which was making for the island tossed and pitched so fiercely that the family lay prostrated on the sofas in the miserable cabin of the little steamer, with their feet wrapped in plaids and their eyes shut because of their nausea. The older lady suffered, as she thought, most; several times she was overcome with sea-sickness, and it seemed to her then she was dying, but the chambermaid, who repeatedly brought her the basin, and who for many years, in heat and in cold, had been tossing on these waves, ever on the alert, ever kindly to all,—the chambermaid only laughed. The lady's daughter was frightfully pale and kept a slice of lemon between her teeth. Not even the hope of an unexpected meeting with the prince at Sorrento, where he planned to arrive on Christmas, served to cheer her. The Gentleman from San Francisco, who was lying on his back, dressed in a large overcoat and a big cap, did not loosen his jaws throughout the voyage. His face grew dark, his moustache white, and his head ached heavily; for the last few days, because of the bad weather, he had drunk far too much in the evenings.

And the rain kept on beating against the rattling window panes, and water dripped down from them on the sofas; the howling wind attacked the masts, and sometimes, aided by a heavy sea, it laid the little steamer on its side, and then something below rolled about with a rattle.

While the steamer was anchored at Castellamare and Sorrento, the situation was more cheerful; but even here the ship rolled terribly, and the coast with all its precipices, gardens and pines, with its pink and white hotels and hazy mountains clad in curling verdure, flew up and down as if it were on swings. The rowboats hit against the sides of the steamer, the sailors and the deck passengers shouted at the top of their voices, and somewhere a baby screamed as if it were being crushed to pieces. A wet wind blew through the door, and from a wavering barge flying the flag of the Hotel Royal, an urchin kept on unwearyingly shouting "Kgoyal-al! Hotel Kgoyal-al! . . ." inviting tourists. And the Gentleman from San Francisco felt like the old man that he was,—and it was with weariness and animosity that he thought of all these "Royals," "Splendids," "Excelsiors," and of all those greedy bugs, reeking with garlic, who are called Italians. Once, during a stop, having opened his eyes and half-risen from the sofa, he noticed in the shadow of the rock beach a heap of stone huts, miserable, mildewed through and through, huddled close by the water, near boats, rags, tin-boxes, and brown fishing nets,—and as he remembered that this was the very Italy he had come to enjoy, he felt a great despair. . . . Finally, in twilight, the black mass of the island began to grow nearer, as though burrowed through at the base by red fires, the wind grew softer, warmer, more fragrant; from the dock-lanterns huge golden serpents flowed down the tame waves which undulated like black oil. . . . Then, suddenly, the anchor rumbled and fell with a splash into the water, the fierce yells of the boatman filled the air,—and at once everyone's heart grew easy. The electric lights in the cabin grew more brilliant, and there came a desire to eat, drink, smoke, move. . . . Ten minutes later the family from San Francisco found themselves in a large ferry-boat; fifteen minutes later they trod the stones of the quay, and then seated themselves in a small lighted car, which, with a buzz, started to ascend the slope, while vineyard stakes, half-ruined stone fences, and wet, crooked lemon-trees, in spots shielded by straw sheds, with their glimmering orange-colored fruit and thick glossy foliage, were sliding down past the open car windows. . . . After rain, the earth smells sweetly in Italy, and each of her islands has a fragrance of its own.

The Island of Capri was dark and damp on that evening. But for a while it grew animated and let up, in spots, as always in the hour of the steamer's arrival. On the top of the hill, at the station of the *funiculaire,* there stood already the crowd of those whose duty it was to receive properly the Gentleman from San Francisco. The rest of the tourists hardly deserved any attention. There were a few Russians, who had settled on Capri, untidy, absent-minded people, absorbed in their bookish thoughts, spectacled, bearded, with the collars of their cloth overcoats raised. There was also a company of long-legged, long-necked, round-headed German youths in Tyrolean costume, and with linen bags on their backs, who need no one's services, are everywhere at home, and are by no means liberal in their expenses. The Gentleman from San Francisco, who kept quietly aloof from both the Russians and the Germans, was noticed at once. He and his ladies were hurriedly helped from the car, a man ran before them to show them the way, and they were again surrounded by boys and those thickset Caprean peasant women, who carry on their heads the trunks and valises of wealthy travelers. Their tiny, wooden, foot-stools rapped against the pavement of the small square, which looked almost like an opera square, and over which an electric lantern swung in the damp wind; the gang of urchins whistled like birds and turned somersaults, and as the Gentleman from San Francisco passed among them, it all looked like a stage scene; he went first under some kind of mediaeval archway, beneath houses huddled close together, and then along a steep echoing lane which led to the hotel entrance, flooded with light. At the left, a palm tree raised its tuft above the flat roofs, and higher up, blue stars burned in the black sky. And again things looked as though it was in honor of the guests from San Francisco that the stony damp little town had awakened on its rocky island in the Mediterranean, that it was they who had made the owner of the hotel so happy and beaming, and that the Chinese gong, which had sounded the call to dinner through all the floors as soon as they entered the lobby, had been waiting only for them.

The owner, an elegant young man, who met the guests with a polite and exquisite bow, for a moment startled the Gentleman from San Francisco. Having caught sight of him, the Gentleman from San Francisco suddenly recollected that on the previous night, among other confused images which disturbed his sleep, he had seen this very man. His vision resembled the hotel keeper to a dot, had the same head, the same hair, shining and scrupulously combed, and wore the same frock-coat with rounded skirts. Amazed, he almost stopped for a while. But as there was not a mustard-seed of what is called mysticism in his heart, his surprise subsided at once; in passing the corridor of the hotel he jestingly told his wife and daughter about this strange coincidence of dream and reality. His daughter alone glanced at him with alarm, longing suddenly compressed her heart, and such a strong feeling of solitude on this strange, dark island seized her that she almost began to cry. But, as usual, she said nothing about her feeling to her father.

A person of high dignity, Rex XVII, who had spent three entire weeks on Capri, had just left the island, and the guests from San Francisco were given the apartments he had occupied. At their disposal was put the most handsome and skillful chambermaid, a Belgian, with a figure rendered slim and firm by her corset, and with a starched cap, shaped like a small, indented crown; and they had the privilege of being served by the most well-appearing and portly footman, a black, fiery-eyed Sicilian, and by the quickest waiter, the small, stout Luigi, who was a fiend at cracking jokes and had changed many places in his life. Then the maître-d'hôtel, a Frenchman, gently rapped at the door of the American gentleman's room. He came to ask whether the gentleman and the ladies would dine, and in case they would, which he did not doubt, to report that there was to be had that day lobsters, roast beef, asparagus, pheasants, etc., etc.

The floor was still rocking under the Gentleman from San Francisco—so sea-sick had the wretched Italian steamer made him— yet, he slowly, though awkwardly, shut the window which had banged when the maître-d'hôtel entered, and which let in the smell of the distant kitchen and wet flowers in the garden, and answered with slow distinctiveness, that they would dine, that their table must be placed farther away from the door, in the depth of the hall, that they would have local wine and champagne, moderately dry and but slightly cooled. The maître-d'hôtel approved the words of the guest in various intonations, which all meant, however, only one thing; there is and can be no doubt that the desires of the Gentleman from San Francisco are right, and that everything would be carried out, in exact conformity with his words. At last he inclined his head and asked delicately:

"Is that all, sir?"

And having received in reply a slow "Yes," he added that to-day they were going to have the tarantella danced in the vestibule by Carmella and Giuseppe, known to all Italy and to "the entire world of tourists."

"I saw her on post-card pictures," said the Gentleman from San Francisco in a tone of voice which expressed nothing. "And this Giuseppe, is he her husband?"

"Her cousin, sir," answered the maître-d'hôtel.

The Gentleman from San Francisco tarried a little, evidently musing on something, but said nothing, then dismissed him with a nod of his head.

Then he started making preparations, as though for a wedding: he turned on all the electric lamps, and filled the mirrors with reflections of light and the sheen of furniture, and opened trunks; he began to shave and to wash himself, and the sound of his bell was heard every minute in the corridor, crossing with other impatient calls which came from the rooms of his wife and daughter. Luigi, in his red apron, with the ease characteristic of stout people, made funny faces at the chambermaids, who were dashing by with tile buckets in their hands, making them laugh until the tears came. He rolled head over heels to the door, and, tapping with his knuckles, asked with feigned timidity and with an obsequiousness which he knew how to render idiotic:

"*Ha sonata, Signore?*" (Did you ring, sir?)

And from behind the door a slow, grating, insultingly polite voice, answered:

"Yes, come in."

What did the Gentleman from San Francisco think and feel on that evening forever memorable to him? It must be said frankly: absolutely nothing exceptional. The trouble is that everything on this earth appears too simple. Even had he felt anything deep in his heart, a premonition that something was going to happen, he would have imagined that it was not going to happen so soon, at least not at once. Besides, as is usually the case just after sea-sickness is over, he was very hungry, and he anticipated with real delight the first spoonful of soup, and the first gulp of wine; therefore, he was performing the habitual process of dressing, in a state of excitement which left no time for reflection.

Having shaved and washed himself, and dexterously put in place a few false teeth, he then, standing before the mirror, moistened and vigorously plastered what was left of his thick pearly-colored hair, close to his tawny-yellow skull. Then he put on, with some effort, a tight-fitting undershirt of cream-colored silk, fitted tight to his strong, aged body with its waist swelling out because of an abundant diet; and he pulled black silk socks and patent-leather dancing shoes on his dry feet with their fallen arches. Squatting down, he set right his black trousers, drawn high by means of silk suspenders, adjusted his snow-white shirt with its bulging front, put the buttons into the shining cuffs, and began the painful process of hunting up the front button under the hard collar. The floor was still swaying under him, the tips of his fingers hurt terribly, the button at times painfully pinched the flabby skin in the depression under his Adam's apple, but he persevered, and finally, with his eyes shining from the effort, his face blue because of the narrow collar which squeezed his neck, he triumphed over the difficulties—and all exhausted, he sat down before the pier-glass, his reflected image repeating itself in all the mirrors.

"It's terrible!" he muttered, lowering his strong, bald head and making no effort to understand what was terrible; then, with a careful and habitual gesture, he examined his short fingers with gouty callosities in the joints, and their large, convex, almond-colored nails, and repeated with conviction, "It's terrible!"

But here the stentorian voice of the second gong sounded throughout the house, as in a heathen temple. And having risen hurriedly, the Gentleman from San Francisco drew his tie more taut and firm around his collar, and pulled together his abdomen by means of a tight waistcoat, put on a dinner-coat, set to rights the cuffs, and for the last time he examined himself in the mirror. . . . This Carmella, tawny as a mulatto, with fiery eyes, in a dazzling dress in which orange-color predominated, must be an extraordinary dancer, —it occurred to him. And cheerfully leaving his room, he walked on the carpet, to his wife's chamber, and asked in a loud tone of voice if they would be long.

"In five minutes, papa!" answered cheerfully and gaily a girlish voice. "I am combing my hair."

"Very well," said the Gentleman from San Francisco.

And thinking of her wonderful hair, streaming on her shoulders, he slowly walked down along corridors and staircases, spread with red velvet carpets,—looking for the library. The servants he met hugged the walls, and he walked by as if not noticing them. An old lady, late for dinner, already bowed with years, with milk-white hair, yet bare-necked, in a light-gray silk dress, hurried at top speed, but she walked in a mincing, funny, hen-like manner, and he easily overtook her. At the glass door of the dining hall where the guests had already gathered and started eating, he stopped before the table crowded with boxes of matches and Egyptian cigarettes, took a great Manilla cigar, and threw three liras on the table. On the winter veranda he glanced into the open window; a stream of soft air came to him from the darkness, the top of the old palm loomed up before him afar-off, with its boughs spread among the stars and looking gigantic, and the distant even noise of the sea reached his ear. In the library-room, snug, quiet, a German in round silver-bowed glasses and with crazy, wondering eyes—stood turning the rustling pages of a newspaper. Having coldly eyed him, the Gentleman from San Francisco seated himself in a deep leather arm-chair near a lamp under a green hood, put on his pince-nez and twitching his head because of the collar which choked him, hid himself from view behind a newspaper. He glanced at a few head-lines, read a few lines about the interminable Balkan war, and turned over the page with an habitual gesture. Suddenly, the lines blazed up with a glassy sheen, the veins of his neck swelled, his eyes bulged out, the pince-nez fell from his nose. . . . He dashed forward, wanted to swallow air—and made a wild, rattling noise; his lower jaw dropped, dropped on his shoulder and began to shake, the shirt-front bulged out,—and the whole body, writhing, the heels catching in the carpet, slowly fell to the floor in a desperate strug-gle with an invisible foe. . . .

Had not the German been in the library, this frightful accident would have been quickly and adroitly hushed up. The body of the Gentleman from San Francisco would have been rushed away to some far corner—and none of the guests would have known of the occurrence. But the German dashed out of the library with out-cries and spread the alarm all over the house. And many rose from their meal, upsetting chairs, others growing pale, ran along the corridors to the library, and the question, asked in many languages, was heard: "What is it? What has happened?" And no one was able to answer it clearly, no one understood anything, for until this very day men still wonder most at death and most absolutely refuse to believe in it. The owner rushed from one guest to another, trying to keep back those who were running and soothe them with hasty assurances, that this was nothing, a mere trifle, a little fainting-spell by which a Gentleman from San Francisco, had been over-come. But no one listened to him, many saw how the footmen and waiters tore from the gentleman his tie, collar, waistcoat, the rumpled evening coat, and even—for no visible reason—the dancing shoes from his black silk-covered feet. And he kept on writhing. He obstinately struggled with death, he did not want to yield to the foe that attacked him so unexpectedly and grossly. He shook his head, emitted rattling sounds like one throttled, and turned up his eye-balls like one drunk with wine. When he was hastily brought into Number Forty-three,—the smallest, worst, dampest, and coldest room at the end of the lower corridor,—and stretched on the bed, —his daughter came running, her hair falling over her shoulders, the skirts of her dressing-gown thrown open, with bare breasts raised by the corset. Then came his wife, big, heavy, almost completely dressed for dinner, her mouth round with terror.

In a quarter of an hour all was again in good trim at the hotel. But the evening was irreparably spoiled. Some tourists returned to the dining-hall and finished their dinner, but they kept silent, and it was obvious that they took the accident as a personal insult, while the owner went from one guest to another, shrugging his shoulders in impotent and appropriate irritation, feeling like one innocently victimized, assuring everyone that he understood perfectly well "how disagreeable this is," and giving his word that he would take all "the measures that are within his power" to do away with the trouble. Yet it was found necessary to cancel the tarantella. The unnecessary electric lamps were put out, most of the guests left for the beer-hall, and it grew so quiet in the hotel that one could dis-tinctly hear the tick-tock of the clock in the lobby, where a lonely parrot babbled something in its expressionless manner, stirring in its cage, and trying to fall asleep with its paw clutching the upper perch in a most absurd manner. The Gentleman from San Francisco lay stretched in a cheap iron bed, under coarse woolen blankets, dimly lighted by a single gas-burner fastened in the ceiling. An ice-bag slid down on his wet, cold forehead. His blue, already lifeless face grew gradually cold; the hoarse, rattling noise which came from his mouth, lighted by the glimmer of the golden fillings, gradually weakened. It was not the Gentleman from San Francisco that was emitting those weird sounds; he was no more,—someone else did it. His wife and daughter, the doctor, the servants were standing and watching him apathetically. Suddenly, that which they expected and feared happened. The rattling sound ceased. And slowly, slowly, in everybody's sight a pallor stole over the face of the dead man, and his features began to grow thinner and more luminous, beautiful with the beauty that he had long shunned and that became him well. . . .

The proprietor entered. *"Gia e morto,"* whispered the doctor to him. The proprietor shrugged his shoulders indifferently. The older lady, with tears slowly running down her cheeks, approached him and said timidly that now the deceased must be taken to his room.

"O, no, madam," answered the proprietor politely, but without any amiability and not in English, but in French. He was no longer interested in the trifle which the guests from San Francisco could now leave at his cash-office. "This is absolutely impossible," he said, and added in the form of an explanation that he valued this apartment highly, and if he satisfied her desire, this would become known over Capri and the tourists would begin to avoid it.

The girl, who had looked at him strangely, sat down, and with her handkerchief to her mouth, began to cry. Her mother's tears dried up at once, and her face flared up. She raised her tone, began to demand, using her own language and still unable to realize that the respect for her was absolutely gone. The proprietor, with polite dignity, cut her short: "If madam does not like the ways of this hotel, he dare not detain her." And he firmly announced that the corpse must leave the hotel that very day, at dawn, that the police had been informed, that an agent would call immediately and attend to all the necessary formalities. . . . "Is it possible to get on Capri at least a plain coffin?" madam asks. . . . Unfortunately not; by no means, and as for making one, there will be no time. It will be necessary to arrange things some other way. . . . For instance, he gets English soda-water in big, oblong boxes. . . . The partitions could be taken out from such a box. . . .

By night, the whole hotel was asleep. A waiter opened the window in Number 43—it faced a corner of the garden where a consumptive banana-tree grew in the shadow of a high stone wall set with broken glass on the top—turned out the electric light, locked the door, and went away. The deceased remained alone in the darkness. Blue stars looked down at him from the black sky, the cricket in the wall started his melancholy, care-free song. In the dimly lighted corridor two chambermaids were sitting on the window-sill, mending something. Then Luigi came in, in slippered feet, with a heap of clothes on his arm.

"*Pronto?*"—he asked in a stage whisper, as if greatly concerned, directing his eyes toward the terrible door, at the end of the corridor. And waving his free hand in that direction, "*Partenza!*" he cried out in a whisper, as if seeing off a train,—and the chambermaids, choking with noiseless laughter, put their heads on each other's shoulders.

Then, stepping softly, he ran to the door, slightly rapped at it, and inclining his ear, asked most obsequiously in a subdued tone of voice:

"*Ha sonata, Signore?*"

And, squeezing his throat and thrusting his lower jaw forward, he answered himself in a drawling, grating, sad voice, as if from behind the door:

"Yes, come in. . . ."

At dawn, when the window panes in Number Forty-three grew white, and a damp wind rustled in the leaves of the banana-tree, when the pale-blue morning sky rose and stretched over Capri, and the sun, rising from behind the distant mountains of Italy, touched into gold the pure, clearly outlined summit of Monte Solaro, when the masons, who mended the paths for the tourists on the island, went out to their work,—an oblong box was brought to room number forty-three. Soon it grew very heavy and painfully pressed against the knees of the assistant doorman who was conveying it in a one-horse carriage along the white highroad which winded on the slopes, among stone fences and vineyards, all the way down to the seacoast. The driver, a sickly man, with red eyes, in an old short-sleeved coat and in worn-out shoes, had a drunken headache; all night long he had played dice at the eatinghouse—and he kept on flogging his vigorous little horse. According to Sicilian custom, the animal was heavily burdened with decoration: all sorts of bells tinkled on the bridle, which was ornamented with colored woolen fringes; there were bells also on the edge of the high saddle; and a bird's feather, two feet long, stuck in the trimmed crest of the horse, nodded up and down. The driver kept silence: he was depressed by his wrongheadedness and vices, by the fact that last night he had lost in gambling all the copper coins with which his pockets had been full,—neither more nor less than four liras and forty centesimi. But on such a morning, when the air is so fresh, and the sea stretches nearby, and the sky is serene with a morning serenity,—a headache passes rapidly and one becomes carefree again. Besides, the driver was also somewhat cheered by the unexpected earnings which the Gentleman from San Francisco, who bumped his dead head against the walls of the box behind his back, had brought him. The little steamer, shaped like a great bug, which lay far down, on the tender and brilliant blue filling to the brim the Neapolitan bay, was blowing the signal of departure,—and the sounds swiftly resounded all over Capri. Every bend of the island, every ridge and stone was seen as distinctly as if there were no air between heaven and earth. Near the quay the driver was overtaken by the head doorman who conducted in an auto the wife and daughter of the Gentleman from San Francisco. Their faces were pale and their eyes sunken with tears and a sleepless night. And in ten minutes the little steamer was again stirring up the water and picking its way toward Sorrento and Castellamare, carrying the American family away from Capri forever. . . . Meanwhile, peace and rest were restored on the island.

Two thousand years ago there had lived on that island a man who became utterly entangled in his own brutal and filthy actions. For some unknown reason he usurped the rule over millions of men and found himself bewildered by the absurdity of this power, while the fear that someone might kill him unawares, made him commit deeds inhuman beyond all measure. And mankind has forever retained his memory, and those who, taken together, now rule the world, as incomprehensibly and, essentially, as cruelly as he did,— come from all the corners of the earth to look at the remnants of the stone house he inhabited, which stands on one of the steepest cliffs of the island. On that wonderful morning the tourists, who had come to Capri for precisely that purpose, were still asleep in the various hotels, but tiny long-eared asses under red saddles were already being led to the hotel entrances. Americans and Germans, men and women, old and young, after having arisen and breakfasted heartily, were to scramble on them, and the old beggar-women of Capri, with sticks in their sinewy hands, were again to run after them along stony, mountainous paths, all the way up to the summit of Monte Tiberia. The dead old man from San Francisco, who had planned to keep the tourists company but who had, instead, only scared them by reminding them of death, was already shipped to Naples, and soothed by this, the travelers slept soundly, and silence reigned over the island. The stores in the little town were still closed, with the exception of the fish and greens market on the tiny square. Among the plain people who filled it, going about their buisness, stood idly by, as usual, Lorenzo, a tall old boatman, a carefree reveller and once a handsome man, famous all over Italy, who had many times served as a model for painters. He had brought and already sold—for a song—two big sea-crawfish, which he had caught at night and which were rustling in the apron of Don Cataldo, the cook of the hotel where the family from San Francisco had been lodged,—and now Lorenzo could stand calmly until nightfall, wearing princely airs, showing off his rags, his clay pipe with its long reed mouth-piece, and his red woolen cap, tilted on one ear. Meanwhile, among the precipices of Monte Solare, down the ancient Phoenician road, cut in the rocks in the form of a gigantic staircase, two Abruzzi mountaineers were coming from Anacapri. One carried under his leather mantle a bagpipe, a large goat's skin with two pipes; the other, something in the nature of a wooden flute. They walked, and the entire country, joyous, beautiful, sunny, stretched below them; the rocky shoulders of the island, which lay at their feet, the fabulous blue in which it swam, the shining morning vapors over the sea westward, beneath the dazzling sun, and the wavering masses of Italy's mountains, both near and distant, whose beauty human word is powerless to render. . . . Midway they slowed up. Overshadowing the road stood, in a grotto of the rock wall of Monte Solare, the Holy Virgin, all radiant, bathed in the warmth and the splendor of the sun. The rust of her snow-white plaster-of-Paris vestures and queenly crown was touched into gold, and there were meekness and mercy in her eyes raised toward the heavens, toward the eternal and beatific abode of her thrice-blessed Son. They bared their heads, applied the pipes to their lips, and praises flowed on, candid and humbly-joyous, praises to the sun and the morning, to Her, the Immaculate Intercessor for all who suffer in this evil and beautiful world, and to Him who had been born of her womb in the cavern of Bethlehem, in a hut of lowly shepherds in distant Judea.

As for the body of the dead Gentleman from San Francisco, it was on its way home, to the shores of the New World, where a grave awaited it. Having undergone many humiliations and suffered much human neglect, having wandered about a week from one port warehouse to another, it finally got on that same famous ship which had brought the family, such a short while ago and with such a pomp, to the Old World. But now he was concealed from the living: in a tar-coated coffin he was lowered deep into the black hold of the steamer. And again did the ship set out on its far sea journey. At night it sailed by the island of Capri, and, for those who watched it from the island, its lights slowly disappearing in the dark sea, it seemed infinitely sad. But there, on the vast steamer, in its lighted halls shining with brilliance and marble, a noisy dancing party was going on, as usual.

On the second and third night there was again a ball—this time in mid-ocean, during the furious storm sweeping over the ocean, which roared like a funeral mass and rolled up mountainous seas fringed with mourning silvery foam. The Devil, who from the rocks of Gibraltar, the stony gateway of two worlds, watched the ship vanish into night and storm, could hardly distinguish from behind the snow the innumerable fiery eyes of the ship. The Devil was as huge as a cliff, but the ship was even bigger, a many-storied, many-stacked giant, created by the arrogance of the New Man with the old heart. The blizzard battered the ship's rigging and its broad-necked stacks, whitened with snow, but it remained firm, majestic —and terrible. On its uppermost deck, amidst a snowy whirlwind there loomed up in loneliness the cozy, dimly lighted cabin, where, only half awake, the vessel's ponderous pilot reigned over its entire mass, bearing the semblance of a pagan idol. He heard the wailing moans and the furious screeching of the siren, choked by the storm, but the nearness of that which was behind the wall and which in the last account was incomprehensible to him, removed his fears. He was reassured by the thought of the large, armored cabin, which now and then was filled with mysterious rumbling sounds and with the dry creaking of blue fires, flaring up and exploding around a man with a metallic headpiece, who was eagerly catching the indistinct voices of the vessels that hailed him, hundreds of miles away. At the very bottom, in the under-water womb of the "Atlantis," the huge masses of tanks and various other machines, their steel parts shining dully, wheezed with steam and oozed hot water and oil; here was the gigantic kitchen, heated by hellish furnaces, where the motion of the vessel was being generated; here seethed those forces terrible in their concentration which were transmitted to the keel of the vessel, and into that endless round tunnel, which was lighted by electricity, and looked like a gigantic cannon barrel, where slowly, with a punctuality and certainty that crushes the human soul, a colossal shaft was revolving in its oily nest, like a living monster stretching in its lair. As for the middle part of the "Atlantis," its warm, luxurious cabins, dining-rooms, and halls, they radiated light and joy, were astir with a chattering smartly-dressed

crowd, were filled with the fragrance of fresh flowers, and resounded
with a string orchestra. And again did the slender supple pair of
hired lovers painfully turn and twist and at times clash convulsively
amid the splendor of lights, silks, diamonds, and bare feminine
shoulders: she—a sinfully modest pretty girl, with lowered eyelashes
and an innocent hair-dressing, he—a tall, young man, with black
hair, looking as if it were pasted, pale with powder, in most exquisite patent-leather shoes, in a narrow long-skirted dresscoat,—
a beautiful man resembling a leech. And no one knew that this
couple had long since been weary of torturing themselves with a
feigned beatific torture under the sounds of shamefully-melancholy
music; nor did any one know what lay deep, deep, beneath them,
on the very bottom of the hold, in the neighborhood of the gloomy
and sultry maw of the ship, that heavily struggled with the ocean,
the darkness, and the storm. . . .

—Translated by A. Yarmolinsky

MIKHAIL SHOLOKHOV

****

*Ranked by the Russians themselves as the leading contemporary
writer in the Soviet Union, some sixteen million seven hundred and
nine thousand copies of his two-volume novel,* The Silent Don, *having
been published since 1925, Mikhail Sholokhov is represented by
a chapter, "Civil War," from the first volume* And Quiet Flows
the Don. *Not concerned with the chief characters in the book, this
unit deals with the return to his Don River village of the soldier
Bunchuk at a time when Kerensky is momentarily in power in
Petrograd and civil war has been unleashed between the Red
Guards and the counter-revolutionists.*

****

Civil War

THE TOWN of Novocherkassk became the centre of attraction for all
who had fled from the Bolshevik Revolution. Important generals
who formerly had been arbiters of the destiny of the Russian armies
poured down into the lower regions of the Don, hoping to find support for their activities among the reactionary Don Cossacks and to
develop an offensive against Sovietized Russia. On November 15
General Alexeev arrived in the town. After talks with Kaledin he
set to work to organize volunteer detachments. The backbone of the
future Volunteer Army was provided by officers, Junkers, and others
who had fled from the north. Within three weeks an unwholesome
flesh had grown around this framework, consisting of students,
soldiers, the most active of the counter-revolutionary Cossacks, and
men seeking adventure and higher pay even in Kerensky rubles.

At the beginning of December more generals arrived, and on
December 19 Kornilov himself appeared in the town. By this time
Kaledin had succeeded in withdrawing almost all the Cossack regiments from the Rumanian and Austro-German fronts and had distributed them along the main railway lines of the Don province. But
the Cossacks, wearied with three years of war and returning from

the front in a revolutionary mood, showed no great desire to fight the Bolsheviks. The regiments were left with hardly a third of their normal complement, for the home fires beckoned powerfully, and there was no power on earth that could have restrained the Cossacks from their elemental movement homeward.

When Kaledin made a first attempt in December to send front-line detachments against revolutionary Rostov, the Cossacks refused to attack and turned back after going a little distance. But the widely developed organization for consolidating the fragmentary divisions began to have its results. By the middle of December, Kaledin had several reliable volunteer detachments at his command.

But from three sides columns of Red Guards were approaching the province. In Kharkov and Voronezh forces were being assembled to strike a blow against the counter-revolutionaries in the Don. Clouds hung and deepened and blackened over the Don. The winds from the Ukraine were already bringing the sound of the gun-thunder accompanying the first clashes. Gloomy days were coming to the Don; an evil time was approaching.

Yellow-white, billowing clouds were floating slowly over Novocherkassk. In the height of the heaven right above the glittering dome of the Cathedral, a grey, fluffy scrawl of feathery cloud hung in an expanse of cloudless blue, its long tail drooping and gleaming a rosy silver.

One morning in November, Ilia Bunchuk arrived at Novocherkassk by the Moscow train. He was the last to leave the car, pulling down the edges of his old overcoat and feeling a little awkward and strange in his civilian clothing.

He went out into the town, carrying his cheap, shabby suitcase under his arm. He met hardly anyone along the whole of the road, although he crossed the town from one side to the other. After half an hour's walk he halted before a small, dilapidated house. It had not been repaired for years; time had set its hands upon it, and the roof was sinking, the walls were awry, the shutters hung loosely, and the windows squinted. As he opened the wicket gate Bunchuk ran his eyes over the house and the tiny yard; then he hurried up the steps.

He found half the narrow corridor of the house occupied by a chest piled with lumber. In the darkness he knocked his knee against one corner, but threw open the door, not feeling the pain. There was no one in the first, low room. He went towards the second, halting on the threshold. His head swam with the terribly familiar scent peculiar to this one house. His eyes took in all the room: the ikon in the corner, the bed, the table, the small, speckled mirror above it, some photographs, several rickety chairs, a sewing-machine, and a tarnished samovar standing on the stove. With heart suddenly, violently beating, he threw down his suitcase and stared around the kitchen. The tall, green-washed stove had a welcoming look; from behind a blue cotton curtain peeped an old tabby-cat, its eyes gleaming with almost human curiosity. An unwashed utensil lay untidily on the table, and a ball of wool and four gleaming knitting-needles carrying an unfinished stocking had been left on a stool.

He ran out on the steps. From the door of a shed in the far corner of the yard emerged an old, bowed woman. "Mother! But is it? Is it she?" His lips trembling, he ran to meet her, tearing the cap from his head as he went.

"Who do you want?" the old woman asked cautiously, standing with her palm shading her eyes.

"Mother!" the words burst hoarsely from Bunchuk's throat. "Don't you know me?"

He went stumbling towards her and saw her sway at his shout as though before a blow. She wanted to run, but her strength failed her and she came in little spurts, as though battling against a wind. He caught her in his arms, he kissed her furrowed face and her eyes, dull with fear and gladness, while his own eyes blinked helplessly.

"Ilia! Iliusha! My little son! I didn't know you. . . . Lord, where have you come from?" the old woman whispered.

They went into the house. He threw off his overcoat with a sigh of relief and sat down at the table.

"I never thought I should see you again. . . . It's so many years. . . . My dear—how could I know you when you had grown so much and looked so much older?" she said.

"Well, but how are you, Mother?" he asked with a smile.

As she disconnectedly replied she bustled about, clearing the table, putting charcoal into the samovar. With streaming eyes she ran back again and again to her son to stroke his head and press him to her. She boiled water and gave him a meal, herself washed his head, took some clean underwear, yellow with age, from the bottom of the chest, and sat until midnight with her eyes fixed on him, questioning him and bitterly shaking her head.

Two o'clock had just struck in the neighbouring belfry when Bunchuk lay down to sleep. He dropped off at once, and dreamed that he was once more a pupil at the craft school, tired out with play and dozing over his books, while his mother opened the door from the kitchen and asked sternly: "Ilia, have you learned your lessons for tomorrow?" He slept with a fixed, tensely happy smile on his face.

His mother went to him more than once during the night, straightening the blanket and pillow, kissing his great forehead, and quietly going out again.

He spent only one day at home. In the morning a comrade in a soldier's greatcoat came and talked with him in undertones. After the man had gone he bustled about, swiftly packed his suitcase, and drew on his ill-fitting overcoat. He took a hurried farewell of his mother, promising to see her again within a month.

"Where are you off to now, Ilia?" she asked.

"To Rostov, Mother, to Rostov. I'll be back soon. . . . Don't you fret, Mother . . . don't fret," he cheered her.

She hurriedly removed a small cross from her neck, and as she kissed her son she slipped the string over his head. As with trembling fingers she adjusted it around his neck, she whispered:

"Wear this, Ilia. Defend him and save him, Lord; cover him with Thy wings. He is all I have in the world. . . ." As she passionately embraced him she could not control herself, and the corners of her lips quivered and drooped bitterly. Like spring rain one warm tear after another fell on to Bunchuk's hairy hand. He unfastened her hands from his neck and ran with clouded face out of the house.

The crowd was packed like sardines at Rostov station, and the floors were littered ankle-deep with cigarette-ends and the husks of sunflower-seeds. In the station square the soldiers from the town garrison were trading their equipment, tobacco, and articles they had stolen. A swarming throng of the many nationalities to be found in the southern seaport towns moved slowly about. Bunchuk pressed through the crowd, sought out the party committee room, and made his way upstairs. His further progress was barred by a Red Guard armed with a rifle of Japanese pattern. A knife was tied to its barrel instead of a bayonet.

"Who do you want, comrade?" the guard asked.

"I want Comrade Abramson. Is he here?"

"Third room on the left."

Bunchuk opened the door of the room indicated, and found a short, big-nosed, black-haired man talking to an elderly railwayman. His left hand was thrust into his jacket, his right waved methodically in the air.

"That's not good enough!" the black-haired man was declaring.

"That isn't organization! If you carry on your agitation like this you'll get exactly opposite results to those we want."

Judging from the anxiously guilty look on the railwayman's face, he wanted to say something in justification, but the other man would not let him open his mouth. Evidently irritated to the last degree, he shouted:

"Remove Mitchenko from the work at once! This is not to be endured! We cannot allow what is going on among you. Vierkhovietsky will have to answer for it to the revolutionary tribunal. Is he arrested? Yes? I shall insist on his being shot!" he ended harshly. Still not completely in control of himself, he turned his angry face in Bunchuk's direction and asked sharply: "What do you want?"

"Are you Comrade Abramson?" Bunchuk asked.

"Yes."

Bunchuk handed him documents from the Petrograd party committee and sat down on the window-ledge. Abramson carefully read the letters, then said, smiling morosely:

"Wait a bit; we'll have a talk in a moment or two."

He dismissed the railwayman and went out, returning a few minutes later with a well-built, clean-shaven, non-commissioned officer bearing the mark of a sabre-cut across his lower jaw.

"This is a member of our Military-Revolutionary Committee," Abramson said to Bunchuk. "And you, Comrade Bunchuk, are a machine-gunner, aren't you?"

"Yes."

"You're just the man we're wanting," the non-commissioned officer smiled.

"Can you organize machine-gun detachments from the worker Red Guards for us? As soon as possible?" Abramson asked.

"I'll try. It's a question of time."

"Well, how long do you need? A week—two, three?" Smiling expectantly, the other man bent towards Bunchuk.

"Several days."

"Excellent!"

Abramson rubbed his forehead and said with obvious annoyance:

"Part of the town garrison is badly demoralized, and they are not to be relied on. Like everywhere else, I suppose, Comrade Bunchuk, our hopes here are in the workers. The sailors too; but as for the soldiers—" He tugged at his beard, and asked: "How are you off in regard to supplies? Well, we'll arrange that. Have you had anything to eat today? No, of course not."

"You must have starved a bit in your time, brother, if you can

tell at a glance whether a man is full or hungry," Bunchuk thought.
As he went with a guide to Abramson's room, his mind still turned
on him: "He's a brave lad, he's a true Bolshevik! Hard, yet there's
something good and human in him. He doesn't think twice about
the death-sentence for some saboteur, yet he can see to the needs of
his comrades."

Still under the warm impression of his meeting, he reached
Abramson's quarters and had some dinner, then lay down to rest on
the bed in the little book-filled room. He fell straight off to sleep.

For the next four days Bunchuk was occupied from early morning
till nightfall with the workers assigned to him by the party committee. There were sixteen all together, men of the most varied
peace-time occupations, ages, and even nationalities. There were two
stevedores, a Ukrainian named Khvilichko, and a Russianized
Greek, Mikhalidze; a compositor, Stepanov; eight metal-workers;
a miner, Zelenkov, from the Paramonov mines; a weak-looking
Armenian baker, Gievorkiantz; a Russianized German and skilled
locksmith named Rebinder; and two workers from the railway workshops.

A seventeenth requisition was brought to Bunchuk by a woman
attired in a padded soldier's greatcoat and boots too large for her
feet. As he took the sealed letter from her, he asked: "On your way
back can you call at the staff for me?"

She smiled, embarrassedly tidied a thick lock of hair that had
fallen below her kerchief, and replied nervously:

"I have been sent to you—" then, overcoming her momentary
confusion, she added: "as a machine-gunner."

Bunchuk flushed heavily. "Have they gone out of their minds?
Is it a woman's battalion I've got to organize? Excuse me, but this
isn't fit work for you; it's heavy and calls for a man's strength. No,
I can't accept you."

Still frowning, he opened the letter and hurriedly scanned its
contents. The requisition itself merely stated that the party member
Anna Pogoodko had been assigned to the machine-gun section, but
attached to it was a letter from Abramson, which read:

Dear Comrade Bunchuk:

*We are sending you a good comrade in Anna Pogoodko. We have
yielded to her insistent demand, and hope that you will make a
fighting machine-gunner of her. I know the girl. I can warmly recommend her, she is a valuable worker, and I ask you only to watch*

one thing: she is fiery and a little exalted in temperament (she hasn't yet outgrown her youth). Keep her from thoughtless actions, and look after her.

Speed up the training. We hear that Kaledin is preparing to attack us.

With comradely greeting,

Abramson

Bunchuk stared at the girl standing before him. The dim light of the cellar which had been allotted to him for headquarters shadowed her face and concealed its lines.

"Oh well," he said ungraciously, "if it's your own wish—and Abramson asks, you can stay."

They crowded around the machine-gun, hung in clusters over it, leaning on one another's backs and watching with inquisitive eyes as under Bunchuk's skilful hands it came to pieces. Then he re-assembled it, explaining the nature and function of each section, showing them how to handle it, to load it, sight it, determine the trajectory and the range. Then he showed them how to protect themselves from the enemy fire, pointed out the necessity of setting up the gun at a point of vantage and of arranging the ammunition cases correctly.

All seventeen learned quickly with the exception of the baker, Gievorkiantz. No matter how many times Bunchuk showed him, he could not remember, and he lost his head, muttering in his confusion:

"Why doesn't it come out right? Ah—I'm a fool—this bit ought to be there. . . . And now it isn't right!" he cried in despair. "Why isn't it?"

"This is why!" The swarthy Bogovoi imitated his tone. "It doesn't come right because you're stupid. That's how it goes." He confidently put the section in its proper place.

"He's extraordinarily stupid," the phlegmatic German, Rebinder, agreed.

Only Stepanov shouted with annoyance, his face flushing:

"You ought to show your comrade and not snarl at him!"

He was supported by Krutogorov, a great, big-limbed worker from the railway workshops:

"You stand there laughing, you fools, and the work can wait! Comrade Bunchuk, instruct your waxwork gallery or else send them packing! The Revolution is in danger, and they stand there laughing! And they're party men too!" He waved his sledge-hammer fist.

Anna Pogoodko inquired about everything with keen curiosity. She attached herself importunately to Bunchuk, seized his sleeve, and could not be displaced from the side of the machine-gun.

"And what would happen if the water were to freeze in the water-jacket?" "What deviation has to be allowed for in a strong wind?" she plied him with questions, expectantly raising her black eyes to his.

In her presence he felt awkward, and as though in revenge he grew more exacting in regard to her and was exaggeratedly cool in his manner. But when each morning punctually at seven she entered the cellar, her hands thrust into the sleeves of her jacket, the soles of her great soldier's boots shuffling, he was troubled with an unusual, agitating feeling. She was rather shorter than he, of a full, healthy figure, perhaps a little round-shouldered, and not particularly beautiful except for her great, strong eyes, which endowed all her face with a wild beauty.

During the first four days he hardly had an opportunity to look at her. The cellar was badly lighted, and even if he had had time to study her face he would have felt too uncomfortable to do so. On the evening of the fifth day they left together. She went in front, but as she stood on the topmost step, she turned back to him with some query. She stood waiting for the answer, her head slightly tilted, her eyes bent on him, her hand brushing back her hair. But he did not catch her question. He slowly mounted the stairs, gripped by a pleasantly painful feeling. He knew it well; he had experienced its prick at all important turns in his life. Now he felt it again as he stared at the swarthily rosy cheeks of this girl, at the June azure in the whites of her eyes, and the bottomless depths of her black irises. She found it difficult to adjust her hair without removing her kerchief, and in her concentration her rosy nostrils quivered a little. The lines of her mouth were strong, yet childishly tender. On her raised upper lip there was a fine down, which showed dark against her skin. As simple as a fairy-story she stood before him, holding her hairpins in her silvery-white teeth, her arched brow quivering; and it seemed that she would melt away like a sound at dawn in a pine wood.

A wave of rapture and heavy joy carried Bunchuk away. He bowed his head as though before a blow and said half-seriously, half in jest:

"Anna Pogoodko, you're as good as someone's happiness."

"Nonsense!" she said firmly, and smiled. "Nonsense, Comrade

Bunchuk! I was asking at what time we go to shooting practice tomorrow.'

Her smile made her appear more simple, approachable, and earthly. He stopped at her side, gazing abstractedly down the street to where the stranded sun was flooding everything with a livid hue. He quietly replied:

"Tomorrow at eight. Which way do you go? Where do you live?"

She mentioned the name of some little street on the outskirts of the town. They went together, walking for some distance without speaking. At last she gave him a sidelong glance and asked:

"Are you a Cossack?"

"Yes."

"And you've been an officer?"

"Me an officer!"

"What is your native district?"

"Novocherkassk."

"Have you been long in Rostov?"

"Several days."

"And before that?"

"I was in Petrograd."

"When did you join the party?"

"In 1913."

"And where is your family?"

"In Novocherkassk," he said hurriedly, and imploringly stretched out his hand. "Stop a minute and let me do some questioning now. Were you born in Rostov?"

"No. I was born in Yekaterinoslav province, but I have lived here for some time."

"Are you a Ukrainian?"

She hesitated for a moment, then firmly replied:

"No."

"A Jewess?"

"Yes. But how did you know? Do I talk like one?"

"No."

"Then how did you guess I was a Jewess?"

He reduced the length of his stride in an attempt to fall into step with her and answered:

"Your ear—the shape of your ears, and your eyes. Otherwise you show little sign of your nationality." He thought for a moment, then added: "It's good that you're with us."

"Why?" she asked inquisitively.

"Well, the Jews have a certain reputation. And I know that many

workers believe it to be true—you see I am a worker, too—that the
Jews only do all the ordering and never go under fire themselves.
That is not true, and you will prove splendidly that it isn't true."

They walked slowly. She deliberately took a longer way home
and, after telling him a little more about herself, began to question
him again about the Kornilov attack, the attitude of the Petrograd
workers, and the November Revolution. From somewhere on the
quays came the sound of a rifle-shot, then a machine-gun disturbed
the silence. She at once asked him:

"What make is that?"

"A Lewis."

"How much of the belt has been used?"

He did not reply. He was admiring the orange feeler of a search-
light stretching from an anchored trawler into the height of the
flaming evening sky.

They wandered about the deserted town for some three hours and
separated at last at the gate of her dwelling.

He returned home glowing with an inward satisfaction.

"She's a fine comrade and an intelligent girl! It was good to have
a talk with her. I've grown boorish during these last years, and
friendly intercourse with people is necessary, otherwise one gets as
worm-eaten as soldiers' biscuit," he thought, deliberately deceiving
himself.

Abramson, just returned from a session of the Military-Revolutionary Committee, began to question him about the training of the
machine-gun detachments and asked about Anna.

"How is she getting on? If she isn't suitable we can easily put her
to other work," he said.

"Oh no!" Bunchuk took alarm. "She's a very capable girl."

He felt an almost irresistible desire to go on talking about her and
mastered his inclination only with a great effort of his will.

On December 8 Kaledin began to fling troops into an attack upon
Rostov. Thin chains of Alexeev's officers' detachment moved along
the railway line, supported on the right flank by a denser body of
Junkers, and on the left by partisans of Popov's detachment.

The line of Red Guards scattered around the outskirts of the town
was possessed with restless anxiety. Some of the workers, many of
whom had rifles in their hands for the first time in their lives, were
terror-stricken and pressed close to the muddy ground; while others
raised their heads and stared at the distant tiny figures of the oncoming Whites.

Unable to endure the tense silence, the Red Guards opened fire without waiting for the word of command. When the first shot rang out, Bunchuk, kneeling at the side of his machine-gun, cursed, jumped to his feet, and shouted:

"Cease fire!"

His cry was lashed by the sputter of shots. He waved his hand, tried to outshout the firing, and ordered Bogovoi to open fire with the machine-gun. Bogovoi set his smiling, muddy face close to the breech and put his hand on the firing lever. The familiar sound of the spurting machine-gun bullets penetrated Bunchuk's ears. He stared in the direction of the enemy, attempting to determine the accuracy of the range, then ran along the line towards the other machine-guns.

"Fire!" he shouted.

"Right-o! Ho-ho-ho-ho!" Khvilichko howled, turning a frightened but happy face towards him.

The third machine-gun from the centre was manned by not altogether reliable elements. Bunchuk ran towards it. He stopped halfway and, bending, stared through his glasses. He could clearly see the spurting grey mounds cast up by the bullets in the distance. He lay down and assured himself that the range of the third machine-gun was hopelessly inaccurate.

"Lower, you devils!" he cried, crawling along the line. Bullets whistled close above him. The enemy was firing as perfectly as if at exercise.

The gun muzzle was tilted at a ridiculous angle; around it the gunners lay on top of one another. The Greek Mikhalidze was firing without pause, uselessly expending all his reserves of ammunition. Close to him was the terrified Stepanov, and behind, with head thrust into the ground and back humped like a tortoise, was one of the railwaymen.

Thrusting Mikhalidze aside, Bunchuk took long and careful sight. When the bullets began to spurt once more from the gun, they immediately had effect. A group of Junkers who had been coming on at a run turned and fled back down the slope, leaving one of their number on the clayey ground.

Handing the machine-gun over, Bunchuk returned to his own gun and found Bogovoi lying on his side, cursing and binding up a wound in his leg. Rebinder had taken his place and was firing intelligently and economically, without a trace of excitement.

From the left flank Gievorkiantz came leaping like a hare, dropping at every shot that passed over his head, groaning and shouting:

"I can't. . . . I can't. . . . It won't shoot! It's jammed!"

Bunchuk ran along the line to the disabled gun. When still a little way off, he saw Anna on her knees at its side, staring under her palm at the advancing enemy chain.

"Lie down!" he shouted, his face darkening with fear for her. "Lie down, I tell you!"

She glanced at him and continued to kneel. Curses as heavy as stones fell from his lips. He ran up to her and flung her forcibly to the ground.

Krutogorov was wheezing by the shield.

"It's had enough! It won't work!" he muttered to Bunchuk and, looking round for Gievorkiantz, burst into a shout: "He's run away, damn him! Your antediluvian monster has run away. . . . He's completely upset me with his groans. . . . He wouldn't let a man work properly!"

Gievorkiantz crawled up, writhing like a serpent, mud clinging to the black scrub of his beard. Krutogorov stared at him for a moment, then howled above the roar of the firing:

"What have you done with the ammunition belts? You animal! Bunchuk, take him away or I shall kill him!"

Bunchuk examined the machine-gun. A bullet struck hard against the shield, and he removed his hand as though burned. He put the gun in order, and himself directed the firing, forcing the oncoming Alexeev men to lie down. Then he crawled away, looking for cover.

The chains of the enemy drew closer. Their fire grew heavier. In the Red Guard ranks three men were hit, and their comrades took their rifles and cartridges: dead men have no need of weapons. Right in the eyes of Anna and Bunchuk, as they lay at the side of Krutogorov's gun, a young Red Guard was struck by a bullet. He writhed and groaned, digging into the earth with his feet, and finally, raising himself on his hands, coughed and gasped in air for the last time. Bunchuk glanced sidelong at Anna. A fleeting terror lurked in her great, dilated eyes as she stared unwinkingly at the feet of the dead lad, not hearing Krutogorov's shout:

"A belt—a belt! Girl, give me a fresh belt!"

By a deep flanking movement the Kaledin troops pushed the Red Guard ranks back. The black greatcoats and tunics of the retreating workers began to dribble through the streets of the suburb. The machine-gun on the extreme right fell into the hands of the Whites. The Greek Mikhalidze was shot down by a Junker, a second gunner was transfixed with bayonets, and only the compositor, Stepanov, managed to escape.

The retreat was halted when the first shells began to fly from the Red trawlers in the port. The Red Guards hesitated and turned, then advanced into the attack. Bunchuk had gathered Anna, Krutogorov, and Gievorkiantz around him. Suddenly Krutogorov pointed to a distant fence with little grey human figures assembled behind it.

"There they are!" he shouted.

Bunchuk swung the gun round in that direction. Anna sat down and saw all movement die away behind the fence. After a moment, the Whites opened a measured fire, and the bullets sped over them, tearing invisible holes in the misty canvas of the sky. The belt rattled like a kettle-drum as it ran through the machine-gun. The shells fired by the Black Sea fleet sailors in the trawlers went screaming overhead. The sailors had now got the range and were carrying on a concentrated fire. Isolated groups of the retreating Kaledin troops were covered by the bursting shrapnel. One of the shells burst right in the midst of one group, and the brown column of the explosion scattered the men in all directions. Anna dropped her field-glasses and groaned, covering her terror-stricken eyes with dirty palms.

"What's the matter?" Bunchuk shouted, bending towards her.

She compressed her lips, and her dilated eyes glazed.

"I can't . . ."

"Be brave! You—Anna, do you hear? Do you hear? You mustn't do that! You mustn't . . ." the authoritative voice of command beat at her ear.

On the right flank some of the enemy had gathered in a valley and on the slopes of a rise. Bunchuk noticed them, ran with the machine-gun to a more convenient spot, and opened fire on the valley.

Towards evening a first fine snow began to whirl down over the harsh earth. Within an hour the wet, sticky snow had completely enveloped the field and the muddy black bundles of the dead. The Kaledin troops withdrew.

Bunchuk spent the night in the machine-gun outpost. Krutogorov chewed away at some stringy meat, spitting and cursing. Huddled in the gateway of a yard, Gievorkiantz warmed his blue hands over a cigarette. Bunchuk sat on an ammunition-case, wrapping the trembling Anna in his greatcoat, tearing her damp hands from her eyes and kissing them. The words of unaccustomed tenderness came with difficulty from his lips.

"Now, now; how could you take on so? . . . You were hard. . . . Anna, listen, take yourself in hand! Anna—dear—you'll get used to

it. If your pride will not allow you to go back, you must be different.
You can't look on the dead like that. Don't let your thoughts turn
that way! Take them in hand. You see now; although you said you
were brave, the woman in you has won."

Anna was silent. Her hands smelt of the wintry earth and of
womanly warmth.

The falling snow concealed the sky in a dense gracious blanket.
The yard, the fields, the town lurking like a beast in the darkness
were wrapped in drowsy slumber.

Six days the struggle continued around and in Rostov. Fighting
went on in the streets and at the crossroads. Twice the Red Guards
surrendered the station, and twice they drove the enemy out again.
During those six days there were no prisoners taken by either side.

Late one afternoon Bunchuk and Anna were passing the freight
station and saw two Red Guards shoot a captured officer. Bunchuk
said almost challengingly to Anna, who had turned away:

"That's sensible! They must be killed, wiped out without mercy.
They show us no mercy, and we don't ask for it. So why should we
show them mercy? This filth must be raked off the earth. There can
be no sentimentality, once it is a question of the fate of the Revolution. Those workers are right!"

On the third day of the struggle he was taken ill. But he kept on
his feet for some days, feeling a continually increasing nausea and
weakness in all his body. His head rang and was unbearably heavy.

The Red Guard detachments abandoned the town at dawn on
December 15. Bunchuk, supported by Anna and Krutogorov, walked
behind a wagon containing wounded and a machine-gun. He bore
his helpless body along with the utmost difficulty, put forward his
iron-heavy feet as though asleep, and heard Anna say from a great
distance off:

"Get into the wagon, Ilia. Do you hear? Do you understand what
I say? I ask you to get in; you're ill."

But he did not understand her words, nor did he understand that
he was broken and in the grip of typhus. He clutched his head and
pressed his hairy hands to his burning, flaming face. He felt as
though blood were dripping from his eyes, and all the world, boundless and unstable, cut off from him by an invisible curtain, were
rearing and tearing under his feet. In his delirium his imagination
began to conjure up incredible visions. He stopped again and again,
struggling with Krutogorov, who was trying to put him into the
wagon.

rattled from artillery fire. She would take her granddaughter on her knee and say: "Don't be afraid, it's war."

Suddenly on a bright autumn morning she saw Germans coming down Saksagansky Street. She had expected everything, but not this. Hadn't Osip written that they would be beaten? But the Germans came along, young, merry, laughing, chewing something as they went. She became flustered like a hen, shielded Alya. A German caught sight of her, laughed, and took aim at her with his tommy gun; his comrades also laughed. Hannah barely managed to reach her house. She sat down beside Alya and said: "That's nothing. It was done on purpose to trap them. Our men will come soon. Papa will come soon." She was comforting not her granddaughter, but herself.

When Hannah went to the market with little Alya a week after the Germans came, she saw a notice posted on the wall. "Jews of the City of Kiev and its environs. On Monday, September 29, 7 A.M., you must present yourselves with your belongings, papers and warm clothing in Dorogozhitskaya Street, near the Jewish cemetery. Penalty for non-appearance—death."

An elderly man stood next to her; Hannah asked him: "Can you make out what they're up to?"

The man looked round furtively and went away. A woman nearby said: "It's obvious. They're going to deport the Jews."

Hannah slowly walked home. She had aged much during that week, her head trembled, she could barely drag her feet. Where can those brutes send us to? And winter coming soon. Hannah looked at her grandchild with tenderness and grief. What will become of the child? I've lived long enough, it's time for me to die. How save Alya?

She decided to go and see Vera. "I'll ask her to take the child until our men come back." The door was opened by a strange woman who glared angrily at Hannah.

"She's not here any more. They took her away. They've taken all the Communists away."

Hannah understood. Now nobody would save them. She must submit to fate. Perhaps they won't send them far. There must be some decent people even among the Germans, they'll take pity on the child.

And Hannah made preparations for a journey. Alya's warm coat was torn, she must mend it. I'll bake some flatcakes. Domestic cares took her mind off her gloomy thoughts.

In the morning Hannah began to pack, but seeing the street

crammed with people, she realized that there was no need to hurry
—it will be good if we get there by evening.

Lvov Street was jammed. Many aged people, many children.
Hannah asked herself: "Where are the young people?" and remembered, the young are fighting. Two bearded old men were carrying
a paralyzed woman on a blanket. A man with an artificial leg was
pushing a baby carriage. Children lost their mothers and cried. The
old men prayed; and the mournful strains of Oriental chanting
mingled with the wailing of women. Alya became frightened and
tightly hugged her big doll. Suddenly Hannah caught sight of Dr.
Weinberg in the crowd. With difficulty she pushed her way toward
him.

"Where are they sending us, Doctor?"

He looked at her with his kind, mournful eyes and bending over
toward her whispered in reply: "To our graves."

She shrieked and clutched Alya. "That can't be! The child?"

The doctor waved his hand, took off his spectacles; Hannah saw
tears in his eyes.

German patrols were lined up on the pavement. Now and again
Hannah heard disjointed phrases from the house gates, street doors,
and open windows. "Lord, how many of them! Where are they
sending them?" "To work, they say." "It's terrible to look at!"

Alya could not walk any more, she cried. Hannah picked her up,
but she had not the strength to carry her. Somebody said: "Put the
child on this cart." The old man who was driving it kept mumbling
to himself. Perhaps he was praying? Or had he gone out of his
mind?

Perhaps the doctor was exaggerating? Once he said Raya had
pneumonia, whereas it was just an ordinary 'flu.

A woman walking at Hannah's side said: "People say they'll send
us to different small towns."

Of course the doctor's exaggerating. They can't kill little children.

But those Germans had shameless eyes, they looked on and
laughed. Where are our men? Where's Osip? Of course our side
will win, but when?

Where were they? Still in Lvov Street. In that house Hannah's
elder sister, Fenya, once lived. When Hannah became acquainted
with Nahum she went to her sister and asked for her blessing, as if
she were her mother. Nahum was a kindhearted man, only crazy.
When he went away she had a hard time. She worked as a washer-
woman. In spite of all, she put Osip on his feet. Léo had an easier
time, of course, but Osip has a clear head. He's respected, he's an

officer. Raya did right in going to the war, everybody must fight, since they're such brutes.

The highroad. She had been here long ago—when she and Nahum went to Rosa's wedding. Nahum had danced so comically. And she too had danced. Now life was behind her. But Alya? She must not leave Alya.

Now all around them was vacant land, a hill, a ravine, and sand. The Germans ordered them to halt. Dusk was falling. Desks were set up on the trampled grass, an outdoor office. People were called up in groups—thirty at a time.

A German took Hannah's passport. He threw it on the ground and shouted: "Don't talk! Your valuables!"

Hannah proffered her wedding ring and three silver spoons. "Is that all?"

They were told to go further. Another German yelled: "Undress!"

Hannah stood stock-still. The German struck her. "Undress! Undress the child!"

What are they up to! Brutes! Hannah began to undress Alya. The child cried: "I don't want to bathe, Granny! It's cold, Granny."

An old man refused to undress. The German struck him in the face; he staggered, but did not fall; his eyes became bloodshot and in a shrill guttural voice he cried out: "Be accursed, you, and your family, and your house!"

Another German ran up and crushed the old man's skull with the butt of his tommy gun.

Alya cried: "Granny, I'm frightened."

"Kill me, but spare the child!" pleaded Hannah.

"Dont talk!"

As two girls undressed, the Germans looked at them with greedy, vicious eyes. But the girls stepped forward and to the surprise of all broke into song:

Arise ye prisoners of starvation . . .

Hannah saw a ravine. Her mind still grasped the words spoken by the woman next to ser: "This is Babi Yar." Then a German snatched Alya out of her arms and swung the child into the ravine. Hannah uttered a frantic shriek, turned round to the German and raising her arm high shouted: "Osip will come! The Red Army will come! You'll answer for everything, you brutes!"

They were driven right to the edge of the ravine, and then—a round of tommy-gun bullets.

The Germans quarreled near the heaps: "That watch is mine."

Among the rings was the one which a long time ago the young, dreaming tailor had slipped on Hannah's finger. None of the Germans wanted Alya's coat which Hannah had mended yesterday.

The firing was so heavy Osip opened his mouth, and his eyes bulged. Looking at him Minayev wanted to laugh, but didn't. Later Minayev said: "That was some music, eh?" But at that moment Minayev, like the rest of the men, was not thinking about anything. They were not even conscious of the cold. When Minayev climbed to the top of the steep hill his will was as strong as if he had been waiting for this moment all his life—from the time he played his boyish games, from the time he read his first book. That moment had been preceded by so much tearless suffering, so many lost friends and grim communiqués. They had grown to love and to hate this steppe. Over a hundred days. And at last the offensive had started.

Millions had prepared for this moment. In the rear, drilling soldiers had stormed heights, crossed fields, and lain flat in hollows. In the factories women with pallid faces, as if the war had squeezed the life out of them, had worked like mad. Weary engine drivers had driven heavily laden trains under a hail of bombs. Sappers had trained to clear passages through mine fields. Logs had been accumulated for future river crossings. Curly-haired traffic girls were prepared for roads on which the Germans were still strutting. Cases of canned food, cots for the wounded, fuel tanks, felt snow boots, thousands of maps. The Generals, Colonel Ignatov, Osip—all pored over maps on which the positions of the enemy's divisions and regiments were marked. They knew where the Italians were, the Rumanians, the Germans; and what kind of Germans—fresh or battered, SS men or reserves. They knew that the Italians in the Ravenna Division were asking: "Why have we come here?" and that the German Seventy-First Division had come from Reims. Intelligence knew the names of the Reichswehr generals, the German second echelons, read letters in which Lieutenant Schmidt informed his wife that all leaves had been stopped. Editors of Front, Army, and Divisional newspapers prepared special issues calling for the "decisive blow." Political instructors read aloud from diaries of the German butchers; tested hearts as a mechanic tests a motor. A top-rank general who suffered from a liver ailment made a tour of the positions, concealing from the others that he had just had an attack.

Colonel Ignatov said to Osip: "At six nought-nought." Stalin, his pupils dilated from lack of sleep, pored over the map. He had to foresee that some German generals would favor retreat while others would oppose it, that Field Marshal Fritz Erich von Mannstein, with many tanks at his command, would prove a pedant; he had to foresee everything, from late rains to an early ice-break, to the influence of the moon, blunders, and accident.

In the meanwhile the battalion now under Osip's command was subjected to hurricane fire, repulsed German attacks, counterattacked to avoid being pushed back. Few were left of those who on that sultry August day had first seen this cheerless place. Here lay buried Lieutenant Zarubin, anti-tank gunners Shapovalov, Zagvozdev, Magaradze, Butenko, Brodsky and many others.

All was ready, and it started exactly on time. For the men of the battalion it started at the first gun pit in which the historical scout Lubimov, ex-barber at the Sochi sanatorium, killed two Germans with the butt of his rifle. When Minayev, seriously·this time, said "a historical moment," Lubimov turned away in disgust.

What was sometimes called the "romance of war"—the hazard of the game, love of danger, unhabitual mode of life—marches, campfires, tents in the forest, living without women, with that constant longing for a woman that was like an unbearable itch, with tender letters and coarse oaths—all this was nothing to Osip. He dreamed of the day when the war would end and it would be possible to work, to build, to organize; he longed for home life; he admired Raya, but when he looked at her sniper photograph he would sigh: to think that a woman like that should be fighting; that's what the Germans have done! He hated the Germans also for the fact that they had marred the life of a little child—torn Alya from her mother for a year, maybe years. For him the war was a disgusting disease which the people's body must overcome. This, perhaps, explains why Osip became so friendly with his men who, like him, longed for their families and hated the Germans for, among other things, turning their lives upside down. Speaking of their commander the men said: "He understands."

The attack was hard going. It was said things were easier on the right where the Rumanians were. The Germans were putting up a desperate resistance. The advance was slow, and at the cost of heavy casualties. The men were tired and glum, but within them flickered the hope: it was in earnest this time.

Minayev the jokester, asserted: "The Germans deliberately aban-

doned the Rumanians—they have no time for music now"; laughed
over the reports about the war in Africa: "The Bey of Algiers got a
bump on the the head long ago."

A few days later things came easier: they had only Rumanians
against them. Minayev gave out slips of paper bearing the inscription: such and such a number of fiddlers for dispatch to P.O.W.
camp—he couldn't bother to send a convoy with them! The
Rumanians cheerfully marched off to the rear and Minayev exclaimed in admiration: "Look at them! Merry as if they were hurrying to a wedding."

Later, forty Germans headed by a lieutenant, put up their hands.
This was something new. But there was no time to ponder over it.
The Seventh Department will deal with them; they dabble in psy-
choanalysis there.

A railway station. Hundreds of railway cars—German, French,
Belgian, Polish, Czech—pale lions, crowns, tricolor cockades and a
brand new black eagle. The whole of Europe had come rolling to
this cheerless steppe. Automobiles of every make; cases of French
wine, sardines, asparagus, chocolate, cigarette lighters; a dead
German gazing down the long road with his one remaining eye, and
tears in that eye.

There will be no mail for a long time. Minayev reread an old
letter from his mother and said to Osip:

"My little mother is always inventing something. Now it's a cage
to put Hitler in and exhibit him in all countries. Imagine what the
English would do if they heard of it. They'd form a Society for the
Protection of Hitler."

Osip managed to write a letter to Raya: *"Everything is going
splendidly out here as you'll soon read in the newspapers. I've never
been in better health, I'm only anxious about you. Rayechka, I was
never able to tell you the most important thing, I'm incapable of
formulating it, but believe me, I don't forget you for a moment. I'm
anxious about Mama and Alya. I'm told the climate where they are
is hard for those unaccustomed to it. Send me Mama's letters. I ardently embrace my dear sergeant!"*

Ignatov summoned Osip. "We must dig in now. The Fritzes will
try to break through, they have no alternative."

He told his orderly to bring some champagne. "Trophies from
France. I've never tasted it before, let's try it. We've got something
to drink to."

He drew his finger over the map. "This is the horseshoe."

When Osip got back to the battalion Minayev gasped with astonishment: "Where did you get the vodka?"

"Vodka, nothing! It's champagne. Do you know what's happened. We've encircled them!"

"I said you were drunk! What're you talking about? How can they be encircled; they pulled back four miles yesterday."

"I don't mean those opposite us, I mean their whole army! It's absolutely true. I can't get over it myself."

Usually cool and dispassionate, he flung his arms around Minayev's neck. And Minayev, laughing with joy, said: "My little mother was right. We'll put him in a cage!"

RETURN TO KIEV

Osip was smiling, everything delighted him—especially the fact that they were drawing near to Kiev. Sometimes the Germans retreated so hurriedly they had no time to burn the houses and drive off the inhabitants. In living villages, girls with roguish and tender eyes, and hospitable housewives, who regaled their guests with homebrew, cream and boiled pumpkin, told them how the mighty Germans had begun to sigh and pray to God.

One old woman kept making the sign of the cross at the passing tanks, artillery, and trucks. She said: "They keep on coming and coming, and the Germans said the Russians had no soldiers." Yesterday's "sons-in-law" now claimed to be partisans. The genuine partisans came out of the forests, and gazing at them, Osip felt his eyes moist with affection.

Then came the areas of German devastation; glare of burning villages. It was difficult to breathe. Osip saw felled apple trees, their leaves, which had not yet had time to fade, still trembling on their branches. Osip turned away, heartsick at that blind human fury.

Wounded Sergeant Seletsky refused to go to the battalion hospital base; he said to Osip: "I want to drive them out." That's what everybody was living for now—to drive them out.

Minayev had never seen Osip in such a mood. They were celebrating the anniversary of the October Revolution and the capture of Kiev. Chaly, editor of the divisional paper, told a funny story: "One American asked another: Why are the Russians such good fighters. The second American answered: 'It's easy for them— they're not afraid of the Reds.'" Then they danced and sang. Osip recalled Kiev, and suddenly, without preface, he told Minayev:

"When I first became acquainted with my wife we went to a concert. We were listening to the orchestra, when she bent over toward me and asked: 'Do you recognize it?' I didn't know anything about music, but I was ashamed to confess it, so I answered: 'Yes.' During the intermission she asked me: 'Well, what was that piece they were playing?' It was something lively—so I said Carmen. 'You have a wonderful ear, you have!' she said. Actually, it was Beethoven, some symphony or other. How was I to know? But it upset me. When I got home I had a look at myself in the glass—she was right, my ears were nothing to boast about. I had just had my hair cut, and they were sticking out something awful. Of course, I knew that Raya did not mean that, but I went and asked my mother: are my ears normal ears or not? My mother answered: 'They're like your father's.' Later, after we were married, I told Raya about it and she teased me for years afterward. She doesn't write often. I can't force myself to write either, and things are easier for me. She's a sergeant, her conditions are different. But I'm homesick. Anything for a peep at Kiev! We're near it. But my people aren't there. They went away with the evacuees."

Later Minayev said to Olga: "He's a fine chap. It took me some time to learn what he was like. He used to get on my nerves. He'd speak in quotations; if I talked about cabbages he'd come on with dialectics. But you mustn't think he's just a dry stick, he's not. It's his nature. I, for example, go into raptures, but he's shy. Do you know why a tortoise has a shell? Because it has a sensitive body."

Olga said: "He's a nice man, but unhappy."

"Unhappy? Did you see how he cut up yesterday?"

She smiled, but said obstinately: "He was gay, but still, he's unhappy."

About ten days later Osip's dream came true. They were transferred to the Zhitomir highroad and he saw Kiev. But he was amazed—the Kiev of his memories was not there. Dark ruins loomed through the cold rain. Before him lay not Kiev, but war. . . .

He walked to Saksagansky Street. To his delight he saw that the house he had lived in was still standing. He knocked at his neighbors', the Yakovenkos. Yakovenko was in the army. Their daughter Ninochka had been sent away to work by the Germans. Only Mrs. Yakovenko and her lame daughter Glasha remained.

"Sit down in this armchair. I have nothing to treat you to, we became very poor under the Germans." Then she began to weep.

"I'm thinking of your mother. Poor woman, she came to me and said: 'They're sending us away. Please keep an eye on our things until my children come back.' We didn't know then what those beasts were up to. Later Ninochka said: 'They've slaughtered them all, the children too.' Whenever I hear Babi Yar mentioned I can't keep back my tears. They gave your room to a rat who kept nosing around to see who could be sent to Germany. He did my Ninochka in."

Osip sat motionless; his face expressed such grief that Mrs. Yakovenko stopped talking and Glasha ran into the kitchen and burst into sobs.

Going down the stairs the thought occurred to Osip: Perhaps she's got it all mixed up? Raya had written that they had gone with the evacuees. He knocked at the Kulikovs'. An old woman opened the door.

"I'm Alpert. Have you seen my mother?"

His tone was despairing. Mrs. Kulikov thought that he was accusing her. She cried: "We couldn't do a thing. Do you think they consulted us?"

"All I'm asking you is: did you see my mother and my little daughter?"

"I saw them the evening before they were taken away."

He went toward Babi Yar. His mind was a blank, he was not yet fully conscious of the immensity of his bereavement; he breathed with difficulty; he heard nothing; he just walked on and on. A thought flashed through his mind: how long Lvov Street is! He did not know that that very thought had passed through his mother's mind going to her death with Alyenka.

Not a soul was about. Suddenly a man with the bleary eyes of a drunkard emerged from a hovel. Osip hailed him: "Where's Babi Yar?"

"Turn to the right and you'll see it. I suppose you have relatives there. Other soldiers have passed here and asked. Only, you won't find anything. When the Germans started to clear out, they had a lot of war prisoners dig everything up to leave no trace. They burned the corpses day and night; it was impossible to breathe."

He reached Babi Yar. In places it was no longer a yar (ravine), it had been filled in. Sand, ashes, small, charred bones. Osip went down on his knees and pressed his face to the cold, wet sand.

Darkness had set in, but he could not tear himself away. He now thought of Raya, of the love which had prompted her to the white lie. She had taken the whole burden of grief upon herself to save his peace of mind.

How long we lived together, and yet I did not know the woman

she was. I was surprised when she went to the front, fearing neither
a soldier's life nor death. What must she, the mother, have felt
writing me about Alya?

And thinking of Raya, life triumphed. It is possible to kill a
defenseless person and, in fear of retribution, burn the body, scatter
the ashes and put the witnesses out of the way; but it is impossible
to kill the loftiest thing in man—love. Raya proved stronger than
the murderers.

Two days later he wrote to Raya:

*"Raya, my darling Raya, forgive me for having tormented you
with questions. I know everything now. I have been to Babi Yar.
Raya, we two must live through this, words will not help either of
us, but I want to take you by the hand and say—we two are alone,
a terrible thing has happened, but you and I will live, we will forget
nothing, we will live with this thing in our hearts. I now know the
strength of your character. I don't know how many were killed in
Kiev, they say seventy thousand, but figures convey nothing, they
killed human beings. This cannot be forgiven. My darling, be
strong! After what I have lived through in Babi Yar I am not afraid
of words, I want to say we two are bound together forever, and that
is stronger than death. Osip."*

When Minayev saw Osip, he guessed at once that something had
happened. Several days later, Osip said: "Both my mother and
Alya. In Babi Yar."

In the ensuing weeks it looked as though the spirit of the Germans
had revived. The German Command had replaced the battered
divisions with divisions brought from the West.

Their counteroffensive opened successfully; after fierce fighting
the Germans forced their way into Zhitomir and advanced on Kiev.
The Divisional Commander, General Zykov, ordered Osip to hold.
The general said: "The chief thing is the shovel."

Minayev reported to Osip that all was quiet on his sector, except
that "they were hammering away as they did on that mound, they've
gone crazy." Communication with Polishchuk was cut, but a signal-
man managed to crawl through from that sector to report that the
Germans had reached the trenches but had been swept back; the
Third Battalion was standing fast. At a quarter past ten, seven
Tigers approached the mound where Staff Headquarters were situated. The Divisional Commander called Osip to the telephone.
"How is it at your end?"

"We're holding. Twenty-six tanks passed through Leonidze's sector. Seven Tigers here, outside the line. The Katyushas are having a go at them."

Two Tigers were wrecked, the rest veered to the right against Polishchuk, whose battalion retreated. After the tanks a wave of infantry forced Minayev to retreat. By nightfall the regimental staff and two companies were surrounded. Osip smiled grimly: like 1941; instead of a regiment, I'll have to command two companies. They held on for twenty-four hours. Osip received a concussion, his head ached and he wanted to vomit. A tank attack was repulsed with incendiary bottles. Toward the end of the day self-propelled guns, dispatched by the General, and Minayev's battalion broke through to the Headquarters. Osip went off to Leonidze's sector to cheer up the men. Next morning the battalion launched a counterattack and recovered a small village. Osip reported to General Zykov: all points had been recovered, except that Polishchuk had yet to retake a farm —it stood on an eminence and was a good position. But Polishchuk had sustained heavy losses. If the reserve battalion were. . . .

"What's the matter with you?" the general asked. "You're not looking so well."

"I had a concussion. It's not serious."

"Take a nap for an hour or two."

"No. I'll go and see Polishchuk."

"Wait, have a bite first."

As the general poured out the vodka, he saw that Osip was asleep. Hell, how worn out the men are! A little later, though he had not slept for three nights, Osip jumped up and went off to Polishchuk.

Fierce fighting raged another four days: attack and counterattack. The Germans gave up thoughts of Kiev. Osip slept six hours, got up, washed in ice-cold water—the frost had set in—and then suddenly felt anxious: why no letters from Raya? He wrote to her: alive and well, waiting for letters—"my whole life centers in you now."

—Translated by J. Feinberg

IV

****

ASIA

****

CHINA · 1059

INDIA · 1078

LIN YUTANG

****

*Lin Yutang, who has written several books in an effort to tell
"exactly how he feels about China," and is now concluding some
years of work on one in which he is telling how America appears to
a Chinese, has written a number of essays which his friend Pearl
Buck has described as "short and pungent pieces . . . an instinctive
expression of the working of his mind, glancing, darting, penetrating, laughing. . . ." When Dr. Lin selected this piece, from a book
of such pieces, he said he felt it needed no explanatory comment, it
expressed his thoughts as much then as when he wrote it several
years ago. Besides, he said, he was busy in New York inventing a
Chinese typewriter. When the book was put to press, another effort
was made to see if Dr. Lin cared to make any belated comment, but
by then the learned doctor was somewhere in France busy composing another book, indicating that with him the Importance of Living
Is Writing Itself, as well as Living, and, for the time being, he was
not answering the mail.*

****

The End of Living is Living Itself

IN THE PROGRESS of human civilization the arts of living and the
arts of killing—artcraft and warcraft—have always existed side by
side. No history of any nation shows that a period of peace without
domestic or foreign wars ever existed for more than 300 years. This
seems to derive from the fact that man is both a fighting and a
peaceful animal. In him the fighting instinct and the instinct for
peaceful living—which I call the carnivorous and the herbivorous
instincts—are strangely mixed.

This is not to imply a state of human imperfection; it may be
questioned whether the kind of civilization wherein man is so
thoroughly tamed and domesticated that there is no more fight left
in him would be worth having at all. Life is, or should be, accompanied by struggle, or else the racial fiber degenerates, which hap-

pens within the amazingly short period of a few generations as in a well-provided family.

I am not trying to condone war, but am merely pointing out our biological heritage. In the world of nature the warring instinct and the instinct to live are different aspects of the same thing. Those primeval biological instincts go deeper than any temporary ideologies or political creeds. In the biological world merciless wars have always existed side by side with the most persistent displays of love for the young and all those manifestations of courtship which produce beauty and which we know as the charm and fragrance of the flower, the caroling of the lark, and the song of the cricket.

If it is somewhat disheartening to the student of nature that the most ruthless war is going on above ground and underground day and night in what is apparently a peaceful forest, or to reflect that the kingfisher sitting on a branch so peacefully in a sunset has just returned from murder of an innocent minnow, it is also a source of comfort to know that nature's instinct to live is always overpowering and manages to stage a most impressive comeback after a natural disaster. Anybody who visited the coasts of Long Island Sound and saw the green trees and peaceful landscapes after the disastrous hurricane of the autumn before, cannot help being impressed by nature's persistent urge to live.

Today, once more, Europe is ravaged by war. To every observer war seemed inevitable after Munich, because peace was so much like war that, to the average Frenchman or Englishman, a temporary peace seemed infinitely more devastating. . . . To add to the confusion the fighting man still parades as a lover of peace, and aggressors accuse their victims as "warmongers."

What is the meaning of all this? Has man's instinct for peaceful living been temporarily inhibited, overshadowed, and perhaps destroyed by the warring instinct? And will civilization—meaning the arts, the religions, the common faiths of mankind, the modern conquests of science, and the arts of living—will this modern civilization be destroyed? Let us take up the second proposition first.

Many people are horrified by the thought of great cities demolished by air bombing, and many foremost thinkers of today are rather inclined to believe that modern civilization as we know it will be destroyed. I beg profoundly to differ.

Knowing that the warring instinct is but another aspect of the instinct for living, and believing that no man going to battle has ever renounced the desire to live, I think the instinct for living is the stronger of the two and hence cannot be destroyed. Since that instinct cannot be destroyed, civilization, too, or the arts of living, cannot be destroyed. What do we mean when we say that by this war modern civilization will be destroyed?

Physically the arts and sciences may receive a temporary setback, but I wager that after the war hens will still lay eggs and men will still not have forgotten how to make omelettes. Sheep will still grow wool and English mills will still turn out tweeds and homespuns. The physical features of a city may be altered under the most ruthless bombing, and conceivably some old manuscripts or even the Magna Carta, in the British Museum, may be lost or go up in flames. Some English poets and French scientists may have been killed by shrapnel and some valuable laboratory equipment, or even all of Oxford, may be wiped out. Still, the underground Bodleian Library cannot be destroyed. Still, the scientific method will survive; it is inconceivable that all treatises and textbooks of science will disappear. Gramophone records and Chopin's music will still be there, because the love for music will still be there.

The quality of manhood may suffer perceptibly from the slaughter of the flower of the nation. But so long as a nation is not completely annihilated with the worst aerial bombings, modern civilization and all the heritage of the arts and the sciences will be carried on. After war and destruction the generous instinct for peaceful living, the creative forces of human ingenuity will restore Europe in an amazingly short period.

The lesson seems plain that mere physical violence never accomplishes anything. China provides a good example. The destruction of Chinese schools, universities, and cultural institutions by the Japanese in the present war could never be more systematic, more thorough and more physically complete. Yet it would be far-fetched to say that modern Chinese culture is thereby destroyed. The professors and students of a university in Chekiang marched a thousand miles overland from the southeast and reopened their classes in Southwest Yunnan.

Nothing is lost if man is not lost. Devotees of China's ancient culture may express an exquisite regret that the world's only extant imperial library of Yunglo was burned during the sack of Peking by English and French troops in 1859. But what of it for the Chinese nation as a whole? The most ruthless destruction of Confucian books and persecution of Confucianists under the dictator Ch'in Shihhwang (builder of the Great Wall) failed to destroy the Confucian culture.

This leads to the subtler, nonphysical aspects of the question and the positive side of human living. Modern civilization would be destroyed if the things that make for civilization, the things we take for granted—freedom of belief, the rights and liberties of the individual, democracy, and that now tottering faith in the common man—if these things were destroyed. Without war, a totalitarian State which deprives men of these gifts of civilization and sets men as spies upon their fellow men has already begun to destroy civilization. With a nation not so easily regimented, where the spirit of man still remains free, that civilization cannot be destroyed by a war.

It is, in fact, entirely possible for civilization to destroy itself by subordinating the instinct for peaceful living to the other instinct for killing. Civilizaton can be destroyed unless these simple values of human life are more jealously guarded and the simple liberties and privileges of living are more consciously appreciated. There is every sign of the danger that in contemporary thinking and contemporary life such common privileges of living are increasingly giving way to the claims of the State-monster. The citizen of a totalitarian State in Europe has already lost certain privileges and liberties of thinking and living which the savages of Africa have always enjoyed and are still enjoying.

In fact, we have already traveled a long way from civilization as ordinarily understood. All nature loafs. Then civilization came, offering man certain comforts of living in exchange for certain restrictions of liberty, generally called a sense of duty. No horse has a sense of duty, and every carrier-pigeon flies home just because he likes it. But man was put to work.

First, he was told to work for a living. Next he was told to war for a living in defense of his right to work. And then we were told to put guns before butter and regard it as a nobler form of death to die with one's army boots on than with one's boots off in bed. We are going back to nature without the natural liberties of nature. Man has ration cards and a sense of duty. A million automatons, completely trained and regimented to think in one direction, either curse or praise the Soviet Union as their master tells them to do.

And so what threatens civilization is not war itself or the destruction of war but the changing conceptions of life values entailed by certain types of political doctrines. These doctrines directly impinge upon man's ordinary, natural privileges of living and subordinate them to the needs of national killing. The importance of killing supersedes the importance of living, from the totalitarian standpoint.

It cannot be denied that from the point of view of the State, organized for war and conquest, totalitarianism has everything to be said for it, but from the standpoint of the individual as the ultimate aim served by civilization, and for the purpose of enjoying the ordinary blessings of living, it has nothing to be said on its side. It is neither the machine nor war that is destroying modern civilization but the tendency to surrender the rights of the individual to the State which is such a powerful factor in contemporary thinking.

The Roman Empire was probably destroyed by rats or by mosquitoes and ultimately by a deterioration in manhood. Modern civilization can possibly be destroyed by the kind of peace that causes a similar racial deterioration, either in the physical sense, as Professor Hooton suggests, or in the spiritual sense of loss of ordinary human liberties. Physically the twentieth-century man wearing a gas-mask snout is horrifying enough to frighten a caveman; spiritually, in certain countries, I doubt that he is more respectable to look at.

The contempt for the common man has gone far enough. In a totalitarian world Whitman's "Song of the Open Road" will read like a forgotten dream.

> Afoot and light-hearted I take to the
>   open road,
> Healthy, free, the world before me,
> The long brown path before me leading
>   wherever I choose.

And his warning will not be lost:

> O highway I travel, do you say to me,
>   *Do not leave me?*
> Do you say, *Venture not—if you leave
>   me you are lost?*

Only by recapturing that dream of human freedom and restoring the value and importance of the common man's rights and liberties of living can that undermining threat to modern civilization be averted. More than ever I believe that the Great Vagabond who proudly refuses to give up an inch of his liberties will be the savior of the world.

I started out by saying that the warring instinct and the instinct for peaceful living are different aspects of the same thing. It is seldom realized that the volunteer who enlists to go to the front is as much following an instinct for new venture upon the open road as the more noble desire to seek death at the cannon's mouth.

It is not a true picture of war at the front to say that the soldier is more excited by the capture of an enemy than by the capture of a stray chicken for the evening meal. The exact reverse is true. Out there on the open road one suddenly realizes that the gift of life is all the more precious, that life is all the sweeter in the presence of death. Out in the trenches people do not brood over their enemies until they get up enough hatred to go out and kill the enemy.

An amateur poet reads his newly inspired limerick at the expense of the field rat or the village maiden; a corporal smokes his pipe and says not a word, while the company listens to the reading of an old novel, perhaps of Bulwer-Lytton, by a comrade; a white-faced, sensitive young man of eighteen comes in with his amazing discovery of violets in the neighboring battered village; someone takes a guitar and sings. At the front the caroling of the lark in the sky and the song of the cricket underground seem more enchanting, more appreciated.

All of a sudden the soldier sees the great naked truth that life is worth living for its own sake. As he looks back upon the people living in the rear, silly common aspects of ordinary living assume an exaggerated importance and a strange fascination. In the first flush of war excitement a volunteer may jump into his khaki shirt and uniform with glee, but after two or three years in the trenches, wearing a red tie and walking with one's sweetheart leisurely of a Sunday afternoon seem to be the only things worth living for. The importance of wearing a red tie is fully appreciated when you cannot wear it. To the soldier returning on leave the most common sights of city or country life—a hot-dog stand, the neon lights at night, even the traffic lights—seem good and reassuring. Even being a lazy louse lying in bed without the hallucination of the reveille seems to constitute an august virtue and a permanent achievement of human civilization.

In fact, one suddenly realizes that all the good things of life—the morning coffee, fresh air, a stroll in the afternoon, even dashing for the subway or dodging friends among commuters in the morning train—constitute civilization because they constitute the very end of living. War makes us realize the importance of things we ordinarily take for granted. No one values a luxurious shave in a barber shop more than a soldier returning from the front.

That the end of living is just living itself is so obvious that we never thought of it, and in times of peace we even question it.

Moralists, for example, seem to despise the act of lying in bed, and theologians used to think that to be uncomfortable was to be virtuous. But in the soldier at the front the conviction must sooner or later grow that lying in bed is one of the supreme gifts of civilization and that to sleep with one's boots off is an incomparably truer form of living than sleeping with one's boots on.

HU SHIH

****

NEW YORK CITY
MAY 28TH, 1949

This essay in English was written in 1927 and first published in 1928 as a chapter in a symposium on the future of modern civilization edited by the late Professor Charles A. Beard under the title, Whither Mankind. *I have selected this piece (with few deletions, minor changes, and some added foot-notes) for several reasons.*

First, because it was based chiefly on an original Chinese essay which I had published in June 1926, and which embodied some of my conclusions drawn from years of observation and thinking. Those conclusions were strengthened by my trip to Europe in 1926 and to the United States in 1927.

In the second place, because this essay expresses a philosophical position distinct and free from the usual "pose" of apologetic writers from the Orient.

And lastly, because I sincerely believe that the central theme of the essay—an eulogistic appraisal of the modern civilization of Science, Technology and Democracy—may still deserve some attention at the present time. Professor Beard's symposium appeared exactly a year before the stock-market crash of October, 1929. In his preface, Beard announced that "the volume as a whole rejects the pessimistic views of writers like Chesterton, Belloc, and Spengler," and that "for visions of despair, it substitutes a more cheerful outlook upon the future of modern civilization."

The years of the Depression and of the Second World War may seem to many to have vindicated the pessimists. But have they been really vindicated? As I reread these pages on one of the darkest mornings in the history of my own people, I am still inclined to agree with my optimistic views of twenty-one years ago. I do not recant my main thesis in this essay. So here, with the permission of the editor, will it stand as my renewed and considered tribute to this modern civilization of scientific and technological progress and democratic control of power.

HU SHIH

****

The Civilizations of the East and West

IN RECENT YEARS the despondent mood of a number of European writers has led to the revival of such old myths as the bankruptcy of the material civilization of the West and the superiority of the spiritual civilization of the Oriental nations. When I was in Germany last year, a German savant most solemnly assured me that the civilization of the East was based on spiritual principles. "In the East," said my enthusiastic friend, "even souls are selected on the basis of moral fitness. For does not the doctrine of the transmigration of souls imply the idea of moral selection?" Although these expressions represent nothing more than the pathological mentality of war-stricken Europe, they have already had the unfortunate effect of gratifying the vanity of Oriental apologists and thereby strengthening the hand of reaction in the East. In the West, too, one could see, as I have seen during my recent travels, that such loose thinking was leading not a few people away from a proper understanding of their own civilization which is fast becoming the world civilization. It is in the hope of furnishing a new point of view and a new basis of discussion that I now offer these few reflections on the civilizations of the East and the West.

I

AS A TRUE CHINESE, I must begin with Confucius. According to Confucius, all implements of civilization are spiritual in origin: they all come from "ideas." "When conceived, they are called ideas. When materially embodied, they are called implements. When instituted for general use, they are called forms or patterns. When wrought into the everyday life of all the people, they marvel at them and call them the work of the gods."* Confucius cited many examples to illustrate this point of view. Man saw wood floating on water and invented ships; he saw wood submerged under water and, caring for the preservation of the bodies of his dead parents, invented coffins and tombs. He saw rain fall from the heavens and, thinking probably of the work of time obliterating all traces of human memory, invented writing to take the place of knotted cords.

* The Book of Change, *Chapter 11 of Appendix I, traditionally attributed to Confucius.*

Needless to say, this view of Confucius was supported by Plato and Aristotle in the West. Human tools and institutions had their origin in the "ideas" or ideal patterns which Aristotle called the "formal causes." Confucius and Plato and Aristotle lived in those good old days when the human mind was not yet troubled by the medieval dualism of matter and spirit and was therefore able to recognize the ideality underlying the material embodiment of human inventions.

Indeed there is no such thing as a purely material civilization. Every tool of civilization is produced by human intelligence making use of the matter and energy in the natural world for the satisfaction of a want, a desire, an esthetic feeling or an intellectual curiosity. A clay pot is no more material than a love lyric; nor is St. Paul's Cathedral less material than the Woolworth Building. Indeed when man first made fire by accidentally drilling wood, the invention was regarded as such a spiritual thing as to be attributed to one of the greatest gods. In the East, all the legendary kings of China were not priest-philosophers, but inventors. Such, for example, were Sui-jen, the discoverer of fire, You-tsao, the first builder of houses, and Shen-nung, the first teacher of agriculture and medicine.

Our forefathers were quite right in deifying the creators of tools. Man is a tool-making animal, and it is tool-making which constitutes civilization. The invention of fire created a new epoch in the history of human civilization; agriculture, another; the invention of writing, a third; printing, a fourth. It was the inventon of the telescope and the steam-engine and the discovery of electricity and radioactivity that have made the modern world what it is today. And if the priests of the Medieval Age were justly canonized as saints, Galileo, Watt, Stephenson, Morse, Bell, Edison, and Ford certainly deserve to be honored as gods and enshrined with Prometheus and Cadmus. They represent that which is most divine in man, namely, that creative intelligence which provides implements and makes civilization possible.

The civilization of a race is simply the sum-total of its achievement in adjusting itself to its environment. Success or failure in that adjustment depends upon the ability of the race to use intelligence for the invention of necessary and effective tools. Advancement in civilization depends upon the improvement of tools. Such terms as the Stone Age, the Bronze Age, the Iron Age and the Steam and Electricity Age tell the tale of the development of civilization. And what is true of the historical development of civilization, is no less true of the geographical distribution of the different civilizations. The difference between the Eastern and Western civilizations is primarily a difference in the tools used. The West has during the last two hundred years moved far ahead of the East merely because certain Western nations have been able to devise new tools for the conquest of nature and for the multiplication of the power to do work. The East, whence have come a number of the epoch-making tools of ancient civilization, has failed to carry on that great tradition and is left behind in the stage of manual labor while the Western world has long entered the age of steam and electricity.

This, then, is the real difference between the Oriental and the Western civilizations. The Oriental civilization is built primarily on human labor as the source of power whereas the modern civilization of the West is built on the basis of the power of machinery. As one of my American friends has put it, "each man, woman and child in America possesses from twenty-five to thirty mechanical slaves, while it is estimated that each man, woman and child in China has at his command but three quarters of one mechanical slave."* An American engineer has stated the case in almost the same language: "Every person in the United States has thirty-five invisible slaves working for him. . . . The American workman is not a wage slave, but a boss of a considerable force, whether he realizes it or not."** Herein lies the real explanation of the difference between the two civilizations. It is a difference in degree which in the course of time has almost amounted to a difference in kind.

II

In July, 1926, I arrived at Harbin, in Northern Manchuria, on my way to Europe. The modern city of Harbin was formerly a Russian Concession which grew up from a small trading center into what is now called the "Shanghai of North China." With the development of the Russian Concession, there grew up, a few miles away, the native city of Harbin which was once only a group of peasant villages. While I was touring through the city, I was struck by one interesting fact: whereas practically all the vehicles of locomotion in the native city were jinrickshas, or carriages pulled by human power, no 'ricksha was allowed to operate in the former Russian

* Julian Arnold, *"Some Bigger Issues in China's Problems,"* The Commercial Press, Shanghai.
** Thomas T. Read, *"The American Secret,"* The Atlantic Monthly, March, 1927.

City which, though now under Chinese administration, still retained much of Russian influence and tradition. Transportation and traveling in the modern city of Harbin were by tramways and taxicabs; 'rickshas carrying passengers from the native city must leave without a fare.

Here I made my great discovery in modern geography—I discovered the borderline between the Eastern and Western civilizations. The city of Harbin separates the East from the West by separating the jinricksha (man-power-carriage) civilization from the motor-car civilization!

Let all apologists for the spiritual civilization of the East reflect on this. What spirituality is there in a civilization which tolerates such a terrible form of human slavery as the 'ricksha coolie? Do we seriously believe that there can be any spiritual life left in those poor human beasts of burden who run and toil and sweat under that peculiar bondage of slavery which knows neither the minimum wage nor any limit of working hours? Do we really believe that the life of a 'ricksha coolie is more spiritual or more moral than that of the American workman who rides to and from his work in his own motor-car, who takes his whole family out picnicking on Sundays in distant parks and woods, who listens to the best music of the land on the radio for almost no cost, and whose children are educated in schools equipped with the most modern library and laboratory facilities?

It is only when one has fully realized what misery and acute suffering the life of 'ricksha-pulling entails and what effects it produces on the bodily health of those human beasts of burden—it is only then that one will be truly and religiously moved to bless the Hargreaveses, the Cartwrights, the Watts, the Fultons, the Stephensons, and the Fords who have devised machines to do the work for man and relieve him from much of the brutal suffering to which his Oriental neighbor is still subject.

Herein, therefore, lies the real spirituality of the material civilization, of mechanical progress *per se*. Mechanical progress means the use of human intelligence to devise tools and machines to multiply the working ability and productivity of man so that he may be relieved from the fate of toiling incessantly with his unaided hands, feet and back without being able to earn a bare subsistence, and so that he may have enough time and energy left to seek and enjoy the higher values which civilization can offer him. Where man has to sweat blood in order to earn the lowest kind of livelihood, there is little *life* left, letting alone civilization. A civilization to be worthy of its name must be built upon the foundation of material progress. As the Chinese statesman Kuan Chung (died 645 B.C.) said twenty-six centuries ago, "When food and clothing are sufficiently provided for, honor and disgrace can be distinguished; and when granaries are full, the people will know good manners." This is not to drag in the so-called economic interpretation of history: it is simple commonsense. Picture a civilization where boys and girls and old women with bamboo baskets tied to their backs and with pointed sticks in hand, flock to every dumping place of refuse and search for a possible torn piece of rag or a half-burnt piece of coal. How can we expect a moral and spiritual civilization to grow up in such an atmosphere?

Then people may point to the religious life in those regions where the material civilization is low. What spirituality is there, let us say, in the old beggar-woman who dies in the direst destitution, but who dies while still mumbling, '*Namo Amita Buddha!*'* and in the clear conviction that she will surely enter that blissful paradise presided over by the Amita Buddha? Do we earnestly think it moral or spiritual to inculcate in that beggar-woman a false belief which shall so hypnotize her as to make her willingly live and die in such dire conditions where she ought not to have been had she been born in a different civilization?

No! All those hypnotic religions belong to an age when man had reached senility and felt himself impotent in coping with the forces of nature. Therefore he gave up the fight in despair and, like the disappointed fox in the ancient fable who declared the grapes sour because he could not reach them, began to console himself and teach the world that wealth and comfort are contemptible and that poverty and misery are something to be proud of. From this it was only a step to the idea that life itself was not worth living and that the only desirable thing was the blissful existence in the world beyond. And when wise men calmly taught these ideas, fanatics went further and practised self-denial, self-torture, and even suicide. In the West, saints prayed, fasted, slept on pillars, and whipped themselves at regular intervals. In medieval China, monks prayed, fasted, and, feeding themselves daily with fragrant oil and tying their bodies with oiled cloth, gladly burned themselves to death as offerings to some deity of Mahayana Buddhism.

It took over a thousand years for a portion of mankind to emerge from the civilization which glorifies poverty and sanctifies disease,

---

* *This sentence, meaning "Homage to the Amita Buddha," is daily recited by followers of the Paradise (Pure Land) Sect of Buddhism.*

and slowly build up a new civilization which glorifies life and combats poverty as a crime. As we look around today, the religions of the Middle Ages are still there, the churches and cathedrals are still there, the monasteries and nunneries are still there. How is it that the outlook upon life has so radically changed? The change has come because in the last two centuries men have hit upon a few key-inventions out of which a vast number of tools and machines have been constructed for the control of the resources and powers in nature. By means of these machines men have been able to save labor and reduce distance, to fly in the air, tunnel the mountains and sail underneath the deep seas, to enslave lightning to pull our carriages and employ "ether" to deliver our messages throughout the world. Science and machinery seem to meet no resistance from nature. Life has become easier and happier, and man's confidence in his own powers has greatly increased. Man has become the master of himself and of his own destiny. Thus a revolutionary poet sings:

> I fight alone, and win or sink,
> I need no one to make me free;
> I want no Jesus Christ to think
> That he could ever die for me.*

Thus the new civilization of the new age has given to men a new religion, the religion of self-reliance as contrasted with the religion of defeatism of the Middle Ages.

III

I BEGAN by pointing out the spirituality of the most material phase of modern Western civilization, namely, its technological phase. Modern technology is highly spiritual because it seeks, through human ingenuity and intelligence, to relieve human energy from the unnecessary hardships of life and provide for it the necessary conditions for the enjoyment of life. Whatever be the use man may make of the resultant comfort and leisure, the relief of suffering and hardship is in itself spiritual.

I shall now try to show the spirituality of the other phases of the Western civilization. I shall leave out art, music, and literature, for it is evident to all that the West has its art and literature which are at least comparable with those found in the East, and its music

* Proem, in "Arrows in the Gale," by Arturo Giovannitti, 1914.

which is certainly far more advanced than any which the Oriental countries can boast.

Let us begin with Science. Whatever may be our divergent views regarding the exact definition of the life of the spirit, probably no one today will deny that the desire to know is one of the legitimate spiritual demands of mankind. Yet practically all the older civilizations have tried to suppress this intellectual longing of man. According to the Book of Genesis, the Fall of Man was caused, not by Woman, but by the acquisition of Knowledge. Most of the Oriental religions taught such slogans as "No knowledge, no desire"; "Know nothing and follow the plan of God"; "Abandon wisdom and shun sagacity." A great sage of the East, Chuang Tzu, declared: "Life is finite and knowledge is infinite. How hazardous it is to pursue the infinite with the finite!" Thereupon those teachers of man turned away from the strenuous path of knowledge-seeking and resorted to the various ways of introspection, meditation, and contemplation in search for what they conceived to be "deeper wisdom." Some taught the ways of direct communion with God through devout contemplation. Others elaborated the stages of dhyana by means of which one might attain the magic powers of the gods.

As recently as January, 1927, an Egyptian fakir tried to demonstrate to an American audience in Englewood, N.J., that he could prove the superiority of the spiritual civilization of the East by allowing himself to be buried alive for two hours and 52 minutes five feet under the ground. He bettered the record set by the great magician, Houdini, by 82 minutes, but failed to secure a vaudeville contract with the Loew's Company which feared that the theatre audience might not have the patience to sit three hours for the Oriental wise man to revive.*

After all, there is very little spirituality in such small tricks of spiritualism, which are still commonly practised by mendicant priests of the East. Do not most animals succeed in doing this during their period of hibernation? On the other hand, there is genuine spiritual joy in the work of the scientists who seek to wring from nature her little secrets by means of rigid methods of study and experimentation. Truth is deeply hidden and never reveals itself to those insolent souls who approach nature with unaided hands and untrained sense-organs. Science trains our intelligence and equips it with necessary tools and methods. It teaches us not to despair of the infinity of knowledge, for it is only through piecemeal accumulation of fragmentary information that we can hope to arrive at some knowledge

* The New York Times, *January 21, 1927.*

of nature at all. Every piecemeal acquisition is progress, and every little step in advance gives to the worker a genuinely spiritual rapture. When Archimedes, on jumping into the bath tub, suddenly found the solution of the scientific problem that had troubled him, he was so overjoyed that he ran naked into the streets and shouted to everybody: "Eureka! Eureka!" This has been the spiritual joy that has constantly visited every research-worker in science, every Galileo, Newton, Pasteur, and Edison—a state of rapturous spirituality totally unknown to the pseudo-prophets of the old civilization, who professed to seek the higher knowledge of the totality of things by inward contemplation and self-hypnotism.

The most spiritual element in science is its skepticism, its courage to doubt everything and believe nothing without sufficient evidence. This attitude is not merely negative, although on the negative side it has performed very great service in liberating the human mind from slavish subjection to superstition and authority. The attitude of doubt is essentially constructive and creative: it is the only legitimate road to belief; it aims at conquering doubt itself and establishing belief on a new basis. It has not only fought the old beliefs with the irresistible weapon, "Give me evidence," but also raised new problems and led to new discoveries by the same insistence on evidence. It is this spirit of "creative doubt" which has made the biographies of the great scientists such as Darwin, Huxley, Pasteur, and Koch, the most inspiring of all human records. Just as credulity has made our medieval saints, so has doubt made our modern gods who overcame nature and blessed man.

IV

BUT THE MOST spiritual phase of the modern civilization of the West is its new religion which, in the absence of a better name, I shall term the religion of Democracy.

Modern civilization did not begin with religion, but it has resulted in a new religion; it did not much trouble about morals, but it has achieved a new system of morals. The European powers of the fifteenth and sixteenth centuries were frankly states of piracy. The great heroes of the age, Columbus, Magellan, Drake, and their like, were great pirates who braved the stormy and unknown seas in search of gold, silver, ivory, spices, and slaves. Their adventures were usually supported by genuine royal or imperial patronage, and their glory and spoils were justly shared by their state and sovereign. They had no scruples for their religion which taught love for all men, or for their morals which condemned even usury.

Those acts of piracy opened up the new continents to European trade and colonization which in turn greatly enhanced the material wealth and power of some of the European states and furnished tremendous stimulus to production and invention. The Industrial Revolution which followed, fundamentally transformed the methods of production and multiplied the productive powers of the European states. With the increase in the material enjoyment and the rise of a large middle class, there has been simultaneously an expansion in man's imaginative power and sympathy. And with the restoration of man's confidence in himself as the agent to control his own destinies, there have developed the various types of social consciousness and social virtues. All this leads to the rise of the new religion of democracy, by which I mean to include the individualistic ideals of the eighteenth century and the socialistic ideals of the last hundred years.

The new religion of the eighteenth century was Liberty. The new religion since the middle of the last century has been Socialism. Both are spiritual forces rarely if ever dreamed of by older civilizations. It is true that there were in the East religions which taught universal love and there were schools of thought which advocated equal distribution of land and property. But these have remained paper doctrines which never became real factors in social life and political organization.

Not so in the West. The fight for Freedom and the Rights of Man became the war-cry of the American Revolution, the French Revolution, and the revolutions of 1848, and have vibrated through all the later revolutions. They have worked themselves into the constitutions of the new republics. They have brought about the downfall of monarchies, empires, and aristocracies. They have given to man equality before the law and freedom of thought, speech, publication, and religious belief. Above all, they have emancipated the women and made universal education a reality.

The ideals of Socialism are merely supplementary to the earlier and more individualistic ideas of democracy. They are historically part of the great democratic movement. By the middle of the nineteenth century, the *laissez-faire* policy was no longer sufficient to achieve the desired results of equality and liberty under the highly organized and centralized economic system. Compulsory education was opposed as an infringement of liberty, and legislation regulating wages and factory conditions was branded as class legislation. The time had come for a new social and political philosophy which would meet the needs of the new economic life of the age. Hence the rise of the socialistic movments which when freed from their distracting theories of economic determinism and class war, simply mean the emphasis on the necessity of making use of the collective power of society or of the state for the greatest happiness of the greatest number. In practice, the movement has taken two main directions. On one hand, there has been the strong tendency to organize labor as the effective means for the protection of the interests of the working class, and collective bargaining and strikes have been the chief weapons. On the other hand, there has been an equally strong tendency on the part of all modern democratic governments to forestall the wasteful methods of class struggle by assimilating and putting into practice a number of socialistic ideas such as taxation on inheritance, progressive income tax, compulsory insurance of workmen against accident and old age, regulation of working hours, fixing of minimum wages, and others. By one way or another or by both, many ideas which were once regarded as dangerously socialistic, have become an integral part of the legislative and governmental program of every modern state. One may still believe in the sacred right of property, but the tax on income and inheritance has become a most important source of revenue for most governments. One may still condemn the idea of class war, but organized labor has become a fact and strikes are almost universally legalized. England, the mother country of capitalism, has had a Labor Government and may soon have another. The United States of America, the champion of individual liberty, is trying to enforce national prohibition. The world is becoming socialistic without being aware of it.

This religion of Democracy which not only guarantees one's own liberty, nor merely limits one's liberty by respecting the liberty of other people, but endeavors to make it possible for every man and every woman to live a free life; which not only succeeds through science and machinery in greatly enhancing the happiness and comfort of the individual, but also seeks through organization and legislation to extend the goods of life to the greatest number—this is the greatest spiritual heritage of the Western civilization. Is it necessary for me to remind my readers that neither the emancipation of women, nor democratic government, nor universal education has come from the so-called spiritual civilizations of the East?

V

I CANNOT THINK of a more fitting conclusion . . . than proposing to reconsider the much misused and therefore very confusing phrases "spiritual civilization," "material civilization," and "materialistic civilization." The term "material civilization" ought to have a purely neutral meaning, for all tools of civilization are material embodiments of ideas and the wheelbarrow civilization of the East is no less material than the motor-car civilization of the West. The term "materialistic civilization," which has often been applied to stigmatize the modern civilization of the West, seems to me to be a more appropriate word for the characterization of the backward civilizations of the East. For to me that civilization is materialistic which is limited by matter and incapable of transcending it; which feels itself powerless against its material environment and fails to make full use of human intelligence for the conquest of nature and for the improvement of the conditions of man. Its sages and saints may do all they can to glorify contentment and hypnotize the people into a willingness to praise their gods and abide by their fate. But that very self-hypnotizing philosophy is more materialistic than the dirty houses they live in, the scanty food they eat, and the clay and wood with which they make the images of their gods.

On the other hand, that civilization which makes the fullest possible use of human ingenuity and intelligence in search of truth in order to control nature and transform matter for the service of mankind, to liberate the human spirit from ignorance, superstition, and slavery to the forces of nature, and to reform social and political institutions for the benefit of the greatest number—such a civilization is highly idealistic and spiritual. This civilization will continue to grow and improve itself. But its future growth and improvement will be brought about only through conscious and deliberate endeavors in the direction of more fully realizing those truly spiritual potentialities which the progress of this civilization has indicated.

JAWAHARLAL NEHRU

✳✳

Jawaharlal Nehru is represented by three selections from The Discovery of India *which he allowed his publisher, Richard Walsh of the John Day Company, to select for him. This book, by the man who later became the Prime Minister of India, was written by Nehru in Ahmadnagar Fort prison from April to September, 1944. That confinement like those during nine other years of his life resulted from his Ghandi-associated activities against the British in the long struggle for a free India. Of* The Discovery of India *as a whole, Mr. Nehru has said, "I do not know how other authors feel about their writings, but always I have a strange sensation when I read something that I had written some time previously. That sensation is heightened when the writing has been done in the close and abnormal atmosphere of prison and the subsequent reading has taken place outside. I recognize it, of course, but not wholly; it seems almost as if I am reading some familiar piece written by another, who is near to me and yet who is different. Perhaps that is the measure of the change that has taken place in me.*

"So I have felt about this book also. It is mine and not wholly mine, as I am constituted today; it represents rather some past self of mine which has already joined that long succession of other selves that existed for a while and faded away, leaving only a memory behind."

✳✳

Time in Prison

I. THE URGE TO ACTION

TIME seems to change its nature in prison. The present hardly exists, for there is an absence of feeling and sensation which might separate it from the dead past. Even news of the active, living and dying world outside has a certain dreamlike unreality, an immobility and an unchangeableness as of the past. The outer objective time ceases to be, the inner and subjective sense remains but at a lower level, except when thought pulls it out of the present and experiences a kind of reality in the past or in the future. We live, as Auguste Comte said, dead men's lives, encased in our pasts, but this is especially so in prison where we try to find some sustenance for our starved and locked-up emotions in memory of the past or fancies of the future.

There is a stillness and everlastingness about the past; it changes not and has a touch of eternity, like a painted picture or a statue in bronze or marble. Unaffected by the storms and upheavals of the present, it maintains its dignity and repose and tempts the troubled spirit and the tortured mind to seek shelter in its vaulted catacombs. There is peace there and security, and one may even sense a spiritual quality.

But it is not life, unless we can find the vital links between it and the present with all its conflicts and problems. It is a kind of art for art's sake without the passion and the urge to action which are the very stuff of life. Without that passion and urge, there is a gradual oozing out of hope and vitality, a settling down on lower levels of existence, a slow merging into non-existence. We become prisoners of the past and some part of its immobility sticks to us. This passage of the mind is all the easier in prison where action is denied and we become slaves to the routine of jail life.

Yet the past is ever with us and all that we are and that we have comes from the past. We are its products and we live immersed in it. Not to understand it and feel it as something living within us is not to understand the present. To combine it with the present and extend it to the future, to break from it where it cannot be so united, to make of all this the pulsating and vibrating material for thought and action—that is life.

Any vital action springs from the depths of the being. All the long past of the individual and even of the race has prepared the background for the psychological moment of action. All the racial memories, influences of heredity and environment and training, subconscious urges, thoughts and dreams and actions from infancy and childhood onward, in their curious and tremendous mix-up, inevitably drive to that new action, which again becomes yet another factor influencing the future. Influencing the future, partly determining it, possibly even largely determining it, and yet, surely, it is not all determinism.

Aurobindo Ghose writes somewhere of the present as "the pure and virgin moment," that razor's edge of time and existence which divides the past from the future, and is, and yet, instantaneously is not. The phrase is attractive, and yet what does it mean? The virgin moment emerging from the veil of the future in all its naked purity, coming into contact with us, and immediately becoming the soiled and stale past. Is it we that soil it and violate it? Or is the moment not so virgin after all, for it is bound up with all the harlotry of the past?

Whether there is any such thing as human freedom in the philosophic sense or whether there is only an automatic determinism, I do not know. A very great deal appears certainly to be determined by the past complex of events which bear down and often overwhelm the individual. Possibly even the inner urge that he experiences, that apparent exercise of free will, is itself conditioned. As Schopenhauer says: "A man can do what he will, but not will as he will." A belief in an absolute determinism seems to me to lead inevitably to complete inaction, to death in life. All my sense of life rebels against it, though of course that very rebellion may itself have been conditioned by previous events.

I do not usually burden my mind with such philosophical or metaphysical problems, which escape solution. Sometimes they come to me almost unawares in the long silences of prison, or even in the midst of an intensity of action, bringing with them a sense of detachment or consolation in the face of some painful experience. But usually it is action and the thought of action that fill me, and when action is denied, I imagine that I am preparing for action.

The call of action has long been with me; not action divorced from thought, but rather flowing from it in one continuous sequence. And when, rarely, there has been full harmony between the two, thought leading to action and finding its fulfillment in it, action leading back to thought and a fuller understanding—then I have sensed a certain fullness of life and a vivid intensity in that moment of existence. But such moments are rare, very rare, and usually one outstrips the other and there is a lack of harmony, and vain efforts to bring the two in line. There was a time, many years ago, when I lived for considerable periods in a state of emotional exaltation, wrapped up in the action which absorbed me. Those days of my youth seem far away now, not merely because of the passage of years but far more so because of the ocean of experience and painful thought that separates them from today. The old exuberance is much less now, the almost uncontrollable impulses have toned down, and passion and feeling are more in check. The burden of thought is often a hindrance, and in the mind where there was once certainty, doubt creeps in. Perhaps it is just age, or the common temper of our day.

And yet, even now, the call of action stirs strange depths within me and, after a brief tussle with thought, I want to experience again "that lovely impulse of delight" which turns to risk and danger and faces and mocks at death. I am not enamored of death, though I do not think it frightens me. I do not believe in the negation of or abstention from life. I have loved life and it attracts me still, and in my own way I seek to experience it, though many invisible barriers have grown up which surround me. But that very desire leads me to play with life, to peep over its edges, not to be a slave to it, so that we may value each other all the more. Perhaps I ought to have been an aviator, so that when the slowness and dullness of life overcame me I could have rushed into the tumult of the clouds and said to myself:

> I balanced all, brought all to mind,
> The years to come seemed waste of breath,
> A waste of breath the years behind
> In balance with this life, this death.

II. THE PAST IN ITS RELATION TO THE PRESENT

THIS URGE to action, this desire to experience life through action, has influenced all my thought and activity. Even sustained thinking, apart from being itself a kind of action, becomes part of the action to come. It is not something entirely abstract, in the void, unrelated to action and life. The past becomes something that leads up to the present, the moment of action, the future something that flows from it; and all three are inextricably intertwined and interrelated.

Even my seemingly actionless life in prison is tacked on somehow, by some process of thought and feeling, to coming or imagined action, and so it gains for me a certain content without which it would be a vacuum in which existence would become intolerable. When actual action has been denied me, I have sought some such approach to the past and to history. Because my own personal experiences have often touched historic events and sometimes I have even had something to do with the influencing of such events in my own sphere, it has not been difficult for me to envisage history as a living process with which I could identify myself to some extent.

I came late to history, and even then not through the usual direct road of learning a mass of facts and dates and drawing conclusions and inferences from them unrelated to my life's course. So long as I did this, history had little significance for me. I was still less interested in the supernatural or problems of a future life. Science and the problems of today and of our present life attracted me far more.

Some mixture of thought and emotion and urges of which I was only dimly conscious led me to action, and action, in its turn, sent me back to thought and a desire to understand the present. The roots of that present lay in the past and so I made voyages of discovery into the past, ever seeking a clue in it, if any such existed, to the understanding of the present. The domination of the present never left me even when I lost myself in musings of past events and of persons far away and long ago, forgetting where or what I was. If I felt occasionally that I belonged to the past, I felt also that the whole of the past belonged to me in the present. Past history merged into contemporary history: it became a living reality tied up with sensations of pain and pleasure.

If the past had a tendency to become the present, the present also, sometimes receded into the distant past and assumed its immobile, statuesque appearance. In the midst of an intensity of action itself, there would suddenly come a feeling as if it were some past event and one was looking at it, as it were, in retrospect.

It was this attempt to discover the past in its relation to the present that led me twelve years ago to write *Glimpses of World History* in the form of letters to my daughter. I wrote rather superficially and as simply as I could, for I was writing for a girl in her early teens, but behind that writing lay that quest and voyage of discovery. A sense of adventure filled me, and I lived successively different ages and periods and had for companions men and women who had lived long ago. I had leisure in jail; there was no sense of hurry or of completing a task within an allotted period of time. So I let my mind wander or take root for a while, keeping in tune with my mood, allowing impressions to sink in and fill the dry bones of the past with flesh and blood.

It was a similar quest, though limited to recent and more intimate times and persons, that led me later to write my autobiography.

I suppose I have changed a good deal during these twelve years. I have grown more contemplative. There is perhaps a little more poise and equilibrium, some sense of detachment, a greater calmness of spirit. I am not overcome now to the same extent as I used to be by tragedy or what I conceived to be tragedy. The turmoil and disturbance are less, and are more temporary, even though the tragedies have been on a far greater scale. Is this, I have wondered, the growth of a spirit of resignation, or is it a toughening of the texture? Is it just age and a lessening of vitality and of the passion of life? Or is it due to long periods in prison and life slowly ebbing away, and the thoughts that fill the mind passing through, after a brief stay, leaving only ripples behind? The tortured mind seeks some mechanism of escape, the senses get dulled from repeated shocks, and a feeling comes over one that so much evil and misfortune shadow the world that a little more or less does not make much difference. There is only one thing that remains to us, that cannot be taken away: to act with courage and dignity and to stick to the ideals that have given meaning to life. But that is not the politician's way.

Someone said the other day: Death is the birthright of every person born. A curious way of putting an obvious thing. It is a birthright which nobody has denied or can deny, and which all of us seek to forget and escape so long as we may. And yet there was something novel and attractive about the phrase. Those who complain so bitterly of life have always a way out of it, if they so choose. That is always in our power to achieve. If we cannot master life we can at least master death. A pleasing thought lessening the feeling of helplessness.

III. LIFE'S PHILOSOPHY

SIX OR SEVEN years ago an American publisher asked me to write an essay on my philosophy of life for a symposium he was preparing. I was attracted to the idea but I hesitated, and the more I thought over it, the more reluctant I grew. Ultimately I did not write that essay.

What was my philosophy of life? I did not know. Some years earlier I would not have been so hesitant. There was a definiteness about my thinking and objectives then which has faded away since. The events of the past few years in India, China, Europe, and all over the world have been confusing, upsetting and distressing, and the future has become vague and shadowy and has lost that clearness of outline which it once possessed in my mind.

This doubt and difficulty about fundamental matters did not come in my way in regard to immediate action, except that it blunted somewhat the sharp edge of that activity. No longer could I function, as I did in my younger days, as an arrow flying automatically to the target of my choice, ignoring all else but that target. Yet I functioned, for the urge to action was there and a real or imagined co-ordination of that action with the ideals I held. But a growing distaste for politics, as I saw them, seized me, and gradually my whole attitude to life seemed to undergo a transformation.

The ideals and objectives of yesterday were still the ideals of today but they had lost some of their luster, and even as one seemed to go toward them, they lost the shining beauty which had warmed the heart and vitalized the body. Evil triumphed often enough, but what was far worse was the coarsening and distortion of what had seemed so right. Was human nature so essentially bad that it would take ages of training, through suffering and misfortune, before it could behave reasonably and raise man above that creature of lust and violence and deceit that he now was? And meanwhile was every effort to change it radically in the present or the near future doomed to failure?

Ends and means: were they tied up inseparably, acting and reacting on each other, the wrong means distorting and sometimes even destroying the end in view? But the right means might well be beyond the capacity of infirm and selfish human nature. What then was one to do? Not to act was a complete confession of failure and a submission to evil; to act meant often enough a compromise with some form of that evil, with all the untoward consequences that such compromises result in.

My early approach to life's problems had been more or less scientific, with something of the easy optimism of the science of the nineteenth and early twentieth century. A secure and comfortable existence, and the energy and self-confidence I possssed, increased that feeling of optimism. A kind of vague humanism appealed to me.

Religion, as I saw it practiced, and accepted even by thinking minds, whether it was Hinduism or Islam or Buddhism or Christianity, did not attract me. It seemed to be closely associated with superstitious practices and dogmatic beliefs, and behind it lay a method of approach to life's problems which was certainly not that of science. There was an element of magic about it, an uncritical credulousness, a reliance on the supernatural.

Yet it was obvious that religion had supplied some deeply felt inner need of human nature, and that the vast majority of people all over the world could not do without some form of religious belief. It had produced many fine types of men and women, as well as bigoted, narrow-minded, cruel tyrants. It had given a set of values to human life, and though some of these values had no appli-

cation today, or were even harmful, others were still the foundation
of morality and ethics.

In the wider sense of the word, religion dealt with the uncharted
regions of human experience, uncharted, that is, by the scientific
positive knowledge of the day. In a sense it might be considered an
extension of the known and charted region, though the methods of
science and religion were utterly unlike each other, and to a large
extent they had to deal with different kinds of media. It was obvious
that there was a vast unknown region all around us, and science,
with its magnificent achievements, knew little enough about it,
though it was making tentative approaches in that direction. Probably also the normal methods of science, its dealings with the visible
world and the processes of life, were not wholly adapted to the
psychical, the artistic, the spiritual, and other elements of the invisible world. Life does not consist entirely of what we see and hear
and feel, the visible world which is undergoing change in time and
space. It is continually touching an invisible world of other, and possibly more stable or equally changeable elements, and no thinking
person can ignore this invisible world.

Science does not tell us much, or for the matter of that, anything,
about the purpose of life. It is now widening its boundaries and it
may invade the so-called invisible world before long and help us to
understand this purpose of life in its widest sense, or at least give us
some glimpses which illumine the problem of human existence. The
old controversy between science and religion takes a new form—
the application of the scientific method to emotional and religious
experiences.

Religion merges into mysticism and metaphysics and philosophy.
There have been great mystics, attractive figures, who cannot easily
be disposed of as self-deluded fools. Yet mysticism (in the narrow
sense of the word) irritates me; it appears to be vague and soft
and flabby, not a rigorous discipline of the mind but a surrender
of mental faculties and a living in a sea of emotional experience.
The experience may lead occasionally to some insight into inner
and less obvious processes, but it is also likely to lead to self-delusion.

Metaphysics and philosophy, or a metaphysical philosophy, have
a greater appeal to the mind. They require hard thinking and the
application of logic and reasoning, though all this is necessarily
based on some premises which are presumed to be self-evident, and
yet which may or may not be true. All thinking persons, to a greater
or less degree, dabble in metaphysics and philosophy, for not to do
so is to ignore many of the aspects of this universe of ours. Some

may feel more attracted to them than others, and the emphasis on them may vary in different ages. In the ancient world, both in Asia and in Europe, all the emphasis was laid on the supremacy of the inward life over things external, and this inevitably led to metaphysics and philosophy. The modern man is wrapped up much more in these things external, and yet even he, in moments of crisis and mental trouble, often turns to philosophy and metaphysical speculations.

Some vague or more precise philosophy of life we all have, though most of us accept unthinkingly the general attitude which is characteristic of our generation and environment. Most of us accept also certain metaphysical conceptions as part of the faith in which we have grown up. I have not been attracted toward metaphysics; in fact I have had a certain distaste for vague speculation. And yet I have sometimes found a certain intellectual fascination in trying to follow the rigid lines of metaphysical and philosophic thought of the ancients or the moderns. But I have never felt at ease there and have escaped from their spell with a feeling of relief.

Essentially I am interested in this world, in this life, not in some other world or a future life. Whether there is such a thing as a soul, or whether there is a survival after death or not, I do not know; and important as these questions are, they do not trouble me in the least. The environment in which I have grown up takes the soul (or rather the *atma*) and a future life, the karma theory of cause and effect, and reincarnation for granted. I have been affected by this, and so, in a sense, I am favorably disposed toward these assumptions. There might be a soul which survives the physical death of the body, and a theory of cause and effect governing life's actions seems reasonable, though it leads to obvious difficulties when one thinks of the ultimate cause. Presuming a soul, there appears to be some logic also in the theory of reincarnation.

But I do not believe in any of these or other theories and assumptions as a matter of religious faith. They are just intellectual speculations in an unknown region about which we know next to nothing. They do not affect my life, and whether they were proved right or wrong subsequently, they would make little difference to me.

Spiritualism with its séances and its so-called manifestations of spirits and the like has always seemed to me a rather absurd and impertinent way of investigating psychic phenomena and the mysteries of the afterlife. Usually it is something worse and is an exploitation of the emotions of some overcredulous people who seek relief or escape from mental trouble. I do not deny the possibility of some of these psychic phenomena having a basis of truth, but the approach appears to me to be all wrong and the conclusions drawn from scraps and odd bits of evidence to be unjustified.

Often, as I look at this world, I have a sense of mysteries, of unknown depths. The urge to understand it, in so far as I can, comes to me; to be in tune with it and to experience it in its fullness. But the way to that understanding seems to me essentially the way of science, the way of objective approach, though I realize that there can be no such thing as true objectiveness. If the subjective element is unavoidable and inevitable, it should be conditioned as far as possible by the scientific method.

What the mysterious is I do not know. I do not call it God because God has come to mean much that I do not believe in. I find myself incapable of thinking of a deity or of any unknown supreme power in anthropomorphic terms, and the fact that many people think so is continually a source of surprise to me. Any idea of a personal God seems very odd to me. Intellectually, I can appreciate to some extent the conception of monism, and I have been attracted toward the Advaita (nondualist) philosophy of the Vedanta, though I do not presume to understand it in all its depth and intricacy, and I realize that merely an intellectual appreciation of such matters does not carry one far. At the same time the Vedanta, as well as other similar approaches, rather frighten me with their vague formless incursions into infinity. The diversity and fullness of nature stir me and produce a harmony of the spirit, and I can imagine myself feeling at home in the old Indian or Greek pagan and pantheistic atmosphere, but minus the conception of god or gods that was attached to it.

Some kind of ethical approach to life has a strong appeal for me, though it would be difficult for me to justify it logically. I have been attracted by Gandhiji's stress on right means, and I think one of his greatest contributions to our public life has been this emphasis.* The idea is by no means new, but this application of an ethical doctrine to large scale public activity was certainly novel. It is full of difficulty, and perhaps ends and means are not really separable and form together one organic whole. In a world which thinks almost exclusively of ends and ignores means, this emphasis on means

---

* *The suffix in the form Gandhiji is sometimes mistaken by American and English readers to be an affectionate diminutive. On the contrary, it is the simplest of numerous terms of respect used in the Hindustani language and was preferred by Gandhi over the title Mahatma. It amounted to calling him "Mr. Gandhi."—Ed.*

seems odd and remarkable. How far it has succeeded in India I cannot say. But there is no doubt that it has created a deep and abiding impression on the minds of large numbers of people.

A study of Marx and Lenin produced a powerful effect on my mind and helped me to see history and current affairs in a new light. The long chain of history and of social development appeared to have some meaning, some sequence, and the future lost some of its obscurity. The practical achievements of the Soviet Union were also tremendously impressive. Often I disliked or did not understand some development there and it seemed to me to be too closely concerned with the opportunism of the moment or the power politics of the day. But despite all these developments and possible distortions of the original passion for human betterment, I had no doubt that the Soviet revolution had advanced human society by a great leap and had lit a bright flame which could not be smothered, and that it had laid the foundations for that "new Civilization" toward which the world would advance. I am too much of an individualist and believer in personal freedom to like overmuch regimentation. Yet it seemed to me obvious that in a complex social structure individual freedom had to be limited, and perhaps the only way to real personal freedom was through some such limitation in the social sphere. The lesser liberties may often need limitation in the interest of the larger freedoms.

Much in the Marxist philosophical outlook I could accept without difficulty: its monism and nonduality of mind and matter, the dynamics of matter and the dialectic of continuous change by evolution as well as leap, through action and interaction, cause and effect, thesis, antithesis, and synthesis. It did not satisfy me completely, nor did it answer all the questions in my mind, and almost unawares a vague idealist approach would creep into my mind, something rather akin to the Vedanta approach. It was not a difference between mind and matter but rather of something that lay beyond the mind. Also there was the background of ethics. I realized that the moral approach is a changing one and depends upon the growing mind and an advancing civilization; it is conditioned by the mental climate of the age. Yet there was something more to it than that, certain basic urges which had greater permanence. I did not like the frequent divorce in communist, as in other, practice between action and these basic urges or principles. So there was an odd mixture in my mind which I could not rationally explain or resolve. There was a general tendency not to think too much of those fundamental questions which appear to be beyond reach, and rather to concentrate on the problems of life—to understand in the narrower and more immediate sense what should be done and how. Whatever ultimate reality may be, and whether we can ever grasp it in whole or in part, there certainly appear to be vast possibilities of increasing human knowledge, even though this may be partly or largely subjective, and of applying this to the advancement and betterment of human living and social organization.

There has been in the past, and there is to a lesser extent even today among some people, an absorption in finding an answer to the riddle of the universe. This leads them away from the individual and social problems of the day, and when they are unable to solve that riddle they despair and turn to inaction and triviality, or find comfort in some dogmatic creed. Social evils, most of which are certainly capable of removal, are attributed to original sin, to the unalterableness of "human nature," or the social structure, or (in India) to the inevitable legacy of previous births. Thus one drifts away from even the attempt to think rationally and scientifically and takes refuge in irrationalism, superstition, and unreasonable and inequitable social prejudices and practices. It is true that even rational and scientific thought does not always take us as far as we would like to go. There is an infinite number of factors and relations which influence and determine events in varying degrees and it is impossible to grasp all of them. Still we can try to pick out the dominating forces at work and by observing external material reality, and by experiment and practice, trial and error, grope our way to ever-widening knowledge and truth.

For this purpose, and within these limitations, the general Marxist approach, fitting in as it more or less did with the present state of scientific knowledge, seemed to me to offer considerable help. But even accepting that approach, the consequences that flow from it and the interpretation of past and present happenings were by no means always clear. Marx's general analysis of social development seems to have been remarkably correct, and yet many developments took place later which did not fit in with his outlook for the immediate future. Lenin successfully adapted the Marxian thesis to some of these subsequent developments, and again since then further remarkable changes have taken place—the rise of fascism and nazism and all that lay behind them. The very rapid growth of technology and the practical application of vast developments in scientific knowledge are now changing the world picture with an amazing rapidity, leading to new problems.

And so while I accepted the fundamentals of the socialist theory,

I did not trouble myself about its numerous inner controversies. I had little patience with leftist groups in India, spending much of their energy in mutual conflict and recrimination over fine points of doctrine which did not interest me at all. Life is too complicated, and as far as we can understand it in our present state of knowledge, too illogical for it to be confined within the four corners of a fixed doctrine.

The real problems for me remain problems of individual and social life, of harmonious living, of a proper balancing of an individual's inner and outer life, of an adjustment of the relations between individuals and between groups, of a continuous becoming something better and higher, of social development, of the ceaseless adventure of man. In the solution of these problems the way of observation and precise knowledge and deliberate reasoning, according to the method of science, must be followed. This method may not always be applicable in our quest of truth, for art and poetry and certain psychic experiences seem to belong to a different order of things and to elude the objective methods of science. Let us therefore not rule out intuition and other methods of sensing truth and reality. They are necessary even for the purposes of science. But always we must hold to our anchor of precise objective knowledge tested by reason and even more so by experiment and practice, and always we must beware of losing ourselves in a sea of speculation unconnected with the day-to-day problems of life and the needs of men and women. A living philosophy must answer the problems of today.

It may be that we of this modern age, who so pride ourselves on the achievements of our times, are prisoners of our age, just as the ancients and the men and women of medieval times were prisoners of their respective ages. We may delude ourselves, as others have done before us, that our way of looking at things is the only right way, leading to truth. We cannot escape from that prison or get rid entirely of that illusion, if illusion it is.

Yet I am convinced that the methods and approach of science have revolutionized human life more than anything else in the long course of history, and have opened doors and avenues of further and even more radical change, leading up to the very portals of what has long been considered the unknown. The technical achievements of science are obvious enough; its capacity to transform an economy of scarcity into one of abundance is evident; its invasion of many problems which have so far been the monopoly of philosophy is becoming more pronounced. Space-time and the quantum theory utterly changed the picture of the physical world. More recent researches into the nature of matter, the structure of the atom, the transmutation of the elements, and the transformation of electricity and light, either into the other, have carried human knowledge much further. Man no longer sees nature as something apart and distinct from himself. Human destiny appears to become a part of nature's rhythmic energy.

All this upheaval of thought due to the advance of science, has led scientists into a new region verging on the metaphysical. They draw different and often contradictory conclusions. Some see in it a new unity, the antithesis of chance. Others, like Bertrand Russell, say: "Academic philosophers ever since the time of Parmenides have believed the world is unity. The most fundamental of my beliefs is that this is rubbish." Or again: "Man is the product of causes which had no prevision of the end they were achieving; his origin, his growth, his hopes and fears, his loves and beliefs are but the outcome of accidental collocations of atoms." And yet the latest developments in physics have gone a long way to demonstrate a fundamental unity in nature. "The belief that all things are made of a single substance is as old as thought itself; but ours is the generation which, first of all in history, is able to perceive the unity of Nature not as a baseless dogma or a hopeless aspiration, but a principle of science based on proof as sharp and clear as anything which is known."*

Old as this belief is in Asia and Europe, it is interesting to compare some of the latest conclusions of science with the fundamental ideas underlying the Advaita Vedantic theory. These ideas were that the universe is made of one substance whose form is perpetually changing, and further that the sum total of energies remains always the same. Also that "the explanations of things are to be found within their own nature, and that no external beings or existences are required to explain what is going on in the universe," with its corollary of a self-evolving universe.

It does not very much matter to science what these vague speculations lead to, for meanwhile it forges ahead in a hundred directions, in its own precise experimental way of observation, widening the bounds of the charted region of knowledge, and changing human life in the process. It may be on the verge of discovering vital mysteries, and yet they may elude it. Still it will go on along its appointed path, for there is no end to its journeying. Ignoring for the moment the *Why?* of philosophy, it will go on asking *How?*,

* *Karl K. Darrow,* The Renaissance of Physics *(New York, 1936), p. 301.*

and as it finds this out it gives greater content and meaning to life, and perhaps takes us some way in answering the why.

Or perhaps we cannot cross that barrier, and the mysterious will continue to remain the mysterious, and life with all its changes will still remain a bundle of good and evil, a succession of conflicts, a curious combination of incompatible and mutually hostile urges.

Or again, perhaps the very progress of science, unconnected with and isolated from moral discipline and ethical considerations, will lead to the concentration of power and the terrible instruments of destruction which it has made in the hands of evil and selfish men, seeking the domination of others—and thus to the destruction of its own great achievements. Something of this kind we see happening now, and behind this war there lies this internal conflict of the spirit of man.

How amazing is this spirit of man! In spite of innumerable failings, man, throughout the ages, has sacrificed his life and all he held dear for an ideal, for truth, for faith, for country and honor. That ideal may change, but that capacity for self-sacrifice continues, and because of that, much may be forgiven to man, and it is impossible to lose hope for him. In the midst of disaster he has not lost his dignity or his faith in the values he cherished. Plaything of nature's mighty forces, less than the speck of dust in this vast universe, he has hurled defiance at the elemental powers, and with his mind, cradle of revolution, sought to master them. Whatever gods there be, there is something godlike in man, as there is also something of the devil in him.

The future is dark, uncertain. But we can see part of the way leading to it and can tread it with firm steps, remembering that nothing that can happen is likely to overcome the spirit of man which has survived so many perils. Remembering also that life, for all its ills, has joy and beauty, and we can always wander, if we know how to, in the enchanted woods of nature.

> What else is Wisdom? What of man's endeavor
> Or God's high grace, so lovely and so great?
> To stand from fear set free, to breathe and wait;
> To hold a hand uplifted over Hate;
> And shall not Loveliness be loved for ever?*

* *Chorus from the* Bacchae *of Euripides—Gilbert Murray's translation.*

SRI AUROBINDO

****

Nominated for this volume by Indian scholars, Sri Aurobindo is considered one of the most outstanding of living Indo-Anglians, a poet, a playwright, a critic and a philosopher. The Life Divine *is a philosophical treatise and has been called a prose symphony, containing 1600 pages as a plea and program to divinize man. The section representing him here constitutes the final pages of the work.*

****

The Life Divine:
The Present Evolutionary Crisis

AT PRESENT mankind is undergoing an evolutionary crisis in which is concealed a choice of its destiny; for a stage has been reached in which the human mind has achieved in certain directions an enormous development while in others it stands arrested and bewildered and can no longer find its way. A structure of the external life has been raised up by man's ever-active mind and life-will, a structure of an unmanageable hugeness and complexity, for the service of his mental, vital, physical claims and urges, a complex political, social, administrative, economic, cultural machinery, an organised collective means for his intellectual, sensational, æsthetic and material satisfaction. Man has created a system of civilisation which has become too big for his limited mental capacity and understanding and his still more limited spiritual and moral capacity to utilise and manage, a too dangerous servant of his blundering ego and its appetites. For no greater seeing mind, no intuitive soul of knowledge has yet come to his surface of consciousness which could make this basic fullness of life a condition for the free growth of something that exceeded it. This new fullness of the means of life might be, by its power for a release from the incessant unsatisfied stress of his economic and physical needs, an opportunity for the full pursuit of other and greater aims surpassing the material existence, for the

discovery of a higher truth and good and beauty, for the discovery
of a greater and diviner spirit which would intervene and use life
for a higher perfection of the being: but it is being used instead
for the multiplication of new wants and an aggressive expansion
of the collective ego. At the same time Science has put at his disposal many potencies of the universal Force and has made the life
of humanity materially one; but what uses this universal Force is a
little human individual or communal ego with nothing universal
in its light of knowledge or its movements, no inner sense or power
which would create in this physical drawing together of the human
world a true life unity, a mental unity or a spiritual oneness. All that
is there is a chaos of clashing mental ideas, urges of individual and
collective physical want and need, vital claims and desires, impulses
of an ignorant life-push, hungers and calls for life satisfaction of
individuals, classes, nations, a rich fungus of political and social and
economic nostrums and notions, a hustling medley of slogans and
panaceas for which men are ready to oppress and be oppressed, to
kill and be killed, to impose them somehow or other by the immense and too formidable means placed at his disposal, in the belief
that this is his way out to something ideal. The evolution of human
mind and life must necessarily lead towards an increasing universality; but on a basis of ego and segmenting and dividing mind this
opening to the universal can only create a vast pullulation of un-
accorded ideas and impulses, a surge of enormous powers and desires, a chaotic mass of unassimilated and intermixed mental, vital
and physical material of a larger existence which, because it is not
taken up by a creative harmonising light of the spirit, must welter
in a universalised confusion and discord out of which it is impossible
to build a greater harmonic life. Man has harmonised life in the past
by organised ideation and limitation; he has created societies based
on fixed ideas or fixed customs, a fixed cultural system or an organic life-system, each with its own order; the throwing of all these
into the melting-pot of a more and more intermingling life and a
pouring in of ever new ideas and motives and facts and possibilities
call for a new, a greater consciousness to meet and master the increasing potentialities of existence and harmonise them. Reason and
Science can only help by standardising, by fixing everything into an
artificially arranged and mechanised unity of material life. A greater
whole-being, whole-knowledge, whole-power is needed to weld all
into a greater unity of whole-life.

A life of unity, mutuality and harmony born of a deeper and
wider truth of our being is the only truth of life that can success-

fully replace the imperfect mental constructions of the past which were a combination of association and regulated conflict, an accommodation of egos and interests grouped or dovetailed into each other to form a society, a consolidation by common general life-motives, a unification by need and the pressure of struggle with outside forces. It is such a change and such a reshaping of life for which humanity is blindly beginning to seek, now more and more with a sense that its very existence depends upon finding the way. The evolution of mind working upon life has developed an organisation of the activity of mind and use of Matter which can no longer be supported by human capacity without an inner change. An accommodation of the egocentric human individuality, separative even in association, to a system of living which demands unity, perfect mutuality, harmony, is imperative. But because the burden which is being laid on mankind is too great for the present littleness of the human personality and its petty mind and small life-instincts, because it cannot operate the needed change, because it is using this new apparatus and organisation to serve the old infraspiritual and infrarational life-self of humanity, the destiny of the race seems to be heading dangerously, as if impatiently and in spite of itself, under the drive of the vital ego seized by colossal forces which are on the same scale as the huge mechanical organisation of life and scientific knowledge which it has evolved, a scale too large for its reason and will to handle, into a prolonged confusion and perilous crisis and darkness of violent shifting incertitude. Even if this turns out to be a passing phase or appearance and a tolerable structural accommodation is found which will enable mankind to proceed less catastrophically on its uncertain journey, this can only be a respite. For the problem is fundamental and in putting it evolutionary Nature in man is confronting herself with a critical choice which must one day be solved in the true sense if the race is to arrive or even to survive. The evolutionary nisus is pushing towards a development of the cosmic Force in terrestrial life which needs a larger mental and vital being to support it, a wider mind, a greater wider more conscious unanimised Life-Soul, Anima, and that again needs an unveiling of the supporting Soul and spiritual Self within to maintain it.

A rational and scientific formula of the vitalistic and materialistic human being and his life, a search for a perfected economic society and the democratic cultus of the average man are all that the modern mind presents us in this crisis as a light for its solution. Whatever the truth supporting these ideas, this is clearly not enough to meet the need of a humanity which is missioned to evolve beyond itself or, at any rate, if it is to live, must evolve far beyond anything that it at present is. A life-instinct in the race and in the average man himself has felt the inadequacy and has been driving towards a reversal of values or a discovery of new values and a transfer of life to a new foundation. This has taken the form of an attempt to find a simple and ready-made basis of unity, mutuality, harmony for the common life, to enforce it by a suppression of the competitive clash of egos and so to arrive at a life of identity for the community in place of a life of difference. But to realise these desirable ends the means adopted have been the forcible and successful materialisation of a few restricted ideas or slogans enthroned to the exclusion of all other thought, the suppression of the mind of the individual, a mech-anised compression of the elements of life, a mechanised unity and drive of the life-force, a coercion of man by the State, the substitut-tion of the communal for the individual ego. The communal ego is idealised as the soul of the nation, the race, the community; but this is a colossal and may turn out to be a fatal error. A forced and imposed unanimity of mind, life, action raised to their highest tension under the drive of something which is thought to be greater, the collective soul, the collective life, is the formula found. But this obscure collective being is not the soul or self of the community; it is a life-force that rises from the subconscient and, if denied the light of guidance by the reason, can be driven only by dark massive forces which are powerful but dangerous for the race because they are alien to the conscious evolution of which man is the trustee and bearer. It is not in this direction that evolutionary Nature has pointed mankind; this is a reversion towards something that she had left behind her.

Another solution that is attempted reposes still on the material-istic reason and a unified organisation of the economic life of the race; but the method that is being employed is the same, a forced compression and imposed unanimity of mind and life and a mech-anical organisation of the communal existence. A unanimity of this kind can only be maintained by a compression of all freedom of thought and life, and that must bring about either the efficient stability of a termite civilisation or a drying up of the springs of life and a swift or slow decadence. It is through the growth of con-sciousness that the collective soul and its life can become aware of itself and develop; the free play of mind and life is essential for the growth of consciousness: for mind and life are the soul's only instru-mentation until a higher instrumentation develops; they must not be inhibited in their action or rendered rigid, unplastic and unprogressive. The difficulties or disorders engendered by the growth of the individual mind and life cannot be healthily removed by the suppression of the individual; the true cure can only be achieved by his progression to a greater consciousness in which he is fulfilled and perfected.

An alternative solution is the development of an enlightened reason and will of the normal man consenting to a new socialised life in which he will subordinate his ego for the sake of the right arrangement of the life of the community. If we inquire how this radical change is to be brought about, two agencies seem to be suggested, the agency of a greater and better mental knowledge, right ideas, right information, right training of the social and civic individual and the agency of a new social machinery which will solve everything by the magic of the social machine cutting humanity into a better pattern. But it has not been found in experience, whatever might have once been hoped, that education and intellectual training by itself can change man; it only provides the human individual and collective ego with better information and a more efficient machinery for its self-affirmation, but leaves it the same unchanged human ego. Nor can human mind and life be cut into perfection—even into what is thought to be perfection, a constructed substitute,—by any kind of social machinery; matter can be so cut, thought can be so cut, but in our human existence matter and thought are only instruments for the soul and the life-force. Machinery cannot form the soul and life-force into standardised shapes; it can at best coerce them, make soul and mind inert and stationary and regulate the life's outward action; but if this is to be effectively done, coercion and compression of the mind and life are indispensable and that again spells either unprogressive stability or decadence. The reasoning mind with its logical practicality has no other way of getting the better of Nature's ambiguous and complex movements than a regulation and mechanisation of mind and life. If that is done, the soul of humanity will either have to recover its freedom and growth by a revolt and a destruction of the machine into whose grip it has been cast or escape by a withdrawal into itself and a rejection of life. Man's true way out is to discover his soul and its self-force and instrumentation and replace by it both the mechanisation of mind and the ignorance and disorder of life-nature. But there would be little room and freedom for such a movement of self-discovery and self-effectuation in a closely regulated and mechanised social existence.

There is the possibility that in the swing back from a mechanistic

idea of life and society the human mind may seek refuge in a return
to the religious idea and a society governed or sanctioned by religion. But organised religion, though it can provide a means of
inner uplift for the individual and preserve in it or behind it a way
for his opening to spiritual experience, has not changed human life
and society; it could not do so because, in governing society, it had
to compromise with the lower parts of life and could not insist on
the inner change of the whole being; it could insist only on a credal
adherence, a formal acceptance of its ethical standards and a conformity to institution, ceremony and ritual. Religion so conceived
can give a religio-ethical colour or surface tinge,—sometimes, if it
maintains a strong kernel of inner experience, it can generalise to
some extent an incomplete spiritual tendency; but it does not transform the race, it cannot create a new principle of the human existence. A total spiritual direction given to the whole life and the
whole nature can alone lift humanity beyond itself. Another possible
conception akin to the religious solution is the guidance of society
by men of spiritual attainment, the brotherhood or unity of all in
the faith or in the discipline, the spiritualisation of life and society
by the taking up of the old machinery of life into such a unification
or inventing a new machinery. This too has been attempted before
without success; it was the original founding idea of more than one
religion: but the human ego and vital nature were too strong for a
religious idea working on the mind and by the mind to overcome its
resistance. It is only the full emergence of the soul, the full descent
of the native light and power of the Spirit and the consequent replacement or transformation and uplifting of our insufficient mental
and vital nature by a spiritual and supramental supernature that
can effect this evolutionary miracle.

At first sight this insistence on a radical change of nature might
seem to put off all the hope of humanity to a distant evolutionary
future; for the transcendence of our normal human nature, a transcendence of our mental, vital and physical being, has the appearance of an endeavour too high and difficult and at present, for man
as he is, impossible. Even if it were so, it would still remain the sole
possibility for the transmutation of life; for to hope for a true
change of human life without a change of human nature is an irrational and unspiritual proposition; it is to ask for something unnatural and unreal, an impossible miracle. But what is demanded by
this change is not something altogether distant, alien to our existence
and radically impossible; for what has to be developed is there in
our being and not something outside it: what evolutionary Nature

presses for, is an awakening to the knowledge of self, the discovery of self, the manifestation of the self and spirit within us and the release of its self-knowledge, its self-power, its native self-instrumentation. It is, besides, a step for which the whole of evolution has been a preparation and which is brought closer at each crisis of human destiny when the mental and vital evolution of the being touches a point where intellect and vital force reach some acme of tension and there is a need either for them to collapse, or sink back into a torpor of defeat or a repose of unprogressive quiescence or to rend their way through the veil against which they are straining. What is necessary is that there should be a turn in humanity felt by some or many towards the vision of this change, a feeling of its imperative need, the sense of its possibility, the will to make it possible in themselves and to find the way. That trend is not absent and it must increase with the tension of the crisis in human world-destiny; the need of an escape or a solution, the feeling that there is no other solution than the spiritual cannot but grow and become more imperative under the urgency of critical circumstance. To that call in the being there must always be some answer in the Divine Reality and in Nature.

The answer might, indeed, be only individual; it might result in a multiplication of spiritualised individuals or even, conceivably though not probably, a gnostic* individual or individuals isolated in the unspiritualised mass of humanity. Such isolated realised beings must either withdraw into their secret divine kingdom and guard themselves in a spiritual solitude or act from their inner light on mankind for what little can be prepared in such conditions for a happier future. The inner change can begin to take shape in a collective form only if the gnostic individual finds others who have the same kind of inner life as himself and can form with them a group with its own autonomous existence or else a separate community or order of beings with its own inner law of life. It is this need of a separate life with its own rule of living adapted to the inner power or motive force of the spiritual existence and creating for it its native atmosphere that has expressed itself in the past in the formation of the monastic life or in attempts of various kinds at a new separate collective living self-governed and other in its spiritual principle than the ordinary human life. The monastic life is in its nature an association of other-worldly seekers, men whose whole attempt is to find and realise in themselves the spiritual reality and who form their common existence by rules of living which help them in that

---

* *defined more fully four paragraphs further on.—Editor.*

endeavour. It is not usually an effort to create a new life-formation which will exceed the ordinary human society and create a new world-order. A religion may hold that eventual prospect before it or attempt some first approach to it, or a mental idealism may make the same endeavour. But these attempts have always been overcome by the persistent inconscience and ignorance of our human vital nature; for that nature is an obstacle which no mere idealism or incomplete spiritual aspiration can change in its recalcitrant mass or permanently dominate. Either the endeavour fails by its own imperfection or it is invaded by the imperfection of the outside world and sinks from the shining height of its aspiration to something mixed and inferior on the ordinary human level. A common spiritual life meant to express the spiritual and not the mental, vital and physical being must found and maintain itself on greater values than the mental, vital, physical values of the ordinary human society; if it is not so founded, it will be merely the normal human society with a difference. An entirely new consciousness in many individuals transforming their whole being, transforming their mental, vital and physical nature-self, is needed for the new life to appear; only such a transformation of the general mind, life, body nature can bring into being a new worthwhile collective existence. The evolutionary nisus must tend not merely to create a new type of mental beings but another order of beings who have raised their whole existence from our present mentalised animality to a greater spiritual level of the earth-nature.

Any such complete transformation of the earth-life in a number of human beings could not establish itself altogether at once; even when the turning-point has been reached, the decisive line crossed, the new life in its beginnings would have to pass through a period of ordeal and arduous development. A general change from the old consciousness taking up the whole life into the spiritual principle would be the necessary first step; the preparation for this might be long and the transformation itself once begun proceed by stages. In the individual it might after a certain point be rapid and even effect itself by a bound, an evolutionary saltus; but an individual transformation would not be the creation of a new type of beings or a new collective life. One might conceive of a number of individuals thus evolving separately in the midst of the old life and then joining together to establish the nucleus of the new existence. But it is not likely that Nature would operate in this fashion, and it would be difficult for the individual to arrive at a complete change while still enclosed in the life of the lower nature. At a certain stage it might be necessary to follow the age-long device of the separate community, but with a double purpose, first to provide a secure atmosphere, a place and life apart, in which the consciousness of the individual might concentrate on its evolution in surroundings where all was turned and centred towards the one endeavour and, next, when things were ready, to formulate and develop the new life in those surroundings and in this prepared spiritual atmosphere. It might be that, in such a concentration of effort, all the difficulties of the change would present themselves with a concentrated force; for each seeker, carrying in himself the possibilities but also the imperfections of a world that has to be transformed, would bring in not only his capacities but his difficulties and the oppositions of the old nature and, mixed together in the restricted circle of a small and close common life, these might assume a considerably enhanced force of obstruction which would tend to counterbalance the enhanced power and concentration of the forces making for the evolution. This is a difficulty that has broken in the past all efforts of mental man to evolve something better and more true and harmonious than the ordinary mental and vital life. But if Nature is ready and has taken her evolutionary decision or if the power of the Spirit descending from the higher planes is sufficiently strong, the difficulty would be overcome and a first evolutionary formation or formations would be possible.

But if an entire reliance upon the guiding Light and Will and a luminous expression of the truth of the Spirit in life are to be the law, that would seem to presuppose a gnostic world, a world in which the consciousness of all its beings was founded on this basis; there it can be understood that the life-interchange of gnostic individuals in a gnostic community or communities would be by its very nature an understanding and harmonious process. But here, actually, there would be a life of gnostic beings proceeding within or side by side with a life of beings in the Ignorance, attempting to emerge in it or out of it, and yet the law of the two lives would seem to be contrary and to offend against each other. A complete seclusion or separation of the life of a spiritual community from the life of the Ignorance would then seem to impose itself: for otherwise a compromise between the two lives would be necessary and with the compromise a danger of contamination or incompleteness of the greater existence; two different and incompatible principles of existence would be in contact and, even though the greater would influence the lesser, the smaller life would also have its effect on the greater, since such mutual impact is the law of all contiguity and

interchange. It might even be questioned whether conflict and collision would not be the first rule of their relation, since in the life of
the Ignorance there is present and active the formidable influence
of those forces of Darkness, supporters of evil and violence, whose
interest it is to contaminate or destroy all higher Light that enters
into the human existence. An opposition and intolerance or even a
persecution of all that is new or tries to rise above or break away
from the established order of the human Ignorance, or if it is victorious, an intrusion of the lower forces into it, an acceptance by the
world more dangerous than its opposition, and in the end an extinction, a lowering or a contamination of the new principle of life, have
been a frequent phenomenon of the past; that opposition might be
still more violent and a frustration might be still more likely if a
radically new light or new power were to claim the earth for its
heritage. But it is to be supposed that the new and completer light
would bring also a new and completer power. It might not be necessary for it to be entirely separate; it might establish itself in so many
islets and from there spread through the old life, throwing out upon
it its own influences and filtrations, gaining upon it, bringing to it
a help and illumination which a new aspiration in mankind might
after a time begin to understand and welcome.

But these are evidently problems of the transition, of the evolution before the full and victorious reversal of the manifesting Force
has taken place and the life of the gnostic becomes as much as that
of the mental being an established part of the terrestrial world-order.
If we suppose the gnostic consciousness to be established in the
earth-life, the power and knowledge at its disposal would be much
greater than the power and knowledge of mental man, and the life
of a community of gnostic beings, supposing it to be separate, would
be as safe against attack as the organised life of man against any
attack by a lower species. But as this knowledge and the very principle of the gnostic nature would ensure a luminous unity in the
common life of gnostic beings, so also it would be sufficient to ensure
a dominating harmony and reconciliation between the two types of
life. The influence of the supramental principle on earth would fall
upon the life of the Ignorance and impose harmony on it within its
limits. It is conceivable that the gnostic life would be separate, but
it would surely admit within its borders as much of human life as
was turned towards spirituality and in progress towards the heights;
the rest might organise itself mainly on the mental principle and on
the old foundations, but, helped and influenced by a recognisable
greater knowledge, it would be likely to do so on lines of a completer

harmonisation of which the human collectivity is not yet capable. Here also, however, the mind can only forecast probabilities and possibilities; the supramental principle in Supernature would itself determine according to the truth of things the balance of a new world-order.

A gnostic Supernature transcends all the values of our normal ignorant Nature; our standards and values are created by ignorance and therefore cannot determine the life of Supernature. At the same time our present nature is a derivation from Supernature and is not a pure ignorance but a half-knowledge; it is therefore reasonable to suppose that whatever spiritual truth there is in or behind its standards and values will reappear in the higher life, not as standards, but as elements transformed, uplifted out of the Ignorance and raised into the true harmony of a more luminous existence. As the universalised spiritual individual sheds the limited personality, the ego, as he rises beyond mind to a completer knowledge in Supernature, the conflicting ideals of the mind must fall away from him, but what is true behind them will remain in the life of Supernature. The gnostic* consciousness is a consciousness in which all contradictions are cancelled or fused into each other in a higher light of seeing and being, in a unified self-knowledge and world-knowledge. The gnostic being will not accept the mind's ideals and standards; he will not be moved to live for himself, for his ego, or for humanity or for others or for the community or for the State; for he will be aware of something greater than these half-truths, of the Divine Reality, and it is for that he will live, for its will in himself and in all, in a spirit of large universality, in the light of the will of the Transcendence. For the same reason there can be no conflict between self-affirmation and altruism in the gnostic life, for the self of the gnostic being is one with the self of all,—no conflict between the ideal of individualism and the collective ideal, for both are terms of a greater Reality and only in so far as either expresses the Reality or their fulfilment serves the will of the Reality, can they have a value for his spirit. But at the same time what is true in the mental ideals and dimly figured in them will be fulfilled in his existence; for while his consciousness exceeds the human values so that he cannot substitute mankind or the community or the State or others or himself for God, the affirmation of the Divine in himself and a sense of the Divine in others and the sense of oneness with humanity, with all other beings, with all the world because of the Divine in them and a lead towards a greater and better affirmation of the

See footnote page 1099.

growing Reality in them will be part of his life action. But what he shall do will be decided by the Truth of the Knowledge and Will in him, a total and infinite Truth that is not bound by any single mental law or standard but acts with freedom in the whole reality, with respect for each truth in its place and with a clear knowledge of the forces at work and the intention in the manifesting Divine Nisus at each step of cosmic evolution and in each event and circumstance.

All life for the achieved spiritual or gnostic consciousness must be the manifestation of the realised truth of spirit; only what can transform itself and find its own spiritual self in that greater Truth and fuse itself into its harmony can be accorded a life-acceptance. What will so survive the mind cannot determine, for the supramental gnosis will itself bring down its own truth and that truth will take up whatever of itself has been put forth in our ideals and realisations of mind and life and body. The forms it has taken there may not survive, for they are not likely to be suitable without change or replacement in the new existence; but what is real and abiding in them or even in their forms will undergo the transformation necessary for survival. Much that is normal to human life would disappear. In the light of gnosis the many mental idols, constructed principles and systems, conflicting ideals which man has created in all domains of his mind and life, could command no acceptance or reverence; only the truth, if any, which these specious images conceal, could have a chance of entry as elements of a harmony founded on a much wider basis. It is evident that in a life governed by the gnostic consciousness war with its spirit of antagonism and enmity, its brutality, destruction and ignorant violence, political strife with its perpetual conflict, frequent oppression, dishonesties, turpitudes, selfish interests, its ignorance, ineptitude and muddle could have no ground for existence. The arts and the crafts would exist, not for any inferior mental or vital amusement, entertainment of leisure and relieving excitement or pleasure, but as expressions and means of the truth of the spirit and the beauty and delight of existence. Life and the body would be no longer tyrannous masters demanding nine tenths of existence for their satisfaction, but means and powers for the expression of the spirit. At the same time, since the matter and the body are accepted, the control and the right use of physical things would be a part of the realised life of the spirit in the manifestation in earth-nature.

It is almost universally supposed that spiritual life must necessarily be a life of ascetic spareness, a pushing away of all that is not

absolutely needed for the bare maintenance of the body; and this is
valid for a spiritual life which is in its nature and intention a life of
withdrawal from life. Even apart from that ideal, it might be
thought that the spiritual turn must always make for an extreme
simplicity, because all else would be a life of vital desire and physical
self-indulgence. But from a wider standpoint this is a mental standard based on the law of the Ignorance of which desire is the
motive; to overcome the Ignorance, to delete the ego, a total reject-
tion not only of desire but of all the things that can satisfy desire
may intervene as a valid principle. But this standard or any mental
standard cannot be absolute nor can it be binding as a law on the
consciousness that has arisen above desire; a complete purity and
self-mastery would be in the very grain of its nature and that would
remain the same in poverty or in riches: for if it could be shaken
or sullied by either, it would not be real or would not be complete.
The one rule of the gnostic life would be the self-expression of the
Spirit, the will of the Divine Being; that will, that self-expression
could manifest through extreme simplicity or through extreme complexity and opulence or in their natural balance,—for beauty and
plenitude, a hidden sweetness and laughter in things, a sunshine and
gladness of life are also powers and expressions of the Spirit. In all
directions the Spirit within determining the law of the nature would
determine the frame of the life and its detail and circumstance. In
all there would be the same plastic principle; a rigid standardisation,
however necessary for the mind's arrangement of things, could not
be the law of the spiritual life. A great diversity and liberty of self-
expression based on an underlying unity might well become manifest; but everywhere there would be harmony and truth of order.

A life of gnostic beings carrying the evolution to a higher supramental status might fitly be characterised as a divine life; for it
would be a life in the Divine, a life of the beginnings of a spiritual
divine light and power and joy manifested in material Nature. That
might be described, since it surpasses the mental human level, as a
life of spiritual and supramental supermanhood. But this must not
be confused with past and present ideas of supermanhood; for
supermanhood in the mental idea consists of an overtopping of the
normal human level, not in kind but in degree of the same kind, by
an enlarged personality, a magnified and exaggerated ego, an increased power of mind, an increased power of vital force, a refined
or dense and massive exaggeration of the forces of the human
Ignorance; it carries also, commonly implied in it, the idea of a
forceful domination over humanity by the superman. That would

mean a supermanhood of the Nietzschean type; it might be at its worst the reign of the "blonde beast" or the dark beast or of any and every beast, a return to barbaric strength and ruthlessness and force: but this would be no evolution; it would be a reversion to an old strenuous barbarism. Or it might signify the emergency of the Rakshasa or Asura out of a tense effort of humanity to surpass and transcend itself, but in the wrong direction. A violent and turbulent exaggerated vital ego satisfying itself with a supreme tyrannous or anarchic strength or self-fulfilment would be the type of a Rakshasic supermanhood: but the giant, the ogre or devourer of the world, the Rakshasa, though he still survives, belongs in spirit to the past; a larger emergence of that type would be also a retrograde evolution. A mighty exhibition of an overpowering force, a self-possessed, self-held, even, it may be, an ascetically self-restrained mind-capacity and life-power, strong, calm or cold or formidable in collected vehemence, subtle, dominating, a sublimation at once of the mental and vital ego, is the type of the Asura. But earth has had enough of this kind in her past and its repetition can only prolong the old lines; she can get no true profit for her future, no power of self-exceeding, from the Titan, the Asura: even a great or supernormal power in it could only carry her on larger circles of her old orbit. But what has to emerge is something much more difficult and much more simple; it is a self-realised being, a building of the spiritual self, an intensity and urge of the soul and the deliverance and sovereignty of its light and power and beauty,—not an egoistic supermanhood seizing on a mental and vital domination over humanity, but the sovereignty of the Spirit over its own instruments, its possession of itself and its possession of life in the power of the spirit, a new consciousness in which humanity itself shall find its own self-exceeding and self-fulfilment by the revelation of the divinity that is striving for birth within it. This is the sole true supermanhood and the one real possibility of a step forward in evolutionary Nature.

This new status would indeed be a reversal of the present law of human consciousness and life, for it would reverse the whole principle of the life of the Ignorance. It is for the taste of the Ignorance, its surprise and adventure, one might say, that the soul has descended into the Inconscience and assumed the disguise of Matter, for the adventure and the joy of creation and discovery, an adventure of the spirit, an adventure of the mind and life and the hazardous surprises of their working in Matter, for the discovery and conquest of the new and the unknown; all this constitutes the enterprise of life and all this, it might seem, would cease with the cessation of the Ignorance. Man's life is made up of the light and the darkness, the gains and losses, the difficulties and dangers, the pleasures and pains of the Ignorance, a play of colours moving on a soil of the general neutrality of Matter which has as its basis the nescience and insensibility of the Inconscient. To the normal life-being an existence without the reactions of success and frustration, vital joy and grief, peril and passion, pleasure and pain, the vicissitudes and uncertainties of fate and struggle and battle and endeavour, a joy of novelty and surprise and creation projecting itself into the unknown, might seem to be void of variety and therefore void of vital savour. Any life surpassing these things tends to appear to it as something featureless and empty or cast in the figure of an immutable sameness; the human mind's picture of heaven is the incessant repetition of an eternal monotone. But this is a misconception; for an entry into the gnostic consciousness would be an entry into the Infinite. It would be a self-creation bringing out the Infinite infinitely into form of being, and the interest of the Infinite is much greater and multitudinous as well as more imperishably delightful than the interest of the finite. The evolution in the Knowledge would be a more beautiful and glorious manifestation with more vistas ever unfolding themselves and more intensive in all ways than any evolution could be in the Ignorance. The delight of the Spirit is ever new, the forms of beauty it takes innumerable, its godhead ever young and the taste of delight, *rasa,* of the Infinite eternal and inexhaustible. The gnostic manifestation of life would be more full and fruitful and its interest more vivid than the creative interest of the Ignorance; it would be a greater and happier constant miracle.

If there is an evolution in material Nature and if it is an evolution of being with consciousness and life as its two key-terms and powers, this fullness of being, fullness of consciousness, fullness of life must be the goal of development towards which we are tending and which will manifest at an early or later stage of our destiny. The self, the spirit, the reality that is disclosing itself out of the first inconscience of life and matter, would evolve its complete truth of being and consciousness in that life and matter. It would return to itself—or, if its end as an individual is to return into its Absolute, it could make that return also,—not through a frustration of life but through a spiritual completeness of itself in life. Our evolution in the Ignorance with its chequered joy and pain of self-discovery and world-discovery, its half fulfilments, its constant finding and missing, is only our first state. It must lead inevitably towards an evolution in the Knowledge, a self-finding and self-unfolding of the Spirit, a self-revelation of the Divinity in things in that true power of itself in Nature which is to us still a Supernature.

BIOGRAPHIES AND BIBLIOGRAPHIES

****

MAXWELL ANDERSON, playwright and poet, was born in Atlantic, Pennsylvania, on December 15, 1888, son of a minister. He spent his boyhood in Pennsylvania, Ohio and Iowa, and went in 1907 to North Dakota, from whose state university he was graduated in 1911. He married Margaret Haskett in 1911, received his M.A. from Stanford in 1914, taught school for several years in California and North Dakota, and finally entered on a career of journalism, at first in San Francisco and after 1918 in New York, where he worked as an editorial writer for the *New Republic*, *Evening Globe*, and *Morning World* until 1924.

Mr. Anderson wrote his first play, *White Desert*, in 1923, and followed it the next year with the immensely successful *What Price Glory?*, written in collaboration with Laurence Stallings. In 1933 he was awarded the Pulitzer Prize for his *Both Your Houses*, a satire of political corruption in Congress and both *Winterset* and *High Tor* won the Critics' Prize.

He was married for the second time in 1933 to Gertrude Maynard, and is the father of four children. He lives now at New City, Rockland County, New York. His *Anne of the Thousand Days* enjoyed a long run on Broadway, opening in December, 1948.

You Who Have Dreams, Simon & Schuster, 1925

Three American Plays, Harcourt, Brace, 1926

Saturday's Children, Longmans, Green, 1927

Gods of the Lightning, and *Outside Looking In* (former with HAROLD HICKERSON), Longmans, Green, 1928

Elizabeth the Queen (verse play), Longmans, Green, 1930

Night over Taos (verse play), French, 1932

Both Your Houses, French, 1933

Mary of Scotland (verse play), Doubleday, Doran, 1934

Valley Forge (verse play), Anderson House, 1934

Winterset (verse play), Anderson House, Washington, 1936

The Masque of Kings (verse play), Anderson House, Washington, 1936

The Wingless Victory (verse play), Anderson House, Washington, 1936

High Tor (verse play), Anderson House, Washington, 1937

The Star-Wagon, Anderson House, Washington, 1937

Knickerbocker Holiday (musical comedy, music by KURT WEILL), Anderson House, Washington, 1938

The Feast of Ortolans (radio play), Dramatists Play Service, 1938

The Essence of Tragedy (essays) Anderson House, Washington, 1939

Key Largo (verse play), Anderson House, Washington, 1940

Eleven Verse Plays, Harcourt, Brace, 1940

Second Overture, Dramatists Play Service, 1940

Journey to Jerusalem, Anderson House, Washington, 1940

Candle in the Wind, Anderson House, Washington, 1941

The Eve of St. Mark, Anderson House, Washington, 1942

Storm Operation, Anderson House, 1944

Truckline Cafe (not published), 1945

Joan of Lorraine, Anderson House, 1946

Off Broadway (essays), William Sloane Associates, 1947

Anne of the Thousand Days, William Sloane Associates, 1948

Lost in the Stars (musical play, music by KURT WEILL), not published, 1949

Unless there is indication to the contrary, all of Mr. Anderson's works are prose drama.

LOUIS ARAGON, French poet and novelist, was born in 1897 and was first widely known in letters for his connection with the Surrealist school of art and writing in Paris, a cult of creative effort on a level of expression not directed to ready comprehension except on the personal level of expression or that of some subconscious intuitive level of appreciation of an audience.

This period, which followed after his service in the First World War, was succeeded by a revolt against Surrealism and active engagement in politics as a member of the Communist party. In 1932 he received a five-year suspended sentence for a poem, *Red Front*, thought to have insulted the French flag. In 1936 he received the *Prix Renaudot* for the literary quality of his novels. In 1939 he was managing editor of the afternoon Communist paper in Paris, *Ce Soir*, which was suppressed just before Aragon was drafted into the French Army. In the Second World War Aragon was in a surrounded division and was taken prisoner at Angoulème, but escaped, leading others with him. For his military service he was awarded a *croix de guerre*, a second with palms, and the *medaille militaire*.

After the French armistice, Aragon acted as an organizer for the underground movement and wrote and published six books of poetry on clandestine presses. *Le Crève-Coeur* (Heartbreak) was printed legally in France during the occupation but was suppressed by the Germans. In total these books of poems are considered to be "a record of the wartime emotions of French soldiers and civilians, such as no other poet has even attempted to give"—to quote Malcolm Cowley's introduction to *Aragon, Poet of the French Resistance*. He is married to Elsa Triolet, a Russian writer of a number of books including a biography of the Russian poet Mayakovsky. She has been identified with the Existentialists.

Red Front (poem, translated by E. E. CUMMINGS), 1933
The Bells of Basel (novel), Harcourt, Brace, 1936
Residential Quarter (novel), Harcourt, Brace, 1938
The Century Was Young (novel), Duell, Sloan & Pearce, 1941
Aragon, Poet of the French Resistance (poems and prose; edited by MALCOLM COWLEY), Duell, Sloan and Pearce, 1945
Aurelien (novel), Duell, Sloan and Pearce, 1947

W. H. (Wystan Hugh) AUDEN was born February 21, 1907 in York, son of a retired medical officer. After leaving Oxford he was for a time a schoolmaster. In 1937 he was an ambulance driver for the Loyalists in the Spanish War and that same year received the King's Poetry Medal on his return to England. In 1939 he came to the United States to become a permanent resident. He is married to Erika Mann, the writer and daughter of Thomas Mann.

Some of his writing has been in collaboration with Christopher Isherwood and Louis MacNeice.

Auden's *Age of Anxiety* inspired a symphony by Leonard Bernstein and a ballet with choreography by Jerome Robbins which was produced in 1950 by the New York City Ballet Company.

Poems, 1930
The Orators (prose and verse), 1932
The Dance of Death (poems), 1933
The Dog Beneath the Skin or, *Where is Francis* (play), 1935
Look Stranger (poems), 1936
The Ascent of F.6 (play, with CHRISTOPHER ISHERWOOD), 1936
Letters From Iceland (prose, with LOUIS MACNEICE), 1937
Spain, 1937
The Oxford Book of Light Verse (editor: anthology), Oxford Press, 1938
On The Frontier (play, with ISHERWOOD), Random House, 1939
Journey to a War (prose, with ISHERWOOD), Random House, 1939
Another Time (poems), Random House, 1940
The Double Man (poems), Random House, 1941
New Year Letter (poems), Faber and Faber, 1941
For The Time Being (poems), Random House, 1944
The Collected Poetry of W. H. Auden, Random House, 1945
The Age of Anxiety (poetry), Random House, 1947
The Portable Greek Reader (editor: anthology), Viking, 1948
The Enchafed Flood, Random House, 1950

SRI AUROBINDO, considered by English and Indian scholars as the most outstanding of the Indo-Anglians now writing, is a master of many languages and ranges of knowledge. His works included a seven-hundred page volume of *Collected Poems and Plays* (1942); *Letters to His Disciples* (essays and criticism); *The Future Poetry* (literary criticism); and *The Life Divine* (1300 pages, a philosophical treatise).

The Life Divine was brought out in America in 1949 by The Greystone Press, and it is from this volume that Sri Aurobindo is represented in *The World's Best*. The book is prescribed for study at Harvard, Syracuse, Cornell and Stanford Universities. The writer's contention in that book is that in unified cooperative movement, helping man to divest himself of separative, communalistic and nationalistic tendencies, lies mankind's hope of regaining a living faith in the ideal unity of all life.

The author is seventy-eight years old, and lives in a small town in Southeastern India. He was educated at London and Cambridge. He was nominated in 1950 for the Nobel Peace Prize.

MARIANO AZUELA was born in 1873 and lives in Mexico City. A doctor by profession, he has written many novels. He became internationally famous for his sensational novel of Mexican Revolution *Los de Abajo*, written from his experiences as comrade of the revolutionist, Julian Medina. He was Director General of Public Education in Jalisco in 1915.

The Under Dogs (novel), Brentano's, 1929

PIO BAROJA (y Nessi) was born in San Sebastian, Spain, in 1873, the son of a Basque mining engineer. His career began as a doctor of medicine, which he abandoned to run a bakery. At twenty-six he left Spain to travel through Europe. He is a free-thinker, an anti-clerical and a great realist. He has been widely translated. He has never married. Of Baroja, H. L. Mencken once wrote, "He stands for the modern Spanish mind at its most enlightened...the Spanish of education and worldly wisdom, detached from the medieval imbecility of the old regime and yet aloof from the worst follies of the demagogues. . . ."

Of his eighty-odd books, all but twelve (of essays) are novels. Among those translated into English are:

Youth And Egolatry (autobiography), 1920
The Quest (novel), 1922
Weeds (novel), 1923
The Lord of Labray (novel), 1926
The Tree Of Knowledge (novel), 1928
(All published by Knopf)

HILAIRE BELLOC. Anglo-French historian, essayist, novelist and poet, was born July 27, 1870 at Saint-Cloud, Paris, the son of a French barrister and his English wife. At Oxford he won a history scholarship and was graduated with honors in 1895. His first book was *Verses and Sonnets*, followed by children's books and later by historical biographies. From 1906 to 1910 Belloc was a Liberal member of Parliament. He is a Catholic and in 1934 received the Papal honor of Knight Commander with Star of the Order of St. Gregory the Great. His wife, who died in 1914, was an American. One son died in the First World War and a second in the Second World War.

Verses and Sonnets, 1895
The Bad Child's Book of Beasts, 1896
The Path to Rome, 1902
On Nothing, 1908
On Everything, 1909
On Anything, 1910
On Something, 1911
The Jews, 1922
On, 1923
History of England (4 vols.), 1925-1927
Richelieu, 1929
Wolsey, 1930
The Man Who Made Gold, 1931
Oliver Cromwell, 1931
Napoleon, Lippincott, 1932
Charles II: The Last Rally, Harper, 1939
Cautionary Verses, Knopf, 1941
Places (essays), Sheed and Ward, 1942
Elizabeth: Creature of Circumstance, Harper, 1942
The Servile State, Holt, 1946

WILLIAM ROSE BENÉT was born February 2, 1886, at Fort Hamilton in New York Harbor of a family military for generations. He was graduated from the Sheffield Scientific School at Yale in 1907. After a period spent in California with his family, he got a job on *The Century Magazine*, as reader from 1911 to 1914, and assistant editor 1914 to 1917. He married Teresa Frances Thompson, sister of the novelist, Kathleen Norris, and became the father of three children.

In the First World War, Mr. Benét was commissioned a second lieutenant in the Air Service (non-flying). After the war an advertising job and a position as assistant editor of *The Nation's Business* followed; and in 1920 he helped found *The Literary Review* of the New York *Evening Post*, of which he was associate editor until 1923. At that time Henry Seidel Canby reorganized the Review as *The Saturday Review of Literature* and established it independently. All the old staff transferred to the new venture, of which Mr. Benét remained an associate editor. In 1929-30 he was also editor of the publishing firm of Brewer and Warren.

William Rose Benét was best known for his poetry. *The Dust Which Is God* received the Pulitzer Prize for poetry in 1942. His other works included a novel, essays, children's books, and he compiled and edited several distinguished anthologies. Being the literary executor of his second wife, Elinor Wylie, he collected, and wrote the foreword to, her *Collected Poems*, and, in her *Collected Prose*, wrote the preface to the "Fugitive Prose" section. He also edited *Last Poems* by Elinor Wylie, (poems transcribed from MSS. by Jane D. Wise and other poems hitherto unpublished in book form) and wrote the Foreword (Alfred A. Knopf, 1943). Mr. Benét's third wife was Lora Baxter, the actress. His fourth wife was Marjorie Flack, writer and illustrator of children's books.

While Mr. Benét made his own choice for THE WORLD'S BEST before the book was published and is thus included, he died at the age of 64 of a heart attack in New York on May 4, 1950.

Merchants from Cathay, Century, 1913
The Falconer of God, and Other Poems, Century, 1914
The East I Know (translation from the French; with TERESA FRANCES BENÉT), Yale University Press, New Haven, Conn., 1914
The Great White Wall, Yale University Press, New Haven, Conn., 1916
The Burglar of the Zodiac, and Other Poems, Yale University Press, New Haven, Conn., 1918
Perpetual Light: A Memorial, Yale University Press, New Haven, Conn., 1919
Moons of Grandeur, Doran, 1920
Saturday Papers (essays on literature; with HENRY SEIDEL CANBY and AMY LOVEMAN), Macmillan, 1921
The First Person Singular (novel), Doran, 1922
Poems for Youth (anthology), Dutton & Company, 1925
The Flying King of Kurio (juvenile), Doran, 1926
Wild Goslings (essays), Doran, 1927
Man Possessed (selected poetry), Doran, 1927
Sagacity, Random House, 1929
Twentieth-Century Poetry (anthology; with HENRY SEIDEL CANBY and JOHN DRINKWATER), Houghton Mifflin, Boston, 1929
Adventures in English Literature (anthology text book; with others), Harcourt, Brace, 1931
Collected Poems and Collected Prose of Elinor Wylie (editor), Knopf, 1932

Rip Tide (novel in verse), Duffield & Green, 1932
Starry Harness, Duffield & Green, 1933
Fifty Poets (anthology), Duffield & Green, 1933
Reviewing Ten Years ("a personal record of *The Saturday Review of Literature*"), Saturday Review Publishers, 1933
The Prose and Poetry of Elinor Wylie (essay),Wheaton College Press, Norton, Mass., 1934
The Pocket University (guide to daily reading; editor), Doubleday, Doran, Garden City, N. Y., 1934
Emblems and Electra (drawings by W. A. DWIGGINS), Mergenthaler Linotype Co., Brooklyn, N. Y., 1935
Golden Fleece, Dodd, Mead, 1935
Harlem, and Other Poems, Methuen, London, 1935
From Robert & Elizabeth Browning (correspondence), Murray, London, 1936
Mother Goose (a new collection; illustrations by ROGER DUVOISIN), Heritage Press, 1936
The Oxford Anthology of American Literature (anthology; with NORMAN HOLMES PEARSON), Oxford University Press, 1938
Poems for Modern Youth (anthology; with ADOLF GILLIS), Houghton Mifflin, Boston, 1938
Day's End: A Fantasia in One Act: Dock Street Theatre, Charleston, S. C. (Nat. Playwrighting Award, produced May 8, 1939. In *The Best One-Act Plays of 1939*. Edited by MARGARET MAYORGA), Dodd, Mead, 1940
With Wings as Eagles, Dodd, Mead, 1940
Adolphus or The Adopted Dolphin and the Pirate's Daughter (juvenile verses; pictures by MARJORIE FLACK), Houghton Mifflin, Boston, 1941
The Dust Which is God (semi-autobiographical novel in verse), Dodd, Mead, 1941
My Brother Steve (Introduction to *Twenty-Five Short Stories by Stephen Vincent Benét*), The Sun Dial Press, 1943
Day of Deliverance, A Book of Poems in Wartime, Knopf, 1944
The Poetry of Freedom (anthology; edited with NORMAN COUSINS), Random House, 1945
Anthology of Famous English and American Poetry (ed. with CONRAD AIKEN), Modern Library, 1945
The Stairway of Surprise (poems), Knopf, 1947
Timothy's Angels (juvenile verses; pictures by ALAJALOV), Crowell, 1947

The Reader's Encyclopedia; An Encyclopedia of World Literature and the Arts
(editor), Crowell, 1948

ELIZABETH BOWEN, Anglo-Irish novelist, was born June 7, 1899, in Dublin,
on both sides of Anglo-Irish descent.
While she has lived for years in London,
Oxford, or in Italy, her family home,
Bowen's Court, Kildorrery, County Cork,
which was given to her ancestors by
Cromwell, is her property and her residence a good deal of the time.

She began writing at twenty, and has
written many distinguished short stories
and several novels, usually concerned with
the upper middle class.

The House in Paris, 1916
To the North, 1933
The Death of the Heart, 1939
Look at All Those Roses (stories), 1941
Bowen's Court, 1942
Ivy Gripped the Steps, 1946
The Heat of the Day, 1949
(all published by Knopf)

VAN WYCK BROOKS, American critic,
was born in Plainfield, New Jersey, on
February 16, 1886. He graduated from
Harvard in 1908 and since then has kept
in close touch with the literary life of
America. His first book, *The Wine of
the Puritans* (1909) was recognized as
a brilliant study, and it was followed by
the author's appointment as an instructor
at Leland Stanford University (1911-1913).
After this he taught for a year in England. From 1915 to 1918 he was connected
with the Century Company, and in 1920
he became associate editor of *The Freeman.* He edited Randolph Bourne's *The
History of a Literary Radical* (1920) and
has done several translations.

The 1923 *Dial* prize of $2000 was pre-
sented to Mr. Brooks in recognition of
his having created a new point of view
in criticism in this country. In 1937 he
received the Gold Medal for Essays and
Criticism of the National Institute of Arts
and Letters.

He now lives in Bridgewater, Connecticut.

The Wine of the Puritans, Kennerley, 1909
The Malady of the Ideal, Fifield, London,
1913
John Addington Symonds, Kennerley, 1914
The World of H. G. Wells, Kennerley, 1915

America's Coming of Age, Huebsch, 1915
Letters and Leadership, Huebsch, 1918
The Ordeal of Mark Twain, Dutton, 1920
The Pilgrimage of Henry James, Dutton,
1925
Emerson and Others, Dutton, 1927
The Life of Emerson, Dutton, 1932
Sketches in Criticism, Dutton, 1932
Three Essays on America, Dutton, 1934
*The Flowering of New England (1815-
1865)*, Dutton, 1936
*New England: Indian Summer (1865-
1915)*, Dutton, 1940
On Literature Today, Dutton, 1941
Opinions of Oliver Allston, Dutton, 1941
The World of Washington Irving, Dutton,
1944
The Times of Melville and Whitman, Dut-
ton, 1947
A Chilmark Miscellany, Dutton, 1948

PEARL BUCK, winner of both the Nobel
and the Pulitzer Prizes, spent a great
deal of her life in the China of which
she writes so eloquently. She was born
in Hillsboro, West Virginia, on June 26,
1892, but when she was a few months
old she was taken to China, where her
parents were missionaries. She returned
to America to enter Randolph-Macon College, graduated in 1914, and returned to
China. She came to America again in
1925, for one year, to study at Cornell
for her master's degree. For a number
of years she taught English at Southeastern University and Chung Yang University, both of Nanking.

Her first book was published in 1930,
and *The Good Earth*, which was awarded
the Pulitzer Prize, appeared in 1931. In
1938 she received the Nobel Prize in
literature, for the bulk of her work.

She came to the United States in 1934,
and makes her home in the countryside
of Pennsylvania. She is married to Richard J. Walsh, New York publisher.

East Wind: West Wind (novel), Day,
1930
The Good Earth (novel), Day, 1931
Sons (novel), Day, 1932
Is There a Case for Foreign Missions?
(pamphlet), Day, 1932
The First Wife, and Other Stories, Day,
1933
All Men Are Brothers (translation from
the Chinese), Day, 1933
The Mother (novel), Day, 1934
A House Divided (novel), Day, 1935
The Exile (biography), Day, 1936
Fighting Angel (biography), Day, 1936

This Proud Heart (novel), Day, 1938
The Patriot (novel), Day, 1939
The Chinese Novel (lecture), Day, 1939
Other Gods (novel), Day, 1940
Stories for Little Children, Day, 1940
Dragon Seed (novel), Day, 1940
Today and Forever (short stories), Day, 1941
Of Men and Women (essays), Day, 1941
American Unity and Asia (essays and lectures), Day, 1942
The Chinese Children Next Door, 1942
What America Means to Me, 1943
The Water-Buffalo Children, 1943
The Promise, 1944
The Dragon Fish, 1944
Tell the People (with JAMES YEN), American Institute of Pacific Relations, 1945
Yu Lan: Flying Boy of China, 1945
Portrait of a Marriage, 1945
Talk About Russia (with MARSHA SCOTT), 1945
Pavilion of Women (novel), 1946
How It Happens (with ERNA VON PUSTAU), 1947
Far And Near; Stories of Japan, China and America, 1947
The Big Wave, 1948
Peony, 1948
American Argument (with ESLANDA GOODE ROBESON), 1949
Kinfolk, 1949
(All books published by John Day Co. unless otherwise noted)

IVAN BUNIN was born in Voronezh, of Russian land-owning nobility, October 22, 1870. His first book of poems appeared in 1891. He won the Pushkin Prize in 1903. He has translated Byron, Tennyson and Longfellow into Russian. He left Russia in 1919 to live in France. In 1933 he won the Nobel prize, his *The Gentleman From San Francisco* being specifically cited in the award.

His first fictional work was *The Village* (1910), which Gorki praised for its "bold truth" about the Russian peasants' mode of life and for its having resisted the fashionable temptation of idealizing the peasantry.

The Gentleman From San Francisco (stories), Knopf, 1923
The Dreams of Chang (stories), Knopf, 1923
The Village (novel), Knopf, 1923
Mitya's Love (novel), 1926
The Well of Days (novel), Knopf, 1934
Grammar of Love (stories), 1934

The Eleaghin Affair (stories), Knopf, 1935
The Liberation of Tolstoy (not published in the United States), 1937
Dark Avenues (stories), John Lehmann (London), 1949

JAMES BRANCH CABELL was born in Richmond, Virginia, on April 14, 1879, of a family which has lived in Virginia since colonial days. He was graduated from William and Mary in 1898, where as an undergraduate he taught French and Greek for two years. His first position was on the *Richmond Times*. The following year he went to New York and reported on the *New York Herald* from 1899 to 1901, when he returned to Richmond and worked on the *News*. He spent the period from 1902 to 1910 in writing, and his first magazine stories and books appeared in these years.

Mr. Cabell worked in the coal mines of West Virginia from 1911 to 1913, and upon his return to Virginia interested himself in genealogical and historical research and in his writing. He was editor of *The Reviewer* in 1921 and of the *American Spectator* from 1932 to 1935.

In 1913 he was married to Priscilla Bradley who died in 1949; he has one son, and lives in Richmond.

Most of Mr. Cabell's books belong to a series which is referred to collectively as the *Biography of Manuel*. It is the history of an imaginary but perfectly constructed medieval country, Poictesme, which Mr. Cabell sees so minutely in his mind that he has drawn maps of it. In 1930, with the publication of *Townsend of Lichfield*, the Dom Manuel biography was complete.

The Eagle's Shadow, Doubleday, Page, 1904
The Line of Love (short stories), Harpers, 1905
Gallantry (short stories), Harpers, 1907
Chivalry (short stories), Harpers, 1909
The Cords of Vanity, Doubleday, Page, 1909
The Soul of Melicent, Stokes, 1913
The Rivet in Grandfather's Neck, McBride, 1915
The Majors and Their Marriages (genealogy), privately printed, 1915
The Certain Hour (short stories), McBride, 1916
From the Hidden Way (poetry), McBride, 1916

The Cream of the Jest, McBride, 1917
Beyond Life (criticism), McBride, 1919
Jurgen, McBride, 1919
The Judging of Jurgen (criticism), Book-
 fellows, Chicago, 1920
Domnei (reissue of *The Soul of Melicent*),
 McBride, 1920
Figures of Earth, McBride, 1921
The Jewel Merchants (one-act play),
 McBride, 1921
Joseph Hergesheimer (criticism), Book-
 fellows, Chicago, 1921
Taboo (criticism), McBride, 1921
The Lineage of Lichfield (criticism), Mc-
 Bride, 1922
The High Place, McBride, 1923
Straws and Prayer-Books (criticism),
 McBride, 1924
The Silver Stallion, McBride, 1926
The Music from Behind the Moon, Day,
 1926
Something About Eve, McBride, 1927
Ballades from the Hidden Way (reprinted
 poetry, with introduction), Crosby Gaige,
 1928
The White Robe, McBride, 1928
The Way of Ecben, McBride, 1929
Sonnets from Antan (poetry), Fountain
 Press, 1929
Townsend of Lichfield (miscellanies), Mc-
 Bride, 1930
The Works of James Branch Cabell, eight-
 een volumes, with revised texts, Mc-
 Bride, 1927-1930.
Between Dawn and Sunrise (selections
 edited by JOHN MACY), McBride, 1930
Some of Us (criticism), McBride, 1930
These Restless Heads (autobiography), Mc-
 Bride, 1932
Special Delivery (series of letters), Mc-
 Bride, 1933
Smirt, McBride, 1934
Ladies and Gentlemen (series of letters),
 McBride, 1934
Smith, McBride, 1935
Preface to the Past (collected prefaces
 to *The Works*), McBride, 1936
Smire, Doubleday, Doran, Garden City,
 N. Y., 1937
The Nightmare Has Triplets (criticism),
 Doubleday, Doran, Garden City, N.Y.,
 1937
Of Ellen Glasgow, an Inscribed Portrait
 (with ELLEN GLASGOW), privately print-
 ed, 1938
The King Was in His Counting House,
 Farrar & Rinehart, 1938
Hamlet Had an Uncle, Farrar & Rinehart,
 1940
The First Gentleman of America, Farrar
 & Rinehart, 1942

The St. Johns (with A. J. HANNA; Rivers
 of America Series), Farrar & Rinehart,
 1943
There Were Two Pirates, Farrar, Straus,
 1946
Let Me Lie, (Virginia commentaries),Far-
 rar, Straus, 1947
The Witch-Woman, Farrar, Straus, 1948
The Devil's Own Dear Son, Farrar, Straus,
 1949
   All of Mr. Cabell's works, unless otherwise specified, are novels.

ERSKINE CALDWELL was born in
White Oak, Georgia, on December 17,
1902. He was educated at Erskine College, the University of Virginia, and the
University of Pennsylvania. He has been
three times married and has three children by his first wife, Helen Lannigan.
His second wife, Margaret Bourke-White,
whom he married in 1939, was his picture collaborator on several books about
the American scene and one on Europe.
He has worked as a cotton picker, stage-
hand, professional football player, newspaper reporter, book reviewer, lecturer,
editor, and screen writer and was war
correspondent for *PM* and Columbia
Broadcasting System in Russia in 1941.
Novels and volumes of short stories have
been published abroad in following translations: French, German, Italian, Czech,
Norwegian, Swedish, Danish, Russian,
Georgian, Ukrainian, Japanese, Chinese,
Spanish, and Portuguese. He lives now
in Arizona.
   "County Full of Swedes" received the
Yale Review $1000 Award for fiction in
1933. Many of his books concern poor
whites of the South, and his novel *Tobacco Road*, dramatized by Jack Kirk-
land, brought to Broadway the plight of
these people in a play which had a longer
run on Broadway than any other play
in history. His short stories, a form in
which he is ranked among the leading
practitioners in America, have been collected in the volume *Jackpot*.

The Bastard (novelette), Heron Press,
 1929
Poor Fool (novelette), Rariota Press,
 1930
American Earth (short stories), Scrib-
 ners, 1931
Mama's Little Girl, privately printed,
 Mount Vernon, Me., 1932
Tobacco Road (novel), Scribners, 1932

God's Little Acre (novel), Viking Press, 1933

We Are the Living (short stories), Viking Press, 1933

A Message for Genevieve, privately printed, Mount Vernon, Me., 1933

Journeyman (novel), Viking Press, 1935

Kneel to the Rising Sun (short stories), Viking Press, 1935

Tenant Farmer (pamphlet), Phalanx Press, 1935

Some American People (vignettes), McBride, 1935

The Sacrilege of Alan Kent (novelette), Falmouth Book House, Portland, Me., 1936

You Have Seen Their Faces (documentary; with MARGARET BOURKE-WHITE), Viking Press, 1937

Southways (short stories), Duell, Sloan & Pearce, 1938

North of the Danube (documentary; with MARGARET BOURKE-WHITE), Duell, Sloan & Pearce, 1938

Trouble in July (novel), Duell, Sloan and Pearce, 1940

Jackpot (complete short stories), Duell, Sloan & Pearce, 1940

Say! Is This the U.S.A.? (documentary; with MARGARET BOURKE-WHITE), Duell, Sloan & Pearce, 1941

All Out on the Road to Smolensk (autobiography), Duell, Sloan & Pearce, 1942

All Night Long (novel), Duell, Sloan & Pearce, 1942

Georgia Boy (novel), Duell, Sloan & Pearce, 1943

Tragic Ground (novel), Duell, Sloan & Pearce, 1944

A House in the Uplands (novel), Duell, Sloan & Pearce, 1946

Caldwell Caravan (collected stories), World Publishing, 1946

The Sure Hand of God (novel), Duell, Sloan & Pearce, 1947

This Very Earth (novel), Duell, Sloan & Pearce, 1948

A Place Called Estherville (novel), Duell, Sloan & Pearce, 1949

MORLEY CALLAGHAN is of Irish descent. He was born in Toronto, Canada, in 1903, and was graduated from St. Michael's College of the University of Toronto. After graduation he was a reporter on the Toronto *Daily Star*, and later the proprietor of a lending library in his native city. He was graduated from the law school there and has become a member of the Canadian bar.

Mr. Callaghan was encouraged in his writing career by Ernest Hemingway and Ezra Pound, both of whom were instrumental in having his early stories published. His first novel, *Strange Fugitive*, was published in 1928. Since then he has written more novels and three collections of short stories.

He was married in 1929 to Loretta Dee, and has two children. He lives in Toronto, Canada.

Strange Fugitive (novel), Scribners, 1928

A Native Argosy (short stories), Scribners, 1929

It's Never Over (novel), Scribners, 1930

No Man's Meat (short stories), E. W. Titus, Paris, 1931

A Broken Journey (novel), Scribners, 1932

Such Is My Beloved (novel), Scribners, 1934

They Shall Inherit the Earth (novel), Random House, 1935

Now That April's Here (short stories), Random House, 1936

More Joy in Heaven (novel), Random House, 1937

ALBERT CAMUS was born in Algiers in 1913 and spent the early part of his life in North Africa. He worked at odd jobs to pay his way through the University of Algiers. In 1940 he quit journalism and moved to France. During the Nazi occupation he started, with others, the underground paper *Combat*. He is the author of many pamphlets.

The Stranger (novel), Knopf, 1946

The Plague (novel), Knopf, 1948

Caligula; and *Cross Purpose* (plays), New Directions, 1948

WINSTON (Leonard Spencer) CHURCHILL, English statesman, soldier, historian and biographer, is the third son of the late Lord Randolph Churchill and grandson of the seventh Duke of Marlborough. He was born November 30, 1874. His mother was an American, the former Jennie Jerome of New York. He was educated at Harrow and Sandhurst, going thence into the army. In the South African war he was a war correspondent for the London *Morning Post*, was captured by the Boers and escaped.

He entered Parliament as a conservative member in 1900, joined the Liberals in 1904 and in 1906 was Under-Secretary for the Colonies. He was Home Secretary in

1910 and in 1911 was First Lord of the Admiralty, preparing the British fleet for its part in the war beginning in August 1914. In 1917 he was Minister of Munitions and Minister for War and Air in 1919-1921. He was defeated by his constituencies in 1923 and 1924. He was Chancellor of the Exchequer until 1929 and on the resignation of Neville Chamberlain in 1940, he became Prime Minister, directing England's part in the Second World War until its conclusion, working with Roosevelt and Stalin through several international conferences. After the Second World War he was out of official politics until he contested the English election of 1950 with Clement Attlee, in an election which returned him to Parliament and depreciated the Labor majority to a scant few.

Beginning with *The Story of the Malakand Field Force* in 1898, Churchill produced many works of history and biography including his noted *Marlborough* in several volumes. In the field of oratory he has been unexcelled in modern times. In 1950 he was nominated for The Nobel Peace Prize.

HISTORICAL AND DESCRIPTIVE

The Story of the Malakand Field Force, 1898
The River War (2 vols.), 1899
Hamilton's March, 1900
London to Ladysmith via Pretoria, 1900
Mr. Brodrick's Army, 1903
My African Journey, 1908
The World Crisis (6 vols.), 1923-31
The Gathering Storm, Houghton, Mifflin, 1948
Their Finest Hour, Houghton, Mifflin, 1949
The Grand Alliance, Houghton, Mifflin, 1950

BIOGRAPHICAL

Lord Randolph Churchill (2 vols.), 1906
Marlborough; His Life and Times (4 vols.), 1933-38
Great Contemporaries, 1937

POLITICAL

For Free Trade (speeches), 1906
Liberalism and the Social Problem (speeches), 1909
The People's Rights (speeches), 1910
Thoughts and Adventures, 1923
India: Speeches and an Introduction, 1931
Arms and the Covenant (speeches), 1938
While England Slept, Putnam, 1938

MISCELLANEOUS

Savrola, 1900

My Early Life (also published as *A Roving Commission*), 1930
Step by Step: 1936-1939, Putnam, 1939
Blood, Sweat, and Tears (speeches), Putnam, 1941
The End of the Beginning (speeches), Little, Brown, 1943
Onwards to Victory (speeches), Little, Brown, 1944
The Dawn of Liberation (speeches), Little, Brown, 1945
Secret Session Speeches, Simon and Schuster, 1946
Victory; War Speeches, Little, Brown, 1946
Maxims and Reflections (edited by COLIN COOTE), Houghton, Mifflin, 1949

PAUL CLAUDEL, French poet and playwright, was born August 6, 1868, in a small village in Aisne, the son of a father who dealt in mortgages and a mother whose family were mainly Catholic farmers and priests. He went to law school and later to the École des Sciences Politiques.

In 1886 he experienced a literary revelation with the discovery of Rimbaud, which released him from "a prison of inflexible laws," and on Christmas the same year he became a Roman Catholic convert. He was eighteen.

Four years later he passed examinations for the French diplomatic service, and the same year his first drama was published in Paris anonymously.

For many years Claudel lived a very active diplomatic life, beginning with his appointment as consulate assistant in New York in 1893, and consul pro tem. in Boston the following year. He was consul at Shanghai, Fuchow, and other cities in China. In 1906 he married a Frenchwoman and their first child was born in China.

After service in Prague, Frankfort and elsewhere, he went to Brazil as Minister Plenipotentiary, his secretary Darius Milhaud accompanying him. Milhaud set many of Claudel's poems to music and wrote the score for his *Book of Christopher Columbus,* produced in 1929 at the Berlin Opera House. He was French Ambassador to Japan 1921 to 1925, to the United States 1933 to 1935 and in 1939 he was with the French Ministry of Propaganda.

He has five children and several grandchildren, and is now living in France. He has been often called the greatest living French poet. His plays have a Greek grandeur. His poems are mystical, religious and Catholic.

The East I Know, Yale University Press, 1914
The Tidings Brought to Mary (play), 1916
The Hostage (play), 1917
Tête d'Or (play), 1919
Three Poems of the War, 1919
The City (play), 1920
Proteus (play), 1921
Letters to a Doubter, 1927
The Book of Christopher Columbus (play), 1930
The Satin Slipper (play), 1931
Ways and Crossways, 1933
Coronal (poems), Pantheon Books, 1943
Poetic Art, Philosophical Library, 1948
The Eye Listens, Philosophical Library, 1950

JEAN COCTEAU was born July 5, 1891 near Paris and is one of the most versatile men in French letters: novelist, dramatist, scenario writer, critic, poet, essayist, actor, director, stage designer and producer. He lives in Paris. He visited America in 1949 in connection with one of his film premieres.

Thomas the Impostor (novel), 1925
The Grand Écart (novel), 1925
Enfants Terribles (novel), 1925
The Call to Order (essays), 1927
Opium: The Diary of an Addict (essays), 1932
Orphée (play), 1933
The Infernal Machine (play), 1936
Round the World Again in Eighty Days (essays), Routledge (London), 1937
The Eagle Has Two Heads (play), Funk, 1948
Art and Faith (letters, with JACQUES MARITAIN), Philosophical Library, 1948
Blood of a Poet (film), Bodley Press, 1949

COLETTE (Mme. Maurice Goudeket, formerly Colette-Willy), is the outstanding living French woman novelist. She was born January 28, 1873, in a small town in Burgundy, France. Baptized Gabrielle Sidonie Colette, she kept only her family name for writing. While she has not been extensively translated and sold in America, she has written a great many novels and some essays. A play made from her novel *Chéri* is now running in Paris. Early in 1950 Americans saw a French motion picture from her novel *Gigi*. She began her writing under the influence of her first husband, Willy, whom she divorced when she was thirty-

three. She lives with her fourth husband in an apartment in the Palais Royal, a neighbor of Cocteau. In 1927 the poet Paul Claudel, spoke of her as "the greatest living writer" in France. Her work consists of fifty-odd books being brought out in 1950 in a fifteen-volume collection in Paris. She is President of the Goncourt Academy, one of the highest honors a woman writer can attain to in France.

Chéri, Boni, 1929
Mitsou, Boni, 1930
Claudine at School, Boni, 1930
The Gentle Libertine, Farrar & Rinehart, 1931
Recaptured, Doubleday, 1932
The Last of Chéri, Putnam, 1932
A Lesson In Love, Farrar and Rinehart, 1932
The Innocent Wife, Farrar and Rinehart, 1934
Duo, Farrar and Rinehart, 1935

PADRAIC COLUM, Irish-American poet and dramatist, was born Dec. 8, 1881. He came to America in 1914 for the first time and save for a visit to Hawaii in 1923 to write stories for Hawaiian children, based on native folklore, and trips to Europe, he has lived here since. In 1912 he married Mary Gunning Maguire of Dublin who, as Mary Colum, is a well-known literary critic. Colum came of age in Dublin at the time of the Celtic Revival and his first play was produced when he was twenty. His second, *The Land*, was the first success of the Irish Theatre. In 1916 he founded *The Irish Review* with James Stephens and Thomas MacDonagh. He was President of the Poetry Society of America in 1938 and 1939 and is a member of the Academy of Irish Letters.

Wild Earth (poems), 1907
My Irish Year, 1912
A Boy in Eirinn, 1913
Three Plays, 1916
The King of Ireland's Son, 1916
Mogu, the Wanderer (plays), 1917
The Adventures of Odysseus and the Tale of Troy, 1918
The Boy Who Knew What the Bird Said, 1918
The Girl Who Sat by the Ashes, 1919
The Children of Odin, 1920
The Boy Apprenticed to an Enchanter, 1920
The Golden Fleece, 1921
Dramatic Legends (poems), 1922

The Children Who Followed the Piper, 1923

Castle Conquer, 1923

The Island of the Mighty, At The Gateways of the Day (Hawaiian Stories), 1924

The Voyagers, The Forge in the Forest, The Bright Islands (Hawaiian Stories), 1925

The Road Round Ireland, 1926

Creatures (verse) ; *The Fountain of Youth*, 1927

Balloon (a comedy in four acts) ; *Orpheus* (Stories from the Mythologies of the World), 1929

Old Pastures, 1931

Poems, 1932

A Half-Day's Ride (A Book of Essays), 1932

The Big Tree of Bunlahy (stories), 1933

The Legend of Saint Columba, 1935

The Story of Lowry Maen (narrative poem), 1937

Where the Winds Never Blew and the Cocks Never Crew, Macmillan, 1940

The Frenzied Prince, McKay, 1943

Anthology of Irish Verse (ed.), Black and Gold Library, 1948

Most of the above were published by Macmillan.

NOEL COWARD, the English playwright, composer, lyricist, actor, director, producer, scenario writer and motion picture actor, was born in Teddington, December 16, 1899 and was educated privately and at Croydon, receiving his dramatic training at the leading dramatic school in England, the Italia Conti Academy. He made his debut in 1910 in a show with Gertrude Lawrence. He was then eleven. He served in the army during the First World War. Two Coward productions, *This Happy Breed* (play) and *In Which We Serve* (a motion picture), were among Coward's by-product contributions to the Second World War. He has written flippant society comedies, serious dramas, musical plays and patriotic pageants. One of his most recent activities was appearing in the British full-length film version of one of his one act plays, *The Astonished Heart*. He lives in Paris, London and the British West Indies. He has covered many phases of a very active life in his witty autobiography *Present Indicative*.

Easy Virtue, Harper, 1926

Bitter Sweet, and other Plays, 1929

Collected Sketches and Lyrics, 1932

Design For Living, 1933

Cavalcade, 1933

Play Parade, 1933

Conversation Piece, 1934

Point Valaine, 1935

Tonight At 8:30, 1936

Present Indicative (autobiography), 1937

To Step Aside (stories), 1939

Curtain Calls, 1940

Blithe Spirit, 1941

Present Laughter, 1947

This Happy Breed, 1947

(All the above are plays, and published by Doubleday, unless otherwise specified.)

BENEDETTO CROCE, Italian philosopher, historian and critic, was born of an Abruzzese family, Feb. 25, 1866. He lost his parents and only sister in the earthquake of 1883 and was himself dug out of the ruins. In his studies he turned to Marx, Hegel and Vico and in 1903 founded and directed *La Critica*, which he continued until 1937. From 1920 to 1921 he was Minister of Education. He was also Minister Without Portfolio in the Badoglio Cabinet in 1944 and the Bonomi Cabinet, from which he resigned. In 1943 he was taken prisoner by the Nazis and freed by the British. He has written scores of books on poetry, aesthetics, philosophy and history. He lives in Naples, is married and has had four children.

History as the Story of Liberty, Norton, 1941

Germany and Europe, Random House, 1944

Politics and Morals, Philosophical Library, 1945

My Philosophy (essays), Macmillan, 1950

ARCHIBALD JOSEPH CRONIN, Scottish novelist and physician, was born in Dumbartonshire, July 19, 1896. He studied medicine at Glasgow University and was a surgeon sub-lieutenant in the British Navy in the First World War. For many years he practiced in Wales and London but when his health broke in 1930 he wrote *Hatter's Castle*. The success of this book in several languages enabled him to devote himself to writing. He now lives in Connecticut with his wife who is also a physician.

Hatter's Castle, 1931

Three Loves, 1932

Grand Canary, 1933

The Stars Look Down, 1935
The Citadel, 1937
Jupiter Laughs (play), 1940
The Keys of the Kingdom, 1941
The Green Years, 1944
Shannon's Way, 1948

All except *Jupiter Laughs* are novels, all published by Little, Brown & Company.

WALTER DE LA MARE, English poet, novelist and anthologist, was born April 25, 1873 in a village in Kent. His father was a church warden and his mother was the daughter of a naval surgeon and author. He is related on his mother's side to Robert Browning.

At sixteen, while at St. Paul's School, he founded a school magazine and wrote most of its copy. After his formal education, he became a bookkeeper in the Anglo-American Standard Oil Company but meantime wrote considerable poetry. In 1908 he was granted a hundred pounds a year pension by the Asquith Government to write and has been writing since.

POETRY

Songs of Childhood, 1902
Poems, 1906
The Return, 1910
The Listeners and Other Poems, 1912
A Child's Day, 1912
Peacock Pie, 1913
Motley and Other Poems, 1918
Flora, 1919
The Veil and Other Poems, 1921
Down-adown-Derry, 1922
Come Hither (anthology), 1923
Ding Dong Bell, 1924
Stuff and Nonsense, 1927
Poems for Children, 1930
The Fleeting and Other Poems, 1933
A Forward Child, 1934
Early One Morning, 1935
The Wind Blows Over, 1936
This Year, Next Year, 1937
Memory and Other Poems, Holt, 1938
Behold, This Dreamer! (anthology),Knopf, 1939
Collected Poems, Holt, 1941
Burning-glass and Other Poems, Viking, 1945
Peacock Pie; a Book of Rhymes, Faber and Faber (London), 1946
Rhymes and Verses; Collected Poems For Children, Holt, 1947

PROSE

Henry Brocken, 1904

The Three Mulla-Mulgars, 1910
Crossings (play), 1921
Memoirs of a Midget, 1921
The Riddle and Other Stories, 1923
Broomsticks and Other Tales, 1925
The Connoisseur and Other Stories, 1926
Told Again, 1927
Stories From the Bible, 1929
Desert Islands, 1930
On the Edge, 1930
The Eighteen-Eighties, 1931
Lewis Carroll, 1932
The Lord Fish and Other Stories, 1933
Animal Stories, Scribner, 1940
Pleasures and Speculations, Faber and Faber (London), 1940
Bells and Grass, Viking, 1942
Mr. Bumps and His Monkey, Winston, 1942
Dutch Cheese, and Other Stories, Faber and Faber (London), 1946
Collected Tales, Knopf, 1950

Love [a garland of prose and poetry] (ed. anthology), Morrow, 1946

MAZO DE LA ROCHE, Canadian novelist, was born in Toronto in 1885 and spent her childhood on a fruit farm in Ontario. She began to write, first novels, then plays, while at the University of Toronto and rose to fame with a $10,000 *Atlantic Monthly* prize in 1927 with her novel *Jalna.* Since then she has done a large number of books in the *Jalna* series and most of her writing has had a Canadian countryside background. In 1938 she received the Lorna Pierce medal of the Royal Society of Canada.

Explorers of the Dawn, 1922
Possession, Macmillan, 1923
Delight, Macmillan, 1925
Low Life & Other Plays, 1929
Portrait of A Dog, 1930
Lark Ascending, 1932
Beside a Norman Tower, 1934
Whiteoaks (play), 1936
The Very House, 1937
Growth of a Man, 1938
The Sacred Bullock (short stories), 1939
Quebec, Historic Seaport, Doubleday, 1944

WHITEOAK SERIES

Jalna, 1927
Whiteoaks of Jalna, 1929
Finch's Fortune, 1931
The Master of Jalna, 1933
Young Renny, 1935
Whiteoak Harvest, 1936

Whiteoak Heritage, 1940
Wakefield's Course, 1941
Building of Jalna, 1944
Return to Jalna, 1946
Mary Wakefield, 1949
(Published by Little, Brown, unless otherwise noted)

JOHN DEWEY, educator and philosopher, leading exponent of the pragmatic school since the death of William James, was born in Burlington, Vermont, on October 20, 1859. He received his A.B. from the University of Vermont in 1879 and his Ph.D. from Johns Hopkins University in 1884.

His long and distinguished academic career took him first to the University of Michigan, where he was assistant professor of philosophy until 1888; thereafter he was chairman of the Philosophy Department until 1894. From that year until 1904 he was head of the combined departments of Psychology, Philosophy and Education at the University of Chicago; in connection with the latter department, he founded one of the first experimental schools in the country, developing educational ideas which, through his writings, have had manifold influence in this and foreign countries, notably China and Turkey. Since 1904 he has been a professor of philosophy at Columbia, becoming "emeritus" in 1931.

He has called his own philosophy "empirical naturalism." His special theory of knowledge, which he has developed on a basis of thorough-going naturalism, he has called "instrumentalism," since it treats intelligence and experimental science as the sole dependable agencies for promotion and realization of values esthetic, economic, political and moral in all phases of human life. He has insisted especially upon the function of intelligence, backed by scientific knowledge, in formation of new ends and new types of value. In consequence, his philosophy is often known as "experimentalism."

He married Alice Chapman in 1886 and is the father of five children. He lives now in Manhattan. In 1946 he married a second time, to Mrs. Roberta Grant.

Psychology, Harpers, 1886
Leibnitz, Griggs, Chicago, 1888
Outlines of a Critical Theory of Ethics, Register Publishing Co., Ann Arbor, Mich., 1891
A Study of Ethics, Register Publishing Co., Ann Arbor, Mich., 1894

School and Society, University of Chicago Press, Chicago, 1899
Studies in Logical Theory, University of Chicago Press, Chicago, 1903
How We Think, Heath, 1909
The Influence of Darwin on Philosophy, and Other Essays, Holt, 1910
German Philosophy and Politics, Holt, 1915
Essays in Experimental Logic, University of Chicago Press, Chicago, 1916
Democracy and Education, Macmillan, 1916
Reconstruction in Philosophy, Holt, 1920
Human Nature and Conduct, Holt, 1922
Experience and Nature, Open Court, Chicago, 1925
The Public and Its Problems, Holt, 1927
The Philosophy of John Dewey (selections), Holt, 1928
The Quest for Certainty, Minton, Balch, 1929
Characters and Events (essays), Holt, 1929
Experience and Nature, Norton, 1929
Impressions of Soviet Russia and the Revolutionary World, Mexico—China—Turkey, New Republic, 1929
The Sources of a Science of Education (lecture), Liveright, 1929
Construction and Criticism (lecture), Columbia University Press, 1930
Individualism, Old and New, Minton, Balch, New York, 1930
The Way Out of Educational Confusion (lecture), Harvard University Press, Boston, 1931
Philosophy and Civilization, Minton, Balch, 1931
Art as Experience, Minton, Balch, 1934
A Common Faith, Yale University Press, New Haven, 1934
Liberalism and Social Action, Putnam, 1935
Logic, the Theory of Inquiry, Holt, 1938
Experience and Education (lecture), Macmillan, 1938
Freedom and Culture, Putnam, 1939
Intelligence in the Modern World (selections; edited by JOSEPH RATNER), Modern Library, 1939
Theory of Valuation, University of Chicago Press, 1939
A Bibliography of John Dewey, 1882-1939, by MILTON HALSEY THOMAS, with an introduction by HERBERT W. SCHNEIDER, Columbia University Press, 1939
The Living Thoughts of Thomas Jefferson (selections, with essay), Longmans, Green, 1940
Education Today, Putnam, 1940
Problems of Men, Philosophical Library, 1946

The Wit and Wisdom of John Dewey (edited by A. H. JOHNSON), Beacon Press, 1949

Knowing and the Known (with A. F. BENTLEY), Beacon Press, 1949

ISAK DINESEN is the pen name of Baronesse Karen Blixen and under it she wrote *Seven Gothic Tales*, a group of stories which brought her literary fame. They were written in English although the Baronesse is Danish. She was born in 1885 in Denmark, studied painting in Copenhagen and later in Paris and Rome. In 1914 she married a cousin and went to British East Africa, now the Kenya Colony, where her family bought a coffee plantation. After divorcing her husband in 1921, she ran the plantation herself until 1931, when the drop in coffee prices forced her to give up the farm and return to Denmark. It was while in Africa that she began seriously to write, and among the work she produced then was her distinguished *Out of Africa*, an account of her years in Kenya. Her father Captain A. W. Dinesen was a naval officer who once lived three years as a trapper with the Indians in Minnesota, and later wrote about his experiences. Her former husband, a cousin of King Christian of Denmark, has written on big game hunting.

Seven Gothic Tales, Random House, 1934
Out of Africa, Random House, 1938
Winter's Tales, Random House, 1943
The Angelic Avengers (pseud. PIERRE ANDREZEL), Random House, 1947

JOHN DOS PASSOS has combined in his writing a keen social consciousness and sympathy for the victims of injustice. He was born in Chicago on January 14, 1896. After his graduation from Harvard he went to Spain to study architecture, but he soon entered the World War as a member of the French ambulance service, later joining the U. S. medical corps. His experiences during this period furnished the material for his first book, *One Man's Initiation—1917*, a semi-autobiographical novel about an ambulance driver.

On his return to the United States Mr. Dos Passos married Katherine Smith who was killed in an automobile accident in September, 1947. He has lived in Chicago, New York, Washington, Cambridge, London, Brussels, Madrid, and Paris. In 1930

he published *The 42nd Parallel*, the first novel in his U.S.A. trilogy (collected 1937), which also includes *1919* and *The Big Money*. These novels tell the story of the first three decades of the 20th century in a wide panorama of American life and are outstanding especially for their experiments in form. In 1949 Mr. Dos Passos married Elizabeth Holdridge.

Aside from his other novels Mr. Dos Passos has published volumes of poetry, essays, travel, and plays.

One Man's Initiation—1917 (novel), Allen & Unwin, London, 1920
Three Soldiers (novel), Doran, 1921
A Pushcart at the Curb (poetry), Doran, 1922
Rosinante to the Road Again (essays), Doran, 1922
Streets of Night (novel), Doran, 1923
Manhattan Transfer (novel), Harpers, 1925
The Garbage Man (play), Harpers, 1926
Orient Express (travel diary), Harpers, 1927
Airways, Inc. (play), Macaulay, 1928
The 42nd Parallel (novel), Harpers, 1930
1919 (novel), Harcourt, Brace, 1932
In All Countries (travel), Harcourt, Brace, 1934
Three Plays, Harcourt, Brace, 1934
The Big Money (novel), Harcourt, Brace, 1936
U.S.A. (trilogy), Harcourt, Brace, 1937
Journeys Between Wars (travel and current history), Harcourt, Brace, 1938
Adventures of a Young Man (novel), Harcourt, Brace, 1939
The Living Thoughts of Tom Paine (selections, with essay), Longmans, Green, 1940
The Ground We Stand On (political essays), Harcourt, Brace, 1941
Number One (novel), Houghton, Mifflin, 1943
State of the Nation, Houghton, Mifflin, 1944
First Encounter, Philosophical Library, 1945
Tour of Duty, Houghton, Mifflin, 1946
The Grand Design (novel), Houghton, Mifflin, 1949
The Prospect Before Us, Houghton, Mifflin, 1950

LORD DUNSANY, Edward John Moreton Drax Plunkett, 18th Baron, the Irish dramatist and story writer, was born in London, though of an Irish family, son of the 17th Baron Dunsany, July 24, 1878. He was trained at Sandhurst, the British equivalent of West Point, and succeeded his father at the latter's death in 1899. He served in the Boer War in the Coldstream Guards and in the First World War. He was a captain and was wounded in 1916.

He was discovered as a literary figure by the Abbey Theatre, Dublin, in 1909 when they produced his play *The Glittering Gates*. In 1904 he married Lady Beatrice Valliers, daughter of the Earl of Jersey, and they have one son.

Fiction of an imaginative nature, fantasy, plays comic and mythological, and short stories compose most of his output, although he has also written a number of essays, poems, and his autobiography, *Patches of Sunlight*, which appeared in 1938. He is six feet four, and according to his own reckoning, has spent ninety-seven per cent of his life, not in writing, but in sport or soldiering.

The Sword of Welleran, 1908
The Gods of Pegana, 1911
Time and the Gods, 1913
Five Plays, 1914
Fifty-one Tales, 1915
A Dreamer's Tales, 1916
A Night at an Inn (play), 1916
The Last Book of Wonder, 1916
Plays of God and Men, 1917
Tales of War, 1918
Tales of Three Hemispheres, 1919
Unhappy Far-off Things (essays), 1919
If (play), 1921
The Chronicle of Rodriguez, 1922
The King of Elfland's Daughter, 1924
The Charwoman's Shadow, 1926
The Evil Kettle, 1926
The Old King's Tale, 1926
The Blessing of Pan, 1927
Seven Modern Comedies (plays), 1929
Fifty Poems, 1929
The Old Folk of the Centuries, 1930
Travel Tales of Mr. Joseph Jorkens, 1931
The Curse of the Wise Woman, 1933
Jorkens Remembers Africa, 1934
Up in the Hills, 1935
Mr. Faithful (play), 1935
Rory and Bran, 1936
My Talks with Dean Spanley, 1936
My Ireland, 1937
Plays for Earth and Air, 1937
Patches of Sunlight (autobiography), Reynal, 1938
Mirage Waters (poems), 1938
The Story of Mona Sheehy, Harper, 1940
Jorkens Has a Large Whiskey, Putnam, 1940

ILYA EHRENBURG, Russian novelist, journalist and poet, was born of poor Jewish parents January 27, 1891 in Russia and joined the Bolshevik Party in 1906. In 1909 he traveled through Europe, subsequently spending a good deal of time until 1941 in Paris. He went back to Russia to participate in the revolution in 1917. In the last war he was a war correspondent. He received the Stalin Award for Literature in 1942, the Order of Lenin in 1944, and was made an officer of the Legion of Honor in Paris in 1945. He lives in Moscow.

The Face of War (history), 1920
The Love of Jeanne Ney, 1929
Adventures of Julio Jurenito (novel), 1930
A Street in Moscow (novel), 1932
Out of Chaos (novel), 1934
What a Man Needs (articles), 1937
Fall of Paris (novel), 1943
Russia at War (history), 1943
The Tempering of Russia, Knopf, 1944
European Crossroad, Knopf, 1947
The Storm (novel), Gaer Associates, 1949

ALBERT EINSTEIN, theoretical physicist, discoverer and exponent of the theory of relativity, who was awarded the Nobel Prize in 1922, was born at Ulm, Germany March 14, 1879 and educated in Munich and Switzerland. In 1940 he became a United States citizen. He was appointed a life member of the Institute for Advanced Study, Princeton, New Jersey, in 1933 and still lives there. He has been twice married and has two children.

Dr. Einstein is a member of the Institut de France and has received many decorations and honorary degrees from dozens of universities throughout the world for his scientific work.

Relativity; the special and general theory, Holt, 1920
Meaning of Relativity, 1923
Sidelights on Relativity, 1923
Investigation on the Theory of the Brownian Movement, 1926
About Zionism, 1931
Living Philosophies (with others), Tower Books, 1931
Builders of the Universe, 1932
On the Method of Theoretical Physics, 1933
Why War? (with SIGMUND FREUD), 1933
The World As I See It, 1934
Evolution of Physics (with LEOPOLD INFELD), Simon and Schuster, 1938

Out of My Later Years, Philosophical Library, 1950

T. S .ELIOT, (christened Thomas Stearns) was born September 26, 1888 in St. Louis, Missouri, of a distinguished Boston family of which President Charles W. Eliot of Harvard was another member, but became a British subject in 1927. He entered Harvard in 1906 finishing his undergraduate work in three years and taking his M.A. in his fourth, member of the same class as John Reed, Heywood Broun, Hamilton Fish, Jr., Walter Lippmann, and Stuart Chase. He contributed poems to the *Harvard Advocate* between 1907 and 1910 and penned the class ode. He also spent a year at the Sorbonne but returned to Harvard to take his Ph.D. in philosophy. In 1915 he married a London woman, Vivienne Haigh-Wood.

In 1922 his poem, *The Waste Land*, won him the $2,000 *Dial* Award and it was translated soon into many languages. Also in 1922, Eliot established *The Criterion*, a journal of literary and philosophical criticism which continued for seventeen years. For many years he has worked as literary editor for the London publishing house of Faber and Faber. In 1932 he returned to America for the first time in nearly a score of years and served as Charles Eliot Norton professor of poetry at Harvard. For a time in the late forties he lived at Princeton University. One of his ventures into the theatre, *The Cocktail Party*, opened in New York early in 1950 to both critical and popular acclaim. He is now living in England.

Selected Poems, 1932
Selected Essays, 1932
The Rock (pageant play), 1934
After Strange Gods, 1934
Murder in The Cathedral (play), 1935
Collected Poems, 1936
Essays Ancient and Modern, 1936
Anabasis (translation of poem by ST.-JOHN PERSE), 1938
The Family Reunion (play), 1939
Old Possum's Book of Practical Cats (poems), 1939
The Idea of a Christian Society, 1940
Four Quartets, 1943
A Choice of Kipling's Verse (editor), Scribners, 1943
Notes Toward The Definition of Culture, 1949
The Cocktail Party (play), 1950

(All published by Harcourt, Brace unless otherwise noted.)

WILLIAM FAULKNER [also spelled Falkner] has been compared to Dostoevsky for the intensity of his interest in the psychological aspects of humanity. He was born in New Albany, Mississippi, on September 25, 1897, and attended school in Oxford, Mississippi. His studies at the State University were interrupted when he went to France to serve with the British Royal Air Force in the First World War, where he was wounded in a crash.

On his return he served as a postmaster for two years in Mississippi, and then went to New Orleans, where he became friendly with Sherwood Anderson while working on his first novel, *Soldier's Pay*, and writing occasional sketches for the New Orleans Sunday *Times-Picayune*. In 1929 Mr. Faulkner was married to Estelle Franklin. He is a particular enemy of crowds and cities, and lives in the small town of Oxford, Mississippi.

The Marble Faun (poetry), Four Seas, Boston, 1924
Soldier's Pay (novel), Boni & Liveright, 1926
Mosquitos (novel), Boni & Liveright, 1927
Sartoris (novel), Harcourt, Brace, 1929
The Sound and the Fury (novel), Smith & Haas, 1929
As I Lay Dying (novel), Smith & Haas, 1930
Sanctuary (novel), Smith & Haas, 1931
Idyll in the Desert (short story), Random House, 1931
These Thirteen (short stories), Smith & Haas, 1931
Light in August (novel), Smith & Haas, 1931
Miss Zylphia Gant (short stories), Book Club of Texas, Dallas, 1932
Salmagundi (essays and poems), Casanova Press, Milwaukee, 1932
This Earth (poem), Equinox Cooperative Press, 1932
A Green Bough (poetry), Smith & Haas, 1933
Dr. Martino, and Other Stories, Smith & Haas, 1934
Pylon (novel), Smith & Haas, 1935
Absalom, Absalom! (novel), Random House, 1936
The Unvanquished (short stories), Random House, 1938
The Wild Palms (novel), Random House, 1939
The Hamlet (novel), Random House, 1940
Go Down Moses and Other Stories, Random House, 1942
The Portable Faulkner (edited by MALCOLM COWLEY), Viking, 1946

Intruder in the Dust (novel), Random House, 1948

Knight's Gambit (long stories), Random House, 1949

DOROTHEA FRANCES CANFIELD FISHER, known to readers of her novels and short stories as Dorothy Canfield, was born February 17, 1879. Her family had lived, since the founding of the town in 1764, in Arlington, Vermont, where Mrs. Fisher has her home. For twenty years, during her childhood and youth, her father was on the faculty of one or another State University. Her education was received alternately in France, in the middle-western towns where her father's profession took the family, and in New York, where for a decade her father was Librarian of Columbia University. In 1907 she married John Redwood Fisher of New York and Philadelphia. Three years of war work were done by the Fishers in France between 1915 and 1918, Mr. Fisher having served during those years in the American Ambulance Field Service.

Most of Mrs. Fisher's novels deal with the problems of the adjustment to life, especially to family life under modern conditions, by modern women of intelligence and vitality.

She has been one of the judges of the Book of the Month Club since its beginning 25 years ago.

Corneille and Racine in England, Macmillan, 1904

English Rhetoric and Composition (with G. R. CARPENTER), Macmillan, 1906

What Shall We Do Now? (with others), Stokes, 1906

Gunhild (novel), Holt, 1907

The Squirrel Cage (novel), Holt, 1912

The Montessori Mother (book on child training), Holt, 1913

Mothers and Children (book on child training), Holt, 1914

Hillsboro People (short stories), Holt, 1915

The Bent Twig (novel), Holt, 1915

The Real Motive (short stories), Holt, 1916

Fellow Captains (prose and poetry; with SARAH N. CLEGHORN), Holt, 1916

Understood Betsy (juvenile), Holt, 1917

Home Fires in France (short stories), Holt, 1918

The Day of Glory (novel), Holt, 1919

The Brimming Cup (novel), Harcourt, Brace, 1921

Rough Hewn (novel), Harcourt, Brace, 1922

Raw Material (sketches), Harcourt, Brace, 1923

The Home-Maker (novel), Harcourt, Brace, 1924

Made-to-Order Stories, Harcourt, Brace, 1925

Her Son's Wife (novel), Harcourt, Brace, 1926

Why Stop Learning? (book on adult education), Harcourt, Brace, 1927

Self-Reliance (child psychology), Harcourt, Brace, 1929

The Deepening Stream (novel), Harcourt, Brace, 1930

Learn or Perish (lecture), Liveright, 1930

Basque People (short stories), Harcourt, Brace, 1931

Bonfire (novel), Harcourt, Brace, 1933

Tourists Accommodated (drama), Harcourt Brace, 1934

Fables for Parents (short stories), Harcourt, Brace, 1937

Seasoned Timber (novel), Harcourt, Brace, 1939

Election of Academy Hill (story), Harcourt, Brace, 1939

Tell Me a Story (stories for children), University Publishing Co., Lincoln, Neb., 1940

Nothing Ever Happens (stories; with SARAH N. CLEGHORN), Beacon Press, Boston, 1940

Our Young Folks, Harcourt, Brace, 1943

American Portraits, Holt, 1946

Four-Square, Harcourt, Brace, 1949

Something Old, Something New, Scott, 1949

E. M. FORSTER (Edward Morgan), was born in 1879 and educated in Kings College, Cambridge. After graduation he lived in Italy where his first two novels were written. In 1911 he went to India with G. Lowes Dickinson, one of his teachers at Cambridge, and on this trip he accumulated material for *A Passage to India*, usually considered his major work. It won the Femina Vie Heureuse and James Tait Black Memorial prizes in 1925. The novel was based on material gathered on his first trip as well as additional work done on a second visit in 1921. Among his other books, he is widely known for *Aspects of the Novel* which grew out of his Clark lectures at Cambridge in 1927.

Where Angels Fear To Tread (novel), Knopf, 1920

Howards End (novel), Knopf, 1921
The Longest Journey (novel), Knopf, 1922
A Room With a View (novel), Knopf, 1923
A Passage to India (novel), Harcourt, Brace, 1924
Letters of Mrs. Fay, 1925
Aspects of The Novel (criticism), 1927
Collected Tales, Knopf, 1927
The Eternal Moment, 1928
Goldsworthy Lowes Dickinson (biography), 1934
Abinger Harvest (criticism), 1936
Virginia Woolf (lecture), 1942

ROBERT (Lee) FROST was born in San Francisco on March 26, 1875. It was an accident of circumstance that he was born in the West: his family was of New England, and at the age of ten he returned to the New England farm country with which his poetry is identified.

He entered Dartmouth College in 1892 but so disliked academic life that he left after a few months and took a job in a mill. A later attendance at Harvard terminated also in his leaving to take up various occupations, including shoemaking, editing a country newspaper, teaching, and farming. Tiring of these, he left for England in 1912, taking with him his wife, Eleanor White Frost, whom he had married in 1895, and his four children.

His first book of verse, *A Boy's Will*, was published in England in 1913. Returning to America in 1915, he taught for four years at Amherst College, and from 1921 to 1923 he was "poet in residence" at the University of Michigan. Since then his teaching career has taken him to many institutions, including Amherst, Harvard, Yale, and Middlebury.

Mr. Frost received the Loines Prize for Poetry in 1931, the Mark Twain Medal in 1937, and awards from the National Institute of Arts and Letters, the Poetry Society of America; Limited Editions Club, and Author-Meets-the Critics in 1949. And he has had the unique distinction of receiving four Pulitzer prizes for poetry, in 1924, 1931, 1937 and 1943.

A Boy's Will, Nutt, London, 1913; Holt, 1915
North of Boston, Nutt, London, 1914; Holt, 1914
Mountain Interval, Holt, 1916
New Hampshire, Holt, 1923

Selected Poems, Holt, 1923 (enlarged 1928, 1934, and by Cape, London, in 1936)
West-Running Brook, Holt, 1929
A Way Out, Harbor Press, 1929
The Cow's in the Corn (verse play), Slide Mountain Press, Gaylordsville, Vt., 1929
The Lovely Shall be Choosers, Random House, 1929
Collected Poems, Holt, 1930
The Lone Striker, Knopf, 1933
Gold Hesperidee, Bibliophile Press, Cortland, N. Y., 1935
Three Poems, Daniel Oliver Associates, Hanover, N. H., 1935
From Snow to Snow, Holt, 1936
A Further Range, Holt, 1936
Collected Poems, Holt, 1939
A Witness Tree, Holt, 1942
Come In (edited by LOUIS UNTERMEYER), 1943
A Masque of Reason, Holt, 1945
A Masque of Mercy, Holt, 1947
Steeple Bush, Holt, 1947
Complete Poems of Robert Frost, Holt, 1949

All of Mr. Frost's works, unless otherwise indicated are poetry.

ANDRÉ GIDE, French novelist, critic, essayist and dramatist, awarded the Nobel Prize for Literature in 1947, was born Nov. 22, 1869, in Paris from Huguenots on his father's side and Norman Catholics converted to Protestantism on his mother's. Critics and Gide himself have referred to these "divergent influences" as the source of his intellectual contradictions and the reason for his writing, since, as Professor Justin O'Brien says, "only in art could he harmonize his opposing tendencies."

He studied under private tutors and at the École Alsacienne, his father's death in 1880 having left him in the care of his mother, an aunt and an Englishwoman. His first writings were in *Les Cahiers d'André Walter* in 1891, begun at 18 and published anonymously as the posthumous diary of a youth. After several other books which identified him with French symbolism, he went to North Africa, became ill, and on his return to Paris in 1895 broke with symbolism, and with his book *Nourritures Terrestres* began to preach the joy of living by the senses. He married his cousin and wrote and traveled extensively.

Gide has participated in civic affairs at times, for he was mayor of a commune in Normandy in 1896, a juror in

Rouen in 1912 and a special envoy of the Colonial Ministry in 1925 and 1926 on a trip to the Congo after which his books *Voyage au Congo* and *Retour du Chad* led to legal reforms. In the early 1930's he went to Russia, pro-Soviet before going, and anti-Soviet upon returning. His defense of personal freedom has included dialogues on homosexuality, in *Corydon*. His most famous novel is *The Counterfeiters*. He has written his memoirs in *Si le grain ne meurt*, and three volumes of his journals have thus far been translated into English. He has been a marked influence on a number of French writers, including Mauriac, Lacretelle, and Martin du Gard, as well as Giono, Green, Malraux and Saint Exupery. In 1909 he founded the *Nouvelle Revue Française*, which was a focal point in contemporary French literature. Fifteen volumes of his works had been collected in French up to 1939, which did not include the several volumes of his *Journal*, still in progress. In recent years he has been living in Switzerland and Paris.

Strait is the Gate, Knopf, 1924
Lafcadio's Adventures, Knopf, 1925
Dostoievsky, Knopf, 1926
The Counterfeiters, Knopf, 1928
Travels in the Congo, Knopf, 1929
The School for Wives, 1930
The Immoralist, Knopf, 1930
Two Symphonies, Knopf, 1931
If it Die, Random House, 1935
Return From the U.S.S.R., Knopf, 1937
Imaginary Interviews, Knopf, 1944
The Journals of Andre Gide,
    Vol. I, 1889-1913, Knopf, 1947
    Vol. II, 1914-1927, Knopf, 1948
    Vol. III, 1928-1939, Knopf, 1949
Oscar Wilde, Philosophical Library, 1949
The Fruits of the Earth, Knopf, 1949
Anthology of French Verse (editor), Pantheon, 1949
Notes on Chopin, Philosophical Library, 1949
Corydon, Farrar, Straus, 1950
Autumn Leaves, Philosophical Library, 1950

GRAHAM GREENE, English novelist, was born October 2, 1904 in Hertfordshire, son of the headmaster of the Berkhamstead School. He is a relative of Robert Louis Stevenson. Educated at Oxford, he was a sub-editor of the London *Times* from 1926 to 1930, and after his marriage in 1927 traveled considerably in Mexico, America and Africa. He has a son and daughter. A convert to Catholicism, his novels and stories have had religious implications which, in the case of one of his latest novels, *The Heart of the Matter*, characterized the entire book. He has written several tense crime novels he calls "entertainments" and a number of distinguished short stories, the first to appear in America having been printed in STORY. Films have been made from a number of his books, including *This Gun For Hire*, *Orient Express*, *Brighton Rock*, and a play from *The Heart of the Matter*. The picture *Fallen Idol* is based on his short story *The Basement Room*.

Brighton Rock, 1938
Another Mexico, 1939
The Confidential Agent, 1939
The Labyrinthine Ways (reissued in 1946 as *The Power and The Glory*), 1940
The Ministry of Fear, 1943
The Heart of the Matter, 1948
Nineteen Stories, 1949
    (all published by Viking Press)

JOHN GUNTHER, internationally known not only as a reporter of events but as a reporter of entire continents since the publication of his famous "inside" volumes, [*Inside Europe*, *Inside Asia*, and *Inside Latin America*, *Inside U.S.A.*, *Behind the Curtain*, etc.] was born in Chicago August 30, 1901 and began his literary life at four as a bookworm; at six he was particularly fond of the *Iliad*, which he knew by heart; and at eleven he had written his own personal digest of Ridpath's *Universal History*.

He went to college in Chicago, hoping to be a chemist, but in 1924 he joined the Chicago *Daily News* and has been a writer of either fact or fiction ever since. He has worked in every country in Europe and he went around the world in connection with *Inside Asia*. For the Latin American book he flew 18,000 miles and visited twenty countries. He covered the outbreak of the war in London in 1939, was a war correspondent accredited to General Eisenhower's headquarters at Malta and represented the combined American press at the invasion of Sicily, 1943.

He married Frances Gunther in 1927. Their son John, who died of a brain tumor at 17, in 1947 was the subject of one of his finest books, *Death Be Not Proud*, proceeds of which he devoted to cancer research.

Mr. Gunther lives in New York City when he is not on the wing somewhere and is now married to Jane Parry Vandercook.

The Red Pavilion (novel), Harper, 1926
Eden for One (novel), Harper, 1927
The Golden Fleece (novel), Harper, 1929
The Bright Nemesis (novel), Bobbs-Merrill, Indianapolis, 1932
Inside Europe (current history), Harper, 1936; revised eds., 1937, 38, 39, 40.
Inside Asia (current history), Harper, 1939; revised 1942.
The High Cost of Hitler (broadcasts), Hamilton, London, 1939
Inside Latin America (current history), Harper, 1941
D Day (current history), Harper, 1944
The Troubled Midnight (novel), Harper, 1945
Inside U.S.A. (current history), Harper, 1947
Death Be Not Proud (biography), Harper, 1949
Behind the Curtain (current history), Harper, 1949
Roosevelt in Retrospect (biography), Harper, 1950

KNUT HAMSUN, Norwegian Nobel Prize winner in 1920 for his peasant novels, particularly *Growth of the Soil*, was born August 4, 1859 of peasant stock. After working at various jobs in Norway, he made two trips to America, which he attacked in his first book *The Cultural Life in Modern America*. His first novel was *Hunger* (1890). He has written some poetry, and a few plays which were not successful. His most outstanding novels were *Children of the Age*, *Segelfoss Town* and *Growth of the Soil*. As a very old man, Hamsun approved of the Nazi invasion of Norway, as he had approved of Prussian militarism in the first World War. He still lives in Norway in retirement.

Shallow Soil, 1914
Segelfoss Town, 1915
Hunger, 1920
Growth of the Soil, 1921
Dreamers, 1921
Wanderers, 1922
Victoria, 1923
In the Grip of Life, 1924
Children of the Age, 1924
Rosa, 1926
Mysteries, 1927
The Women at the Pump, 1928

Chapter the Last, 1929
Benom and Rosa, 1932
Look Back on Happiness, Coward-McCann, 1940
(All published by Knopf, unless otherwise noted)

ERNEST HEMINGWAY is the son of a doctor and was born in Oak Park, Illinois, on July 21, 1898. While attending school he made frequent hunting and fishing expeditions in northern Michigan, and these early experiences are reflected in the vigor of his writing.

After working as a reporter in Kansas City, he joined a volunteer ambulance unit in France druing the First World War, and later transferred to the Italian Arditi where he saw front-line action and was seriously wounded. The Italian Government decorated him with two of the highest medals of the country.

At the close of the war, Mr Hemingway reentered newspaper work as a foreign correspondent, in which capacity he reported battles in the Near East. He then settled in Paris as a member of the expatriate group which included Ezra Pound and Gertrude Stein, and within a short time had begun to exercise a tremendous influence in American letters. He became the leading spokesman for the "lost generation," expressing the loss of faith and hope which succeeded the War and urging a return to primal emotions.

Since 1927 his restless vitality, expressed in skiing, fishing, and hunting have led him on journeys throughout the world. He covered the Spanish Civil War for the North American Newspaper Alliance and he was a war correspondent in Europe during the Second World War. He lives now on his ranch in Cuba.

Three Stories and Ten Poems, Contact Publishing Co., Paris, 1923
In Our Time (short shories), Three Mountains Press, Paris, 1924
In Our Time (short stories), Boni & Liveright, 1925 (revised and enlarged by Scribners, 1930)
The Torrents of Spring (novel), Scribners, 1926
The Sun Also Rises (novel), Scribners, 1926
Today Is Friday (play), As Stable Press, Englewood, N. J., 1926
Men Without Women, Scribners, 1927
Fiesta, Scribners, 1927
A Farewell to Arms, Scribners, 1929
Death In the Afternoon, Scribners, 1932

God Rest You Merry, Gentlemen (short story), House of Books, 1933

Winner Take Nothing (short stories), Scribners, 1933

The Green Hills of Africa (travel), Scribners, 1935

Gattorno (pictures and commentary), Ucar, Garcia, Havana, 1935

To Have and Have Not (novel), Scribners, 1937

The Fifth Column and the First Forty-Nine Stories, Scribners, 1938

Spanish Earth (commentary and narrative for film), J. B. Savage, Cleveland, 1938

The Spanish War (collected newspaper articles), Fact Publishing Co., London, 1938

The Fifth Column (play), Scribners, 1940

For Whom the Bell Tolls (novel), Scribners, 1940

Men at War (editor), Crown, 1942

Across The River and Into the Trees, Scribners, 1950

JOHN HERSEY was born in Tientsin, China, June 17, 1914 and spent the first ten years of his life there before his parents returned with him to the United States. He is the son of Roscoe Monroe Hersey and Grace (Baird) Hersey. He was a student at Hotchkiss School and graduated from Yale in 1936, going to England for a year at Cambridge. The summer of 1937 he served as private secretary to Sinclair Lewis.

In 1940 he married Frances Ann Cannon and the couple have three children, Martin Cannon, John R. Jr., and Ann Baird, and live in Connecticut.

Mr. Hersey was a war correspondent in the Pacific theater of war in 1942, the Mediterranean in 1943, Russian 1944 and 1945, and China and Japan both before the Second World War and in 1945, 1946. He has been a writer, editor and war correspondent for *Time* and *Life*, a contributor to the *New Yorker*, and an editor of '47.

His observations in the Pacific, Italy, Japan, Poland and Esthonia have been utilized by him in his books which in the order of publication are:

Men on Bataan, Knopf, 1942

Into the Valley, Knopf, 1943

A Bell for Adano, Knopf, 1944

Hiroshima, Knopf, 1946

The Wall, Knopf, 1950

HERMANN HESSE, German-Swiss poet and novelist, was born in Wurttemberg July 2, 1877. He was the son of an Estonian who had for some years been a missionary in India and later became an official in the Office of Foreign Missions at Basel, Switzerland. Here Hesse went to school. He has become a Swiss citizen and lives now in Lugano. His first book of poetry, *Romantic Songs*, was published in 1899 and his first novel in 1904. In 1913 he published a travel book on India and another in 1922. In 1946 he received the Nobel prize for literature and the Goethe Prize in Frankfurt.

In The Old Sun, 1913

Gertrude and I, 1915

Inside of Chaos, 1923

Demian, Holt, 1923

Steppenwolf, 1929

Death and the Lover, 1932

Magister Ludi (novel), Holt, 1949

HU SHIH, one of China's greatest scholars, was born in Shanghai in 1891, of an Anhwei family of scholars. He studied in America, received his B. A. from Cornell and Ph. D. from Columbia. He was the leading figure in the "literary revolution" and the "new thought" movement while serving on the faculty of the National University of Peking.

In 1928 Hu Shih started a monthly magazine, *Crescent Moon*, which stood for fundamental re-thinking, civil rights, liberty and good government. It was suspended in 1933 and was replaced by the *Independent Critic*, an organ of debate and untrammeled criticism. From 1938 to 1942 he served as China's Ambassador to the United States, but thereafter returned to China. When the Chiang Kai-shek government lost to the Communists, he left and is now in the United States.

He is the author of many articles in Chinese and English, all characterized by his liberal viewpoint. His best known books in Chinese are *History of Chinese Philosophy, Vol. I; Experiments*, poems written in *pai hua*, and *The Collected Writings of Hu Shih*.

The Development of Logical Method in Ancient China

Chinese Renaissance

ALDOUS LEONARD HUXLEY was born July 26, 1894, the third son of Leonard Huxley (eldest son and biographer of the scientist Thomas Huxley) and Julia Arnold (niece of Matthew Arnold and sister of Mrs. Humphrey Ward). He was educated at Eton, which he left at seventeen owing to an affliction of the eyes. Later he went to Oxford, where he took his degree in English literature.

In 1919 he joined the editorial staff of the *Athenaeum* under J. Middleton Murry. He married (1919) Maria Nys. Most of Mr. Huxley's earlier novels were written in Italy and the South of France; his later books in New Mexico and California. Huxley has been extraordinarily prolific as a writer. After having contributed to *Oxford Poetry* (1916) of which he was one of the editors, and to *Wheels*, an anthology edited by Edith Sitwell, he published his first book, *The Burning Wheel* (1916), a volume of poems. *The Defeat of Youth* (1918) and *Leda* (1920), were also collections of his verse, as was *Jonah* (1917), a privately printed unbound volume of poems in French and English.

His first prose volume was *Limbo* (1920) consisting of seven experimental prose narratives. Although Huxley was attending to his editorial duties on Condé Nast's London *House and Garden* at this time, he managed to publish in quick succession *Crome Yellow* (1921), his first novel ("in the manner of Peacock," he said) ; *Mortal Coils* (1922), another brilliant experimental collection like *Limbo; On The Margin* (1923), another collection of essays, most of which had appeared in the London *Athenaeum* as *Marginalia* by Autolycus; *Antic Hay* (1923), his second novel. His next books were *Little Mexican and Other Stories* (1924) ; and *Young Archimedes and Other Sketches; Those Barren Leaves,* a novel (1925) ; *Along the Road,* essays (1925) ; *Two Or Three Graces,* short stories (1925) ; *Jesting Pilate,* essays (1926) ; *Proper Studies,* essays (1927) ; *Point Counterpoint,* a novel (1928) ; *Arabia Infelix,* (1929) poems, limited edition ; *Holy Face And Other Essays,* limited edition (1929) ; *Brief Candles,* short stories (1930) ; and *Music At Night,* essays (1931). *Texts and Pretexts,* an anthology with commentaries, was published in 1933. Meanwhile he had edited the letters of his friend, D. H. Lawrence.

The Cicadas, a collection of poems, *Eyeless in Gaza,* a novel (1936) and *The Olive Tree,* a volume of essays (1937) followed, and in 1937, while living on D. H. Lawrence's old ranch, near Taos in New Mexico, he wrote *Ends and Means,* a study of politics, economics and education in the light of what has been called the Perennial Philosophy. A fantastic novel, *After Many A Summer Dies the Swan,* was published in 1940 ; and in 1941 he produced *Grey Eminence,* a study of the relations between politics and mystical religion written in the form of a biography of Richelieu's coadjutor, Father Joseph.

There followed *The Art of Seeing* (1942), a discussion of the theoretical bases of Dr. Bates's unorthodox method of visual education. *Time Must Have a Stop* (1944), *Science, Liberty and Peace* (1946), *The Perennial Philosophy* (1945) and an omnibus of his work, *World of Aldous Huxley,* edited by Charles J. Rolo (1947). *Mortal Coils,* a play based on his early story *The Gioconda Smile,* appeared in 1938 and was made into a film. *Ape and Essence,* a novel, followed. *Themes and Variations* appeared in 1950.

The American editions of Huxley's books are published by Harper's.

JULIAN HUXLEY was born in London June 22, 1887, the second son of the late Leonard Huxley, grandson of T. H. Huxley and great-grandson of Thomas Arnold. He is the nephew of Mrs. Humphrey Ward and a brother of Aldous Huxley.

He was educated at Eton and Balliol College, Oxford, where he won the Newdigate Prize for verse. He was a Professor at Rice Institute in Houston, Texas for three years.

During the First World War, Huxley served in Italy. After the war he was a Fellow of New College, Oxford, till 1925, when he was appointed Professor of Zoology in King's College, at the University of London.

Huxley was married in 1919, and has two sons. He has made many lecture tours in America and has been a member of numerous committees and organizations. In 1946 he was appointed Executive Director of the Preparatory Commission of Unesco and in November 1946 was elected Director General of Unesco itself.

He is the author of *Essays in Popular Science,* and *Essays of a Biologist,* and is co-author with H. G. Wells of *Science of Life.* Among his books are: *Africa View* (Harper, 1931) ; *What Dare I Think?* (1931) ; *A Scientist Among the Soviets* (1932) ; *Captive Shrew* (1933) ; *If I Were Dictator* (1934) ; *Simple Science* (1935) ; *Science and Social Needs* (Harper, 1935) ; *The Stream of Life* (Harper, 1927) ; *We Europeans* (with A. C. Haddon, 1936) ; *Man Stands Alone* (Harper, 1941) ; *Democracy Marches, Evolution*

(Harper, 1943) ; *On Living in a Revolution* (Harper, 1944) ; *Touchstone for Ethics* (editor ; Harper, 1947) ; *Religion Without Revelation* (Harper, 1927) ; and *Heredity, East and West* (Schuman, 1949).

ROBINSON JEFFERS has said that during his college years he was "not deeply interested in anything but poetry." He adds that poetry runs pretty thin under such a limitation, and he had passed thirty before he wrote anything worth reading. He was born in Pittsburgh, Pennsylvania, on January 10, 1887, the son of a scholar. His ancestral stock, he says, was "all pre-revolutionary American, except paternal grandfather from North Ireland." He went to school in Europe, and on his return to this country was graduated from Occidental College, Los Angeles, at eighteen. Subsequently he spent what he calls "desultory years" at the University of Zurich and the University of Southern California Medical School.

Mr. Jeffers married Una Call Kuster in 1913, and settled in Carmel, California, building his own house of sea boulders. In 1916 he became the father of twin sons, Garth and Donnan.

His first volume of poetry to attract wide attention was *Tamar and Other Poems*, published in 1924. Through this and his subsequent works he has earned the title of the poet of tragic terror. His poetry is characterized by emotional violence and an intense revulsion from society. "Cut humanity out of my being," he has written, "that is the wound that festers."

Flagons and Apples, Grafton Press, Los Angeles, 1912
Californians, Macmillan, 1916
Tamar and Other Poems, Peter Boyle, 1924
Roan Stallion, Tamar, and Other Poems, Boni & Liveright, 1925
The Women at Point Sur, Liveright, 1927
Poems, Book Club of California, San Francisco, 1928
Cawdor, and Other Poems, Liveright, 1928
Dear Judas, and Other Poems, Liveright, 1929
Descent to the Dead, Random House, 1931
Thurso's Landing, and Other Poems, Liveright, 1932
Give Your Heart to the Hawks, and Other Poems, Random House, 1933
Solstice, and Other Poems, Random House, 1935

Such Counsels You Gave to Me, and Other Poems, Random House, 1937
Selected Poetry, Random House, 1938
Be Angry at the Sun, Random House, 1941
Medea (adaptation), Random House, 1946
The Double Axe, Random House, 1948
All of Mr. Jeffer's work is poetry. A large number of limited editions have been omitted from the bibliography on his own request.

JOHANNES V. JENSEN, Danish novelist, poet and essayist, 1944 Nobel Prize winner for his six volume anthropological-historical-novel *The Long Journey*, was born in Himmerland, Denmark Jan. 20, 1873. Son of a veterinarian, he studied medicine and although he never practiced a scientific interest pervades his writing. He has traveled extensively and some of his work is set in America (*The Wheel*, etc.).

Fire And Ice, Volume I of the trilogy *The Long Journey*, 1923
The Cimbrians, Volume II of the trilogy *The Long Journey*, 1923
Christopher Columbus, Volume III of the trilogy *The Long Journey*, 1924
The Long Journey, One Volume edition, 1933
(All published by Knopf)

C. E. M. JOAD, head of the Department of Philosophy, Birkbeck College, former Chairman of the National Peace Council, member of the staff of the Ministry of Labor from 1914 to 1930, was born in London August 12, 1891. He lives in Hampstead. Joad, who has been called the Mencken of England, was a pacifist and socialist in Oxford, a conscientious objector in the First World War, a feminist and then more or less of an anti-feminist and a student of psychic phenomena. He wrote several early novels. His books of philosophy began in 1919 with *Essays in Common Sense Philosophy*, followed by *Common Sense Ethics* (1921), *Common Sense Theology* (1922). In 1933 he wrote *A Belligerent Autobiography;* in 1936 a *Guide to Philosophy;* in 1940 *Philosophy for Our Times*. This list is interspersed with numerous other books on Christianity, liberty, Indian civilization, morals, politics, etc.

God and Evil, Harper, 1943
Adventures of the Young Soldier in Search of a Better World, Arco, 1944

Philosophy, McKay, 1945
How Our Minds Work (psychology), Philosophical Library, 1947
Decadence (philosophy), Philosophical Library, 1948

ARTHUR KOESTLER, Hungarian novelist, playwright and journalist, was born in 1905 in Budapest and educated in Vienna. He was a foreign correspondent, in the Middle East and later in Paris, of the *Vossische Zeitung* from 1926 to 1930; a journalist in Berlin until 1932; and, as a correspondent in the U.S.S.R., traveled through Soviet Central Asia in 1932 and 1933. He did free lance work throughout Europe and was a special correspondent for the *News Chronicle,* London, in the Spanish civil war, Egypt and Palestine, etc., from 1936 to 1938. He was a private in the British army in the Second World War.

The Gladiators, 1939
Scum of the Earth, 1941
Darkness at Noon, 1941
Dialogue with Death, 1942
Arrival and Departure, 1943
Twilight Bar (play), 1945
The Yogi and the Commissar, 1945
Thieves in the Night, 1946
Insight and Outlook, 1949
Promise and Fulfilment, 1949
(All published by Macmillan)

HALLDÓR LAXNESS, Icelandic novelist, poet and playwright, was born at Laxnes, near Reykjavik, in 1902. His father was a farmer. Laxness is considered the greatest and most consistently modern of the youngest generation of Icelandic writers. Only one of his books has been published in America, *Independent People* (Knopf 1946), which is one of three volumes on a grand scale dealing with the life of the independent cottage farmer. Another novel, in four volumes, *The Light of the World,* has as a central character a poet of the people.

Laxness spent part of his youth in Germany, and has experimented with Catholicism, Surrealism and Communism. He lives in Iceland.

SINCLAIR LEWIS, the first American author to be awarded the Nobel Prize for distinction in world literature, (1930) was born in Sauk Centre, Minnesota, on February 7, 1885, the son of a doctor. His boyhood was typically middle-western, but he insisted on attending Yale University, and came East in 1903. His college career was interrupted for a year in 1906-7, when he spent a couple of months in Upton Sinclair's Helicon Hall, the co-operative colony at Englewood, New Jersey, wandered down to the Panama Canal by steerage and vainly tried to find a job there, lived on the East Side of New York trying to freelance, and for a few months was assistant editor of *Translantic Tales,* a magazine of translations.

After graduation from Yale, in 1908, he worked on newspapers in Iowa and San Francisco, for the Associated Press in the latter, and on a magazine for the deaf in Washington, D. C., and finally found a measure of security as editor for the publishers Frederick A. Stokes and then George H. Doran. In 1914 he married Grace Hegger, and became in 1917 the father of Wells Lewis, who was killed while serving in the U. S. Army during the Second World War.

He left his job at the Doran Company in 1915, for freelancing, and in 1920 achieved recognition with *Main Street,* his seventh novel. This was followed in 1922 by *Babbitt,* a satirical portrayal of an American businessman, and in 1925 by *Arrowsmith,* chronicling a man of science. It was awarded the Pulitzer Prize, which Mr. Lewis refused as a protest against the restrictive terms of the award.

In 1928 Mr. Lewis was divorced from his first wife and married Dorothy Thompson, the political commentator; in 1930 they had a son. And in 1930 Mr. Lewis received the Nobel Prize. In his speech of acceptance he devoted himself to an attack on the American Academy of Arts and Letters (of which he is now a member) for its conventional standards of taste and morals.

Aside from his novels, Mr. Lewis has written several plays, including *Hobohemia,* and the dramatization of his own novel *It Can't Happen Here,* which showed a shift from the social analysis of most of his novels to political concern with the danger of Fascism in this country. *Jayhawker,* a play which he wrote with Lloyd Lewis, deals with Abolitionist days and *Angela Is Twenty-Two,* in which Mr. Lewis himself appeared, is a comedy of May and December.

Our Mr. Wrenn, Harpers, 1914
The Trail of the Hawk, Harpers, 1915
The Job, Harpers, 1917
The Innocents, Harpers, 1917

Free Air, Harcourt, Brace, 1919

Main Street, Harcourt, Brace, 1920

Babbitt, Harcourt, Brace, 1922

Arrowsmith, Harcourt, Brace, 1925

Mantrap, Harcourt, Brace, 1926

John Dos Passos' Manhattan Transfer (criticism), Harpers, 1926

Elmer Gantry, Harcourt, Brace, 1927

The Man Who Knew Coolidge, Harcourt, Brace, 1928

Dodsworth, Harcourt, Brace, 1929

Cheap and Contented Labor (tract), Women's Trade Union League, Philadelphia, 1930

Launcelot (poem), Harvey Taylor, 1932

Sinclair Lewis on The Valley of the Moon, Harvey Taylor, 1932

Ann Vickers, Doubleday, Doran, Garden City, N. Y., 1933

Work of Art, Doubleday, Doran, Garden City, N. Y., 1934

It Can't Happen Here, Doubleday, Doran, Garden City, N. Y., 1935

Selected Short Stories, Doubleday, Doran, Garden City, N. Y., 1935

Jayhawker (drama; with LLOYD LEWIS), Doubleday, Doran, Garden City, N. Y., 1935

Prodigal Parents, Doubleday, Doran, Garden City, N. Y., 1938

It Can't Happen Here (a play from the novel), Dramatists Play Service, 1938

Bethel Merriday, Doubleday, Doran, 1940

Gideon Planish, Random House, 1943

Cass Timberlane, Random House, 1945

Kingsblood Royal Random House, 1947

The God-seeker Random House, 1949

All of Mr. Lewis's works unless otherwise specified are novels.

LIN YUTANG, Chinese philologist, essayist and novelist, was born in South China in 1895. His father was a Christian pastor and the son became a Christian for a time. He married in China and completed his education at St. John's, Harvard and Leipzig Universities. The couple returned to China to have their first child born in China. For a time Lin Yutang was a member of the new Revolutionary Government but "got tired of that and saw through the farce of the revolution and graduated into an author, partly by inclination and partly by necessity."

He has three daughters and has lived many years in New York, but is now in France. He is the inventor of the Chinese index system and has invented a Chinese typewriter.

My Country And My People (essays), John Day, 1935, 1937, 1939

The Importance of Living, John Day, 1937

Moment In Peking (novel), John Day, 1940

With Love And Irony (essays), John Day, 1940

A Leaf In The Storm (novel), John Day, 1941

The Wisdom Of China and India (editor), Random House, 1942

Between Tears And Laughter, John Day, 1943

Vigil Of a Nation, John Day, 1945

The Gay Genius — The Life and Times of Su Tungpo, John Day, 1947

Chinatown Family, John Day, 1948

The Wisdom Of Confucius (editor and translator), Modern Library, 1948

On The Wisdom Of America (editor), John Day, 1950

A History of the Press and Public Opinion in China, University of Chicago Press

ARCHIBALD MACLEISH was born on May 7, 1892, in Glencoe, Illinois, near Lake Michigan. He was graduated from Yale in 1915 and received his LL.B. from Harvard in 1919, but in the meantime had married Ada Hitchcock in 1916 and had seen action in France in the First World War, entering the army as a private and leaving it a captain. Since then, Mr. MacLeish has become the father of three children and the recipient of honorary degrees from many universities.

After practicing law for three years, Mr. MacLeish began his poetic career in 1923 when he went to France, where he remained until 1928. His poetry of this period expressed the individual's hopelessness in the face of post-war chaos and was subjective in character.

On his return to the United States his poetry began to show a growing awareness of his national and cultural heritage, and with *Conquistador*, an epic of the conquest of Mexico, he won the 1933 Pulitzer Prize for poetry. Since then he has turned his attention more and more to the immediate social issues of the American scene and to the problems facing American democracy in the modern world. His interest in these matters has expressed itself primarily in verse plays, several of them written specifically for radio presentation.

Mr. MacLeish was one of the editors of *Fortune* from its beginning to 1938. He set up the Nieman Fellowships in Journalism at the Harvard School of Journalism. In 1939 he was appointed Librarian of Congress, a position he held until 1944, and from October, 1941 to June, 1942, he served, in addition, as Director of the United States Office of Facts and Figures. He was assistant director of the Office of War Information, June 1942-February 1943, and American delegate to the Conference of Allied Ministers of Education, London, 1944. From 1944 to 1945 he was an assistant Secretary of State. In 1949 he resigned as deputy Chairman of the American Delegation to the first General Conference of UNESCO, Paris.

Songs for a Summer Day, Yale University Press, New Haven, Conn., 1915
Tower of Ivory, Yale University Press, New Haven, Conn., 1917
The Happy Marriage, Houghton Mifflin, Boston, 1924
The Pot of Earth, Houghton Mifflin, Boston, 1925
Nobodaddy (drama), Dunster House, Boston, 1926
Streets in the Moon, Houghton Mifflin, Boston, 1926
The Hamlet of A. MacLeish, Houghton Mifflin, Boston, 1928
Einstein, Black Sun Press, Paris, 1929
New Found Land, Black Sun Press, Paris, 1930
Before March, Knopf, 1932
Conquistador, Houghton Mifflin, Boston, 1932
Frescoes for Mr. Rockefeller's City, Day, 1933
Selected Poems of Archibald MacLeish 1924-1933, Houghton Mifflin, Boston, 1933
Panic (drama), Houghton Mifflin, Boston, 1935
Public Speech, Farrar & Rinehart, 1936
The Fall of the City (verse play for radio), Farrar & Rinehart, 1937
Land of the Free, Harcourt, Brace, 1938
Air Raid (verse play for radio), Harcourt, Brace, 1938
America Was Promises, Duell, Sloan, & Pearce, 1939
The Irresponsibles, Duell, Sloan, & Pearce, 1940
The States Talking (pamphlet), Free Company, 1941
The American Cause (essay), Duell, Sloan, & Pearce, 1941
Prophets of Doom (lecture), University of Pennsylvania Press, Philadelphia, 1941
A Time to Speak (selected prose), Houghton Mifflin, Boston, 1941

American Opinion and the War (lecture), Macmillan, 1942
A Time to Act, (selected addresses), Houghton, Mifflin, 1943
American Story (broadcasts), Duell, Sloan, and Pearce, 1944
Act Five (poems), Random House, 1948
Unless otherwise indicated, Mr. MacLeish's works are poetry.

SALVADOR DE MADARIAGA, Spanish essayist and poet, was born in Galicia July 23, 1886, and was educated at Madrid and Paris. He received an honorary M. A. from Oxford in 1928. He worked as a mining engineer for the Spanish railways, but went to London in 1916 and entered journalism. In 1921 he became associated with the League of Nations Secretariat, and from 1922 to 1927 was director of the disarmament section. From 1928 to 1931 he occupied the chair of Spanish studies at Oxford. In 1931 he was Spanish Ambassador to the United States and from 1932 to 1934 Ambassador to France.

De Madariaga writes in Spanish, French and English and translations of his books are his own. His work has been founded upon the principles of the liberty of the individual and the solidarity of mankind and he has long been actively associated with work devoted to the solutions of international problems and relations.

He is married to a Scotswoman, a classical scholar, and they have two daughters.

Shelley and Calderon (essays), 1920
Spanish Folksongs, 1922
The Genius of Spain, 1923
The Sacred Giraffe, 1926
Englishmen, Frenchmen, Spaniards, 1928
Disarmament, 1929
Spain (Scribners; republished by Creative Age, 1943), 1930
Sir Bob, 1930
Don Quixote, 1934
Anarchy or Hierarchy, 1937
Theory and Practice in International Relations (lectures), University of Pennsylvania Press, 1937
The World's Design, Allen, 1938
Christopher Columbus (biography), Macmillan, 1940
Hernán Cortés: Conqueror of Mexico (biography), Macmillan, 1941
Heart of Jade, Creative Age, 1944
Victors, Beware, Jonathan Cape (London), 1946

Rise of the Spanish American Empire,
Macmillan, 1947
The Fall of the Spanish American Empire,
Macmillan, 1948

EDUARDO MALLEA, generally recognized as the outstanding novelist of Argentina and by many as the outstanding novelist of South America, was born in
1903 in the city of Bahía Blanca, son of
a leading surgeon. He published his first
book at the age of 23, after finishing
his work at the Colegio Nacional in Buenos Aires and studying law for two years
at the University. For eight years after
that he lived and traveled in Europe, returning to Argentina in the early 1930's,
where for some years he has been literary editor of the newspaper *La Na-
ción*, and editorial board member of the
magazine *Sur*.

Mallea received the Buenos Aires Municipal Prize for Prose in 1935 and the
National Prize for Literature in 1937.
He has written four novels and several
volumes of essays and short stories, and
much criticism. His first work to appear in the United States was his novella
Fiesta in November, in 1942. *The Bay of
Silence* introduced him in 1944 as a
novelist.

Fiesta in November (novella), Houghton
Mifflin, 1942
The Bay of Silence (novel), Knopf, 1944

ANDRÉ MALRAUX, French novelist and
critic, was born in Paris the son of a
civil servant, on November 3rd, 1895 and
studied in the Paris School of Oriental
Languages. In Indo-China in 1923 on an
archaeological expedition, he joined the
Young Annam League in its fight for
dominion status and later joined the
Committee of Twelve and became Propaganda Commissioner, in 1926, in Shanghai in a coalition of the Kuomintang and
Communist Parties, using his experience
for his first three novels. He became
famous with the publication of *Man's
Fate*, which won the Goncourt Prize. In
the Franco revolution in 1936, Malraux
organized an air corps for the Loyalists
and in the course of 65 flights was twice
wounded. In 1939 he volunteered in the
French tank corps, was captured and
escaped.

Nearly all of his work in fiction has
portrayed phases of revolution. He was
Minister of Information in France in 1945

and 1946 and since then has been associated with the French leader De Gaulle.
He lives in Paris.

The Conquerors, Harcourt, Brace, 1929
The Royal Way, Smith and Haas, 1935
Days of Wrath, 1936
Man's Hope, 1938
The Case for De Gaulle, 1948
Psychology of Art, Bollingen Series-Pan-
theon, 1949
(published by Random House, unless
otherwise noted)

THOMAS MANN, greatest living German
language author, and 1929 winner of the
Nobel Prize for literature, was born in
Lübeck, son of a prosperous mercantile
family, on June 6, 1875. It is the Lübeck locale which served him for *Buddenbrooks*, the novel of a conservative German family and its disintegration, the
book especially cited in his Nobel award
and the one from which a fragment was
taken for *THE WORLD'S BEST*.

Thomas Mann was slated to be a merchant, but at school he began writing and
after the death of his father in 1890 the
family moved to Munich. At nineteen
he was working temporarily in the insurance business. After a year he left
to take up work at the University and
later joined his brother Heinrich in Rome.
There he worked on *Buddenbrooks*, which
appeared in Berlin in 1900, and the 25-
year-old author was soon after acclaimed
a literary success.

Until 1933, Thomas Mann wrote and
lived in Germany, leaving it for lectures
in various countries. In 1905 he had married Katja Pringsheim, daughter of a
Munich merchant, and the couple had six
children, among whom Erika, actress and
writer, and Klaus Mann, also a writer,
became widely known in literary circles.
Erika is now the wife of W. H. Auden,
the poet; Klaus died in 1949.

Besides a number of distinguished short
stories and many novels, including *The
Magic Mountain*, one of the greatest contemporary novels, Thomas Mann has
written critical and political essays of
wide influence.

Dr. Mann left Germany with the rise
of Hitler, living in Switzerland from
1933 to 1938, and in the United States
since that time. He is now an American
citizen.

Royal Highness, 1916
Buddenbrooks, 1924

Death in Venice, 1924
The Magic Mountain, 1927
Children and Fools, 1928
Early Sorrow, 1930
A Man and His Dog, 1930
Mario and the Magician, 1931
Past Masters and Other Papers, 1933
Joseph and His Brothers, 1934
Young Joseph, 1935
Stories of Three Decades, 1936
An Exchange of Letters, 1937
Joseph in Egypt, 1938
Living Thoughts of Schopenhauer (editor), Longmans Green, 1939
The Beloved Returns, 1940
The Transposed Heads, 1941
Order of the Day, 1942
Listen, Germany!, 1943
Joseph the Provider, 1944
The Tables of the Law, 1945
Essays of Three Decades, 1947
Doctor Faustus, 1948
Joseph and His Brothers (one-volume edition), 1948
(All published by Knopf, except as otherwise noted)

JACQUES MARITAIN, French philosopher and Catholic writer, was born in Paris November 18, 1882, and educated at the Sorbonne. He is married to Raïssa Maritain, herself a writer, who has collaborated with him on several books.

In 1913 Maritain became professor of modern history and philosophy at the *Institut Catholique* in Paris, founded to offset "skeptical tendencies" of the Sorbonne. Reared as a Protestant, and a student of Bergson while at the Sorbonne, Maritain wrote his first book in 1917 as an attack on Bergsonism. Maritain has referred to himself as an anti-modernist, and he is the leading interpreter of the thought of St. Thomas Aquinas, and advocate of Catholic revival in France.

After the fall of France in 1940 the Maritains came to America. Dr. Maritain served as professor at the Institute of Medieval Studies at Toronto and visiting professor at Columbia and Princeton, and has been French Ambassador to the Vatican since 1945.

The Life of Prayer (with R. MARITAIN), 1928
Three Reformers: Luther, Descartes, Rousseau, 1928
The Things That Are Not Caesar's, 1930
Art and Scholasticism, 1930
An Introduction to Philosophy, 1930
Primacy of the Mind, 1930

The Angelic Doctor, Sheed and Ward, 1931
Théonas, 1933
Freedom in the Modern World, 1935
Temporal Power and Liberty, 1935
An Introduction to Logic, Sheed and Ward, 1937
The Degrees of Knowledge, Scribner, 1938
True Humanism, Scribners, 1938
Anti-Semitism, 1939
Preface to Metaphysics: Seven Lectures on Being, Sheed and Ward, 1939
Scholasticism and Politics, 1940
Science and Wisdom, Scribners, 1940
Religion in the Modern World, U. of Pa. Press, 1941
The Living Thoughts of St. Paul (editor), Longmans Green, 1941
France, My Country, Through the Disaster, Longmans Green, 1941
Ransoming the Time, Scribners, 1941
Art and Poetry, Philosophical Library, 1943
The Twilight of Civilization, Sheed and Ward, 1943
The Rights of Man and Natural Law, Scribners, 1943
Education at the Crossroads, Yale University Press, 1943
Christianity and Democracy, Scribners, 1944
The Dream of Descartes, Philosophical Library, 1945
The Person and the Common Good, Scribners, 1947
Art and Faith (letters: with JEAN COCTEAU), Philosophical Library, 1948
Existence and the Existent, Pantheon, 1948

JOHN P. MARQUAND was born in Wilmington, Delaware, on November 10, 1893, and received his A.B. from Harvard in 1915. After two years as assistant managing editor of the Boston *Transcript*, he saw action on the front as a first lieutenant in the Field Artillery, and returned in 1919 to resume his newspaper career, this time with the New York *Herald*. He married Christina Sedgwick in 1922, and was remarried in 1937 to Adelaide Hooker; he is now the father of five children.

Mr. Marquand has led a literary double life, writing on the one hand popular detective stories centering around the character of Mr. Moto and on the other hand a number of searching novels set in New England. His *The Late George Apley*, a novel in the form of a memoir satirizing the life of a Boston Brahmin, was awarded the 1938 Pulitzer Prize. He did confidential work for the War Department during the Second World War. He has been for some time one of the five judges of the Book-of-the-Month Club.

The Unspeakable Gentleman, Scribners, 1922
Four of a Kind, Scribners, 1923
The Black Cargo, Scribners, 1925
Lord Timothy Dexter, Minton, Balch, 1925
Warning Hill, Little, Brown, 1930
Haven's End, Little, Brown, 1935
Ming Yellow, Little, Brown, 1935
No Hero, Little, Brown, 1935
Thank You, Mr. Moto, Little, Brown, **1937**
The Late George Apley, Little, Brown, 1937
Think Fast, Mr. Moto, Little, Brown, 1937
Mr. Moto Is So Sorry, Little, Brown, 1938
Wickford Point, Little, Brown, 1939
Mr. Moto Takes a Hand, Robert Hale (London), 1940
Don't Ask Questions, Robert Hale (London), 1941
H. M. Pulham, Esq., Little, Brown, 1941
Last Laugh, Mr. Moto, Little, Brown, 1942
So Little Time, Little, Brown, 1943
Repent in Haste, Little, Brown, 1945
B. F.'s Daughter, Little, Brown, 1946
The Late George Apley (play; with S. J. KAUFMAN), Dramatists Guild, 1946
Point of No Return, Little, Brown, 1949
All of Mr. Marquand's works are novels except as otherwise noted.

was killed in action in 1942. He has written scores of volumes of poetry, plays and novels. A selection of his publications in America, issued through Macmillan, follows.

Salt-Water Poems and Ballads, 1913
Poems, 1921
Selected Poems, 1923
Sailor's Garland (editor), 1924
Trial of Jesus, 1925
Verse Plays, 1925
Sea Life in Nelson's Time, 1925
Tristan and Isolt, 1927
Midnight Folk, 1927
Midsummer Night and Other Tales in Verse, 1928
Coming of Christ, 1928
Wanderer of Liverpool, 1930
Chaucer, 1931
Poetry, 1932
The Taking of the Gry, 1934
Poems; Complete Edition With Recent Poems, 1935
Dead Ned, 1938
Live and Kicking Ned, 1939
Basilissa; a Tale of the Empress Theodora, 1940
Some Memories of W. B. Yeats, 1940
In the Mill, 1941
Gautama the Enlightened, and other Verse, 1941
The Nine Days Wonder, 1941
The Bird of Dawning, 1942
Wonderings, 1943
A Generation Risen, 1943
New Chum, 1945
A Macbeth Production, 1945
Thanks Before Going, 1947
A Play of St. George, 1948
On The Hill, 1950

JOHN MASEFIELD, poet laureate of England since 1930, is not only a narrative poet, but a novelist and playwright. He was born June, 1878 in England, son of a Herefordshire solicitor and a clergyman's daughter. He was apprenticed aboard a windjammer at the age of fifteen. On one of his voyages, he stopped off in New York for three years, working in a bakery, a livery stable, a saloon and at one time a carpet factory in Yonkers. In 1897 he returned to London. His first collection of poems, *Salt Water Ballads*, came out in 1902, and from this he chose for THE WORLD'S BEST the memorable lyric *Sea Fever*, among other later poems. He worked on various newspapers and magazines, and was in the Red Cross service in the First World War. In 1935 he received the Order of Merit. His son

EDGAR LEE MASTERS was born at Garnett, Kansas, on August 23, 1869, the son of a lawyer. When he was eleven his family moved from Petersburg to Lewistown, Illinois, where he attended high school. After four years of work on the local weekly, during which time he contributed stories and poems to various magazines, he entered Knox College, Illinois, for a year. Returning to Lewistown, he studied law, was admitted to the bar in 1891, and for a year was in partnership with his father. Then he went to Chicago, where he opened a law office, and practiced until 1922.

Mr. Masters achieved first fame with his *Spoon River Anthology* in 1915. He then published many volumes, including poetry, drama, novels, and biography. He was awarded the first $5,000 fellowship granted by the Academy of American Poets, 1946.

While Mr. Masters made his own choice for THE WORLD'S BEST before the book was published and is thus included, he died at the age of 81 in Melrose Park near Philadelphia on March 6, 1850.

A Book of Verses, Way & Williams, Chicago, 1898

Maximilian (blank verse drama), Badger, Boston, 1902

The New Star Chamber, and Other Essays, Hammersmark Publishing Co., Chicago, 1904

Blood of the Prophets (poetry), Hammersmark Publishing Co., Chicago, 1905

Althea (play), Rooks Press, Chicago, 1907

The Trifler (play), Rooks Press, Chicago, 1908

Songs and Sonnets, Rooks Press, Chicago, 1910

Eileen (play), Rooks Press, Chicago, 1910

The Leaves of the Tree (play), Rooks Press, Chicago, 1910

The Locket (play), Rooks Press, Chicago, 1910

The Bread of Idleness (play), Rooks Press, Chicago, 1911

Spoon River Anthology (poetry), Macmillan, 1915

Spoon River Anthology, with Additional Poems, Macmillan, 1916

Songs and Satires (poetry), Macmillan, 1916

The Great Valley (poetry), Macmillan, 1916

Toward the Gulf (poetry), Macmillan, 1918

Starved Rock (poetry), Macmillan, 1919

Mitch Miller (novel), Macmillan, 1920

Domesday Book (poetry), Macmillan, 1920

The Open Sea (poetry), Macmillan, 1921

Children of the Market Place (novel), Macmillan, 1922

Skeeters Kirby (novel), Macmillan, 1923

The Nuptial Flight (novel), Liveright, 1923

Mirage (novel), Liveright, 1924

The New Spoon River (poetry), Liveright, 1924

Selected Poems, Macmillan, 1925

Lee, a Dramatic Poem, Macmillan, 1926

Kit O'Brien (novel), Liveright 1927

Jack Kelso (dramatic poem), Appleton, 1928

The Fate of the Jury (poetry), Appleton, 1929

Gettysburg, Manila, Acoma (poetry), Liveright, 1930

Lichee Nuts (poetry), Liveright, 1930

Lincoln the Man (biography), Dodd, Mead, 1931

Godbey (dramatic poem), Dodd, Mead, 1931

The Serpent in the Wilderness (poetry), Dick, 1933

The Tale of Chicago (history), Putnam, 1933

Dramatic Dialogues (plays), French, 1934

Richmond (dramatic poem), French, 1934

Invisible Landscapes (poetry), Macmillan, 1935

Vachel Lindsay (biography), Scribners, 1935

Poems of People, Appleton-Century, 1936

The Golden Fleece of California (poetry), Countryman Press, Weston, Vt., 1936

Across Spoon River (autobiography), Farrar & Rinehart, 1936

Walt Whitman (biography), Scribners, 1937

The New World (poetry), Appleton-Century, 1937

The Tide of Time (novel), Farrar & Rinehart, 1937

Mark Twain (biography), Scribners, 1938

More People (poetry), Appleton-Century, 1939

The Living Thoughts of Emerson (selections, with essay), Longmans, Green, 1940

Illinois Poems, Press of James A. Decker, Prairie City, Ill., 1941

The Sangamon (regional history), Farrar & Rinehart, 1942

Along the Illinois (poetry), Decker, Prairie City, Ill., 1942

Spoon River Anthology has been translated into Swedish by Bertel Gripenberg (Holger Schlidts Forlag, Helsingfors, 1927), into Danish by Ova Brusendorf (Jespersen Og Forlag, Copenhagen, 1935), into Dutch (Bij De Boekengilde, Antwerp), into Japanese by Gan Yamaoka (Tokio, 1931), and into Norwegian.

The Nuptial Flight was translated into German by Anna Nusbaum, with an introduction by Upton Sinclair (F. G. Speidelsch, Vienna and Leipzig, 1929).

WILLIAM SOMERSET MAUGHAM, English novelist and dramatist, was born in Paris January 25, 1874, the son of a solicitor to the British Embassy, youngest of six sons; one brother, Lord Maugham, became Lord Chief Justice of England.

Maugham's mother died of tuberculosis when he was eight and his father two years later of cancer; and the boy lived for a while with an uncle, a clergyman in Kent, providing a background for the opening portion of his novel, *Of Human Bondage*. Plans were for his schooling to prepare him to enter the church but his desire to write occasioned his being sent to Heidelberg instead of Oxford. He later chose medicine as a career but never practiced.

In Paris he wrote for nearly ten years without notable success, until in 1907 *Lady Frederick* was produced as a successful play. He had several plays produced before he became widely known as a novelist.

In the First World War he enlisted with a Red Cross ambulance unit and was later tranferred to the Intelligence Department of the British Army. He married in 1915, and had one daughter. In the Second World War he was assigned to special work at the British Ministry of Information in Paris, where the Nazi advance brought him the loss of his villa and all his belongings.

For several years he has spent a great deal of his time in the United States. Many of his books have been filmed, including four of his short stories in one film, *Quartet*.

NOVELS AND SHORT STORIES

Of Human Bondage, Doran, 1915
The Moon and Sixpence, Doran, 1919
Mrs. Craddock, Doran, 1920
The Trembling of a Leaf, Doran, 1921
The Painted Veil, Doran, 1925
The Casuarina Tree, Doran, 1926
Ashenden, or the British Agent, Doubleday, Doran, 1928
Cakes and Ale, Doubleday, Doran, 1930
First Person Singular, Doubleday, Doran, 1931
The Narrow Corner, Doubleday, Doran, 1932
Ah King, Doubleday, Doran, 1933
East and West (collected stories), Doubleday, Doran, 1934
Cosmopolitans, Doubleday, Doran, 1936
Theatre, Doubleday, Doran, 1937
Favorite Stories of W. Somerset Maugham, Doubleday, Doran, 1937
Christmas Holiday, Doubleday, Doran, 1939
The Mixture as Before, Doubleday, 1940
Up at the Villa, Doubleday, 1941
The Hour Before Dawn, Doubleday, 1942
The Razor's Edge, Doubleday, 1944
Then and Now, Doubleday, 1946
Creatures of Circumstance, Doubleday, 1947
Catalina, Doubleday, 1948
Quartet, Doubleday, 1949

ESSAYS AND TRAVEL

The Land of the Blessed Virgin (Andalusia), Knopf, 1920
On a Chinese Screen, Doran, 1922
The Gentleman in the Parlour, Doubleday, Doran, 1930
Don Fernando, Doubleday, Doran, 1935
Books and You, Doubleday, 1940
Great Novelists and Their Novels, Winston, 1948

AUTOBIOGRAPHY

The Summing Up, Doubleday, Doran, 1938
Strictly Personal, Doubleday, 1941
A Writer's Notebook, Doubleday, 1949

ANTHOLOGIES

The Traveller's Library, Doubleday, Doran, 1933
Fifty Modern English Writers, Doubleday, Doran, 1933
Tellers of Tales, Doubleday, Doran, 1939
Introduction to Modern English and American Literature, New Home Library, 1943

PLAYS

Collected Edition of the Plays of William Somerset Maugham, Heinemann (London), 1931-4
Six Comedies, Doubleday, Doran, 1937

FRANÇOIS MAURIAC, French novelist, critic and poet, and member of the French Academy, was born in Bordeaux, October 11, 1885. The region around Bordeaux, where he was raised as an orthodox Catholic by his mother following his father's death when François was two months old, has been the background for much of his novel writing. His first books however were poetry, and it was not until 1913 that he brought out his first novel.

In 1925 Mauriac was awarded the *Grand Prix du Roman* by the French Academy for a series of novels which included *Genetrix*, *The Desert of Love* and *Thérèse*. His Catholic point of view was more fully demonstrated in later novels, *The Viper's Tangle*, and others.

In 1932 Mauriac was elected President of the Société des Gens de Lettres and in 1933 he was chosen to occupy Eugene Brieux's place in the French Academy. He has written a *Life of Jesus*, among his numerous other works, and a play, *Asmodée*, or *The Intruder*.

Woman of the Pharisees, Holt, 1946
The Unknown Sea, Holt, 1948

Proust's Way (biography), Philosophical Library, 1950

ANDRÉ MAUROIS was born July 26, 1885 at Elbeuf, a small city in Normandy, and educated at the College of Rouen. He hoped to be a professor of philosophy and passed all the examinations. However, his father, uncles and great uncles were all manufacturers, owning woolen mills in Normandy, and the family pressure on him to follow a career in the mills was difficult to resist. Following his military service, he spent several years in Normandy, directing spinning and weaving operations. Nevertheless, he had a strong desire to write and it was the First World War which finally permitted him to follow his vocation.

Because he knew English, André Maurois was attached as liaison officer to the British troops. His wartime experiences formed the basis of *Les Silences Du Colonel Bramble,* which was extremely successful on its publication in 1918.

He wrote a sequel to *Les Silences Du Colonel Bramble — Les Discours Du Docteur O'Grady:* a short novel, *Ni Ange, Ni Bête;* then *Ariel, Ou La Vie De Shelley,* a biography in a new form which was praised not only by French critics, but by English and American critics. Since then Maurois has written other biographies, among them those of Disraeli, of Byron, Marshal Lyautey, and Edward VII.

In France, André Maurois is known above all for his novels, of which the most popular are *Climats: Le Cercle De Famille, Bernard Quesnay* and *L' Instinct Du Bonheur.* He has written also fantastic stories recalling the early novels of Wells, for example: *Le Preseur D'Ames.* On June 23, 1940 Mr. Maurois was elected to the French Academy to succeed René Doumic. He is an Officer of the Legion of Honor, recipient of the British Military Medal, Commander of the British Empire.

Dickens, 1935
Prophets and Poets, 1935
The Miracle of England, 1937
Ricochets, 1937
Chateaubriand, Harper, 1938
The Thought-Reading Machine, Harper, 1938
The Living Thoughts of Voltaire (editor), Longmans Green, 1939
The Battle of France, Lane (London), 1940

Tragedy in France, Harper, 1940
The Art Of Living, Harper, 1940
Byron, Jonathan Cape (London), 1940
Frédéric Chopin, Harper, 1942
I Remember, I Remember, Harper, 1942
The Miracle of America, Harper, 1944
Seven Faces of Love, Didier, 1944
Franklin, The Life of an Optimist, Didier, 1945
The Woman Without Love, Harper, 1945
Washington: The Life of a Patriot, Didier, 1946
The Miracle of France, Harper, 1948
From My Journal, Harper, 1948
Proust: Portrait of a Genius, Harper 1950

H. L. MENCKEN, journalist, critic, and essayist, was born in Baltimore, Maryland, on September 12, 1880. His German grandfather had come to the United States n 1848 and had founded a tobacco business, which Mr. Mencken's father wished him to carry on; but he was determined to become a journalist, and after his schooling at the Baltimore Polytechnic he became a reporter on the Baltimore *Morning Herald.* By 1903, when he was only twenty-three, he was city editor. In that year he published his first book, *Ventures into Verse.*

Mr. Mencken was editor of the *Evening Herald* in 1905 and 1906, on the staff of the Baltimore *Sun* from 1906 until 1941. Meanwhile he had become literary critic for *The Smart Set,* and from 1914 on he was co-editor of the magazine with George Jean Nathan. In 1924 he founded with Nathan *The American Mercury,* of which he was sole editor from 1925 to 1933.

In 1930 he married Sara Haardt, the author, who died in 1935. He lives in Baltimore.

Ventures into Verse, Marshall, Beek, & Gordon, 1903
George Bernard Shaw—His Plays, Luce, Boston, 1905
The Philosophy of Friedrich Nietzsche, Luce, Boston, 1908
Men Versus the Man (with R. R. LA-MONTE), Holt, 1910
The Artist (drama), Luce, Boston, 1912
Europe After 8:15 (travelogue; with GEORGE JEAN NATHAN and W. H. WRIGHT), Lane, 1914
A Book of Burlesques (sketches), Knopf, 1916
A Little Book in C Major (epigrams), Knopf, 1916

A Book of Prefaces (essays), Knopf, 1917

In Defense of Women, Knopf, 1918

Damn—A Book of Calumny (essays), Knopf, 1918

The American Language (philology), Knopf, 1919

Prejudices (essays), Knopf
—*First Series*, 1919
—*Second Series*, 1920
—*Third Series*, 1922
—*Fourth Series*, 1924
—*Fifth Series*, 1926
—*Sixth Series*, 1927

The American Credo (essays; with GEORGE JEAN NATHAN), Knopf, 1920

Heliogabalus (drama; with GEORGE JEAN NATHAN), Knopf, 1920

Americana (Selections from the American Mercury Americana Department, edited by H. L. MENCKEN), Knopf, 1925

Americana 1926, Knopf, (same as above)

Notes on Democracy, Knopf, 1926

James Branch Cabell, McBride, 1927

Selected Prejudices (essays), Knopf, 1927

Menckeniana, a Schimpflexicon (comments on H. L. MENCKEN), Knopf, 1928

Treatise on the Gods, Knopf, 1930

Lo, the Poor Bookseller (pamphlet), Stanley Rose, Hollywood, Cal., 1930

Making a President, Knopf, 1932

Treatise on Right and Wrong, Knopf, 1934

Happy Days, 1880-1892 (autobiography), Knopf, 1940

Newspaper Days, 1899-1906 (autobiography), Knopf, 1941

A New Dictionary of Quotations, Knopf, 1942

Heathen Days, 1890-1936, Knopf, 1943

The American Language: Supplement One, Knopf, 1945

Christmas Story, 1946

The Days of H. L. Mencken (one volume consisting of *Happy Days, Newspaper Days* and *Heathen Days*), Knopf, 1947

The American Language: Supplement Two, Knopf, 1948

A Mencken Chrestomathy (selections), Knopf, 1949

EDNA ST. VINCENT MILLAY has been a poet since childhood: before she reached high school her verses were published in *St. Nicholas.* She was born in Rockland, Maine, on February 22, 1892, and spent her early years in New England. At the age of nineteen, while still a schoolgirl, she wrote her first long poem, *Renascence,* which won for her nation-wide fame and admiration.

After a brief period at Barnard College Miss Millay went to Vassar, where she won the cup awarded in the Intercollegiate Poetry Contest, and from which she was graduated in 1917. Her first volume of poetry, *Renascence and Other Poems,* was published the same year. After graduation she moved to New York, wrote and acted for the Provincetown Players, and took part in productions of the Theatre Guild; and to support herself she published short stories over the pseudonym "Nancy Boyd." She wrote and published poetry and experimented in poetic plays, of which she published three in 1921. In 1925 the Metropolitan Opera Association commissioned her to write the book for an opera, the music to be written by Deems Taylor; and *The King's Henchman,* produced in 1927, was perhaps the most successful American opera given in New York to that date.

In 1920 *Poetry* gave Miss Millay a cash prize, and in 1931 it awarded her the Helen Haire Levinson Prize. *The Harp-Weaver and Other Poems* received the 1923 Pulitzer Prize for poetry.

In 1923 she married the late Eugen Jan Boissevain. She lives now, for the most part, at her farm, Steepletop, Austerlitz, New York.

Renascence and Other Poems, Kennerley, 1917

Possession, a Sonnet, privately printed, 1918

A Few Figs from Thistles, Shay, 1920 (enlarged 1920, 1921)

Aria da Capo (play), Harper, 1920

Second April, Kennerley, 1921

The Lamp and the Bell (poetic drama), Harper, 1921

Two Slatterns and a King (poetic drama), Stewart, Kidd, Cincinnati, 1921

The Ballad of the Harp-Weaver, Shay, 1922

The Harp-Weaver and Other Poems, Harper, 1923

Poems, Harper, 1923

Renascence, Fredrick & Bertha Goudy, 1924

Distressing Dialogues (humor), Harper, 1924

The King's Henchman (libretto), 1926 (complete edition without music)

Three Plays, Harper, 1926

The Pamphlet Poets: Edna St. Vincent Millay, Simon & Schuster, 1927

The Buck in the Snow & Other Poems, Harper, 1928

Edna St. Vincent Millay's Poems Selected for Young People, Harper, 1929

Fatal Interview, Harper, 1931

The Princess Marries the Page (poetic
drama), Harper, 1932
Wine from These Grapes, Harper, 1934
Epitaph for the Race of Man (Vol. 2 of
the limited edition of *Wine from These
Grapes*), Harper, 1934
Vacation Song, Harper, 1936
Flowers of Evil (translation from the
French of Baudelaire; with GEORGE DIL-
LON), Harper, 1936
Conversation at Midnight, Harper, 1937
Huntsman, What Quarry?, Harper, 1939
Make Bright the Arrows, Harper, 1940
There Are No Islands Any More, Harper,
1940
Collected Sonnets, Harper, 1941
Murder of Lidice, Harper, 1942
Collected Lyrics, Harper, 1943

Unless otherwise indicated, all Miss Millay's works are poetry. Not included in
the bibliography are the large number
of her verses which have been set to
music and published as sheet music.

GABRIELA MISTRAL, Chilean poetess,
was born in 1889, the daughter of a
school teacher who was a poet. She began writing at fifteen, after happening
upon some poems of her father whom
she had not seen since she was three.
For many years she taught school and
in later years she has been with the Chilean
consular service. She was two years in
Mexico on an educational project and
taught at Columbia University, Vassar,
and Middlebury. She is at present in the
Chilean consular service in Los Angeles,
California. She was awarded the Nobel
Prize for literature in 1945. She has done
considerable writing, but very little of it
has been translated into English, because
of her rather elusive style. The excerpt
by which she is represented in this volume
had to be especially translated for this
book. Gabriela Mistral is a pen name,
her real name being Lucila Godoy Alca-
yaga.

FERENC MOLNÁR, Hungarian dramatist and novelist, was born in Hungary,
January 12, 1878, the son of a physician,
and educated for the law in Budapest
and Geneva. He never practiced, but went
into newspaper work in Hungary where
he began writing humorous articles and
plays. He was a war correspondent from
1914 to 1918. His first play to gain him
renown was *The Devil* in 1907, followed
by *Liliom* in 1909. He married Lili Darvas,
a noted actress.

In 1940, he left Hungary to escape
Nazism—Molnár is of Jewish origin—
and has been living in New York near
Central Park. His latest book, *Companion
in Exile*, was devoted to his secretary,
who left Hungary with him, and died in
this country.

Liliom, 1921
Fashions for Men, 1922
The Swan, 1922
The Guardsman, 1924
Olympia, 1928
Plays, 1929
The Good Fairy, 1932
Delicate Story, French, 1941
(The above are plays)
Husbands and Lovers (sketches), 1924
Prisoners (fiction), 1925
Eva and the Derelict Boat (stories), 1926
Paul Street Boys (novel), 1927
Farewell My Heart, Simon and Schuster,
1945
The Captain of St. Margaret's (mem-
oirs), Duell, Sloan and Pearce, 1945
Companion in Exile (biography), Horizon
Press, 1950

JAWAHARLAL NEHRU, Indian political leader and Prime Minister of India,
was born in 1889 in India, the son of
a lawyer. He was educated in England at
Harrow and Cambridge and was a bar-
rister-at-law in the Inner Temple. He
joined Gandhi's non-cooperation movement in 1920 and was President of the
Indian National Congress 1929, 1936, 1937,
and 1946. He was imprisoned for political activities many times and in confinement wrote a number of books including
Glimpses of World History and his autobiography. He became Prime Minister of
India in August, 1947. He visited the
United States in behalf of his country
in 1949, and in 1950 he was nominated
for the Nobel Peace Prize. His writings
were introduced into America partly as
a result of John Gunther's encountering
Nehru and his influence in India in connection with Gunther's *Inside Asia*. His
books have all been published by The
John Day Company, New York.

Toward Freedom, 1941
Glimpses of World History, 1942
The Unity of India, 1942
Nehru On Gandhi, 1948
Visit To America, 1950
Independence and After, 1950
The above does not include some early
works of Nehru published in India.

PABLO NERUDA, Chilean poet and political figure, considered one of the most outstanding living poets in the Spanish language, was born in Parral, Chile, in 1904, and drew attention to his poetic talent with his first book of poems in 1921, *La Canción de la Fiesta*. For many years he was in the Chilean diplomatic service, serving in Burma, Ceylon, Java, Argentina, Spain, France and Mexico. He has been a Chilean senator since 1945.

Neruda was in Madrid during the Spanish Civil War, and the experience has been reflected in many of his poems. He was recently awarded the Chilean National Prize for his poetry.

A good representation of his writing is contained in the one book of his many volumes which has been translated into English, *Residence on Earth* (New Directions, 1946), translated by his authorized American translator and representative, Angel Flores, of Queens College, New York. Mr. Flores did the special translation of Neruda's latest work—one of his longest poems—*The Summits of Macchu Picchu*, for THE WORLD'S BEST.

SEAN O'CASEY was born in Dublin in 1884, youngest of a fairly large family. He is self-educated, largely, he has written, through picking up second-hand books in Dublin shops. As a laborer he became interested in the Irish National Movement and learned Gaelic.

His first play was produced by the Abbey Theatre though it was the fourth one he had written after three earlier rejections. The play was *The Shadow of a Gunman*.

He married an actress, Eileen Reynolds (stage name Eileen Carey) in 1928 and has two sons. He was an organizer of the Irish Citizen Army.

I Knock at the Door (autobiography), 1939
Pictures in the Hallway (autobiography), 1942
Red Roses for Me (play), 1943
Drums Under The Windows, 1946
Oak Leaves and Lavender (play), 1947
Inishfallen, Fare Thee Well (autobiography), 1949
Cock-a-doodle Dandy (play), 1950
Collected Plays, 1950
(All published by Macmillan)

LIAM O'FLAHERTY, the Irish novelist and short story writer, was born in the Aran Islands off County Galway, in 1897 and completed his education at the National University in Dublin. He was originally intended for priesthood but, after forming a company of Irish Volunteers at Black Rock College, he resumed a martial career with the Irish Guards in 1915 and was shell-shocked in Belgium in 1917. He took part in the Irish Civil War. He began writing in 1921 and his books and stories have mainly concerned Dublin or the Aran Islands.

The Informer, Harcourt, Brace, 1925
Spring Sowing, Knopf, 1926
The Life of Tim Healy, Harcourt, Brace, 1927
The Assassin, Harcourt, Brace, 1928
The House of Gold, Harcourt, Brace, 1929
The Mountain Tavern and Other Stories, Harcourt, Brace, 1929
Two Years, Harcourt, Brace, 1930
The Return of the Brute, Harcourt, Brace, 1930
I Went to Russia, Harcourt, Brace, 1931
The Puritan, Harcourt, Brace, 1932
Skerrett, Smith, 1932
The Martyr, Harcourt, Brace, 1933
Famine, Random House, 1937
Land, Random House, 1946

EUGENE O'NEILL, playwright and winner of the Nobel Prize for Literature in 1936, (the second American to receive this honor) has had an intensely vivid and varied career. Born in an hotel on what is now Times Square in New York on October 16, 1888, a son of the famous romantic actor, James O'Neill, he has been in intimate touch with the theatre since earliest childhood.

A college career at Princeton ended after one year. He then worked in a small mail-order house in New York for a year and a half. In 1909 he went on a gold-prospecting trip to Honduras, where he found no gold but contracted malaria. He returned to this country, and after a short period as assistant manager of *The White Sister*, in which his father was one of the stars, he sailed on a Norwegian barque to Buenos Aires, where he worked for short periods with the Westinghouse Electrical Co., Swift Packing Co., and Singer Sewing Machine Co. Then he went to sea again as ordinary seaman on a British tramp steamer, and later as an able bodied seaman on transatlantic American Line ships. His ambition at this time, as he says, was "to be a Jack London 'he-man' sailor."

In 1912, he acted for part of a season with his father, and later worked as a reporter on a New London, Connecticut, newspaper. At the end of that year he suffered a physical breakdown and was forced to go to a tuberculosis sanatorium for six months. This period of rest cure he acknowledges as a turning point of his life: it was then, he has said, that he first began "thinking it over," and a few months after he left the sanatorium he wrote his first play. In 1914-15 he studied the technique of playwrighting for one year in Baker's famous "47 Workshop" at Harvard. In 1916 he joined the Provincetown Players, and for many years it was this group which gave him his chance to be heard in the theatre, and produced almost all of his work.

Recognition as the foremost American playwright came in 1920 with the Pulitzer Prize for his *Beyond the Horizon*. Since then he has been awarded the Pulitzer Prize twice, in 1922 for *Anna Christie* and in 1928 for *Strange Interlude*.

Thirst, and Other One-Act Plays, Badger, Boston, 1914

Before Breakfast, Frank Shay, 1916

The Moon of the Caribbees, and Other One-Act Plays of the Sea, Liveright, 1919

Gold, Liveright, 1920

Beyond the Horizon, Liveright, 1921

The Emperor Jones; Diff'rent; The Straw, Liveright, 1921

The Hairy Ape; Anna Christie; The First Man, Liveright, 1922

All God's Chillun Got Wings; Welded, Liveright, 1924

Complete Works, two volumes, Boni & Liveright, 1924

Desire Under the Elms, Liveright, 1925

The Great God Brown; The Fountain; The Moon of the Caribbees, and Other Plays, Liveright, 1926

Lazarus Laughed, Liveright, 1927

Marco Millions, Liveright, 1927

Strange Interlude, Liveright, 1928

Dynamo, Liveright, 1929

Mourning Becomes Electra, Liveright, 1931

Nine Plays, Random House, 1932

Ah, Wilderness!, Random House, 1934

Days Without End, Random House, 1934

Plays, three volumes, Random House, 1941

The Iceman Cometh, Random House, 1946

All of Mr. O'Neill's works are plays.

JOSÉ ORTHEGA Y GASSET, Spanish philosopher and critic, was born, May 9th, 1883, and lives in Buenos Aires as an emigré. He is chiefly known in the United States for *The Revolt of the Masses*, which has aroused controversy from both right and left for its analysis of society, in the terms of what he considers loss of cultural values through the rise of a mass mind.

He was born in Madrid, son of an important Madrid newspaper editor and was educated by private tutors and at a Jesuit school. He was graduated from the University of Madrid where he later became Professor of Metaphysics. He has founded several magazines including *Europa*, *El Sol*, a liberal newspaper, and *La Revista del Occidente*.

He participated in the overthrow of the Spanish monarchy and in 1931 was elected deputy. He became a voluntary exile in Argentina and in 1941 was appointed Professor of Philosophy at the University of San Marcos, in Lima, Peru.

The Revolt of the Masses, Norton, 1932

The Modern Theme, Norton, 1933

Invertebrate Spain, Norton, 1937

Toward a Philosophy of History, Norton, 1941

The Mission of the University, Princeton University Press, 1944

Concord and Liberty, Norton, 1946

The Dehumanization of Art; and Notes on the Novel, Princeton University Press, 1948

ST. JOHN PERSE is the pen name of the distinguished French poet and diplomat, Alexis Saint-Léger Léger, or more commonly, Alexis Léger, formerly Permanent Secretary of the French Foreign Office, one of the principal officers of the Third Republic, and now an exile in America, whose citizenship was revoked and all of whose property was seized by the Vichy Government.

The poet was born on a small coral island in the French Antilles in 1889, son of a family which, during the war in the Dominican Republic, had moved to New Orleans and contributed three sons and three ships to the Confederacy.

Léger was sent to Paris for his education, entered the diplomatic service, and went to China. In 1919 he was Secretary of the embassy in Peking and has held the following other posts: Expert for Political Questions at Washington Conference, 1921; Director, Asiatic and Oceania Departments at Ministry of Foreign Affairs, 1925; *Chef de Cabinet* 1925-1931;

Assistant Director, Political and Commercial Affairs 1927-1929 and Director 1929; member Delegation to The Hague International Conference 1929; member Delegation to London Naval Conference 1930; Ambassador; Secretary-General for Foreign Affairs 1933-1940.

T. S. Eliot has translated his long poem *Anabase*, declaring it of the same importance as the later work of James Joyce.

M. Léger is at present consultant on French literature in the Library of Congress.

Anabase (translated by T. S. ELIOT), Harcourt, Brace, 1938

Éloges (translated by LOUISE VARESE), Norton, 1944

Exile and Other Poems, Pantheon-Bollingen Series, 1949

JOHN BOYNTON PRIESTLEY was born in Bradford, Yorkshire in 1894, the son of a schoolmaster. He served throughout the First World War in the Infantry, and afterwards went to Cambridge University where he took honors in English Literature and Modern European History. He then went to London, establishing himself as an essayist, reviewer and critic.

His most successful novel was *The Good Companions*, a long picaresque humorous tale, which has been translated into many languages. He has written many plays, including *Dangerous Corner*, *Laburnum Grove*, *Johnson Over Jordan* and *The Inspector Calls*.

He has been twice married and has several daughters and a son. His house is in Highgate Village, London, which was once the home of Samuel Taylor Coleridge, the poet. He also has a house in the Isle of Wight.

Talking, Harpers, 1926
The Old Dark House, Harper, 1928
The Good Companions, Harper, 1929
Angel Pavement, Harper, 1930
The Balconinny, Harper, 1931
Faraway, Harper, 1932
Self-selected Essays, Harper, 1933
Wonder Hero, Harper, 1933
English Journey, Harper, 1934
Three Plays and a Preface, 1935
Laburnum Grove, French, 1936
They Walk in the City, Harper, 1936
The English Comic Characters, Lane (London), 1937
Midnight on the Desert, Harper, 1937
I Have Been Here Before, Harper, 1938

The Doomsday Men, Harper, 1938
Time and the Conways, French, 1939
Johnson Over Jordan, Harper, 1939
Rain Upon Godshill, Harper, 1939
Britain Speaks, Harper, 1940
Let The People Sing, Harper, 1940
Out of the People, Harper, 1941
Britain at War, Harper, 1942
Black-out in Gretley, Harper, 1943
Daylight on Saturday, Harper, 1943
Four Plays, Harper, 1944
Three Men in New Suits, Harper, 1945
Bright Day, Harper, 1946
Jenny Villiers, Harper, 1947
The Linden Tree and *The Inspector Calls*, 1948
Delight, Harper, 1949

ERICH MARIA REMARQUE, German novelist, was born in 1898 in Osnabrück, Westphalia, in a family of Roman Catholics. At eighteen he was drafted into the German army during the First World War and was wounded five times. After his discharge he was for a time a teacher, test driver for a Berlin tire company, and then a sports editor. His first novel, written at this time, was an immediate success. *All Quiet on the Western Front* sold more than a million copies in Germany the year of its publication, and was translated into many languages and made into a motion picture.

Remarque left Germany for Switzerland to live away from the publicity his book occasioned. In 1938 the Nazis deprived him of citizenship. In 1939 he came to America to take out American citizenship and has lived here intermittently since.

All Quiet on the Western Front, 1929
The Road Back, Little, Brown, 1931
Three Comrades, Little, Brown, 1937
Flotsam, Little, Brown, 1941
Arch of Triumph, Appleton-Century, 1946

JULES ROMAINS, pseudonym of Louis Farigoule, French novelist, dramatist, essayist and poet, was born in a village of Le Velay, in the Cevennes Mountains, August 26, 1885. He passed his childhood in Paris where his father was a teacher. He received his degree in philosophy and science from the Sorbonne in 1909 and was made the same year a professor of philosophy at the Lycée of Brest; later he taught at Laon, Nice and Paris.

Romain's first book of poems was published when he was sixteen, *La Vie Una-nime,* the central thought of which he later expanded into a literary theory, "unanism," or the oneness of life, holding that collective emotions transcend those of the individual and the poet gives groups a keener awareness of their personality. His playwrighting talent came to the fore with the success of his farces, *Knock, ou le Triomphe de la médecine,* translated as *Dr. Knock,* and others, produced by Louis Jouvet.

In 1923 his many-volumed novel began to appear, *Men of Good Will,* aiming to depict modern French life in about 30 volumes.

From 1938 to 1941 he was international president of the P. E. N. Club. In 1946 he was elected to the French Academy. He is married and now lives in Paris.

The Death of a Nobody, 1914 (re-issued Knopf 1944)
Eyeless Sight: Study of Extra Retinal Vision, 1924
Lucienne, 1925
Dr. Knock (play), 1925
Six Gentlemen in a Row, 1927
The Body's Rapture, 1933
The Seven Mysteries of Europe, Knopf, 1940
Stefan Zweig: Great European, Viking, 1941
Salsette Discovers America, Knopf, 1942

"MEN OF GOOD WILL" SERIES (Knopf)

Men of Good Will (The 6th of October, Quinette's Crime), 1933
Passion's Pilgrims (Childhood's Loves, Eros in Paris), 1934
The Proud and the Meek (The Proud, The Meek), 1935
The World From Below (The Lonely, The Provincial Interlude), 1935
The Earth Trembles (Flood Warning, The Powers That Be), 1936
The Depths and the Heights (To the Gutter, To the Stars), 1937
The Death of a World (Mission to Rome, The Black Flag), 1938
Verdun (The Prelude, The Battle), 1939
Aftermath (Vorge Against Quinette, The Sweets of Life), 1941
The New Day (Promise of Dawn, The World Is Your Adventure), 1942
Work and Play (Mountain Days, Work and Play), 1944
The Wind is Rising (Gathering of the Gangs, Offered in Evidence), 1945

Escape in Passion (The Magic Carpet, Françoise), 1946
The Seventh of October, 1946
The Short Novels of Balzac (editor), Dial Press, 1948

BERTRAND RUSSELL, (Bertrand Arthur William), 3rd Earl Russell, Viscount Amberley, the English philosopher, mathematician and sociologist, was born May 18, 1872, at Trelleck, Wales, a member of one of the oldest families in England. The first Earl was created by Queen Victoria in whose government he was twice prime minister. Bertrand Russell was orphaned at three and reared by Lord John Russell's widow. He was educated at home until he entered Trinity College, Cambridge. There he distinguished himself in the study of mathematics and he turned down an opportunity to enter a political career to write, his first book being on German Social Democracy, followed by four on mathematics.

The First World War he opposed, although he was over military age himself. He was dismissed from Trinity College in 1916 as lecturer on mathematics, and sentenced to four months in prison where he wrote his *Introduction to Mathematical Philosophy.* He strongly supported the democracies in the Second World War.

In 1920 he was professor of philosophy at the University of Peking and in 1922 and 1923 he ran, but failed, to get elected as a Labor Member of Parliament. He and his second wife ran a school on progressive lines in Sussex from 1927 to 1932, and in 1938 he began teaching in America, first at the University of Chicago, then at the University of California, and in 1940 was appointed William James Lecturer in Philosophy at Harvard and professor of philosophy at the College of the City of New York, where his views on sex caused protests, and he left for Marion, Pa., as lecturer on the history of culture at the Barnes Foundation. He has been married three times, and now lives in England. He has written a score of books.

Why Men Fight, Century, 1917
Political Ideals, Century, 1917
The Problem of China, Century, 1922
The Prospects of Industrial Civilization, Century, 1923
Sceptical Essays, Norton, 1928

The Scientific Outlook, Free Press, 1931
Power; a New Social Analysis, Norton, 1938
An Inquiry Into Meaning and Truth, Norton, 1940
The Philosophy of Bertrand Russell (edited by P. A. SCHILPP), Northwestern University, 1944
A History of Western Philosophy, Simon and Schuster, 1945
Human Knowledge; its Scope and Limits, Simon and Schuster, 1948

VICTORIA MARY SACKVILLE-WEST, English poet and novelist who signs her books V. Sackville-West, was born in March, 1892 at Knole Castle, once the seat of the Archbishops of Canterbury, given by Queen Elizabeth to her cousin, Lord Treasurer Thomas Sackville. Victoria Mary Sackville-West's father was the third Baron Sackville; her parents were first cousins, and her maternal grandmother was a Spanish gypsy. She was educated at home and in 1913 married Harold Nicolson, the author and diplomat; they have two sons. She lives at Sissinghurst, Kent, and is a Fellow of the Royal Society of Literature. Her books are numerous.

Heritage (fiction), 1919
Challenge (fiction), 1923
Knole and The Sackvilles (genealogy), 1923
Gray Wethers (fiction), 1923
The Heir & Other Stories (fiction), 1924
The Dairy of Lady Ann Clifford, 1924
Seducers in Ecuador (fiction), 1925
The Land (poetry), 1927
Passenger to Teheran (travel), 1927
Twelve Days (fiction), 1929
The Edwardians (fiction), 1930
King's Daughter (poetry), 1930
All Passion Spent (fiction), 1931
Thirty Clocks Strike the Hour (fiction), 1932
Collected Poems, 1934
The Dark Island (fiction), 1934
St. John's Avenue, 1936
Family History (fiction), 1937
Pepita (biography), 1937
Solitude (poetry), 1939
Country Notes in Wartime (essays), 1941
Grand Canyon (fiction), 1942
The Eagle and The Dove, 1944
The Garden (poetry), 1946
Devil At Westease, 1947
(All published by Doubleday)

CARL SANDBURG, who has been called the folk singer of America, was born in Galesburg, Illinois, January 6, 1878. His parents were Swedish immigrants, and his family name was Johnson until his father had it changed to Sandburg to avoid confusion with the many other Johnsons in the town.

He left school at thirteen to do odd jobs such as driving a milk wagon, helping out in a barber shop, shifting scenery, truck driving, dish washing, house painting, and carpentering. In 1898 he enlisted with the Sixth Illinois Volunteers and saw active service in Puerto Rico in the Spanish-American War. On his return he worked his way through Lombard College in Galesburg, and in 1902 became an advertising writer, journalist, and organizer for the Social-Democratic Party in Wisconsin. He was secretary to the Socialist mayor of Milwaukee from 1910 to 1912.

Mr. Sandburg then entered journalism as associate editor of *System*, a magazine in Chicago. In 1917 he joined the Chicago *Daily News*, and in 1918 visited Norway and Sweden as correspondent for the Newspaper Enterprise Association. Upon his return he became associated with the *Daily News* as editorial writer.

His earliest poems were privately printed in 1904. In 1914 he won his first literary award, the Levinson Prize. Since then his reputation has become international. *Cornhuskers*, a book of verse, shared the prize of the Poetry Society of America in 1918, and his *Abraham Lincoln: The War Years*, the second part of his six-volume biography of Lincoln, was awarded the Pulitzer Prize in 1940.

Mr. Sandburg has traveled throughout America, collecting and singing native ballads and folk songs, which he has published in book form as *The American Songbag* (1927).

Mr. Sandburg was married in 1908 to Lillian Steichen, and is the father of three daughters. During the war he made foreign broadcasts for the Office of War Information, and wrote the commentary for the U. S. Government film, *Bomber*, and a weekly newspaper column on current problems.

In Reckless Ecstasy, privately printed, Galesburg, Ill., 1904
Chicago Poems, Holt, 1916
Cornhuskers (poetry), Holt, 1918
The Chicago Race Riots (history), Harcourt, Brace & Howe, 1919
Smoke and Steel (poetry), Harcourt,

Brace & Howe, 1920. Reprinted with the next title by Harcourt, Brace, in 1938. Reprinted with the next title and *Good Morning, America* by Harcourt, Brace, in 1942

Slabs of the Sunburnt West (poetry), Harcourt, Brace, 1922. Reprinted with *Smoke and Steel* by Harcourt, Brace, in 1938. Reprinted with *Smoke and Steel* and *Good Morning, America* by Harcourt, Brace, in 1942

Rootabaga Stories (juvenile), Harcourt, Brace, 1922. Reprinted with the next title in 1936

Rootabaga Pigeons (juvenile), Harcourt, Brace, 1923. Reprinted with *Rootabaga Stories* in 1936

Selected Poems (edited by REBECCA WEST), Harcourt, Brace, 1926

Abraham Lincoln: The Prairie Years (biography), two volumes, Harcourt, Brace, 1926

The American Songbag (anthology of folk songs), Harcourt, Brace, 1927

Good Morning, America (poetry), Harcourt, Brace, 1928. Reprinted with *Smoke and Steel* and *Slabs of the Sunburnt West* by Harcourt, Brace, in 1942

Abe Lincoln Grows Up (selection for young folks from *Abraham Lincoln: The Prairie Years*), Harcourt, Brace, 1928

Rootabaga Country (selections from *Rootabaga Stories* and *Rootabaga Pigeons*), Harcourt, Brace, 1929

Steichen, the Photographer (biography), Harcourt, Brace, 1929

Potato Face (juvenile), Harcourt, Brace, 1930

Early Moon (selected poems, especially for children), Harcourt, Brace, 1930

Mary Lincoln, Wife and Widow (biography; Part II by PAUL ANGLE), Harcourt, Brace, 1932

...The People, Yes (poetry), Harcourt, Brace, 1936

Lincoln and Whitman Miscellany, Holiday Press, Chicago, 1938

Abraham Lincoln: The War Years (biography), four volumes, Harcourt, Brace, 1939

Storm Over the Land: A Profile of the Civil War, Harcourt, Brace, 1942

Home Front Memo, 1943

The Photographs of Abraham Lincoln (with FREDERICK HILL MESERVE), 1944

Remembrance Rock (novel), Harcourt, Brace, 1948

Lincoln Collector, Harcourt, Brace, 1949

GEORGE SANTAYANA, poet and philosopher, born in Madrid, Spain, December 16, 1863, was a graduate of Harvard in 1886, studied in Berlin and England and from 1872 on until 1911 spent most of his time in the United States; he is considered Spanish-American although he has never given up his Spanish citizenship and for many years has been living in Rome. From 1889 to 1911 he was professor of philosophy at Harvard. He has written one novel, *The Last Puritan* (1936), and two volumes of autobiography, *Persons And Places* (1944) and *The Middle Span* (1945). The rest of his books are philosophy or poetry, including *The Life Of Reason* in five volumes (1905-1906); the four-volume *Realms Of Being* (1928-40); *Poems*, selected by the author and revised 1923; *Dialogues In Limbo* (1925), and many other volumes. Nearly all Santayana's works have been published in the United States by Charles Scribner's Sons. All his books have been written in the English language. He says of himself that he figures in the English speaking world "as a sort of permanent guest, familiar, appreciative, and I hope discreet, but still foreign. This is no less true of me intellectually than it is socially, and should not be ignored in considering my work."

His maternal grandfather was from Catalonia. This ancestor left Spain in 1823 with his family for Scotland where Santayana's mother was born. The family moved to Virginia where she spent her early childhood. Eventually she married a Boston merchant in Manila. After his death she returned to Spain on the outbreak of the Civil War and married the man who became Santayana's father. After Santayana's birth in Madrid, the family moved to Boston where young Santayana began his schooling in the Boston Latin School.

JEAN-PAUL SARTRE was born in Paris in 1905. Critic, novelist and dramatist, Sartre was a teacher of philosophy for many years at the Lycées of Laon, Le Havre, and later at Lycée Condorcet in Paris. Between 1936 and 1940 he wrote a number of short volumes on the imagination and the emotions, followed by critical studies, and in 1938 by his first novel, *Nausea*. The despair of his first work, in which he declared nothing justified man's existence, gave way to an active participation in the French resistance movement, and in 1943 he published in French a seven-hundred page philosophical treatise which is eventually to be brought out in America.

Interpretation of the "existential philosophy" has been much debated, but its meaning has emerged as less a denial of the value of existence than as a voluntary acceptance, without illusions, of personal responsibility. His books have been brought out by different publishers in the United States, and are still appearing.

The Age of Reason, (novel), Knopf, 1947
The Reprieve, Knopf, 1947
No Exit and *The Flies* (plays), Knopf, 1947
Existentialism, Philosophical Library, 1947
The Emotions, Philosophical Library, 1948
Anti-Semite and Jew, Schocken, 1948
The Chips Are Down (play), Lear, 1948
The Psychology of Imagination, Philosophical Library, 1948
The Wall, and Other Stories, New Directions, 1948
What is Literature?, Philosophical Library, 1949
Three Plays (Dirty Hands, The Respectful Prostitute, and The Victors) (plays), Knopf, 1949
Nausea (novel), New Directions, 1949

SIEGFRIED (Lorraine) SASSOON, English poet and novelist, was born in London, September 8th, 1886, descendant of a wealthy family of Spanish Jews, resident first in Persia, Bombay and finally England. His mother, an artist, was a sister of the sculptor, Sir Hamo Thornycroft. He was educated at Cambridge and served in the First World War, an experience which made him a pacifist and directed his life to poetry. In 1928 he published his first prose work, a fictionalized autobiography, anonymously: *Memoirs of a Fox-Hunting Man.* It won the Hawthornden and the James Tait Black Memorial Prizes. In 1933 he married and has one son, and lives in Wiltshire.

Satirical Poems, 1926
Vigils (poems), 1936
The Old Century and Seven More Years (memoirs), 1939
Rhymed Ruminations, 1941
The Weald of Youth (memoirs), 1942
Siegfried's Journey: 1916-1920 (memoirs), 1946
Meredith (biography), 1948
Collected Poems, 1949
   (All published by Viking Press)

ALBERT SCHWEITZER, philosopher, missionary, doctor, writer and musician, was born in upper Alsace in 1875, the second child of Louis Schweitzer, an evangelical pastor. His paternal grandfather was a schoolmaster and organist and three of his grandfather's brothers occupied similar double posts. His mother was the daughter of a pastor.

Albert Schweitzer says of himself he was a dull student and a bad piano practicer. Nevertheless at the age of eighteen he entered the University of Strasbourg to major in philosophy and theology; and at twenty-one he decided to devote himself to science and art until he was thirty, when he would devote himself to the "direct service of humanity."

At twenty-four his philosophical book, *The Religious Philosophy Of Kant,* was published and he became a preacher in Strasbourg's Church of St. Nicholas. In 1903 he was appointed Principal of Strasbourg's Theological College and began work on a book which made him an international reputation, *The Quest Of The Historical Jesus.* In 1905 he began to study medicine with a view to spending the rest of his life as a doctor in equatorial Africa. While studying for his M.D. he continued preaching and played at the organ concerts of the Bach Society in Paris each winter. He wrote a book on organ building and a major theological work, *Paul And His Interpreters.*

In June, 1912, Dr. Schweitzer married Hélène Bresslau, daughter of a Strasbourg historian, who prepared herself for a life as a trained nurse. In 1913 they left for Africa where at Lambaréné the couple founded a hospital and treated two thousand cases during the first nine months. It was there Dr. Schweitzer began his multiple volume work, *The Philosophy Of Civilization,* the core of which is based upon a reverence for life. In 1949 Dr. Schweitzer came to America to take part in the Goethe festival in Colorado. He had been prevailed upon to make the visit on the promise of a gift from the University of Chicago of two million francs to the Lambaréné hospital.

He is at present back in Africa, and early in 1950 he was nominated for the Nobel Peace Prize.

African Notebook, Holt, 1939
Albert Schweitzer; an Anthology (edited by CHARLES R. JOY), Harper, 1947
On the Edge of the Primeval Forest, Macmillan, 1948
Goethe: Four Studies, Beacon Press, 1949

Memoirs of Childhood and Youth, Macmillan, 1949

Out of My Life and Thought, Holt, 1949

The Philosophy of Civilization, Macmillan, 1949

The Wit and Wisdom of Albert Schweitzer (edited by CHARLES R. JOY), Beacon Press, 1949

VINCENT SHEEAN was born in Pana, Illinois, on December 5, 1899, and was educated at the University of Chicago. During his career as foreign correspondent, at first for the Chicago *Tribune* and later for news syndicates, he reported the Fascist march on Rome, the French and Spanish wars on the Rif tribes, the overthrow of the Hankow government in China, and the Palestine riots of 1929. In *Personal History* (1935) he recorded the development of his views through these experiences of the post-war decades, and *Not Peace But a Sword*, published in 1939, was a survey of European conditions in that year. Mr. Sheean has also written six novels, a book of short stories, and a play.

In 1935 he married Diana, daughter of Sir Johnston and Lady Forbes-Robertson, and is the father of two daughters. He was a captain in the Army Air Force from May 1942 to August 1944. His latest book, on India, followed à visit to Ghandi, and he was there when the popular leader was assassinated.

An American Among the Riffi (current history), Harcourt, Brace, 1926

The Anatomy of Virtue (novel), Harcourt, Brace, 1927

The New Persia (current history), Harcourt, Brace, 1927

Gog and Magog (novel), Harcourt, Brace, 1930

The Tide (novel), Doubleday, Doran, 1933

Personal History (autobiography), Doubleday, Doran, 1935

Sanfelice (novel), Doubleday, Doran, 1936

The Pieces of a Fan (short stories), Doubleday, Doran, 1937

A Day of Battle (novel), Doubleday, Doran, 1938

Not Peace But a Sword (history), Doubleday, Doran, 1939

Bird of the Wilderness (novel), Random House, 1941

Between the Thunder and the Sun, Random House, 1943

This House Against This House (current history), Random House, 1946

A Certain Rich Man (novel), Random House, 1947

Lead Kindly Light, Random House, 1949

ROBERT E. SHERWOOD, three times winner of the Pulitzer Prize for drama, and once for his history-biography, *Roosevelt and Hopkins*, was born in New Rochelle, New York, on April 4, 1896, and educated at Harvard. He interrupted his college career to enlist with the Black Watch of the Canadian Expeditionary Force in 1917, and saw service overseas. Returning to New York in 1919, he was first the dramatic editor of *Vanity Fair*, then associate editor of *Life*, and from 1924 to 1928 editor. Since his first play, *The Road to Rome*, which he wrote in 1927, Mr. Sherwood has devoted the greater part of his energies to the stage. *Idiot's Delight*, *Abe Lincoln in Illinois*, and *There Shall Be No Night* were all awarded Pulitzer Prizes. In 1941 he received the Gold Medal for drama from the National Institute of Arts and Letters, and in 1946 his movie script for *The Best Years of Our Lives* won him an Academy Award. In 1949 he was the author of a musical play, *Miss Liberty*.

Mr. Sherwood has also written one novel, *The Virtuous Knight* (1931). He was special assistant to the Secretary of War in 1940, and to the Secretary of the Navy in 1945. He served as director of the overseas branch of the Office of War Information, resigning in 1944. He was long a close friend of President Roosevelt. He now lives in New York City with his second wife, Madeline Hurlock Sherwood.

The Road to Rome, Scribners, 1927

The Queen's Husband, Scribners, 1928

Waterlooo Bridge, Scribners, 1930

This is New York, Scribners, 1931

The Virtuous Knight (novel), Scribners, 1931

Reunion in Vienna, Scribners, 1932

Unending Crusade, Heinemann, London, 1932

The Petrified Forest, Scribners, 1935

Idiot's Delight, Scribners, 1937

Abe Lincoln in Illinois, Scribners, 1939

There Shall Be No Night, Scribners, 1940

The Rugged Path (play), 1945

Roosevelt and Hopkins (history), Harper, 1948

WILLIAM L. SHIRER was born in Chicago on February 23, 1904, and received his early schooling in Cedar Rapids, Iowa. After graduating from Coe College and working for a time on Cedar Rapids newspapers, he went to New York to continue journalism, but his next job did not materialize until he reached Paris in 1925. After a year on the Paris edition of the *Chicago Tribune*, he joined the European staff of the paper and was chief of the *Chicago Tribune's* Central European bureau from 1929 to 1932 with headquarters in Vienna.

After a year in India and another loafing on the Catalan coast, he went to Berlin in 1934 as correspondent for the Universal Service. In 1937 he joined the Columbia Broadcasting System and had perhaps the largest audience of listeners of any European radio correspondent. He was a war correspondent from 1939 to 1945, and radio news commentator from 1945 to 1947. He is a member of the editorial board of the *United Nations World*. He lives in New York City.

In Vienna he married Therese Stiberitz and has two daughters, Eileen Inga and Linda. His day-by-day notes as foreign correspondent in Berlin from 1934 to 1941, published as *Berlin Diary*, was his first book. It had the largest reading audience of any American journalist's book of the Second World War. It was followed by a sequel in 1947.

Berlin Diary (journal, 1934-1941), Knopf, 1941
End of a Berlin Diary (journal), Knopf, 1947

MIKHAIL SHOLOKHOV, considered the most widely read author in the U.S.S.R., was born in 1905 in a village in the Don River region. His parents were poor, but they managed to send him to school in Moscow. He returned to his native village at fifteen to become a schoolteacher, and later a town official, where he and his father were the only men remaining in the town during the Civil War of 1920-23.

He began his writing career at 18, and did war correspondence during the Nazi invasion of 1941. His mother was killed in a German bombing raid.

Sholokhov's fame rests on two huge novels recording the life of the Don Cossacks, work on his major opus occupying him fourteen years. The books, published in America in two consecutive volumes, are said to have sold many millions of copies in Russia, and to have been printed in thirty-eight languages in the U.S. S.R. The books delineate the change that occurs when one way of life, the simple peasant primitive mode, is shaken by history into a new form.

Sholokhov was awarded the Stalin Prize of one hundred thousand rubles, and the Order of Lenin. He is a member of the Academy of Sciences, and was elected a deputy to the Supreme Soviet of the U.S.S.R.

And Quiet Flows the Don, 1934
Seeds Of Tomorrow, 1935
The Don Flows Home To The Sea, 1941
The Silent Don (And Quiet Flows The Don and The Don Flows Home To The Sea in one volume), 1942
(All published by Knopf)

ANGELOS SIKELIANOS was born in Lekkas, one of the Ionian Islands, in 1884, and left college at Athens to devote himself to poetry. With his American wife, Eva Palmer, who now lives in New York, he recreated the Delphic Festivals on the slopes of Mount Parnassus, reviving the ancient theatre at Delphi for summer seasons between 1927 and 1930. An even larger cultural idea was behind the Delphic revival, which was "to found in Delphi an international center for the cultural collaboration of peoples," including the ceding by the government of lands to foreign nations for the establishing of "a spiritual center for each country." The movement was favored in its theatrical phase only and the larger objective was killed by politics. He was nominated for the Nobel Prize in 1947.

Alaphroiskiotos (the Seer), 1907
Verses, 1916
Prologue to Life (five volumes), 1915-1920
Dedication, 1927
Lyrical Life (three volumes including 18 poems of Resistance written under the German occupation of Greece)
Dithyramb of the Rose (translated by FRANCES SIKELIANOS)
The Sibyl
Daedalus in Crete, Christ in Rome, Death of Digenis (all poetical dramas translated into English by EVA SIKELIANOU)
Proanakrousma (the Awakener), prose
Akritan Songs, Spap Co., 1944

FRANS EEMIL SILLANPÄÄ, awarded the Nobel Prize in 1939, is Finland's leading novelist and short story writer, a position established by him in 1919 with the publication of his novel *Meek Heritage* which won him a government pension for life. His novel *The Maid Silja* was widely translated into other languages. He was born September 16, 1888 of a family of farmers and studied at the State University, but left without a degree in order to return home and write. Physically he is a huge man, weighing more than 250 pounds. He is married and has seven children and lives in Helsinki. His only works available in English are the two novels mentioned above.

IGNAZIO SILONE was born in Pescina, a small town in the mountains near Rome, May 1, 1900, son of a small landowner and a mother who was a weaver, one of six brothers all of whom, he says, "succumbed to illness or other misfortunes, the last was killed in prison by the Fascists." When he was three months old part of his home town was destroyed by flood; when he was fifteen it was entirely destroyed by an earthquake.

As a boy he was schooled for the clergy, but in 1917 he joined the Peasant League and later became editor of a leftist weekly opposed to Italy's entering the war. He was editor of a Trieste newspaper wrecked by the Fascists in 1922, and after the Fascists marched on Rome he was forced to leave Italy. He returned as a militant Communist, was jailed both in Italy and in Spain, and left the Communist Party in 1930 to live in Switzerland and write.

Ignazio Silone is a pen name, his real name being Secondo Tranquilli. He is married and his wife, Darina, made the translations of the hitherto unpublished material used in THE WORLD'S BEST.

Fontamara (novel), McBride, 1934
Mr. Aristotle (short stories), McBride, 1935
Bread and Wine (novel), Story Press-Harper, 1936
The School for Dictators, Story Press-Harper, 1938
The Living Thoughts of Mazzini (editor), Longmans Green, 1939
The Seed Beneath the Snow (novel), Harper, 1942
And He Hid Himself (play), Harper, 1945
The God That Failed (a chapter in that book), Harper, 1950

UPTON SINCLAIR was born in Baltimore, Maryland, on September 20, 1878.

His book about the Chicago stockyards, *The Jungle*, has been compared with *Uncle Tom's Cabin* and some of the novels of Charles Dickens for its influence on legislation and its help in improving the conditions of the poor.

Mr. Sinclair worked his way through the College of the City of New York by writing dime novels, and received his A.B. in 1897. He did post-graduate work at Columbia for four years. In 1906 he participated in the government investigation of the Chicago stockyards, and after publication of *The Jungle* he founded the Helicon Home Colony in Englewood, New Jersey, an experiment in practical Socialism in which Sinclair Lewis also took part.

He has said that the three men who shaped his thought were Jesus, Hamlet, and Shelley, and that he has "written exclusively in the cause of human welfare." All of his books have had as their purpose the elimination of social ills.

It was his interest in the welfare of society also which lay behind his entrance into politics on the Socialist ticket. He was a Socialist candidate for Congress from New Jersey in 1906, from California in 1920, and for the United States Senate in 1922. He was the Socialist candidate for the governorship of California in 1926 and 1930, and the Democratic candidate in 1934. At the start of the last campaign he founded the famous EPIC league—"End Poverty in California." He was also the founder of the American Civil Liberties Union, Southern California branch.

In 1913 Mr. Sinclair married Mary Craig Kimbrough, the poet. He lives now in California, where he publishes many of his own writings. His novel *Dragon's Teeth* received the Pulitzer Prize in 1943.

Springtime and Harvest (novel), publisher unknown, 1901
King Midas (reissue of *Springtime and Harvest*), Funk & Wagnalls, 1901
†*The Journal of Arthur Stirling* (novel), Appleton, 1903
Prince Hagen, a Phantasy (novel), Page, Boston, 1903
†*Manassas* (novel), Macmillan, 1904
Our Bourgeois Literature: The Reason and the Remedy (pamphlet), Kerr, Chicago, 1905
A Captain of Industry (novel), Haldeman-Julius, Girard, Kans., 1906
††*The Jungle* (novel), Doubleday, Page, Garden City, N. Y., 1906
What Life Means to Me (autobiography; pamphlet), Kerr, Chicago, 1906

A Home Colony (prospectus), Helicon Home Colony, Englewood, N. J., 1906

The Industrial Republic (social study), Doubleday, Page, Garden City, N. Y., 1907

The Helicon Home Colony (prospectus), Helicon Home Colony, Englewood, N. J., 1907

The Overman (short story), Doubleday, Page, Garden City, N. Y., 1907

†*The Metropolis* (novel), Moffat Yard, Boston, 1908

†*The Moneychangers* (novel), Dodge, New York, 1908

Good Health and How We Won It (health study; with MICHAEL WILLIAMS), Stokes, 1909

††*Prince Hagen* (play), 1909

†*Samuel the Seeker* (novel), Dodge, New York, 1910

†*Love's Pilgrimage* (novel), Kennerley, 1911

†*The Fasting Cure* (health study), Kennerley, 1911

Plays of Protest, Kennerley, 1912

†*Damaged Goods* (novel), Winston, Philadelphia, 1913

†*Sylvia* (novel), Winston, Philadelphia, 1913

†*Sylvia's Marriage* (novel), Winston, Philadelphia, 1914

Sinclair-Astor Letters (correspondence), National Civic Federation, 1914

†*The Cry for Justice* (anthology of the literature of social protest), Winston, Philadelphia, 1915

†*King Coal* (novel), Macmillan, New York, 1917

The Price I Paid (pamphlet), Sinclair, Pasadena, Cal., 1917

The Profits of Religion (economic study of the church), Sinclair, Pasadena, Cal., 1918

The Brass Check (study of American journalism), Sinclair, Pasadena, Cal., 1919

†*Jimmie Higgins* (novel), Boni & Liveright, New York, 1920

100%: The Story of a Patriot (novel), Sinclair, Pasadena, Cal., 1920

National News (pamphlet), Sinclair, Pasadena, Cal., 1920

The Book of Life, Mind, and Body (study in the conduct of life), Macmillan, 1921 (Part I), Sinclair, Pasadena, Cal., 1922 (Part II)

The Associated Press and Labor (seven chapters from *The Brass Check*), Sinclair, Pasadena, Cal., 1921

The Crimes of the "Times" (pamphlet), Sinclair, Pasadena, Cal., 1921

McNeal-Sinclair Debate on Socialism (pamphlet), Haldeman-Julius, Girard, Kans., 1921

They Call Me Carpenter (novel), Sinclair, Pasadena, Cal., 1922

Hell (verse drama and photoplay), Sinclair, Pasadena, Cal., 1923

The Goose-Step (study of American education), Sinclair, Pasadena, Cal., 1923

To the Chief of Police of Los Angeles (pamphlet), Sinclair, Pasadena, Cal., 1923

The Millennium (novel), three pamphlets, Sinclair, Pasadena, Cal., 1924

The Pot Boiler (play), Haldeman-Julius, Girard Kans., 1924

The Naturewoman (play), Haldeman-Julius, Girard, Kans., 1924

Singing Jailbirds (play), Sinclair, Pasadena, Cal., 1924

My Life and Diet (health study), Sinclair, Pasadena, Cal., 1924

The Goslings (study of the American schools), Sinclair, Pasadena, Cal., 1924

Mammonart (social study), Sinclair, Pasadena, Cal., 1925

Bill Porter (play), Sinclair, Pasadena, Cal., 1925

What's the Use of Books? (pamphlet), Vanguard Press, 1926

Letters to Judd, an American Workingman (pamphlet), Sinclair, Pasadena, Cal., 1926

The Spokesman's Secretary (fiction), Sinclair, Pasadena, Cal., 1926

†*Oil!* (novel), Boni, New York, 1927

†*Money Writes!* (social study), Boni, New York, 1927

†*Boston* (novel), two volumes, Boni, New York, 1928

Oil! (a play from the novel), Sinclair, Pasadena, Cal., 1929

†*Mountain City* (novel), Boni, New York, 1930

†*Mental Radio* (study in telepathy), Boni, New York, 1930

Books of Upton Sinclair in Translations and Foreign Editions (bibliography), Sinclair, Pasadena, Cal., 1930 (enlarged, 1938)

†*Roman Holiday* (novel), Farrar & Rinehart, New York, 1931

†*The Wet Parade* (novel), Farrar & Rinehart, New York, 1931

Socialism and Culture (pamphlet), Haldeman-Julius, Girard, Kans., 1931

Books of Upton Sinclair in Russia (pamphlet), Sinclair, Pasadena, Cal., 1931

†*American Outpost* (reminiscences), Farrar & Rinehart, New York, 1932

I, Governor of California: And How I Ended Poverty (political pamphlet), Farrar & Rinehart, New York, 1933

Upton Sinclair Presents William Fox (biography), Sinclair, Pasadena, Cal., 1933

††*The Way Out: What lies Ahead for America* (political and social study), Farrar & Rinehart, New York, 1933

EPIC Answers: How to End Poverty in California (political pamphlet), Sinclair, Pasadena, Cal., 1934

The Lie Factory Starts (political pamphlet), Sinclair, Pasadena, Cal., 1934

Immediate EPIC: The Final Statement of the Plan (political pamphlet), Sinclair, Pasadena, Cal., 1934

†*An Upton Sinclair Anthology* (selected works, compiled by I. O. Evans), Farrar & Rinehart, New York, 1934

Depression Island (play), Sinclair, Pasadena, Cal., 1935

I, Candidate for Governor: And How I Got Licked (political pamphlet), Sinclair, Pasadena, Cal., 1935

We, People of America: And How We Ended Poverty (political pamphlet), Sinclair, Pasadena, Cal., 1935

†*Co-Op* (novel), Farrar & Rinehart, New York, 1936

†*What God Means to Me* (study of religion), Farrar & Rinehart, New York, 1936

†*The Gnomobile* (juvenile), Farrar & Rinehart, New York, 1936

Wally for Queen! (play), Sinclair, Pasadena, Cal., 1936

The Flivver King (pamphlet novel), Sinclair, Pasadena, Cal., 1937

No Pasarán! (pamphlet novel), Sinclair, Pasadena, Cal., 1937

†*Our Lady* (novel), Rodale Press, Emmaus, Pa., 1938

†*Little Steel* (novel), Farrar & Rinehart, New York, 1938

Terror in Russia? Two Views by Upton Sinclair and Eugene Lyons (political study), Richard R. Smith, New York, 1938

What Can Be Done About America's Economic Troubles? (pamphlet), Sinclair, Pasadena, Cal., 1939

Your Million Dollars (pamphlet), Sinclair, Pasadena, Cal., 1939

†*Marie Antoinette* (play), Vanguard Press, New York, 1939

Expect No Peace (pamphlet of essays), Sinclair, Pasadena, Cal., 1939

Telling the World (previously published essays), Laurie, London, 1940

World's End (novel), Viking Press, New York, 1940

Between Two Worlds (novel), Viking Press, New York, 1941

Peace or War in America (debate with PHILIP LaFOLLETTE), Sinclair, Pasadena, Cal., 1941

Dragon's Teeth (novel), Viking Press, 1942

Wide Is the Gate (novel), Viking Press, 1943

Presidential Agent (novel), Viking Press, 1944

Dragon Harvest (novel), Viking Press, 1945

A World to Win (novel), Viking Press, 1946

Presidential Mission (novel), Viking Press, 1947

One Clear Call (novel), Viking Press, 1948

O Shepherd, Speak! (novel), Viking Press, 1949

One dagger (†) before a title in the above bibliography indicates that Mr. Sinclair published his own edition at some time later than the other publisher mentioned.

Two daggers (††) before a title indicate that Mr. Sinclair published his own edition at the same time as the other publisher.

EDITH SITWELL, one of the three Sitwells composing the present-day poets and prose writers of a notable old English family, was born in 1887 and lives at the ancestral home Renishaw near Sheffield, England. Her first poetry appeared when she was twenty-four, and in 1916, five years later, she became leader of a group of younger English poets establishing an annual anthology of verse, entitled, *Wheels*. Osbert and Sacheverell, her brothers, were frequent contributors. In 1923, she conducted a poetic recital to musical accompaniment and has lectured a great deal since. She lectured in the United States in the winter of 1949 and was acclaimed for her readings of *Façade* (originally written for a ballet with music by William Walton).

The Sleeping Beauty (poetry), Knopf, 1924

Troy Park (poetry), Knopf, 1925

Rustic Elegies (poetry), Knopf, 1927

Gold Coast Customs (poetry), Houghton Mifflin, 1929

Collected Poems, Houghton Mifflin, 1930

Alexander Pope, Cosmopolitan, 1930

English Eccentrics, Houghton Mifflin, 1933

The Pleasures of Poetry (editor: anthology), Norton, 1934

Selected Poems, Houghton Mifflin, 1937

I Live Under a Black Sun, Doubleday, 1938

Fanfare for Elizabeth, Macmillan, 1946
Song of the Cold, Vanguard, 1948
Canticle of the Rose (poetry), Vanguard, 1949

JOHN STEINBECK, whose *Grapes of Wrath* is one of the great books in American literature for its awakening of the public to an awareness of a social problem, is of mixed German and Irish stock. His father's family pioneered in the Big Sur region of California, where he was born on February 27, 1902. His early education was conventional, although, after being graduated from Salinas High School, he enrolled at Stanford University, where his attendance was irregular and extended over a period of eight years. He never received a degree.

Coming to New York as a young man he found a job as reporter on one of the Metropolitan newspapers, but his friends say that he was fired because he was unable to write his stories without infusing them with the sympathy with underprivilege which has since distinguished most of his writing. For a while he worked as a bricklayer during the erection of Madison Square Garden, and later as a chemist and a painter's apprentice. Then he returned to his home in California to write his novels. He married Carol Henning in 1930 and married a second time, to Gwyn Conger in 1943. They were later divorced.

The Grapes of Wrath was awarded the Pulitzer Prize for 1940. During the Second World War, Steinbeck was a war columnist overseas.

Cup of Gold (fictionalized biography), McBride, 1929
The Pastures of Heaven (short stories), Brewer, Warren, & Putnam, 1932
To a God Unknown (novel), Ballou, 1933
Tortilla Flat (novel), Covici Friede, 1935
In Dubious Battle (novel), Covici Friede, 1936
Nothing So Monstrous (story), privately printed, 1936
Saint Katy the Virgin (short story), Covici Friede, 1936
The Red Pony (story), Covici Friede, 1937
Of Mice and Men (novel), Covici Friede, 1937
Of Mice and Men (play), Covici, Friede, 1937
The Long Valley (short stories), Viking, 1938
Their Blood is Strong (pamphlet), Simon

J. Lubin Society of California, San Francisco, 1938
The Grapes of Wrath (novel), Viking, 1939
Steinbeck Replies (pamphlet), Friends of Democracy, 1940
The Forgotten Village (documentary narrative), Viking, 1941
Sea of Cortez (travel; with E. F. RICKETTS), Viking, 1941
The Moon is Down (novel), Viking, 1942
The Moon is Down (play), Viking, 1942
Bombs Away: The Story of a Bomber Team (photographs by JOHN SWOPE), Viking, 1942
The Portable Steinbeck (selected by PASCAL COVICI with an introduction by LEWIS GANNETT), Viking, 1943
Cannery Row (novel), 1945
The Wayward Bus (novel), 1947
The Pearl (fiction), Viking, 1947
A Russian Journal (personal narrative, illustrated with 70 photographs by ROBERT CAPA), Viking, 1948

JAMES THURBER, writer, cartoonist, and playwright, was born in Columbus, Ohio, December 8, 1894. He studied at Ohio State University. After two years as a code clerk in the United States State Department he began journalistic work. From 1920 to 1924 he was a reporter for the Columbus *Dispatch*, and then for two years with the Chicago *Tribune* in Paris. In 1926 he became a member of the staff of the New York *Evening Post*, and since 1927 he has been a regular contributor of both writing and drawings to *The New Yorker*.

Mr. Thurber collaborated with Elliott Nugent on *The Male Animal* in 1940, a comedy which ran on Broadway and was made into a movie. Other of his stories, *The Secret Life of Walter Mitty*, and *The Catbird Seat* have been cinematized.

Is Sex Necessary? (with E. B. WHITE), Harper, 1929, reissued 1950
The Owl in the Attic and Other Perplexities, Harper, 1931
The Seal in the Bedroom and Other Predicaments, Harper, 1932
My Life and Hard Times, Harper, 1933
The Middle Aged Man on the Flying Trapeze, Harper, 1935
Let Your Mind Alone!, Harper, 1937
The Cream of Thurber (selections), Hamilton, London, 1939
The Last Flower, Harper, 1939
Fables for Our Time, Harper, 1940

The Male Animal (play; with ELLIOT NU-
GENT), Random House, 1940
My World — And Welcome to It, Har-
court, Brace, 1942
Many Moons, Harcourt, Brace, 1943
Men, Women and Dogs, Harcourt, Brace,
1943
The Great Quillow, Harcourt, Brace, 1944
The Thurber Carnival, Harper, 1945
The White Deer (fantasy), Harcourt,
Brace, 1945
The Beast In Me and Other Animals,
Harcourt, Brace, 1948
   Unless otherwise noted, Mr. Thurber's
works are collections of humorous stories
and sketches.

ARNOLD JOSEPH TOYNBEE, British historian, was born April 14, 1889 and educated at Oxford. He was a Fellow and Tutor
at Balliol College from 1912 to 1915, a member of the staff of the Political Institute
of the Foreign Office in 1918, and a member of the British delegation to the Peace
Conference. He was a professor at London University from 1919 to 1924 in Greek
literature and history, and Director of
Studies of the Royal Institute of International Affairs from 1925 on. He was
Director of the Research Department of
the Foreign Office from 1943 to 1946. His
major work is a six-volume study of history, considering the chief societies or
civilizations in existence today—Western,
the Orthodox Christian, the Islamic, the
Hindu, and the Far Eastern. He lives in
London and has visited the United States
in recent years.

Published in England:
Nationality and the War, 1915
*The Western Question in Greece and Tur-
key*, 1922
A Survey of International Affairs, 1924
A Journey to China, 1931
A Study of History (6 vols.), 1934-1939

Published in the United States (Oxford
University Press)
A Study of History (Abridgement of Vols.
I-VI by D. C. SOMERVELL), 1947
Civilization on Trial, 1948

SIGRID UNDSET, Norwegian novelist
who was born in a small Danish town
May 20, 1882 and taken in 1884 to Chris-
tiania, died at 67 on June 10, 1949 in
Lillehammer, after she had made her selection personally, and written her comment for *THE WORLD'S BEST*. She was

then living in her village home in Norway after some years in Brooklyn, N. Y.
   For many years Sigrid Undset held the
position of the most distinguished of present-day Scandinavian fiction writers. The
section she chose is from *The Longest
Years*, (Knopf, 1935), reflecting her early childhood. She was the daughter of a
well-known archaeologist, who died when
she was eleven, and she began supporting
herself when she was sixteen. In 1928 she
was awarded the Nobel Prize in literature
for her many novels of family life and
her ethical-religious-historical novels, her
two best known being the trilogy *Kristin
Lavransdatter*, and the four-volume *The
Master of Hestviken*, translated into
English 1928-1930.
   She was a convert to the Catholic
church.

Jenny, 1921
Kristin Lavransdatter, 1929, 1935
The Wild Orchid, 1931
The Burning Bush, 1932
Ida Elisabeth, 1933
Stages on the Road, 1934
The Master of Hestviken, 1935
The Longest Years, 1935
Gunnar's Daughter, 1936
The Faithful Wife, 1937
Images in a Mirror, 1938
Men, Women, and Places, 1939
Madame Dorthea, 1940
Return to the Future, 1942
Happy Times in Norway (juvenile), 1942
Sigurd and His Brave Companions (juve-
nile), 1943
True and Untrue and Other Norse Tales
(juvenile), 1945
   (All published by Knopf)

CARL VAN DOREN, teacher, editor, and
writer, was born in Hope, Illinois, Sept.
10, 1885, received his A.B. degree from
the University of Illinois in 1907 and
taught there for a year as assistant in
rhetoric. After receiving his Ph.D. from
Columbia in 1911 he was a member of
the English department till 1916 and part-
time lecturer till 1930. He was headmaster
of the Brearley School in New York City
from 1916 to 1919.
   Mr. Van Doren was literary editor of
The Nation from 1919 to 1922 and of *The
Century Magazine* from 1922 to 1925, edi-
tor-in-chief of the Literary Guild from
1926 through 1934, chairman of the editorial committee of the Readers Club from
1941 and editor of The Living Library
since 1946. He was also managing editor

of *The Cambridge History of American Literature* (published 1917-21).

His works include biographies (primarily), histories of literature, critical studies, anthologies, a novel (*The Ninth Wave*, 1926), a collection of short stories (*Other Provinces*, 1925), and an autobiography (*Three Worlds*, 1936). In 1939 his *Benjamin Franklin* was awarded the Pulitzer Prize for biography and the Franklin medal 1943, of the American Philosophical Society.

He was married twice and has three married daughters.

The Life of Thomas Love Peacock, Dutton, 1911
The American Novel, Macmillan, 1921 (revised 1940)
Contemporary American Novelists: 1900-1920, Macmillan, 1922
The Roving Critic, Knopf, 1923
Many Minds (critical studies), Knopf, 1924
James Branch Cabell, McBride, 1924 (revised 1932)
Other Provinces (short stories), Knopf, 1925
American and British Literature Since 1890 (with MARK VAN DOREN), Appleton-Century, 1925, revised 1939
The Ninth Wave (novel), Harcourt, Brace, 1926
Swift (biography), Viking Press, 1930
American Literature: An Introduction, U. S. Library Association, Los Angeles, 1933
Sinclair Lewis, Doubleday, Doran, 1933
Modern American Prose (anthology), Harcourt, Brace, 1934
An Anthology of World Prose, Reynal & Hitchcock, 1935
What Is American Literature? (reissue of *American Literature: An Introduction*), Morrow, 1935
The Borzoi Reader (anthology), Knopf, 1936
Three Worlds (autobiography), Harpers, 1936
Benjamin Franklin, Viking Press, 1938
An Illinois Boyhood (first part of *Three Worlds*), Viking Press, 1939
Secret History of the American Revolution, Viking Press, 1941
Mutiny in January (history), Viking Press, 1943
Portable Library Carl Van Doren (selections), Viking Press, 1945
Benjamin Franklin's Autobiographical Writings (Editor), Viking Press, 1945
American Scriptures (Edited with CARL CARMER), Boni and Gaer, 1946

Letters and Papers of Benjamin Franklin and Richard Jackson, American Philosophical Society, 1947
The Great Rehearsal, Viking, 1948

PIERRE VAN PAASSEN (Pieter Antenie Laurusse van Paassen) was born in Gorcum, The Netherlands, on February 7, 1895, and was a student in schools there until 1913. His family moved to Canada when he was nineteen, and from 1914 to 1916 he attended Victoria College in Toronto. After that he served with the Canadian forces in France until the end of the first World War. Returning to Canada, he was a reporter for the Toronto *Globe* for two years, and from 1921 to 1924 for the Atlanta *Constitution* of Atlanta, Georgia.

From 1924 to the outbreak of World War II Mr. van Paassen was a columnist and roving foreign correspondent for the New York *Evening World* and, when that paper ceased to exist, for the North American Newspaper Alliance, the Toronto *Star* and a number of other American and Canadian newspapers. He is one of the most traveled of present-day writers, having visited and revisited Palestine, Spain, Russia, Ethiopia, Germany and Italy. During this time he studied intermittently at the *École Pratique des Hautes Études* in Paris, and in 1934 he received the degree of Bachelor of Theology from the *Faculté Libre Protestante*. He was ordained to the Unitarian Ministry in 1946, and is a professor of education in the American Unitarian Association. He is an Honorary Citizen of Tel Aviv, Israel.

Mr. van Paassen is married to the former Cornelia Sizoo, and is the father of two children. He lives in Bronxville, New York.

Évolution de la Conception de la Cité de Dieu, 1934
Nazism: an Assault on Civilization (with JAMES WATERMAN WISE), 1934
Days of Our Years (autobiography), Dial Press, 1939
That Day Alone (current history), Dial Press, 1941
The Time is Now! (essay), Dial Press, 1941
The Forgotten Ally, Dial Press, 1943
Earth Could Be Fair, Dial Press, 1946
The Tower of Terzel, Dial Press, 1948
Why Jesus Died, Dial Press, 1949

REBECCA WEST, British novelist and journalist, was born December 25, 1892.

in Ireland, the daughter of an army officer and war correspondent and a Scottish mother who was a musician. She was educated in Edinburgh and London where for a time she appeared on the stage and took her present pseudonym from the name of the heroine in Ibsen's *Rosmersholm*. She began journalistic writing at twenty on the staff of the *Free Woman*. In 1930 she married a banker, Henry Maxwell Andrews.

Rebecca West has been frequently called the world's greatest woman reporter but she has written much criticism, novels and one huge two-volume work on Yugoslavia, a travel diary which is considered a masterpiece.

Return Of The Soldier (novel), Doubleday, 1918

The Judge (novel), Doubleday, 1922

The Strange Necessity, Doubleday, 1928

Harriet Hume: A London Fantasy (novel), Doubleday, 1929

Ending In Earnest: A Literary Log (essays), Doubleday, 1931

The Harsh Voice (four short novels), Doubleday, 1935

The Thinking Reed (novel), Viking, 1936

Black Lamb And Grey Falcon (history and travel), Viking, 1941

The Meaning Of Treason, Viking, 1947

THORNTON WILDER, three times winner of the Pulitzer Prize—once for a novel and twice for plays—has said that all his works deal "with the mystery of death and judgment, the tragedy of beauty, and pity of ending of life's comedy." He was born in Madison, Wisconsin, on April 17, 1897, the son of a newspaper editor. When he was nine years old, his father went to China as American consul-general at Hong Kong and Shangai; Thornton Wilder attended school at Chefoo, and continued his education in this country after his return, graduating from Yale in 1920.

After one year of graduate study at the American Academy in Rome, Mr. Wilder was house master and teacher of French at Lawrenceville School in New Jersey until 1928. Meanwhile in 1927 he achieved a wide popularity with *The Bridge of San Luis Rey*, which was awarded the Pulitzer Prize. The following year he spent in Europe, working on his third novel, returning in 1929 to make a lecture tour, and from 1930 to 1936 he was on the faculty of the University of Chicago.

Much of Mr. Wilder's interest has lain in the theatre. He published several collections of one-act plays, and attained outstanding success with *Our Town*, which received the 1939 Pulitzer Prize and in 1942 his play *The Skin of Our Teeth* won him a second Pulitzer Prize. He served in the U. S. Air Corps Intelligence from June 1942, and was a Lieutenant Colonel from Sept. 1944 until his discharge in Sept. 1945. He received several military decorations.

Mr. Wilder is unmarried, and lives in New Haven, Connecticut.

The Cabala (novel), Boni, 1926

The Bridge of San Luis Rey (novel), Boni, 1927

The Angel That Troubled the Waters (one-act plays), Coward-McCann, 1928

The Woman of Andros (novel), Boni, 1930

The Long Christmas Dinner and other Plays, Coward-McCann, 1931

Lucrece (play, translated from ANDRÉ OBEY'S *Le Viol de Lucrèce*), Houghton Mifflin, Boston, 1933

Heaven's My Destination (novel), Harper, 1935

Our Town (play), Coward-McCann, 1938

The Merchant of Yonkers (play), Harper, 1939

The Skin of Our Teeth (play), Harper, 1942

The Ides of March (novel), Harper, 1948

RICHARD WRIGHT, was born near Natchez, Mississippi, on September 4, 1908, and attended school there. He began working at the age of fifteen in Memphis, Tennessee, and later did odd jobs in Chicago.

Mr. Wright was on the Federal Writers Project in Chicago in 1935 and in New York in 1938. It was at this time that he began writing for magazines and contributing to *The New Masses* and the New York *Daily Worker*. His *Uncle Tom's Children*, a collection of four stories, received in 1938 the *Story Magazine* prize of $500 for the best book submitted by anyone associated with the Federal Writers Project: and in 1939 he won a Guggenheim Fellowship, and in 1941 the Spingarn Medal.

Native Son, a Book-of-the-Month Club choice, was dramatized by Mr. Wright and Paul Green in 1941. Mr. Wright was once a Communist but disavowed its party aims. He is married, has a small daughter, and has lived some years in Paris.

Uncle Tom's Children (four novellas), Story Press-Harper, 1938

Native Son (novel), Harper, 1940

How "Bigger" Was Born (pamphlet), Harper, 1940

Native Son (play from the novel; with PAUL GREEN), Harper, 1941

Bright and Morning Star (short story), International Publishers, 1941

12 Million Black Voices (Negro folk history), Viking Press, 1941

Black Boy (autobiography), Harper, 1945

ACKNOWLEDGMENTS

✸✸

THE EDITOR and publishers wish to acknowledge with gratitude the helpful cooperation of authors, publishers and agents throughout the world for permission to reprint, or in some instances, print for the first time in book form or in first English translation, the material in this book as follows:

Anderson, Maxwell: *A Faith in the Theater* (Off Broadway) from *Off Broadway*, copyright 1947, by Maxwell Anderson. By permission of the author and Anderson House, Washington, D. C.

Aragon, Louis: *Poems in Wartime* (four) from *Aragon: Poet of the Resistance*. Reprinted by permission of the publishers, Duell, Sloan and Pearce, Inc. Copyright 1945, by Duell, Sloan and Pearce, Inc.

Auden, W. H.: *Massacre of the Innocents* from *Collected Poetry of W. H. Auden*, copyright 1945, by W. H. Auden. Reprinted by permission of the author and the publisher, Random House, Inc.

Aurobindo, Sri: *The Present Evolutionary Crisis* from *The Life Divine*, copyright 1949, by the Sri Aurobindo Library, Inc. By permission of the publishers, The Greystone Press, N. Y.

Azuela, Mariano: *The Under Dogs* from *The Under Dogs*, copyright 1929, by Brentano's, Inc. By permission of the author.

Baroja, Pio: *Youth and Egolatry*, reprinted from *Youth and Egolatry*. Translated by Jacob S. Fassett, Jr. and Frances L. Phillips. By permission of the author and Alfred A. Knopf, Inc. Copyright 1920, by Alfred A. Knopf, Inc.

Belloc, Hilaire: *Heroic Poem in Praise of Wine* from *Sonnets and Verse*, published and copyright 1939 by Sheed and Ward, New York. By permission of the author and A. D. Peters, London.

Benét, William Rose: *Fire and Glass* from *Golden Fleece*, copyright 1935, by Dodd, Mead and Company, Inc. By permission of the author and Dodd, Mead and Company, Inc. *Where All Is Glacier* from *The Dust Which Is God*, copyright 1941, by William Rose Benét, published by Dodd, Mead and Company, Inc., by permission of the author. *Harmony, Wound in Secret* reprinted from *The Stairway of Surprise*. By permission of the author and Alfred A. Knopf, Inc. Copyright 1935, 1942, 1943, 1944, 1945, 1946, 1947 by William Rose Benét.

Bowen, Elizabeth: *The Easter Egg Party*, reprinted from *Look at All Those Roses*. By permission of the author and Alfred A. Knopf, Inc. Copyright 1941, by Elizabeth Bowen.

Brooks, Van Wyck: *Edwin Arlington Robinson* from *A Chilmark Miscellany,* copyright 1948, by Van Wyck Brooks. By permission of the author and publisher, E. P. Dutton and Co., Inc., New York.

Buck, Pearl: *Fighting Angel* (Chapter 7 of *Fighting Angel*) by Pearl S. Buck. Copyright 1936 by Pearl S. Buck, published by the John Day Co., N. Y. Reprinted by permission of author and publisher, and the author's agent, David Lloyd, New York.

Bunin, Ivan: *The Gentleman from San Francisco.* Translated by Avrahm Yarmolinsky. By permission of author and Dr. Michael A. Hoffman, Paris.

Cabell, James Branch: *Is of Southern Ladies* from *Let Me Lie,* copyright 1947, by James Branch Cabell. By permission of the author and Farrar, Straus and Co., publishers, New York.

Caldwell, Erskine: *Yellow Girl* reprinted from *Jackpot,* by permission of the author and of the publishers, Duell, Sloan and Pearce, Inc. Copyright 1931, 1933, 1935, 1938, 1940, by Erskine Caldwell.

Callaghan, Morley: *Rigmarole* from *Now That April's Here,* copyright 1936, by Random House, Inc. By permission of the author and Harold Matson, the author's agent. Published by Random House, Inc.

Camus, Albert: *Sentence of Death* reprinted from *The Stranger* by Albert Camus. Translated by Stuart Gilbert. By permission of the author and Alfred A. Knopf, Inc. Copyright 1946 by Alfred A. Knopf, Inc.

Churchill, Winston: *Dunkirk: The Miracle of the Evacuation.* By permission of the British Information Service.

Claudel, Paul: *Here and There* from *The East I Know,* by Paul Claudel, translated by Teresa Frances and William Rose Benét. Copyright 1914 by the Yale University Press. By permission of the author and the publishers.

Cocteau, Jean: *Proust and Laughter,* by Jean Cocteau. Copyright 1949, The Condé Nast Publications Inc. Reprinted from August 15, 1949 *Vogue,* by permission of the author and publisher.

Colette: *Reading and Writing* (How I Began to Write). Copyright 1948 by *Mademoiselle.* Reprinted from *Mademoiselle,* September 1948.

Colum, Padraic: *What the Shuiler Said* from *Wild Earth,* copyright 1916 by The Macmillan Co. *Folding Hour* from *Poems,* copyright 1932 by The Macmillan Co. *Scanderbeg* from *Old Pastures,* copyright 1930 by The Macmillan Co. *I Shall Not Die for Thee* from *Wild Earth and Other Poems,* copyright 1916 by The Macmillan Co. *The Seer* hitherto unpublished. Reprinted by permission of the author and publishers.

Coward, Noel: *Hands Across the Sea* from *Tonight at 8:30* by Noel Coward. Copyright 1935, 1936, by Noel Coward. Reprinted by permission of the author and Doubleday and Company, Inc., publishers.

Croce, Benedetto: *Soliloquy of an Old Philosopher,* from *My Philosophy,* by Benedetto Croce, copyright 1950 by The Macmillan Company, and *My Philosophy,* selected by R. Klibansky, translated by E. F. Carritt, George Allen & Unwin Ltd., London, 1949. Used with permission of

The Macmillan Company and George Allen & Unwin Ltd., London.

Cronin, A. J.: *Birth,* from *The Citadel,* by A. J. Cronin. Copyright 1937 by A. J. Cronin. By permission of the author and Little, Brown and Co., publishers.

De la Mare, Walter: *Dreams, Fare Well* from *Collected Poems, 1901-1918.* Copyright, 1920, by Henry Holt & Co., Inc. Copyright, 1948, by Walter de la Mare. Used by permission of the publishers and the author's representative Rupert Thompson.

De la Roche, Mazo: *Death of a Centenarian,* from *Whiteoaks of Jalna,* by Mazo de la Roche, copyright 1929 by Little, Brown and Co. By permission of the author and Little, Brown & Co. publishers.

Dewey, John: *The Unity of the Human Being,* from *Intelligence in the Modern World, John Dewey's Philosophy,* edited by Joseph Ratner, copyright 1939, by Random House, Inc. By permission of the author.

Dinesen, Isak: *The Pearls* from *Winter's Tales,* copyright 1942 by Random House, Inc. By permission of the publishers.

Dos Passos, John: *Art and Isadora,* from *The Big Money,* copyright 1933, 1934, 1935, 1936, by John Dos Passos. Published by Harcourt, Brace and Company. By permission of the author.

Dunsany, Lord: *Business in Ireland,* from *My Ireland,* copyright 1937 by Funk & Wagnalls Co. By permission of the author and publishers.

Ehrenburg, Ilya: *The Storm* from *The Storm,* copyright 1949 by Gaer Associates, Inc., translated by J. Fineberg. By permission of the author and publishers.

Einstein, Albert: *Science and Life,* sections 1, 2, 16 and 34 from *Out of My Later Years,* copyright 1950 by Philosophical Library, publishers. By permission of the author and publishers.

Eliot, T. S.: *Burnt Norton,* from *Collected Poems, 1909-1935,* by T. S. Eliot. Copyright 1936, by Harcourt, Brace and Co., Inc. Reprinted by permission of the author and publishers.

Faulkner, William: *Sunday Morning at the Compsons,* from *The Sound and the Fury.* Copyright 1929, by William Faulkner. Copyright 1946, by Random House, Inc. By permission of the publishers.

Fisher, Dorothy Canfield: *A Drop in the Bucket,* from *Hillsboro People,* by Dorothy Canfield. Copyright, 1915, by Henry Holt and Co., Inc. Copyright, 1942, by Dorothy Canfield Fisher. Used by permission of the author and publishers.

Forster, E. M.: *The Trial* from *A Passage to India* by E. M. Forster, copyright, 1924, by Harcourt, Brace and Company, Inc. By permission of the author and publishers.

Frost, Robert: *The Need of Being Versed in Country Things, The Mountain, The Road Not Taken, The Grindstone, The Gift Outright, One Step Backward Taken,* from *Complete Poems of Robert Frost.* Copyright 1930, 1939, 1943, 1947, 1949 by Henry Holt and Company, Inc. Copyright 1936, 1942 by Robert Frost. Used by permission of the author and publishers.

Gide, André: *Fruits of the Earth* and *New Fruits* reprinted from *The Fruits of the Earth,* by André Gide, translated by Dorothy Bussy. By permission of Alfred A. Knopf, Inc., publishers. Copyright 1949 by Alfred A. Knopf, Inc.

Greene, Graham: *The Hint of an Explanation,* from *Nineteen Stories,* copyright 1936, 1941, 1942, 1946, 1947, 1949 by Graham Greene. By permission of the author, his agents Mary Pritchett and Barbara Brandt, and the publishers, The Viking Press, Inc.

Gunther, John: *Death Be Not Proud: The Graduation,* from *Death Be Not Proud,* by John Gunther, copyright, 1949, by John Gunther. By permission of the author and the publishers, Harper & Brothers.

Hamsun, Knut: *The Wonderful New Machine,* reprinted from *Growth of the Soil,* translated by W. W. Worster. By permission of the author and publishers, Alfred A. Knopf, Inc. Copyright, 1921, 1949, by Alfred A. Knopf, Inc.

Hemingway, Ernest: *The Snows of Kilimanjaro,* reprinted from *The Fifth Column and The First Forty-nine Stories* by Ernest Hemingway, copyright 1938 by Ernest Hemingway; used by permission of the author and publishers, Charles Scribner's Sons.

Hersey, John: *Moment of Judgment,* reprinted from *The Wall,* by John Hersey. By permission of the author and Alfred A. Knopf, Inc., publishers. Copyright, 1950, by John Hersey.

Hesse, Hermann: *Within and Without,* translated for this volume by Thomas K. Brown, III. By permission of the author.

Hu Shih: *The Civilizations of the East and West,* by Hu Shih, copyright 1930 by the Forum Publishing Co., copyright 1931 by Simon and Schuster, Inc. By permission of the author.

Huxley, Aldous: *The Tillotson Banquet,* from *Mortal Coils,* copyright 1920, 1948, by Aldous Huxley. By permission of the author and the publishers, Harper & Brothers.

Huxley, Julian: *The Uniqueness of Man,* from *Man Stands Alone,* by Julian Huxley, copyright 1941, by Julian S. Huxley. By permission of the author and publishers, Harper & Brothers.

Jeffers, Robinson: *Life from the Lifeless,* from *Selected Poetry of Robinson Jeffers,* copyright 1938 by Robinson Jeffers, by permission of the author and the publishers, Random House, Inc. *Cassandra,* from *A Little Treasury of Modern Poetry,* an anthology published 1946 by Charles Scribner's Sons. By permission of the author. *Their Beauty Has More Meaning,* from October 1947 issue of *Poetry,* copyright October 1947 by Modern Poetry Association. By permission of the author and *Poetry* magazine, Chicago.

Jensen, Johannes V.: *Columbus in the Trade Wind,* reprinted from *The Long Journey,* by Johannes V. Jensen, translated by Arthur G. Chater, by permission of Alfred A. Knopf, Inc. Copyright 1924, 1945 by Alfred A. Knopf, Inc.

Joad, C. E. M.: *The Function of Philosophy, The Culture of the Many,* from *Decadence,* by C. E. M. Joad, copyright, 1949, by Philosophical Library, Inc. By permission of the author and publisher.

Koestler, Arthur: *Apage Satanas!* from *Darkness at Noon* by Arthur Koestler, translated by Daphne Hardy, copyright, 1941, by The Macmillan Co. and used with their permission and that of the author.

Laxness, Halldór: *An Icelandic Pioneer,* reprinted from *Independent People* by Halldór Laxness, translated by J. A. Thompson. By permission of the author and Alfred A. Knopf, Inc. Copyright 1946 by Halldór Laxness.

Lewis, Sinclair: *An Assemblage of Husbands and Wives,* from *Cass Timberlane* by Sinclair Lewis. Copyright, 1945, by Sinclair Lewis. By permission of the author and the publisher, Random House, Inc.

Lin Yutang: *The End of Living Is Living Itself* from *With Love and Irony* (there as *The Real Threat: Not Bombs, but Ideas*). Copyright 1934, 1936, 1937, 1938, 1939, 1940, by Lin Yutang. By permission of the author and John Day Co., publishers.

MacLeish, Archibald: *Epistle to Be Left in the Earth, You Andrew Marvell,* from *Selected Poems, 1924-1933,* by Archibald MacLeish, copyright 1933 by Archibald MacLeish. Reprinted by permission of the author and by permission of and arrangement with Houghton Mifflin Company, the authorized publishers. *The Flesh That Once Sang, The Cat in the Wood, Winter Is Another Country, Years of the Dog,* and *Poem in Prose,* from *Actfive,* by Archibald MacLeish, copyright, 1948, by Archibald MacLeish. By permission of the author and publishers, Random House, Inc.

Madariaga, Salvador de: *Dedicated to Women,* from *The World's Design* by Salvador de Madariaga. By permission of the author and the publishers George Allen & Unwin Ltd. Published 1938 by George Allen & Unwin Ltd.

Mallea, Eduardo: *Pillars of Society,* from *Fiesta in November,* by Eduardo Mallea, translated from the Spanish by Alis De Sola. Copyright, 1942, by Houghton Mifflin Company. By permission of the author and the editors of the book, *Fiesta in November,* Angel Flores and Dudley Poore.

Malraux, André: *The Essential Problems* from *Man's Hope,* by André Malraux, translated from the French by Stuart Gilbert and Alastair MacDonald. Copyright 1938 by Random House, Inc. By permission of the author and publishers.

Mann, Thomas: *The Masters of Buddenbrooks,* reprinted from *Buddenbrooks,* by Thomas Mann, translated by H. T. Lowe-Porter. By permission of the author and Alfred A. Knopf, Inc. Copyright, 1936, by Alfred A. Knopf, Inc.

Maritain, Jacques: *Art and Beauty* from *Art and Scholasticism* by Jacques Maritain, translated from the French by J. F. Scanlan. Published, 1946, by Charles Scribner's Sons. By permission of the author and publishers in the United States, Charles Scribner's Sons.

Marquand, John P.: *Yoicks—and Away* from *H. M. Pulham, Esquire,* by John P. Marquand. Copyright, 1940, 1941, by John P. Marquand and Adelaide H. Marquand. By permission of the author and publisher, Little, Brown and Company, Boston.

Masefield, John: *The Rider at the Gate* from *The Dream and Other Poems,* by John Masefield, copyright 1923, by John Masefield. Used with the permission of the author and The Macmillan Company. *On Growing Old* from *Enslaved,* copyright 1920, 1948, by John Masefield. By permission of the author and The Macmillan Company. *Sea-Fever* from *Story of the Round House,* copyright 1912, 1940, by The Macmillan Company and used with permission of the author and The Macmillan Company.

Masters, Edgar Lee: *Five From Spoon River,* from *Spoon River Anthology* and *New Spoon River.* Copyright 1914, 1915, by William Marion Reedy, copyright 1915, 1919, by The Macmillan Company. By permission of the author.

Maugham, W. Somerset: *Truth, Beauty and Goodness* from *The Summing Up,* by W. Somerset Maugham. Copyright 1938 by W. Somerset Maugham, reprinted by permission of the author and Doubleday & Company, Inc.

Mauriac, François: *Thérèse and the Doctor,* from *Thérèse,* by François Mauriac, translated by Gerard Hopkins. Copyright, 1947, by Henry Holt and Co. By permission of Eyre & Spottiswoode, Ltd., London.

Maurois, André: *The Kingdom of God,* from *I Remember, I Remember,* by André Maurois, translated from the French by Denver and Jane Lindley. Copyright, 1942, by André Maurois. By permission of the author and the publishers, Harper and Brothers.

Mencken, H. L.: *The Poetry of Christianity,* reprinted from *Treatise on the Gods,* by H. L. Mencken. By permission of the author and Alfred A. Knopf, Inc. Copyright, 1930, by Alfred A. Knopf, Inc.

Millay, Edna St. Vincent: *I Shall Forget* from *A Few Figs From Thistles,* copyright, 1918, 1919, 1922, by Edna St. Vincent Millay. *Cherish You Then* from *Second April,* copyright, 1921, by Edna St. Vincent Millay. *Pity Me Not, Euclid Alone* from *The Harp-Weaver and Other Poems,* copyright, 1920, 1921, 1922, 1923, by Edna St. Vincent Millay. *On Hearing a Symphony* from *The Buck in the Snow,* copyright, 1928, by Edna St. Vincent Millay. *Where Can the Heart, Only the Diamond* from *Wine From These Grapes,* copyright, 1934, by Edna St. Vincent Millay. All others from *Fatal Interview,* copyright, 1931, by Edna St. Vincent Millay. Published by Harper & Brothers, N. Y. By permission of the author and Brandt & Brandt.

Mistral, Gabriela: Three Poems, *Intimate, The Footprint, Poem of the Son,* translated from the Spanish by Frances P. Mousseau, for *THE WORLD'S BEST,* by permission of the author and her agent, Doris Dana, New York.

Molnár, Ferenc: *Liliom's Return,* from *Liliom,* by Ferenc Molnár, copyright, 1921, by United Plays, Inc. By permission of Liveright Publishing Corporation, Paramount Pictures, the author and Dr. Edmund Pauker.

Nehru, Jawaharlal: *Time in Prison,* and *Life's Philosophy* from *The Discovery of India* by Jawaharlal Nehru. Copyright, 1946, by The John Day Co. By permission of the publishers.

Neruda, Pablo: *Summits of Macchu Picchu,* by Pablo Neruda, translated from the Spanish by Angel Flores. Printed by permission of the author.

O'Casey, Sean: From *The Plough and the Stars,* by Sean O'Casey, copyright, 1926, by The Macmillan Co., and used with their permission and that of the author.

O'Flaherty, Liam: *The Challenge,* copyright, 1948, by *Story* Magazine. By permission of the author and *Story* Magazine.

O'Neill, Eugene: *The Hunted,* from *Mourning Becomes Electra,* copyright, 1931, by Eugene O'Neill. By permission of the author and the publishers, Random House, Inc.

Ortega y Gasset, José: *The Coming of the Masses,* from *The Revolt of the Masses,* by Ortega y Gasset, copyright, 1932, by W. W. Norton & Company, Inc. By permission of the publishers.

Perse, St. John: *Snows* (*Neiges* by St. John Perse, translated by Denis Devlin), from *Exile,* by St. John Perse, copyright, 1949, by Bollingen Foundation, Inc. By permission of the author and publisher.

Priestley, J. B.: *The Grand Canyon* from *Midnight on the Desert,* by J. B. Priestley. Copyright, 1937, by J. B. Priestley. By permission of the author and Harper & Brothers, publishers.

Remarque, Erich Maria: *Darkness in Paris* from *Arch of Triumph* by Erich Maria Remarque, translated from the German by Walter Sorell and Denver Lindley, copyright, 1945, by Erich Maria Remarque. By permission of the author and the publishers, Appleton-Century-Crofts, Inc.

Romains, Jules: *On the College Roof,* reprinted from *Passion's Pilgrims* by Jules Romains, translated by Warre B. Wells. By permission of the author and Alfred A. Knopf, Inc. Copyright 1934 by Alfred A. Knopf, Inc.

Russell, Bertrand: *Education* from *Why Men Fight,* copyright, 1917, Century Co. By permission of the author and Appleton-Century-Crofts, Inc.

Sackville-West, V.: *The Duchess Dresses for Dinner,* from *The Edwardians* by V. Sackville-West, copyright, 1930, by Doubleday, Doran & Co. By permission of the author.

Sandburg, Carl: *Abraham Lincoln Speaks at Gettysburg,* condensed from *Abraham Lincoln: The War Years,* by Carl Sandburg, copyright, 1939, by Harcourt, Brace and Company, Inc. By permission of the author and publishers.

Santayana, George: *Normal Madness,* from *Dialogues in Limbo,* by George Santayana, copyright 1948 by Daniel M. Cory. Used by permission of the author and publishers, Charles Scribner's Sons.

Sartre, Jean-Paul: *The Art of Prose* from *What Is Literature?* by Jean-Paul Sartre, translated from the French by Bernard Frechtman, copyright, 1949, by Philosophical Library. By permission of the author and publisher.

Sassoon, Siegfried: *The Weald of Youth,* from *The Weald of Youth,* by Siegfried Sassoon, copyright, 1942, by Siegfried Sassoon. Reprinted by permission of the author and publishers, The Viking Press, Inc.

Schweitzer, Albert: *Out of My Life and Thought* from *Out of My Life and Thought,* by Albert Schweitzer, translated by C. T. Campion. Copyright, 1933, 1949, by Henry Holt and Company, Inc. By permission of the publishers.

Sheean, Vincent: *Valediction to Churchill* by Vincent Sheean, copyright 1945, by Editorial Publications, Inc. By permission of the author and *The New Republic,* from the issue of August 13, 1945.

Sherwood, Robert: *The Titans Meet at Teheran* from *Roosevelt and Hopkins, an Intimate History,* by Robert E. Sherwood, copyright, 1948, by Robert E. Sherwood. By permission of the author and publishers, Harper & Brothers.

Shirer, William L.: *The Prisoners at Nuremberg,* reprinted from *End of a Berlin Diary,* by William L. Shirer. By permission of the author and Alfred A. Knopf, Inc. Copyright, 1947, by William L. Shirer.

Sholokhov, Mikhail: *Civil War,* reprinted from *And Quiet Flows the Don,* by Mikhail Sholokhov, translated by Stephen Garry. By permission of Alfred A. Knopf, Inc. Copyright, 1934, by Alfred A. Knopf, Inc.

Sikelianos, Angelos: *March of the Spirit* and *The Sacred Way* from *Modern Greek Poetry,* translated by Rae Dalven, copyright, 1949, by Gaer Associates, Inc. Reprinted by permission of Eva Sikelianos and the publishers.

Sillanpää, F. E.: *The Night of the Harvest Festival* from *The Maid Silja* by F. E. Sillanpää, translated from the Finnish by Alexander Matson. Copyright 1933 by The Macmillan Company and used with permission of the author and The Macmillan Company.

Silone, Ignazio: *The Seed Beneath the Snow,* unpublished and hitherto untranslated parts, translated by Darina Silone for *THE WORLD'S BEST*. By permission of the author.

Sinclair, Upton: *The Hog Squeal of the Universe* from *The Jungle,* copyright, 1905, 1906, 1933, 1946, by Upton Sinclair. By permission of the author.

Sitwell, Edith: *Still Falls the Rain, Heart and Mind, The Bee-Keeper, The Coat of Fire* and *The Canticle of the Rose,* reprinted from *Canticle of the Rose, Poems, 1917-1949,* copyright 1949 by Edith Sitwell, by permission of the author and The Vanguard Press.

Steinbeck, John: *Easter Sunday: Sea of Cortez* from *Sea of Cortez,* by John Steinbeck and E. F. Ricketts. Copyright 1941 by John Steinbeck and Edward F. Ricketts. Reprinted by permission of the author and The Viking Press, Inc.

Thurber, James: *More Alarms at Night* from *My Life and Hard Times* by James Thurber, copyright, 1933, by James Thurber. By permission of the author and the publishers, Harper & Brothers.

Toynbee, Arnold J.: *Civilization on Trial* from *Civilization on Trial* by Arnold J. Toynbee, copyright 1948 by Oxford University Press, Inc. By permission of the author and publisher.

Undset, Sigrid: *The Loss and the Healing*, reprinted from *The Longest Years,* by Sigrid Undset, translated by Arthur G. Chater. By permission of the author and Alfred A. Knopf, Inc. Copyright 1935 by Alfred A. Knopf, Inc.

Van Doren, Carl: *Franklin and French Ladies* from *Benjamin Franklin* by Carl Van Doren, copyright 1938 by Carl Van Doren. By permission of the author and The Viking Press, Inc.

Van Paassen, Pierre: *Uncle Kees Protests* from *Earth Could Be Fair,* copyright 1946 by Pierre van Paassen. By permission of the author and the publishers, The Dial Press, Inc.

West, Rebecca: *The Meaning of Treason* from *Harper's Magazine,* later incorporated as epilogue to *The Meaning of Treason* by Rebecca West, copyright, 1947, by Rebecca West. Reprinted by permission of the author and The Viking Press, Inc.

Wilder, Thornton: *From a Journal-Letter of Julius Caesar* from *The Ides of March* by Thornton Wilder, copyright 1948 by Thornton Wilder. By permission of the author and the publishers, Harper & Brothers.

Wright, Richard: *American Hunger* from *American Hunger* by Richard Wright. Reprinted from *Mademoiselle,* September 1945. By permission of the author and the publishers *Mademoiselle.*

****

THE EDITOR wishes to thank the individuals who took their time to study a list of 457 world authors and to sign their names to their ballots on which they recorded their choices of those authors they thought most suitable for inclusion in this volume of the world's greatest living authors:

AUTHORS

Ballot Group # 1 (96 signed ballots)

Louis Adamic, Milford, N. J.; Conrad Aiken, Brewster, Mass.; Gertrude Atherton, San Francisco, Cal.; Pio Baroja, Madrid; Ludwig Bemelmans, New York; William Rose Benét, New York; Kay Boyle, New York; Louis Bromfield, Mansfield, O.; Van Wyck Brooks, New York; Tom K. Brown, III, New York; Struthers Burt, Southern Pines, N. C.;

James Cain, Hollywood, Cal.; Erskine Caldwell, Tucson, Ariz.; Taylor Caldwell, Eggertsville, N. Y.; Henry Seidel Canby, New York; Carl Carmer, New York; Mary Ellen Chase, Northampton, Mass.; Mazo de la Roche, Toronto; John Dos Passos, Provincetown, Mass.;

Irwin Edman, New York; Walter D. Edmonds, Boonville, N. Y.; John Erskine, New York; James T. Farrell, New York; Edna Ferber, Stepney, Conn.; Dorothy Canfield Fisher, Arlington, Vt.; Henry James Forman, New York;

Jean Giono, Manosque, France; Robert Graves, Mallorca, Spain; Julian Green, Paris, France; John Gunther, New York; Albert Halper, Brooklyn, N. Y.; Ernest Hemingway, San Francisco de Paula, Cuba; Lillian Hellman, New York; Josephine Herbst, Erwinna, Pa.; Joseph Hergesheimer, Stone Harbor, N. J.; Hermann Hesse, Montagnola, Switzerland; J. G. Hitrec, New York;

K. R. Srinivasa Iyengar, Andhra University, Waltair, S. India; Stasa Jilovska, Prague; McKinlay Kantor, New York; Arthur Koestler, New York; Manuel Komroff, New York; Alfred Kreymborg, New York; Oliver LaFarge, Santa Fe, N. M.; Halldór Laxness, Iceland; Henry Goddard Leach, New York; Francis Leary, New York; Sinclair Lewis, Williamstown, Mass.; Lin Yutang, New York; Emil Ludwig, Ascona, Switzerland;

Archibald MacLeish, Conway, Mass.; Maurice Maeterlinck,

Nice, France; Albert Maltz, Los Angeles, Cal.; Jacques Maritain, Rome; Gabriela Mistral, Santa Barbara, Cal.; Ferenc Molnár, New York; John Middleton Murry, West Suffolk, England; George Jean Nathan, New York; Robert Nathan, Truro, Mass.; Pablo Neruda, Santiago, Chile;

Clifford Odets, New York; Sean O'Faolain, Dublin; Frederic Prokosch, Rome; Samuel Putnam, Lambertville, N. J.; Marjorie Kinnan Rawlings, Hawthorn, Fla.; Elmer Rice, Stamford, Conn.; Conrad Richter, Pine Grove, Pa.; Kenneth Roberts, Kennebunkport, Me.; Muriel Rukeyser, New York;

Hon. V. Sackville-West, Sissinghurst, Kent, England; George Santayana, Rome; Siegfried Sassoon, Wiltshire, England; Gladys Schmitt, Pittsburgh, Pa.; Evelyn Scott, London; Vincent Sheean, New York; Ignazio Silone, Rome; Upton Sinclair, Monrovia, Cal.; Betty Smith, Chapel Hill, N. C.; Wallace Stegner, Stanford University, Cal.; Phil Stong, Washington, Conn.; Jesse Stuart, Riverton, Ky.; Raymond Swing, Washington, D. C.;

Genevieve Taggard, East Jamaica, Vt.; Dorothy Thompson, New York; Sigrid Undset, Lillehammer, Norway;

Carl Van Doren, New York; Mark Van Doren, New York; R. G. Waldeck, New York; Robert Penn Warren, New York; Glenway Wescott, Hampton, N. J.; Rebecca West, London; Margaret Widdemer, New York; Thornton Wilder, Hamden, Conn.; William Carlos Williams, Rutherford, N. J.; Avrahm Yarmolinsky, New York; Frank Yerby, Jackson Heights, N. Y.

MEMBERS OR OFFICERS OF P. E. N. CLUBS OUTSIDE THE UNITED STATES
Ballot Group # 2 (30 signed ballots)

Miss Dot Allan, Glasgow, Scotland; Raoul Auernheimer, Los Angeles, Cal.; Ruth M. Bedford, Sydney, Australia; Ferdinand Bruckner, New York; Yolanda Bedregal de Conitzer, La Paz, Bolivia; Edgard de Roche Miranda of Brazil; José Miguel Ferrer, Secretary P. E. N., *Ministerio de Relationes Exteriores,* Caracas, Venezuela; Richard Friedenthal, Editor, *Die Neue Rundschau,* London, England; Reuben Grossman, Tel Aviv, Israel; Percy N. Jacobson, West Montreal, Canada; Professor Wilhelm Keilhau, Oslo, Norway; Majid Khadduri, Secretary Baghdad P.E.N., Baghdad, Iraq; Pat A. Lawlor, New Zealand; Joseph Leftwich, London, England; John McKellar, Secretary P.E.N., Melbourne, Australia; Henri Membré, Paris, France; May Morton, Belfast, N. Ireland;

Hermon Ould, International Secretary, P.E.N., London, England; Professor William Moses Rubinyi, Vice President, Hungarian P.E.N., Budapest, Hungary; M. Soucková, Czechoslovak Consulate, New York; Sophia Wadia, Editor of the Indian P.E.N. and *The Aryan Path,* Bombay, India; and the following members of the Syndicate of Czechoslovakian Writers: Frantisek Halas, President; Jinrich Chalupecky, Zirina Hankova, Dr. Josef Knap, Jiri Kolar, Paul Levit, Dr. Bohemil Bovak, Rudolf Sturm, and Dr. Josef Trager, all of Prague, Czechoslovakia.

MEMBERS OF THE P.E.N. CLUB
(Poets, Editors, Novelists) of the United States
Ballot Group # 3 (36 signed ballots)

Leonard Bacon, Peace Dale, R. I.; Mrs. Betty Kirk Boyer, Norristown, Pa.; Herschel Brickell, Editor, O. Henry Memorial Prize Stories, Christian, Miss.; Whit Burnett, Former Secretary, P.E.N. Club of America; Melville Cane, New York; Prof. J. M. Clark, Columbia University, New York; Robert P. Tristram Coffin, Bowdoin College, Brunswick, Me.; Russel Crouse, New York; Helene Eliat, New York; Joseph Freeman, New York; Susan Glaspell, Provincetown, Mass.; Dorothy Graham, New York; Jane Hudson, Executive Secretary, P.E.N., New York; Langston Hughes, New York; Inez Haynes Irwin, New York; Rita Halle Kleeman, New York; Clare Leighton, Durham, N. C.; Eva Lips, New York; Constance Darcy Mackey, New York; Neil MacNeil, *The New York Times,* New York; Madeline Mason, New York; Caroline B. Packer, Editor, *Church Music,* New York; Genevieve Parkhurst, New York; Virgilia Sapieha, New York; Robert Pick, New York; Rebecca N. Porter, Santa Barbara, Cal.; Harvena A. Richter, Pine Grove, Pa.; Constance Robertson, Kenwood, Oneida, N. Y.; William Sloane, William Sloane Associates, New York; Agnes Smedley, Yaddo, Saratoga Springs, N. Y.; Chard Powers Smith, Falls Village, Conn.; William Soskin, New York; Gladys Taber, Southbury, Conn.; Emily Kimbrough, Haverford, Pa.; Sophie Kerr Underwood, New York; Karolina Vining, Baltimore, Md.

GROUP OF EDITORS OF THE COLUMBIA DICTIONARY OF MODERN EUROPEAN LITERATURE
Ballot Group #4 (70 signed ballots)

Richard Alewyn, Queens College; Hermann Barnstorff, University of Missouri; Jean-Albert Bédé, Columbia University; Adolph

B. Benson, Yale University; Thomas G. Bergin, Cornell University; John G. Blankenagel, Wesleyan University; Hermann Boeschenstein, University College, Toronto, Canada; Paul Bonnet, University of California; Claude L. Bourciet, French Summer School, Middlebury, Vt.; Friedrich Bruns, University of Wisconsin; Adolf Busse, Hunter College; Joaquin Casalduero, Smith College; Halina Chybowska, New York; Federico De Onis, Columbia University; John C. Di Lorenzo, New York; Nelo Drizari, Columbia University; Leon Feraru, Long Island University; M. Fischer, New York; E. M. Fleissner, Wells College; Eugenio Florit, Barnard College; Charlotte E. Forsyth, College of Notre Dame of Maryland; Margaret Gilman, Bryn Mawr College; Stanley Burnshaw, The Dryden Press, New York; Einar Haugen, University of Wisconsin; Edith F. Helman, Simmons College; Harvey W. Hewett-Thayer, Princeton, N. J.; Andrés Iduarte, Columbia University; J. F. Jackson, University of Illinois; Watson Kirkconnell, McMaster University, Hamilton, Ont., Canada; Leon Kochnitzky, New York; Victor Lange, Cornell University; Nancy Lenkeith, New York; Sol Liptzin, City College, New York; Bluma Renée Long, Wells College; Evelyn Beatrice Macht, New York; Harold M. March, Swarthmore College; Howard R. Marraro, Columbia University; Ferdinand D. Maurino, Triple Cities College of Syracuse University; Franz H. Mautner, Ohio Wesleyan University; Sister M. Serafina Mazza, Seton Hall College; Karl H. Menges, Columbia University; Claire Murray, The Reader's Digest; Werner Neuse, Middlebury College; William A. Nitze, University of California; Justin O'Brien, Columbia University; Wolfgang Paulsen, University of Iowa; Maria Pei, Columbia University; Henri Peyre, Yale University; William K. Pfeiler, University of Nebraska; Kurt Pinthus, Library of Congress; Paul R. Pope, Cornell University; J. A. Posin, Leland Stanford University; Walter A. Reichart, University of Michigan; Joseph Remenyi, Western Reserve University; Anthony C. Rinaldini, New York; Ernst Rose, New York University; Aaron Schaffer, University of Texas; Alfred Senn, University of Pennsylvania; C. S. Singleton, Johns Hopkins University; Sigmund Skard, University of Oslo, Norway; Robert K. Spaulding, University of California; Charles Wharton Stork, Harcum Junior College; Norman L. Torrey, Columbia University; Dr. Louis E. Van Norman, President, World Peace Research, San Diego, Cal.; J. B. C. Watkins, The American-Scandinavian Foundation, Ottawa, Canada; Rene Wellek, Yale University; Francis J. Whitfield, The University of Chicago; Mrs.

B. F. Whitmore, Smith College; Albin Widen, Minneapolis, Minn.; Edmund Zawacki, University of Wisconsin.

EDITORS
Ballot Group #5 (24 signed ballots)

Riley H. Allen, Editor, *Honolulu Star-Bulletin;* Carl Alpert, Managing Editor, *The New Palestine;* Charles Angoff, *The American Mercury;* May Lamberton Becker, Readers Guide, *New York Herald Tribune;* Edith O'Dell Black, Ex-Editor, *The Golden Book;* Bruce Bliven, Editorial Director, *The New Republic;* Evelyn Boyce, Assistant Editor, Columbia University Press; William Bridgwater, Editor, Columbia University Press; A. S. Burack, Editor, *The Writer;* Hallie S. Burnett, Co-Editor, *Story;* Carolyn Coggins, *New York Herald Tribune;* Margaret Cousins, Managing Editor, *Good Housekeeping;* Clifton Fadiman, Editor and Critic; Muriel Fuller, Editor, Thomas Nelson & Sons; Eleanor Gilchrist, Assistant Editor, *Story;* J. Laughlin, Editor, New Directions; Fred Melcher, *Publishers Weekly;* Philip Rahv, Editor, *Partisan Review;* Fred Reinfeld, Editor and Author; Alberto Rembao, Editor, *La Nueva Democracia;* Elizabeth J. Sherwood, Managing Editor, Columbia University Press; Dent Smith, former Editor, *Encore;* Harrison Smith, *The Saturday Review;* Pierre Tisseyre, Editor, *Le Monde Français.*

CRITICS, REVIEWERS or NEWSPAPER LITERARY EDITORS
Ballot Group #6 (31 signed ballots)

J. Donald Adams, *New York Times Book Review;* H. Russell Austin, *Milwaukee Journal;* Frederic Babcock, *Magazine of Books, Chicago Tribune;* Elise Beauchamp, *Times Picayune,* New Orleans, La.; Alice Dixon Bond, *Boston Herald;* Warren Bower, New York University; Calvert Carroll, *News-Post,* Baltimore, Md.; John Cournos, *New York Sun;* Malcolm Cowley, Sherman, Conn.; Lewis Gannett, *New York Herald Tribune;* Ralph Habas, *Chicago Times;* M. Harrop, *Times Star,* Cincinnati, O.; Paul Jordan Smith, *Los Angeles Times;* J. M. Lattery, *Washington Post;* Edward A. Laycock, *Boston Globe;* Francis Ludlow, *Retail Bookseller;* John K. M. McCaffery, *The Author Meets the Critics;* Martha MacGregor, *New York Post Home News;* Scott O'Dell, *Los Angeles Daily News;* Olga Owens, *Boston Sunday Post;* Irving M. Peck, *United Press;* Orville Prescott, *New York Times;* Karl Schriftgiesser, *Newsweek;*

Winfield T. Scott, *Providence Journal;* John K. Sherman, *Minneapolis Star and Tribune;* Robert I. Snajdr, *Cleveland Plain Dealer;* J. Lon Tinkle, *Dallas Morning News;* W. A. White, *Pittsburgh Press;* Frank Winn, *Deseret News,* Salt Lake City; Norman J. Wright, Honolulu, T. H.; Ballot signed with request that name be withheld: Reviewer, New York.

COLLEGE PRESIDENTS, EDUCATORS
Ballot Group #7 (121 signed ballots)

Harlen M. Adams, Chico State College; W. S. Allen, John B. Stetson University; Sister M. Amatora, O. S. F., St. Francis College, Fort Wayne, Ind.; Winslow S. Anderson, Whitman College; Ray N. Baker, Bethel College; Maurice Baudin, Jr., New York University; Horace M. Bond, Lincoln University; George W. Bowman, Wilmington College; Charles A. Brady, Kenmore, N. Y.; Irma Brandeis, Bard College; Mrs. James P. Brawley, Clark College, Atlanta, Ga.; Wiley G. Brooks, Nebraska State Teachers College; Earl E. Clarke, Polytechnic Institute of Puerto Rico; Rufus E. Clement, Atlanta University; Sister Colette, Marywood School, Evanston, Ill.; Mother Loretta Corcoran, Manhattanville College of the Sacred Heart, New York; Lewis T. Corlett, Northwest Nazarene College; R. W. Cowden, Director of Avery Hopwood Awards, University of Michigan; James E. Cox, Oakland City College; H. L. Creek, Purdue University; Josiah Crudup, Gainesville, Ga.; Ruby G. Crumm, Altoona, Pa.; Carlton F. Culmsee, Utah State Agricultural College; John J. Curran, Quincy, Ill.; Carter Davidson, Union College; Rose M. Davis, Moravian College for Women, Bethlehem, Pa.; Sister M. Dignu, O.S.B., College of St. Scholastica; Theodore A. Distler, Franklin and Marshall College; Bertram W. Doyle, Professor of Sociology, Louisville, Ky.; Karl W. Dykema, Director, Division of Language and Literature, Youngstown College, Youngstown, O.; William W. Edel, President, Dickinson College, Carlisle, Pa.; Joseph H. Edge, former President, Dakota Wesleyan (Mitchell, S. D.), Nashville, Tenn.; Mrs. L. R. Elliott, Fort Worth, Tex.; Edward Engson, Los Angeles, Cal.; Sister Eugenia, Saint Mary-of-the-Woods College; Mother M. Erskine, College of the Sacred Heart, Grand Coteau, La.; Edward A. Fitzpatrick, Mount Mary College, Milwaukee, Wis.; Anthony Frederick, S.M., St. Mary's University, San Antonio, Tex.; Robert F. Galbreath, D.D., S.S.D., S.H.D., New Wilmington, Pa.; Herman Gimmestad, Midland College; Eric F. Goldman, Princeton University; Mrs. D. R. Grace, Dorris, Cal.; G. C. Graham, College President, Hankton, S. D.; Maurice J. Grajewski, St. Francis College, Burlington, Wis.; C. H. Gray, Rensselaer Polytechnic Institute; John J. Gross, Lewis and Clark College; Albert Guerard, Sr., Stanford University; Emmett W. Gulley, Pacific College; Frances W. Hadley, Milwaukee-Downer College; Rev. Ansgar Hallén, O.S.B., St. Martins College, Lacey, Wash.; Walter Havighurst, Miami University; Ira Hayward, Utah State Agricultural College; George Harris Healey, Cornell University; Fred G. Holloway, Western Maryland College; John S. Holten, University of Minnesota; Virginia O. Hudson, Radford College; Herbert L. Hughes, Louisiana Polytechnic Institute; Percival Hunt, University of Pittsburgh; Sister Mary Jerome, O.P., Siena Heights College; L. Clark Keating, George Washington University; Charles B. Ketcham, Mount Union College; Herbert Krause, Augustana College; Wilson C. La Due, Bethany-Peniel College; Walter C. Langsam, Wagner College; Beach Langston, University of New Hampshire; Ruth R. Lewis, San Bernardino, Cal.; Thomas A. Little, Walla Walla College; A. T. MacAllister, Princeton University; J. R. McCain, Decatur, Ga.; C. S. McClain, Olivet Nazarene College; N. E. McClure, Ursinus College; William F. McConn, Marion College; Howard McDonald, Brigham Young University; Richard I. McKinney, Storer College; Cora M. Mattison, William Penn College; Benjamin E. Mays, Morehouse College; H. G. Merriam, Montana State University; Hugh M. Milton, II, New Mexico A & M State College; B. Q. Morgan, Stanford University; Sister Mary Louise Morgan, Ursuline College; Marie Odéïde Mouton, Maryville College; William M. Murphy, Union College; W. Coleman Neirls, University of Scranton; E. G. O'Neill, Yale University; Henry Olson, Buena Vista College; Mildred Mihills Owens, Central College; Sister Mary Paul, Barry College; Mrs. Elsie H. Pine, Emporia, Kan.; James Pine, Rear Admiral, U. S. Coast Guard, Supt. Coast Guard Academy, New London, Conn.; John W. Randolph, Westminster College; W. H. Ready, Los Angeles College; Audrey Reiter, Loretto Heights College; Emmet J. Riley, Carroll College, Helena, Mont.; David A. Robertson, Goucher College; Mother V. Rogers, Duchesne College; Herbert Jackson Root, Kansas Wesleyan University; H. E. Rosenberger, Kletzing College; Evelyn B. Rowe, Nasson College; Helen Santmyer, Cedarville College; P. L. Schact, Capital University; John W. Shank, Lake Forest Academy; Walter L. Simmons, Rhode Island State College; Harold E. B. Speight, Elmira College; Marian

M. Speight, Bethune-Cookman College; Jack M. Stein, Columbia University; S. D. Stephens, Newark College of Rutgers; Irving C. Story, Pacific University; Hugh C. Stuntz, Scarritt College; English Faculty, College of St. Francis, Joliet, Ill.; Thomas H. Taylor, Howard Payne College; Ruth Z. Temple, Russell Sage College; Sister Helen Therese, Ursuline College, Cleveland, O.; R. H. Vining, Montgomery, W. Va.; Gilbert P. Voigt, Wittenberg College; Chad Walsh, Beloit College; Adolph M. Wasilifsky, St. Joseph's College, Emmitsburg, Md.; C. Hoyt Watson, Seattle Pacific College; Bertha M. Watts, Canterbury College; W. M. Whyburn, Texas Technological College; Professor Arthur Herman Wilson, Susquehanna University; Ballot signed with request that name be withheld: High School Principal, Brooklyn, N. Y.; and, many others in this field who made out ballots but did not care to sign their names.

LIBRARIANS
Ballot Group # 8 (108 signed ballots)

Paul Ahorn, Storrs, Conn.; Faith Armstrong, Public Library, Rockford, Ill.; Sister Mary Aurelius, BVM, Mundelein College; William Bacon, Public Library, Erie, Pa.; May E. Baillet, Free Public Library, Irvington, N. J.; Louise Parks Banes, Kern County Free Library, Bakersfield, Cal.; Luis E. Bejarano, United States Merchant Marine Academy, Kings Point, N. Y.; Fleming Bennett, West Virginia University Library; Sarah H. Bilby, Public Library, Bexley, Columbus, O.; Paul Bixler, Antioch College; Eleanor A. Blanchard, Central College Library; Louis H. Bolander, U. S. Naval Academy; Helen I. Borneman, Wilson College; Dorrice Bratcher, Southeast Missouri State College; Richard L. Brown, Public Library, Reading, Pa.; Dorothy H. Bruno, Sacramento City Library; J. E. Burchard, Massachusetts Institute of Technology; Emily Carle, Public Library, Birmingham, Ala.; Mary O. Carmody, Mechanics' Institute, San Francisco, Cal.; Lucile Cavenaugh, St. Francis College, Brooklyn, N. Y.; William B. Child, New York; Sister M. Claudia, Marygrove College; Irving S. Cole, Public Library, Melden, Mass.; Alice Collins, Dorothea Bignell, Mahala Saville, Librarians, University of Mississippi; Charles H. Compton, St. Louis Public Library; Berenice Cooper, State College, Superior, Wis.; Helen Dysart, San Diego Public Library; A. R. Eaton, Harrisburg Public Library; Josephine H. Edwards, Public Library, New Rochelle, N. Y.; Elizabeth, N. J. Public Library Staff; Leo R. Etzkorn, Public Library, Paterson, N. J.; Eleanor W. Folley, Baltimore,

Md.; Blanche Galloway, Madera, Cal.; William A. Gillard, St. John's University Library; Lucille Gottry, Public Library, Rochester, Minn.; Ruth W. Gregory, Waukegan, Ill.; Nora Dell Hacker, Long Beach Public Library, Long Beach, Cal.; Grace Helliwell, Public Library, Palo Alto, Cal.; Robt. W. Henderson, New York Public Library; Edward A. Henry, University of Cincinnati; Reverend Irenalus Herscherofer, St. Bonaventure's Church, St. Bonaventure, N. Y.; Laurel C. Hjelte, Plumas County Free Library, Quincy, Cal.; Dorothy Hovde, Cedar Rapids, Ia.; James Humphry, III, Colby College; Ida M. Husted, Philadelphia, Pa.; Dorothy L. Huth, Gilbert M. Simmons Library, Kenosha, Wis.; John Hall Jacobs, New Orleans Public Library; Delbert R. Jeffers, Monterey, Cal.; Margaret M. Jemison, Emory University; David Jolly, Hampton Institute; Kings County Public Library, Hanford, Cal.; L. H. Kirkpatrick, Librarian, University of Utah; Dorothea M. Krause, Wanson, Wis.; Magnus K. Kristoffersen, Hartford Public Library; Los Angeles Public Library; Flora B. Ludington, Mount Holyoke College; Georgie G. McAfee, Lima, Ohio; Mildred P. McKay, Concord, N. H.; Mrs. J. M. McLean, Ayer, Mass.; Harriet D. MacPherson, Smith College; Rev. Vincent B. Maloney, St. Michael's College, Winooski Park, Vt.; Louise E. Maltby, New Haven Public Library; Esther L. Mardon, Woodland, Cal.; Elizabeth Martin, Public Library, Davenport, Ia.; Mead Public Library, Sheboygan, Wis.; Muriel Mitchell, Siskiyou County Free Library, Yreka, Cal.; Ray N. Newell, Atlantic City, N. J.; Robert G. Newman, Berkshire Athenaeum, Pittsfield, Mass.; Mrs. Elsie K. Newtoft, American Scandinavian Foundation; Margaret Nordholm, Public Library, Waterloo, Ia.; Jerrold Orne, Washington University; Sue Osmotherly, Winnetka, Ill.; M. L. Pearson, Ball State Teachers College; Joseph H. Reason, Howard University Library; Louise Richardson, Florida State University; Edith Ridgeway, Kansas State College; Rev. Arthur J. Riley, St. John's Seminary, Brighton, Mass.; J. L. Roden, Librarian, Norman, Okla.; Mrs. J. E. Rogers, Public Library, Oshkosh, Wis.; Sgt. Charles M. Roske, Camp Cook, Cal.; M. L. Samson, U. S. Military Academy Library; Staff Members, Public Library, San Jose, Cal.; Avis E. Schroeder, Parlin Memorial Library, Everett, Mass.; George Seibel, Allegheny Free Library, Pittsburgh, Pa.; Clarence E. Sherman, Public Library, Providence, R. I.; Wayne Shirley, Dean, Pratt Institute Library School, Brooklyn, N. Y.; Katharine Abigail Shorey, Martin Memorial Library, York, Pa.; Wendell W. Smiley, East Carolina Teachers

College; Alice B. Story, Cedar Rapids, Ia.; Morris Swett, Library of The Artillery School, Fort Sill, Okla.; A. Marjorie Taylor, Public Library, Rochester, N. Y.; Florence S. Taylor, Public Library, Omaha, Neb.; Charles Thorburn, Muskogee, Okla.; Nathan Van Patten, Leland Stanford University, Palo Alto, Cal.; Helen E. Vogleson, Los Angeles County Public Library; R. L. Walkley, Tufts College; Agnes Walsh, Public Library, Vallejo, Cal.; Luke White, Jr., Public Library, Plainfield, N. J.; Frank H. Whitmore, Public Library, East Chicago, Ind.; Jerome K. Wilcox, College of the City of New York; Mrs. Walter M. Wilkins, Public Library, Lackawanna, N. Y.; Mrs. Grinnell Willis, Ferguson Library, Stamford, Conn.; Mary C. Wilson, Public Library, Indianapolis, Ind.; Donald Wing, Yale University; Charles F. Woods, Public Library, Riverside, Cal.; Ola M. Wyeth, Public Library, Savannah, Ga.; Lee F. Zimmerman, Minnesota Department of Education; Ballot signed with request that name be withheld: Librarian, Boston, Mass.; and scores of other librarians who completed their ballots but did not sign their names.

MISCELLANEOUS PUBLIC FIGURES
(Ballot Group #9 — 22 signed ballots)

Leonard Amster, New York; Mrs. Charles H. Arnold, Commissioner, Winsted Girl Scouts, Winsted, Conn.; Dr. Touvia Ashkenazi, Authority Near Eastern Languages, Pittsburgh, Pa.; Helen Black, American Representative, Literary-Musical Agency of Moscow, U.S.S.R., New York; Francis Burr, Smithtown Branch, L. I., N. Y.; Huntington Cairns, Secretary, Treasurer and General Counsel, National Gallery of Art, Washington, D. C.; Jacques Chambrun, Literary Agent, New York; Jacques Mercier Cointreau, Executive-President Cointreau, Ltd., New York; H. William Fitelson, Attorney, New York; Rose Husik Forman, Musician, New York; Leon W. Frost, General Secretary, Children's Aid Society, Detroit, Mich.; T. Ross Hicks, Minister, Northampton, Mass.; Halvdan Koht, Doctor of Literature, Lysaker, Norway; Helen L. Leary, New York; Mary Margaret McBride, Radio — WNBC and NBC, New York; Nolan Miller, Writer-in-Residence, Antioch College, Yellow Springs, O.; Phyllis Moir, Author's Representative, Paris; John Reynolds, Attorney, New York; Julius Rothenberg, Lithographer, New York; Maurice J. Speiser, Attorney, New York; James Stevenson, Student, Yale, New Haven, Conn.; Winthrop Taylor, Attorney, St. James, L. I., N. Y.

BOOK STORE PERSONNEL

(Ballot Group #10 — 23 signed ballots)

Arthur B. Bensinger, Louisville, Ky.; M. van Bronkhorst, Doubleday Bookshop, Penn Station, New York; K. F. Brown, Long Beach, Cal.; Harry Burton, Longmans Green & Co., Toronto, Ont., Canada; Peak Crawford, Doubleday Book Shop, Broad Street, Philadelphia, Pa.; Robert Edgerton, Fresno Book Shop, Fresno, Cal.; Katharin Flowers, McClelland's, Columbus, O.; Lillian H. Friedman, Stix, Baer & Fuller, St. Louis, Mo.; Frigate Book Shop, Baltimore, Md.; Mrs. Edith Guiffin, The Village Book Shop, Carmel, Cal.; Fred B. Hampel, Hampel's Book Shop, Milwaukee, Wis.; Ralph B. Henry, Carson Pirie Scott & Co., Chicago, Ill.; Harold C. Holmes, The Holmes Book Co., Oakland, Cal.; Alan C. Hood, The Baker & Taylor Co., New York; Jean Kelley, Campbell's Book Store, Los Angeles, Cal.; Teresa Moore, St. Louis, Mo.; Lyman W. Newlin, Minnesota Book Store, Minneapolis, Minn.; W. Pettibone, Scruggs Vandervoort Barney, St. Louis, Mo.; Philip Sipser, Duttons, Park Avenue, New York; Edward J. Strecker, Albany, N. Y.; A. v. A. van Duym, New York; C. W. Welch, Jr., Stewart Dry Goods, Louisville, Ky.; Mary C. Welch, J. L. Hudson Co., Detroit, Mich.; (plus 6 unsigned).

GENERAL READERS

(Subscribers to the Saturday Review of Literature)

(Ballot Group #11 — 82 signed ballots)

T. B. Anderson, Litchfield, Conn; Miss E. Beatty, Washington, D. C.; Henri A. Berens, Fremont, Nebr.; Mrs. Cobbett Biemiller, Morristown, N. J.; Ivan Black, New York; Irwin R. Blacker, Cleveland, O.; Mrs. H. Bragdon, Poestenkill, N. Y.; A. J. Burkhardt, Chicago, Ill.; Henrietta C. Byrne, San Francisco, Cal.; Kenneth D. Carlcon, Bank Clerk, Minneapolis, Minn.; B. B. Comer Memorial Library (Three Librarians), Sylacauga, Ala.; Charles A. Cuneo, Writer, Medford, Mass.; Isabel Doughty, Woodstock, N. Y.; J. Downing, M.D., Los Angeles, Cal.; Bess M. Duffy, Teacher, Wyandotte, Mich.; Mildred Crozier Duplechid, High School Librarian, Eunice, La.; A. Harry Eisenberg, Los Angeles, Cal.; Mrs. Margaret B. Ekholm, former teacher, Escalon, Cal.; Frances H. Fenn, Writer, Los Angeles, Cal.; Mrs. H. J. Field, Teacher, Melstone, Montana; Oscar Fleishaker, Rabbi, Rock Island, Ill.; Rebecca George, Teacher, Panama City, Fla.; Mary Butler Goodier.

Fair Oaks, Cal.; Eleanor G. Hall, Richmond, Va.; G. A. Hartwig, Chicago, Ill.; Mrs. John J. Hauser, Bronx, N. Y.; Weare Holbrook, Writer, Hartsdale, N. Y.; Mary M. Hollis, Terra Haute, Ind.; Walter Hopkins, Teacher, Everett, Wash.; Ethel Ireland, Chicago, Ill.; Elizabeth E. Irvin, Teacher of English, Warren, Ohio; Arthur E. Isham, Public Relations Director, Redlands, Cal.; Chas. E. Jennings, Chicago, Ill.; Mrs. A. L. Katz, Rice Lake, Wis.; Izle Kneen, Mt. Union, Ia.; Minna Kushner, Almonesson, N. J.; Louise Lipscomb, Wichita Falls, Tex.; Alfred Lipsey, M.D., Chicago, Ill.; Esther Longfellow, Palo Alto, Cal.; Mrs. Jack Macdonald, Dundee, Ill.; Mrs. Viola W. McKinney, Bishop, Texas; Lynne Malmquist, Bookseller, Sioux City, Ia.; Mrs. Louis E. Marchi, Pittsburgh, Pa.; Mrs. Ida Maron, Salem, Mass.; John C. Martin, Leonia, N. J.; Donn Marvin, S. D. Pictures, Ossining, N. Y.; Mrs. J. S. Mayfield, Columbia, Miss.; F. S. Miller, Designer and Engineer, Akron, O.; M. James Morley, Kenosha, Wis.; Mabel E. Mulock, Allentown, Pa.; John D. Murphy, Mgr. Book Dept., Fayetteville, Ark.; W. C. Nicol, Peoria, Ill.; Mrs. Fred B. Noble, Editor, Jacksonville, Fla.; Helen B. Northcross, Hampton, Va.; Mrs. Albert S. Parish, Knoxville 15, Tenn.; L. A. Pennington, Urbana, Ill.; Miss Gerardine Pritchard, Teacher of English, Cumberland, Md.; Wilhelm Reith, M.D., Forest Hills, N. Y.; Mrs. M. Runkel, 12th Naval District Librarian; Anita E. H. Russel, Portland, Ore.; Carl Schilter, Tyler, Tex.; Milton Schwartz, Brooklyn, N. Y.; Flora Warner Seymour, Editor, Chicago, Ill.; Milford E. Shields, Author, Durango, Colo.; Anna Simpson, Akron, O.; Dr. A. J. Stanley, University of Oklahoma, Oklahoma City, Okla.; Mildred A. Stemper, Cottage School, Pleasantville, N. Y.; Raymond F. Stewart, Graduate Student, Lamont, Ia.; Esther Taylor, Avon, N. Y.; George Tennyson, Editor, Washington, D. C.; Mrs. B. F. Thomas, Arlington, Tenn.; Harlin E. Tillberg, Evanston, Ill.; Esther C. Tovey, Des Moines, Ia.; Lee S. Trimble, Atlanta, Ga.; Donovan A. Turk, Consultant, Public Relations, Indianapolis, Ind.; John Coburn Turner, Manager of *Script,* American Broadcasting Co., New York; Rosella Upperstrom, English Teacher, Schenectady, N. Y.; Minnie Warren, Teacher, Snow Hill, Md.; Donald E. Wightman, Little Silver, N. J.; Lawrence E. Witte, New York, N. Y.; Doris M. Wordell, Teacher of English, Quincy, Mass.; J. P. Wozencraft, M.D., Rochester, Minn.

INDEX OF AUTHORS

Anderson, Maxwell, 173
Aragon, Louis, 750
Auden, W. H., 479
Aurobindo, Sri, 1093
Azuela, Mariano, 339

Baroja, Pio, 959
Belloc, Hilaire, 472
Benét, William Rose, 225
Bowen, Elizabeth, 623
Brooks, Van Wyck, 141
Buck, Pearl, 131
Bunin Ivan, 1008

Cabell, James Branch, 268
Caldwell, Erskine, 237
Callaghan, Morley, 333
Camus, Albert, 736
Churchill, Winston, 541
Claudel, Paul, 720
Cocteau, Jean, 714
Colette, 747
Colum, Padraic, 618
Coward, Noel, 510
Croce, Benedetto, 912
Cronin, A. J., 587

De la Mare, Walter, 457
De la Roche, Mazo, 323
Dewey, John, 111
Dinesen, Isak, 862
Dos Passos, John, 124
Dunsany, Lord, 592

Ehrenburg, Ilya, 1044
Einstein, Albert, 824
Eliot, T. S., 393

Faulkner, William, 155
Fisher, Dorothy Canfield, 255
Forster, E. M., 435
Frost, Robert, 52

Gide, André, 645
Greene, Graham, 566
Gunther, John, 221

Hamsun, Knut, 852
Hemingway, Ernest, 16
Hersey, John, 297
Hesse, Hermann, 830
Hu Shih, 1066
Huxley, Aldous, 400
Huxley, Julian, 490

Jeffers, Robinson, 248
Jensen, Johannes V., 876
Joad, C. E. M., 556

Koestler, Arthur, 977

Laxness, Halldór, 898
Lewis, Sinclair, 38
Lin Yutang, 1059

MacLeish, Archibald, 188
Madariaga, Salvador de, 95
Mallea, Eduardo, 368
Malraux, André, 677
Mann, Thomas, 757
Maritain, Jacques, 685
Marquand, John P., 279
Masefield, John, 431
Masters, Edgar Lee, 184

Maugham, W. Somerset, 420
Mauriac, François, 696
Maurois, André, 670
Mencken, H. L., 148
Millay, Edna St. Vincent, 98
Mistral, Gabriela, 349
Molnár, Ferenc, 993

Nehru, Jawaharlal, 1078
Neruda, Pablo, 355

O'Casey, Sean, 599
O'Flaherty, Liam, 634
O'Neill, Eugene, 3
Ortega y Gasset, José, 945

Perse, St. John, 731
Priestley, J. B., 536

Remarque, Erich Maria, 797
Romains, Jules, 655
Russell, Bertrand, 447

Sackville-West, V., 466
Sandburg, Carl, 77
Santayana, George, 936

Sartre, Jean-Paul, 726
Sassoon, Siegfried, 529
Schweitzer, Albert, 809
Sheean, Vincent, 309
Sherwood, Robert, 204
Shirer, William L., 314
Sholokhov, Mikhail, 1029
Sikelianos, Angelos, 971
Sillanpää, F. E., 889
Silone, Ignazio, 919
Sinclair, Upton, 196
Sitwell, Edith, 502
Steinbeck, John, 61

Thurber, James, 250
Toynbee, Arnold J., 577

Undset, Sigrid, 841

Van Doren, Carl, 228
Van Paassen, Pierre, 965

West, Rebecca, 548
Wilder, Thornton, 104
Wright, Richard, 303